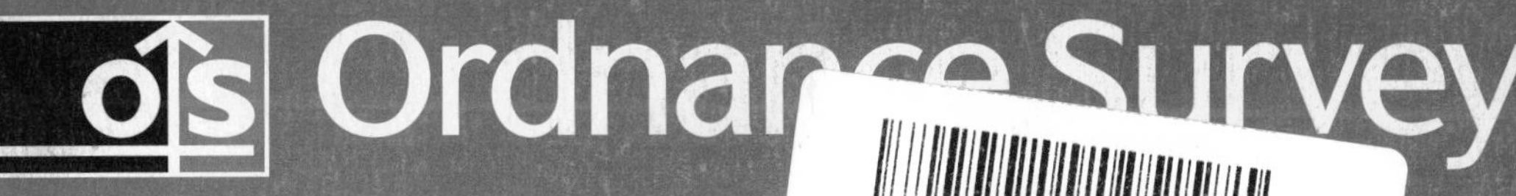

Ordnance Survey

STREET ATLAS
Cheshire

Contents

PHILIP'S

First edition published 1995
First colour edition published 1998 by

Ordnance Survey®   and George Philip Ltd
Romsey Road   an imprint of Reed Consumer Books Ltd
Maybush   Michelin House, 81 Fulham Road,
Southampton   London SW3 6RB
SO16 4GU   and Auckland and Melbourne

ISBN 0-540-07507-8 (hardback)
ISBN 0-540-07508-6 (wire-o)

To the best of the Publishers' knowledge, the information in this
atlas was correct at the time of going to press. No responsibility
can be accepted for any errors or their consequences.

The representation in this atlas of a road, track or path is no
evidence of the existence of a right of way.

**The mapping between pages 1 and 237 (inclusive) in this atlas
is derived from Ordnance Survey® Large Scale and Landranger®
mapping; pages 238-242 (inclusive) are derived from Ordnance
Survey® OSCAR® and Land-line® data, and Landranger® mapping.**

Ordnance Survey, OSCAR, Land-Line and Landranger are registered
trade marks of Ordnance Survey, the National Mapping Agency of
Great Britain.

Printed and bound in Spain by Cayfosa

Digital Data

The exceptionally high-quality mapping
found in this book is available as digital
data in TIFF format, which is easily
convertible to other bit-mapped (raster)
image formats.

The index is also available in digital form
as a standard database table. It contains
all the details found in the printed index
together with the National Grid reference
for the map square in which each entry
is named and feature codes for places
of interest in eight categories such as
education and health.

For further information and to discuss
your requirements, please contact the
Ordnance Survey Solutions Centre on
01703 792929.

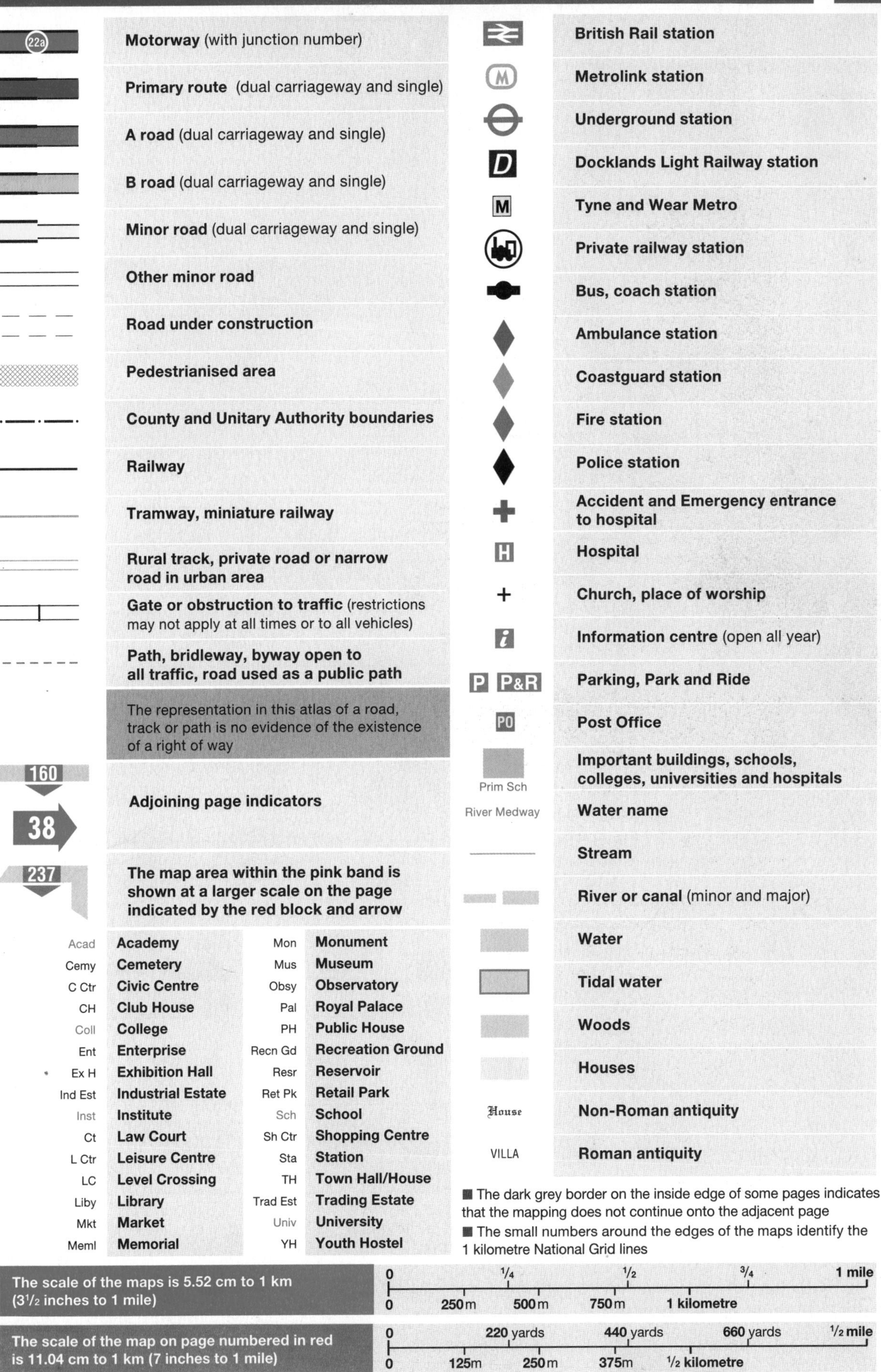

Motorway (with junction number)	British Rail station
Primary route (dual carriageway and single)	Metrolink station
A road (dual carriageway and single)	Underground station
B road (dual carriageway and single)	Docklands Light Railway station
Minor road (dual carriageway and single)	Tyne and Wear Metro
Other minor road	Private railway station
Road under construction	Bus, coach station
Pedestrianised area	Ambulance station
County and Unitary Authority boundaries	Coastguard station
Railway	Fire station
Tramway, miniature railway	Police station
Rural track, private road or narrow road in urban area	Accident and Emergency entrance to hospital
Gate or obstruction to traffic (restrictions may not apply at all times or to all vehicles)	Hospital
Path, bridleway, byway open to all traffic, road used as a public path	Church, place of worship
The representation in this atlas of a road, track or path is no evidence of the existence of a right of way	Information centre (open all year)
Adjoining page indicators	Parking, Park and Ride
	Post Office
The map area within the pink band is shown at a larger scale on the page indicated by the red block and arrow	Important buildings, schools, colleges, universities and hospitals

160
38
237

Acad	Academy	Mon	Monument
Cemy	Cemetery	Mus	Museum
C Ctr	Civic Centre	Obsy	Observatory
CH	Club House	Pal	Royal Palace
Coll	College	PH	Public House
Ent	Enterprise	Recn Gd	Recreation Ground
Ex H	Exhibition Hall	Resr	Reservoir
Ind Est	Industrial Estate	Ret Pk	Retail Park
Inst	Institute	Sch	School
Ct	Law Court	Sh Ctr	Shopping Centre
L Ctr	Leisure Centre	Sta	Station
LC	Level Crossing	TH	Town Hall/House
Liby	Library	Trad Est	Trading Estate
Mkt	Market	Univ	University
Meml	Memorial	YH	Youth Hostel

Prim Sch	
River Medway	Water name
	Stream
	River or canal (minor and major)
	Water
	Tidal water
	Woods
	Houses
House	Non-Roman antiquity
VILLA	Roman antiquity

■ The dark grey border on the inside edge of some pages indicates that the mapping does not continue onto the adjacent page
■ The small numbers around the edges of the maps identify the 1 kilometre National Grid lines

The scale of the maps is 5.52 cm to 1 km (3½ inches to 1 mile)

0		¼		½		¾		1 mile
0	250m	500m	750m	1 kilometre				

The scale of the map on page numbered in red is 11.04 cm to 1 km (7 inches to 1 mile)

0		220 yards		440 yards		660 yards		½ mile
0	125m	250m	375m	½ kilometre				

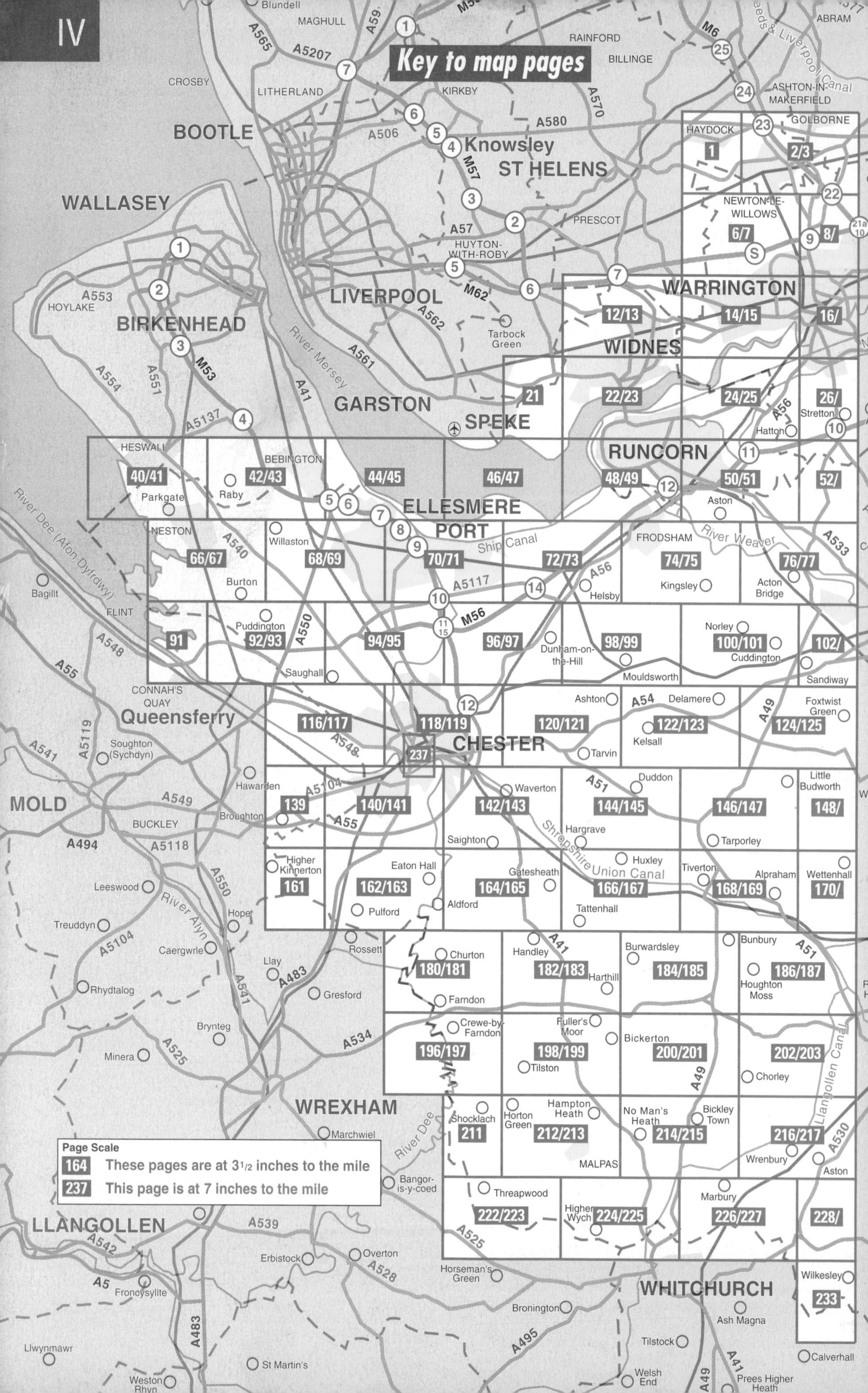
Key to map pages
Page Scale
164 These pages are at 3 1/2 inches to the mile
237 This page is at 7 inches to the mile
Blundell
MAGHULL
RAINFORD
BILLINGE
ABRAM
CROSBY
LITHERLAND
KIRKBY
ASHTON-IN-MAKERFIELD
GOLBORNE
HAYDOCK
BOOTLE
Knowsley
ST HELENS
WALLASEY
PRESCOT
NEWTON-LE-WILLOWS
HUYTON-WITH-ROBY
HOYLAKE
BIRKENHEAD
LIVERPOOL
WARRINGTON
Tarbock Green
WIDNES
River Mersey
GARSTON
SPEKE
Stretton
Hatton
RUNCORN
HESWALL
BEBINGTON
Parkgate
Raby
ELLESMERE PORT
Aston
NESTON
Willaston
Ship Canal
FRODSHAM
River Weaver
River Dee (Afon Dyfrdwy)
Burton
Helsby
Kingsley
Acton Bridge
Bagillt
FLINT
Puddington
Norley
Dunham-on-the-Hill
Cuddington
Saughall
Mouldsworth
Sandiway
CONNAH'S QUAY
Queensferry
Ashton
Delamere
Foxtwist Green
CHESTER
Kelsall
Tarvin
Soughton (Sychdyn)
Hawarden
Duddon
Little Budworth
MOLD
Waverton
Broughton
BUCKLEY
Hargrave
Saighton
Tarporley
Shropshire Union Canal
Higher Kinnerton
Eaton Hall
Gatesheath
Huxley
Tiverton
Alpraham
Wettenhall
Leeswood
River Alyn
Hope
Pulford
Aldford
Tattenhall
Treuddyn
Rossett
Churton
Handley
Burwardsley
Bunbury
Caergwrle
Llay
Harthill
Houghton Moss
Rhydtalog
Gresford
Farndon
Brynteg
Crewe-by-Farndon
Fuller's Moor
Bickerton
Minera
Tilston
Chorley
Llangollen Canal
WREXHAM
Shocklach
Horton Green
Hampton Heath
No Man's Heath
Bickley Town
Marchwiel
River Dee
MALPAS
Wrenbury
Aston
Bangor-is-y-coed
Threapwood
Higher Wych
Marbury
LLANGOLLEN
Erbistock
Overton
Froncysyllte
Horseman's Green
WHITCHURCH
Wilkesley
Bronington
Ash Magna
Llwynmawr
Tilstock
Calverhall
St Martin's
Weston Rhyn
Welsh End
Prees Higher Heath
1 2/3 6/7 8/ 12/13 14/15 16/ 21 22/23 24/25 26/ 40/41 42/43 44/45 46/47 48/49 50/51 52/ 66/67 68/69 70/71 72/73 74/75 76/77 91 92/93 94/95 96/97 98/99 100/101 102/ 116/117 118/119 120/121 122/123 124/125 237 139 140/141 142/143 144/145 146/147 148/ 161 162/163 164/165 166/167 168/169 170/ 180/181 182/183 184/185 186/187 196/197 198/199 200/201 202/203 211 212/213 214/215 216/217 222/223 224/225 226/227 228/ 233
M6 M53 M57 M62 M56 A59 A565 A5207 A570 A580 A506 A57 A553 A554 A551 A562 A561 A41 A5137 A540 A5117 A56 A533 A550 A548 A55 A5119 A541 A549 A5104 A494 A5118 A54 A49 A51 A483 A534 A525 A539 A542 A5 A528 A495 A530

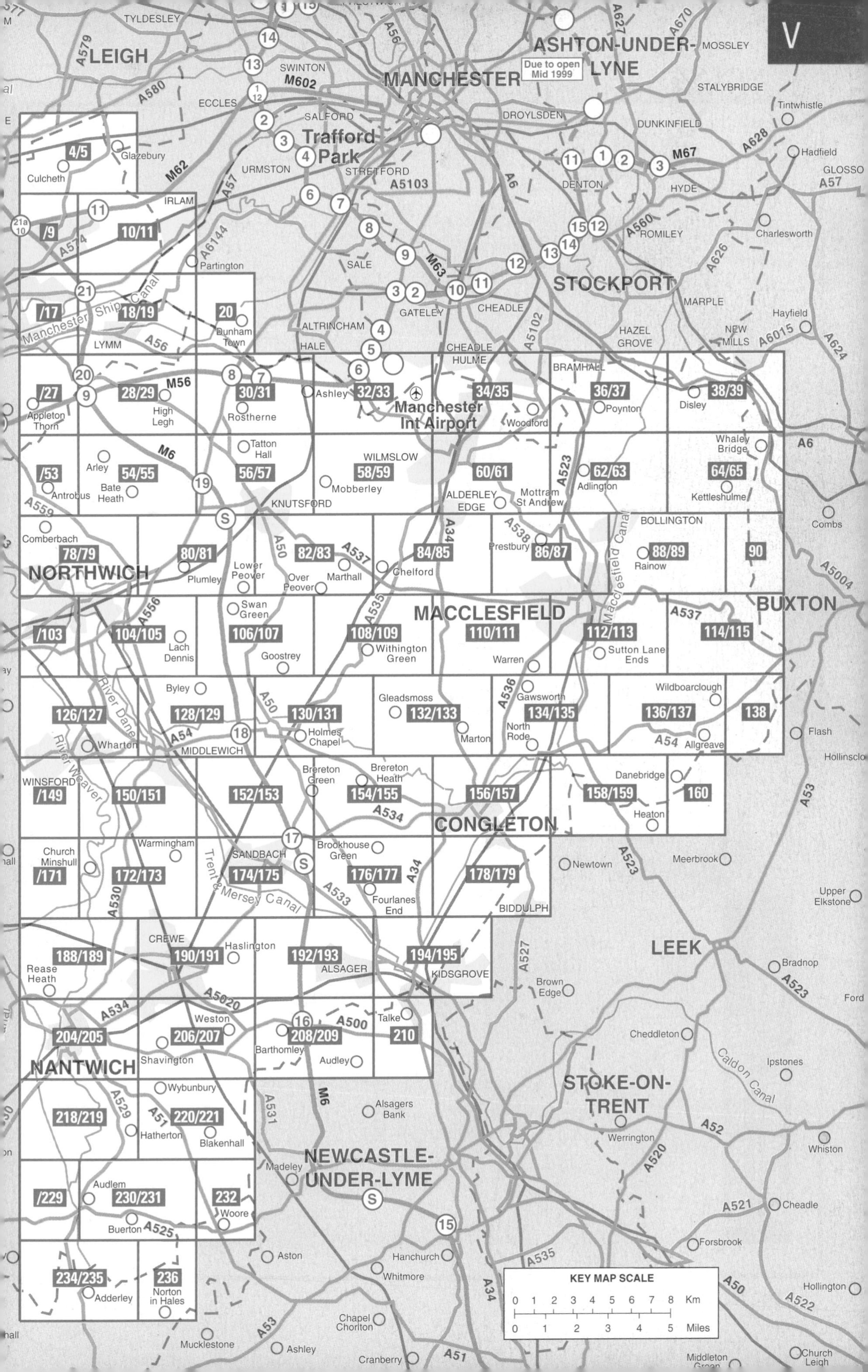
V
TYLDESLEY
LEIGH
A579
A580
ECCLES
SWINTON
M602
MANCHESTER
ASHTON-UNDER-LYNE
Due to open Mid 1999
MOSSLEY
A627
A670
A56
STALYBRIDGE
SALFORD
Trafford Park
DROYLSDEN
DUNKINFIELD
Tintwhistle
URMSTON
STRETFORD
A5103
M67
A628
Hadfield
GLOSSOP
A57
DENTON
HYDE
A6
Culcheth
Glazebury
M62
IRLAM
A57
A574
A6144
Partington
A560
ROMILEY
Charlesworth
SALE
M63
STOCKPORT
A626
MARPLE
GATELEY
CHEADLE
Manchester Ship Canal
LYMM
A56
Dunham Town
ALTRINCHAM
HALE
CHEADLE HULME
A5102
HAZEL GROVE
Hayfield
NEW MILLS
A6015
A624
BRAMHALL
M56
Appleton Thorn
High Legh
Rostherne
Ashley
Manchester Int Airport
Woodford
Poynton
Disley
Whaley Bridge
A6
M6
Arley
Antrobus
Bate Heath
Tatton Hall
WILMSLOW
Mobberley
KNUTSFORD
ALDERLEY EDGE
Mottram St Andrew
A523
Adlington
Kettleshulme
Combs
A559
Comberbach
NORTHWICH
Plumley
Lower Peover
A50
Over Peover
Marthall
A537
Chelford
A34
A538
Prestbury
BOLLINGTON
Rainow
Macclesfield Canal
A5004
BUXTON
A556
Swan Green
Lach Dennis
Goostrey
A535
MACCLESFIELD
Withington Green
Warren
Sutton Lane Ends
A537
River Dane
Byley
Wharton
A54
MIDDLEWICH
Holmes Chapel
Gleadsmoss
Marton
A536
Gawsworth
North Rode
Wildboarclough
Allgreave
Flash
Hollinsclough
River Weaver
WINSFORD
Brereton Green
Brereton Heath
A534
CONGLETON
Danebridge
Heaton
A53
Church Minshull
Warmingham
SANDBACH
Trent & Mersey Canal
Brookhouse Green
A533
Fourlanes End
BIDDULPH
Newtown
A523
Meerbrook
Upper Elkstone
A530
CREWE
Haslington
ALSAGER
KIDSGROVE
A527
LEEK
Rease Heath
Bradnop
A523
Ford
A534
A5020
Weston
A500
Talke
Brown Edge
Shavington
Barthomley
Audley
Cheddleton
NANTWICH
Caldon Canal
Ipstones
Wybunbury
A529
A51
A531
M6
Alsagers Bank
STOKE-ON-TRENT
Hatherton
Blakenhall
Werrington
A52
Whiston
A520
Madeley
NEWCASTLE-UNDER-LYME
Audlem
Woore
Buerton
A525
A521
Cheadle
Forsbrook
Aston
Hanchurch
Whitmore
A535
A34
Adderley
Norton in Hales
Hollington
A50
A522
Chapel Chorlton
A53
Mucklestone
Ashley
Cranberry
A51
Middleton Green
Church Leigh
KEY MAP SCALE
0 1 2 3 4 5 6 7 8 Km
0 1 2 3 4 5 Miles
4/5
/9
10/11
/17
18/19
20
/27
28/29
30/31
32/33
34/35
36/37
38/39
/53
54/55
56/57
58/59
60/61
62/63
64/65
78/79
80/81
82/83
84/85
86/87
88/89
90
/103
104/105
106/107
108/109
110/111
112/113
114/115
126/127
128/129
130/131
132/133
134/135
136/137
138
/149
150/151
152/153
154/155
156/157
158/159
160
/171
172/173
174/175
176/177
178/179
188/189
190/191
192/193
194/195
204/205
206/207
208/209
210
218/219
220/221
/229
230/231
232
234/235
236

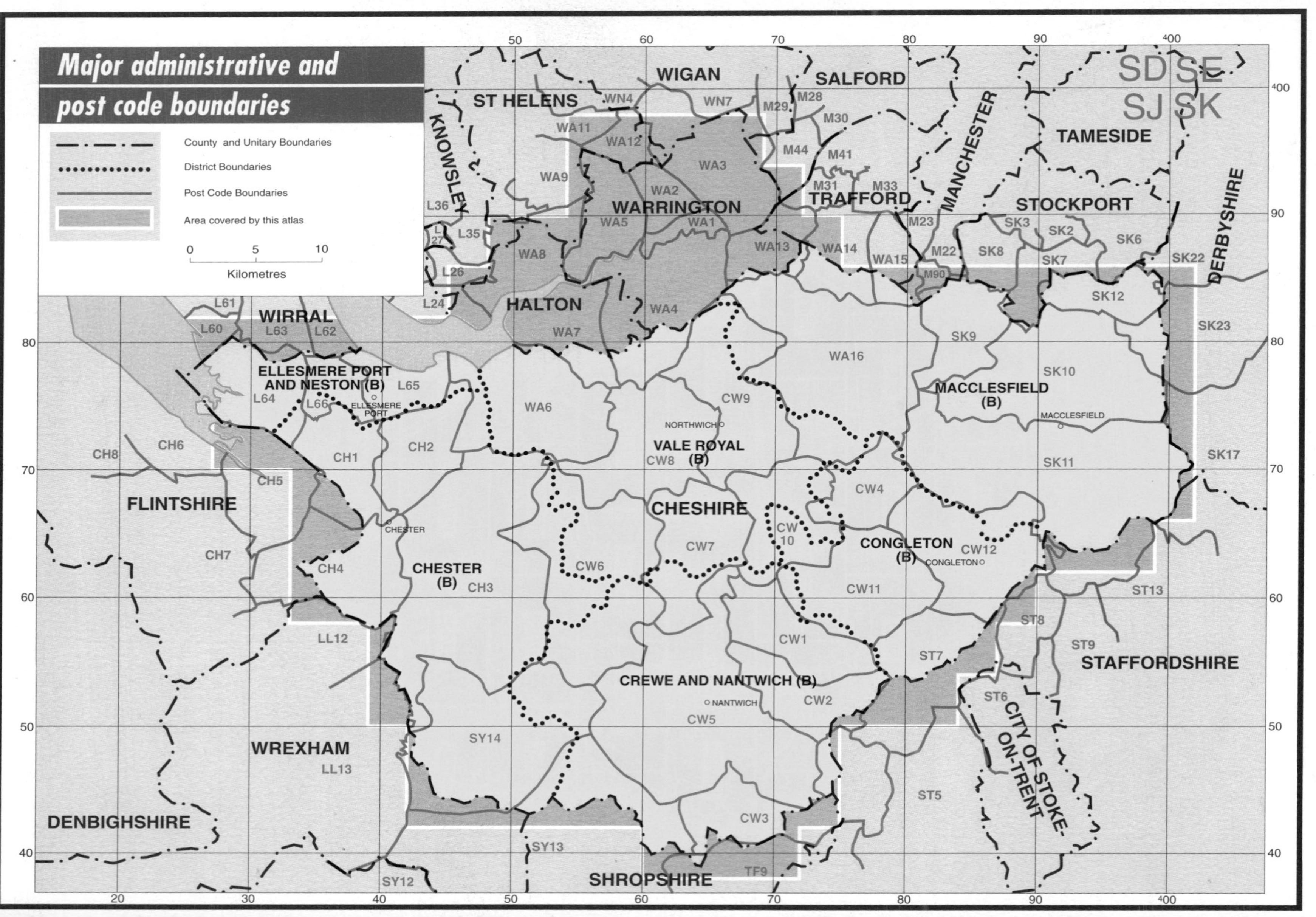
Major administrative and post code boundaries
County and Unitary Boundaries
District Boundaries
Post Code Boundaries
Area covered by this atlas
0
5
10
Kilometres
SD
SE
SJ
SK
WIGAN
SALFORD
ST HELENS
KNOWSLEY
MANCHESTER
TAMESIDE
WARRINGTON
TRAFFORD
STOCKPORT
DERBYSHIRE
HALTON
WIRRAL
ELLESMERE PORT AND NESTON (B)
ELLESMERE PORT
MACCLESFIELD (B)
MACCLESFIELD
VALE ROYAL (B)
NORTHWICH
CHESHIRE
FLINTSHIRE
CHESTER
CHESTER (B)
CONGLETON (B)
CONGLETON
CREWE AND NANTWICH (B)
NANTWICH
STAFFORDSHIRE
CITY OF STOKE-ON-TRENT
WREXHAM
DENBIGHSHIRE
SHROPSHIRE
WN4
WN7
M28
M29
M30
M44
M41
M31
M33
M23
M22
M90
WA1
WA2
WA3
WA4
WA5
WA6
WA7
WA8
WA9
WA11
WA12
WA13
WA14
WA15
WA16
L24
L26
L27
L35
L36
L60
L61
L62
L63
L64
L65
L66
SK2
SK3
SK6
SK7
SK8
SK9
SK10
SK11
SK12
SK17
SK22
SK23
CW1
CW2
CW3
CW4
CW5
CW6
CW7
CW8
CW9
CW10
CW11
CW12
CH1
CH2
CH3
CH4
CH5
CH6
CH7
CH8
LL12
LL13
SY12
SY13
SY14
TF9
ST5
ST6
ST7
ST8
ST9
ST13
20
30
40
50
60
70
80
90
400

2

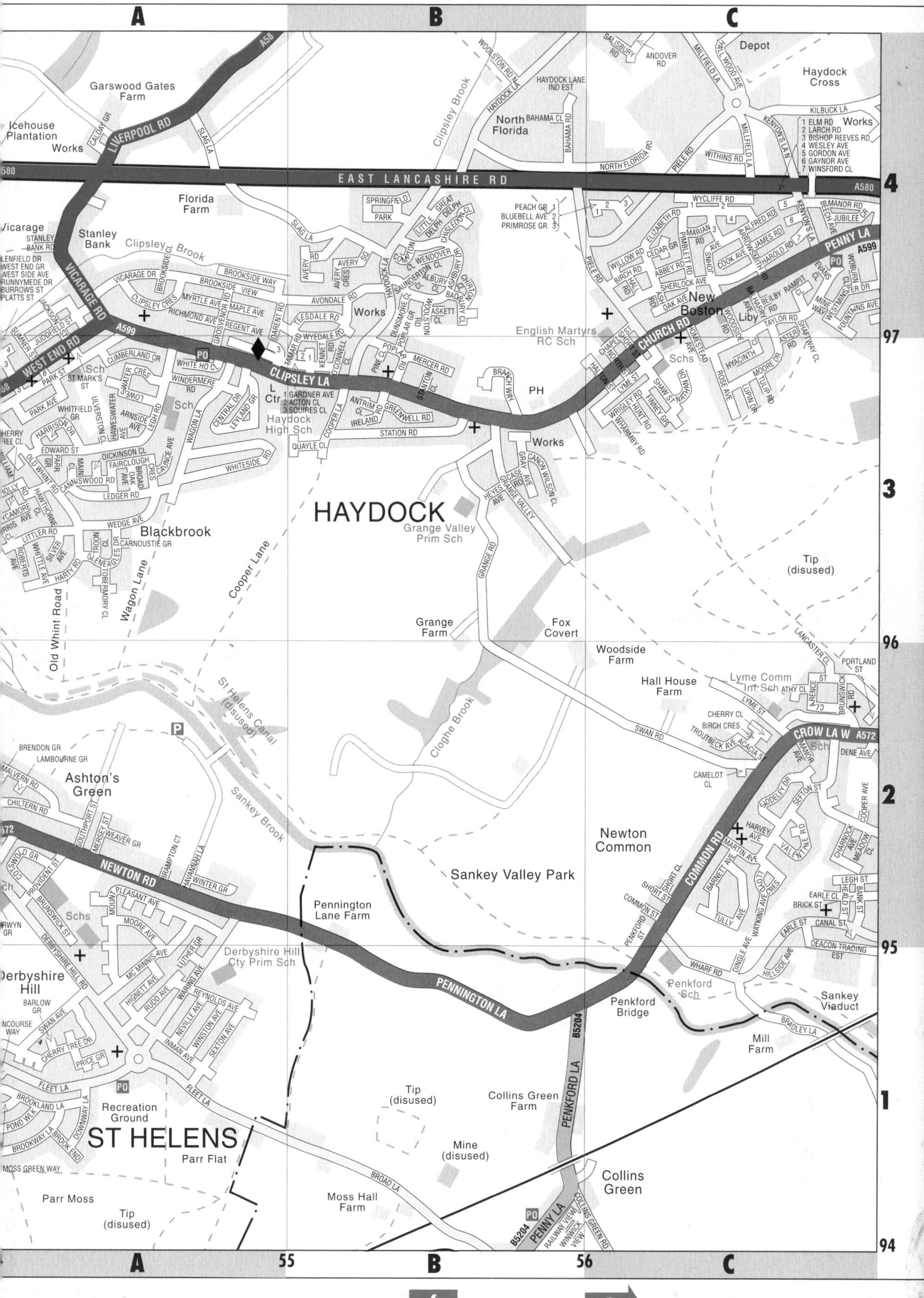
A
B
C
Garswood Gates Farm
Icehouse Plantation
Works
LIVERPOOL RD
SLAG LA
Clipsley Brook
HAYDOCK LA
HAYDOCK LANE IND EST
North Florida
BAHAMA CL
BAHAMA RD
NORTH FLORIDA RD
SALISBURY RD
ANDOVER RD
Depot
Haydock Cross
KILBUCK LA
1 ELM RD
2 LARCH RD
3 BISHOP REEVES RD
4 WESLEY AVE
5 GORDON AVE
6 GAYNOR AVE
7 WINSFORD CL
Works
WITHINS RD
PIELE RD
MILLFIELD LA
KENYON'S LA N
EAST LANCASHIRE RD
A580
4
Florida Farm
Vicarage
Stanley Bank
Clipsley Brook
SPRINGFIELD PARK
PEACH GR 1
BLUEBELL AVE 2
PRIMROSE GR 3
WYCLIFFE RD
MANOR RD
JUBILEE
PENNY LA
A599
VICARAGE RD
VICARAGE DR
BROOKSIDE WAY
BROOKSIDE VIEW
CLIPSLEY CRES
MYRTLE AVE
MAPLE AVE
RICHMOND AVE
REGENT AVE
AVONDALE RD
TEESDALE RD
WYEDALE RD
Works
AVERY RD
AVERY SQ
AVERY CRES
WENDOVER CL
SAUNDERTON CL
ALBURY CL
ASKETT CL
WILLOW RD
BIRCH RD
CEDAR GR
ABBEY RD
SHERLOCK AVE
OAK AVE
New Boston
Liby
CHURCH RD
English Martyrs RC Sch
Schs
97
WEST END RD
A599
Sch
CUMBERLAND CR
PO
WHITE HO CL
WINDERMERE RD
CLIPSLEY LA
1 GARDNER AVE
2 ACTON CL
3 SQUIRES CL
L Ctr
Haydock High Sch
Sch
MERCER RD
PINE CL
POPLAR RD
ANTRIM CL
IRELAND
GREENWELL RD
STATION RD
QUAYLE CL
BRANCH WAY
PH
Works
HYACINTH
MOORE DR
TULIP RD
TAYLOR RD
PARK AVE
EDWARD ST
DICKINSON CL
FAIRCLOUGH CRES
WHITESIDE RD
CANNISWOOD RD
LEDGER RD
3
HAYDOCK
Grange Valley Prim Sch
GRANGE VALLEY
HEYES AVE
Blackbrook
WEDGE AVE
LITTLER RD
CARNOUSTIE GR
Tip (disused)
Cooper Lane
Wagon Lane
Old Whint Road
GRANGE RD
Grange Farm
Fox Covert
96
Woodside Farm
Hall House Farm
Lyme Comm Inf Sch
LANCASTER CL
PORTLAND ST
St Helens Canal (disused)
P
Cloghe Brook
SWAN RD
CHERRY CL
BIRCH CRES
TROUTBECK AVE
ACACIA ST
CROW LA W
A572
Sch
DENE AVE
BRENDON GR
LAMBOURNE GR
Ashton's Green
MALVERN RD
CHILTERN RD
Sankey Brook
CAMELOT CL
2
SOUTHPORT ST
MERSEY ST
WEAVER GR
BRAMPTON CT
HAVANNAH LA
WINTER GR
Newton Common
COMMON RD
NEWTON RD
Sankey Valley Park
Pennington Lane Farm
SHORT CL
SHORT ST
COMMON ST
PENKFORD ST
LEGH ST
EARLE CL
BRICK ST
CANAL ST
EARLE ST
DEACON TRADING EST
95
PROVIDENT ST
BRUNSWICK ST
Schs
PLEASANT AVE
MOORE AVE
DERBYSHIRE HILL RD
Derbyshire Hill Cty Prim Sch
PENNINGTON LA
Penkford Bridge
Penkford Sch
WHARF RD
HILLSIDE AVE
Sankey Viaduct
BRADLEY LA
Mill Farm
Derbyshire Hill
SWAN AVE
CHERRY TREE DR
PRICE GR
PO
FLEET LA
B5204
PENKFORD LA
Tip (disused)
Collins Green Farm
1
Recreation Ground
BROOKLAND LA
DOWNWAY LA
BROOKWAY LA
BROOK END
ST HELENS
Parr Flat
Mine (disused)
Collins Green
MOSS GREEN WAY
BROAD LA
Parr Moss
Tip (disused)
Moss Hall Farm
PO
PENNY LA
RAILWAY VIEW
WINWICK VIEW
COLLINS GREEN RD
94
55
56

6

2

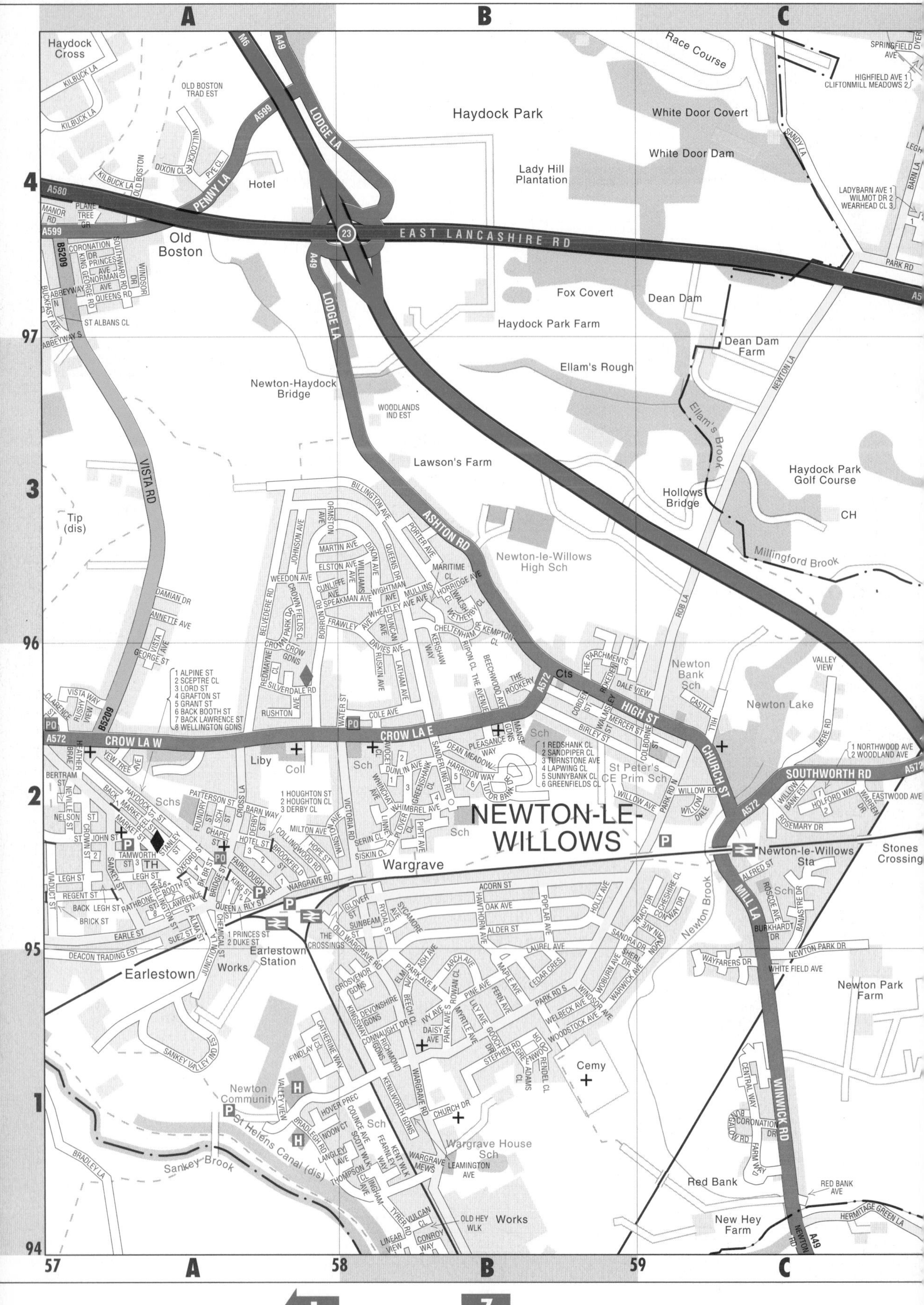
A
B
C
4
97
3
96
2
95
1
94
57
58
59
Haydock Cross
OLD BOSTON TRAD EST
Haydock Park
Race Course
White Door Covert
White Door Dam
Lady Hill Plantation
Hotel
Old Boston
EAST LANCASHIRE RD
LODGE LA
PENNY LA
Fox Covert
Dean Dam
Haydock Park Farm
Dean Dam Farm
Ellam's Rough
Newton-Haydock Bridge
WOODLANDS IND EST
Lawson's Farm
VISTA RD
Tip (dis)
Hollows Bridge
Haydock Park Golf Course
CH
Millingford Brook
Ellam's Brook
ASHTON RD
Newton-le-Willows High Sch
Newton Bank Sch
Newton Lake
Cts
HIGH ST
CROW LA W
CROW LA E
CHURCH ST
SOUTHWORTH RD
Liby
Coll
Sch
Schs
St Peter's CE Prim Sch
NEWTON-LE-WILLOWS
Wargrave
Newton-le-Willows Sta
Stones Crossing
MILL LA
Earlestown Station
Earlestown
Works
THE CROSSINGS
DEACON TRADING EST
Newton Brook
Newton Park Farm
Cemy
Newton Community
St Helens Canal (dis)
Sankey Brook
Wargrave House Sch
Red Bank
New Hey Farm
WINWICK RD
Works

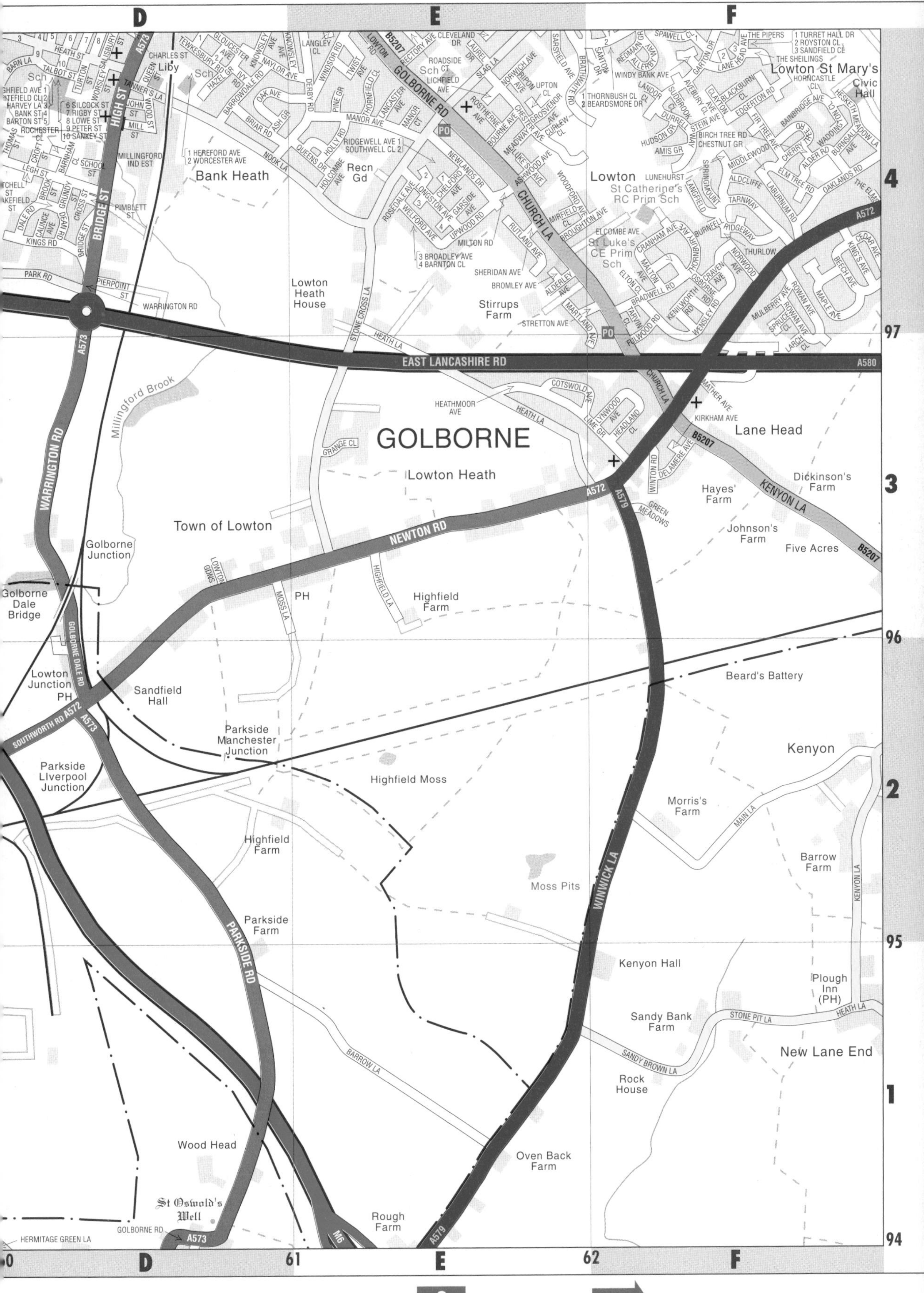
D
E
F
GOLBORNE
Lowton St Mary's
Civic Hall
Lowton
St Catherine's RC Prim Sch
St Luke's CE Prim Sch
Bank Heath
Recn Gd
Lowton Heath House
Stirrups Farm
EAST LANCASHIRE RD
A580
A572
Lane Head
Lowton Heath
Hayes' Farm
Dickinson's Farm
KENYON LA
B5207
Johnson's Farm
Five Acres
Town of Lowton
Golborne Junction
NEWTON RD
WARRINGTON RD
A573
Golborne Dale Bridge
PH
Highfield Farm
Millingford Brook
Lowton Junction
Sandfield Hall
Parkside Manchester Junction
Beard's Battery
Kenyon
Parkside Liverpool Junction
Highfield Moss
Morris's Farm
Barrow Farm
Highfield Farm
Moss Pits
WINWICK LA
A579
Parkside Farm
PARKSIDE RD
Kenyon Hall
Plough Inn (PH)
Sandy Bank Farm
New Lane End
Rock House
BARROW LA
SANDY BROWN LA
STONE PIT LA
KENYON LA
MAIN LA
Wood Head
Oven Back Farm
St Oswold's Well
Rough Farm
M6
HIGH ST
BRIDGE ST
CHURCH LA
GOLBORNE RD
HEATH LA
STONE CROSS LA
MOSS LA
HIGHFIELD LA
GOLBORNE DALE RD
SOUTHWORTH RD
HERMITAGE GREEN LA
4
3
2
1
97
96
95
94
61
62

3

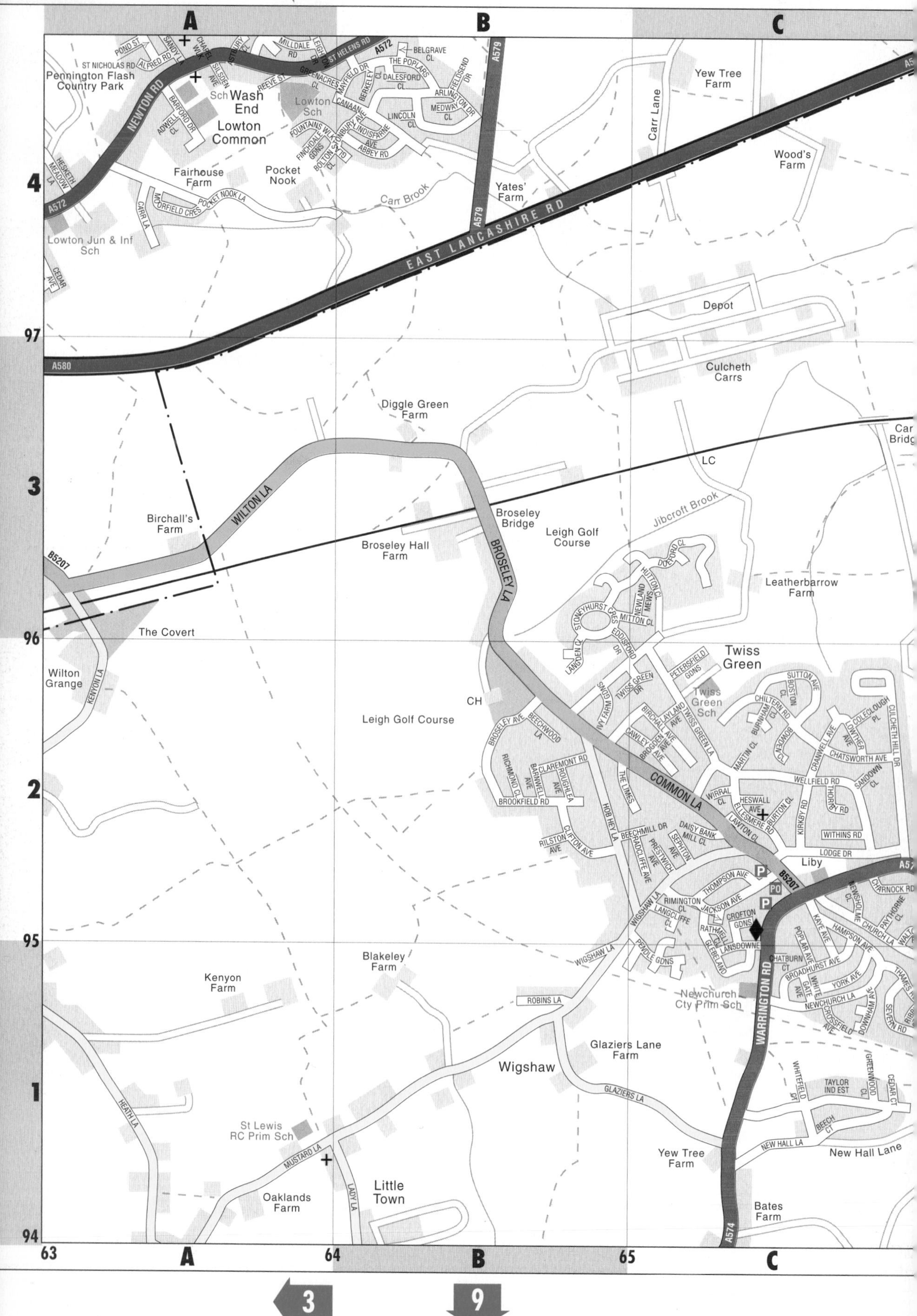
A
B
C
4
97
3
96
2
95
1
94
63
64
65
Pennington Flash Country Park
NEWTON RD
A572
ST NICHOLAS RD
ALFRED RD
POND ST
SANDY LA
CHAPEL WLK
SILSDEN AVE
ASTBURY CL
MILLDALE RD
LEIGH DR
ST HELENS RD
BELGRAVE CL
THE POPLARS
MAYFIELD DR
BERKELEY CL
DALESFORD CL
FIELDSEND DR
ARLINGTON DR
MEDWAY CL
LINCOLN CL
GREENACRES CL
REEVE ST
CANAAN
LINDISFARNE AVE
ABBEY RD
FOUNTAINS WLK
FINCHDALE GDNS
BOLTON CL
STONEBURY AVE
Sch
Wash End
Lowton Common
Lowton Sch
BARFORD DR
ADWELL CL
HESKETH MEADOW LA
Fairhouse Farm
Pocket Nook
POCKET NOOK LA
MOORFIELD CRES
CARR LA
Carr Brook
Lowton Jun & Inf Sch
CEDAR AVE
A579
Yates' Farm
EAST LANCASHIRE RD
Yew Tree Farm
Carr Lane
Wood's Farm
Depot
Culcheth Carrs
A580
Diggle Green Farm
Carr Bridge
LC
WILTON LA
Birchall's Farm
B5207
Broseley Bridge
Leigh Golf Course
Jibcroft Brook
Broseley Hall Farm
BROSELEY LA
DOTFORD CL
HUTTON CL
NEWLAND MEWS
MITTON CL
STONEYHURST CRES
LANGDEN CL
EDDISFORD DR
Leatherbarrow Farm
The Covert
Wilton Grange
KENYON LA
Twiss Green
PETERSFIELD GDNS
Twiss Green Sch
CH
IVY FARM GDNS
TWISS GREEN DR
BIRCHALL AVE
LAYLAND AVE
TWISS GREEN LA
CAWLEY AVE
BROGDEN AVE
SUTTON AVE
BOSTON CL
CHILTERN RD
BURNHAM CL
BOWDEN CL
MARTIN CL
CRANWELL AVE
LOWTHER AVE
COLECLOUGH PL
CULCHETH HILL DR
CHATSWORTH AVE
WELLFIELD RD
SANDOWN CL
THORNBY RD
Leigh Golf Course
BROSELEY AVE
BEECHWOOD LA
RICHMOND CL
BARNWELL AVE
CLAREMONT RD
ROUGHLEA AVE
BROOKFIELD RD
THE TIMES
COMMON LA
WIRRAL CL
HESWALL AVE
BURTON CL
ELLESMERE RD
LAWTON CL
KIRKBY RD
WITHINS RD
HOB HEY LA
BEECHMILL DR
DAISY BANK MILL CL
SEPHTON AVE
PRESTWICH AVE
RADCLIFFE AVE
RILSTON AVE
CLIFTON AVE
LODGE DR
Liby
P
PO
THOMPSON AVE
RIMINGTON CL
JACKSON AVE
WIGSHAW LA
LANGCLIFFE CL
CROFTON GDNS
RATHMELL
CLEBELAND
LANSDOWNE
PENDLE GDNS
WIGSHAW LA
A57
CHARNOCK RD
NEWSHOLME CL
PAYTHORNE CL
CHURCH LA
KAYE AVE
HAMPSON AVE
POPLAR AVE
CHATBURN CT
BROADHURST AVE
WHITE GATE
YORK AVE
THAMES AVE
NEWCHURCH LA
DOWNHAM AVE
CROSSFIELD AVE
SEVERN RD
Newchurch Cty Prim Sch
WARRINGTON RD
Blakeley Farm
Kenyon Farm
ROBINS LA
Glaziers Lane Farm
Wigshaw
GLAZIERS LA
WHITEFIELD DR
TAYLOR IND EST
GREENWOOD CL
CEDAR CT
BEECH CT
NEW HALL LA
New Hall Lane
Yew Tree Farm
HEATH LA
St Lewis RC Prim Sch
MUSTARD LA
Little Town
LADY LA
Oaklands Farm
Bates Farm
A574

3
9

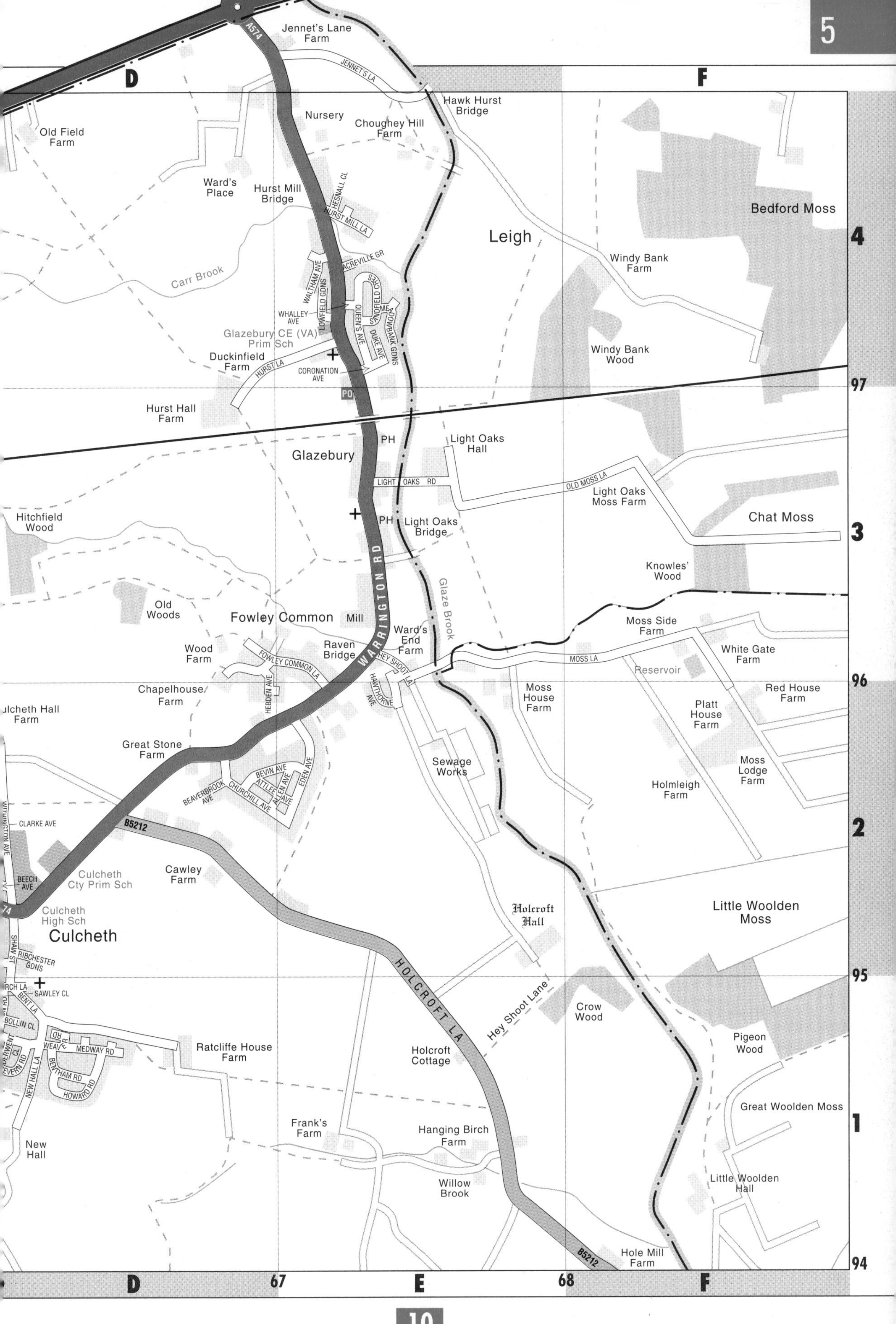

Jennet's Lane Farm

Old Field Farm

Ward's Place

Nursery

Choughey Hill Farm

Hawk Hurst Bridge

Bedford Moss

Hurst Mill Bridge

Carr Brook

Windy Bank Farm

Leigh

4

WALTHAM AVE

ACREVILLE GR

LOWFIELD GDNS

HESNALL CL

HURST MILL LA

QUEEN'S AVE

DUKE AVE

SOMERSET AVE

DOWBANK GDNS

WHALLEY AVE

Glazebury CE (VA) Prim Sch

Duckinfield Farm

HURST LA

CORONATION AVE

PO

Windy Bank Wood

97

Hurst Hall Farm

PH

Light Oaks Hall

Glazebury

LIGHT OAKS RD

OLD MOSS LA

Light Oaks Moss Farm

Chat Moss

Hitchfield Wood

PH

Light Oaks Bridge

WARRINGTON RD

3

Old Woods

Fowley Common

Mill

Glaze Brook

Knowles' Wood

Wood Farm

Raven Bridge

Ward's End Farm

Moss Side Farm

White Gate Farm

FOWLEY COMMON LA

HEY SHOOT LA

HEBDEN AVE

HAWTHORNE AVE

MOSS LA

Reservoir

Red House Farm

96

Chapelhouse Farm

Culcheth Hall Farm

Moss House Farm

Platt House Farm

Moss Lodge Farm

Great Stone Farm

BEVIN AVE

ATTLEE AVE

EDEN AVE

ALLEN AVE

Sewage Works

Holmleigh Farm

CLARKE AVE

BEAVERBROOK AVE

CHURCHILL AVE

WITHINGTON AVE

B5212

2

BEECH AVE

Cawley Farm

Culcheth Cty Prim Sch

Little Woolden Moss

A574

Culcheth High Sch

Holcroft Hall

Culcheth

SHAW ST

RIBCHESTER GDNS

BIRCH LA

SAWLEY CL

HOLCROFT LA

Hey Shoot Lane

95

BOLLIN CL

DERWENT CL

NEW HALL LA

BENTHAM RD

WEAVER RD

MEDWAY RD

HOWARD RD

Ratcliffe House Farm

Crow Wood

Pigeon Wood

Holcroft Cottage

New Hall

Frank's Farm

Hanging Birch Farm

Great Woolden Moss

1

Willow Brook

Little Woolden Hall

B5212

Hole Mill Farm

94

1

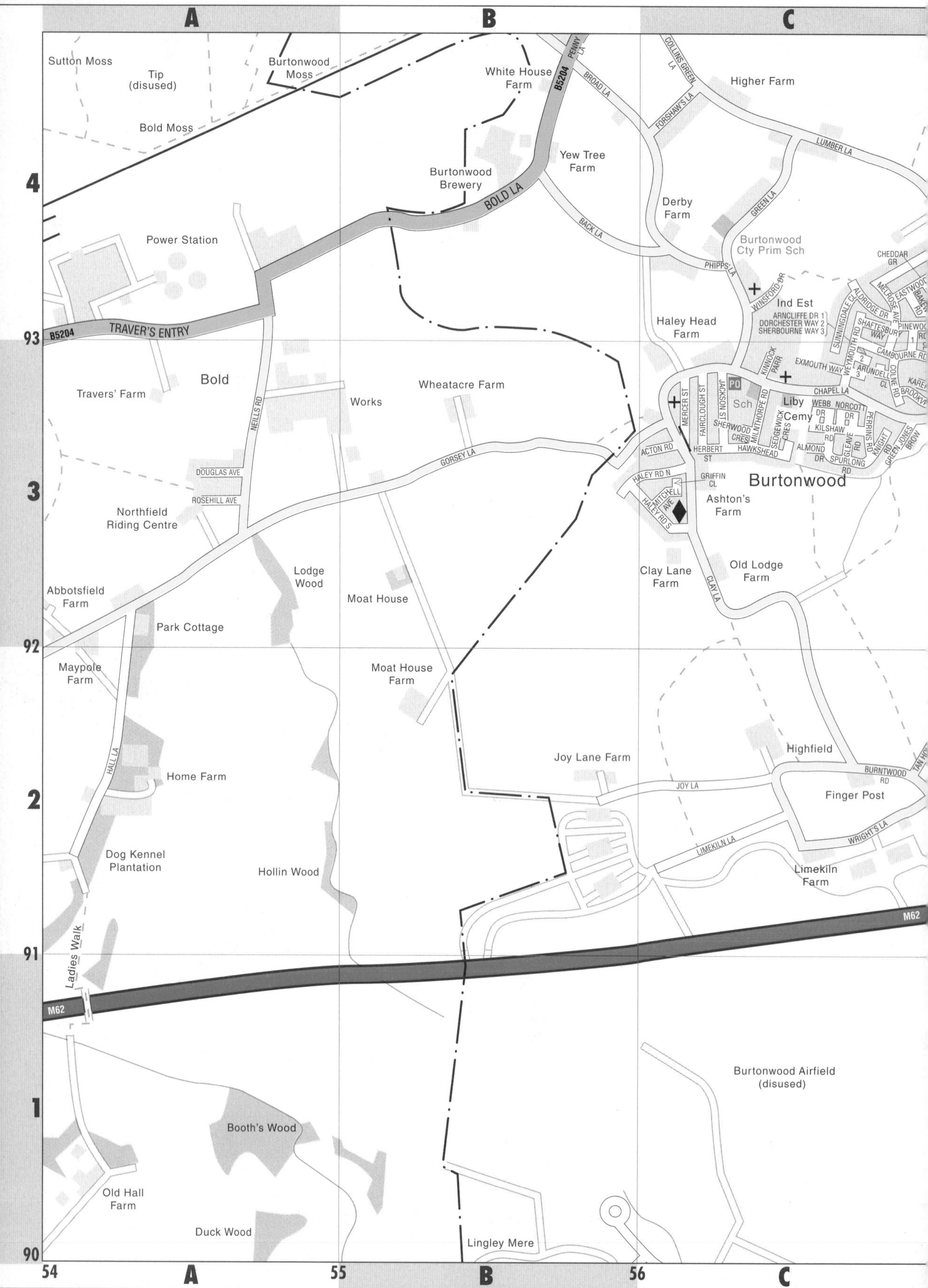
A
B
C
4
3
2
1
93
92
91
90
54
55
56
Sutton Moss
Tip
(disused)
Burtonwood
Moss
Bold Moss
White House
Farm
PENNY LA
B5204
BROAD LA
COLLINS GREEN LA
Higher Farm
FORSHAW'S LA
LUMBER LA
Yew Tree
Farm
Burtonwood
Brewery
BOLD LA
Derby
Farm
GREEN LA
BACK LA
Power Station
Burtonwood
Cty Prim Sch
PHIPPS LA
CHEDDAR GR
WINSFORD DR
Ind Est
ARNCLIFFE DR 1
DORCHESTER WAY 2
SHERBOURNE WAY 3
B5204
TRAVER'S ENTRY
Haley Head
Farm
KINNOCK PARK
EXMOUTH WAY
ARUNDELL CL
CHAPEL LA
Bold
Travers' Farm
Wheatacre Farm
Works
NEILLS RD
MERCER ST
FAIRCLOUGH ST
JACKSON ST
PO
Sch
MILNTHORPE RD
SEDGEWICK CRES
Liby
Cemy
WEBB DR
NORCOTT DR
KILSHAW RD
PERRINS RD
SHERWOOD CRES
HAWKSHEAD
ALMOND DR
SPURLONG RD
GLEAVE RD
KNIGHT RD
GREEN JONES BROW
GORSEY LA
ACTON RD
HERBERT ST
DOUGLAS AVE
ROSEHILL AVE
HALEY RD N
GRIFFIN CL
MITCHELL AVE
HALEY RD S
Burtonwood
Ashton's
Farm
Northfield
Riding Centre
Lodge
Wood
Clay Lane
Farm
Old Lodge
Farm
Abbotsfield
Farm
Moat House
CLAY LA
Park Cottage
Maypole
Farm
Moat House
Farm
Highfield
Joy Lane Farm
BURNTWOOD RD
HALL LA
Home Farm
JOY LA
Finger Post
WRIGHT'S LA
LIMEKILN LA
Dog Kennel
Plantation
Hollin Wood
Limekiln
Farm
M62
Ladies Walk
M62
Burtonwood Airfield
(disused)
Booth's Wood
Old Hall
Farm
Duck Wood
Lingley Mere

14

2
8

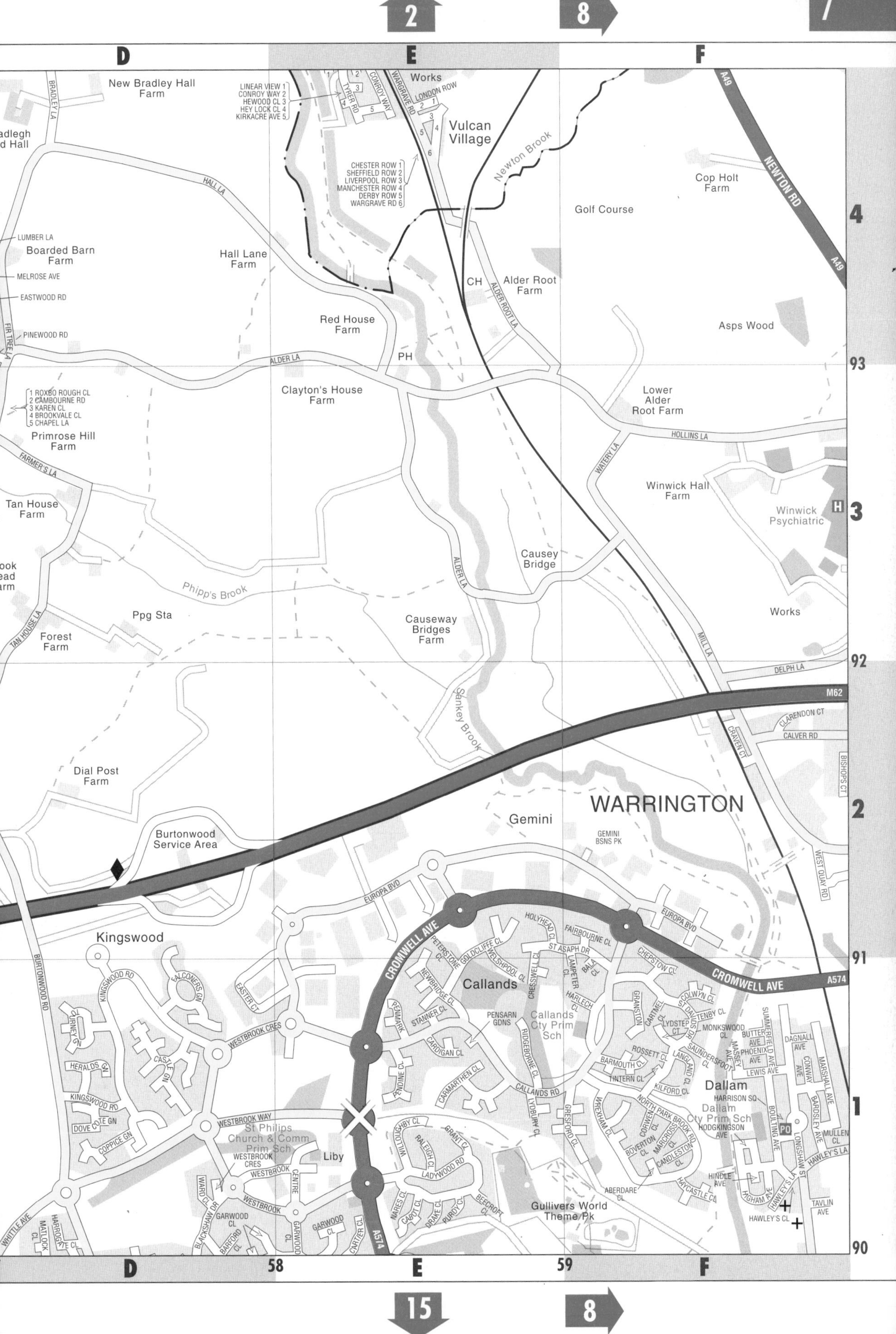
D
E
F
New Bradley Hall Farm
Works
Vulcan Village
Newton Brook
Cop Holt Farm
NEWTON RD
A49
Golf Course
LINEAR VIEW 1
CONROY WAY 2
HEWOOD CL 3
HEY LOCK CL 4
KIRKACRE AVE 5
CHESTER ROW 1
SHEFFIELD ROW 2
LIVERPOOL ROW 3
MANCHESTER ROW 4
DERBY ROW 5
WARGRAVE RD 6
HALL LA
LUMBER LA
Boarded Barn Farm
MELROSE AVE
EASTWOOD RD
PINEWOOD RD
FIR TREE LA
Hall Lane Farm
Red House Farm
CH
Alder Root Farm
ALDER ROOT LA
Asps Wood
PH
ALDER LA
Clayton's House Farm
Lower Alder Root Farm
HOLLINS LA
1 ROXBO ROUGH CL
2 CAMBOURNE RD
3 KAREN CL
4 BROOKVALE CL
5 CHAPEL LA
Primrose Hill Farm
FARMER'S LA
WATERY LA
Winwick Hall Farm
Winwick Psychiatric
H
Tan House Farm
Causey Bridge
Phipp's Brook
ALDER LA
Works
Ppg Sta
Forest Farm
TAN HOUSE LA
Causeway Bridges Farm
MILL LA
DELPH LA
M62
Sankey Brook
CLARENDON CT
CALVER RD
CRAVEN CT
BISHOPS CT
Dial Post Farm
WARRINGTON
Gemini
GEMINI BSNS PK
Burtonwood Service Area
WEST QUAY RD
EUROPA BVD
Kingswood
CROMWELL AVE
A574
Callands
Callands Cty Prim Sch
Dallam
Dallam Cty Prim Sch
BURTONWOOD RD
KINGSWOOD RD
FALCONERS GN
EASTER CT
WESTBROOK CRES
HERALDS GN
CASTLE GN
KINGSWOOD RD
DOVE COTE GN
COPPICE GN
WESTBROOK WAY
St Philips Church & Comm Prim Sch
Liby
Gullivers World Theme Pk
PO
58
59
90
91
92
93
1
2
3
4

15
8

7
3

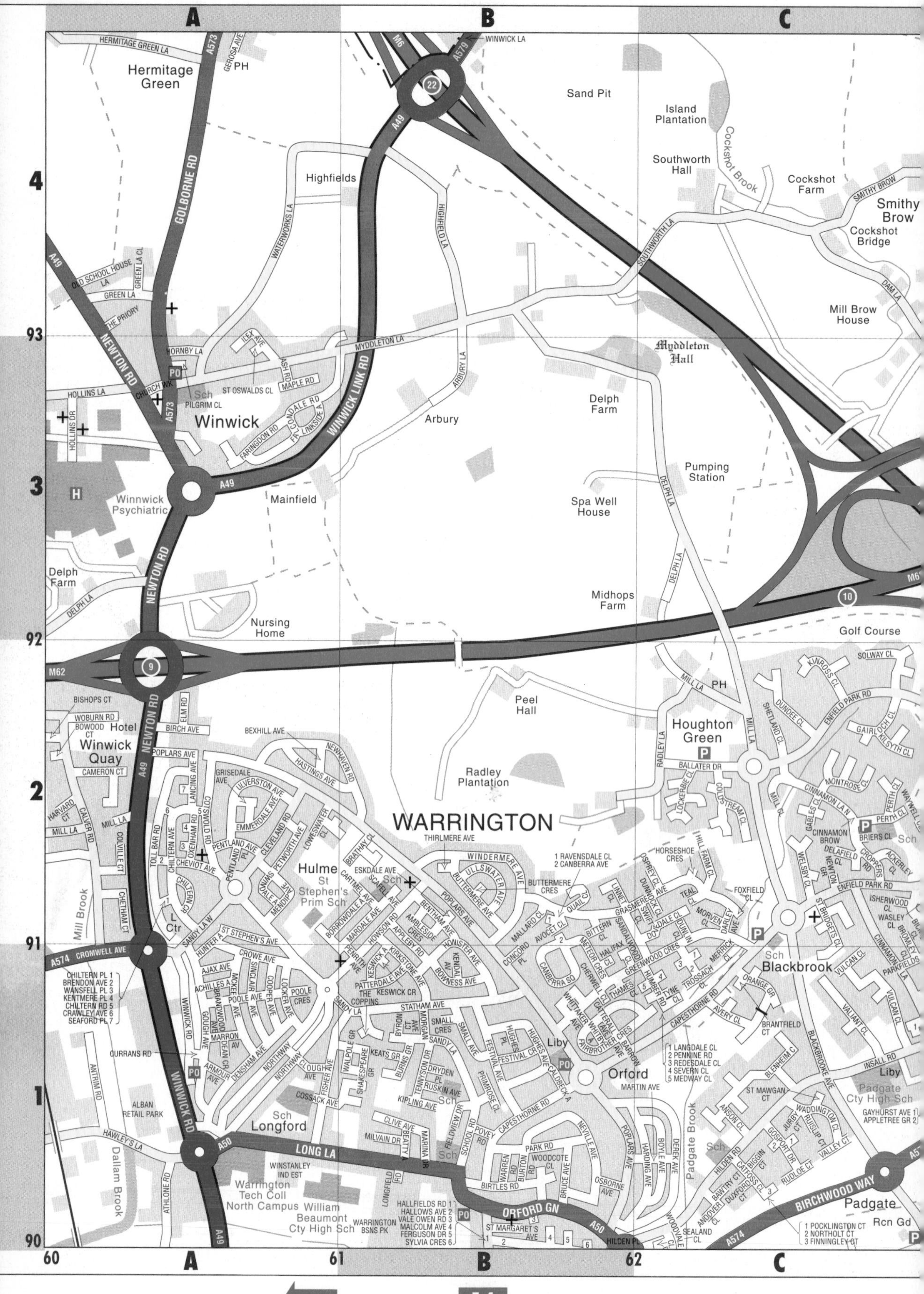
A
B
C
4
93
3
92
2
91
1
90
60
61
62
Hermitage Green
HERMITAGE GREEN LA
GEROSA AVE
PH
GOLBORNE RD
A573
M6
A579
WINWICK LA
22
A49
Sand Pit
Island Plantation
Southworth Hall
Cockshot Brook
Cockshot Farm
SMITHY BROW
Smithy Brow
Cockshot Bridge
DAM LA
Mill Brow House
Highfields
HIGHFIELD LA
WATERWORKS LA
SOUTHWORTH LA
OLD SCHOOL HOUSE LA
GREEN LA CL
GREEN LA
THE PRIORY
NEWTON RD
HORNBY LA
ILEX AVE
ASH RD
MAPLE RD
MYDDLETON LA
Myddleton Hall
ARBURY LA
Arbury
HOLLINS LA
CHURCH WK
PO
Sch
ST OSWALDS CL
PILGRIM CL
HOLLINS DR
Winwick
FARINGDON RD
FALCONDALE RD
LINKSIDE A
WINWICK LINK RD
Delph Farm
Pumping Station
Spa Well House
DELPH LA
H
Winnwick Psychiatric
Mainfield
Delph Farm
DELPH LA
Nursing Home
Midhops Farm
M6
10
Golf Course
M62
9
Peel Hall
MILL LA
PH
SOLWAY CL
KINROSS CL
DUNDEE CL
SHETLAND CL
ENFIELD PARK RD
GAIRLOCH CL
KILSYTH CL
BISHOPS CT
WOBURN RD
BOWOOD CT
Hotel
Winwick Quay
ELM RD
BIRCH AVE
POPLARS AVE
CAMERON CT
BEXHILL AVE
NEWHAVEN RD
HASTINGS AVE
Houghton Green
RADLEY LA
P
BALLATER DR
Radley Plantation
LOCKERBIE CL
COLDSTREAM CL
MILL CL
MONTROSE CL
CINNAMON LA N
PERTH CL
WAYWELL CL
GRISEDALE AVE
ULVERSTON AVE
LANCING AVE
HARVARD CT
CALVER RD
MILL LA
COLVILLE CT
WARRINGTON
THIRLMERE AVE
EMMERDALE AVE
CLEVELAND RD
PENTWORTH AVE
LOWESWATER CL
BRATHAY CL
TOLL BAR RD
CHILTERN AVE
OXENHAM RD
COTSWOLD RD
PENTLAND AVE
CHEVIOT AVE
Hulme
St Stephen's Prim Sch
ESKDALE AVE
SCAFELL AVE
CARTMEL AVE
WINDERMERE AVE
ULLSWATER AVE
BUTTERMERE AVE
1 RAVENSDALE CL
2 CANBERRA AVE
HORSESHOE CRES
HILL FARM CL
GABLES CL
CINNAMON BROW
BRIERS CL
Sch
DELAFIELD CL
CROPPERS RD
ACKERLEY CL
Mill Brook
CHETHAM CT
CHILTERN CR
L Ctr
SANDY LA W
HUNTER A
ST STEPHEN'S AVE
MENDIP AVE
QUANTOCK AVE
BORROWDALE AVE
MARDALE AVE
HOWSON RD
AMBLESIDE CRES
BENTHAM AVE
POPLARS AVE
BUTTERMERE CRES
MALLARD CL
AVOCET CL
QUAIL CL
OSPREY CL
DUNNOCK CL
SWIFT CL
LINNET CL
GRASMERE AVE
TEAL CL
MORVEN CL
DARLEY AVE
FOXFIELD CL
WELSBY CL
NEWTON GR
ENFIELD PARK RD
ISHERWOOD CL
WASLEY CL
BROMLEY CL
ST BRIDGETS CL
A574
CROMWELL AVE
CROWE AVE
AJAX AVE
ACHILLES AVE
PENRITH AVE
KESWICK A
KIRKSTONE AVE
APPLEBY RD
HONISTER AVE
KENDAL AV
BOWNESS AVE
CONCORD PL
CANBERRA SQ
BITTERN CL
SANDALWOOD CL
HALIFAX CL
METEOR CRES
CHERWELL CL
THAMES CL
GREENWOOD CRES
HUMBER RD
TYNE CL
DOVEDALE CL
DUNLIN CL
TROSSACH CL
MERRICK CL
P
Sch
Blackbrook
CINNAMON LA
PARKFIELDS LA
VULCAN CL
CHILTERN PL 1
BRENDON AVE 2
WANSFELL PL 3
KENTMERE PL 4
CHILTERN RD 5
CRAWLEY AVE 6
SEAFORD PL 7
SINCLAIR AVE
COOPER AVE
LOCKER AVE
POOLE CRES
POOLE AVE
MCKEE AVE
BRANDWOOD AVE
GOUGH AVE
MARRON AV
PATTERDALE AVE
THE COPPINS
KESWICK CR
SANDY LA
STATHAM AVE
BYRON AVE
MORGAN CT
SMALL CRES
SMALL AVE
CAPESTHORNE RD
AVERY CL
ORANGE GR
BRANTFIELD CT
VALIANT CL
VULCAN CL
WINWICK RD
CURRANS RD
DENSHAM AVE
ARMOUR AVE
DEAN CR
NORTHWAY
CLOUGH AVE
WALPOLE GR
KEATS GR
SHAKESPEARE GR
BURNS GR
TENNYSON DR
DRYDEN PL
RUSKIN AVE
SANDY LA
FESTIVAL AVE
HUGHES PL
FESTIVAL CR
HUGHES AVE
Liby
PO
CALDBECK A
WHITTAKER AVE
CATTERALL AVE
WHITBURN AVE
FAIRBROTHER CRES
BARROW AVE
Orford
MARTIN AVE
1 LANGDALE CL
2 PENNINE RD
3 REDESDALE CL
4 SEVERN CL
5 MEDWAY CL
BLENHEIM CL
BLACKBROOK AVE
INSALL RD
Liby
Padgate Cty High Sch
GAYHURST AVE 1
APPLETREE GR 2
PO
ANTRIM RD
ALBAN RETAIL PARK
Sch
Longford
COSSACK AVE
FISHER AVE
KIPLING AVE
Sch
PRIMROSE CL
ST MAWGAN CT
ANSON CL
GOSPORT DR
JURBY CL
RUISLIP CT
WADDINGTON CL
VALLEY CT
HAWLEY'S LA
A50
LONG LA
CLIVE AVE
MILVAIN DR
BEATTY A
MARINA DR
FIELDVIEW DR
SCHOOL RD
POVEY RD
CAPESTHORNE RD
PARK RD
WOODCOTE CL
WARREN RD
BURTON RD
NEVILLE AVE
POPLARS AVE
HARDING AVE
BOYLE AVE
DEREK AVE
Padgate Brook
Sch
HILDEN RD
CATFOSS CL
BIGGIN CT
RUDLOE CT
Dallam Brook
WINSTANLEY IND EST
Warrington Tech Coll North Campus
William Beaumont Cty High Sch
LONGFIELD RD
BIRTLES RD
BRUCE AVE
OSBORNE AVE
BAWTRY CT
DUXFORD CT
ANDOVER CL
BIRCHWOOD WAY
A574
Padgate
Rcn Gd
P
ATHLONE RD
WINWICK RD
HALLFIELDS RD 1
HALLOWS AVE 2
VALE OWEN RD 3
MALCOLM AVE 4
FERGUSON DR 5
SYLVIA CRES 6
WARRINGTON BSNS PK
PO
ORFORD GN
ST MARGARET'S AVE
A50
HILDEN PL
WOODVALE
SEALAND CL
1 POCKLINGTON CT
2 NORTHOLT CT
3 FINNINGLEY CT

7
16

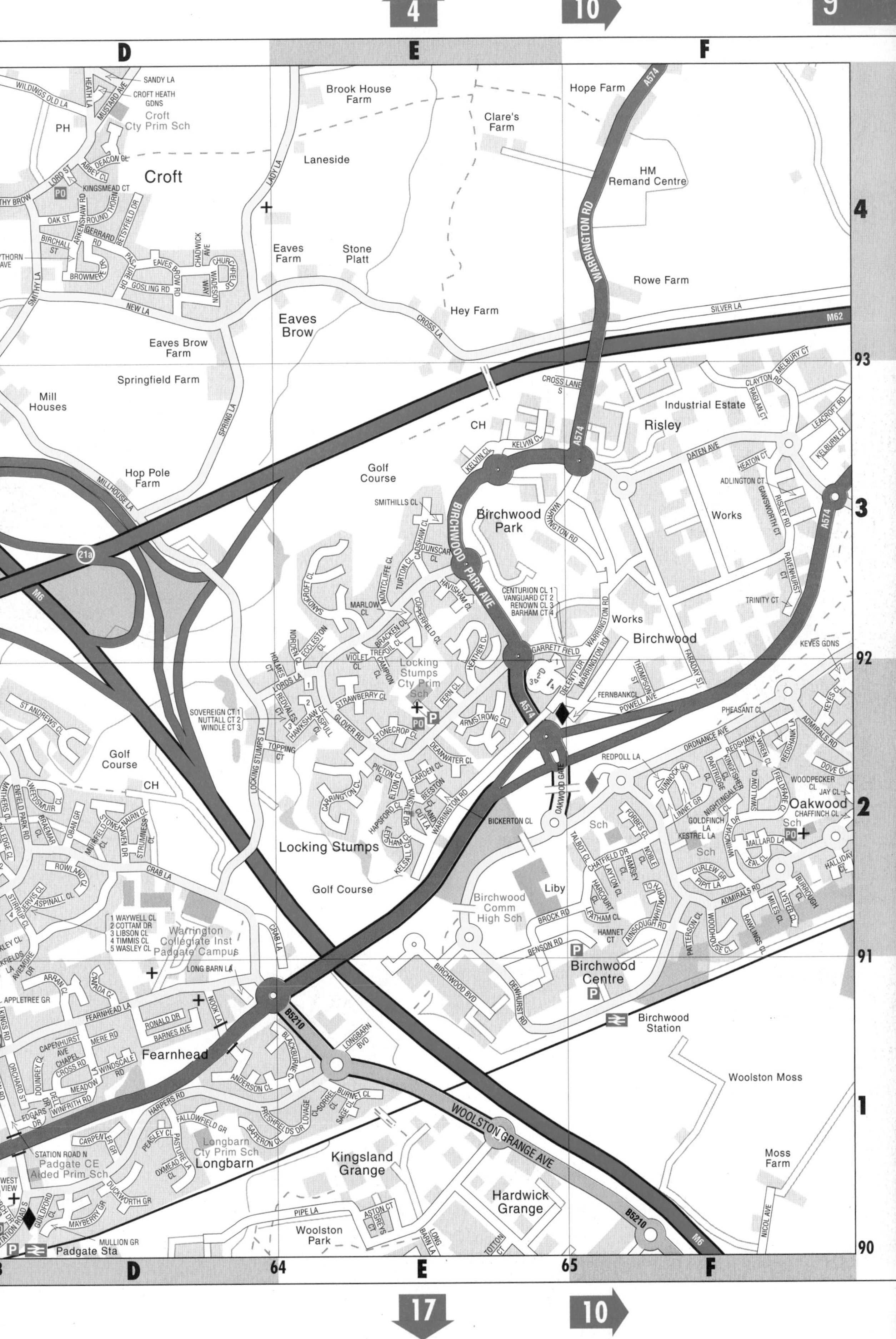

4
10
D
E
F
Croft
Croft Cty Prim Sch
PH
PO
Brook House Farm
Hope Farm
Clare's Farm
Laneside
HM Remand Centre
Eaves Farm
Stone Platt
Rowe Farm
Hey Farm
Eaves Brow
Eaves Brow Farm
Springfield Farm
Mill Houses
Hop Pole Farm
Golf Course
CH
Industrial Estate
Risley
Birchwood Park
Works
Birchwood
Locking Stumps Cty Prim Sch
Locking Stumps
Golf Course
Golf Course
Warrington Collegiate Inst Padgate Campus
Sch
Oakwood
Liby
Birchwood Comm High Sch
Birchwood Centre
Birchwood Station
Woolston Moss
Fearnhead
Longbarn Cty Prim Sch
Longbarn
Padgate CE Aided Prim Sch
Padgate Sta
Kingsland Grange
Hardwick Grange
Woolston Park
Moss Farm
WARRINGTON RD
BIRCHWOOD · PARK AVE
WOOLSTON GRANGE AVE
SILVER LA
CROSS LA
NEW LA
LADY LA
SPRING LA
MILLHOUSE LA
CRAB LA
LOCKING STUMPS LA
ORDNANCE AVE
DATEN AVE
OAKWOOD GATE
BIRCHWOOD BVD
LONGBARN BVD
PIPE LA
A574
M62
M6
B5210
21a
CENTURION CL 1
VANGUARD CT 2
RENOWN CL 3
BARHAM CT 4
SOVEREIGN CT 1
NUTTALL CT 2
WINDLE CT 3
1 WAYWELL CL
2 COTTAM DR
3 LIBSON CL
4 TIMMIS CL
5 WASLEY CL
4
3
2
1
93
92
91
90
64
65
17
10

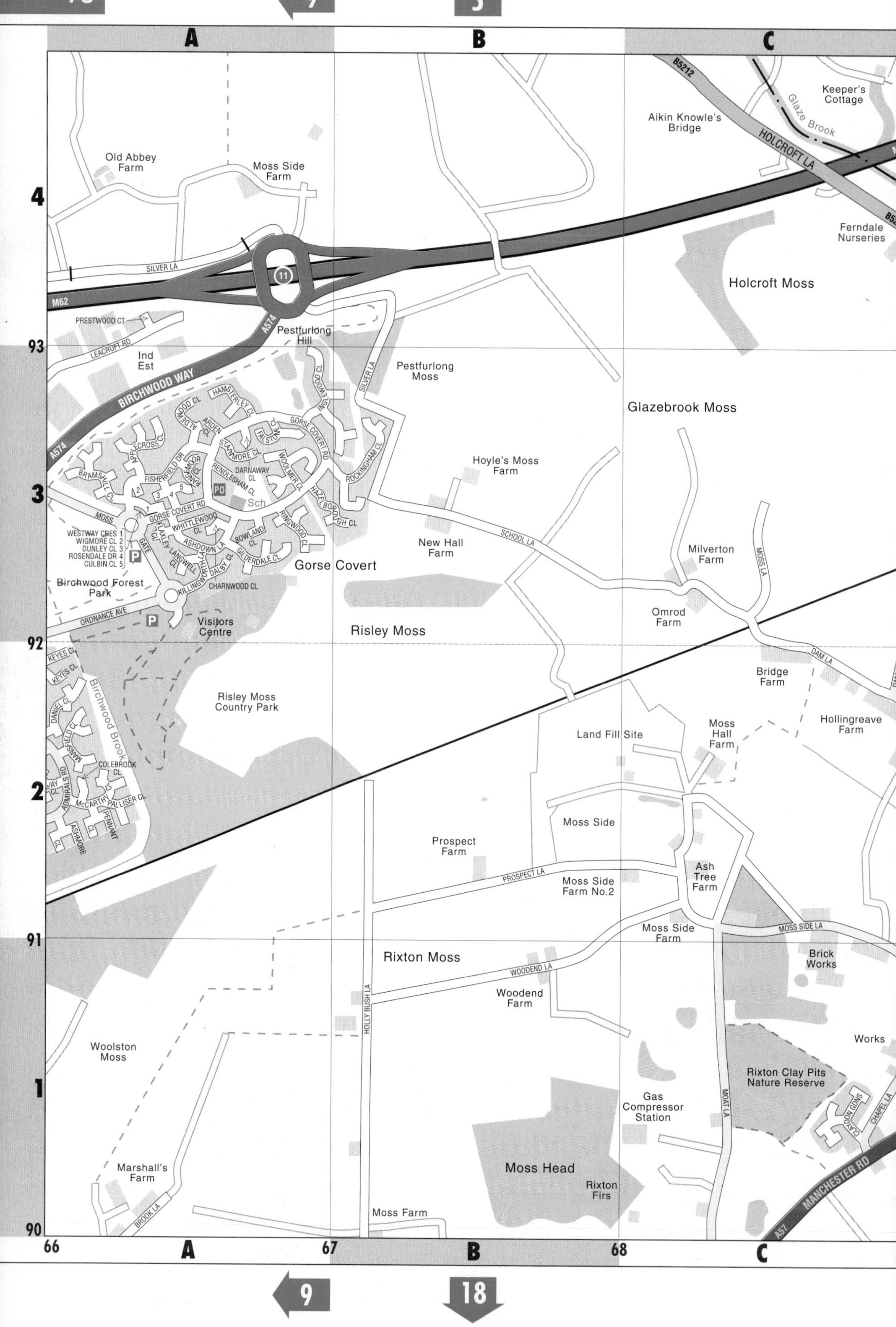

A   B   C

Keeper's Cottage
B5212
Glaze Brook
Aikin Knowle's Bridge
HOLCROFT LA
B52

Old Abbey Farm
Moss Side Farm

4

Ferndale Nurseries

Holcroft Moss

SILVER LA
M62
A574
PRESTWOOD CT
LEACROFT RD
Ind Est

93

Pestfurlong Hill
Pestfurlong Moss

Glazebrook Moss

BIRCHWOOD WAY
A574

Hoyle's Moss Farm

Moss
HAMSPLEY CL
GORSE COVERT RD
ROCKINGHAM CL
SILVER LA

3

FISHERFIELD DR
DARNAWAY CL
RENDLESHAM CL
HAZELBOROUGH CL
WOOLMER CL
TELSTON

SCHOOL LA
Milverton Farm
MOSS LA

PO
Sch

WESTWAY CRES 1
WIGMORE CL 2
DUNLEY CL 3
ROSENDALE DR 4
CULBIN CL 5
GATE
GORSE COVERT RD
WHITTLEWOOD
ASHDOWN LA
LANGWELL
BOWLAND CL
GILDERDALE CL
RINGWOOD CL

New Hall Farm

Gorse Covert

Omrod Farm

Birchwood Forest Park
CHARNWOOD CL
KILLINGS
DALEY CL

ORDNANCE AVE
P
Visitors Centre

Risley Moss

DAM LA

Bridge Farm

92

KEYES CL
KEYES CL
BIRCHWOOD BROOK
Risley Moss Country Park

Land Fill Site
Moss Hall Farm
Hollingreave Farm

DANIEL CL
MANSFIELD CL
COLEBROOK CL
WAY CL
KIRKWHARFE CL
McCARTH
PALLISER CL
PENNANT
ASHMORE

Moss Side

2

Prospect Farm
Ash Tree Farm

PROSPECT LA
Moss Side Farm No.2
MOSS SIDE LA

Moss Side Farm

91

Rixton Moss
WOODEND LA

Brick Works

HOLLY BUSH LA
Woodend Farm

MOAT LA
CHAPEL LA
Works

Woolston Moss

Rixton Clay Pits Nature Reserve
CLAY MOOR GDNS

1

Gas Compressor Station

Marshall's Farm
BROOK LA

Moss Head
Rixton Firs
MANCHESTER RD
A57

Moss Farm

90

66   A   67   B   68   C

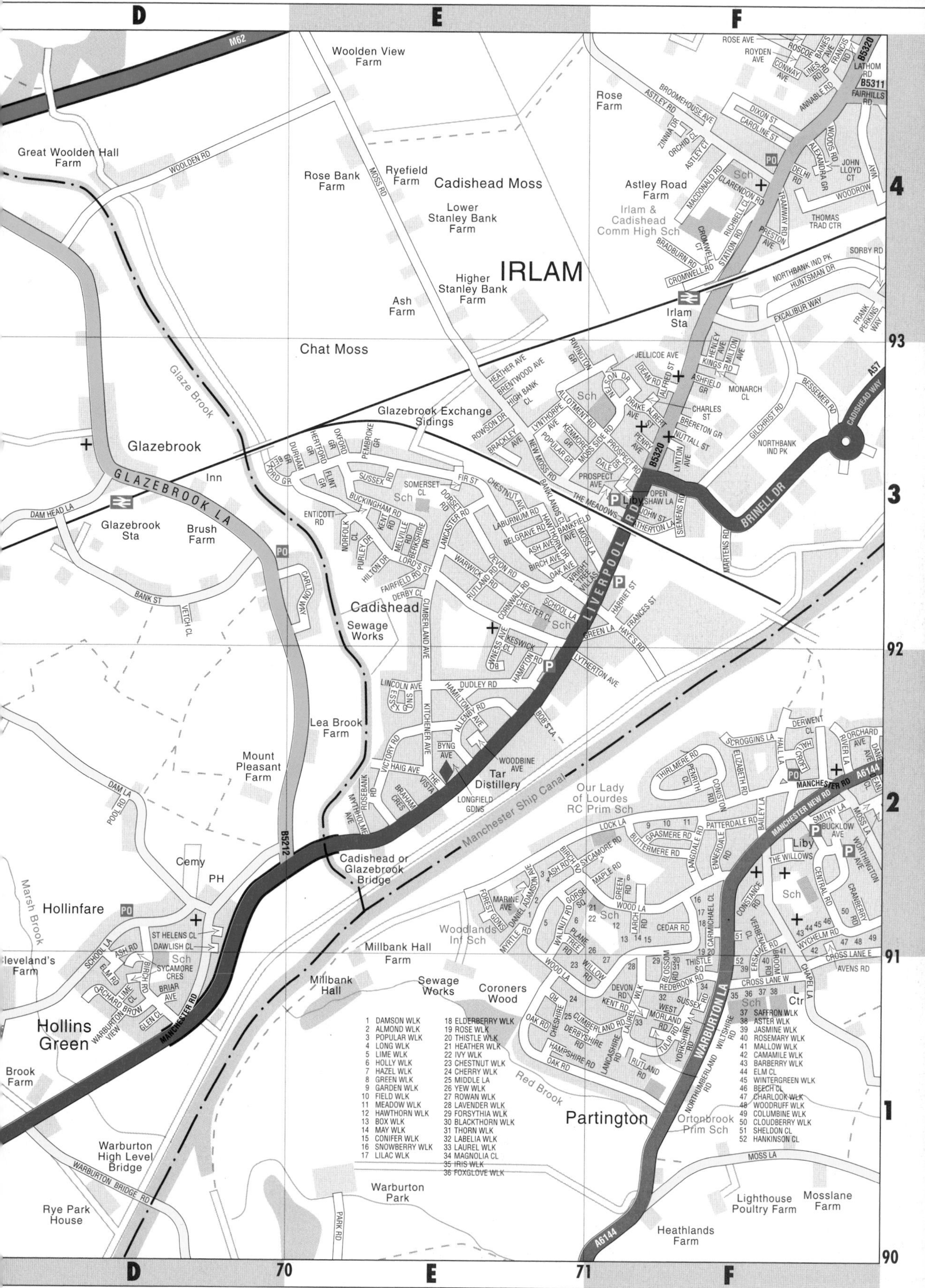

D
E
F
M62
Woolden View Farm
Great Woolden Hall Farm
WOOLDEN RD
Rose Bank Farm
MOSS RD
Ryefield Farm
Cadishead Moss
Lower Stanley Bank Farm
Rose Farm
Astley Road Farm
Irlam & Cadishead Comm High Sch
IRLAM
Higher Stanley Bank Farm
Ash Farm
Irlam Sta
Chat Moss
Glaze Brook
Glazebrook Exchange Sidings
Glazebrook
GLAZEBROOK LA
Inn
Glazebrook Sta
Brush Farm
DAM HEAD LA
BANK ST
VETCH CL
CARLTON WAY
Cadishead
Sewage Works
Lea Brook Farm
Mount Pleasant Farm
Tar Distillery
LIVERPOOL RD
B5320
B5212
B5311
A57
A6144
BRINELL DR
CADISHEAD WAY
NORTHBANK IND PK
HUNTSMAN DR
EXCALIBUR WAY
FRANK PERKINS WAY
SORBY RD
BESSEMER RD
GILCHRIST RD
MONARCH CL
THOMAS TRAD CTR
JOHN LLOYD CT
WOODROW
ROSE AVE
ROYDEN AVE
LATHOM RD
FAIRHILLS RD
ANNABLE RD
BROOMEHOUSE AVE
ASTLEY RD
CAROLINE ST
DIXON ST
STATION RD
CROMWELL RD
Manchester Ship Canal
Our Lady of Lourdes RC Prim Sch
Cadishead or Glazebrook Bridge
Cemy
PH
Hollinfare
Marsh Brook
Cleveland's Farm
Hollins Green
Brook Farm
MANCHESTER RD
Millbank Hall Farm
Millbank Hall
Sewage Works
Coroners Wood
Woodlands Inf Sch
Red Brook
Partington
Ortonbrook Prim Sch
WARBURTON LA
MANCHESTER NEW RD
MOSS LA
Warburton High Level Bridge
WARBURTON BRIDGE RD
Rye Park House
Warburton Park
PARK RD
Heathlands Farm
Lighthouse Poultry Farm
Mosslane Farm
1 DAMSON WLK
2 ALMOND WLK
3 POPULAR WLK
4 LONG WLK
5 LIME WLK
6 HOLLY WLK
7 HAZEL WLK
8 GREEN WLK
9 GARDEN WLK
10 FIELD WLK
11 MEADOW WLK
12 HAWTHORN WLK
13 BOX WLK
14 MAY WLK
15 CONIFER WLK
16 SNOWBERRY WLK
17 LILAC WLK
18 ELDERBERRY WLK
19 ROSE WLK
20 THISTLE WLK
21 HEATHER WLK
22 IVY WLK
23 CHESTNUT WLK
24 CHERRY WLK
25 MIDDLE LA
26 YEW WLK
27 ROWAN WLK
28 LAVENDER WLK
29 FORSYTHIA WLK
30 BLACKTHORN WLK
31 THORN WLK
32 LABELIA WLK
33 LAUREL WLK
34 MAGNOLIA CL
35 IRIS WLK
36 FOXGLOVE WLK
37 SAFFRON WLK
38 ASTER WLK
39 JASMINE WLK
40 ROSEMARY WLK
41 MALLOW WLK
42 CAMAMILE WLK
43 BARBERRY WLK
44 ELM CL
45 WINTERGREEN WLK
46 BEECH CL
47 CHARLOOK WLK
48 WOODRUFF WLK
49 COLUMBINE WLK
50 CLOUDBERRY WLK
51 SHELDON CL
52 HANKINSON CL
4
93
3
92
2
91
1
90
70
71

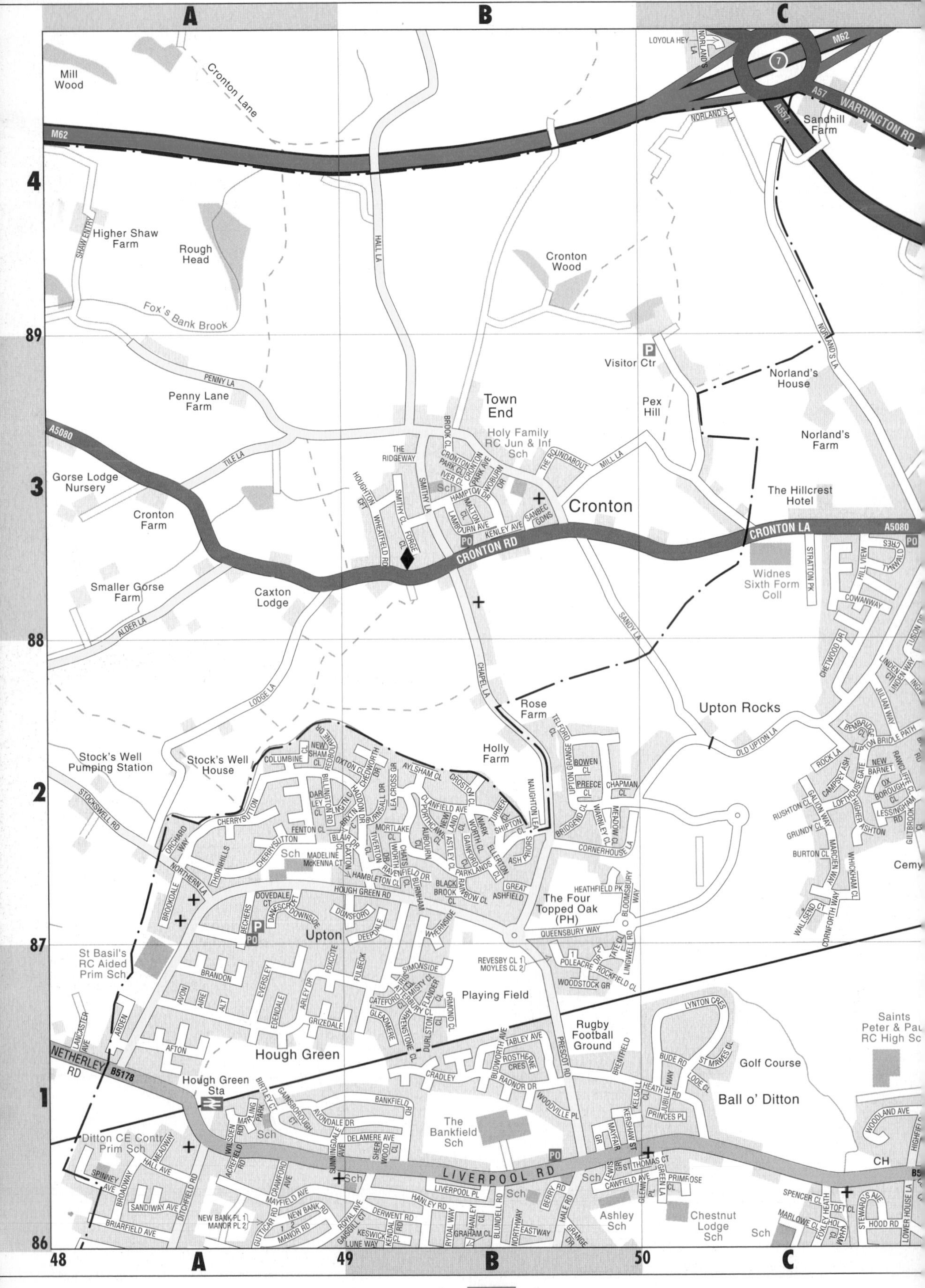
A
B
C
Mill Wood
Cronton Lane
M62
LOYOLA HEY
NORLAND'S LA
7
A57 WARRINGTON RD
A557
Sandhill Farm
4
SHAW ENTRY
Higher Shaw Farm
Rough Head
HALL LA
Cronton Wood
Fox's Bank Brook
89
P
Visitor Ctr
Norland's House
PENNY LA
Penny Lane Farm
Town End
Pex Hill
A5080
BROOK CL
Holy Family RC Jun & Inf Sch
Norland's Farm
THE RIDGEWAY
CRONTON PARK CL
CRONTON PARK AVE
WOBURN DR
THE ROUNDABOUT
MILL LA
TILE LA
Gorse Lodge Nursery
3
HOUGHTON CFT
SMITHY CL
SMITHY LA
IVER CL
Sch
HAMPTON DR
MALTON CL
Cronton
The Hillcrest Hotel
Cronton Farm
WHEATFIELD RD
FORGE CL
LAMBOURN AVE
KENLEY AVE
SANBEC GDNS
CRONTON LA
PO
CRONTON RD
STRATTON PK
HILL VIEW
Widnes Sixth Form Coll
Smaller Gorse Farm
Caxton Lodge
COWANWAY
ALDER LA
88
SANDY LA
CHETWOOD DR
CHAPEL LA
LINDEN WAY
JULIAN WAY
LODGE LA
Rose Farm
TELFORD CL
Upton Rocks
OLD UPTON LA
UPTON BRIDLE PATH
Stock's Well Pumping Station
Stock's Well House
COLUMBINE CL
NEW SHAM CL
OXTON CL
Holly Farm
BOWEN CL
UPTON GRANGE
ROCK LA
AYLSHAM CL
LEA CROSS GR
CROSTON CL
NAUGHTON LA
PREECE CL
CHAPMAN CL
RUSHTON CL
STOCKSWELL RD
2
CHERRYSUTTON
BILLINGTON RD
HADDON DR
BURNSALL DR
CLANFIELD AVE
TURNER CL
BRIDGEND CL
WARWLEY CL
MEADOW CL
GRUNDY CL
LOFTHOUSE GATE
ORCHARD WAY
FENTON CL
MORTLAKE CL
SHIPTON CL
MARK WORTH CL
ASTLEY CL
GAINFORD CL
CORNERHOUSE LA
BURTON CL
MARCIEN WAY
WHICKHAM CL
Cemy
THORNHILLS
CHERRYSUTTON
Sch
MADELINE McKENNA CT
BLAIR DR
CAXTON CL
TIVERTON CL
CHATSWORTH CL
RAVENFIELD DR
ASH PRIORS
PARKLANDS CL
NORTHERN LA
HAMBLETON CL
BURNHAM CL
BLACKBROOK CL
RAINBOW CL
GREAT ASHFIELD
HEATHFIELD PK
BLOOMSBURY WAY
BROOKDALE
DOVEDALE CL
HOUGH GREEN RD
The Four Topped Oak (PH)
WALLSEND CT
CORNFORTH WAY
BECHERS
DANESCROFT
DOWNSIDE
DUNSFORD
DEEPDALE
Upton
WHERNSIDE
QUEENSBURY WAY
87
St Basil's RC Aided Prim Sch
FOXCOTE
FULBECK
SIMONSIDE
REVESBY CL 1
MOYLES CL 2
POLEACRE DR
TATE CL
ROCKFIELD CL
LINGWELL RD
BRANDON
EVERSLEY
WOODSTOCK GR
AVON
AIRE
ALT
EDENDALE
ARLEY DR
CATEFORD CL
FLANDER CL
ORMOND CL
Playing Field
LYNTON CRES
Saints Peter & Paul RC High Sch
LANCASTER AVE
ARDEN
GRIZEDALE
GLEADMERE
DURLSTON CL
Rugby Football Ground
TABLEY AVE
BUDWORTH AVE
ROSTHERNE CRES
PRESCOT RD
BRENTFIELD
BUDE RD
ST MAWES CL
AFTON
Hough Green
Golf Course
NETHERLEY RD
B5178
CRADLEY
RADNOR DR
HEATHER RD
JUBILEE WAY
LOOE CL
Hough Green Sta
Ball o' Ditton
1
BIRTLEY CT
GAINSBOROUGH CT
BANKFIELD RD
WOODVILLE PL
KELSALL CL
KERSHAW ST
PRINCES PL
WOODLAND AVE
AVONDALE DR
The Bankfield Sch
Sch
Ditton CE Contr Prim Sch
MEADWAY
HALL AVE
WILSDEN RD
ACREFIELD RD
DELAMERE AVE
SHERWOOD CL
MAYFAIR GR
PO
ST THOMAS CT
CH
SPINNEY AVE
BROADWAY
SUNNINGDALE AVE
Sch
LIVERPOOL RD
Sch
CAWFIELD AVE
PRIMROSE CL
CRAWFORD AVE
MAYFIELD AVE
LIVERPOOL PL
Sch
SPENCER CL
SANDIWAY AVE
DITCHFIELD RD
NEW BANK PL 1
MANOR PL 2
NEW BANK RD
MANOR RD
ROYAL AVE
DERWENT RD
HANLEY RD
BLUNDELL RD
BERRY RD
HALE RD
Ashley Sch
Chestnut Lodge Sch
MARLOWE CL
TOFT CL
STEWARDS AVE
HOOD RD
LOWER HOUSE LA
BRIARFIELD AVE
GUTTICAR RD
GARSGILL CT
KESWICK CL
KENDAL RD
RYDAL WAY
HANLEY CL
GRAHAM CL
NORTHWAY
EASTWAY
GRANGE DR
Sch
86
48
A
49
B
50
C

14

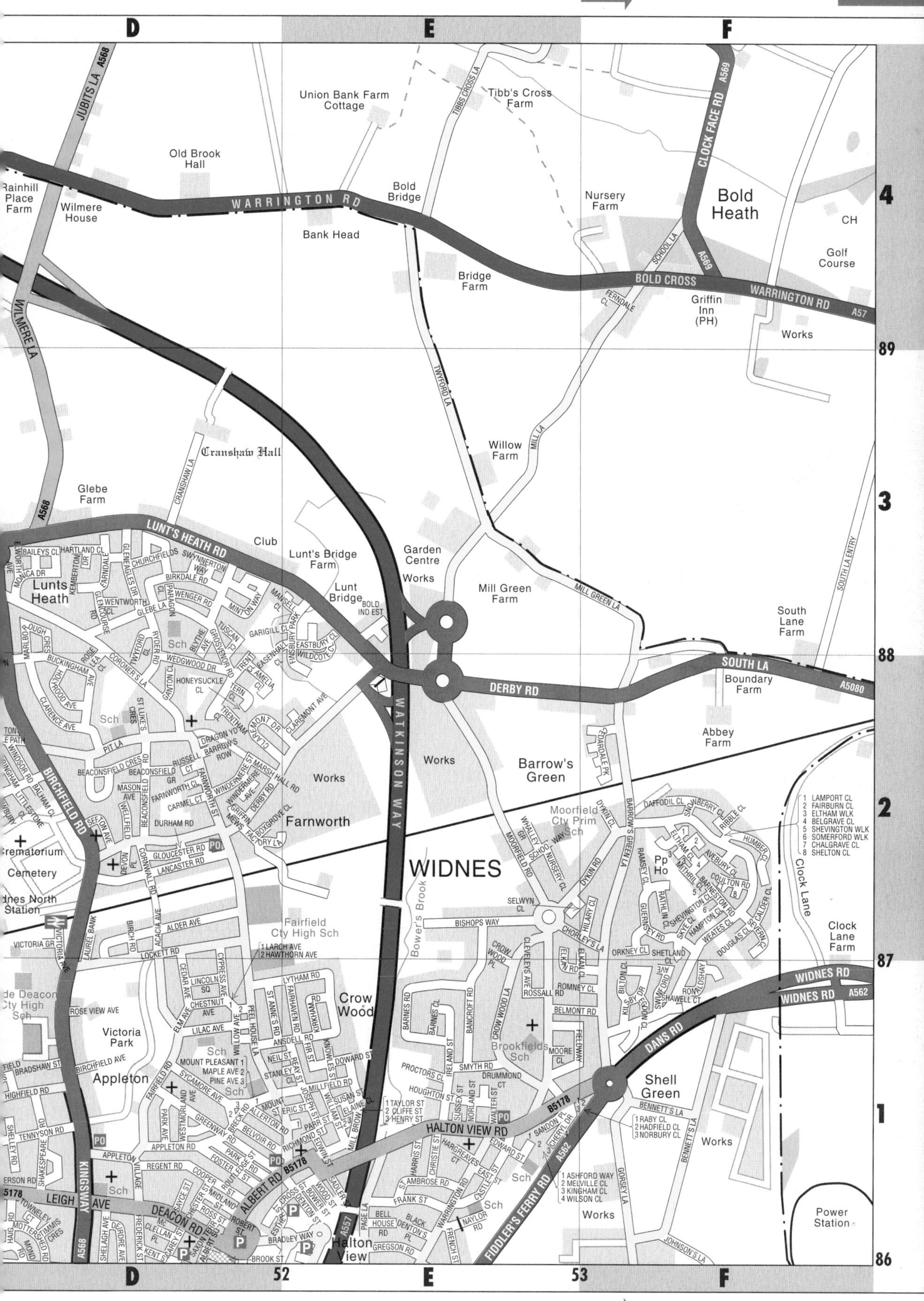
D
E
F
Union Bank Farm Cottage
Tibb's Cross Farm
Old Brook Hall
Rainhill Place Farm
Wilmere House
WARRINGTON RD
Bank Head
Bold Bridge
Nursery Farm
Bold Heath
CLOCK FACE RD
A569
CH
Golf Course
BOLD CROSS
WARRINGTON RD
A57
Griffin Inn (PH)
Works
Bridge Farm
WILMERE LA
JUBITS LA
A568
Cranshaw Hall
Glebe Farm
Willow Farm
MILL LA
TWYFORD LA
LUNT'S HEATH RD
Club
Lunt's Bridge Farm
Garden Centre
Works
Lunt Bridge
Mill Green Farm
MILL GREEN LA
South Lane Farm
SOUTH LANE ENTRY
Lunts Heath
SOUTH LA
A5080
Boundary Farm
DERBY RD
WATKINSON WAY
Abbey Farm
Works
Barrow's Green
Works
Farnworth
WIDNES
BIRCHFIELD RD
Crematorium
Cemetery
Widnes North Station
Moorfield Cty Prim Sch
1 LAMPORT CL
2 FAIRBURN CL
3 ELTHAM WLK
4 BELGRAVE CL
5 SHEVINGTON WLK
6 SOMERFORD WLK
7 CHALGRAVE CL
8 SHELTON CL
Clock Lane
Clock Lane Farm
Fairfield Cty High Sch
Bower's Brook
Crow Wood
Victoria Park
Appleton
WIDNES RD
A562
DANS RD
Shell Green
Brookfields Sch
HALTON VIEW RD
B5178
1 RABY CL
2 HADFIELD CL
3 NORBURY CL
1 TAYLOR ST
2 CLIFFE ST
3 HENRY ST
1 ASHFORD WAY
2 MELVILLE CL
3 KINGHAM CL
4 WILSON CL
Works
Power Station
KINGSWAY
LEIGH AVE
DEACON RD
ALBERT RD
FIDDLER'S FERRY RD
A557
Halton View
4
89
3
88
2
87
1
86
52
53

23

14

A B C

Lingley Mere
North West Water Authority HQ
Billington CL
Finch's Plantation
Whittle Brook
Great Sankey L Ctr
Great Sankey Cty High Sch
Golf Course
South Park Plantation
Eccles Plantation
Park Farm
Barrow Hall Cty Prim Sch
Brow Farm
Wensleydale CL
Airedale CL
Kingsdale CL
Twyntowndale Dr
Coldale
Widdale CL
Barrowdale
Cordale
Fordale CL
Bisby
Teesdale CL 1
Garsdale CL 2
Swaledale CL
Halton Dr
Lilford
Conifer
Woodside
Wilmot Ave
Foreland CL
Bembridge CL
Godshill CL
Whitkirk CL
Freshwater CL
Leon
Totland CL
Mayfair CL
1 Coogee Ave
2 Clovelly Ave
Cronulla Dr
1 2
Warwick
Stanley
York
Princess
Ave
North View
Hall Terr
Rowan
Cedar
Vine Cres
Bargyloo
A57 WARRINGTON RD
Dawson House
Shank La
Shorewell CL
Ruscolm CL
Muriel CL
Audre CL
Lingley Rd
Keith Ave
Bromfield Way
Wroxham Rd
Sunnyside
Park Rd
The Rd
Ranworth Rd
North CL
Lingwood Rd
Jonesbury Dr
Campbell Cres
89
PH
Pyecroft CL
Hilary CL
Pyecroft Rd
Sanderson CL
PH
Victoria Ave
Kircaldy CL
Kintore CL
Park Road Cty Prim Sch
Dilcance
Thetford Rd
Laburnum Farm
Liverpool Rd
Henderson CL
Edward Rd
Friends La
LIVERPOOL RD
Sheringham
Yarmouth Rd
Sankey Sta
Station Rd
Hayfield Farm
Sandy La
Brightwell CL
Kingston Ave 1
Southfields Ave 2
Beechwood Dr
The Dale
Greenside Farm
Sch
St Vincent Rd
St Mary's Rd
3
Sandy Lane Farm
LABURNUM LA
St Joseph's CL
Walton Ave
Friars Ave
St Alban Rd
St Stephen's Rd
South La
Cunningham
Burnham
Upton
Sch
Susan Dr
Groarke CL
Kenyon Dr
Denise Ave
Norton Ave
Larch Ave
Windmill La
City Rd
1 Helston CL
2 William Penn CL
Heath Rd
Holly Terr
88
A5080
SOUTH LA
Stocks La
Coniston Ave
Dartmouth Rd
Meeting La
Combe Rd
Barbauld CL
Paignton CL
Bideford CL
Honiton Way
Jubilee Ave
PO
1 2
Liby
Gerry
Formby
Coronation Dr
Four Top'd Oak
Avon Ave
Daisy Bank Rd
Cherry Tree Ave
Hillside
Ainsdale CL
Hesketh
Penketh Cty Prim Sch
Ellesmere Dr
Lynton
Barnstaple Way
Porlock CL
Arlington Dr
Denby
Oak Dr
Denehurst Dr
Recn Gd
A5
Brook Farm
Greenall Ave
Greenall CL
Victoria CL
Bank
Avistock Dr
WARRINGTON RD
2
FARNWORTH RD
A5080
WIDNES RD
A562
Padstow CL
Beadnell Dr
Pewrth
PO
Fenham Dr
Pop Ar Ave
Oak CL
Maple CL
Hall Nook
Southlands Ave
Marston CL
Hamble
Doe Green
Cuerdley Rd
Beech Ave
Newlyn Gdns
Harlyn Gdns
Penrose CL
Tannery La
Rothay Dr
Roeburn
Station Rd
St Brides CL
Falmouth CL
Brimeleigh Cres
Walkers La
St Austel CL
Bramble CL
Ditchfield
Finlay Ave
Radlett CL
Chapel
Schs
Penketh
LC
MOWCROFT LA
Back La
87
Cuerdley Green
Cuerdley Cross
A562
WIDNES RD
PH
Wrights Lane
Taylor's Lane
Marsh End Farm
Marsh La
Fiddler's Ferry
St Helens Canal (dis)
PH
LC
River Mersey
Mersey Way
Fiddler's Ferry Reach
Power Station
1
86

54 A 55 B 56 C

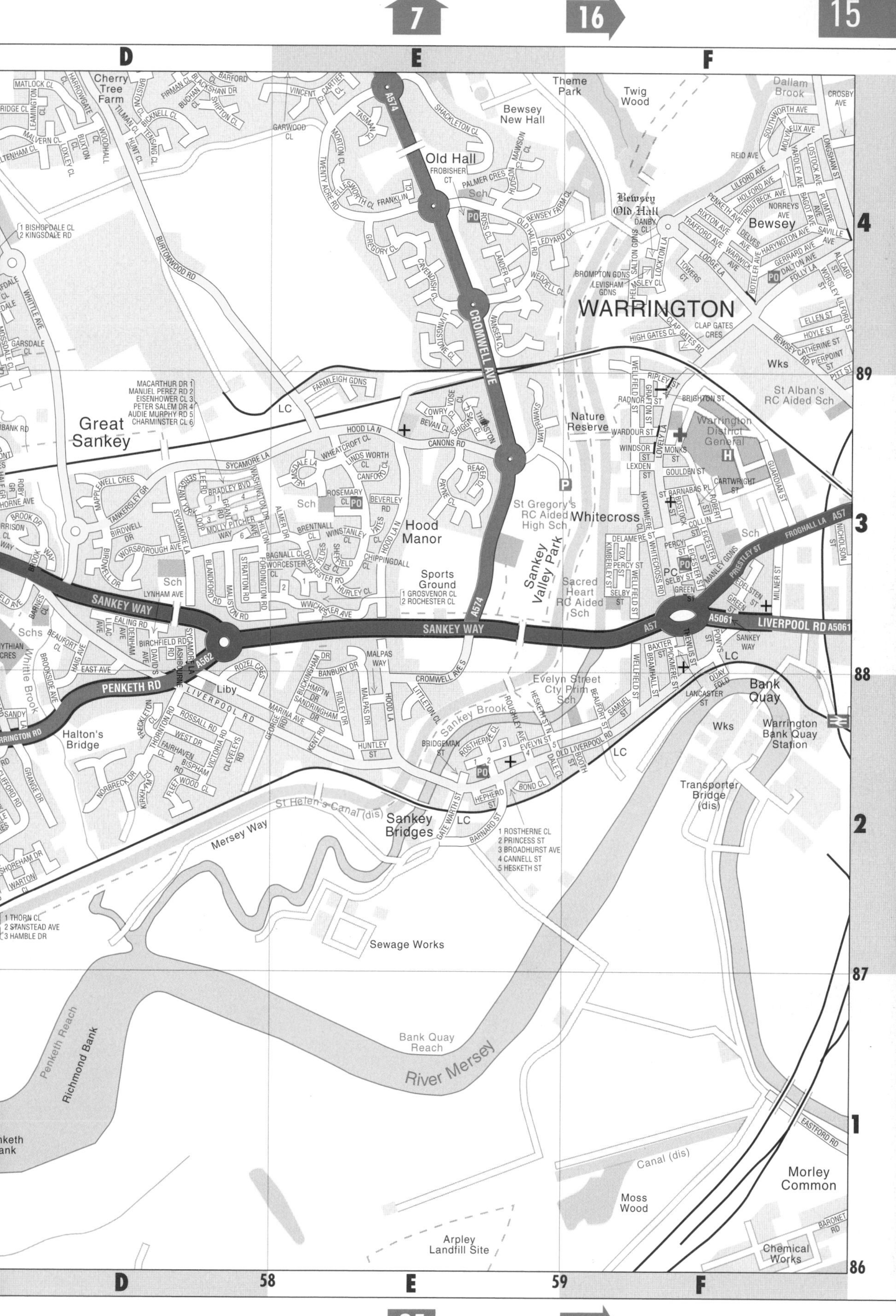

D
E
F

4

89

3

88

2

87

1

86

WARRINGTON

Theme Park

Twig Wood

Dallam Brook

Crosby Ave

Cherry Tree Farm

Old Hall

Bewsey New Hall

Bewsey Old Hall

Bewsey

St Alban's RC Aided Sch

Warrington District General H

Great Sankey

Nature Reserve

St Gregory's RC Aided High Sch

Whitecross

Hood Manor

Sports Ground
1 GROSVENOR CL
2 ROCHESTER CL

Sankey Valley Park

Sacred Heart RC Aided Sch

SANKEY WAY

SANKEY WAY

PENKETH RD

LIVERPOOL RD A5061

Bank Quay

Warrington Bank Quay Station

Liby

Halton's Bridge

Evelyn Street City Prim Sch

Sankey Brook

Transporter Bridge (dis)

Sankey Bridges

St Helen's Canal (dis)

Mersey Way

1 ROSTHERNE CL
2 PRINCESS ST
3 BROADHURST AVE
4 CANNELL ST
5 HESKETH ST

Wks

1 THORN CL
2 STANSTEAD AVE
3 HAMBLE DR

Sewage Works

Penketh Reach

Richmond Bank

Bank Quay Reach

River Mersey

Morley Common

Canal (dis)

Moss Wood

Chemical Works

Arpley Landfill Site

Eastford Rd

1 BISHOPDALE CL
2 KINGSDALE RD

MACARTHUR DR 1
MANUEL PEREZ RD 2
EISENHOWER CL 3
PETER SALEM DR 4
AUDIE MURPHY RD 5
CHARMINSTER CL 6

CROMWELL AVE

A574

A574

A57

A562

A5061

LC

LC

LC

LC

LC

PO

PO

PO

PO

PO

15
8

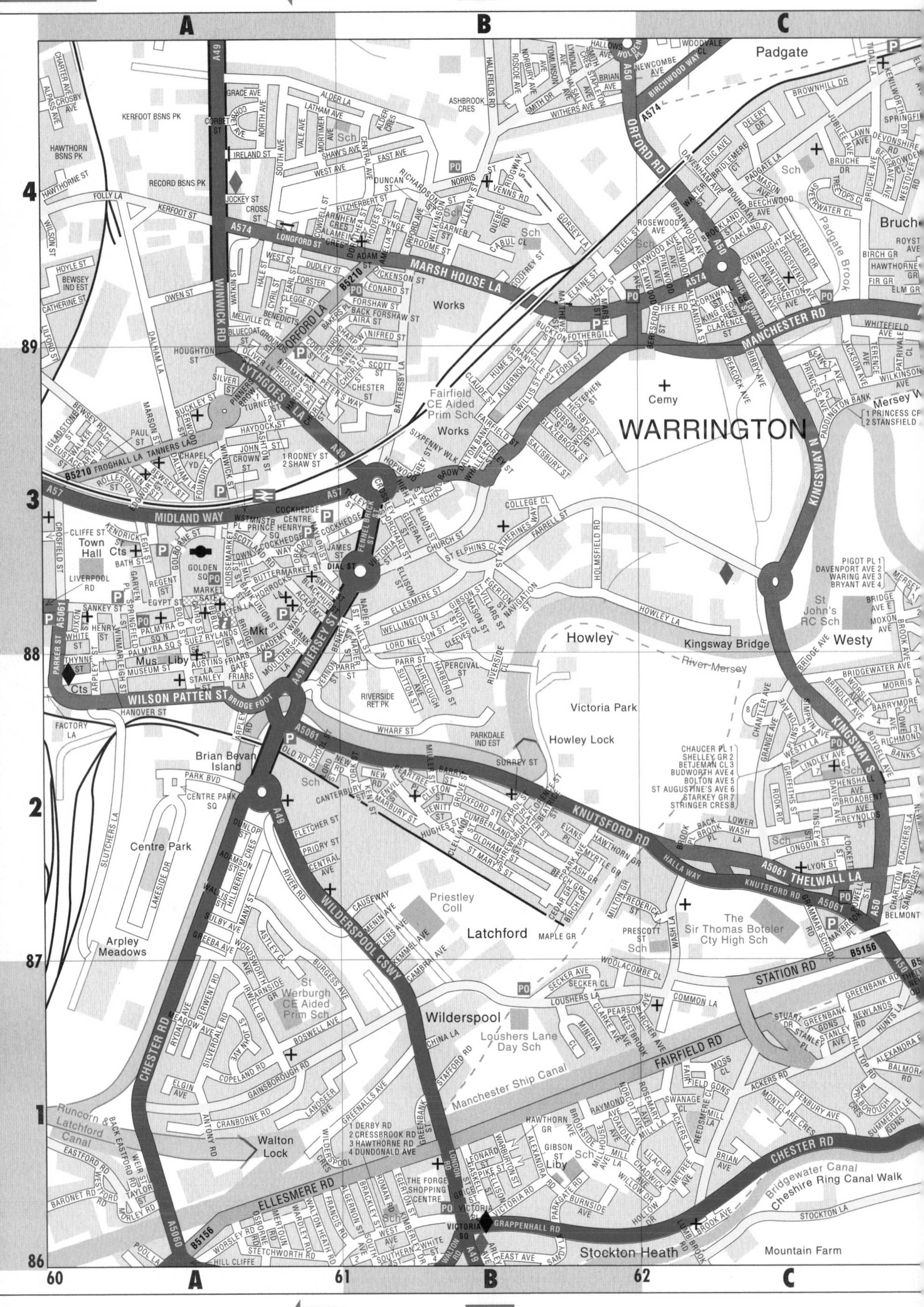
A
B
C
4
3
2
1
89
88
87
86
60
61
62
WARRINGTON
Padgate
Bruche
Howley
Westy
Latchford
Wilderspool
Stockton Heath
Mountain Farm
Victoria Park
Howley Lock
Kingsway Bridge
River Mersey
Cemy
Works
Town Hall
Cts
Mus. Liby
Mkt
Golden Sq
Brian Bevan Island
Centre Park
Arpley Meadows
Walton Lock
Runcorn & Latchford Canal
Manchester Ship Canal
Bridgewater Canal
Cheshire Ring Canal Walk
Fairfield CE Aided Prim Sch
St John's RC Sch
Priestley Coll
St Werburgh CE Aided Prim Sch
Loushers Lane Day Sch
The Sir Thomas Boteler Cty High Sch
Padgate Brook
Riverside Ret Pk
Parkdale Ind Est
Kerfoot Bsns Pk
Hawthorn Bsns Pk
Record Bsns Pk
Bewsey Ind Est
WINWICK RD
MIDLAND WAY
MARSH HOUSE LA
MANCHESTER RD
ORFORD RD
KINGSWAY N
KINGSWAY S
KNUTSFORD RD
THELWALL LA
WILSON PATTEN ST
MERSEY ST
LYTHGOES LA
WILDERSPOOL CSWY
CHESTER RD
FAIRFIELD RD
STATION RD
ELLESMERE RD
GRAPPENHALL RD
LONGFORD ST
FROGHALL LA
BIRCHWOOD WAY

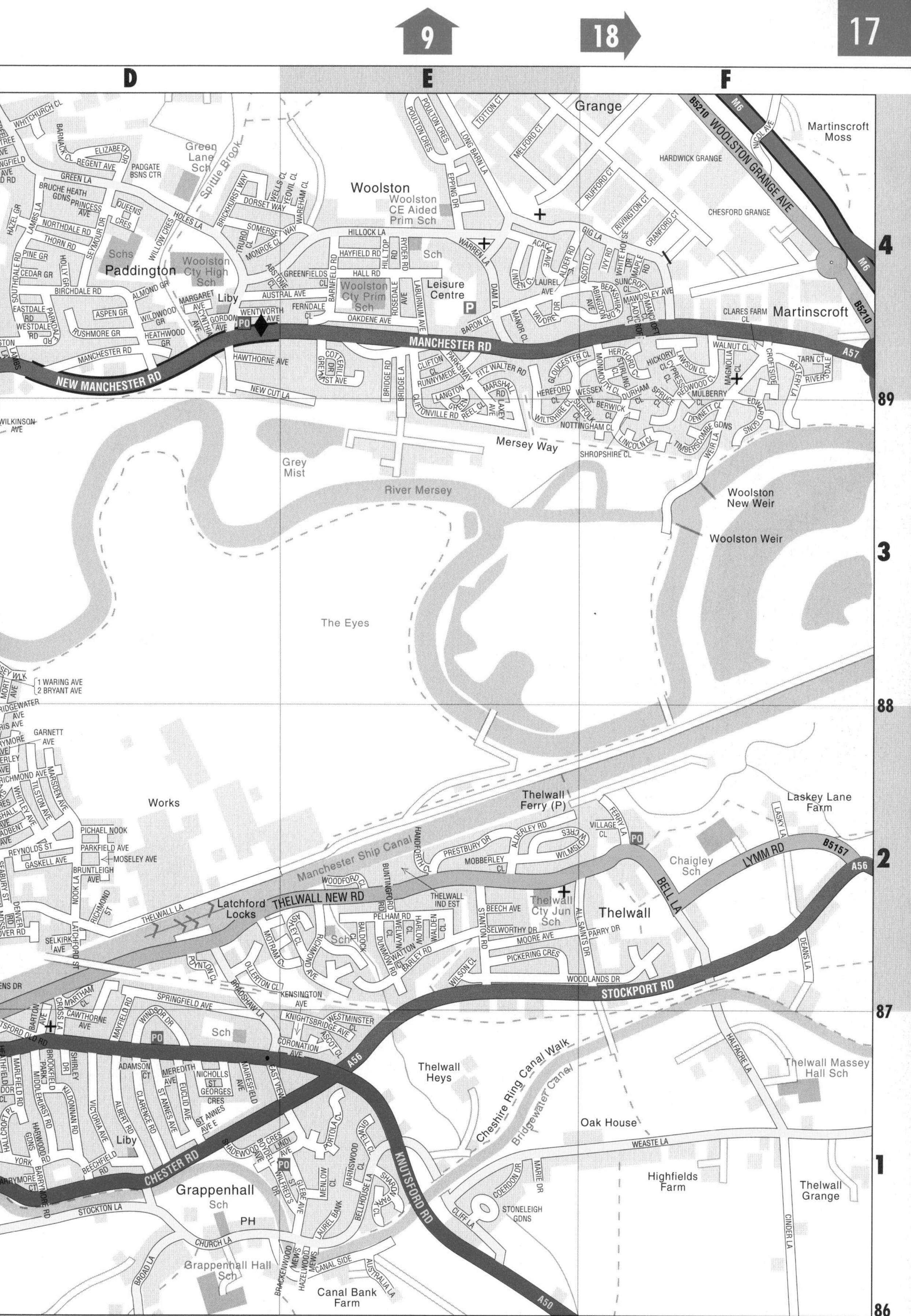

D   E   F

WHITCHURCH CL

Green Lane Sch

Grange

Martinscroft Moss

B5210 WOOLSTON GRANGE AVE

Hardwick Grange

M6

Spittle Brook

Woolston

Woolston CE Aided Prim Sch

Chesford Grange

Paddington

Woolston Cty High Sch

Woolston Cty Prim Sch

Leisure Centre

Clares Farm

Martinscroft

4

M6

B5210

A57

MANCHESTER RD

89

NEW MANCHESTER RD

Mersey Way

Grey Mist

Woolston New Weir

Woolston Weir

3

River Mersey

The Eyes

88

Works

Thelwall Ferry (P)

Laskey Lane Farm

Manchester Ship Canal

Chaigley Sch

LYMM RD

B5157

A56

2

Latchford Locks

THELWALL NEW RD

Thelwall Ind Est

Thelwall Cty Jun Sch

Thelwall

Cheshire Ring Canal Walk

STOCKPORT RD

87

Thelwall Heys

Bridgewater Canal

Thelwall Massey Hall Sch

Oak House

CHESTER RD

KNUTSFORD RD

Weaste La

Highfields Farm

Thelwall Grange

1

Grappenhall

Sch

PH

Stoneleigh Gdns

A50

Grappenhall Hall Sch

Canal Bank Farm

86

D   64   E   65   F

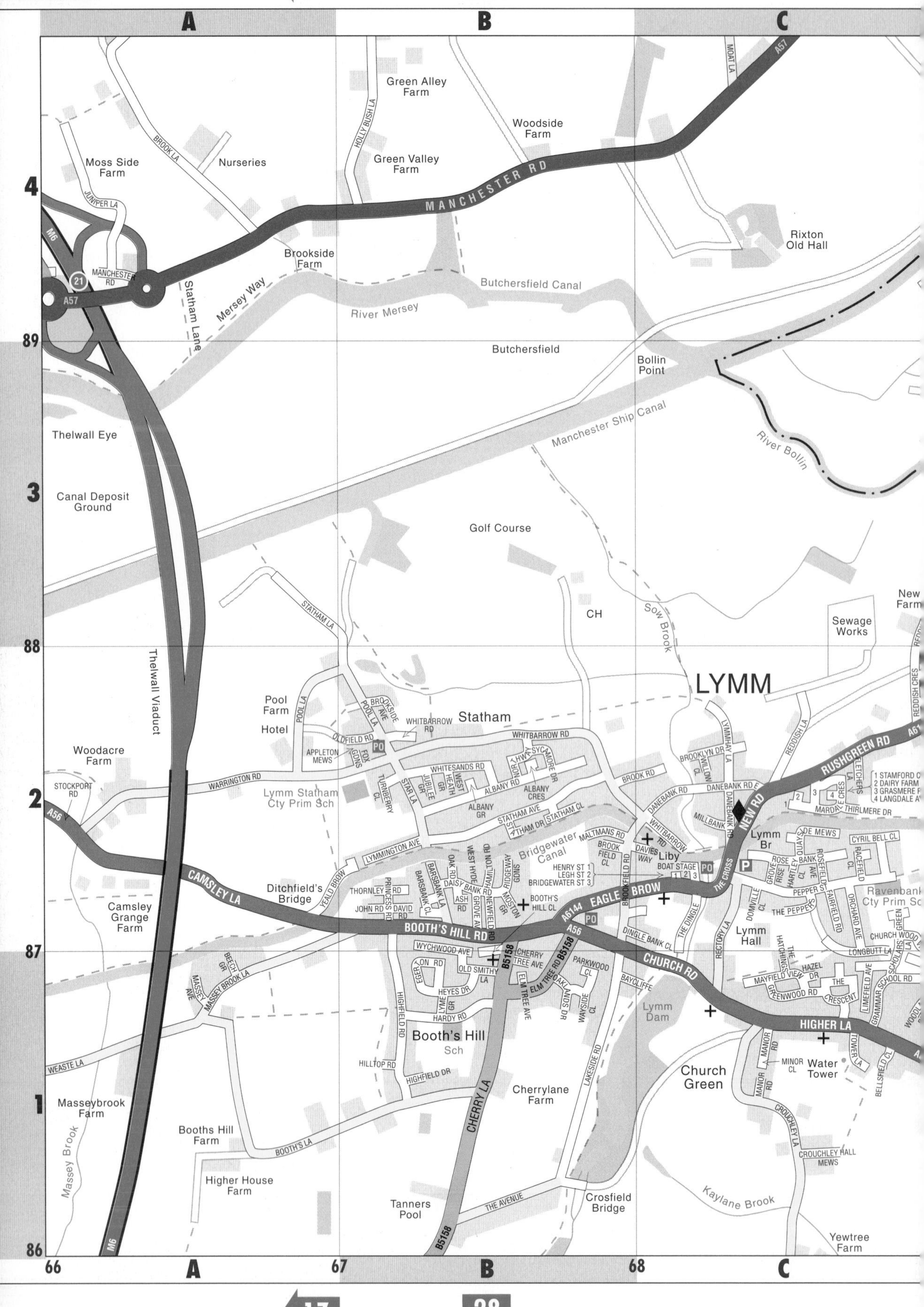

A   B   C

4
Moss Side Farm
Nurseries
Green Alley Farm
Woodside Farm
Rixton Old Hall
BROOK LA
HOLLY BUSH LA
Green Valley Farm
MANCHESTER RD
MOAT LA
A57
JUNIPER LA
MANCHESTER RD
Brookside Farm
Butchersfield Canal
21
M6
Statham Lane
Mersey Way
River Mersey
Butchersfield
Bollin Point
A57

89
Thelwall Eye
Manchester Ship Canal
River Bollin

3
Canal Deposit Ground
Golf Course
CH
Sow Brook
New Farm
Sewage Works

STATHAM LA
Thelwall Viaduct

88
Pool Farm Hotel
Statham
LYMM
POOL LA
POOL LA
BROOKSIDE AVE
WHITBARROW RD
WHITBARROW RD
LYMMAY LA
REDDISH LA
RUSHGREEN RD
A6144
REDDISH CRES
Woodacre Farm
OLDFIELD RD
FOX COVNS
APPLETON MEWS
PO
WHITESANDS RD
WEST HEATH
ALBANY RD
SYCAMORE DR
HWY
BROOK RD
BROOKLYN DR
WILLOW
LETCHERS LA
1 STAMFORD O
2 DAIRY BANK
3 GRASMERE R
4 LANGDALE A

2
STOCKPORT RD
A56
WARRINGTON RD
Lymm Statham Cty Prim Sch
TURBERRY CL
STAR LA
JUBILEE
ALBANY GR
ALBANY CRES
STATHAM AVE
THAM DR STATHAM CL
MALTMANS RD
BROOK
FIELD CL
DANEBANK AVE
DANEBANK RD E
MILLBANK
NEW RD
MARDA
THIRLMERE DR
DE MEWS
Lymm Br
ROSE
HARTLEY
RISE
PEPPER CL
CYRIL BELL CL
RACEFIELD
RAVENBANK
Cty Prim Sch
Camsley Grange Farm
CAMSLEY LA
Ditchfield's Bridge
TEAL D BROW
LYMMINGTON AVE
OLD HYDE RD
WEST HYDE RD
RENWELL RD
KIDSWAY
Bridgewater Canal
HENRY ST 1
LEGH ST 2
BRIDGEWATER ST 3
DAVIES WAY
BOAT STAGE
Liby
WHITBARROW RD
THE CROSS
EAGLE BROW
PO
A6144
THE DINGLE
DOMVILLE
LYMM HALL
THE PEPPERS
ORCHARD AVE
CHURCH WOOD
LONGBUTT LA
THORNLEY RD
PRINCESS RD
DAVID
JOHN RD
BARSBANK CL
OAK RD
DAISY BANK RD
ASH RD
HUSTON
BOOTH'S HILL CL
BROOKFIELD RD
DINGLE BANK CL
RECTORY LA
MAYFIELD VIEW
HATCHINGS
THE
GRENWOOD RD
HAZEL DR
LIMEFIELD AVE
THE CRESCENT

87
THORNLEY RD
WYCHWOOD AVE
OLD SMITHY LA
B5158
CHERRY TREE AVE
PARKWOOD CL
CHURCH RD
BAYCLIFFE
Lymm Dam
Church Green
GRAMMAR SCHOOL RD
SCHOLARS CL
MANOR RD
HIGHER LA
WOOL
A6
HEYES DR
LYME GR
HARDY RD
ELM TREE AVE
ELM TREE RD
JACKSON DR
WAYSIDE CL
LAKESIDE RD
MANOR CL
Water Tower
CROWLEY LA
HAZEL RD
BELLSFIELD CL
HIGHFIELD RD
Booth's Hill Sch
HIGHFIELD DR
CHERRY LA
Cherrylane Farm
MINOR CL

1
Masseybrook Farm
WEASTE LA
HILLTOP RD
MASSEY BROOK LA
MASSEY AVE
BEECH GR
Booths Hill Farm
BOOTH'S LA
Higher House Farm
Tanners Pool
B5158
THE AVENUE
Crosfield Bridge
Kaylane Brook
Yewtree Farm

86
66   67   68
A   B   C
Massey Brook
M6

11
20

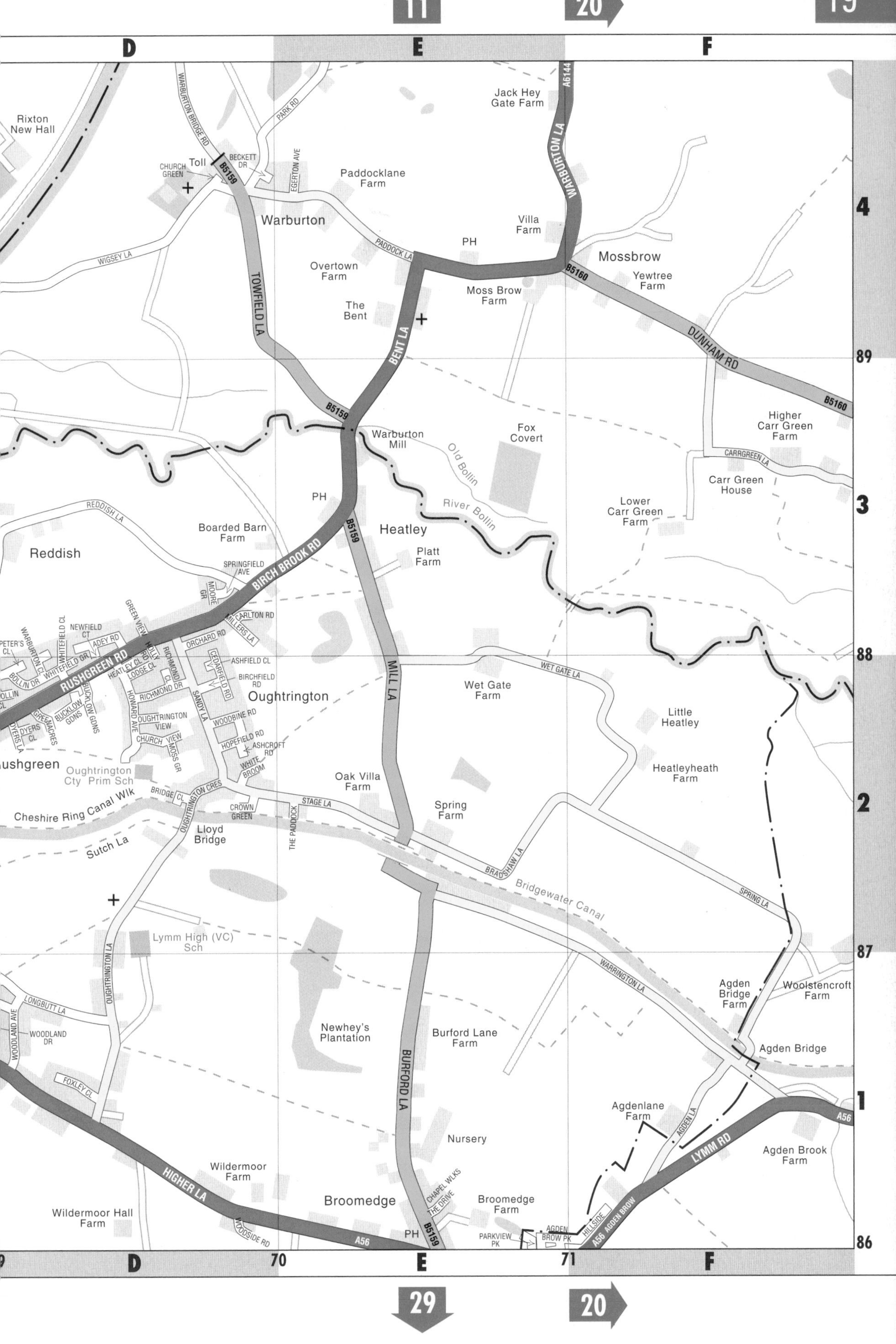
D
E
F
Rixton New Hall
Toll
Church Green
Beckett Dr
Warburton Bridge Rd
Park Rd
Egerton Ave
Paddocklane Farm
Jack Hey Gate Farm
A6144
Warburton La
B5159
Warburton
Wigsey La
Paddock La
PH
Villa Farm
Mossbrow
Overtown Farm
B5160
Yewtree Farm
Moss Brow Farm
Towfield La
The Bent
Bent La
Dunham Rd
Warburton Mill
Old Bollin
Fox Covert
Higher Carr Green Farm
Carrgreen La
Carr Green House
River Bollin
Lower Carr Green Farm
Reddish La
Boarded Barn Farm
Heatley
Platt Farm
Reddish
Birch Brook Rd
Springfield Ave
Moore Gr
Carlton Rd
Millers La
Rushgreen Rd
Orchard Rd
Ashfield Cl
Birchfield Rd
Cedarfield Rd
Oughtrington
Mill La
Wet Gate La
Wet Gate Farm
Little Heatley
Heatleyheath Farm
Sandy La
Woodbine Rd
Hopefield Rd
Ashcroft Rd
White Broom
Richmond Dr
Richmond Cl
Heatley Cl
Lodge Cl
Howard Ave
Oughtrington View
Church View
Moss Gr
Bucklow Gdns
Greenacres
Dyers Cl
Dyers La
Green View
Holly Rd
Newfield Ct
Adey Rd
Whitefield Cl
Whitefield Gr
Warburton Cl
Peter's Cl
Bollin Dr
ushgreen
Oughtrington Cty Prim Sch
Oughtrington Cres
Bridge Cl
Crown Green
Stage La
The Paddock
Oak Villa Farm
Spring Farm
Cheshire Ring Canal Wlk
Lloyd Bridge
Sutch La
Bradshaw La
Bridgewater Canal
Spring La
Lymm High (VC) Sch
Oughtrington La
Warrington La
Agden Bridge Farm
Woolstencroft Farm
Agden Bridge
Longbutt La
Woodland Ave
Woodland Dr
Newhey's Plantation
Burford Lane Farm
Burford La
Foxley Cl
Agdenlane Farm
Agden La
Lymm Rd
A56
Agden Brook Farm
Nursery
Higher La
Wildermoor Farm
Broomedge
Chapel Wlks
The Drive
Broomedge Farm
Wildermoor Hall Farm
Woodside Rd
PH
Parkview Pk
Agden Brow Pk
Hillside
A56 Agden Brow
4
89
3
88
2
87
1
86
70
71

29
20

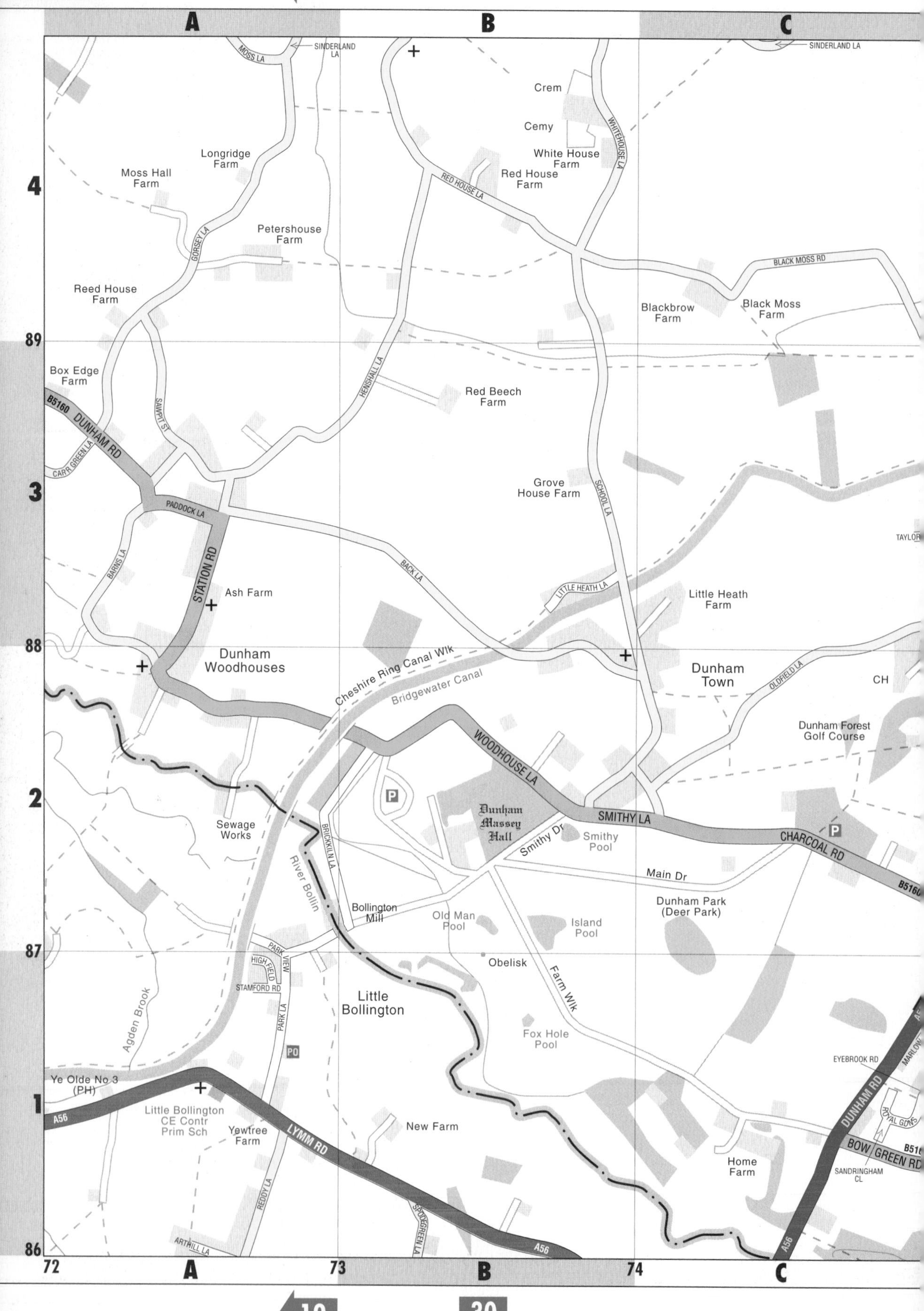

A　　　　　　B　　　　　　C

MOSS LA

SINDERLAND LA

SINDERLAND LA

Crem

Cemy

WHITEHOUSE LA

White House Farm

Longridge Farm

Moss Hall Farm

Red House LA

Red House Farm

4

GORSEY LA

Petershouse Farm

BLACK MOSS RD

Reed House Farm

Blackbrow Farm

Black Moss Farm

89

SAWPIT ST

Box Edge Farm

HENSHALL LA

B5160

DUNHAM RD

Red Beech Farm

CARR GREEN LA

PADDOCK LA

Grove House Farm

SCHOOL LA

TAYLOR

3

BARNS LA

STATION RD

BACK LA

Ash Farm

LITTLE HEATH LA

Little Heath Farm

Dunham Woodhouses

Cheshire Ring Canal Wlk

Dunham Town

OLDFIELD LA

CH

88

Bridgewater Canal

Dunham Forest Golf Course

WOODHOUSE LA

2

P

Sewage Works

BRICKKILN LA

Dunham Massey Hall

Smithy Dr

SMITHY LA

Smithy Pool

CHARCOAL RD

P

B5160

River Bollin

Main Dr

Dunham Park (Deer Park)

Bollington Mill

Old Man Pool

Island Pool

87

PARK VIEW

Obelisk

Farm Wlk

HIGH FIELD

STAMFORD RD

Agden Brook

PARK LA

Little Bollington

Fox Hole Pool

EYEBROOK RD

MARLOW

PO

DUNHAM RD

Ye Olde No 3 (PH)

ROYAL GONS

1

A56

REDDY LA

LYMM RD

Little Bollington CE Contr Prim Sch

Yewtree Farm

New Farm

BOW GREEN RD

B516

Home Farm

SANDRINGHAM CL

ARTHILL LA

SONGGREEN LA

A56

A56

86

72　　　　A　　　　73　　　　B　　　　74　　　　C

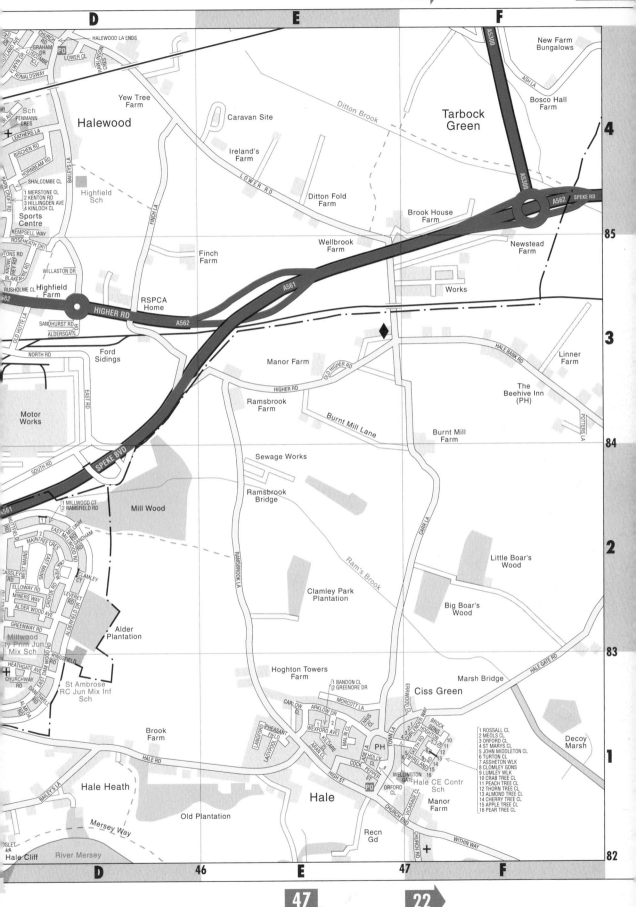

D
E
F
Halewood
Yew Tree Farm
Caravan Site
Ireland's Farm
Ditton Brook
Tarbock Green
New Farm Bungalows
Bosco Hall Farm
A5300
ASH LA
LOWER RD
Ditton Fold Farm
Brook House Farm
A562
SPEKE RD
Highfield Sch
Sports Centre
Finch Farm
Wellbrook Farm
Newstead Farm
Works
A561
Highfield Farm
HIGHER RD
RSPCA Home
Ford Sidings
Manor Farm
HALE BANK RD
Linner Farm
The Beehive Inn (PH)
Motor Works
Ramsbrook Farm
Burnt Mill Lane
Burnt Mill Farm
POTTERS LA
Sewage Works
SPEKE BVD
Ramsbrook Bridge
Mill Wood
CARR LA
Little Boar's Wood
Ram's Brook
RAMSBROOK LA
Clamley Park Plantation
Big Boar's Wood
Alder Plantation
Millwood Cty Prim Jun Mix Sch
St Ambrose RC Jun Mix Inf Sch
Hoghton Towers Farm
Marsh Bridge
Ciss Green
HALE GATE RD
Brook Farm
HALE RD
PH
Decoy Marsh
Hale Heath
Hale
Hale CE Contr Sch
Manor Farm
Old Plantation
Mersey Way
Recn Gd
WITHIN WAY
Hale Cliff
River Mersey
1 MILLWOOD CT
2 RAMSFIELD RD
1 BANDON CL
2 GREENORE DR
1 ROSSALL CL
2 MEOLS CL
3 ORFORD CL
4 ST MARYS CL
5 JOHN MIDDLETON CL
6 TURTON CL
7 ASSHETON WLK
8 CLOMLEY GDNS
9 LUMLEY WLK
10 CRAB TREE CL
11 PEACH TREE CL
12 THORN TREE CL
13 ALMOND TREE CL
14 CHERRY TREE CL
15 APPLE TREE CL
16 PEAR TREE CL
1 MERSTONE CL
2 KENTON RD
3 HILLINGDEN AVE
4 KINLOCH CL
4
85
3
84
2
83
1
82
46
47

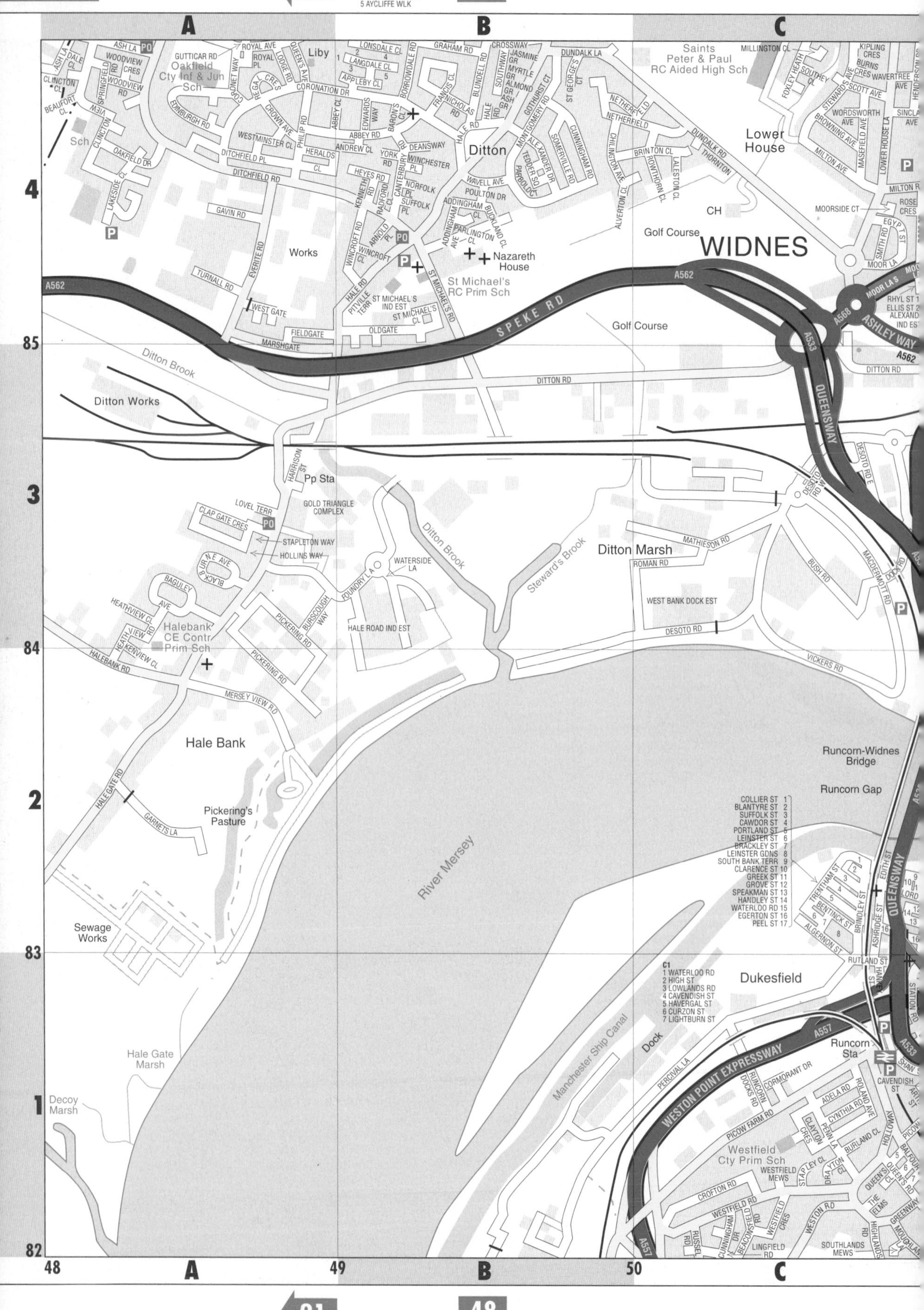
A
B
C
4
85
3
84
2
83
1
82
48
49
50
Oakfield Cty Inf & Jun Sch
Liby
Saints Peter & Paul RC Aided High Sch
Lower House
Ditton
WIDNES
Golf Course
CH
Works
Nazareth House
St Michael's RC Prim Sch
ST MICHAEL'S IND EST
SPEKE RD
A562
DITTON RD
Ditton Brook
Ditton Works
Pp Sta
GOLD TRIANGLE COMPLEX
HALE ROAD IND EST
WATERSIDE LA
Ditton Marsh
Steward's Brook
WEST BANK DOCK EST
DESOTO RD
VICKERS RD
MATHIESON RD
ROMAN RD
BUSH RD
MACDERMOTT RD
QUEENSWAY
A533
A568
ASHLEY WAY
MOOR LA S
Halebank CE Contr Prim Sch
HALEBANK RD
MERSEY VIEW RD
PICKERING RD
Hale Bank
HALE GATE RD
GARNETS LA
Pickering's Pasture
Sewage Works
River Mersey
Hale Gate Marsh
Decoy Marsh
Runcorn-Widnes Bridge
Runcorn Gap
COLLIER ST 1
BLANTYRE ST 2
SUFFOLK ST 3
CAWDOR ST 4
PORTLAND ST 5
LEINSTER ST 6
BRACKLEY ST 7
LEINSTER GDNS 8
SOUTH BANK TERR 9
CLARENCE ST 10
GREEK ST 11
GROVE ST 12
SPEAKMAN ST 13
HANDLEY ST 14
WATERLOO RD 15
EGERTON ST 16
PEEL ST 17
C1
1 WATERLOO RD
2 HIGH ST
3 LOWLANDS RD
4 CAVENDISH ST
5 HAVERGAL ST
6 CURZON ST
7 LIGHTBURN ST
Dukesfield
Manchester Ship Canal
Dock
WESTON POINT EXPRESSWAY
A557
Runcorn Sta
Westfield Cty Prim Sch
WESTON RD
SOUTHLANDS MEWS

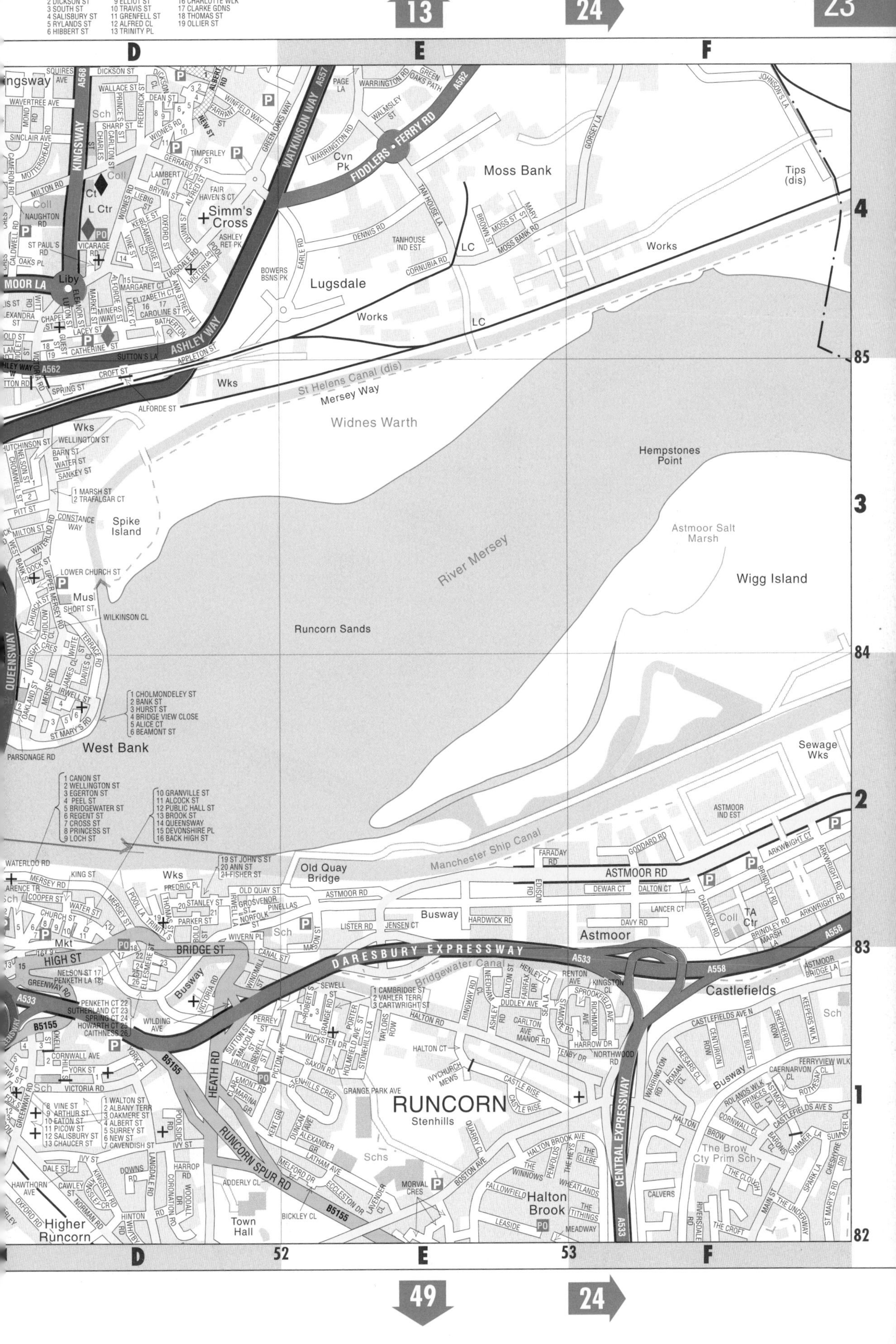

D1
1 ALBERT SQ
2 DICKSON ST
3 SOUTH ST
4 SALISBURY ST
5 RYLANDS ST
6 HIBBERT ST
7 DEAN CL
8 GLADSTONE ST
9 ELLIOT ST
10 TRAVIS ST
11 GRENFELL ST
12 ALFRED CL
13 TRINITY PL
14 EMILY ST
15 MAJOR CROSS ST
16 CHARLOTTE WLK
17 CLARKE GDNS
18 THOMAS ST
19 OLLIER ST
13
24
D
E
F
4
3
2
1
85
84
83
82
52
53
Moss Bank
Simm's Cross
Lugsdale
Works
Tips (dis)
WATKINSON WAY
A557
A562
FIDDLERS FERRY RD
KINGSWAY
ASHLEY WAY
St Helens Canal (dis)
Mersey Way
Widnes Warth
Hempstones Point
Spike Island
Astmoor Salt Marsh
Wigg Island
River Mersey
Runcorn Sands
West Bank
1 CHOLMONDELEY ST
2 BANK ST
3 HURST ST
4 BRIDGE VIEW CLOSE
5 ALICE CT
6 BEAMONT ST
1 CANON ST
2 WELLINGTON ST
3 EGERTON ST
4 PEEL ST
5 BRIDGEWATER ST
6 REGENT ST
7 CROSS ST
8 PRINCESS ST
9 LOCH ST
10 GRANVILLE ST
11 ALCOCK ST
12 PUBLIC HALL ST
13 BROOK ST
14 QUEENSWAY
15 DEVONSHIRE PL
16 BACK HIGH ST
19 ST JOHN'S ST
20 ANN ST
21 FISHER ST
Sewage Wks
ASTMOOR IND EST
Manchester Ship Canal
Old Quay Bridge
ASTMOOR RD
Busway
Astmoor
DARESBURY EXPRESSWAY
A533
A558
Bridgewater Canal
Castlefields
1 CAMBRIDGE ST
2 VAHLER TERR
3 CARTWRIGHT ST
RUNCORN
Stenhills
CENTRAL EXPRESSWAY
RUNCORN SPUR RD
B5155
Halton Brook
The Brow Cty Prim Sch
Higher Runcorn
Town Hall
1 WALTON ST
2 ALBANY TERR
3 OAKMERE ST
4 ALBERT ST
5 SURREY ST
6 NEW ST
7 CAVENDISH ST
8 VINE ST
9 ARTHUR ST
10 EATON ST
11 PICOW ST
12 SALISBURY ST
13 CHAUCER ST
49
24

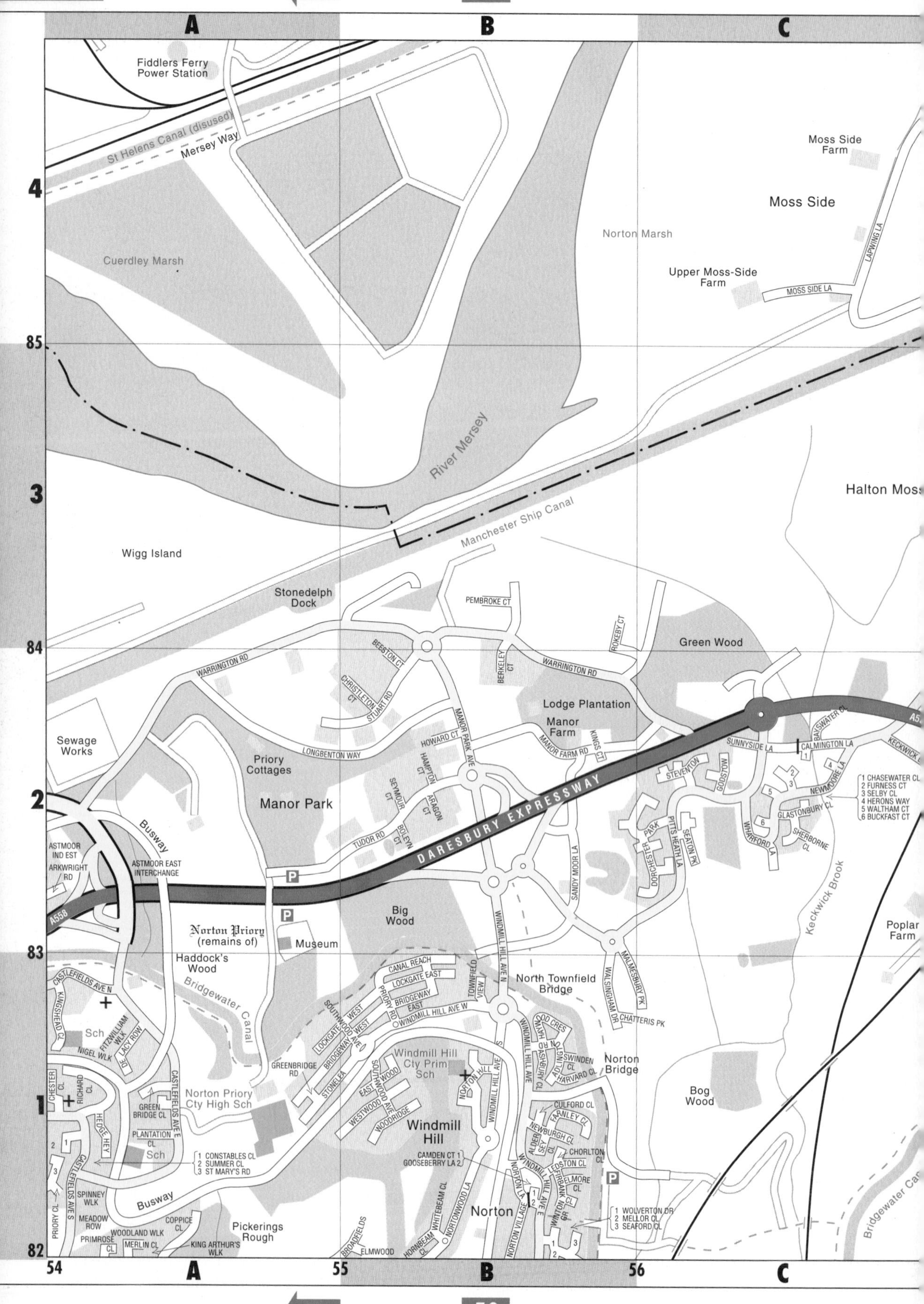

A   B   C

4

85

3

84

2

83

1

82

54   A   55   B   56   C

Fiddlers Ferry
Power Station

St Helens Canal (disused)

Mersey Way

Moss Side
Farm

Moss Side

Norton Marsh

Cuerdley Marsh

Upper Moss-Side
Farm

MOSS SIDE LA

LAPWING LA

River Mersey

Halton Moss

Manchester Ship Canal

Wigg Island

Stonedelph
Dock

PEMBROKE CT

Green Wood

BEESTON CT

BERKELEY
CT

ROXBY CT

WARRINGTON RD

WARRINGTON RD

Sewage
Works

CHRISTLETON
CT

STUART RD

Priory
Cottages

LONGBENTON WAY

HOWARD CT

MANOR PARK AVE

Lodge Plantation

Manor
Farm

MANOR FARM RD

KINGS CT

SUNNYSIDE LA

BAYSWATER CT

CALMINGTON LA

KESWICK

A5

Manor Park

HAMPTON
CT

ARAGON
CT

SEYMOUR
CT

GLEN
CT

STEVENTON

GLOSSOP

NEWMORE LA

1 CHASEWATER CL
2 FURNESS CT
3 SELBY CL
4 HERONS WAY
5 WALTHAM CT
6 BUCKFAST CT

TUDOR RD

DARESBURY EXPRESSWAY

SANDY MOOR LA

PARK
BELSHER

PITTS HEATH LA

SEXTON PK

DORCHESTER LA

GLASTONBURY CL

SHERBORNE
CL

WHARFORD LA

Keckwick Brook

Poplar
Farm

ASTMOOR
IND EST

ARKWRIGHT
RD

Busway

ASTMOOR EAST
INTERCHANGE

A558

P

P

Norton Priory
(remains of)

Museum

Big
Wood

WINDMILL HILL AVE N

MALMESBURY PK

WALSINGHAM DR

CHATTERIS PK

Bog
Wood

Haddock's
Wood

Bridgewater Canal

CANAL REACH

LOCKGATE EAST

BRIDGEWAY
EAST

North Townfield
Bridge

Norton
Bridge

SOUTHDOWN WEST

PRIORY RD

WINDMILL HILL AVE W

TOWNFIELD
VIEW

ODD CRES

Bridgewater Can

Sch

CHESTER CL

KINSHEAD CL

RICHARD CL

FITZWILLIAM
WLK

LACY ROW

DE LACY ROW

NIGEL WLK

CASTLEFIELDS AVE E

Greenbridge
RD

STONE LA

SOUTHDOWN
CL

WESTWOOD
AVE

EAST WOOD

SWINDEN
CL

HARVARD CL

Norton Priory
Cty High Sch

GREEN
BRIDGE CL

PLANTATION
CL

Sch

1 CONSTABLES CL
2 SUMMER CL
3 ST MARY'S RD

Windmill Hill
City Prim
Sch

Windmill
Hill

NORTON HILL AVE

WINDMILL HILL AVE

CULFORD CL

FARNLEY CL

NEWBURGH CL

CHORLTON
CL

LEDSTON CL

Norton

1 CAMDEN CT
2 GOOSEBERRY LA

1 WOLVERTON DR
2 MELLOR CL
3 SEAFORD CL

P

SPINNEY
WLK

MEADOW
ROW

WOODLAND WLK

PRIMROSE
CL

MERLIN CL

COPPICE
CL

KING ARTHUR'S
WLK

Pickerings
Rough

Busway

PRIORY CL

CASTLEFIELDS AVE S

HEDGE HEY

BROADFIELDS

ELMWOOD

HORNBEAM CL

WHITEBEAM CL

NORTONWOOD LA

NORTON VILLAGE

WINDMILL HILL AVE E

WINTON CL

FERNLEE CL

ELMORE
CL

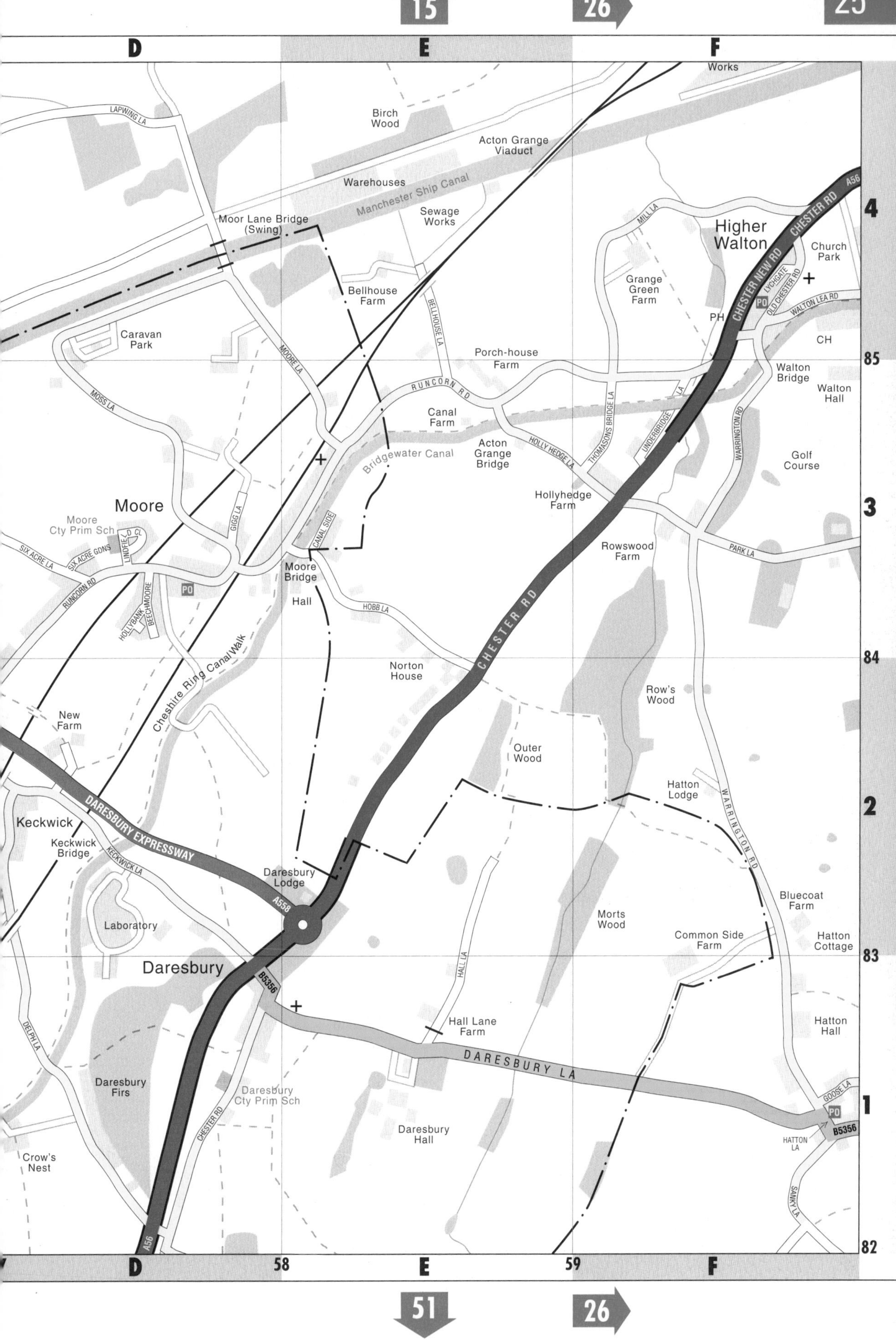

Works

Lapwing La

Birch Wood

Acton Grange Viaduct

Warehouses

Manchester Ship Canal

Sewage Works

Mill La

Higher Walton

Chester New Rd

Chester Rd

A56

4

Moor Lane Bridge (Swing)

Bellhouse Farm

Caravan Park

Moss La

Moore La

Bellhouse La

Grange Green Farm

Lydgate

PO

Old Chester Rd

Church Park

PH

CH

Walton Lea Rd

Runcorn Rd

Porch-house Farm

Walton Bridge

85

Walton Hall

Canal Farm

Bridgewater Canal

Acton Grange Bridge

Holly Hedge La

Thomasons Bridge La

Lingerbridge La

Warrington Rd

Golf Course

Moore

Moore Cty Prim Sch

Lindfield Cl

Gigg La

Hollyhedge Farm

Rowswood Farm

Park La

3

Six Acre La

Six Acre Gdns

Canal Side

Runcorn Rd

PO

Hollybank

Beechmoore

Moore Bridge

Hall

Hobb La

Cheshire Ring Canal Walk

Norton House

Row's Wood

84

New Farm

Outer Wood

Hatton Lodge

Warrington Rd

2

Keckwick

Daresbury Expressway

A558

Keckwick Bridge

Keckwick La

Daresbury Lodge

Bluecoat Farm

Laboratory

Morts Wood

Common Side Farm

Hatton Cottage

Daresbury

B5356

83

Gepr La

Hall La

Hall Lane Farm

Hatton Hall

Daresbury La

Daresbury Firs

Chester Rd

Daresbury Cty Prim Sch

Daresbury Hall

Goose La

PO

B5356

1

Crow's Nest

Hatton La

Sanky La

A56

82

25
16

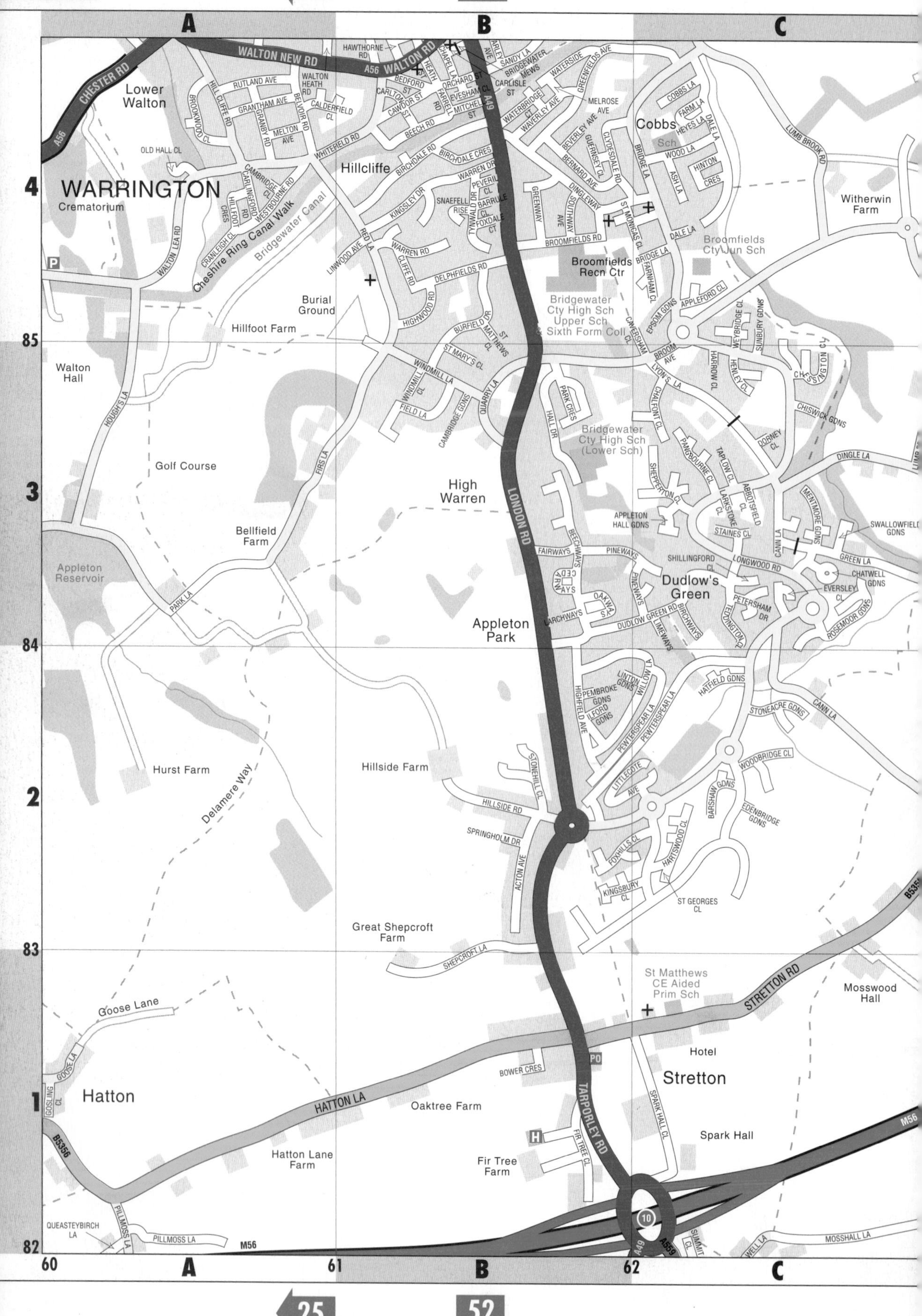
A
B
C
4
3
2
1
85
84
83
82
60
61
62
WARRINGTON
Crematorium
Lower Walton
CHESTER RD
A56
WALTON NEW RD
A56 WALTON RD
HAWTHORNE RD
RUTLAND AVE
GRANTHAM AVE
MELTON AVE
CALDERFIELD CL
BROOKWOOD CL
HILL CLIFFE RD
GRANBY RD
BELVOIR RD
WALTON HEATH RD
BEDFORD ST
CARLTON ST
CAWDOR ST
BEECH RD
FARRELL RD
EVESHAM CL
MITCHELL ST
ORCHARD ST
CARLISLE ST
SANDY LA
BRIDGEWATER MEWS
WATERSIDE
GREENFIELDS AVE
WATERBRIDGE CT
WAVERLEY AVE
MELROSE AVE
A49
OLD HALL CL
WHITEFIELD RD
Hillcliffe
BIRCHDALE RD
BIRCHDALE CRES
WARREN DR
PEVERIL CL
SNAEFELL RISE
BARRULE CL
FOXDALE CT
TYNWALD DR
KINGSLEY DR
CAMBRIDGE CL
CARLINGFORD CL
WESTBOURNE RD
HILLFOOT CRES
CRANLEIGH CL
WALTON LEA RD
Cheshire Ring Canal Walk
Bridgewater Canal
P
LINWOOD AVE
RED LA
WARREN RD
CLIFFE RD
DELPHFIELDS RD
HIGHWOOD RD
Burial Ground
Hillfoot Farm
GREENWAY
SOUTHWAY AVE
DINGLEWAY
BEVERLEY AVE
BERNARD AVE
GUERNSEY CL
CLYDESDALE RD
BROOMFIELDS RD
ST MONICAS CL
Cobbs
Sch
COBBS LA
FARM LA
HEYES LA
DALE LA
WOOD LA
ASH LA
HINTON CRES
BRIDGE LA
DALE LA
Broomfields Recn Ctr
Broomfields Cty Jun Sch
FARNHAM CL
EPSOM GDNS
APPLEFORD CL
CAVERSHAM CL
Bridgewater Cty High Sch Upper Sch & Sixth Form Coll
LUMB BROOK RD
Witherwin Farm
WEYBRIDGE CL
SUNBURY GDNS
CHESSINGTON CL
BROOM AVE
LYON'S LA
HARROW CL
HENLEY CL
CHISWICK GDNS
BURFIELD DR
ST MATTHEWS CL
ST MARY'S CL
WINDMILL LA
WINDMILL CL
FIELD LA
CAMBRIDGE GDNS
QUARRY LA
Walton Hall
HOUGH'S LA
PARK CRES
HALL DR
Bridgewater Cty High Sch (Lower Sch)
CHALFONT CL
PANGBOURNE CL
TAPLOW CL
DORNEY CL
DINGLE LA
Golf Course
FIRS LA
High Warren
LONDON RD
SHEPPERTON CL
APPLETON HALL GDNS
LARKSTOKE CL
ABBOTSFIELD CL
STAINES CL
CANN LA
MENTMORE GDNS
SWALLOWFIELD GDNS
Bellfield Farm
Appleton Reservoir
PARK LA
FAIRWAYS
BEECHWAYS
PINEWAYS
SHILLINGFORD CL
LONGWOOD RD
GREEN LA
CHATWELL GDNS
Dudlow's Green
EVERSLEY CL
PETERSHAM DR
TEDDINGTON CL
ROSEMOOR GDNS
OAKWAYS
LARCHWAYS
DUDLOW GREEN RD
LIMEWAYS
BIRCHWAYS
Appleton Park
LINTON GDNS
WILLOW LA
HATFIELD GDNS
PEMBROKE GDNS
ILFORD GDNS
HIGHFIELD AVE
PEWTERSPEAR LA
STONEACRE GDNS
CANN LA
Hurst Farm
Delamere Way
Hillside Farm
STONEHILL CL
LITTLECOTE AVE
WOODBRIDGE CL
BARSHAW GDNS
EDENBRIDGE GDNS
HILLSIDE RD
SPRINGHOLM DR
ACTON AVE
FOXHILLS CL
HARTSWOOD CL
KINGSBURY CL
ST GEORGES CL
B5356
Great Shepcroft Farm
SHEPCROFT LA
St Matthews CE Aided Prim Sch
STRETTON RD
Mosswood Hall
Goose Lane
GOOSE LA
GOSLING CL
Hatton
HATTON LA
BOWER CRES
PO
Hotel
Stretton
Oaktree Farm
TARPORLEY RD
SPARK HALL CL
Spark Hall
M56
B5356
H
Hatton Lane Farm
Fir Tree Farm
FIR TREE CL
10
QUEASTEYBIRCH LA
PILLMOSS LA
M56
A49
A559
SUMMIT CL
MOSSHALL LA

25
52

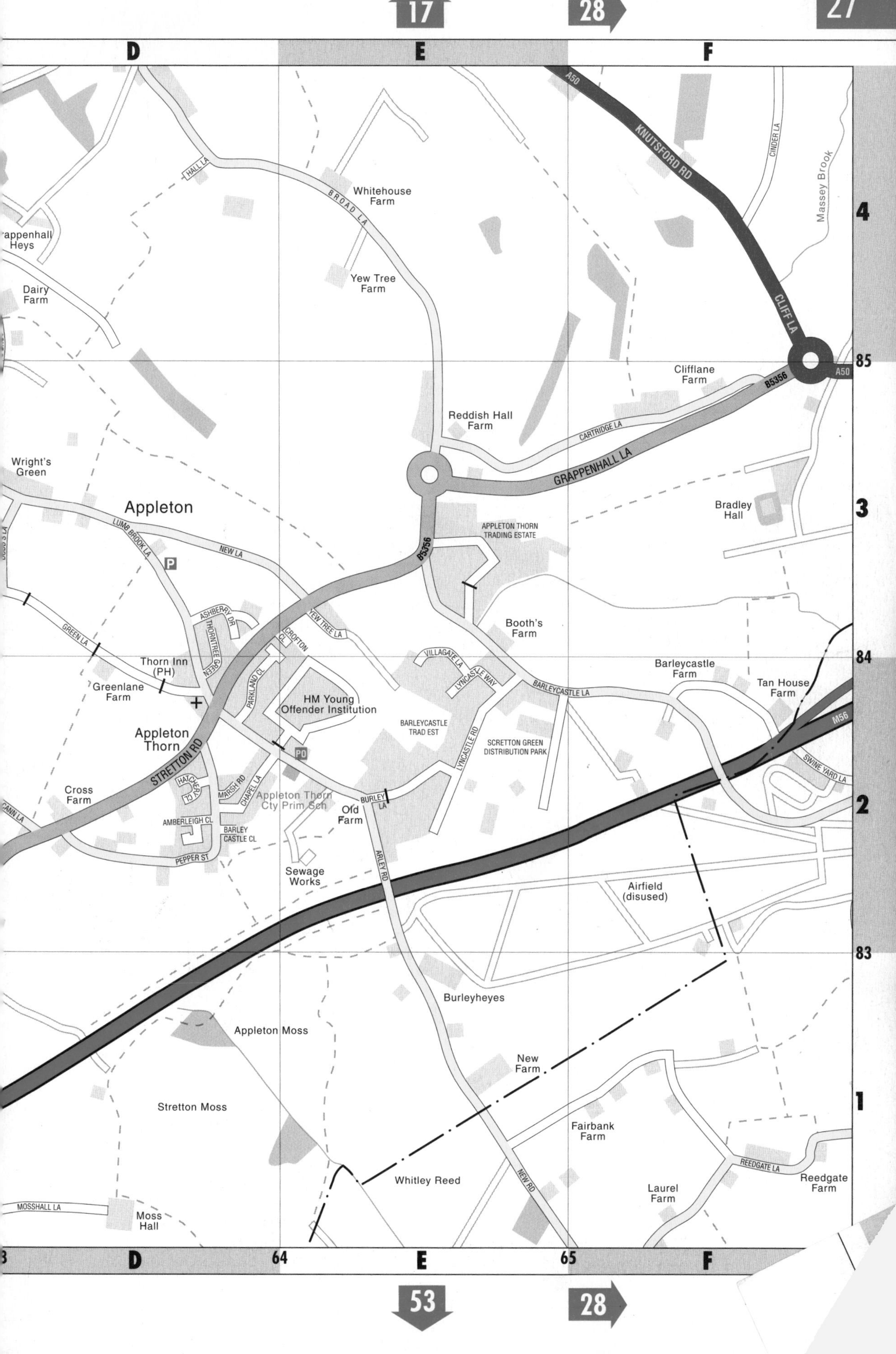

4

85

3

84

2

83

1

Massey Brook

A50
KNUTSFORD RD
CINDER LA
CLIFF LA
B5356
A50
Clifflane Farm
CARTRIDGE LA
GRAPPENHALL LA
Bradley Hall

HALL LA
BROAD LA
Whitehouse Farm
Yew Tree Farm
Reddish Hall Farm

Grappenhall Heys

Dairy Farm

Wright's Green

Appleton

LUMB BROOK LA
NEW LA
P

B5356

APPLETON THORN TRADING ESTATE

Booth's Farm

Barleycastle Farm

Tan House Farm

M56

Thorn Inn (PH)
Greenlane Farm

GREEN LA

ASHBERRY DR
THORNTREE GRN

CROFTON CL
PARKLND CL
YEW TREE LA

VILLAGATE LA
DALE WAY
LYNDALE WAY
BARLEYCASTLE LA

Appleton Thorn

STRETTON RD

HM Young Offender Institution

BARLEYCASTLE TRAD EST

LYNCASTLE RD

SCRETTON GREEN DISTRIBUTION PARK

SWINE YARD LA

Cross Farm

ANN LA

AMBERLEIGH CL
HATCH LA
MARSH RD
CHAPEL LA
BARLEY CASTLE CL
PEPPER ST

PO

Appleton Thorn Cty Prim Sch
Old Farm

BURLEY LA

ARLEY RD

Sewage Works

Airfield (disused)

Appleton Moss

Burleyheyes

New Farm

Fairbank Farm

REEDGATE LA

Reedgate Farm

Stretton Moss

Whitley Reed

NEW RD

Laurel Farm

MOSSHALL LA
Moss Hall

27
18

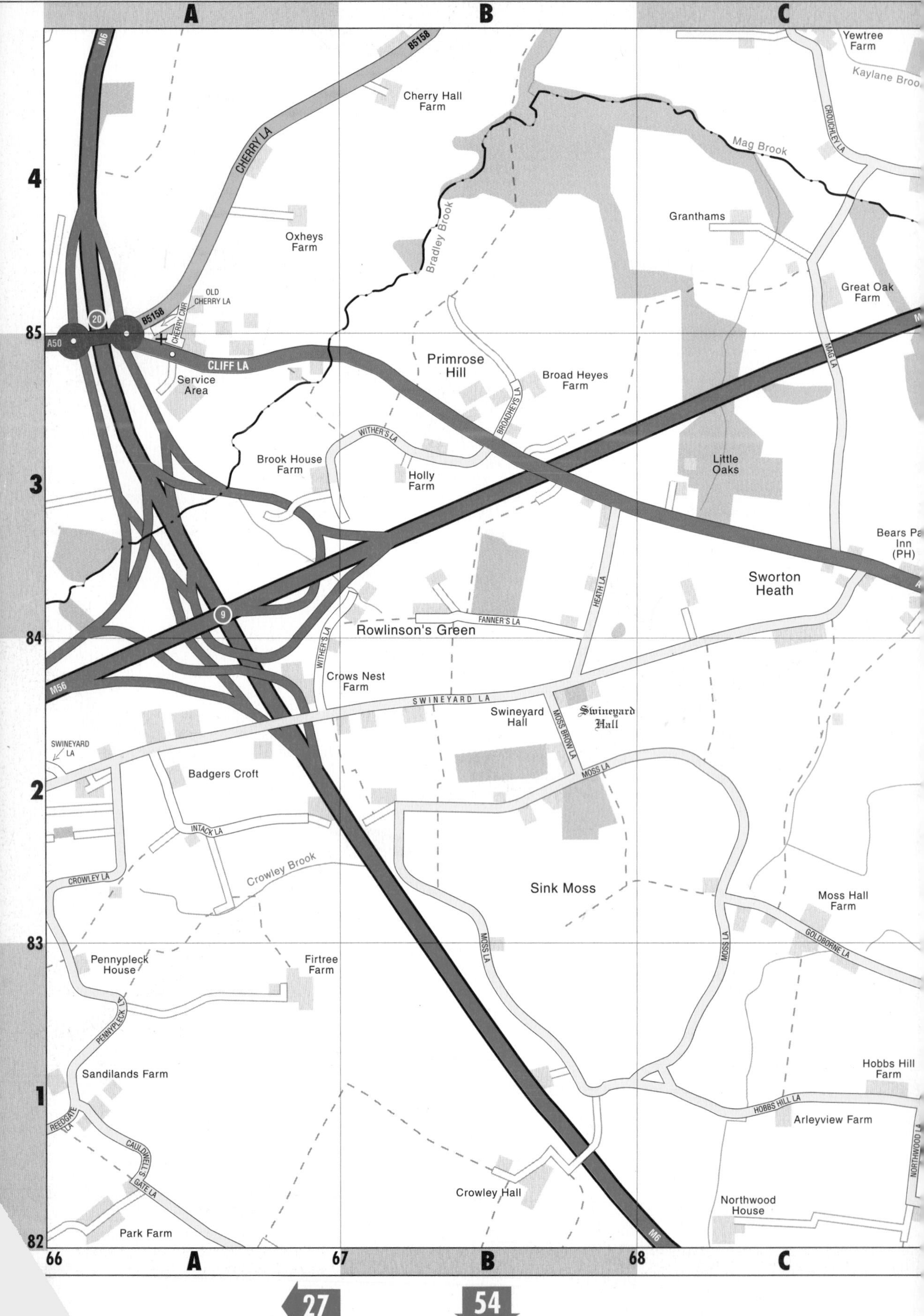
A
B
C
4
85
3
84
2
83
1
82
66
67
68
M6
B5158
Cherry Hall Farm
Yewtree Farm
Kaylane Brook
CROUCHLEY LA
Mag Brook
CHERRY LA
Oxheys Farm
Granthams
Bradley Brook
Great Oak Farm
OLD CHERRY LA
CHERRY CNR
20
A50
CLIFF LA
Service Area
Primrose Hill
Broad Heyes Farm
MAG LA
BROADHEYS LA
WITHER'S LA
Brook House Farm
Holly Farm
Little Oaks
Bears Pa
Inn (PH)
HEATH LA
Sworton Heath
9
FANNER'S LA
Rowlinson's Green
M56
Crows Nest Farm
SWINEYARD LA
Swineyard Hall
MOSS BROW LA
SWINEYARD LA
Badgers Croft
MOSS LA
INTACK LA
Crowley Brook
CROWLEY LA
Sink Moss
Moss Hall Farm
GOLDBORNE LA
Pennypleck House
Firtree Farm
PENNYPLECK LA
Sandilands Farm
Hobbs Hill Farm
HOBBS HILL LA
Arleyview Farm
REEDGATE LA
CAULDWELL'S GATE LA
Crowley Hall
Northwood House
NORTHWOOD LA
Park Farm

27
54

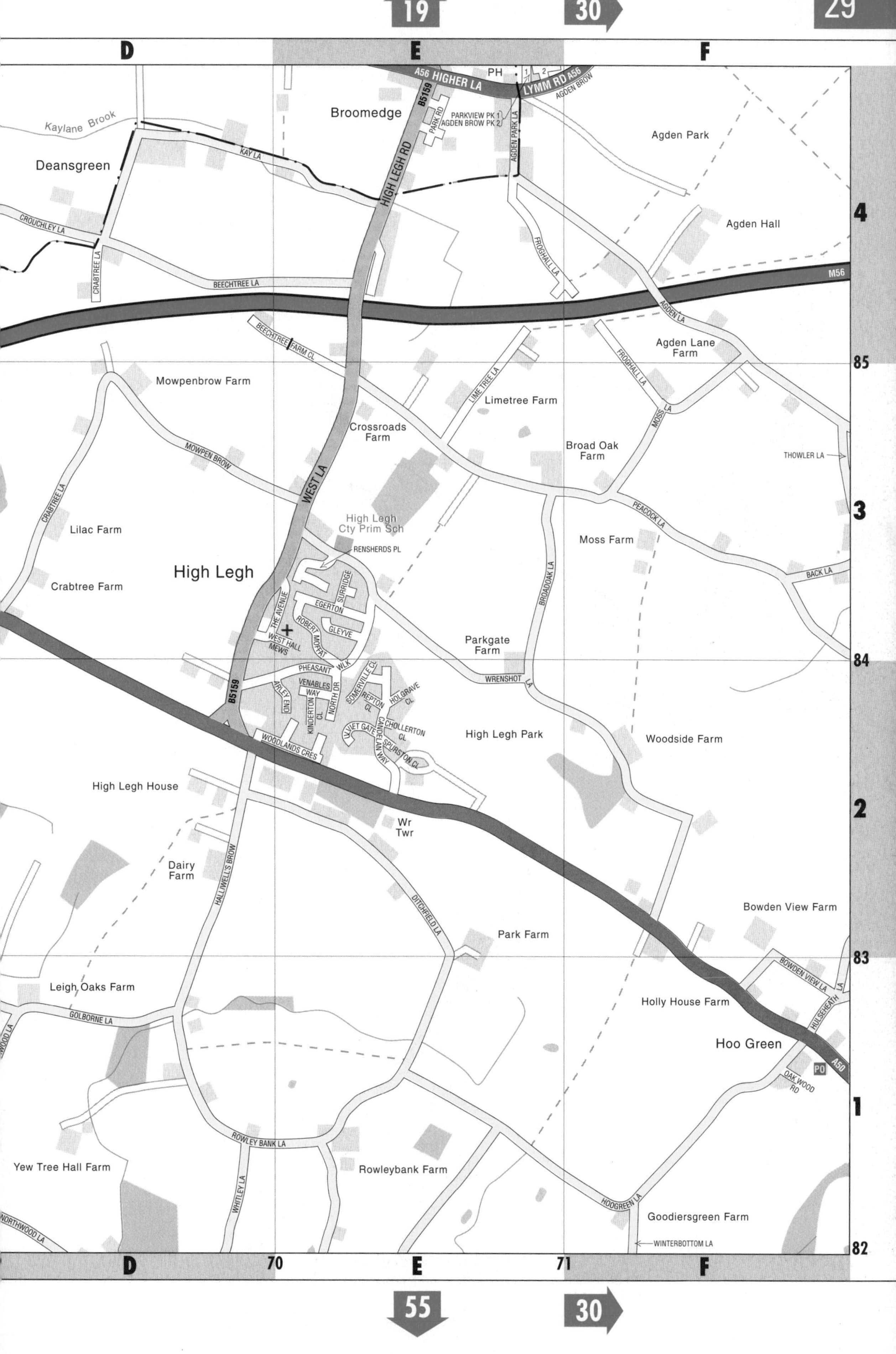
D
E
F
A56 HIGHER LA
LYMM RD A56
AGDEN BROW
PH
B5159
Broomedge
PARKVIEW PK 1
AGDEN BROW PK 2
PARK RD
AGDEN PARK LA
Agden Park
Kaylane Brook
Deansgreen
KAY LA
HIGH LEGH RD
CROUCHLEY LA
CRABTREE LA
BEECHTREE LA
FROGHALL LA
Agden Hall
M56
AGDEN LA
Agden Lane Farm
BEECHTREE FARM CL
LIME TREE LA
Limetree Farm
Mowpenbrow Farm
Crossroads Farm
MOSS LA
Broad Oak Farm
THOWLER LA
MOWPEN BROW
WEST LA
PEACOCK LA
CRABTREE LA
Lilac Farm
High Legh Cty Prim Sch
RENSHERDS PL
Moss Farm
BACK LA
High Legh
Crabtree Farm
SURRIDGE
EGERTON
BROADOAK LA
THE AVENUE
ROBERT MOFFAT
GLEYVE
WEST HALL MEWS
Parkgate Farm
PHEASANT WLK
WRENSHOT LA
SOMERVILLE CL
VENABLES WAY
HOLGRAVE CL
ARLEY END
KINDERTON CL
NORTH DR
REPTON CL
CHOLLERTON CL
VIVIET GATE
CANDELAN WAY
SPURSTON CL
High Legh Park
Woodside Farm
WOODLANDS CRES
High Legh House
Wr Twr
Dairy Farm
HALLIWELL'S BROW
DITCHFIELD LA
Bowden View Farm
Park Farm
BOWDEN VIEW LA
Leigh Oaks Farm
Holly House Farm
HULSEHEATH LA
GOLBORNE LA
Hoo Green
A50
PO
OAK WOOD RD
ROWLEY BANK LA
Yew Tree Hall Farm
Rowleybank Farm
WHITLEY LA
HOOGREEN LA
Goodiersgreen Farm
NORTHWOOD LA
WINTERBOTTOM LA
4
85
3
84
2
83
1
82
70
71

A B C

4

85

3

84

2

83

1

82

72 73 74

A B C

Arthill Farm

ARTHILL LA

Arthill

REDDY LA

Spodegreen Farm

SPODEGREEN LA

COE LA

A56

LYMM RD

A56

DUNHAM RD

M56

A56

Castle Hill

Yarwood Heath Farm

YARWOODHEATH LA

Nags Head (PH)

8

Booth Bank

M56

Booth Bank Farm

BOOTHBANK LA

Hope Cottage

Mereside Farm

Cherrytree Farm

TOM LA

DIRTY LA

Bowden View Farm

Stonedelph Farm

MILLINGTON LA

Newhall Farm

CHESTER RD

Harpers Bank Wood

Rostherne Mere

THOWLER LA

Millington Hall

MILLINGTON HALL LA

Moss House Farm

BACK LA

PEACOCK LA

Hulseheath

Heath Mount

CHAPEL LA

THE CRESCENT

WHITEHOUSE RD

CRESCENT RD

Denfield Hall Farm

Rostherne Brook

NEW RD

Rostherne

PO

MARSH LA

Marsh Farm

HULSEHEATH LA

Swan Hotel

A5034

CICELY MILL LA

Cicely Mill Farm

BUCKLOWHILL LA

Bucklow Hill

Burnthouses

Mere

THE CIRCLE

A50

Hulme Barns Farm

MERESIDE RD

Mere Farm

ASHLEY RD

Tatton Dale

Home Farm

Rostherne Drive

Tatton Park

Loc

A56

Golf Course

Little Mere

A5034

Mereside Farm

The Mere

A50

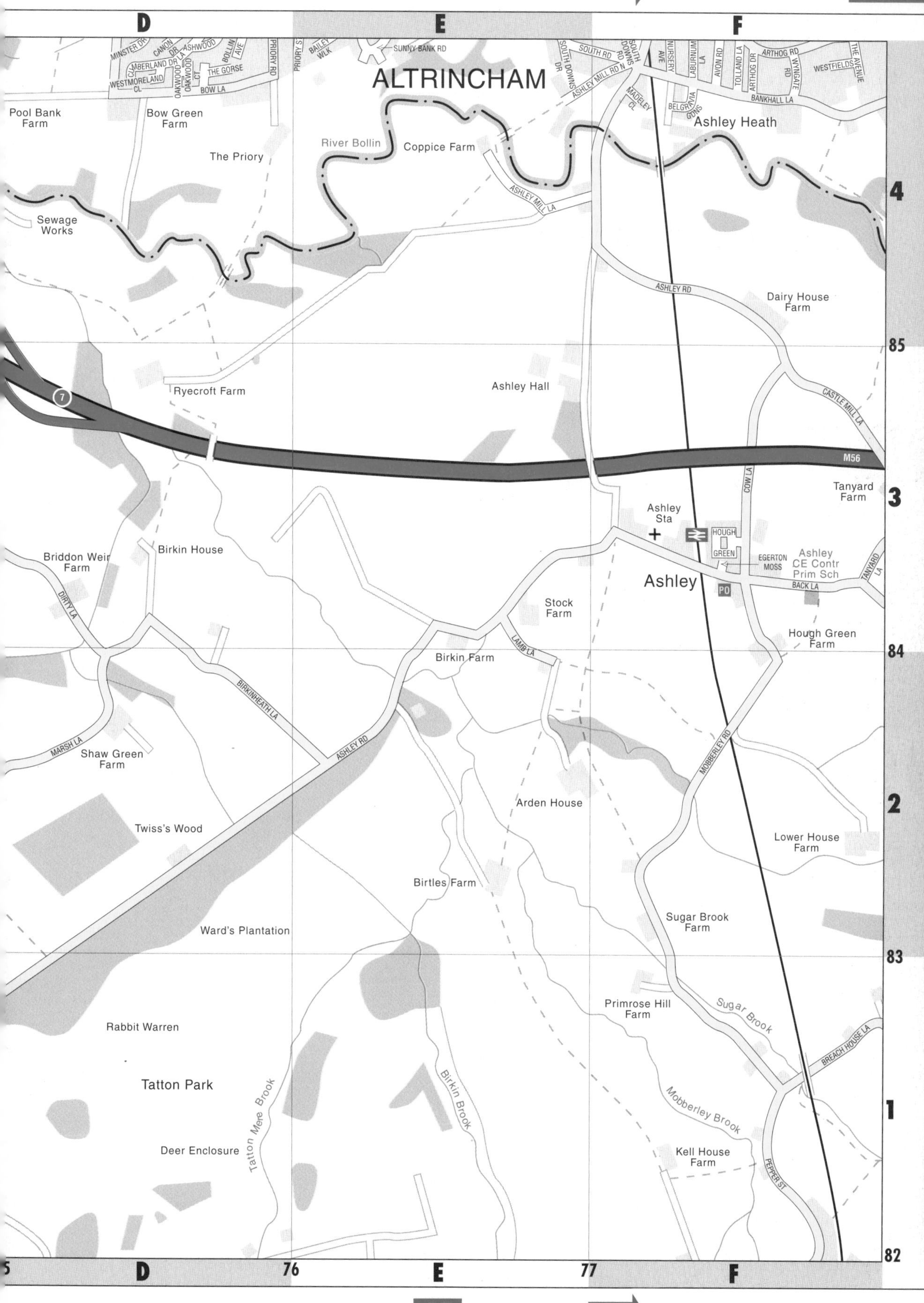
D
E
F
ALTRINCHAM
Pool Bank Farm
Bow Green Farm
The Priory
River Bollin
Coppice Farm
Ashley Heath
Sewage Works
ASHLEY MILL LA
ASHLEY RD
Dairy House Farm
Ryecroft Farm
Ashley Hall
CASTLE MILL LA
M56
Tanyard Farm
COW LA
Ashley Sta
HOUGH GREEN
EGERTON MOSS
Ashley CE Contr Prim Sch
Ashley
BACK LA
TANYARD LA
PO
Briddon Weir Farm
Birkin House
DIRTY LA
Stock Farm
Hough Green Farm
Birkin Farm
LAMB LA
BIRKINHEATH LA
MARSH LA
Shaw Green Farm
MOBBERLEY RD
Arden House
Twiss's Wood
Lower House Farm
Birtles Farm
Sugar Brook Farm
Ward's Plantation
Primrose Hill Farm
Sugar Brook
Rabbit Warren
BREACH HOUSE LA
Tatton Park
Birkin Brook
Mobberley Brook
Tatton Mere Brook
Deer Enclosure
Kell House Farm
PEPPER ST
4
85
3
84
2
83
1
82
76
77

31

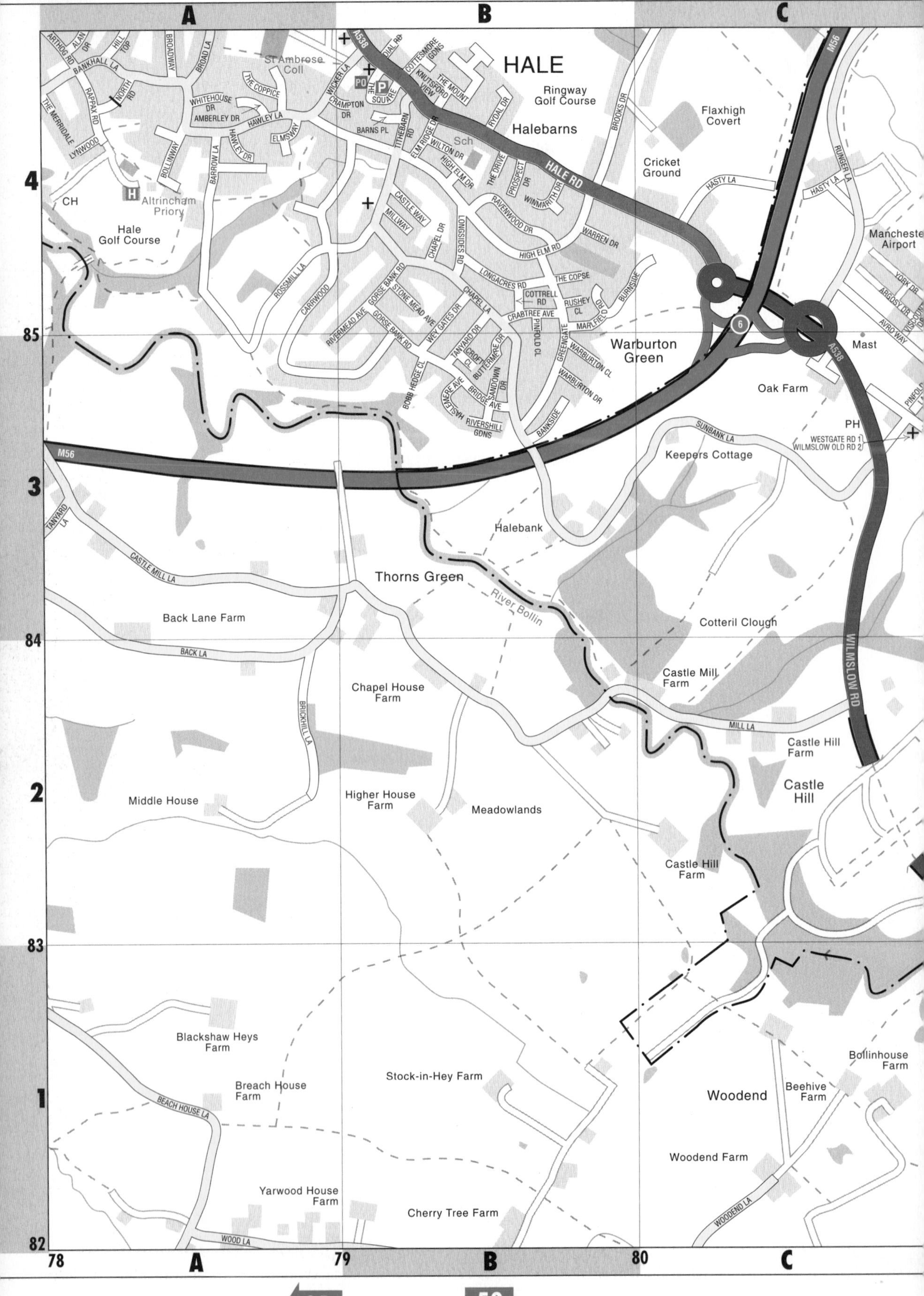
A
B
C
HALE
Ringway Golf Course
Halebarns
Flaxhigh Covert
Cricket Ground
St Ambrose Coll
Altrincham Priory
Hale Golf Course
CH
Sch
HALE RD
Manchester Airport
Warburton Green
Mast
Oak Farm
PH
Keepers Cottage
Halebank
Thorns Green
River Bollin
Back Lane Farm
Cotteril Clough
Castle Mill Farm
Chapel House Farm
Castle Hill Farm
Castle Hill
Middle House
Higher House Farm
Meadowlands
Blackshaw Heys Farm
Breach House Farm
Stock-in-Hey Farm
Woodend
Beehive Farm
Bollinhouse Farm
Woodend Farm
Yarwood House Farm
Cherry Tree Farm
M56
A538
WILMSLOW RD
CASTLE MILL LA
BACK LA
BRICKHILL LA
MILL LA
SUNBANK LA
HASTY LA
BEACH HOUSE LA
WOOD LA
WOODEND LA
TANYARD LA
WESTGATE RD 1
WILMSLOW OLD RD 2
4
3
2
1
85
84
83
82
78
79
80

31
58

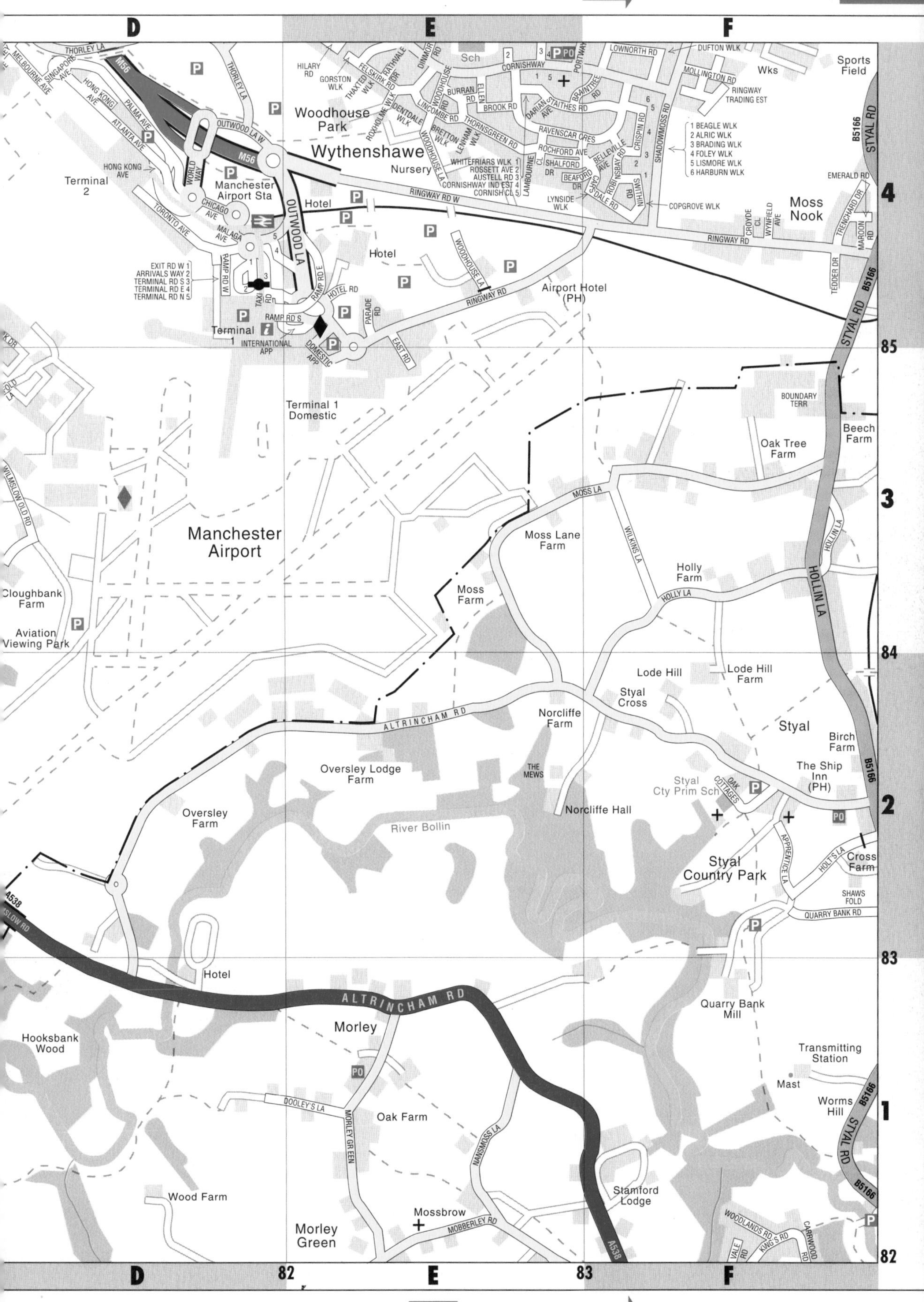

D   E   F

THORLEY LA

MELBOURNE AVE
SINGAPORE AVE
HONG KONG AVE
ATLANTA AVE
PALMA AVE
THORLEY LA

M56

OUTWOOD LA

Woodhouse
Park

HILARY RD
GORSTON WLK
FELSKIRK WLK
FIRTHVALE WLK
FOXWOOD WLK
DENTDALE WLK
LINCOMBE RD
BRETTON WLK
LENHAM WLK
THORNSGREEN RD

DINMOOR RD
WOODHOUSE LA
BURRAN WLK
BROOK RD

Sch

CORNISHWAY

PORTLAN

PO

LOWNORTH RD
DUFTON WLK
MOLLINGTON RD

Wks

RINGWAY
TRADING EST

Sports
Field

STYAL RD
B5166

Wythenshawe

Nursery

WHITEFRIARS WLK 1
ROSSETT AVE 2
AUSTELL RD 3
CORNISHWAY IND EST 4
CORNISH CL 5

Ringway Rd W

DARIAN AVE
STAITHES RD
RAVENSCAR CRES
ROCHFORD AVE
SHALFORD DR
BEAFORD DR

BELLEVILLE AVE
RINGSBY DR
CRISPIN RD
SHADOWMOSS RD
SWITHIN RD
SDALE RD

1 BEAGLE WLK
2 ALRIC WLK
3 BRADING WLK
4 FOLEY WLK
5 LISMORE WLK
6 HARBURN WLK

EMERALD RD
TRENCHARD DR
MARON RD

Moss
Nook

4

Terminal
2

HONG KONG
WAY

HONG KONG
AVE

P

P

CHICAGO
AVE

TORONTO AVE

MALAGA
AVE

Manchester
Airport Sta

OUTWOOD LA

Hotel

P

P

WOODHOUSE LA

P

LYNSIDE
WLK

LYNSIDE
WLK

COPGROVE WLK

CROYDE
CL
WYFIELD
AVE

RINGWAY RD

TEDDER DR

85

EXIT RD W 1
ARRIVALS WAY 2
TERMINAL RD S 3
TERMINAL RD E 4
TERMINAL RD N 5

RAMP RD W

RAMP RD E

Hotel

P

Hotel

P

RINGWAY RD

Airport Hotel
(PH)

B5166

STYAL RD

Terminal
1

TAXI
RD

RAMP RD S

HOTEL RD

PARADE RD

EAST RD

P

P

INTERNATIONAL
APP

DOMESTIC
APP

i

Terminal 1
Domestic

BOUNDARY
TERR

Oak Tree
Farm

Beech
Farm

MOSS LA

WILKINS LA

Holly
Farm

HOLLIN LA

3

Manchester
Airport

K DR

WILMSLOW OLD RD

Cloughbank
Farm

Aviation
Viewing Park

P

P

Moss Lane
Farm

Moss
Farm

Holly La

Lode Hill

Lode Hill
Farm

Styal
Cross

84

ALTRINCHAM RD

Norcliffe
Farm

THE
MEWS

Styal

Birch
Farm

HOLLY LA

B5166

Oversley Lodge
Farm

Norcliffe Hall

Styal
Cty Prim Sch

OAK
COTTAGES

P

The Ship
Inn
(PH)

PO

2

A538

WILMSLOW RD

Oversley
Farm

River Bollin

Styal
Country Park

APPRENTICE LA

HOLT'S LA

Cross
Farm

SHAWS
FOLD

QUARRY BANK RD

P

83

Hotel

ALTRINCHAM RD

Morley

PO

Quarry Bank
Mill

Transmitting
Station

Hooksbank
Wood

DOOLEY'S LA

MORLEY GR EEN

Oak Farm

MARSHMOSS LA

Mast

Worms
Hill

B5166

STYAL RD

1

Wood Farm

Mossbrow

MOBBERLEY RD

Stamford
Lodge

A538

WOODLANDS RD

VALE
RD

KING'S RD

CARRWOOD
RD

P

Morley
Green

82

D   82   E   83   F

← 33

B3
1 SIDDINGTON RD
2 KELSALL WAY
3 CUDDINGTON WAY
4 OVERTON WAY
5 STRETTON WAY
6 BIRTLES WAY

7 WILLASTON WAY
8 NORBURY WAY
9 EASTHAM WAY
10 UPTON WAY
11 ASTON WAY
12 CRANAGE WAY
13 HOOTON WAY

14 OLLERTON RD
15 CHRISTLETON WAY

C3
1 SUTTON WAY
2 CHELFORD CT
3 PEOVER WAY

4 MARTON WAY
5 NANTWICH WAY
6 HASSALL WAY

B2
1 SEALAND WAY
2 ECCLESTON WAY

3 GAWESWORTH WAY
4 WEAVERHAM WAY
5 FRODSHAM WAY
6 ELWORTH WAY
7 WARBURTON RD
8 DAVENHAM RD
9 PARKGATE WAY

10 CHURCH TERR
11 BROOKE WAY
12 ANDERTON WAY
13 NESTON WAY

Map grid references: A, B, C (columns) / 4, 85, 3, 84, 2, 83, 1, 82 (rows)

Key place names: Heald Green Sta, Heald Green Rec Gd, Wood Farm, Bolshaw Cty Prim Sch, Outward Farm, Yew Tree Farm, Bolshaw Farm, CHEADLE, Cheadle Etchells Prim Sch, Outwood Prim Sch, Outwood House, Griffin Farm, The Royal Sch for the Deaf, Stanley Green, Gill Bent Farm, Gillbent, Stanley Green Ind Est, Stanley Green Ret Pk, Bollinhey Farm, The Grange, Handforth, Parkfield, Deandale Farm, Knowle House, Langley House, Knowle Green, Styal Sta, Highfield, Linney's Bridge, Styal Green, Bollin Cross Sch, HM Prison, Wks, Lacey Green Cty Prim Sch, Lacey Green, Finney Green, Handforth Sta, Handforth Bridge, Trading Est, Colshaw Cty Prim Sch, St Benedicts RC Aided Prim Sch, Brooke Farm, Ind Est, Lower Meadow, Handforth Hall, Hall Wood, Resrs, Cemy, River Dean

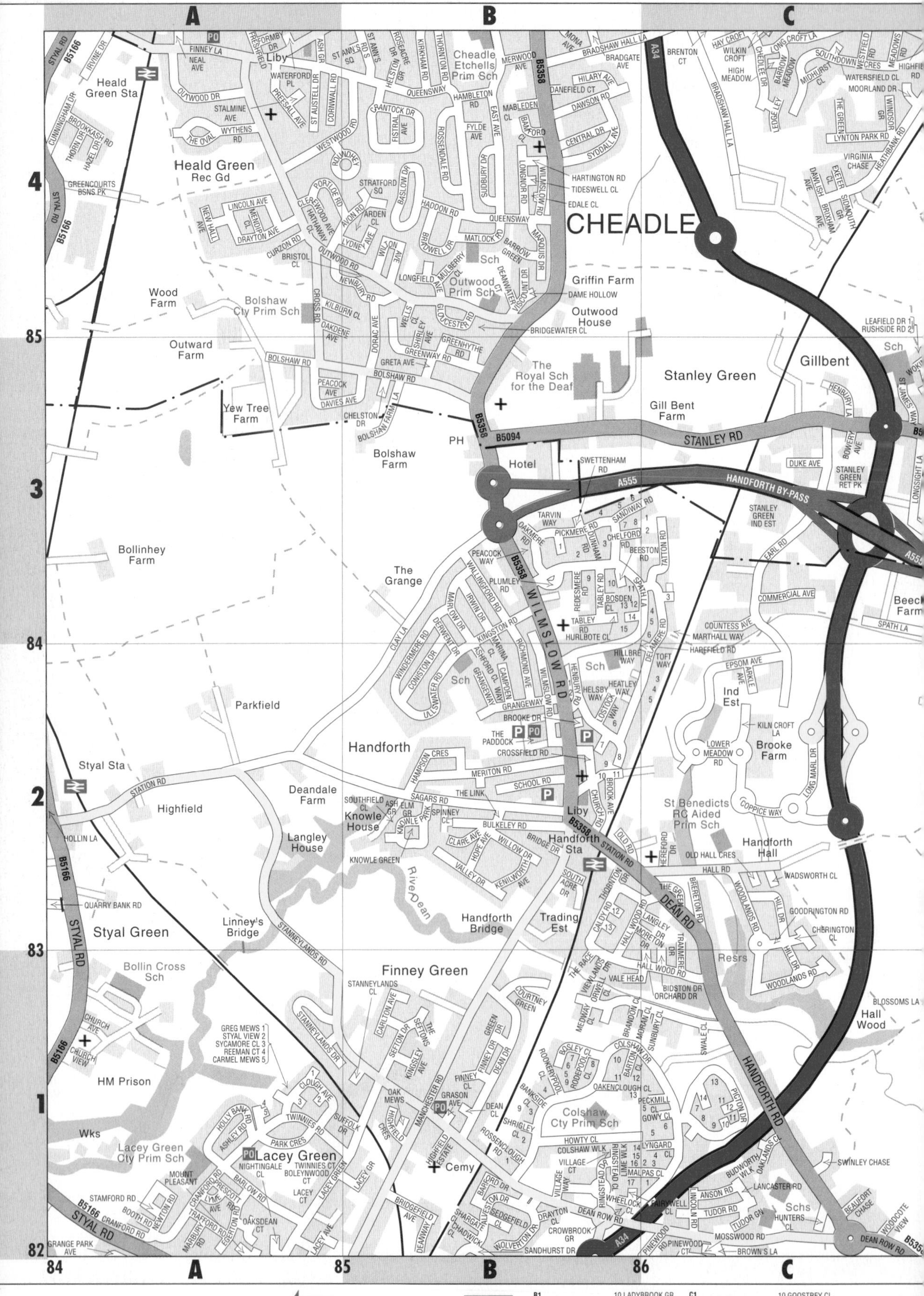

← 33

↓ 60

B1
1 SHELLBROOK GR
2 REDBROOK GR
3 MILLBROOK GR
4 TIMBERSBROOK GR
5 CARDENBROOK GR
6 BENSON WLK
7 TORBROOK GR
8 CLIFFBROOK GR
9 BLACKDEN WLK

10 LADYBROOK GR
11 FODEN WLK
12 BENBROOK GR
13 TAME WLK
14 DAIRYBROOK GR
15 APPLETON WLK
16 WADEBROOK GR
17 RAINOW WAY

C1
1 SALTERSBROOK GR
2 DINGLEBROOK GR
3 RAINOW WAY
4 MOORSBROOK GR
5 TILSTON WLK
6 SNAPEBROOK GR
7 KETTLESHULME WLK
8 WOODCOTT GR
9 EDLESTONE GR

10 GOOSTREY CL
11 TARPARLEY WLK
12 ARCLID CL
13 BRINDLEY GR
14 CHESTER CL

36

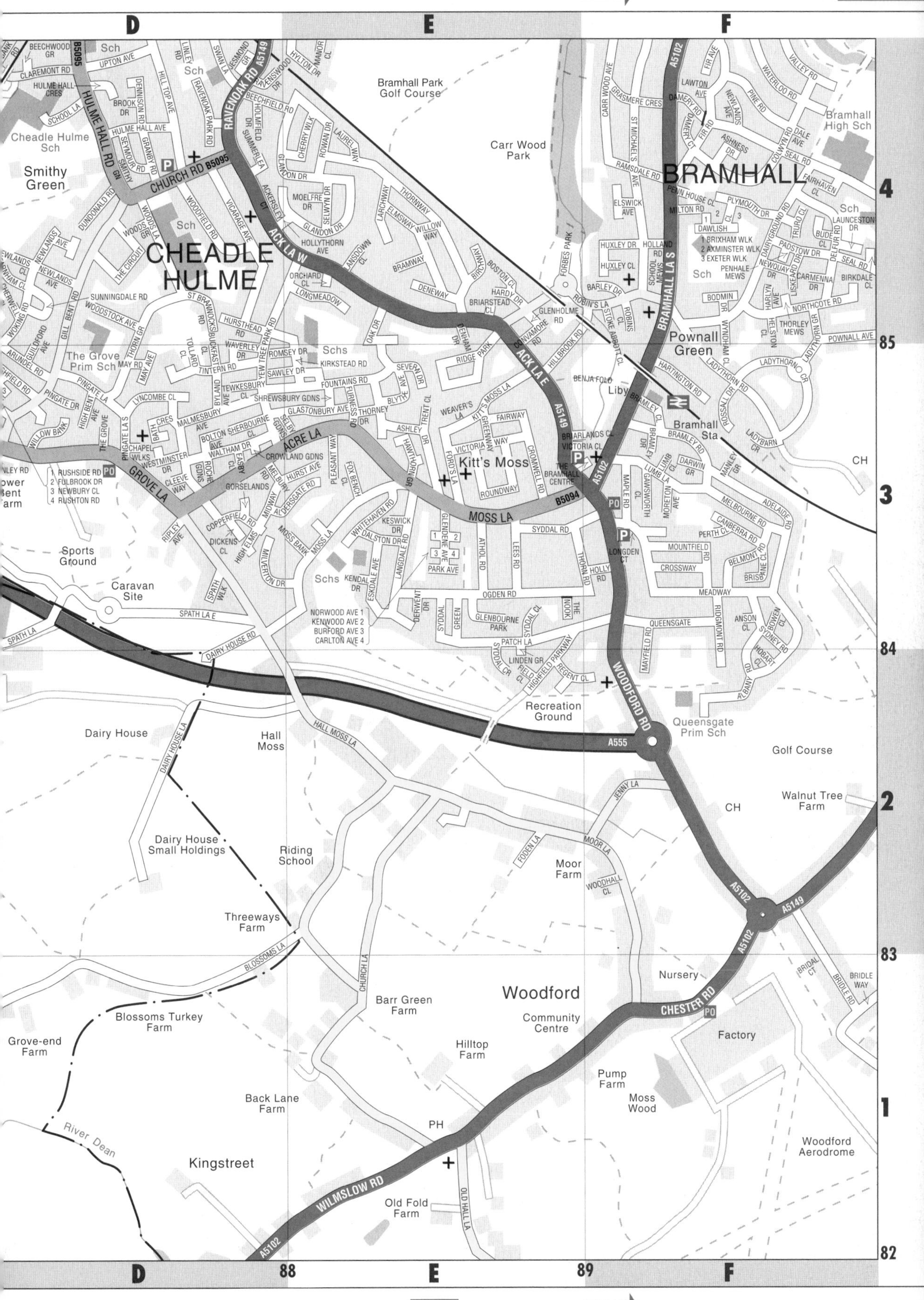
D
E
F
CHEADLE HULME
BRAMHALL
Bramhall Park Golf Course
Carr Wood Park
Bramhall High Sch
Cheadle Hulme Sch
Smithy Green
The Grove Prim Sch
Pownall Green
Bramhall Sta
Kitt's Moss
Sports Ground
Caravan Site
Recreation Ground
Queensgate Prim Sch
Golf Course
Walnut Tree Farm
Dairy House
Hall Moss
Dairy House Small Holdings
Riding School
Moor Farm
Threeways Farm
Woodford
Community Centre
Nursery
Factory
Barr Green Farm
Blossoms Turkey Farm
Grove-end Farm
Hilltop Farm
Pump Farm
Moss Wood
Back Lane Farm
River Dean
Kingstreet
Old Fold Farm
Woodford Aerodrome
HULME HALL RD
CHURCH RD
RAVENOAK RD
ACK LA W
ACK LA E
ACRE LA
GROVE LA
MOSS LA
BRAMHALL LA S
WOODFORD RD
CHESTER RD
WILMSLOW RD
HALL MOSS LA
SPATH LA E
DAIRY HOUSE RD
DAIRY HOUSE LA
BLOSSOMS LA
CHURCH LA
OLD HALL LA
MOOR LA
JENNY LA
FODEN LA
WOODHALL CL
BRIDLE WAY
A5102
A5149
A555
B5094
B5095
4
85
3
84
2
83
1
82
88
89
1 RUSHSIDE RD
2 FULBROOK DR
3 NEWBURY CL
4 RUSHTON RD
NORWOOD AVE 1
KENWOOD AVE 2
BURFORD AVE 3
CARLTON AVE 4
1 BRIXHAM WLK
2 AXMINSTER WLK
3 EXETER WLK

61

36

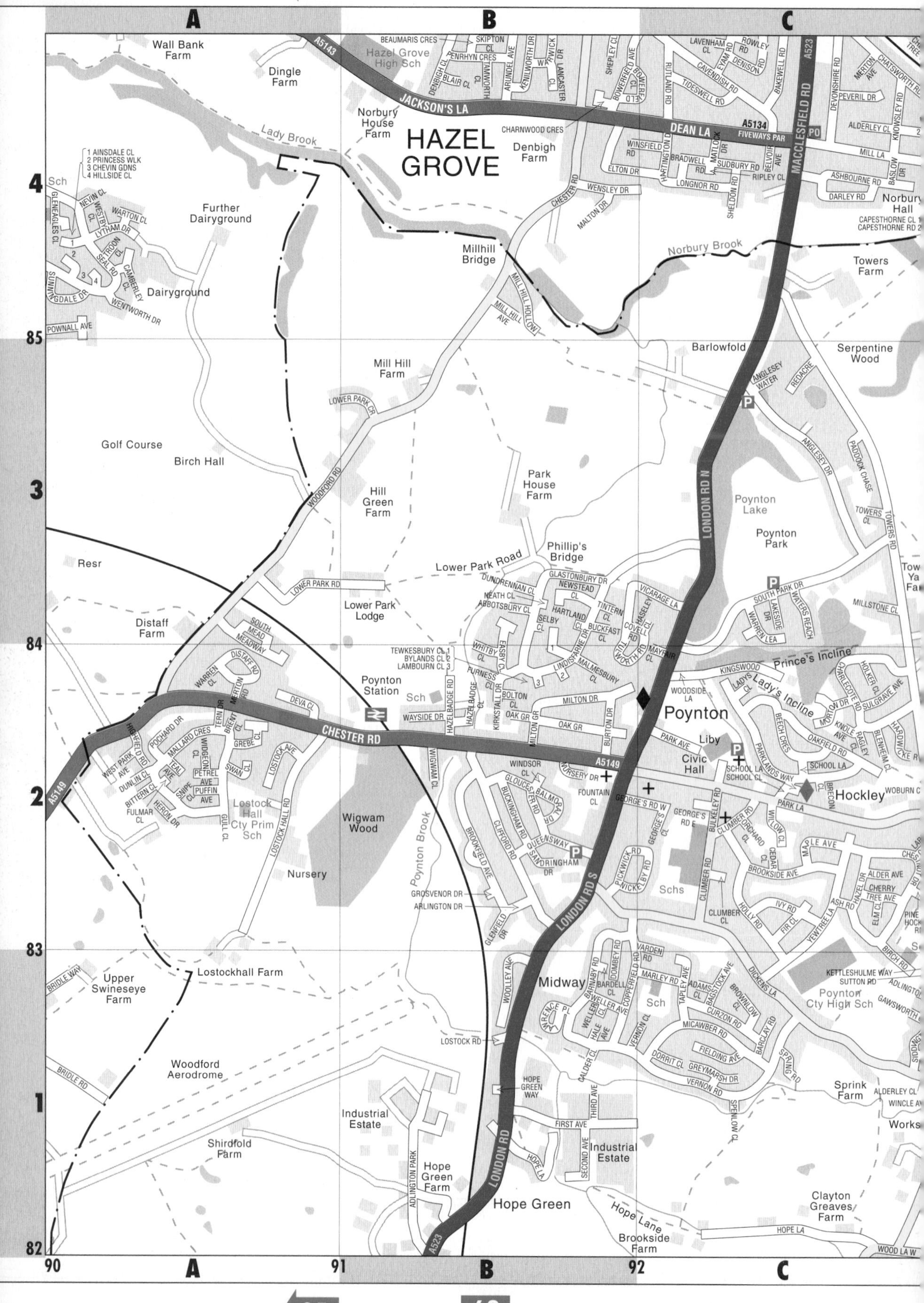

A   B   C

Wall Bank Farm

Dingle Farm

A5143

BEAUMARIS CRES

SKIPTON CL

PENRHYN CRES

Hazel Grove High Sch

JACKSON'S LA

DEAN LA

A5134

FIVEWAYS PAR

MACCLESFIELD RD

A523

PO

Norbury House Farm

HAZEL GROVE

Charnwood Cres

CHARNWOOD CRES

Denbigh Farm

Lady Brook

4

1 AINSDALE CL
2 PRINCESS WLK
3 CHEVIN GDNS
4 HILLSIDE CL

Sch

NEVIN CL

WESTBOURNE CL

WARTON CL

LYTHAM DR

Further Dairyground

Millhill Bridge

Norbury Brook

Towers Farm

CAPESTHORNE CL 1
CAPESTHORNE CL 2

Norbury Hall

GLENEAGLES CL

SUNNINGDALE DR

CAMBERLEY DR

SEAL RD

WENTWORTH DR

Dairyground

POWNALL AVE

85

Mill Hill Farm

MILL HILL HOLLOW AVE

Barlowfold

Serpentine Wood

LOWER PARK CR

WOODFORD RD

Park House Farm

ANGLESEY WATER

P

REDACRE

ANGLESEY DR

LONDON RD N

Poynton Lake

Poynton Park

TOWERS RD

Towers Farm

3

Golf Course

Birch Hall

Hill Green Farm

Lower Park Road

Phillip's Bridge

SOUTH PARK DR

LAKESIDE

WARREN LEA

P

WATERS REACH

Millstone CL

Resr

Tow Ya Fa

LOWER PARK RD

DUNDRENNAN CL

NEWSTEAD CL

GLASTONBURY DR

NEATH CL

ABBOTSBURY CL

HARTLAND

SELBY

TINTERN CL

BUCKFAST CL

Prince's Incline

KINGSWOOD

Lady's Incline

HOLKER DR

CHARLESTON DR

SULGRAVE AVE

Distaff Farm

Lower Park Lodge

SOUTH MEAD

MEADWAY

DISTAFF RD

TEWKESBURY CL 1
BYLANDS CL 2
LAMBOURN CL 3

WHITBY CL

FURNESS

LINDISFARNE DR

MALMESBURY CL

COVELL

TAILWORTH CL

MAYBUR

LADYS

WOODSIDE LA

MORTON DR

KNOLE RD

RADLEY CL

BLENHEIM CL

84

WARREN CL

RIVERTON RD

POCHARD DR

DEVA CL

Poynton Station

HAZEL BADGE RD

BOLTON CL

OAK GR W

OAK GR E

MILTON DR

BURTON DR

Poynton

Liby

Civic Hall

BEECH CRES

OAKFIELD RD

MOWBRAY DR

School La

Hockley

WOBURN C

HERFORD RD

WEST PARK RD

DUNLIN CL

MALLARD CRES

WIDGEON CL

PETREL AVE

PUFFIN AVE

SWAN

LOSTOCK AVE

Sch

WAYSIDE DR

KIRKS TAILOR

MILTON DR

PARK AVE

SCHOOL CL

PARKLANDS WAY

PARK LA

CEDAR RD

A5149

BITTERN CL

FULMAR CL

HERON DR

Lostock Hall Cty Prim Sch

LOSTOCK HALL RD

Wigwam Wood

Poynton Brook

WINDSOR CL

GLOUCESTER RD

BALMORAL

A5149

FOUNTAIN CL

GEORGE'S RD W

GEORGE'S RD E

BUCKLEY RD

CLUMBER RD

WILLOW CL

ORCHARD CL

Brookside Ave

ASH RD

HOLLY RD

FIR CL

MAPLE AVE

ALDER AVE

CHERRY TREE AVE

ELM CL

YEWTREE LA

PINE RD

Nursery

CLIFFORD RD

BROOKSIDE RD

QUEENSWAY

SPRINGBANK DR

P

LONDON RD S

PICKWICK RD

NICKLEBY RD

Schs

CLUMBER RD

IVY RD

BIRCH RD

KETTLESHULME WAY

SUTTON RD

83

BRIDLE WAY

Upper Swineseye Farm

Lostockhall Farm

GLENFIELD DR

WOOLLEY AVE

GROSVENOR DR

ARLINGTON DR

LOSTOCK RD

Midway

WINSBURY RD

BARDELL CL

BOOMBY RD

COPPERFIELD

YARDEN RD

MARLEY RD

ADAMSON CL

TAPLEY AVE

BROWNLOW AVE

Sch

CURZON RD

BARCLAY RD

DICKENS DR

AOLINGTON

Poynton Cty High Sch

GAWSWORTH

Sprink Farm

ALDERLEY CL

WINCLE CL

Works

2

1

BRIDLE RD

Woodford Aerodrome

Shirdfold Farm

Industrial Estate

ADLINGTON PARK

Hope Green Farm

LONDON RD

A523

HOPE GREEN WAY

FIRST AVE

SECOND AVE

THIRD AVE

HOPE LA

Industrial Estate

LAWRENCE PL

WELLER AVE

HALE AVE

VERNON CL

MICAWBER DR

DORRIT CL

FIELDING AVE

GREYMARSH DR

VERNON RD

SPENLOW CL

Clayton Greaves Farm

82

90

A

91

B

92

C

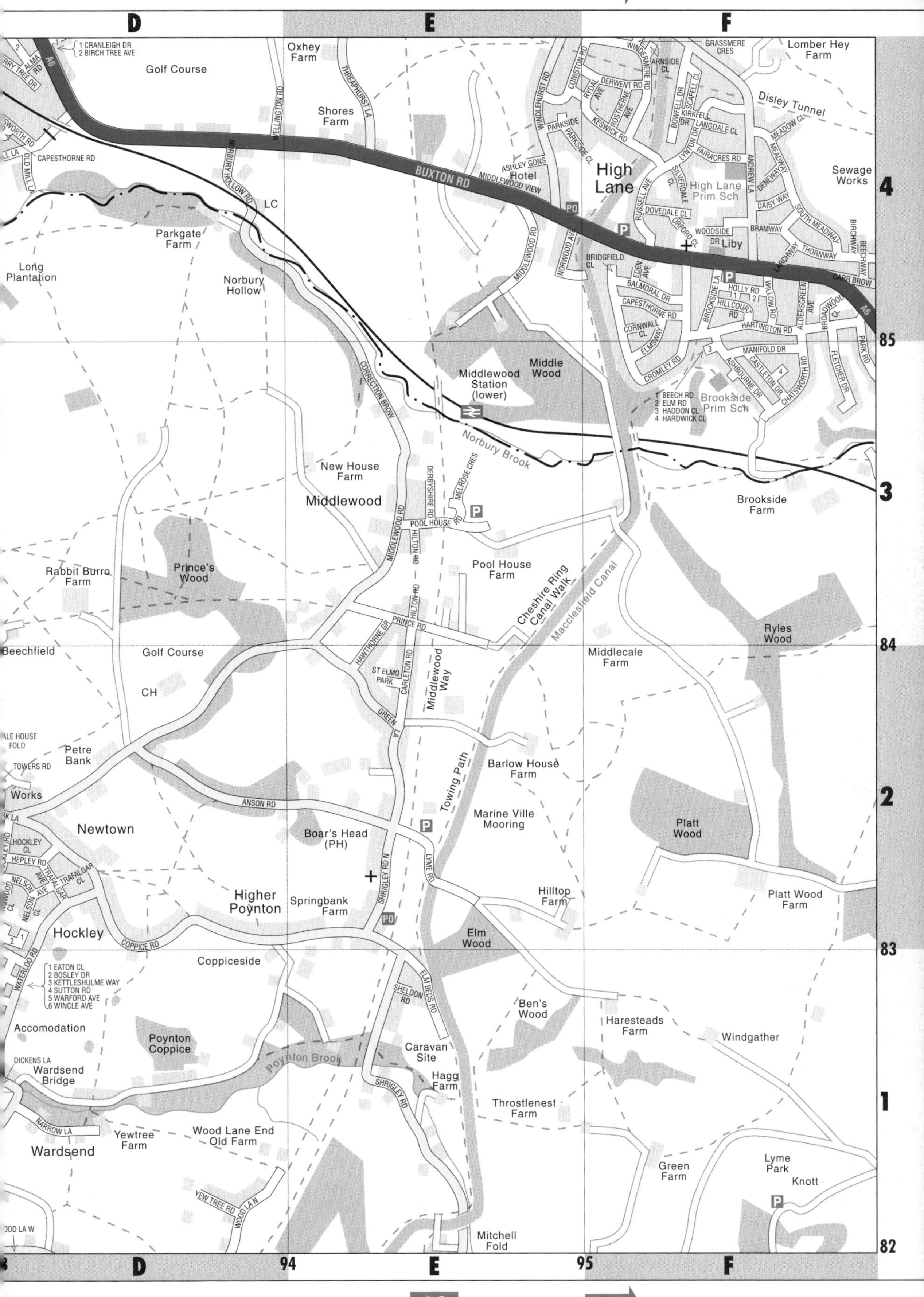
D
E
F
1 CRANLEIGH DR
2 BIRCH TREE AVE
Golf Course
Oxhey Farm
THREAPHURST LA
Shores Farm
WELLINGTON RD
A6
CAPESTHORNE RD
OLD MILL LA
NORBURY HOLLOW RD
LC
Parkgate Farm
Long Plantation
Norbury Hollow
BUXTON RD
ASHLEY GDNS
Hotel
MIDDLEWOOD VIEW
WINDLEHURST RD
CONISTON RD
WINDERMERE RD
ARNSIDE CL
GRASSMERE CRES
Lomber Hey Farm
Disley Tunnel
RYDAL AVE
DERWENT RD
ROSTHERNE AVE
KESWICK RD
PARKSIDE
PARKSIDE CL
BOWFELL DR
SCAFELL CL
KIRKFELL DR
LANGDALE CL
LYNTON DR
FAIRACRES RD
MEADOW CL
MEADWAY
DENEWAY
DAISY WAY
SOUTH MEADWAY
Sewage Works
High Lane
High Lane Prim Sch
RUSSELL AVE
SILVERDALE CL
ANDREW LA
DOVEDALE CL
ORFORD CL
WOODSIDE DR
Liby
BRAMWAY
THORNWAY
BIRCHWAY
BEECHWAY
CARR BROW
PO
P
MIDDLEWOOD RD
NORWOOD AVE
BRIDGFIELD CL
EDEN AVE
BALMORAL DR
CAPESTHORNE RD
CORNWALL CL
ELMSWAY
CROMLEY RD
BROOKSIDE LA
HOLLY RD
HILLCOURT RD
WILLOW RD
HARTINGTON RD
ALDERSGREEN AVE
BROADWOOD CL
MANIFOLD DR
ASHBOURNE DR
CASTLETON DR
CHATSWORTH RD
FLETCHER DR
PARK RD
1 BEECH RD
2 ELM RD
3 HADDON CL
4 HARDWICK CL
Brookside Prim Sch
Middle Wood
Middlewood Station (lower)
CORRECTION BROW
Norbury Brook
New House Farm
Middlewood
DERBYSHIRE RD
MELROSE CRES
POOL HOUSE RD
HILTON RD
Brookside Farm
Rabbit Burro Farm
Prince's Wood
Pool House Farm
Cheshire Ring Canal Walk
Macclesfield Canal
PRINCE RD
HAWTHORNE GR
ST ELMO PARK
CARLETON RD
Middlewood Way
GREEN LA
Ryles Wood
Beechfield
Golf Course
CH
Middlecale Farm
Petre Bank
TOWERS RD
Works
Barlow House Farm
Towing Path
ANSON RD
Newtown
Boar's Head (PH)
Marine Ville Mooring
Platt Wood
HOCKLEY CL
HEPLEY RD
NELSON AVE
TRAFALGAR CL
SHRIGLEY RD N
LYME RD
Higher Poynton
Springbank Farm
Hilltop Farm
Platt Wood Farm
Hockley
COPPICE RD
Elm Wood
WATERLOO RD
Coppiceside
1 EATON CL
2 BOSLEY DR
3 KETTLESHULME WAY
4 SUTTON RD
5 WARFORD AVE
6 WINCLE AVE
SHELDON RD
ELM BEDS RD
Ben's Wood
Haresteads Farm
Windgather
Accomodation
Poynton Coppice
Caravan Site
DICKENS LA
Wardsend Bridge
Poynton Brook
Hagg Farm
SHRIGLEY RD
Throstlenest Farm
NARROW LA
Wardsend
Yewtree Farm
Wood Lane End Old Farm
Green Farm
Lyme Park
Knott
YEW TREE RD
WOOD LA N
Mitchell Fold
4
85
3
84
2
83
1
82
94
95

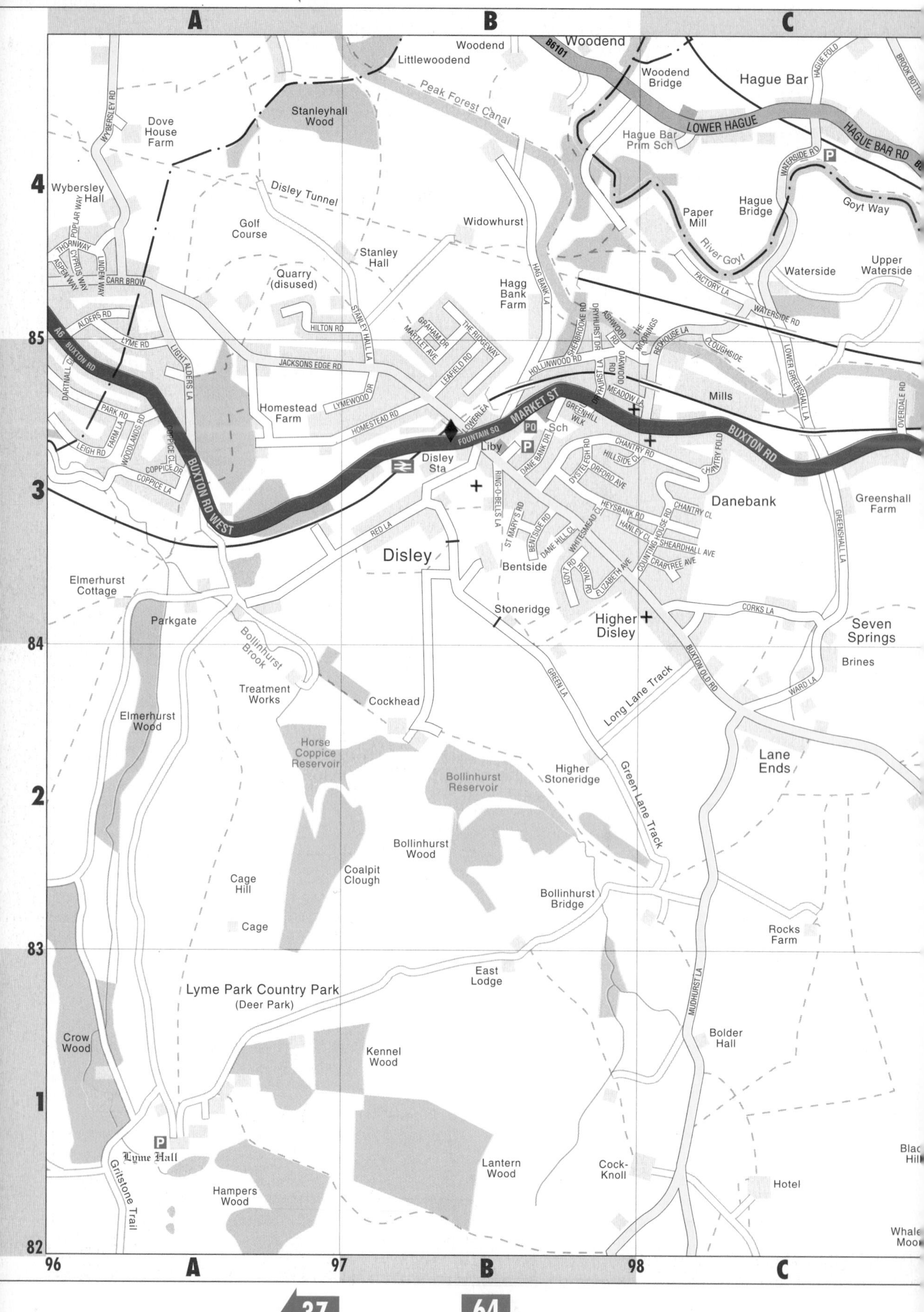

37

A   B   C

Woodend
Littlewoodend
Woodend
B6101
Woodend
Woodend Bridge
Hague Bar
Hague Fold
BROOK BOTTOM
Peak Forest Canal
LOWER HAGUE
Hague Bar Prim Sch
HAGUE BAR RD
WYBERSLEY RD
Dove House Farm
Stanleyhall Wood
WATERSIDE RD
P
Paper Mill
Hague Bridge
Goyt Way

4
Wybersley Hall
POPLAR WAY
Disley Tunnel
CITRUS WAY
THORNWAY
LINDEN WAY
ASPEN WAY
Golf Course
Widowhurst
River Goyt
Waterside
Upper Waterside

Stanley Hall
HAG BANK LA
FACTORY LA
WATERSIDE RD
DARTNALL
CARR BROW
ALDERS RD
LYME RD
Quarry (disused)
Hagg Bank Farm
SCHOOL BROOME RD
DRIMHURST DR
ASHWOOD
THE DOWNINGS
REDHOUSE LA
CLOUGHSIDE

85
A6
BUXTON RD
LIGHT ALDERS LA
HILTON RD
STANLEY HALL LA
JACKSONS EDGE RD
GRAHAM DR
MARTLET AVE
THE RIDGEWAY
LEAFELD RD
HOLLINWOOD RD
HURST LA
OAKWOOD
MEADOW LA
LOWER GREENSHALL LA
Mills
OVERDALE RD

PARK RD
LEIGH RD
WOODLANDS RD
COPPICE DR
COPPICE CL
HOMESTEAD RD
LYMEWOOD DR
Homestead Farm
FOUNTAIN SQ
FOWNLEA
MARKET ST
PO
P Sch
GREENHILL WLK
CHANTRY RD
HILLSIDE CL
CHANTRY FOLD
BUXTON RD
Danebank
Greenshall Farm

FARM LA
COPPICE LA
BUXTON RD WEST
Disley Sta
Liby
P
DANE BANK DR
D'ETELEIGH
ORFORD AVE
HOUSE RD
CHANTRY CL
GREENSHALL LA

3
RED LA
RING-O-BELLS LA
MARY'S RD
BENTSIDE RD
DANE HILL CL
HEYSBANK RD
HANLEY RD
COUNTING HOUSE RD
SHEARDHALL AVE
CHANTRY CL
Danebank

Disley
Bentside
GREEN LA
WHITESHEAD
ROYAL RD
CRABTREE AVE
CORKS LA
Seven Springs

Elmerhurst Cottage
Stoneridge
ELIZABETH AVE
Higher Disley
WARD LA
Brines

Parkgate
BUXTON OLD RD
Lane Ends
84
Bollinhurst Brook
Long Lane Track

Treatment Works
Cockhead
Higher Stoneridge
Green Lane Track

Elmerhurst Wood
Horse Coppice Reservoir
Bollinhurst Reservoir
MUDHURST LA

2
Bollinhurst Wood
Rocks Farm

Cage Hill
Coalpit Clough
Bollinhurst Bridge
Bolder Hall

Cage
East Lodge
83
Lyme Park Country Park
(Deer Park)

Crow Wood
Kennel Wood
Black Hill

1
P
Gritstone Trail
Lyme Hall
Lantern Wood
Cock-Knoll
Hotel
Whaley Moor

Hampers Wood

82
96   A   97   B   98   C

37   64

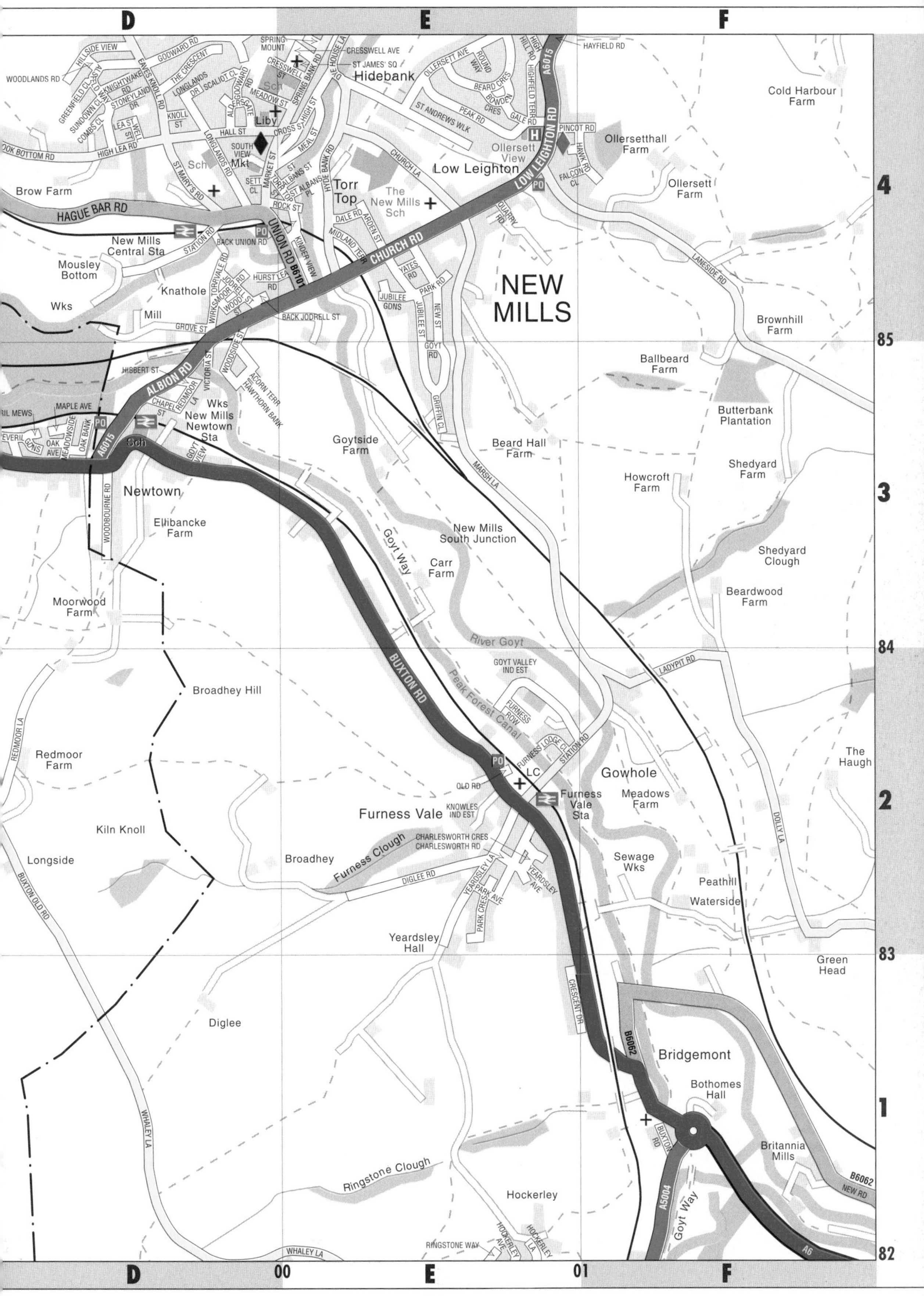
D
E
F
NEW MILLS
Hidebank
Low Leighton
Torr Top
The New Mills Sch
New Mills Central Sta
Mousley Bottom
Knathole
Brow Farm
Wks
Mill
Cold Harbour Farm
Ollersetthall Farm
Ollersett View
Ollersett Farm
Brownhill Farm
Ballbeard Farm
Butterbank Plantation
Shedyard Farm
Howcroft Farm
Beard Hall Farm
Goytside Farm
New Mills Newtown Sta
Newtown
Ellibancke Farm
Moorwood Farm
New Mills South Junction
Carr Farm
Goyt Way
River Goyt
Shedyard Clough
Beardwood Farm
Broadhey Hill
Redmoor Farm
Kiln Knoll
Longside
Broadhey
Furness Vale
Furness Clough
Furness Vale Sta
Gowhole
Meadows Farm
Sewage Wks
Peathill
Waterside
The Haugh
Yeardsley Hall
Green Head
Diglee
Bridgemont
Bothomes Hall
Britannia Mills
Ringstone Clough
Hockerley
Peak Forest Canal
HAGUE BAR RD
CHURCH RD
LOW LEIGHTON RD
ALBION RD
UNION RD
BUXTON RD
A6015
B6101
B6062
A5004
A6
LANESIDE RD
LADYPIT RD
DOLLY LA
MARSH LA
STATION RD
WHALEY LA
BUXTON OLD RD
REDMOOR LA
WOODBOURNE RD
CRESCENT DR
DIGLEE RD
HAYFIELD RD
NEW RD
00
01
85
84
83
82
4
3
2
1

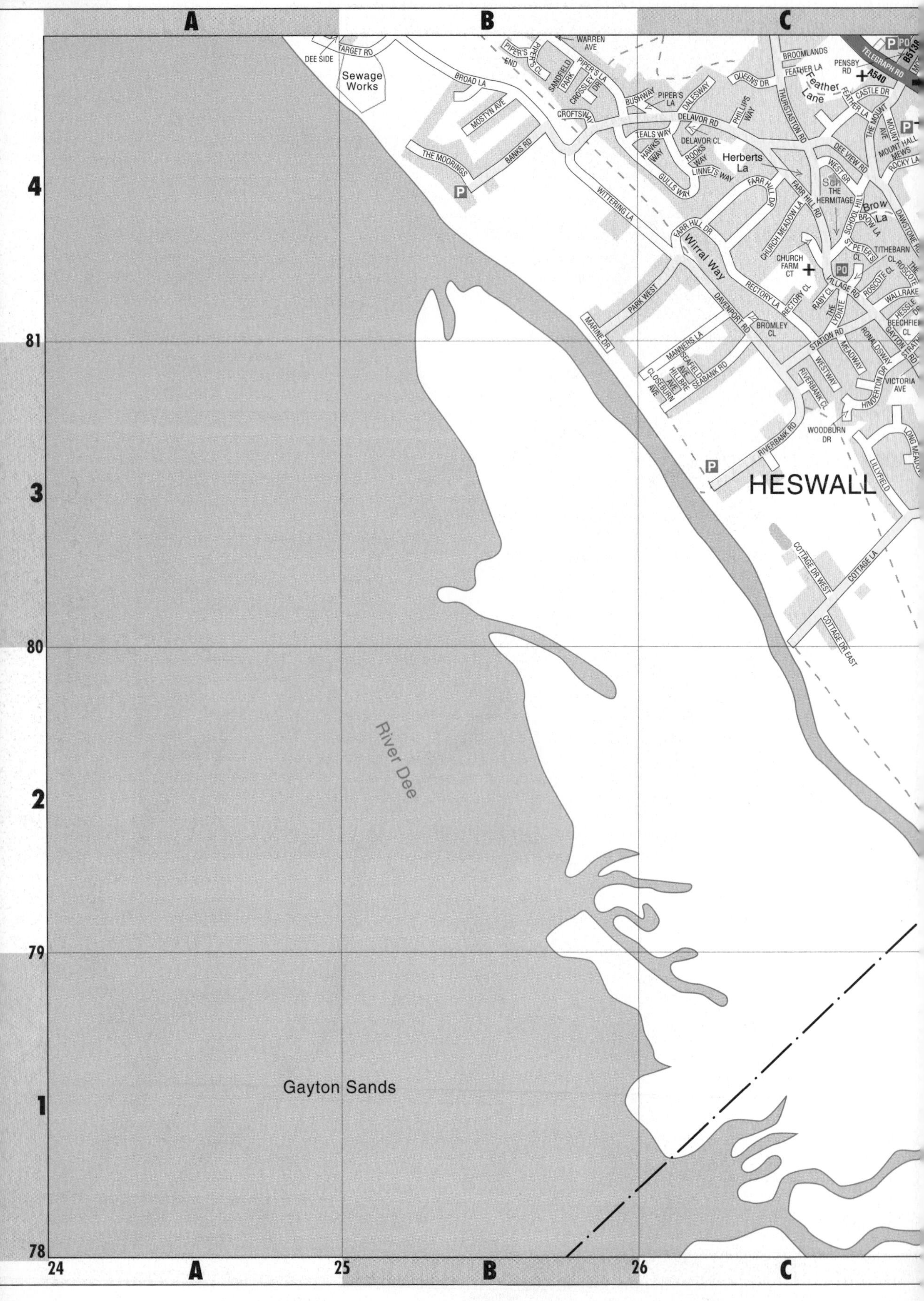

A | B | C

HESWALL

River Dee

Gayton Sands

Sewage Works

DEE SIDE

TARGET RD

BROAD LA

WARREN AVE

PIPER'S END

PIPER'S CL

SANDFIELD PARK

PIPER'S LA

CROSSFIELD CL

BUSHWAY

PIPER'S LA

TALESWAY

QUEENS DR

BROOMLANDS

FEATHER LA

PENSBY RD

TELEGRAPH RD

B5136

Feather Lane

A540

MOSTYN AVE

CROFTSWAY

PHILLIPS WAY

DELAVOR RD

CASTLE DR

FEATHER LA

MOUNT HALL

MOUNT MEWS

THE MOORINGS

BANKS RD

HAWKS WAY

TEALS WAY

DELAVOR CL

ROOKS WAY

DEE VIEW RD

WESTGR

ROCKY LA

WITTERING LA

GULLS WAY

LINNETS WAY

Herberts La

THE HERMITAGE

THE MOUNT

Wirral Way

FARR HILL DR

FARR HILL RD

SCHOOL HILL

Brow La

BROW LA

DANSTONE CL

CHURCH MEADOW LA

CHURCH FARM CT

RECTORY RD

ST PETER'S CL

VILLAGE RD

TITHEBARN

PO

ROSCOTE CL ROSCOTE

WALLRAKE

HESSLE

PARK WEST

DAVENPORT RD

RABY CL

RECTORY LA

THE UPLANDS

STATION RD

ROMAN ROAD

GAYTON RD

BEECHFIELD CL

STRAI

MARINE DR

BROMLEY CL

MANNERS LA

CLOSEFIELD

HILLBRE

SEABANK RD

MEADOWAY

WESTWAY

HINVERTON DR

VICTORIA AVE

LONG MEADOW

CLOSEBURN AVE

RIVERBANK WAY

RIVERBANK RD

WOODBURN DR

LILYFIELD

COTTAGE LA

COTTAGE DR WEST

COTTAGE DR EAST

P

D E F

Heswall Sta
Hilldene
Thornton Manor
Manor Wood
Barnston Prim Sch
Windmill (dis)
The Beacons
Gayton
Gayton Prim Sch
New Hall Farm
Club House
Gayton Wood
Golf Course
Hotel
Westwood Farm
Westwood Grange Country Club
Backwood Hall Farm
Backwood Hall
Leighton Hall Farm
Ashfield Farm
Ashfield Hall Farm
Fiveways
Cedar Court
The Wirral Ctry Pk
Wirral Way
Oakland Farm
Brook House
CLAYHILL LIGHT IND PK
Neston St Mary's CE Contr Prim Sch
Parkgate Cty Prim Sch
Parkgate
Neston Cty High Sch
THE SQUARE
Sch

TELEGRAPH RD
BARNSTON RD
BRIMSTAGE RD
CHESTER RD
CHESTER HIGH RD
BOATHOUSE LA
NESTON RD
LIVERPOOL RD
PARKGATE LA
THE PARADE
NORTH PARADE
LEIGHTON RD
WOOD LA
GAYTON LA
GAYTON PARKWAY
WELL LA
DOVESMEAD RD
BRIMSTAGE GN
COTESMORE DR
WIDGEONS COVERT
RABY PARK RD
THE RUNNELL
FAIRHOLME AVE
LEIGHTON CHASE
THE PRIORY
ABBOTS WAY
BROOKLANDS RD
TITHEBARN DR
THE LOOMS
BEVYL RD
MOORINGS CL
LONG ACRES RD
WATER TOWER RD
MAYFIELD GDNS
COALBROOKDALE RD

A551 A5137 A540 B5135 B5136

4
81
3
80
2
79
1
78

D 28 E 29 F

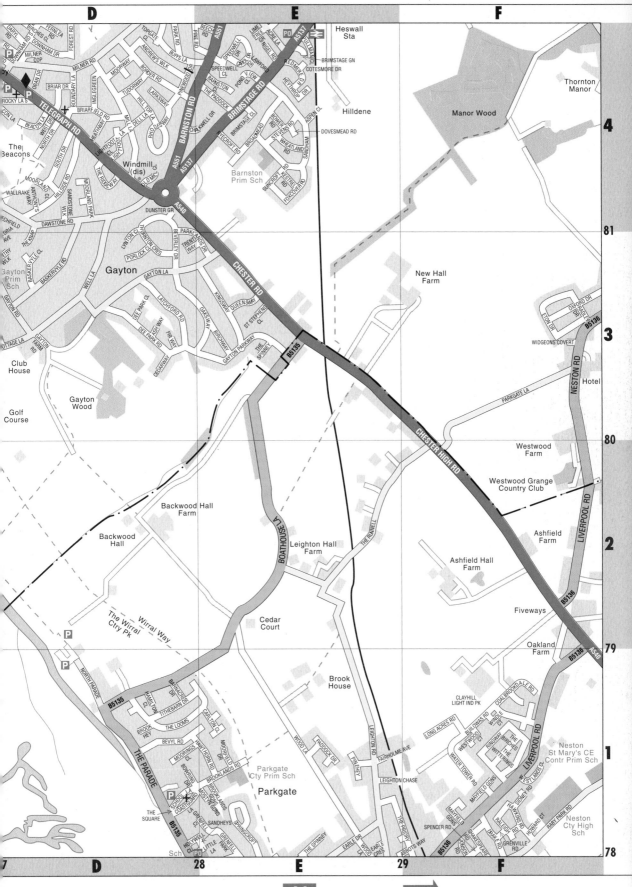

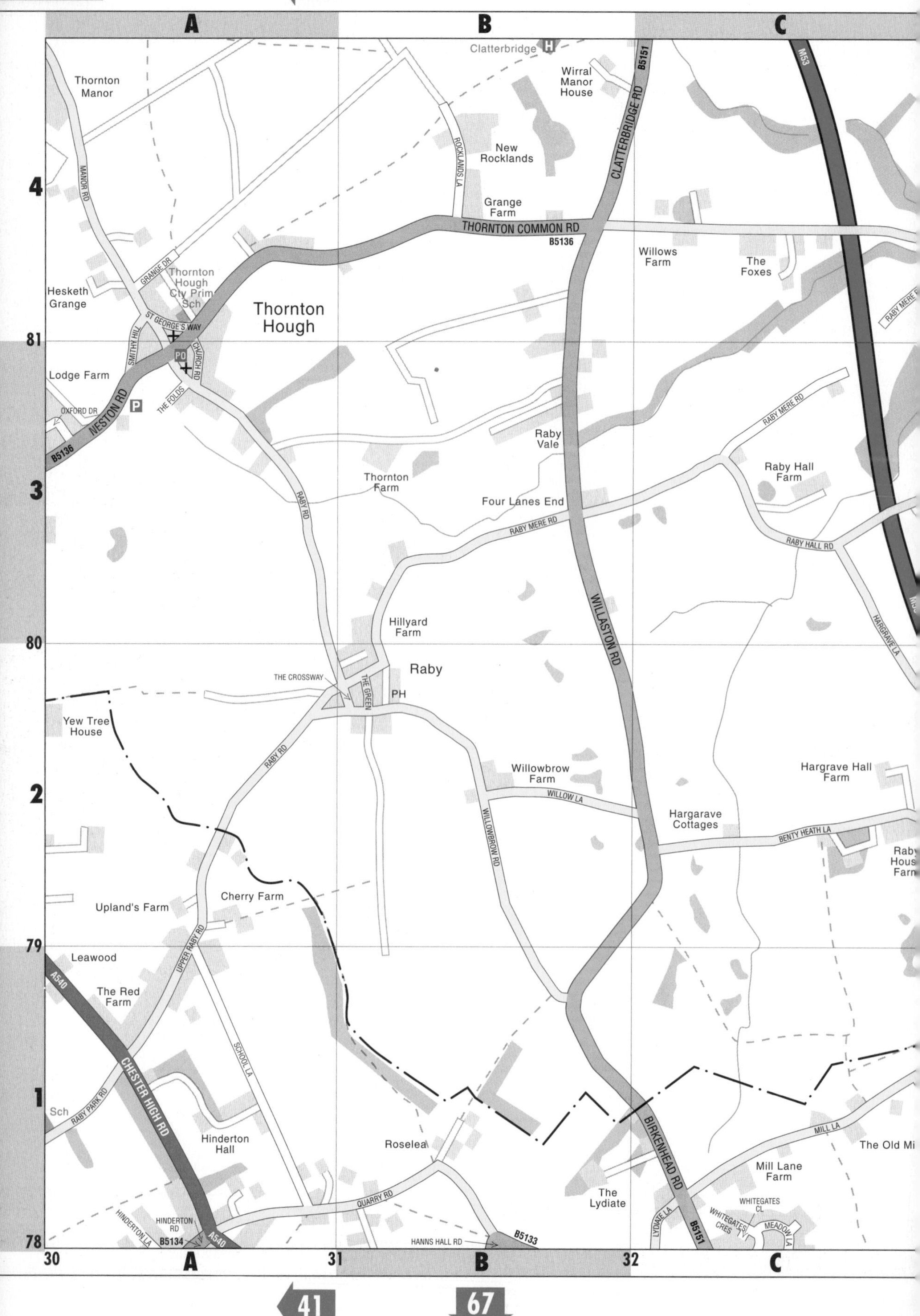

Thornton Manor

Clatterbridge

Wirral Manor House

New Rocklands

ROCKLANDS LA

CLATTERBRIDGE RD

B5151

M53

Grange Farm

THORNTON COMMON RD
B5136

Willows Farm

The Foxes

RABY MERE RD

Hesketh Grange

MANOR RD

GRANGE DR

Thornton Hough Cty Prim Sch

ST GEORGE'S WAY

SMITHY HILL

CHURCH RD

Thornton Hough

Raby Vale

Raby Hall Farm

RABY MERE RD

Lodge Farm

NESTON RD

PO

THE FOLDS

Thornton Farm

Four Lanes End

RABY MERE RD

RABY HALL RD

OXFORD DR

P

RABY RD

Raby Hall Farm

HARGRAVE LA

B5136

Hillyard Farm

Yew Tree House

THE CROSSWAY

THE GREEN

Raby

PH

WILLASTON RD

Willowbrow Farm

Hargrave Hall Farm

Upland's Farm

Cherry Farm

RABY RD

WILLOWBROW RD

WILLOW LA

Hargarave Cottages

BENTY HEATH LA

Raby House Farm

Leawood

A540

UPPER RABY RD

The Red Farm

Raby Park Rd

Sch

CHESTER HIGH RD

SCHOOL LA

Hinderton Hall

Roselea

BIRKENHEAD RD

Mill Lane Farm

MILL LA

The Old Mi

The Lydiate

LYDIATE LA

B5151

WHITEGATES CRES

WHITEGATES CL

MEADOW LA

HINDERTON LA

HINDERTON RD

B5134

A540

QUARRY RD

HANNS HALL RD

B5133

D E F

Bromborough Rake Sta
The Vineyard Farm
Lancelyn Farm
Poulton Hall
Raby Mere
Acre Lane
Civic Hall
Liby
Mendell Prim Sch
Wirral Ed Ctr
Bromborough Sta
Raeburn Prim Sch
BEBINGTON
Cemy
Golf Course
Raby Hall
Eastham
Heygarth Prim Sch
Brookhurst
Bromborough Golf Course
Hargrave House Farm
Eastham Glenburn Cty Inf Sch
South Wirral High Sch
Schs
Eastham Rake Sta
Street Hey
Hooton
Hooton Bridge
Hooton Farm
Hooton Sta
ROFTEN IND EST
HOOTON RD
B5133
M53
A41
NEW CHESTER RD
Green Lane
Clatter Brook
Dibbinsdale

4 81 3 80 2 79 1 78
34 35

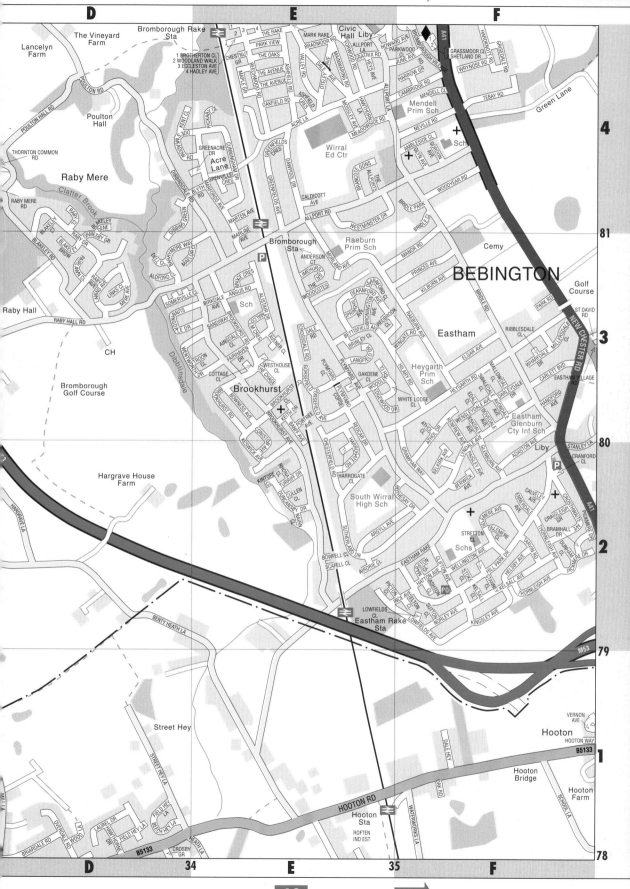

43

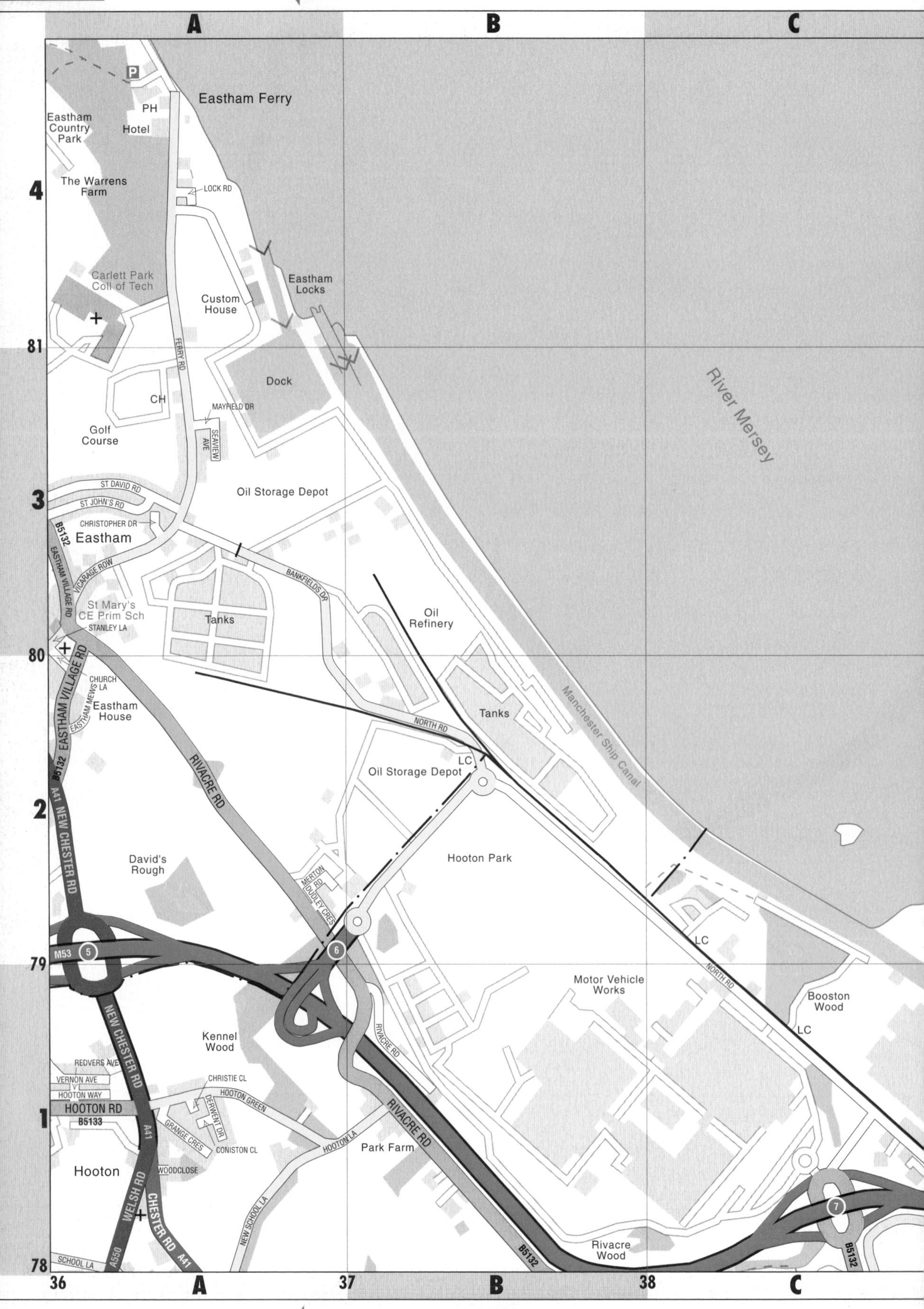
A
B
C
Eastham Ferry
PH
Hotel
Eastham Country Park
The Warrens Farm
LOCK RD
Carlett Park Coll of Tech
Custom House
Eastham Locks
FERRY RD
Dock
CH
MAYFIELD DR
SEAVIEW AVE
Golf Course
River Mersey
ST DAVID RD
ST JOHN'S RD
CHRISTOPHER DR
Oil Storage Depot
B5132
Eastham
EASTHAM VILLAGE RD
VICARAGE ROW
BANKFIELDS DR
St Mary's CE Prim Sch
STANLEY LA
Tanks
Oil Refinery
CHURCH LA
EASTHAM MEWS
Eastham House
Tanks
Manchester Ship Canal
NORTH RD
LC
Oil Storage Depot
RIVACRE RD
A41 NEW CHESTER RD
David's Rough
Hooton Park
MERTON RD
DUDLEY CRES
M53
5
6
LC
Motor Vehicle Works
NORTH RD
Booston Wood
LC
Kennel Wood
RIVACRE RD
REDVERS AVE
VERNON AVE
HOOTON WAY
HOOTON RD
B5133
CHRISTIE CL
HOOTON GREEN
DERWENT DR
GRANGE CRES
CONISTON CL
HOOTON LA
Park Farm
RIVACRE RD
Hooton
WOODCLOSE
NEW SCHOOL LA
WELSH RD
A550
CHESTER RD
A41
7
B5132
Rivacre Wood
B5132
SCHOOL LA
4
81
3
80
2
79
1
78
36
37
38

43

69

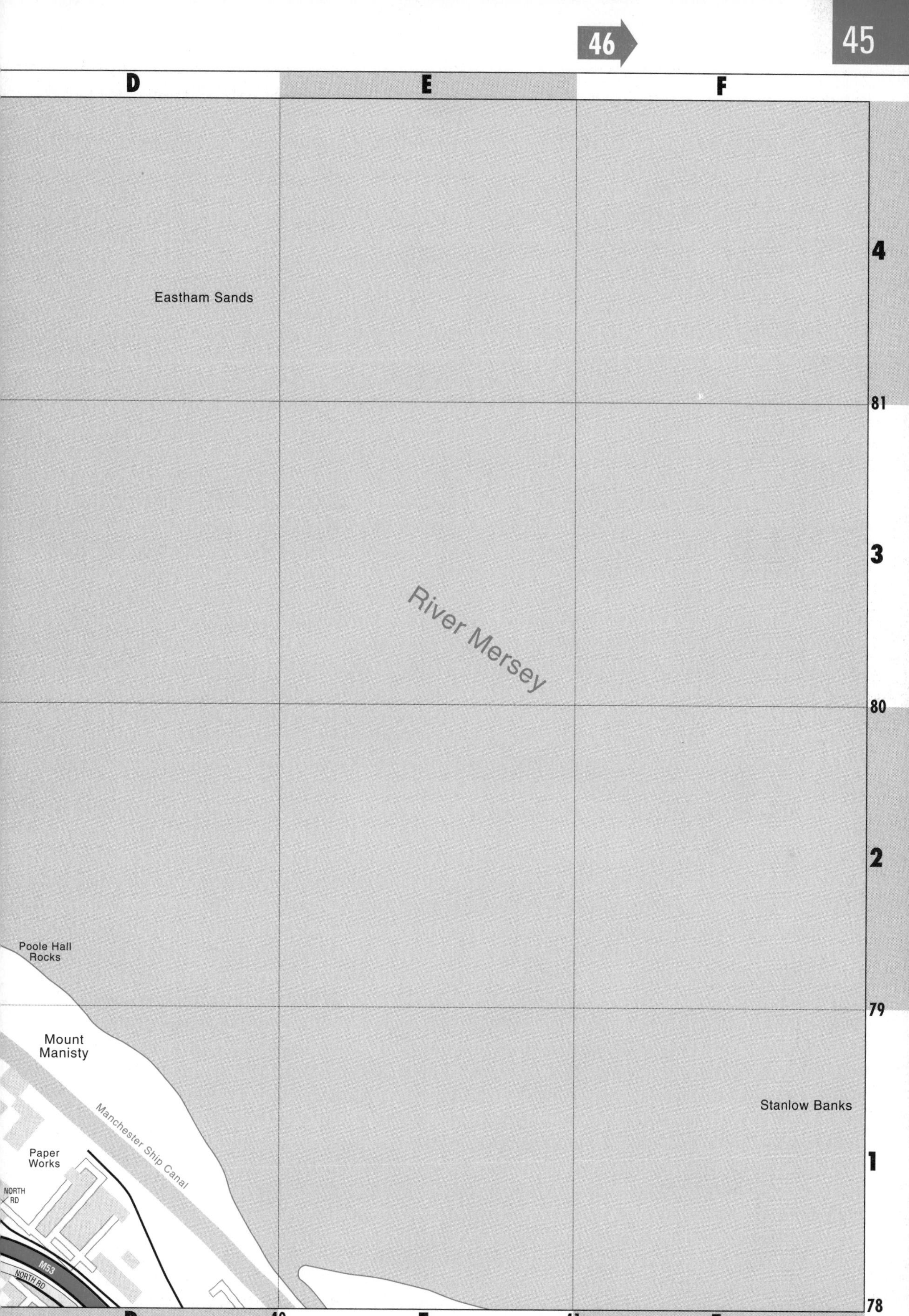

4

81

3

River Mersey

80

2

Eastham Sands

Poole Hall
Rocks

79

Mount
Manisty

Stanlow Banks

Manchester Ship Canal

Paper
Works

1

NORTH
RD

M53

NORTH RD

78

45

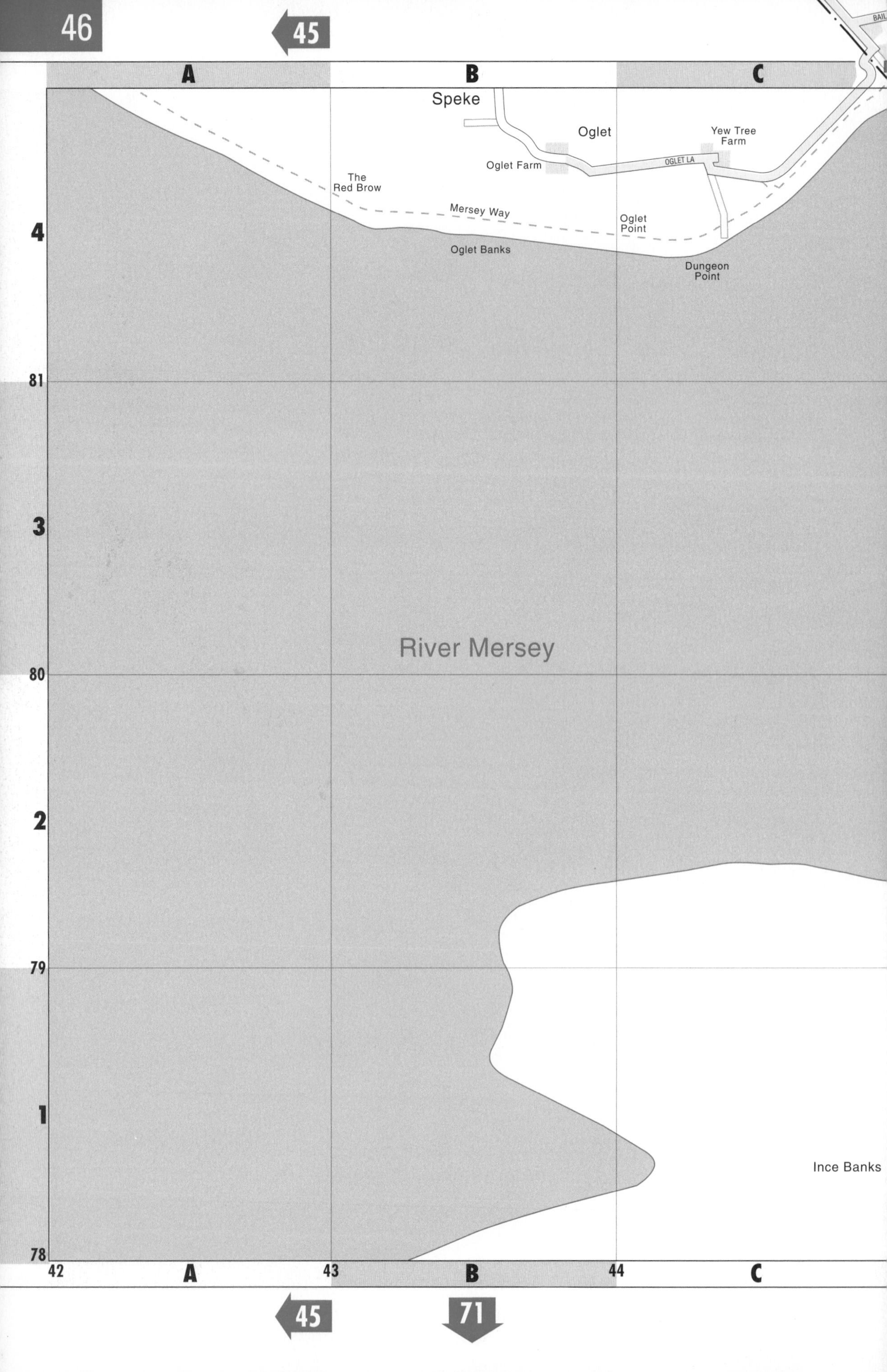

A
B
C

Speke

Oglet

Yew Tree
Farm

The
Red Brow

Oglet Farm

OGLET LA

Oglet
Point

Mersey Way

Oglet Banks

Dungeon
Point

4

81

3

River Mersey

80

2

79

1

Ince Banks

78

42
A
43
B
44
C

71

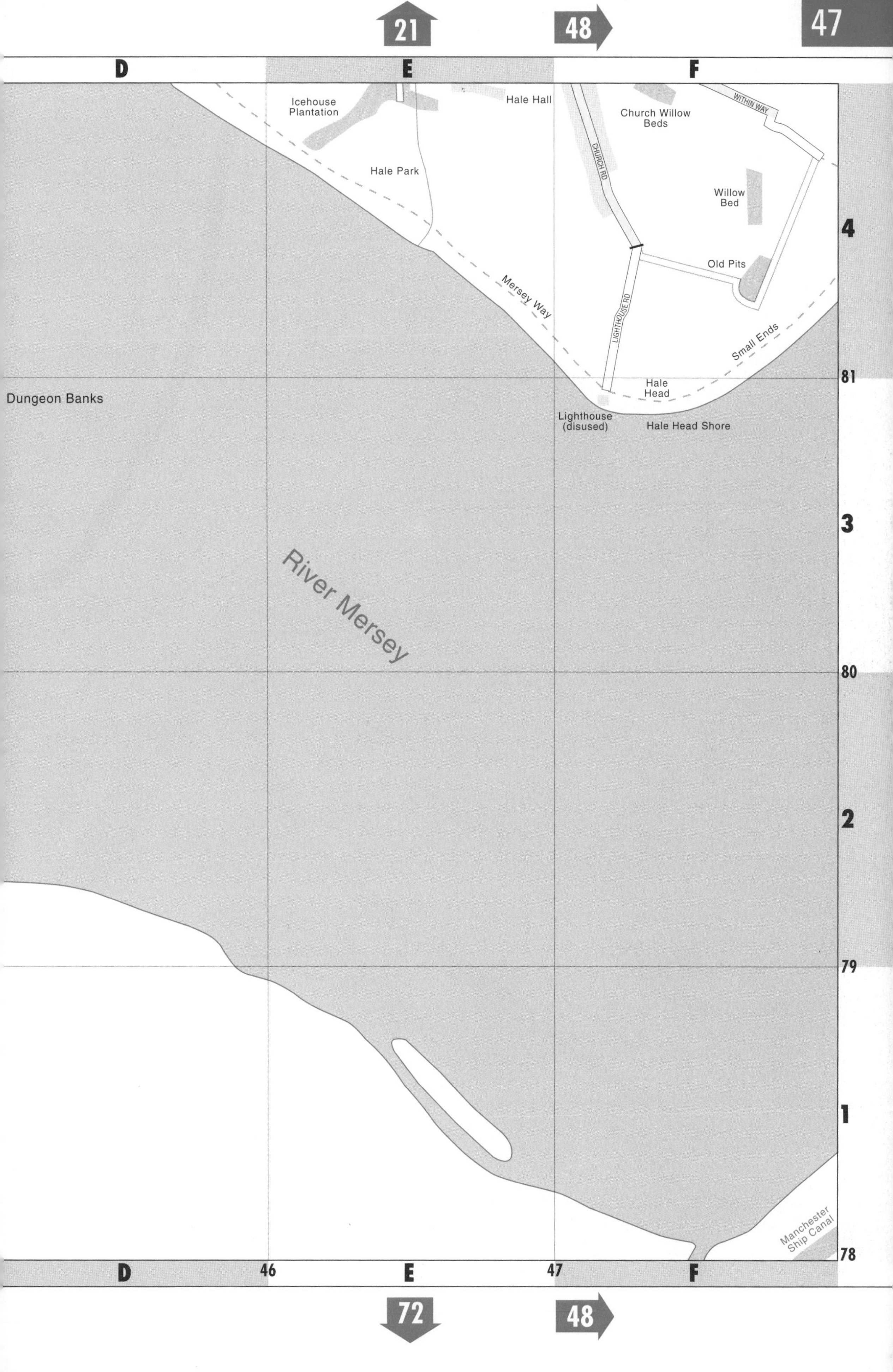

D

E

F

Icehouse
Plantation

Hale Hall

Church Willow
Beds

WITHIN WAY

CHURCH RD

Hale Park

Willow
Bed

4

LIGHTHOUSE RD

Old Pits

Mersey Way

Small Ends

81

Dungeon Banks

Hale
Head

Lighthouse
(disused)

Hale Head Shore

River Mersey

3

80

2

79

1

Manchester
Ship Canal

78

D

46

E

47

F

A   B   C

4

81

3

80

2

79

1

78

Docks

Runcorn & Western
Canal (disused)

Mersey View

Works

PICOW FARM RD

A557

BEACONSFIELD RD

CUNNINGHAM DR

HALE RD
HILLSIDE AVE
RUSSELL RD
CAMERON AVE
HAZEL AVE
PERRIN AVE
MINSTER CT

Beacon Hill

P

Runcorn Hill
(Public Park)

HIGHLANDS RD
COOK
ROYD
PAI

Recn
Gd

CLARKS TERR

PO

BEACON HILL
VIEW

SANDY LA

LC

Lancaster
Ave

WESTON POINT EXPRESSWAY

Weston
Point Cty Prim
Sch

COMPANY'S CL 1
MONTPELIER AVE 2
LAMBSICKLE CL 3

WESTON RD

Weston
Mersey Locks

Swing
Bridge

WEST RD

SOUTH PM

CANAL SIDE

BAKER RD
KELLY RD
CULLEN RD

LEONARD ST

SYDNEY ST

MATHER AVE

CASTNER AVE
ROSCOE CRES

LYDIATE LA

COLLIER'S ROW

PO

WESTON CT

Sewage
Works

Weston
Point

Manchester Ship Canal

Works

Weaver Navigation

BANKS LA

CHESHYRE'S LA

LC

CHESHYRE'S LA

Weston

ASHTON CL
CRESTA DR
MARION DR

HEATH RD SW

LAMBSICK
TILDSLE

River Mersey

Weaver
Sluices

BANKES LA

CAV
FA

Works

Weston Marsh
Lock

River Weaver

ALDER LA

Frodsham Marsh
Farm

Frodsham Marsh

BROOK FURLONG

Frodsham Score

Manchester Ship Canal

Canal Deposit Dump

Jetties

MOORDITCH LA

TADGERS LA

MOORDITCH LA

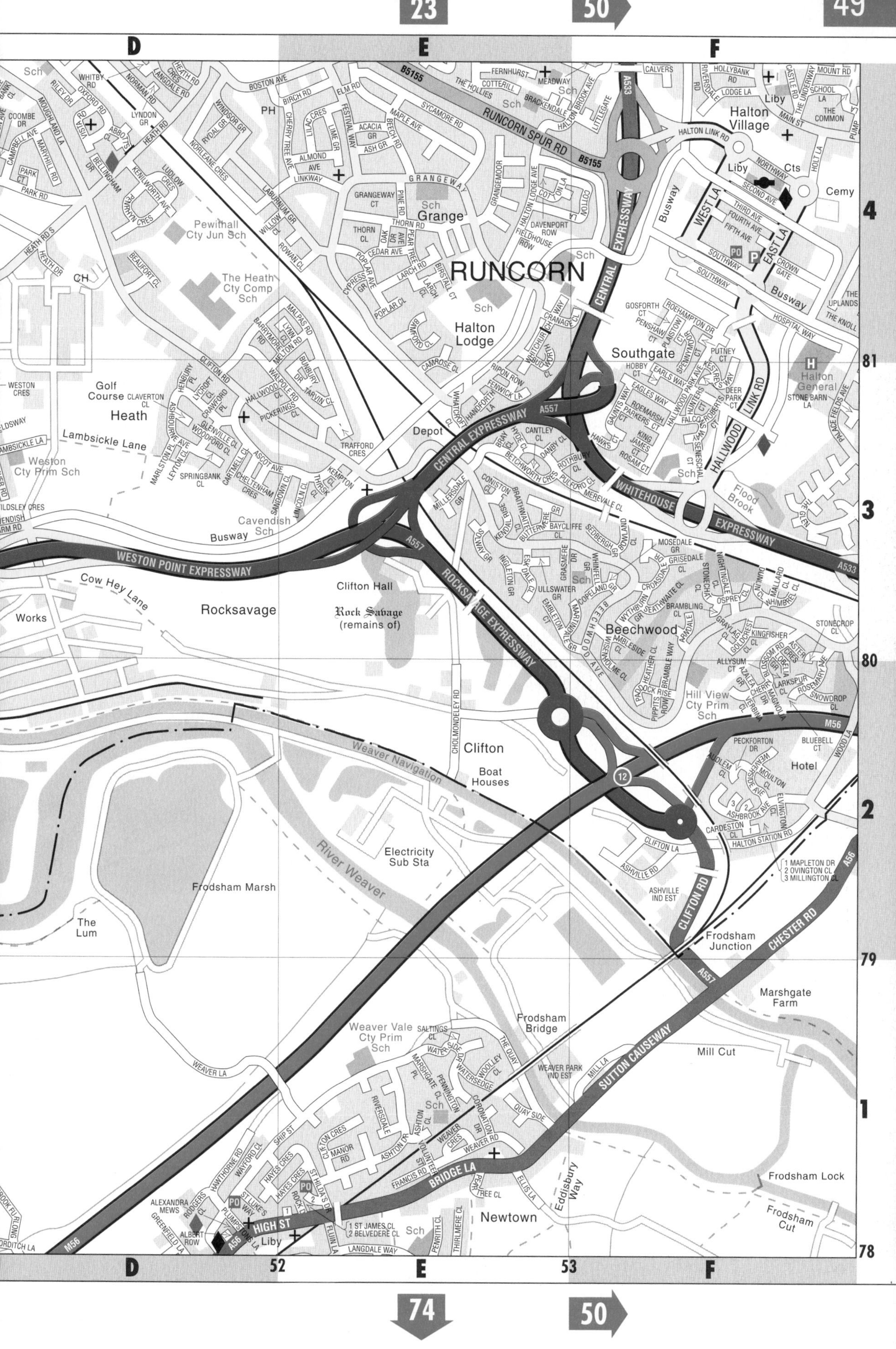

23
50
D
E
F
RUNCORN
Halton Village
Grange
Halton Lodge
Southgate
Heath
Golf Course
Pewithall Cty Jun Sch
The Heath Cty Comp Sch
Weston Cty Prim Sch
Cavendish Sch
Depot
Halton General
Rocksavage
Clifton Hall
Rock Savage (remains of)
Beechwood
Hill View Cty Prim Sch
Clifton
Boat Houses
Hotel
Works
Frodsham Marsh
The Lum
Electricity Sub Sta
River Weaver
Weaver Navigation
Frodsham Junction
Marshgate Farm
Frodsham Bridge
Weaver Vale Cty Prim Sch
Mill Cut
Frodsham Lock
Frodsham Cut
Newtown
Eddisbury Way
WESTON POINT EXPRESSWAY
CENTRAL EXPRESSWAY
ROCKSAVAGE EXPRESSWAY
WHITEHOUSE EXPRESSWAY
RUNCORN SPUR RD
SUTTON CAUSEWAY
CHESTER RD
BRIDGE LA
HIGH ST
CLIFTON RD
HALLWOOD LINK RD
Lambsickle Lane
Cow Hey Lane
Busway
1 MAPLETON DR
2 OVINGTON CL
3 MILLINGTON CL
1 ST JAMES CL
2 BELVEDERE CL
4
81
3
80
2
79
1
78
52
53
74
50

49   24

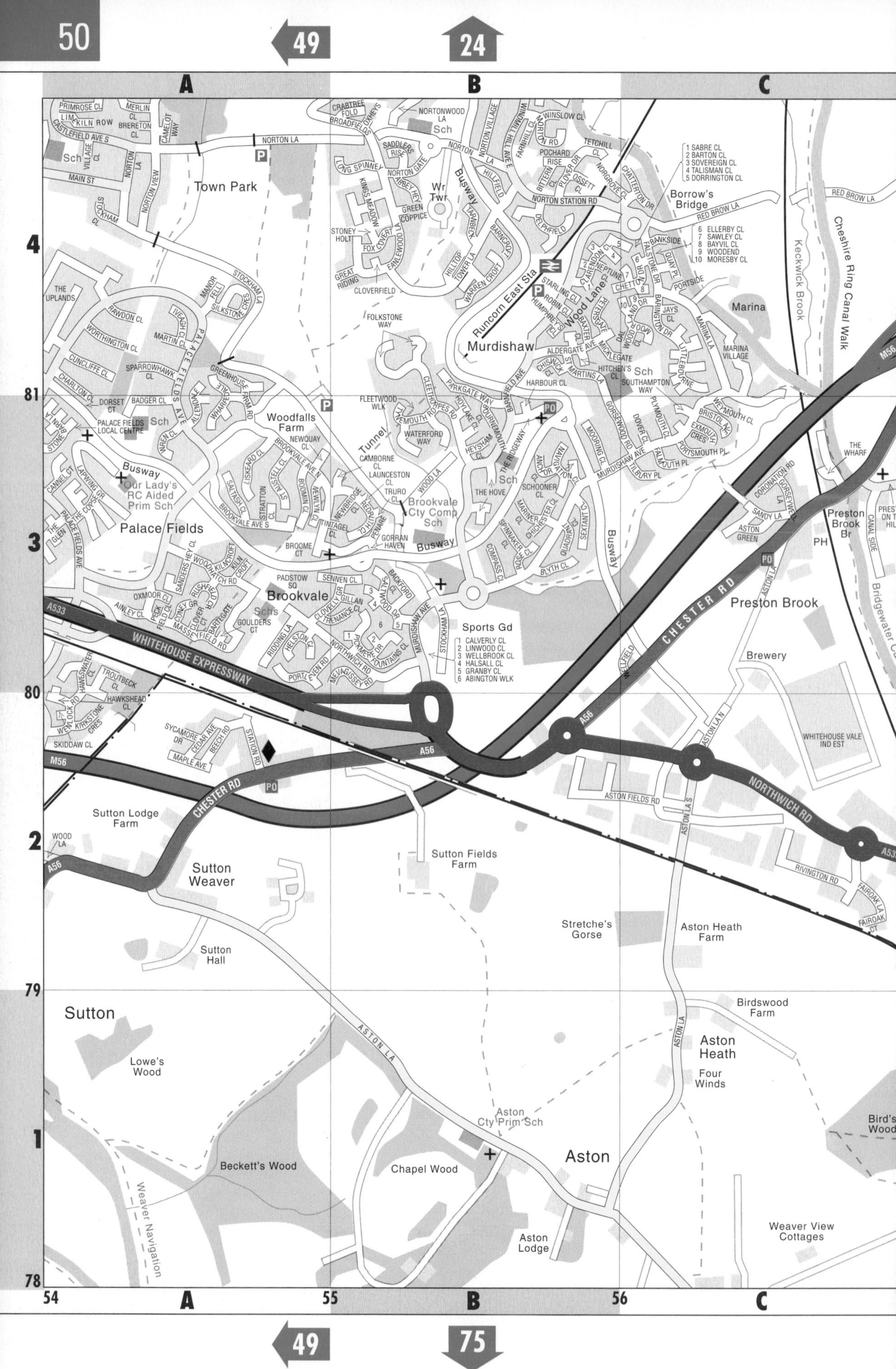

A   **B**   **C**

PRIMROSE CL
MERLIN CL
LIM KILN ROW
BRERETON CL
CASTLEFIELD AVE S
CAMELOT WAY
VILLAGE CL
NORTON LA
Sch
MAIN ST
STOCKHAM LA
NORTON VIEW
Town Park
NORTON LA
P
CRABTREE FOLD
BROADFIELDS
NORTONWOOD LA
NORTON VILLAGE
WINSLOW CL
NORTON RD
TETCHILL
Sch
LONG SPINNEY
SADDLERS RISE
NORTON GATE
KINGS MEADOW
NORTON HILL AVE
NORTON LA
FARNHILL
POCHARD RISE
NORGROVE CL
CHATTERTON DR

1 SABRE CL
2 BARTON CL
3 SOVEREIGN CL
4 TALISMAN CL
5 DORRINGTON CL

Borrow's Bridge
RED BROW LA
RED BROW LA
Cheshire Ring Canal Walk
Keckwick Brook

THE UPLANDS
RAWDON CL
WORTHINGTON CL
CUNCLIFFE CL
CHARLTON CL
DORSET CT
BADGER CL
Sch
MANOR FELL
STOCKHAM LA
SILKSTONE CRES
GREENHOUSE FARM RD
WHARFE
ALLENBY SQ
Woodfalls Farm
P
NEWQUAY CL
FOLKSTONE WAY
CLOVERFIELD
GREAT RIDING
STONEY HOLT
FOX COVERT
EARLSWOOD
HILLTOP
WARREN CROFT
HILLFIELD
BARNFIELD
BARNACRE
DELLFIELD
Wr Twr
Busway
Runcorn East East Sta
NORTON STATION RD
STARLING CL
ROBIN CL
P
HUMPHREY
Wood Lane
PLOVER CL
BITTERN CL
OSSETT CL
NEPTUNE
BANKSIDE
FALSTINE DR
PORTSIDE
QUAY CL
Marina
WT
MEYMOUTH CL

6 ELLERBY CL
7 SAWLEY CL
8 BAYVIL CL
9 WOODEND
10 MORESBY CL

Murdishaw
Marina Village
RED BROW LA

PALACE FIELDS LOCAL CENTRE
PALACE FIELDS AVE
Busway
Our Lady's RC Aided Prim Sch
LAPWING GR
COPSE
CANNEL CT
Palace Fields
THE GLEN
THE PALACE FIELDS AVE
WARREN CT
Sch
Tunnel
FLEETWOOD WLK
CAMBORNE CL
LAUNCESTON CL
TRURO
NEWBRIDGE CL
STRATTON CL
TINTAGEL CL
BROOME CT
WATERFORD WAY
HEYSHAM CL
WOOD LA
THE HOVE
Brookvale Cty Sch
PARKGATE WAY
CLEETHORPES RD
HOYLAKE
THE RINGWAY
Sch
SCHOONER CL
ANCHOR CL
MARINER CT
AGINCOURT CL
Southampton Way
HITCHEN'S LA
HARBOUR CL
ALDERGATE AVE
MARTINS LA
BRISTOL CL
PLYMOUTH CL
PORTSMOUTH PL
MURDISHAW AVE
DOVER CL
GORSEWOOD CL
FALMOUTH CL
TILBURY PL
MOVING CL
EXMOUTH CRES

OXMOOR CL
AINLEY CL
BADGERS HEY
WOODHATCH RD
KILKRUTH RD
CLOVELL'S GILLAN
TRENANCE CL
SENNEN CL
PADSTOW SQ
GORRAN HAVEN
BACKFORD
Brookvale
Schs
GOULDERS CT
RIDDING LA
HESTON CL
NORTHWICH RD
PICKMERE PORT
THE FOUNTAINS
MEVAGISSEY RD
STOCKHAM LA
Busway
BLYTH CL
COMPASS CL
SEXTANT CL
QUARRY CL
SPINNAKER CL
CHICHESTER CL

Sports Gd
1 CALVERLY CL
2 LINWOOD CL
3 WELLBROOK CL
4 HALSALL CL
5 GRANBY CL
6 ABINGTON WLK

CHESTER RD
Preston Brook
CORONATION RD
GORSEY WEY
ASTON GREEN
SANDY LA
P
THE WHARF
PH
Preston Brook Br
CANAL SIDE
PRESTON ON TH...
Bridgewater Can...
M56

A533
WHITEHOUSE EXPRESSWAY
M56
TROUTBECK CL
HAWKSWATER CL
HAWKSHEAD CL
WOOD LA
SKIDDAW CL
KIRKSTONE CRES
A56
SYCAMORE DR
CEDAR AVE
BEECH RD
MAPLE AVE
STATION RD
P
PO
CHESTER RD
A56
WHITEFIELD
Sutton Lodge Farm
ASTON FIELDS RD
ASTON LA
A56
NORTHWICH RD
Brewery
WHITEHOUSE VALE IND EST
RIVINGTON RD
FAIROAK LA
FAIROAK CT
A533

Sutton Weaver
Sutton Hall
Sutton Fields Farm
Stretche's Gorse
Aston Heath Farm
Aston Heath
Birdswood Farm
Four Winds

Sutton
Lowe's Wood
Beckett's Wood
Chapel Wood
Aston Cty Prim Sch
Aston
Bird's Wood
Weaver Navigation
ASTON LA
Aston Lodge
Weaver View Cottages

81   4
3
2
1
80
79
78

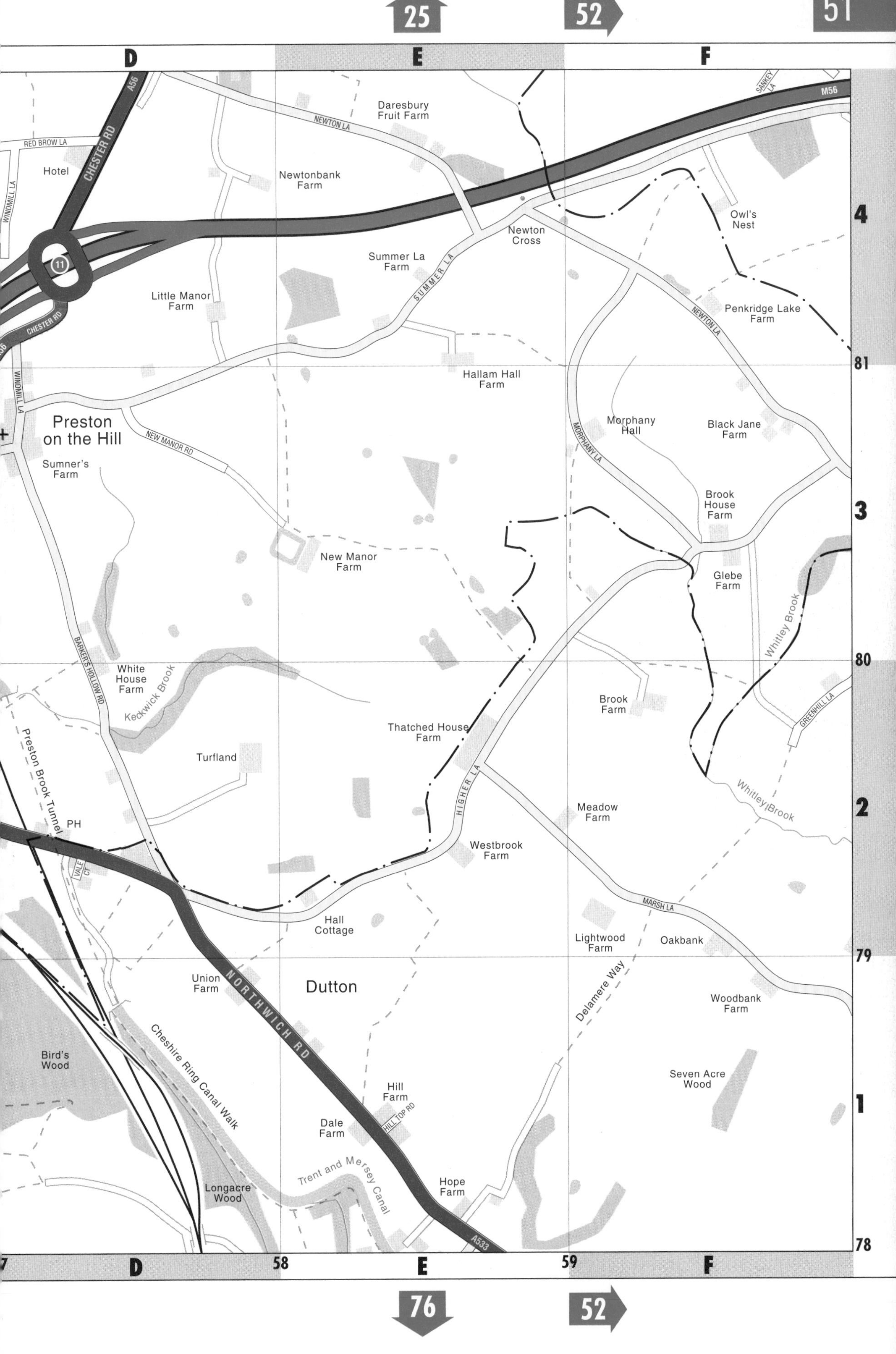

D E F

Daresbury
Fruit Farm

NEWTON LA

Newtonbank
Farm

CHESTER RD

A56

RED BROW LA

Hotel

WINDMILL LA

Summer La
Farm

SUMMER LA

Newton
Cross

Owl's
Nest

SANKEY LA

M56

4

Little Manor
Farm

11

CHESTER RD

A56

WINDMILL LA

Penkridge Lake
Farm

NEWTON LA

81

Preston
on the Hill

NEW MANOR RD

Hallam Hall
Farm

Morphany
Hall

Black Jane
Farm

MORPHANY LA

Sumner's
Farm

New Manor
Farm

Brook
House
Farm

3

BARKERS HOLLOW RD

White
House
Farm

Keckwick Brook

Glebe
Farm

Whitley Brook

GREENHILL LA

Turfland

Thatched House
Farm

Brook
Farm

80

Preston Brook Tunnel

Whitley Brook

HIGHER LA

Meadow
Farm

2

PH

VALE CT

Westbrook
Farm

Hall
Cottage

MARSH LA

Lightwood
Farm

Oakbank

79

Bird's
Wood

Cheshire Ring Canal Walk

NORTHWICH RD

Union
Farm

Dutton

Delamere Way

Woodbank
Farm

Hill
Farm

HILL TOP RD

Seven Acre
Wood

1

Dale
Farm

Trent and Mersey Canal

Hope
Farm

Longacre
Wood

A533

78

7 D 58 E 59 F

51
26

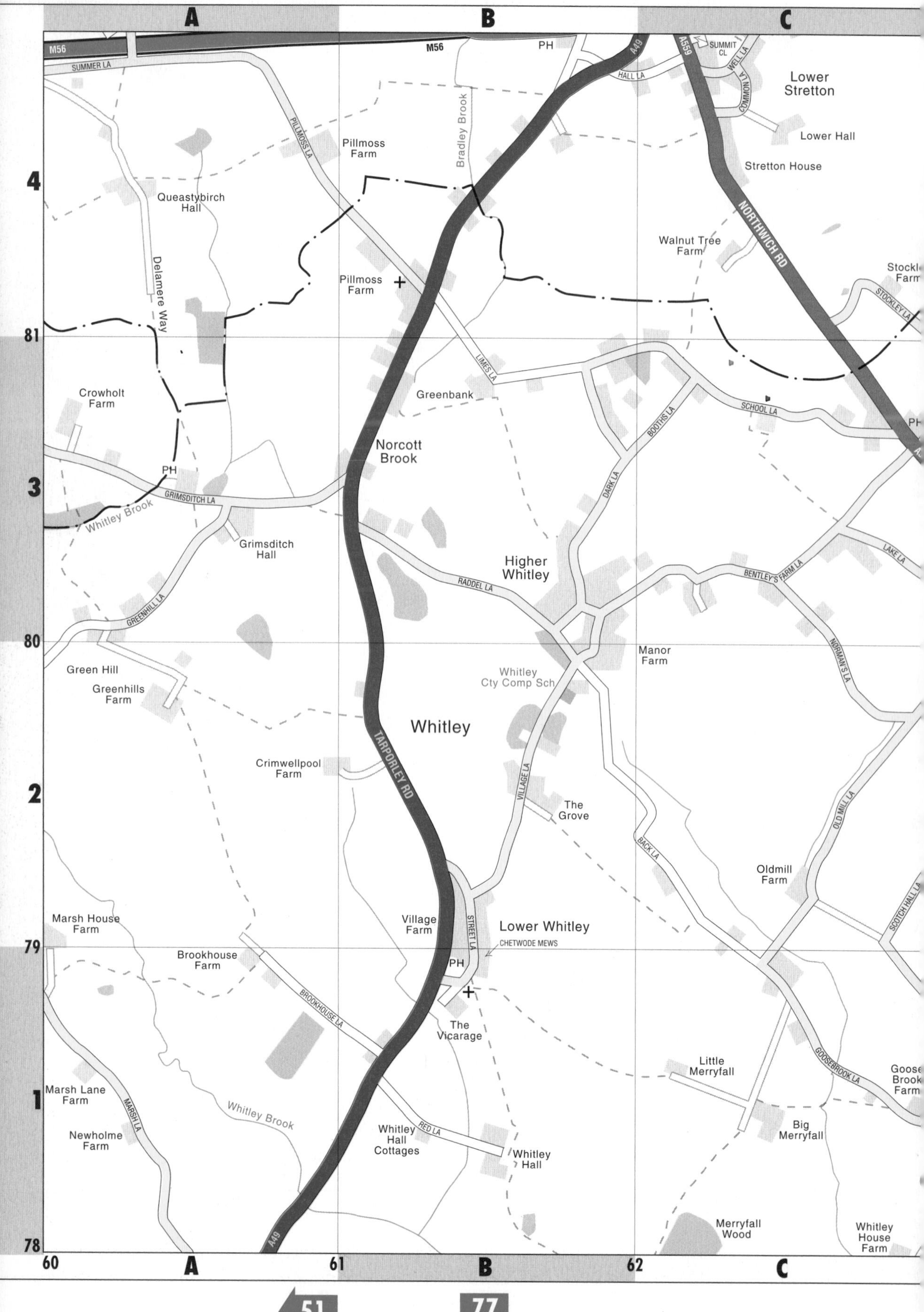
A
B
C
M56
M56
SUMMER LA
PH
A49
HALL LA
A559
SUMMIT CL
WELL LA
COMMON LA
Lower Stretton
Lower Hall
Stretton House
PILLMOSS LA
Pillmoss Farm
Bradley Brook
Queastybirch Hall
Delamere Way
Walnut Tree Farm
NORTHWICH RD
Stockl Farm
STOCKLEY LA
Pillmoss Farm
LIMES LA
Crowholt Farm
Greenbank
SCHOOL LA
BOOTHS LA
PH
Norcott Brook
PH
GRIMSDITCH LA
Whitley Brook
DARK LA
Grimsditch Hall
Higher Whitley
LAKE LA
RADDEL LA
BENTLEY'S FARM LA
GREENHILL LA
Green Hill
Greenhills Farm
Manor Farm
Whitley Cty Comp Sch
NORMAN'S LA
Whitley
TARPORLEY RD
Crimwellpool Farm
VILLAGE LA
The Grove
OLD MILL LA
BACK LA
Oldmill Farm
Marsh House Farm
Village Farm
STREET LA
Lower Whitley
CHETWODE MEWS
SCOTCH HALL LA
Brookhouse Farm
PH
BROOKHOUSE LA
The Vicarage
Little Merryfall
GOOSEBROOK LA
Goose Brook Farm
Marsh Lane Farm
Whitley Brook
MARSH LA
Newholme Farm
Whitley Hall Cottages
RED LA
Whitley Hall
Big Merryfall
Merryfall Wood
Whitley House Farm
A49
4
81
3
80
2
79
1
78
60
61
62

51
77

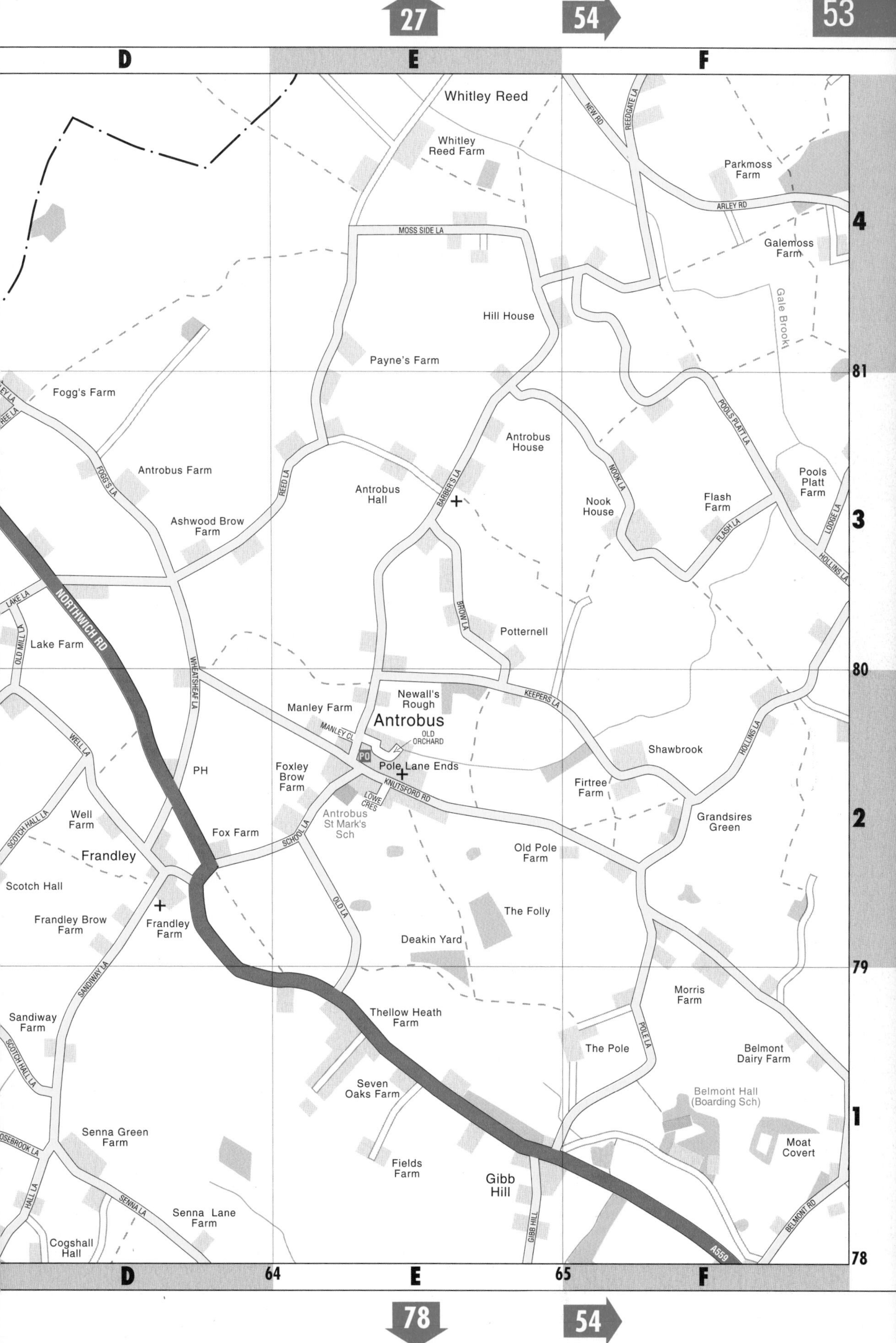
D
E
F
Whitley Reed
Whitley Reed Farm
NEW RD
REEDGATE LA
Parkmoss Farm
ARLEY RD
Galemoss Farm
MOSS SIDE LA
Gale Brook
Hill House
Payne's Farm
Fogg's Farm
POOLS PLATT LA
Antrobus House
Antrobus Farm
FOGG'S LA
REED LA
Antrobus Hall
BARBER'S LA
NOOK LA
Nook House
Flash Farm
FLASH LA
Pools Platt Farm
LODGE LA
HOLLINS LA
Ashwood Brow Farm
LAKE LA
NORTHWICH RD
Lake Farm
OLD MILL LA
BROW LA
Potternell
WHEATSHEAF LA
KEEPERS LA
Newall's Rough
Manley Farm
Antrobus
MANLEY CL
OLD ORCHARD
WELL LA
PO
Pole Lane Ends
Shawbrook
PH
Foxley Brow Farm
KNUTSFORD RD
Firtree Farm
LOWE CRES
Well Farm
SCOTCH HALL LA
Antrobus St Mark's Sch
Grandsires Green
Fox Farm
SCHOOL LA
Frandley
Old Pole Farm
Scotch Hall
Frandley Brow Farm
Frandley Farm
OLD LA
The Folly
Deakin Yard
SANDIWAY LA
Morris Farm
Sandiway Farm
Thellow Heath Farm
POLE LA
The Pole
Belmont Dairy Farm
SCOTCH HALL LA
Seven Oaks Farm
Belmont Hall (Boarding Sch)
Senna Green Farm
Moat Covert
ROSEBROOK LA
Fields Farm
Gibb Hill
HALL LA
SENNA LA
Senna Lane Farm
BELMONT RD
Cogshall Hall
GIBB HILL
A559
4
81
3
80
2
79
1
78
64
65

A   B   C

The Firs

M6

Crowley Grange

Stockley Farm

4

Garland Hall

CALDWELL'S GATE LA

BACK LA

Arley

The Dairy

ARLEY RD

The Ashe

⊹ Arley Hall

PO

Arley
Cty Prim
Sch

Arley
Green

81

Lady Park

LODGE LA

Crowley Lodge

SACK LA

HOLLINS LA

Hollies
Farm

Big
Wood

3

Arley Park

Alderhedge
Wood

80

The Belts

Reed House
Farm

The Kennels

CANN LA

Cannla
Farm

New Farm

2

Arley Brook

The
Slacks

Willowbed
Wood

Willow
Lodge

Bate Heath

COLLIERS LA

79

ARLEY MOSSEND LA

Arley Moss Farm

BUDWORTH RD

Kays Fa

Hilltop
Farm

Moss End

Yewtree
Farm

Fields Farm

1

KNUTSFORD RD

KNUTSFORD RD

George's Lane
Farm

Budworth
Heath

HEATH LA

BUDWORTH HEATH LA

GEORGE'S LA

Wathall Farm

Aston Park

Gravestones Farm

78

66   A   67   B   68   C

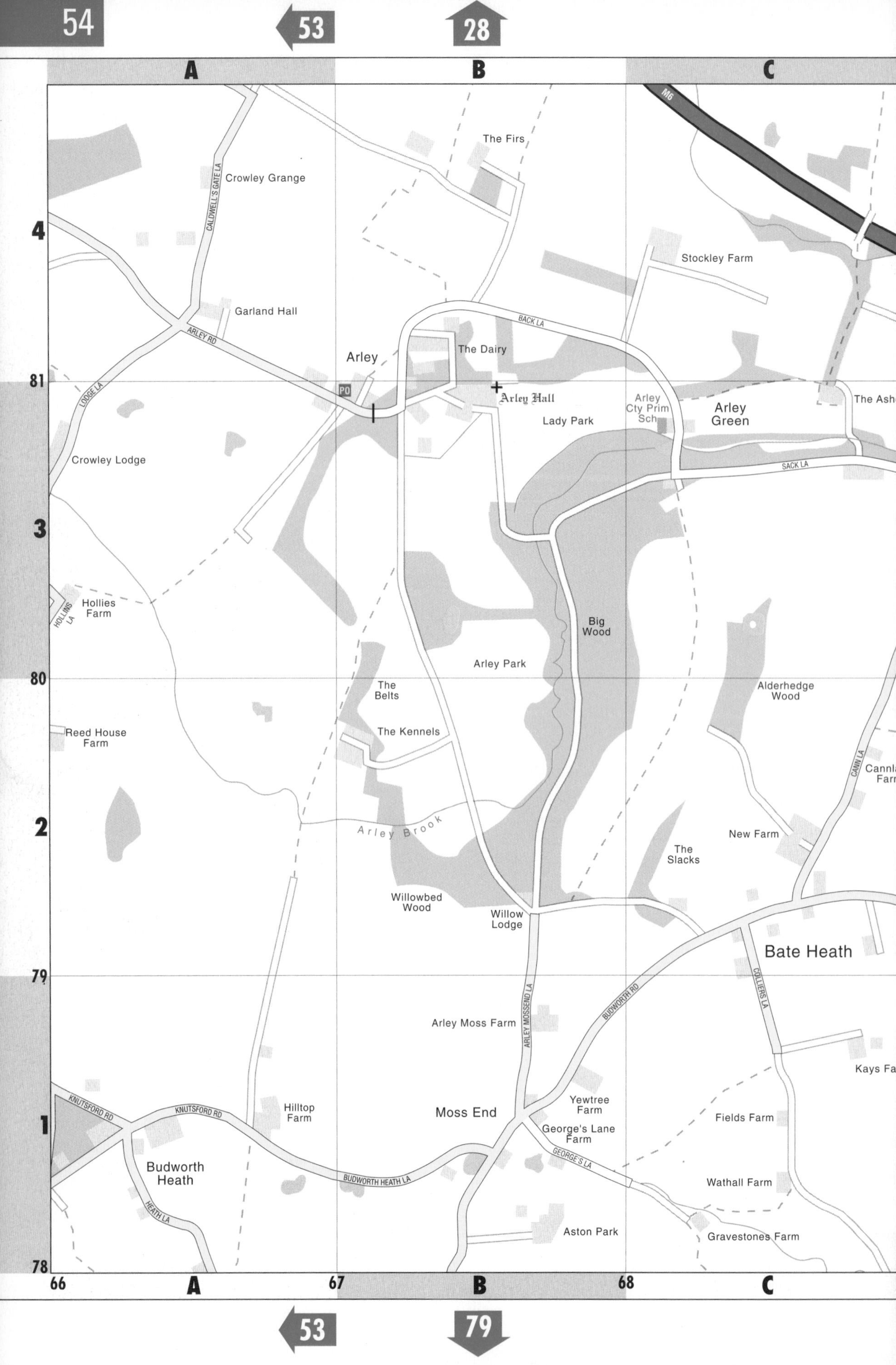

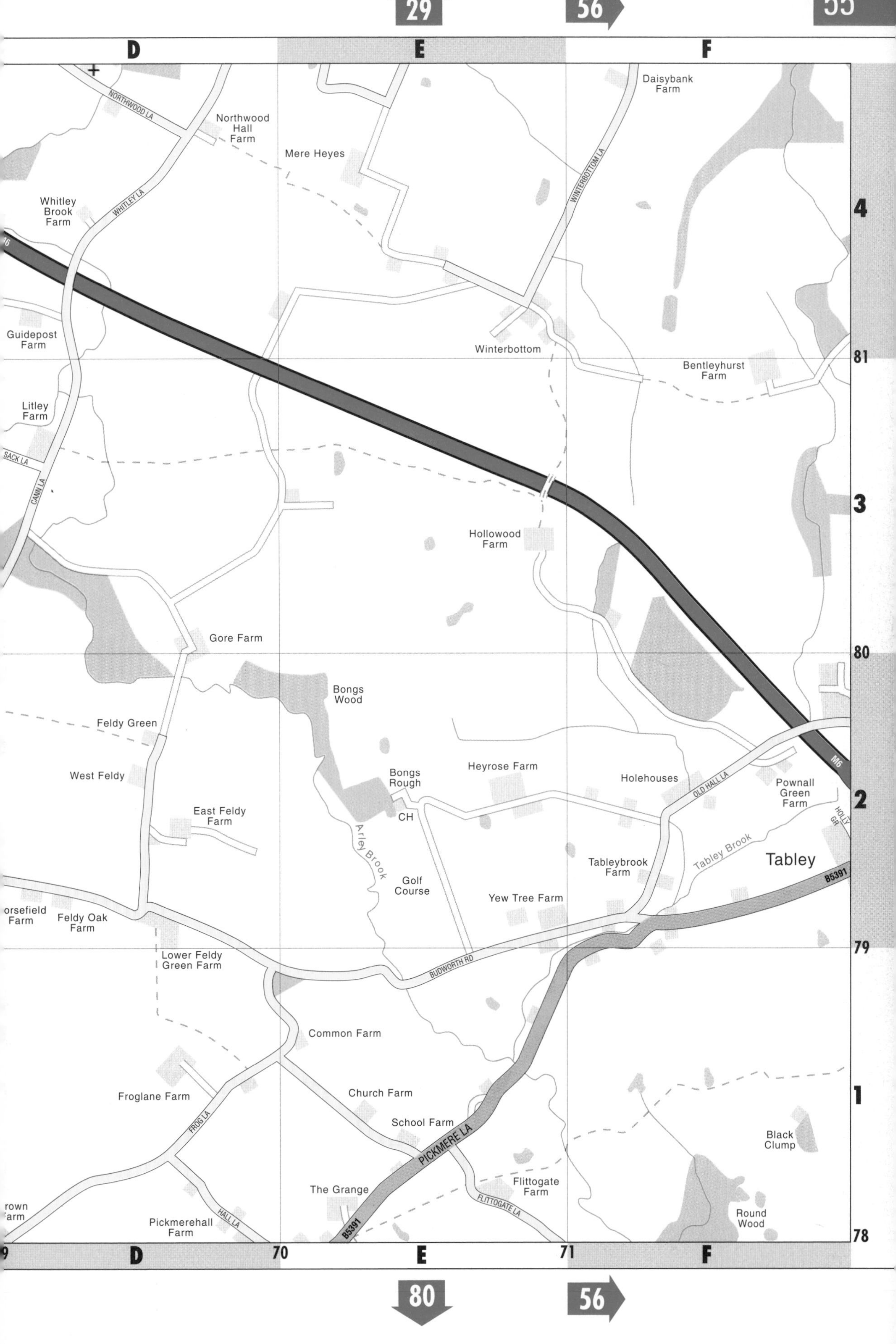
29
56
D
E
F
NORTHWOOD LA
Northwood Hall Farm
Mere Heyes
Daisybank Farm
WINTERBOTTOM LA
Whitley Brook Farm
WHITLEY LA
M6
Guidepost Farm
Winterbottom
Bentleyhurst Farm
Litley Farm
SACK LA
CANN LA
Hollowood Farm
Gore Farm
Bongs Wood
Feldy Green
West Feldy
Bongs Rough
Heyrose Farm
Holehouses
OLD HALL LA
Pownall Green Farm
HOLLY GR
East Feldy Farm
CH
Arley Brook
Golf Course
Tableybrook Farm
Tabley Brook
Tabley
B5391
orsefield Farm
Feldy Oak Farm
Yew Tree Farm
Lower Feldy Green Farm
BUDWORTH RD
Common Farm
Froglane Farm
Church Farm
School Farm
FROG LA
PICKMERE LA
Black Clump
The Grange
Flittogate Farm
FLITTOGATE LA
rown arm
Pickmerehall Farm
HALL LA
Round Wood
B5391
4
81
3
80
2
79
1
78
9
70
71
80
56

55
30

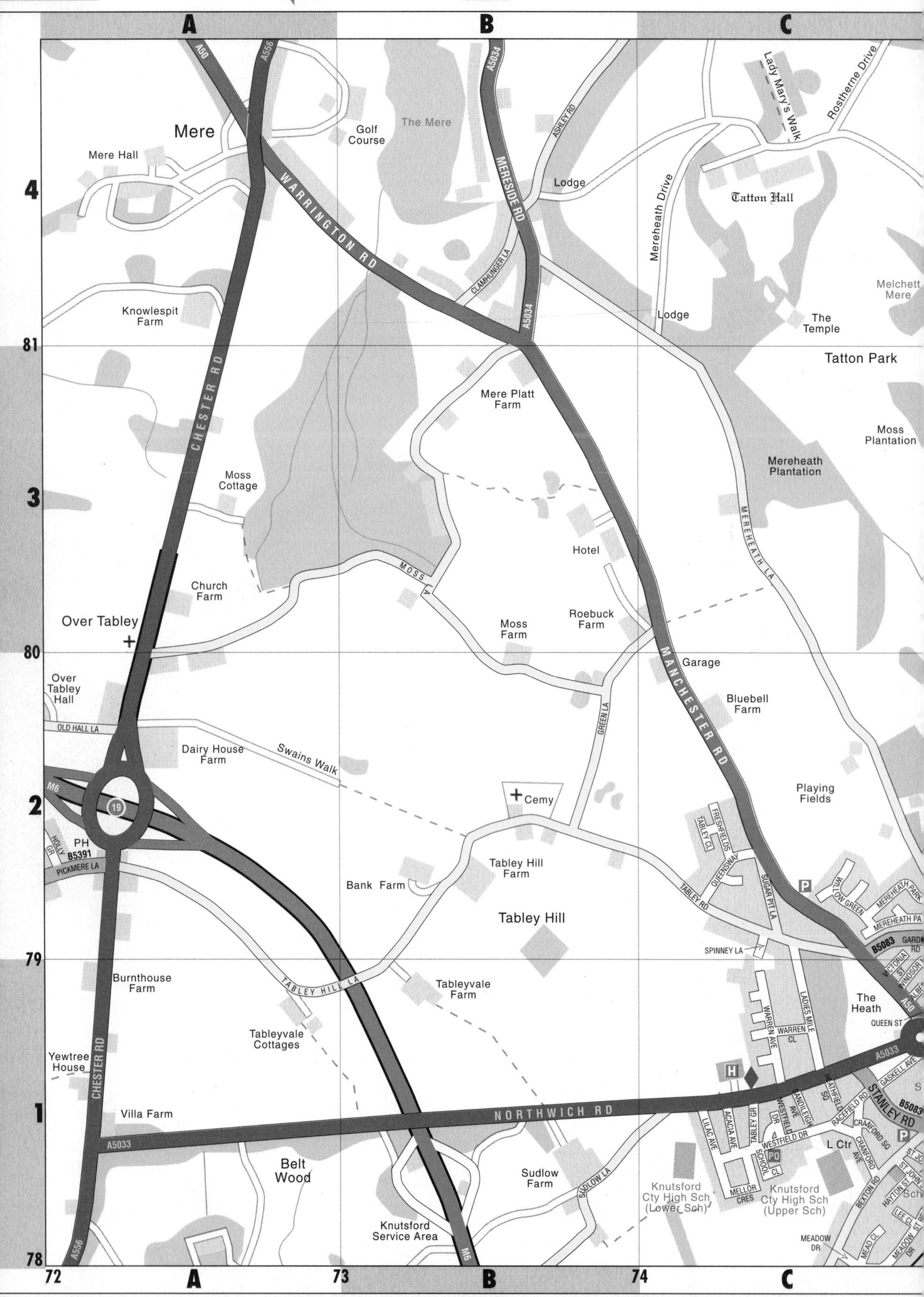
A
B
C
4
3
2
1
81
80
79
78
72
73
74
Mere
Mere Hall
Golf Course
The Mere
Lodge
Tatton Hall
Lady Mary's Walk
Rostherne Drive
Mereheath Drive
WARRINGTON RD
MERESIDE RD
ASHLEY RD
CLAMHUNGER LA
Knowlespit Farm
Melchett Mere
The Temple
Tatton Park
Mere Platt Farm
Moss Plantation
Mereheath Plantation
CHESTER RD
Moss Cottage
Hotel
MEREHEATH LA
Church Farm
MOSS LA
Over Tabley
Moss Farm
Roebuck Farm
Garage
Over Tabley Hall
OLD HALL LA
Bluebell Farm
Dairy House Farm
Swains Walk
GREEN LA
MANCHESTER RD
Playing Fields
Cemy
M6
19
HOLLY GR
PH
B5391
PICKMERE LA
Tabley Hill Farm
Bank Farm
TABLEY RD
QUEENSWAY
FRESHFIELDS
TABLEY CL
SUGAR PIT LA
WILLOW GREEN
MEREHEATH PARK
MEREHEATH PA
Tabley Hill
SPINNEY LA
B5083
VICTORIA ST
WINDSOR
TABLEY HILL LA
Burnthouse Farm
Tableyvale Farm
WARREN AVE
LADIES MILE
WARREN CL
The Heath
QUEEN ST
A50
Tableyvale Cottages
Yewtree House
A5033
GASKELL AVE
STANLEY RD
NORTHWICH RD
Villa Farm
LILAC AVE
ACACIA AVE
TABLEY GR
WESTFIELD DR
SANDILEIGH AVE
HEATHFIELD SQ
RACEFIELD RD
CRANFORD SQ
CRANFORD AVE
L Ctr
SCHOOL CL
PO
A556
A5034
Belt Wood
Sudlow Farm
SUDLOW LA
Knutsford Cty High Sch (Lower Sch)
MELLOR CRES
Knutsford Cty High Sch (Upper Sch)
BEXTON RD
HAYTON ST
ST JOHN
Knutsford Service Area
MEADOW DR
MEAD CL
LEE CL
Sch

55
81

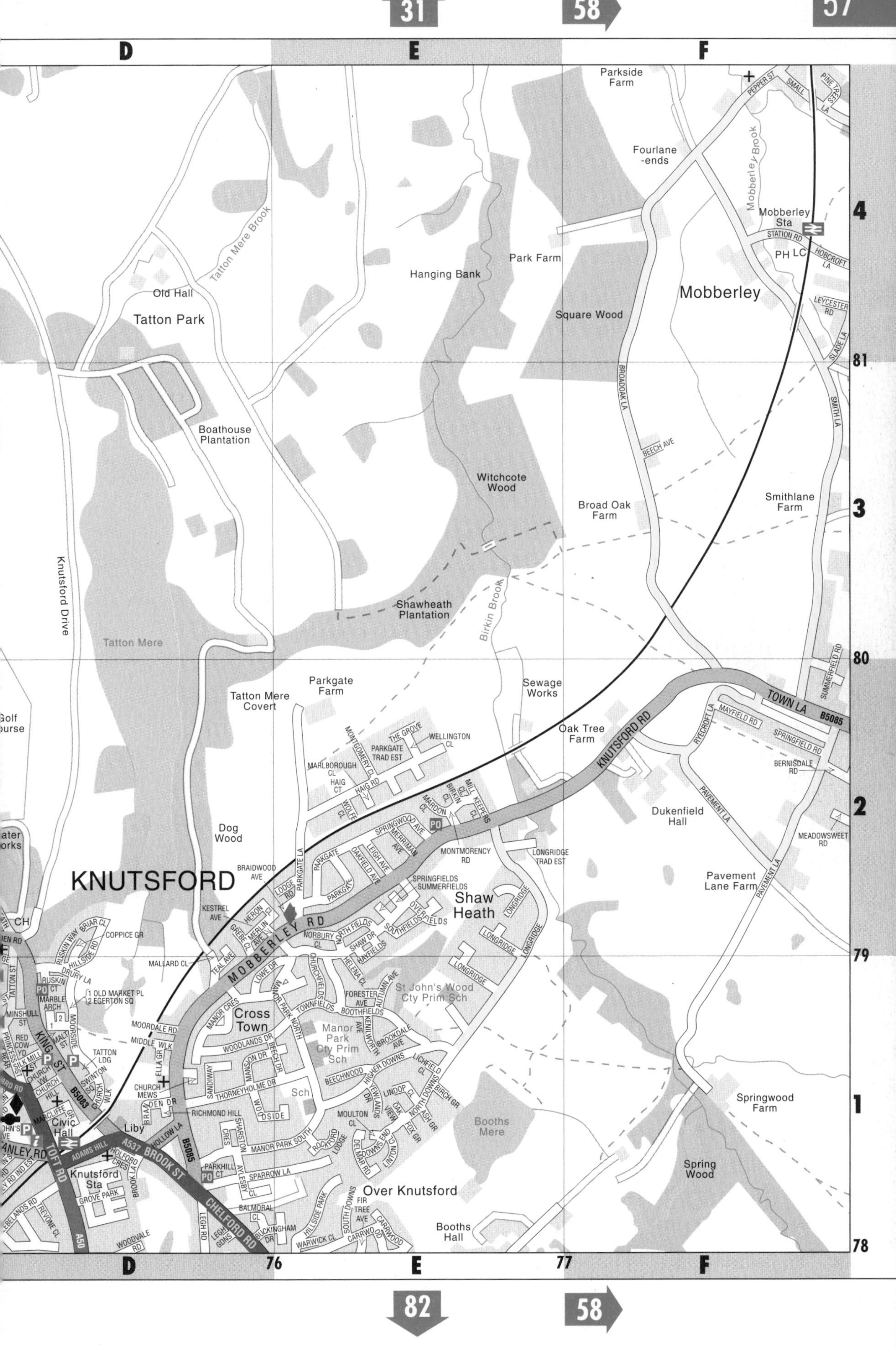
D
E
F
Parkside Farm
Fourlane -ends
Mobberley Brook
Mobberley Sta
STATION RD
HOBCROFT LA
PH LC
Mobberley
LEYCESTER RD
SLADE LA
SMITH LA
Tatton Mere Brook
Old Hall
Tatton Park
Hanging Bank
Park Farm
Square Wood
BROADOAK LA
BEECH AVE
Boathouse Plantation
Witchcote Wood
Broad Oak Farm
Smithlane Farm
Knutsford Drive
Shawheath Plantation
Birkin Brook
Tatton Mere
Parkgate Farm
Tatton Mere Covert
Sewage Works
Oak Tree Farm
KNUTSFORD RD
TOWN LA
B5085
SUMMERFIELD RD
MAYFIELD RD
SPRINGFIELD RD
RYECROFT LA
BERNISDALE RD
PAVEMENT LA
Dukenfield Hall
MEADOWSWEET RD
Pavement Lane Farm
THE GROVE
WELLINGTON CL
PARKGATE TRAD EST
MARLBOROUGH CL
HAIG CT
HAIG RD
WOLFE CL
MONTGOMERY CL
MILL KEEPERS
Dog Wood
MONTMORENCY RD
LONGRIDGE TRAD EST
KNUTSFORD
BRAIDWOOD AVE
PARKGATE LA
SPRINGFIELDS
SUMMERFIELDS
Shaw Heath
LONGRIDGE
KESTREL AVE
MOBBERLEY RD
COPPICE GR
MALLARD CL
TEAL AVE
1 OLD MARKET PL
2 EGERTON SQ
St John's Wood Cty Prim Sch
Cross Town
Manor Park Cty Prim Sch
MOORDALE RD
MIDDLE WLK
TATTON LDG
KING ST
B5083
CHURCH MEWS
Sch
RICHMOND HILL
Booths Mere
Springwood Farm
Civic Hall
Liby
A537 BROOK ST
B5085
Spring Wood
Knutsford Sta
GROVE PARK
Over Knutsford
CHELFORD RD
Booths Hall
WOODVALE RD
TOFT RD
A50
Golf Course
CH

4
81
3
80
2
79
1
78

D 76 E 77 F

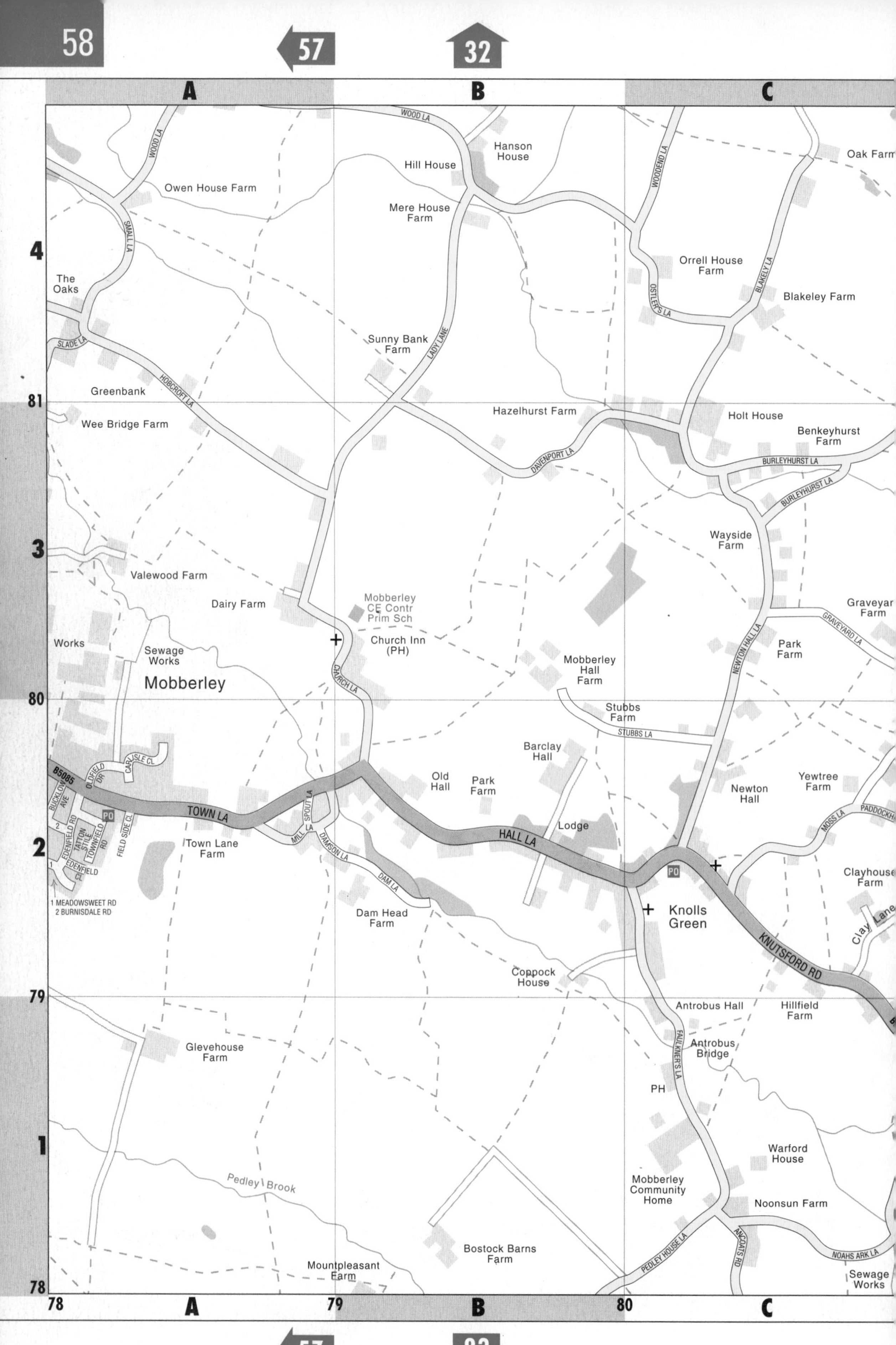

A B C

4

81

3

80

2

1

79

78

78 A 79 B 80 C

The Oaks

Owen House Farm

Hill House

Hanson House

Oak Farm

Mere House Farm

WOOD LA

WOODEND LA

Orrell House Farm

OSTLERS LA

BLAKELY LA

Blakeley Farm

Sunny Bank Farm

LADY LANE

Greenbank

HOBCROFT LA

SLADE LA

SMALL LA

Wee Bridge Farm

Hazelhurst Farm

DAVENPORT LA

Holt House

BURLEYHURST LA

Benkeyhurst Farm

BURLEYHURST LA

Wayside Farm

Valewood Farm

Dairy Farm

Mobberley CE Contr Prim Sch

Church Inn (PH)

Mobberley Hall Farm

NEWTON HALL LA

Park Farm

Graveyar Farm

GRAVEYARD LA

Works

Sewage Works

Mobberley

CHURCH LA

Stubbs Farm

STUBBS LA

B5085

OLD FIELD DR

CARLISLE CL

Barclay Hall

Newton Hall

Yewtree Farm

PADDOCKH

BUCKLOW AVE

EDENFIELD RD

TATTON STILE

TOWNFIELD RD

FIELD SIDE CL

TOWN LA

Town Lane Farm

MILL LA

SPOUT LA

DAMSON LA

Old Hall

Park Farm

Lodge

HALL LA

PO

MOSS LA

Clayhouse Farm

Clay Lane

EDENFIELD CL

1 MEADOWSWEET RD
2 BURNISDALE RD

Dam Head Farm

DAM LA

Knolls Green

PO

KNUTSFORD RD

Coppock House

Antrobus Hall

Hillfield Farm

Glevehouse Farm

FAULKNER'S LA

Antrobus Bridge

PH

Warford House

Pedley Brook

Mobberley Community Home

Noonsun Farm

Bostock Barns Farm

PEDLEY HOUSE LA

ANCOATS RD

NOAHS ARK LA

Mountpleasant Farm

Sewage Works

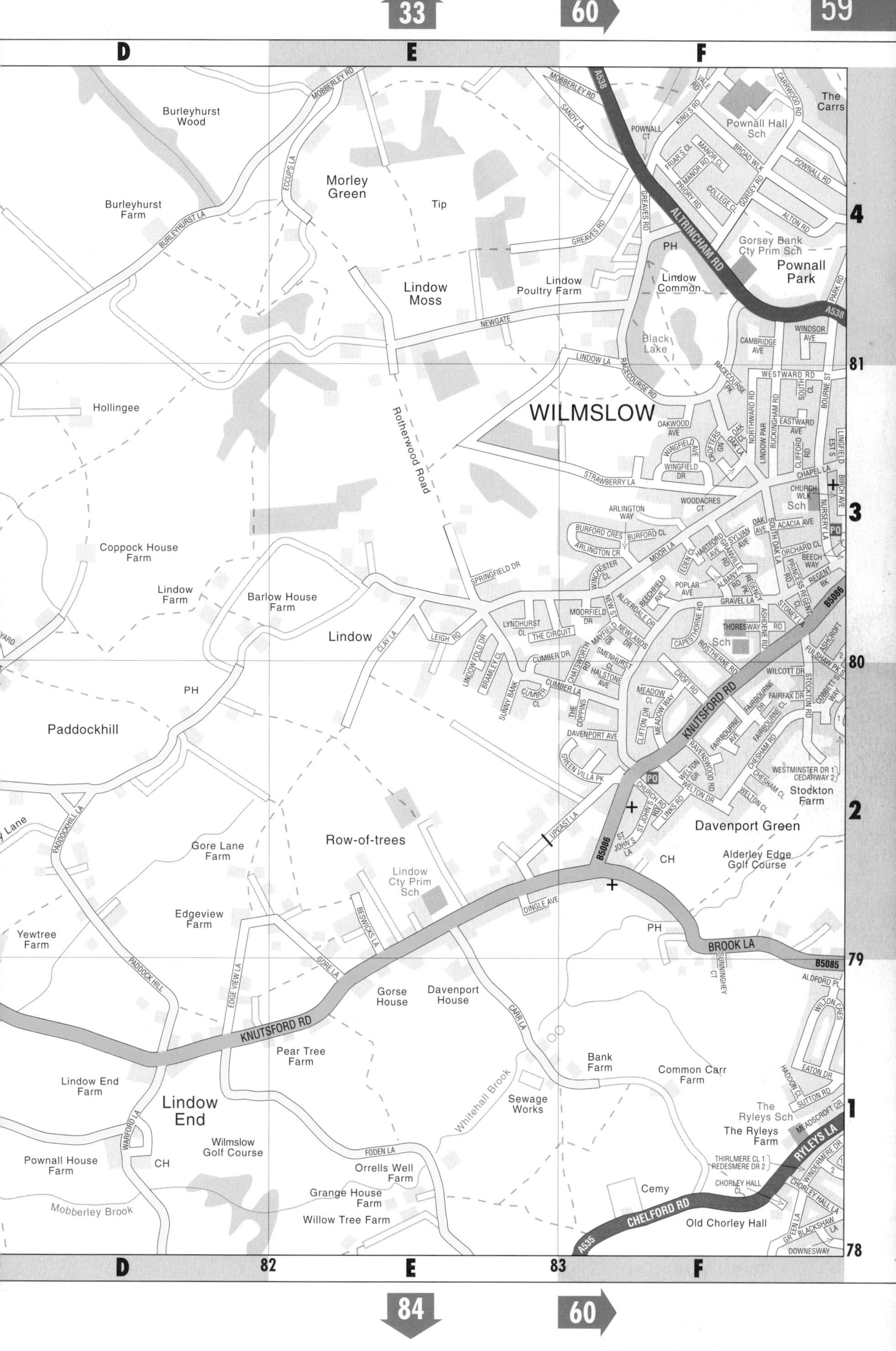

D
E
F

The Carrs

Burleyhurst Wood

Morley Green

Tip

MOBBERLEY RD

MOBBERLEY RD

SANDY LA

ECCUPS LA

GREAVES RD

A538

ALTRINCHAM RD

POWNALL CT

FRIARS CL

KING'S RD

VALE

Pownall Hall Sch

BROAD WLK

MANOR CL

PRIORY RD

COLLEGE CL

CARWOOD RD

POWNALL RD

ALTON RD

GORSEY RD

4

Burleyhurst Farm

BURLEYHURST LA

GREAVES RD

PH

Gorsey Bank Cty Prim Sch

Pownall Park

Lindow Poultry Farm

Lindow Moss

NEWGATE

Lindow Common

Lindow La

RACECOURSE RD

Black Lake

WINDSOR AVE

CAMBRIDGE AVE

RACECOURSE PK

PARK RD

A538

81

Hollingee

Rotherwood Road

WILMSLOW

WESTWARD RD

EASTWARD AVE

OAKWOOD AVE

CROFTERS

LINDOW PAR

NORTHWARD RD

BUCKINGHAM RD

SOUTH RD

BOURNE ST

CLIFFORD RD

LINGFIELD EST S

BIRCH RD

NURSERY LA

Sch

CHURCH WLK

3

STRAWBERRY LA

WINGFIELD AVE

WINGFIELD DR

WOODACRES CT

CHAPEL LA

OAK LA

OAK LA

PO

Coppock House Farm

ARLINGTON WAY

BURFORD CRES

BURFORD CL

ARLINGTON CR

MOOR LA

EDEN CL

HARTFORD

DALE

GRANVILLE RD

REGENCY

SYLVAN AVE

OAK AVE

ACACIA AVE

ORCHARD CL

BEECH WAY

REGENT

B5086

Lindow Farm

Barlow House Farm

SPRINGFIELD DR

WINCHESTER CL

NEW ST

NEWLANDS

BEECHFIELD

ALDERDALE DR

POPLAR AVE

ALBANY RD

PRINCESS RD

REGENT

GRAVEL LA

STONEY

ASHTREE RD

BK

Lindow

CLERK LA

LEIGH RD

LINDOW FOLD DR

LYNDHURST CL

THE CIRCUIT

MOORFIELD DR

CHESWORTH CL

MANFIELD CL

SMENHURST CL

HALSTONE AVE

CAPESTHORNE CL

Sch

ROSTHERNE RD

THORESWAY RD

ASHFIELD

FULSHAW PK

80

CUMBER DR

SUNNY BANK

CUMBER CL

CUMBER LA

THE COPPINS

DAVENPORT AVE

MEADOW CL

CLIFTON DR

CROFT RD

MEADOW WAY

KNUTSFORD RD

FAIRBOURNE CL

FAIRBOURNE AVE

WILCOTT DR

FAIRFAX RD

STOCKTON RD

CONNERY WAY

ASHCROFT

PH

Paddockhill

PADDOCKHILL LA

GREEN VILLA PK

PO

CHURCH GRN

ST JOHN'S RD

ST JOHN'S RD

RAVENSWOOD RD

WELTON DR

LINKS RD

WELTON CL

WELTON DR

CHESHAM RD

CHESHAM CL

WESTMINSTER DR 1

CEDARWAY 2

Stockton Farm

2

Row-of-trees

B5086

UPCAST LA

B5086

Davenport Green

CH

Alderley Edge Golf Course

Lindow Cty Prim Sch

Gore Lane Farm

Edgeview Farm

BESWICKS LA

DINGLE AVE

PH

BROOK LA

B5085

79

Yewtree Farm

ley Lane

PADDOCK HILL

EDGE VIEW LA

GORE LA

Gorse House

Davenport House

CARR LA

Whitehall Brook

SUNNINGHEY CT

ALDFORD PL

WILSON CRES

HADDON RD

EATON DR

SUTTON RD

KNUTSFORD RD

Pear Tree Farm

Bank Farm

Common Carr Farm

The Ryleys Sch

The Ryleys Farm

MEADSCROFT DR

RYLEYS LA

1

Lindow End Farm

WARFORD LA

Lindow End

Sewage Works

THIRLMERE CL 1

REDESMERE DR 2

WINDERMERE DR

Pownall House Farm

CH

Wilmslow Golf Course

FODEN LA

Orrells Well Farm

Cemy

CHORLEY HALL CL

CHORLEY HALL LA

GREEN LA

BLACKSHAW

Mobberley Brook

Grange House Farm

Willow Tree Farm

CHELFORD RD

A535

Old Chorley Hall

DOWNESWAY

78

D
82
E
83
F

59
34

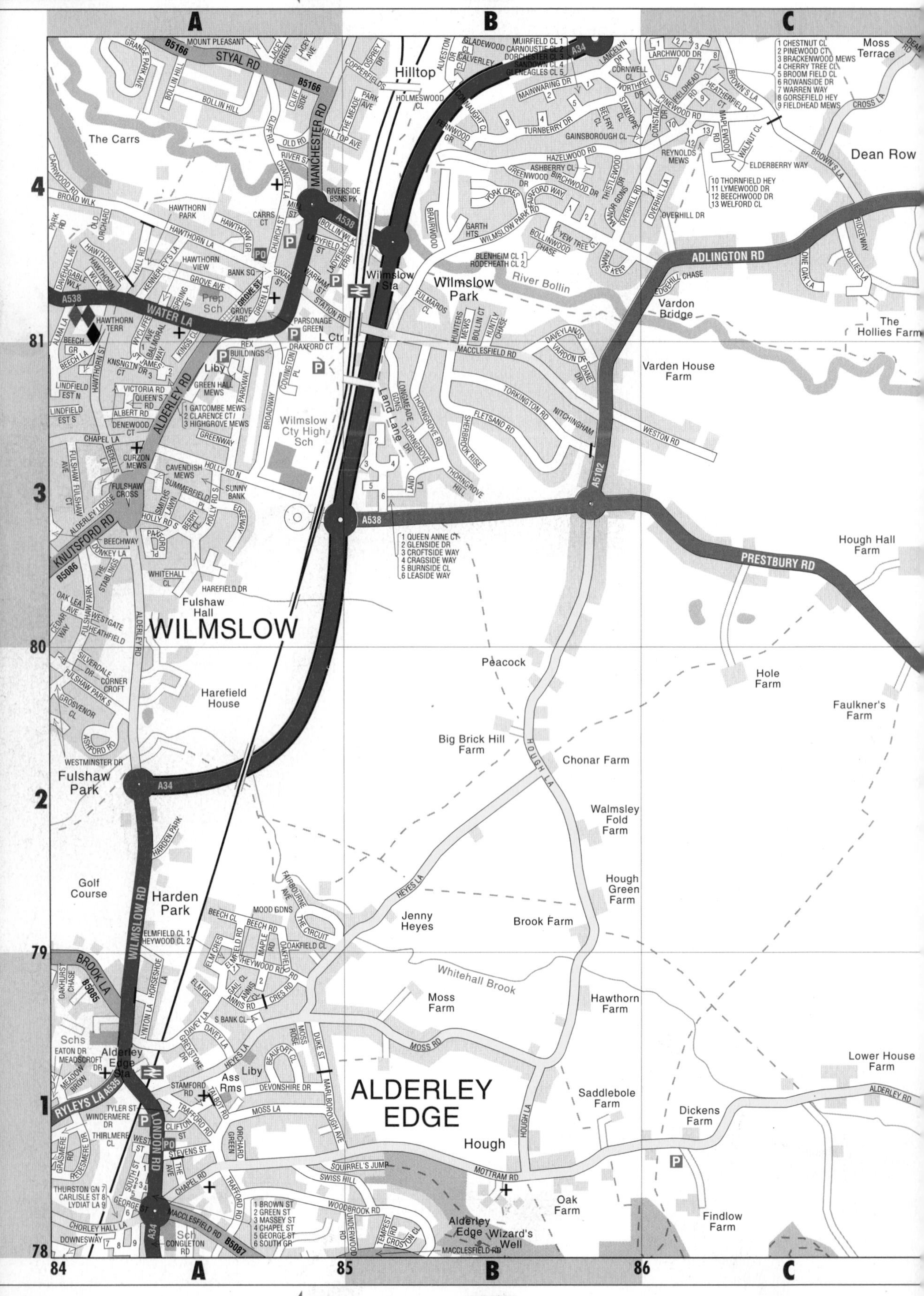
WILMSLOW
ALDERLEY EDGE
Wilmslow Park
Hilltop
The Carrs
Dean Row
Fulshaw Park
Harden Park
Golf Course
Peacock
Big Brick Hill Farm
Chonar Farm
Walmsley Fold Farm
Hough Green Farm
Brook Farm
Jenny Heyes
Moss Farm
Hawthorn Farm
Saddlebole Farm
Dickens Farm
Hough
Oak Farm
Findlow Farm
Lower House Farm
Faulkner's Farm
Hole Farm
Hough Hall Farm
Varden House Farm
Vardon Bridge
The Hollies Farm
Moss Terrace
Harefield House
Fulshaw Hall
Wilmslow Cty High Sch
Alderley Edge Wizard's Well
River Bollin
Whitehall Brook
ADLINGTON RD
PRESTBURY RD
WILMSLOW RD
LONDON RD
STYAL RD
MANCHESTER RD
WATER LA
ALDERLEY RD
KNUTSFORD RD
BROOK LA
RYLEYS LA
HOUGH LA
HEYES LA
MOSS RD
MOTTRAM RD
MACCLESFIELD RD
ALDERLEY RD
1 CHESTNUT CL
2 PINEWOOD CT
3 BRACKENWOOD MEWS
4 CHERRY TREE CL
5 BROOM FIELD CL
6 ROWANSIDE DR
7 WARREN WAY
8 GORSEFIELD HEY
9 FIELDHEAD MEWS
10 THORNFIELD HEY
11 LYMEWOOD DR
12 BEECHWOOD DR
13 WELFORD CL
1 QUEEN ANNE CT
2 GLENSIDE DR
3 CROFTSIDE WAY
4 CRAGSIDE WAY
5 BURNSIDE CL
6 LEASIDE WAY
1 GATCOMBE MEWS
2 CLARENCE CT
3 HIGHGROVE MEWS
1 BROWN ST
2 GREEN ST
3 MASSEY ST
4 CHAPEL ST
5 GEORGE ST
6 SOUTH GR
A
B
C
4
81
3
80
2
79
1
78
84
85
86

59
85

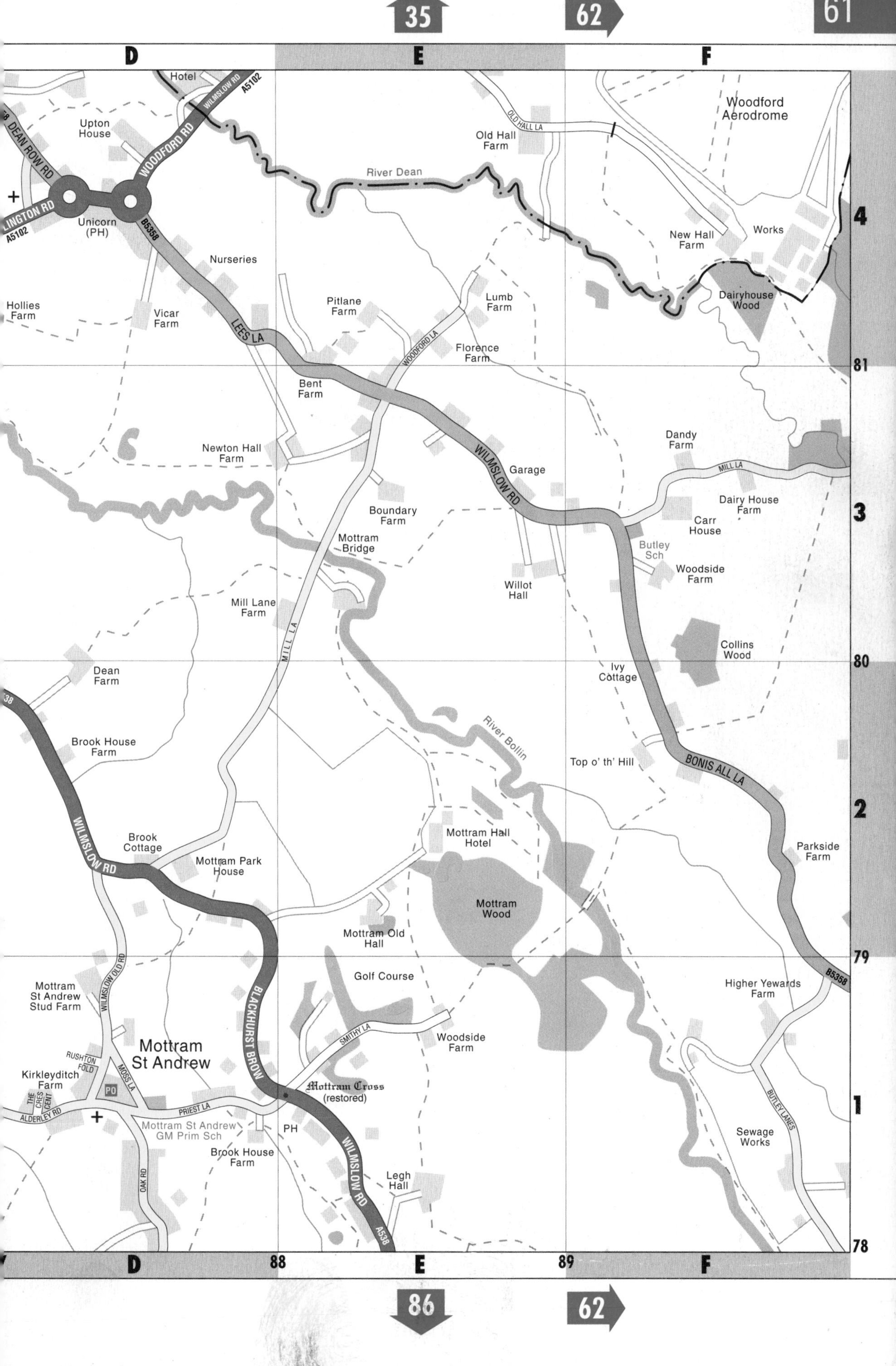

D
E
F

Hotel

Upton
House

WOODFORD RD

WILMSLOW RD

A5102

DEAN ROW RD

LINGTON RD

A5102

Unicorn
(PH)

B5358

Nurseries

Hollies
Farm

Vicar
Farm

LEES LA

Pitlane
Farm

Bent
Farm

Newton Hall
Farm

WOODFORD LA

River Dean

Old Hall
Farm

OLD HALL LA

Woodford
Aerodrome

New Hall
Farm

Works

Dairyhouse
Wood

4

Lumb
Farm

Florence
Farm

81

Garage

WILMSLOW RD

Dandy
Farm

MILL LA

Dairy House
Farm

Carr
House

Butley
Sch

Woodside
Farm

3

Boundary
Farm

Mottram
Bridge

Willot
Hall

Mill Lane
Farm

MILL LA

Collins
Wood

80

Ivy
Cottage

Dean
Farm

Brook House
Farm

WILMSLOW RD

38

Brook
Cottage

Mottram Park
House

River Bollin

Mottram Hall
Hotel

Top o' th' Hill

BONIS ALL LA

Parkside
Farm

2

Mottram
Wood

B5358

79

Mottram
St Andrew
Stud Farm

WILMSLOW OLD RD

MOSS LA

Mottram
St Andrew

BLACKHURST BROW

Mottram Old
Hall

Golf Course

SMITHY LA

Woodside
Farm

Higher Yewards
Farm

BUTLEY LANES

Kirkleyditch
Farm

THE CRESCENT

RUSHTON
FOLD

PO

ALDERLEY RD

PRIEST LA

Mottram Cross
(restored)

PH

Mottram St Andrew
GM Prim Sch

Brook House
Farm

OAK RD

WILMSLOW RD

Legh
Hall

A538

Sewage
Works

1

78

D
88
E
89
F

61
36

A   **B**   **C**

A523

Streetlane
Farm

STREET LA

Starkie House

Oak Farm

Skellorngreen
Farm

Ash Tree
Farm

Skellorn Green

4

Sandholes
Moss

Sandholes
Farm

Gibson
Wood

Marfields
Farm

Gorsewood
Farm

Pedleyhill
Farm

PEDLEY HILL

Isles
Wood

Boothgreen
Farm

Booth Green

81

Water
Treatment
Plant

MILL LA

Redbrook
Bridge

Red Brook

Redbrook
Farm

Roundylane
Farm

Roundy
House

SPRING BANK LA

ROUNDY LA

3

Adlington
Hall

The Garden
House

Adlington
Sta

Adlington

WYCH LA

BROOKLEDGE LA

Adlington
Cty Prim
Sch

+

REDBROOK WAY

LEIGH RD

BROUGHTON RD

LONDON RD

Mauern
Hall

Brookledge
Farm

HARROP LA

The
Wilderness

Wych Wood

Barton's
Clough

80

River Dean

Harropgreen
Farm

Middlewood Way

Cheshire Ring Canal Walk

Macclesfield Canal

2

Brook House
Farm

Issues
Wood

Wych Farm

Higher Doles
Farm

Cla
Gre
Fa

Towing Path

Millhouse Bridge

Bonis
Wood

Oakdene

Mill House

79

Bonis Hall

New Mill
House

PEGGIE S LA

Whitehall
Farm
Green
Farm

Ashley
Farm

PH

Lane
Head

B5358

BONIS HALL LA

B5358

**Whiteley
Green**

Whiteley
Heys

HOLEHOUSE LA

1

Plant
House

A523

Howlanehead
Sandyhead
Farm

WELL LA

78

90   **A**   91   **B**   92   **C**

61
87

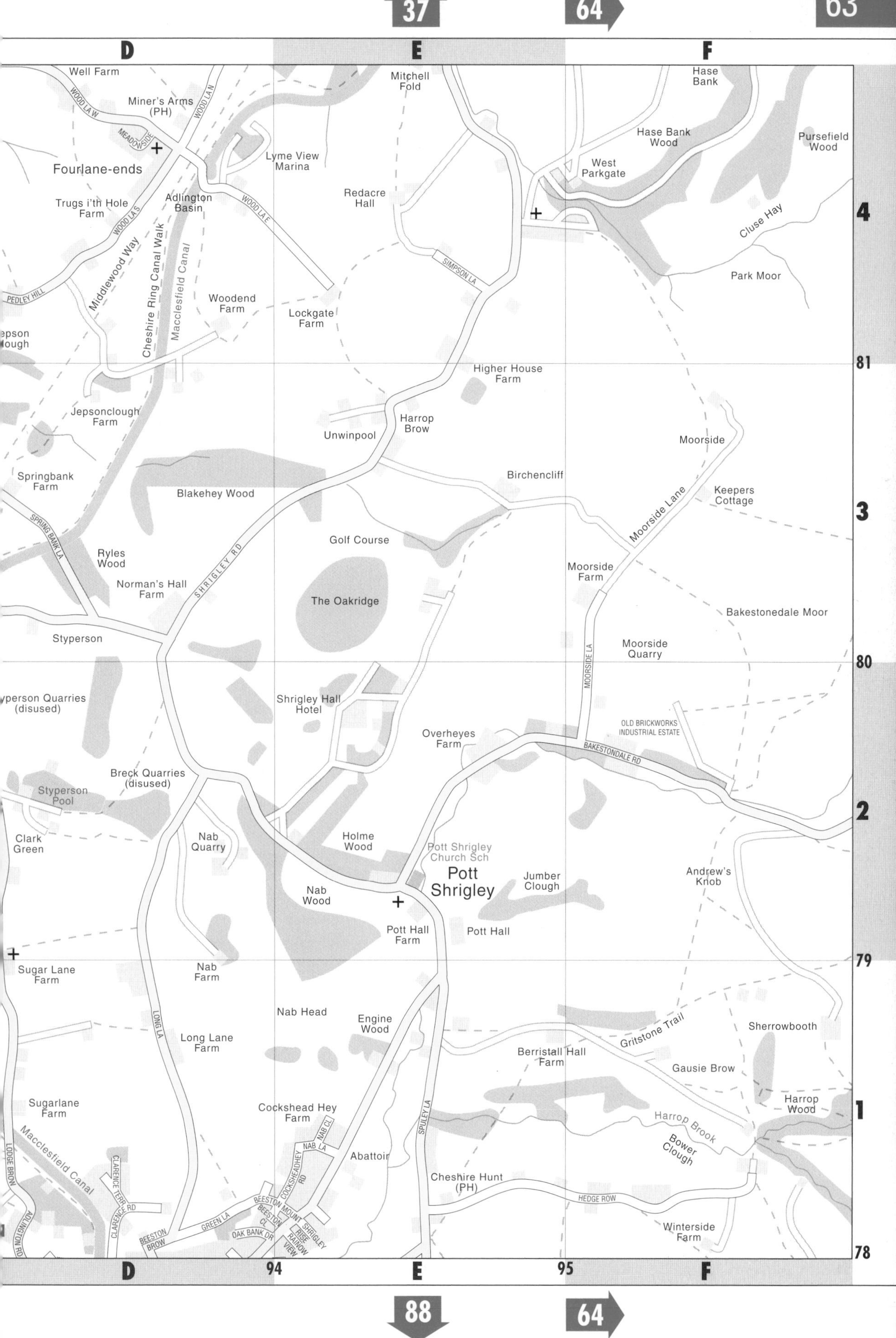

Well Farm

Miner's Arms (PH)

WOOD LANE

WOOD LA W

MEADOWS LA

Lyme View Marina

Mitchell Fold

Hase Bank

Hase Bank Wood

Pursefield Wood

Fourlane-ends

Adlington Basin

WOOD LA E

Redacre Hall

West Parkgate

Cluse Hay

4

Trugs i'th Hole Farm

WOOD LA S

Middlewood Way

Cheshire Ring Canal Walk

Macclesfield Canal

Woodend Farm

Lockgate Farm

SIMPSON LA

Park Moor

PEDLEY HILL

81

impson lough

Jepsonclough Farm

Higher House Farm

Harrop Brow

Moorside

Unwinpool

Birchencliff

Moorside Lane

Keepers Cottage

Springbank Farm

SPRING BANK LA

Blakehey Wood

Golf Course

Moorside Farm

Bakestonedale Moor

3

Ryles Wood

SHRIGLEY RD

The Oakridge

Norman's Hall Farm

MOORSIDE LA

Moorside Quarry

Styperson

80

yperson Quarries (disused)

Shrigley Hall Hotel

Overheyes Farm

OLD BRICKWORKS INDUSTRIAL ESTATE

BAKESTONDALE RD

Breck Quarries (disused)

Styperson Pool

Nab Quarry

Holme Wood

Pott Shrigley Church Sch

Jumber Clough

Andrew's Knob

2

Clark Green

Nab Wood

Pott Shrigley

Sugar Lane Farm

Nab Farm

LONG LA

Pott Hall Farm

Pott Hall

79

Long Lane Farm

Nab Head

Engine Wood

SPULEY LA

Berristall Hall Farm

Gritstone Trail

Gausie Brow

Sherrowbooth

Harrop Wood

1

Sugarlane Farm

Macclesfield Canal

CLARENCE TERRACE RD

Cockshead Hey Farm

NAB LA

Abattoir

Cheshire Hunt (PH)

Harrop Brook

Bower Clough

ADLINGTON RD

LODGE BROW

COCKSHEADHEY RD

BEESTON MOUNT

GREEN LA

BEESTON BROW

OAK BANK DR

SHRIGLEY RISE

RAINOW VIEW

HEDGE ROW

Winterside Farm

78

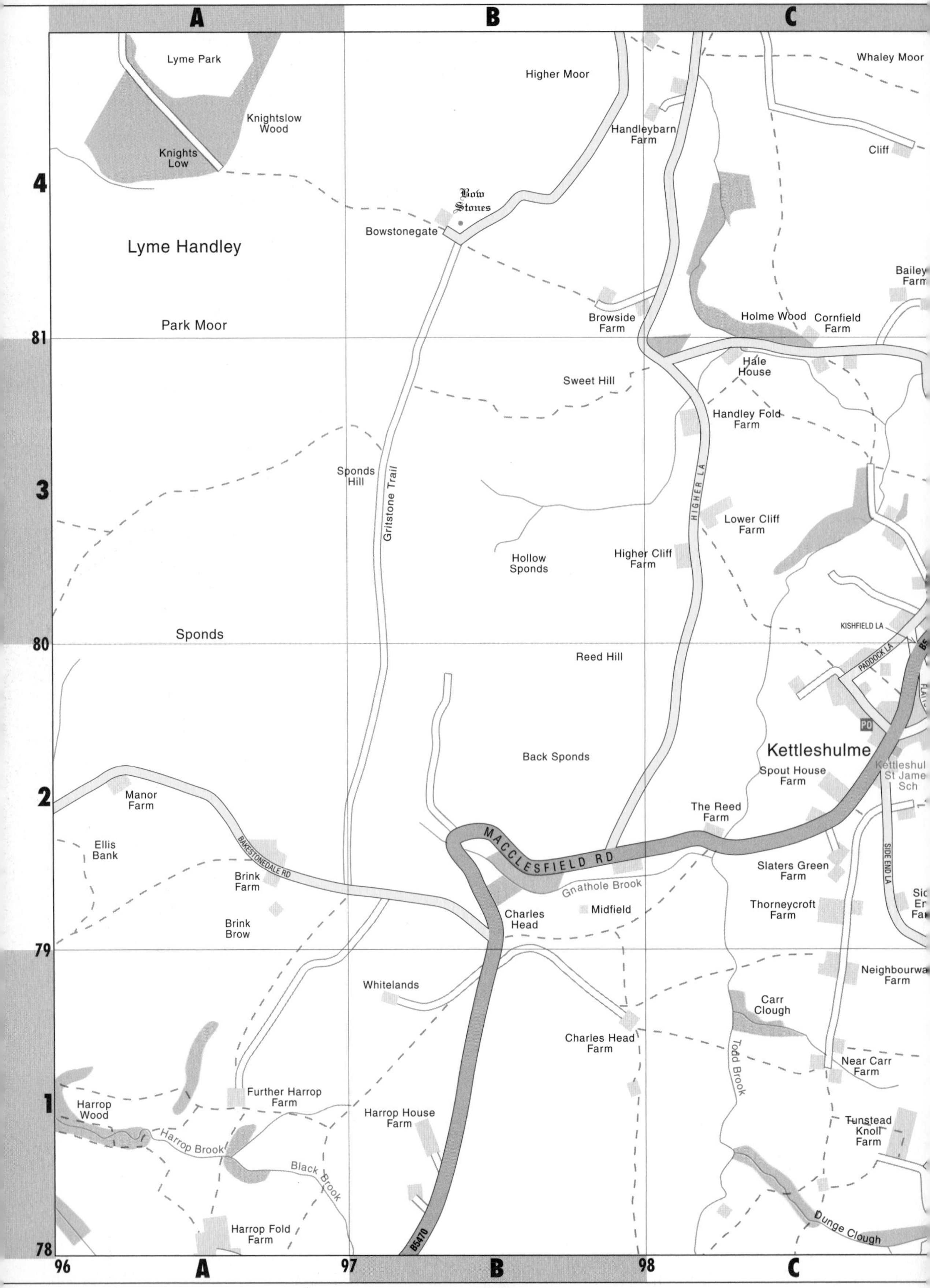

A

B

C

Lyme Park

Knightslow
Wood

Knights
Low

Whaley Moor

Higher Moor

Handleybarn
Farm

Cliff

4

Bow
Stones

Lyme Handley

Bowstonegate

Bailey
Farm

Browside
Farm

Holme Wood

Cornfield
Farm

Park Moor

81

Hale
House

Sweet Hill

Handley Fold
Farm

HIGHER LA

Sponds
Hill

Gritstone Trail

Lower Cliff
Farm

3

Higher Cliff
Farm

Hollow
Sponds

KISHFIELD LA

80

Reed Hill

Sponds

PADDOCK LA

Kettleshulme

Back Sponds

Spout House
Farm

Kettleshul
St Jame
Sch

Manor
Farm

The Reed
Farm

PO

2

Ellis
Bank

Slaters Green
Farm

Brink
Farm

MACCLESFIELD RD

Thorneycroft
Farm

Si
Er
Fa

Brink
Brow

Gnathole Brook

SIDE END LA

Charles
Head

Midfield

79

Neighbourwa
Farm

Whitelands

Carr
Clough

Charles Head
Farm

Near Carr
Farm

Todd Brook

1

Harrop
Wood

Further Harrop
Farm

Tunstead
Knoll
Farm

Harrop House
Farm

Harrop Brook

Black
Brook

Dunge Clough

B5470

Harrop Fold
Farm

78

96

A

97

B

98

C

BAKESTONEDALE RD

39

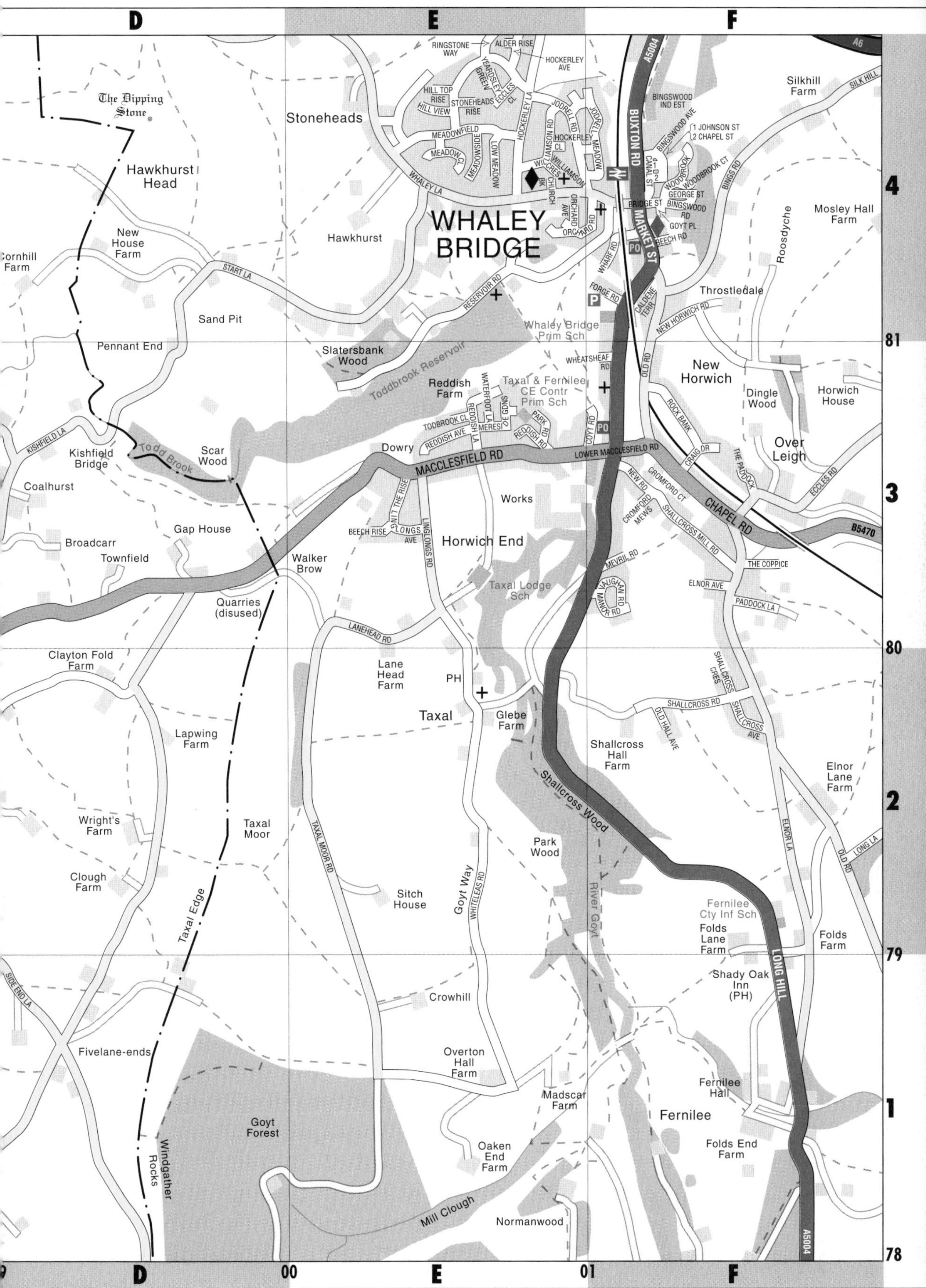
D
E
F
The Dipping Stone
Stoneheads
Hawkhurst Head
New House Farm
Cornhill Farm
Hawkhurst
WHALEY BRIDGE
START LA
Sand Pit
Pennant End
Slatersbank Wood
Toddbrook Reservoir
Reddish Farm
Whaley Bridge Prim Sch
Taxal & Fernilee CE Contr Prim Sch
New Horwich
Dingle Wood
Horwich House
Over Leigh
KISHFIELD LA
Kishfield Bridge
Todd Brook
Scar Wood
Dowry
MACCLESFIELD RD
LOWER MACCLESFIELD RD
CHAPEL RD
Coalhurst
Gap House
Broadcarr
Townfield
Walker Brow
Works
Horwich End
Taxal Lodge Sch
Quarries (disused)
LANEHEAD RD
Clayton Fold Farm
Lane Head Farm
PH
Taxal
Glebe Farm
SHALLCROSS RD
Shallcross Hall Farm
Lapwing Farm
Shallcross Wood
Elnor Lane Farm
Wright's Farm
Taxal Moor
TAXAL MOOR RD
Park Wood
Clough Farm
Taxal Edge
Sitch House
Goyt Way
WHITELEAS RD
River Goyt
Fernilee Cty Inf Sch
Folds Lane Farm
Folds Farm
LONG HILL
Shady Oak Inn (PH)
SIDE END LA
Crowhill
Fivelane-ends
Overton Hall Farm
Madscar Farm
Fernilee Hall
Fernilee
Goyt Forest
Oaken End Farm
Folds End Farm
Windgather Rocks
Mill Clough
Normanwood
A5004
A6
B5470
BUXTON RD
MARKET ST
Silkhill Farm
Mosley Hall Farm
Roosdyche
Throstledale
BINGSWOOD IND EST
1 JOHNSON ST
2 CHAPEL ST
4
81
3
80
2
79
1
78
00
01

90

41

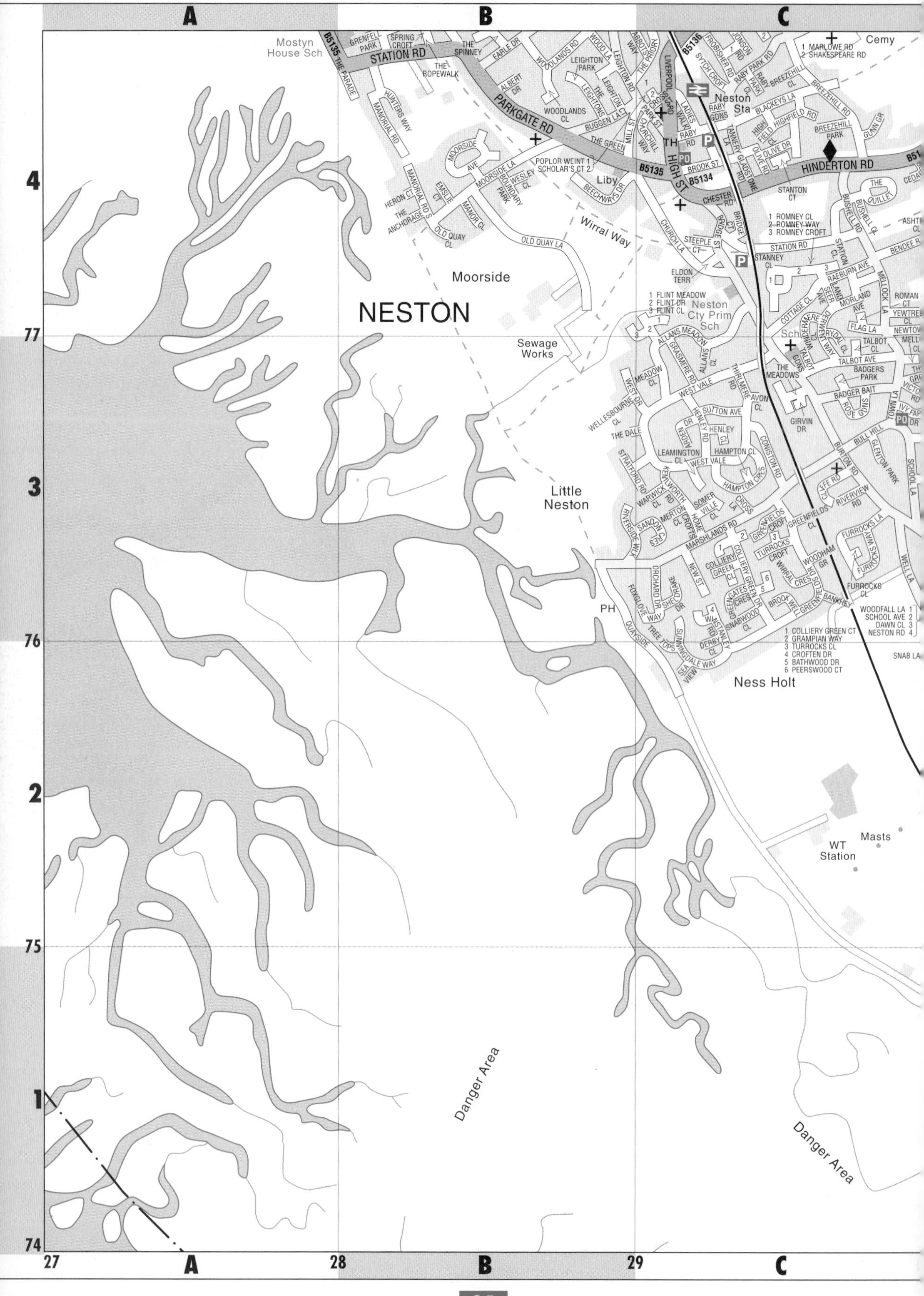
A
B
C
NESTON
Moorside
Little Neston
Ness Holt
Mostyn House Sch
Neston Sta
Neston Cty Prim Sch
Sewage Works
Wirral Way
Cemy
Liby
PH
WT Station
Masts
Danger Area
Danger Area
STATION RD
PARKGATE RD
HINDERTON RD
HIGH ST
CHESTER RD
OLD QUAY LA
MOORSIDE LA
B5135
B5134
B5136
1 MARLOWE RD
2 SHAKESPEARE RD
1 ROMNEY CL
2 ROMNEY WAY
3 ROMNEY CROFT
1 FLINT MEADOW
2 FLINT DR
3 FLINT CL
POPLOR WEINT 1
SCHOLAR'S CT 2
WOODFALL LA 1
SCHOOL AVE 2
DAWN CL 3
NESTON RD 4
1 COLLIERY GREEN CT
2 GRAMPIAN WAY
3 TURROCKS CL
4 CROFTEN DR
5 BATHWOOD DR
6 PEERSWOOD CT
4
77
3
76
2
75
1
74
27
28
29

91

42
68

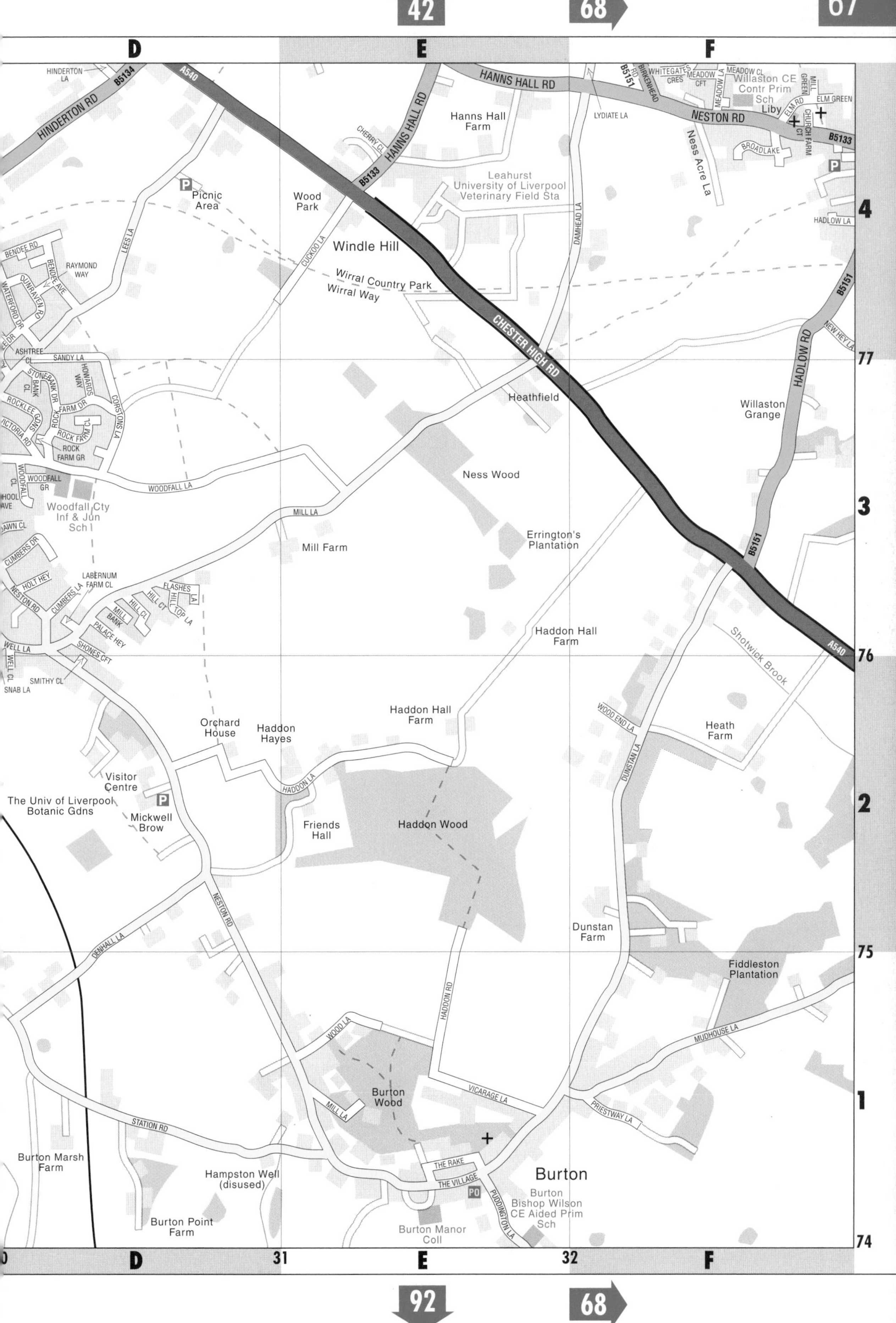
D
E
F
HINDERTON RD
HINDERTON LA
B5134
A540
HANNS HALL RD
Hanns Hall Farm
NESTON RD
B5133
Willaston CE Contr Prim Sch
Liby
Leahurst University of Liverpool Veterinary Field Sta
Picnic Area
Wood Park
Windle Hill
Wirral Country Park
Wirral Way
CHESTER HIGH RD
Heathfield
Ness Wood
Willaston Grange
HADLOW RD
B5151
Errington's Plantation
Mill Farm
MILL LA
WOODFALL LA
Woodfall Cty Inf & Jun Sch
Haddon Hall Farm
Orchard House
Haddon Hayes
Visitor Centre
The Univ of Liverpool Botanic Gdns
Mickwell Brow
Friends Hall
Haddon Wood
Heath Farm
Shotwick Brook
DUNSTAN LA
Dunstan Farm
Fiddleston Plantation
MUDHOUSE LA
HADDON RD
Burton Wood
Burton
Burton Bishop Wilson CE Aided Prim Sch
Burton Manor Coll
Burton Marsh Farm
Hampston Well (disused)
Burton Point Farm
STATION RD
NESTON RD
DENHALL LA
4
3
2
1
77
76
75
74
31
32

92
68

A

B

C

HOOTON RD B5133

B5133

MILL LA

NESTON RD

HADLOW RD B5151

DELAMERE ACRE

BRIARDALE RD

OLD FARM CL

THE HOWE

OLD VICARAGE RD

PEMBERTON CL

OSSOM BENNET CL

PARK RD

CHANGE LA

CROSBY GR

BARFORD GRANGE

Willaston

ASHTREE FARM CT

ASHTREE

WALLCROFT

INTAKE CL

SMITHY LA

4

Wirral Country Park

Wirral Way

P Picnic Area

ADFALENT LA

Picnic Area

Works

Heath Farm

WATERWORKS LA

OAKFIELD RD

The Oaklands Hotel

Mayfield

Heath Lodge

The Grange

HEATH LA

MARGARET'S LA

77

NEW HEY LA

HOWGILL CL

BERWICK

STIPERS CL

Dehon House Youth Centre

BEN NEVIS DR

PENDLE

ULLAPOOL

ROYBURGH

PEEBLES

CREAM DR

COLDS

Hotel

Leaswood Farm

Oaks Farm

+

PH

LEDSHAM RD

B5463

JEDBUR

SELKIRK

3

BADGERSRAKE LA

Ledsham Hall Farm

76

A540

CHESTER HIGH RD

Hallwood Farm

HALLWOOD DR

Inglewood

LEDSHAM HALL LA

WELSH RD

Foxes Farm

BADGERSRAKE LA

Cross Lanes Farm

Bank Farm

Garden Centre

2

MUDHOUSE LA

Badger's Rake House

Badgersrake Covert

75

PARKGATE RD

LEDSHAM LA

Aviary Farm

Ledsham

Manor House Farm

PUDDINGTON LA

Daisy Bank Farm

Court Farm

1

Hotel

A550

A540

RECTORY L

Whitegates Farm

PIPERS LA

Heath Hey

The Tudor Rose

Millhey

74

33

A

34

B

35

C

D E F

4 3 2 1

77 76 75 74

37 38

Childer Thornton
Childer Thornton Cty Prim Sch
The Moorings
Meadow Bank
Golf Course
Clayhill Wood
Rivacre Valley Country Park
Church Wood
Rossmore Cty Prim Sch
Rivacre Valley Cty Prim Sch
Overpool
Cemy
Liby
Little Sutton Sta
Little Sutton CE Contr Prim Sch
Pius XII RC Aided Prim Sch
Overpool Sta
Westminster Industrial Park
Little Sutton
Parklands Cty Prim Sch
Sutton Cty High Sch
Schs
Sutton New Hall Farm
ELLESMERE PORT
Water Treatment Works
Brookside Cty Inf Sch
Great Sutton
Gorsthills Cty Prim Sch
St Saviour's RC Aided Inf & Jun Sch
Sutton Green
Capenhurst Grange Sch
Meadow Cty Prim Sch
Works
Farm Meadow
Capenhurst Station

A41
A550
M53
B5132
B5463
WELSH RD
RIVACRE RD
NETHERPOOL RD
ROSSMORE RD W
ROSSMORE RD E
STATION RD
LEDSHAM RD
OVERPOOL RD
CHESTER RD
SUTTON WAY
CAPENHURST LA

1 BREDON CL
2 HAMBLEDON CL
3 BLACKDOWN CL
4 HAWICK CL

BIRCHWOOD CL 1
LAURELWOOD DR 2
BRISTOL DR 3

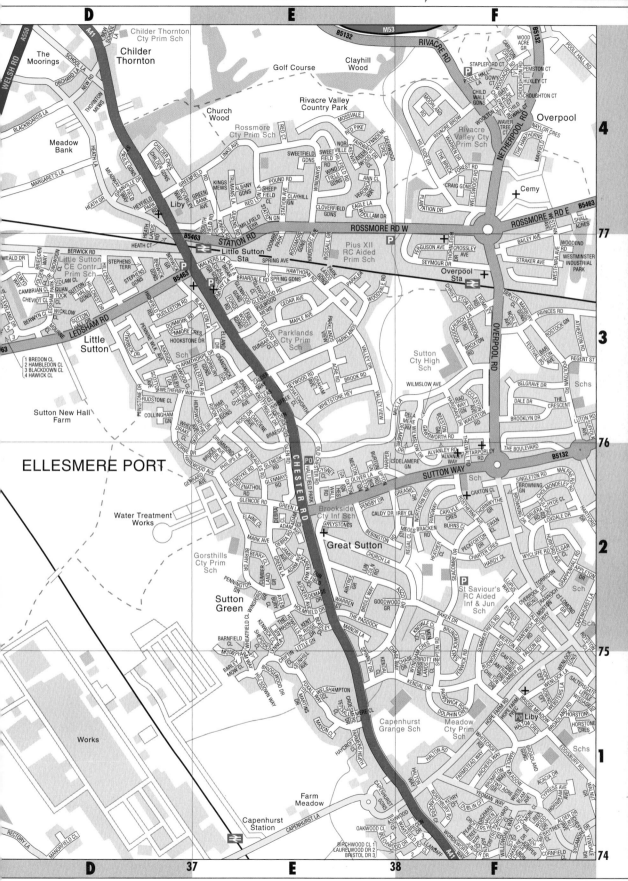

A   B   C

River Mersey

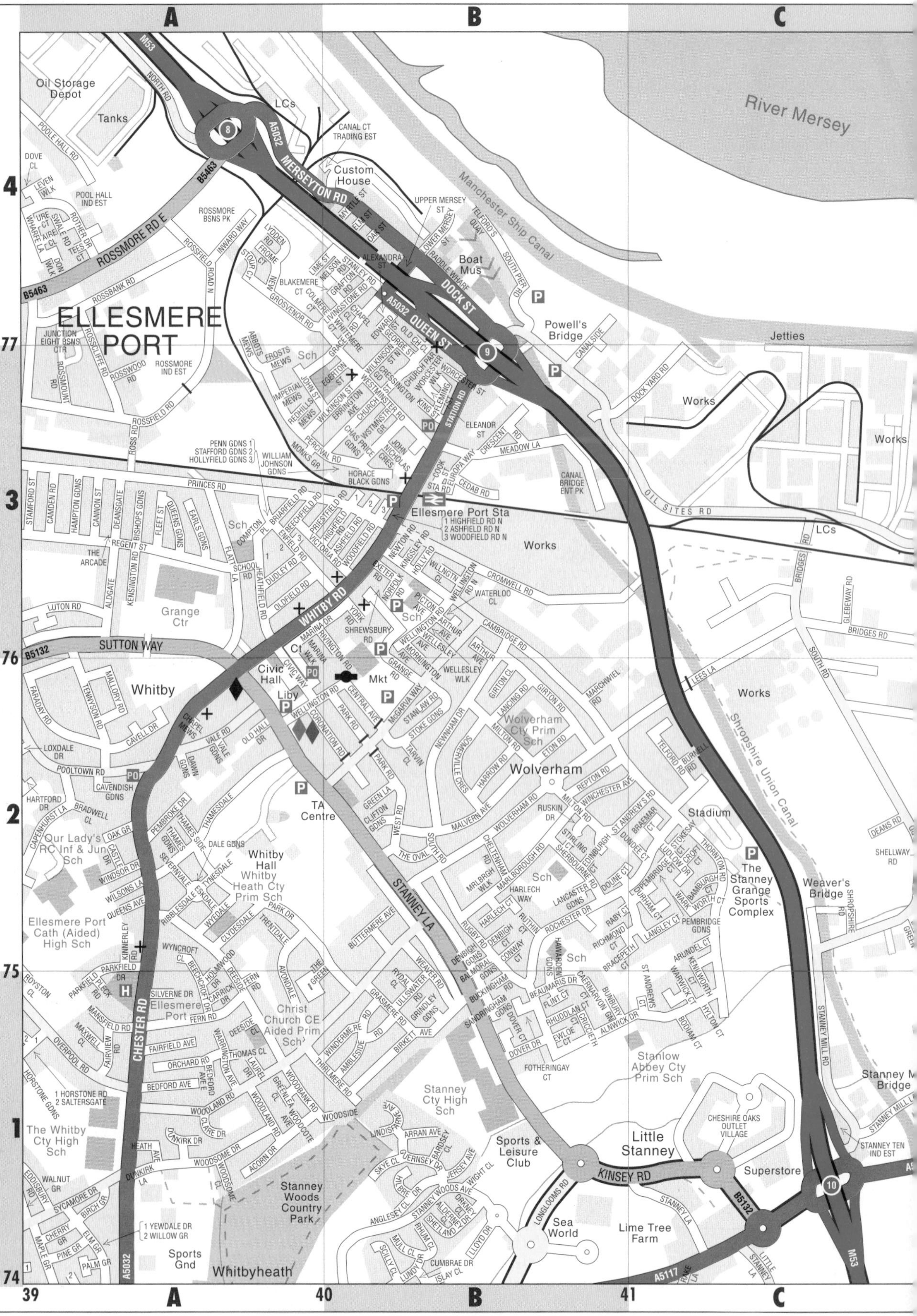

Oil Storage Depot

Tanks

LCs

M53

NORTH RD

A5032

POOLE HALL RD

DOVE CL

LEVEN WLK

URE WHARF LA

AIRE RD

TEES CT

POOL HALL IND EST

ROSSMORE RD E

B5463

ROSSMORE BSNS PK

ROSSMORE ROAD N

INWARD WAY

LYDDEN RD

FROME RD

NEW GROSVENOR RD

STOUR CT

BLAKEMERE CT

COLMERE CT

CANAL CT TRADING EST

Custom House

MERSEYTON RD

DOCK ST

UPPER MERSEY ST

LEYLAND ST

NELSON ST

STANLEY RD

GRATTON ST

ALEXANDRA ST

UPPER MERSEY ST

LOWER MERSEY ST

Boat Mus

A5032 QUEEN ST

Manchester Ship Canal

TELFORD'S Q

SOUTH PIER RD

8

9

Powell's Bridge

CANAL SIDE

P

P

Jetties

ELLESMERE PORT

JUNCTION EIGHT BSNS CTR

B5463

ROSS RD

ROSSFIELD RD

ROSSWOOD RD

ROSSMOUNT RD

ROSSBANK RD

Rossmore Ind Est

ABBOTS MEWS

FROSTS MEWS

IMPERIAL MEWS

REDHILLS MEWS

Sch

LIVINGSTONE RD

EDWARD ST

OLD CH RD

GRACE RD

WELLINGTON RD

KENSINGTON AVE

ERNLEIGH AVE

CHURCH ST

WESTMINSTER AVE

KING ST

WORCESTER ST

CHURCHILL ST

STATION RD

POO

ELEANOR ST

CRESCENT

MEADOW LA

Dock Yard Rd

Works

Works

77

PENN GDNS 1
STAFFORD GDNS 2
HOLLYFIELD GDNS 3

WILLIAM JOHNSON GDNS

MONKS GR

PERCIVAL RD

CHAS MEWS ST

JOHN ST

HORACE ST

BLACK GDNS

HENRY NICHOLAS ST

CEDAB RD

CANAL BRIDGE ENT PK

OIL SITES RD

LCs

BRIDGES RD

3

STAMFORD ST

CAMDEN RD

HAMPTON GDNS

CANNON ST

FLEET ST

QUEENS GDNS

EARLE GDNS

DEANSGATE

BISHOPS GDNS

PRINCES RD

BRIARFIELD RD

BEECHFIELD RD

PRIESTFIELD RD

HIGHFIELD RD

ASHFIELD RD

WOODFIELD RD

NEWTON RD

WELLINGTON RD

Ellesmere Port Sta
1 HIGHFIELD RD N
2 ASHFIELD RD N
3 WOODFIELD RD N

Works

THE ARCADE

REGENT ST

KENSINGTON RD

ALDGATE

LUTON RD

Grange Ctr

COMPTON RD

SCHOOL LA

HEATHFIELD RD

DUDLEY RD

WHITBY RD

EXETER RD

NORFOLK RD

MOLESLEY RD

WELNGTN RD

WELLINGTON RD

WATERLOO CL

CAMBRIDGE RD

CROMWELL RD

Sch

BRIDGES RD

GLEBEWAY RD

FARADAY RD

TENNYSON RD

MILTON RD

MARINA DR

MANRINGTON DR

SHREWSBURY RD

Civic Hall

Liby

BURTON CL

ST ARTHUR

ARTHUR ST

GRANGE

WELLESLEY AVE

WELLESLEY WLK

GIRTON RD

GIRTON RD

MARCHWIEL

Works

B5132 SUTTON WAY

76

Whitby

CAVELL DR

VALE RD

OLD HALL RD

MAGARIA WAY

STANLAW RD

STOKE GDNS

NEWHAM RD

LANCING RD

MILTON RD

Wolverham City Prim Sch

EATON RD

TELFORD RD

BURNELL RD

LEES LA

SOUTH RD

Works

LOXDALE DR

POOLTOWN RD

CAVENDISH GDNS

DAWN GDNS

CORONATION RD

PARK RD

GREEN LA

CLIFTON GDNS

WEST RD

LARWH

MALVERN AVE

WOLVERHAM RD

RUSKIN DR

REPTON RD

WINCHESTER AVE

Wolverham

Stadium

The Stanney Grange Sports Complex

Shropshire Union Canal

2

Our Lady's RC Inf & Jun Sch

OAK LA

PEMBROKE DR

THAMES RD

THAMES SIDE

SEVENVALE

TYNESDALE

DALE GDNS

TA Centre

Whitby Hall

Whitby Heath Cty Prim Sch

THE OVAL

CHELTENHAM RD

MARLBOROUGH RD

STIRLING RD

ST ANDREWS RD

DUNDEE CT

BRAEMAR CT

THORNTON RD

STOKESAY

BAMBURGH CT

The Stanney Grange Sports Complex

P

DEANS RD

SHELLWAY RD

Weaver's Bridge

STANNEY MILL RD

Ellesmere Port Cath (Aided) High Sch

KINNERLEY RD

QUEENS AVE

WINDSOR LA

WILSONS LA

RIBBLESDALE

ESKDALE

WYEDALE

CLYDESDALE

TEASDALE

MRLBRGH WLK

HARLECH WAY

LANCASTER GDNS

RUGBY RD

ST ANDREWS

WARWICK CT

75

STANNEY LA

ROYSTON CL

PARKFIELD PK

PARKFIELD DR

SILVERNE DR

Ellesmere Port

FERN RD

CARRICK DR

AVONDALE

WINDERMERE RD

WEAVER RD

RYDAL ST

ULLSWATER RD

GRASMERE RD

BIRKETT AVE

DENBIGH RD

BAMORAL

CONWAY RD

RUTHIN

ROCHESTER DR

RICHMOND

RABY CT

LANGLEY CT

ARUNDEL CT

BURBURY

WARWICK

ALNWICK DR

HILTON CT

BIDDAM CT

H

CHESTER RD

MANSFIELD RD

MAXWELL CL

FAIRVIEW

OVERPOOL RD

FAIRFIELD AVE

ORCHARD RD

BEDFORD AVE

THOMAS CL

DEESIDE

WOODLAND RD

CLARE DR

WOODSOME

LINDISFARNE

ARRAN AVE

Stanney Cty High Sch

Christ Church CE Aided Prim Sch

BUCKINGHAM GDNS

SANDRINGHAM GDNS

DOVER DR

FOTHERINGAY CT

Stanlow Abbey Cty Prim Sch

Little Stanney

CHESHIRE OAKS OUTLET VILLAGE

Superstore

STANNEY MILL RD

Stanney Bridge

STANNEY TEN IND EST

1

The Whitby Cty High Sch

WALNUT GR

SYCAMORE DR

CHERRY TREE

PINE GR

BIRCH GR

HEATH AVE

DUNKIRK AVE

WOODSOME DR

ACORN DR

Stanney Woods Country Park

ANGLESEY GDNS

SKYE CL

GUERNSEY DR

JERSEY RD

SHETLAND

STANNEY WOODS AVE

ALTRINCHAM DR

WIGHT CL

Sea World

Sports & Leisure Club

KINSEY RD

LONGLOWS RD

STANNEY LA

LITTLE STANNEY LA

Lime Tree Farm

10

M53

A5117

A5032

MAPLE GR

PALM GR

ELM GR

EDGBURY

Sports Gnd

Whitbyheath

1 YEWDALE DR
2 WILLOW GR

MULL CL

ANGLESEY CL

CUMBRAE CL

ISLAY CL

LLOYD CL

B5132

LITTLE STANNEY LA

74

39   A   40   B   41   C

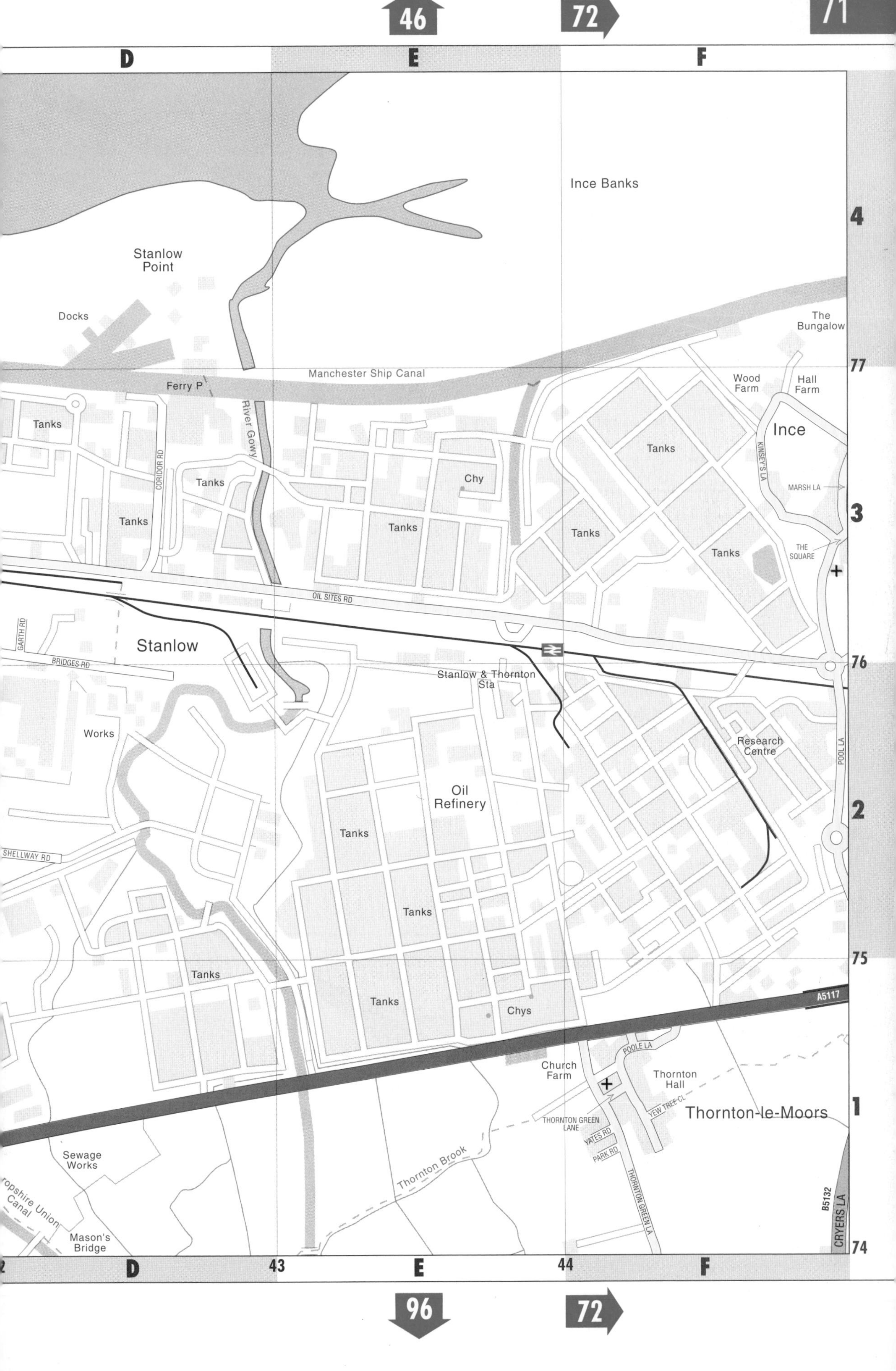

D

E

F

4

Ince Banks

Stanlow
Point

Docks

The
Bungalow

77

Manchester Ship Canal

Ferry P

Wood
Farm

Hall
Farm

CORDOR RD

River Gowy

Tanks

Tanks

Chy

Tanks

Tanks

Ince

KINSEY'S LA

MARSH LA

3

Tanks

Tanks

Tanks

Tanks

THE
SQUARE

+

GARTH RD

OIL SITES RD

Stanlow

BRIDGES RD

Stanlow & Thornton
Sta

76

Research
Centre

POOLE LA

Works

Oil
Refinery

2

SHELLWAY RD

Tanks

Tanks

Tanks

75

A5117

Tanks

Tanks

Chys

Church
Farm

+

Thornton
Hall

POOLE LA

YEW TREE CL

Thornton-le-Moors

1

Sewage
Works

THORNTON GREEN
LANE

YATES RD

PARK RD

ropshire Union
Canal

Thornton Brook

THORNTON GREEN LA

B5132

CRYERS LA

Mason's
Bridge

74

D

43

E

44

F

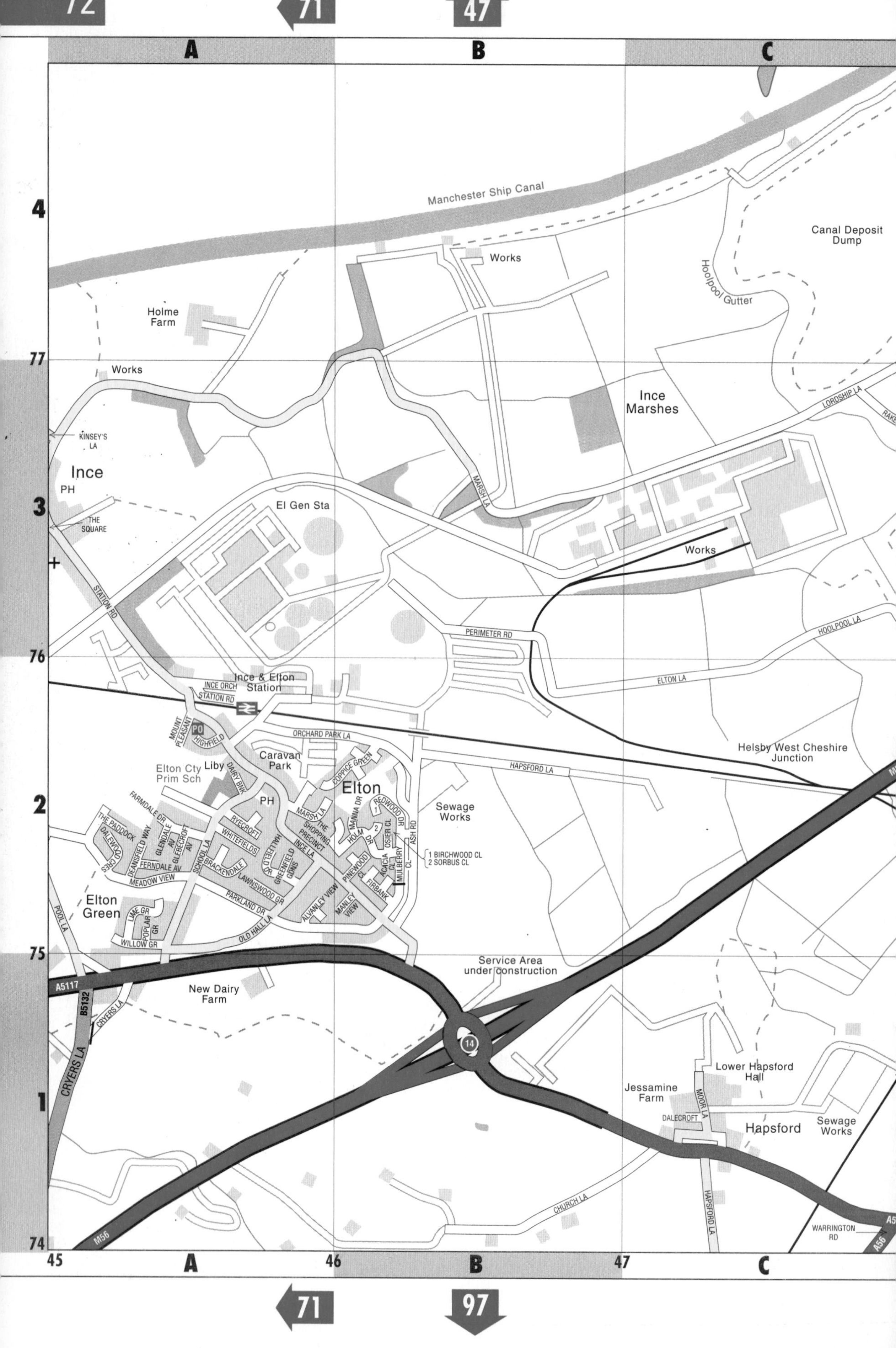

A   B   C

4

Manchester Ship Canal

Canal Deposit
Dump

Hoolpool Gutter

Works

Holme
Farm

77

Works

KINSEY'S
LA

Ince Marshes

Ince

PH

LORDSHIP LA

RAKE

3

THE
SQUARE

El Gen Sta

MARSH LA

Works

STATION RD

HOOLPOOL LA

PERIMETER RD

76

Ince & Elton
Station

INCE ORCH
STATION RD

ELTON LA

Helsby West Cheshire
Junction

MOUNT
PLEASANT

PO

HIGHFIELD

ORCHARD PARK LA

Caravan
Park

Liby

Elton Cty
Prim Sch

DAIRY BRK

HAPSFORD LA

2

PH

Elton

MARSH LA

COPPICE GREEN

Sewage
Works

FARMDALE DR

GLENDALE AV

SHOPPING
PRECINCT

MANNA DR

REDWOOD CL

1 BIRCHWOOD CL
2 SORBUS CL

THE PADDOCK

OAKWAY

RYECROFT

HOLM DR

HO

OSIER CL

2

HEADSFIELD WAY

GLEBECROFT

WHITEFIELDS

HALLFIELD

GREENFIELD

INCE LA

ACACIA CL

MULBERRY CL

ASH RD

FERNDALE AV

SCHOOL LA

BRACKENDALE

LAWISWOOD GR

PINEWOOD

FIRBANK

MEADOW VIEW

PARKLAND DR

ALVANLEY VIEW

MANLEY
VIEW

**Elton
Green**

LIME GR

POPLAR GR

OLD HALL LA

POOL LA

WILLOW GR

75

Service Area
under construction

A5117

New Dairy
Farm

CRYERS LA

B5132

14

Lower Hapsford
Hall

Jessamine
Farm

MOOR LA

1

DALECROFT

Hapsford

Sewage
Works

HAPSFORD LA

CHURCH LA

A5

M56

74

WARRINGTON
RD

A56

45   A   46   B   47   C

48
74

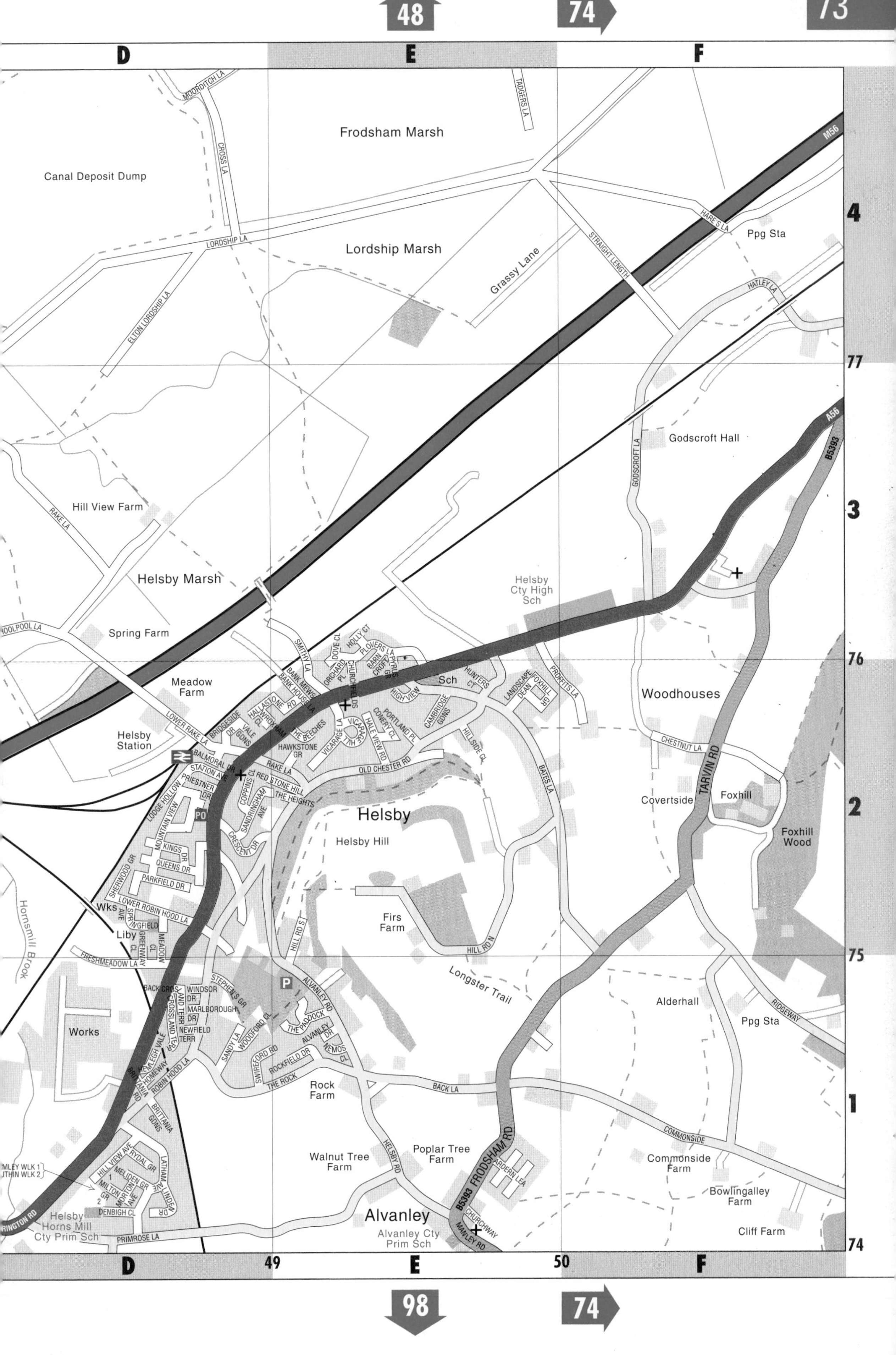
D
E
F
Frodsham Marsh
Canal Deposit Dump
Lordship Marsh
Grassy Lane
Ppg Sta
Godscroft Hall
Hill View Farm
Helsby Marsh
Spring Farm
Helsby Cty High Sch
Meadow Farm
Helsby Station
Woodhouses
Sch
Covertside
Foxhill
Foxhill Wood
Helsby
Helsby Hill
Wks
Liby
Hornsmill Brook
Firs Farm
Longster Trail
Alderhall
Ppg Sta
Works
Rock Farm
Walnut Tree Farm
Poplar Tree Farm
Commonside Farm
Bowlingalley Farm
Alvanley
Alvanley Cty Prim Sch
Helsby Horns Mill Cty Prim Sch
Cliff Farm
MOORDITCH LA
CROSS LA
TADGERS LA
LORDSHIP LA
ELTON LORDSHIP LA
STRAIGHT LENGTH
HARE'S LA
HATLEY LA
M56
A56
B5393
GODSCROFT LA
RAKE LA
HOOLPOOL LA
LOWER RAKE LA
SMITHY LA
BANK MEWS
BANK HOUSE LA
DOVE CL
HOLLY CT
ORCHARD PL
CHURCHFIELDS
PLOVERS LA
BARN CROFT
PYRUS GR
HIGH VIEW
HUNTERS CT
LANDSCAPE DEAN
FOXHILL GR
PROFFITS LA
CAMBRIDGE GDNS
HILLSIDE CL
PORTLAND PL
COMERY CL
HALE VIEW RD
VICARAGE HILL
VICARAGE LA
THE BEECHES
HAWKSTONE GR
HALLASTONE RD
WROXHAM CL
BRIDGESIDE
VALE GDNS
RAKE LA
OLD CHESTER RD
RED STONE HILL
THE HEIGHTS
BALMORAL DR
STATION AVE
PRIESTNER DR
LODGE HOLLOW
MOUNTAIN VIEW
COPPINS CL
SANDRINGHAM AVE
CRESCENT DR
BATES LA
CHESTNUT LA
TARVIN RD
KINGS DR
QUEENS DR
PARKFIELD DR
SHERWOOD GR
LOWER ROBIN HOOD LA
SPRINGFIELD CL
GREENWAY CL
MEADOW CL
FRESHMEADOW LA
HILL RD S
HILL RD N
BACK CROSS LA
WINDSOR DR
MARLBOROUGH DR
NEWFIELD TERR
CROSSLAND TERR
STEPHENS GR
ALVANLEY RD
THE PADDOCK
ALVANLEY DR
NEMOS CL
WOODFORD CL
SANDY LA
SWIREFORD RD
ROCKFIELD DR
THE ROCK
BACK LA
RIDGEWAY
COMMONSIDE
BRITTANIA RD
HOMEWAY
ROBIN HOOD LA
BRITTANIA GDNS
HILL VIEW AVE
RYDAL GR
MELIDEN GR
MILTON GR
MORTON AVE
DENBIGH CL
LATHAM AVE
LINDEN DR
HELSBY RD
FRODSHAM RD
ARDERN LEA
CHURCHWAY
MANLEY RD
PRIMROSE LA
WARRINGTON RD
MLEY WLK 1
THIN WLK 2
P
PO
4
77
3
76
2
75
1
74
49
50

98
74

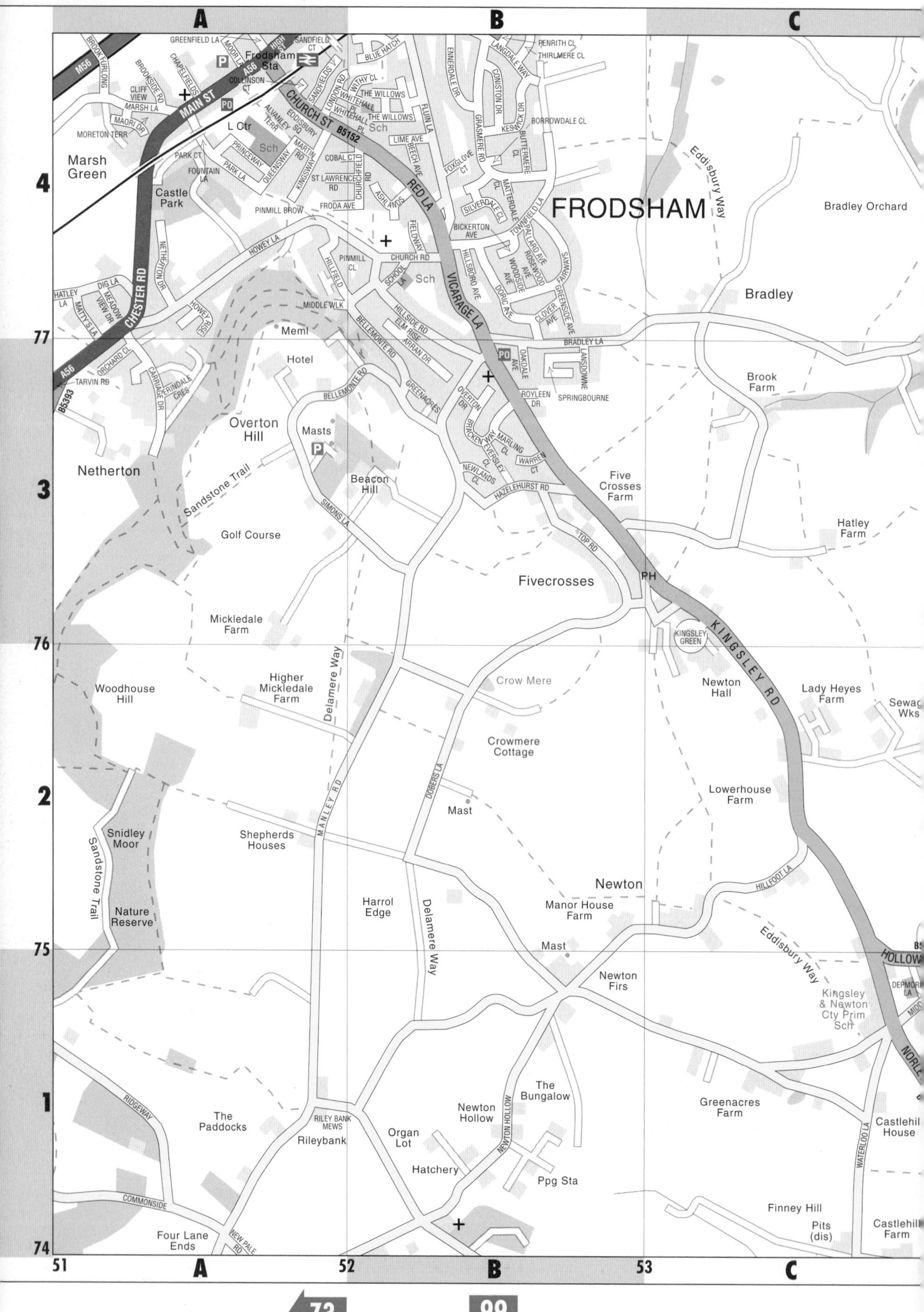

A   B   C

4

Marsh
Green

M56

BROOK FURLONG
BROOKSIDE RD
CLIFF VIEW
MARSH LA
MAORI DR
MORETON TERR

CHAPELFIELDS
MOORE CL
COLLINSON CT
MAIN ST
A56

GREENFIELD LA
SANDFIELD CT
Frodsham Sta
P
PO
BLUE HATCH

Castle
Park

CHESTER RD
A56

NETHERTON
DIG LA
MATTY S LA
HATLEY LA
NEW DR
MEADOW

ORCHARD CL
TARVIN RD
B5393

PARK CT
PRINCEWAY
QUEENSWAY
KINGSWAY
PARK LA
FOUNTAIN LA

CHURCH ST
B5152
L Ctr
Sch
EDDISBURY SQ
ALVANLEY TERR
MARTIN

ST LAWRENCE RD
CHURCHFIELD RD
COBAL CT
FRODA AVE
ASHLANDS

PINMILL BROW
HOWEY LA
HOWEY RD
PINMILL CL
HILLFIELD

CANDFIELDS
WITHY CL
WHITEHALL PL
THE WILLOWS
LONDON RD
THE WILLOWS

RED LA
FIELDWAY

SCHOOL LA
CHURCH RD
MIDDLE WLK
Sch

FLUIN LA
LIME BEECH AVE
FOXGLOVE CT

ENNERDALE DR
GRASMERE RD
WATTENDALE CL
SILVERDALE CL
BICKERTON AVE

LANGDALE E WAY
CONISTON DR
KESWICK RD
BORROWDALE CL

HO KESWICK
BUTTERMERE CL

PENRITH CL
THIRLMERE CL

FRODSHAM

Bradley Orchard

77

Meml
Hotel

Overton
Hill
Masts
P

BELLEMONTE RD
HILLSIDE RD
ELM ARBAN DR

GREENACRES
OVERTON DR
BRACKEN PL
SEELEY
NEWLANDS CL

HAZELEHURST RD
WARREN CT

HILLSBORO AVE
WOODSIDE AVE
LODGE AVE
CLOVER AVE
GREENSIDE AVE

VICARAGE LA

PO
OAKDALE AVE
ROYLEEN DR
SPRINGBOURNE

SUMMERFIELD RD
ROSEWOOD

BRADLEY LA
LANSDOWNE

Bradley

Brook
Farm

3

Netherton

Sandstone Trail

Golf Course

Beacon
Hill

SIMONS LA

TOP RD

Five
Crosses
Farm

Hatley
Farm

Mickledale
Farm

Fivecrosses

PH

KINGSLEY
GREEN
KINGSLEY RD

76

Woodhouse
Hill

Higher
Mickledale
Farm

DELAMERE WAY

Crow Mere

Crowmere
Cottage

Newton
Hall

Lady Heyes
Farm

Sewage
Wks

2

Sandstone Trail

Snidley
Moor

Nature
Reserve

MANLEY RD

Shepherds
Houses

BEBBERS LA

Mast

DELAMERE WAY

Lowerhouse
Farm

HILLFOOT LA

Newton

EDDISBURY WAY

75

Harrol
Edge

Mast

Manor House
Farm

Newton
Firs

Kingsley
& Newton
Cty Prim
Sch

HOLLOW

DEPMORE
LA

NORLE

MIDD

BS

1

RIDGEWAY

The
Paddocks

RILEY BANK
MEWS
Rileybank

COMMONSIDE

Four Lane
Ends

NEW PALE RD

Organ
Lot

Hatchery

Newton
Hollow

NEWTON HOLLOW

DELAMERE WAY

The
Bungalow

Ppg Sta

Greenacres
Farm

WATERLOO LA

Finney Hill
Pits
(dis)

Castlehill
House

Castlehill
Farm

74

51   A   52   B   53   C

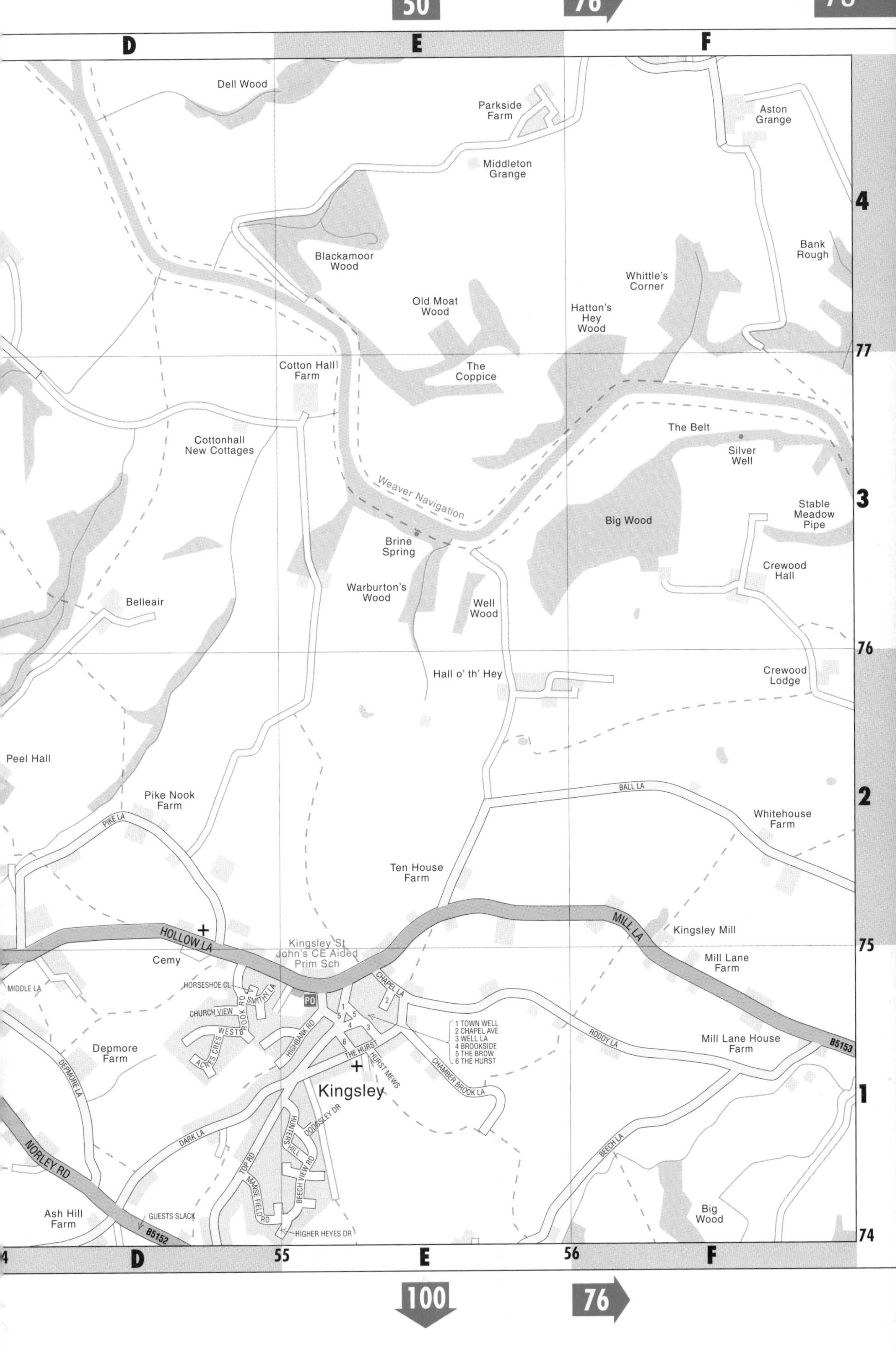

D
E
F

Dell Wood

Parkside Farm

Aston Grange

Middleton Grange

4

Blackamoor Wood

Bank Rough

Old Moat Wood

Whittle's Corner

Hatton's Hey Wood

77

Cotton Hall Farm

The Coppice

Cottonhall New Cottages

The Belt

Silver Well

Weaver Navigation

3

Big Wood

Stable Meadow Pipe

Brine Spring

Crewood Hall

Warburton's Wood

Well Wood

Belleair

76

Hall o' th' Hey

Crewood Lodge

Peel Hall

BALL LA

2

Pike Nook Farm

Whitehouse Farm

PIKE LA

Ten House Farm

HOLLOW LA

MILL LA

Kingsley Mill

75

Cemy

Kingsley St John's CE Aided Prim Sch

Mill Lane Farm

MIDDLE LA

HORSESHOE CL

CHAPEL LA

PO

CHURCH VIEW

WEST G

HIGHBANK RD

SMITHY LA

RODDY LA

Mill Lane House Farm

B5153

1 TOWN WELL
2 CHAPEL AVE
3 WELL LA
4 BROOKSIDE
5 THE BROW
6 THE HURST

Depmore Farm

THE HURST

HURST MEWS

CHAMBER BROOK LA

1

NORLEY RD

DEPMORE LA

Kingsley

DARK LA

HUNTS LA

DODGSLEY DR

TOP RD

BEECH VIEW RD

MAISE FIELD RD

HINTS HILL

BEECH LA

Big Wood

Ash Hill Farm

GUESTS SLACK

B5152

HIGHER HEYES DR

74

4
D
55
E
56
F

75 51

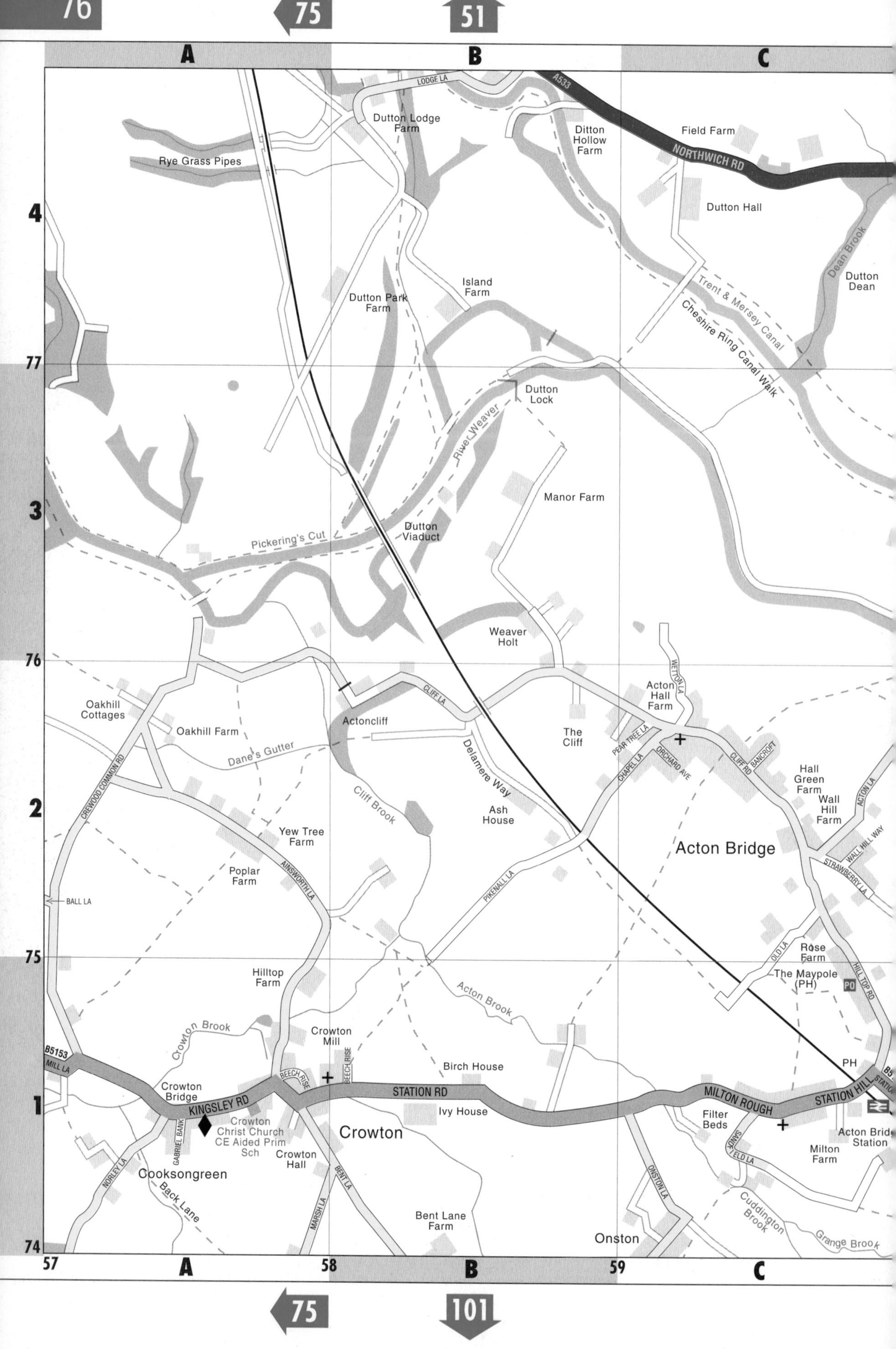
A
B
C
4
3
2
1
77
76
75
74
57
58
59
Lodge La
A533
Northwich Rd
Dutton Lodge Farm
Ditton Hollow Farm
Field Farm
Rye Grass Pipes
Dutton Hall
Dean Brook
Dutton Dean
Dutton Park Farm
Island Farm
Trent & Mersey Canal
Cheshire Ring Canal Walk
Dutton Lock
River Weaver
Manor Farm
Pickering's Cut
Dutton Viaduct
Weaver Holt
Wetton La
Acton Hall Farm
The Cliff
Cliff La
Oakhill Cottages
Oakhill Farm
Actoncliff
Dane's Gutter
Pear Tree La
Chapel La
Orchard Ave
Cliff Rd
Bancroft
Hall Green Farm
Wall Hill Farm
Acton La
Delamere Way
Crewood Common Rd
Cliff Brook
Ash House
Yew Tree Farm
Acton Bridge
Wall Hill Way
Strawberry La
Poplar Farm
Ainsworth La
Pikenall La
Ball La
Old La
Rose Farm
Hill Top Rd
The Maypole (PH)
PO
Hilltop Farm
Acton Brook
Crowton Brook
Crowton Mill
B5153
Mill La
Birch House
PH
Beech Rise
Crowton Bridge
Station Rd
Milton Rough
Station Hill
Kingsley Rd
Ivy House
Filter Beds
Crowton Christ Church CE Aided Prim Sch
Crowton
Gabriel Bank
Sandy La
Acton Bridge Station
Milton Farm
Crowton Hall
Eld La
Norley La
Cooksongreen
Bent La
Onston La
Back Lane
Cuddington Brook
Marsh La
Bent Lane Farm
Onston
Grange Brook

75 101

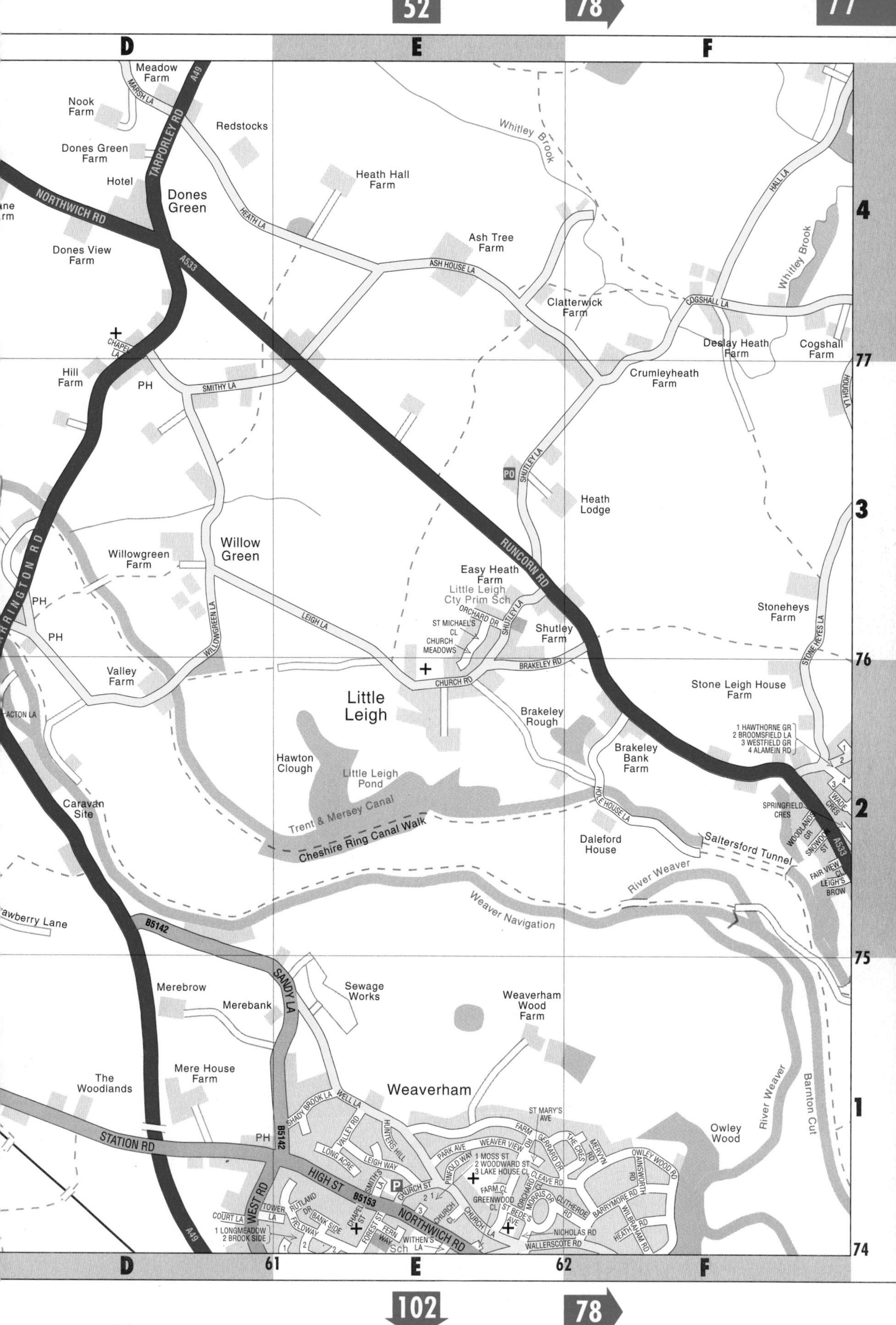
52
78
D
E
F
Meadow Farm
Nook Farm
MARSH LA
A49
TARPORLEY RD
Redstocks
Dones Green Farm
Hotel
Dones Green
NORTHWICH RD
Heath Hall Farm
Whitley Brook
HEATH LA
Dones View Farm
A533
Ash Tree Farm
ASH HOUSE LA
Clatterwick Farm
COGSHALL LA
HALL LA
Whitley Brook
Deslay Heath Farm
Cogshall Farm
CHAPEL LA
Hill Farm
PH
SMITHY LA
Crumleyheath Farm
HOUGH LA
SHUTLEY LA
PO
Heath Lodge
Willow Green
Willowgreen Farm
RUNCORN RD
Easy Heath Farm
Little Leigh Cty Prim Sch
ORCHARD DR
ST MICHAEL'S CL
CHURCH MEADOWS
SHUTLEY LA
Shutley Farm
Stoneheys Farm
STONE HEYES LA
PH
PH
LEIGH LA
WILLOWGREEN LA
Valley Farm
BRAKELEY RD
CHURCH RD
Little Leigh
Stone Leigh House Farm
ACTON LA
Brakeley Rough
1 HAWTHORNE GR
2 BROOMSFIELD LA
3 WESTFIELD GR
4 ALAMEIN RD
Hawton Clough
Little Leigh Pond
Brakeley Bank Farm
Caravan Site
Trent & Mersey Canal
Cheshire Ring Canal Walk
HOLE HOUSE LA
SPRINGFIELD CRES
WADE CRES
WOODLANDS GR
SNOWDON ST
A533
Daleford House
Saltersford Tunnel
FAIR VIEW CL
LEIGH'S BROW
River Weaver
Weaver Navigation
awberry Lane
B5142
SANDY LA
Sewage Works
Merebrow
Merebank
Weaverham Wood Farm
The Woodlands
Mere House Farm
Weaverham
ST MARY'S AVE
WELL LA
SHADY BROOK LA
VALLEY RD
HUNTERS HILL
FARM
GERRARD DR
THE CRES
MERVYN RD
OWLEY WOOD RD
Owley Wood
River Weaver
Barnton Cut
STATION RD
PH
B5142
LONG ACRE
LEIGH WAY
PARK AVE
WEAVER VIEW
1 MOSS ST
2 WOODWARD ST
3 LAKE HOUSE CL
PINFOLD WAY
HIGH ST
SMITH'S LA
P
CHURCH ST
CLEAVE RD
AINSWORTH RD
B5153
FARM CL
GREENWOOD CL
ORCHARD
MORRIS DR
CLITHEROE RD
BARRYMORE RD
WEST RD
TOWER LA
RUTLAND DR
BANK SIDE
CHAPEL ST
FOREST ST
NORTHWICH RD
CHURCH CL
CHURCH LA
ST BEDE'S AVE
WILBRAHAM RD
HEATH RD
COURT LA
1 LONGMEADOW
2 BROOK SIDE
FIELDWAY
FERN WAY
WITHEN'S LA
NICHOLAS RD
WALLERSCOTE RD
Sch
A49
4
77
3
76
2
75
1
74
61
62
102
78

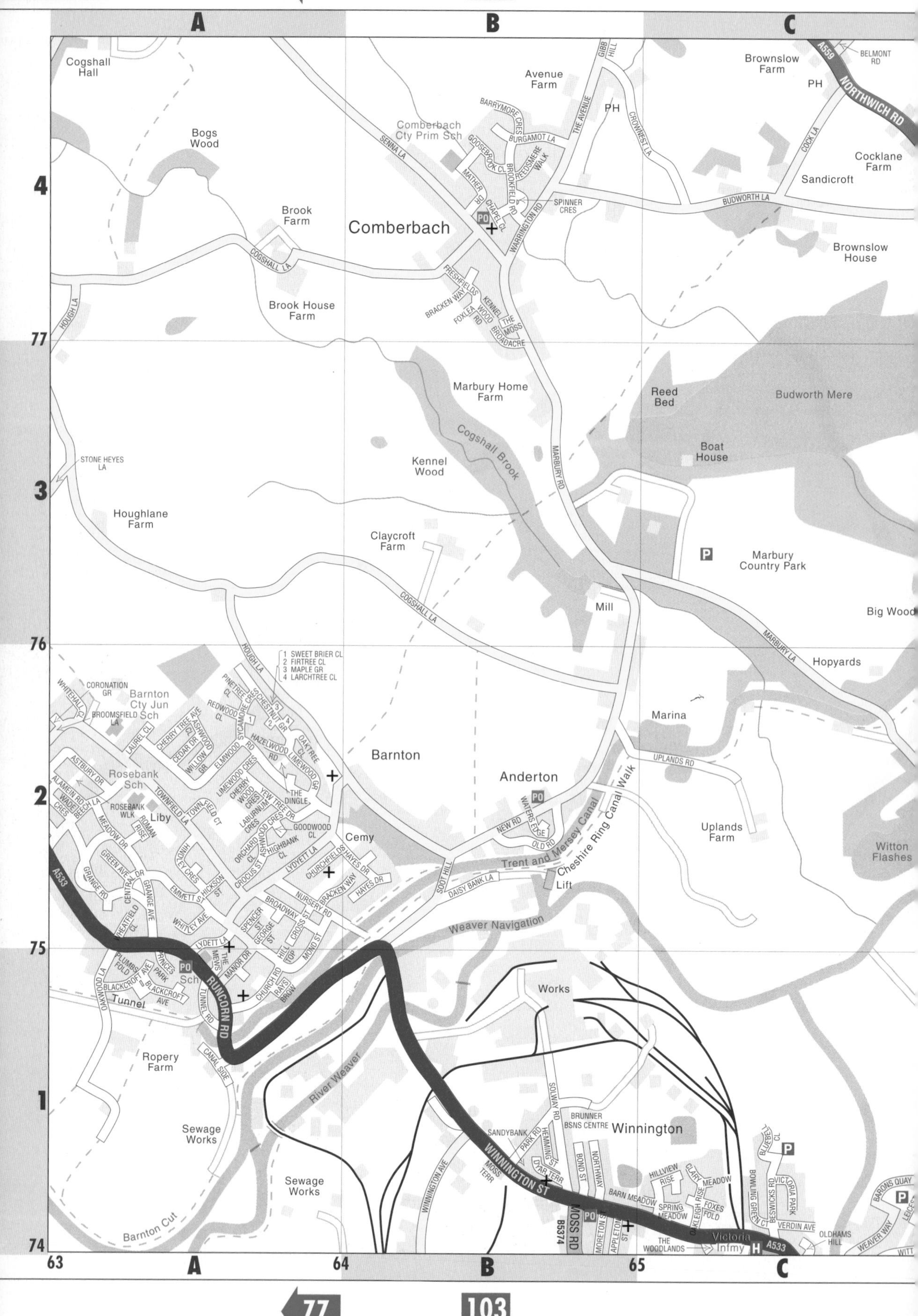

A   B   C

4

77

3

76

2

75

1

74

63   A   64   B   65   C

Cogshall Hall
Bogs Wood
Brook Farm
Comberbach
Avenue Farm
Comberbach Cty Prim Sch
Brownslow Farm
PH
PH
BELMONT RD
A559
NORTHWICH RD
Cocklane Farm
Sandicroft
BUDWORTH LA
Brownslow House
Brook House Farm
HOUGH LA
COGSHALL LA
Marbury Home Farm
Reed Bed
Budworth Mere
Cogshall Brook
Boat House
Kennel Wood
MARBURY RD
Stone Heyes La
Houghlane Farm
Claycroft Farm
P
Marbury Country Park
COGSHALL LA
Mill
MARBURY LA
Big Wood
Hopyards
1 SWEET BRIER CL
2 FIRTREE CL
3 MAPLE GR
4 LARCHTREE CL
CORONATION GR
Barnton Cty Jun Sch
Broomsfield Sch
WHITEHALL LA
ROUGH LA
Barnton
Marina
UPLANDS RD
Rosebank Sch
Liby
Anderton
PO
Uplands Farm
Witton Flashes
The Dingle
Cemy
New Rd
WATERS EDGE
OLD RD
Trent and Mersey Canal
Cheshire Ring Canal Walk
A533
RUNCORN RD
Tunnel
Sch
PO
SPOT HILL
DAISY BANK LA
Lift
Weaver Navigation
Works
Ropery Farm
CANAL SIDE
River Weaver
Sewage Works
WINNINGTON AVE
Sandybank
BRUNNER BSNS CENTRE
Winnington
SOLWAY RD
P
Sewage Works
Barnton Cut
WINNINGTON ST
MOSS TERR
Hillview Rise
Spring Meadow
Barn Meadow
Foxes Fold
VERDIN AVE
Oldhams Hill
WITT
MOSS RD
B5374
PO
The Woodlands
Victoria Infmy
H
A533
Barons Quay
LEGE'S

54
80

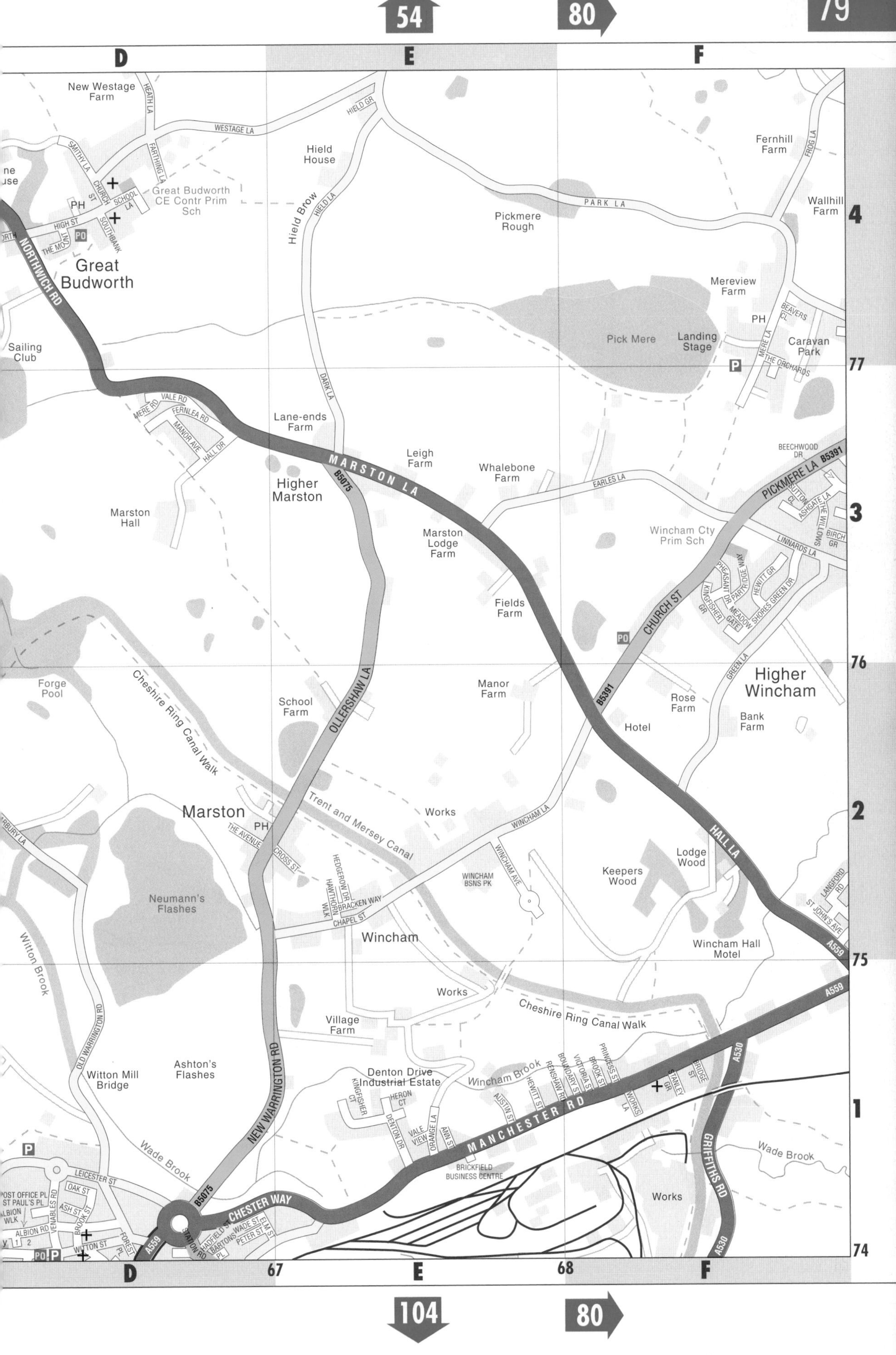
D
E
F
New Westage Farm
HEATH LA
WESTAGE LA
HIELD GR
Hield House
SMITHY LA
FARTHING LA
CHURCH ST
SCHOOL LA
Great Budworth CE Contr Prim Sch
PH
HIGH ST
PO
SOUTHBANK
THE MOUNT
Hield Brow
HIELD LA
NORTHWICH RD
Great Budworth
PARK LA
Pickmere Rough
Fernhill Farm
FROG LA
Wallhill Farm
4
Mereview Farm
BEAVERS CL
Sailing Club
Pick Mere
Landing Stage
Caravan Park
MERE LA
THE ORCHARDS
P
77
VALE RD
MERE RD
FERNLEA RD
MANOR AVE
HALL DR
DARK LA
Lane-ends Farm
Leigh Farm
MARSTON LA
B5075
Higher Marston
Whalebone Farm
EARLES LA
BEECHWOOD DR
PICKMERE LA
B5391
Marston Hall
Marston Lodge Farm
Wincham Cty Prim Sch
SUTTON CL
ASHGATE LA
THE WILLOWS
BIRCH GR
LINNARDS LA
3
PHEASANT DR
PARTRIDGE WAY
KINGFISHER GR
HEWITT GR
SHORES GREEN DR
MEADOW GATE
Fields Farm
CHURCH ST
PO
Forge Pool
Cheshire Ring Canal Walk
OLLERSHAW LA
Manor Farm
GREEN LA
Higher Wincham
76
School Farm
Rose Farm
Bank Farm
Hotel
Marston
PH
THE AVENUE
CROSS ST
Trent and Mersey Canal
Works
WINCHAM LA
WINCHAM AVE
WINCHAM BSNS PK
HALL LA
2
Lodge Wood
Keepers Wood
LANGFORD RD
ST JOHN'S AVE
Neumann's Flashes
HEDGEROW DR
HAWTHORN WALK
BRACKEN WAY
CHAPEL ST
Wincham
Wincham Hall Motel
A559
75
Witton Brook
Works
Cheshire Ring Canal Walk
Village Farm
OLD WARRINGTON RD
Witton Mill Bridge
Ashton's Flashes
NEW WARRINGTON RD
Denton Drive Industrial Estate
Wincham Brook
KINGFISHER CT
HERON CT
DENTON DR
VALE VIEW
ORANGE LA
ANN ST
AUSTIN ST
HEWITT ST
RENSHAW RD
BOUNDARY ST
VICTORIA ST
BROOK ST
PRINCESS ST
WORKS LA
STANLEY GR
BRIDGE ST
A530
MANCHESTER RD
1
GRIFFITHS RD
Wade Brook
Wade Brook
BRICKFIELD BUSINESS CENTRE
Works
P
LEICESTER ST
OAK ST
POST OFFICE PL
ST PAUL'S PL
ALBION WLK
VENABLES RD
ASH ST
BROOK ST
ALBION RD
WITTON ST
FOREST PL
B5075
CHESTER WAY
A559
STATION RD
HADFIELD ST
BARTONS WADE ST
ELM ST
PETER ST
PL
PO
P
74
67
68
D
E
F

104
80

A B C

Rinks Pool

Brook Farm

Roses Farm

Rinks Wood

Nether Tabley

Pickmeremoss Wood

Tanyard Farm

Clay House Farm

Tabley (rems

Dogkenne Wood

Pickmere

Providence Farm

The Hut

Crow Wood

Manor Farm

Tabley Grange

Smoker Hill Farm

Leonard's Wood

Waterless Brook

Home Farm

Smoker Brook

Smoker Wood

White Hou Farm

The Smoker (PH)

Hopley's Pipes

Wincham Brook

Peas Wood

Halford Farm

Maltkiln Farm

Winnington Wood

Mill Wood

Holford Hall

Peover Eye

Lostock Gralam

Brookhouse Farm

Mushro Farm

Long Wood

Sch

Reservoir

Lostock Gralam Station

Holford Moss

Home Farm

Wade Brook

Fieldhouse Farm

Lostock

Langford Farm

HALL LA, B5391, PICKMERE LA, MILLEY LA, FLITTOGATE LA, PO, PARK LA, MERE CL, WELL FIELD CL, MEREHAVEN CL, PH, SPINK LA, GREEN LA, ORCHARD CL, PEAR TREE DR, THE WOODLANDS, SHELLEY AVE, JOHN FRYER AVE, MILTON CL, KEATS LA, CHESTER RD, LINNARDS LA, WHITEHOUSE LA, PLUMLEY MOOR RD, MALT KILN, YEWTREE RD, OAK FIELD RD, HOLLYTREE RD, MOORCROFT, TROUTHALL LA, ASCOL DR, A559, A556, CEDAR CL, LANGFORD RD, WARREN AVE, GROVE AVE, HESKETH DR, TOWNSHEND RD, HIGHFIELD AVE, HOLFORD AVE, FRYER RD, GIBBON DR, WILSON CRES, MANCHESTER RD, SMITHY LA, SCHOOL LA, LODGE LA, STUBBS LA, AITCHISON RD, BATEMAN RD, FITTON ST, HERBERT ST, ARTHUR ST, STATION RD, ROBERTS RD, HARRIS RD, PAULDEN RD, MOSS LA, LOSTOCK HOLLOW, BIRCHES LA

4 77 3 76 2 75 1 74

69 A 70 B 71 C

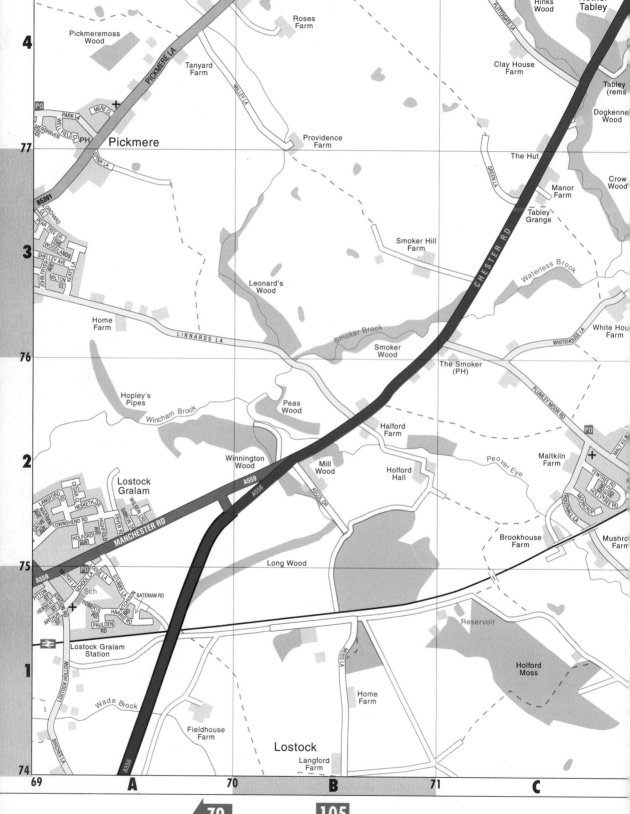

D E F

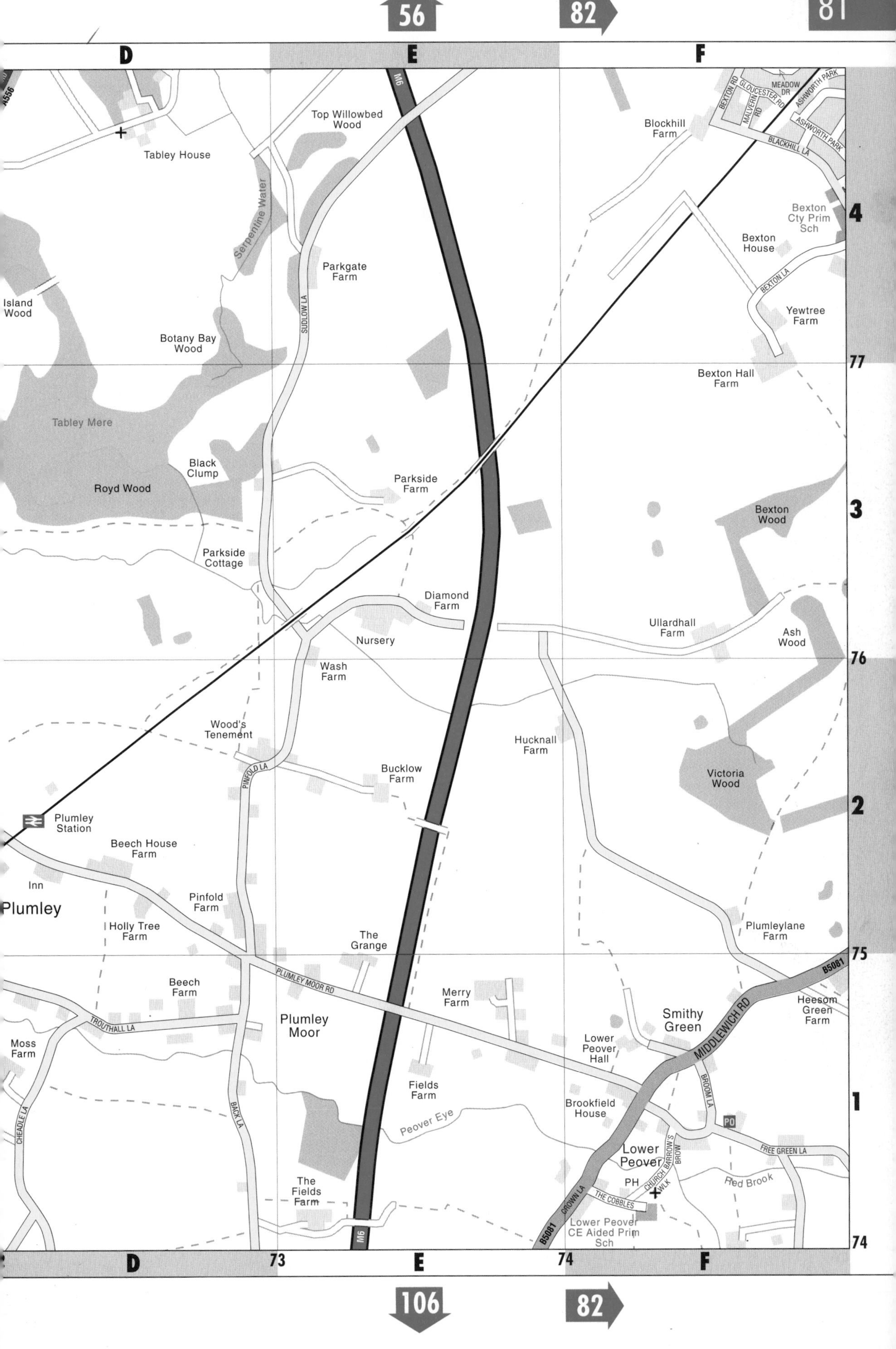
M6
A556
Top Willowbed Wood
Tabley House
Serpentine Water
Blockhill Farm
BEXTON RD
GLOUCESTER RD
MALVERN RD
MEADOW DR
ASHWORTH PARK
BLACKHILL LA
Bexton Cty Prim Sch
Bexton House
BEXTON LA
Yewtree Farm
Parkgate Farm
SUDLOW LA
Island Wood
Botany Bay Wood
Bexton Hall Farm
Tabley Mere
Black Clump
Royd Wood
Parkside Farm
Bexton Wood
Parkside Cottage
Diamond Farm
Ullardhall Farm
Ash Wood
Nursery
Wash Farm
Wood's Tenement
Hucknall Farm
Bucklow Farm
PINFOLD LA
Victoria Wood
Plumley Station
Beech House Farm
Inn
Plumley
Pinfold Farm
Holly Tree Farm
The Grange
Plumleylane Farm
Beech Farm
PLUMLEY MOOR RD
Merry Farm
B5081
MIDDLEWICH RD
Heesom Green Farm
Smithy Green
TROUTHALL LA
Plumley Moor
Moss Farm
Lower Peover Hall
BROOM LA
Fields Farm
Brookfield House
BACK LA
CHEADLE LA
Peover Eye
PO
FREE GREEN LA
Lower Peover
BARROW'S BROW
Red Brook
CHURCH WLK
PH
The Fields Farm
THE COBBLES
CROWN LA
Lower Peover CE Aided Prim Sch
4
77
3
76
2
75
1
74
73

D E F

81
57

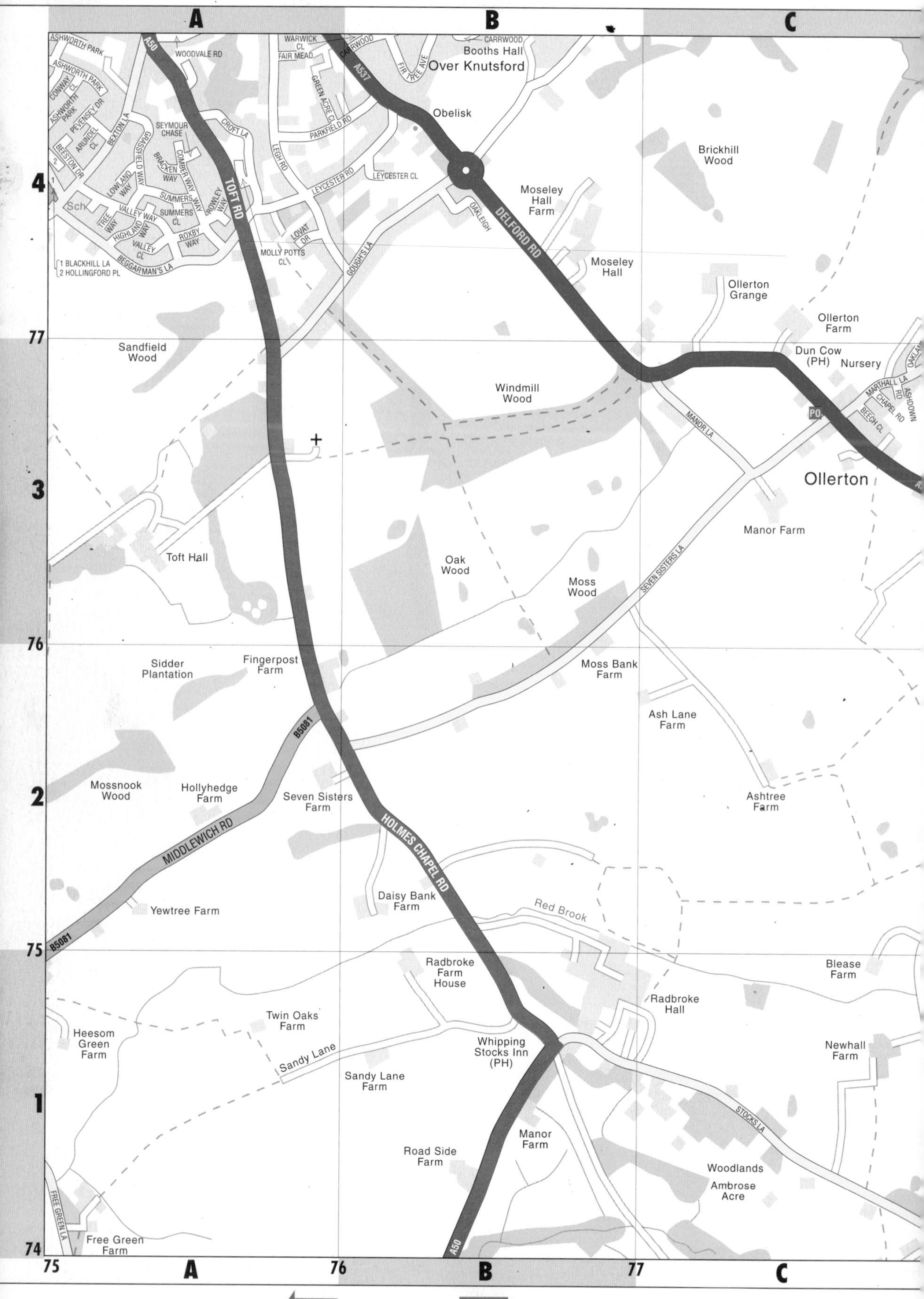
Over Knutsford
Booths Hall
Obelisk
Brickhill Wood
Moseley Hall Farm
Moseley Hall
Ollerton Grange
Ollerton Farm
Dun Cow (PH)
Nursery
Sandfield Wood
Windmill Wood
Ollerton
Manor Farm
Toft Hall
Oak Wood
Moss Wood
Sidder Plantation
Fingerpost Farm
Moss Bank Farm
Ash Lane Farm
Mossnook Wood
Hollyhedge Farm
Seven Sisters Farm
Ashtree Farm
Yewtree Farm
Daisy Bank Farm
Red Brook
Radbroke Farm House
Blease Farm
Radbroke Hall
Heesom Green Farm
Twin Oaks Farm
Sandy Lane
Whipping Stocks Inn (PH)
Newhall Farm
Sandy Lane Farm
Manor Farm
Road Side Farm
Woodlands
Ambrose Acre
Free Green Farm
TOFT RD
DELFORD RD
HOLMES CHAPEL RD
MIDDLEWICH RD
SEVEN SISTERS LA
MANOR LA
STOCKS LA
GOUGH'S LA
LEYCESTER RD
LEYCESTER CL
PARKFIELD RD
CARRWOOD
FIR TREE AVE
GREEN ACRE CL
LEGH RD
WARWICK CL
FAIR MEAD
WOODVALE RD
CROFT LA
ASHWORTH PARK
SEYMOUR CHASE
LOWLAND WAY
VALLEY WAY
SUMMERS WAY
SUMMERS CL
ROWLEY WAY
ROXBY WAY
HIGHLAND WAY
VALLEY CL
BEGGARMAN'S LA
MOLLY POTTS CL
LOVAT DR
OAKLEIGH
MARTHALL LA
CHAPEL RD
BEECH CL
ASHDOWN
FREE GREEN LA
1 BLACKHILL LA
2 HOLLINGFORD PL
A50
A537
B5081
PO
Sch
A
B
C
4
3
2
1
77
76
75
74

81
107

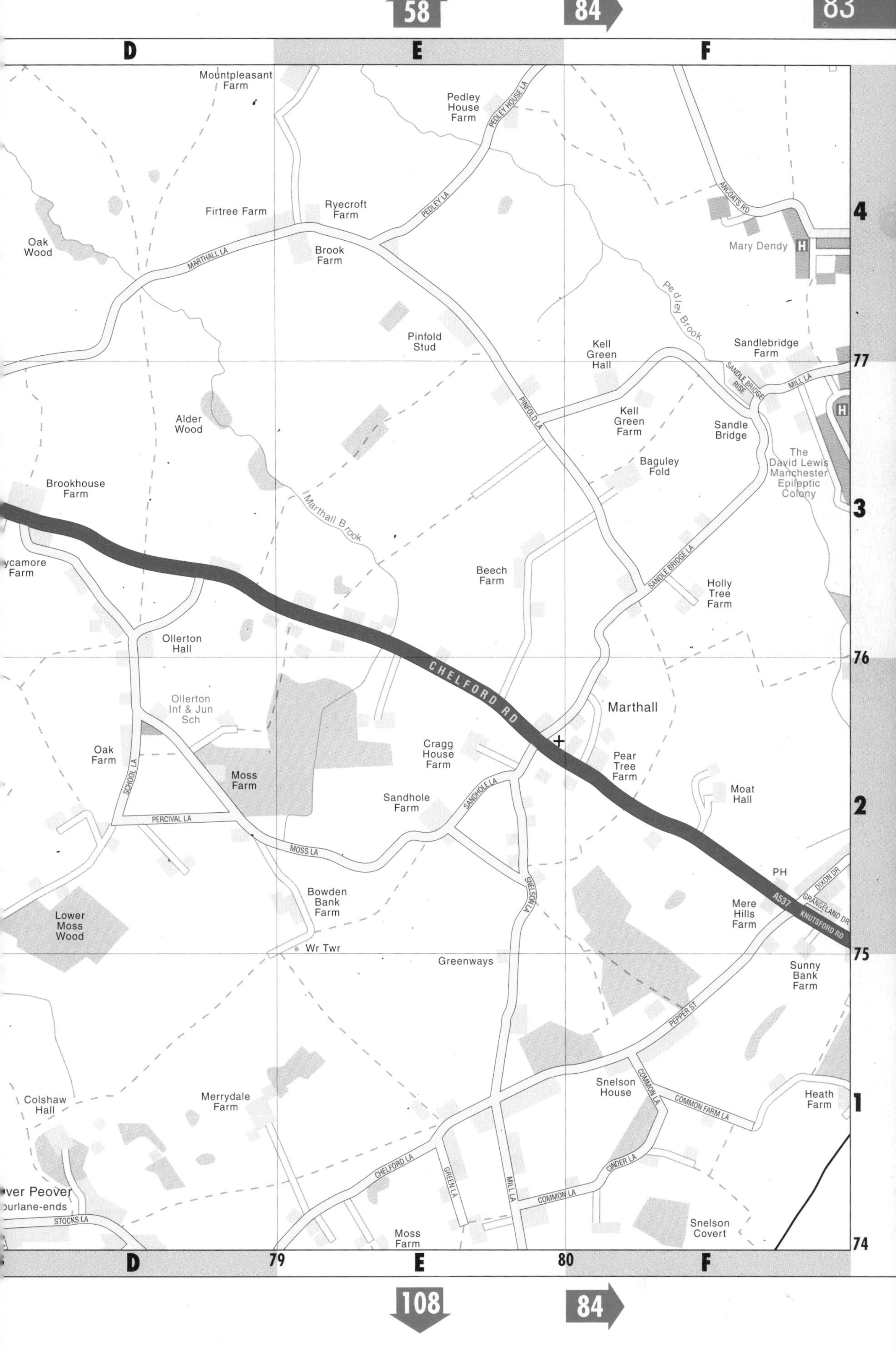
D
E
F
Mountpleasant Farm
Pedley House Farm
PEDLEY HOUSE LA
Firtree Farm
Ryecroft Farm
PEDLEY LA
ANCOATS RD
Mary Dendy
Oak Wood
MARTHALL LA
Brook Farm
Pedley Brook
Pinfold Stud
Kell Green Hall
Sandlebridge Farm
SANDLE BRIDGE RISE
MILL LA
Alder Wood
PINFOLD LA
Kell Green Farm
Sandle Bridge
The David Lewis Manchester Epileptic Colony
Baguley Fold
Brookhouse Farm
Marthall Brook
ycamore Farm
Beech Farm
SANDLE BRIDGE LA
Holly Tree Farm
Ollerton Hall
CHELFORD RD
Ollerton Inf & Jun Sch
Marthall
Oak Farm
Cragg House Farm
Pear Tree Farm
SCHOOL LA
Moss Farm
Moat Hall
Sandhole Farm
SANDHOLE LA
PERCIVAL LA
MOSS LA
PH
DIXON DR
Bowden Bank Farm
SNELSON LA
A537
GRANGELAND DR
KNUTSFORD RD
Mere Hills Farm
Lower Moss Wood
Wr Twr
Greenways
Sunny Bank Farm
PEPPER ST
Colshaw Hall
Merrydale Farm
Snelson House
COMMON LA
COMMON FARM LA
Heath Farm
CHELFORD LA
GREEN LA
CINDER LA
MILL LA
COMMON LA
ver Peover
ourlane-ends
STOCKS LA
Snelson Covert
Moss Farm
4
77
3
76
2
75
1
74
79
80

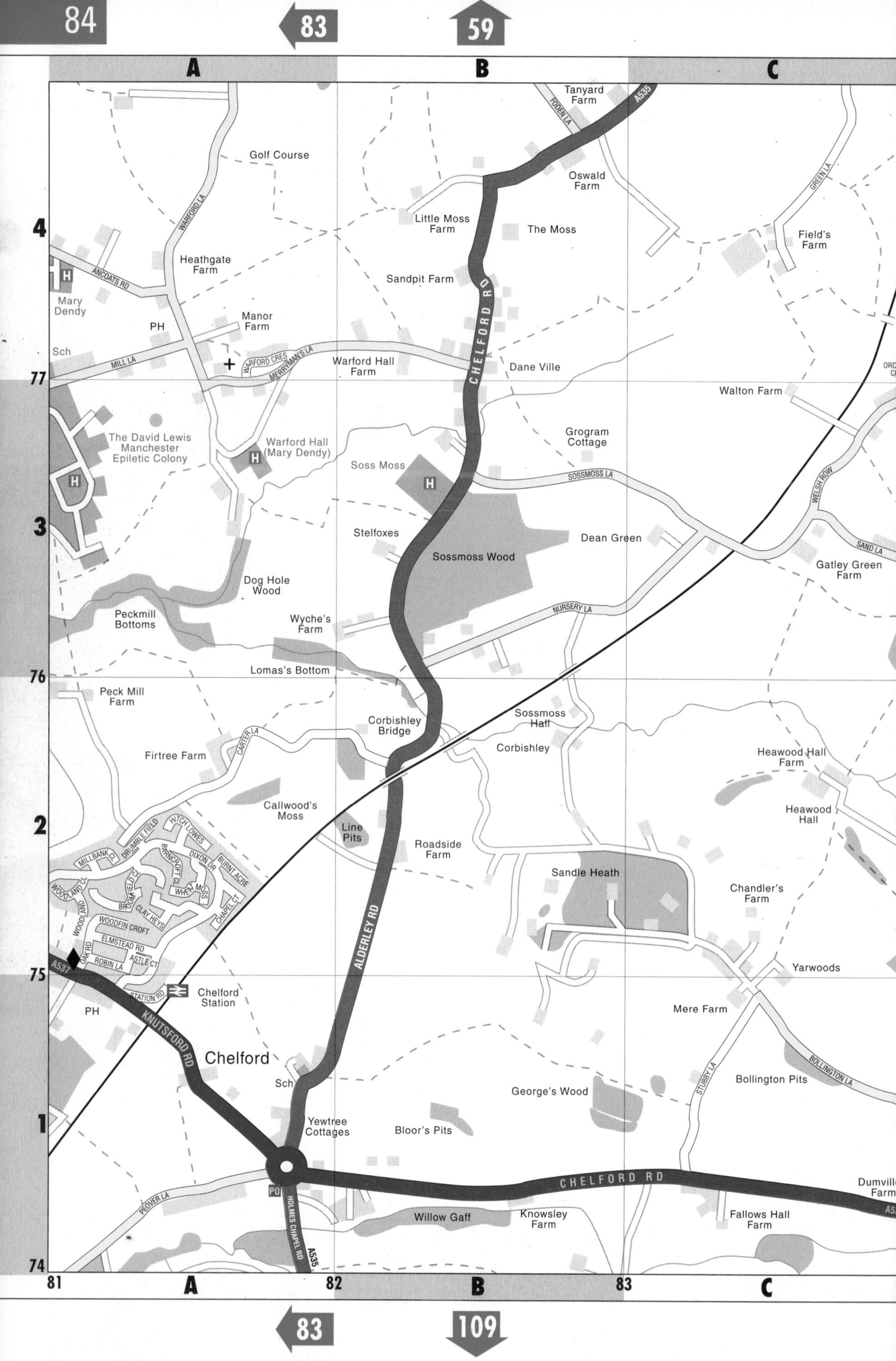

Tanyard Farm

Oswald Farm

Golf Course

Little Moss Farm

The Moss

Field's Farm

4

Heathgate Farm

Sandpit Farm

ANCOATS RD

WARFORD LA

Mary Dendy

H

PH

Manor Farm

Sandpit Farm

CHELFORD RD

Dane Ville

Walton Farm

GREEN LA

Sch

MILL LA

WARFORD CRES

MERRIMAN'S LA

Warford Hall Farm

77

The David Lewis Manchester Epiletic Colony

Warford Hall (Mary Dendy)

H

Soss Moss

H

Grogram Cottage

SOSSMOSS LA

WELSH ROW

ORCH CFT

3

H

Stelfoxes

Sossmoss Wood

Dean Green

Gatley Green Farm

SAND LA

Dog Hole Wood

Peckmill Bottoms

Wyche's Farm

NURSERY LA

76

Lomas's Bottom

Peck Mill Farm

CARTER LA

Corbishley Bridge

Sossmoss Hall

Corbishley

Heawood Hall Farm

Firtree Farm

Callwood's Moss

Line Pits

Roadside Farm

Heawood Hall

2

MILLBANK CL

HTCH LOWES

DRUMBLE FIELD

DIXON DR

BURNT ACRE

WHEN MOSS

BARNCROFT CL

CLAY HEYS

CHAPEL CT

ASTLE CT

Sandle Heath

Chandler's Farm

WOODLAND CL

BRI STONE FIELD CL

WOODFIN CROFT

ELMSTEAD RD

OAK RD

ROBIN LA

ALDERLEY RD

Yarwoods

75

A537

STATION RD

Chelford Station

Mere Farm

STURDY LA

Bollington Pits

BOLLINGTON LA

PH

KNUTSFORD RD

Chelford

Sch

George's Wood

1

Yewtree Cottages

Bloor's Pits

PO

HOLMES CHAPEL RD

A535

CHELFORD RD

Dumville Farm

74

PEOVER LA

Willow Gaff

Knowsley Farm

Fallows Hall Farm

A53

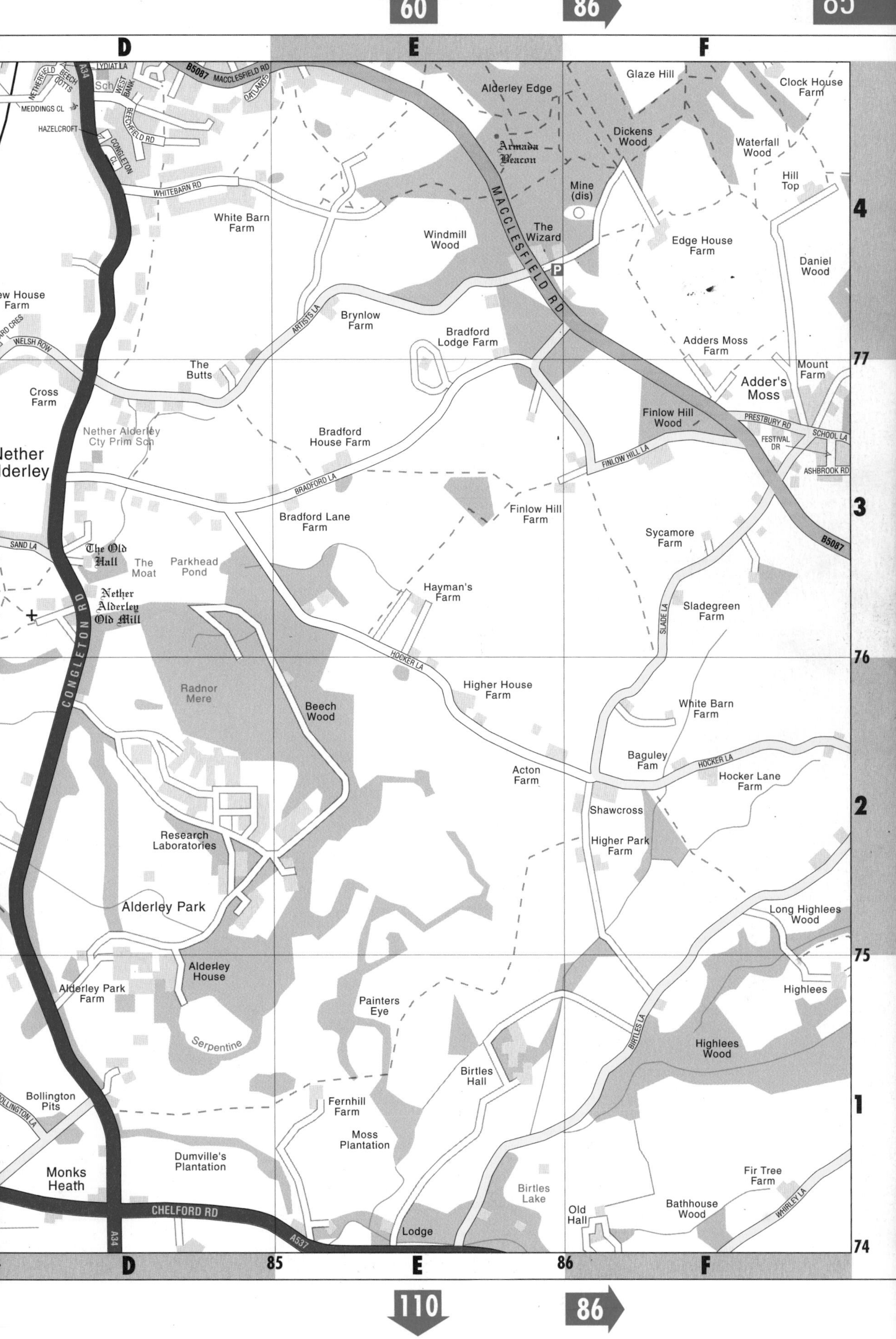
D
E
F
Alderley Edge
Glaze Hill
Clock House Farm
Dickens Wood
Waterfall Wood
Armada Beacon
Hill Top
Mine (dis)
White Barn Farm
Windmill Wood
The Wizard
Edge House Farm
Daniel Wood
MACCLESFIELD RD
B5087 MACCLESFIELD RD
LYDIAT LA
NETHERFIELD
BEECH COTTS
Sch
WEST BANK
OATLANDS
MEDDINGS CL
HAZELCROFT
BEECHFIELD RD
CONGLETON CL
WHITEBARN RD
A34
New House Farm
WELSH ROW
ARTISTS LA
Brynlow Farm
Bradford Lodge Farm
Adders Moss Farm
The Butts
Cross Farm
Mount Farm
Adder's Moss
Finlow Hill Wood
PRESTBURY RD
FESTIVAL DR
SCHOOL LA
ASHBROOK RD
FINLOW HILL LA
Nether Alderley Cty Prim Sch
Bradford House Farm
Nether Alderley
BRADFORD LA
Bradford Lane Farm
Finlow Hill Farm
Sycamore Farm
B5087
SAND LA
The Old Hall
The Moat
Parkhead Pond
Nether Alderley Old Mill
Hayman's Farm
Sladegreen Farm
SLADE LA
HOCKER LA
Radnor Mere
Higher House Farm
CONGLETON RD
Beech Wood
White Barn Farm
Baguley Fam
HOCKER LA
Acton Farm
Hocker Lane Farm
Shawcross
Research Laboratories
Higher Park Farm
Alderley Park
Long Highlees Wood
Alderley House
Alderley Park Farm
Painters Eye
Highlees
BIRTLES LA
Serpentine
Highlees Wood
Birtles Hall
Bollington Pits
BOLLINGTON LA
Fernhill Farm
Moss Plantation
Dumville's Plantation
Monks Heath
Fir Tree Farm
Birtles Lake
Old Hall
Bathhouse Wood
WHIRLEY LA
CHELFORD RD
A537
Lodge
A34
4
77
3
76
2
75
1
74
85
86

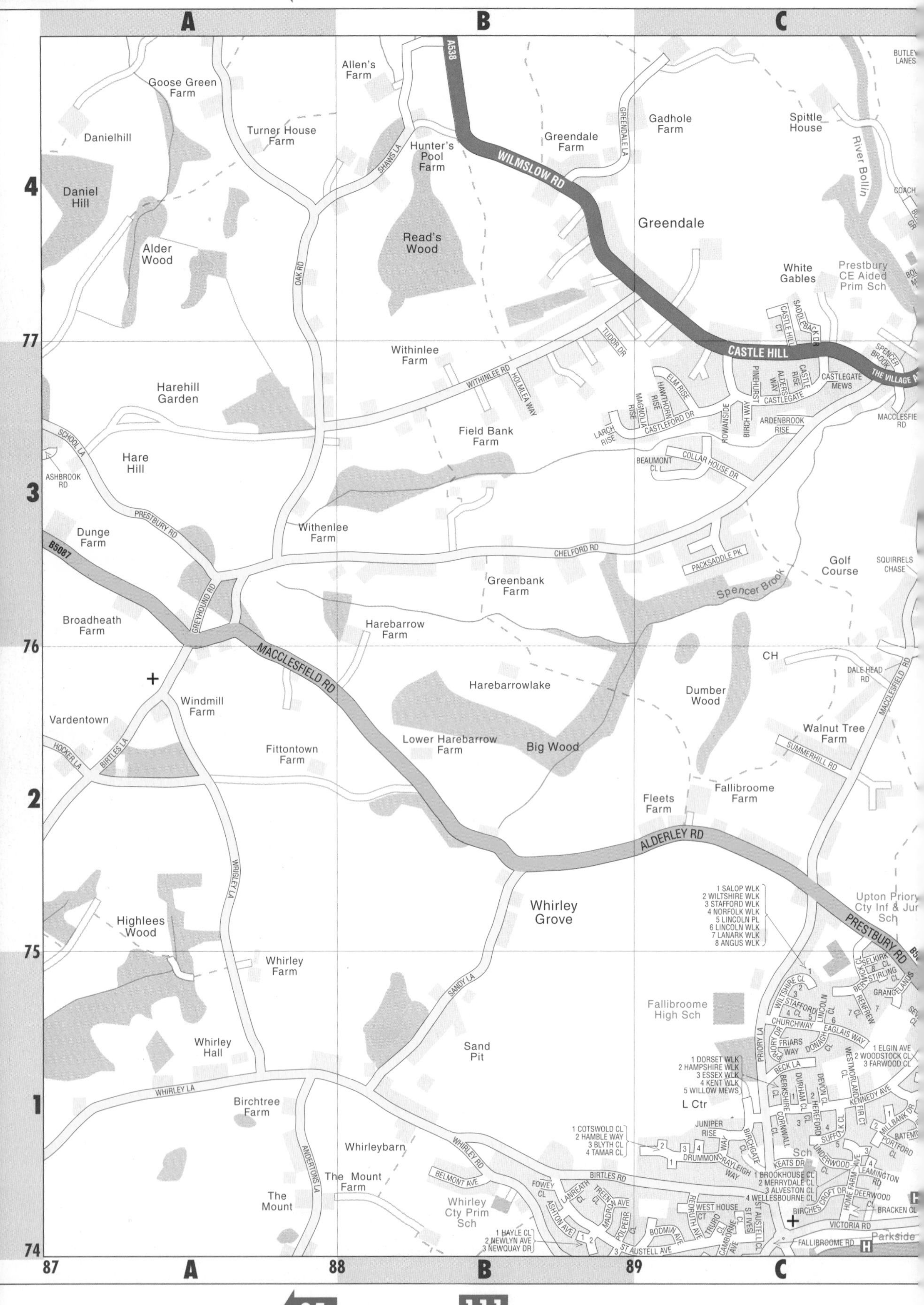

A   B   C

BUTLEY LANES

Goose Green Farm

Allen's Farm

Danielhill

Turner House Farm

Hunter's Pool Farm

Greendale Farm

Gadhole Farm

Spittle House

River Bollin

4

Daniel Hill

Read's Wood

WILMSLOW RD

Greendale

COACH

Alder Wood

GREENDALE LA

White Gables

Prestbury CE Aided Prim Sch

77

Withinlee Farm

CASTLE HILL

The Village

Harehill Garden

WITHINLEE RD

HOLME LA WAY

Field Bank Farm

TUDOR DR

LARCH RISE

ELM RISE

CASTLE RISE

HAWTHORN RISE

MAGNOLIA RISE

CASTLEFORD DR

PINEHURST

ALDERS WAY

CASTLEGATE

ROWANSIDE

HORN RIBH

ARDENBROOK RISE

CASTLEGATE MEWS

SADDLE BACK CR

CASTLE HILL CT

SPENCER BROOK

MACCLESFIE RD

SCHOOL LA

Hare Hill

ASHBROOK RD

PRESTBURY RD

BEAUMONT CL

COLLAR HOUSE DR

3

Dunge Farm

Withenlee Farm

CHELFORD RD

PACKSADDLE PK

Golf Course

SQUIRRELS CHASE

B5087

GREYHOUND RD

Greenbank Farm

Spencer Brook

76

Broadheath Farm

MACCLESFIELD RD

Harebarrow Farm

Harebarrowlake

CH

DALE HEAD RD

MACCLESFIELD RD

+

Windmill Farm

Dumber Wood

Walnut Tree Farm

Vardentown

HOCKERLA

BIRTLES LA

Fittontown Farm

Lower Harebarrow Farm

Big Wood

SUMMERHILL RD

2

WRIGLEY LA

Fleets Farm

Fallibroome Farm

ALDERLEY RD

Highlees Wood

1 SALOP WLK
2 WILTSHIRE WLK
3 STAFFORD WLK
4 NORFOLK WLK
5 LINCOLN PL
6 LINCOLN WLK
7 LANARK WLK
8 ANGUS WLK

Upton Priory Cty Inf & Jur Sch

PRESTBURY RD

75

Whirley Farm

Whirley Grove

Fallibroome High Sch

SANDY LA

WILTSHIRE CL

STAFFORD CL

CHURCHWAY

PRIORY LA

CHURCHWAY

FRIARS WAY

DONAS

EAGLAIS WAY

SELKIRK CL

STIRLING

BEN NEVIS

GRANDE CL

WESTMORLAND

DEVON CL

DURHAM CL

HEREFORD

SUFFK CL

1 ELGIN AVE
2 WOODSTOCK CL
3 FARWOOD CL

KENNEDY AVE

ELGIN FIR CT

Whirley Hall

Sand Pit

BECK LA

CORNWALL

BERKSHIRE CL

1 DORSET WLK
2 HAMPSHIRE WLK
3 ESSEX WLK
4 KENT WLK
5 WILLOW MEWS

L Ctr

MILLBANK DR

BATEMI

1

WHIRLEY LA

Birchtree Farm

1 COTSWOLD CL
2 HAMBLE WAY
3 BLYTH CL
4 TAMAR CL

JUNIPER RISE

DRUMMON

RAYLEIGH WAY

BIRCHATE

KEATS DR

LEAMINGTON

PORTFORD

UNDERWOOD

DEERWOOD

BRACKEN CL

1 BROOKHOUSE CL
2 MERRYDALE CL
3 ALVESTON CL
4 WELLESBOURNE CL

ANDERTONS LA

Whirleybarn

The Mount Farm

The Mount

BELMONT AVE

WHIRLEY RD

BIRTLES RD

FOWEY CL

LANBREATH CL

GREEN AVE

ASHTON AVE

POLPERR

BODMIN AVE

REDRUTH AVE

WEST HOUSE

CAMBRID

ST IVES

ST WEST

CROFT

BIRCHES

Parkside

FALLIBROOME RD

Victoria Rd

+

Whirley Cty Prim Sch

1 HAYLE CL
2 NEWLYN AVE
3 NEWQUAY DR

ST AUSTELL AVE

H

74

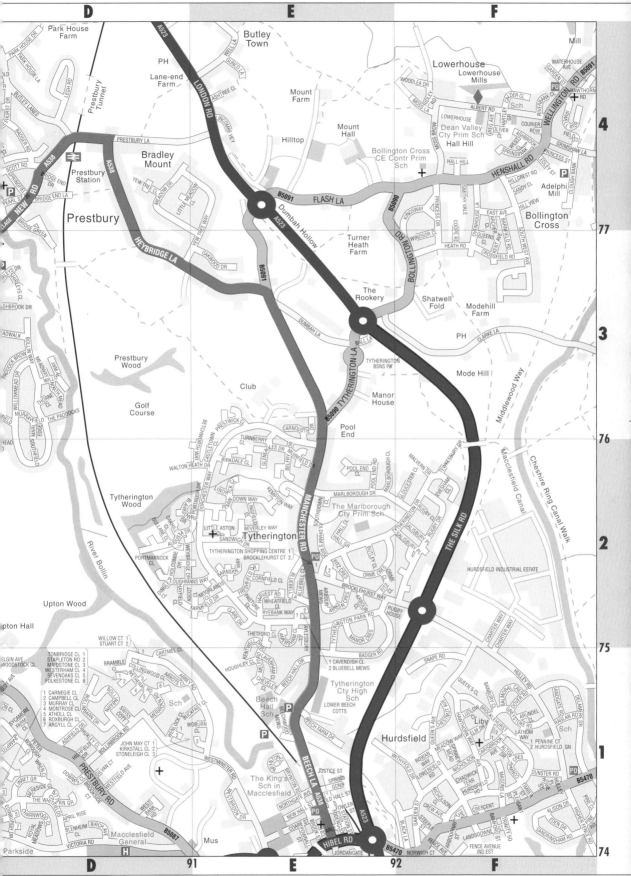
D
E
F
Park House Farm
Butley Town
PH
Lane-end Farm
Prestbury Tunnel
LONDON RD
A523
Mount Farm
Lowerhouse
Lowerhouse Mills
Mill
WATERHOUSE AVE
WELLINGTON RD
B5091
HAWTHORN RD
ALBERT RD
LOWERHOUSE
Dean Valley Cty Prim Sch
Hall Hill
Mount Hall
Hilltop
PRESTBURY LA
A538
Bradley Mount
Prestbury Station
Bollington Cross CE Contr Prim Sch
HENSHALL RD
HALL HILL
Adelphi Mill
Bollington Cross
FLASH LA
B5091
B5090
Dumbah Hollow
Prestbury
HEYBRIDGE LA
Turner Heath Farm
BOLLINGTON RD
The Rookery
Shatwell Fold
Modehill Farm
DUMBAH LA
PH
CLARKE LA
Prestbury Wood
TYTHERINGTON LA
TYTHERINGTON BSNS PK
Mode Hill
Middlewood Way
Club
Manor House
Golf Course
Pool End
MANCHESTER RD
Macclesfield Canal
Cheshire Ring Canal Walk
Tytherington Wood
The Marlborough Cty Prim Sch
THE SILK RD
Tytherington
TYTHERINGTON SHOPPING CENTRE
River Bollin
HURDSFIELD INDUSTRIAL ESTATE
Upton Wood
Upton Hall
TYTHERINGTON PARK RD
RUGBY HOUSE
Tytherington Cty High Sch
LOWER BEECH COTTS
Beech Hall Sch
Sch
Hurdsfield
Liby
PRESTBURY RD
BEECH LA
The King's Sch in Macclesfield
Macclesfield General
Parkside
Mus
HIBEL RD
B5470
B5087
FENCE AVENUE IND EST
4
77
3
76
2
75
1
74
91
92
D
E
F

87
63

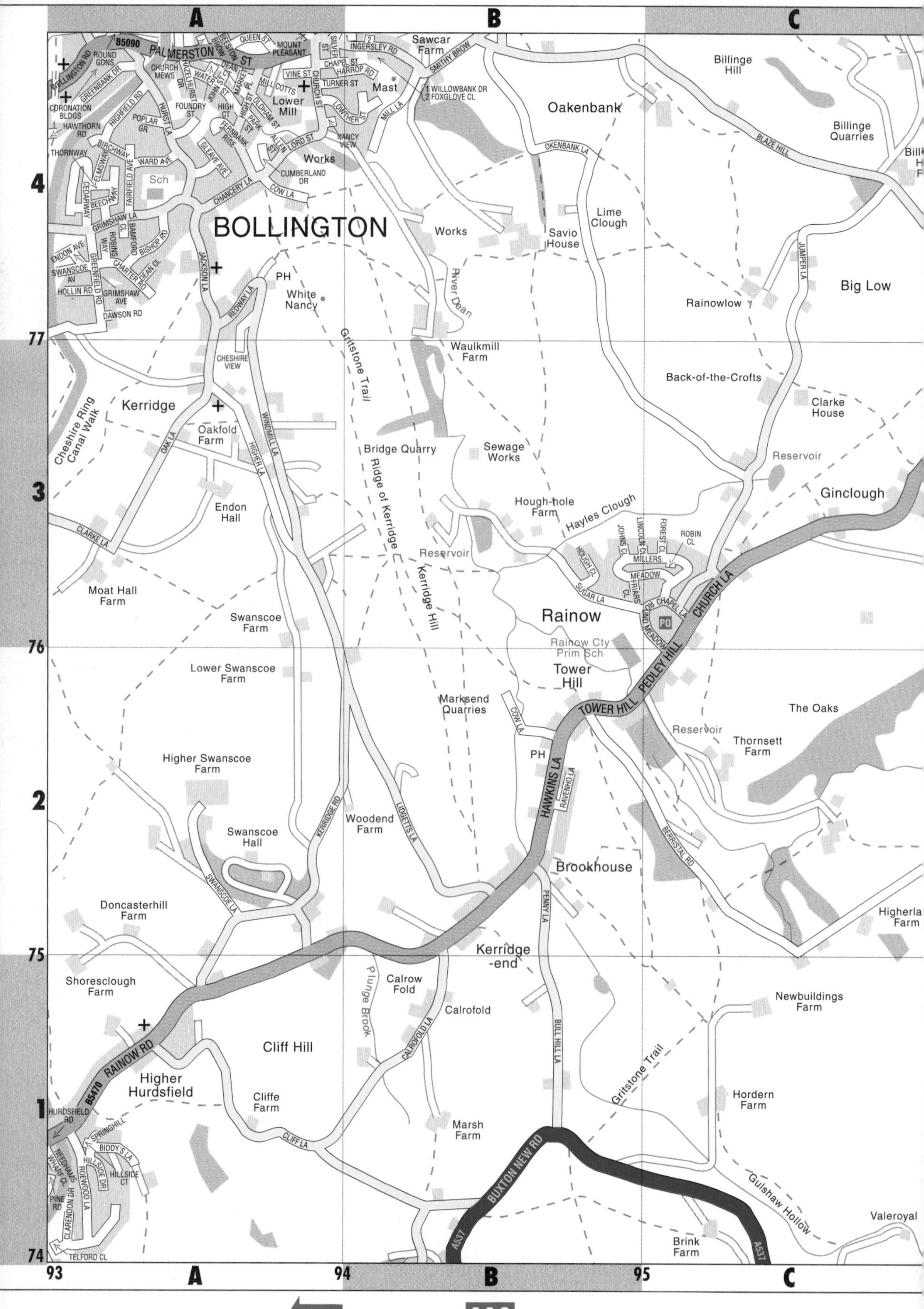
A
B
C
4
77
3
76
2
75
1
74
93
94
95
BOLLINGTON
B5090
PALMERSTON ST
WELLINGTON RD
ROUND GDNS
GREENBANK DR
CHURCH MEWS
HAZELHURST DR
WATER ST
DEAN CT
BEESTON BROW
QUEEN ST
MOUNT PLEASANT
SILVER ST
INGERSLEY RD
Sawcar Farm
SMITHY BROW
CHAPEL ST
HARROP RD
VINE ST
TURNER ST
MILL COTTS
Mast
Lower Mill
1 WILLOWBANK DR
2 FOXGLOVE CL
CORONATION BLDGS
HIGHFIELD RD
HAWTHORN RD
POPLAR GR
HURST LA
FOUNDRY ST
HIGH CT
FERNBANK RISE
OLDHAM ST
PARK ST
JOHN ST
MARKET PL
HIGH ST
ALLEN ST
LORD ST
LOWTHER ST
NANCY VIEW
MILL LA
CHURCH ST
THORNWAY
BIRCHWAY
ELMSWAY
WARD AVE
GLEAVE AVE
Works
CUMBERLAND DR
COW LA
CEDARWAY
BEECHWAY
FAIRFIELD AVE
Sch
CHANCERY LA
GRIMSHAW LA
ROBINS WAY
BAMFORD CL
BISHOP RD
ENDON AVE
SWANSCOE AV
GREENFIELD RD
CHARTER RD
DEAN CL
HOLLIN RD
GRIMSHAW AVE
DAWSON RD
JACKSON LA
REDWAY LA
PH
White Nancy
Works
River Dean
Oakenbank
OKENBANK LA
Lime Clough
Savio House
Billinge Hill
Billinge Quarries
BLAZE HILL
JUMPER LA
Big Low
Rainowlow
CHESHIRE VIEW
Waulkmill Farm
Gritstone Trail
Back-of-the-Crofts
Clarke House
Kerridge
Cheshire Ring Canal Walk
Oakfold Farm
OAK LA
HIGHER LA
WINDMILL LA
Bridge Quarry
Sewage Works
Reservoir
Ginclough
Endon Hall
Ridge of Kerridge
Hough-hole Farm
Hayles Clough
JOHNS CL
LINCOLN CL
FOREST CL
ROBIN CL
HOUGH CL
MILLERS
MEADOW
FRIARS CL
CLARKE LA
Reservoir
SUGAR LA
CHAPEL LA
CHURCH LA
Moat Hall Farm
Kerridge Hill
Rainow
ROUND MEADOW
PO
Swanscoe Farm
Rainow Cty Prim Sch
PEDLEY HILL
Tower Hill
Lower Swanscoe Farm
TOWER HILL
The Oaks
Marksend Quarries
COW LA
Reservoir
Thornsett Farm
PH
Higher Swanscoe Farm
HAWKINS LA
RAVENHO LA
Woodend Farm
KERRIDGE RD
LIDGETTS LA
Swanscoe Hall
BERRISTAL RD
Brookhouse
SWANSCOE LA
PENNY LA
Doncasterhill Farm
Higherla Farm
Kerridge -end
Shoresclough Farm
Calrow Fold
Plunge Brook
Calrofold
Newbuildings Farm
RAINOW RD
B5470
Cliff Hill
CALROFOLD LA
BULL HILL LA
Higher Hurdsfield
Gritstone Trail
Cliffe Farm
Hordern Farm
HURDSFIELD RD
SPRINGHILL
BIDDY'S LA
CLIFF LA
Marsh Farm
NEEDHAMS WHARF CL
HILLSIDE DR
HILLSIDE CT
ROEWOOD LA
BUXTON NEW RD
Gulshaw Hollow
PINE RD
CLARENDON DR
A537
Valeroyal
Brink Farm
A537
TELFORD CL

87
113

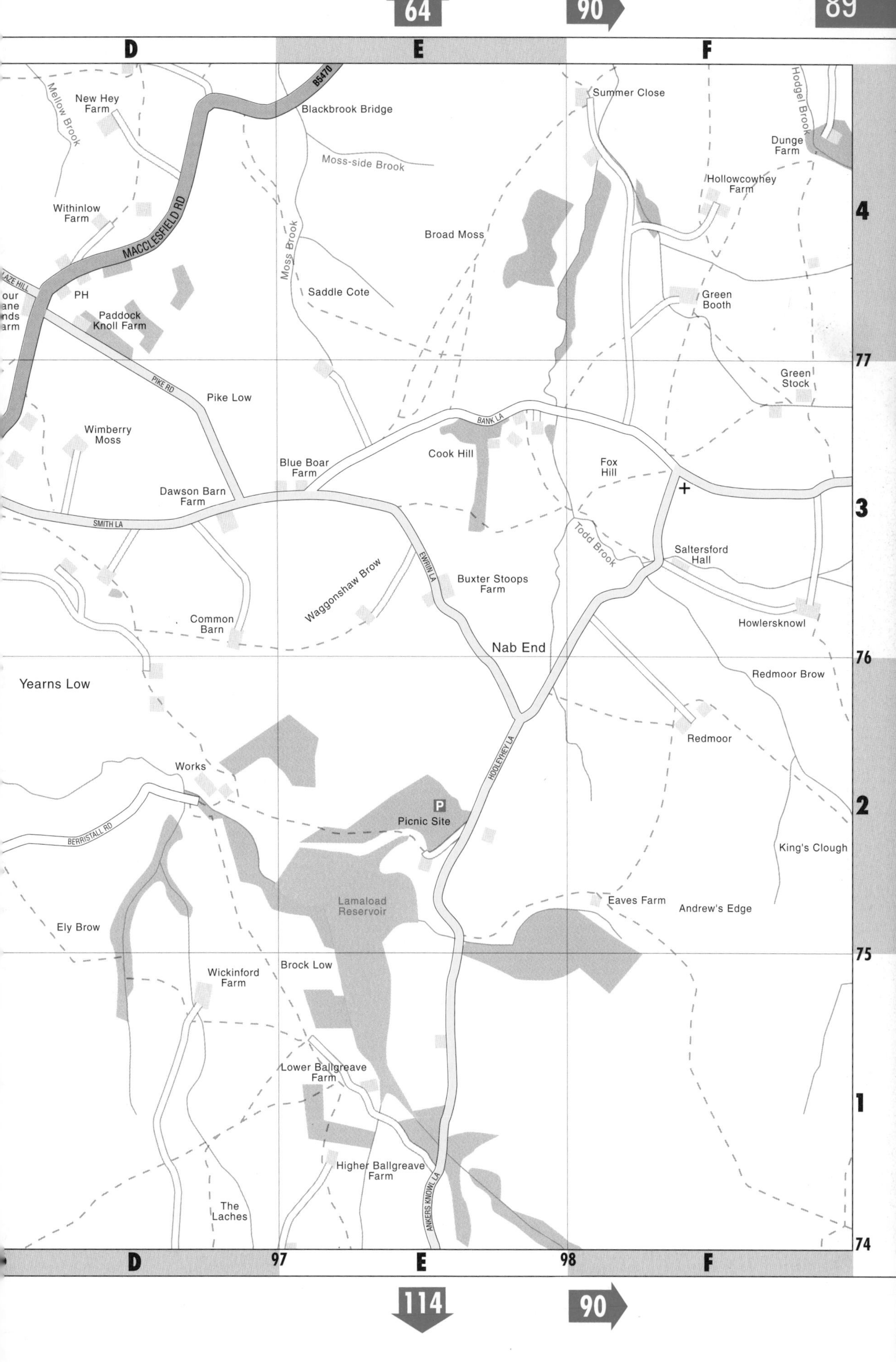

D E F

B5470

Hodgel Brook

New Hey Farm

Mellow Brook

Blackbrook Bridge

Summer Close

Moss-side Brook

Dunge Farm

Hollowcowhey Farm

Withinlow Farm

Moss Brook

Broad Moss

4

MACCLESFIELD RD

Saddle Cote

Green Booth

PH

ur ane nds rm

LAZE HILL

Paddock Knoll Farm

77

Green Stock

PIKE RD

Pike Low

BANK LA

Cook Hill

Fox Hill

+

Wimberry Moss

Blue Boar Farm

Saltersford Hall

3

Dawson Barn Farm

Todd Brook

SMITH LA

EWRIN LA

Buxter Stoops Farm

Howlersknowl

Waggonshaw Brow

Common Barn

Nab End

76

Redmoor Brow

Yearns Low

Redmoor

Works

2

P

King's Clough

BERRISTALL RD

Picnic Site

HODLEYHEY LA

Ely Brow

Lamaload Reservoir

Eaves Farm

Andrew's Edge

75

Brock Low

Wickinford Farm

Lower Ballgreave Farm

1

Higher Ballgreave Farm

ANKERS KNOWL LA

The Laches

74

D 97 E 98 F

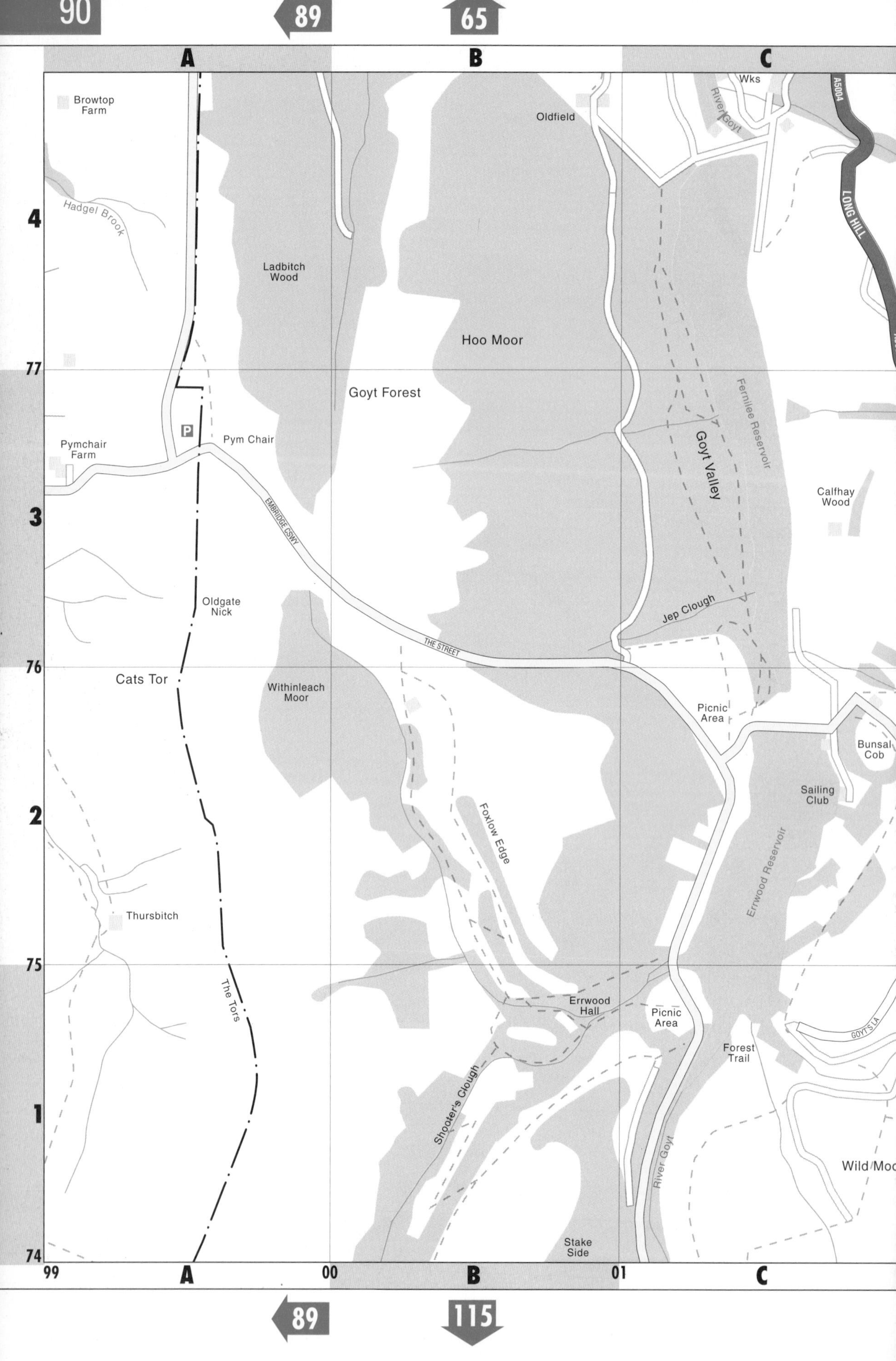
89
65
A
B
C
Browtop Farm
Oldfield
Wks
River Goyt
A5004
LONG HILL
Hadgel Brook
4
Ladbitch Wood
Hoo Moor
77
Goyt Forest
Pym Chair
Pymchair Farm
P
Goyt Valley
Fernilee Reservoir
Calfhay Wood
3
EMBRIDGE CSWY
Oldgate Nick
Jep Clough
THE STREET
76
Cats Tor
Withinleach Moor
Picnic Area
Bunsal Cob
Sailing Club
2
Foxlow Edge
Erwood Reservoir
Thursbitch
75
The Tors
Errwood Hall
Picnic Area
Forest Trail
GOYT'S LA
Shooter's Clough
1
River Goyt
Wild Moo
Stake Side
74
99
00
01
89
115

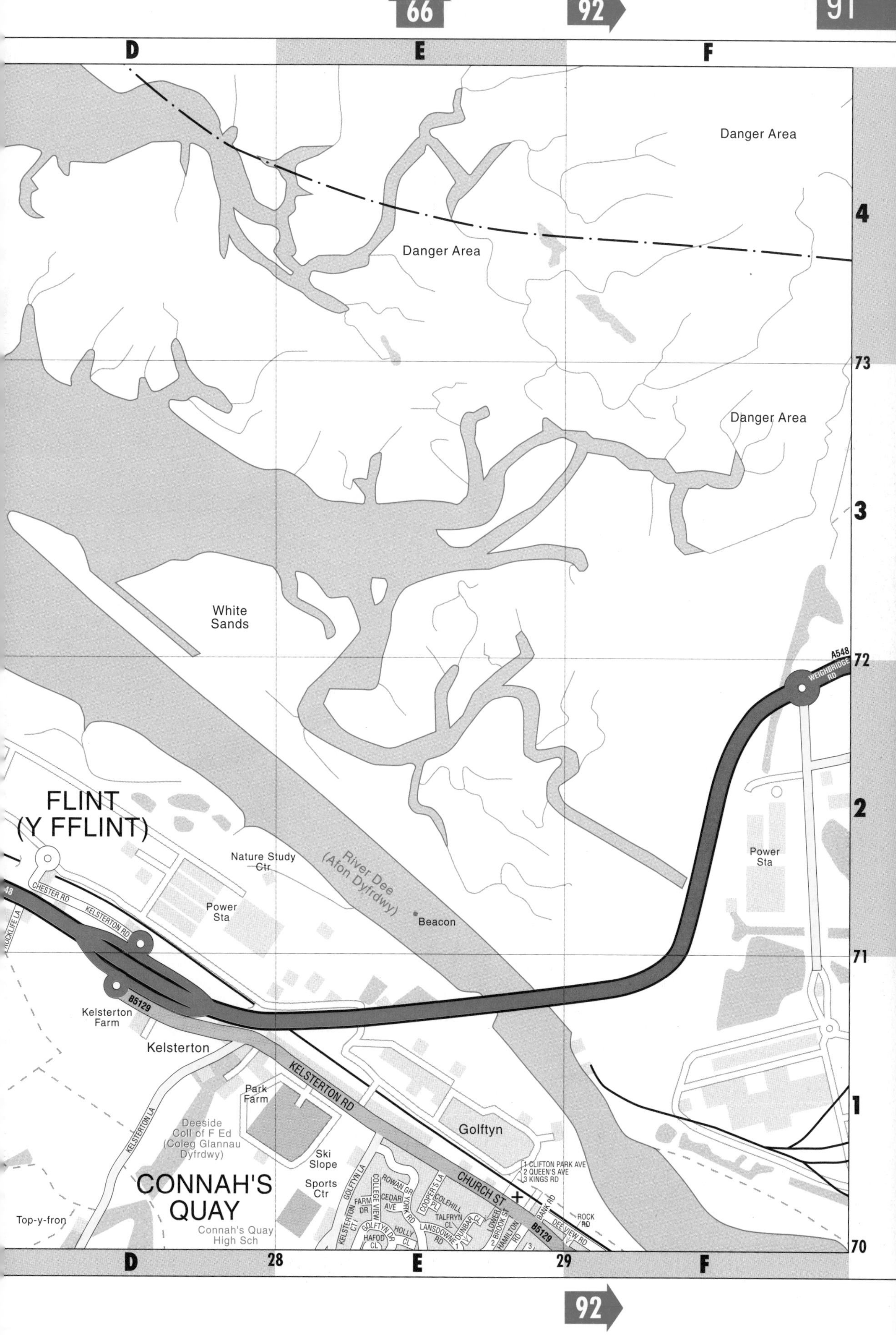
D
E
F
Danger Area
Danger Area
Danger Area
4
73
3
72
2
71
1
70
White Sands
A548
WEIGHBRIDGE RD
FLINT (Y FFLINT)
Nature Study Ctr
River Dee (Afon Dyfrdwy)
Beacon
Power Sta
Power Sta
CHESTER RD
KELSTERTON RD
B5129
Kelsterton Farm
Kelsterton
KELSTERTON RD
Park Farm
Golftyn
KELSTERTON LA
Deeside Coll of F Ed (Coleg Glannau Dyfrdwy)
Ski Slope
Sports Ctr
CONNAH'S QUAY
Connah's Quay High Sch
Top-y-fron
GOLFTYN LA
COLLEGE VIEW
ROWAN GR
CEDAR AVE
YORK RD
COOPER'S LA
COLEHILL PL
FARM DR
TALFRYN CL
DUNBAR CL
LOWER BROOK ST
HAMILTON RD
HOLLY CL
GOLFTYN DR
HAFOD CL
KELSTERTON CT
LANSDOWNE RD
CHURCH ST
BANK RD
DEE VIEW RD
ROCK RD
1 CLIFTON PARK AVE
2 QUEEN'S AVE
3 KINGS RD
D
28
E
29
F

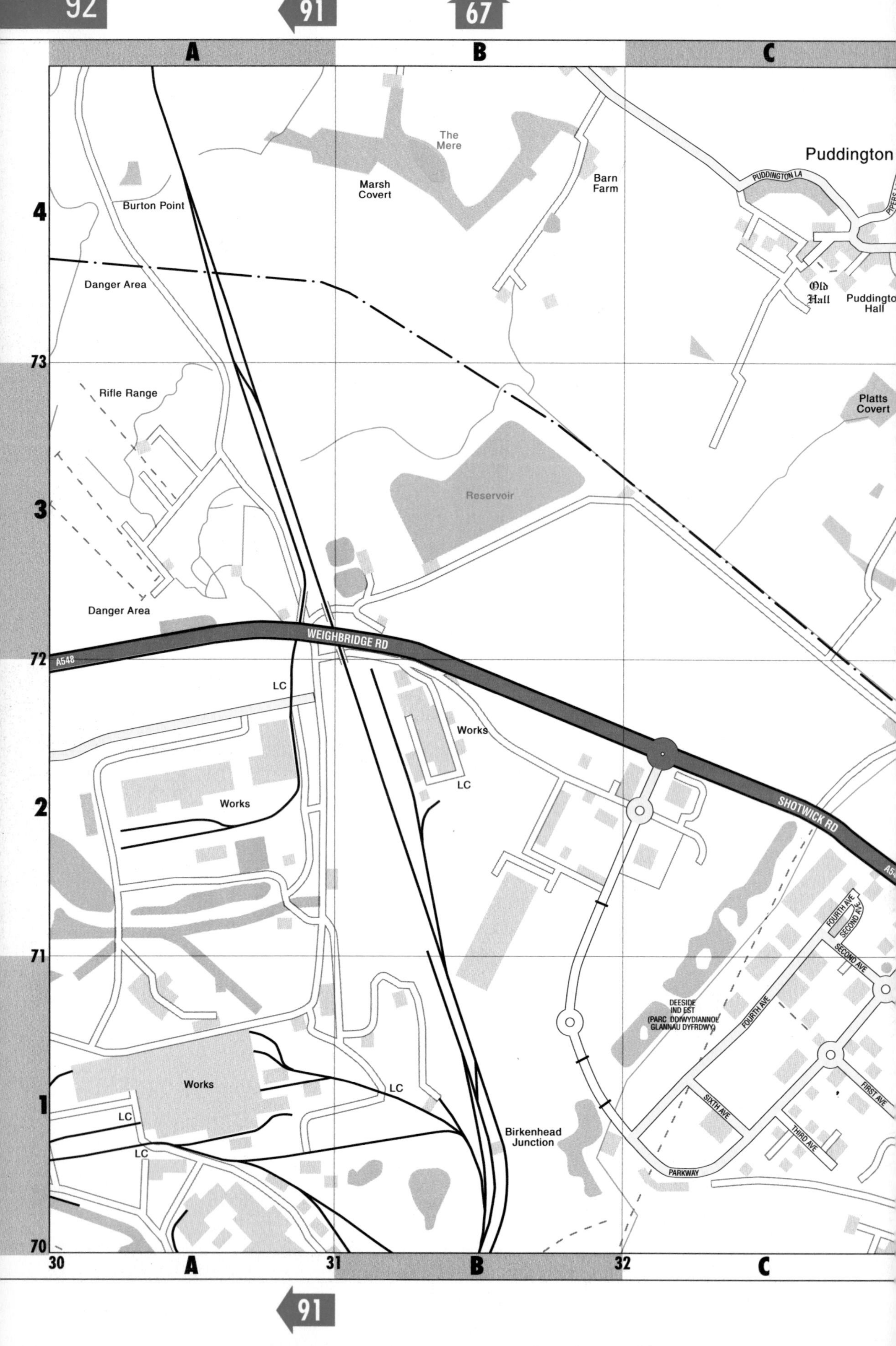

A   B   C

4

Puddington

Burton Point

Marsh
Covert

The
Mere

Barn
Farm

PUDDINGTON LA

Danger Area

Old
Hall

Puddingto
Hall

73

Rifle Range

Platts
Covert

Reservoir

3

Danger Area

WEIGHBRIDGE RD

72

A548

LC

Works

LC

Works

SHOTWICK RD

2

Works

LC

A5

71

FOURTH AVE

SECOND AVE

SECOND AVE

DEESIDE
IND EST
(PARC DDIWYDIANNO
GLANNAU DYFRDWY)

FOURTH AVE

Works

LC

LC

Birkenhead
Junction

FIRST AVE

1

LC

SIXTH AVE

THIRD AVE

PARKWAY

70

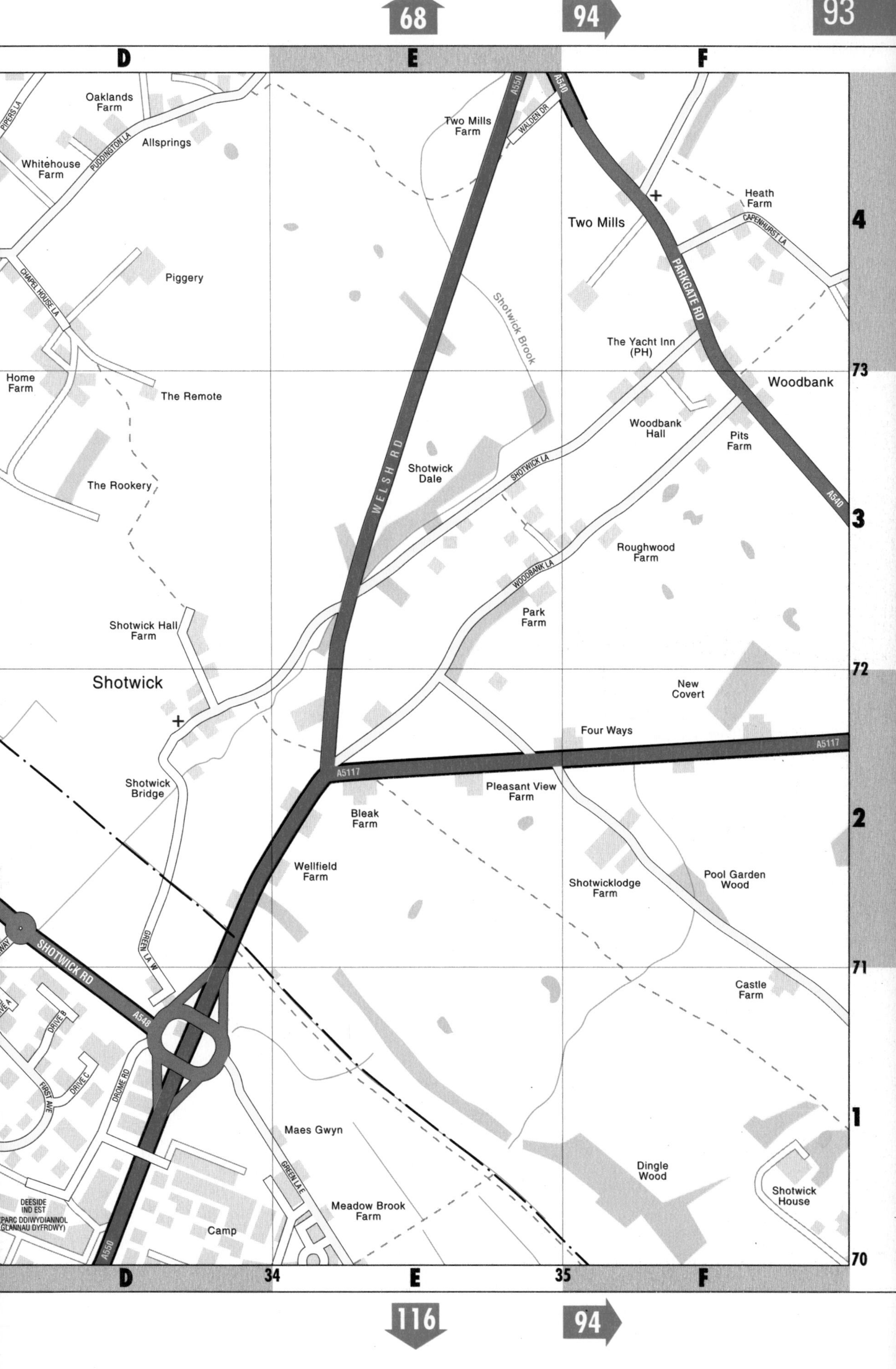
68
94
D
E
F
Oaklands Farm
Whitehouse Farm
Allsprings
PIPERS LA
PUDDINGTON LA
Two Mills Farm
WALDEN DR
A550
A540
Two Mills
Heath Farm
CAPENHURST LA
PARKGATE RD
Piggery
CHAPEL HOUSE LA
Shotwick Brook
The Yacht Inn (PH)
Woodbank
Home Farm
The Remote
Woodbank Hall
Pits Farm
Shotwick Dale
SHOTWICK LA
WELSH RD
The Rookery
Roughwood Farm
WOODBANK LA
Park Farm
Shotwick Hall Farm
Shotwick
New Covert
Four Ways
A5117
Shotwick Bridge
Pleasant View Farm
Bleak Farm
Wellfield Farm
Shotwicklodge Farm
Pool Garden Wood
SHOTWICK RD
GREEN LA W
Castle Farm
A548
DRIVE A
DRIVE B
DRIVE C
FIRST AVE
DROME RD
Maes Gwyn
GREEN LA E
Dingle Wood
Shotwick House
DEESIDE IND EST (PARC DDIWYDIANNOL GLANNAU DYFRDWY)
Meadow Brook Farm
Camp
4
73
3
72
2
71
1
70
34
35
116
94

A   **B**   **C**

Capenhurst

Manor Farm Cres

Capenhurst CE Contr Prim Sch

CAPENHURST LA

New Houses

Lower Brook Farm

PENFOLD CL

RECTORY LA

4

LAURELWOOD DR

BAKEWELL CL
CANNOCK CL
ASHBOURNE CL
LICHFIELD DR
OXFORD CL
CARDIFF CL

LINDEN CL
VINE
HONEY
SUCKLE
CEDAR

OAK WAY
MOLM
TUDOR CL
APPLE
TREE GR
MELROSE DR
LAMBOURNE DR

BRAMLEY CL
LAXTON CL
LARCHDALE

CHESTER RD

PLOUGHMANS CL 1
THE FURROWS 2
PLOUGHMANS WAY 3
BADGERS CL 4

NORWICH DR

ELY CL
COVENTRY
AVE

HEREFORD CL

WILLOWDALE WAY

PARKSIDE
WAY

MARKS CRES

CANTERBURY CL 5
GLOUCESTER CL 6
SALISBURY CL 7
BANGOR CL 8
WELLS CL 9

TEWKESBURY
AVE

SAXON WAY 10
WEST PARK DR 11
GREEN LAWNS DR 12
PARLIAMENT WAY 13
ST GEORGES AVE 14
ST DAVIDS DR 15

SILVERB

Backford Cross

DUNKIRK LA

Old Hall Farm

Dunkirk Farm

Manor Farm

Dunkirk

LIVERPOOL RD

ROSEMERE DR 16
KINNINGTON WAY 17
BACKFORD GDNS 18

Acres Farm

73

Big Wood

Coalpit Lane

Depot

Acres Wood

3

A5117

CHESTER GATES

M56

A540

Ashcroft Farm

POWEY LA

Gibbet Mill

Rendova Farm

Lea Manor Farm

72

A5117

Saughall Nurseries

STRAWBERRY LA

Hill Farm

Gebe Farm

COALPIT LA

Wood Farm

DEMAGE LA

GROVE RD

2

Big Wood

Nursery

PARKGATE RD

TOWNFIELD LA

Grove Farm

STATION RD

71

Green Farm

Parkgate House

LONG LA

Warren Farm

St Oswald's CE Aided Prim Sch

Mollington

The Willows

Lea Far

PO

LODGE LA

PARK AVE

FIELDWAY

MOLLINGTON CL

WITHIN LEA

WELL LA

1

PARK WAY

NEWCROFT

MEADOWCROFT

FIDDLERS LA

Parkside Farm

Astbury House

Wheatsheaf (PH)

OVERWOOD LA

FELLDALE CL

MEADOW CT

The Thomas Wedge CE Contr Jun

PO

CHURCH RD

GREEN WAY

SAUGHALL HEY

KINGSWOOD AVE

HOME PARK

TARRANT CT

Saughall

The Ridings Cty Inf Sch

KINGSWOOD

A540

OVERWOOD AVE

ALDERSEY CL

SMITHY CL

RAKE WAY

CHAPEL CL

THE CLOSE

FAIRHOLME CL

THE RIDINGS

ROSEWOOD GR

70

36   **A**   **37**   **B**   **38**   **C**

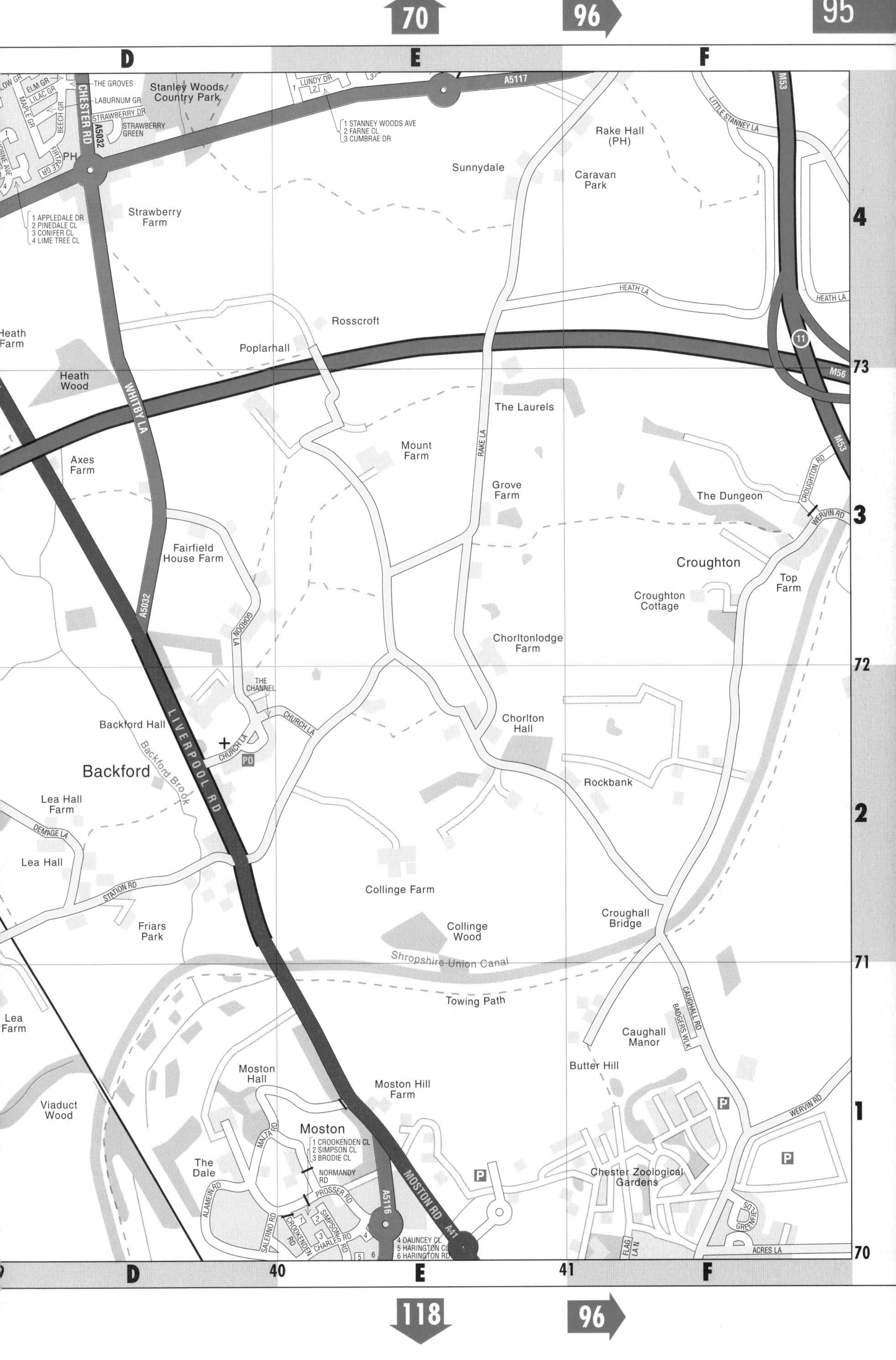
D
E
F
Stanley Woods Country Park
THE GROVES
LABURNUM GR
STRAWBERRY DR
STRAWBERRY GREEN
CHESTER RD
A5032
A5117
LUNDY DR
1 STANNEY WOODS AVE
2 FARNE CL
3 CUMBRAE DR
1 APPLEDALE DR
2 PINEDALE CL
3 CONIFER CL
4 LIME TREE CL
Strawberry Farm
Sunnydale
Rake Hall (PH)
Caravan Park
LITTLE STANNEY LA
M53
HEATH LA
Rosscroft
Poplarhall
Heath Wood
WHITBY LA
M56
The Laurels
Mount Farm
Axes Farm
RAKE LA
Grove Farm
The Dungeon
CROUGHTON RD
WERVIN RD
Croughton
Top Farm
Croughton Cottage
Fairfield House Farm
GORDON LA
A5032
Chorltonlodge Farm
THE CHANNEL
CHURCH LA
Backford Hall
LIVERPOOL RD
Chorlton Hall
Backford Brook
Backford
Rockbank
Lea Hall Farm
DEMAGE LA
Lea Hall
STATION RD
Collinge Farm
Croughall Bridge
Friars Park
Collinge Wood
Shropshire Union Canal
Towing Path
Lea Farm
CAUGHALL RD
BADGERS WLK
Caughall Manor
Butter Hill
Moston Hall
Moston Hill Farm
Viaduct Wood
Moston
1 CROOKENDEN CL
2 SIMPSON CL
3 BRODIE CL
WERVIN RD
The Dale
MALTA RD
NORMANDY RD
PROSSER RD
Chester Zoological Gardens
ALAMEIN RD
A5116
MOSTON RD
SALERNO RD
CROOKENDEN RD
SIMPSON RD
CHARLES RD
A41
4 DAUNCEY CL
5 HARINGTON CL
6 HARINGTON RD
FLAG LA N
ACRES LA
4
73
3
72
2
71
1
70
40
41

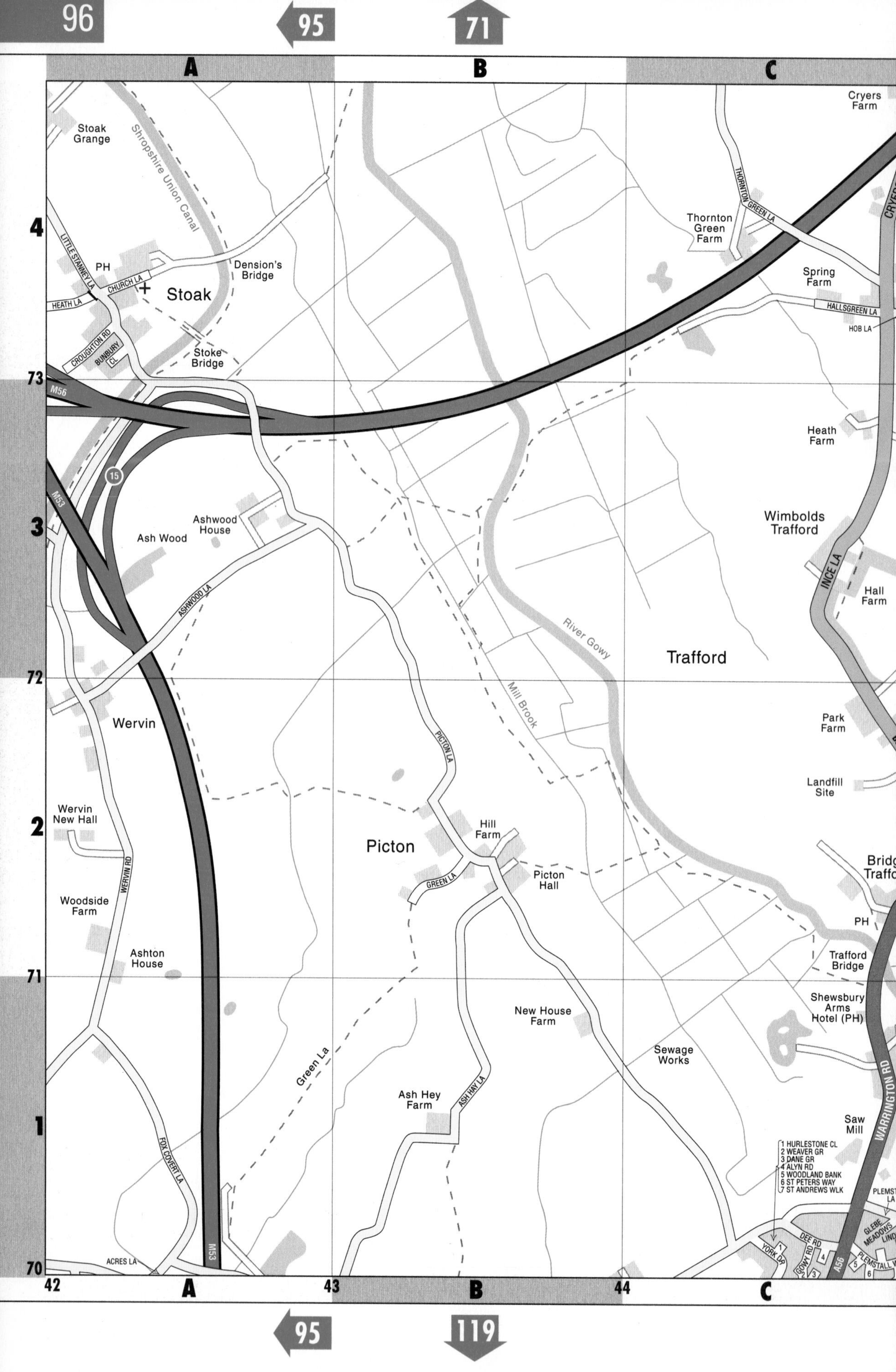

A

B

C

4

Stoak
Grange

Shropshire Union Canal

Little Stanney La

PH

Church La

Heath La

Groughton Rd

Bunbury Cl

Dension's
Bridge

+ Stoak

Stoke
Bridge

Cryers
Farm

Thornton
Green
Farm

Thornton Green La

Spring
Farm

Hallsgreen La

HOB LA

Cryers

73

M56

M53

15

Ash Wood

Ashwood
House

Ashwood La

Heath
Farm

Wimbolds
Trafford

Ince La

Hall
Farm

3

River Gowy

Trafford

72

Wervin

Picton La

Mill Brook

Park
Farm

Landfill
Site

Wervin
New Hall

Hill
Farm

Green La

Picton

Picton
Hall

Bridg
Traffo

PH

2

Woodside
Farm

Wervin Rd

Ashton
House

Trafford
Bridge

71

Shewsbury
Arms
Hotel (PH)

Green La

New House
Farm

Sewage
Works

Warrington Rd

1 HURLESTONE CL
2 WEAVER GR
3 DANE GR
4 ALYN RD
5 WOODLAND BANK
6 ST PETERS WAY
7 ST ANDREWS WLK

Saw
Mill

1

Fox Covert La

M53

Ash Hey
Farm

Ash Hay La

PLEMST
LA

GLEBE
MEADOWS

LINDE

70

Acres La

M56

York Dr

Dee Rd

Gowy Rd

Plemstall La

42

A

43

B

44

C

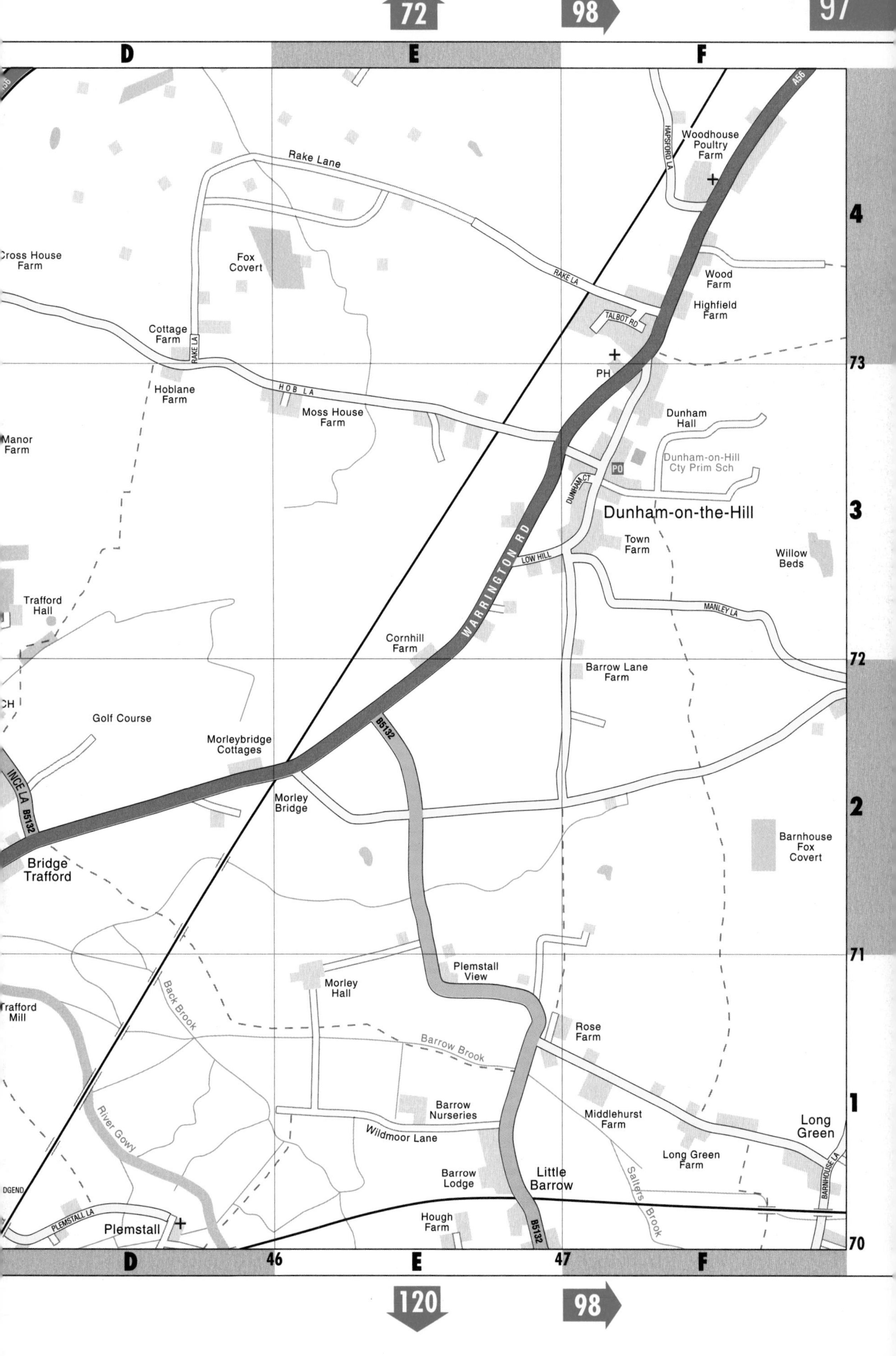

D
E
F

Rake Lane

Woodhouse
Poultry
Farm

+

4

Cross House
Farm

Fox
Covert

RAKE LA

Wood
Farm

Cottage
Farm

RAKE LA

TALBOT RD

Highfield
Farm

+

PH

73

Hoblane
Farm

HOB LA

Dunham
Hall

Manor
Farm

Moss House
Farm

PO

Dunham-on-Hill
Cty Prim Sch

DUNHAM CT

Dunham-on-the-Hill

3

WARRINGTON RD

LOW HILL

Town
Farm

Willow
Beds

Trafford
Hall

MANLEY LA

Cornhill
Farm

Barrow Lane
Farm

72

CH

Golf Course

B5132

Morleybridge
Cottages

INGE LA   B5132

Morley
Bridge

Barnhouse
Fox
Covert

2

Bridge
Trafford

71

Back Brook

Morley
Hall

Plemstall
View

Rose
Farm

Trafford
Mill

Barrow Brook

River Gowy

Barrow
Nurseries

Middlehurst
Farm

Long Green
Farm

Long
Green

1

Wildmoor Lane

Salters Brook

BARNHOUSE LA

DGEND

Barrow
Lodge

Little
Barrow

PLEMSTALL LA

+

Plemstall

Hough
Farm

B5132

70

D
46
E
47
F

A B C

4

3

73

72

71

1

70

48 A 49 B 50 C

Golf Course

CH

PECK MILL LA

Peck Mill Farm

TOWERS LA

Church-house Farm

B5393

Greengate Farm

The Green

MANLEY RD

Alvanley Hall

Crabtree Farm

Moor's Brook

Abbot's Clough Farm

Manley Old Hall

Lowerhall Farm

Lower Farm

Rose Farm

COB HALL LA

SUGAR LA

MANLEY LA

New House Farm

Manor Farm

PO

Manley Hall

MOSS LA

MOSS DR

Dunham Heath

Manley House Farm

Siddall's Hill

Rookery Farm

CHAPEL LA

Grange Farm

Swinford House

Longster Trail

Peckmill Brook

WELL LA

NORTON'S LA

Mouldsworth Hall

SMITHY LA

Mouldsworth

BARNHOUSE LA

Stone House Farm

Motor Mus

Long Wood

GONGAR LA

The Rookery

GRANGE RD

CHURCH RD

B5393

Bakery

Ashton Brook

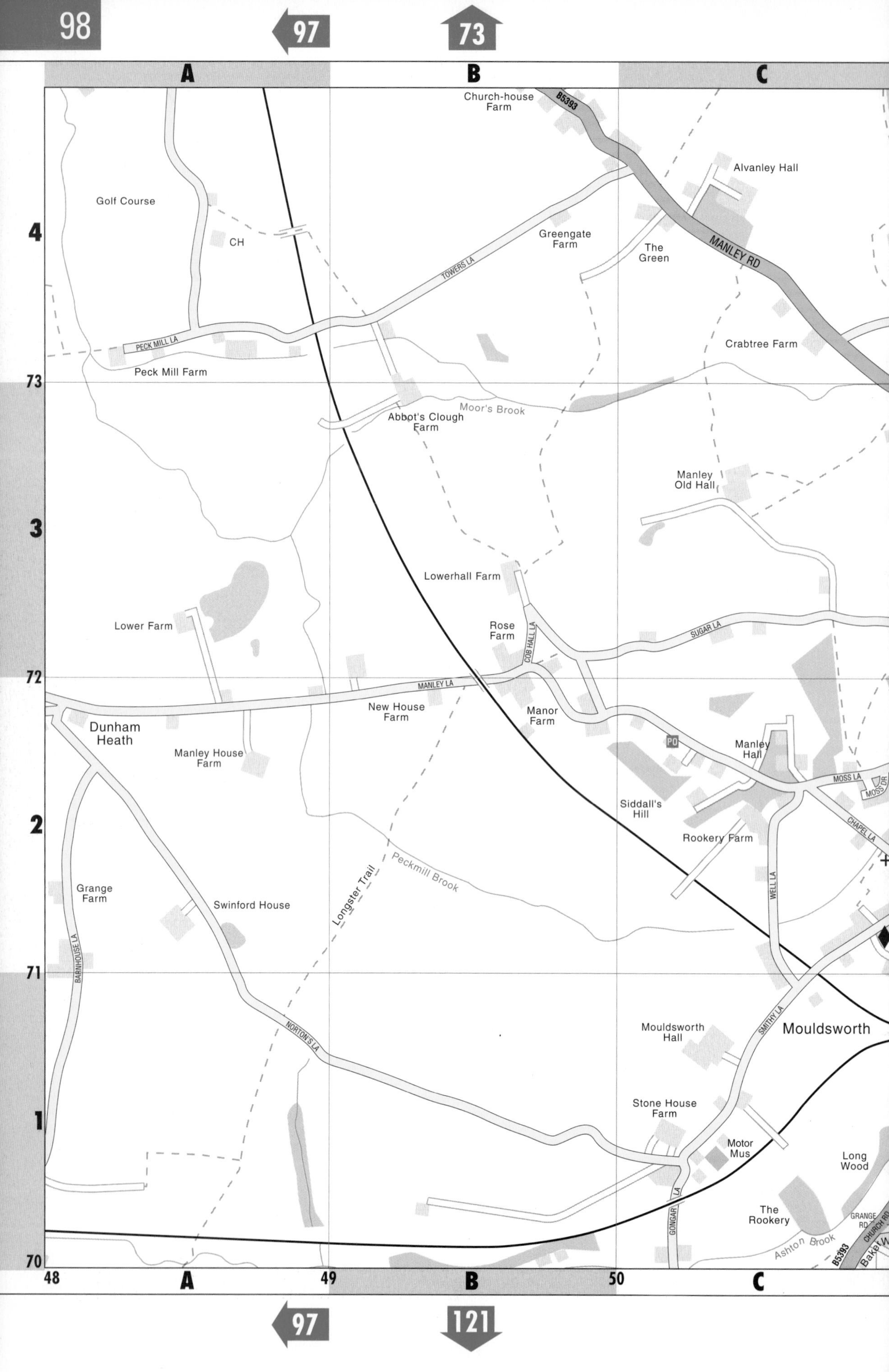

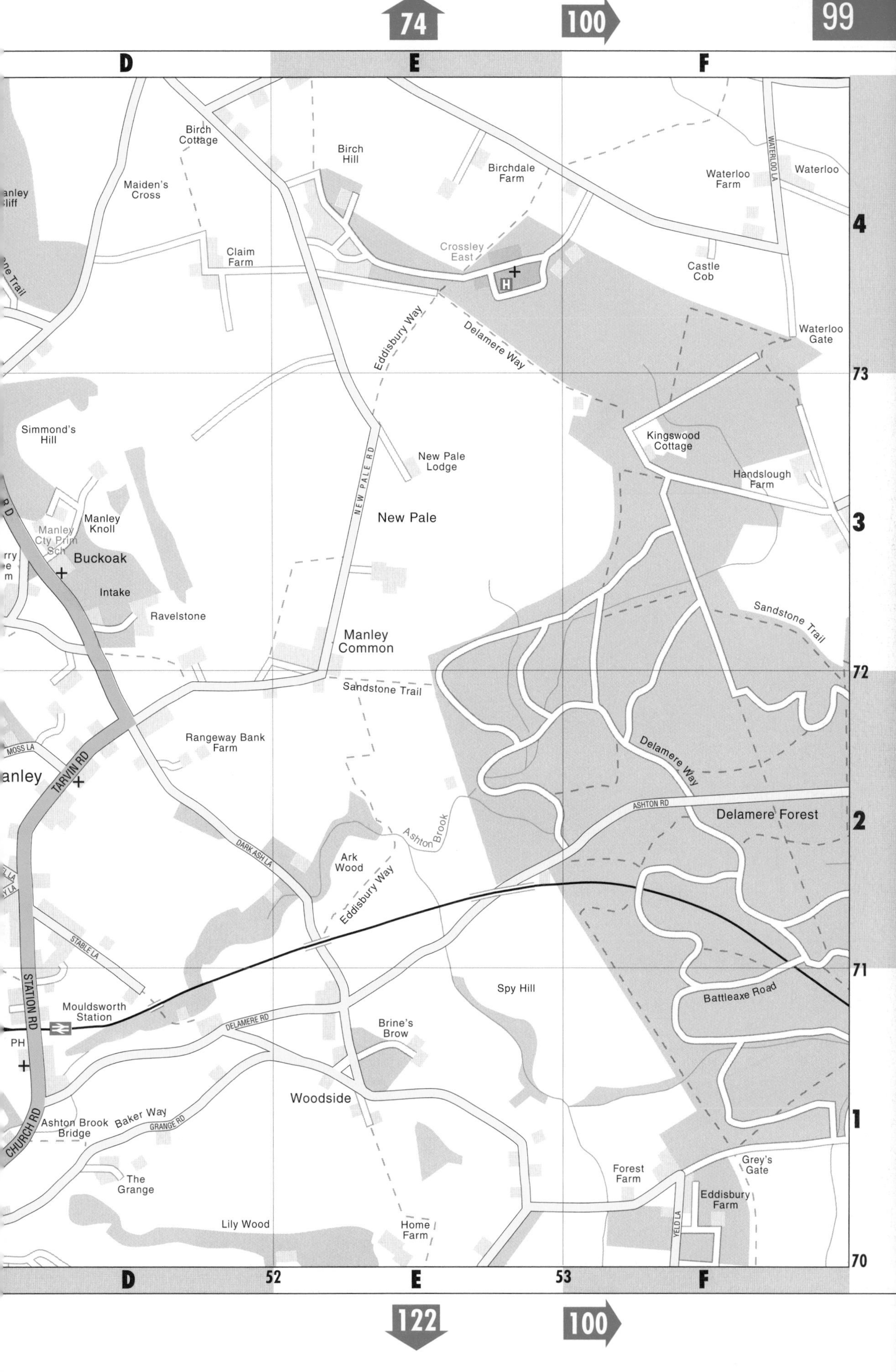
D
E
F
Birch Cottage
Birch Hill
Birchdale Farm
Waterloo Farm
Waterloo
WATERLOO LA
Maiden's Cross
Claim Farm
Crossley East
Castle Cob
Eddisbury Way
Delamere Way
Waterloo Gate
4
73
Simmond's Hill
New Pale Lodge
NEW PALE RD
Kingswood Cottage
Handslough Farm
New Pale
Manley Knoll
Manley Cty Prim Sch
Buckoak
Intake
Ravelstone
3
Sandstone Trail
Manley Common
Sandstone Trail
72
Rangeway Bank Farm
MOSS LA
TARVIN RD
Delamere Way
ASHTON RD
Delamere Forest
2
Ashton Brook
DARK ASH LA
Ark Wood
Eddisbury Way
STABLE LA
Spy Hill
71
Battleaxe Road
STATION RD
Mouldsworth Station
DELAMERE RD
Brine's Brow
PH
Woodside
1
CHURCH RD
Ashton Brook Bridge
Baker Way
GRANGE RD
The Grange
Forest Farm
Grey's Gate
Eddisbury Farm
YELD LA
Lily Wood
Home Farm
70
D
52
E
53
F

99
75

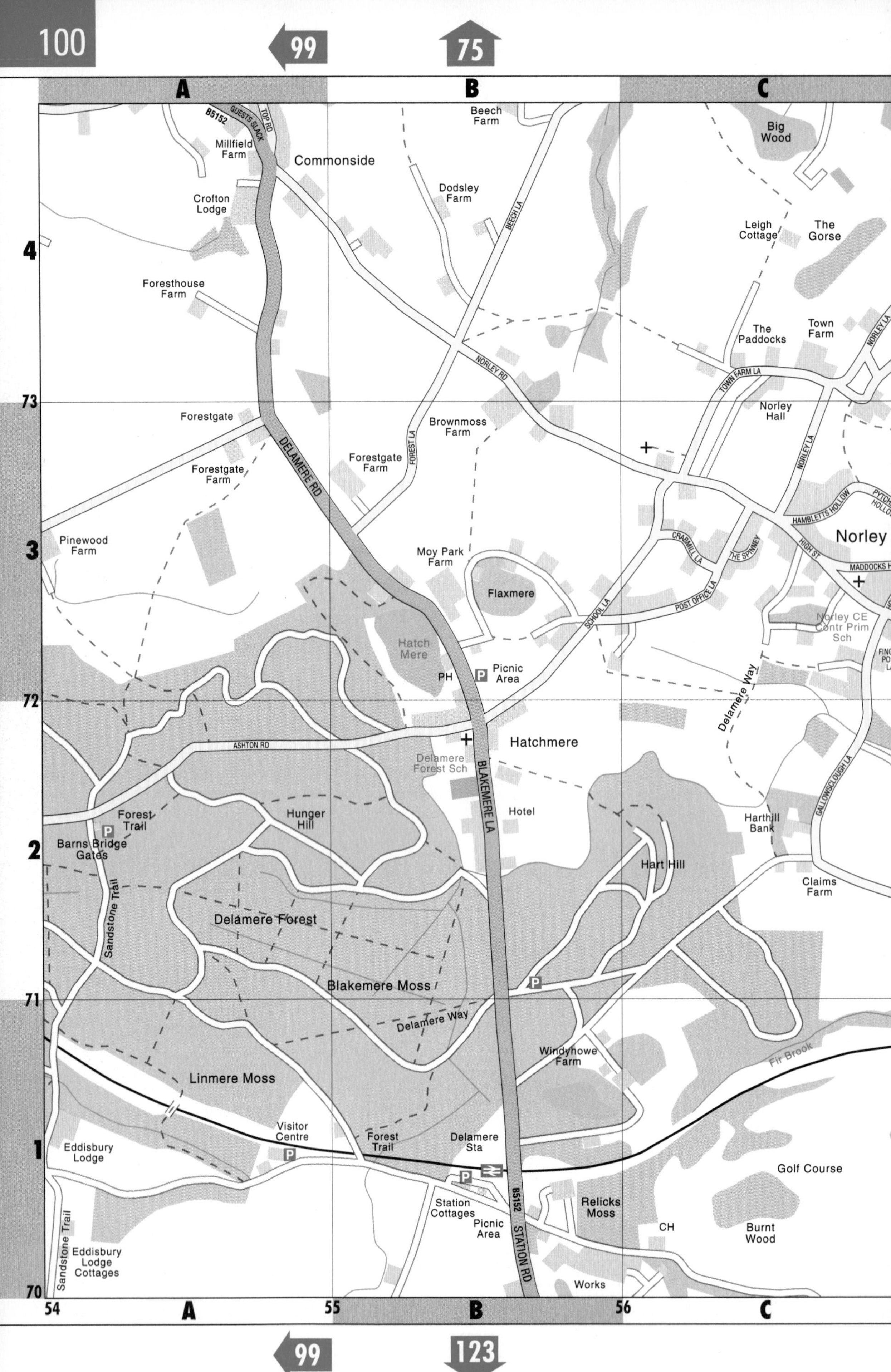
A
B
C
4
73
3
72
2
71
1
70
54
55
56
Beech Farm
Big Wood
B5152
GUESTS SLACK
TOP RD
Millfield Farm
Commonside
Dodsley Farm
Crofton Lodge
BEECH LA
Leigh Cottage
The Gorse
Foresthouse Farm
The Paddocks
Town Farm
NORLEY RD
TOWN FARM LA
NORLEY LA
Forestgate
Brownmoss Farm
Norley Hall
DELAMERE RD
FOREST LA
Forestgate Farm
NORLEY LA
HAMBLETTS HOLLOW
PYTCHES HOLLOW
Pinewood Farm
Moy Park Farm
CRABMILL LA
THE SPINNEY
HIGH ST
Norley
MADDOCKS HILL
Flaxmere
POST OFFICE LA
SCHOOL LA
Norley CE Contr Prim Sch
Hatch Mere
Picnic Area
PH
Delamere Way
ASHTON RD
Hatchmere
Delamere Forest Sch
BLAKEMERE LA
GALLOWSCLOUGH LA
Forest Trail
Hotel
Hunger Hill
Harthill Bank
Barns Bridge Gates
Hart Hill
Claims Farm
Sandstone Trail
Delamere Forest
Blakemere Moss
Delamere Way
Windyhowe Farm
Fir Brook
Linmere Moss
Visitor Centre
Forest Trail
Delamere Sta
Eddisbury Lodge
Golf Course
Station Cottages
B5152
Relicks Moss
Picnic Area
CH
Burnt Wood
STATION RD
Sandstone Trail
Eddisbury Lodge Cottages
Works

99
123

76
102

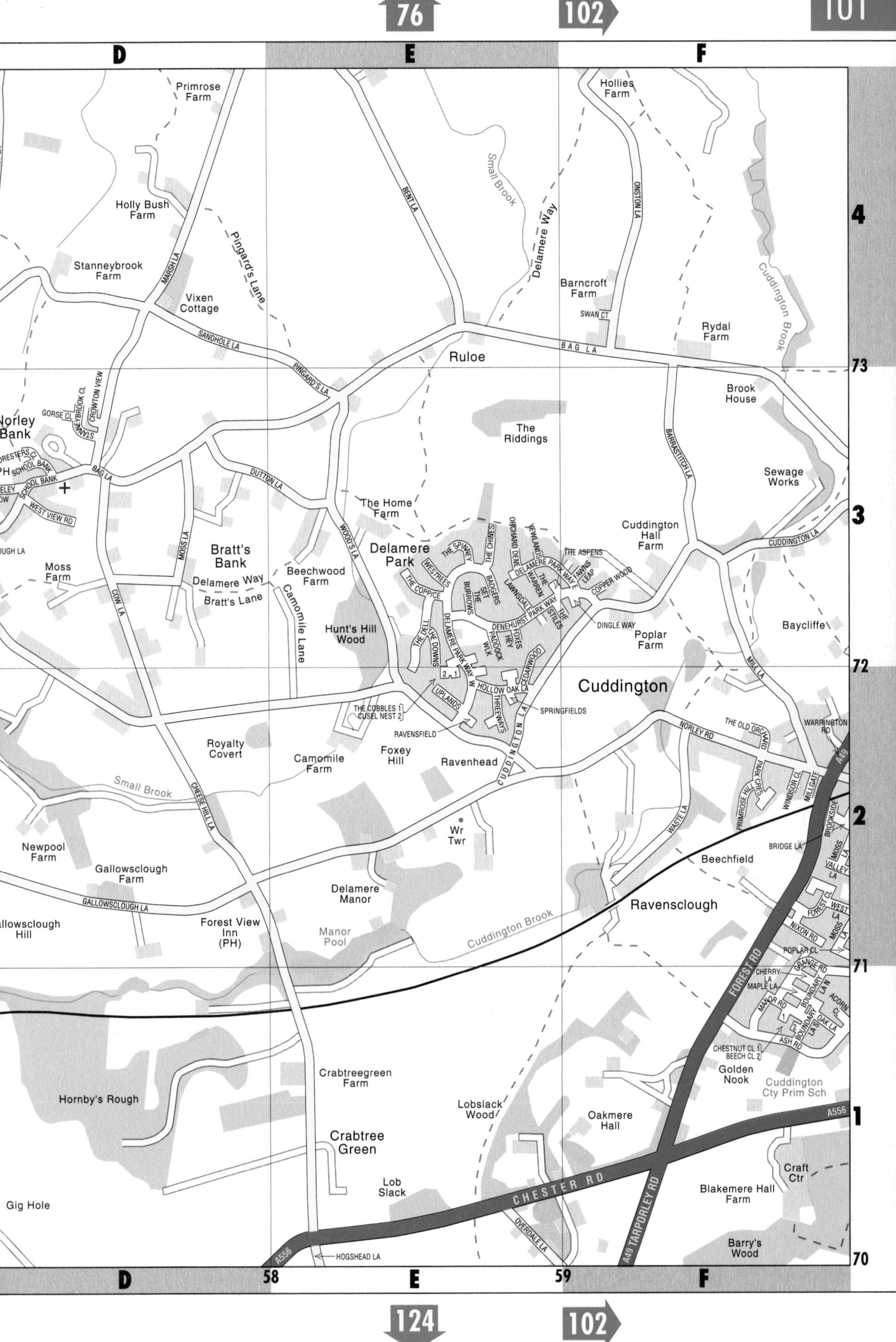
D
E
F
Primrose Farm
Hollies Farm
Small Brook
BENT LA
Delamere Way
ONSTON LA
Holly Bush Farm
Pingard's Lane
Cuddington Brook
Stanneybrook Farm
MARSH LA
Vixen Cottage
Barncroft Farm
SWAN CT
Rydal Farm
SANDHOLE LA
BAG LA
Ruloe
PINGARD'S LA
Brook House
Norley Bank
GORSE CL
STANNEYBROOK CL
CROWTON VIEW
The Riddings
FORESTERS CL
PH
SCHOOL BANK
BAG LA
DUTTON LA
BARRASTITCH LA
Sewage Works
WEST VIEW RD
The Home Farm
Cuddington Hall Farm
CUDDINGTON LA
MOSS LA
Bratt's Bank
WOOD'S LA
Delamere Park
THE SPINNEY
THE CHIMES
ORCHARD DENE
YEWLANDS
THE ASPENS
Moss Farm
Delamere Way
Beechwood Farm
WESTREES
THE WARREN
DELAMERE PARK WAY E
FAWNS LEAP
COPPER WOOD
Bratt's Lane
Camomile Lane
THE COPPICE
THE BURROWS
BADGERS SET
LAWNSDALE
COW LA
Hunt's Hill Wood
DENEHURST PARK WAY
THE STILES
DINGLE WAY
Poplar Farm
Baycliffe
THE DELL
THE DOWNS
DELAMERE PARK WAY W
PADDOCK WLK
FOXES HEY
CEDARWOOD
MILL LA
Cuddington
HOLLOW OAK LA
UPLANDS
THREEWAYS
THE COBBLES 1
CUSEL NEST 2
SPRINGFIELDS
THE OLD ORCHARD
WARRINGTON RD
NORLEY RD
RAVENSFIELD
Royalty Covert
Foxey Hill
Camomile Farm
Ravenhead
CUDDINGTON LA
PARK CRES
Small Brook
CHESE HILL LA
PRIMROSE HILL
WINDSOR CL
MILLGATE
A49
Wr Twr
WASTE LA
BROOKSIDE
Newpool Farm
BRIDGE LA
Beechfield
MOSS LA
Gallowsclough Farm
VALLEY LA
Delamere Manor
GALLOWSCLOUGH LA
Ravensclough
FOREST CL
WEST LA
allowsclough Hill
Forest View Inn (PH)
Manor Pool
Cuddington Brook
NIXON RD
MOSS LA
POPLAR CL
GRANGE RD
FOREST RD
CHERRY LA
MAPLE LA
BOUNDARY LA N
ACORN CL
MANOR RD
OAK LA
BOUNDARY LA S
ASH RD
CHESTNUT CL 1
BEECH CL 2
Crabtreegreen Farm
Golden Nook
Cuddington Cty Prim Sch
Hornby's Rough
Lobslack Wood
Oakmere Hall
A556
Crabtree Green
Craft Ctr
CHESTER RD
Lob Slack
Blakemere Hall Farm
Gig Hole
OVERDALE LA
A49 TARPORLEY RD
Barry's Wood
A556
HOGSHEAD LA
4
73
3
72
2
71
1
70
58
59

124
102

101
77

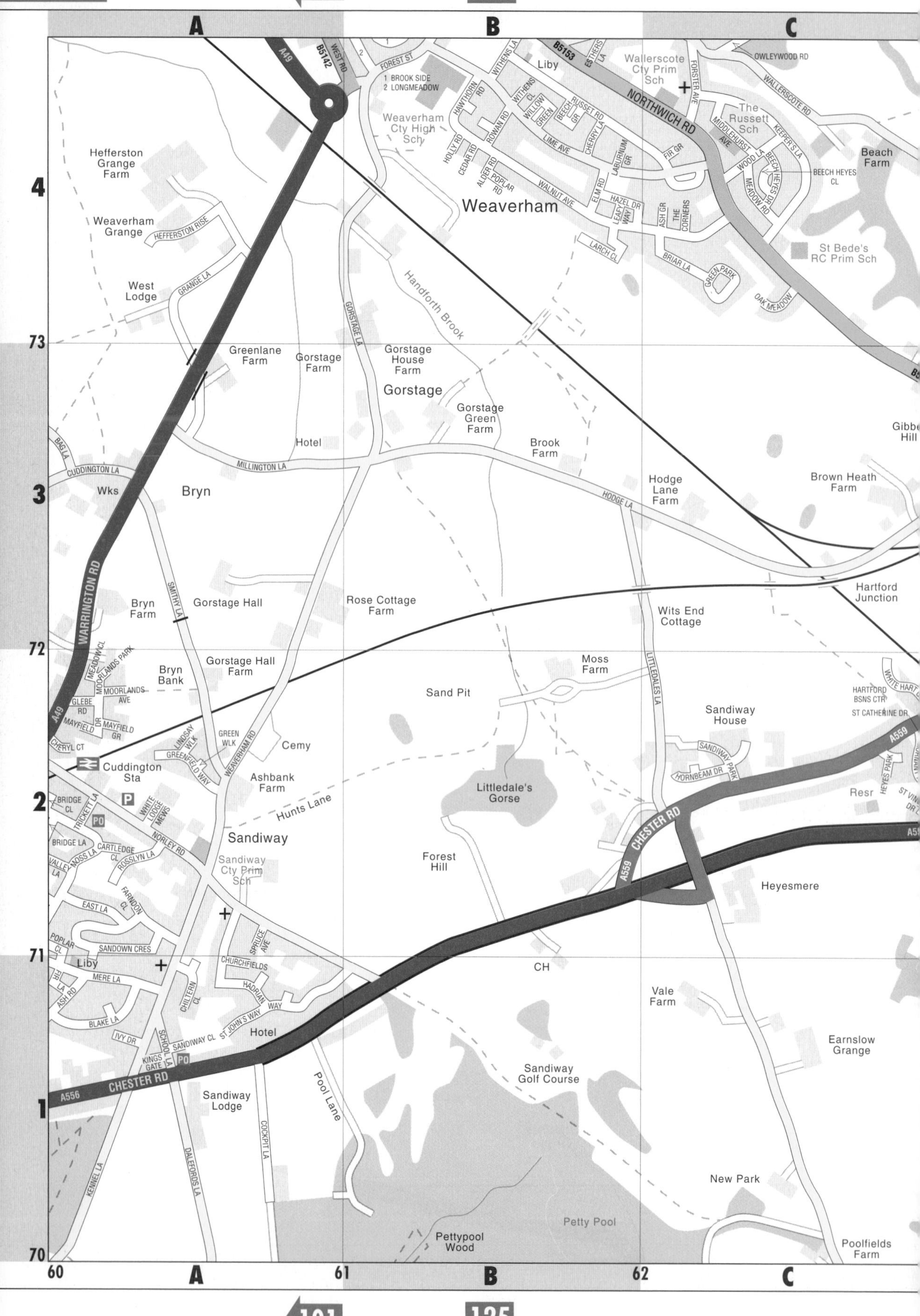
A
B
C
Weaverham
Weaverham Cty High Sch
Wallerscote Cty Prim Sch
The Russett Sch
St Bede's RC Prim Sch
Hefferston Grange Farm
Weaverham Grange
West Lodge
Beach Farm
Greenlane Farm
Gorstage Farm
Gorstage House Farm
Gorstage
Gorstage Green Farm
Handforth Brook
Hotel
Brook Farm
Hodge Lane Farm
Brown Heath Farm
Wks
Bryn
Bryn Farm
Gorstage Hall
Rose Cottage Farm
Wits End Cottage
Hartford Junction
Bryn Bank
Gorstage Hall Farm
Moss Farm
Sand Pit
Sandiway House
Cemy
Cuddington Sta
Ashbank Farm
Hunts Lane
Littledale's Gorse
Resr
Sandiway
Sandiway Cty Prim Sch
Forest Hill
Heyesmere
Liby
CH
Vale Farm
Earnslow Grange
Hotel
Sandiway Golf Course
Sandiway Lodge
Pool Lane
New Park
Petty Pool
Pettypool Wood
Poolfields Farm
WARRINGTON RD
NORTHWICH RD
CHESTER RD
A49
B5142
B5153
A559
A556
1 BROOK SIDE
2 LONGMEADOW
HODGE LA
MILLINGTON LA
CUDDINGTON LA
SMITHY LA
WEAVERHAM RD
LITTLEDALES LA
GORSTAGE LA
NORLEY RD
KENNEL LA
DALEFORDS LA
COCKPIT LA
4
3
2
1
73
72
71
70
60
61
62

101
125

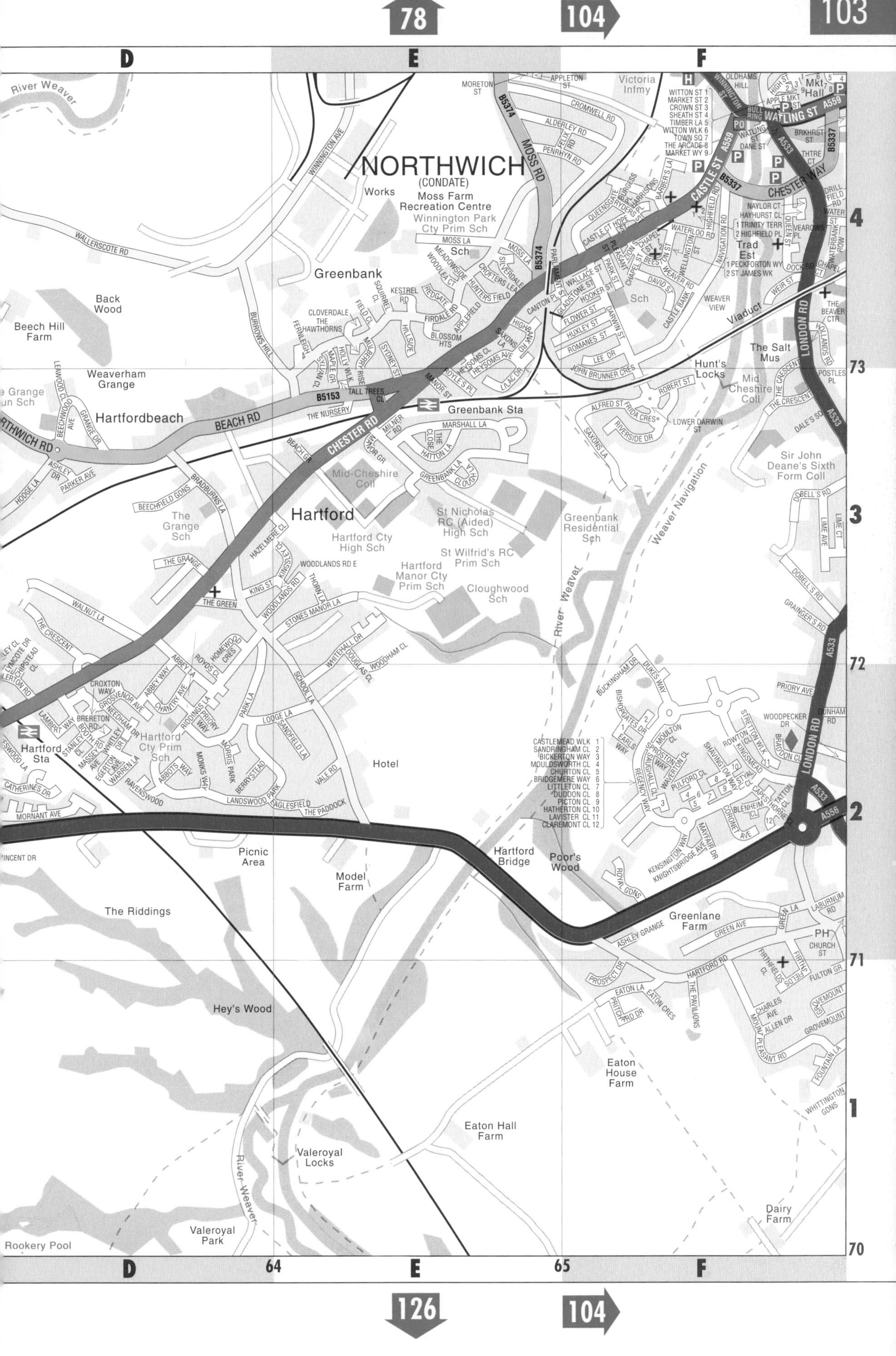
D
E
F
NORTHWICH
(CONDATE)
Works
Moss Farm
Recreation Centre
Winnington Park
Cty Prim Sch
Greenbank
Back
Wood
Beech Hill
Farm
Weaverham
Grange
Hartfordbeach
Greenbank Sta
Mid-Cheshire
Coll
Hartford
The
Grange
Sch
Hartford Cty
High Sch
St Nicholas
RC (Aided)
High Sch
St Wilfrid's RC
Prim Sch
Hartford
Manor Cty
Prim Sch
Cloughwood
Sch
Greenbank
Residential
Sch
Victoria
Infmy
Trad
Est
The Salt
Mus
Mid
Cheshire
Coll
Hunt's
Locks
Viaduct
Weaver Navigation
River Weaver
Sir John
Deane's Sixth
Form Coll
Hartford
Sta
Hartford
Cty Prim
Sch
Hotel
Picnic
Area
Model
Farm
Hartford
Bridge
Poor's
Wood
Greenlane
Farm
The Riddings
Hey's Wood
Eaton
House
Farm
Eaton Hall
Farm
Valeroyal
Locks
Valeroyal
Park
Rookery Pool
Dairy
Farm
River Weaver
WITTON ST 1
MARKET ST 2
CROWN ST 3
SHEATH ST 4
TIMBER LA 5
WITTON WLK 6
TOWN SQ 7
THE ARCADE 8
MARKET WY 9
CASTLEMEAD WLK 1
SANDRINGHAM CL 2
BICKERTON WAY 3
MOULDSWORTH CL 4
CHURTON CL 5
BRIDGEMERE WAY 6
LITTLETON CL 7
DUDDON CL 8
PICTON CL 9
HATHERTON CL 10
LAVISTER CL 11
CLAREMONT CL 12
1 TRINITY TERR
2 HIGHFIELD PL
1 PECKFORTON WY
2 ST JAMES WK
CHESTER RD
BEACH RD
B5153
MOSS RD
B5374
CASTLE ST
A559
WATLING ST
CHESTER WAY
B5337
LONDON RD
A533
A556
WALLERSCOTE RD
WINNINGTON AVE
BURROWS HILL
WALNUT LA
SCHOOL LA
4
73
3
72
2
71
1
70
64
65

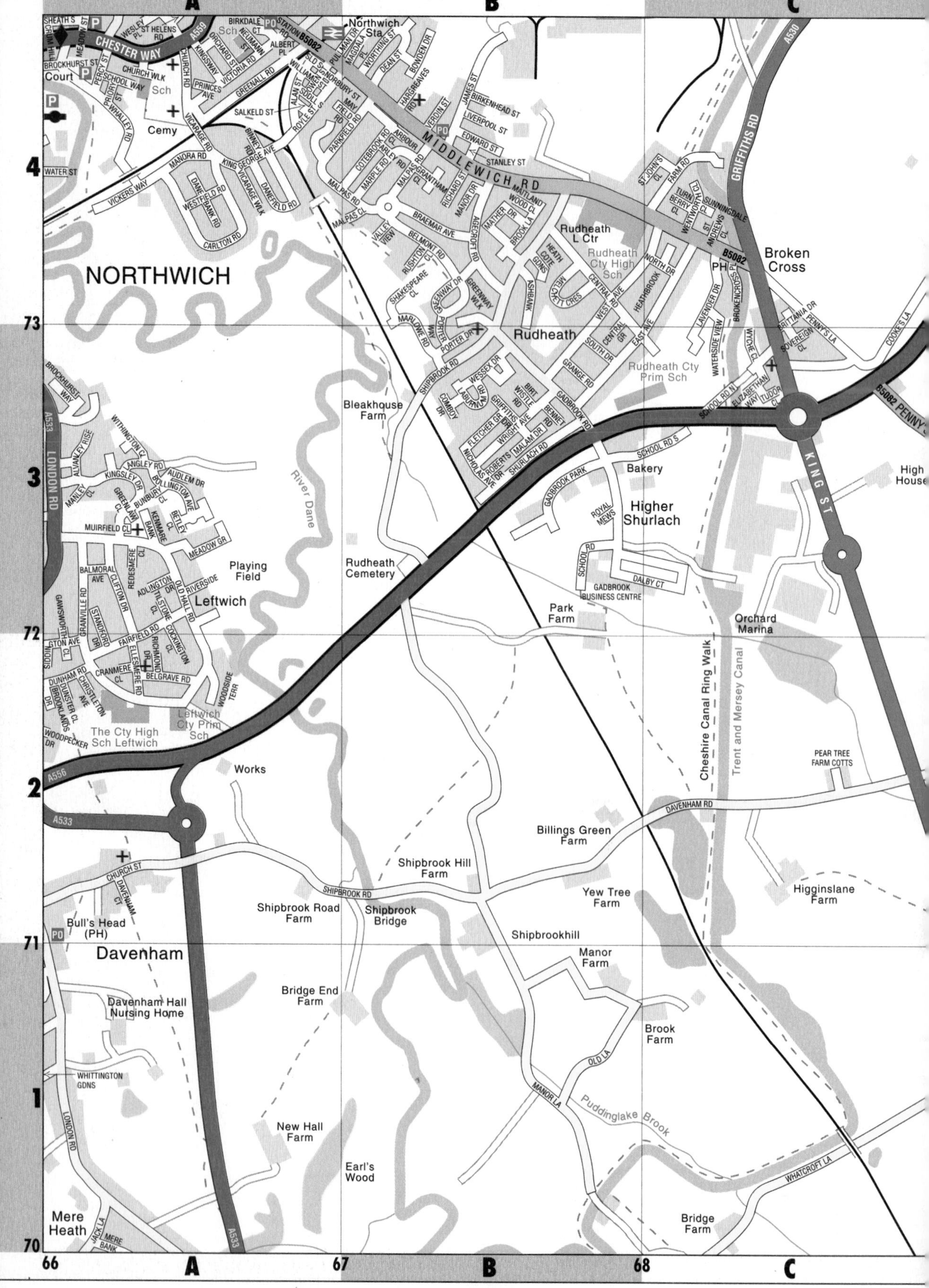
A
B
C
4
73
3
72
2
71
1
70
66
67
68
NORTHWICH
Northwich Sta
CHESTER WAY
MIDDLEWICH RD
Cemy
Court
Rudheath L Ctr
Rudheath Cty High Sch
Broken Cross
Rudheath
Rudheath Cty Prim Sch
Bleakhouse Farm
GRIFFITHS RD
KING ST
High House
Bakery
Higher Shurlach
GADBROOK BUSINESS CENTRE
Park Farm
Orchard Marina
River Dane
Playing Field
Leftwich
Rudheath Cemetery
LONDON RD
The Cty High Sch Leftwich
Leftwich Cty Prim Sch
Works
Cheshire Canal Ring Walk
Trent and Mersey Canal
PEAR TREE FARM COTTS
DAVENHAM RD
Billings Green Farm
Shipbrook Hill Farm
Yew Tree Farm
Higginslane Farm
SHIPBROOK RD
Shipbrook Road Farm
Shipbrook Bridge
Shipbrookhill
Bull's Head (PH)
Davenham
Manor Farm
Bridge End Farm
Davenham Hall Nursing Home
Brook Farm
OLD LA
MANOR LA
Puddinglake Brook
WHITTINGTON GDNS
New Hall Farm
Earl's Wood
WHATCROFT LA
Bridge Farm
Mere Heath
A556
A533
A530
B5082

80
106

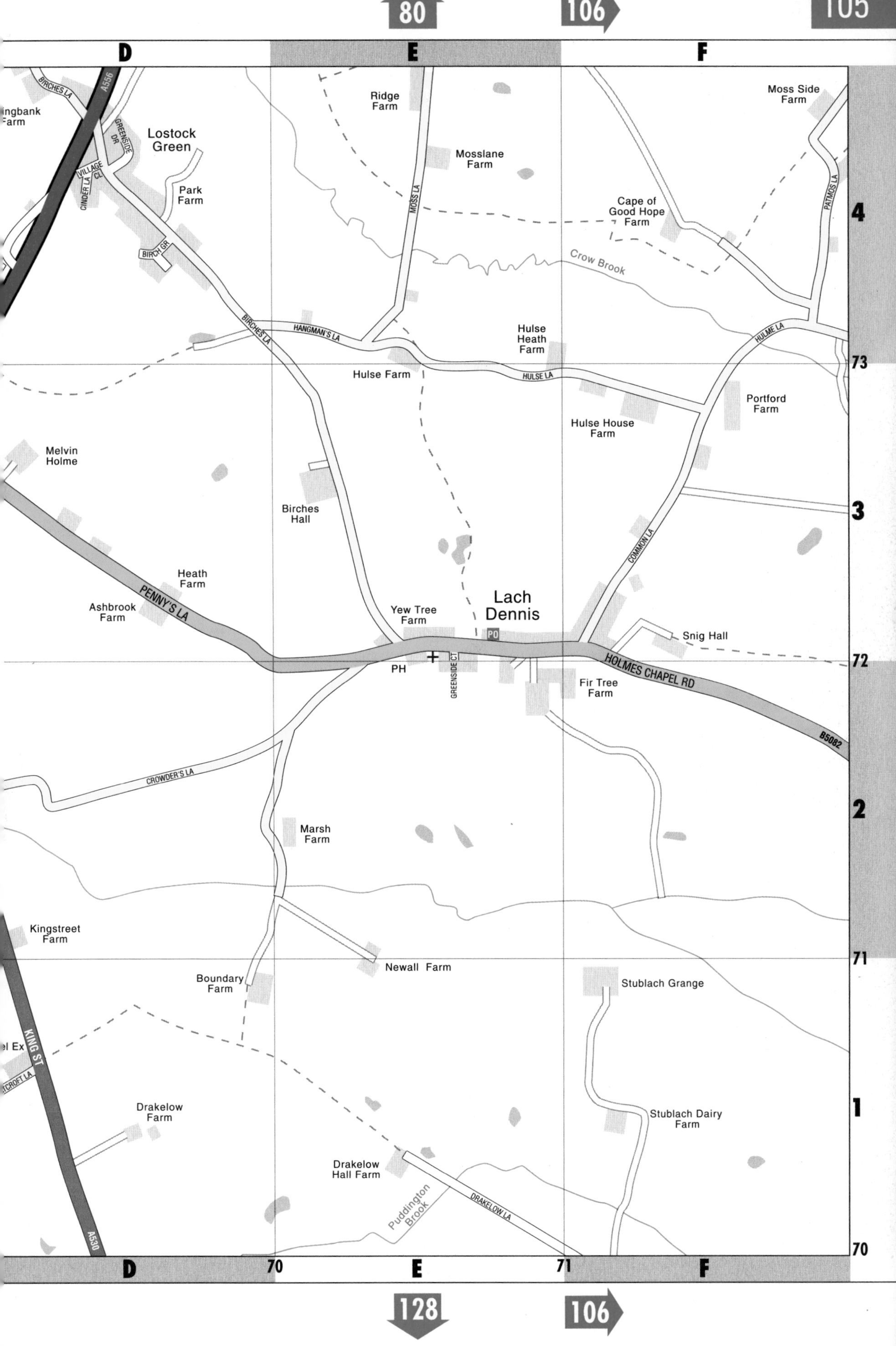
D
E
F
Ridge Farm
Moss Side Farm
ingbank Farm
Lostock Green
Mosslane Farm
Park Farm
Cape of Good Hope Farm
Crow Brook
Hulse Heath Farm
Hulse Farm
Portford Farm
Hulse House Farm
Melvin Holme
Birches Hall
Heath Farm
Ashbrook Farm
Yew Tree Farm
Lach Dennis
PO
Snig Hall
PH
Fir Tree Farm
PENNY'S LA
HOLMES CHAPEL RD
B5082
CROWDER'S LA
Marsh Farm
Kingstreet Farm
Boundary Farm
Newall Farm
Stublach Grange
KING ST
Drakelow Farm
Stublach Dairy Farm
Drakelow Hall Farm
Puddington Brook
DRAKELOW LA
A530
A556
BIRCHES LA
GREENSIDE DR
VILLAGE CL
CINDER LA
BIRCH GR
MOSS LA
HANGMAN'S LA
HULSE LA
HULME LA
PATMOS LA
COMMON LA
GREENSIDE CT
4
73
3
72
2
71
1
70
70
71

128
106

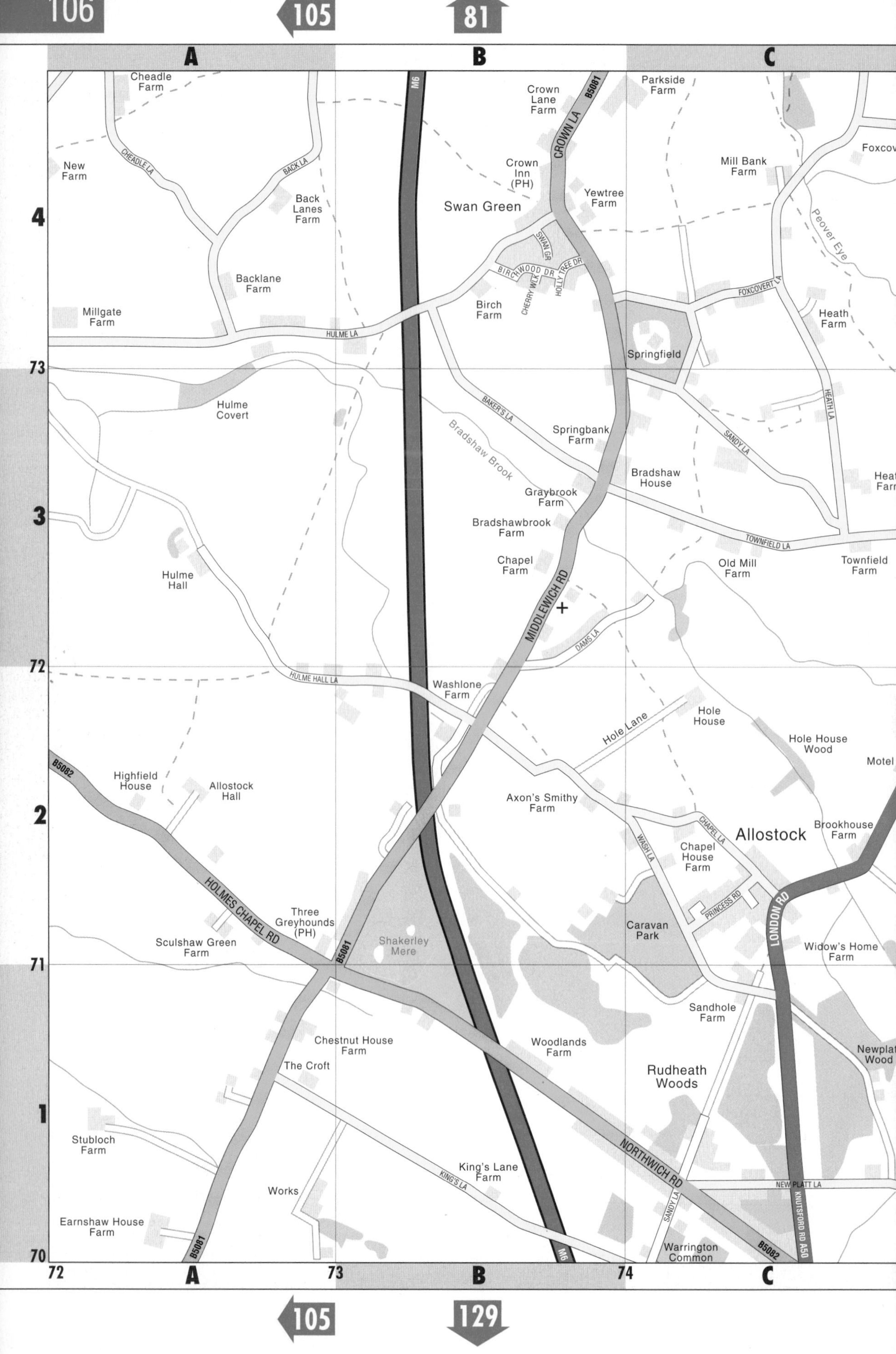

A   B   C

Cheadle Farm

New Farm

CHEADLE LA

BACK LA

Back Lanes Farm

4

Backlane Farm

Millgate Farm

HULME LA

73

Hulme Covert

3

Hulme Hall

72

HULME HALL LA

B5082

Highfield House

Allostock Hall

2

HOLMES CHAPEL RD

Sculshaw Green Farm

Three Greyhounds (PH)

71

B5061

Chestnut House Farm

The Croft

1

Stubloch Farm

Works

Earnshaw House Farm

70

B5081

72   A   73   B   74   C

M6

Crown Lane Farm

B5061

CROWN LA

Crown Inn (PH)

Swan Green

Yewtree Farm

SWAN GR

BIRCHWOOD DR

CHERRY WLK

HOLLY TREE DR

Birch Farm

BAKER'S LA

Bradshaw Brook

Springbank Farm

Graybrook Farm

Bradshawbrook Farm

Chapel Farm

MIDDLEWICH RD

+

DAMS LA

Washlone Farm

Hole Lane

Shakerley Mere

Woodlands Farm

King's Lane Farm

KING'S LA

Parkside Farm

Foxcov

Mill Bank Farm

PEOVER EYE

FOXCOVERT L

Heath Farm

Springfield

HEATH LA

SANDY LA

Bradshaw House

TOWNFIELD LA

Old Mill Farm

Townfield Farm

Heat Farm

Hole House

Hole House Wood

Motel

CHAPEL LA

Allostock

Brookhouse Farm

Axon's Smithy Farm

WASH LA

Chapel House Farm

PRINCESS RD

LONDON RD

Widow's Home Farm

Caravan Park

Sandhole Farm

Newplat Wood

Rudheath Woods

NORTHWICH RD

NEW PLATT LA

SANDY LA

B5082

KNUTSFORD RD A50

Warrington Common

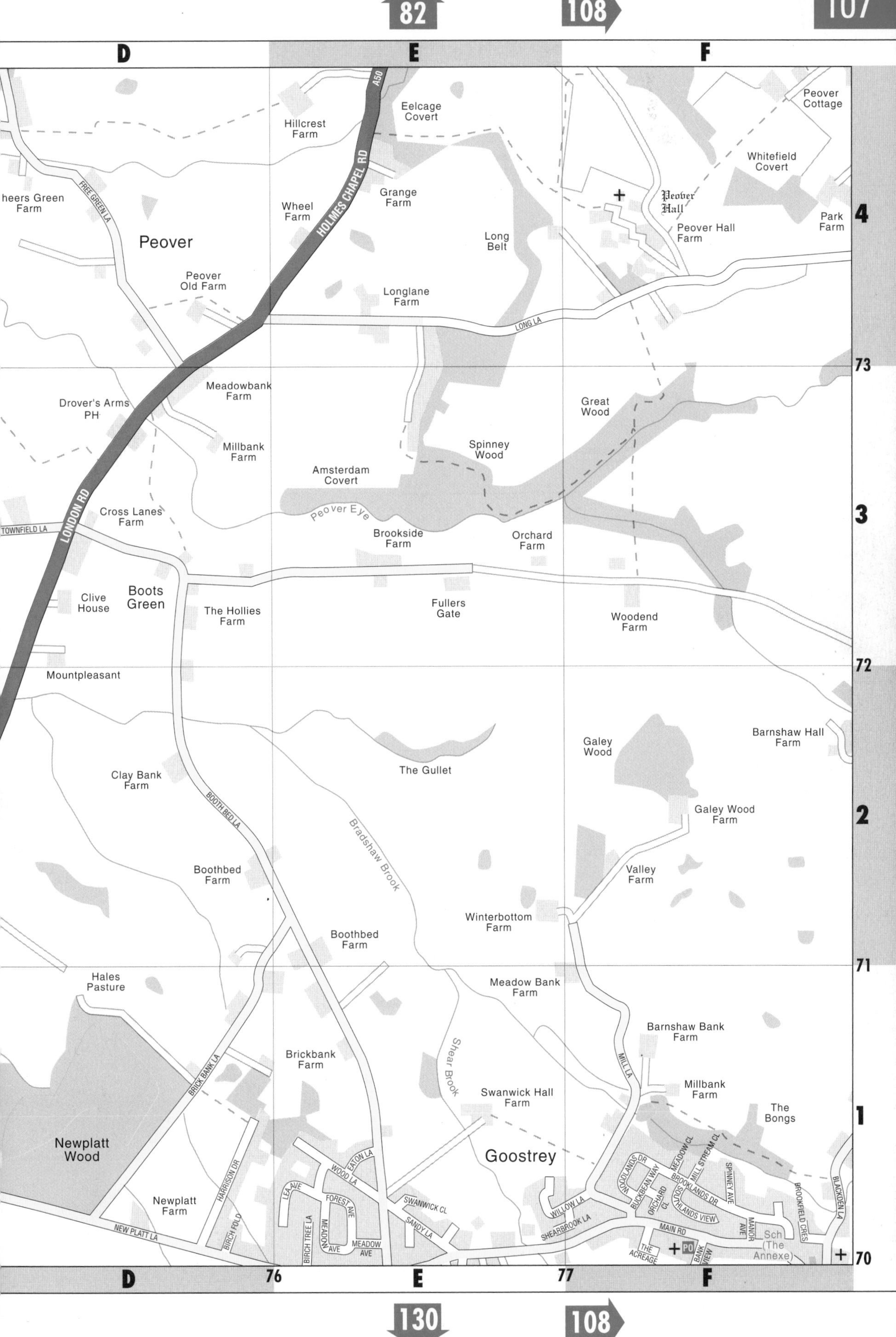

D

E

F

Peover Cottage

Hillcrest Farm

Eelcage Covert

Whitefield Covert

heers Green Farm

FREE GREEN LA

Wheel Farm

Grange Farm

Peover Hall

Peover Hall Farm

Park Farm

4

Peover

HOLMES CHAPEL RD

A50

Long Belt

Peover Old Farm

Longlane Farm

Long La

73

Meadowbank Farm

Great Wood

Drover's Arms PH

Spinney Wood

Millbank Farm

Amsterdam Covert

LONDON RD

Peover Eye

TOWNFIELD LA

Cross Lanes Farm

Brookside Farm

Orchard Farm

3

Clive House

Boots Green

The Hollies Farm

Fullers Gate

Woodend Farm

Mountpleasant

72

Barnshaw Hall Farm

Clay Bank Farm

The Gullet

Galey Wood

Galey Wood Farm

2

BOOTH BED LA

Bradshaw Brook

Boothbed Farm

Valley Farm

Boothbed Farm

Winterbottom Farm

71

Hales Pasture

Meadow Bank Farm

BRICK BANK LA

Brickbank Farm

Shear Brook

Barnshaw Bank Farm

MILL LA

Millbank Farm

The Bongs

Swanwick Hall Farm

1

Newplatt Wood

Goostrey

WOODLANDS DR

MEADOW CL

MILL STREAM CL

SPINNEY AVE

BROOKFIELD CRES

BLACKDEN LA

HARRISON DR

Newplatt Farm

BIRCH FOLD

LEA AVE

EATON LA

WOOD LA

FOREST AVE

SWANWICK CL

WILLOW LA

BULLBEAN WAY

ORCHARD CL

BROOKLANDS DR

WOODLANDS VIEW

MANOR AVE

Sch (The Annexe)

NEW PLATT LA

BIRCH TREE LA

MEADOW AVE

SANDY LA

MEADOW AVE

SHEARBROOK LA

MAIN RD

THE ACREAGE

PO

BANK VIEW

70

D

76

E

77

F

107
83

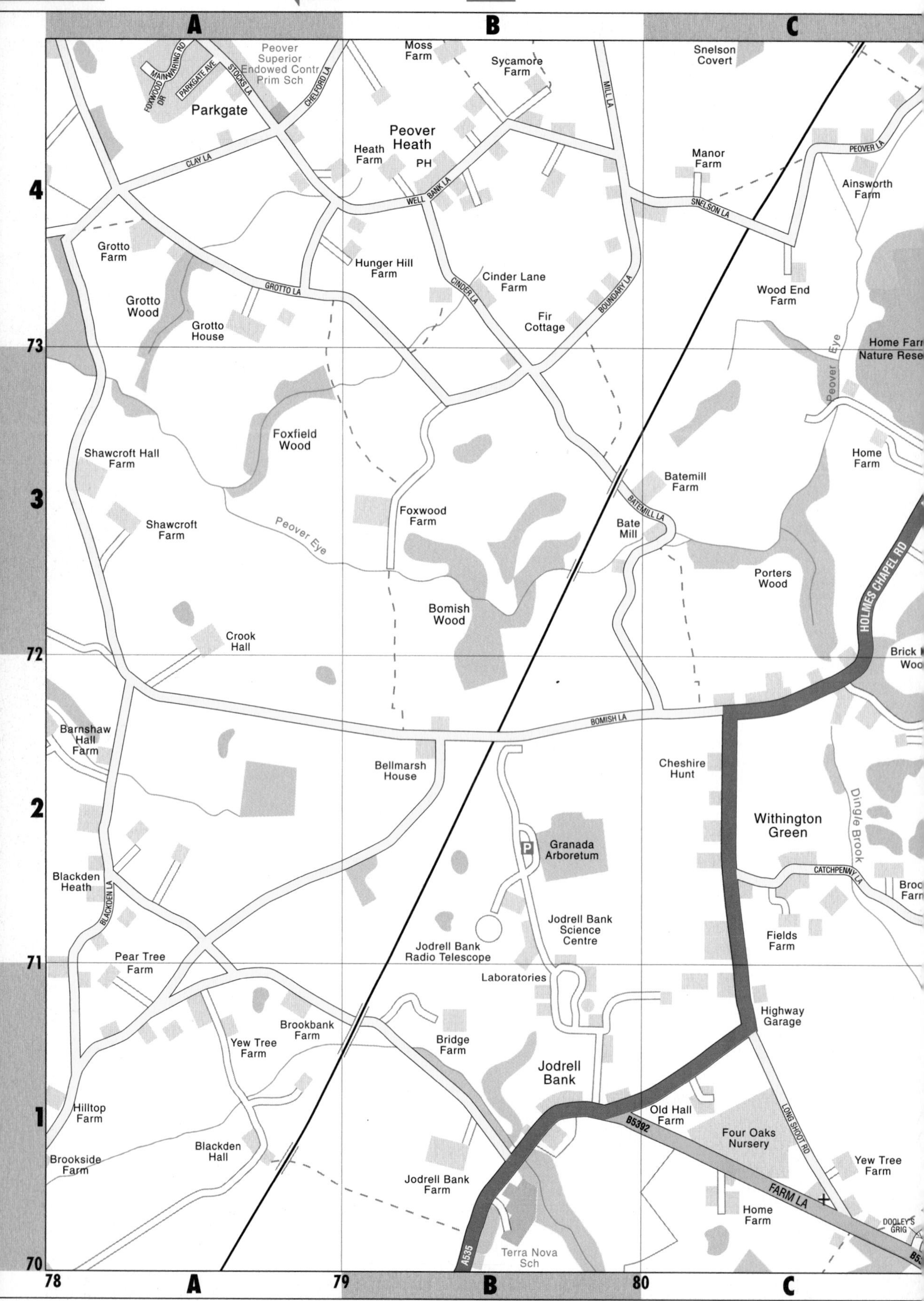
A
B
C
Peover Superior Endowed Contr Prim Sch
Parkgate
Moss Farm
Sycamore Farm
Snelson Covert
Peover Heath
Heath Farm
PH
Manor Farm
Ainsworth Farm
CLAY LA
WELL BANK LA
SNELSON LA
PEOVER LA
MILL LA
STOCKS LA
CHELFORD LA
PARKGATE AVE
MAINWARING RD
FOXWOOD DR
Grotto Farm
Hunger Hill Farm
Cinder Lane Farm
Wood End Farm
Grotto Wood
Grotto House
GROTTO LA
CINDER LA
BOUNDARY LA
Fir Cottage
Home Farm Nature Rese
Peover Eye
Foxfield Wood
Shawcroft Hall Farm
Home Farm
Batemill Farm
BATEMILL LA
Shawcroft Farm
Foxwood Farm
Bate Mill
Porters Wood
HOLMES CHAPEL RD
Bomish Wood
Crook Hall
Brick Woo
BOMISH LA
Barnshaw Hall Farm
Bellmarsh House
Cheshire Hunt
Withington Green
Dingle Brook
P
Granada Arboretum
CATCHPENNY LA
Blackden Heath
BLACKDEN LA
Broo Farm
Jodrell Bank Science Centre
Fields Farm
Jodrell Bank Radio Telescope
Pear Tree Farm
Laboratories
Highway Garage
Brookbank Farm
Yew Tree Farm
Bridge Farm
Jodrell Bank
Hilltop Farm
Old Hall Farm
B5392
Four Oaks Nursery
LONG SHOOT RD
Blackden Hall
Brookside Farm
Yew Tree Farm
Jodrell Bank Farm
FARM LA
Home Farm
DOOLEY'S GRIG
A535
Terra Nova Sch
4
73
3
72
2
71
1
70
78
79
80

107
131

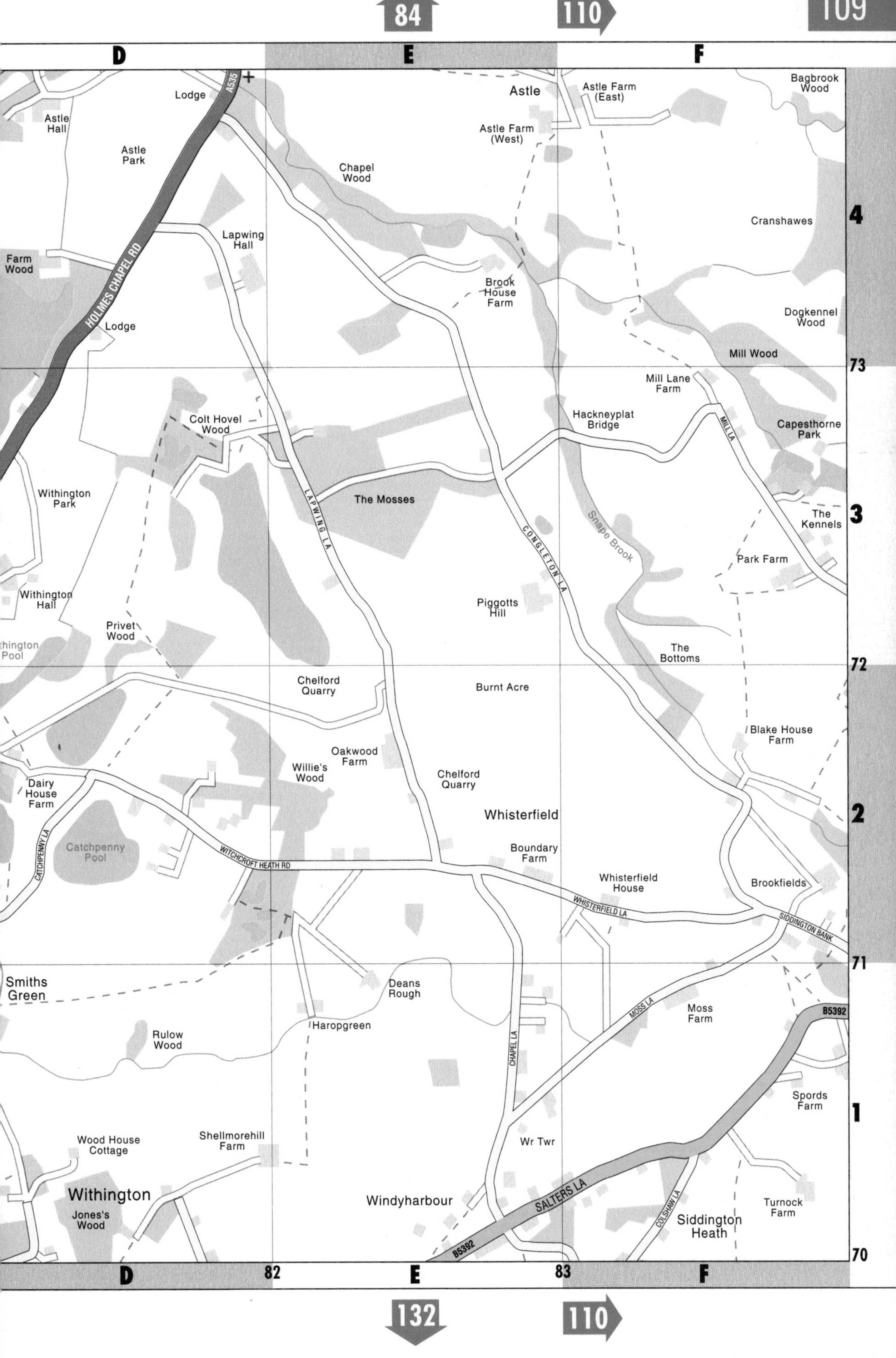
D
E
F
Astle
Astle Farm (East)
Bagbrook Wood
Lodge
A535
Astle Hall
Astle Park
Astle Farm (West)
Chapel Wood
Cranshawes
Lapwing Hall
Farm Wood
HOLMES CHAPEL RD
Brook House Farm
Dogkennel Wood
Lodge
Mill Wood
Mill Lane Farm
Colt Hovel Wood
Hackneyplat Bridge
MILL LA
Capesthorne Park
Withington Park
The Mosses
LAPWING LA
CONGLETON LA
Snape Brook
The Kennels
Park Farm
Withington Hall
Piggotts Hill
Privet Wood
hington Pool
The Bottoms
Chelford Quarry
Burnt Acre
Blake House Farm
Oakwood Farm
Willie's Wood
Chelford Quarry
Dairy House Farm
Whisterfield
CATCHPENNY LA
Catchpenny Pool
WITCHCROFT HEATH RD
Boundary Farm
Whisterfield House
Brookfields
WHISTERFIELD LA
SIDDINGTON BANK
Smiths Green
Deans Rough
Moss Farm
MOSS LA
B5392
Haropgreen
Rulow Wood
CHAPEL LA
Spords Farm
Wr Twr
Wood House Cottage
Shellmorehill Farm
Withington
Jones's Wood
Windyharbour
SALTERS LA
COLSHAW LA
Siddington Heath
Turnock Farm
B5392
4
73
3
72
2
71
1
70
D
82
E
83
F

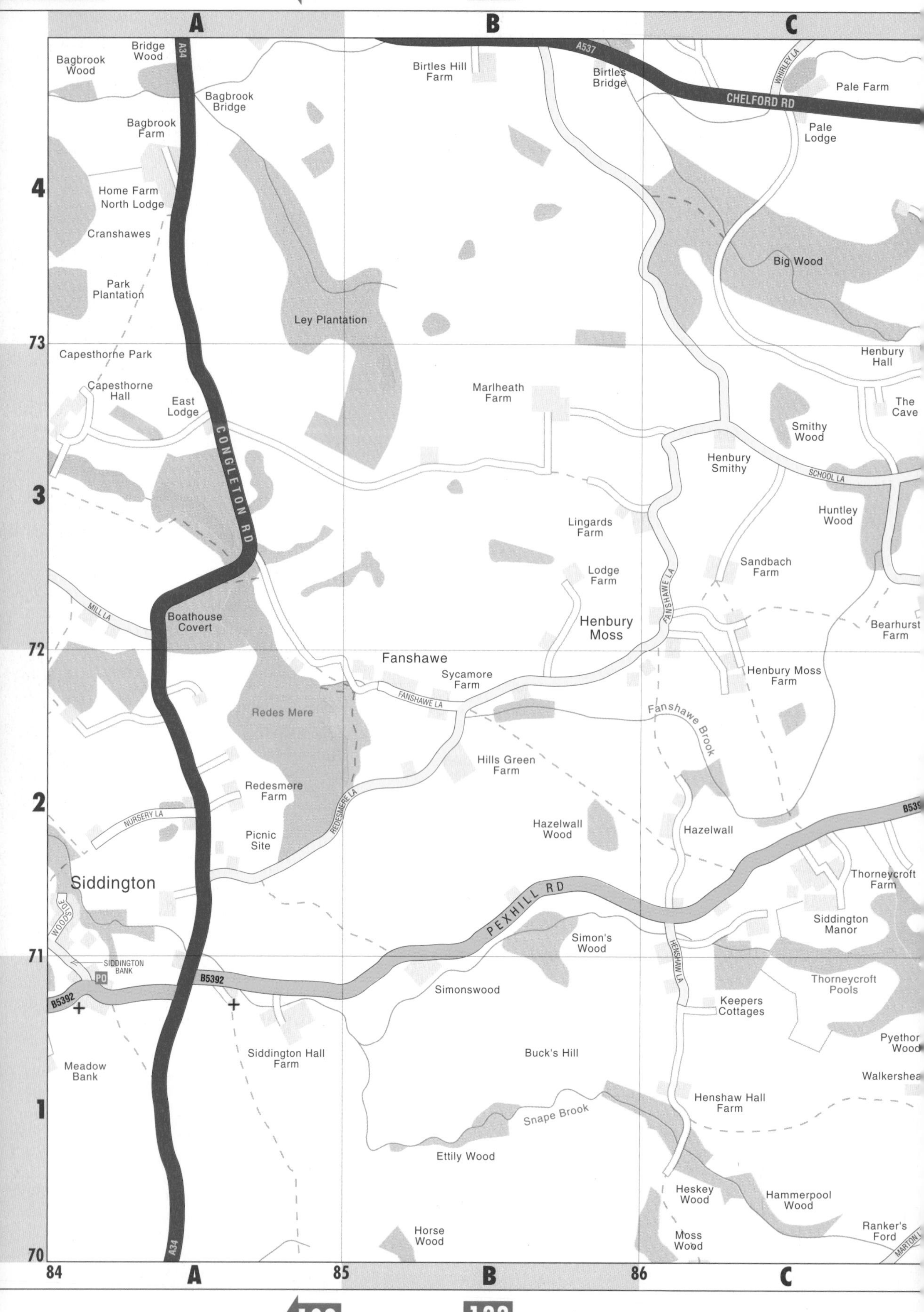

A   B   C

Bagbrook Wood
Bridge Wood
Bagbrook Bridge
A34
Bagbrook Farm
Home Farm
North Lodge
Cranshawes
Park Plantation

Birtles Hill Farm
A537
Birtles Bridge
CHELFORD RD
WHIRLEY LA
Pale Farm
Pale Lodge
Big Wood

4

Ley Plantation

73

Capesthorne Park
Capesthorne Hall
East Lodge
CONGLETON RD

Marlheath Farm

Henbury Hall
Smithy Wood
The Cave
SCHOOL LA
Henbury Smithy
Huntley Wood
Lingards Farm
Sandbach Farm
FANSHAWE LA
Bearhurst Farm

3

MILL LA
Boathouse Covert

Lodge Farm

Henbury Moss
Henbury Moss Farm

72

Fanshawe
Sycamore Farm
FANSHAWE LA
Redes Mere
Fanshawe Brook

Hills Green Farm
Redesmere Farm
REDESMERE LA
Picnic Site
Hazelwall Wood
Hazelwall
B539
Thorneycroft Farm
Siddington Manor

2

NURSERY LA

Siddington
SCHOOL LA
PEXHILL RD
Simon's Wood
HENSHAW LA
Thorneycroft Pools

71

SIDDINGTON BANK
PO
B5392
Simonswood
Keepers Cottages
Pyethor Wood
Walkershead

Meadow Bank
Siddington Hall Farm
Buck's Hill
Henshaw Hall Farm

1

Snape Brook
Ettily Wood
Heskey Wood
Hammerpool Wood
Ranker's Ford
MARTON L
Horse Wood
Moss Wood

70

84   A   85   B   86   C

86
112

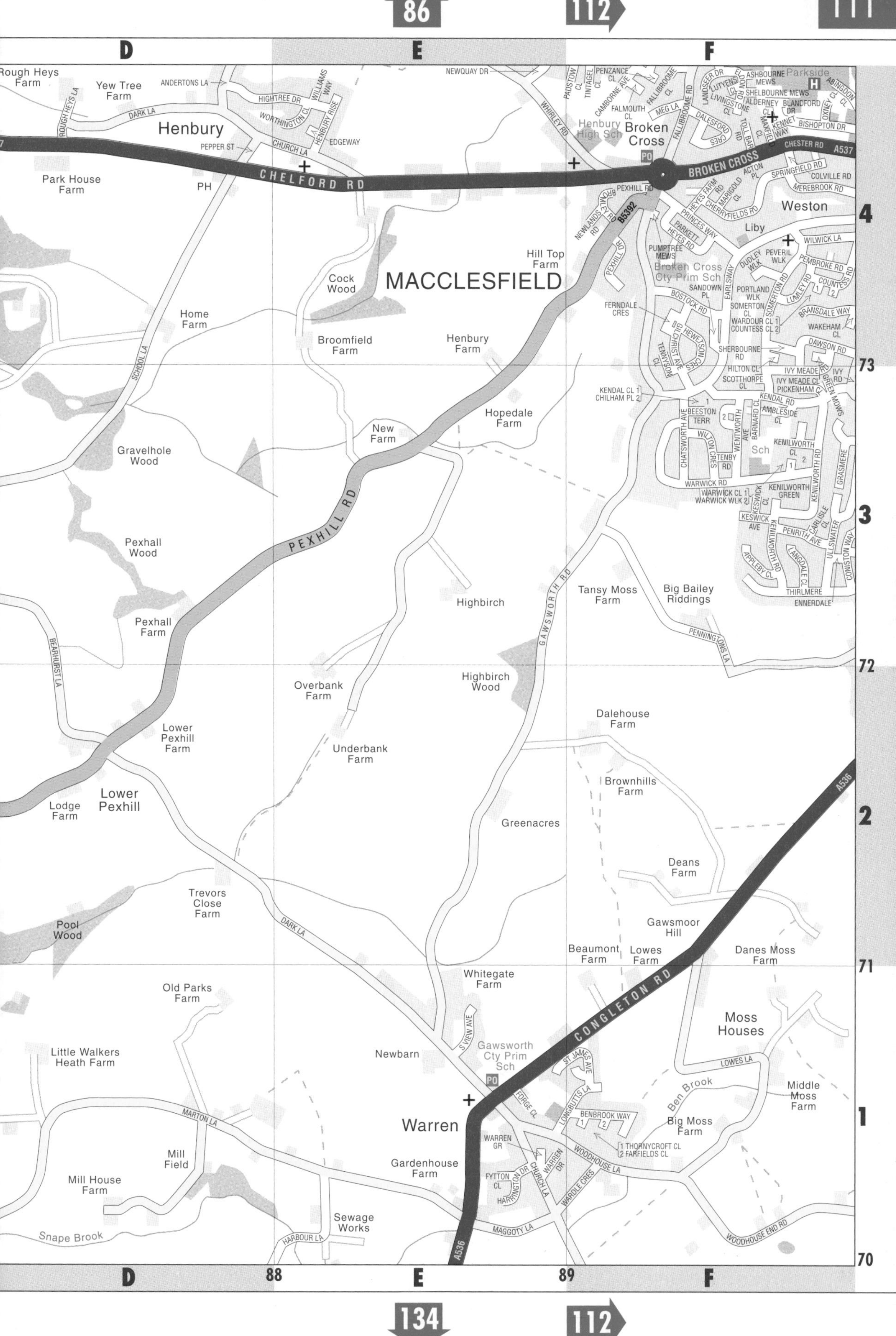
D
E
F
Rough Heys Farm
Yew Tree Farm
Henbury
Park House Farm
PH
CHELFORD RD
MACCLESFIELD
Broken Cross
Weston
Liby
Parkside
Henbury High Sch
Broken Cross Cty Prim Sch
Cock Wood
Hill Top Farm
Home Farm
Broomfield Farm
Henbury Farm
Hopedale Farm
New Farm
Gravelhole Wood
Pexhall Wood
Pexhall Farm
PEXHILL RD
Highbirch
Tansy Moss Farm
Big Bailey Riddings
Highbirch Wood
Overbank Farm
Underbank Farm
Lower Pexhill Farm
Lower Pexhill
Lodge Farm
Dalehouse Farm
Brownhills Farm
Greenacres
Deans Farm
Trevors Close Farm
Pool Wood
Gawsmoor Hill
Beaumont Farm
Lowes Farm
Danes Moss Farm
Whitegate Farm
Old Parks Farm
Moss Houses
Little Walkers Heath Farm
Newbarn
Gawsworth Cty Prim Sch
CONGLETON RD
Middle Moss Farm
Warren
Big Moss Farm
Ben Brook
Mill Field
Mill House Farm
Gardenhouse Farm
Sewage Works
Snape Brook
GAWSWORTH RD
DARK LA
SCHOOL LA
BEARHURST LA
MARTON LA
MAGGOTY LA
WOODHOUSE LA
WOODHOUSE END RD
LOWES LA
PENNINGTONS LA
HARBOUR LA
A536
A537
B5392
BROKEN CROSS
CHESTER RD
4
73
3
72
2
71
1
70
88
89

134
112

MACCLESFIELD

C4
1 NORWICH CT
2 VICTORIA WLK
3 LICHFIELD CT
4 OXFORD CT
5 CANTERBURY CT
6 ELY CT
7 WINCHESTER CT
8 SALISBURY CT
9 LANCASTER CT
10 YORK CT
11 CUCKSTOOLPIT HILL
12 DAINTRY TERR
13 ST PAUL'S RD
14 HALLEFIELD DR
15 HALLEFIELD CRES
16 THORNYCROFT
17 CAWLEY ST
18 LOWER BANK ST
19 BUCKLOW WLK
20 KNUTSFORD ROAD WLK
21 WILMLOW WL
22 ALDERLEY WL
23 PEARSON ST
24 CAPETHORNE

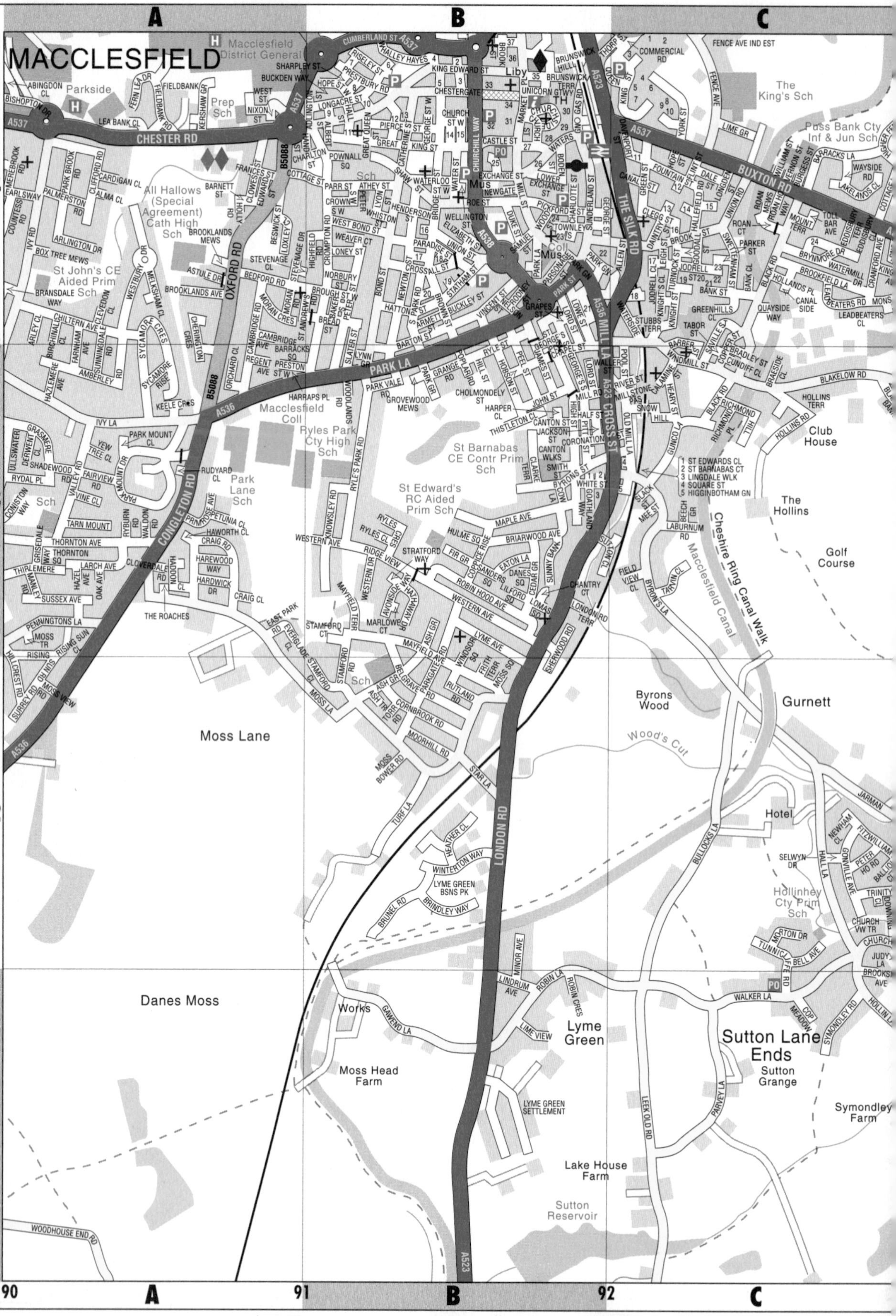

B4
1 TUNNICLIFFE ST
2 KING EDWARD RD
3 LITTLE ST
4 WESTMINSTER RD
5 WESTMINSTER ST
6 GROSVENOR ST
7 WALKER ST
8 BOOTHBY ST
9 POYTON ST
10 ANDERSON ST
11 LANGFORD ST
12 PINFOLD ST
13 FOUNDRY CT
14 CHARLOTTE ST W
15 CHATHAM ST
16 MARSDEN TERR
17 BACK PARADISE ST
18 HOLLAND ST
19 ST JOHN'S RD
20 BLACKSHAW ST
21 BROKEN BANKS
22 MAYDEWS PAS
23 TOWNLEY PL
24 MARLBOROUGH CT
25 EXCHANGE CL
26 QUEEN VICTORIA ST
27 BACK WALLGATE
28 SHORT ST
29 108 STEPS
30 STEP HILL
31 MILL STREET MALL
32 CASTLE STREET MALL
33 FISELEY'S PAS
34 CHESTERGATE MALL
35 BRUNSWICK ST
36 JORDAN GATE
37 CUMBERLAND ST

Danes Moss · Moss Lane · Lyme Green · Sutton Lane Ends · Gurnett · The Hollins · Golf Course · Byrons Wood · Sutton Reservoir · Lake House Farm · Moss Head Farm · Symondley Farm

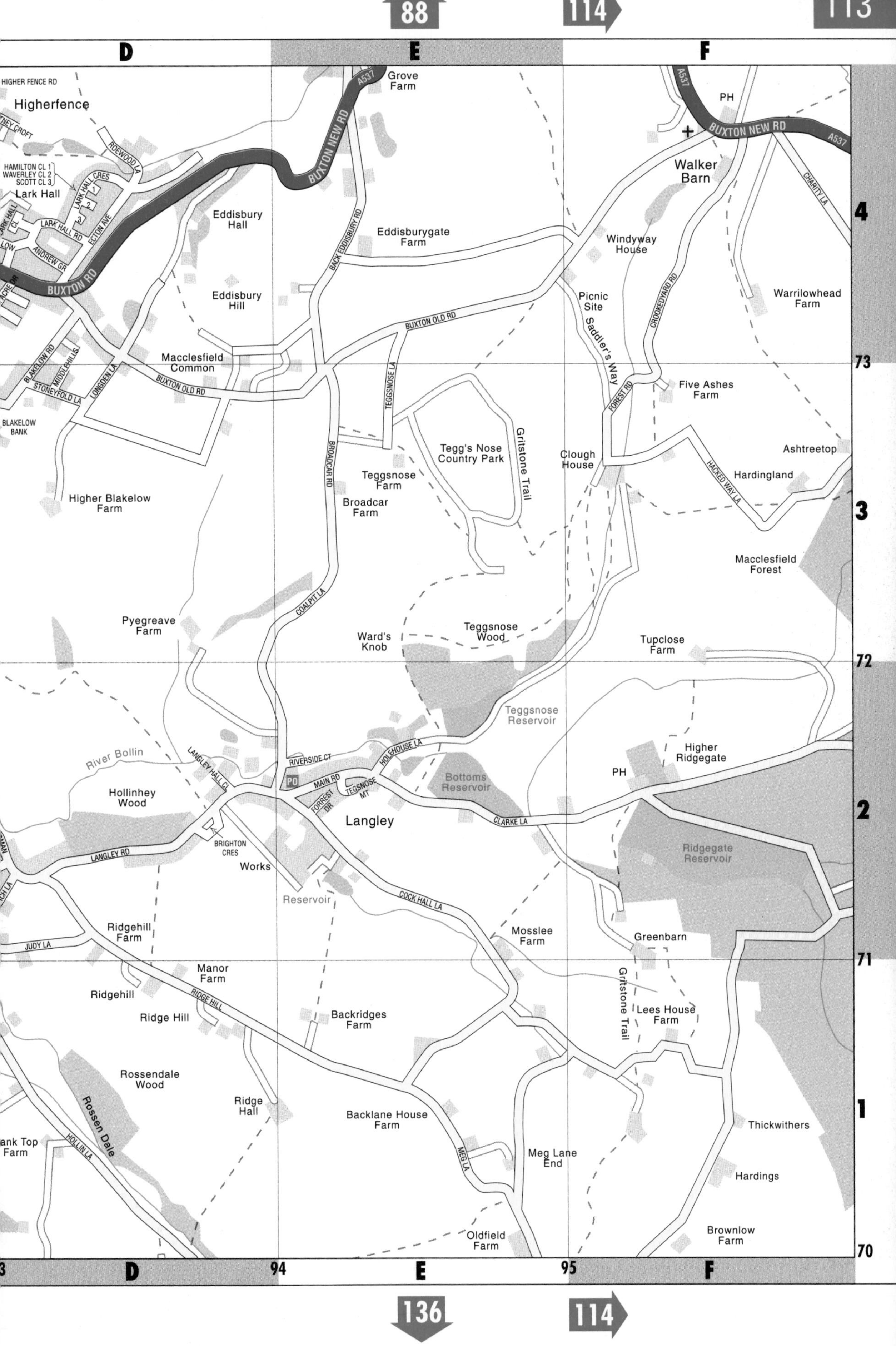

D
E
F

Higherfence

HIGHER FENCE RD
NEY CROFT
Grove Farm
ROEWOOD LA
BUXTON NEW RD
A537
PH
BUXTON NEW RD
A537
CHARITY LA

HAMILTON CL 1
WAVERLEY CL 2
SCOTT CL 3
Lark Hall
LARK HALL CRES
Walker Barn

LARK HALL 1
LOW
ANDREW GR
ACRE RD
LARK HALL RD
ECTON AVE
BUXTON RD
Eddisbury Hall
Eddisburygate Farm
Windyway House
Warrilowhead Farm

BLAKELOW RD
WIDGEHILLS
STONEFOLD LA
LONGDEN LA
BUXTON OLD RD
Eddisbury Hill
Macclesfield Common
BACK EDDISBURY RD
BUXTON OLD RD
Picnic Site
Saddler's Way
CROOKEDYARD RD
FOREST RD
Five Ashes Farm
73

BLAKELOW BANK
BUXTON OLD RD
TEGGSNOSE LA
Tegg's Nose Country Park
Gritstone Trail
Clough House
Ashtreetop
Hardingland

Higher Blakelow Farm
BROADCAR RD
Teggsnose Farm
Broadcar Farm
Macclesfield Forest
3

Pyegreave Farm
COALPIT LA
Ward's Knob
Teggsnose Wood
HACKED WAY LA
Tupclose Farm
72

River Bollin
LANGLEY HALL CL
RIVERSIDE CT
HOLEHOUSE LA
Teggsnose Reservoir
Higher Ridgegate

Hollinhey Wood
PO
MAIN RD
FOREST DR
TEGGSNOSE MT
Bottoms Reservoir
PH
2

Langley
CLARKE LA
Ridgegate Reservoir

LANGLEY RD
Works
Reservoir
COCK HALL LA
Greenbarn

JUDY LA
Ridgehill Farm
Mosslee Farm
Gritstone Trail
71

Ridgehill
RIDGE HILL
Manor Farm
Lees House Farm

Ridge Hill
Backridges Farm
Thickwithers

Rossendale Wood
Ridge Hall
Backlane House Farm
MEG LA
Meg Lane End
Hardings
1

Rossen Dale
HOLLIN LA
ank Top Farm
Oldfield Farm
Brownlow Farm
70

3
D
94
E
95
F

113
89

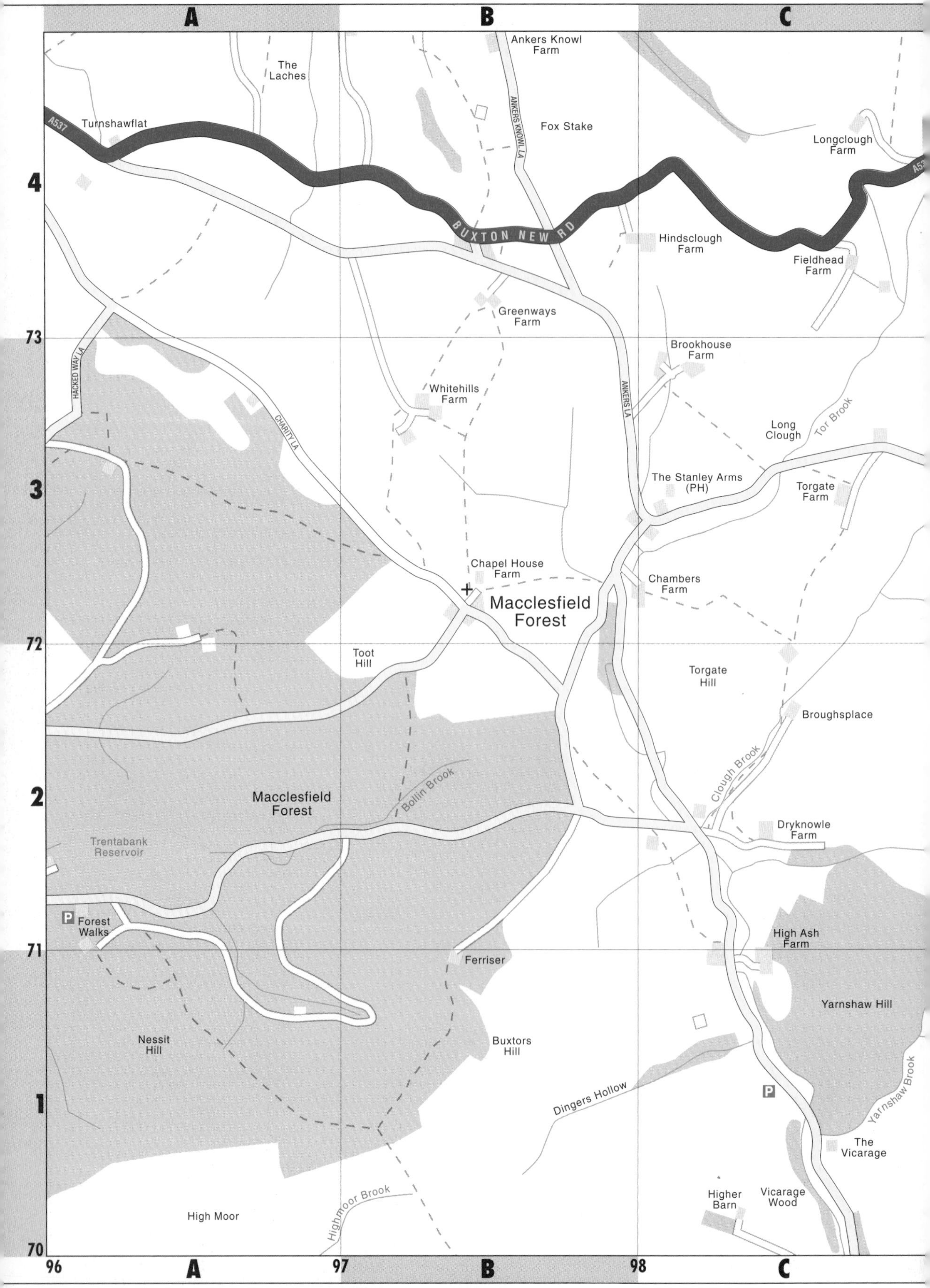

A   **B**   **C**

Ankers Knowl
Farm

The
Laches

Fox Stake

Longclough
Farm

A537

Turnshawflat

BUXTON NEW RD

Hindsclough
Farm

Fieldhead
Farm

4

Greenways
Farm

73

Brookhouse
Farm

HACKED WAY LA

Whitehills
Farm

ANKERS LA

Long
Clough

Tor Brook

CHARITY LA

The Stanley Arms
(PH)

Torgate
Farm

3

Chapel House
Farm

Chambers
Farm

Macclesfield
Forest

72

Toot
Hill

Torgate
Hill

Broughsplace

Macclesfield
Forest

Bollin Brook

Clough Brook

Dryknowle
Farm

2

Trentabank
Reservoir

High Ash
Farm

P Forest
Walks

71

Ferriser

Yarnshaw Hill

Nessit
Hill

Buxtors
Hill

Dingers Hollow

P

Yarnshaw Brook

1

The
Vicarage

Higher
Barn

Vicarage
Wood

High Moor

Highmoor Brook

70

96   **A**   97   **B**   98   **C**

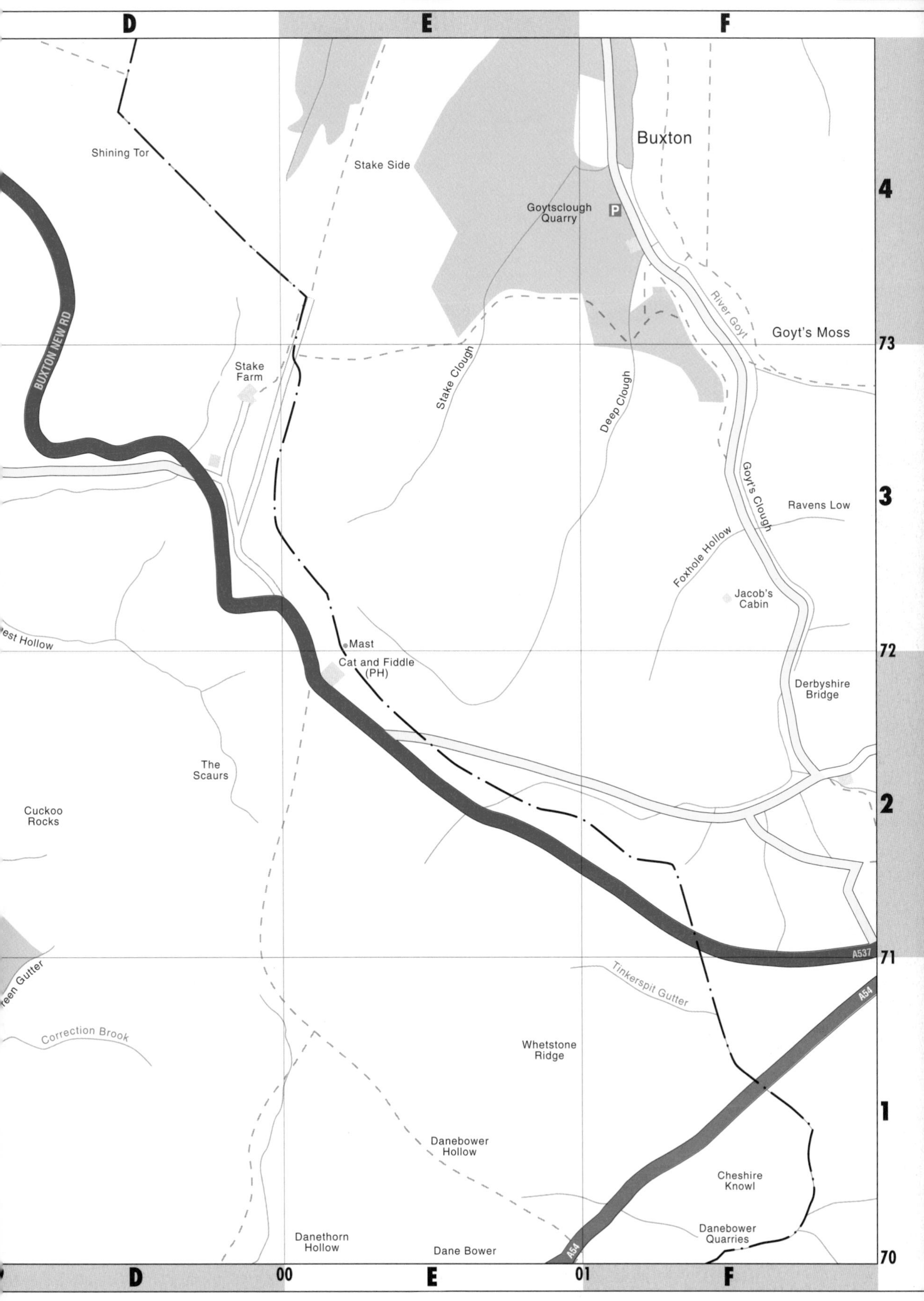

Shining Tor

Stake Side

Buxton

Goytsclough
Quarry

P

River Goyt

Goyt's Moss

BUXTON NEW RD

Stake
Farm

Stake Clough

Deep Clough

Goyt's Clough

Ravens Low

Foxhole Hollow

Jacob's
Cabin

rest Hollow

Mast
Cat and Fiddle
(PH)

Derbyshire
Bridge

The
Scaurs

Cuckoo
Rocks

A537

reen Gutter

Tinkerspit Gutter

A54

Correction Brook

Whetstone
Ridge

Cheshire
Knowl

Danebower
Hollow

Danethorn
Hollow

Dane Bower

A54

Danebower
Quarries

93

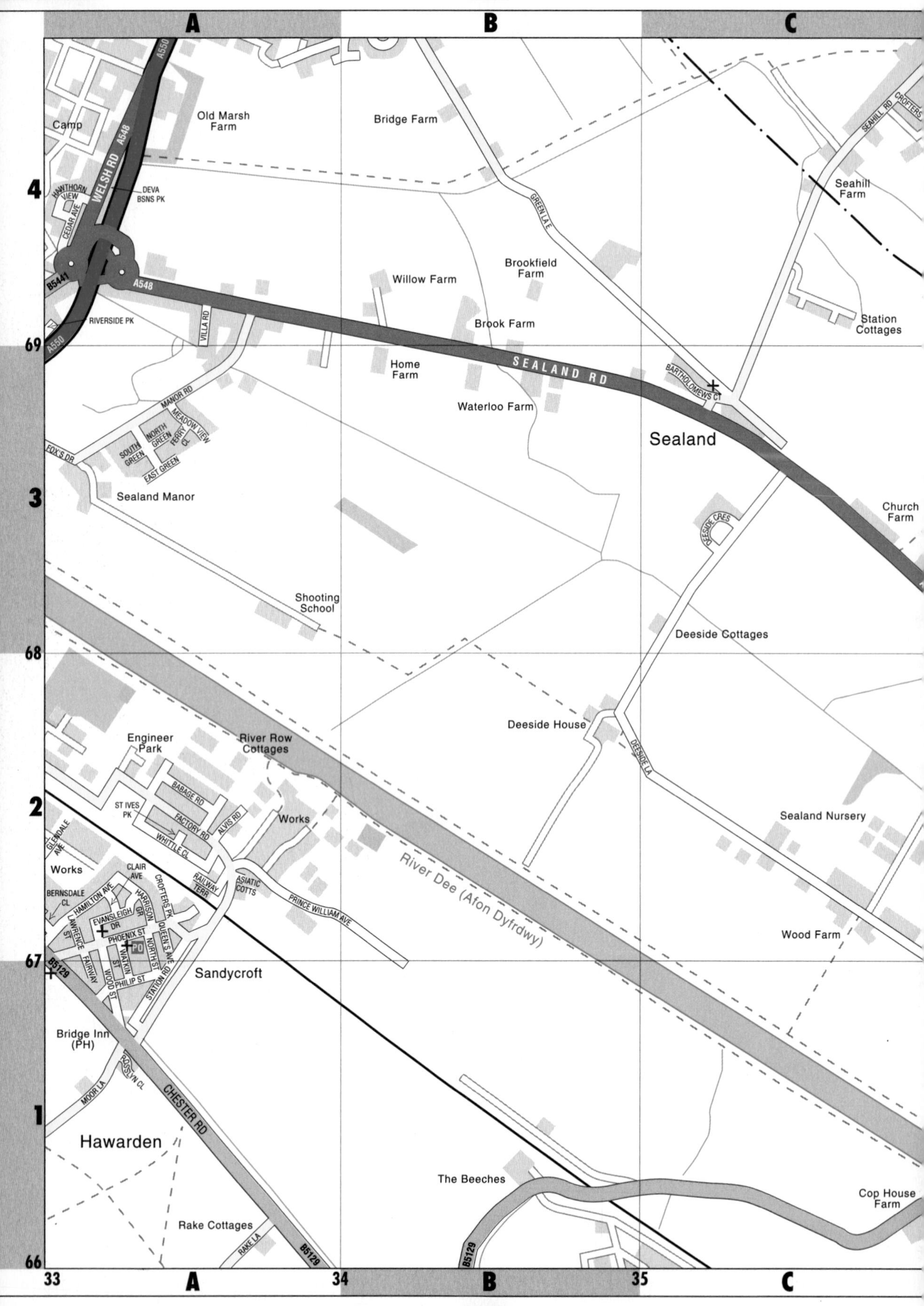

A
B
C
4
3
2
1
69
68
67
66
33
34
35
Old Marsh Farm
Camp
Bridge Farm
WELSH RD
A548
A550
HAWTHORN VIEW
CEDAR AVE
DEVA BSNS PK
B5441
RIVERSIDE PK
VILLA RD
GREEN LAE
Seahill Farm
SEAHILL RD
CROFTERS
Brookfield Farm
Willow Farm
Brook Farm
Station Cottages
Home Farm
SEALAND RD
BARTHOLOMEWS CT
Waterloo Farm
MANOR RD
MEADOW VIEW
NORTH GREEN
TERRY CL
SOUTH GREEN
EAST GREEN
FOX'S DR
Sealand
Sealand Manor
Church Farm
DEESIDE CRES
Shooting School
Deeside Cottages
Deeside House
DEESIDE LA
Engineer Park
River Row Cottages
BARAGE RD
ST IVES PK
FACTORY RD
ALVIS RD
WHITTLE CL
Works
Sealand Nursery
GLENDALE AVE
Works
CLAIR AVE
BERNSDALE CL
HAMILTON AVE
HARRISON GR
CROFTERS PK
RAILWAY TERR
ASIATIC COTTS
PRINCE WILLIAM AVE
River Dee (Afon Dyfrdwy)
LAWRENCE ST
EVANSLEIGH DR
PHOENIX ST
QUEEN'S AVE
NORTH ST
PO
Wood Farm
B5129
FAIRWAY
WATKIN ST
WOOD ST
PHILIP ST
STATION RD
Sandycroft
Bridge Inn (PH)
ROSSLYN CL
MOOR LA
CHESTER RD
Hawarden
The Beeches
Cop House Farm
Rake Cottages
RAKE LA

139

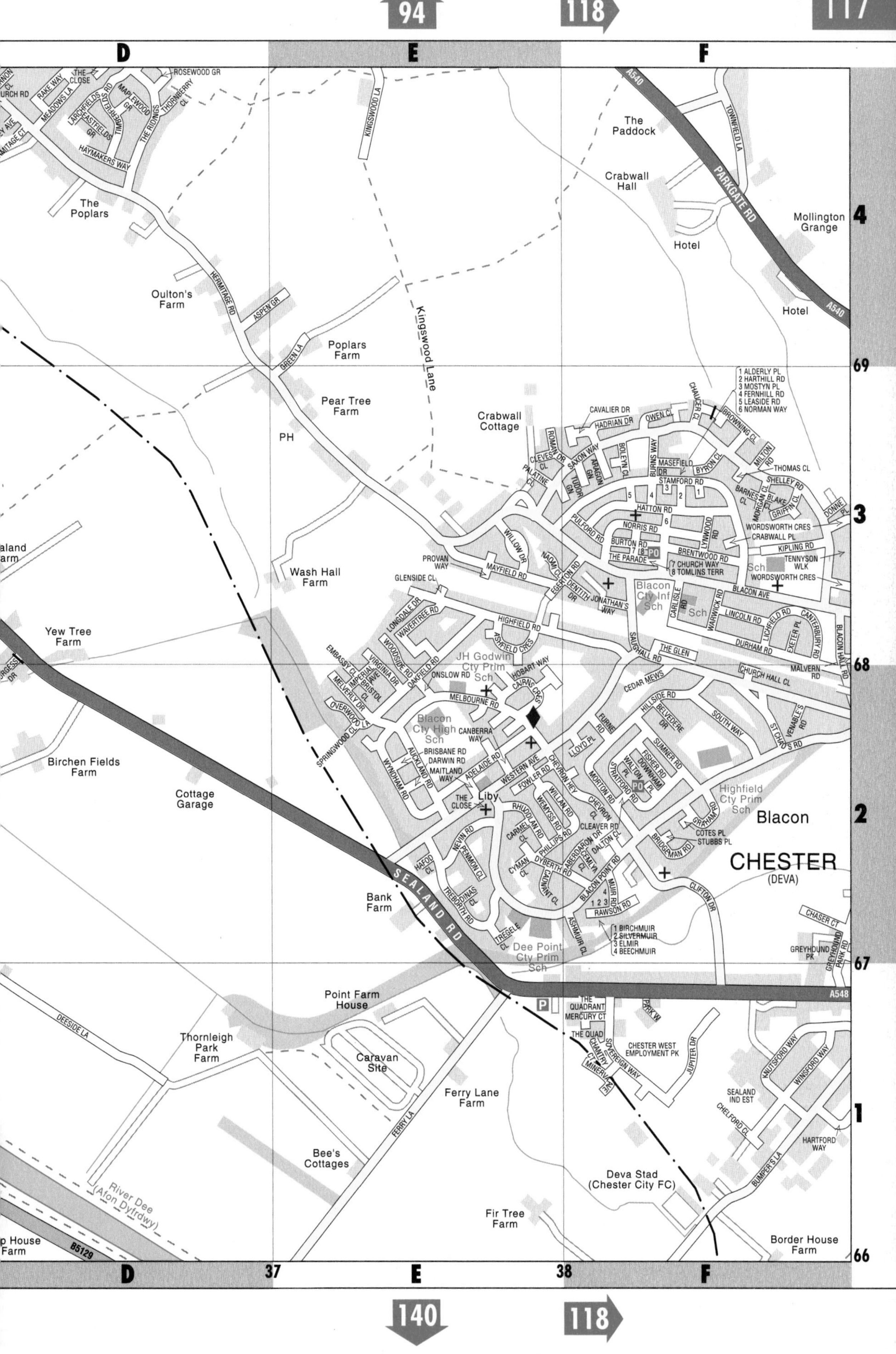

94
118
D
E
F
ROSEWOOD GR
THE CLOSE
RAKE WAY
MEADOWS LA
LARCHFIELDS RD
EASTFIELDS GR
TIMBERFIELD RD
MAPLEWOOD GR
THE RIDINGS
THORNBERRY CL
HAYMAKERS WAY
KINGSWOOD LA
The Paddock
A540
TOWNFIELD LA
Crabwall Hall
PARKGATE RD
Mollington Grange
Hotel
The Poplars
Oulton's Farm
HERMITAGE RD
ASPEN GR
GREEN LA
Poplars Farm
Kingswood Lane
Pear Tree Farm
PH
Crabwall Cottage
1 ALDERLY PL
2 HARTHILL RD
3 MOSTYN PL
4 FERNHILL RD
5 LEASIDE RD
6 NORMAN WAY
CHAUCER CL
CAVALIER DR
HADRIAN DR
OWEN CL
BROWNING CL
ROMAN DR
SAXON WAY
ARAGON GN
BOLEYN CL
BURNS WAY
MASEFIELD DR
BYRON CL
MILTON RD
THOMAS CL
CLEVES CL
PALATINE CL
TUDOR GN
STAMFORD RD
SHELLEY RD
BARNES CL
MORGAN CL
BLAKE CL
GRIFFIN CL
DONNE PL
HATTON RD
NORRIS RD
PULFORD RD
LYNWOOD RD
WORDSWORTH CRES
CRABWALL PL
KIPLING RD
BURTON RD
THE PARADE
PO
BRENTWOOD RD
TENNYSON WLK
7 CHURCH WAY
8 TOMLINS TERR
Sch
WILLOW DR
PROVAN WAY
MAYFIELD RD
NAOMI CL
EGERTON RD
DENTITH DR
JONATHAN'S WAY
Blacon Cty Inf Sch
CARLISLE RD
WARWICK RD
BLACON AVE
LINCOLN RD
LICHFIELD RD
CANTERBURY RD
EXETER PL
BLACON HALL RD
DURHAM RD
Wash Hall Farm
GLENSIDE CL
LONGDALE DR
WAVERTREE RD
HIGHFIELD RD
ASHFIELD CRES
SAIGHALL RD
THE GLEN
MALVERN RD
CHURCH HALL CL
Yew Tree Farm
EMBASSY CL
IMPERIAL AVE
VIRGINIA DR
WOODSIDE RD
OAKFIELD RD
JH Godwin Cty Prim Sch
HOBART WAY
ONSLOW RD
CAIRNS CRES
BRISTOL CL
MELVERLY DR
OVERWOOD LA
MELBOURNE RD
CEDAR MEWS
HILLSIDE RD
BELVEDERE DR
SOUTH WAY
ST CHAD'S RD
VENABLE'S RD
Blacon Cty High Sch
CANBERRA WAY
FURNE RD
SPRINGWOOD CL
LLOYD PL
SUMNER RD
FISHER RD
DOWNHAM PL
WALTON PL
Birchen Fields Farm
AUCKLAND RD
BRISBANE RD
DARWIN RD
MAITLAND WAY
ADELAIDE RD
WESTERN AVE
CHEVRON HEY
WYNDHAM RD
FOWLER RD
MORTON RD
STRATFORD RD
Highfield Cty Prim Sch
Cottage Garage
THE CLOSE
Liby
RHUDDLAN RD
WEMYSS RD
WILLAN RD
CHEVRON CL
CLEAVER RD
GRAHAM CL
Blacon
COTES PL
STUBBS PL
NEVIN RD
PENMON CL
CARMEL CL
PHILLIPS RD
ABERDARON DR
DALTON CL
BRIDGEMAN RD
CHESTER
(DEVA)
HAFOD CL
CYMAN CL
DYBERTH RD
CAIMANT CL
BLACON POINT RD
MUIR RD
CLIFTON DR
SEALAND RD
TREBORTH RD
DINAS CL
Bank Farm
RAWSON RD
CHASER CT
TREGELE CL
ASHMUIR CL
1 BIRCHMUIR
2 SILVERMUIR
3 ELMIR
4 BEECHMUIR
Dee Point Cty Prim Sch
GREYHOUND PK
GREYHOUND PARK RD
A548
Point Farm House
P
THE QUADRANT
MERCURY CT
THE QUAD
PARK W
CHANTRY CT
SOVEREIGN WAY
MINERVA AVE
CHESTER WEST EMPLOYMENT PK
JUPITER DR
KNUTSFORD WAY
WINSFORD WAY
DEESIDE LA
Thornleigh Park Farm
Caravan Site
Ferry Lane Farm
SEALAND IND EST
CHELFORD CL
HARTFORD WAY
FERRY LA
Bee's Cottages
Deva Stad (Chester City FC)
BUMPER'S LA
River Dee (Afon Dyfrdwy)
Fir Tree Farm
Border House Farm
B5129
37
38
4
69
3
68
2
67
1
66
140
118

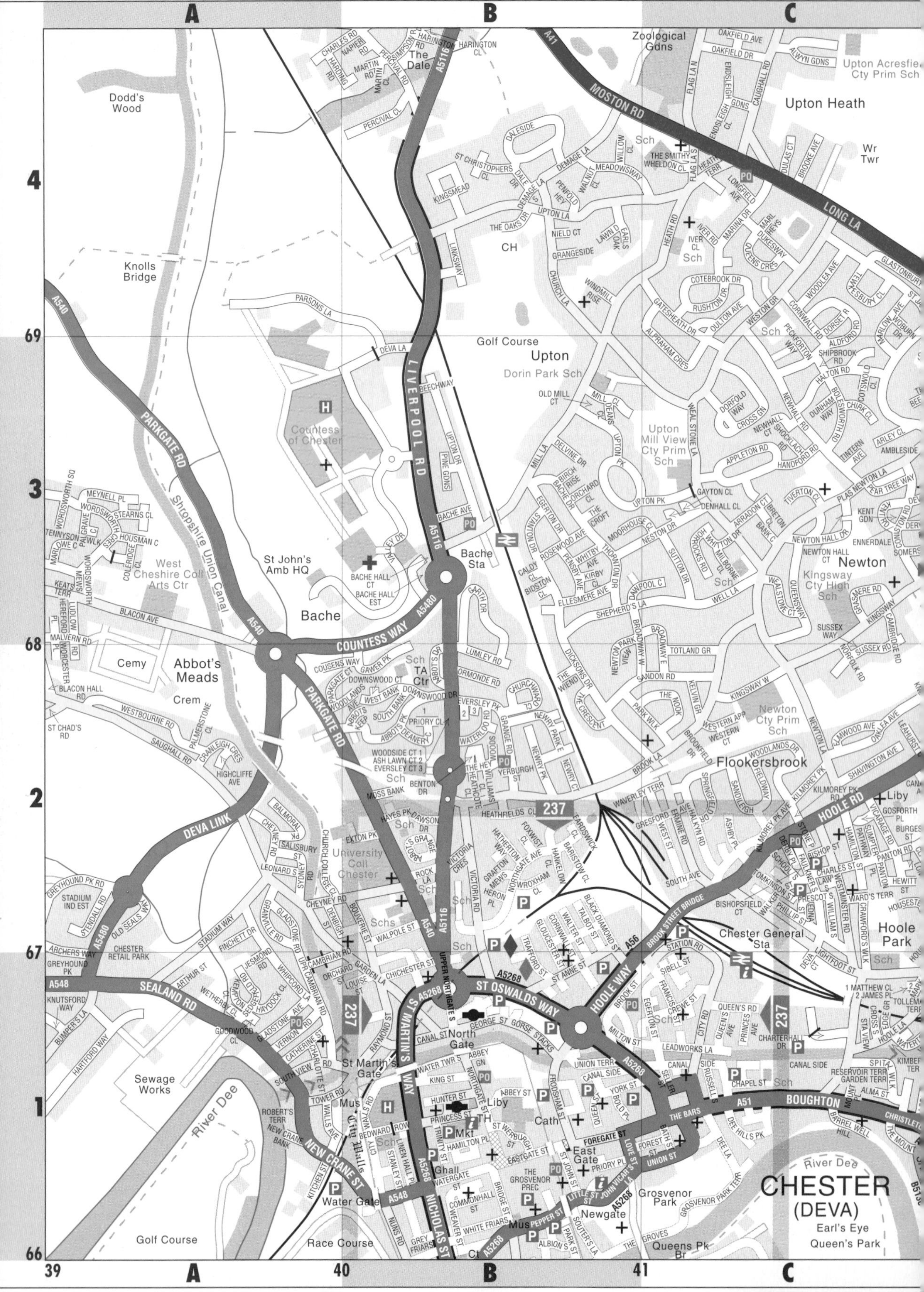

For full street detail of the
highlighted area see page
237.

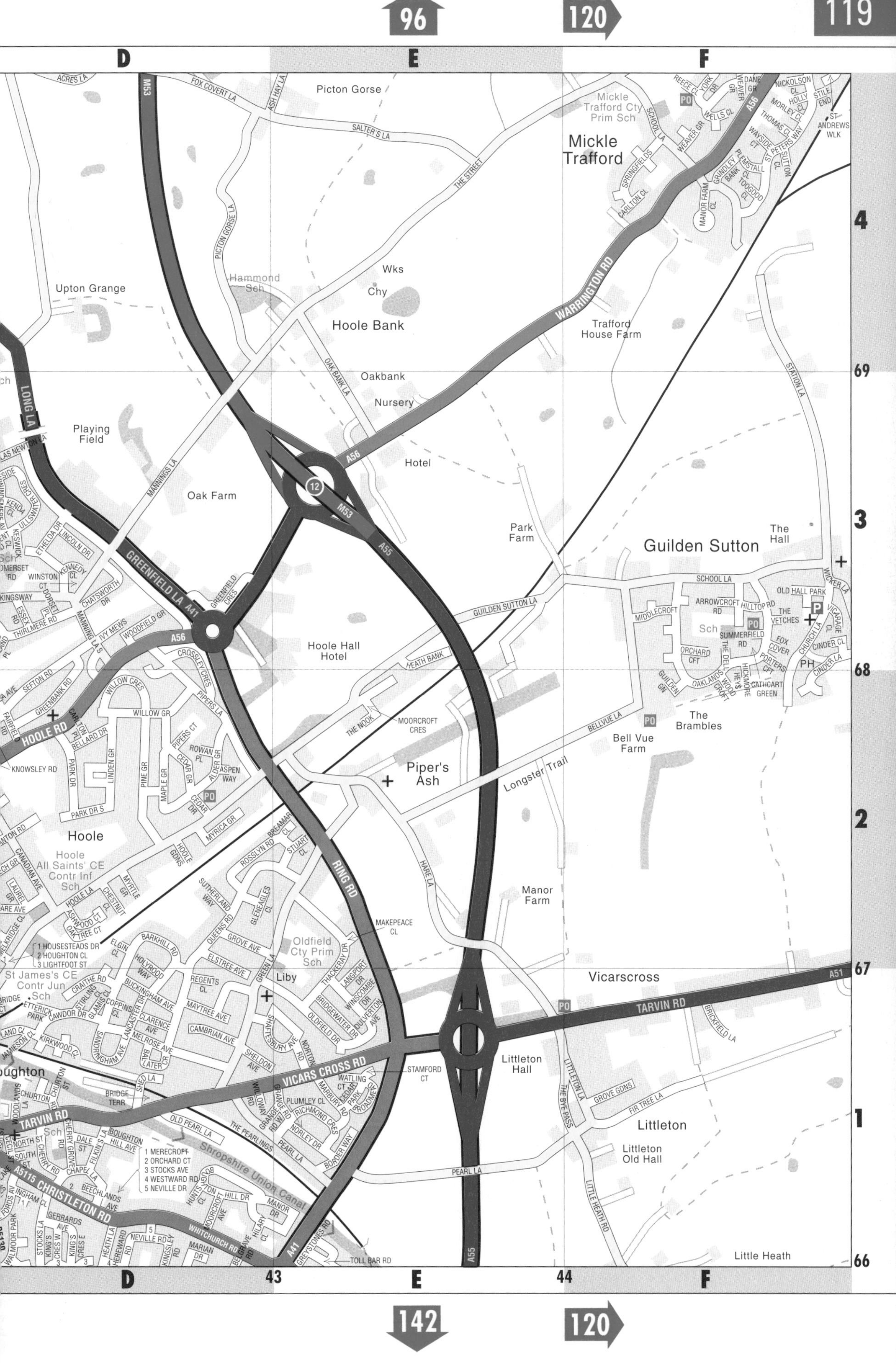
96
120
D
E
F
Picton Gorse
Mickle Trafford
Mickle Trafford Cty Prim Sch
Upton Grange
Hammond Sch
Wks
Chy
Hoole Bank
Trafford House Farm
Oakbank
Nursery
Playing Field
Hotel
Oak Farm
Park Farm
The Hall
Guilden Sutton
Hoole Hall Hotel
The Brambles
Bell Vue Farm
Piper's Ash
Longster Trail
Hoole
Hoole All Saints' CE Contr Inf Sch
Manor Farm
Oldfield Cty Prim Sch
Liby
St James's CE Contr Jun Sch
Vicarscross
Littleton Hall
Littleton
Littleton Old Hall
Shropshire Union Canal
Little Heath
WARRINGTON RD
GREENFIELD LA
HOOLE RD
RING RD
VICARS CROSS RD
TARVIN RD
A5115 CHRISTLETON RD
WHITCHURCH RD
LONG LA
M53
A56
A55
A41
A51
4
3
2
1
69
68
67
66
43
44
142
120

119
97

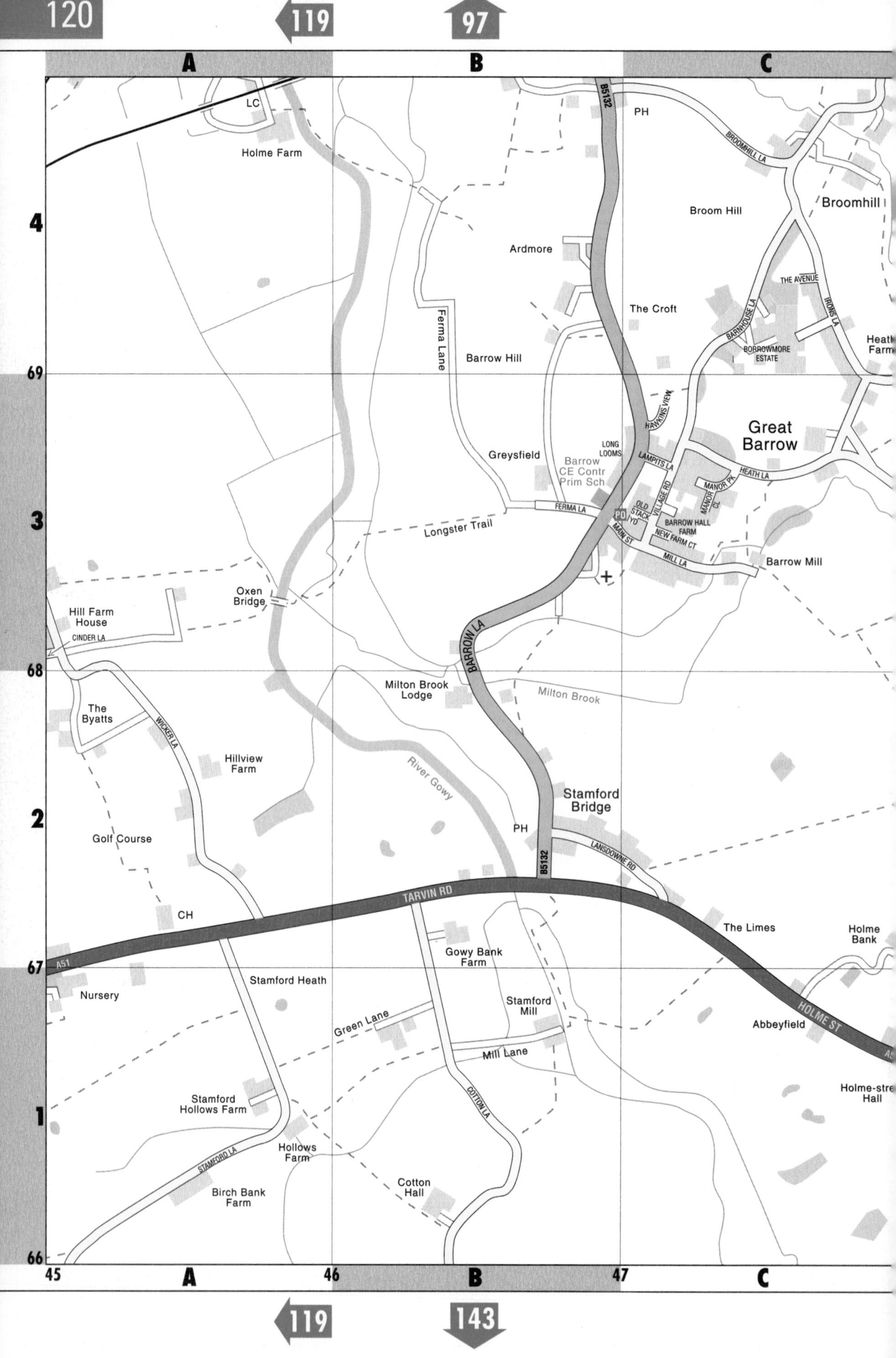
A
B
C
4
69
3
68
2
67
1
66
45
46
47
LC
Holme Farm
PH
BROOMHILL LA
Broomhill
Broom Hill
Ardmore
THE AVENUE
IRONS LA
The Croft
BARNHOUSE LA
Ferma Lane
Barrow Hill
BORROWMORE ESTATE
Heath Farm
HAWKINS VIEW
Great Barrow
LONG LOOMS
LAMPITS LA
Greysfield
Barrow CE Contr Prim Sch
HEATH LA
MANOR PK
VILLAGE RD
MANOR CL
FERMA LA
PO
OLD STACK YD
BARROW HALL FARM
Longster Trail
MAIN ST
NEW FARM CT
MILL LA
Barrow Mill
B5132
Oxen Bridge
Hill Farm House
CINDER LA
BARROW LA
Milton Brook Lodge
Milton Brook
The Byatts
WICKER LA
Hillview Farm
River Gowy
Stamford Bridge
Golf Course
PH
LANSDOWNE RD
CH
TARVIN RD
The Limes
Holme Bank
A51
Gowy Bank Farm
Nursery
Stamford Heath
Stamford Mill
HOLME ST
Green Lane
Abbeyfield
Mill Lane
Stamford Hollows Farm
COTTON LA
Holme-street Hall
Hollows Farm
STAMFORD LA
Cotton Hall
Birch Bank Farm

119
143

98
122

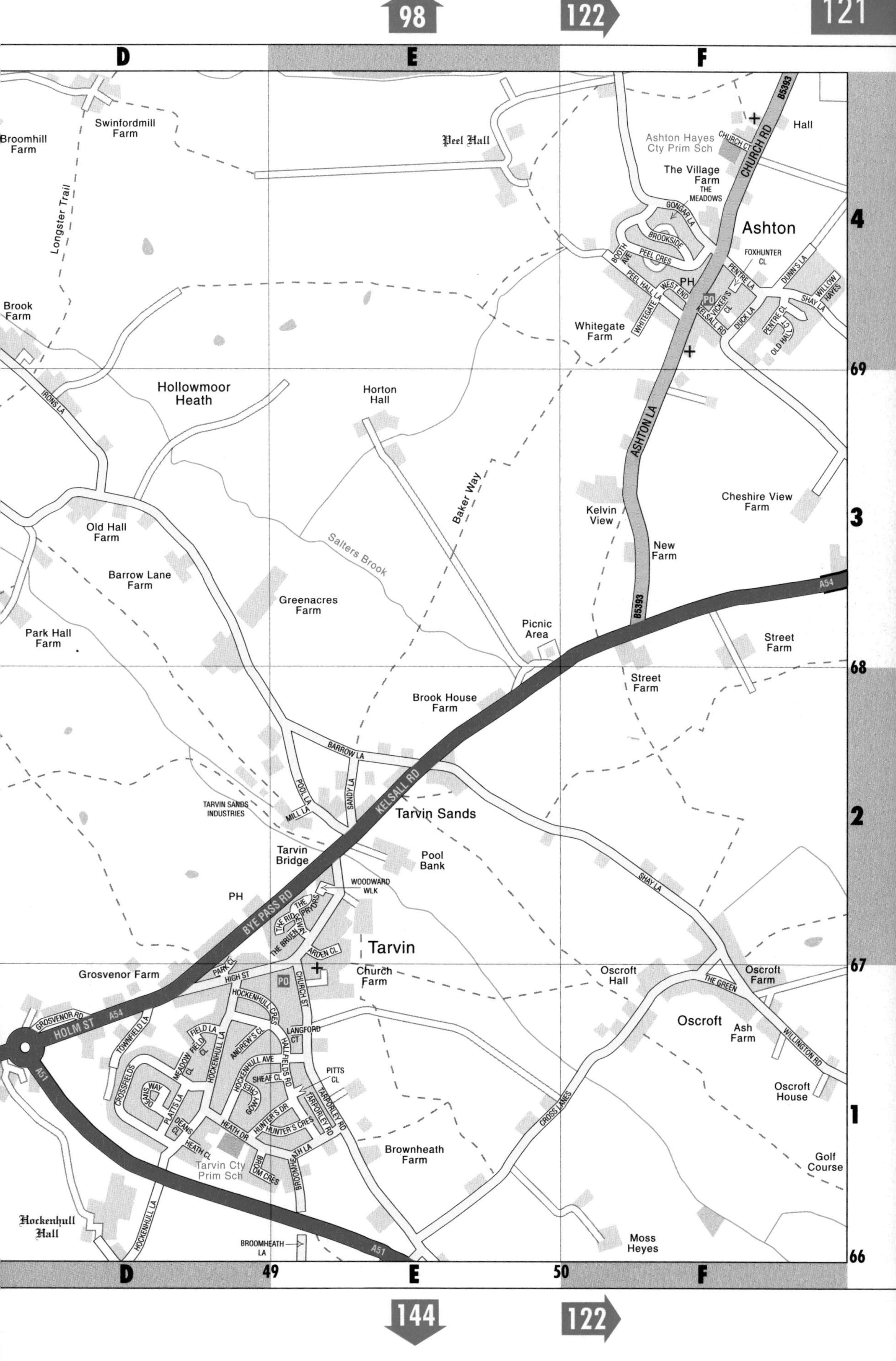
D
E
F
Broomhill Farm
Swinfordmill Farm
Longster Trail
Peel Hall
Ashton Hayes Cty Prim Sch
CHURCH CT
CHURCH RD
B5393
Hall
The Village Farm
THE MEADOWS
GONGAR LA
BROOKSIDE
Ashton
BOOTH AVE
PEEL CRES
FOXHUNTER CL
PENTRE LA
DUNN'S LA
WILLOW HAYES
SHAY LA
PEEL HALL LA
WEST END
PH
PO
VICKER'S CL
KELSALL RD
WHITEGATE
DUCK LA
PENTRE CL
OLD HALL CL
Whitegate Farm
Brook Farm
4
69
IRONS LA
Hollowmoor Heath
Horton Hall
ASHTON LA
Baker Way
Cheshire View Farm
Kelvin View
3
Old Hall Farm
Barrow Lane Farm
Salters Brook
New Farm
Greenacres Farm
B5393
A54
Park Hall Farm
Picnic Area
Street Farm
Street Farm
68
Brook House Farm
BARROW LA
POOL LA
SANDY LA
KELSALL RD
TARVIN SANDS INDUSTRIES
MILL LA
Tarvin Sands
2
Tarvin Bridge
Pool Bank
WOODWARD WLK
PH
BYE PASS RD
THE PRYORS
THE RIDGEWAY
THE BRUEN
SHAY LA
ARDEN CL
Tarvin
Grosvenor Farm
PARK CL
HIGH ST
PO
CHURCH ST
Church Farm
Oscroft Hall
THE GREEN
Oscroft Farm
67
GROSVENOR RD
A54
HOLM ST
TOWNFIELD LA
FIELD LA
HOCKENHULL CRES
MEADOW FIELD CL
HOCKENHULL LA
ANDREW'S CL
LANGFORD CT
HALLFIELDS RD
Oscroft
Ash Farm
WILLINGTON RD
A51
CROSSFIELDS
DEANS WAY
PLATTS LA
HOCKENHULL AVE
SHEAF CL
GOWY CRES
PITTS CL
TARPORLEY RD
Oscroft House
1
DEANS CL
HEATH DR
HUNTER'S DR
HUNTER'S CRES
CROSS LANES
HEATH CL
BROOMHEATH LA
Brownheath Farm
Golf Course
Tarvin Cty Prim Sch
BROOM CRES
Hockenhull Hall
HOCKENHULL LA
BROOMHEATH LA
A51
Moss Heyes
66
D
49
E
50
F

144
122

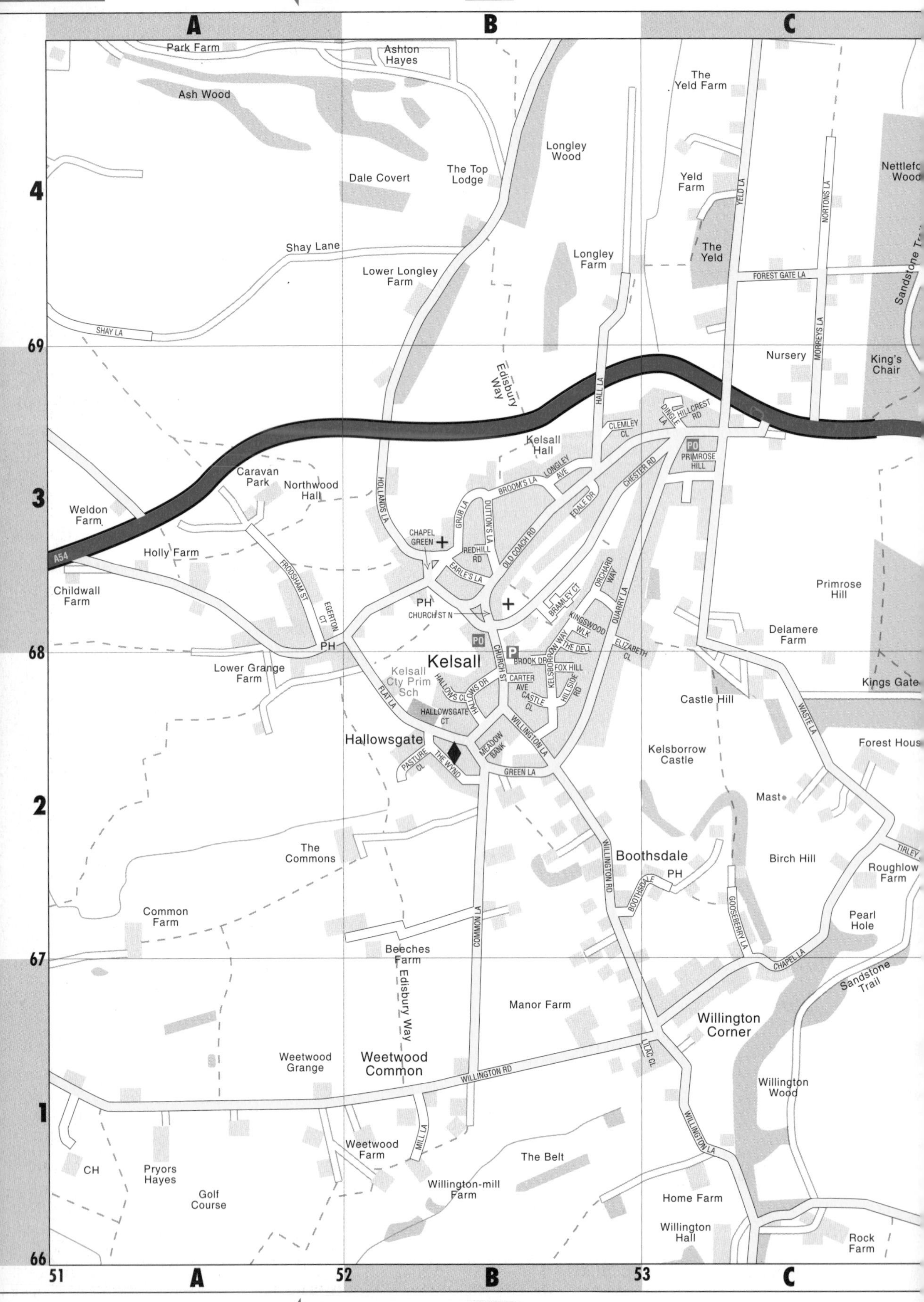

A **B** **C**

4

Park Farm
Ash Wood
Ashton Hayes
Dale Covert
The Top Lodge
Longley Wood
The Yeld Farm
Yeld Farm
Nettlefc Wood
Yeld La
Nortons La
Sandstone Tra

Shay Lane
Lower Longley Farm
Longley Farm
The Yeld
Forest Gate La

69

Shay La
Edisbury Way
Hall La
Nursery
King's Chair
Morreys La

3

Weldon Farm
Caravan Park
Northwood Hall
Kelsall Hall
Clemley Cl
Hillcrest Rd
Dingle La
PO
Primrose Hill
A54
Holly Farm
Chapel Green
Redhill Rd
Grub La
Dutton's La
Broom's La
Longley Ave
Fdale Dr
Old Coach Rd
Chester Rd
Primrose Hill
Childwall Farm
Trousham St
Egerton Ct
Earle's La
Orchard Way
Kingswood Wlk
Quarry La
Delamere Farm

PH
Church St N
Bramley Ct
The Dell
Elizabeth Cl

68

Lower Grange Farm
PH
PO
Kelsall Cty Prim Sch
Church St
P
Brook Dr
Carter Ave
Castle Cl
Kelsborow Way
Fox Hill
Hillside Rd
Kings Gate
Kelsall
Castle Hill

Flat La
Hallows Clows Dr
Hallowsgate Ct
Willington La
Kelsborrow Castle
Waste La
Forest Hous

Hallowsgate
The Wynd
Meadow Bank
Mast
Birch Hill
Tirley
Roughlow Farm

2

Pasture Cl
Green La
Boothsdale
PH
Willington Rd
Boothsdale
Gooseberry La
Chapel La
Pearl Hole

The Commons
Common La
Sandstone Trail

67

Common Farm
Beeches Farm
Edisbury Way
Manor Farm
Willington Corner
Willington Wood

Weetwood Grange
Weetwood Common
Willington Rd
Ludc Cl
Willington La

1

CH
Pryors Hayes
Golf Course
Weetwood Farm
Mill La
The Belt
Home Farm
Rock Farm

Willington-mill Farm
Willington Hall

66

51 **A** **52** **B** **53** **C**

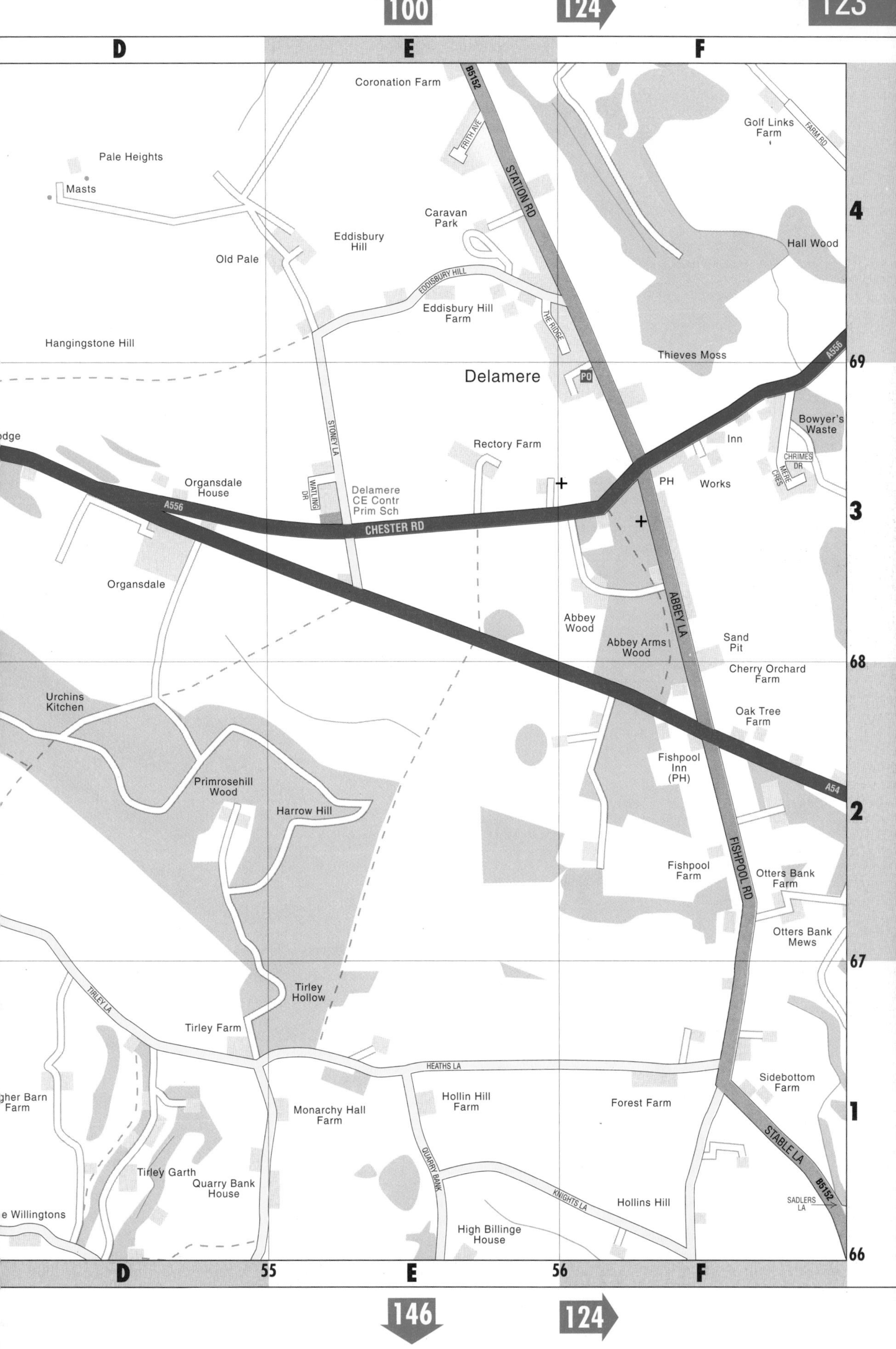
D
E
F
Coronation Farm
B5152
FRITH AVE
STATION RD
Golf Links Farm
FARM RD
Pale Heights
Masts
Caravan Park
Eddisbury Hill
Old Pale
Hall Wood
EDDISBURY HILL
Eddisbury Hill Farm
THE RIDGE
Hangingstone Hill
Thieves Moss
A556
Delamere
PO
Bowyer's Waste
Inn
Rectory Farm
STONEY LA
CHRIMES DR
MERE CRES
PH
Works
Organsdale House
WATLING DR
Delamere CE Contr Prim Sch
A556
CHESTER RD
Organsdale
Abbey Wood
ABBEY LA
Abbey Arms Wood
Sand Pit
Cherry Orchard Farm
Urchins Kitchen
Oak Tree Farm
Fishpool Inn (PH)
Primrosehill Wood
A54
Harrow Hill
Fishpool Farm
FISHPOOL RD
Otters Bank Farm
Otters Bank Mews
TIRLEY LA
Tirley Hollow
Tirley Farm
HEATHS LA
Sidebottom Farm
Monarchy Hall Farm
Hollin Hill Farm
Forest Farm
STABLE LA
QUARRY BANK
Tirley Garth
Quarry Bank House
B5152
KNIGHTS LA
Hollins Hill
SADLERS LA
e Willingtons
High Billinge House
4
69
3
68
2
67
1
66
D
55
E
56
F

123
101

A   B   C

Cheshire
Kennels

Crown Farm

CHESTER RD
FARM RD
A556

Massey's
Lodge

Reekin
Hole

4

Oakmere

Nunsmere

Kennel Lane
OVERDALE LA
A49

HOGSHEAD LA

69

Hogshead
Wood

Shemmy
Moss

Fourways Sand Quarry

Nunsmere
Hall

A556

Waste
Farm

Abbotsmoss
Wood

3

Folly
Farm

Horse Training Ground

Abbotsmoss
Hall

TARPORLEY RD

Keeper's
Cottage

Abbots Moss

68

Polo Ground

Oak Mere

Corner
Farm

Greenlands

Spring
Farm

SHAY'S LA

Shaw's
Farm

Shay's
Farm

A54

2

Cabbage Hall
(PH)

Shay's Lane Brook

Sandymere
Plantation

Sandybrow

Stonehouse
Farm

Common Side

LONGSTONE LA

Sandymere
House

67

Shrewsbury Arms
(PH)

Butts
Farm

+

Moss Hall
Farm

SHOP LA

Heathfield

Oaktree
Farm

RACECOURSE LA

BEECH RD

WHITEHALL LA

Burslem Cottage
Farm

1

Rosebank
Farm

Sunnybank
Farm

PARK RD

Sandiford
Lodge

COACH RD

Polo
Ground

Picnic
Area

White
hall

Poolhead
Farm

SADLERS LA

B5152
STABLE LA

A49

66

57   A   58   B   59   C

123
147

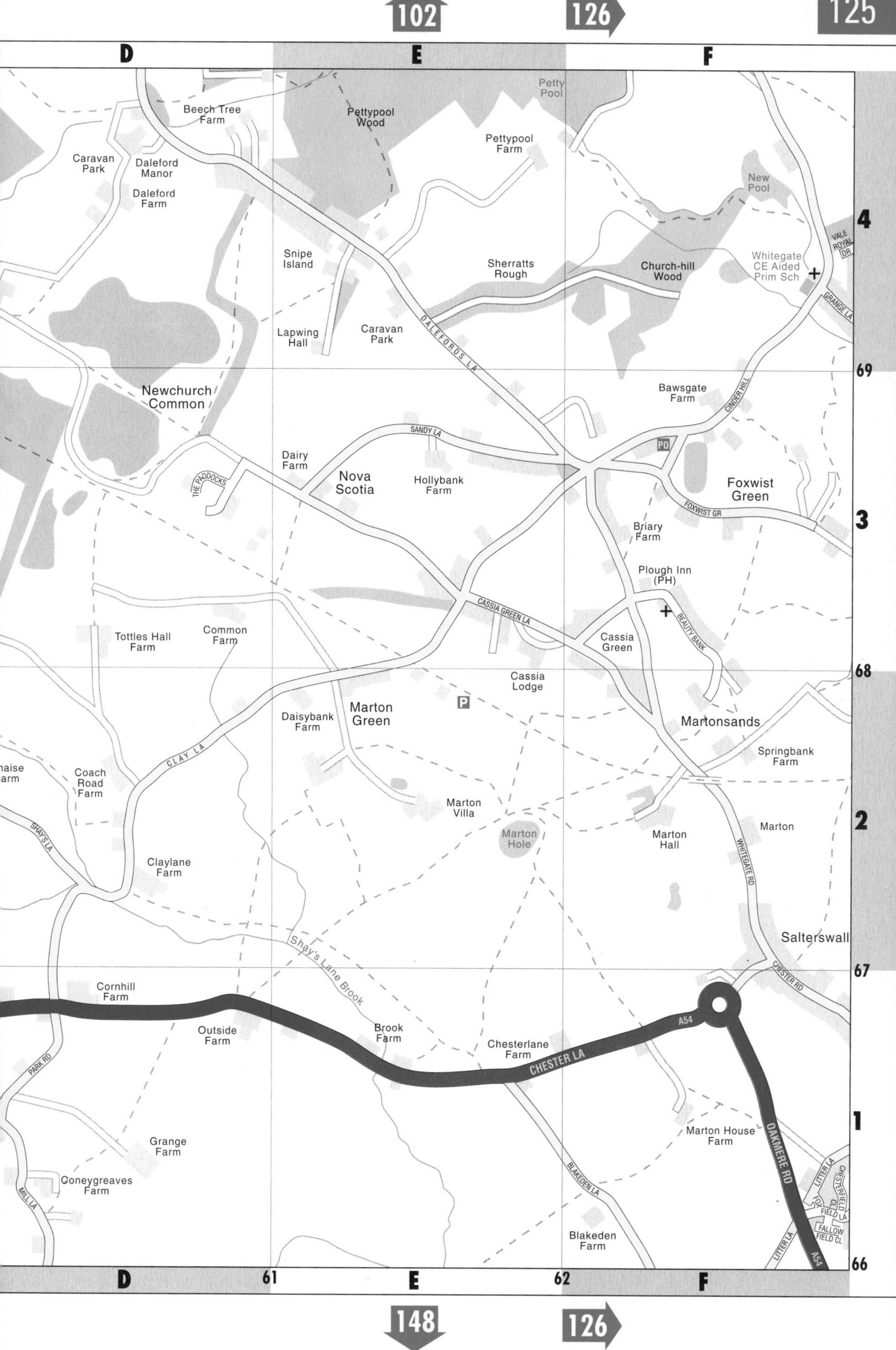

D E F

4

69

3

68

2

67

1

66

Beech Tree Farm
Caravan Park
Daleford Manor
Daleford Farm
Pettypool Wood
Petty Pool
Pettypool Farm
New Pool
Snipe Island
Sherratts Rough
Church-hill Wood
Whitegate CE Aided Prim Sch
VALE ROYAL DR
GRANGE LA
Lapwing Hall
Caravan Park
DALEFORDS LA
Newchurch Common
Bawsgate Farm
CINDER HILL
SANDY LA
PO
Dairy Farm
THE PADDOCKS
Nova Scotia
Hollybank Farm
Foxwist Green
FOXWIST GR
Briary Farm
Plough Inn (PH)
Tottles Hall Farm
Common Farm
CASSIA GREEN LA
BEAUTY BANK
Cassia Green
Cassia Lodge
Daisybank Farm
Marton Green
P
Martonsands
Springbank Farm
CLAY LA
Coach Road Farm
haise arm
Marton Villa
Marton Hole
Marton Hall
WHITEGATE RD
Marton
Claylane Farm
Salterswall
SHAY'S LA
CHESTER RD
Shay's Lane Brook
67
Cornhill Farm
A54
Outside Farm
Brook Farm
Chesterlane Farm
CHESTER LA
PARK RD
OAKMERE RD
Marton House Farm
Grange Farm
BLAKEDEN LA
LITTER LA
CHESTERFIELD CL
FIELD LA
Coneygreaves Farm
MILL LA
LITTER LA
FALLOW FIELD CL
Blakeden Farm
A54

125

103

A

B

C

Vale Royal

Monk's Well

River Weaver

Eaton Bank Wood

Moulton Cty Prim Sch

EATON VIEW

WEAVER GRANGE

THE HOLLIES

BARNSIDE WAY

HARVEST CT

SUMMERFIELD DR

ORCHARD RISE

CHAPEL ST

CHAPEL LA

BEECHFIELD

MAIN RD

WHITLOW LA

CHURCH ST

REGENT ST

JACK LA

POPLAR LA

ANT CT

4

VALE ROYAL DR

Valeroyal Park

LAWRENCE AVE

HILLSIDE LA

WEAVER DR

MEADOW LA

WILSON DR

VICAR LA

PARK LA

Whitegate

BUTTON FIELD

ABBEY CL

Moulton

Valeroyal Cut

Quesse Wood

GRANGE LA

Moultonbank Farm

Hillside Farm

MILL LA

NIDDRIES LA

LODGE DR

LODGE DR

69

Mill Lane Cottages

Parkside Farm

Newbridge Wood

MEADOW HOME PARK

Picnic Site

SMOKEHALL LA

Bark House

Pettypool Brook

Pettypool Brook

Bradford Mill

Foxwist Green Farm

Bogart Brook

Bradford Wood Farm

3

Meadow House Farm

MEADOW GR

SCHOOL RD

Meadowbank

Works

DEAKIN'S LA

SHAW'S LA

UPTON L

68

Brook House

GRANGE LA

EVERFOR

Gale Green Farm

BRADFORD RD

Weaver Navigation

Mills

NAT L

Bradfordwood

Catsclough

Cat's Clough

Golf Course

Sewage Works

Verdin's Cut

2

Knight's Grange (Sports Complex)

BALMORAL CL

MARLBOROUGH AVE

WADES LA

SANDRINGHAM CL

GRANGEBROOK DR

PRIORY CL

ALLANDALE RD

BRAMBLE CL

HAWTHORN CL

ROWAN DR

CLOVER DR

WILLOW CL

SHEPHERDS FOLD DR

KNIGHTS MEADOW

TARN CL

ENNERDALE

RYDAL CL

GRASMERE CR

67

MEADOW CL 1
AMBLESIDE CL 2
ESK DALE CL 3
TURNBERRY CL 4
PRESTWICK CL 5
DALMAHOY CL 6

P

GLENEAGLES

MUIRFIELD DR

BUTTERMERE RD

CONISTON CL

WINDERMERE RD

BOWNESS AVE

TROUTBECK DR

BOWNESS AVE

Roehurst Lane

WINSFORD

WELL BEAU AV

MEDINA AVE

VERDIN CL

ULSWATER DR

HAWESWATER AVE

ROEHURST LA

1 LANGDALE CL
2 KESWICK CL
3 STAVELEY DR
4 CARTMEL CL
5 ARNSIDE CL
6 KENTMERE AVE

CORONATION AVE

LEVEN CT

SPEY CL

WHARTON RD

WHARTON PARK RD

CHESTER RD

PICTON DR

NIXON DR

ALDFORD WAY

BASFORD WAY

ASTON AVE

KINGSLEY WLK

JAYCE AVE

Coll

Sch

QUEENS CT

SADLER CL

COLLINGHAM WAY

SODON CL

A5018

NEW RD

RIVER VIEW

BAKERS LA

WESLEY CT

Barton Stadium

CURZON GF

1

Littler

LITTLER LA

WESTGATE AVE

LITTLER GRANGE CT

BURLAND CL

BROXTON AVE

KINGSLEY WLK

ABBOTTS WAY

COLVERLEY WAY

CROSSWAY

SAXON WAY

CADDY WAY

BRINDLEY AVE

PULP

Sch

Verdin Cty High Sch

ALEXANDRA ST

Guildhall

HIGH ST

LAGOS ST

HIGH ST

OVERWAY

WELLINGTON ST

GEORGE ST

HENLEY DR

KINGSWAY

A54

HARWOOD CL

THORNYCROFT

CARBROOK CL

PIPERS ASH

WOODCOTT AVE

BRAMHALL CL

DELAMERE RISE

PRESTON ST

TATTON CL

HILL TOP AVE

HUNTERS RISE

Sch

Geneva Rd

Civic Hall

DEAN ST

Liby

FOUNTAIN CT

DERNE DR

JUBILEE WAY

PO

DINGLE DR

CLOUGH RD

WILLIAM ST

WEAVER ST

ROYLE ST

MARKET HILL

BARTON ST

River Weaver

FOXFIELD LA

BADGERS CL

BARRIERS WAY

RISE WAY

ST JOHN'S DR

CARLISLE CL

Sch

BRIDGEWATER PL

WHITBY'S LA

PO

1 OTTERS BANK
2 REDSTONE DR

Sch

CHIRK PL

CAMBRIDGE RD

Mkt

THE DRUMBER

LATHAM ST

O'WELL

JOHN ST

QUEENS ST

POOLE ST

STATION RD

66

63

A

64

B

65

C

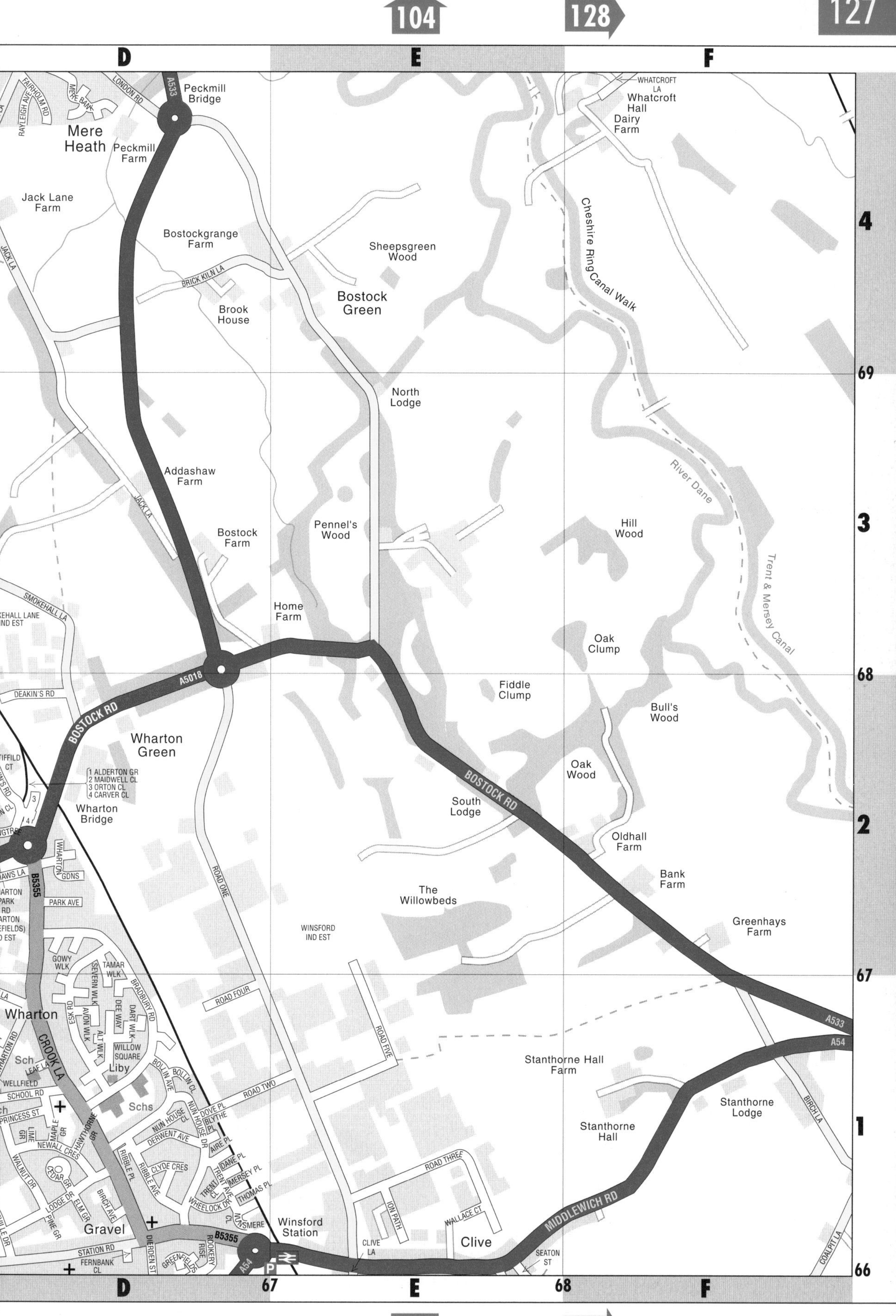
D
E
F
Peckmill Bridge
Mere Heath
Peckmill Farm
Jack Lane Farm
Bostockgrange Farm
BRICK KILN LA
Brook House
Sheepsgreen Wood
Bostock Green
Whatcroft Hall
Dairy Farm
WHATCROFT LA
Cheshire Ring Canal Walk
North Lodge
Addashaw Farm
Bostock Farm
Pennel's Wood
Home Farm
River Dane
Hill Wood
Trent & Mersey Canal
Oak Clump
Fiddle Clump
Bull's Wood
Oak Wood
South Lodge
Oldhall Farm
Bank Farm
Greenhays Farm
The Willowbeds
WINSFORD IND EST
Wharton Green
Wharton Bridge
1 ALDERTON GR
2 MAIDWELL CL
3 ORTON CL
4 CARVER CL
BOSTOCK RD
A5018
A533
A54
B5355
JACK LA
SMOKEHALL LA
DEAKIN'S RD
ROAD ONE
ROAD TWO
ROAD THREE
ROAD FOUR
ROAD FIVE
Wharton
CROOK LA
Liby
Schs
Sch
Gravel
Winsford Station
Clive
MIDDLEWICH RD
Stanthorne Hall Farm
Stanthorne Hall
Stanthorne Lodge
BIRCH LA
COALPIT LA
SEATON ST
CLIVE LA
WALLACE CT
ION PATH
DIERDEN ST
STATION RD
FERNBANK CL
PARK AVE
WHARTON GDNS
SCHOOL RD
PRINCESS ST
NEWALL CRES
HAWTHORNE GR
WALNUT DR
CEDAR GR
LODGE DR
ELM GR
PINE GR
BIRCH AVE
RIBBLE PL
RIBBLE AVE
CLYDE CRES
DERWENT AVE
TRENT AVE
MERSEY PL
THOMAS PL
WHEELOCK DR
DANE PL
AIRE PL
BLYTHE
DOVE PL
NUN HOUSE DR
NUN HOUSE CL
BOLLIN AVE
BOLLIN CL
BRADBURY RD
WILLOW SQUARE
DART WLK
DEE WAY
ALT WLK
AVON WLK
SEVERN WLK
TAMAR WLK
GOWY WLK
ROOKERY RISE
GREENFIELDS
LONDON RD
FAIRHOLM RD
RAYLEIGH AVE
MERE BANK
4
3
2
1
69
68
67
66
67
68

127
105

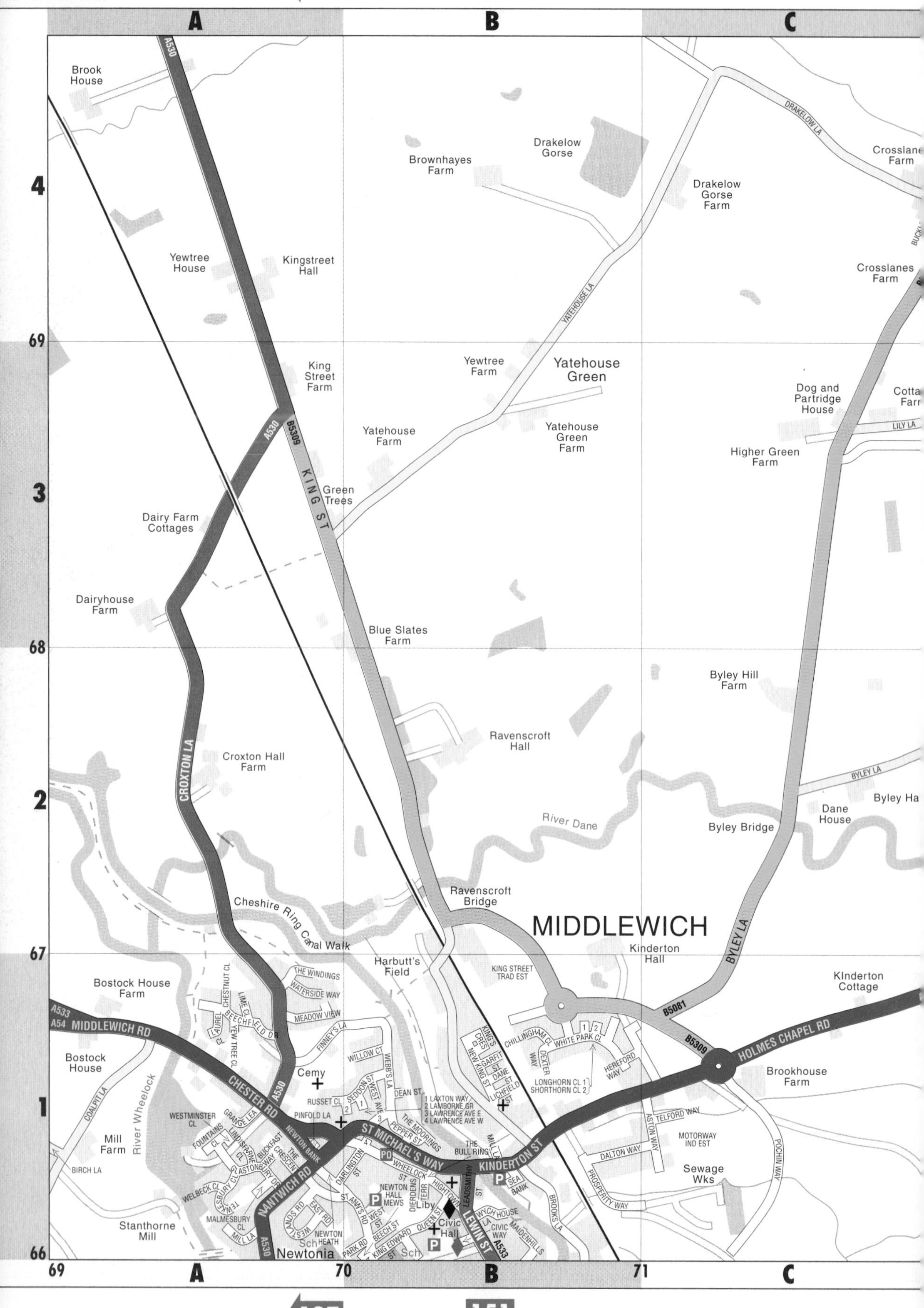
A
B
C
4
69
3
68
2
67
1
66
69
70
71
Brook House
Brownhayes Farm
Drakelow Gorse
Drakelow Gorse Farm
DRAKELOW LA
Crosslanes Farm
Yewtree House
Kingstreet Hall
YATEHOUSE LA
King Street Farm
Yewtree Farm
Yatehouse Green
Dog and Partridge House
Yatehouse Farm
Yatehouse Green Farm
LILY LA
Higher Green Farm
B5309
KING ST
A530
Green Trees
Dairy Farm Cottages
Dairyhouse Farm
Blue Slates Farm
Byley Hill Farm
Ravenscroft Hall
CROXTON LA
Croxton Hall Farm
BYLEY LA
Dane House
River Dane
Byley Bridge
Ravenscroft Bridge
Cheshire Ring Canal Walk
MIDDLEWICH
Kinderton Hall
Harbutt's Field
KING STREET TRAD EST
Bostock House Farm
Kinderton Cottage
B5081
A533
A54 MIDDLEWICH RD
HOLMES CHAPEL RD
Bostock House
Cemy
Brookhouse Farm
CHESTER RD
Mill Farm
River Wheelock
ST MICHAEL'S WAY
KINDERTON ST
NANTWICH RD
MOTORWAY IND EST
Sewage Wks
LEWIN ST
Civic Hall
Liby
Stanthorne Mill
Newtonia
Sch
BIRCH LA
COALPIT LA
WESTMINSTER CL
DEAN ST
1 LAXTON WAY
2 LAMBORNE GR
3 LAWRENCE AVE E
4 LAWRENCE AVE W
LONGHORN CL 1
SHORTHORN CL 2
ASTON WAY
TELFORD WAY
DALTON WAY
PROSPERITY WAY
POCHIN WAY
WHITE PARK CL
CHILLINGHAM CL
HEREFORD WAY
THE WINDINGS
WATERSIDE WAY
MEADOW VIEW
FINNEY'S LA
WILLOW CT
WEBB'S LA
RUSSET CL
SEDDON ST
PINFOLD LA
THE MOORINGS
PEPPER ST
WHEELOCK ST
THE BULL RING
DARLINGTON ST
NEWTON HALL MEWS
WYCH HOUSE LA
CIVIC WAY
MAIDENHILLS
BROOKS LA
SEA BANK
LEADSMITHY ST
QUEEN ST
KING EDWARD ST
NEWTON HEATH
MALMESBURY CL
MILL LA
WELBECK CL

127
151

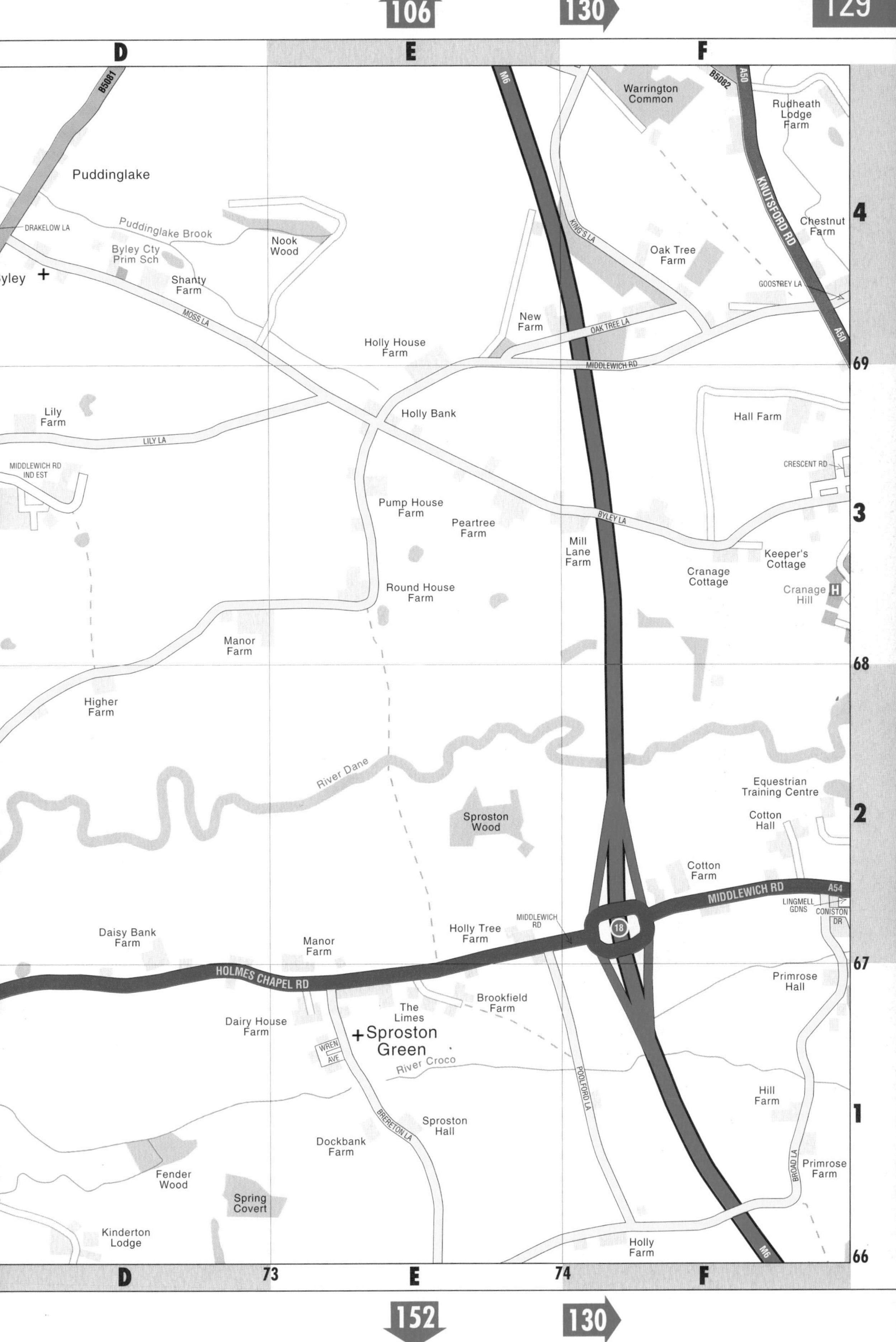
106
130
D
E
F
B5081
Puddinglake
DRAKELOW LA
Puddinglake Brook
Byley Cty
Prim Sch
Byley
Shanty
Farm
Nook
Wood
MOSS LA
Holly House
Farm
New
Farm
M6
Warrington
Common
B5082
A50
Rudheath
Lodge
Farm
KING'S LA
Oak Tree
Farm
KNUTSFORD RD
Chestnut
Farm
GOOSTREY LA
A50
OAK TREE LA
MIDDLEWICH RD
4
69
Lily
Farm
LILY LA
Holly Bank
Hall Farm
MIDDLEWICH RD
IND EST
CRESCENT RD
Pump House
Farm
Peartree
Farm
BYLEY LA
Mill
Lane
Farm
3
Keeper's
Cottage
Cranage
Cottage
Cranage
Hill
Round House
Farm
Manor
Farm
68
Higher
Farm
River Dane
Equestrian
Training Centre
Sproston
Wood
Cotton
Hall
2
Cotton
Farm
MIDDLEWICH RD
A54
LINGMELL
GDNS
CONISTON
DR
MIDDLEWICH
RD
18
Daisy Bank
Farm
Manor
Farm
Holly Tree
Farm
HOLMES CHAPEL RD
67
Primrose
Hall
Brookfield
Farm
The
Limes
Dairy House
Farm
Sproston
Green
WREN
AVE
River Croco
POOLFORD LA
Hill
Farm
1
BRERETON LA
Sproston
Hall
Dockbank
Farm
BROAD LA
Primrose
Farm
Fender
Wood
Spring
Covert
Kinderton
Lodge
Holly
Farm
M6
66
D
73
E
74
F
152
130

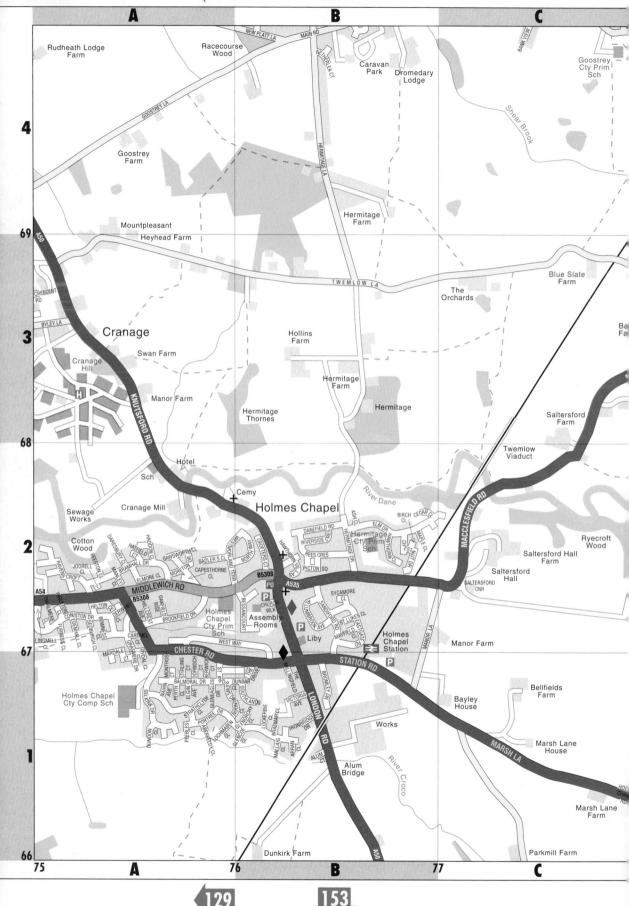

129
107

A   B   C

Rudheath Lodge
Farm

Racecourse
Wood

NEW PLATT LA

MAIN RD

NETHERLEA CT

HERMITAGE LA

Caravan
Park

Dromedary
Lodge

BANK VIEW

Goostrey
Cty Prim
Sch

4

GOOSTREY LA

Goostrey
Farm

Hermitage
Farm

Shear Brook

69

A50

Mountpleasant

Heyhead Farm

TWEMLOW LA

Blue Slate
Farm

The
Orchards

CRESCENT
RD

Cranage

Hollins
Farm

BYLEY LA

3

Cranage
Hill

Swan Farm

Hermitage
Farm

Hermitage

Saltersford
Farm

KNUTSFORD RD

H

Manor Farm

Hermitage
Thornes

Hermitage

68

Hotel

Twemlow
Viaduct

MACCLESFIELD RD

Sch

River Dane

Saltersford
Farm

Ryecroft
Wood

Cemy

Holmes Chapel

Sewage
Works

Cranage Mill

ASH CL

ELM DR

BIRCH
CL

CEDAR
CL

Saltersford Hall
Farm

Saltersford
Hall

2

Cotton
Wood

DANEFIELD RD

Riverside

HERMITAGE DR

Hermitage
Cty Prim
Sch

HAWTHORN CL

MAPLE CL

CHES

SMIT DR

DARESBURY CL

HATFIELD
CT

HADDON CL

GAWSWORTH CL

CRAW
NORTH

REES CRES

SALTERSFORD
CNR

JODRELL
CL

BREESTON CL

BRAMHALL DR

MANLEY CT

ELMORE CL

MORETON
CL

SADLER'S CL

CAPESTHORNE
CL

CROFTERS CT

PICTON SQ

SYCAMORE
CL

RAVENS
CROFT

B5308

ST LUKES CL

A54

MIDDLEWICH RD

A535

SANDIFORD RD

EASTGATE RD

HELTON
CL

CONISTON DR

DERWENT
CL

OAKFIELD
RISE

BROOKFIELD DR

PO

CHURCH
WLK

LIMBROOK AVE

MAYFIELD RD

THIRLMERE
CL

FURNESS CL

BOWNESS CL

Holmes
Chapel
Cty Prim
Sch

BESSANCOURT

Assembly
Rooms

P

Liby

LINGMELL
CL

MARDALE
CT

B5308

HILLCREST

GRASMERE DR

CARTMEL
CL

P

Holmes
Chapel
Station

67

CHESTER RD

STATION RD

P

Manor Farm

Holmes Chapel
Cty Comp Sch

MONTROSE
CT

STIRLING
CT

DORNOCH
DR

BERWICK
CL

ST

THE
DRIVE

DUNBAR
CL

VICTORIA
AVE

LONDON RD

BROMLEY DR

Bayley
House

Bellfields
Farm

NAIRN
AVE

PERTH
CT

ELGIN
AVE

CREWS
SOUTHLANDS

LOCKERBIE
CL

SELKIRK DR

BALMORAL DR

STRATHCLYDE
CL

PORTREE
DR

GLEDEAGLES
DR

GLENDOE
DR

BRAEMAR
CL

IRONBRIDGE DR

Works

Marsh Lane
House

1

DUNOON
CT

PEEBLES
CL

ABERDEEN CL

LOCHMABEN
CL

GLENCOE
DR

MALLAIG
CL

ARRAN
CL

ALUM
CT

Alum
Bridge

River Croco

MARSH LA

Marsh Lane
Farm

66

Dunkirk Farm

A50

Parkmill Farm

75   A   76   B   77   C

129
153

108
132

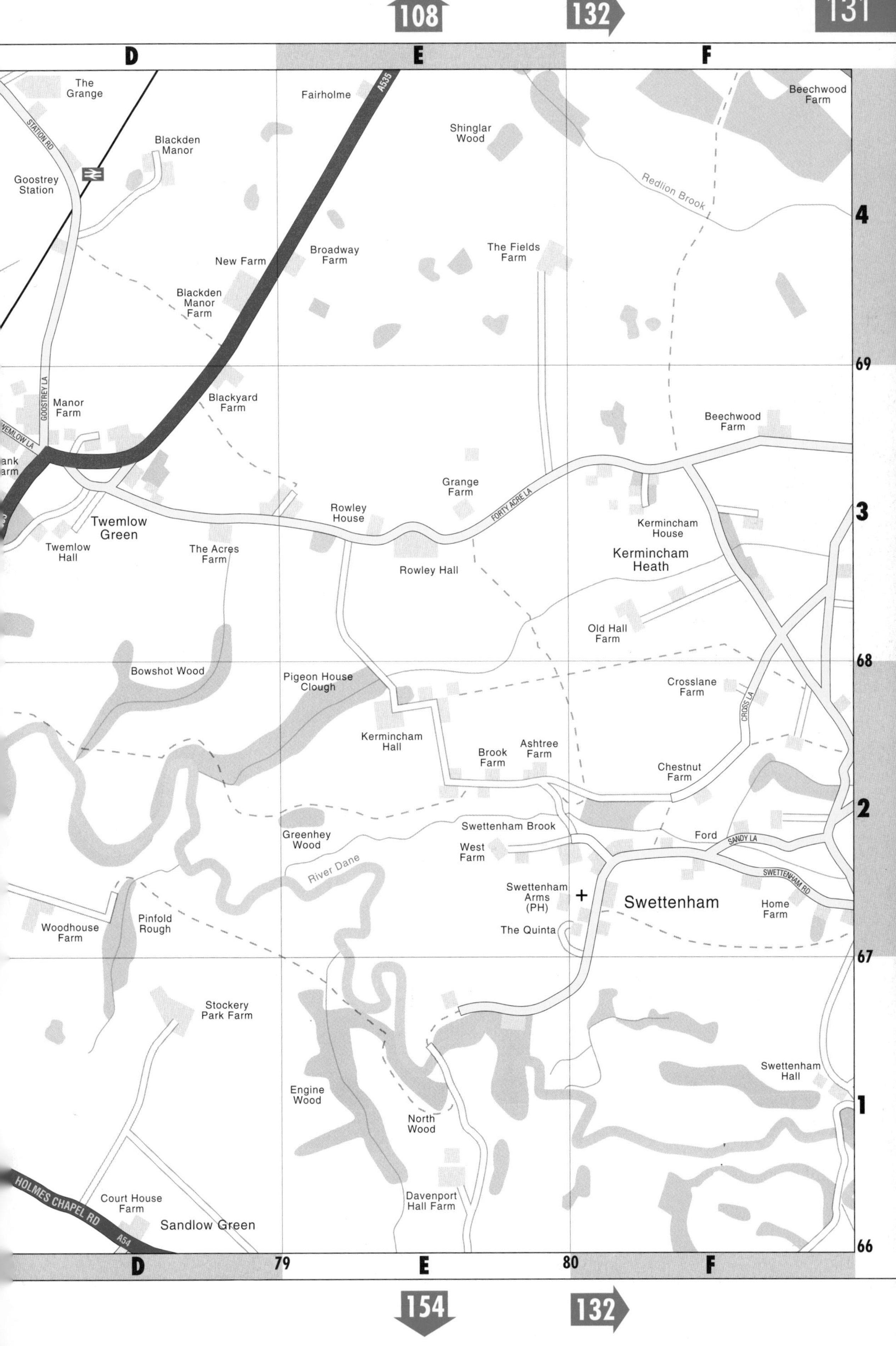
D
E
F
The Grange
Fairholme
A535
Beechwood Farm
Shinglar Wood
STATION RD
Blackden Manor
Goostrey Station
Redlion Brook
4
Broadway Farm
The Fields Farm
New Farm
Blackden Manor Farm
69
GOOSTREY LA
Manor Farm
Blackyard Farm
Beechwood Farm
TWEMLOW LA
Grange Farm
FORTY ACRE LA
3
Rowley House
Twemlow Green
Kermincham House
Twemlow Hall
The Acres Farm
Rowley Hall
Kermincham Heath
Old Hall Farm
68
Bowshot Wood
Pigeon House Clough
Crosslane Farm
CROSS LA
Kermincham Hall
Ashtree Farm
Brook Farm
Chestnut Farm
2
Swettenham Brook
Greenhey Wood
Ford
SANDY LA
West Farm
River Dane
SWETTENHAM RD
Swettenham Arms (PH)
Swettenham
Home Farm
Woodhouse Farm
Pinfold Rough
The Quinta
67
Stockery Park Farm
Swettenham Hall
Engine Wood
1
North Wood
HOLMES CHAPEL RD
Court House Farm
Davenport Hall Farm
A54
Sandlow Green
66
D
79
E
80
F

154
132

131
109

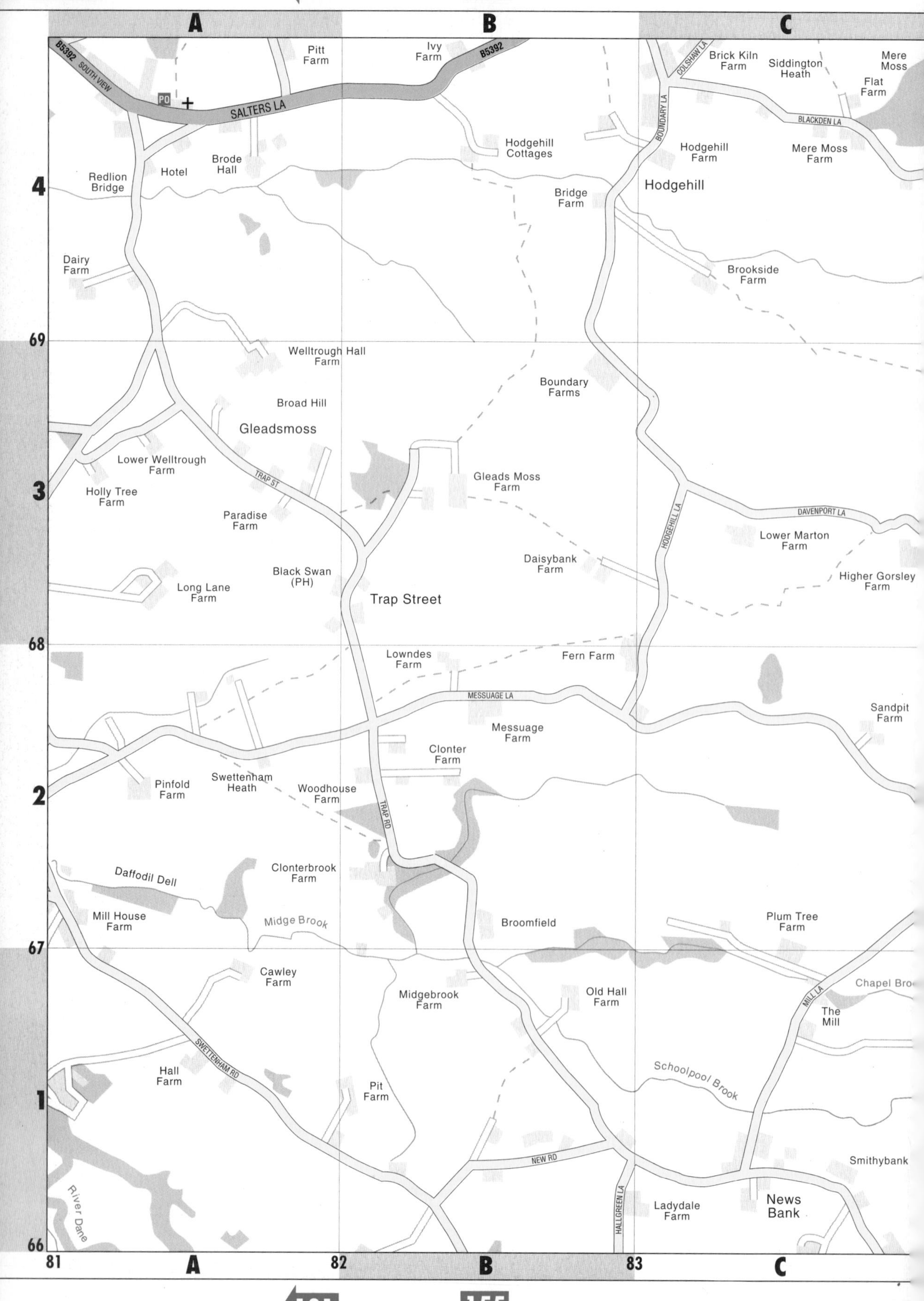
A
B
C
B5392
SOUTH VIEW
SALTERS LA
PO
Pitt Farm
Ivy Farm
Brick Kiln Farm
Siddington Heath
Mere Moss
Flat Farm
COLSHAW LA
BLACKDEN LA
BOUNDARY LA
Hodgehill Cottages
Hodgehill Farm
Mere Moss Farm
Hodgehill
Redlion Bridge
Hotel
Brode Hall
Bridge Farm
Dairy Farm
Brookside Farm
Welltrough Hall Farm
Broad Hill
Boundary Farms
Gleadsmoss
Lower Welltrough Farm
Holly Tree Farm
TRAP ST
Gleads Moss Farm
Paradise Farm
HODGEHILL LA
DAVENPORT LA
Lower Marton Farm
Daisybank Farm
Higher Gorsley Farm
Black Swan (PH)
Long Lane Farm
Trap Street
Lowndes Farm
Fern Farm
MESSUAGE LA
Sandpit Farm
Messuage Farm
Clonter Farm
Pinfold Farm
Swettenham Heath
Woodhouse Farm
TRAP RD
Daffodil Dell
Clonterbrook Farm
Mill House Farm
Midge Brook
Broomfield
Plum Tree Farm
Cawley Farm
Midgebrook Farm
Old Hall Farm
MILL LA
Chapel Bro
The Mill
SWETTENHAM RD
Schoolpool Brook
Hall Farm
Pit Farm
NEW RD
Smithybank
River Dane
HALLGREEN LA
Ladydale Farm
News Bank
4
69
3
68
2
67
1
66
81
82
83

131
155

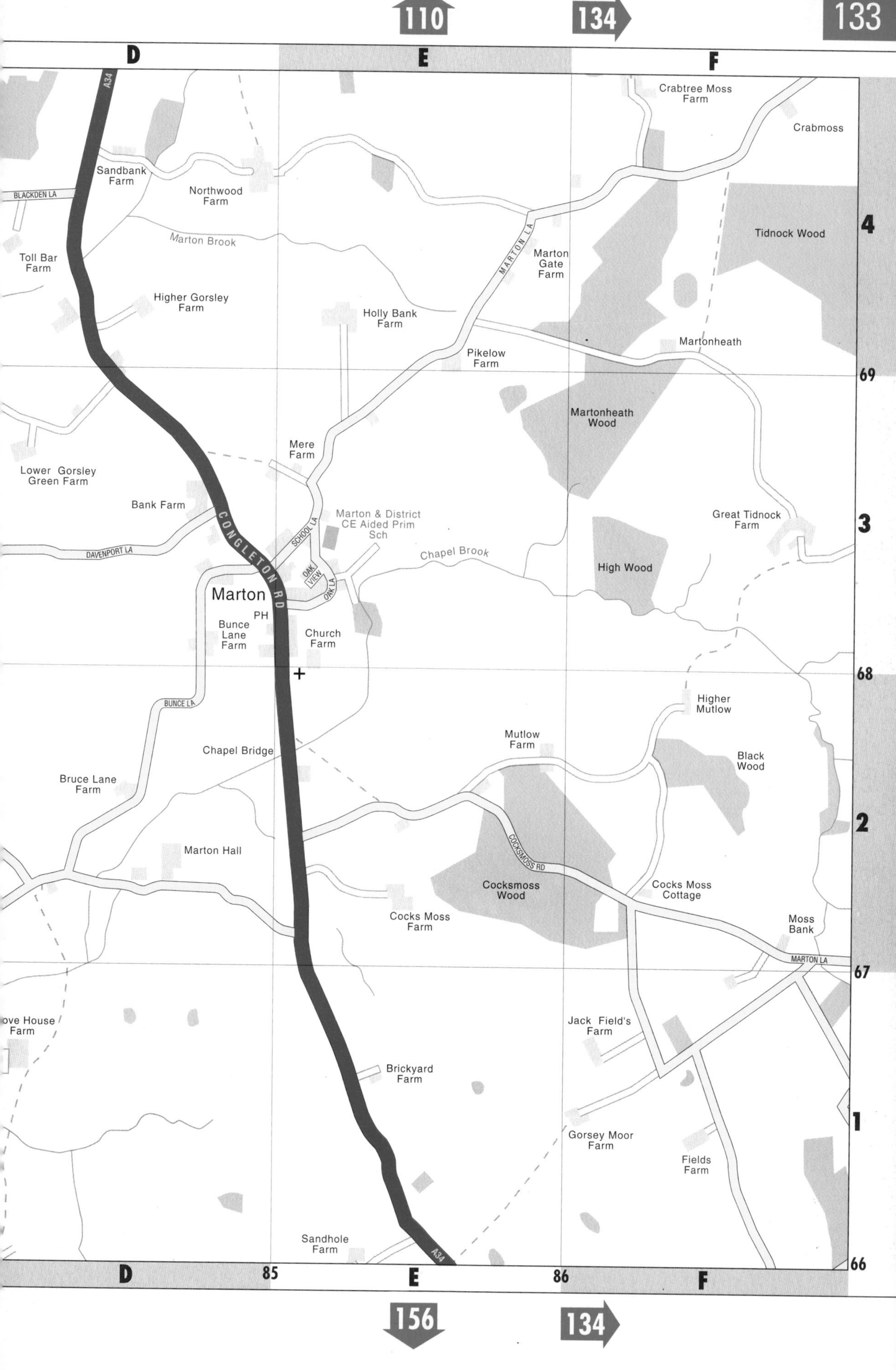

D   E   F

Crabtree Moss Farm

Crabmoss

BLACKDEN LA

Sandbank Farm

Northwood Farm

Marton Brook

Tidnock Wood

4

Toll Bar Farm

MARTON LA

Marton Gate Farm

Higher Gorsley Farm

Holly Bank Farm

Martonheath

Pikelow Farm

69

Mere Farm

Martonheath Wood

Lower Gorsley Green Farm

Bank Farm

Marton & District CE Aided Prim Sch

Chapel Brook

Great Tidnock Farm

3

DAVENPORT LA

SCHOOL LA

High Wood

CONGLETON RD

OAK VIEW

OAK LA

Marton

PH

Bunce Lane Farm

Church Farm

+

68

Higher Mutlow

BUNCE LA

Chapel Bridge

Mutlow Farm

Black Wood

Bruce Lane Farm

Marton Hall

COCKSMOSS RD

2

Cocksmoss Wood

Cocks Moss Cottage

Moss Bank

Cocks Moss Farm

MARTON LA

67

ove House Farm

Jack Field's Farm

Brickyard Farm

Gorsey Moor Farm

1

Fields Farm

Sandhole Farm

A34

66

D   85   E   86   F

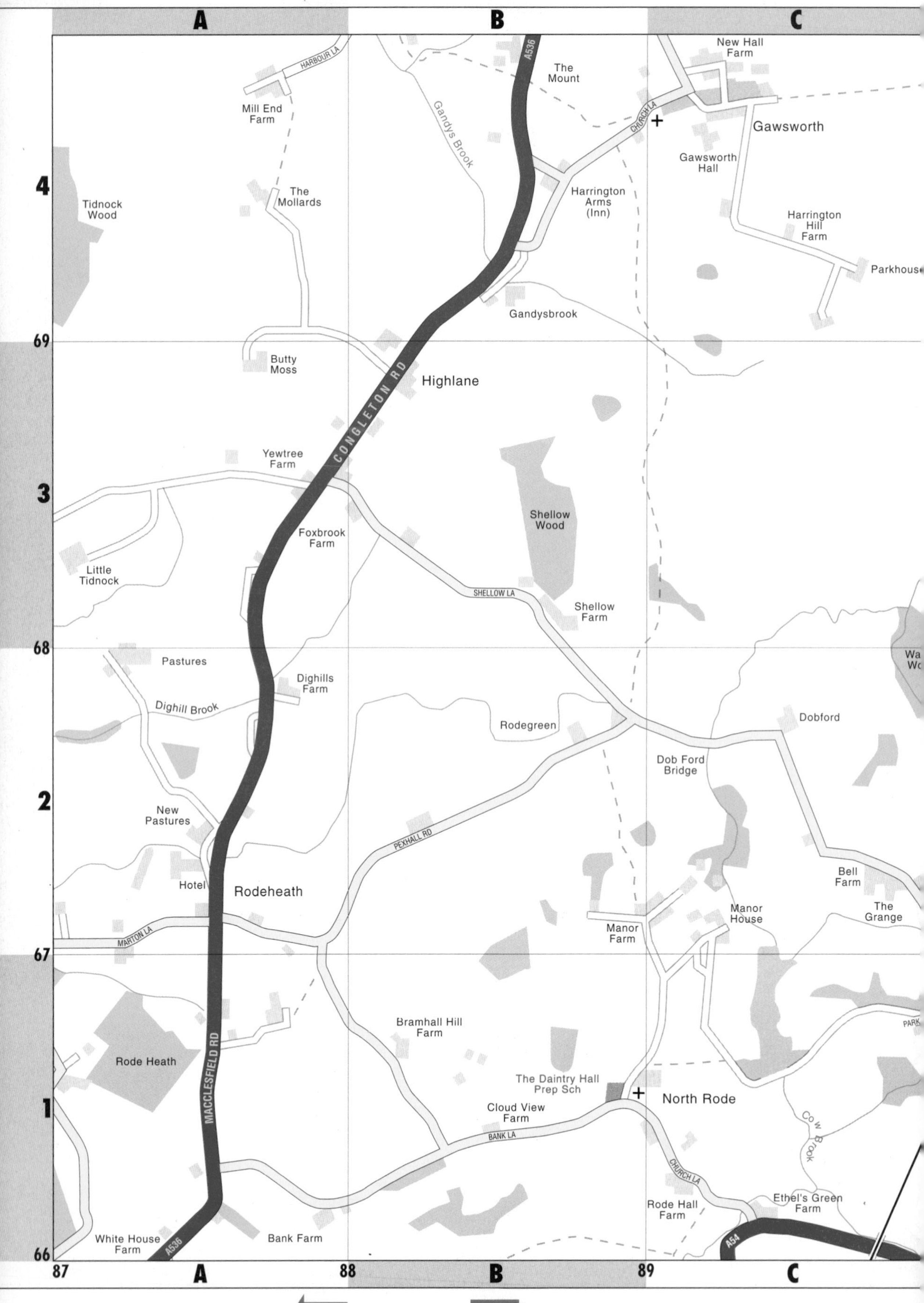

A

B

C

4

Tidnock
Wood

Mill End
Farm

HARBOUR LA

The
Mollards

Gandys Brook

The
Mount

A536

Harrington
Arms
(Inn)

CHURCH LA

New Hall
Farm

✝

Gawsworth

Gawsworth
Hall

Harrington
Hill
Farm

Parkhouse

69

Butty
Moss

CONGLETON RD

Gandysbrook

Highlane

3

Yewtree
Farm

Little
Tidnock

Foxbrook
Farm

SHELLOW LA

Shellow
Wood

Shellow
Farm

Wa
Wo

68

Pastures

Dighill Brook

Dighills
Farm

Rodegreen

Dobford

Dob Ford
Bridge

2

New
Pastures

Hotel

Rodeheath

MARTON LA

PEXHALL RD

Manor
Farm

Manor
House

Bell
Farm

The
Grange

67

MACCLESFIELD RD

Bramhall Hill
Farm

The Daintry Hall
Prep Sch

✝

North Rode

PARK

1

Rode Heath

Cloud View
Farm

BANK LA

Co w Brook

Ethel's Green
Farm

66

White House
Farm

A536

Bank Farm

Rode Hall
Farm

CHURCH LA

A54

87

A

88

B

89

C

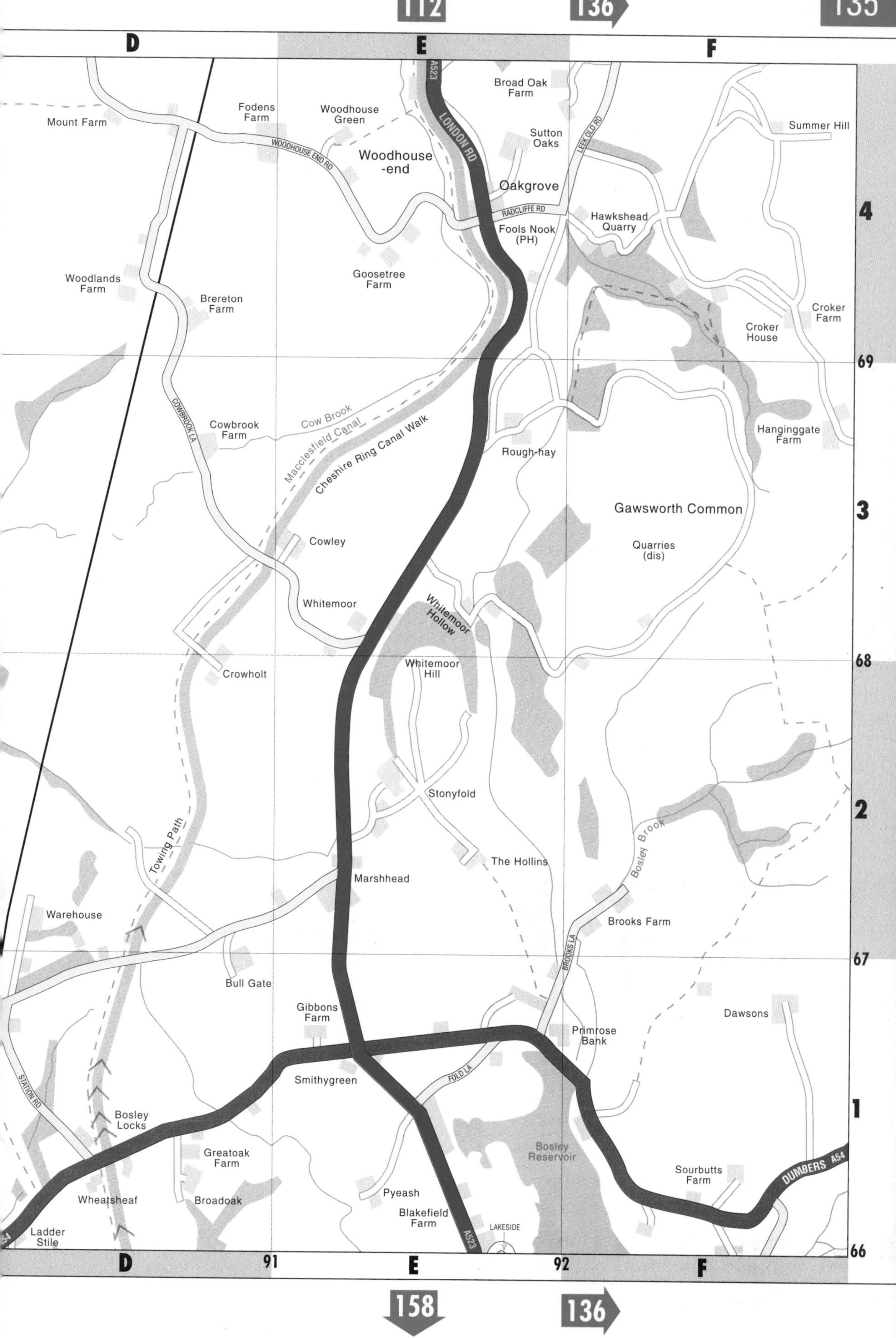

D
E
F

4

69

3

68

2

67

1

66

Mount Farm

Fodens Farm

Woodhouse Green

Broad Oak Farm

Summer Hill

Woodhouse End Rd

LONDON RD

A523

LEEK OLD RD

Sutton Oaks

Woodhouse -end

Oakgrove

RADCLIFFE RD

Hawkshead Quarry

Fools Nook (PH)

Croker House

Croker Farm

Woodlands Farm

Brereton Farm

Goosetree Farm

Cowbrook Farm

COWBROOK LA

Cow Brook

Macclesfield Canal

Cheshire Ring Canal Walk

Rough-hay

Hanginggate Farm

Gawsworth Common

Cowley

Quarries (dis)

Whitemoor

Whitemoor Hollow

Crowholt

Whitemoor Hill

Towing Path

Stonyfold

The Hollins

Bosley Brook

Marshhead

Warehouse

Brooks Farm

BROOKS LA

Bull Gate

Dawsons

Gibbons Farm

Primrose Bank

STATION RD

Smithygreen

FOLD LA

Bosley Locks

Greatoak Farm

Bosley Reservoir

Sourbutts Farm

DUMBERS A54

Wheatsheaf

Broadoak

Pyeash

Blakefield Farm

A523

LAKESIDE

A54

Ladder Stile

D
91
E
92
F

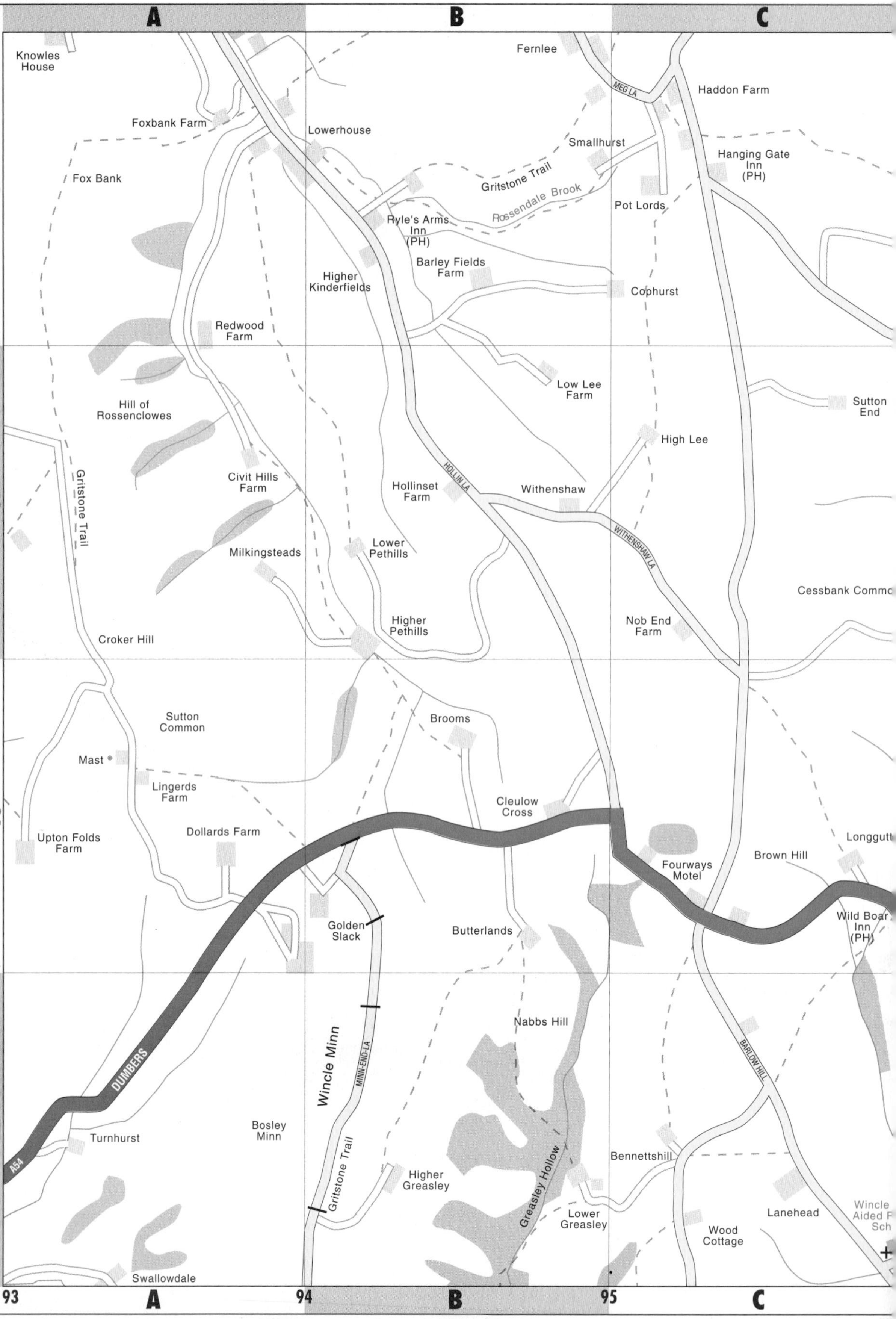

A   B   C

Knowles House

Foxbank Farm

Fox Bank

Lowerhouse

Fernlee

MEG LA

Haddon Farm

Smallhurst

Hanging Gate Inn (PH)

Gritstone Trail

Rossendale Brook

Pot Lords

4

Ryle's Arms Inn (PH)

Barley Fields Farm

Cophurst

Higher Kinderfields

Redwood Farm

Low Lee Farm

69

Sutton End

Hill of Rossenclowes

High Lee

Civit Hills Farm

HOLLIN LA

Hollinset Farm

Withenshaw

WITHENSHAW LA

3

Gritstone Trail

Milkingsteads

Lower Pethills

Cessbank Commo

Croker Hill

Higher Pethills

Nob End Farm

68

Sutton Common

Brooms

Mast

Lingerds Farm

Cleulow Cross

Longgutt

2

Upton Folds Farm

Dollards Farm

Fourways Motel

Brown Hill

Golden Slack

Butterlands

Wild Boar Inn (PH)

67

Nabbs Hill

BARLOW HILL

DUMBERS

Wincle Minn

MINN-END-LA

Greasley Hollow

Bennettshill

Bosley Minn

Wincle Aided P Sch

1

Turnhurst

A54

Gritstone Trail

Higher Greasley

Lower Greasley

Lanehead

Wood Cottage

66

Swallowdale

93   A   94   B   95   C

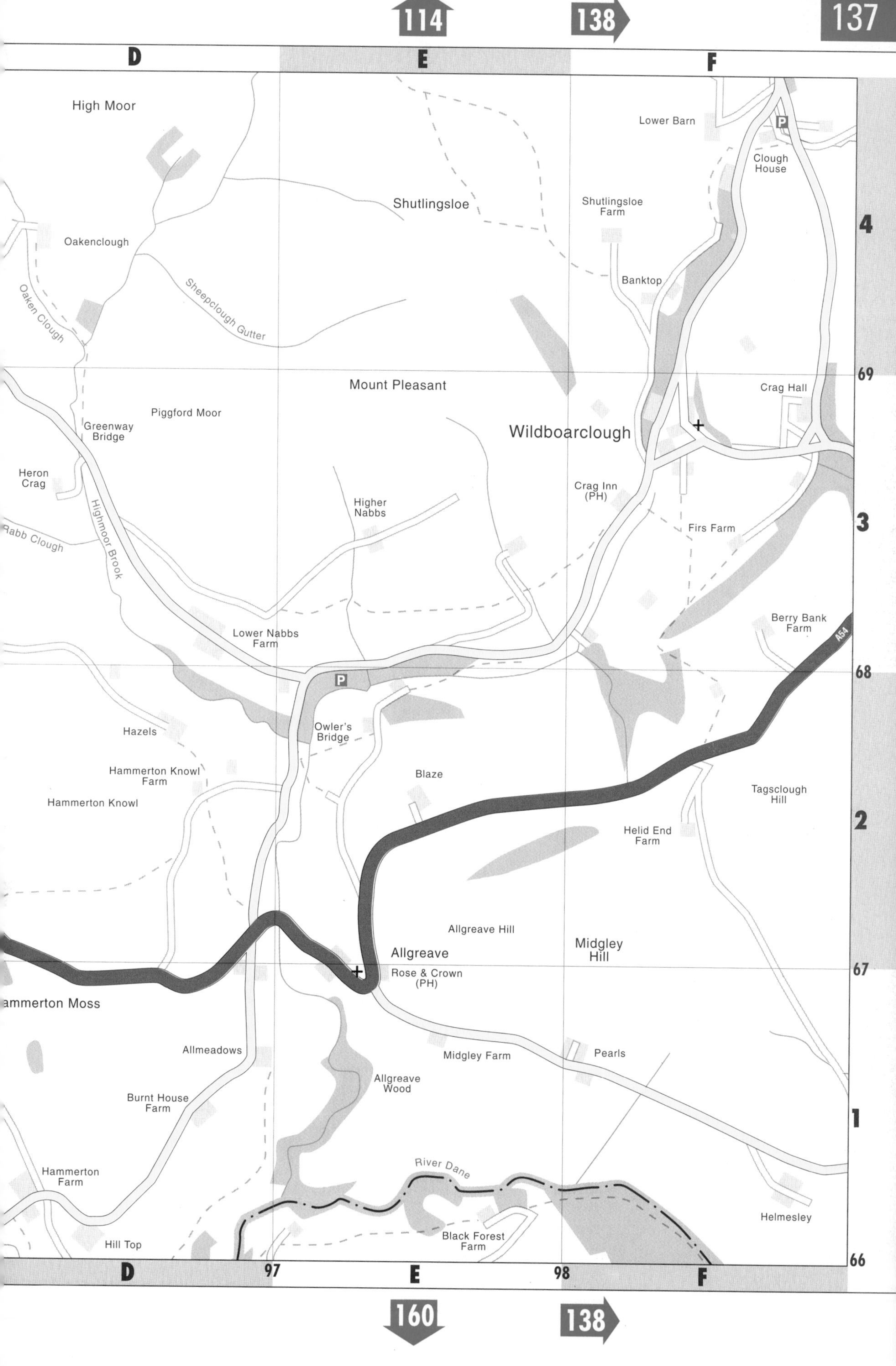

D   E   F

High Moor

Lower Barn

Clough House

Shutlingsloe

Shutlingsloe Farm

Oakenclough

P

Oaken Clough

Banktop

4

Sheepclough Gutter

Mount Pleasant

Crag Hall

69

Piggford Moor

Greenway Bridge

Wildboarclough

Heron Crag

Higher Nabbs

Crag Inn (PH)

Firs Farm

3

Rabb Clough

Highmoor Brook

Berry Bank Farm

Lower Nabbs Farm

454

P

68

Owler's Bridge

Hazels

Blaze

Tagsclough Hill

Hammerton Knowl Farm

Helid End Farm

2

Hammerton Knowl

Allgreave Hill

Midgley Hill

Allgreave

67

Hammerton Moss

Rose & Crown (PH)

Allmeadows

Midgley Farm

Pearls

Allgreave Wood

Burnt House Farm

1

Hammerton Farm

River Dane

Helmesley

Hill Top

Black Forest Farm

66

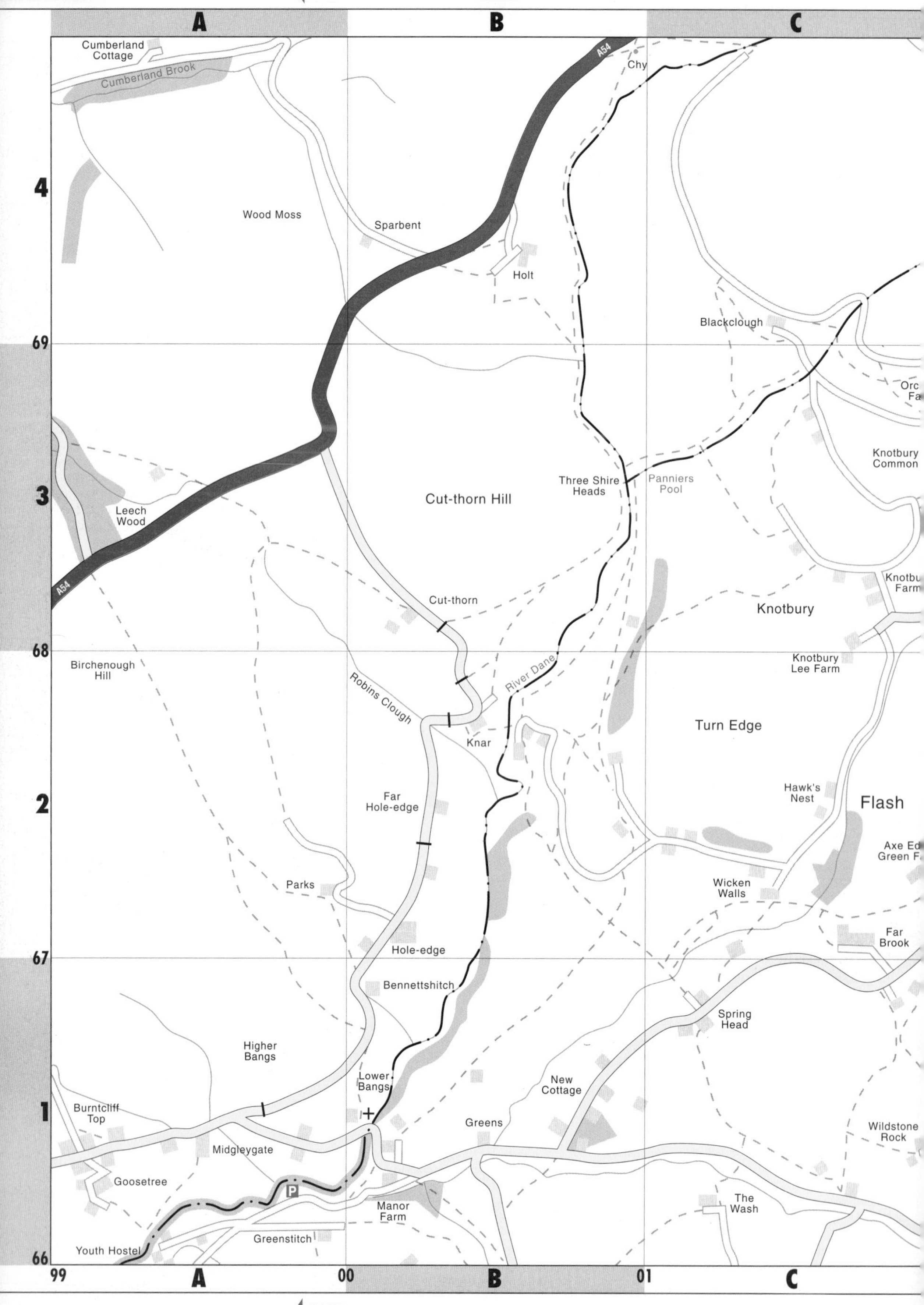

A

B

C

Cumberland
Cottage

Cumberland Brook

Wood Moss

Sparbent

A54

Chy

Holt

Blackclough

Orc
Fa

4

Knotbury
Common

69

Leech
Wood

Cut-thorn Hill

Three Shire
Heads

Panniers
Pool

Knotbu
Farm

A54

Cut-thorn

Knotbury

3

Birchenough
Hill

Robins Clough

Knar

River Dane

Knotbury
Lee Farm

68

Turn Edge

Far
Hole-edge

Hawk's
Nest

Flash

2

Parks

Wicken
Walls

Axe Ed
Green F

Hole-edge

Far
Brook

67

Bennettshitch

Spring
Head

Higher
Bangs

Lower
Bangs

New
Cottage

Wildstone
Rock

1

Burntcliff
Top

Greens

Midgleygate

P

Goosetree

Manor
Farm

The
Wash

Youth Hostel

Greenstitch

66

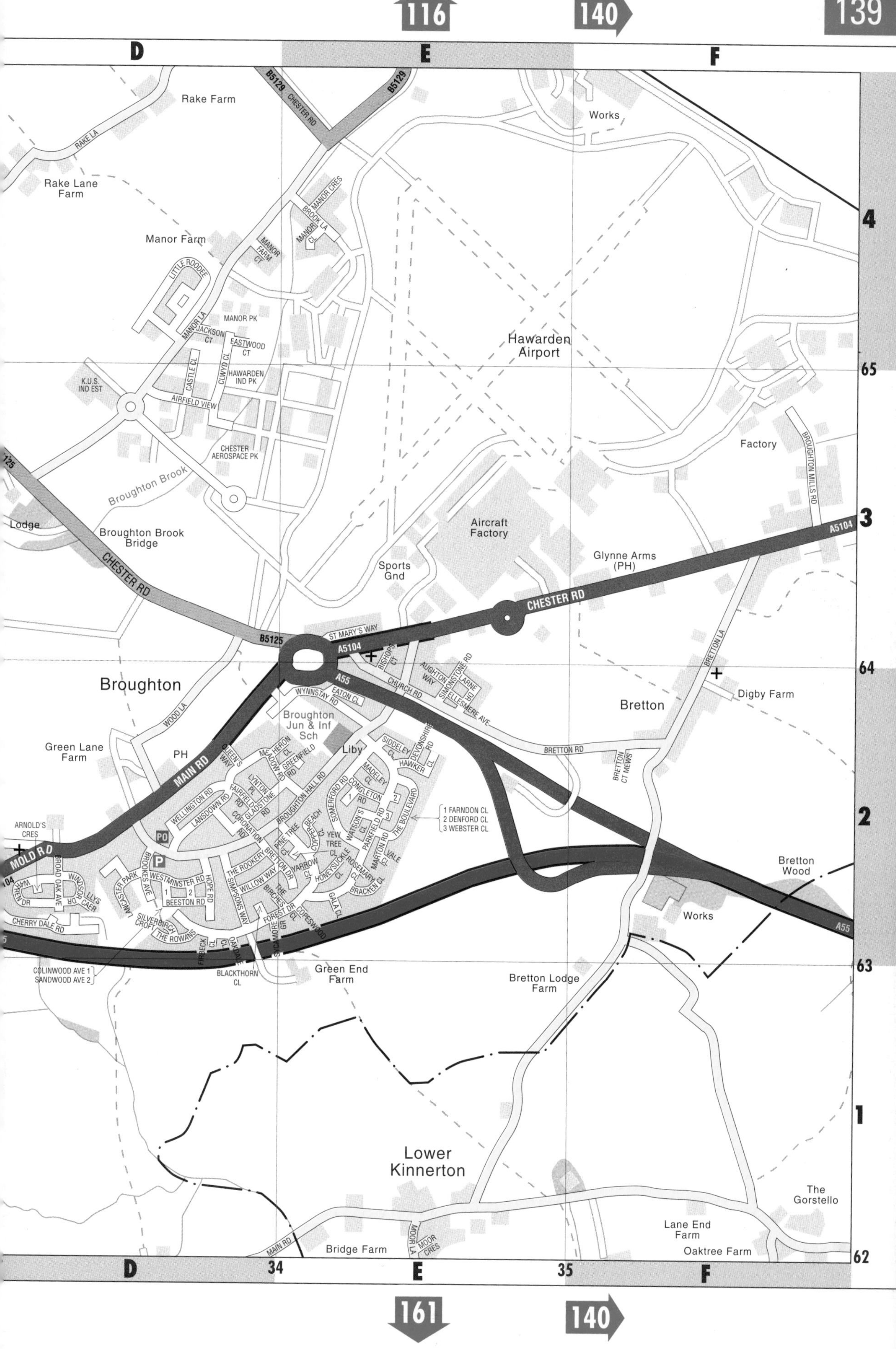
D
E
F
Rake Farm
Rake Lane Farm
Manor Farm
Works
Hawarden Airport
K.U.S. IND EST
CHESTER AEROSPACE PK
Broughton Brook
Lodge
Broughton Brook Bridge
CHESTER RD
Aircraft Factory
Sports Gnd
Factory
Glynne Arms (PH)
Broughton
Green Lane Farm
PH
Broughton Jun & Inf Sch
Liby
Bretton
Digby Farm
Bretton Wood
Works
Green End Farm
Bretton Lodge Farm
Lower Kinnerton
The Gorstello
Lane End Farm
Oaktree Farm
Bridge Farm
1 FARNDON CL
2 DENFORD CL
3 WEBSTER CL
COLINWOOD AVE 1
SANDWOOD AVE 2
A5104
A55
B5125
B5129
4
65
3
64
2
63
1
62
34
35

A   B   C

B5129

Higher Ferry House
Mill Farm
Top Farm
Border House

NORTH ST
EWART ST

River Dee (Afon Dyfrdwy)

Golf Course

MONTROSE CT 1
CHURCHSIDE WLK 2
GLEN ABER DR 3
DONNINGTON WAY 4

4

SALTNEY FERRY RD

BRADSHAW AVE
MAINWARING DR
KYNASTON AVE
BELMONT DR
MAYDOR AVE
ST DAVID'S TERR
DELTA CT
LEYLAND DR
B5129

St David's High Sch
Saltney Ferry Cty Prim Sch

BRYMAU FOUR ESTATE

RIVER LA
KELLAN CT
BRYMAU TWO ESTATE
BRYMAU ONE ESTATE

CENTRAL TRADING ESTATE
BRIDGE ST

MARLEY WAY
A5104
CHESTER ST
HIGH ST
HAINMAKERS ROW

CHESTER RD

Liby
Saltney
Sch   Sch

65

Well House Farm

THE ORCHARDS
MOORCROFT MEWS
SALISBURY AVE
DEVA AVE
THE GR
LIME GR
LINDEN GR
ENGLEFIELD AVE
ALVONLEA RD
CARLTON AVE
HOWARD RD
NORTON AVE
VYRNWY RD
CELYN CRES
CONWAY CL
PADARN
TEG ALED WAY
AWM

George Kenyon Mews
ASHLEIGH
PARK AVE
BELGRAVE AVE
LARCH AVE
ISHELLA
REDWOOD CL
MOUNTAIN VIEW
LABURNUM GR
EATON
IRVING'S CRES
MOSS LGR

Henry Wood CT
Wks
LC

BEAUMONT CL
BARTWOOD DR
GUILDFORD RD 1
DOWNSFIELD RD 2
SUNBURY CRES 3
ABINGDON CRES 4

WREXIN
TELFORD WAY
SHREWSBURY WAY
ST MARKS CL
NEWBURY
HENLEY
MERCER WAY
WILLOW
WITTON
OXFORD RD
ELM RD
OAK RD
POPLAR RD

Sch

3

A5104

Hope's Place

Sandy Lane Farm

SANDY LA
VICTORIA RD
MAPLE GR
BEECHWOOD RD
HAMERTON
TATTON CL
CAPELAND CL
SHERINGHAM CL
SHANNON CL
THURSTON CL
HALKETT CL
STANLEY CL
STANLEY PARK DR
STANLEY PARK CT
TOFT CL
COURTNEY RD
ELMER DR
AVONLEA CL

Lache
COLCHESTER SQ
SYCAMORE CL
DORCHESTER
WINCHESTER
TELFORD
BIRCH RD
DANE FIELD CRES
CLOVELLY
CLOVER PL
KINGS
LARKSPUR

Greenlane Crossing
CIRCULAR DR

LACHE HALL CRES
BARON WAY
FORGE WAY
SMITHY
HAYMAKERS CL
GREEN LA
RAMSDELL CT
GREENACRE RD

64

Bretton Hall

Balderton Brook

The Lache Eyes

2

A55
Bretton Wood

63

Decoy Farm

Common Farm

Balderton

Balderton Lodge

Gorstella

LACHE LA

A55

ROUGHLYN CRES

Caravan Park
Two Mills House

Roughhill

Balderton Dr

LC

1

62

36   A   37   B   38   C

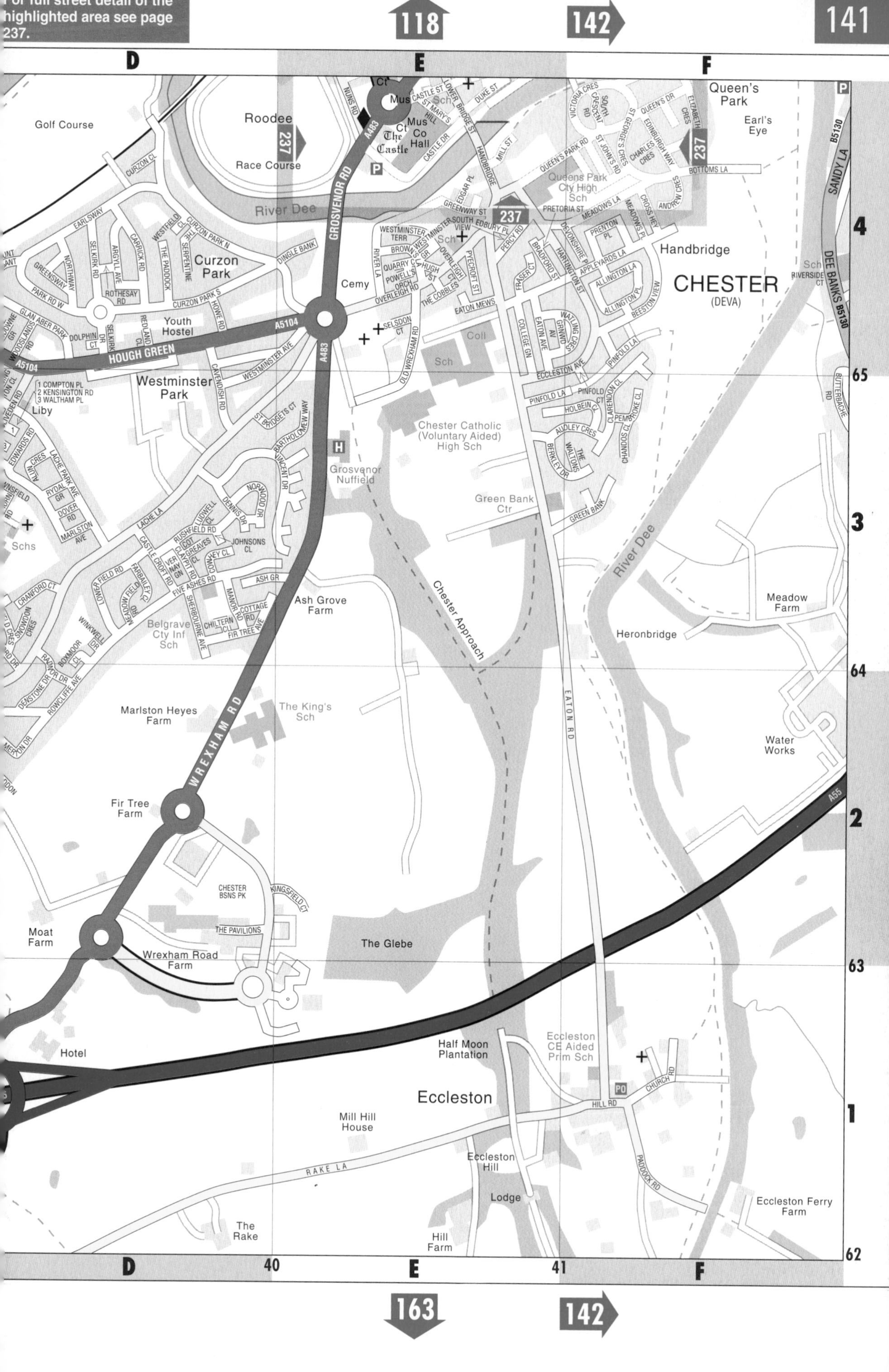

141
119

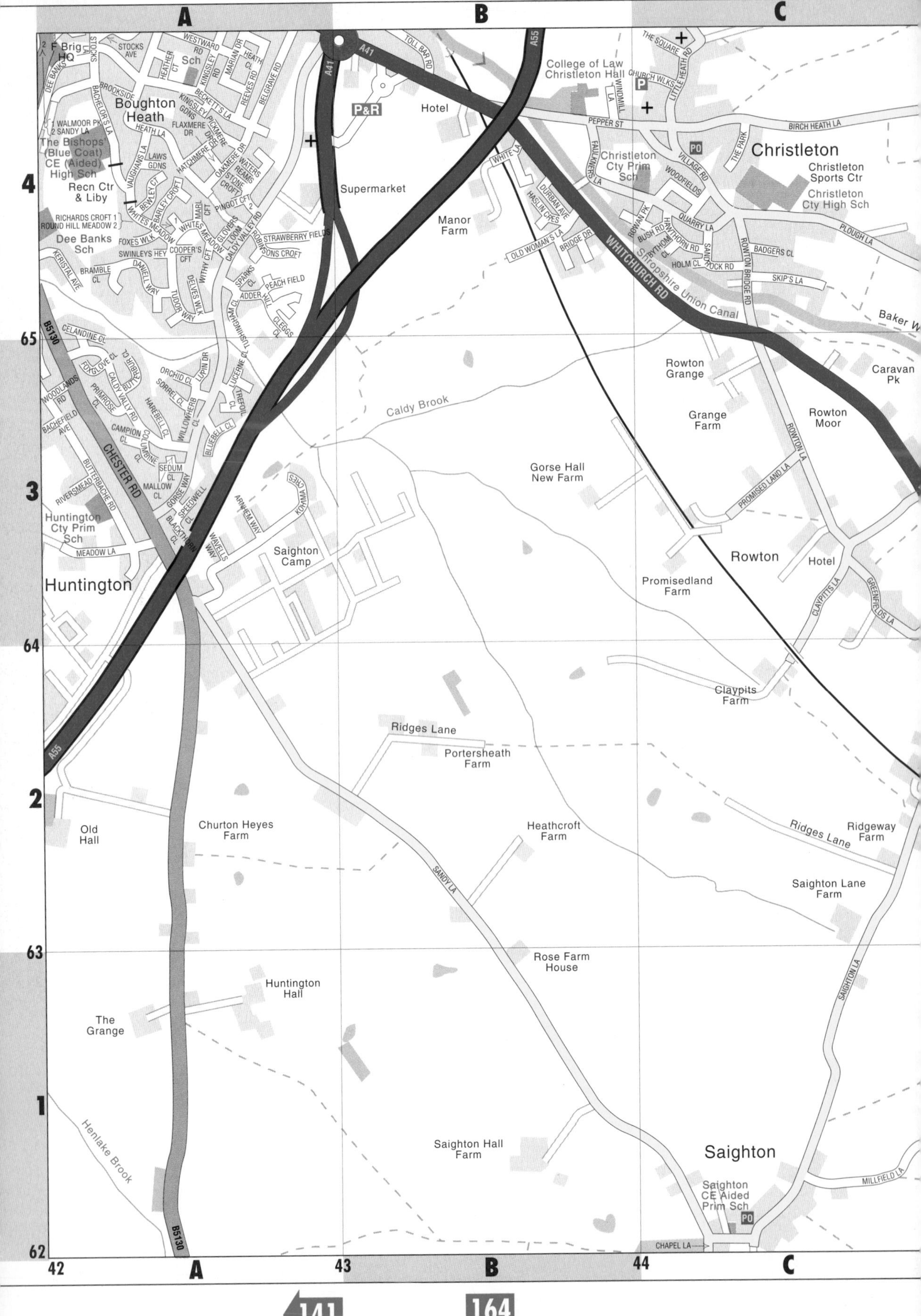
A
B
C
Boughton Heath
Christleton
Huntington
Rowton
Saighton
College of Law Christleton Hall
Hotel
Supermarket
Manor Farm
Christleton Cty Prim Sch
Christleton Sports Ctr
Christleton Cty High Sch
The Bishops' (Blue Coat) CE (Aided) High Sch
Recn Ctr & Liby
Dee Banks Sch
F Brig HQ
Sch
WHITCHURCH RD
Shropshire Union Canal
CHESTER RD
Caldy Brook
Rowton Grange
Grange Farm
Rowton Moor
Caravan Pk
Gorse Hall New Farm
Promisedland Farm
Saighton Camp
Huntington Cty Prim Sch
Claypits Farm
Ridges Lane
Portersheath Farm
Old Hall
Churton Heyes Farm
Heathcroft Farm
Ridgeway Farm
Saighton Lane Farm
Rose Farm House
Huntington Hall
The Grange
Saighton Hall Farm
Saighton CE Aided Prim Sch
Henlake Brook
SANDY LA
SAIGHTON LA
ROWTON LA
MILLFIELD LA
CHAPEL LA
PEPPER ST
BIRCH HEATH LA
PLOUGH LA
BADGERS CL
SKIP'S LA
Baker W
42
43
44
65
64
63
62
4
3
2
1

141
164

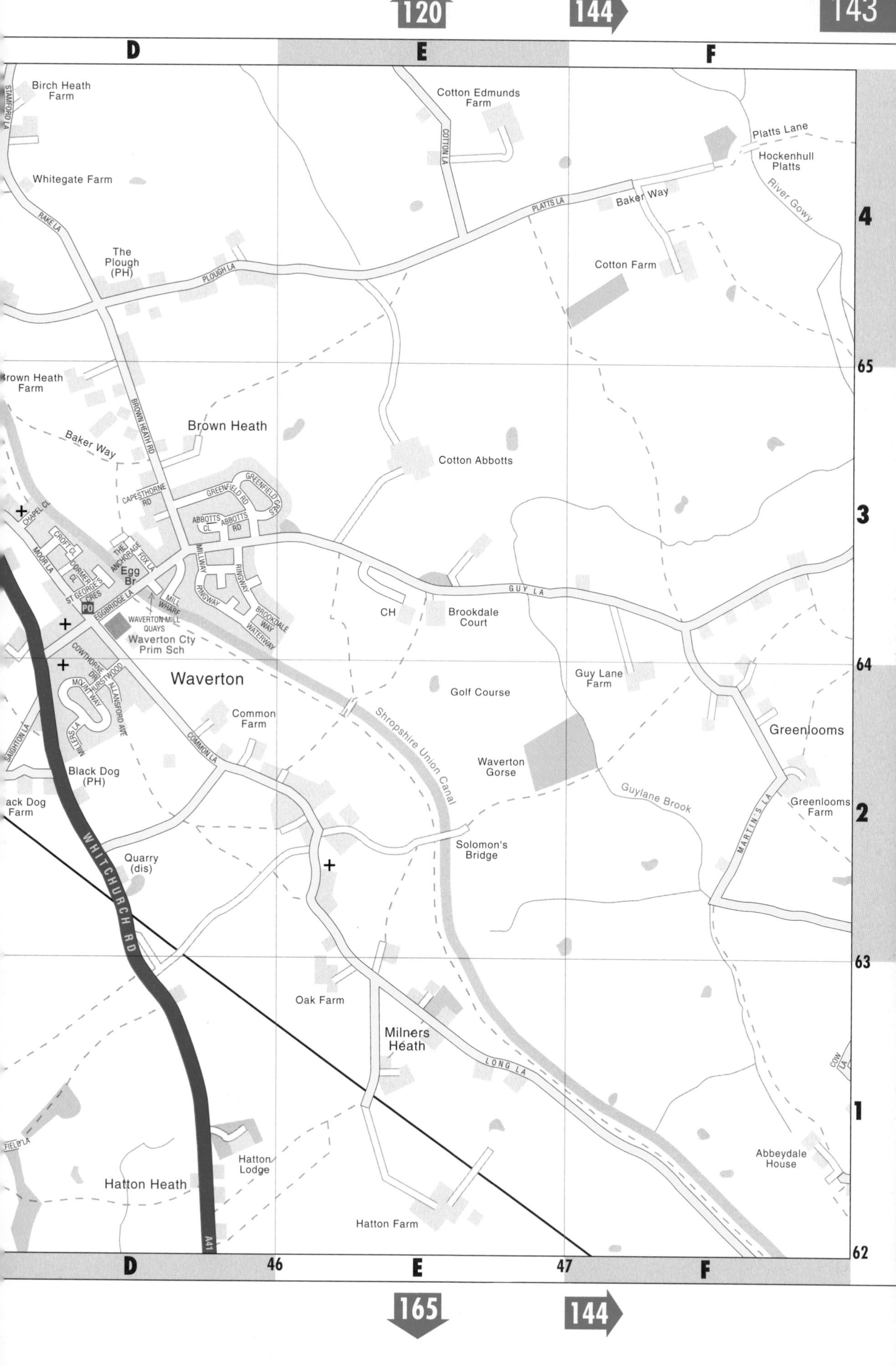

120
144
D
E
F
Birch Heath Farm
Cotton Edmunds Farm
Platts Lane
Hockenhull Platts
River Gowy
Whitegate Farm
PLATTS LA
Baker Way
COTTON LA
RAKE LA
The Plough (PH)
PLOUGH LA
Cotton Farm
Brown Heath Farm
Brown Heath
BROWN HEATH RD
Baker Way
Cotton Abbotts
CAPESTHORNE RD
GREENFIELD RD
GREENFIELD CRES
ABBOTTS CL
ABBOTTS RD
CHAPEL CL
CROFT CL
MOOR LA
DORMER CL
ST GEORGE'S CRES
THE ANCHORAGE
FOX LA
Egg Br
MILLWAY
RINGWAY
MILL WHARF
BROOKDALE WAY
WATERWAY
EGGBRIDGE LA
PO
WAVERTON MILL QUAYS
Waverton Cty Prim Sch
CH
Brookdale Court
GUY LA
Guy Lane Farm
Waverton
COWTHORNE DR
HURSTWOOD
MOUNT WAY
ALLANSFORD AVE
MILLERS LA
SAIGHTON LA
Common Farm
COMMON LA
Golf Course
Shropshire Union Canal
Greenlooms
Waverton Gorse
Guylane Brook
MARTIN'S LA
Greenlooms Farm
Black Dog (PH)
Black Dog Farm
WHITCHURCH RD
Quarry (dis)
Solomon's Bridge
Oak Farm
Milners Heath
LONG LA
COW LA
FIELD LA
Hatton Lodge
Hatton Heath
Abbeydale House
Hatton Farm
A41
4
65
3
64
2
63
1
62
46
47
165
144

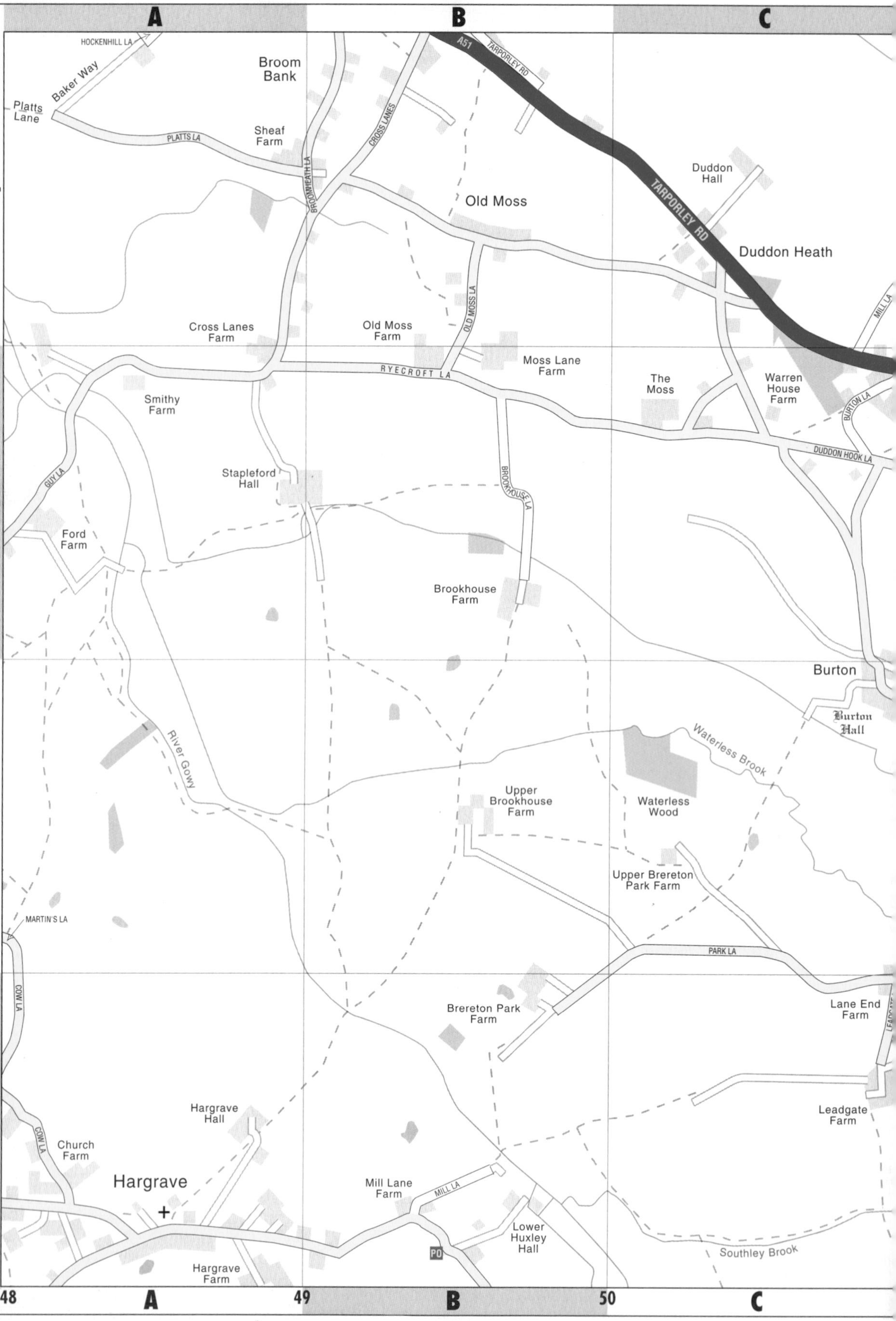

A   B   C

HOCKENHILL LA

Baker Way

Broom Bank

Platts Lane

PLATTS LA

Sheaf Farm

CROSS LANES

A51 TARPORLEY RD

Duddon Hall

BROOMHEATH LA

4

Old Moss

TARPORLEY RD

Duddon Heath

MILL LA

65

Cross Lanes Farm

Old Moss Farm

OLD MOSS LA

Moss Lane Farm

The Moss

Warren House Farm

BURTON LA

RYECROFT LA

Smithy Farm

DUDDON HOOK LA

GUY LA

Stapleford Hall

3

BROOKHOUSE LA

Ford Farm

Brookhouse Farm

64

Burton

Burton Hall

River Gowy

Waterless Brook

Upper Brookhouse Farm

Waterless Wood

2

Upper Brereton Park Farm

MARTIN'S LA

PARK LA

63

COW LA

Brereton Park Farm

Lane End Farm

LEADGATE LA

Hargrave Hall

Leadgate Farm

1

COW LA

Church Farm

Hargrave

Mill Lane Farm

MILL LA

Lower Huxley Hall

PO

Southley Brook

62

Hargrave Farm

48   A   49   B   50   C

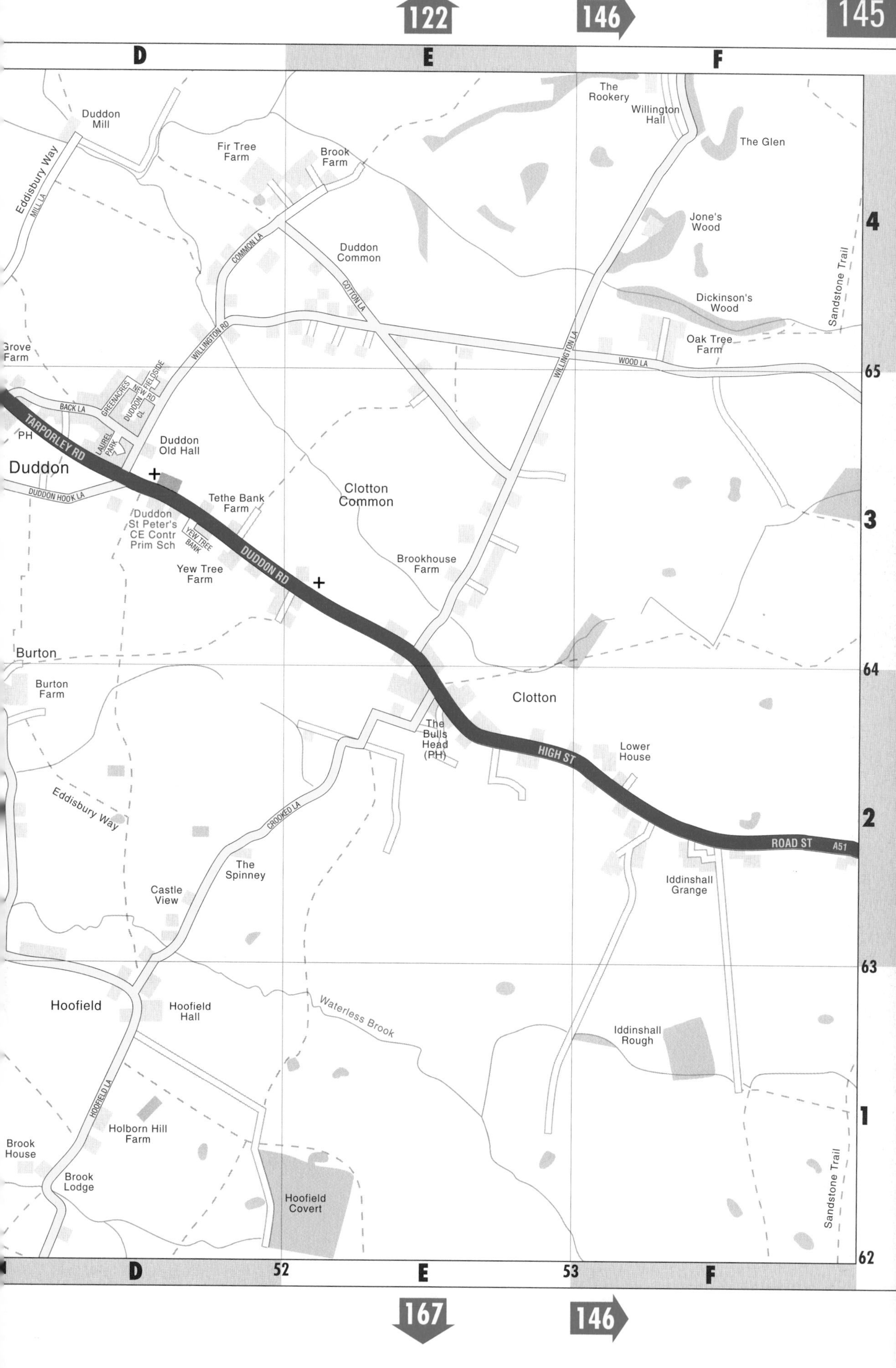

D   E   F

The Rookery

Willington Hall

The Glen

Duddon Mill

Eddisbury Way

MILL LA

Fir Tree Farm

Brook Farm

Jone's Wood

Sandstone Trail

4

COMMON LA

Duddon Common

COTTON LA

Dickinson's Wood

Oak Tree Farm

WILLINGTON LA

WOOD LA

65

Grove Farm

WILLINGTON RD

GREENACRES

NEW FIELDSIDE

DUDDON OLD RD

BACK LA

PH

Duddon

LAUREL PARK

Duddon Old Hall

Clotton Common

3

DUDDON HOOK LA

Tethe Bank Farm

Duddon St Peter's CE Contr Prim Sch

YEW TREE BANK

DUDDON RD

Yew Tree Farm

Brookhouse Farm

Burton

64

Burton Farm

Clotton

Eddisbury Way

The Bulls Head (PH)

HIGH ST

Lower House

2

CROOKED LA

The Spinney

Castle View

ROAD ST   A51

Iddinshall Grange

63

Hoofield

Hoofield Hall

Waterless Brook

Iddinshall Rough

HOOFIELD LA

1

Brook House

Holborn Hill Farm

Brook Lodge

Hoofield Covert

Sandstone Trail

62

D   52   E   53   F

145
123

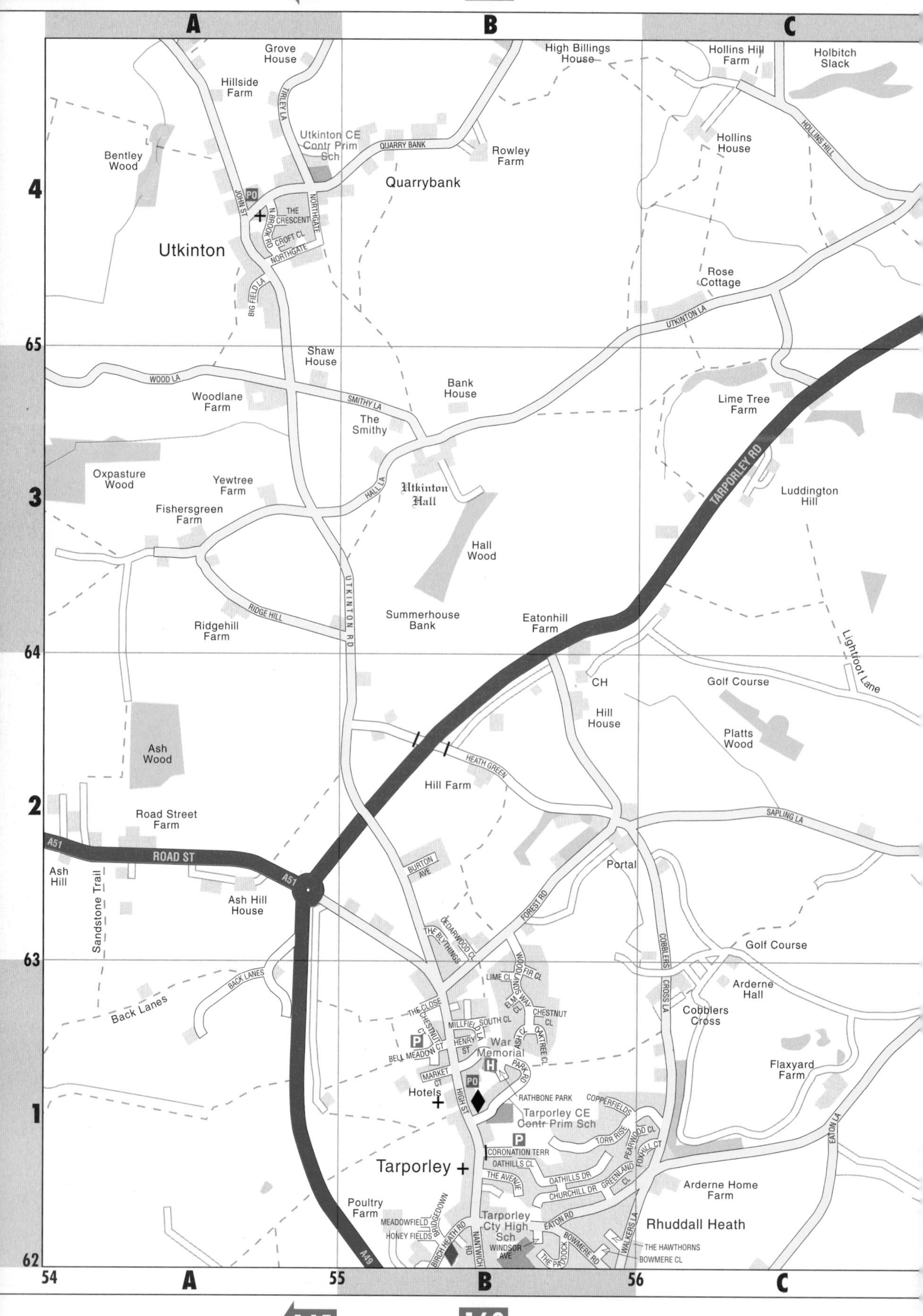
A
B
C
4
65
3
64
2
63
1
62
54
55
56
Grove House
Hillside Farm
High Billings House
Hollins Hill Farm
Holbitch Slack
Bentley Wood
Utkinton CE Contr Prim Sch
Rowley Farm
Hollins House
Quarrybank
Utkinton
Rose Cottage
Shaw House
Bank House
Lime Tree Farm
Woodlane Farm
The Smithy
Oxpasture Wood
Yewtree Farm
Fishersgreen Farm
Utkinton Hall
Luddington Hill
Hall Wood
Ridgehill Farm
Summerhouse Bank
Eatonhill Farm
CH
Golf Course
Lightfoot Lane
Hill House
Platts Wood
Ash Wood
Hill Farm
Road Street Farm
Ash Hill
Sandstone Trail
Ash Hill House
Portal
Golf Course
Back Lanes
Arderne Hall
Cobblers Cross
War Memorial
Flaxyard Farm
Hotels
Tarporley CE Contr Prim Sch
Tarporley
Arderne Home Farm
Poultry Farm
Tarporley Cty High Sch
Rhuddall Heath
TIRLEY LA
QUARRY BANK
JOHN ST
NORTHGATE
THE CRESCENT
N BROOK RD
CROFT CL
BIG FIELD LA
HOLLINS HILL
UTKINTON LA
WOOD LA
SMITHY LA
HALL LA
TARPORLEY RD
RIDGE HILL
UTKINTON RD
HEATH GREEN
SAPLING LA
A51
ROAD ST
BURTON AVE
FOREST RD
CEDARWOOD CL
THE BLYTHINGS
COBBLERS CROSS LA
BACK LANES
LIME CL
WOODLANDS WAY
FIR CL
ELM CL
THE CLOSE
CHESTNUT CL
MILLFIELD LA
SOUTH CL
ASH CL
OAKTREE CL
HENRY ST
BELL MEADOW CT
PARK RD
MARKET CT
HIGH ST
RATHBONE PARK
COPPERFIELDS
TORR RISE
PEARWOOD CL
FOXHILL CT
EATON LA
CORONATION TERR
OATHILLS CL
THE AVENUE
OATHILLS DR
GREENLAND CL
CHURCHILL DR
EATON RD
MEADOWFIELD
BRIDGEDOWN
HONEY FIELDS
BIRCH HEATH RD
NANTWICH RD
WINDSOR AVE
THE PADDOCK
BOWMERE RD
WALKERS LA
THE HAWTHORNS
BOWMERE CL
A49

145
168

D   E   F

STABLE LA

A49

B5152

TARPORLEY RD

PH

Cotebrook

PO

WOODLANDS CL

Tom's Hole

OULTON MILL LA

UTKINTON LA

Alvanley Arms (PH)

Picnic Area   P

BEECH LA

Brownhill

BROWNHILLS RD

Beechlane Farm

EATON LA

Garner House

Red Lion (PH)

LIGHTFOOT LA

ROMAN VILLA (rems of)

SAPLING LA

Eaton   Eaton Farm

LOWER LA   ELM TREE CT

PO

EDGEWELL LA

RIVAL LA

Eaton Cty Prim Sch

WHALLEY DR

N LA

Winterford Farm

WINTERFORD LA

MILL LA

Mill Covert

Hill Top Farm

Mill Pond

Park Place Farm

Little Budworth Country Park

WHITEHALL LA

COACH RD

Rushton

RUSHTON LA

Moss Hall Farm

DOGMORE LA

Motor Racing Circuit

Oulton Park

Oulton Lake

KINGS LA

Parkwall Farm

Hunt's Hill

HICKHURST LA

Boothouse Farm

Philo House

THE HALL LA

Oxheys

PARK RD

Budworth Pool

Egerton Arms (PH)

PINFOLD LA

Little Budworth

VICARAGE LA

BOOTH AVE

ST PE...

WELL LA

MILL LA

PO

ST PETER'S DR

YEW TREE CL

TOWNSFIELD DR

Home Farm

Oulton House

Lower Farm

Hazelhurst Covert

Withey Bed

Old Lanes

Oak Tree Farm

Oultonlowe Farm

Philo Gorse

4

65

3

64

2

63

1

62

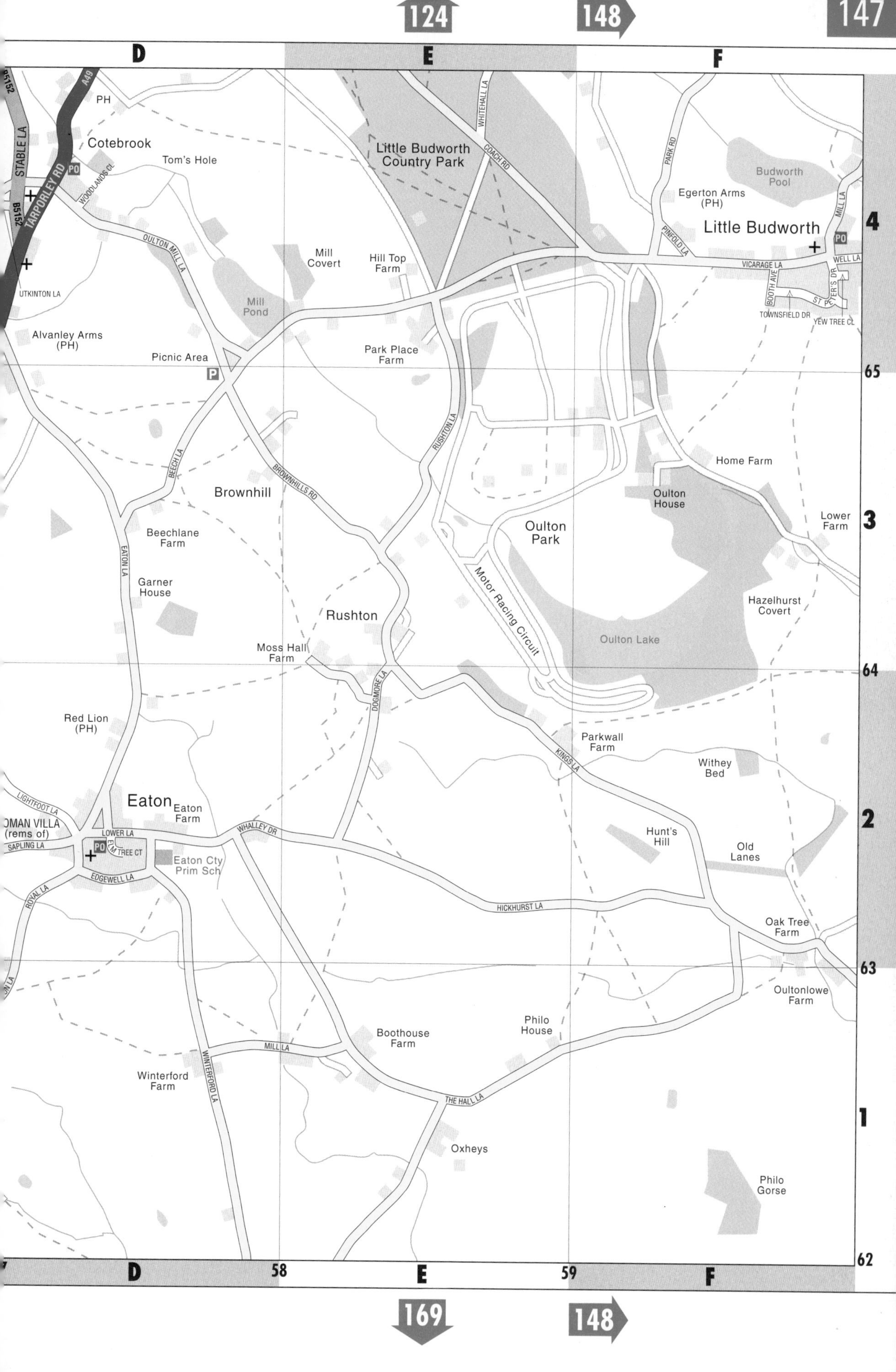

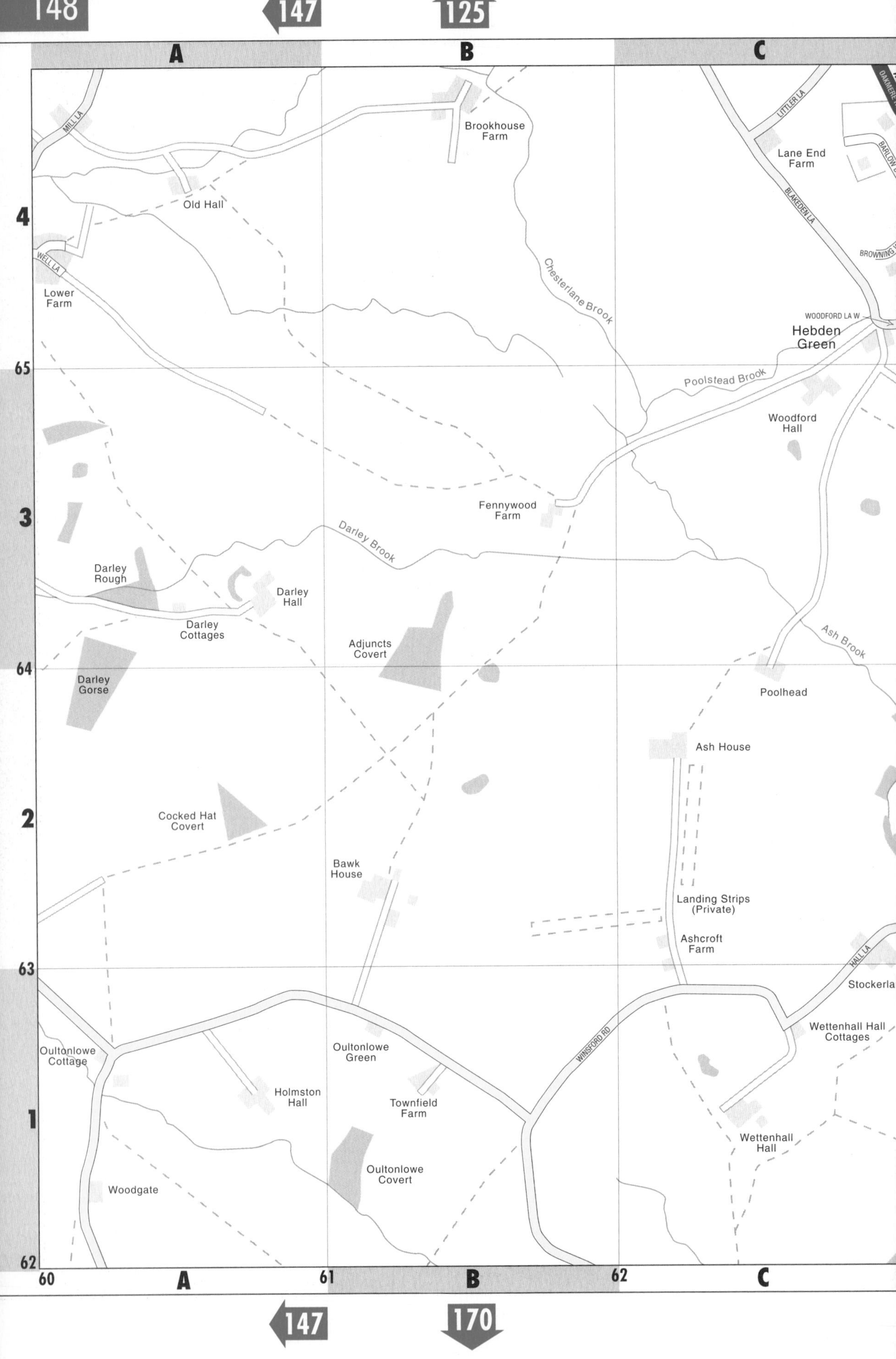

147
125

A

B

C

MILL LA

Brookhouse
Farm

LITTLER LA

OAKMERE RD

BARLOW LA

Lane End
Farm

BLAKEDEN LA

Old Hall

4

BROWNING M

WELL LA

Lower
Farm

Chesterlane Brook

WOODFORD LA W

Hebden
Green

65

Poolstead Brook

Woodford
Hall

3

Fennywood
Farm

Darley Brook

Darley
Rough

Darley
Hall

Ash Brook

Darley
Cottages

Adjuncts
Covert

64

Darley
Gorse

Poolhead

Ash House

2

Cocked Hat
Covert

Bawk
House

Landing Strips
(Private)

Ashcroft
Farm

63

HALL LA

Stockerla

Oultonlowe
Cottage

Oultonlowe
Green

WINSFORD RD

Wettenhall Hall
Cottages

1

Holmston
Hall

Townfield
Farm

Wettenhall
Hall

Woodgate

Oultonlowe
Covert

62

60

A

61

B

62

C

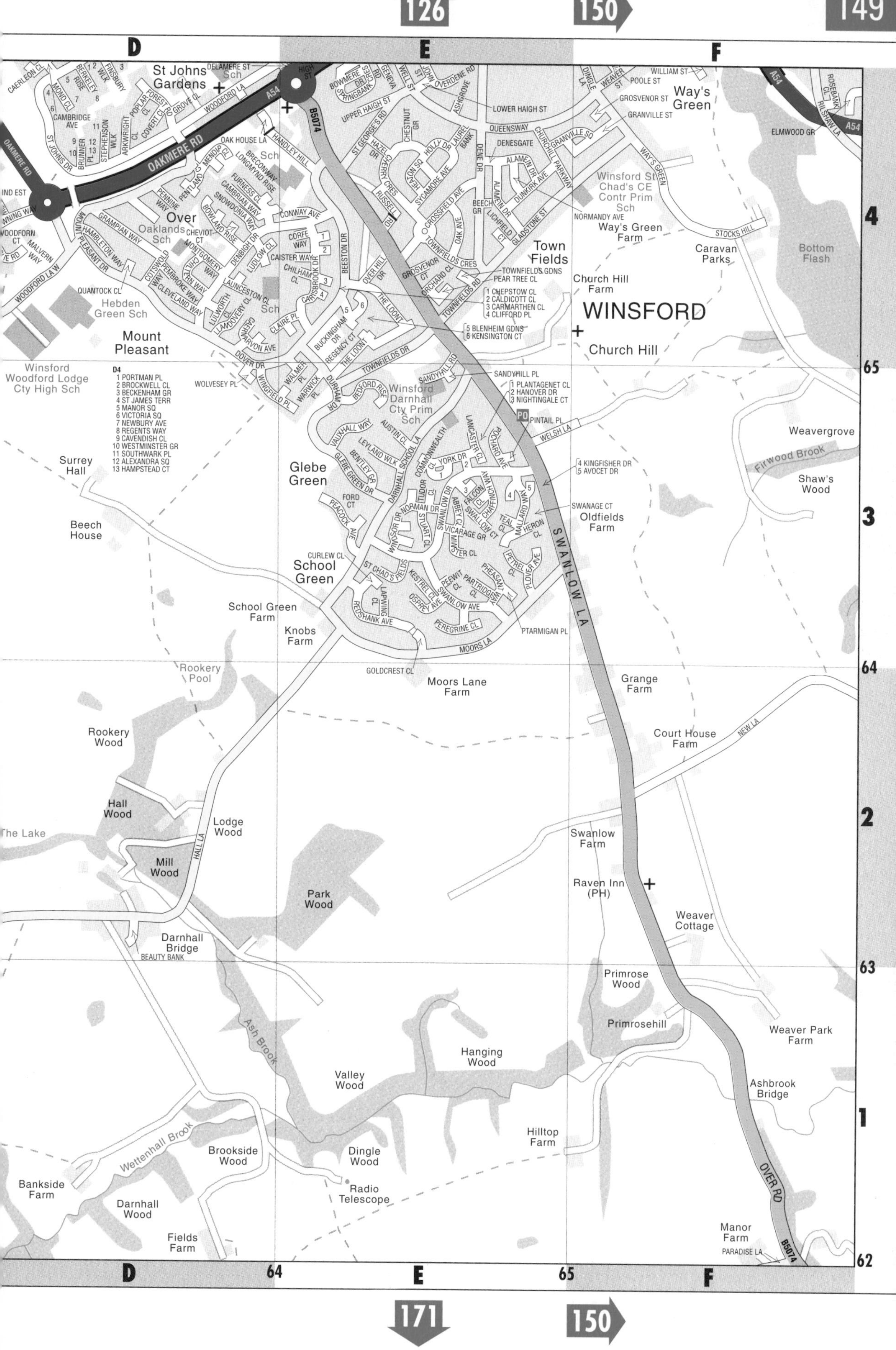
D
E
F
St Johns Gardens
DELAMERE ST
Sch
HIGH ST
B5074
A54
WOODFORD LA
GROVE CL
CAERLEON CL
MOND CL
BERKELEY RISE
FINSBURY WLK
CAMBRIDGE AVE
ST JOHNS DR
BRUNNER PL
STEPHENSON WLK
ARKWRIGHT CL
POPLAR CL
FOREST RD
COVERT CL
OAKMERE RD
OAKMERE RD
IND EST
WOODFORN CT
MALVERN WAY
WOODFORD LA W
OAK HOUSE LA
HANDLEY HILL
MENDIP CL
PENTLAND CL
PENNINE WAY
BRECONWAY
LONGMYND RISE
FURNESS CL
CAMBRIAN WAY
SNOWDONIA WAY
BOWLAND RISE
Over
Oaklands Sch
CHEVIOT CT
GRAMPIAN WAY
HAMBLETON WAY
MOUNT PLEASANT DR
COTSWOLD WAY
PEMBROKE WAY
CHILTERN WAY
MONTGOMERY WAY
DENBIGH DR
LUDLOW CL
CONWAY AVE
CORFE WAY
CAISTER WAY
CHILHAM CL
CARISBROOK DR
BEESTON DR
LAUNCESTON CL
CLEVELAND WAY
LULWORTH CL
LLANDOVERY CL
CAERNARVON AVE
CLAIRE PL
BUCKINGHAM DR
REGENCY CT
THE LOONT
OVER HILL DR
QUANTOCK CL
Hebden Green Sch
Mount Pleasant
Winsford Woodford Lodge Cty High Sch
D4
1 PORTMAN PL
2 BROCKWELL CL
3 BECKENHAM GR
4 ST JAMES TERR
5 MANOR SQ
6 VICTORIA SQ
7 NEWBURY AVE
8 REGENTS WAY
9 CAVENDISH CL
10 WESTMINSTER GR
11 SOUTHWARK PL
12 ALEXANDRA SQ
13 HAMPSTEAD CT
WOLVESEY PL
DOVER DR
WINGFIELD PL
WALMER PL
WARWICK PL
DURHAM DR
TOWNFIELDS DR
BOWMERE RD
SPRINGBANK CRES
GENEVA RD
WELL ST
JOHN ST
OVERDENE RD
ASHGROVE
UPPER HAIGH ST
ST GEORGE'S RD
CHESTNUT GR
HAZEL DR
CHERRY CRES
RUSSELL RD
HOLLY DR
LAUREL BANK
HEWSON SQ
SYCAMORE AVE
CROSSFIELD AVE
OAK AVE
TOWNFIELDS CRES
GROSVENOR CT
ORCHARD CL
TOWNFIELDS RD
LOWER HAIGH ST
QUEENSWAY
DENESGATE
DENE DR
ALAMEIN CL
ALAMEIN DR
DUNKIRK AVE
BEECH GR
LICHFIELD CL
GLADSTONE ST
CHURCHILL PARKWAY
GRANVILLE SQ
NORMANDY AVE
DINGLE LA
WEAVER ST
WILLIAM ST
POOLE ST
GROSVENOR ST
GRANVILLE ST
Way's Green
WAY'S GREEN
Winsford St Chad's CE Contr Prim Sch
Way's Green Farm
STOCKS HILL
Caravan Parks
Town Fields
TOWNFIELDS GDNS
PEAR TREE CL
1 CHEPSTOW CL
2 CALDICOTT CL
3 CARMARTHEN CL
4 CLIFFORD PL
5 BLENHEIM GDNS
6 KENSINGTON CT
Church Hill Farm
WINSFORD
Church Hill
A54
ROSEBANK CL
RILSHAW LA
ELMWOOD GR
Bottom Flash
SANDYHILL RD
SANDYHILL PL
1 PLANTAGENET CL
2 HANOVER DR
3 NIGHTINGALE CT
PO
PINTAIL PL
WELSH LA
BEDFORD RISE
Winsford Darnhall Cty Prim Sch
VAUXHALL WAY
AUSTIN CL
LEYLAND WLK
BENTLEY GR
GLEBE GREEN DR
DARNHALL SCHOOL LA
COMMONWEALTH CL
LANCASTER CL
POCHARD AVE
YORK DR
4 KINGFISHER DR
5 AVOCET DR
Weavergrove
Firwood Brook
Shaw's Wood
Surrey Hall
Glebe Green
FORD CT
PEACOCK AVE
TUDOR CL
NORMAN DR
STUART CL
SWANLOW DR
ABBEY CL
FALCON CL
SWALLOW CT
CHAFFINCH CL
TEAL CL
MALLARD WAY
HERON CL
VICARAGE GR
MINSTER CL
WINDSOR DR
SWANAGE CT
Oldfields Farm
SWANLOW LA
Beech House
CURLEW CL
School Green
ST CHAD'S FIELDS
KESTREL CL
LAPWING CL
PEEWIT CL
PARTRIDGE CL
PHEASANT WLK
PETREL CL
PLOVER AVE
OSPREY AVE
SWANLOW AVE
REDSHANK AVE
PEREGRINE CL
PTARMIGAN PL
School Green Farm
Knobs Farm
MOORS LA
GOLDCREST CL
Moors Lane Farm
Grange Farm
Rookery Pool
Rookery Wood
Court House Farm
NEW LA
Hall Wood
Lodge Wood
HALL LA
The Lake
Mill Wood
Swanlow Farm
Park Wood
Raven Inn (PH)
Weaver Cottage
Darnhall Bridge
BEAUTY BANK
Primrose Wood
Primrosehill
Ash Brook
Weaver Park Farm
Hanging Wood
Valley Wood
Ashbrook Bridge
Hilltop Farm
Wettenhall Brook
Brookside Wood
Dingle Wood
Radio Telescope
Bankside Farm
Darnhall Wood
Fields Farm
OVER RD
Manor Farm
PARADISE LA
B5074
4
65
3
64
2
63
1
62
D
64
E
65
F

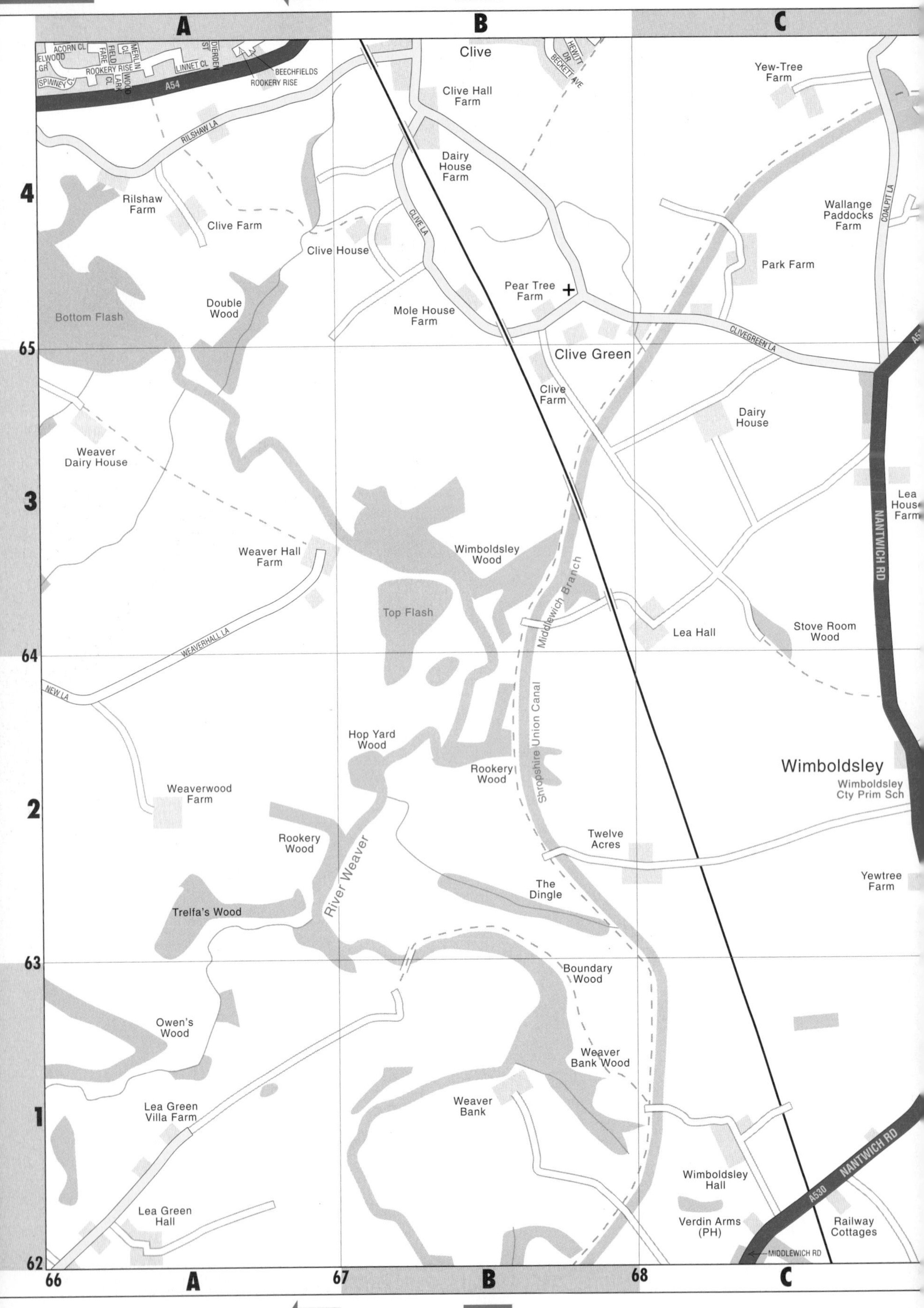

Clive

A

B

C

ELWOOD GR
ACORN CL
SPINNEY CT
MERLIN CL
CLIFE WOOD
DIERDEN ST
ROOKERY RISE
FARE
LINNET CL
FIELD LA
BEECHFIELDS
ROOKERY RISE
A54

Rilshaw Farm

RILSHAW LA

Clive Farm

Clive House

Clive Hall Farm

Dairy House Farm

CLIVE LA

HEWITT DR
BECKETT AVE

Yew-Tree Farm

Bottom Flash

Double Wood

Mole House Farm

Pear Tree Farm

Clive Green

Park Farm

Wallange Paddocks Farm

CLIVEGREEN LA

COLPIT LA

4

65

Clive Farm

Dairy House

Lea House Farm

A530

NANTWICH RD

Weaver Dairy House

Weaver Hall Farm

WEAVERHALL LA

Wimboldsley Wood

Top Flash

Middlewich Branch

Shropshire Union Canal

Lea Hall

Stove Room Wood

3

64

NEW LA

Hop Yard Wood

Rookery Wood

Weaverwood Farm

Rookery Wood

River Weaver

Twelve Acres

Wimboldsley

Wimboldsley Cty Prim Sch

Yewtree Farm

2

The Dingle

Trelfa's Wood

63

Owen's Wood

Boundary Wood

Weaver Bank Wood

Weaver Bank

1

Lea Green Villa Farm

Lea Green Hall

Wimboldsley Hall

Verdin Arms (PH)

A530 NANTWICH RD

Railway Cottages

MIDDLEWICH RD

62

66

67

68

A

B

C

128
152
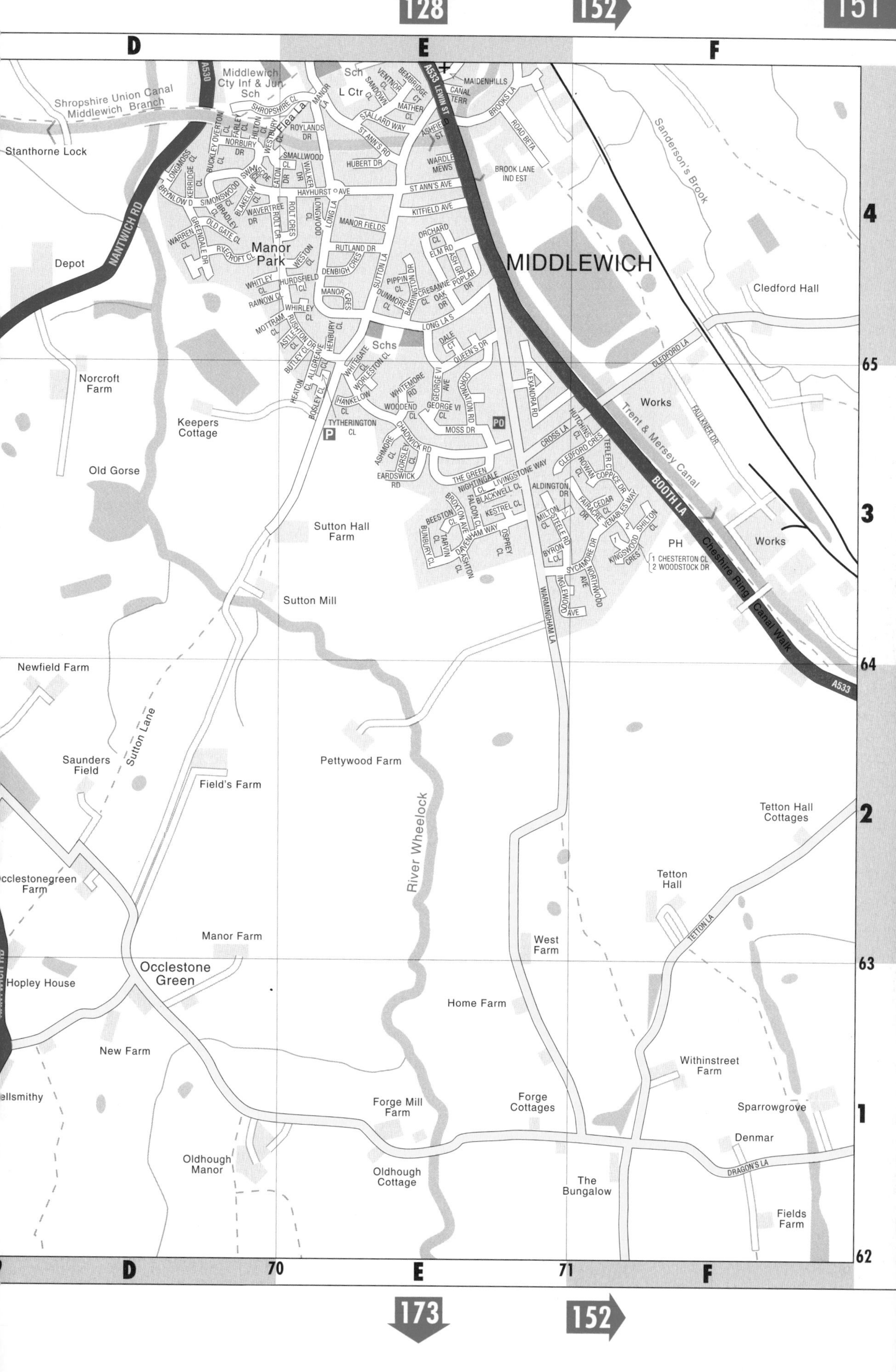
D
E
F
Middlewich Cty Inf & Jun Sch
Shropshire Union Canal Middlewich Branch
Stanthorne Lock
Sch
L Ctr
MAIDENHILLS
CANAL TERR
BROOKS LA
ROAD BETA
BROOK LANE IND EST
Sanderson's Brook
A533 LEWIN ST
A530
NANTWICH RD
Depot
Manor Park
MIDDLEWICH
Cledford Hall
Schs
Norcroft Farm
Keepers Cottage
Old Gorse
Works
Trent & Mersey Canal
CLEDFORD LA
FAULKNER DR
BOOTH LA
Cheshire Ring Canal Walk
A533
Sutton Hall Farm
Sutton Mill
PH
1 CHESTERTON CL
2 WOODSTOCK DR
WARMINGHAM LA
Newfield Farm
Saunders Field
Sutton Lane
Field's Farm
Pettywood Farm
River Wheelock
Tetton Hall Cottages
Tetton Hall
TETTON LA
cclestonegreen Farm
Manor Farm
Occlestone Green
Hopley House
West Farm
Home Farm
New Farm
Withinstreet Farm
ellsmithy
Forge Mill Farm
Forge Cottages
Sparrowgrove
Denmar
DRAGON'S LA
Oldhough Manor
Oldhough Cottage
The Bungalow
Fields Farm
4
65
3
64
2
63
1
62
70
71
173
152

151
129

A **B** **C**

M6

Rookery
Wood

Parkside
Farm

BROAD LA

Broadlane
Farm

Lodge Lane

BRERETON LA

4

Dawfields

Pool
Farm

Brierley Hulme
Farm

Walkers Green

CLEDFORD LA

Briar Pool
Farm

65

Sanderson's Brook

JONE'S LA

Parme Farm

3

Knightshulme
Farm

Curtishulme
Farm

New
Farm

64

Tetton
Bridge

A533

Union
Gorse

Higher
Deleacre

Hollinsgreen

Fousley
Farm

TETTON LA

Bridge
Farm

LC

Hollins Green
Farm

Wood Lane
Farm

Bridge
Farm

2

Trent & Mersey Canal
Cheshire Ring Canal Walk

BOOTH LA

Small Brook

Hollinswood
Farm

WOOD LA

Works

63

Barlow
Wood

Bridge
Cottage

Hollins
Wood

The
Cottage

1

Hilltop
Cottage

Woodville
Farm

DRAGON'S LA

Stud Green

COOKESMERE LA

PLANT LA

Ivy Cottage
Farm

Crow Nest
Bridge

MILL LA

A533

MARSH GREEN RD

Beech Tree
Farm

62

72 **A** 73 **B** 74 **C**

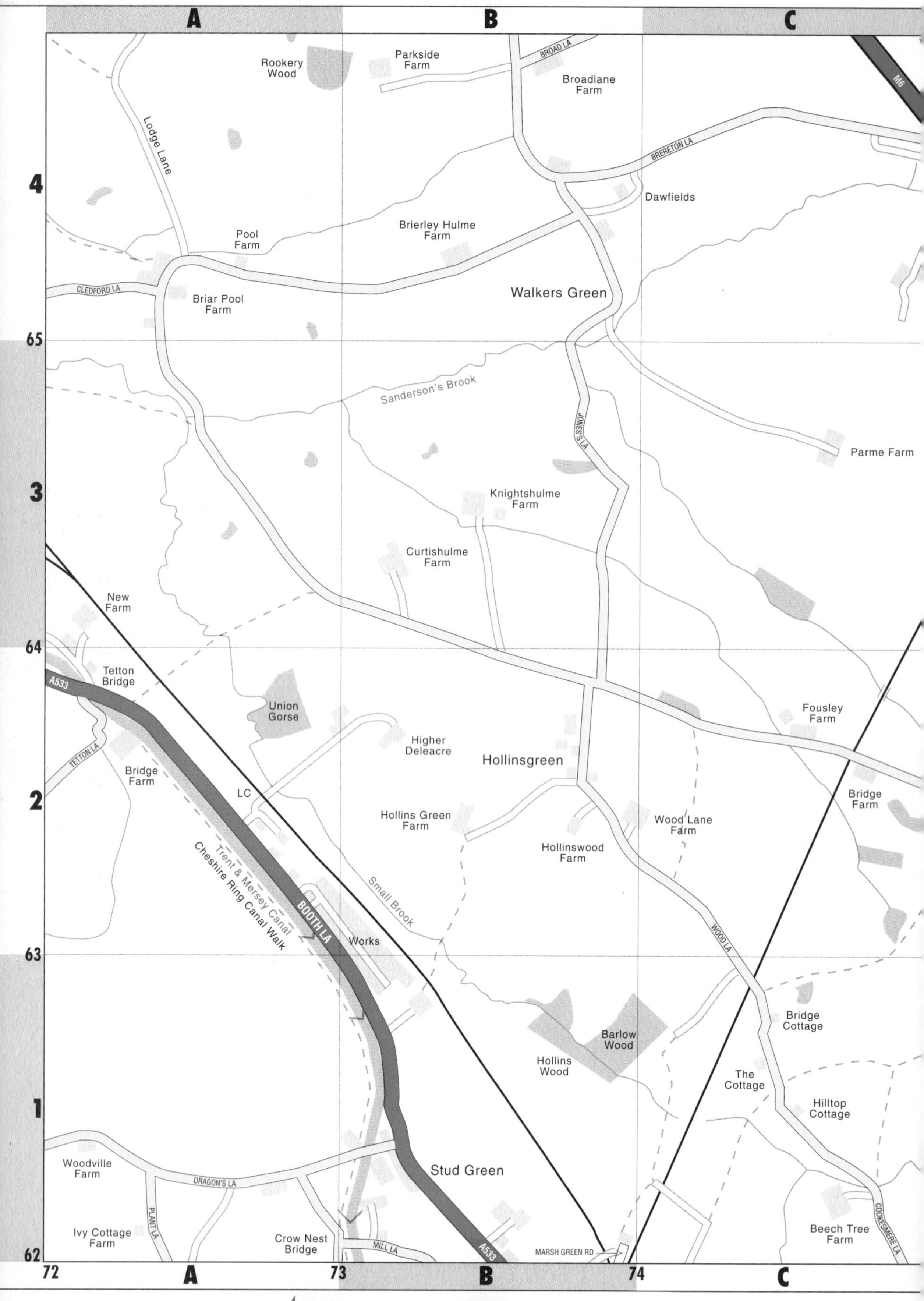

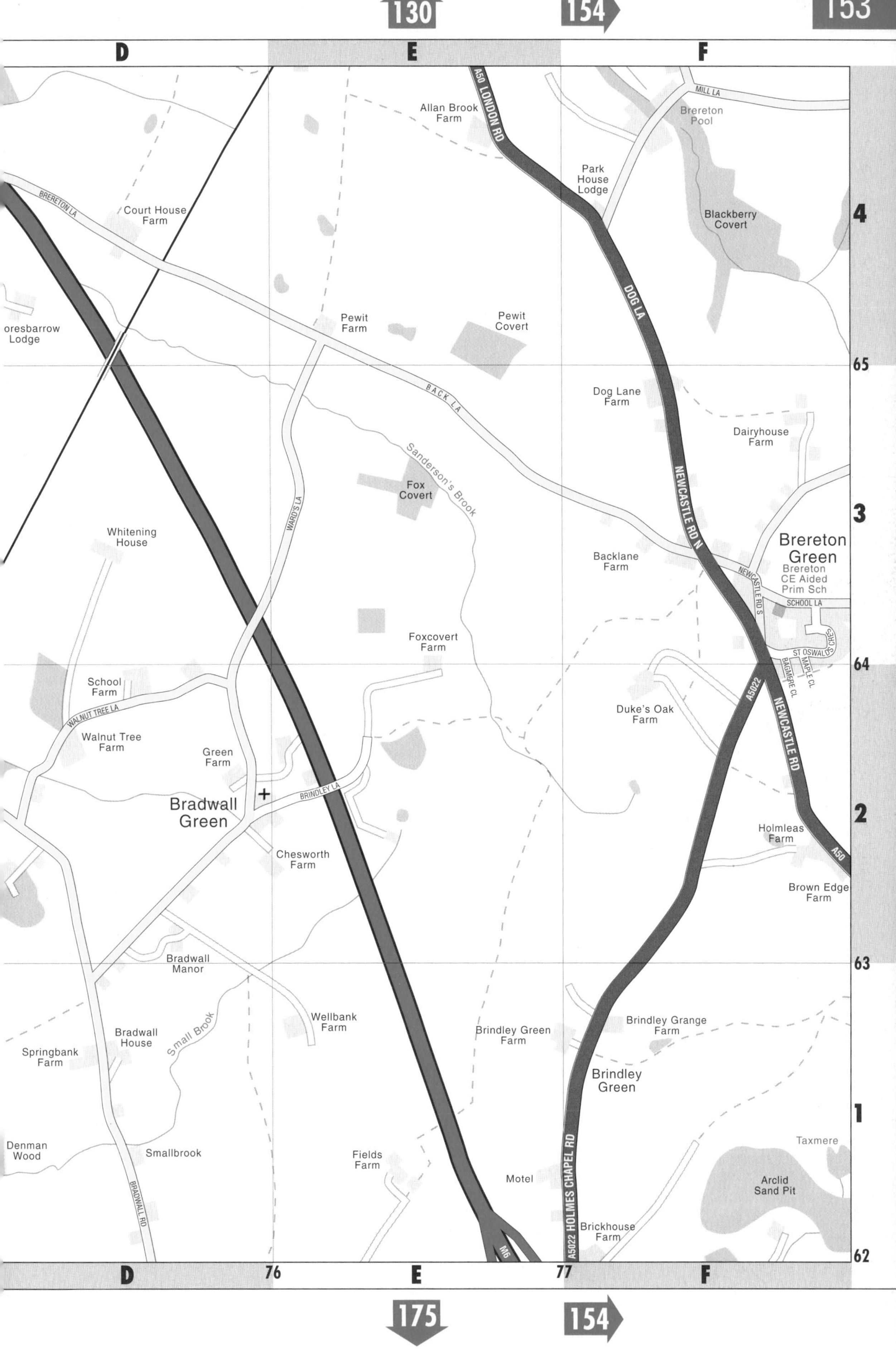

D   E   F

MILL LA

Brereton Pool

Allan Brook Farm

A50 LONDON RD

Park House Lodge

Blackberry Covert

4

BRERETON LA

Court House Farm

oresbarrow Lodge

DOG LA

Dog Lane Farm

Pewit Farm

Pewit Covert

Dairyhouse Farm

65

BACK LA

Sanderson's Brook

Fox Covert

Brereton Green

NEWCASTLE RD N

Backlane Farm

Brereton CE Aided Prim Sch

Whitening House

WARD'S LA

3

NEWCASTLE RD S

SCHOOL LA

Foxcovert Farm

School Farm

ST OSWALD'S

CHS

MAPLE CL

64

Duke's Oak Farm

BADNMERE CL

NEWCASTLE RD

WALNUT TREE LA

Walnut Tree Farm

Green Farm

A5022

Bradwall Green

✚

BRINDLEY LA

Holmleas Farm

2

Chesworth Farm

A50

Brown Edge Farm

Bradwall Manor

63

Small Brook

Wellbank Farm

Brindley Grange Farm

Springbank Farm

Bradwall House

Brindley Green Farm

Brindley Green

Denman Wood

BRADWALL RD

Smallbrook

A5022 HOLMES CHAPEL RD

Taxmere

1

Fields Farm

Motel

Arclid Sand Pit

Brickhouse Farm

M6

62

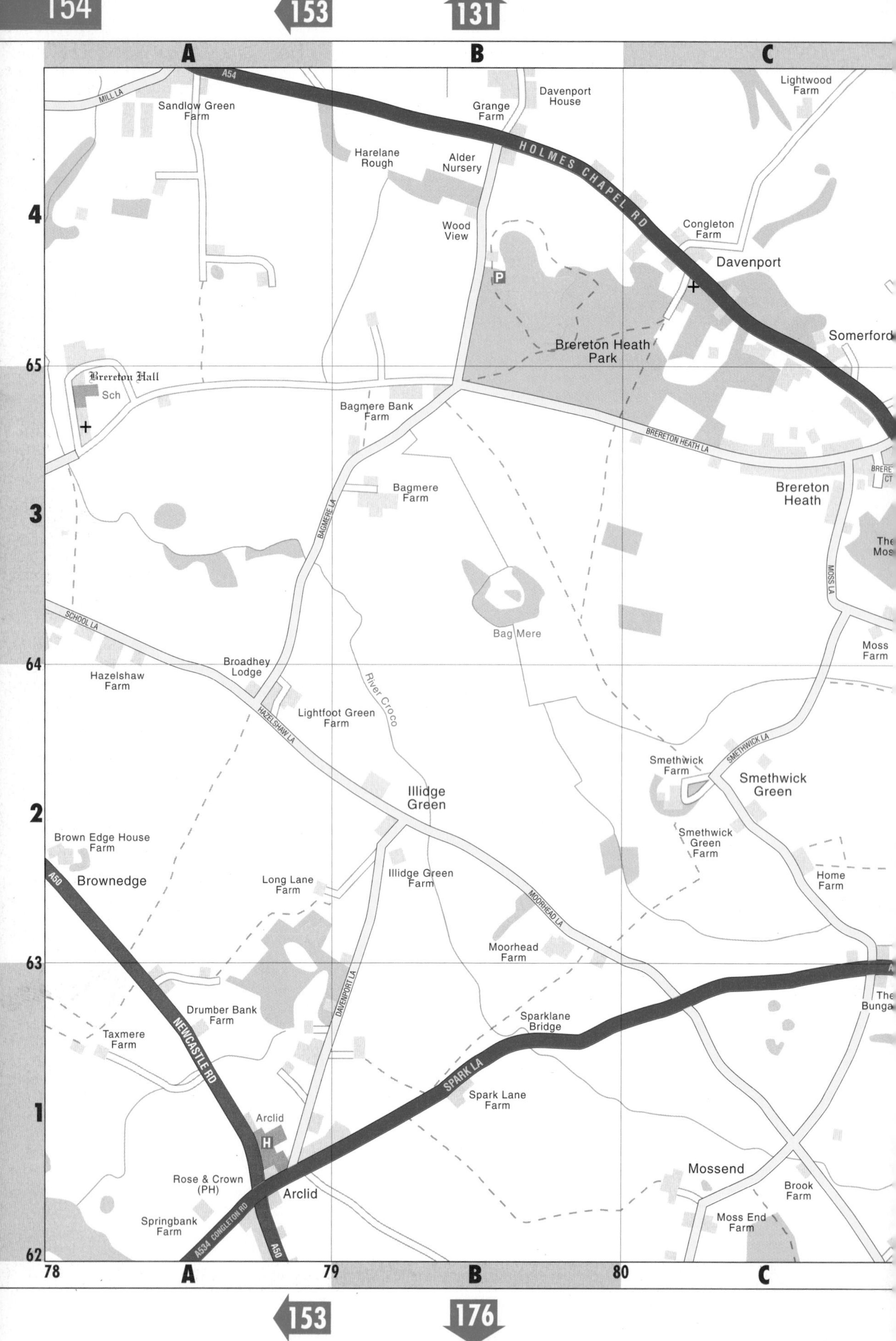

A   B   C

MILL LA

A54

Sandlow Green
Farm

Harelane
Rough

Grange
Farm

Davenport
House

HOLMES CHAPEL RD

Lightwood
Farm

4

Alder
Nursery

Wood
View

Congleton
Farm

Davenport

Brereton Hall

Sch

P

Brereton Heath
Park

Somerford

65

Bagmere Bank
Farm

BRERETON HEATH LA

BRERE
CT

BAGMERE LA

Bagmere
Farm

Brereton
Heath

3

SCHOOL LA

Bag Mere

MOSS LA

The
Mos

Hazelshaw
Farm

Broadhey
Lodge

Moss
Farm

64

HAZELSHAW LA

Lightfoot Green
Farm

River Croco

SMETHWICK LA

Smethwick
Farm

Smethwick
Green

Illidge
Green

2

Brown Edge House
Farm

Long Lane
Farm

Illidge Green
Farm

MOORHEAD LA

Smethwick
Green
Farm

Home
Farm

A50

Brownedge

Moorhead
Farm

63

The
Bunga

NEWCASTLE RD

Drumber Bank
Farm

DAVENPORT LA

Sparklane
Bridge

A

Taxmere
Farm

SPARK LA

Spark Lane
Farm

1

Arclid

H

Mossend

Brook
Farm

Rose & Crown
(PH)

Arclid

Moss End
Farm

Springbank
Farm

A534 CONGLETON RD

A50

62

78   A   79   B   80   C

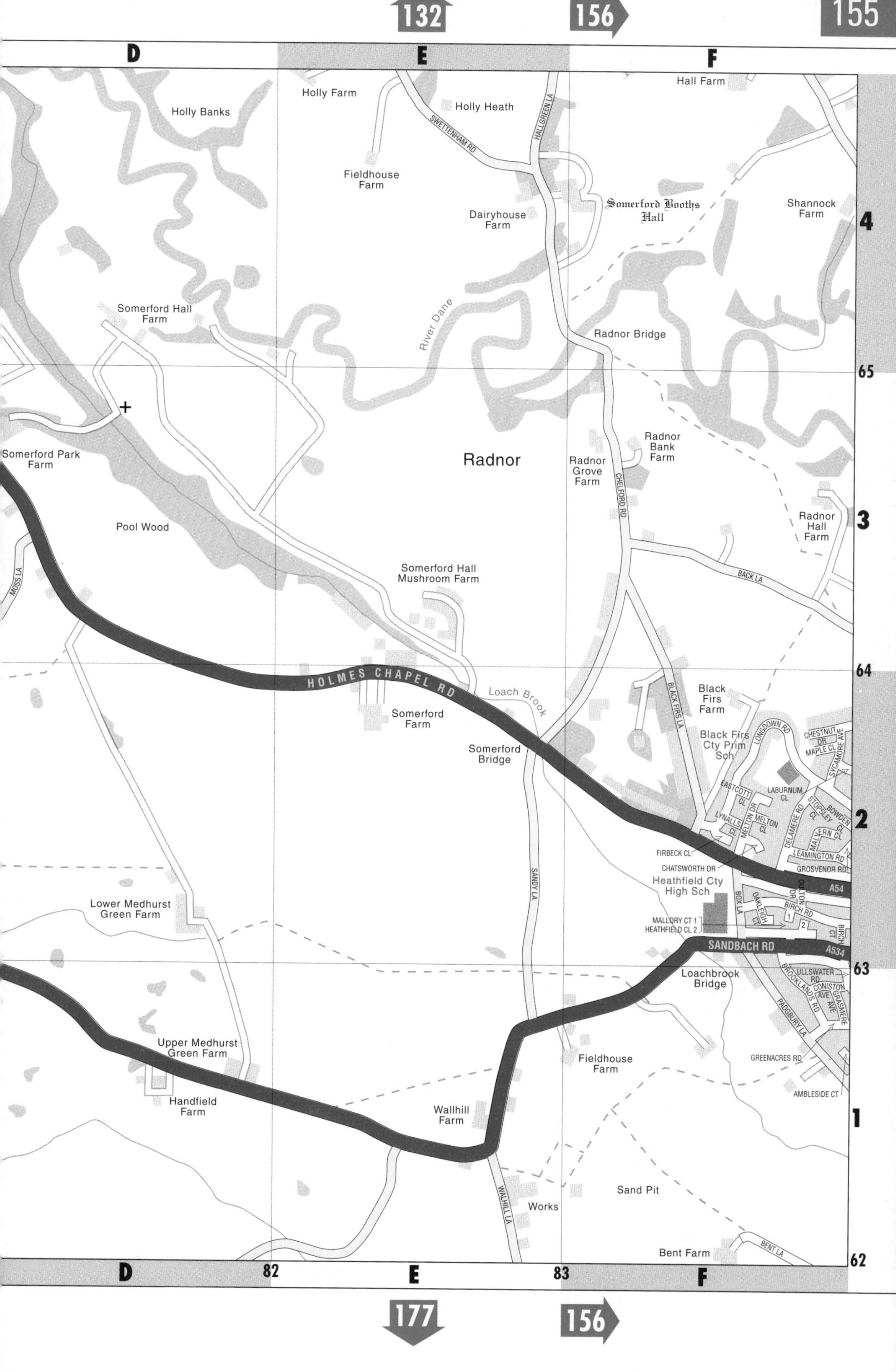

Hall Farm

Holly Farm

Holly Banks

Holly Heath

SWETTENHAM RD

HALGREEN LA

Somerford Booths
Hall

Shannock
Farm

4

Fieldhouse
Farm

Dairyhouse
Farm

River Dane

Radnor Bridge

Somerford Hall
Farm

65

+

Somerford Park
Farm

Radnor

Radnor
Grove
Farm

Radnor
Bank
Farm

CHELFORD RD

Radnor
Hall
Farm

3

MOSS LA

Pool Wood

Somerford Hall
Mushroom Farm

BACK LA

HOLMES CHAPEL RD

Loach Brook

Somerford
Farm

Somerford
Bridge

Black Firs
Farm

BLACK FIRS LA

64

Black Firs
Cty Prim
Sch

LONGDOWN RD

CHESTNUT
DR

MAPLE CL

SYCAMORE AVE

EASTCOTT
CL

LABURNUM
CL

DELAMERE RD

STOSSLEY

BOWDEN
CL

LYNALLS
CL

MELTON DR

MELTON
CL

FERN CL

FIRBECK CL

LEAMINGTON RD

GROSVENOR RD

2

CHATSWORTH DR

Heathfield Cty
High Sch

SANDY LA

MALLORY CT 1
HEATHFIELD CL 2

BOX LA

OAKLEIGH

OULTON RD

BIRCH RD

BIRCH CT

A54

Lower Medhurst
Green Farm

SANDBACH RD

A534

Loachbrook
Bridge

BROOKLAND RD

ULLSWATER
RD

CONISTON
AVE

GRASMERE

PADGBURY LA

63

Upper Medhurst
Green Farm

Fieldhouse
Farm

GREENACRES RD

AMBLESIDE CT

1

Handfield
Farm

Wallhill
Farm

Sand Pit

WALLHILL LA

Works

Bent Farm

BENT LA

62

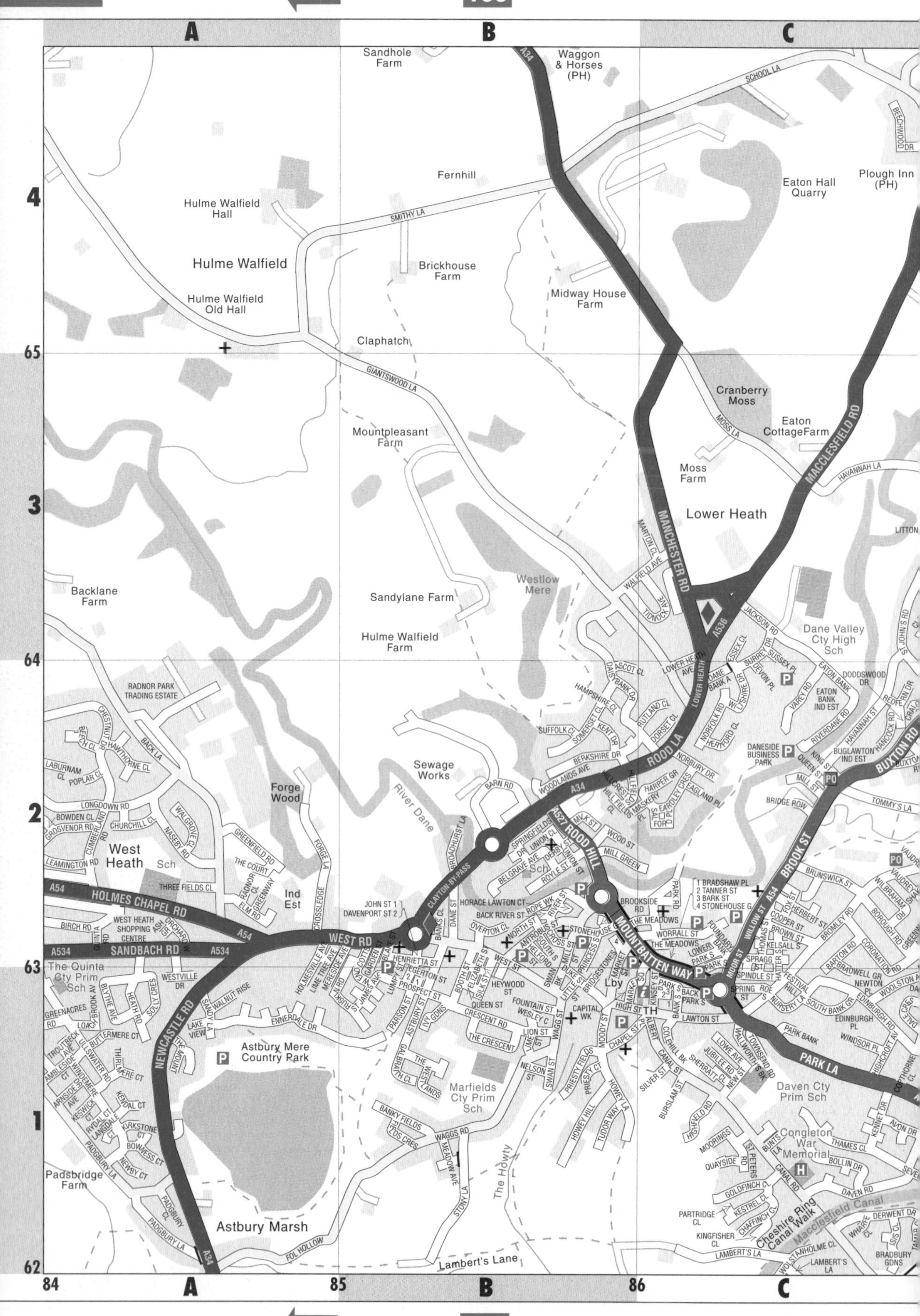
A
B
C
4
65
3
64
2
63
1
62
84
85
86
Sandhole Farm
Waggon & Horses (PH)
Fernhill
Eaton Hall Quarry
Plough Inn (PH)
Hulme Walfield Hall
Hulme Walfield
Brickhouse Farm
Hulme Walfield Old Hall
Midway House Farm
Claphatch
Cranberry Moss
Mountpleasant Farm
Eaton CottageFarm
Moss Farm
Lower Heath
Backlane Farm
Westlow Mere
Sandylane Farm
Dane Valley Cty High Sch
Hulme Walfield Farm
RADNOR PARK TRADING ESTATE
Sewage Works
Forge Wood
River Dane
West Heath
Sch
Ind Est
The Quinta Cty Prim Sch
Astbury Mere Country Park
Marfields Cty Prim Sch
Daven Cty Prim Sch
Congleton War Memorial
Padsbridge Farm
Astbury Marsh
The Howty
Lambert's Lane
Macclesfield Canal
Cheshire Ring Canal Walk
SMITHY LA
GIANTSWOOD LA
SCHOOL LA
MOSS LA
MACCLESFIELD RD
MANCHESTER RD
HAVANNAH LA
ROOD LA
ROOD HILL
HOLMES CHAPEL RD
SANDBACH RD
WEST RD
NEWCASTLE RD
CLAYTON-BY-PASS
MOUNTBATTEN WAY
BROOK ST
PARK LA
BUXTON RD
A34
A536
A54
A534
A527
DANESIDE BUSINESS PARK
EATON BANK IND EST
BUGLAWTON IND EST
1 BRADSHAW PL
2 TANNER ST
3 BARK ST
4 STONEHOUSE G
JOHN ST 1
DAVENPORT ST 2
Lby
TH
FOL HOLLOW
ENNERDALE DR

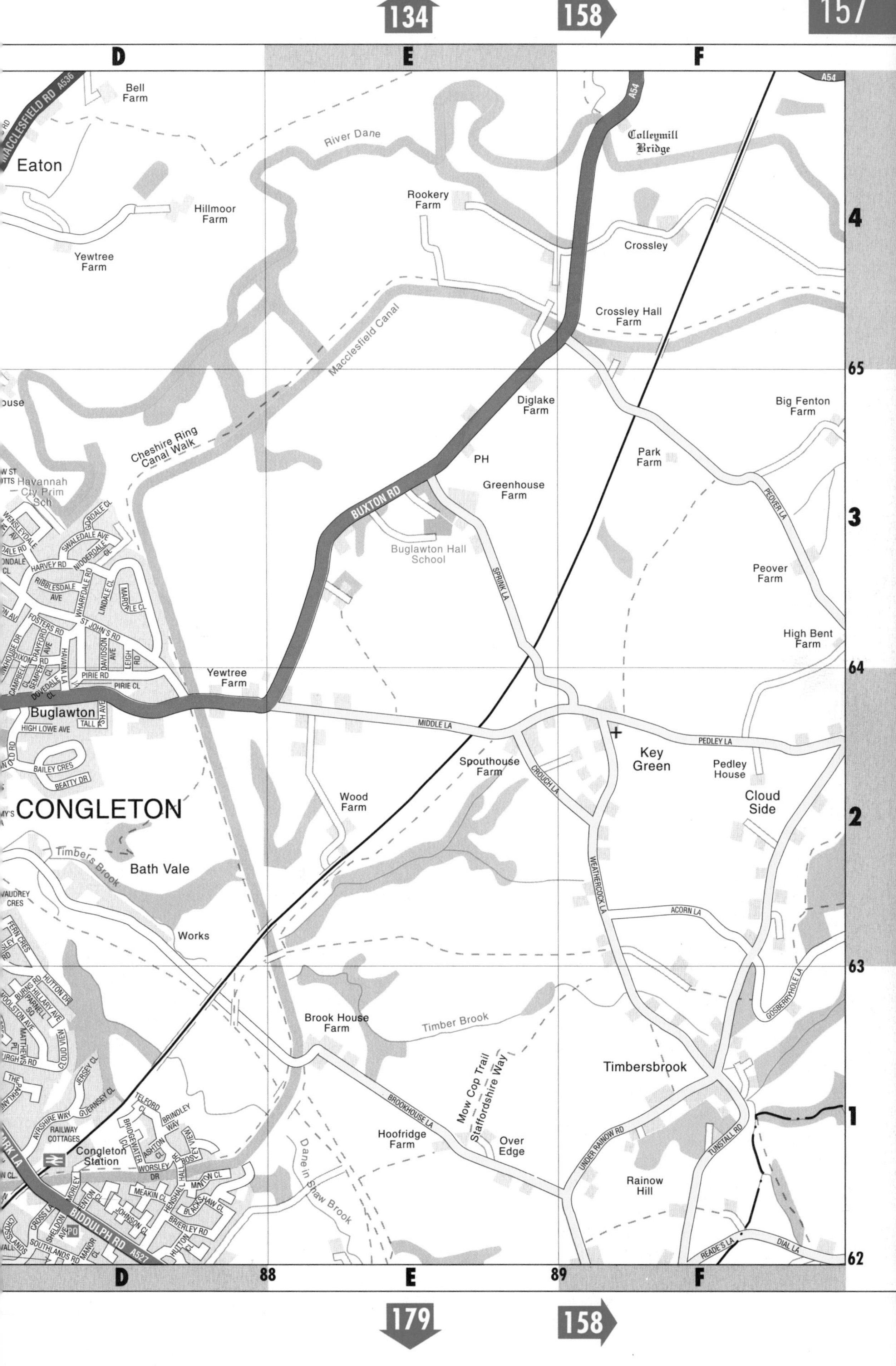
D
E
F
Bell Farm
Eaton
Hillmoor Farm
Yewtree Farm
River Dane
Rookery Farm
Colleymill Bridge
A54
Crossley
Crossley Hall Farm
Macclesfield Canal
Cheshire Ring Canal Walk
Diglake Farm
Big Fenton Farm
Park Farm
PH
Greenhouse Farm
BUXTON RD
Buglawton Hall School
SPRINK LA
PEOVER LA
Peover Farm
High Bent Farm
Havannah City Prim Sch
Yewtree Farm
Buglawton
MIDDLE LA
PEDLEY LA
Key Green
Pedley House
Cloud Side
Spouthouse Farm
CROUCH LA
Wood Farm
CONGLETON
Timbers Brook
Bath Vale
Works
WEATHERCOCK LA
ACORN LA
GOSBERRYHOLE LA
Brook House Farm
Timber Brook
Mow Cop Trail
Staffordshire Way
Timbersbrook
BROOKHOUSE LA
Hoofridge Farm
Over Edge
UNDER RAINOW RD
TUNSTALL RD
Rainow Hill
Dane in Shaw Brook
Congleton Station
BIDDULPH RD A527
READE'S LA
DIAL LA
MACCLESFIELD RD A536
4
65
3
64
2
63
1
62
88
89

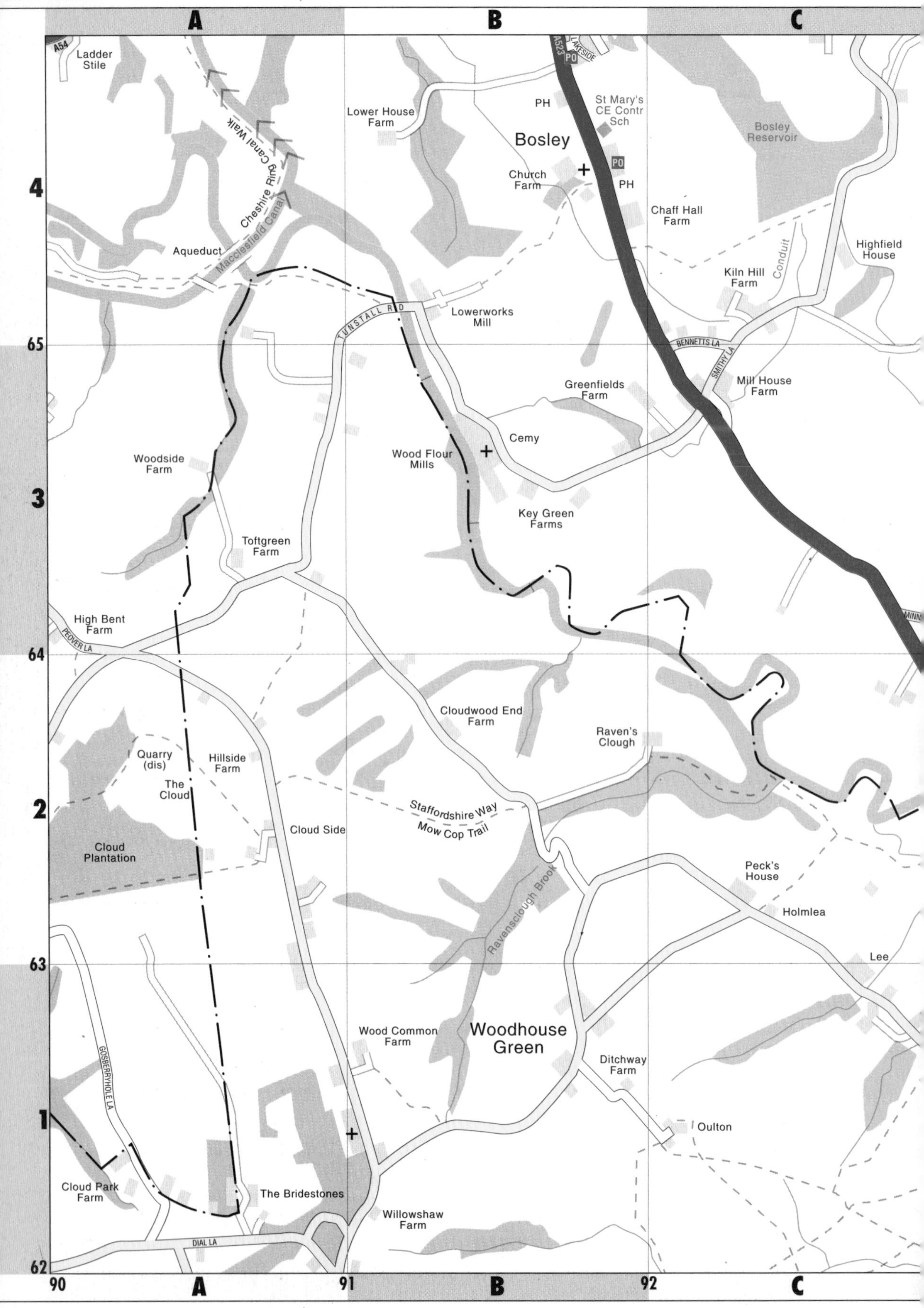

A   B   C

A54

Ladder Stile

Cheshire Ring Canal Walk

Macclesfield Canal

Lower House Farm

St Mary's CE Contr Sch

PH

Bosley

Church Farm

PO

PH

Chaff Hall Farm

Bosley Reservoir

Highfield House

Aqueduct

Conduit

Kiln Hill Farm

BENNETTS LA

SMITH LA

Mill House Farm

4

TUNSTALL RD

Lowerworks Mill

65

Woodside Farm

Greenfields Farm

Cemy

Wood Flour Mills

Key Green Farms

3

Toftgreen Farm

High Bent Farm

PEDVER LA

64

MINN

Cloudwood End Farm

Raven's Clough

Quarry (dis)

Hillside Farm

The Cloud

Cloud Side

Staffordshire Way
Mow Cop Trail

Peck's House

Cloud Plantation

Holmlea

Ravensclough Brook

Lee

63

Wood Common Farm

Woodhouse Green

Ditchway Farm

GOSBERRYHOLE LA

1

Oulton

Cloud Park Farm

The Bridestones

Willowshaw Farm

DIAL LA

62

90   A   91   B   92   C

D E F

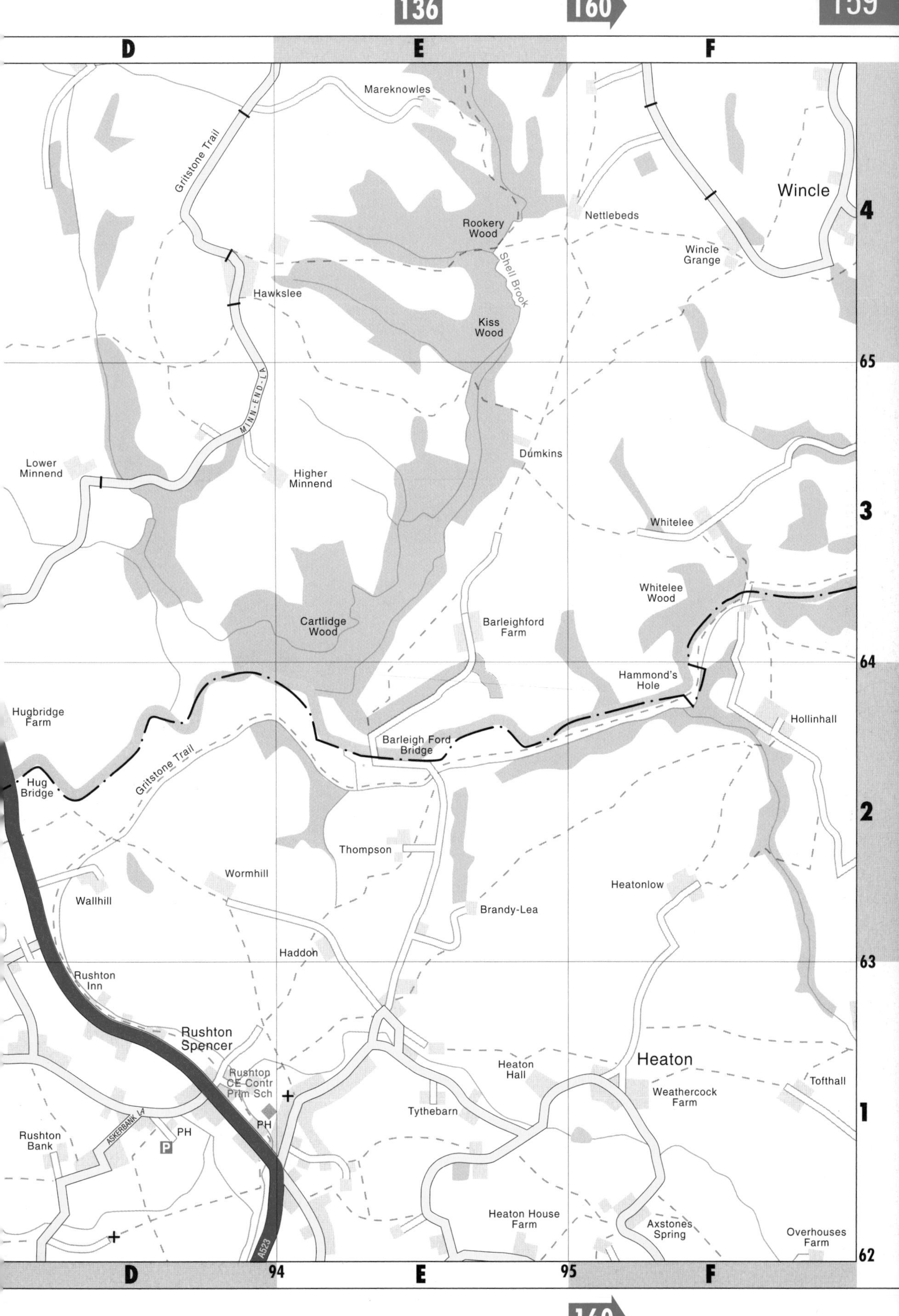
Mareknowles
Gritstone Trail
Wincle
Rookery Wood
Nettlebeds
Wincle Grange
Shell Brook
Hawkslee
Kiss Wood
MINN-END-LA
Dumkins
Lower Minnend
Higher Minnend
Whitelee
Whitelee Wood
Cartlidge Wood
Barleighford Farm
Hammond's Hole
Hugbridge Farm
Hollinhall
Barleigh Ford Bridge
Gritstone Trail
Hug Bridge
Thompson
Wormhill
Heatonlow
Wallhill
Brandy-Lea
Haddon
Rushton Inn
Rushton Spencer
Heaton
Heaton Hall
Tofthall
Rushton CE Contr Prim Sch
Weathercock Farm
Tythebarn
ASKERBANK LA
PH
PH
P
Rushton Bank
Heaton House Farm
Axstones Spring
Overhouses Farm
A523
4
65
3
64
2
63
1
62

D 94 E 95 F

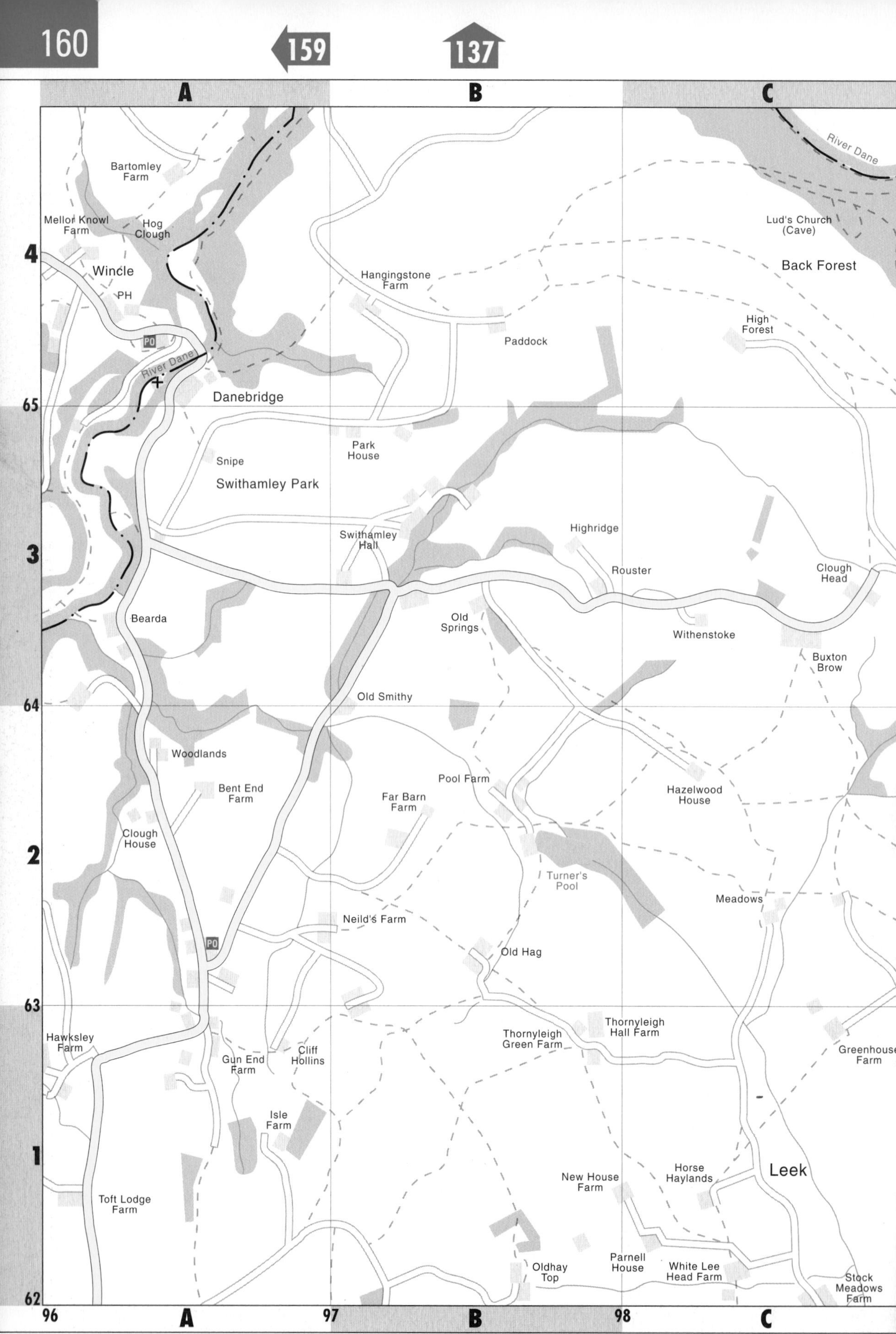

River Dane

Bartomley
Farm

Mellor Knowl
Farm
Hog
Clough

Lud's Church
(Cave)

Back Forest

4

Wincle

Hangingstone
Farm

PH

High
Forest

Paddock

PO

River Dane

Danebridge

65

Park
House

Snipe

Swithamley Park

Highridge

Swithamley
Hall

Rouster

Clough
Head

3

Old
Springs

Withenstoke

Bearda

Buxton
Brow

Old Smithy

64

Woodlands

Pool Farm

Hazelwood
House

Bent End
Farm

Far Barn
Farm

Clough
House

2

Turner's
Pool

Meadows

Neild's Farm

PO

Old Hag

63

Thornyleigh
Hall Farm

Hawksley
Farm

Thornyleigh
Green Farm

Greenhouse
Farm

Gun End
Farm

Cliff
Hollins

Isle
Farm

1

New House
Farm

Horse
Haylands

Leek

Toft Lodge
Farm

Oldhay
Top

Parnell
House

White Lee
Head Farm

Stock
Meadows
Farm

62

D | E | F

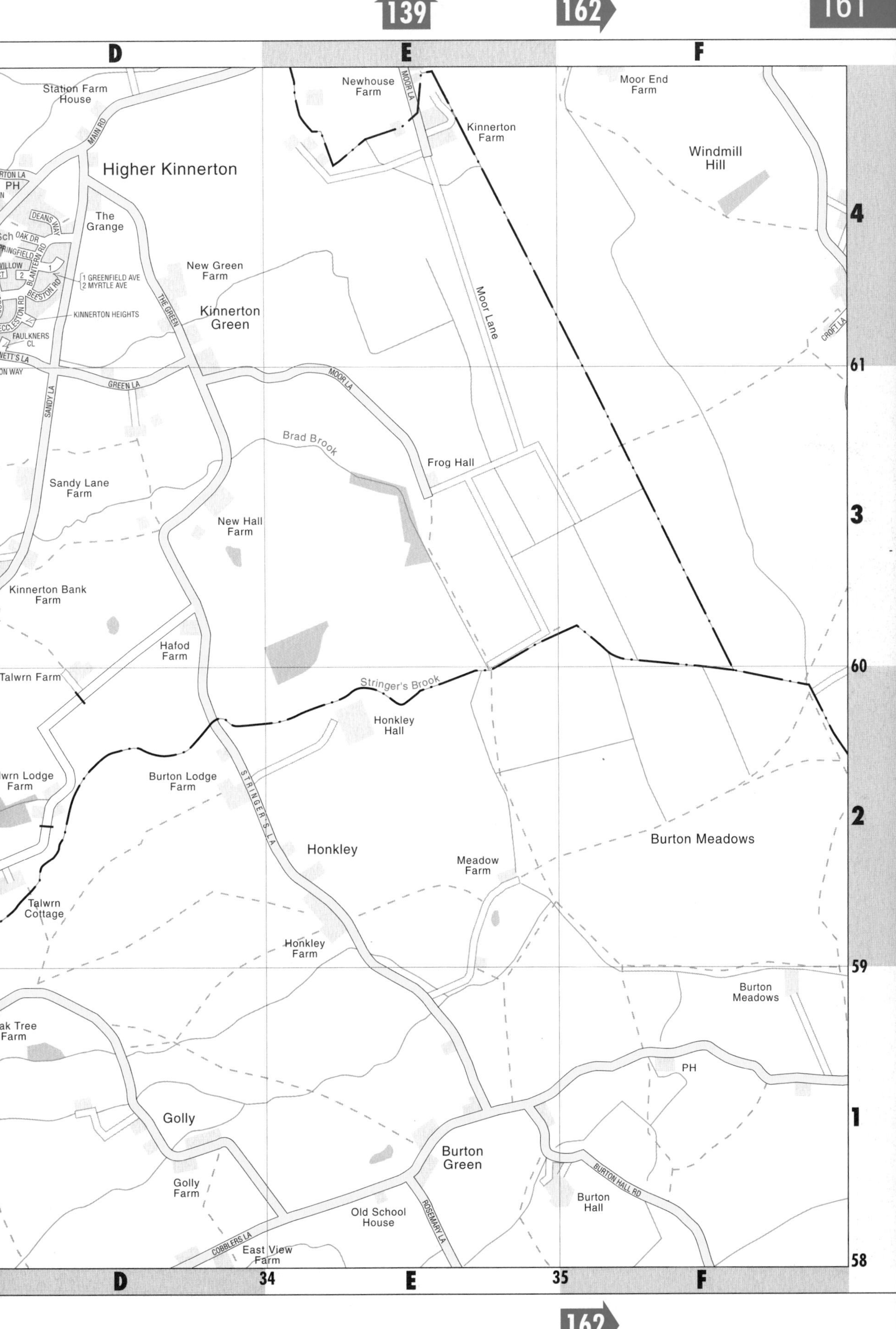

Station Farm House

Higher Kinnerton

The Grange

New Green Farm

1 GREENFIELD AVE
2 MYRTLE AVE

Kinnerton Heights

Kinnerton Green

Sch OAK DR
SPRINGFIELD RD
WILLOW
BLANTERN RD
ECCLESTON RD
BECSTON RD
FAULKNERS CL
NETT'S LA
ON WAY
DEANS WAY
MAIN RD
RTON LA
PH
SANDY LA
THE GREEN
GREEN LA

Newhouse Farm

Kinnerton Farm

Moor End Farm

Windmill Hill

MOOR LA

Moor Lane

CROFT LA

4

MOOR LA

61

Brad Brook

Frog Hall

Sandy Lane Farm

New Hall Farm

Kinnerton Bank Farm

Hafod Farm

3

Talwrn Farm

Stringer's Brook

Honkley Hall

60

wrn Lodge Farm

Burton Lodge Farm

STRINGER'S LA

Honkley

Meadow Farm

Burton Meadows

2

Talwrn Cottage

Honkley Farm

59

Burton Meadows

ak Tree Farm

PH

Golly

Burton Green

BURTON HALL RD

1

Golly Farm

Old School House

ROSEMARY LA

Burton Hall

COBBLERS LA
East View Farm

58

D | 34 | E | 35 | F

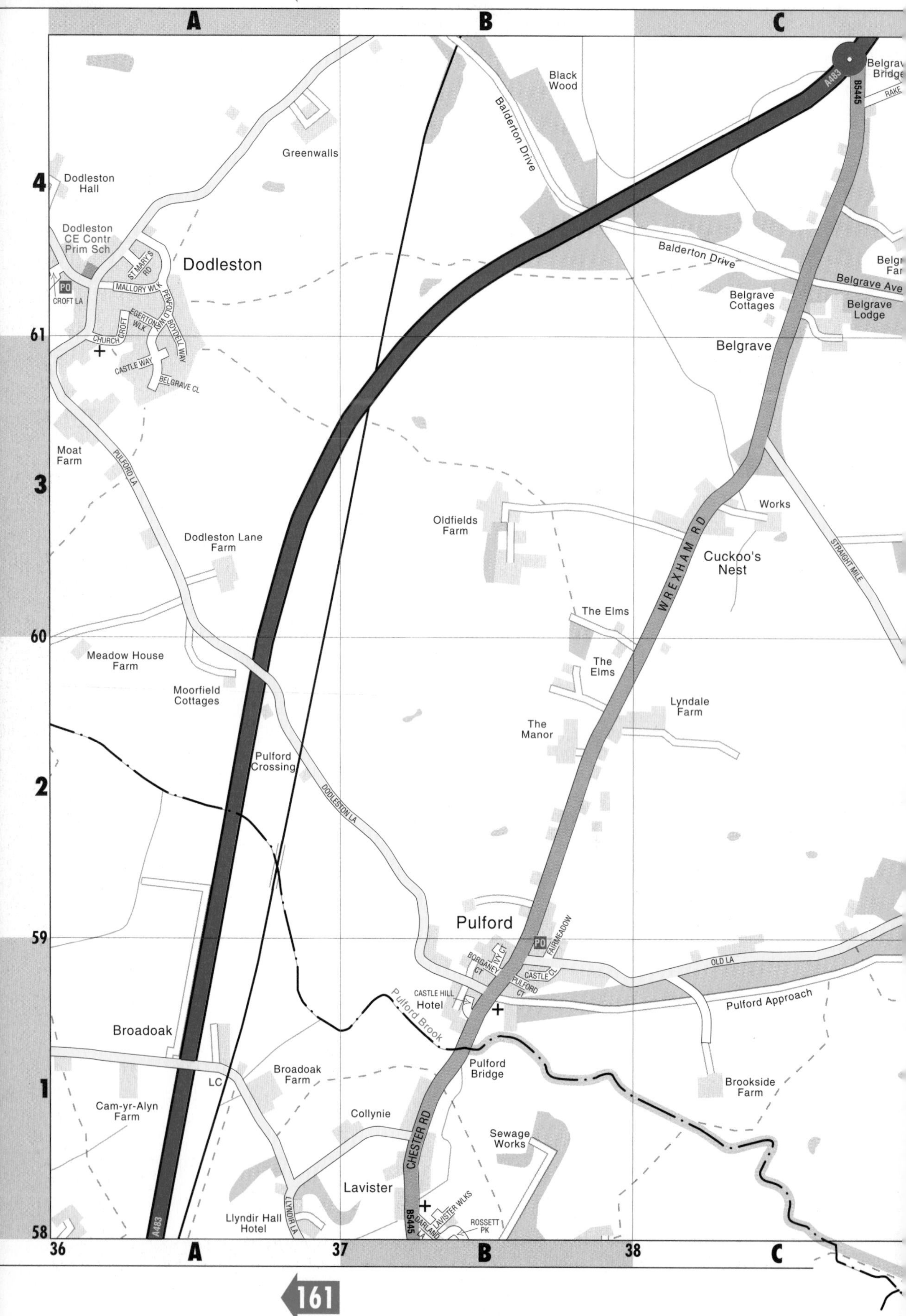

Belgrave Bridge

A483

B5445

RAKE

4

Dodleston Hall

Greenwalls

Black Wood

Balderton Drive

Balderton Drive

Belgr Far

Belgrave Ave

Dodleston CE Contr Prim Sch

Dodleston

Belgrave Cottages

Belgrave Lodge

ST MARY'S RD

PO

MALLORY WLK

PENFOLD BOTTRELL WAY

CROFT LA

EGERTON WLK

CROFT

61

CHURCH

Belgrave

CASTLE WAY

BELGRAVE CL

Moat Farm

PULFORD LA

3

Dodleston Lane Farm

Oldfields Farm

WREXHAM RD

Works

Cuckoo's Nest

STRAIGHT MILE

The Elms

Meadow House Farm

60

The Elms

Moorfield Cottages

Lyndale Farm

Pulford Crossing

DODLESTON LA

The Manor

2

Pulford

PO

FAIRMEADOW

59

BORDANEY CT

IVY CT

CASTLE CL

PULFORD CT

OLD LA

Castle Hill Hotel

Pulford Brook

Pulford Approach

Broadoak

Pulford Bridge

Brookside Farm

1

LC

Broadoak Farm

Cam-yr-Alyn Farm

Collynie

CHESTER RD

Sewage Works

A483

Lavister

B5445

LLYNDIR LA

GARLAND

LAVISTER WLKS

ROSSETT PK

Llyndir Hall Hotel

58

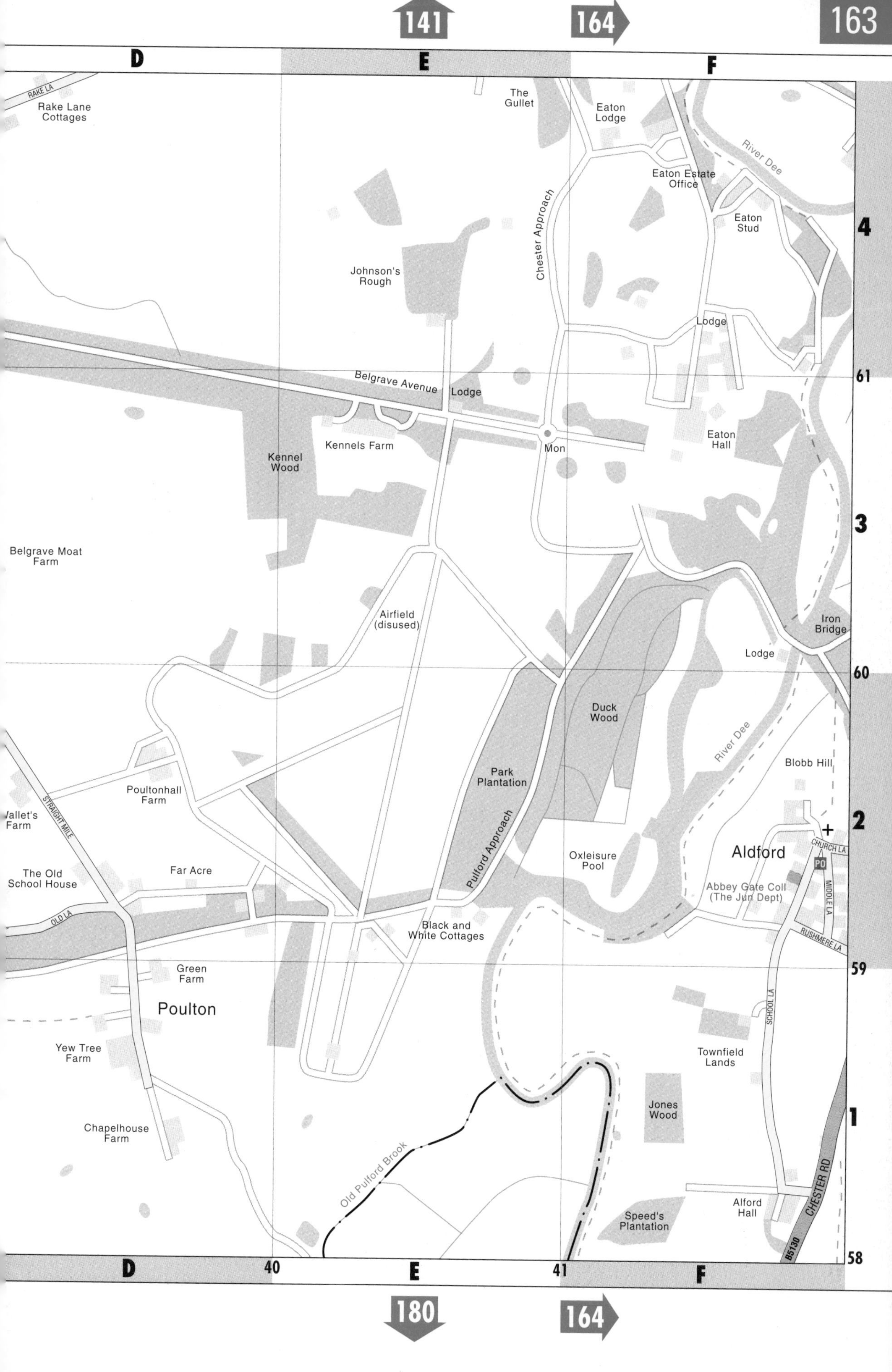

D E F

RAKE LA
Rake Lane
Cottages

The
Gullet

Eaton
Lodge

River Dee

Eaton Estate
Office

Eaton
Stud

4

Chester Approach

Johnson's
Rough

Lodge

Belgrave Avenue   Lodge

61

Kennel
Wood

Kennels Farm

Mon

Eaton
Hall

3

Belgrave Moat
Farm

Airfield
(disused)

Iron
Bridge

Lodge

60

Duck
Wood

River Dee

Blobb Hill

Park
Plantation

Pulford Approach

Poultonhall
Farm

Vallet's
Farm

STRAIGHT MILE

Far Acre

Oxleisure
Pool

Aldford

CHURCH LA

2

PO

MIDDLE LA

The Old
School House

Abbey Gate Coll
(The Jun Dept)

OLD LA

Black and
White Cottages

RUSHMERE LA

Green
Farm

59

Poulton

SCHOOL LA

Yew Tree
Farm

Townfield
Lands

Chapelhouse
Farm

Jones
Wood

1

Old Pulford Brook

Speed's
Plantation

Alford
Hall

CHESTER RD

B5130

D   40   E   41   F   58

A   B   C

B5130

Cheaveley Bridge

Cheaveleyhall Farm

Crook of Dee

4

River Dee

Saighton Grange

Abbey Gate Coll

Powsey Brook

Smithy Farm

Horse Pasture

Powseybrook Bridge

Waverton Approach

61

Buerton Approach

Chapelhouse Farm

Platt's Rough

Sooty Fields Plantation

Bruera

3

CHAPEL LA

Coldharbo Farm

PLATT'S LA

Coldharbo

Buerton Kennels

Churton Heath Farm

Penlington's Wood

60

Newbold

Lea Newbold Farm

Brickyard Farm

2

CHURCH LA

PH

Bank Farm

Brickyard Plantation

LEA LA

Lea Cottages

RUSHMERE LA

59

B5130

CHESTER RD

Leahall Farm

Wim Bridge

1

LOWER LA

Glebe Farm

The Ponderosa

Ford Lane

Ford Lane Farm

58

42   A   43   B   44   C

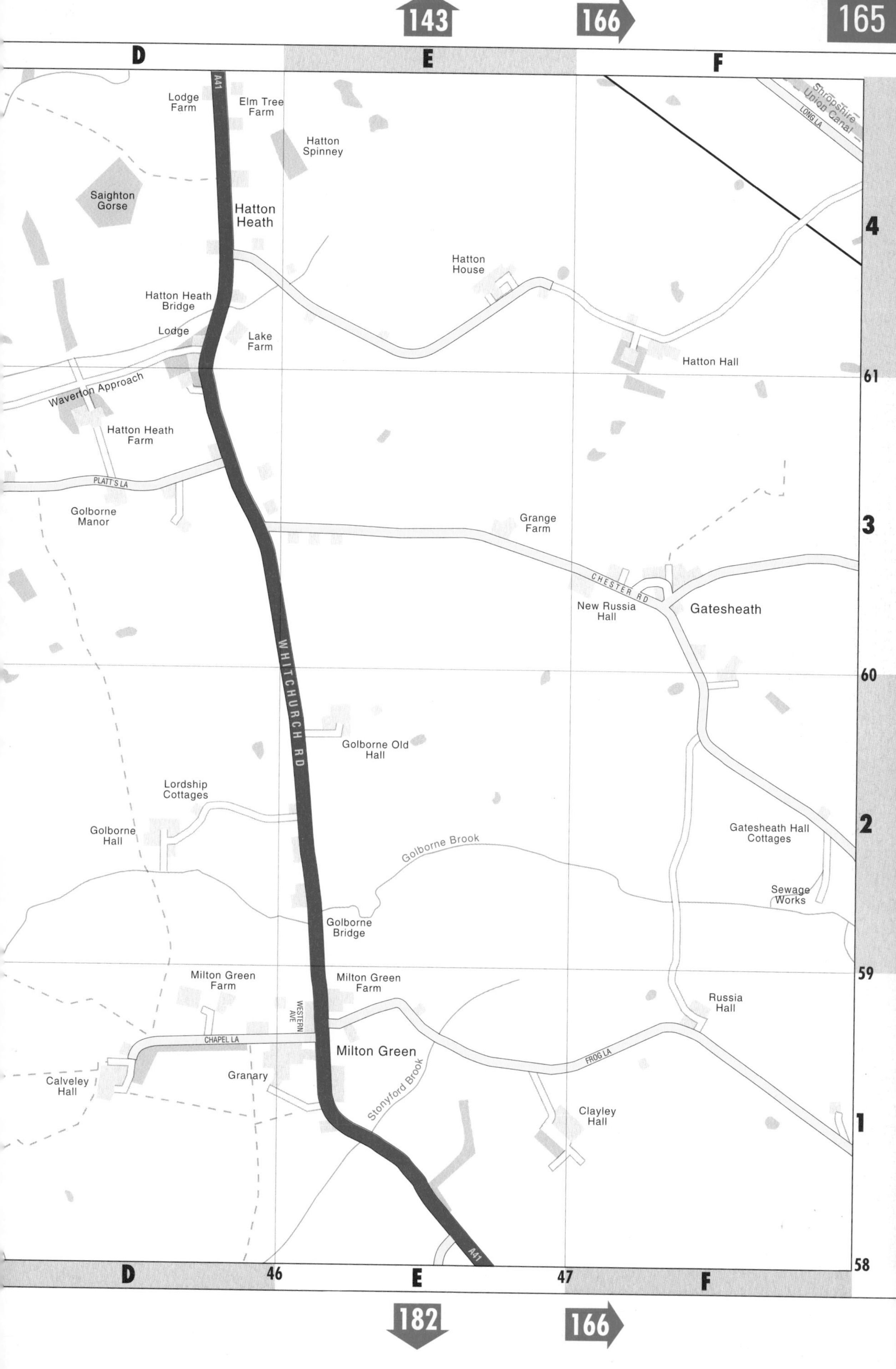

D
E
F

Shropshire Union Canal
LONG LA

Lodge Farm
Elm Tree Farm
Hatton Spinney
A41

Saighton Gorse

Hatton Heath

Hatton House

4

Hatton Heath Bridge
Lodge
Lake Farm
Hatton Hall
61

Waverton Approach

Hatton Heath Farm

PLATT'S LA

Golborne Manor

Grange Farm
3

CHESTER RD

New Russia Hall
Gatesheath

WHITCHURCH RD

Golborne Old Hall
60

Lordship Cottages

Golborne Hall
Gatesheath Hall Cottages
2

Golborne Brook
Sewage Works

Golborne Bridge

Milton Green Farm
Milton Green Farm
59
Russia Hall

WESTERN AVE

CHAPEL LA
Milton Green

Calveley Hall
Granary
FROG LA

Stonyford Brook
Clayley Hall
1

A41

58
D
46
E
47
F

165
144

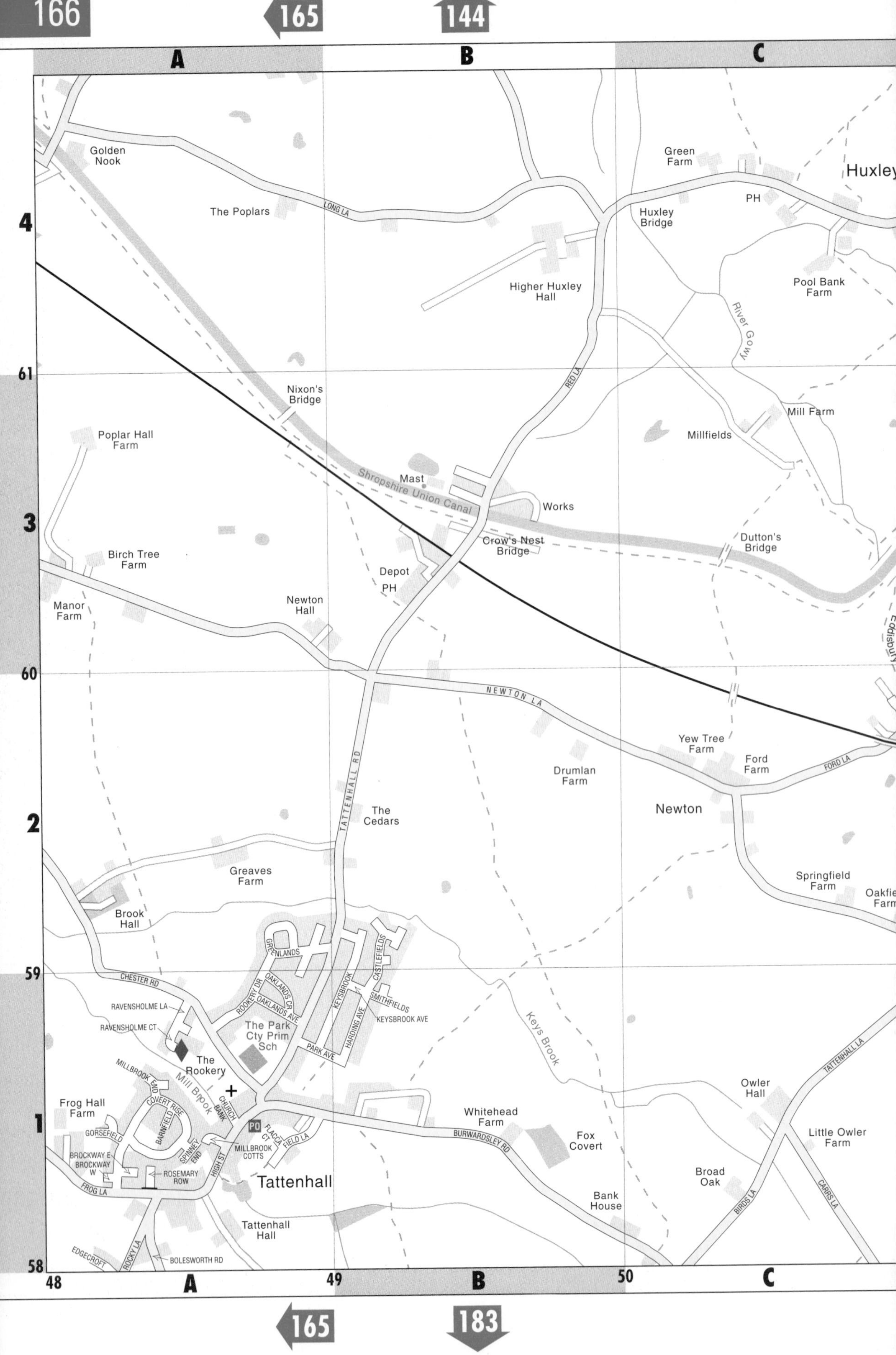
A
B
C
4
61
3
60
2
59
1
58
48
49
50
Golden Nook
The Poplars
LONG LA
Green Farm
Huxley
PH
Huxley Bridge
Higher Huxley Hall
Pool Bank Farm
River Gowy
RED LA
Nixon's Bridge
Mill Farm
Millfields
Poplar Hall Farm
Mast
Shropshire Union Canal
Works
Crow's Nest Bridge
Dutton's Bridge
Birch Tree Farm
Depot
PH
Manor Farm
Newton Hall
Eddisbury
NEWTON LA
Yew Tree Farm
Ford Farm
FORD LA
Drumlan Farm
Newton
TATTENHALL RD
The Cedars
Greaves Farm
Springfield Farm
Oakfie Farm
Brook Hall
GREENLANDS
CASTLEFIELDS
CHESTER RD
ROOKERY DR
OAKLANDS CR
OAKLANDS AVE
KEYSBROOK
SMITHFIELDS
KEYSBROOK AVE
HARDING AVE
RAVENSHOLME LA
RAVENSHOLME CT
The Park Cty Prim Sch
PARK AVE
The Rookery
Keys Brook
TATTENHALL LA
MILLBROOK END
Mill Brook
COVERT RISE
CHURCH BANK
Owler Hall
Frog Hall Farm
BARNFIELD
PO
FLACCA CT
FIELD LA
Whitehead Farm
BURWARDSLEY RD
Fox Covert
Little Owler Farm
GORSEFIELD
SPINNEY END
MILLBROOK COTTS
BROCKWAY E
BROCKWAY W
ROSEMARY ROW
HIGH ST
Tattenhall
Broad Oak
FROG LA
Bank House
BIRDS LA
CARRS LA
Tattenhall Hall
EDGECROFT
ROCKY LA
BOLESWORTH RD

165
183

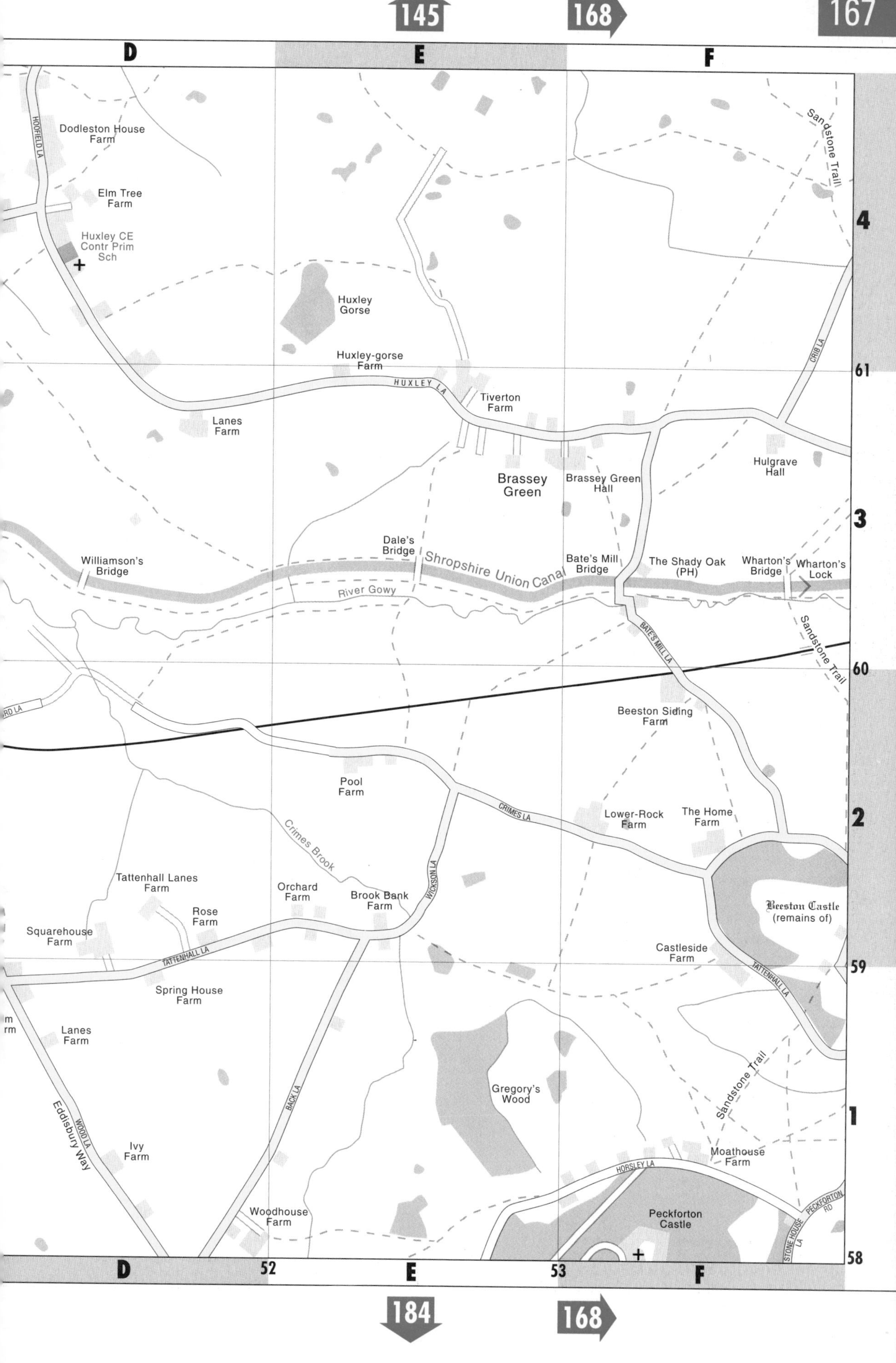

D E F

Sandstone Trail

HOOFIELD LA

Dodleston House Farm

Elm Tree Farm

Huxley CE Contr Prim Sch

4

CRIB LA

Huxley Gorse

61

Huxley-gorse Farm

HUXLEY LA

Tiverton Farm

Lanes Farm

Brassey Green

Brassey Green Hall

Hulgrave Hall

3

Williamson's Bridge

Dale's Bridge

Shropshire Union Canal

Bate's Mill Bridge

The Shady Oak (PH)

Wharton's Bridge

Wharton's Lock

River Gowy

BATE'S MILL LA

Sandstone Trail

60

Beeston Siding Farm

Pool Farm

CRIMES LA

Lower-Rock Farm

The Home Farm

2

Crimes Brook

Beeston Castle (remains of)

Tattenhall Lanes Farm

Rose Farm

Orchard Farm

Brook Bank Farm

WICKSON LA

Squarehouse Farm

TATTENHALL LA

Castleside Farm

TATTENHALL LA

59

Spring House Farm

Lanes Farm

m rm

BACK LA

WOOD LA

Eddisbury Way

Gregory's Wood

Sandstone Trail

1

Ivy Farm

Moathouse Farm

HORSLEY LA

Woodhouse Farm

Peckforton Castle

STONE HOUSE LA

PECKFORTON RD

58

D 52 E 53 F

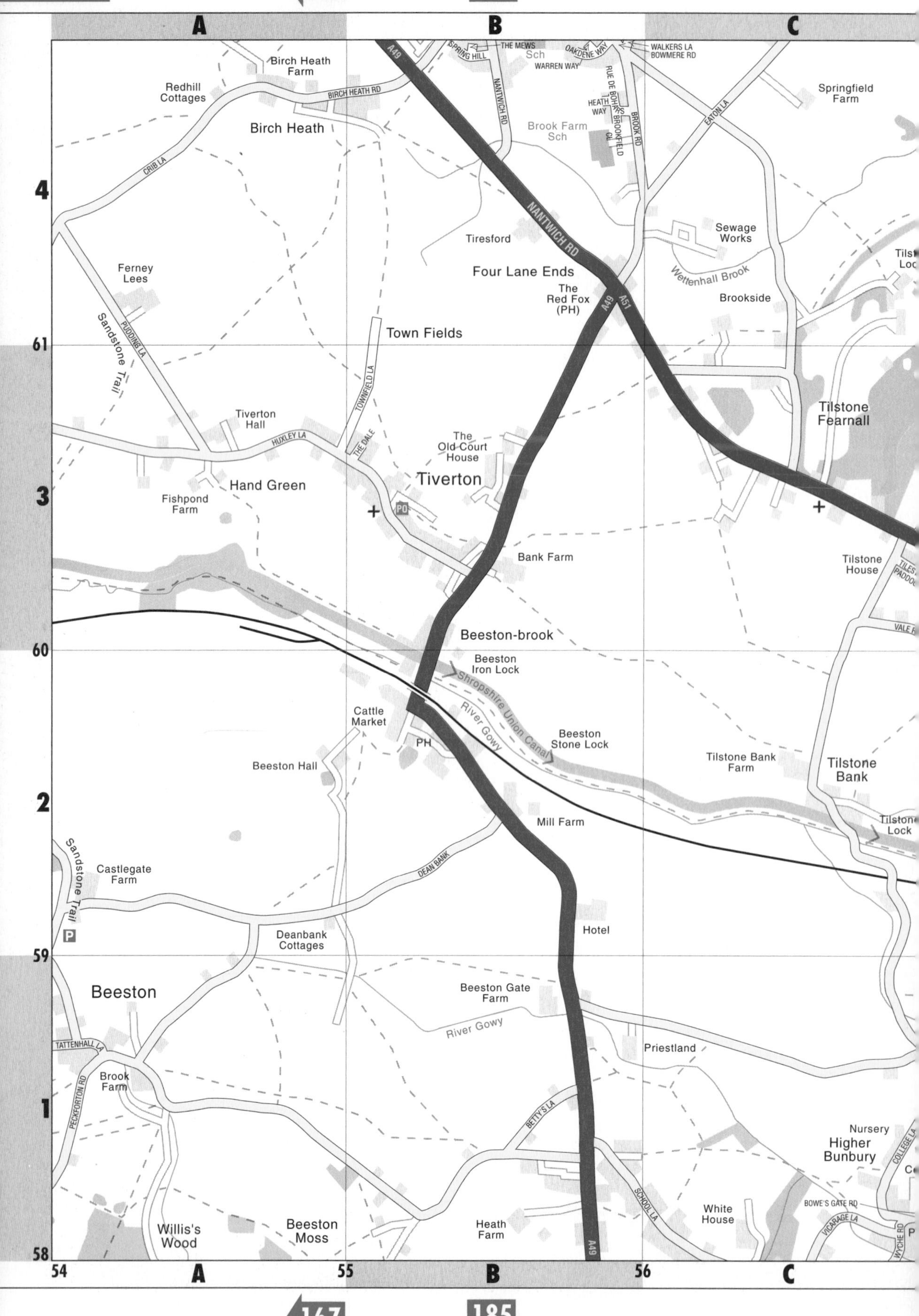
A
B
C
Birch Heath Farm
Redhill Cottages
BIRCH HEATH RD
Birch Heath
CRIB LA
THE MEWS
SPRING HILL
Sch
WARREN WAY
OAKDENE WAY
WALKERS LA
BOWMERE RD
NANTWICH RD
HEATH WAY
RUE DE BOHUN
BROOKFIELD CL
BROOK RD
EATON LA
Springfield Farm
Brook Farm Sch
A49
Tiresford
NANTWICH RD
Sewage Works
Wettenhall Brook
Brookside
Four Lane Ends
The Red Fox (PH)
A51
Ferney Lees
PUDDING LA
Sandstone Trail
Town Fields
TOWNFIELD LA
Tilstone Fearnall
Tiverton Hall
HUXLEY LA
THE DALE
The Old Court House
Tiverton
Hand Green
Fishpond Farm
PO
Bank Farm
Tilstone House
VALE RD
Beeston-brook
Beeston Iron Lock
Shropshire Union Canal
River Gowy
Cattle Market
PH
Beeston Stone Lock
Beeston Hall
Tilstone Bank Farm
Tilstone Bank
Mill Farm
Castlegate Farm
DEAN BANK
Sandstone Trail
P
Deanbank Cottages
Hotel
Beeston
Beeston Gate Farm
River Gowy
Priestland
TATTENHALL LA
Brook Farm
PECKFORTON RD
BETTY'S LA
Nursery
Higher Bunbury
COLLEGE LA
SCHOOL LA
White House
BOWE'S GATE RD
VICARAGE LA
WYCHE RD
Willis's Wood
Beeston Moss
Heath Farm
4
61
3
60
2
59
1
58
54
55
56

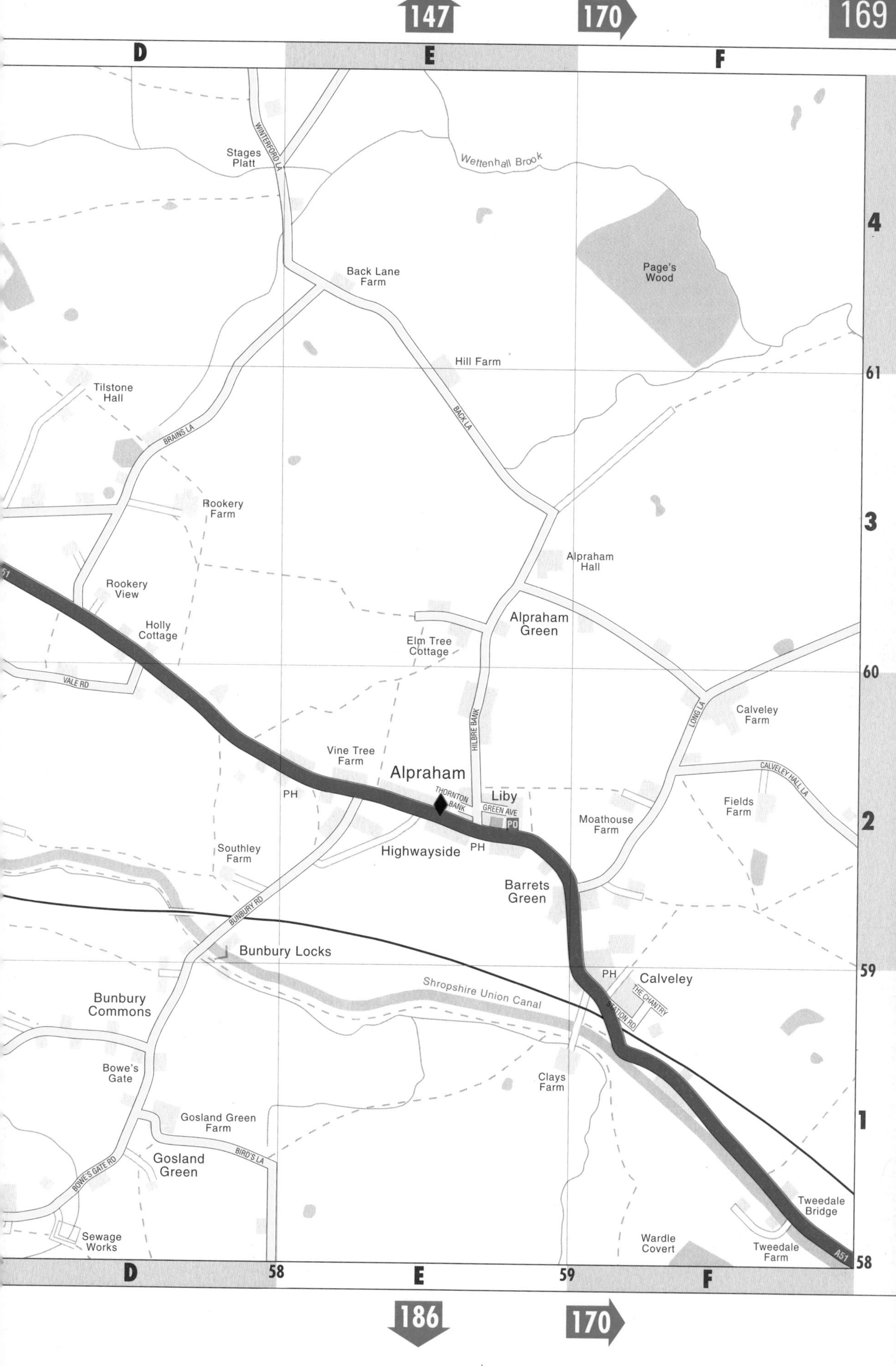

D
E
F

Stages Platt

WINTERFORD LA

Wettenhall Brook

Page's Wood

4

Back Lane Farm

Hill Farm

61

Tilstone Hall

BRAINS LA

BACK LA

Rookery Farm

3

Alpraham Hall

Rookery View

Holly Cottage

Elm Tree Cottage

Alpraham Green

VALE RD

60

HILBRE BANK

Calveley Farm

LONG LA

CALVELEY HALL LA

Vine Tree Farm

Alpraham

Liby

Fields Farm

2

PH

THORNTON BANK

GREEN AVE

PO

Moathouse Farm

Southley Farm

Highwayside

PH

Barrets Green

BUNBURY RD

Bunbury Locks

PH

Calveley

59

Shropshire Union Canal

THE CHANTRY

STATION RD

Bunbury Commons

Bowe's Gate

Clays Farm

Gosland Green Farm

BIRD'S LA

1

A51

BOWE'S GATE RD

Gosland Green

Sewage Works

Wardle Covert

Tweedale Bridge

Tweedale Farm

A51

58

D
58
E
59
F

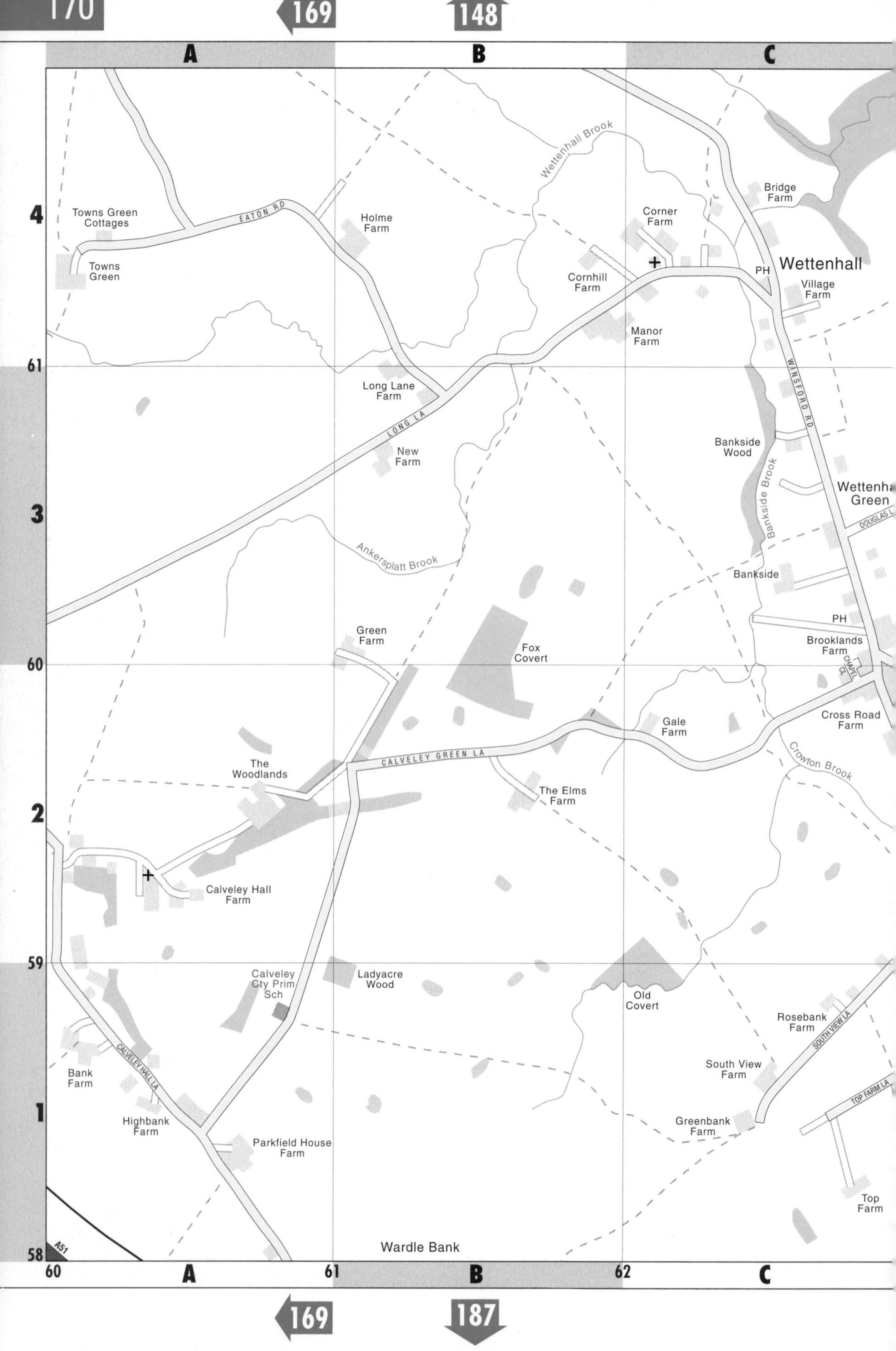

A

B

C

4

Towns Green
Cottages

Towns
Green

EATON RD

Holme
Farm

Wettenhall Brook

Corner
Farm

✛

Cornhill
Farm

PH

Wettenhall

Village
Farm

Bridge
Farm

Manor
Farm

61

Long Lane
Farm

LONG LA

New
Farm

WINSFORD RD

Bankside
Wood

Bankside Brook

Wettenha
Green

DOUGLAS L

3

Ankersplatt Brook

Bankside

Green
Farm

Fox
Covert

PH

Brooklands
Farm

CHAPEL
CL

60

CALVELEY GREEN LA

Gale
Farm

Cross Road
Farm

Crowton Brook

The
Woodlands

The Elms
Farm

2

✛

Calveley Hall
Farm

59

Calveley
Cty Prim
Sch

Ladyacre
Wood

Old
Covert

Rosebank
Farm

SOUTH VIEW LA

South View
Farm

TOP FARM LA

Bank
Farm

CALVELEY HALL LA

1

Highbank
Farm

Parkfield House
Farm

Greenbank
Farm

Top
Farm

A51

58

Wardle Bank

60

A

61

B

62

C

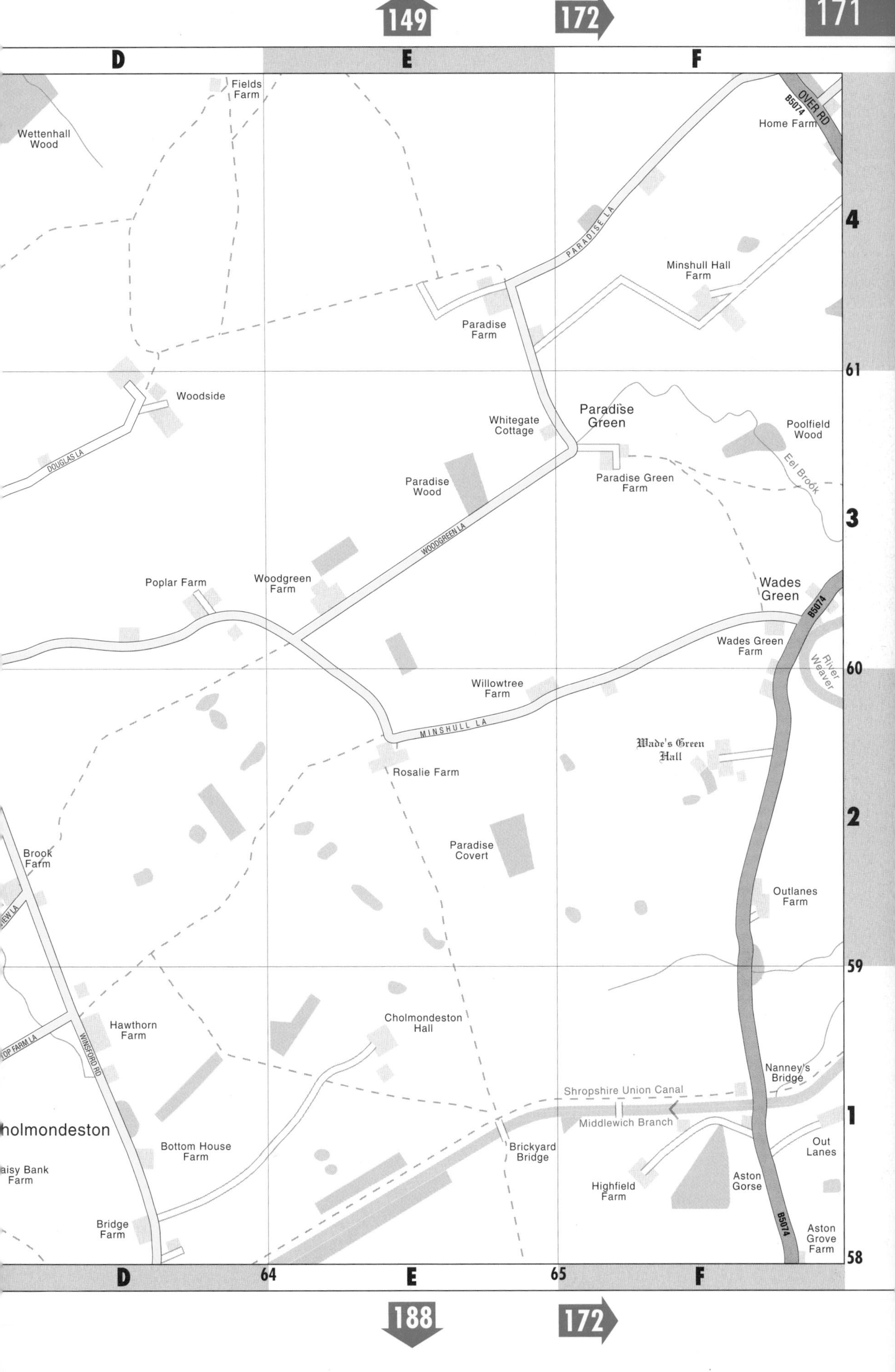

Wettenhall
Wood

Fields
Farm

Home Farm

OVER RD

B5074

PARADISE LA

Minshull Hall
Farm

Paradise
Farm

Woodside

Whitegate
Cottage

Paradise
Green

Paradise Green
Farm

Poolfield
Wood

Eel Brook

DOUGLAS LA

Paradise
Wood

WOODGREEN LA

Poplar Farm

Woodgreen
Farm

Wades
Green

B5074

Wades Green
Farm

River Weaver

Willowtree
Farm

MINSHULL LA

Rosalie Farm

Wade's Green
Hall

Brook
Farm

Paradise
Covert

Outlanes
Farm

VIEW LA

Hawthorn
Farm

Cholmondeston
Hall

Nanney's
Bridge

TOP FARM LA

WINSFORD RD

Shropshire Union Canal

holmondeston

Bottom House
Farm

Brickyard
Bridge

Middlewich Branch

Out
Lanes

aisy Bank
Farm

Highfield
Farm

Aston
Gorse

Bridge
Farm

B5074

Aston
Grove
Farm

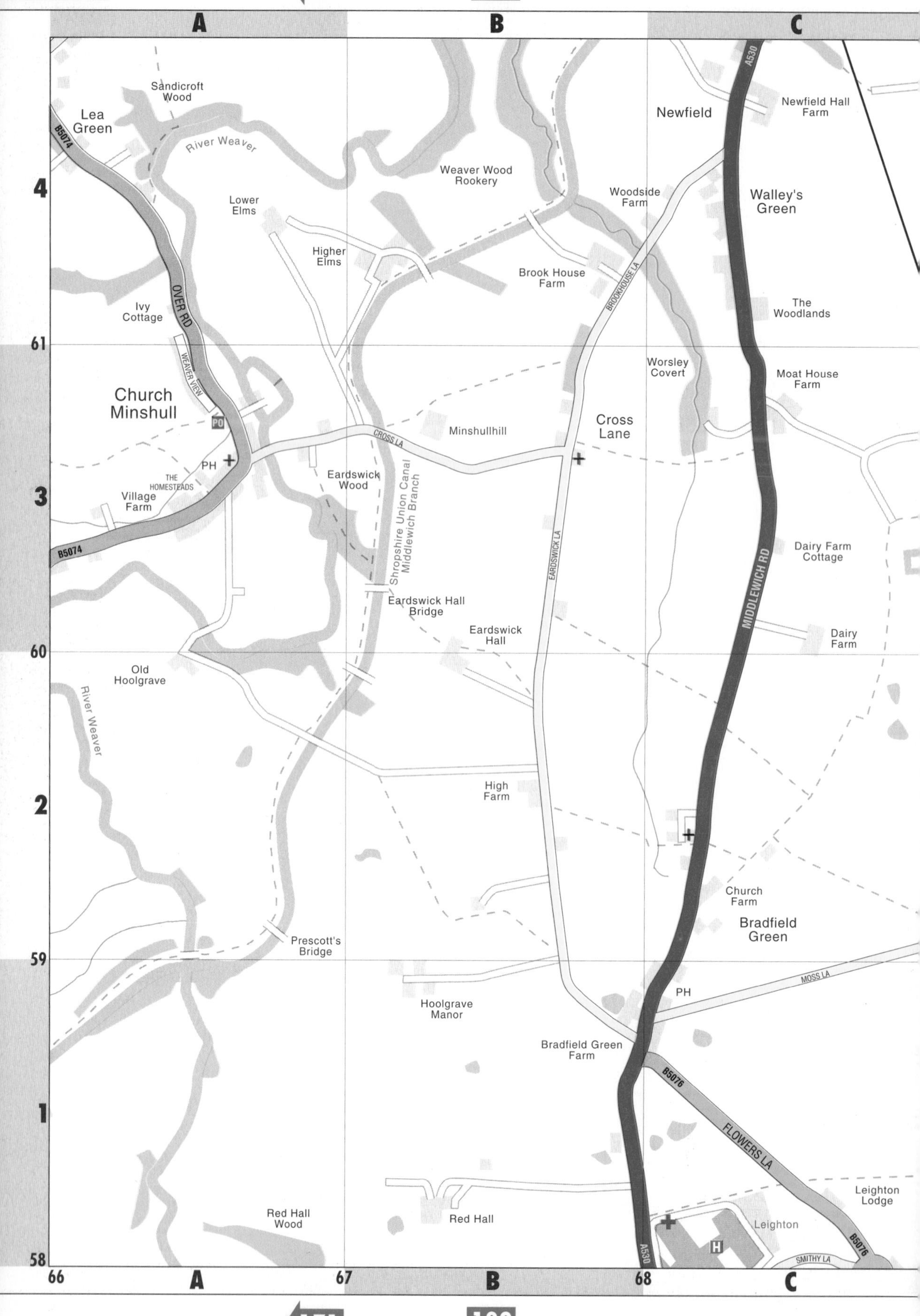

Sandicroft
Wood

Lea
Green

River Weaver

Weaver Wood
Rookery

Newfield

Newfield Hall
Farm

Walley's
Green

Lower
Elms

Woodside
Farm

Higher
Elms

Brook House
Farm

BROOKHOUSE LA

The
Woodlands

OVER RD

Ivy
Cottage

61

Worsley
Covert

Moat House
Farm

WEAVER VIEW

Church
Minshull

PO

CROSS LA

Minshullhill

Cross
Lane

3

PH

THE HOMESTEADS

Village
Farm

Eardswick
Wood

EARDSWICK LA

MIDDLEWICH RD

Dairy Farm
Cottage

B5074

Shropshire Union Canal
Middlewich Branch

Eardswick Hall
Bridge

60

Old
Hoolgrave

Eardswick
Hall

Dairy
Farm

River Weaver

High
Farm

2

Church
Farm

Bradfield
Green

59

Prescott's
Bridge

MOSS LA

PH

Hoolgrave
Manor

Bradfield Green
Farm

B5076

1

FLOWERS LA

Leighton
Lodge

A530

Red Hall
Wood

Red Hall

Leighton

H

B5076

58

SMITHY LA

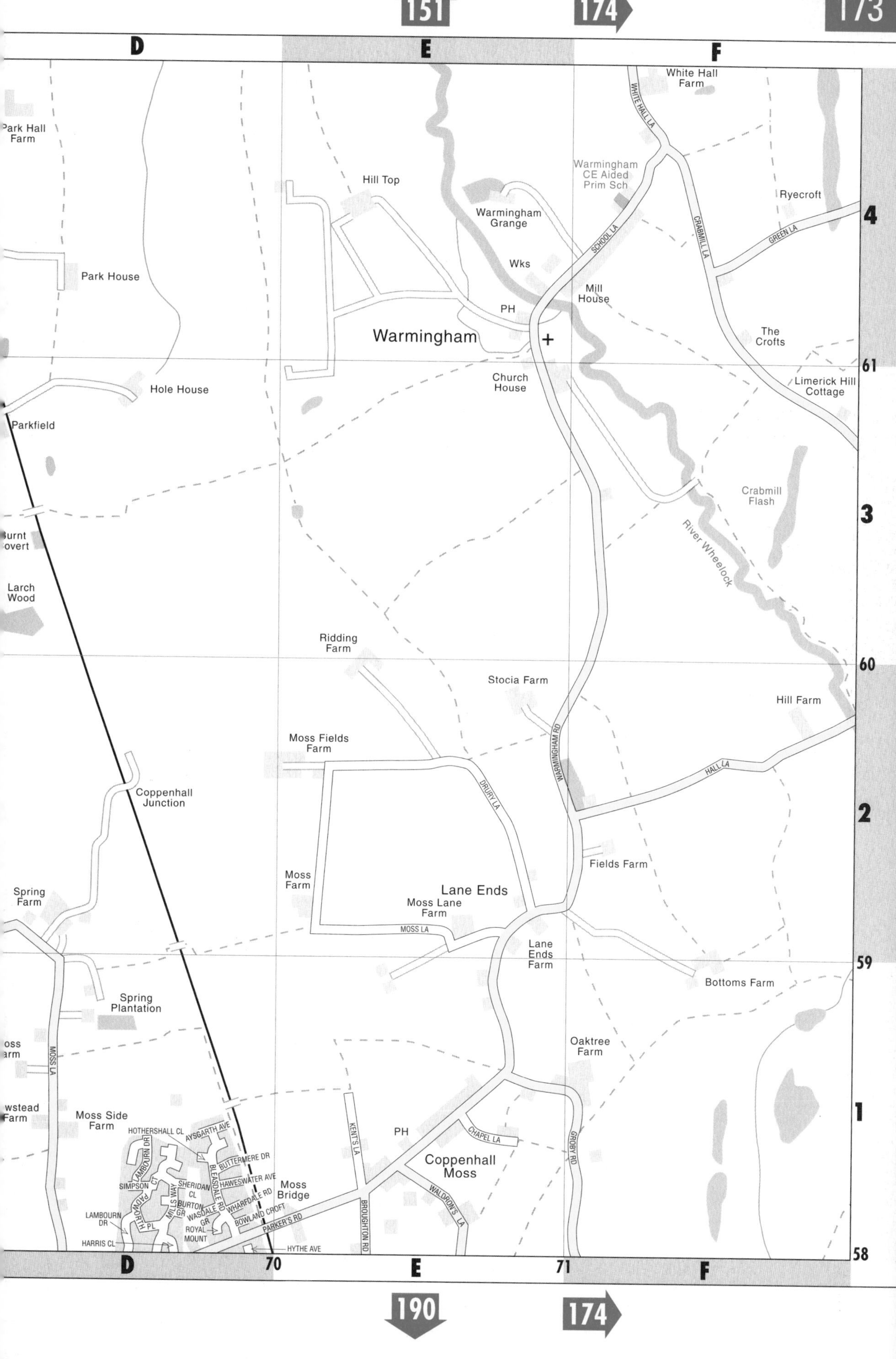

Park Hall Farm

Hill Top

Warmingham CE Aided Prim Sch

Ryecroft

Warmingham Grange

Wks

Mill House

The Crofts

Park House

PH

Warmingham

+

61

Hole House

Church House

Limerick Hill Cottage

Parkfield

4

Burnt Covert

Crabmill Flash

Larch Wood

3

River Wheelock

Ridding Farm

60

Stocia Farm

Hill Farm

Moss Fields Farm

HALL LA

DRURY LA

WARMINGHAM RD

Coppenhall Junction

2

Moss Farm

Fields Farm

Spring Farm

Lane Ends

Moss Lane Farm

MOSS LA

Lane Ends Farm

59

Bottoms Farm

Spring Plantation

Oaktree Farm

Moss Farm

MOSS LA

1

Newstead Farm

Moss Side Farm

HOTHERSHALL CL

AYSGARTH AVE

BUTTERMERE DR

LAMBOURN DR

LAMBOURN CT

BLEASDALE RD

HAWESWATER AVE

WHARFDALE RD

PH

CHAPEL LA

Coppenhall Moss

KENT'S LA

GROBY RD

SIMPSON CT

MILLS WAY

SHERIDAN CL

BURTON GR

WASDALE GR

ROYAL MOUNT

BOWLAND CROFT

Moss Bridge

LAMBOURN DR

PARKDALE PL

HARRIS CL

HYTHE AVE

PARKER'S RD

BROUGHTON RD

WALDRON'S LA

D 70 E 71 F 58

173
152

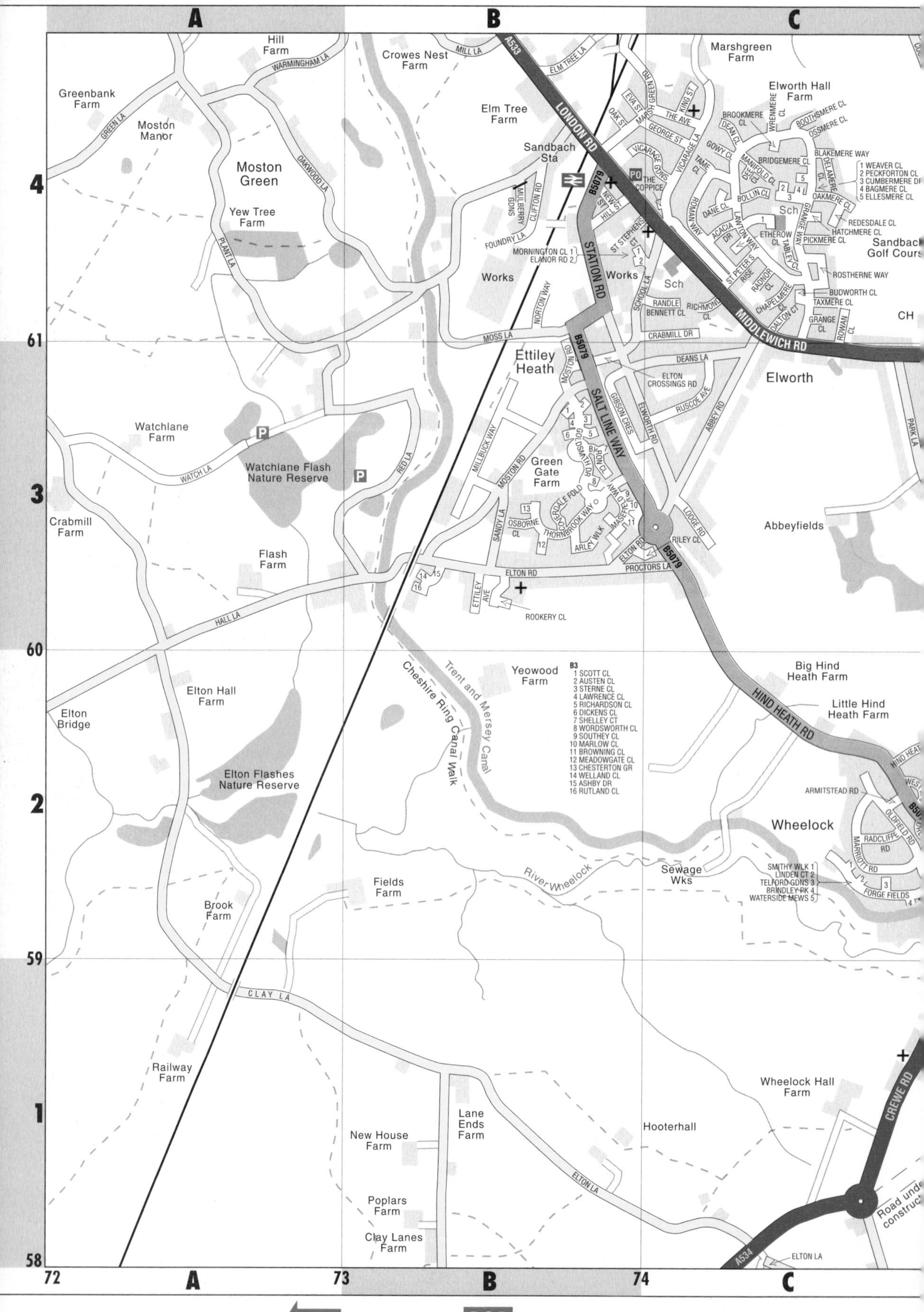
A
B
C
4
61
3
60
2
59
1
58
72
73
74
Hill Farm
WARMINGHAM LA
Crowes Nest Farm
MILL LA
A533
ELM TREE LA
Marshgreen Farm
Greenbank Farm
GREEN LA
Moston Manor
Elm Tree Farm
LONDON RD
Elworth Hall Farm
Sandbach Sta
Moston Green
OAKWOOD LA
Yew Tree Farm
PLANT LA
MULBERRY GDNS
CLIFTON RD
FOUNDRY LA
MORNINGTON CL 1
ELANOR RD 2
STATION RD
B5079
Works
Works
Sch
Sch
NORTON WAY
MOSS LA
RANDLE
BENNETT CL
RICHMOND CL
CRABMILL DR
MIDDLEWICH RD
Sandbach Golf Course
BLAKEMERE WAY
1 WEAVER CL
2 PECKFORTON CL
3 CUMBERMERE DR
4 BAGMERE CL
5 ELLESMERE CL
REDESDALE CL
HATCHMERE CL
PICKMERE CL
ROSTHERNE WAY
BUDWORTH CL
TAXMERE CL
GRANGE CL
ROWAN CL
Ettiley Heath
MOSTON RD
DEANS LA
ELTON CROSSINGS RD
RUSCOE AVE
ABBEY RD
Elworth
PARK LA
Watchlane Farm
WATCH LA
Watchlane Flash Nature Reserve
RED LA
SALT LINE WAY
GIBSON CRES
ELWORTH RD
MILLBUCK WAY
Green Gate Farm
GOLDSMITH DR
THORNBROOK WAY
OSBORNE CL
SANDY LA
ARLEY WLK
LODGE RD
RILEY CL
PROCTORS LA
Abbeyfields
Crabmill Farm
Flash Farm
ELTON RD
ETTILEY AVE
ROOKERY CL
HALL LA
Yeowood Farm
B3
1 SCOTT CL
2 AUSTEN CL
3 STERNE CL
4 LAWRENCE CL
5 RICHARDSON CL
6 DICKENS CL
7 SHELLEY CT
8 WORDSWORTH CL
9 SOUTHEY CL
10 MARLOW CL
11 BROWNING CL
12 MEADOWGATE CL
13 CHESTERTON GR
14 WELLAND CL
15 ASHBY DR
16 RUTLAND CL
Big Hind Heath Farm
Little Hind Heath Farm
HIND HEATH RD
Elton Hall Farm
Elton Bridge
Trent and Mersey Canal
Cheshire Ring Canal Walk
Elton Flashes Nature Reserve
ARMITSTEAD RD
Wheelock
RADCLIFFE RD
SMITHY WLK 1
LINDEN CT 2
TELFORD GDNS 3
BRINDLEY PK 4
WATERSIDE MEWS 5
FORGE FIELDS
River Wheelock
Sewage Wks
Fields Farm
Brook Farm
CLAY LA
Railway Farm
Wheelock Hall Farm
CREWE RD
Lane Ends Farm
New House Farm
Hooterhall
ELTON LA
Poplars Farm
Clay Lanes Farm
Road under construction
A534
ELTON LA

173
191

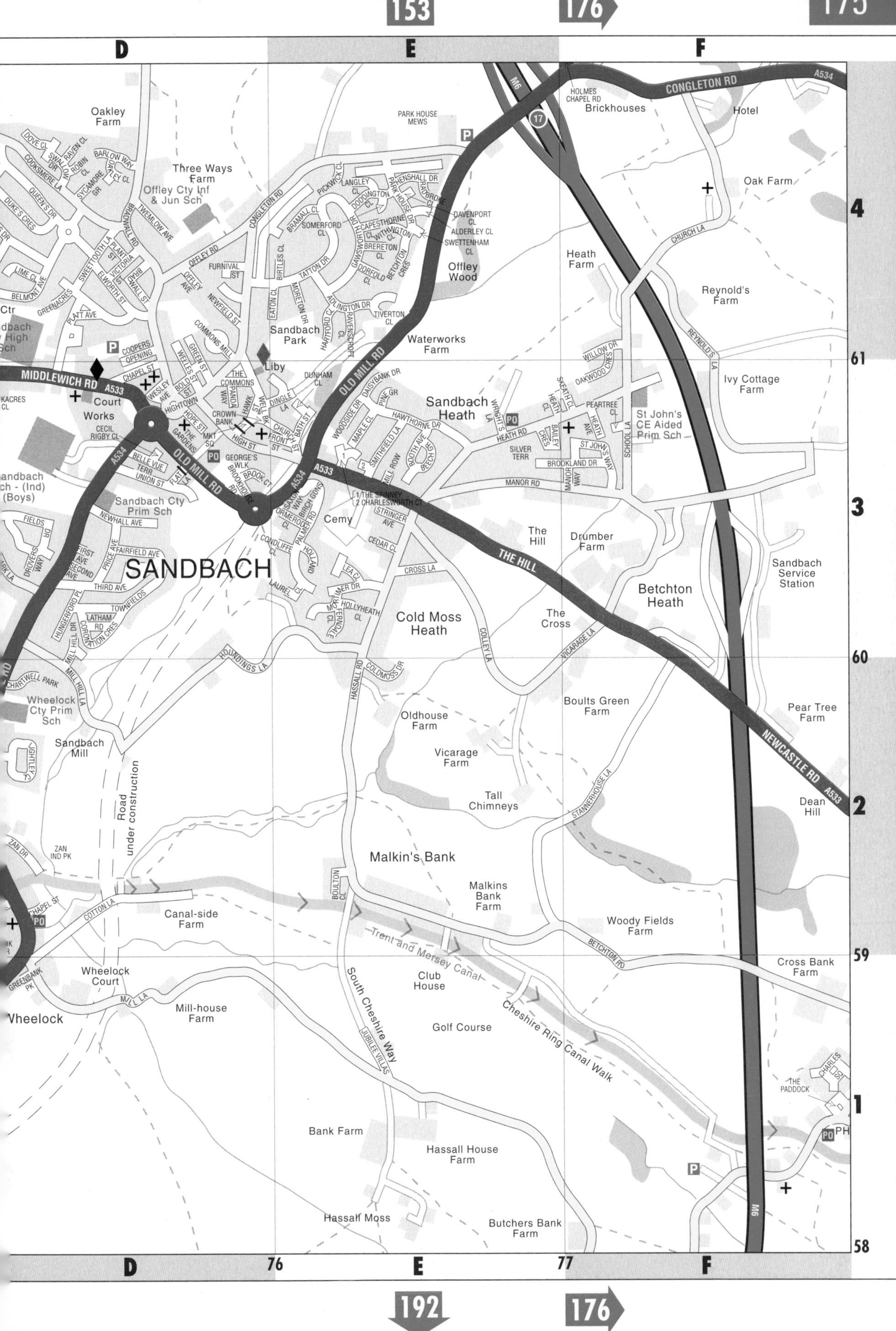
D
E
F
SANDBACH
Oakley Farm
Three Ways Farm
Offley Cty Inf & Jun Sch
Brickhouses
Hotel
Oak Farm
Heath Farm
Offley Wood
Reynold's Farm
Sandbach Park
Waterworks Farm
Liby
Court Works
Sandbach Heath
Ivy Cottage Farm
St John's CE Aided Prim Sch
Sandbach Cty Prim Sch
Cemy
The Hill
Drumber Farm
Sandbach Service Station
Betchton Heath
Cold Moss Heath
The Cross
Wheelock Cty Prim Sch
Sandbach Mill
Oldhouse Farm
Boults Green Farm
Pear Tree Farm
Vicarage Farm
Tall Chimneys
Dean Hill
Road under construction
Malkin's Bank
Malkins Bank Farm
Canal-side Farm
Woody Fields Farm
Trent and Mersey Canal
Cross Bank Farm
Wheelock Court
Club House
Cheshire Ring Canal Walk
Mill-house Farm
Wheelock
Golf Course
South Cheshire Way
Bank Farm
Hassall House Farm
Hassall Moss
Butchers Bank Farm
CONGLETON RD
MIDDLEWICH RD
OLD MILL RD
THE HILL
NEWCASTLE RD
A533
A534
M6
61
60
59
58
4
3
2
1
76
77

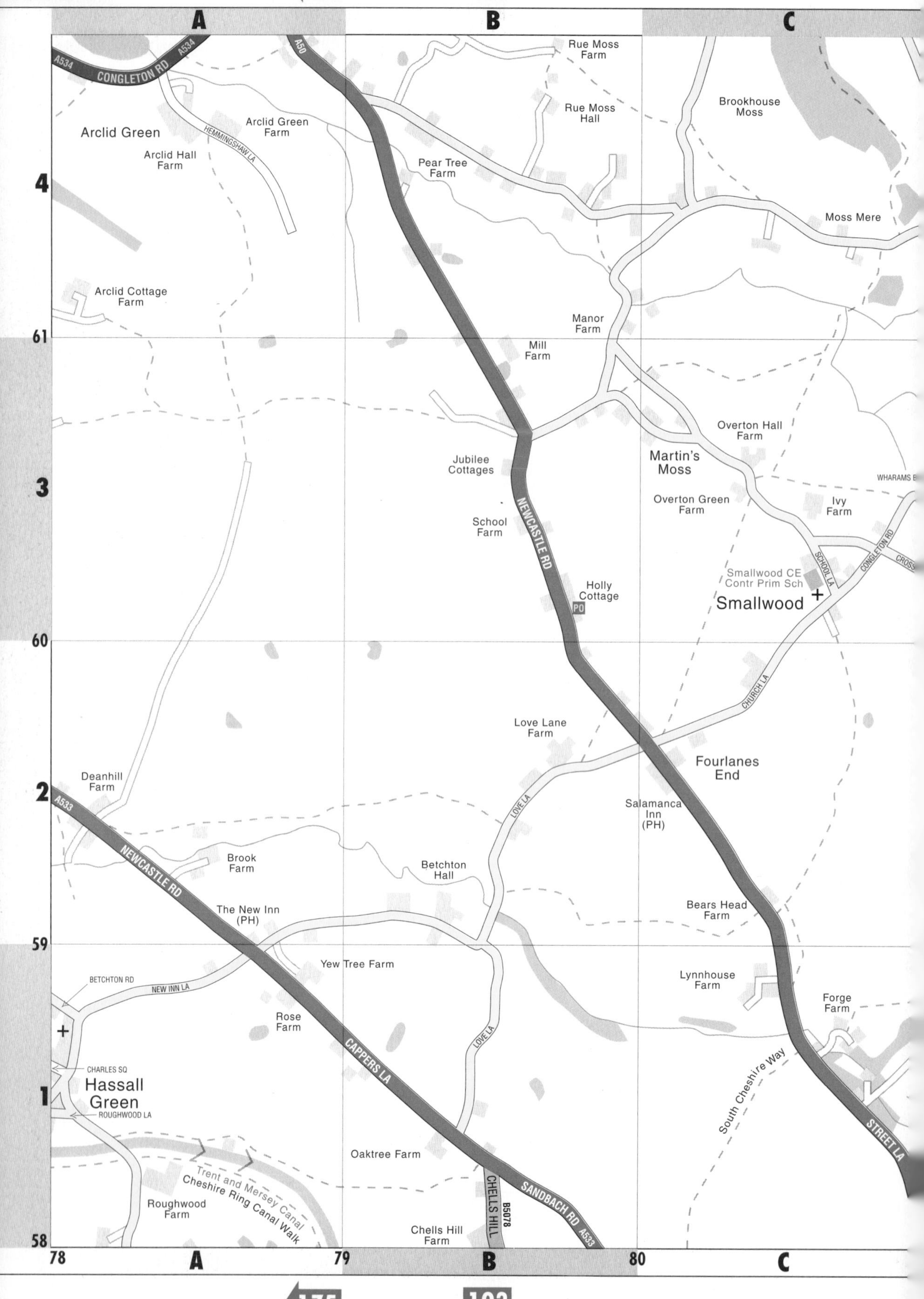

Arclid Green

Arclid Green Farm

CONGLETON RD

A534

A534

HEMMINGSHAW LA

A50

Arclid Hall Farm

Rue Moss Farm

Rue Moss Hall

Brookhouse Moss

Pear Tree Farm

4

Moss Mere

Arclid Cottage Farm

61

Manor Farm

Mill Farm

NEWCASTLE RD

Overton Hall Farm

Jubilee Cottages

Martin's Moss

WHARAMS B

3

Overton Green Farm

Ivy Farm

School Farm

Smallwood CE Contr Prim Sch

SCHOOL LA

CONGLETON RD

CROSS

Holly Cottage

PO

Smallwood

60

CHURCH LA

Love Lane Farm

Fourlanes End

Deanhill Farm

2

A533

Salamanca Inn (PH)

NEWCASTLE RD

Brook Farm

LOVE LA

Betchton Hall

Bears Head Farm

The New Inn (PH)

59

Lynnhouse Farm

BETCHTON RD

NEW INN LA

Yew Tree Farm

Forge Farm

Rose Farm

CAPPERS LA

LOVE LA

SOUTH CHESHIRE WAY

CHARLES SQ

1

Hassall Green

ROUGHWOOD LA

Oaktree Farm

CHELLS HILL

SANDBACH RD

A533

STREET LA

Trent and Mersey Canal

Cheshire Ring Canal Walk

Roughwood Farm

B5078

Chells Hill Farm

58

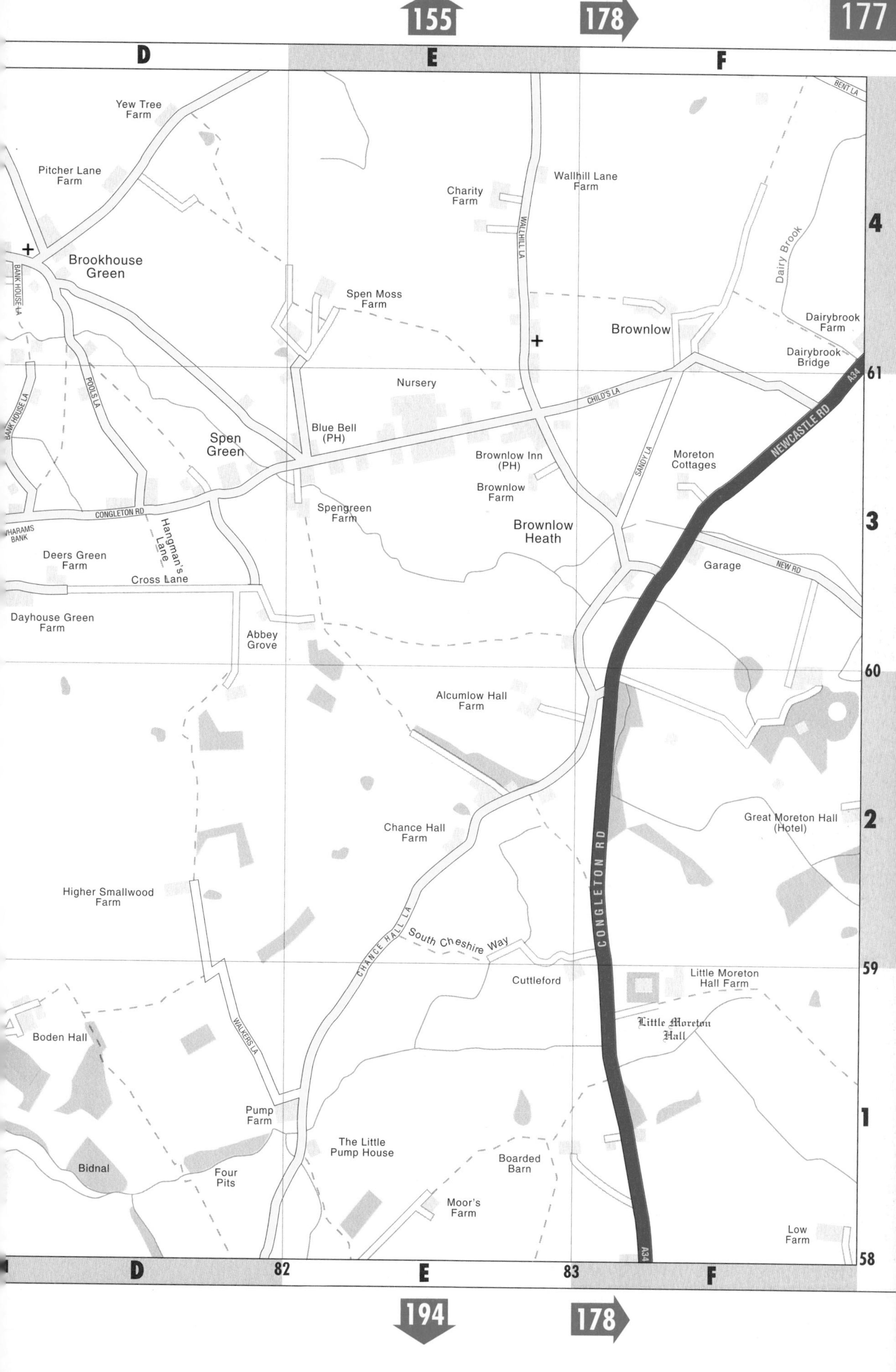

D
E
F

BENT LA

Yew Tree
Farm

Pitcher Lane
Farm

BANK HOUSE LA

✚

Brookhouse
Green

Wallhill Lane
Farm

Charity
Farm

WALLHILL LA

Dairy Brook

Dairybrook
Farm

Brownlow

Dairybrook
Bridge

Spen Moss
Farm

POOLS LA

BANK HOUSE LA

Spen
Green

Blue Bell
(PH)

Nursery

✚

CHILD'S LA

LA TAYLON'S

61

A34

NEWCASTLE RD

Brownlow Inn
(PH)

Brownlow
Farm

Moreton
Cottages

CONGLETON RD

WHARAMS
BANK

Hangman's
Lane

Spengreen
Farm

Brownlow
Heath

3

Deers Green
Farm

Cross Lane

Garage

NEW RD

Dayhouse Green
Farm

Abbey
Grove

60

Alcumlow Hall
Farm

Great Moreton Hall
(Hotel)

2

Chance Hall
Farm

Higher Smallwood
Farm

CHANCE HALL LA

South Cheshire Way

CONGLETON RD

Little Moreton
Hall Farm

59

Cuttleford

Boden Hall

WALKERS LA

Little Moreton
Hall

Pump
Farm

The Little
Pump House

1

Bidnal

Four
Pits

Boarded
Barn

Moor's
Farm

Low
Farm

A34

58

D
82
E
83
F

177
156

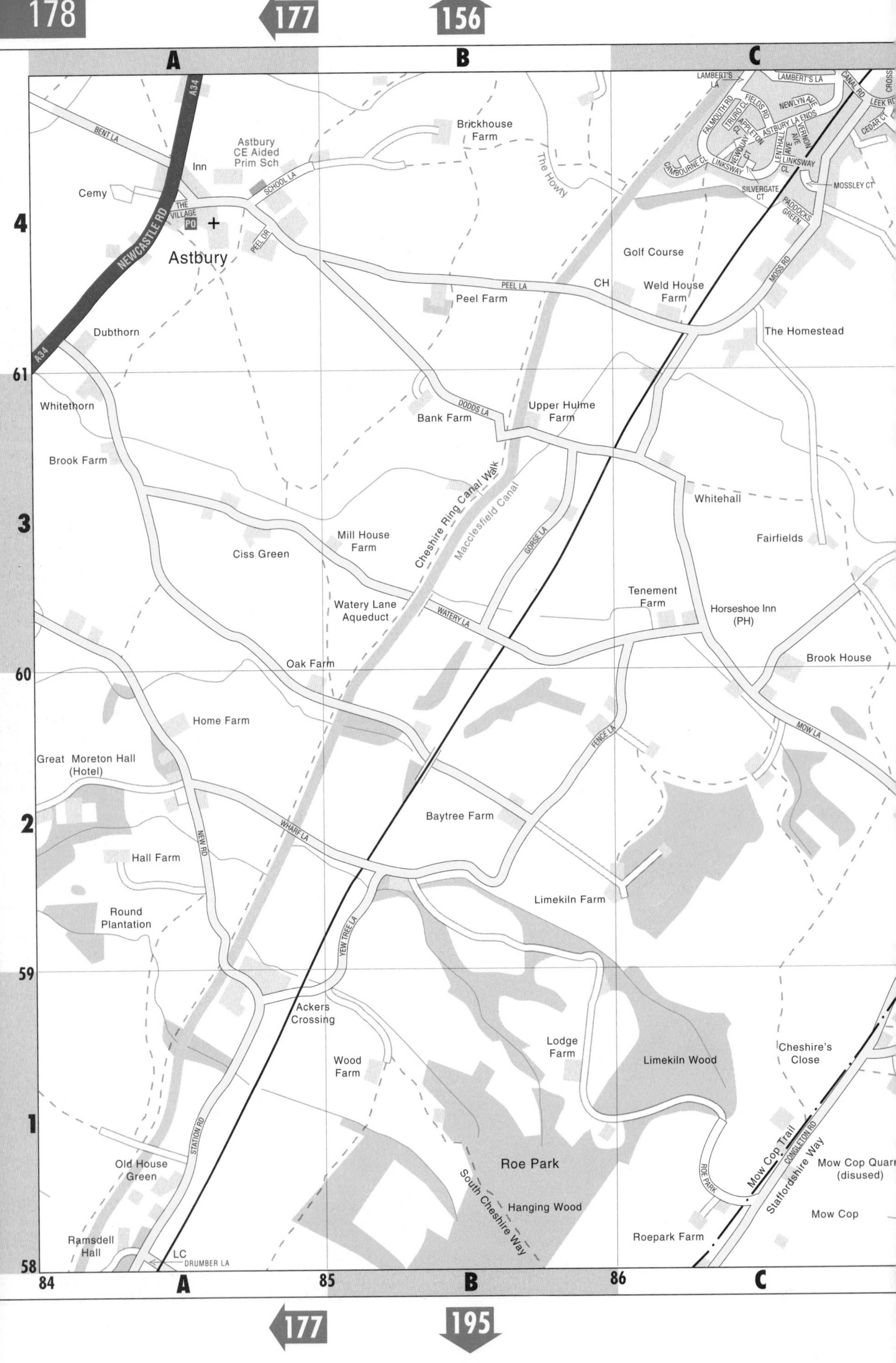
A
B
C
4
3
2
1
61
60
59
58
84
85
86
A34
NEWCASTLE RD
BENT LA
Astbury CE Aided Prim Sch
Inn
Cemy
THE VILLAGE
PO
Astbury
SCHOOL LA
PEEL DR
Brickhouse Farm
The Howty
LAMBERT'S LA
LAMBERT'S LA
CANAL RD
LEEK RD
CEDAR CT
FALMOUTH RD
FIELDS RD
NEWLYN AVE
TRURO CL
APPLETON CL
ASTBURY LA ENDS
VERNON AVE
LENTHALL AVE
NEWQUAY CT
CAMBOURNE CL
LINKSWAY
LINKSWAY CL
SILVERGATE CT
MOSSLEY CT
PADDOCKS GREEN
Golf Course
PEEL LA
CH
Weld House Farm
MOSS RD
Peel Farm
The Homestead
Dubthorn
Whitethorn
DODDS LA
Bank Farm
Upper Hulme Farm
Brook Farm
Cheshire Ring Canal Walk
Macclesfield Canal
Whitehall
Fairfields
GORSE LA
Mill House Farm
Ciss Green
Tenement Farm
Watery Lane Aqueduct
WATERY LA
Horseshoe Inn (PH)
Oak Farm
Brook House
Home Farm
MOW LA
FENCE LA
Great Moreton Hall (Hotel)
Baytree Farm
WHARF LA
NEW RD
Hall Farm
Limekiln Farm
Round Plantation
YEW TREE LA
Ackers Crossing
Wood Farm
Lodge Farm
Limekiln Wood
Cheshire's Close
STATION RD
Roe Park
South Cheshire Way
Hanging Wood
Mow Cop Trail
CONGLETON RD
Staffordshire Way
Mow Cop Quarry (disused)
Mow Cop
ROE PARK
Old House Green
Roepark Farm
Ramsdell Hall
LC
DRUMBER LA

177
195

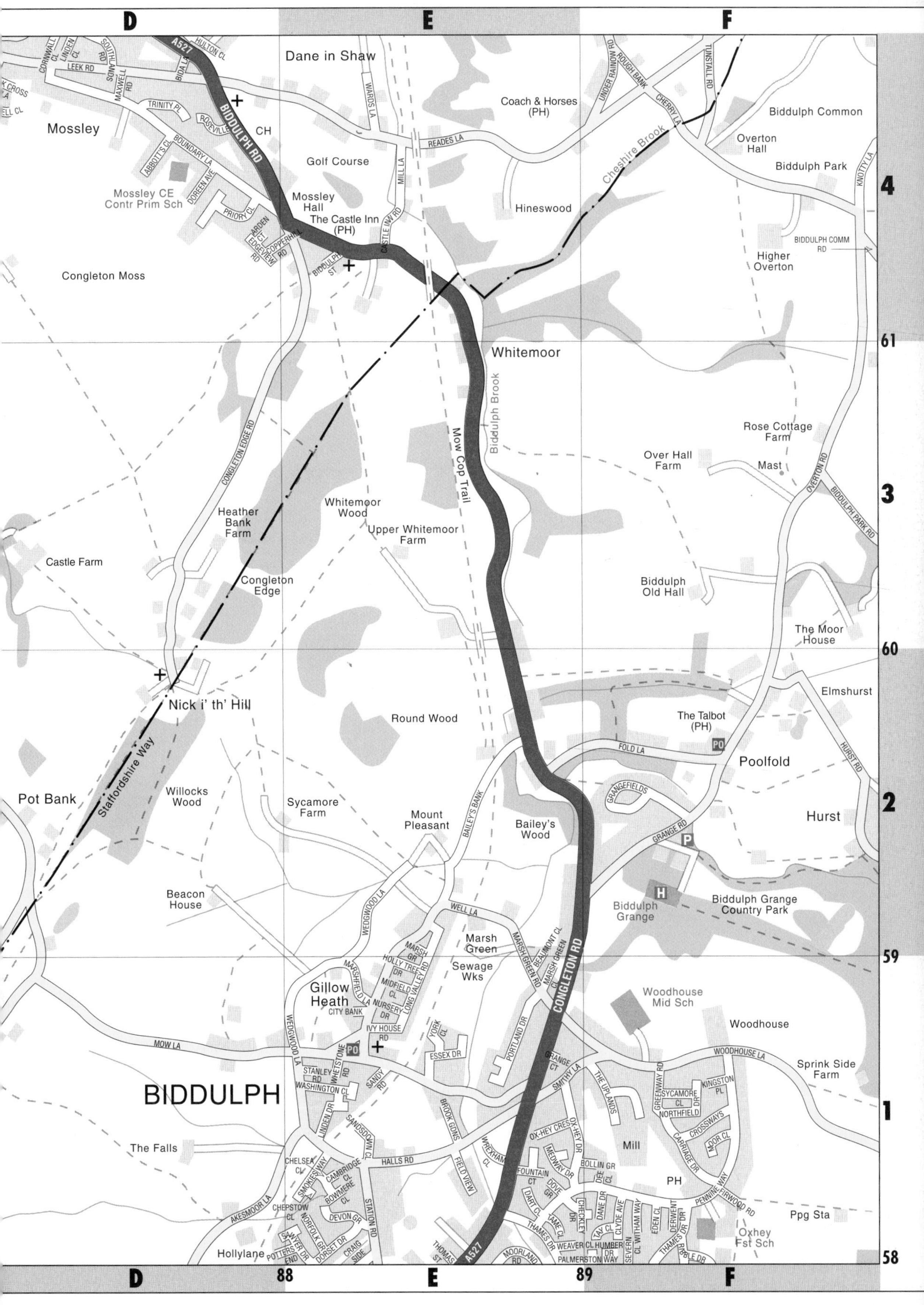
157
D
E
F
Dane in Shaw
Mossley
Mossley CE Contr Prim Sch
Congleton Moss
Golf Course
Mossley Hall
The Castle Inn (PH)
Coach & Horses (PH)
Hineswood
Biddulph Common
Overton Hall
Biddulph Park
Higher Overton
Cheshire Brook
Whitemoor
Biddulph Brook
Mow Cop Trail
Rose Cottage Farm
Over Hall Farm
Mast
Heather Bank Farm
Whitemoor Wood
Upper Whitemoor Farm
Castle Farm
Congleton Edge
Biddulph Old Hall
The Moor House
Elmshurst
Nick i' th' Hill
Round Wood
The Talbot (PH)
Poolfold
Pot Bank
Staffordshire Way
Willocks Wood
Sycamore Farm
Mount Pleasant
Bailey's Wood
Hurst
Beacon House
Biddulph Grange
Biddulph Grange Country Park
Marsh Green
Sewage Wks
Gillow Heath
Woodhouse Mid Sch
Woodhouse
Sprink Side Farm
BIDDULPH
The Falls
Mill
PH
Ppg Sta
Oxhey Fst Sch
Hollylane
BIDDULPH RD
CONGLETON RD
CONGLETON EDGE RD
MOW LA
WOODHOUSE LA
A527
4
61
3
60
2
59
1
58
88
89

163

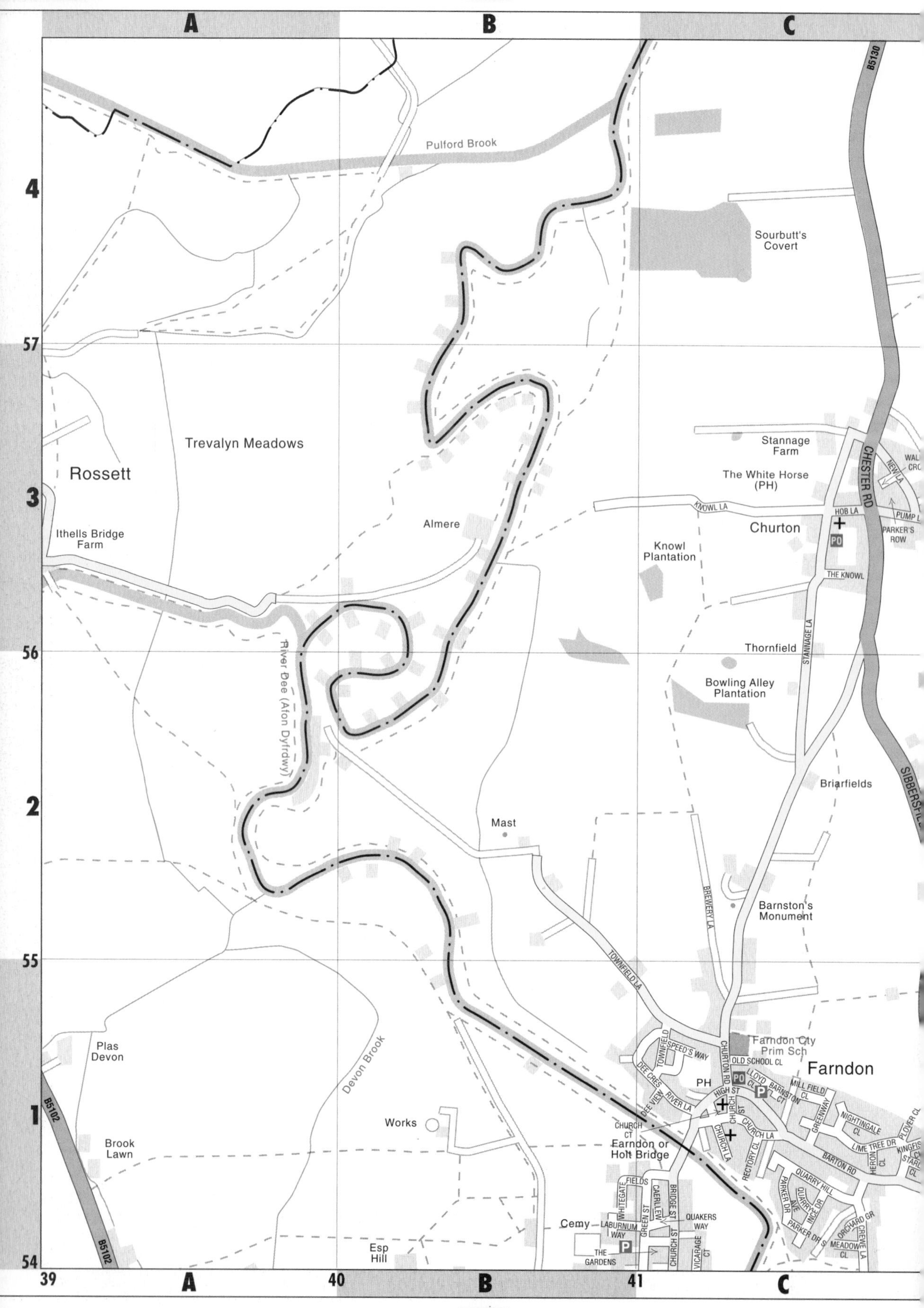
A
B
C
4
57
3
56
2
55
1
54
39
40
41
B5130
Pulford Brook
Sourbutt's Covert
Trevalyn Meadows
Rossett
Ithells Bridge Farm
Almere
Stannage Farm
The White Horse (PH)
CHESTER RD
KNOWL LA
HOB LA
Churton
PO
PARKER'S ROW
PUMP L
Knowl Plantation
THE KNOWL
STANNAGE LA
Thornfield
Bowling Alley Plantation
River Dee (Afon Dyfrdwy)
Briarfields
Mast
SIBBERSFIE
BREWERY LA
Barnston's Monument
TOWNFIELD LA
Plas Devon
Devon Brook
Farndon City Prim Sch
OLD SCHOOL CL
Farndon
TOWNFIELD
SPEED'S WAY
CHURTON RD
DEE CRES
PH
LLOYD CL
BARNSTON CT
MILL FIELD CL
DEE VIEW
RIVER LA
HIGH ST
GREENWAY
NIGHTINGALE CL
PLOVER CL
CHURCH ST
CHURCH LA
CHURCH CT
Farndon or Holt Bridge
LIME TREE DR
BARTON RD
HERON CL
KINGFIS
STARL
B5102
Works
Brook Lawn
RECTORY CL
QUARRY HILL
PARKER DR
QUARRY AVE
INCE DR
ORCHARD GR
CREWE LA
MEADOW CL
FIELDS
WHITEGATE
CAERLLEW
BRIDGE ST
GREEN ST
QUAKERS WAY
Cemy
LABURNUM WAY
P
THE GARDENS
CHURCH ST
VICARAGE CT
Esp Hill

196

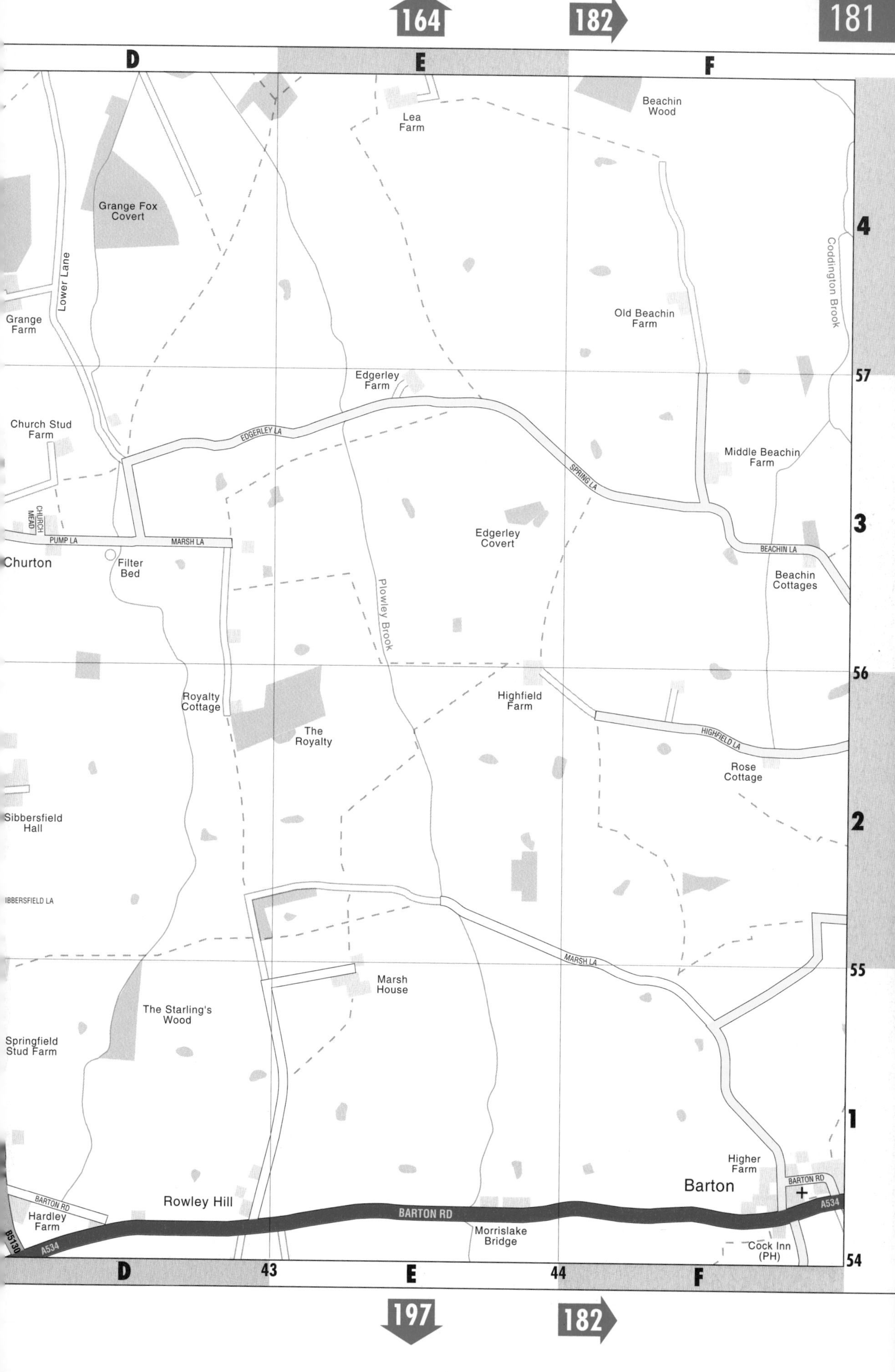
D
E
F
Beachin Wood
Lea Farm
Grange Fox Covert
Lower Lane
Grange Farm
Old Beachin Farm
Coddington Brook
Edgerley Farm
Church Stud Farm
EDGERLEY LA
Middle Beachin Farm
SPRING LA
CHURCH MEAD
PUMP LA
MARSH LA
Edgerley Covert
BEACHIN LA
Churton
Filter Bed
Beachin Cottages
Plowley Brook
Royalty Cottage
Highfield Farm
The Royalty
HIGHFIELD LA
Rose Cottage
Sibbersfield Hall
IBBERSFIELD LA
MARSH LA
Marsh House
The Starling's Wood
Springfield Stud Farm
Higher Farm
Barton
BARTON RD
BARTON RD
Hardley Farm
Rowley Hill
BARTON RD
A534
B5130
A534
Morrislake Bridge
Cock Inn (PH)
4
57
3
56
2
55
1
54
43
44

A **B** **C**

Stonyford Brook

Rectory

Well Farm

Handley

PH

WHITCHURCH RD

A41

Mill Hill

Handley Covert

ROCKY LA

Smellmoor Wood

4

Mere Brook

Pigeonhouse Farm

WHITCHURCH

57

Wind Pump

The Green Farm

Aldersey Green

Golf Course

Square Covert

Aldersey Brook

Coddington Brook

Smithy Farm

Pump Lane Wood

CHOWLEY OAK LA

Chowl

3

Pool Covert

ALDERSEY LA

New Covert

Chowley Collina

GREEN LA

The Cottage

56

Lodge

Slobbercrofts Covert

DOG LA

Holywell Brook

HIGHFIELD LA

BEACHIN LA

Yewtree Farm

Holywell Farm

Holywell Gorse

2

Crook Aldersey

Holy Well

Coddington

Whitegates Farm

Clutton Coverts

55

HOLYWELL LA

Mill Cottages

LOWER HALL MEWS 1
BARNABY CHASE 2
MEADOW RISE 3
BARN CT 4
ASHLEY GDNS 5
SCHOOL GN 6)

Clutton

Clutton Hall Farm

Broxton Bridge

A534

Picnic Area

P

1

Pool Plantation

1 2 3 4
LOWER HALL
5 6

FOLLA

High Cross

BROXTON RD

A534   BARTON RD

Carden Brook

Barton Plantation

TOWNSHIP
CL

Clutton CE Contr Prim Sch

Parker's Hill

Golf Course

Clutton Hill

Hot

54

45   **A**   **46**   **B**   **47**   **C**

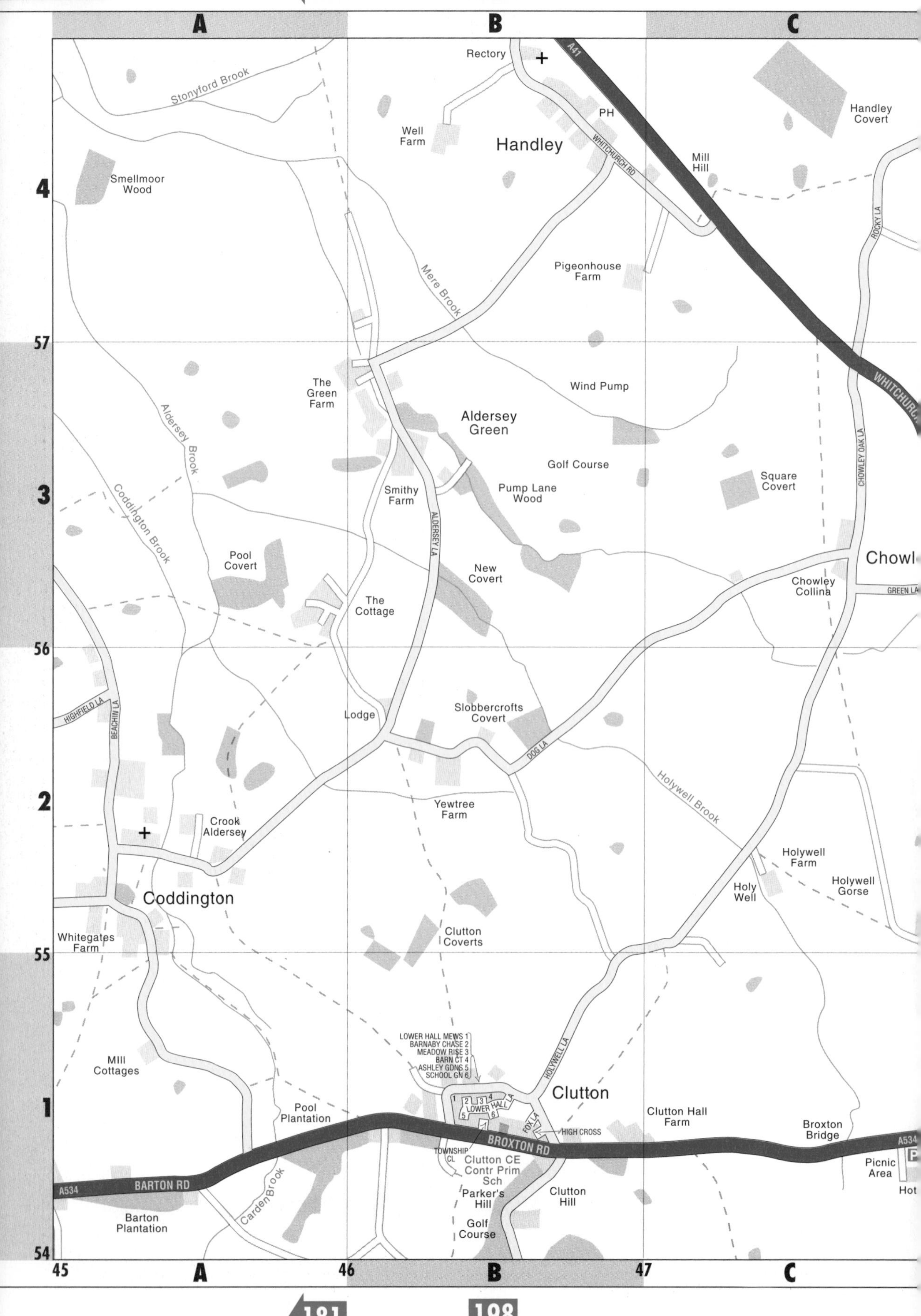

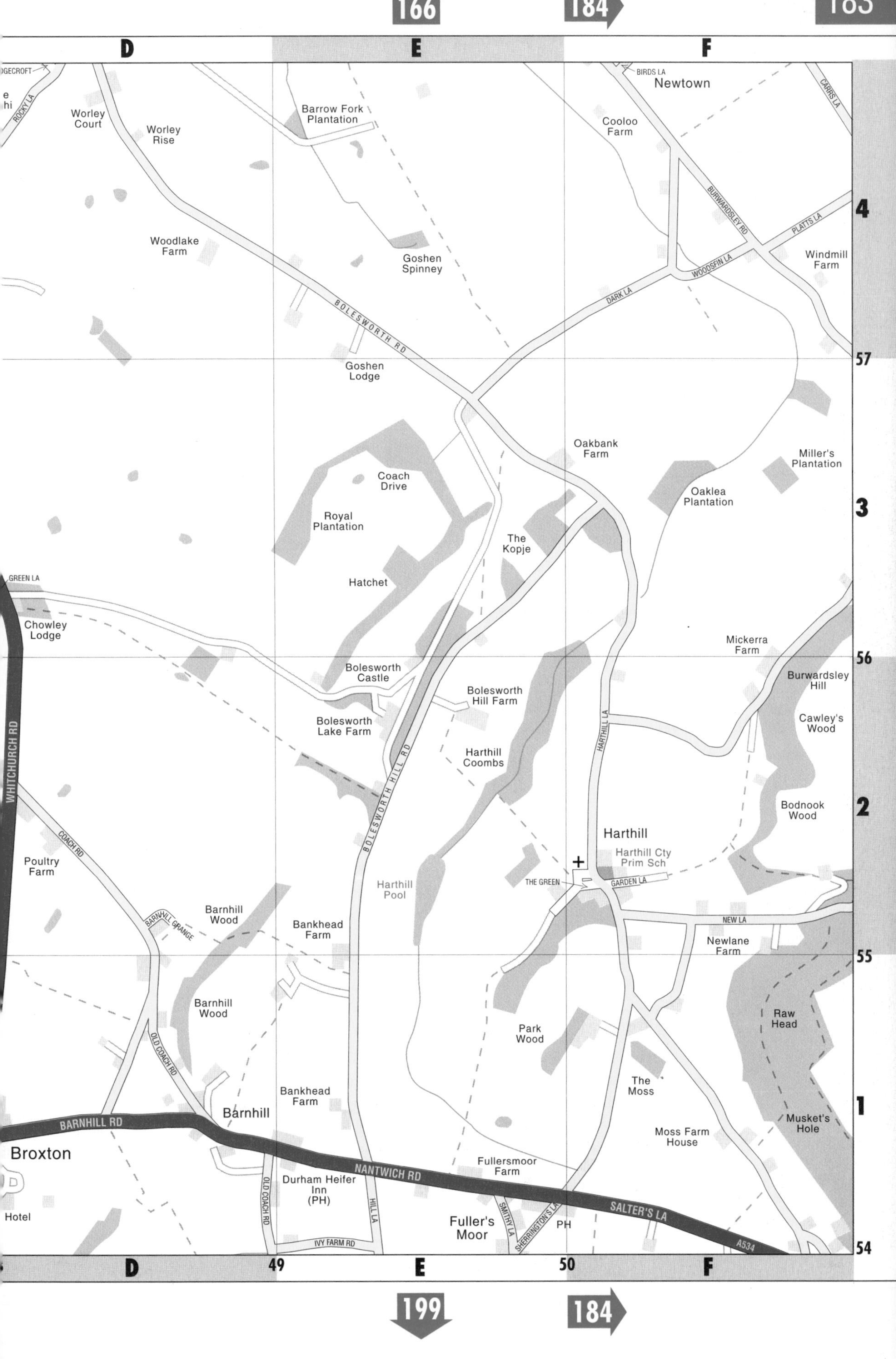
D
E
F
Newtown
Cooloo Farm
Worley Court
Worley Rise
Barrow Fork Plantation
Woodlake Farm
Goshen Spinney
Windmill Farm
BOLESWORTH RD
BURWARDSLEY RD
WOODSFIN LA
PLATTS LA
DARK LA
CARRS LA
BIRDS LA
ROCKY LA
Goshen Lodge
Oakbank Farm
Miller's Plantation
Coach Drive
Oaklea Plantation
Royal Plantation
The Kopje
Hatchet
GREEN LA
Chowley Lodge
Mickerra Farm
Bolesworth Castle
Burwardsley Hill
Bolesworth Hill Farm
Bolesworth Lake Farm
Cawley's Wood
HARTHILL LA
Harthill Coombs
BOLESWORTH HILL RD
WHITCHURCH RD
Bodnook Wood
Harthill
Harthill Cty Prim Sch
THE GREEN
GARDEN LA
COACH RD
Poultry Farm
Harthill Pool
NEW LA
Barnhill Wood
Bankhead Farm
Newlane Farm
BARNHILL GRANGE
Barnhill Wood
Raw Head
Park Wood
OLD COACH RD
The Moss
Bankhead Farm
Barnhill
Musket's Hole
BARNHILL RD
Moss Farm House
Broxton
Fullersmoor Farm
NANTWICH RD
Durham Heifer Inn (PH)
SALTER'S LA
OLD COACH RD
HILL LA
SMITHY LA
SHERRINGTON'S LA
Fuller's Moor
PH
Hotel
IVY FARM RD
A534
4
57
3
56
2
55
1
54
49
50

183
167

A   B   C

4

Wood
Farm

Honeyend
Farm

CARRS LA

PLATTS LA

Fly Fishery

Pennsylvania Wood

EDDISBURY WAY

Stanner
Nab

The Table
Rock

Lodge

River Gowy

57

BURWARDSLEY RD

Hall

Burwardsley
Hall

Broad
Rough

PO

HARTHILL RD

SCHOOL LA

CHURCH RD

Curdlands
House

Cheshire
Workshops

Willow
Hill

OUT LA

Outlanes
Farm

Spring House
Farm

ROCK LA

HILL LA

Waste Hill

CHERRY BANK
COTTS

PECKFO
RAL

3

Burwardsley

BARRACKS LA

PH

Higher Burwardsley

Peckforton Hills

SARRA LA

FOWLERS BENCH LA

Sandstone Trail

STONE HOUSE LA

56

Cawley Lodge
Farm

Willow Hill

Grig Hill
Farm

Peckforton Gap

Stonehouse
Farm

2

NEW LA

Droppingstone
Farm

Sycamore
Farm

Bulkeley Hill

Hillside
Farm

Common
Farm

55

Rawhead
Farm

Bulkeley
Mill

Bulkeley

Brid
Far

1

COPPERMINE LA

Bickerton
Hill

SANDY LA

The
Bickerton Poacher
(PH)

White House
Farm

HITCHENS LA

YEW TREE C

MILL GR

MILL VIEW CL

PO

WREXHAM RD

CHOLMONDELEY LA

A5

54

Tower Wood

Chiflik
Farm

WREXHAM RD

A534

The Grange

51   52   53

A   B   C

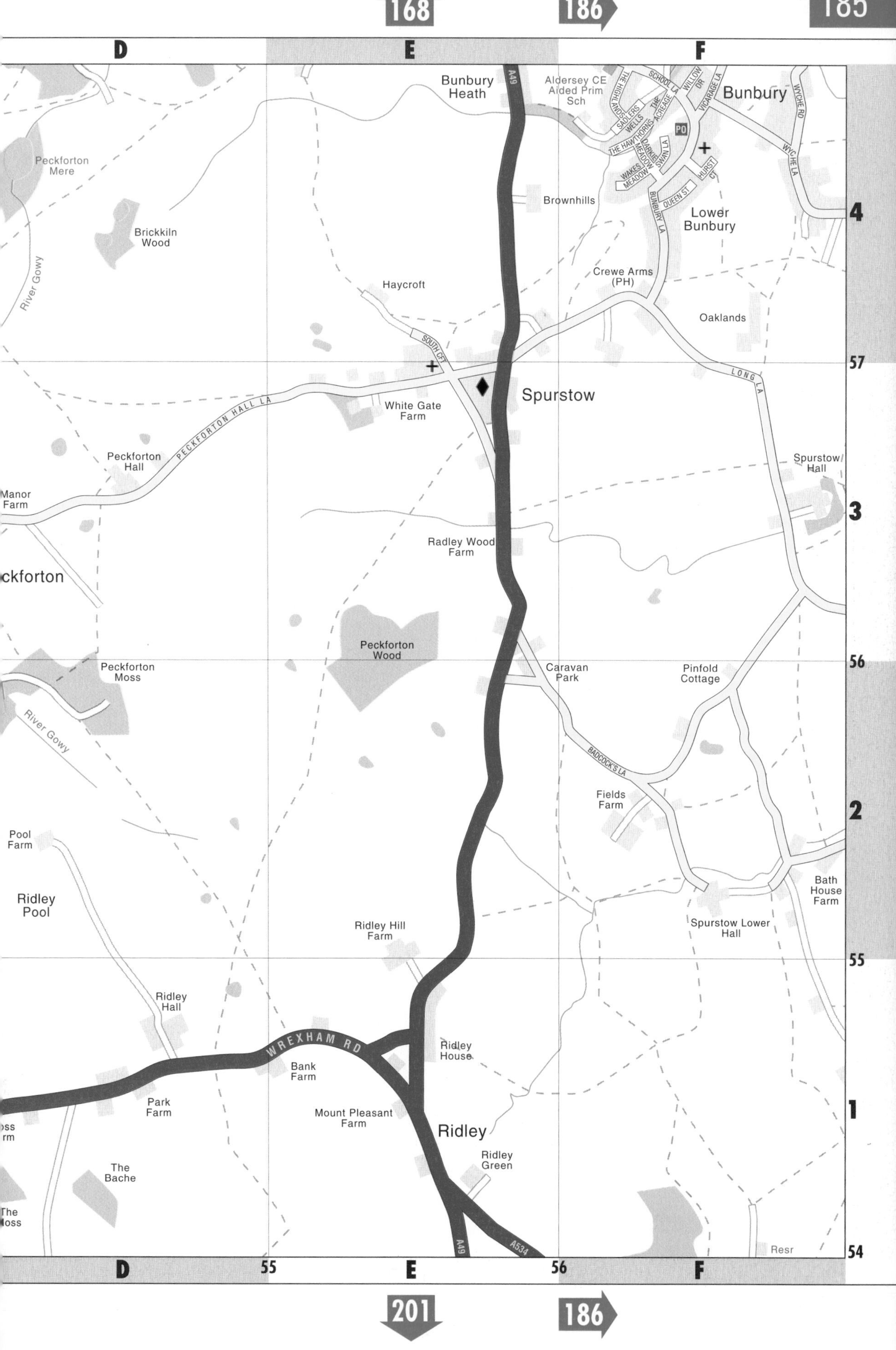

D   E   F

Bunbury
Heath
Aldersey CE
Aided Prim
Sch
Bunbury

Peckforton
Mere

Brickkiln
Wood

THE HIGH ANGLESEY
SCHOOL LA
WILLOW DR
VICARAGE LA
WYCHE RD

THE HAWTHORNES · ACREAGE
SADLERS
WELLS
VYNEW
SWAN
WAKES
MEADOW
ABERDEEN
MEADOW
PO
+
Lower
Bunbury
WYCHE LA

4

Brownhills
QUEEN ST
BUNBURY LA
HURST CT

Haycroft
Crewe Arms
(PH)
Oaklands

River Gowy

SOUTH CT
+
LONG LA
57

White Gate
Farm
Spurstow

Spurstow
Hall

Peckforton
HALL LA
Peckforton
Hall

Manor
Farm

Radley Wood
Farm

3

ckforton

Peckforton
Wood

Peckforton
Moss

Caravan
Park
Pinfold
Cottage
56

River Gowy

BADCOCK'S LA

Fields
Farm

2

Pool
Farm

Bath
House
Farm

Ridley
Pool

Ridley Hill
Farm

Spurstow Lower
Hall

55

Ridley
Hall

WREXHAM RD

Bank
Farm
Ridley
House

Park
Farm

Mount Pleasant
Farm
Ridley

1

oss
rm

Ridley
Green

The
Bache

A49
A534

The
oss

Resr
54

D   55   E   56   F

185
169

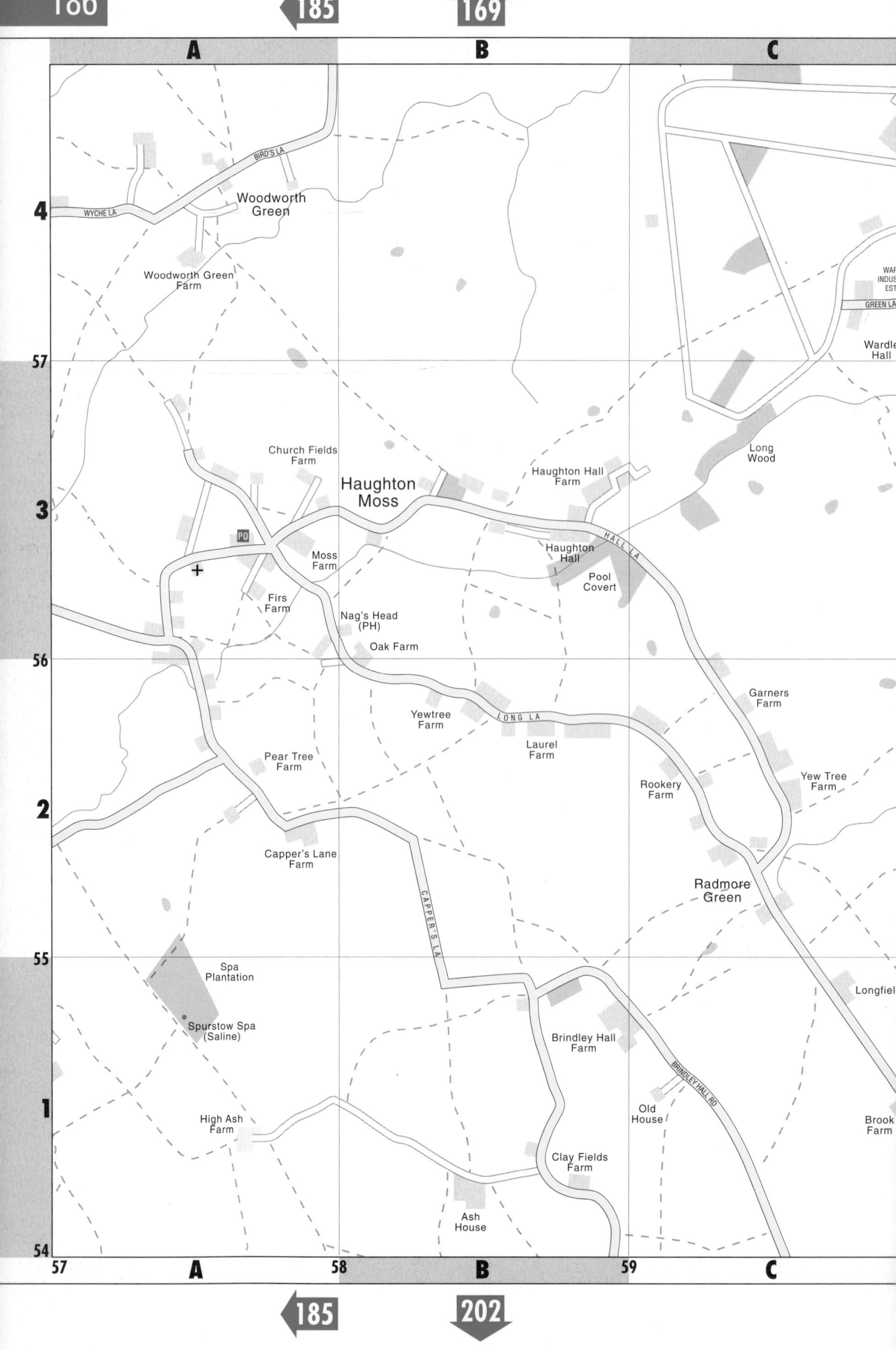
A
B
C
4
57
3
56
2
55
1
54
57
58
59
WYCHE LA
BIRD'S LA
Woodworth Green
Woodworth Green Farm
Church Fields Farm
Haughton Moss
PO
Moss Farm
Firs Farm
Nag's Head (PH)
Oak Farm
Haughton Hall Farm
HALL LA
Haughton Hall
Pool Covert
Long Wood
GREEN LA
Wardle Hall
Yewtree Farm
LONG LA
Laurel Farm
Garners Farm
Pear Tree Farm
Rookery Farm
Yew Tree Farm
Capper's Lane Farm
CAPPER'S LA
Radmore Green
Spa Plantation
Spurstow Spa (Saline)
Brindley Hall Farm
BRINDLEY HALL RD
Longfiel
Old House
High Ash Farm
Clay Fields Farm
Brook Farm
Ash House

185
202

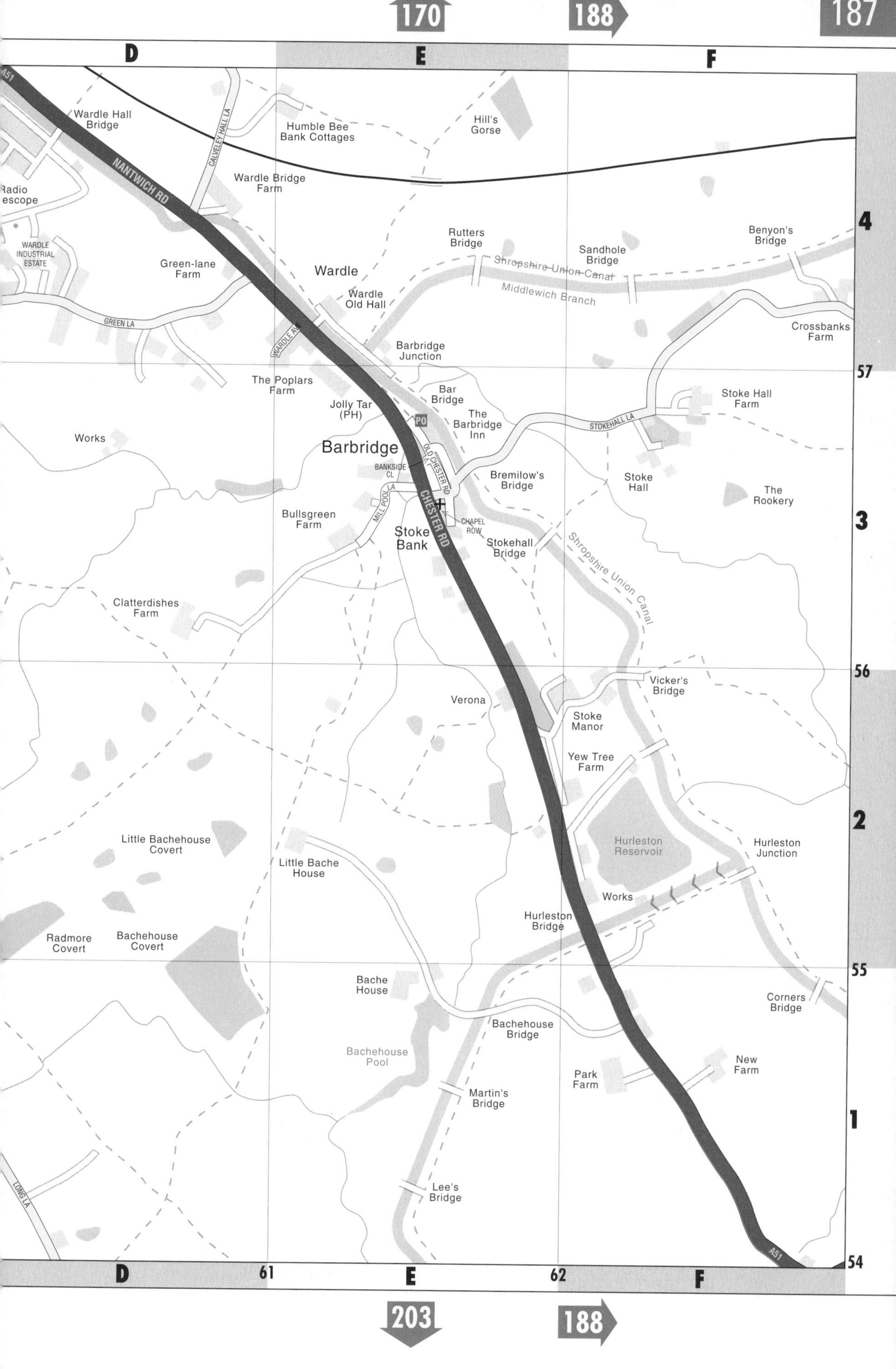
D
E
F
Wardle Hall Bridge
Humble Bee Bank Cottages
Hill's Gorse
CALVELEY HALL LA
NANTWICH RD
A51
Radio Telescope
Wardle Bridge Farm
WARDLE INDUSTRIAL ESTATE
Green-lane Farm
Wardle
Rutters Bridge
Sandhole Bridge
Benyon's Bridge
Shropshire Union Canal
Middlewich Branch
Wardle Old Hall
GREEN LA
WARDLE AVE
Barbridge Junction
Crossbanks Farm
The Poplars Farm
Bar Bridge
Jolly Tar (PH)
The Barbridge Inn
PO
Stoke Hall Farm
STOKEHALL LA
Works
Barbridge
OLD CHESTER RD
BANKSIDE CL
Bremilow's Bridge
Stoke Hall
The Rookery
MILL POOL LA
CHESTER RD
CHAPEL ROW
Bullsgreen Farm
Stoke Bank
Stokehall Bridge
Shropshire Union Canal
Clatterdishes Farm
Vicker's Bridge
Verona
Stoke Manor
Yew Tree Farm
Little Bachehouse Covert
Little Bache House
Hurleston Reservoir
Hurleston Junction
Works
Hurleston Bridge
Radmore Covert
Bachehouse Covert
Bache House
Bachehouse Bridge
Corners Bridge
Bachehouse Pool
Park Farm
New Farm
Martin's Bridge
LONG LA
Lee's Bridge
A51
4
57
3
56
2
55
1
54
61
62

187
171

A
B
C
Shropshire Union Canal
Cholmondeston Bridge
Venetian Marina
WINSFORD RD
Firs Bank Farm
STOKEHALL LA
B5074
Aston New Farm
Ash Villa
Four Oaks Farm
Aston Hall
STATION RD
The Grange
Oak Fields Farm
Green Farm
DAIRY LA
Rose Farm
Aston juxta Mondrum
Worleston CE Contr Prim Sch
CHURCH RD
Lower Hall Farm
Gates Farm
Worleston
MAIN RD
Rookery Hall Farm
Poole Old Hall
Cherry Orchard Farm
Poole Farm
Nursery
Poole Gorse
Poole Bank Farm
The Cottage
Oak Tree Farm
Poole House Farm
Park Farm
Poole Hall
Poole Hills Farm
Shropshire Union Canal
Mile House Farm
Mile End Farm
Rease Heath
CINDER LA
Poolehill
Reaseheath Coll
River Weaver
Hall Farm
Henhullbridge Farm
Henhull Bridge
Reaseheath Old Hall
A51
A51
B5074
4
57
3
56
2
55
1
54
63
64
65

187
204

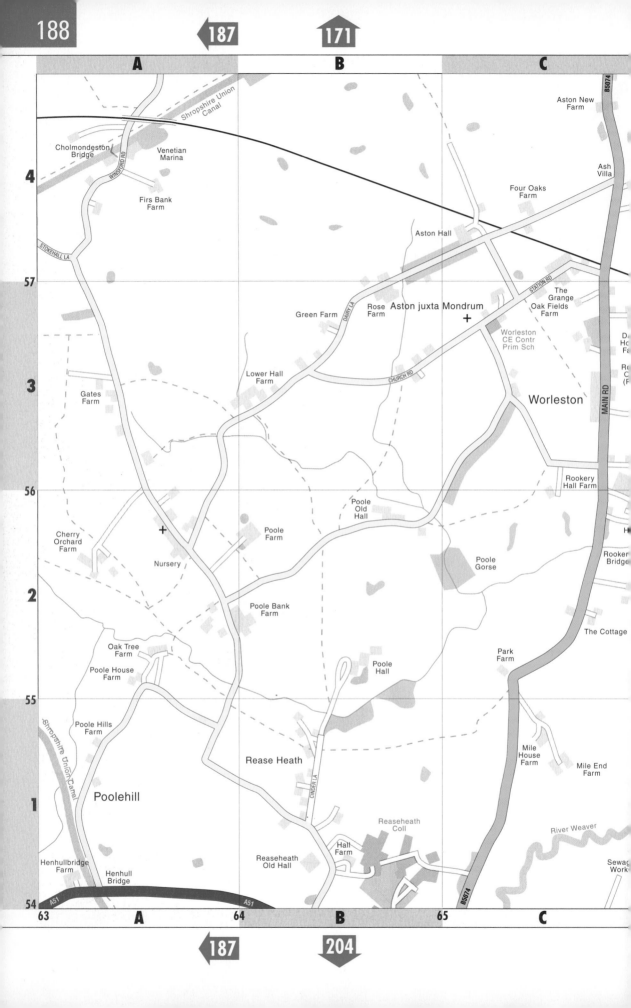

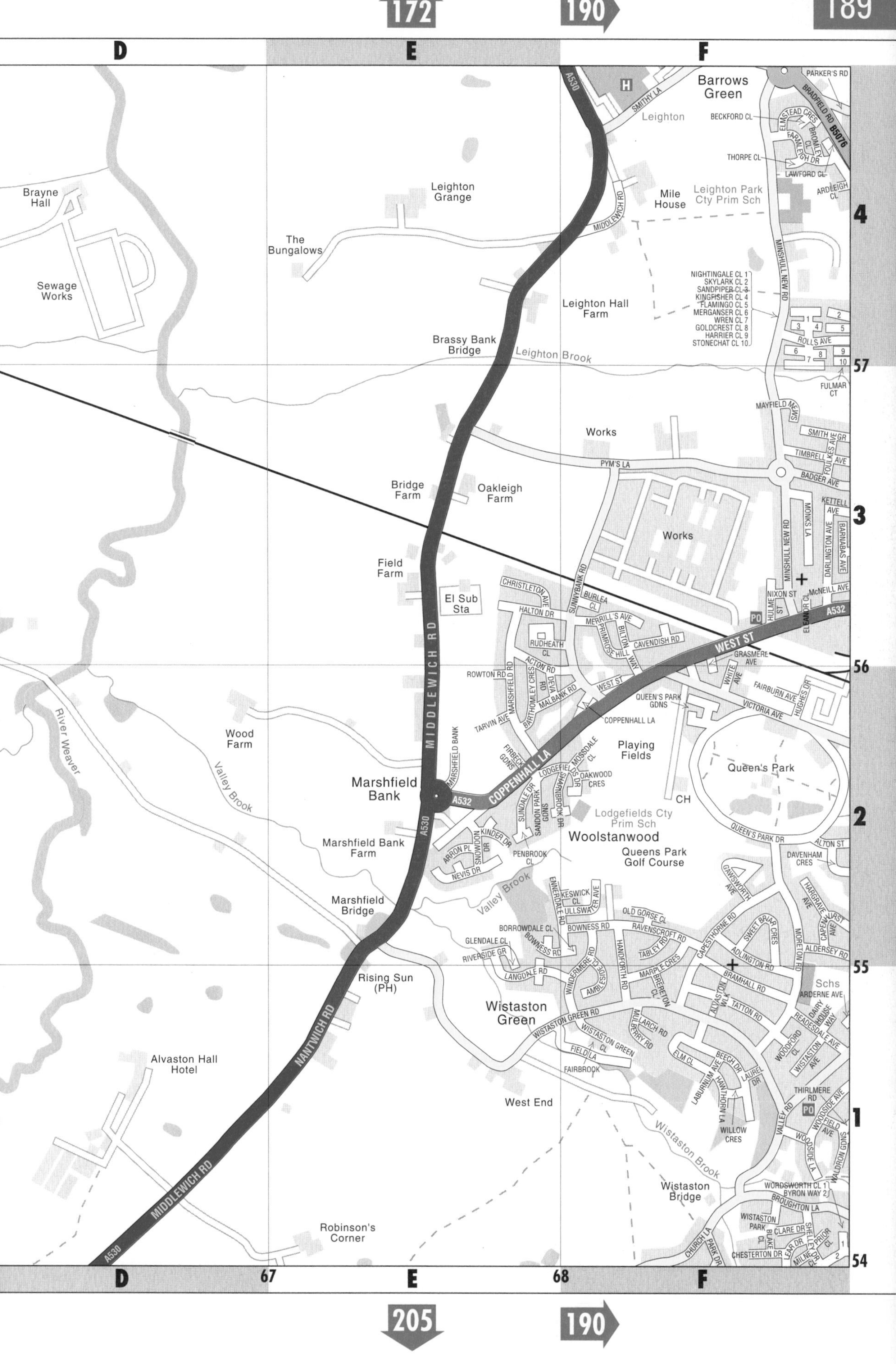
172
190
D
E
F
Barrows Green
Leighton
SMITHY LA
PARKER'S RD
BRADFIELD RD
B5076
BECKFORD CL
ELMSTEAD CRES
BROMLEY CL
FARNLEIGH DR
THORPE CL
LAWFORD CL
ARDLEIGH CL
Brayne Hall
Leighton Grange
Mile House
Leighton Park Cty Prim Sch
MIDDLEWICH RD
A530
The Bungalows
Sewage Works
MINSHULL NEW RD
NIGHTINGALE CL 1
SKYLARK CL 2
SANDPIPER CL 3
KINGFISHER CL 4
FLAMINGO CL 5
MERGANSER CL 6
WREN CL 7
GOLDCREST CL 8
HARRIER CL 9
STONECHAT CL 10
Leighton Hall Farm
ROLLS AVE
Brassy Bank Bridge
Leighton Brook
FULMAR CT
MAYFIELD MEWS
Works
SMITH GR
TIMBRELL AVE
FOULKES AVE
PYM'S LA
BADGER AVE
Bridge Farm
Oakleigh Farm
KETTELL AVE
MONKS LA
DARLINGTON AVE
BARNABAS AVE
Works
Field Farm
El Sub Sta
SUNNYBANK RD
CHRISTLETON AVE
BURLEA CL
NIXON ST
McNEILL AVE
HALTON DR
HULME ST
ELEANOR CL
A532
MERRILL'S AVE
BILTON WAY
PRIMROSE HILL
RUDHEATH CL
CAVENDISH RD
WEST ST
GRASMERE AVE
WHITE AVE
ACTON RD
ROWTON RD
MARSHFIELD RD
BARTHOMLEY CRES
DEVA RD
MALBANK RD
WEST ST
FAIRBURN AVE
HUGHES DR
QUEEN'S PARK GDNS
VICTORIA AVE
COPPENHALL LA
TARVIN AVE
MARSHFIELD BANK
River Weaver
Wood Farm
FIRBECK GDNS
MOSSDALE CL
Playing Fields
Queen's Park
Valley Brook
LODGEFIELDS DR
OAKWOOD CRES
Marshfield Bank
A532
SUNDALE DR
SHAPINBROOK DR
SANDON PARK GDNS
CH
Lodgefields Cty Prim Sch
KINDER DR
ARRON PL
SNOWDON DR
QUEEN'S PARK DR
ALTON ST
Woolstanwood
Marshfield Bank Farm
NEVIS DR
PENBROOK CL
Queens Park Golf Course
DAVENHAM CRES
GAWSWORTH AVE
HARGRAVE AVE
Valley Brook
ENNERDALE RD
KESWICK CL
ULLSWATER AVE
Marshfield Bridge
OLD GORSE CL
RAVENSCROFT RD
CAPESTHORNE RD
SWEET BRIAR CRES
CAPENHURST AVE
BORROWDALE CL
BOWNESS RD
GLENDALE CL
BOWNESS RD
HANDFORTH RD
TABLEY RD
MORETON RD
ALDERSEY RD
RIVERSIDE GR
WINDERMERE RD
ADLINGTON RD
LANGDALE RD
MARPLE CRES
BRERETON CL
BRAMHALL RD
Rising Sun (PH)
AMBLESIDE CL
Schs
ARDERNE AVE
ALVASTON WLK
TATTON RD
DAIRY HOUSE WAY
Wistaston Green
WISTASTON GREEN RD
MULBERRY RD
LARCH RD
READESDALE AVE
WISTASTON GREEN CL
WOODFORD CL
WISTASTON AVE
NANTWICH RD
FIELD LA
ELM CL
BEECH DR
Alvaston Hall Hotel
FAIRBROOK
LABURNUM AVE
LAUREL DR
HAWTHORN LA
THIRLMERE RD
WOODSIDE AVE
West End
VALLEY RD
WILLOW CRES
FIELD AVE
WOODSIDE LA
WALDRON GDNS
Wistaston Brook
Wistaston Bridge
WORDSWORTH CL 1
BYRON WAY 2
BROUGHTON LA
MIDDLEWICH RD
WISTASTON PARK
BLAKE CL
CLARE DR
SHELLEY CL
PRIOR CL
Robinson's Corner
CHURCH LA
PARK DR
CHESTERTON DR
LEAR DR
MILNE CL
A530
4
57
3
56
2
55
1
54
D
67
E
68
F
205
190

CREWE

Coppenhall

Maw Green

Maw Green Landfill Site

Stoneley Farm

Holly Tree Farm

Race Farm

Groby Farm

Monks Coppenhall Cty Prim Sch

Coppenhall Cty High Sch

Sydney Bridge

Playing Field

Cumberland Sports Ctr

Hungerford Cty Prim Sch

Loco Works

Tipkinder Park

The Valley

Valley Brook

Gainsborough Cty Jun Sch

St Thomas More RC (Aided) High Sch

South Cheshire Coll

The Ruskin Cty High Sch

Victoria Centre

The Mkt Centre

Liby Cts

Crewe M Bridge

Manchester Metropolitan Univ, Crewe & Alsager Faculty

Springfield Sch

Crewe BSNS Pk

Crewe Gates Farm Ind Est

Crewe Station

Football Gd

Police Training Centre

Works

BRADFIELD RD

NORTH ST

MIDDLEWICH ST

WEST ST

ALBERT ST

EARLE ST

HUNGERFORD RD

VERNON WAY

MILL ST

EDLESTON RD

NANTWICH RD

GRESTY RD

CREWE RD

WESTON RD

A534 CREWE RD

A532

A5019

A5020

B5076

B5071

B5078

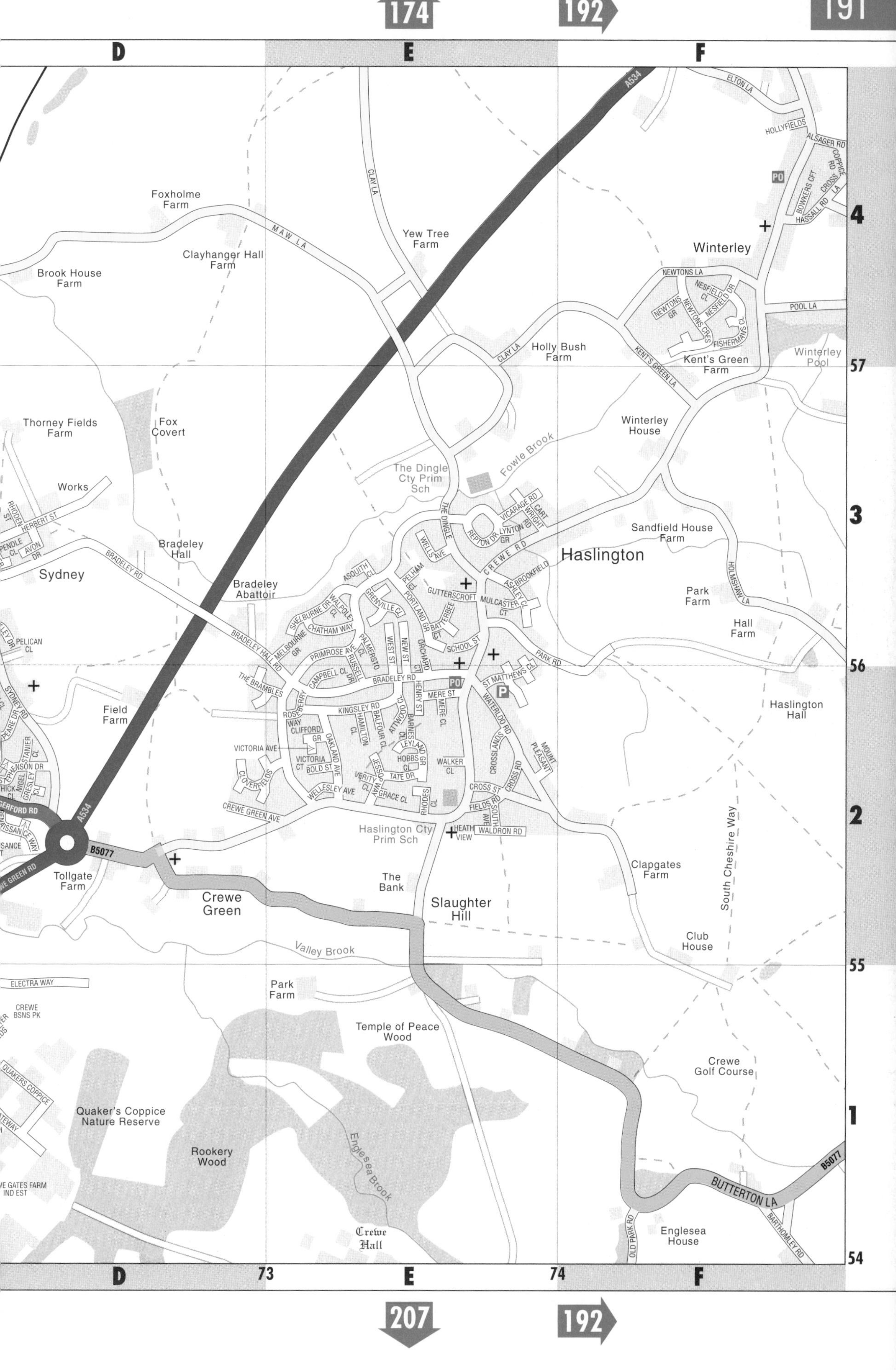

D
E
F

4

Foxholme Farm

Brook House Farm

Clayhanger Hall Farm

MAW LA

CLAY LA

Yew Tree Farm

A34

ELTON LA

HOLLYFIELDS

ALSAGER RD

COPPICE RD

CROSS LA

BUNKERS CFT

HASSALL RD

P

Winterley

NEWTONS LA

NEWTONS GR

NEWTONS DR

NESFIELD CL

NESFIELD DR

FISHERMANS CL

Kent's Green Farm

POOL LA

Winterley Pool

57

Thorney Fields Farm

Fox Covert

Works

Bradeley Hall

Sydney

BRADELEY RD

Bradeley Abattoir

HERBERT ST

PENDLE CL

AVON DR

RHODES

KENT'S GREEN LA

Holly Bush Farm

CLAY LA

Fowle Brook

The Dingle Cty Prim Sch

THE DINGLE

WELLS AVE

VICARAGE RD

LYNTON DR

REPTON DR

CART WRIGHT

CREWE RD

Haslington

Winterley House

Sandfield House Farm

HOLMSHAW LA

Park Farm

Hall Farm

3

BRADELEY HALL RD

ASQUITH CL

PELHAM

SHELBURNE DR

WALPOLE

CHATHAM WAY

MELBOURNE GR

PORTLAND GR

BATTERSEA

PATERSO

PRIMROSE AVE

WEST ST

NEW ST

ORCHARD

CAMPBELL CL

RUSSELL

BRADELEY RD

GUTTERSCROFT

GRENVILLE CL

MULCASTER CT

AG BROOKFIELD

ASHLEY CT

SCHOOL ST

HENRY ST

MERE ST

BARNES GR

ATTENBO

LEYLAND GR

WALKER CL

PARK RD

ST MATTHEWS CL

WINTERFORD RD

CROSSLANDS

MOUNT PLEASANT

Field Farm

PELICAN CL

SYDNEY RD

PEARE RD

STANLEY

NIGEL ST

GRESLEY CL

HICKS

STEPHENSON DR

THE BRAMBLES

ROSEBERRY WAY

KINGSLEY RD

BALFOUR CL

HAMILTON CL

CLIFFORD GR

VICTORIA AVE

VICTORIA CT

OAKLAND AVE

BOLD ST

HOBBS CL

TATE DR

VERITY WAY

GRACE CL

WALKER CL

CROSS FIELDS

CROSS DR

P

PO

MERE CL

CLOVERFIELDS

WELLESLEY AVE

CREWE GREEN AVE

RHODES

HEATH VIEW

WALDRON RD

Haslington Cty Prim Sch

Haslington Hall

56

RUTHERFORD RD

RENAISSANCE WAY

SANCE ST

A34

B5077

Tollgate Farm

Crewe Green

The Bank

Slaughter Hill

Valley Brook

Clapgates Farm

South Cheshire Way

Club House

2

ELECTRA WAY

CREWE BSNS PK

Park Farm

Temple of Peace Wood

Crewe Golf Course

55

QUAKERS COPPICE

GATEWAY

Quaker's Coppice Nature Reserve

Rookery Wood

Englesea Brook

WE GATES FARM IND EST

Crewe Hall

B5077

BUTTERTON LA

OLD PARK RD

BARTHOMLEY RD

Englesea House

1

54

D
73
E
74
F

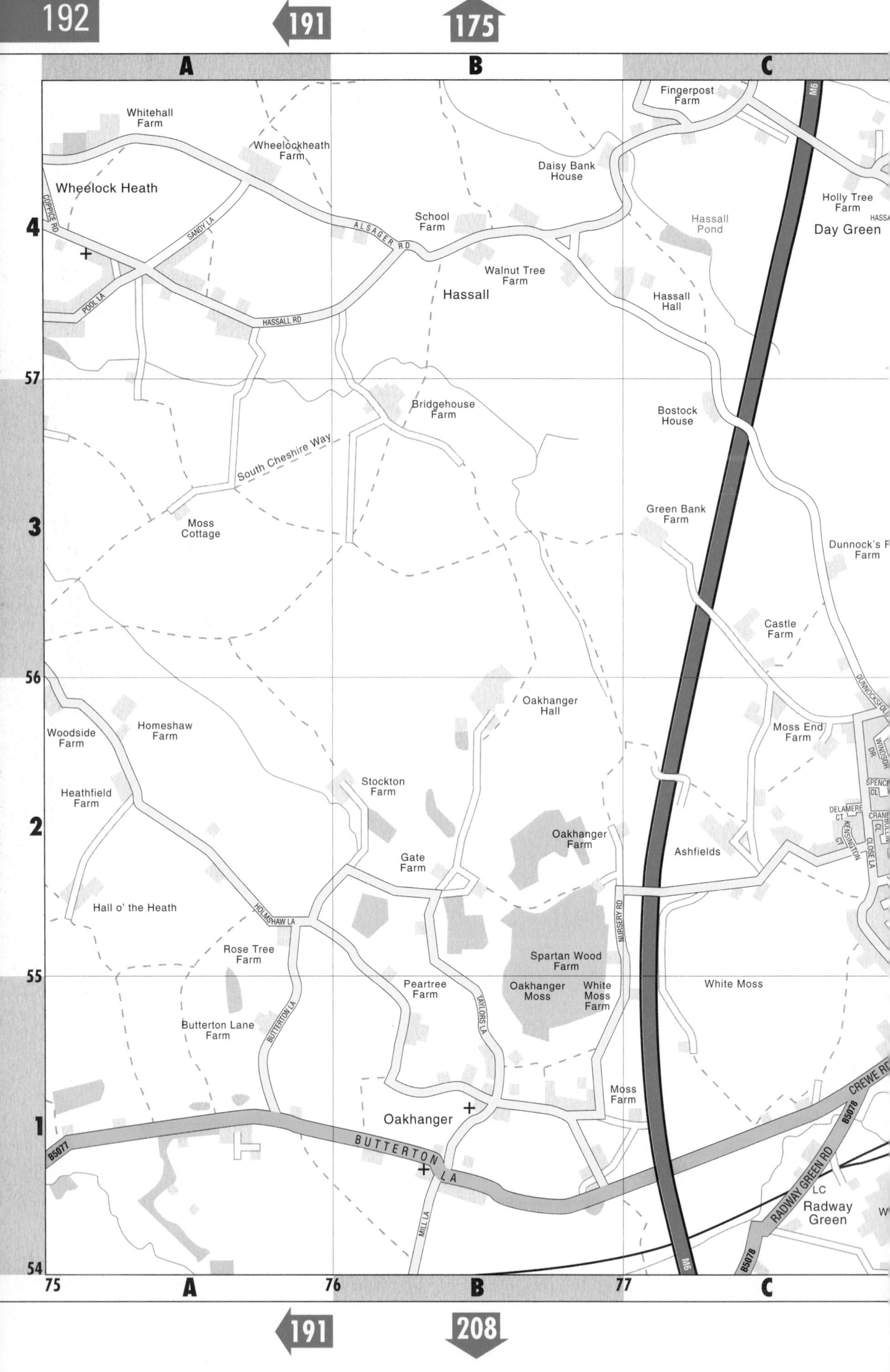

191
175

A **B** **C**

Whitehall Farm

Wheelockheath Farm

Daisy Bank House

Fingerpost Farm

Holly Tree Farm

HASS

Wheelock Heath

ALSAGER RD

School Farm

Hassall Pond

Day Green

4

COPPICE RD

SANDY LA

POOL LA

HASSALL RD

Walnut Tree Farm

Hassall

Hassall Hall

57

Bridgehouse Farm

Bostock House

South Cheshire Way

Green Bank Farm

Dunnock's F Farm

3

Moss Cottage

Castle Farm

DUNNOCKSFOL

56

Woodside Farm

Homeshaw Farm

Oakhanger Hall

Moss End Farm

WINDSOR DR

SPENC CL

Heathfield Farm

Stockton Farm

DELAMERE CT

CRANF KENSINGTON CT CLOSE LA

2

Gate Farm

Oakhanger Farm

Ashfields

HOLMSHAW LA

Hall o' the Heath

Rose Tree Farm

NURSERY RD

Spartan Wood Farm

White Moss

55

BUTTERTON LA

Peartree Farm

TAYLORS LA

Oakhanger Moss

White Moss Farm

CREWE R

B5078

Butterton Lane Farm

Moss Farm

B5078

1

B5071

Oakhanger

BUTTERTON LA

MILL LA

RADWAY GREEN RD

LC

Radway Green

B5078

M6

54

75 **A** **76** **B** **77** **C**

176
194

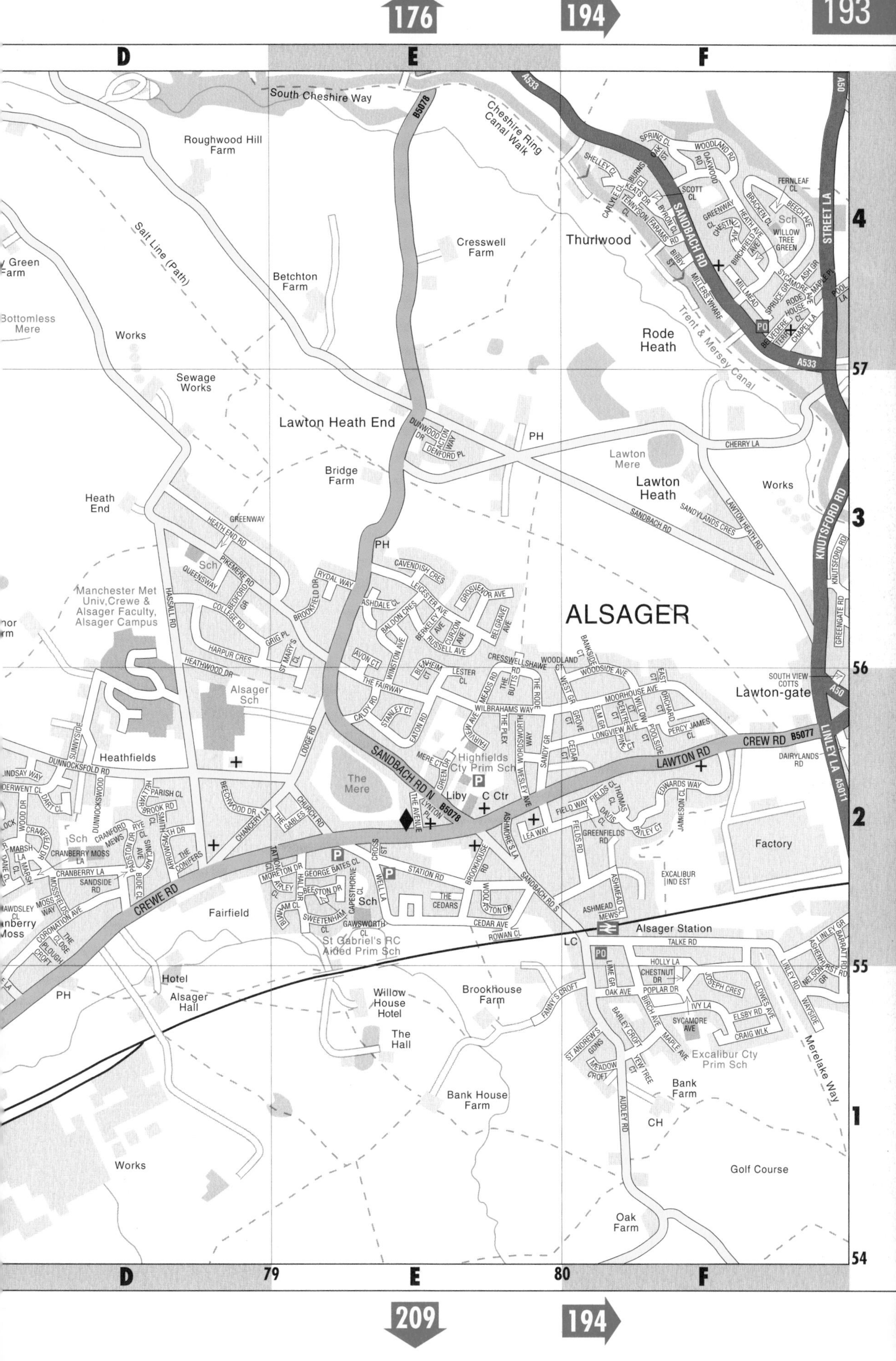
D
E
F
South Cheshire Way
Cheshire Ring Canal Walk
Roughwood Hill Farm
Salt Line (Path)
Cresswell Farm
Thurlwood
Betchton Farm
Bottomless Mere
Works
Rode Heath
Trent & Mersey Canal
Sewage Works
Lawton Heath End
Lawton Mere
Lawton Heath
Bridge Farm
Heath End
Works
Manchester Met Univ,Crewe & Alsager Faculty, Alsager Campus
ALSAGER
Alsager Sch
Lawton-gate
Heathfields
The Mere
Highfields Cty Prim Sch
Liby
C Ctr
Factory
Fairfield
Alsager Station
EXCALIBUR IND EST
St Gabriel's RC Aided Prim Sch
Hotel
Alsager Hall
Willow House Hotel
Brookhouse Farm
The Hall
Excalibur Cty Prim Sch
Bank House Farm
Bank Farm
Merelake Way
Works
Golf Course
Oak Farm
SANDBACH RD
CREWE RD
LAWTON RD
CREW RD
KNUTSFORD RD
STREET LA
LINLEY LA
4
57
3
56
2
55
1
54
79
80

209
194

193
177

A B C

CHANCE HALL LA
Townsend Farm
TOWNSEND LA
Rode Mill
A34
HOLEHOUSE LA
Holehouse Farm
POOL SIDE
Rode Pool
Scholar Green
Kent Green Farm
BARLEYCROFT TERR
4
Works
Rode Hall
Old Wood
STONE CHAIR LA
BARNBRIDGE CL
STATION RD
FOUNDRY LA
HOLLINSHEAD CL
CHURCH LA
WAVERTREE AVE
GRENFELL RD
MEAD AVE
Home Farm
BARBER DR
MARGERY AVE
CINDER HILL LA
ALMA CL
THE MOUNT
57
Bank Farm
Big Barr
Lunts Moss Farm
Scholar Green Cty Prim Sch
PO
Cheshire Ring Canal Walk
Macclesfield Canal
A50
Brick House Farm
PORTLAND DR
Little-moss
Bratt's Wood
CONGLETON RD N
KNUTSFORD RD
Snape's Aqueduct
3
MEADOW WAY
LITTLE MOSS LA
NURSERY RD
CHERRY TREE AVE
BARWOOD AVE
Ashbank Farm
BRATTSWOOD DR
Hall Green
Church Lawton Gate Cty Prim Sch
WOODGATE AVE
BLEEDING WOLF LA
LITTLE MOSS CL
BROWN AVE
Summer House Plantation
LAWTONGATE ESTATE
56
THE GREEN
LAWTON COPPICE
GROVE AVE
MOSS LA
A50
WOODSIDE
THE SPINNEY
Lawton Hall
THE GROVE
Mill Lane Plantation
Moss House Farm
GROVE PARK AVE
ELMWOOD CL
CROSSWAYS RD
LIVERPOOL RD W
DAIRYLANDS RD
Lawton-gate
KNOWSLEY LA
Bridge Farm
2
Church Lawton
A5011
LAWTON AVE
Red Bull
LC
Cheshire Ring Canal Walk
Trent and Mersey Canal
Red Bull Aqueduct
Playi
Fiel
LINLEY GR
FODEN AVE
Works
Rye Low
55
CONGLETON RD S
LIVERPOOL RD E
GLOUCESTER RD
ESSEX DR
LINLEY RD
LIME KILN LA
Training Centre
VICTORIA AV
NORFOLK RD
LINCOLN RD
Pool-lock Aqueduct
Works
SOMERSET AVE
WHITEHALL AVE
HARDINGSWOOD RD
SLACKEN LA
PICKWICK PL
LIVERPOOL RD
WHITE R
OLD BUTT LA
TOWNFIELD CL
LINLEY LA
Toll Gate Farm
Slum Wood
OLD BUTT LA
CHAPEL ST
GLEBE ST
SKELLERN ST
CHURCH ST
WRIGHT ST
WOODLANDS AVE
Harding's Wood
1
STATION RD
MILLSTONE AVE
Kidsgrove Sta
Liby
MEADOWS RD
Butt Lane
PO
WOODSHUTT'S ST
THIRD AVE
The Reginald Mitchell Prim Sch
CONGLETON RD
SECOND AVE
PO
B5371
Linley Hall
WEST AVE
NELSON IND EST
CEDAR AVE
FIFTH AVE
FIFTH AVE
ST SAVIOUR'S ST
BANBURY ST
MITCHELL AVE
BRINDLEY CL
CORONATION CRES
Golf Course
MILL GR
NURSERY CL
ORCHARD CRES
HOLLINS CRES
LOWER ASH RD
GROVE AVE
FIRST AVE
Woodshutts
THE AVENUE
St Saviour's CE Contr Prim Sch
Sch
B5371
FOURTH AVE
LINLEY TRAD EST
A34
MITCHELL DR
HARECASTLE AVE
A5011
54

81 A 82 B 83 C

193
210

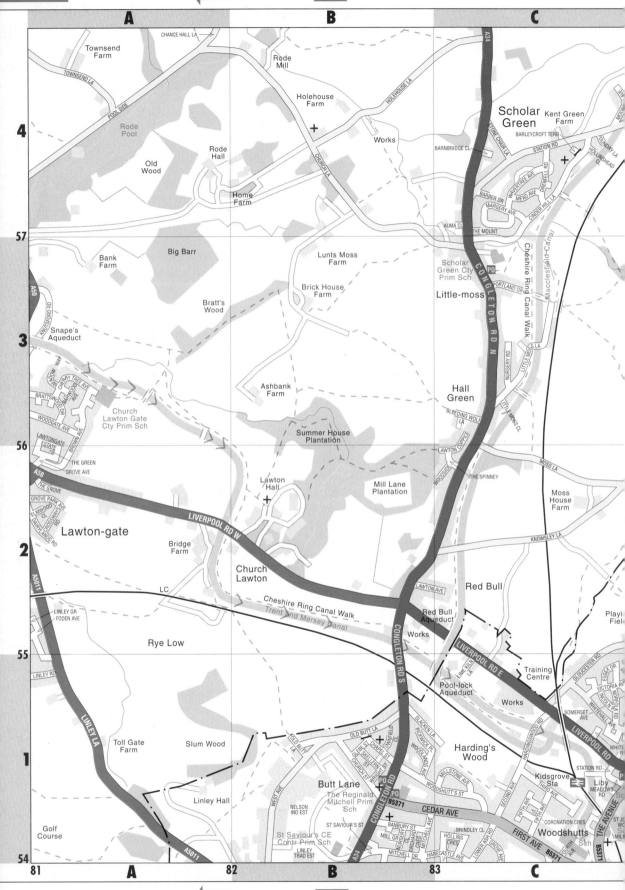

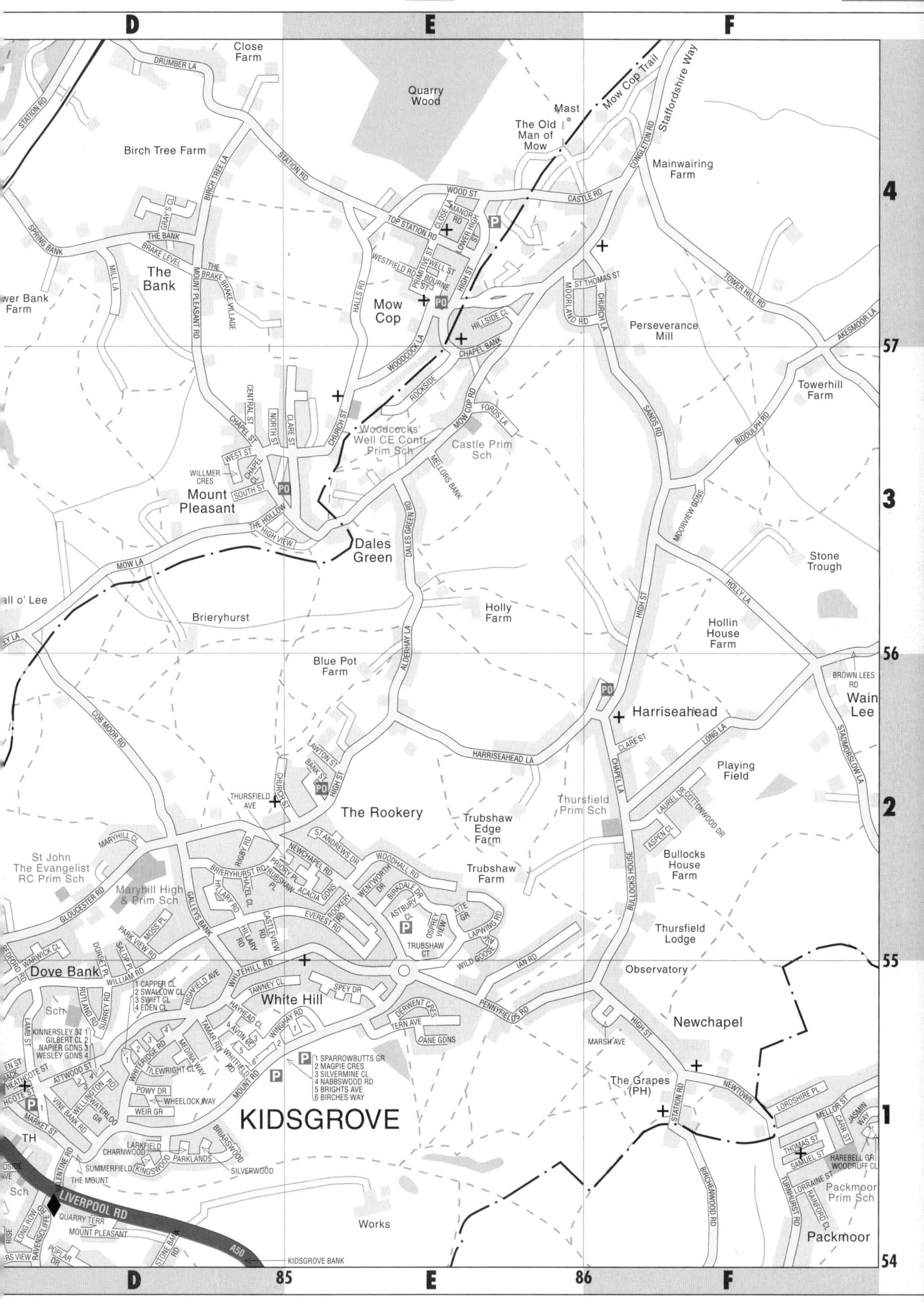
D
E
F
Close Farm
Quarry Wood
Mast
The Old Man of Mow
Mow Cop Trail
Staffordshire Way
Birch Tree Farm
Mainwairing Farm
The Bank
Mow Cop
Perseverance Mill
Towerhill Farm
Woodcocks' Well CE Contr Prim Sch
Castle Prim Sch
Mount Pleasant
Dales Green
Stone Trough
Holly Farm
Brieryhurst
Hollin House Farm
Blue Pot Farm
Harriseahead
Wain Lee
Playing Field
The Rookery
Trubshaw Edge Farm
Thursfield Prim Sch
St John The Evangelist RC Prim Sch
Maryhill High & Prim Sch
Bullocks House Farm
Trubshaw Farm
Thursfield Lodge
Dove Bank
Observatory
White Hill
Newchapel
The Grapes (PH)
KIDSGROVE
Packmoor Prim Sch
Packmoor
Works
LIVERPOOL RD
A50
KIDSGROVE BANK
4
57
3
56
2
55
1
54
85
86

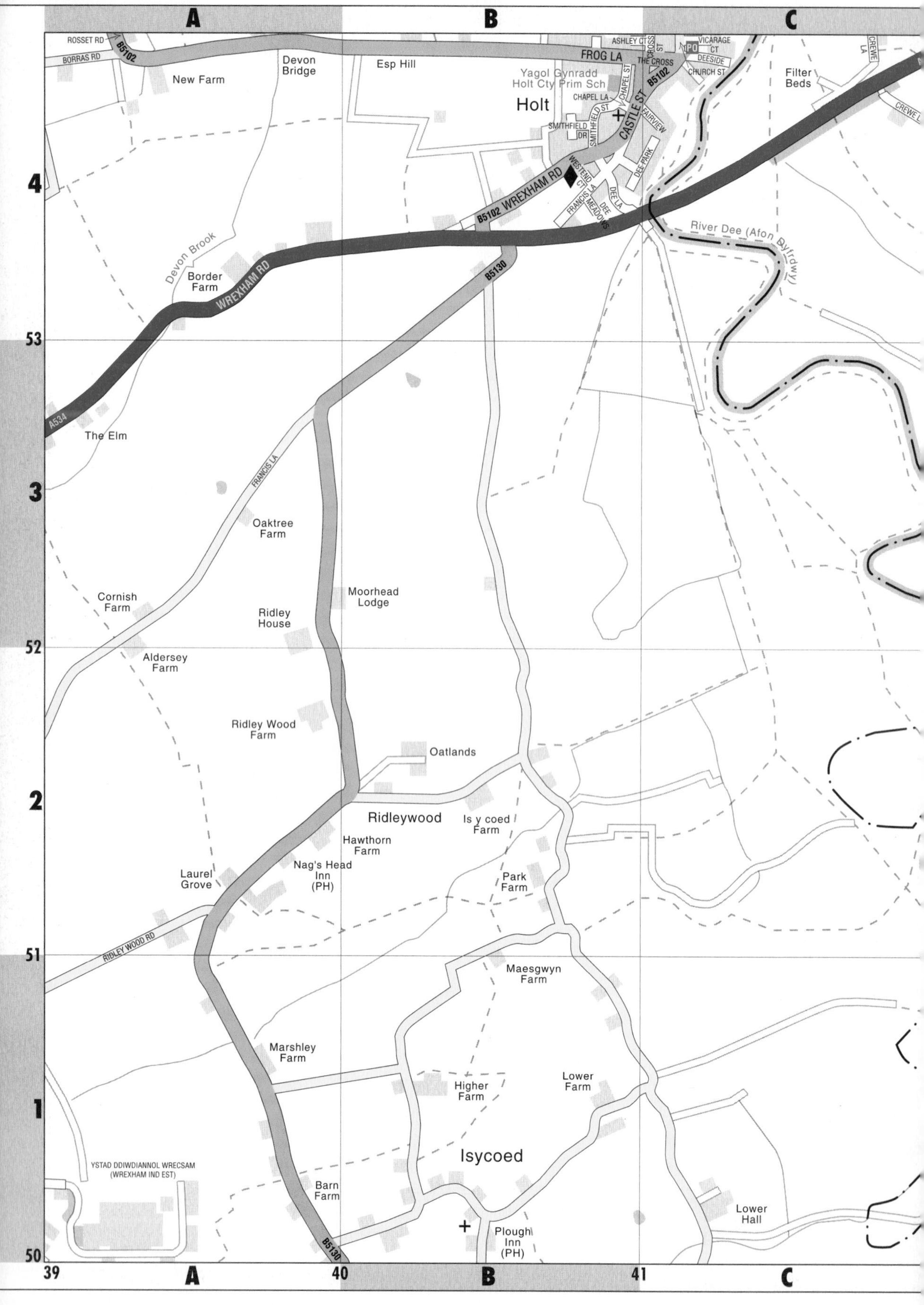

A   B   C

ROSSET RD
BORRAS RD
B5102
New Farm
Devon Bridge
Esp Hill
ASHLEY CT
FROG LA
VICARAGE CT
THE CROSS
DEESIDE
CHURCH ST
MPO
CREWE LA
Yagol Gynradd
Holt Cty Prim Sch
Holt
CHAPEL LA
CASTLE ST
B5102
Filter Beds
CREWE LA
SMITHFIELD DR
SMITHFIELD
WEST END LA
DEE LA
DEE PARK
FRANCIS MEADOWS
B5102 WREXHAM RD
River Dee (Afon Dyfrdwy)

4

Devon Brook
Border Farm
WREXHAM RD
B5130

53

A534
The Elm

FRANCIS LA
Oaktree Farm

3

Moorhead Lodge

Cornish Farm
Ridley House

Aldersey Farm

52

Ridley Wood Farm

Oatlands

2

Ridleywood
Is y coed Farm

Hawthorn Farm

Laurel Grove
Nag's Head Inn (PH)
Park Farm

51

RIDLEY WOOD RD

Maesgwyn Farm

Marshley Farm

Higher Farm
Lower Farm

1

YSTAD DDIWDIANNOL WRECSAM
(WREXHAM IND EST)

Isycoed

Barn Farm

Plough Inn (PH)
Lower Hall

B5130

50

39   A   40   B   41   C

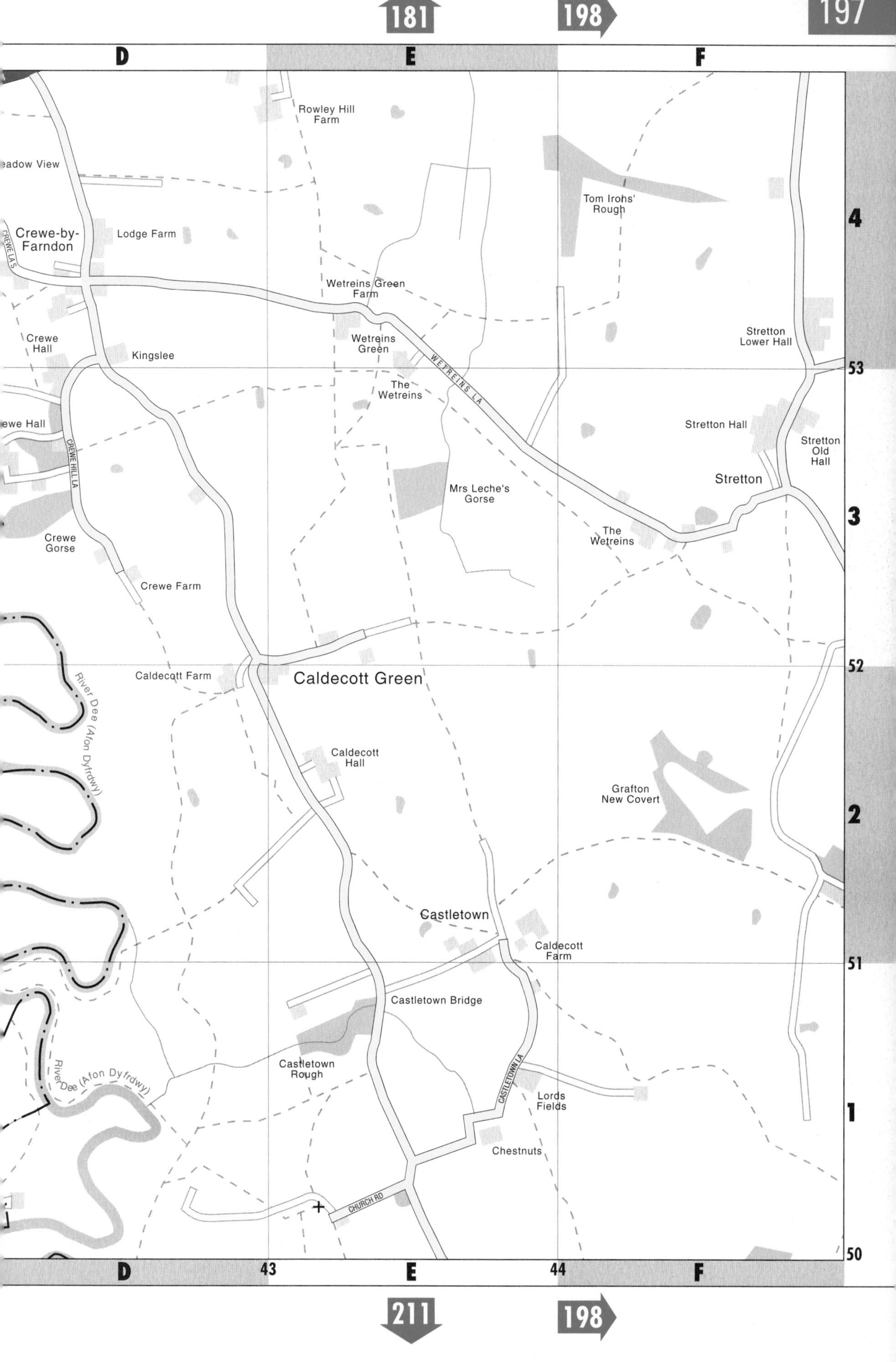

D
E
F

4

Rowley Hill Farm

adow View

Tom Irons' Rough

Crewe-by-Farndon

Lodge Farm

CREWE LA S

Wetreins Green Farm

Stretton Lower Hall

53

Crewe Hall

Kingslee

Wetreins Green

CREWE HILL LA

WETREINS LA

The Wetreins

ewe Hall

Stretton Hall

Mrs Leche's Gorse

Stretton Old Hall

Crewe Gorse

Stretton

The Wetreins

3

Crewe Farm

River Dee (Afon Dyfrdwy)

Caldecott Farm

Caldecott Green

52

Caldecott Hall

Grafton New Covert

2

Castletown

Caldecott Farm

51

Castletown Bridge

River Dee (Afon Dyfrdwy)

Castletown Rough

CASTLETOWN LA

Lords Fields

1

Chestnuts

+ CHURCH RD

50

A

B

C

4

The Birches

Golborne's Wood

Moor Gorse

Round Hill

Carden Brook

Garden Plantation

The Quarries

Cliff Bank

Mill Coppice

Home Farm

Hotel

Carden Marsh

53

Golf Course

Higher Carden

Stretton Mill

HIGHER CARDEN LA

Laurel Grove

Lower Carden

Lower Farm

3

Hook's Rough

Hook's Brook

Lower Carden Hall

Stone House

52

Grafton Lodge

Isle Farm

The Heir's Wood

Hob Hill Farm

2

Hob Hill

Carden Arms Inn (PH)

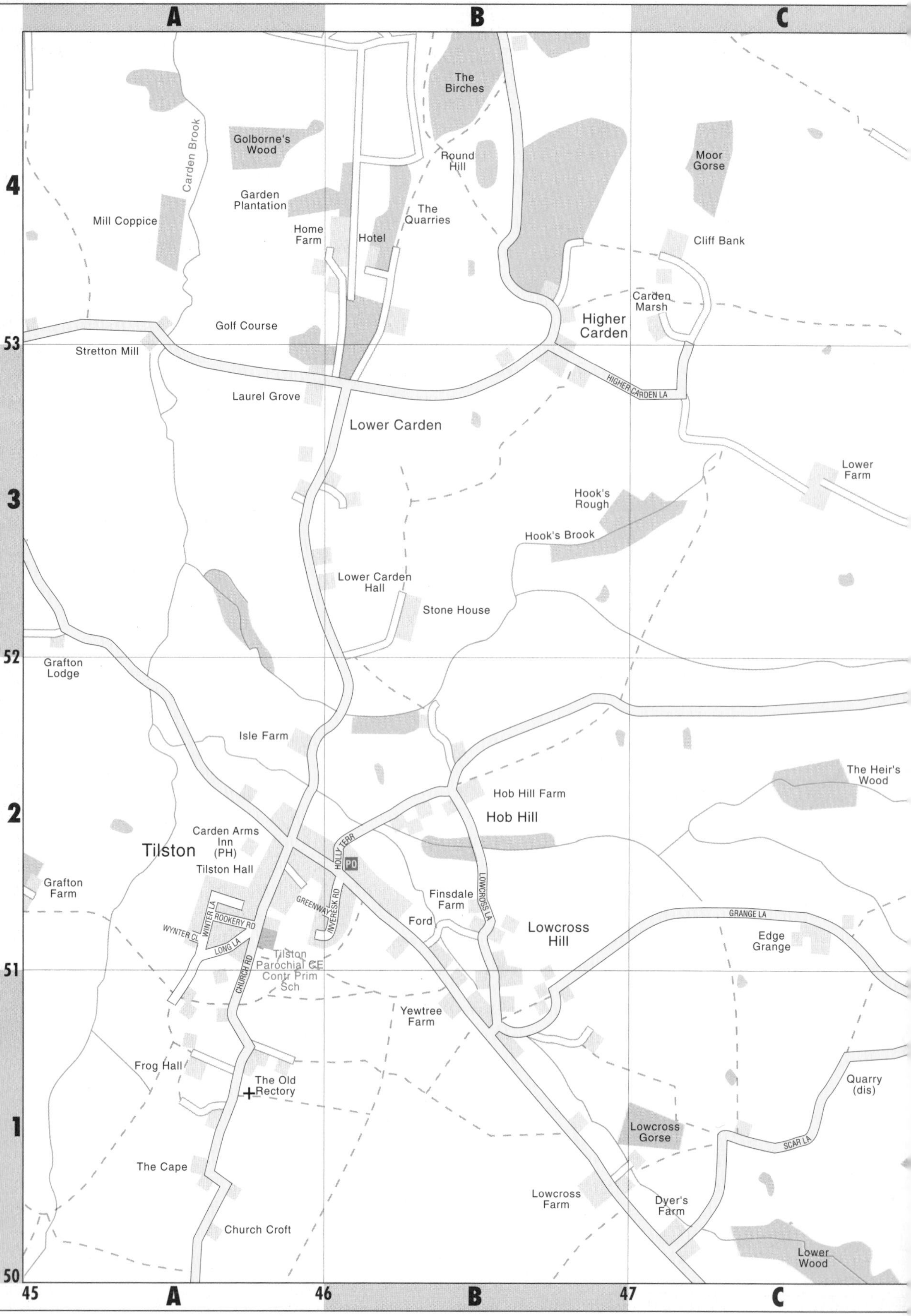

HOLLY TERR

Tilston

Tilston Hall

PO

Grafton Farm

GREENWAY

INVERESK RD

Finsdale Farm

LOWCROSS LA

Lowcross Hill

GRANGE LA

WYNTER CL

WINTER LA

ROOKERY RD

Ford

Edge Grange

LONG LA

CHURCH RD

51

Tilston Parochial CE Contr Prim Sch

Yewtree Farm

Frog Hall

The Old Rectory

Quarry (dis)

1

Lowcross Gorse

SCAR LA

The Cape

Lowcross Farm

Dyer's Farm

Church Croft

Lower Wood

50

45

A

46

B

47

C

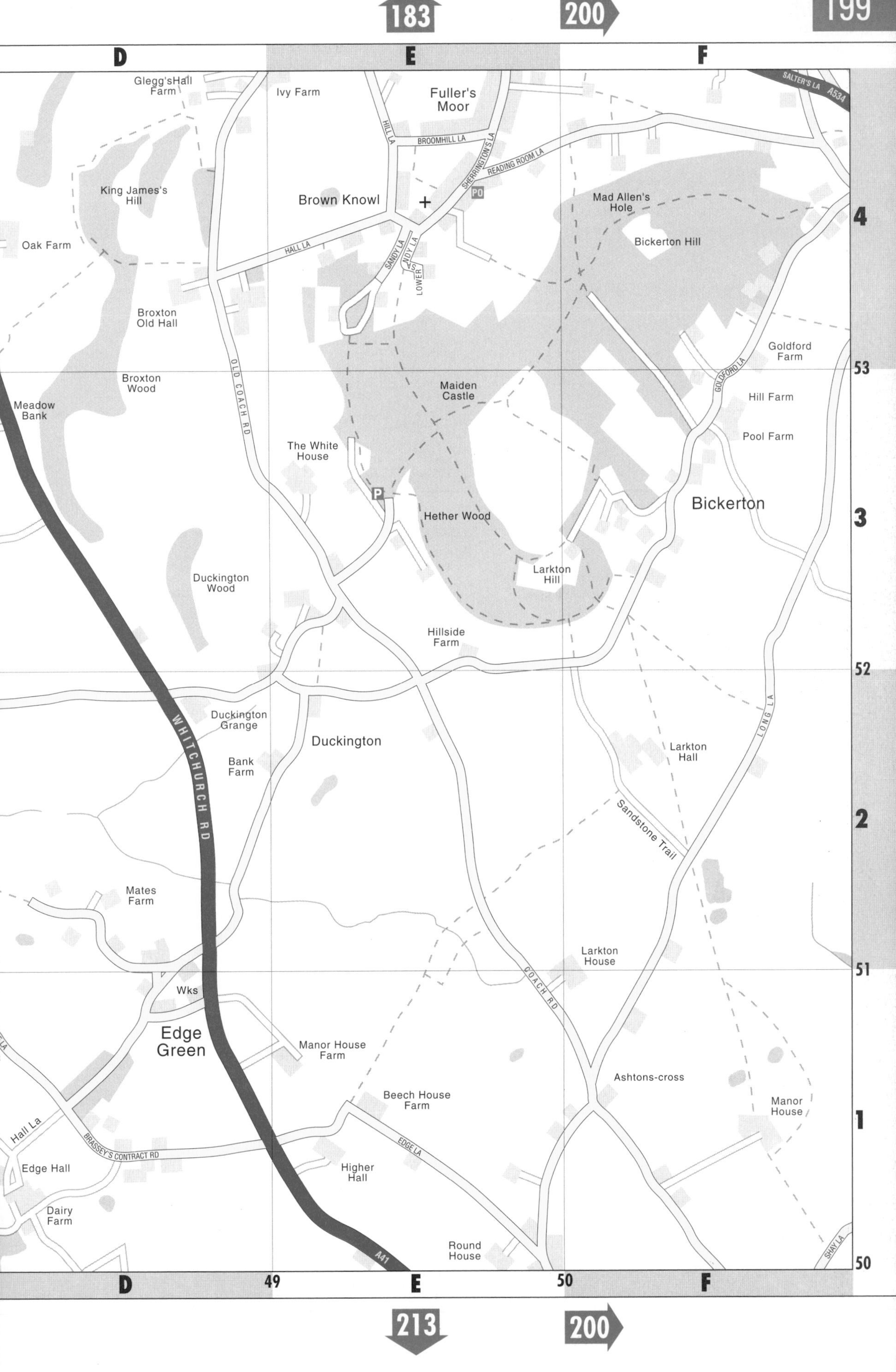

D E F

Salter's La A534

Glegg'sHall Farm

Ivy Farm

Fuller's Moor

Hill La

Broomhill La

Reading Room La

Sherrington's La

King James's Hill

Brown Knowl

PO

+

Mad Allen's Hole

Bickerton Hill

4

Oak Farm

Hall La

Sandy La

Lower Lady La

Broxton Old Hall

Goldford La

Goldford Farm

53

Broxton Wood

Maiden Castle

Hill Farm

Meadow Bank

Pool Farm

The White House

P

Bickerton

3

Hether Wood

Duckington Wood

Larkton Hill

Hillside Farm

52

Duckington Grange

Duckington

Larkton Hall

Long La

Bank Farm

Sandstone Trail

2

Mates Farm

Larkton House

Coach Rd

51

Whitchurch Rd

Wks

Edge Green

Manor House Farm

Ashtons-cross

Manor House

1

Hall La

Brassey's Contract Rd

Beech House Farm

Edge La

Edge Hall

Higher Hall

Dairy Farm

A41

Round House

Shav La

50

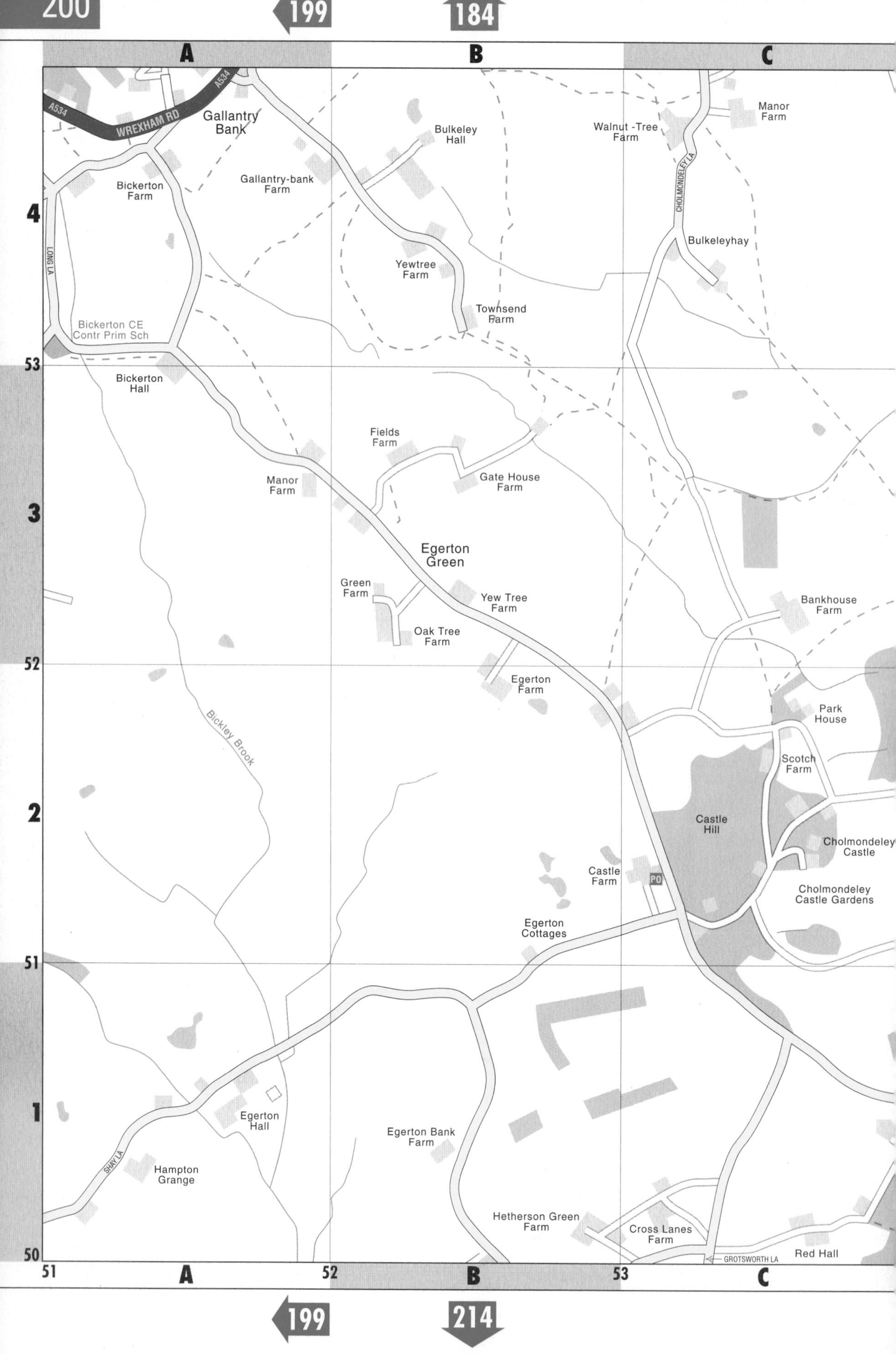

199
184

A   B   C

A534

WREXHAM RD

Gallantry
Bank

Bickerton
Farm

Gallantry-bank
Farm

Bulkeley
Hall

Walnut -Tree
Farm

Manor
Farm

CHOLMONDELEY LA

4

LONG LA

Yewtree
Farm

Townsend
Farm

Bulkeleyhay

Bickerton CE
Contr Prim Sch

53

Bickerton
Hall

Fields
Farm

Manor
Farm

Gate House
Farm

3

Egerton
Green

Green
Farm

Yew Tree
Farm

Bankhouse
Farm

Oak Tree
Farm

52

Egerton
Farm

Park
House

Scotch
Farm

Bickley Brook

2

Castle
Hill

Cholmondeley
Castle

Castle
Farm

PO

Cholmondeley
Castle Gardens

Egerton
Cottages

51

1

Egerton
Hall

Egerton Bank
Farm

SHAY LA

Hampton
Grange

Hetherson Green
Farm

Cross Lanes
Farm

Red Hall

GROTSWORTH LA

50

51   A   52   B   53   C

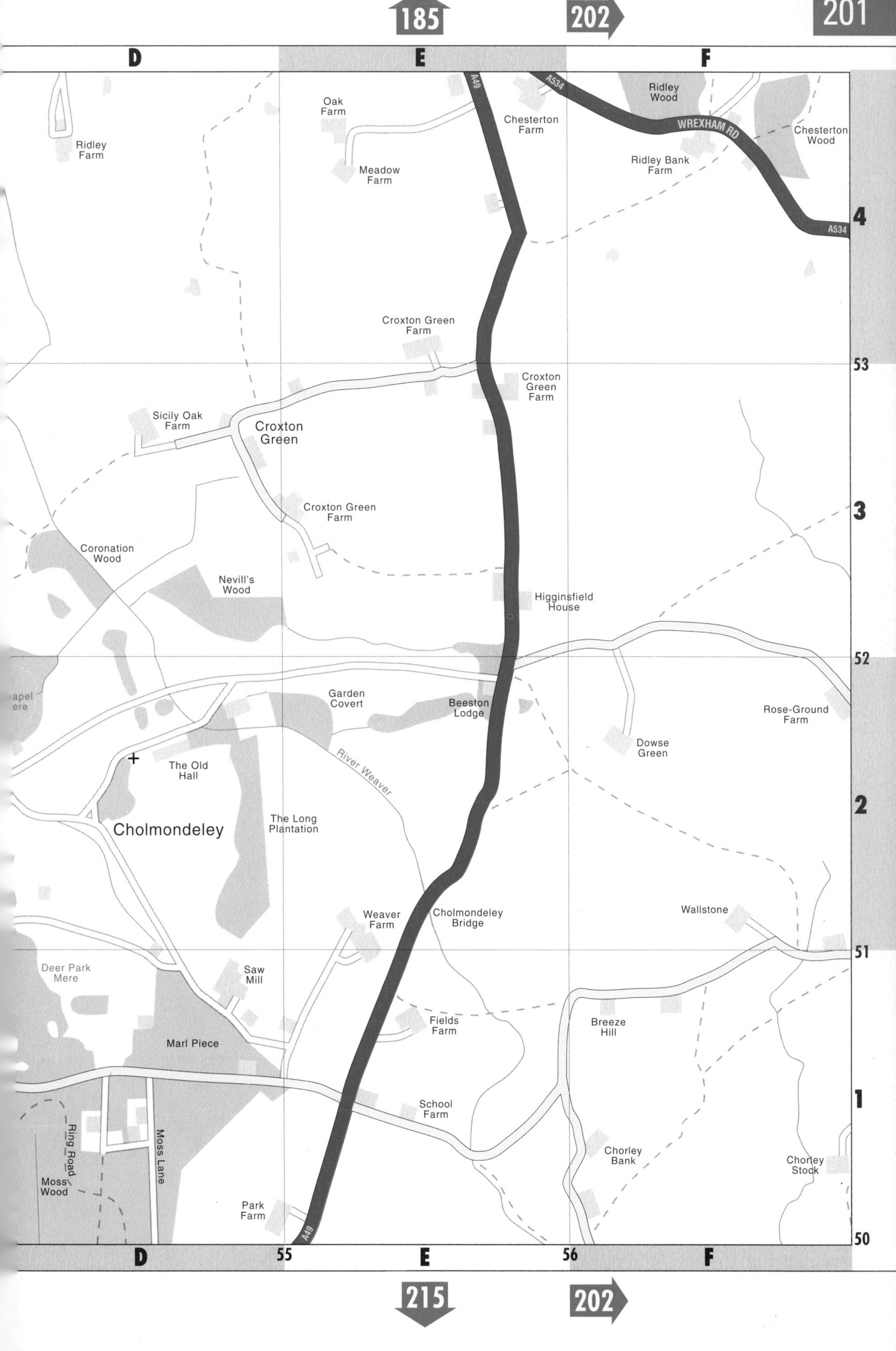

D
E
F

Ridley
Farm

Oak
Farm

Meadow
Farm

Chesterton
Farm

A49

A534

Ridley
Wood

WREXHAM RD

Chesterton
Wood

Ridley Bank
Farm

A534 **4**

Croxton Green
Farm

Croxton
Green
Farm

53

Sicily Oak
Farm

Croxton
Green

Croxton Green
Farm

Coronation
Wood

Nevill's
Wood

Higginsfield
House

3

apel
ere

Garden
Covert

Beeston
Lodge

River Weaver

Rose-Ground
Farm

52

Dowse
Green

The Old
Hall

Cholmondeley

The Long
Plantation

Wallstone

2

Weaver
Farm

Cholmondeley
Bridge

Deer Park
Mere

Saw
Mill

Breeze
Hill

51

Marl Piece

Fields
Farm

Ring Road

Moss Lane

School
Farm

1

Moss
Wood

Chorley
Bank

Chorley
Stock

Park
Farm

A49

50

D
55
E
56
F

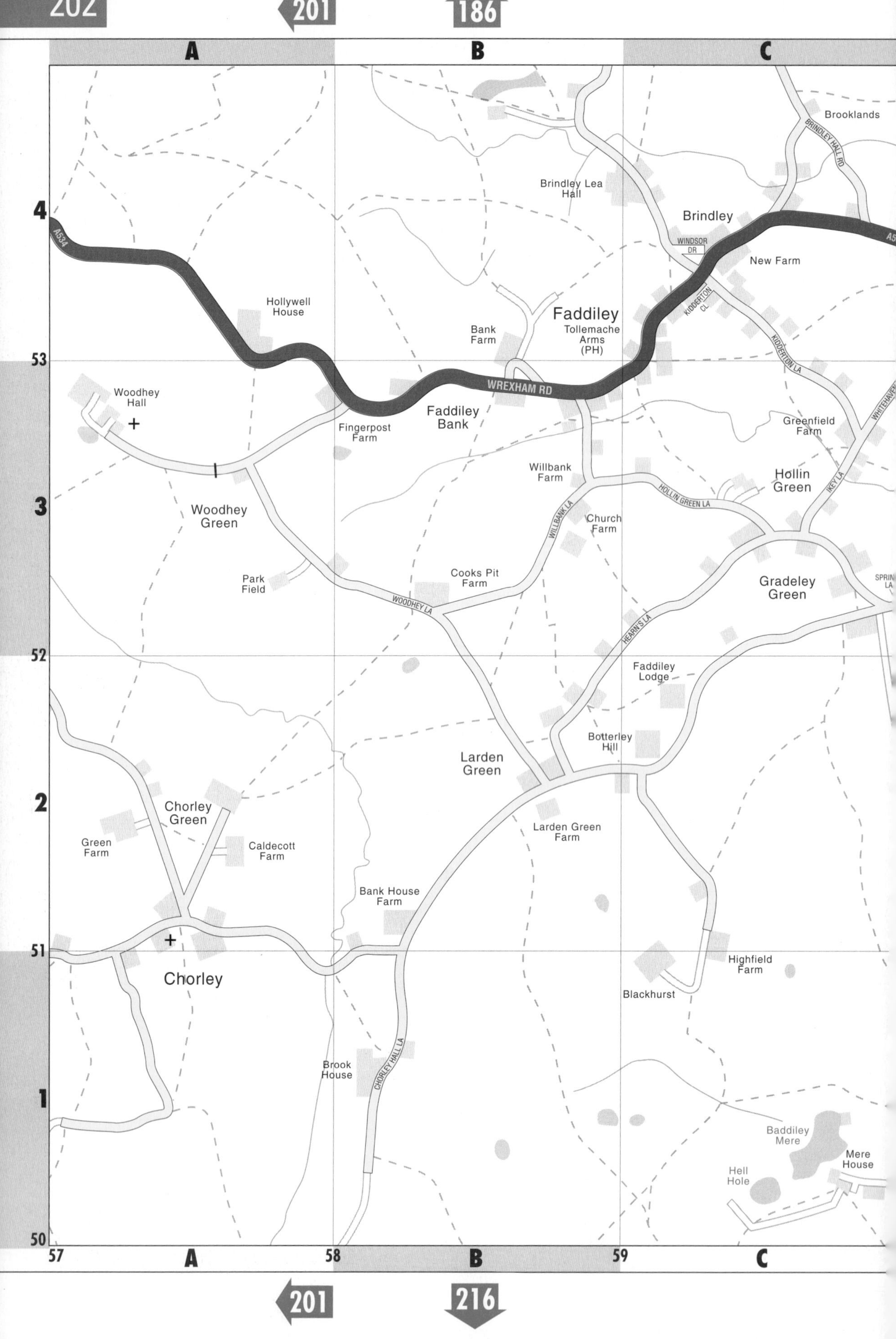
4
53
3
52
2
51
1
50
57
58
59
A534
WREXHAM RD
Brooklands
BRINDLEY HALL RD
Brindley Lea Hall
Brindley
WINDSOR DR
New Farm
Hollywell House
Bank Farm
Faddiley
Tollemache Arms (PH)
KIDDERTON CL
KIDDERTON LA
Woodhey Hall
Fingerpost Farm
Faddiley Bank
Greenfield Farm
WHITEHAVEN
Willbank Farm
Hollin Green
HOLLIN GREEN LA
IKEY LA
Woodhey Green
WILLBANK LA
Church Farm
Park Field
Cooks Pit Farm
WOODHEY LA
Gradeley Green
HEARN'S LA
Faddiley Lodge
Botterley Hill
Larden Green
Chorley Green
Green Farm
Caldecott Farm
Larden Green Farm
Bank House Farm
Chorley
Highfield Farm
Blackhurst
Brook House
CHORLEY HALL LA
Baddiley Mere
Mere House
Hell Hole

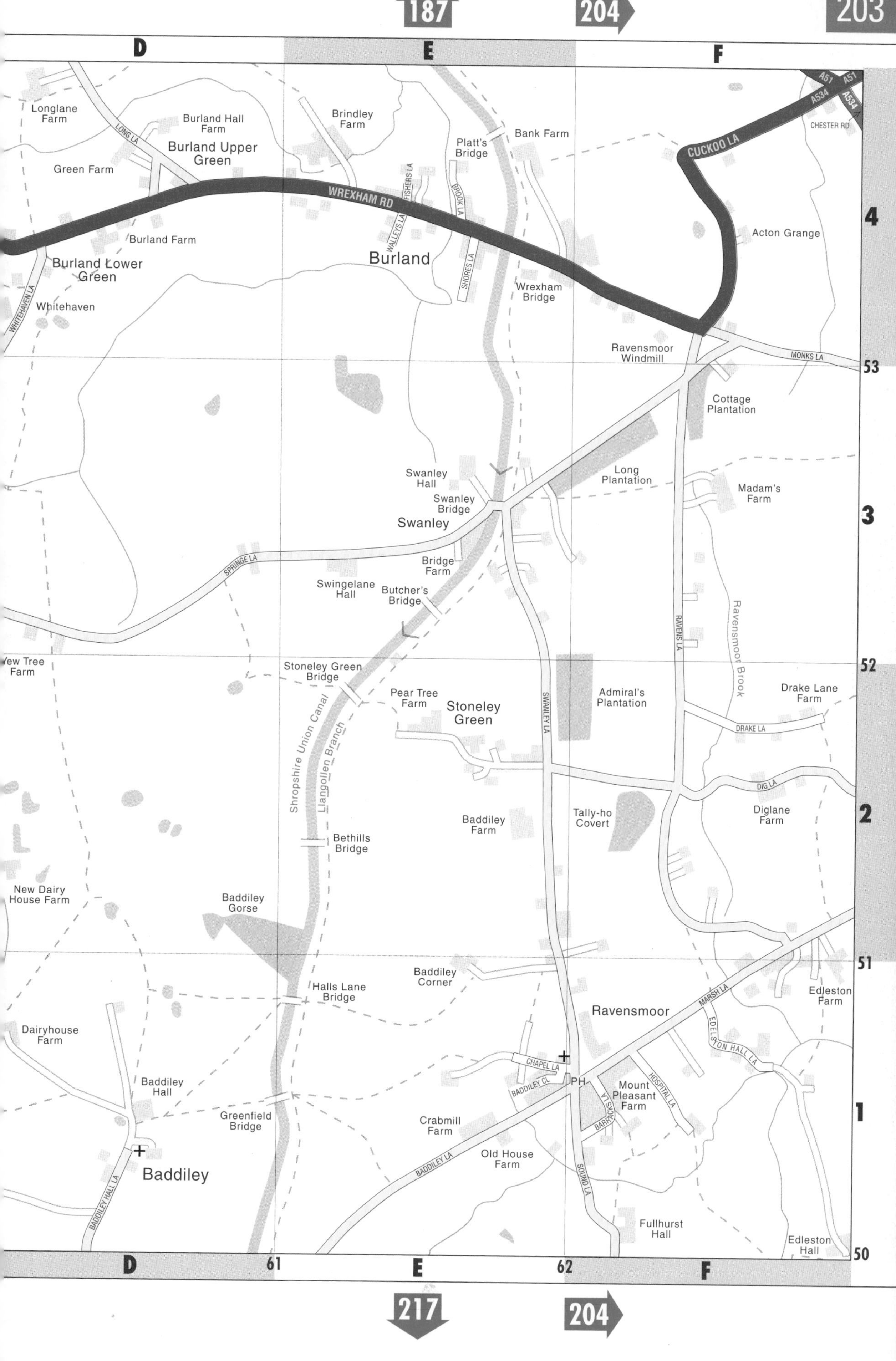

D   E   F

Longlane
Farm
Burland Hall
Farm
Brindley
Farm
Bank Farm
Platt's
Bridge
CUCKOO LA
CHESTER RD
A51 A51
A534 A534
Burland Upper
Green
Green Farm
WREXHAM RD
Acton Grange
4
Burland Farm
Burland
FISHERS LA
WALLEYS LA
BROOK LA
SHORES LA
Burland Lower
Green
Whitehaven
WHITEHAVEN LA
Wrexham
Bridge
Ravensmoor
Windmill
MONKS LA
53
Cottage
Plantation
Swanley
Hall
Long
Plantation
Madam's
Farm
Swanley
Bridge
Swanley
3
SPRINGE LA
Bridge
Farm
Swingelane
Hall
Butcher's
Bridge
RAVENS LA
Ravensmoor Brook
New Tree
Farm
Stoneley Green
Bridge
Pear Tree
Farm
Stoneley
Green
Admiral's
Plantation
Drake Lane
Farm
DRAKE LA
52
Shropshire Union Canal
Llangollen Branch
SWANLEY LA
Baddiley
Farm
Tally-ho
Covert
DIG LA
Diglane
Farm
2
Bethills
Bridge
New Dairy
House Farm
Baddiley
Gorse
51
Halls Lane
Bridge
Baddiley
Corner
Ravensmoor
MARSH LA
Edleston
Farm
EDLESTON HALL LA
Dairyhouse
Farm
Baddiley
Hall
Greenfield
Bridge
CHAPEL LA
BADDILEY CL
PH
Mount
Pleasant
Farm
HOSPITAL LA
1
BADDILEY HALL LA
Baddiley
Crabmill
Farm
BADDILEY LA
Old House
Farm
SOUND LA
BARR LA
Fullhurst
Hall
Edleston
Hall
50

D   61   E   62   F

A   **B**   **C**

A51

Reaseheath
Coll

Cobb's Lane
Farm

A51

The Green

B5074

LARKSPUR CL

ALVASTON
BSNS PK

Bluestone

A534

4

Beam
Bridge

A500

RIVERBANK CL

KINGFISHER CL

MERCER WAY
MEADOWVALE

COBB'S LA

BEAM
HEATHWAY

Acton Bridge

Henhull Hall

Works

THE BARONY EMPLOYMENT PK

MIDDLEWICH RD

RAY AVE

Acton CE Contr
Prim Sch

VAUGHAN RD
ST MARY'S

MANOR RD

WALLFIELDS
CL

BARONY CT

Cemy

BARONY BLDGS

SNIDFORD RD

WHITEHOUSE LA

BRERETON DR

Acton

WILBRAHAM RD

WILBRAHAM
CL

CLAYTONS
ROW

WALL FIELDS RD

A530

BARONY RD

MILLSTONE LA

BIRCHWOOD
DR

PENLINGTON

Kingsleyfield Farm

DAVENPORT AVE

53

ST MARYS
CT

WEAVER RD

The
Barony

PARK VIEW

HEATHSIDE

MONKS LA

CHESTER RD

Star Inn
(PH)

Marina

Nantwich
Junction
Bridge

NANTWICH

JAMES HALL ST

ALBERT ST

Sch

MAISTERSON
CT

PENLINGTON

Snow
Hill

PRINCE EDWARD ST

LADY HELEN WLK

CROMWELL

THE
BROAD

Malbank
Sch

MALBANK

BOWYER AVE

ST LAWRENCE
CT

MOUNT

SWINE MARKET 1
OAT MARKET 2

KING

SCAIFE RD

A530

Haybays

3

Dorfold Hall

Nantwich
Aqueduct

TELFORD RD

NIXON'S
ROW

CHAPEL
ROW

YEW TREE
DR

CROSS
WOOD ST

SECOND
WOOD ST

CHAPEL
MEWS

Liby

C Hall

Gall

Mkt

FACTORY CL

BOWLING GREEN CT

NORTH CROFTS

SOUTH CROFTS

CREWE

BADDOCK
BANK

WELSH ROW

ST ANNE'S LA

WHITEHALL CT

CHRCHYD

MONKS LA

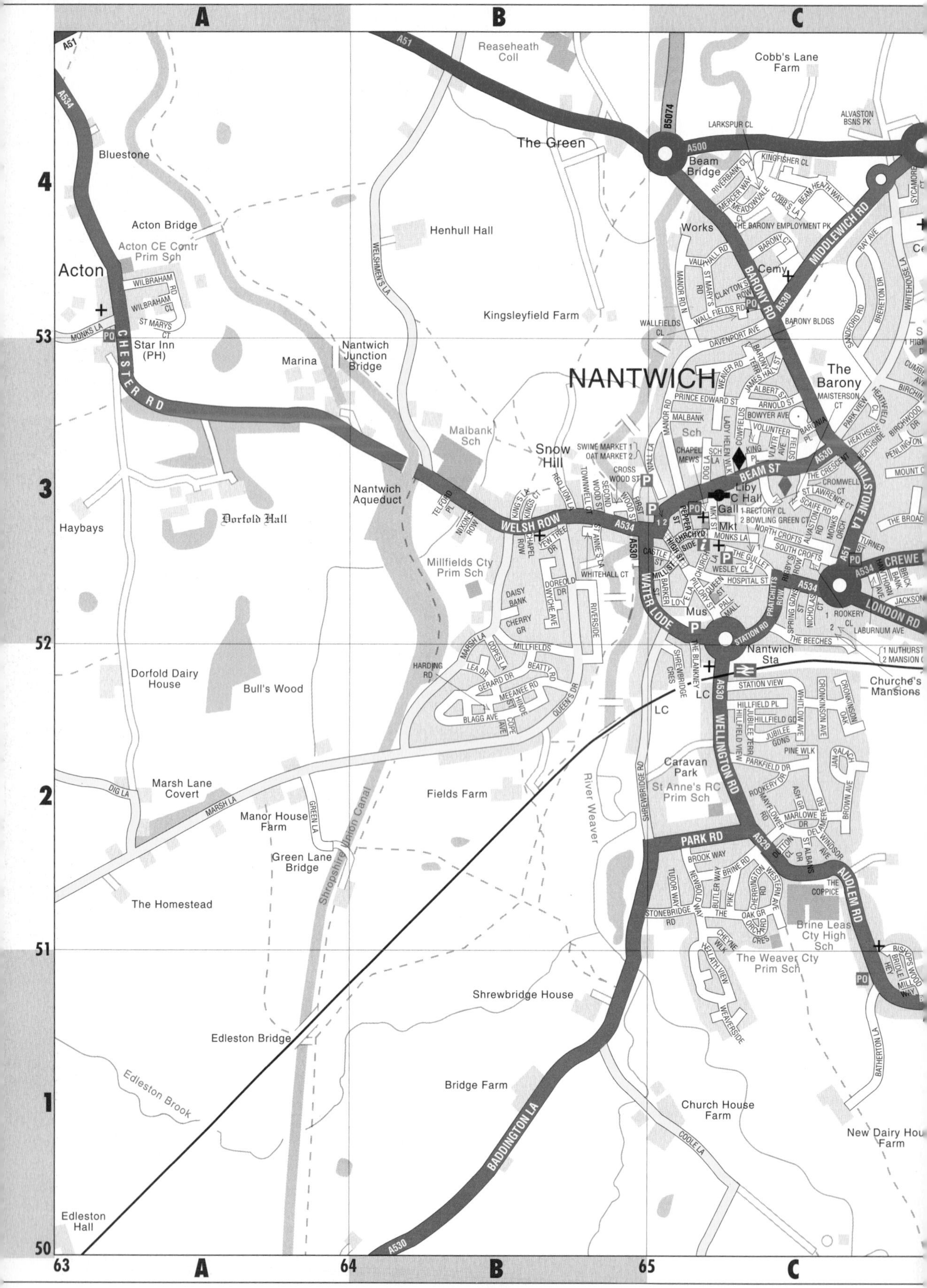

THE GULLET

A534

London RD

JACKSON

Millfields Cty
Prim Sch

DOREOLD
DR

WYCHE AVE

RIVERSIDE

WESLEY CL

A530

QUEEN

PILLORY ST

PALL
MALL

A51

DAISY
BANK

HOSPITAL ST

Mus

ROOKERY
CL

LABURNUM AVE

CHERRY
GR

Millfields

BEATTY RD

Nantwich
Sta

1 NUTHURST
2 MANSION

52

MARSH LA

COPES LA

LEA DR

GERARD DR

HARDING
RD

MEEANEE RD

HINDE

COPE
AVE

BLAGG AVE

QUEEN'S DR

SHREWBRIDGE
CRES

STATION VIEW

LC

Churche's
Mansions

Marsh Lane
Covert

DIG LA

MARSH LA

Manor House
Farm

GREEN LA

Fields Farm

River Weaver

Caravan
Park

St Anne's RC
Prim Sch

HILLFIELD PL

HILLFIELD VIEW

WELLINGTON RD

A530

WHITLOW AVE

CROMINSON AVE

JUBILEE
GDNS

PINE WLK

JAN

ASH GR

BROWN AVE

AUDLEM RD

2

Green Lane
Bridge

Shropshire Union Canal

MARLOWE
DR

PARK RD

A529

ROOKERY DR

ST ALBANS

WINDSOR

THE
COPPICE

The Homestead

BROOK WAY

BRINE RD

PIKE

CHERRINGTON

WESTERN AVE

BISHOPS

Edleston Bridge

TUDOR WAY

NEWBOLD WAY

STONEBRIDGE
RD

BUTLER WAY

OAK GR

CHEYNE

Brine Leas
Cty High
Sch

51

Shrewbridge House

HEATH VIEW

WEAVERSIDE

The Weaver Cty
Prim Sch

PO

BATHERTON LA

BISHOPS WOOD

BRINDLE
HEY

MILL

Edleston Brook

Bridge Farm

Church House
Farm

New Dairy Hou
Farm

1

BADDINGTON LA

COOLE LA

Edleston
Hall

50

A530

63   **A**   **64**   **B**   **65**   **C**

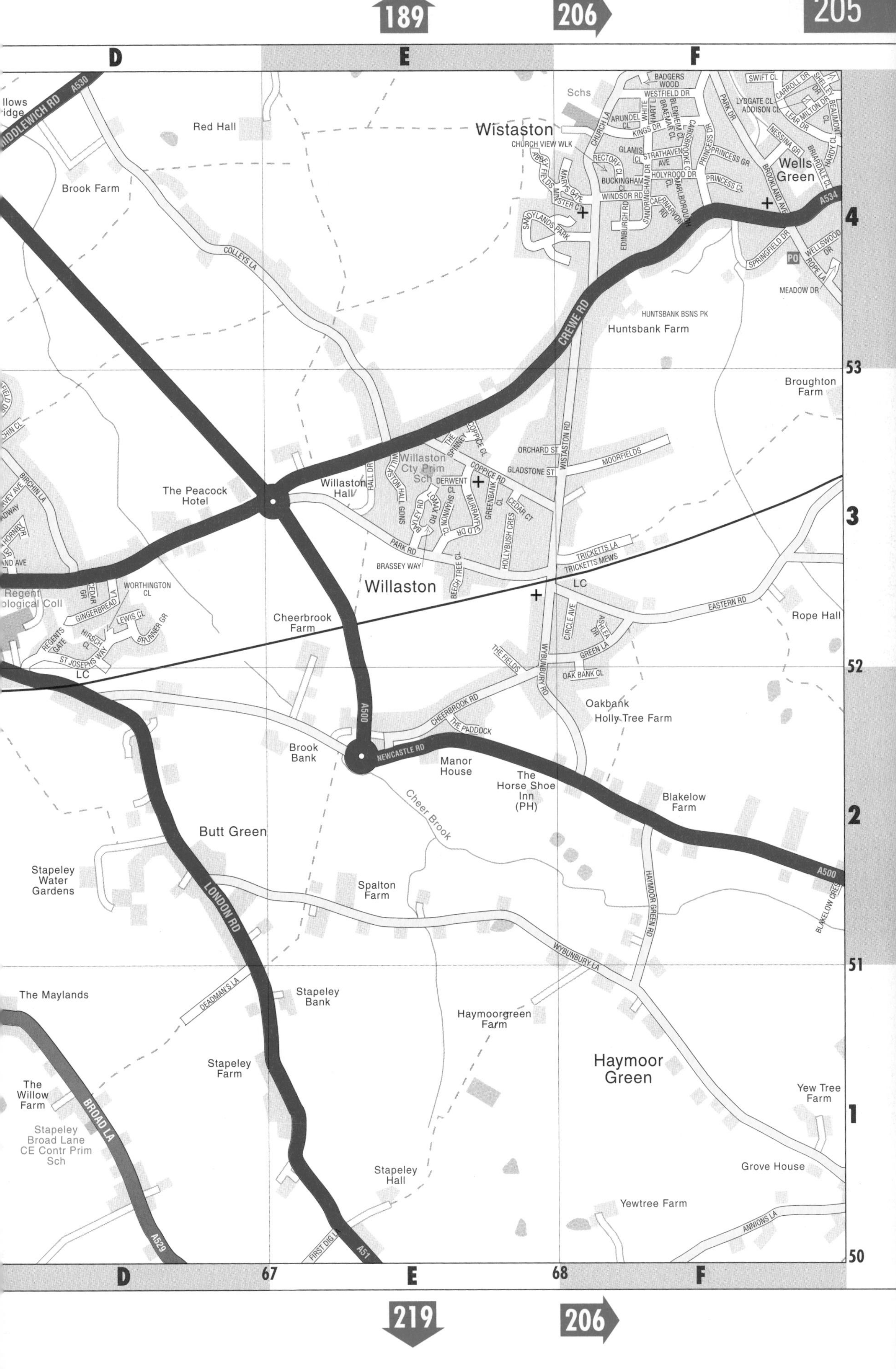
D
E
F
Wistaston
Wells Green
Willaston
Red Hall
Brook Farm
The Peacock Hotel
Willaston Hall
Cheerbrook Farm
Huntsbank Farm
HUNTSBANK BSNS PK
Broughton Farm
Rope Hall
Oakbank
Holly Tree Farm
Brook Bank
Manor House
The Horse Shoe Inn (PH)
Blakelow Farm
Butt Green
Stapeley Water Gardens
Spalton Farm
Cheer Brook
The Maylands
Stapeley Bank
Haymoorgreen Farm
Haymoor Green
Stapeley Farm
The Willow Farm
Stapeley Broad Lane CE Contr Prim Sch
Stapeley Hall
Yew Tree Farm
Grove House
Yewtree Farm
Willaston Cty Prim Sch
Schs
CREWE RD
A500
A530
A534
A529
A51
MIDDLEWICH RD
COLLEYS LA
WISTASTON RD
NEWCASTLE RD
LONDON RD
BROAD LA
WYBUNBURY LA
WYBUNBURY RD
HAYMOOR GREEN RD
EASTERN RD
MOORFIELDS
TRICKETTS LA
TRICKETTS MEWS
CHEERBROOK RD
THE PADDOCK
THE FIELDS
OAK BANK CL
GREEN LA
CIRCLE AVE
ASHLEA DR
DEADMAN'S LA
ANNIONS LA
FIRST DIG LA
BLAKELOW CRES
PARK RD
BRASSEY WAY
BEECH TREE CL
HOLLYBUSH CRES
CEDAR CT
COPPICE RD
COPPICE CL
THE SPINNEY
ORCHARD ST
GLADSTONE ST
DERWENT CL
WILLASTON HALL GDNS
HALL DR
BAYLEY RD
LOMAX RD
SHANNON CL
MURRAYFIELD DR
GREENBANK CL
SANDYLANDS PARK
CHURCH VIEW WLK
ABBEY FIELDS
MARYS GATE
MINSTER CT
CHURCH LA
ARUNDEL CL
KINGS DR
BADGERS WOOD
WESTFIELD DR
BRAEMAR CL
BLENHEIM CL
CARISBROOKE CL
GLAMIS CL
STRATHAVEN AVE
RECTORY CL
BUCKINGHAM CL
HOLYROOD DR
WINDSOR RD
EDINBURGH RD
SANDRINGHAM DR
CAERNARVON RD
MARLBOROUGH
PRINCESS DR
PRINCESS GR
PRINCESS CL
PARK DR
SWIFT CL
LYDGATE CL
ADDISON CL
CARROLL DR
SHELLEY DR
MILTON DR
LEAR DR
BEAUMONT CL
NESSINA GR
BRIARDALE CL
HARDY CL
BROOKLAND AVE
SPRINGFIELD DR
WELLSWOOD DR
ROPE LA
MEADOW DR
PO
WORTHINGTON CL
CEDAR GR
GINGERBREAD LA
LEWIS CL
BRUNNER GR
HIRSCH CL
REGENTS GATE
ST JOSEPHS WAY
BIRCHIN LA
HORNBY DR
LC
53
52
51
50
4
3
2
1
67
68

A B C

Gresty Green Farm

Basford Hall Sorting Sidings

LC

Mill

PH

Greenbank Farm

Wistaston Berkeley Cty Prim Sch

Broughton Farm

Ropegreen Bridge

Brook Farm

Shavington House

Shavington

Green Farm

Shavington Sports Ctr

Shavington Cty High Sch

Shavington Hall

Basford Hall

Basford

Rope Farm

Shavington Farm

Sutch Farm

Shavington Cty Prim Sch

Swill Brook

Shavington Green Farm

Puseydale Farm

PH

GOODALL'S CNR

NEWCASTLE RD

PH

Hough

Hough Manor

Hough Hall

Wybunbury Grange

Clannor Heath

Cockshades Farm

Moss Farm

Hough Common

Yewtree Fa

Dove House Farm

Highfield Farm

Pinfold Farm

Pinfold Corner

Wybunbury Moss

CREWE RD

STOCK LA

GRESTY RD

GRESTY LA

ROPE LA

WESTON LA

BACK LA

CASEY LA

DIG LA

COBBS LA

PIT LA

1 MARTON CL
2 ELLWOOD GREEN

1 COLLINBROOK AVE
2 BALMORAL AVE

4 53 3 52 2 51 1 50

69 70 71

A B C

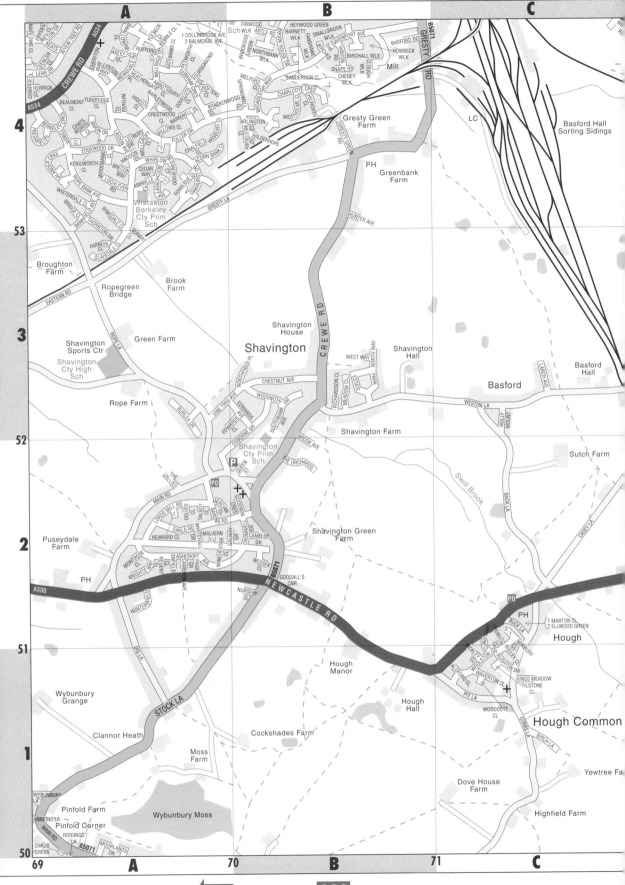

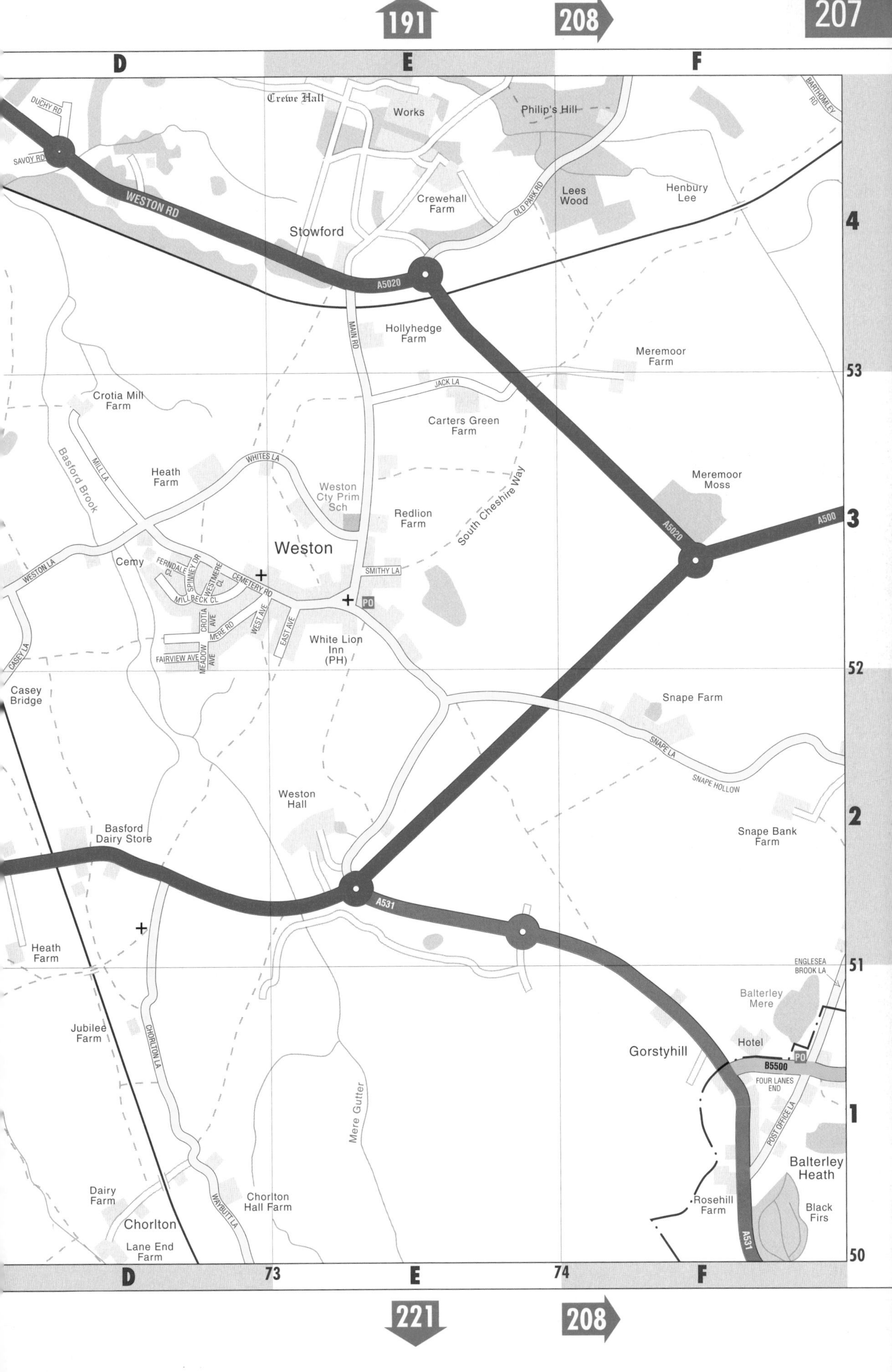
D
E
F
Crewe Hall
Works
Philip's Hill
BARTHOMLEY RD
DUCHY RD
SAVOY RD
WESTON RD
Crewehall Farm
OLD PARK RD
Lees Wood
Henbury Lee
Stowford
A5020
4
Hollyhedge Farm
MAIN RD
Meremoor Farm
53
JACK LA
Crotia Mill Farm
Carters Green Farm
Basford Brook
MILL LA
Heath Farm
WHITES LA
Meremoor Moss
Weston Cty Prim Sch
Redlion Farm
South Cheshire Way
A5020
A500
3
Weston
WESTON LA
Cemy
FERNDALE CL
SPINNEY DR
WESTMERE CL
CEMETERY RD
SMITHY LA
MILLBECK CL
PO
CROTIA AVE
MERE RD
WEST AVE
EAST AVE
White Lion Inn (PH)
CASEY LA
FAIRVIEW AVE
MEADOW AVE
52
Casey Bridge
Snape Farm
SNAPE LA
SNAPE HOLLOW
Weston Hall
2
Basford Dairy Store
Snape Bank Farm
A531
Heath Farm
51
ENGLESEA BROOK LA
Balterley Mere
Jubilee Farm
CHORLTON LA
Gorstyhill
Hotel
B5500
PO
FOUR LANES END
POST OFFICE LA
1
Mere Gutter
Balterley Heath
Rosehill Farm
Black Firs
Dairy Farm
Chorlton Hall Farm
WAYBUTT LA
A531
Chorlton
Lane End Farm
50
D
73
E
74
F

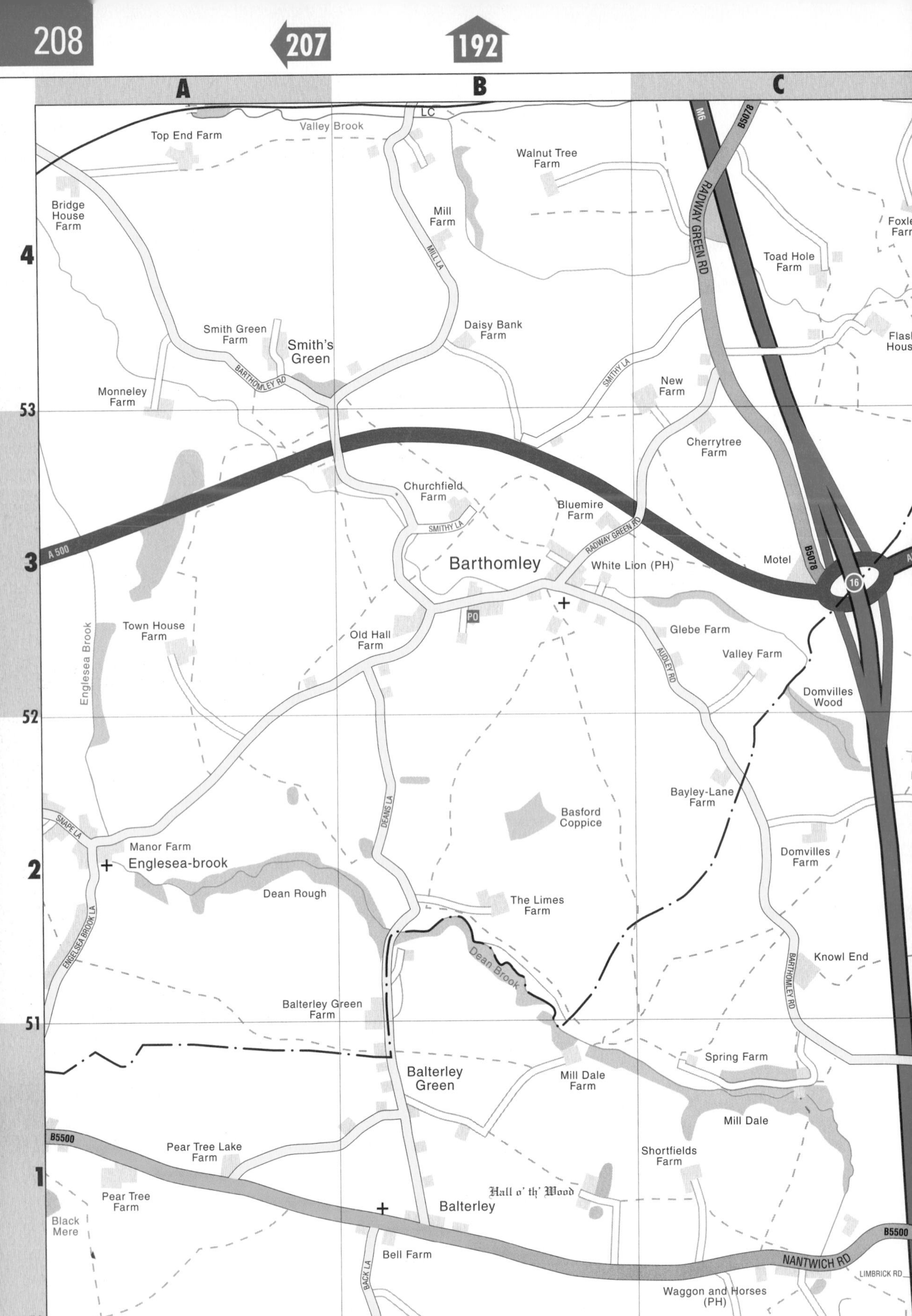

Top End Farm

Valley Brook

LC

Walnut Tree Farm

Bridge House Farm

Mill Farm

Foxle Farm

MILL LA

4

Toad Hole Farm

Smith Green Farm

Daisy Bank Farm

Smith's Green

Flash House

BARTHOMLEY RD

SMITHY LA

New Farm

Monneley Farm

53

Cherrytree Farm

M6

RADWAY GREEN RD

B5078

A 500

Churchfield Farm

SMITHY LA

Bluemire Farm

RADWAY GREEN RD

Motel

B5078

A5

16

3

Barthomley

White Lion (PH)

+

PO

Glebe Farm

Town House Farm

Old Hall Farm

AUDLEY RD

Valley Farm

Englesea Brook

Domvilles Wood

52

Basford Coppice

Bayley-Lane Farm

SNAPE LA

Manor Farm

Englesea-brook

+

Dean Rough

DEANS LA

Domvilles Farm

ENGLESEA BROOK LA

2

BARTHOMLEY RD

The Limes Farm

Dean Brook

Knowl End

Balterley Green Farm

51

Spring Farm

Balterley Green

Mill Dale Farm

Mill Dale

B5500

Pear Tree Lake Farm

Shortfields Farm

1

Pear Tree Farm

+

Hall o' th' Wood

Balterley

Black Mere

B5500

Bell Farm

NANTWICH RD

LIMBRICK RD

BACK LA

Waggon and Horses (PH)

50

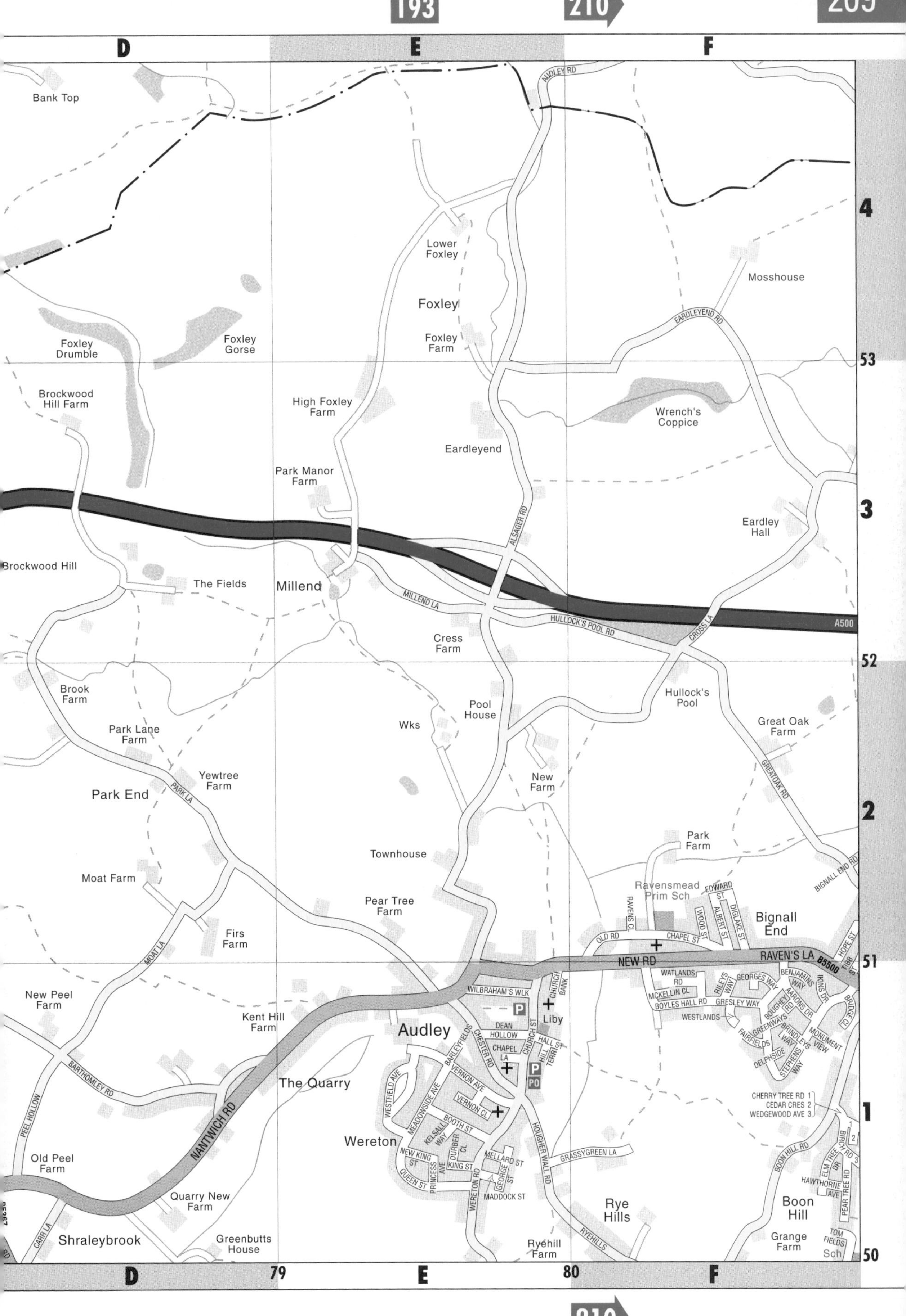
D
E
F
Bank Top
Lower Foxley
Foxley
Foxley Farm
Mosshouse
Foxley Drumble
Foxley Gorse
Brockwood Hill Farm
High Foxley Farm
Wrench's Coppice
Eardleyend
Park Manor Farm
Eardley Hall
Brockwood Hill
The Fields
Millend
Cress Farm
Brook Farm
Hullock's Pool
Pool House
Wks
Great Oak Farm
Park Lane Farm
Yewtree Farm
New Farm
Park End
Townhouse
Park Farm
Moat Farm
Pear Tree Farm
Ravensmead Prim Sch
Bignall End
Firs Farm
New Peel Farm
Kent Hill Farm
Audley
Liby
The Quarry
Wereton
Old Peel Farm
Quarry New Farm
Rye Hills
Boon Hill
Grange Farm
Shraleybrook
Greenbutts House
Ryehill Farm
AUDLEY RD
EARDLEYEND RD
ALSAGER RD
MILLEND LA
HULLOCK'S POOL RD
CROSS LA
A500
GREATOAK RD
PARK LA
BIGNALL END RD
MOAT LA
NEW RD
RAVEN'S LA
B5500
OLD RD
CHAPEL ST
WATLANDS RD
MCKELLIN CL
BOYLES HALL RD
GRESLEY WAY
WESTLANDS
WILBRAHAM'S WLK
CHURCH BANK
DEAN HOLLOW
CHAPEL LA
CHURCH ST
HALL ST
NANTWICH RD
BARTHOMLEY RD
PEEL HOLLOW
CARR LA
HOUGHER WALL RD
GRASSYGREEN LA
RYEHILLS
MADDOCK ST
BOON HILL RD
HAWTHORNE AVE
PEAR TREE RD
TOM FIELDS
CHERRY TREE RD 1
CEDAR CRES 2
WEDGEWOOD AVE 3
4
53
3
52
2
51
1
50
79
80

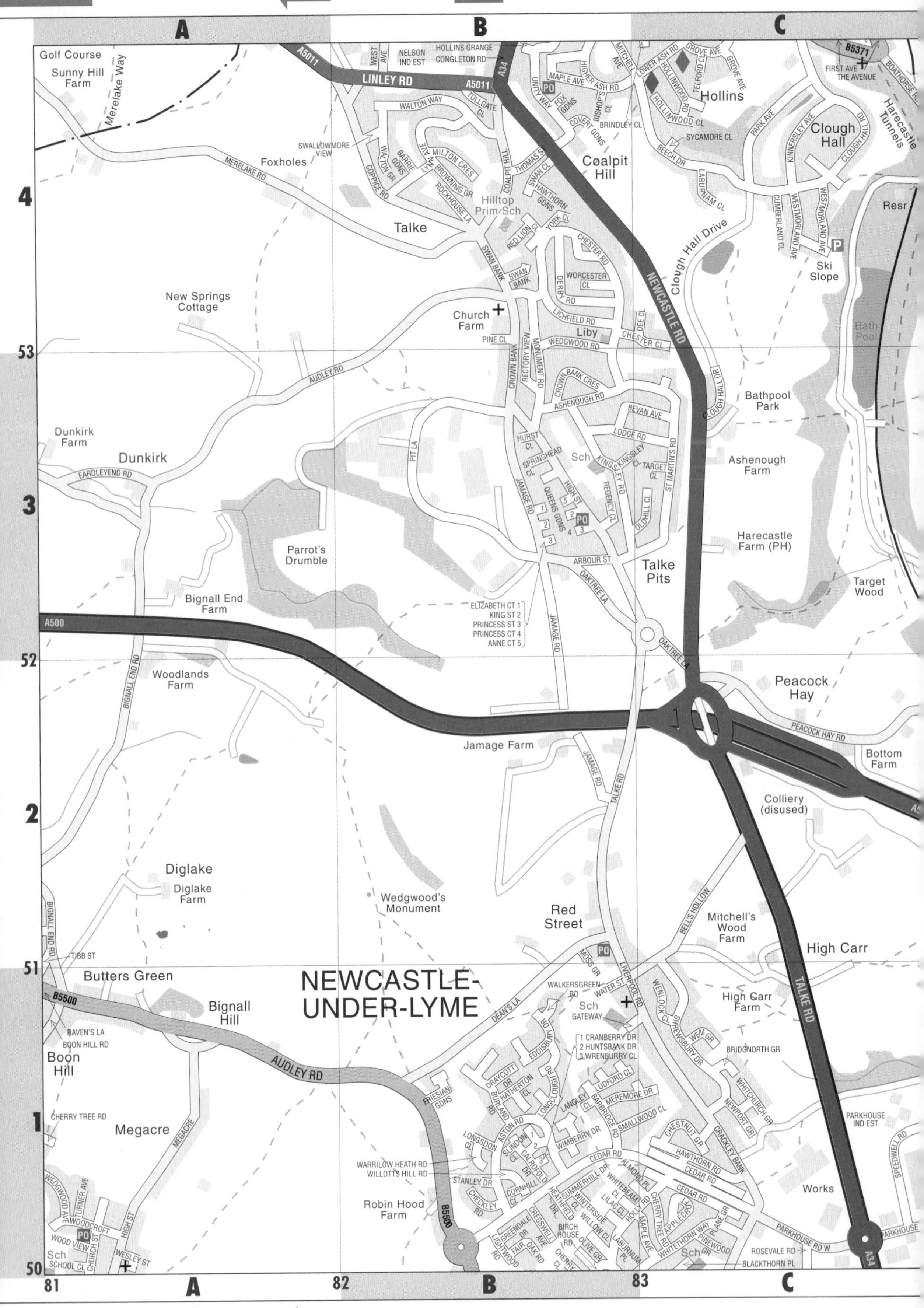

Golf Course
Sunny Hill Farm

Merelake Way

LINLEY RD
A5011

WEST AVE
NELSON AVE
HOLLINS GRANGE
CONGLETON RD
HOLLINS IND EST

MITCHEL RD
LOWER ASH RD
HOLLINWOOD CL
GROVE AVE
GROVE AVE

B5371
FIRST AVE
THE AVENUE

Harecastle Tunnels

Foxholes
MERELAKE RD

WALTON WAY
TOLLGATE

SWALLOWMORE VIEW

WALTER GDNS
BARBEL GDNS
MILTON CRES
COPPICE RD
BROWNING GR
COALPIT HILL
THOMAS ST
SWAN CL
HAWTHORN GDNS

UNITY WAY
MAPLE AVE
FOX GDNS
COVERT GDNS
BISHOP CL
BRINDLEY CL

PARK AVE
SYCAMORE CL
BEECH DR
KINNERSLEY AVE
CLOUGH HALL
Clough Hall

Talke

Hilltop Prim Sch

ROLL LION CL
YORK CL

CHESTER RD
DERBY CL
WORCESTER CL

LABURNUM CL
CUMBERLAND AVE
WESTMORLAND AVE
CUMBERLAND AVE

Ski Slope

Resr

New Springs Cottage

SWAN BANK
SWAN BANK

Church Farm
PINE CL
Liby
LICHFIELD RD
WEDGWOOD RD
CHESTER CL
DEE CL
CHESTER CL

NEWCASTLE RD

CLOUGH HALL DR
Clough Hall Drive

Bathpool Park

Bath Pool

53

AUDLEY RD

CROWN BANK
RECTORY VIEW
MONUMENT RD
CROWN BANK CRES
ASHENOUGH RD
BEVAN AVE
LODGE RD

Ashenough Farm

Dunkirk Farm
Dunkirk
EARDLEYEND RD

PIT LA

HURST CL
SPRINGHEAD
JAMAGE RD
QUEENS GDNS
HIGH ST
KINGSLEY RD
KINGSLEY RD
ST MARTINS RD
TARGET CL
REGENCY CL
OLDHILL CL

Sch

Harecastle Farm (PH)

Target Wood

3

Parrot's Drumble

Bignall End Farm

A500

ARBOUR ST

OAKTREE LA
Talke Pits

ELIZABETH CT 1
KING ST 2
PRINCESS ST 3
PRINCESS CT 4
ANNE CT 5

Woodlands Farm

BIGNALL END RD

JAMAGE RD

Peacock Hay

PEACOCK HAY RD

Bottom Farm

52

Jamage Farm

JAMAGE RD

TALKE RD

Colliery (disused)

2

Diglake
Diglake Farm

Wedgwood's Monument

Red Street

Mitchell's Wood Farm

BELLS HOLLOW

High Carr

BIGNALL END RD

TIBB ST
Butters Green

Bignall Hill

NEWCASTLE-
UNDER-LYME

MOSS GR
WATER ST

WALKERSGREEN RD
Sch GATEWAY

High Carr Farm

TALKE RD

51

B5500

RAVEN'S LA
BOON HILL RD

AUDLEY RD

DEAN'S LA

LIVERPOOL RD
WENLOCK CL
SHREWSBURY DR

WEM GR

1 CRANBERRY DR
2 HUNTSBANK DR
3 WRENBURY CL

BRIDGNORTH GR

WHITCHURCH CL

Boon Hill

FRIESIAN GDNS

GRACCOTT CL
BURLAND CL
HATHERTON

OULTON CL
LANGLEY
GARBORO
LIDFORD CL
MEREMORE DR

NEWPORT CL

PARKHOUSE IND EST

Cherry Tree Rd

Megacre

MEGACRE

LONGSDON CL
ASTON RD
ST THORN
CAL RD
WIMBERRY DR
SMALLWOOD CL

CHESTNUT DR
CRACKLEY BANK

Works

WEDGWOOD AVE
TURNER AVE
WOODCROFT
HIGH ST
WESLEY ST

WARRILOW HEATH RD
WILLOTTS HILL RD
STANLEY DR
CHECKLEY RD
CORNHILL
WIMBERRY DR

CEDAR RD
HAWTHORN DR
CEDAR RD
ALMOND PL
WHITETHORN WAY
PLANE GR
WHITCHURCH

PARKHOUSE RD W
ROSEVALE RD
BLACKTHORN PL

A34
PARKHOUSE

Robin Hood Farm

B5500

GREENDALE
FAIR OAK
LIGHTWOOD
DRESSFIELD AVE
WINTERSIDE
SUMMERHILL GR
WHITEHAM
FIELD
LILAC CL
WILLOW CL
OLIVE GR
CHERRY
BIRCH HOUSE RD
LABURNUM
NEWFOOD
CHERRY TREE DR
MAPLE CL
APPLE CR
Sch

SPEEDWELL

Wood View
Sch
SCHOOL CL

50

81
209

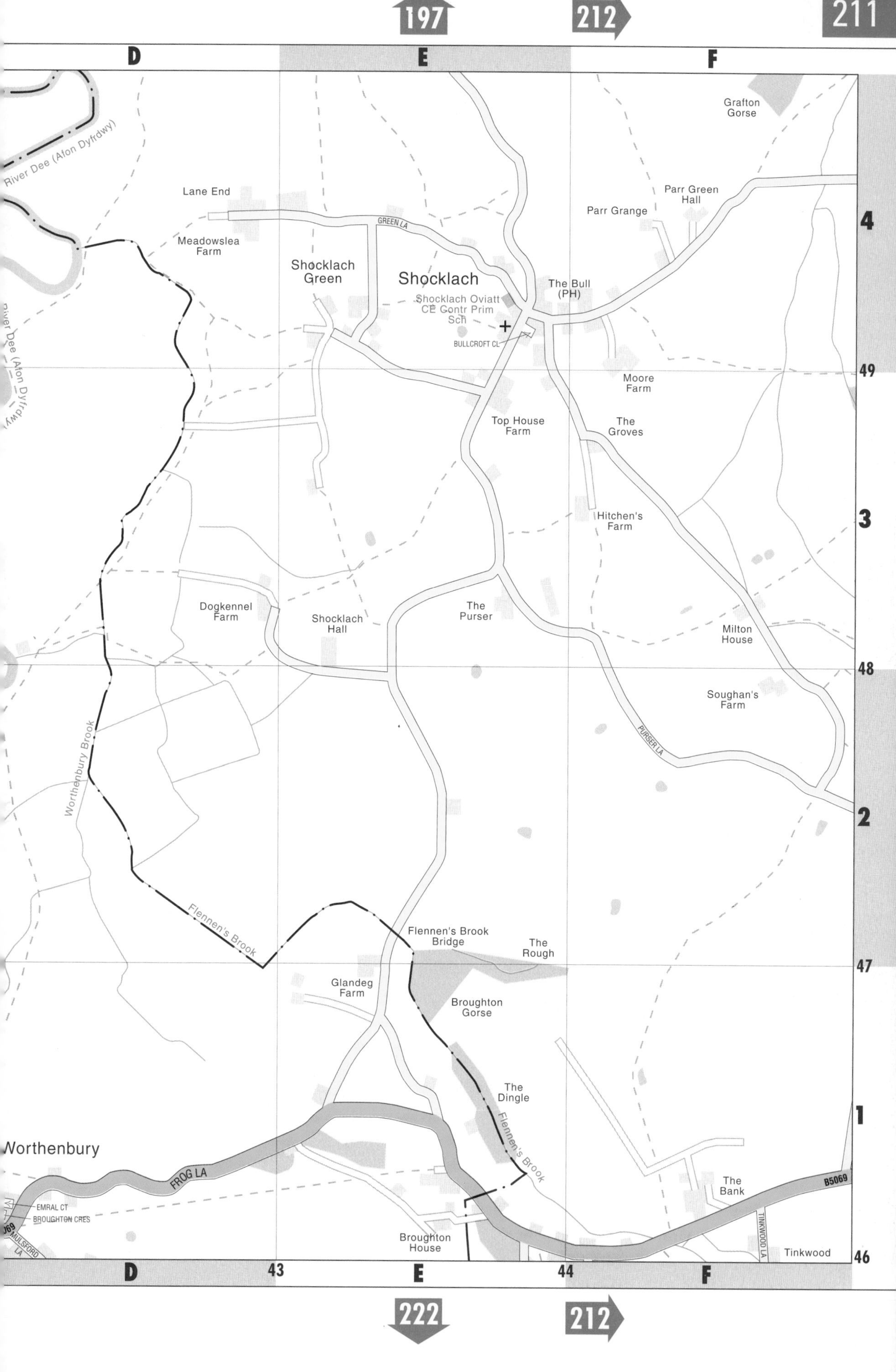

D E F

Grafton
Gorse

Lane End

Parr Green
Hall

Parr Grange

GREEN LA

4

Meadowslea
Farm

Shocklach
Green

Shocklach

The Bull
(PH)

Shocklach Oviatt
CE Contr Prim
Sch

BULLCROFT CL

+

Moore
Farm

49

Top House
Farm

The
Groves

River Dee (Afon Dyfrdwy)

River Dee (Afon Dyfrdwy)

Hitchen's
Farm

3

Dogkennel
Farm

Shocklach
Hall

The
Purser

Milton
House

48

Soughan's
Farm

Worthenbury Brook

PURSER LA

2

Flennen's Brook

Flennen's Brook
Bridge

The
Rough

47

Glandeg
Farm

Broughton
Gorse

The
Dingle

1

Worthenbury

FROG LA

Flennen's Brook

The
Bank

B5069

EMRAL CT

BROUGHTON CRES

U69

MILLSFORD LA

Broughton
House

TINKWOOD LA

Tinkwood

46

D E F

43 44

211
198

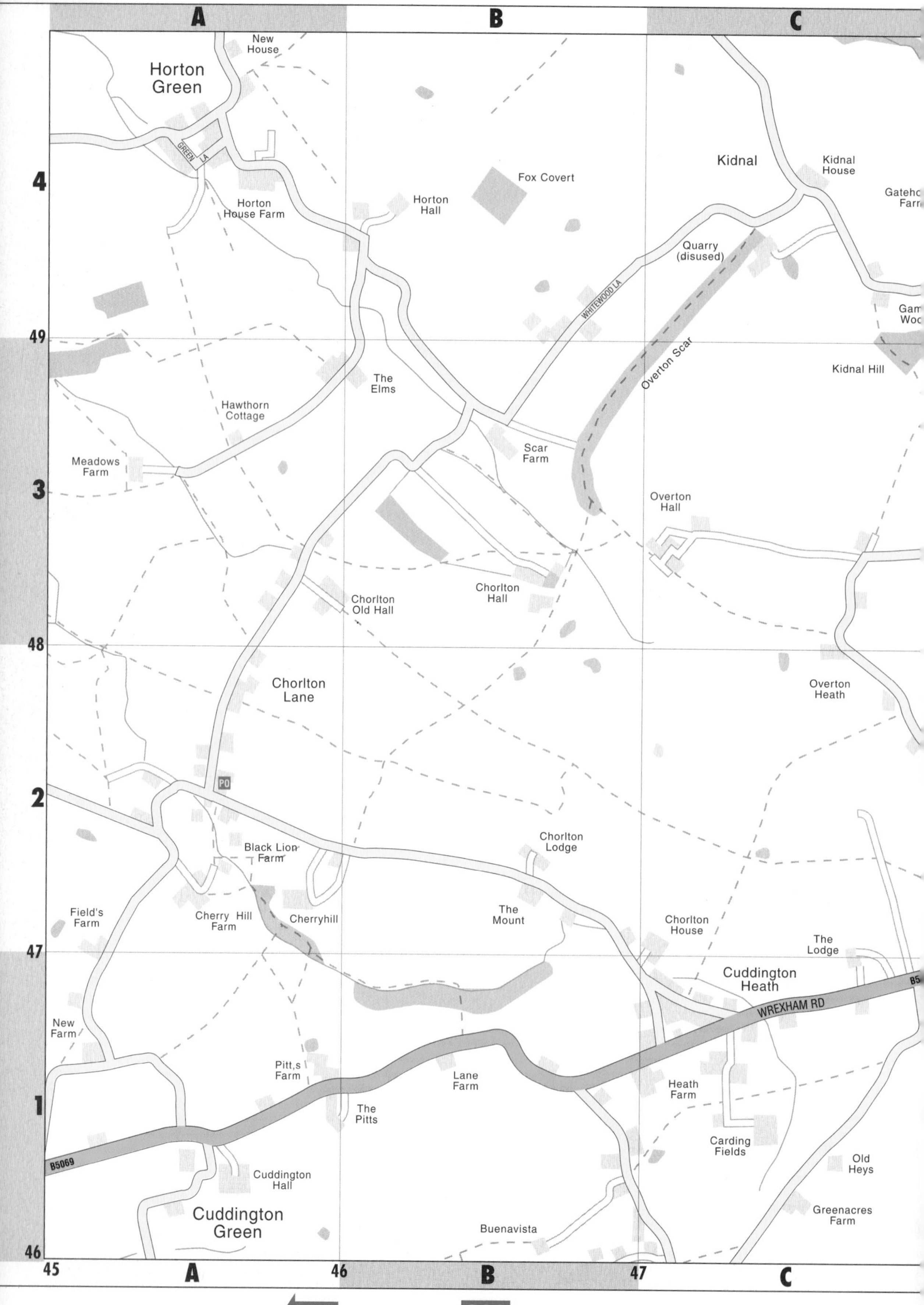

211
223

A   **B**   **C**

4

49

3

48

2

47

1

46

45   **A**   46   **B**   47   **C**

New House

Horton Green

GREEN LA

Horton House Farm

Horton Hall

Fox Covert

Kidnal

Kidnal House

Gateho Farm

Quarry (disused)

WHITEWOOD LA

Overton Scar

Game Wood

Kidnal Hill

The Elms

Hawthorn Cottage

Meadows Farm

Scar Farm

Overton Hall

Chorlton Old Hall

Chorlton Hall

Chorlton Lane

Overton Heath

PO

Black Lion Farm

Chorlton Lodge

Field's Farm

Cherry Hill Farm

Cherryhill

The Mount

Chorlton House

The Lodge

Cuddington Heath

WREXHAM RD

B5

New Farm

Pitt,s Farm

The Pitts

Lane Farm

Heath Farm

Carding Fields

Old Heys

B5069

Cuddington Hall

Cuddington Green

Buenavista

Greenacres Farm

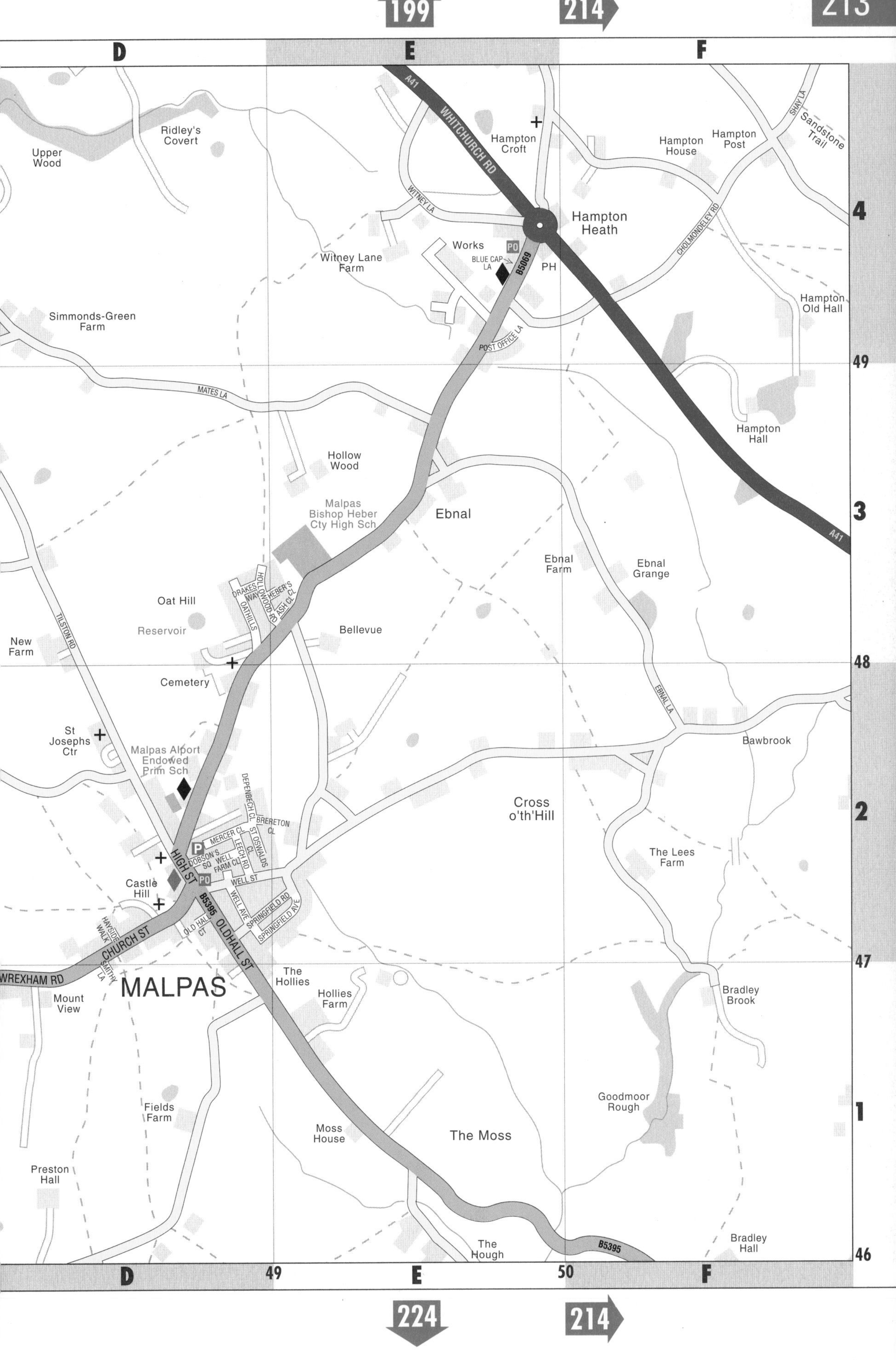

D
E
F

4
49
3
48
2
47
1
46

A41

WHITCHURCH RD

WITNEY LA

Hampton
Croft

Hampton
House

Hampton
Post

Sandstone
Trail

SEAH LA

Hampton Heath

CHOLMONDELEY RD

Hampton
Old Hall

B5069

Works

BLUE CAP LA

PO

PH

POST OFFICE LA

Hampton
Hall

Ridley's
Covert

Upper
Wood

Witney Lane
Farm

Simmonds-Green
Farm

MATES LA

Hollow
Wood

Malpas
Bishop Heber
Cty High Sch

Ebnal

Ebnal
Farm

Ebnal
Grange

A41

New
Farm

TILSTON RD

Oat Hill

Reservoir

DRAKES WAY

HOLLYWOOD RD

HEBER'S
CAITHILS

ASH CL

Bellevue

Cemetery

St
Josephs
Ctr

Malpas Alport
Endowed
Prim Sch

DEFENBECH CL

BRERETON CL

ST OSWALDS

MERCER CL

DOBSON'S
SQ

WELL
FARM CL

LEECH RD

WELL ST

P

PO

Castle
Hill

HIGH ST

HANSIDE
WALK
SMITHY
LA

B5395

CHURCH ST

OLD HALL
CT

OLDHALL ST

WELL AVE

SPRINGFIELD RD

SPRINGFIELD AVE

EBNAL LA

Bawbrook

Cross
o'th'Hill

The Lees
Farm

WREXHAM RD

MALPAS

Mount
View

The
Hollies

Hollies
Farm

Bradley
Brook

Fields
Farm

Moss
House

The Moss

Goodmoor
Rough

Preston
Hall

The Hough

B5395

Bradley
Hall

D
49
E
50
F

A **B** **C**

4

Hampton

Lower House
Farm

Hetherson
Green

Cross Lanes
Cottage

Br
M

Hampton Green

Sunnyside

Middle
House

Broomy
Bank

Pipehouse
Farm

49

Bickley Brook

St WENEFREDES
GREEN

Robber Hill
Farm

Bickley
Town

3

A41

Lower Bickley
Wood Farm

BANK FARM
MEWS

Bickley
Mill

No Man's
Heath

HAMPTON
CRES

DEAN PARK

MEADOW CT

The Wheatsheaf
(PH)

CROSS O' TH' HILL RD

BACK LA

PO

Bickleywood

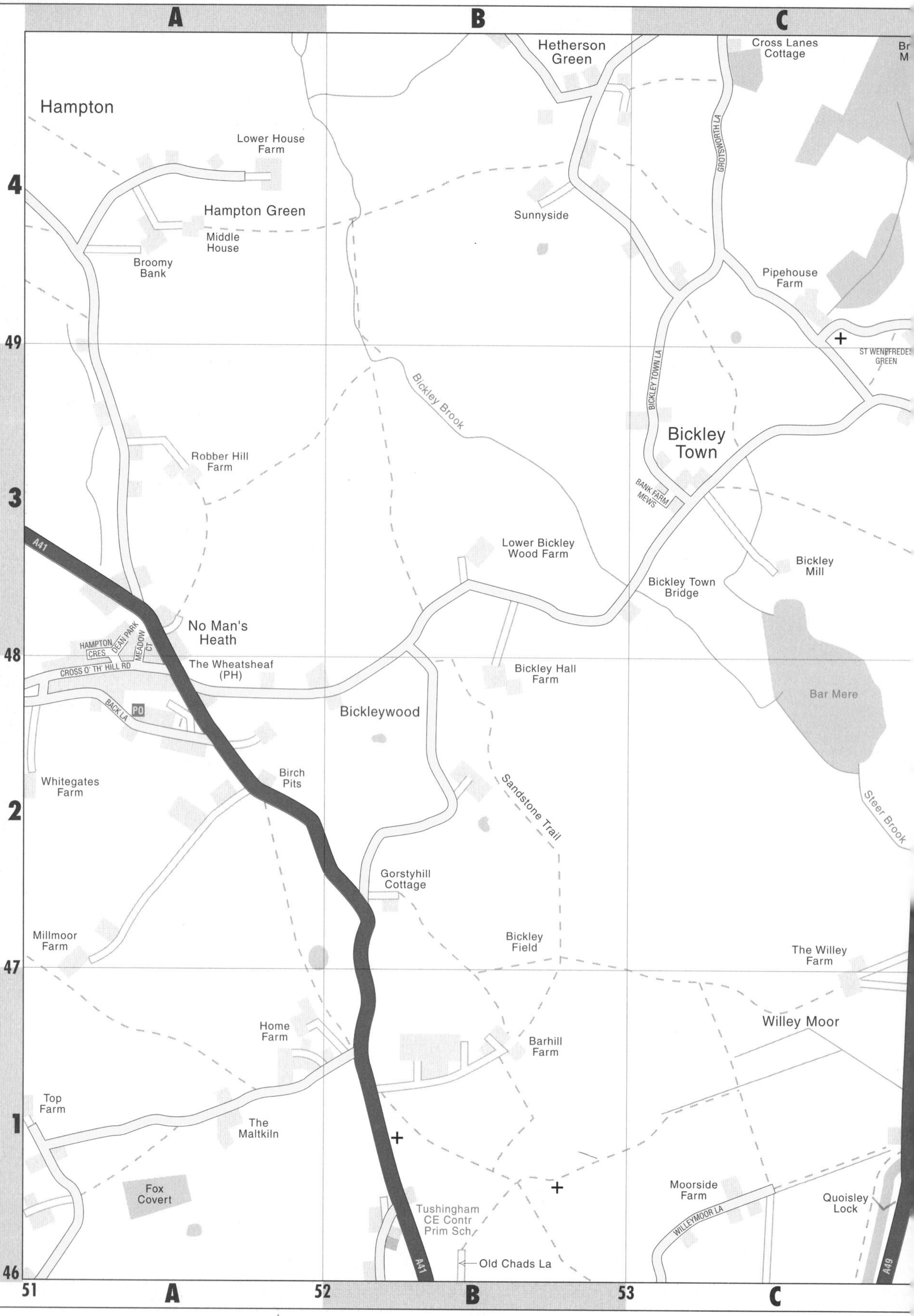

Bickley Town
Bridge

48

Bickley Hall
Farm

Bar Mere

Whitegates
Farm

Birch
Pits

Sandstone Trail

Steer Brook

2

Gorstyhill
Cottage

Millmoor
Farm

Bickley
Field

The Willey
Farm

47

Home
Farm

Willey Moor

Top
Farm

Barhill
Farm

1

The
Maltkiln

Fox
Covert

Moorside
Farm

Quoisley
Lock

Tushingham
CE Contr
Prim Sch

WILLEYMOOR LA

A49

A41

Old Chads La

46

51 **A** 52 **B** 53 **C**

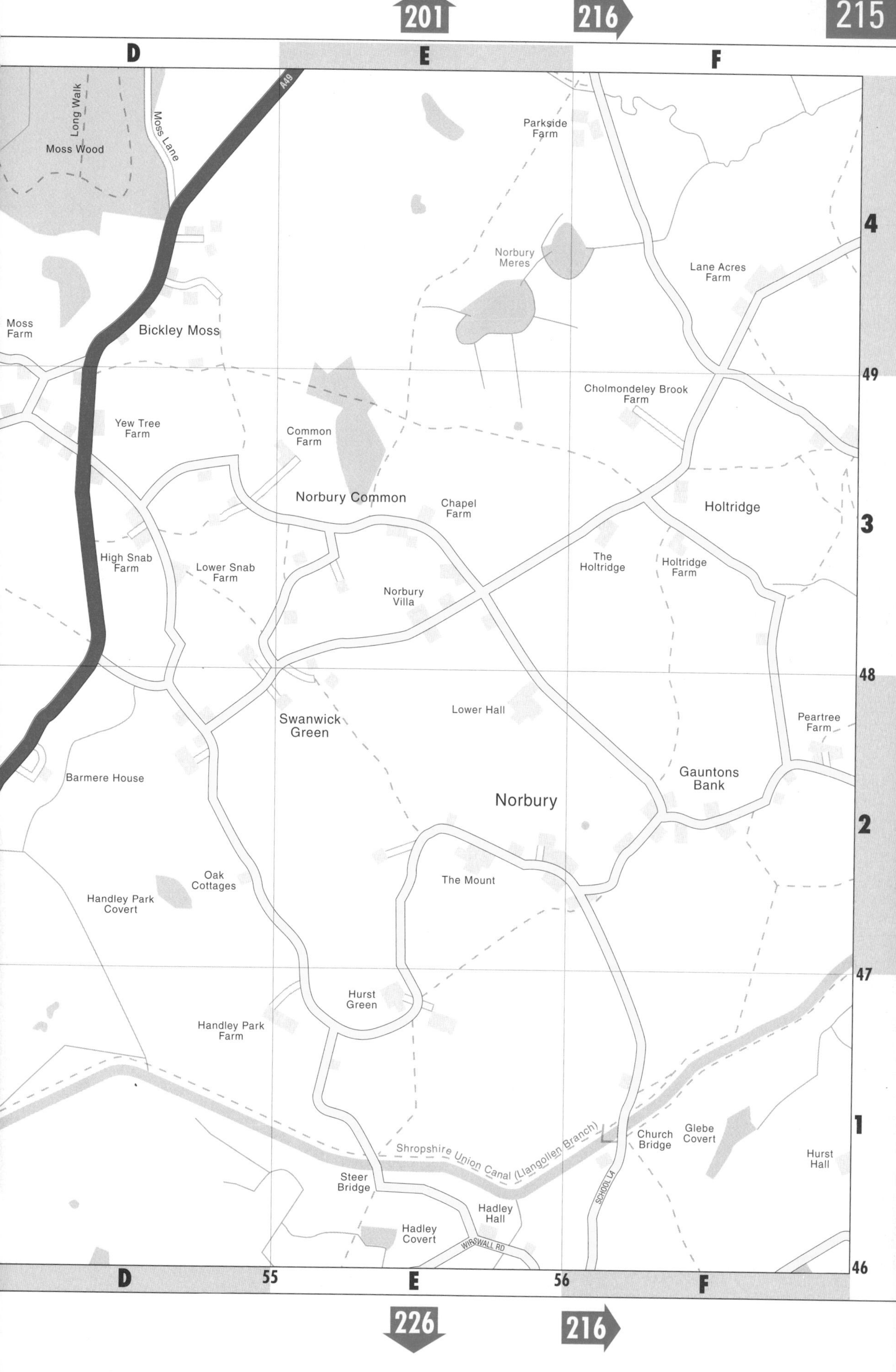
D
E
F
Long Walk
Moss Wood
Moss Lane
A49
Parkside Farm
Norbury Meres
Lane Acres Farm
Moss Farm
Bickley Moss
Cholmondeley Brook Farm
Yew Tree Farm
Common Farm
Norbury Common
Chapel Farm
Holtridge
High Snab Farm
Lower Snab Farm
The Holtridge
Holtridge Farm
Norbury Villa
Lower Hall
Swanwick Green
Peartree Farm
Barmere House
Gauntons Bank
Norbury
The Mount
Oak Cottages
Handley Park Covert
Hurst Green
Handley Park Farm
Shropshire Union Canal (Llangollen Branch)
Church Bridge
Glebe Covert
Hurst Hall
Steer Bridge
SCHOOL LA
Hadley Hall
Hadley Covert
WIRSWALL RD
4
49
3
48
2
47
1
46
D
55
E
56
F

215
202

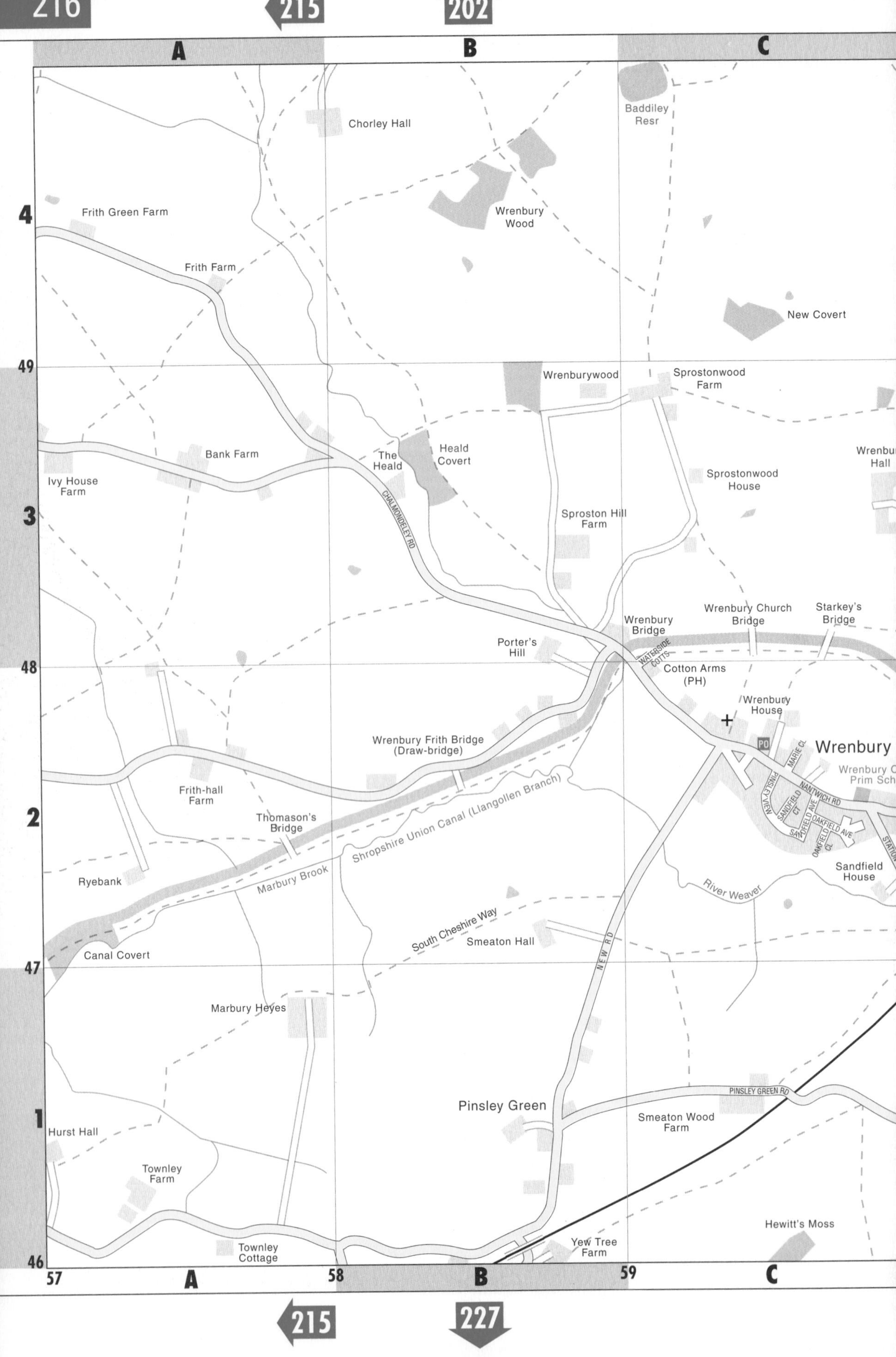
A
B
C
4
49
3
48
2
47
1
46
57
58
59
Chorley Hall
Baddiley Resr
Frith Green Farm
Wrenbury Wood
Frith Farm
New Covert
Wrenburywood
Sprostonwood Farm
Bank Farm
The Heald
Heald Covert
Ivy House Farm
Wrenbury Hall
Sprostonwood House
CHALMONDELEY RD
Sproston Hill Farm
Wrenbury Bridge
Wrenbury Church Bridge
Starkey's Bridge
Porter's Hill
WATERSIDE COTTS
Cotton Arms (PH)
Wrenbury House
PO
Wrenbury
Wrenbury Frith Bridge (Draw-bridge)
MARIE CL
Wrenbury C Prim Sch
NANTWICH RD
PINSLEY VIEW
SANDFIELD CT
SANDFIELD AVE
OAKFIELD AVE
OAKFIELD CL
Frith-hall Farm
Thomason's Bridge
Shropshire Union Canal (Llangollen Branch)
Ryebank
Marbury Brook
Sandfield House
River Weaver
South Cheshire Way
Smeaton Hall
Canal Covert
NEW RD
Marbury Heyes
PINSLEY GREEN RD
Pinsley Green
Smeaton Wood Farm
Hurst Hall
Townley Farm
Hewitt's Moss
Townley Cottage
Yew Tree Farm

215
227

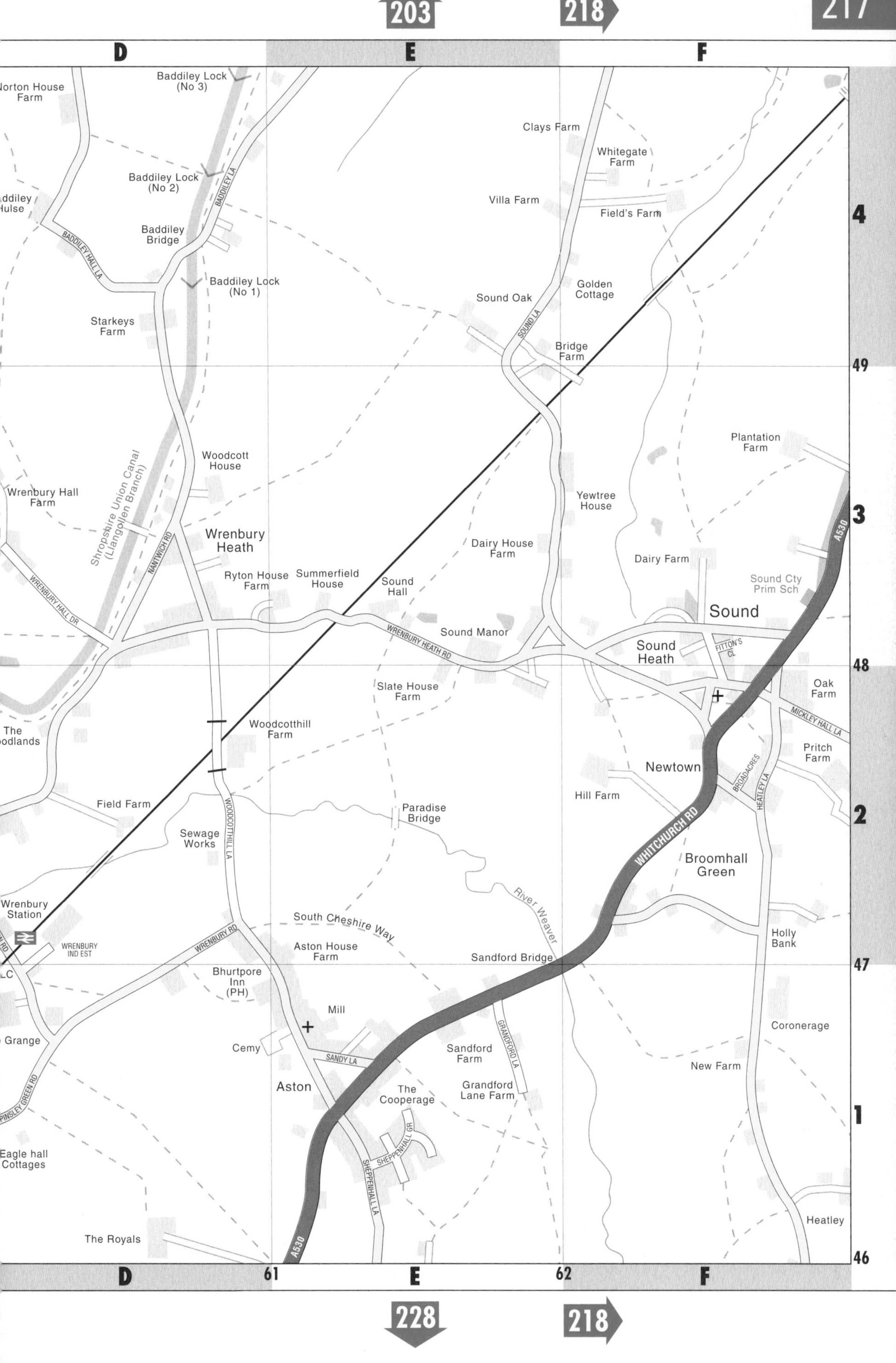
D
E
F
Norton House Farm
Baddiley Lock (No 3)
Baddiley Lock (No 2)
Baddiley Bridge
Baddiley Lock (No 1)
BADDILEY LA
BADDILEY HALL LA
Starkeys Farm
Clays Farm
Whitegate Farm
Villa Farm
Field's Farm
Sound Oak
Golden Cottage
SOUND LA
Bridge Farm
Woodcott House
Wrenbury Hall Farm
Shropshire Union Canal (Llangollen Branch)
NANTWICH RD
Wrenbury Heath
WRENBURY HALL DR
Ryton House Farm
Summerfield House
Sound Hall
Dairy House Farm
Yewtree House
Dairy Farm
Plantation Farm
Sound Cty Prim Sch
A530
Sound
Sound Manor
WRENBURY HEATH RD
Sound Heath
FITTON'S CL
Slate House Farm
Oak Farm
MICKLEY HALL LA
The Woodlands
Woodcotthill Farm
Newtown
Pritch Farm
Hill Farm
BROADACRES
HEATLEY LA
Field Farm
Paradise Bridge
Sewage Works
WOODCOTTHILL LA
WHITCHURCH RD
Broomhall Green
River Weaver
Wrenbury Station
South Cheshire Way
WRENBURY IND EST
WRENBURY RD
Aston House Farm
Sandford Bridge
Holly Bank
Bhurtpore Inn (PH)
Mill
Grange
Cemy
Coronerage
SANDY LA
Sandford Farm
GRANDFORD LA
New Farm
Aston
The Cooperage
Grandford Lane Farm
PINSLEY GREEN RD
SHEPPENHALL GR
SHEPPENHALL LA
Eagle hall Cottages
Heatley
The Royals
4
49
3
48
2
47
1
46
61
62

A   B   C

The Brooklands

Baddington Lane Bridge

Baddington Bank Farm

WHITCHURCH RD

BADDINGTON LA

A530

Batherton Hall

ATCHERLEY CL

CRISHAM AVE

4

Old Hall Austerson

The Grange

Baddington Farm

49

Broomhall Gorse

Hack House Farm

A530

3

Hackgreen Locks

Poplars Farm

Gorse Covert

Hackgreen Bridge

FRENCH LA

Hack Farm

French Lane End

New Farm

Hack Green

Burrow's Bridge

New Cottages

Austerson Farm

Hack House

48

Shropshire Union Canal

MICKLEY HALL LA

2

Mickley Hall

Austerson Hall

COOLE LA

47

Old Hall

South View Farm

South Cheshire Way

Westview Cottages

BRINE PITS LA

Devil's Nest

Mickley Bridge

Austin's Bridge

1

Top of the Town

Top House Farm

Heatley

Finnaker Brook

Cool Lane Bridge

46

63   A   64   B   65   C

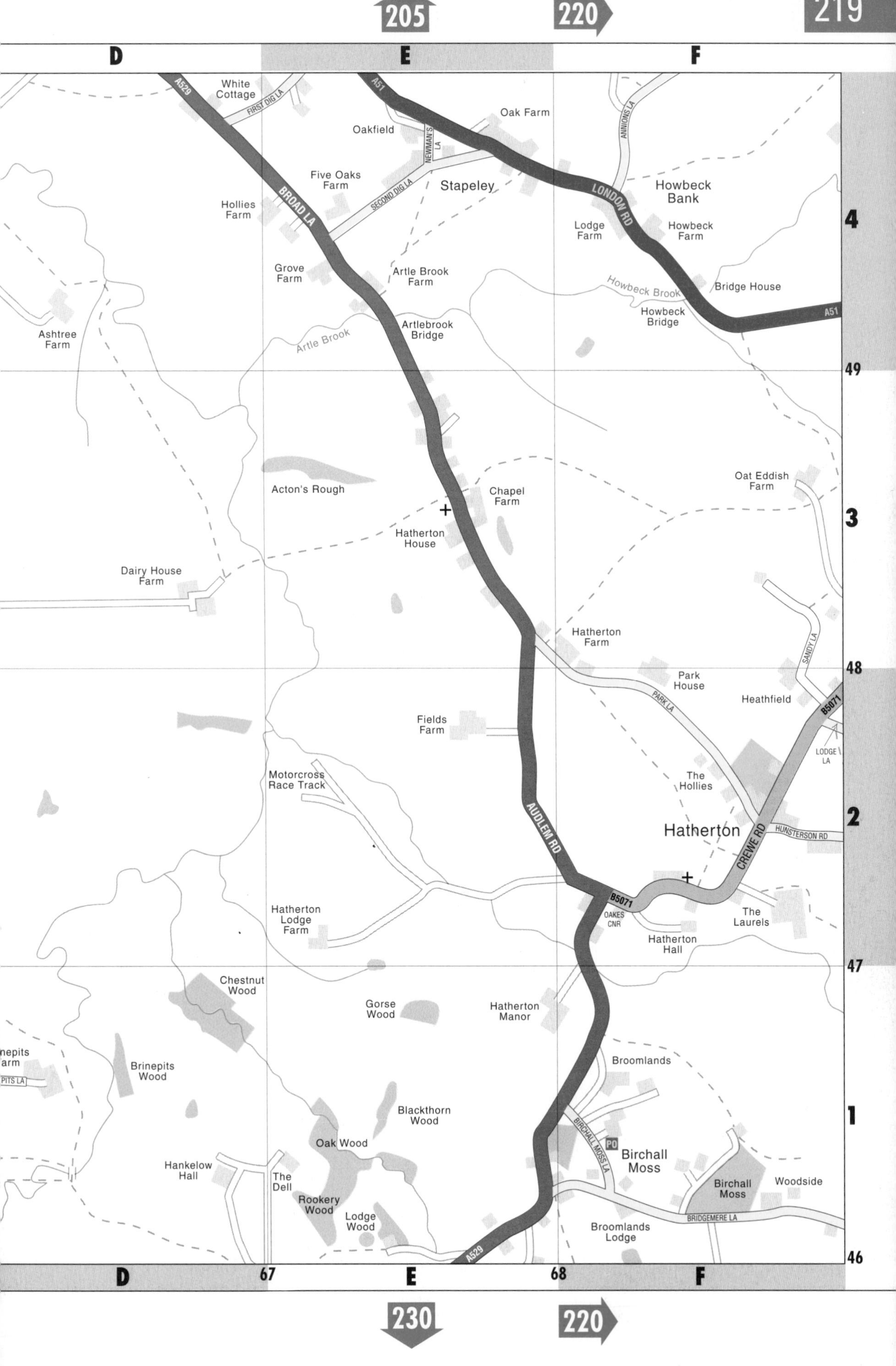
D
E
F
White Cottage
FIRST DIG LA
A529
A51
Oak Farm
Oakfield
NEWMAN'S LA
ANNIONS LA
Five Oaks Farm
SECOND DIG LA
Stapeley
Howbeck Bank
Hollies Farm
BROAD LA
LONDON RD
Lodge Farm
Howbeck Farm
4
Grove Farm
Artle Brook Farm
Howbeck Brook
Bridge House
Howbeck Bridge
Ashtree Farm
Artlebrook Bridge
Artle Brook
49
Oat Eddish Farm
Acton's Rough
Chapel Farm
3
Hatherton House
Dairy House Farm
Hatherton Farm
48
Park House
PARK LA
Heathfield
SANDY LA
B5071
Fields Farm
LODGE LA
Motorcross Race Track
The Hollies
2
Hatherton
CREWE RD
HUNSTERSON RD
AUDLEM RD
B5071
OAKES CNR
The Laurels
Hatherton Lodge Farm
Hatherton Hall
47
Chestnut Wood
Gorse Wood
Hatherton Manor
Broomlands
Brinepits Wood
PITS LA
Blackthorn Wood
1
Oak Wood
BIRCHALL MOSS LA
PO
Birchall Moss
Hankelow Hall
The Dell
Birchall Moss
Woodside
Rookery Wood
Lodge Wood
BRIDGEMERE LA
Broomlands Lodge
A529
46
D
67
E
68
F

219
206
A
B
C
4
49
3
48
2
47
1
46
B5071
MAIN RD
KILN LA
RIDDINGS LA
VALEBROOK DR
ST CHADS CL
GORSEY BANK CRES
CHURCH WAY
WYBECK CRES
GLEBE CL
SOUTHFIELDS CL
FIELDS VIEW CL
CHURCHFIELDS
PO
Red Lion (PH)
The Riddings
Wybunbury
Hall Bank
Vicarage
Cobb's Moss
Cemy
BRIDGE ST
Brook House
COBBS LA
Ellesmere Farm
Wybunbury Delves CE Aided Prim Sch
WRINEHILL RD
A51
Hough Mill Farm
The Cliffe
WYBUNBURY LA
Sand Pit
Jerusalem
Manor Farm
BACK LA
Jericho
Lea Farm
Walgherton
Lea Hall
Lea Forge Farm
Lodge Farm
The Oaks
Hunter's Hill
Forge Bank
HATHERTON RD
Poolbank
Trout Farm
Lea Park
Whispey Hill
George's Wood
Doddington Mill Farm
B5071
Dagfields Farm
CREWE RD
Perry's Rough
LONDON RD
MILL LA
South Cheshire Way
Speakman's Moss
Northwood
LODGE LA
Mill Covert
Hatherton Lodge
George's Wood
Black Mere
Birchenhill Wood
Robin Knight's Rough
Demesne Farm
Sewage Works
HUNSTERSON RD
Black Covert
Hatherton Lodge Farm
The Castle
Doddington Park House
Glover's Moss
Ridley's Pool
Wilbraham's Walk
Lake Lodge
Doddington Hall
Chapel Wood
Pepperstreet Moss
Doddington Pool
Bearcat Fields
Manor Farm
The Duckery
Hunsterson Four Lane End
Ley Ground Farm
BRIDGEMERE LA
PEWIT LA
HUNSTERSON RD
Doddington Park Farm
A51
69
A
70
B
71
C
219
231

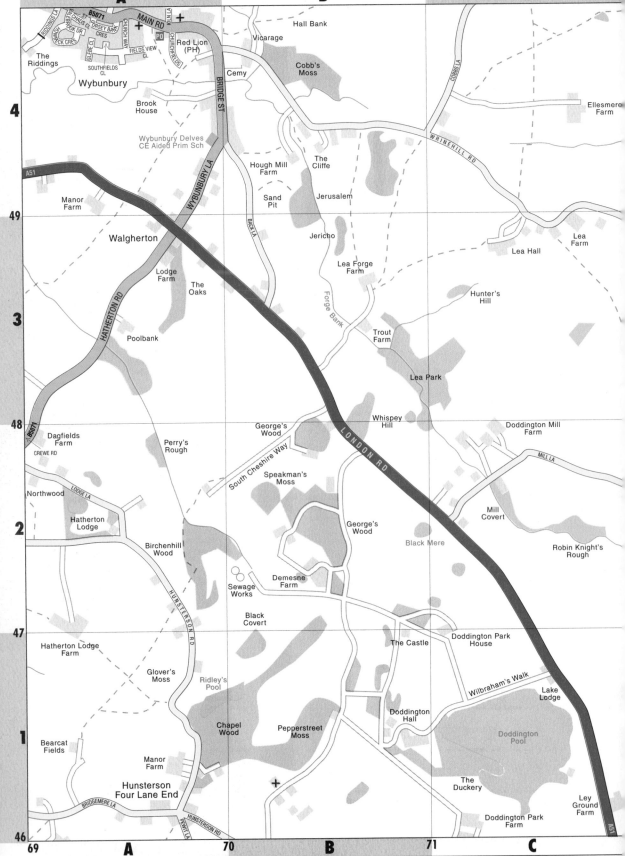

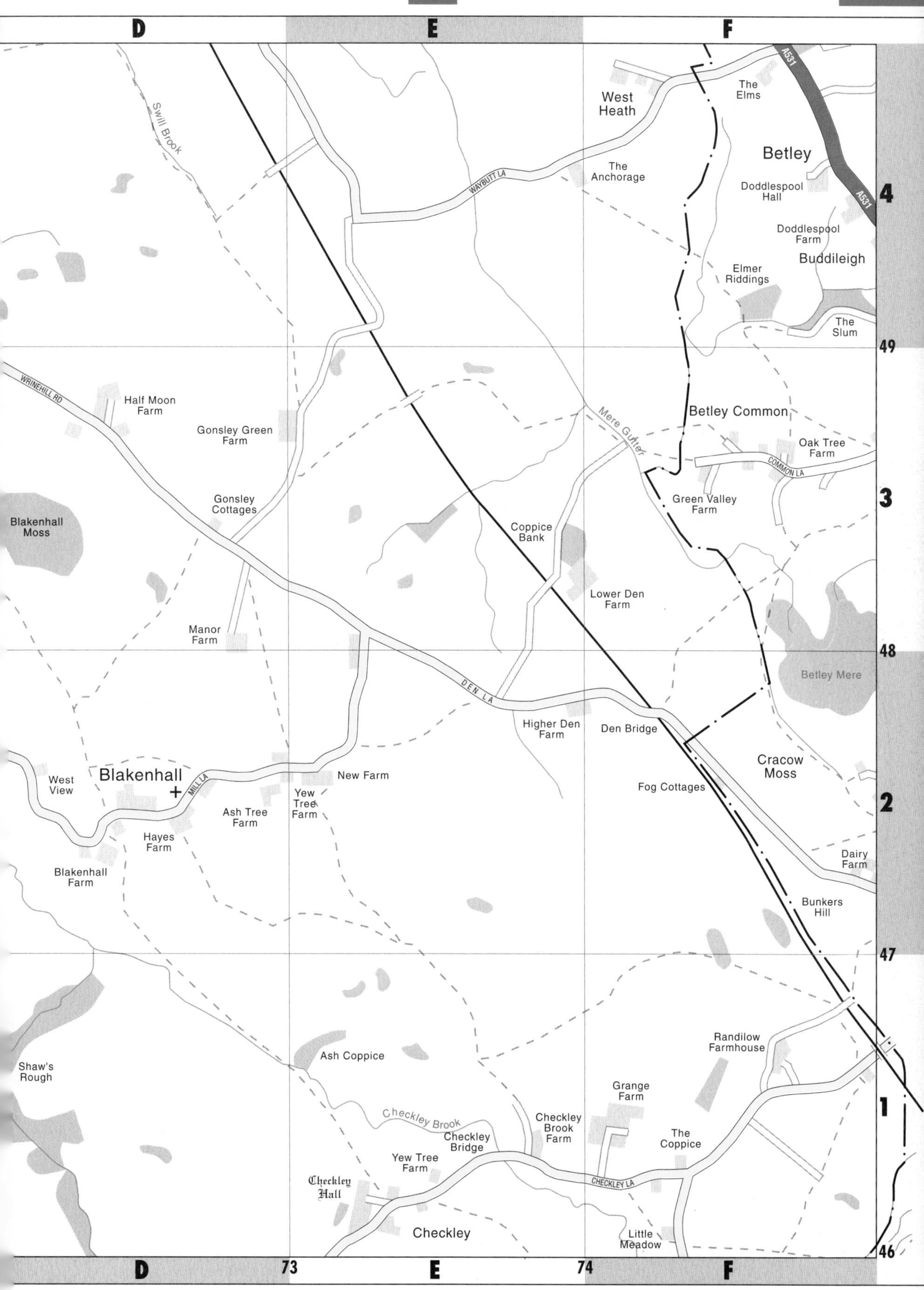
D
E
F
A531
The Elms
West Heath
Swill Brook
Betley
The Anchorage
WAYBUTT LA
Doddlespool Hall
4
A531
Doddlespool Farm
Buddileigh
Elmer Riddings
The Slum
49
WRINEHILL RD
Half Moon Farm
Betley Common
Mere Gutter
Gonsley Green Farm
Oak Tree Farm
COMMON LA
Green Valley Farm
3
Blakenhall Moss
Gonsley Cottages
Coppice Bank
Lower Den Farm
Manor Farm
48
Betley Mere
DEN LA
Higher Den Farm
Den Bridge
Cracow Moss
West View
Blakenhall
MILL LA
New Farm
Fog Cottages
Yew Tree Farm
Ash Tree Farm
2
Hayes Farm
Dairy Farm
Blakenhall Farm
Bunkers Hill
47
Randilow Farmhouse
Ash Coppice
Shaw's Rough
Grange Farm
1
Checkley Brook
Checkley Brook Farm
Checkley Bridge
The Coppice
Yew Tree Farm
CHECKLEY LA
Checkley Hall
Checkley
Little Meadow
46
D
73
E
74
F

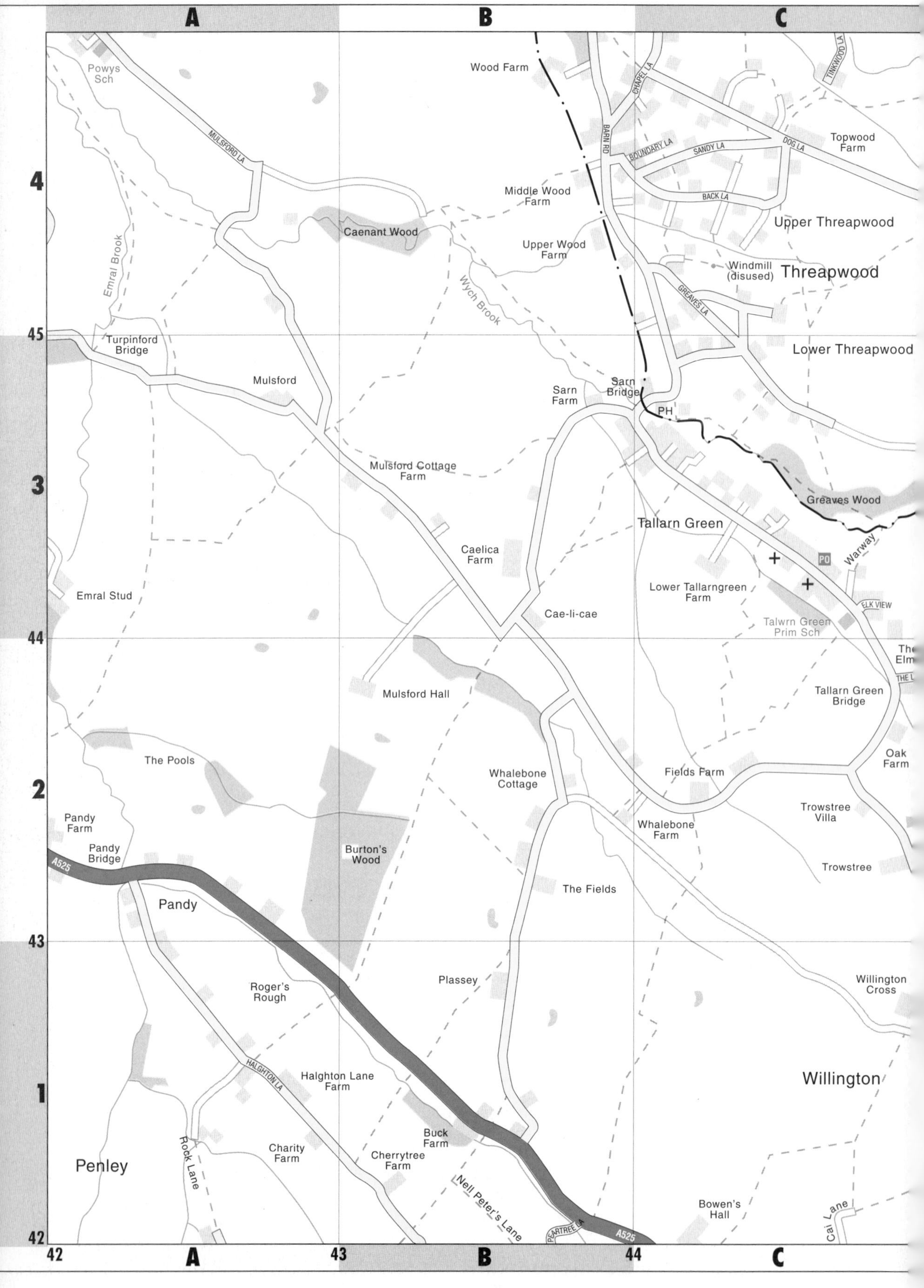

A   B   C

4

Powys
Sch

MULSFORD LA

Wood Farm

Caenant Wood

Middle Wood
Farm

Upper Wood
Farm

Wych Brook

CHAPEL LA

BARN RD

BOUNDARY LA

SANDY LA

BACK LA

DOG LA

TINKWOOD LA

Topwood
Farm

Upper Threapwood

Windmill
(disused)   Threapwood

GREAVES LA

45

Turpinford
Bridge

Emral Brook

Mulsford

Lower Threapwood

Sarn
Farm

Sarn
Bridge

PH

3

Mulsford Cottage
Farm

Caelica
Farm

Cae-li-cae

Tallarn Green

Lower Tallarngreen
Farm

Greaves Wood

PO

Warway

ELK VIEW

Talwrn Green
Prim Sch

44

Emral Stud

Mulsford Hall

The
Elm

THE L

Tallarn Green
Bridge

Oak
Farm

2

The Pools

Whalebone
Cottage

Fields Farm

Whalebone
Farm

Trowstree
Villa

Trowstree

Pandy
Farm

Pandy
Bridge

A525

Burton's
Wood

The Fields

Pandy

43

Roger's
Rough

HALGHTON LA

Plassey

Willington
Cross

1

Penley

Rock Lane

Halghton Lane
Farm

Charity
Farm

Cherrytree
Farm

Buck
Farm

Nell Peter's Lane

PEARTREE

Willington

Bowen's
Hall

Cai Lane

A525

42

42   A   43   B   44   C

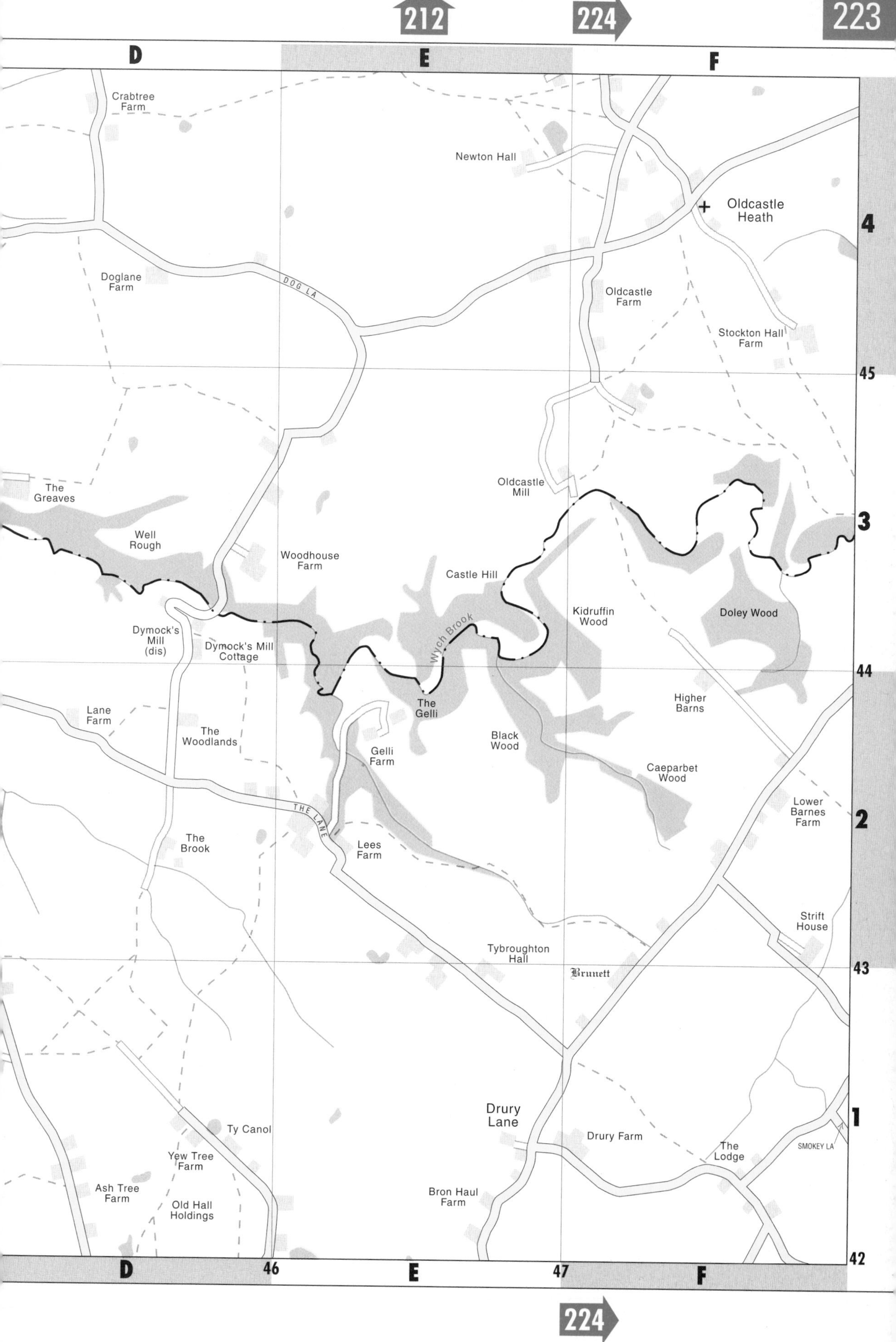
D
E
F
Crabtree Farm
Newton Hall
Oldcastle Heath
4
Doglane Farm
DOG LA
Oldcastle Farm
Stockton Hall Farm
45
The Greaves
Oldcastle Mill
3
Well Rough
Woodhouse Farm
Castle Hill
Kidruffin Wood
Doley Wood
Dymock's Mill (dis)
Dymock's Mill Cottage
Wych Brook
44
The Gelli
Higher Barns
Lane Farm
The Woodlands
Black Wood
Gelli Farm
Caeparbet Wood
Lower Barnes Farm
2
THE LANE
The Brook
Lees Farm
Strift House
Tybroughton Hall
Brunett
43
Drury Lane
1
Ty Canol
Drury Farm
The Lodge
SMOKEY LA
Yew Tree Farm
Ash Tree Farm
Old Hall Holdings
Bron Haul Farm
42
D
46
E
47
F

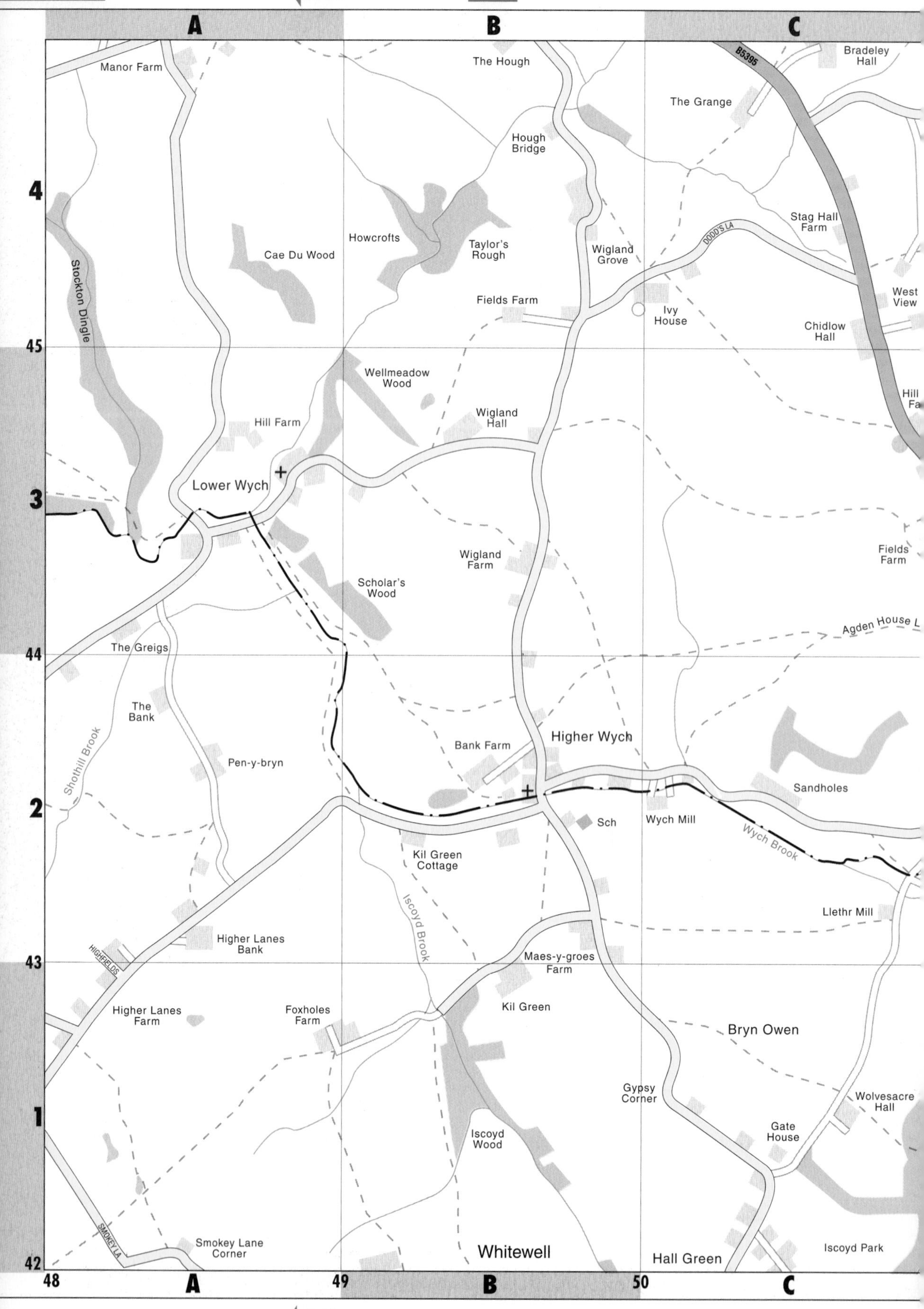

A | B | C

Manor Farm

The Hough

Bradeley Hall

B5395

The Grange

Hough Bridge

Stockton Dingle

Cae Du Wood

Howcrofts

Taylor's Rough

Wigland Grove

DOOD'S LA

Stag Hall Farm

4

West View

Fields Farm

Ivy House

Chidlow Hall

45

Wellmeadow Wood

Wigland Hall

Hill Fa

Hill Farm

Lower Wych

Scholar's Wood

Wigland Farm

Fields Farm

3

Agden House L

The Greigs

44

Shothill Brook

The Bank

Pen-y-bryn

Bank Farm

Higher Wych

Sandholes

2

Kil Green Cottage

Sch

Wych Mill

Wych Brook

Iscoyd Brook

Llethr Mill

HIGHFIELDS

Higher Lanes Bank

43

Maes-y-groes Farm

Kil Green

Higher Lanes Farm

Foxholes Farm

Bryn Owen

1

Gypsy Corner

Wolvesacre Hall

Gate House

Iscoyd Wood

SMOKEY LA

Smokey Lane Corner

Whitewell

Hall Green

Iscoyd Park

42

48 | A | 49 | B | 50 | C

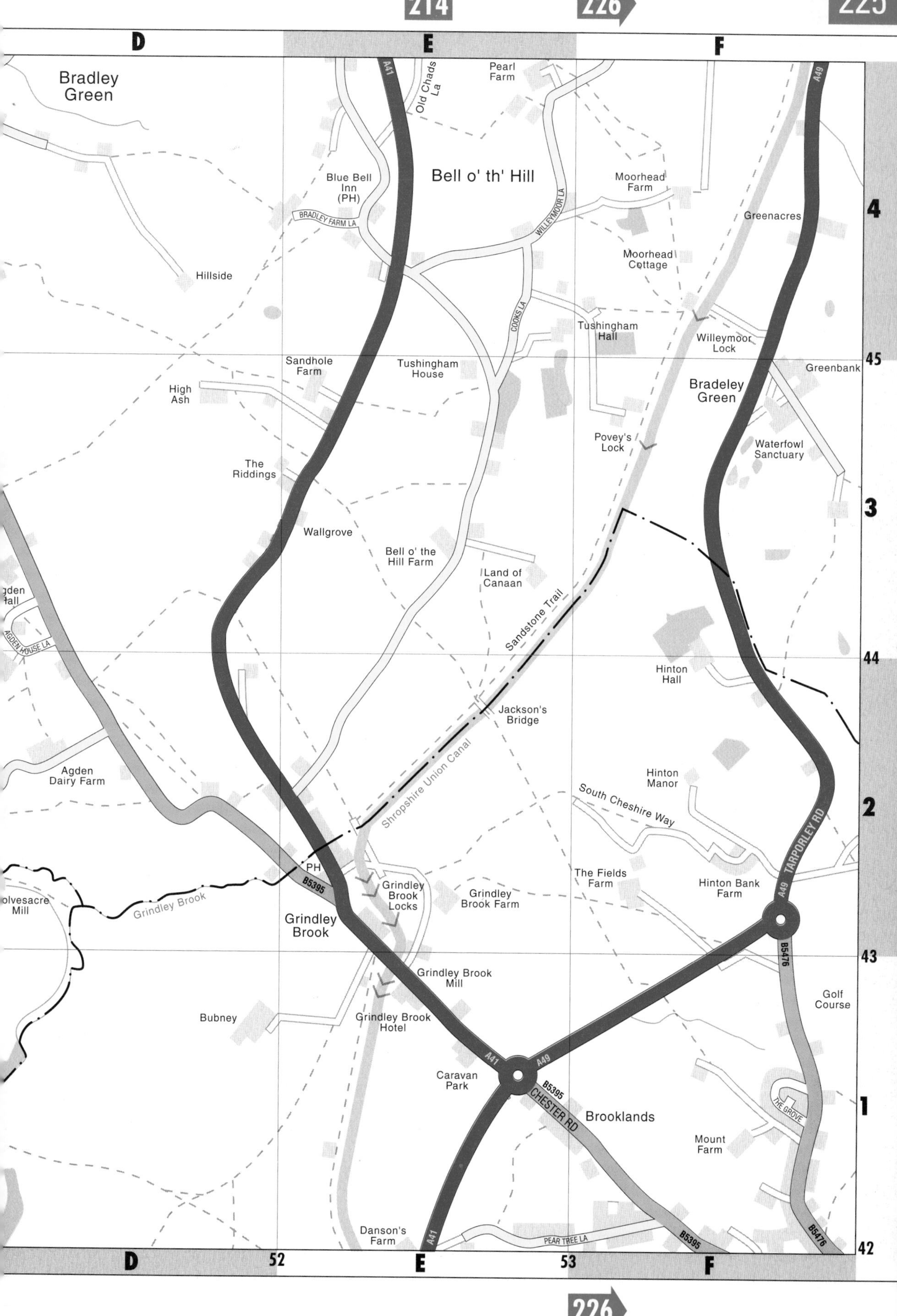

D
E
F

Bradley
Green

A41

Old Chads La

Pearl
Farm

Bell o' th' Hill

Moorhead
Farm

A49

Greenacres

4

Blue Bell
Inn
(PH)

BRADLEY FARM LA

WILLEYMOOR LA

Moorhead
Cottage

Hillside

COOKS LA

Tushingham
Hall

Willeymoor
Lock

Sandhole
Farm

Tushingham
House

45

Bradeley
Green

Greenbank

High
Ash

Povey's
Lock

Waterfowl
Sanctuary

The
Riddings

3

Wallgrove

Bell o' the
Hill Farm

Land of
Canaan

Sandstone Trail

gden
Hall

AGDEN HOUSE LA

Hinton
Hall

44

Shropshire Union Canal

Jackson's
Bridge

Hinton
Manor

South Cheshire Way

2

Agden
Dairy Farm

TARPORLEY RD

A49

The Fields
Farm

Hinton Bank
Farm

olvesacre
Mill

Grindley Brook

PH

B5395

Grindley
Brook
Locks

Grindley
Brook Farm

B5476

43

Grindley
Brook

Golf
Course

Bubney

Grindley Brook
Mill

Grindley Brook
Hotel

Caravan
Park

A41

A49

B5395

CHESTER RD

Brooklands

THE GROVE

Mount
Farm

1

Danson's
Farm

PEAR TREE LA

B5395

B5476

42

D
52
E
53
F

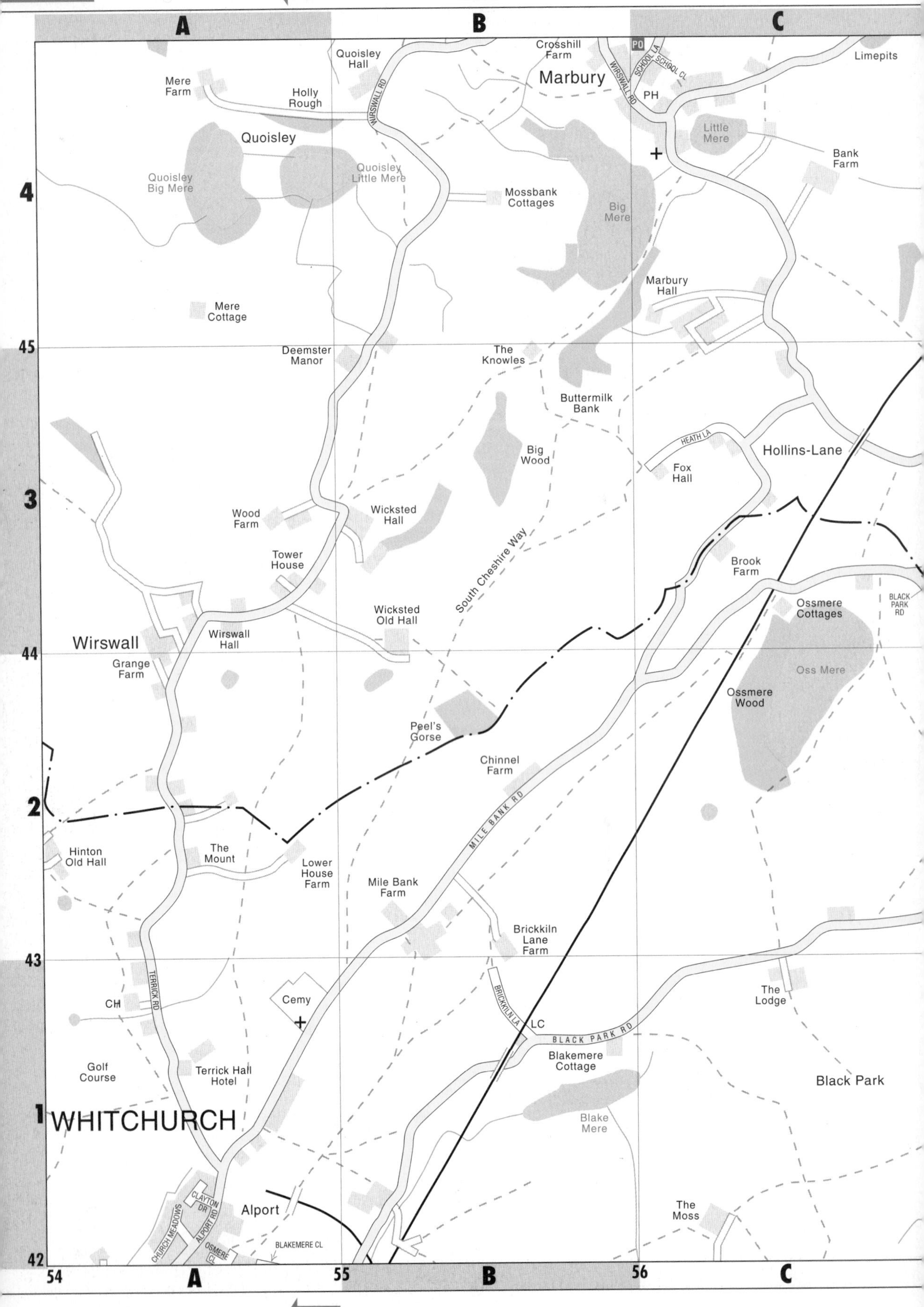

A   B   C

Limepits

Crosshill
Farm

Quoisley
Hall

Marbury

PO

SCHOOL LA   SCHOOL CL

WIRSWALL RD

PH

Mere
Farm

Holly
Rough

WIRSWALL RD

Little
Mere

Bank
Farm

Quoisley

Quoisley
Big Mere

Quoisley
Little Mere

+

Big
Mere

4

Mossbank
Cottages

Mere
Cottage

Marbury
Hall

Deemster
Manor

The
Knowles

45

Buttermilk
Bank

HEATH LA

Hollins-Lane

Big
Wood

Fox
Hall

3

Wood
Farm

Wicksted
Hall

Brook
Farm

Ossmere
Cottages

BLACK
PARK
RD

Tower
House

South Cheshire Way

Wicksted
Old Hall

Oss Mere

Wirswall

Wirswall
Hall

Ossmere
Wood

44

Grange
Farm

Peel's
Gorse

Chinnel
Farm

MILE BANK RD

2

Hinton
Old Hall

The
Mount

Lower
House
Farm

Mile Bank
Farm

Brickkiln
Lane
Farm

BRICKKILN LA

The
Lodge

43

CH

Cemy

+

LC

BLACK PARK RD

Golf
Course

Terrick Hall
Hotel

TERRICK RD

Blakemere
Cottage

Black Park

1

WHITCHURCH

Blake
Mere

CLAYTON DR

CHURCH MEADOWS

ALPORT RD

OSMERE CL

Alport

The
Moss

BLAKEMERE CL

42

54   A   55   B   56   C

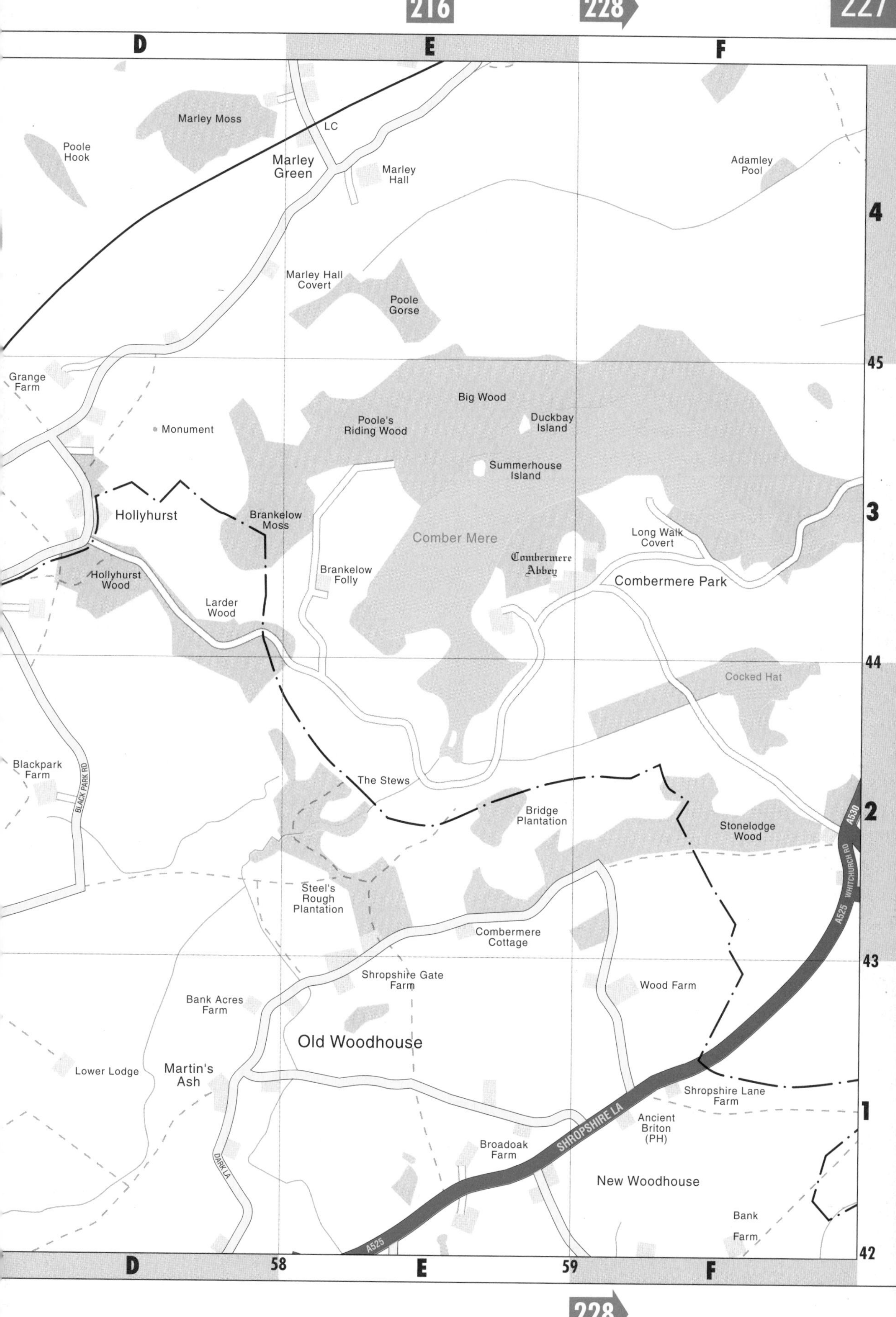

D E F

Marley Moss

Poole
Hook

LC

Marley Green

Marley
Hall

Adamley
Pool

4

Marley Hall
Covert

Poole
Gorse

Grange
Farm

45

Big Wood

Monument

Poole's
Riding Wood

Duckbay
Island

Summerhouse
Island

3

Hollyhurst

Brankelow
Moss

Comber Mere

Long Walk
Covert

Hollyhurst
Wood

Brankelow
Folly

Combermere
Abbey

Combermere Park

Larder
Wood

44

Cocked Hat

Blackpark
Farm

BLACK PARK RD

The Stews

Bridge
Plantation

Stonelodge
Wood

A530 WHITCHURCH RD

2

Steel's
Rough
Plantation

A525

Combermere
Cottage

43

Bank Acres
Farm

Shropshire Gate
Farm

Wood Farm

Lower Lodge

Martin's
Ash

Old Woodhouse

Shropshire Lane
Farm

1

DARK LA

SHROPSHIRE LA

Ancient
Briton
(PH)

Broadoak
Farm

New Woodhouse

Bank
Farm

A525

42

D 58 E 59 F

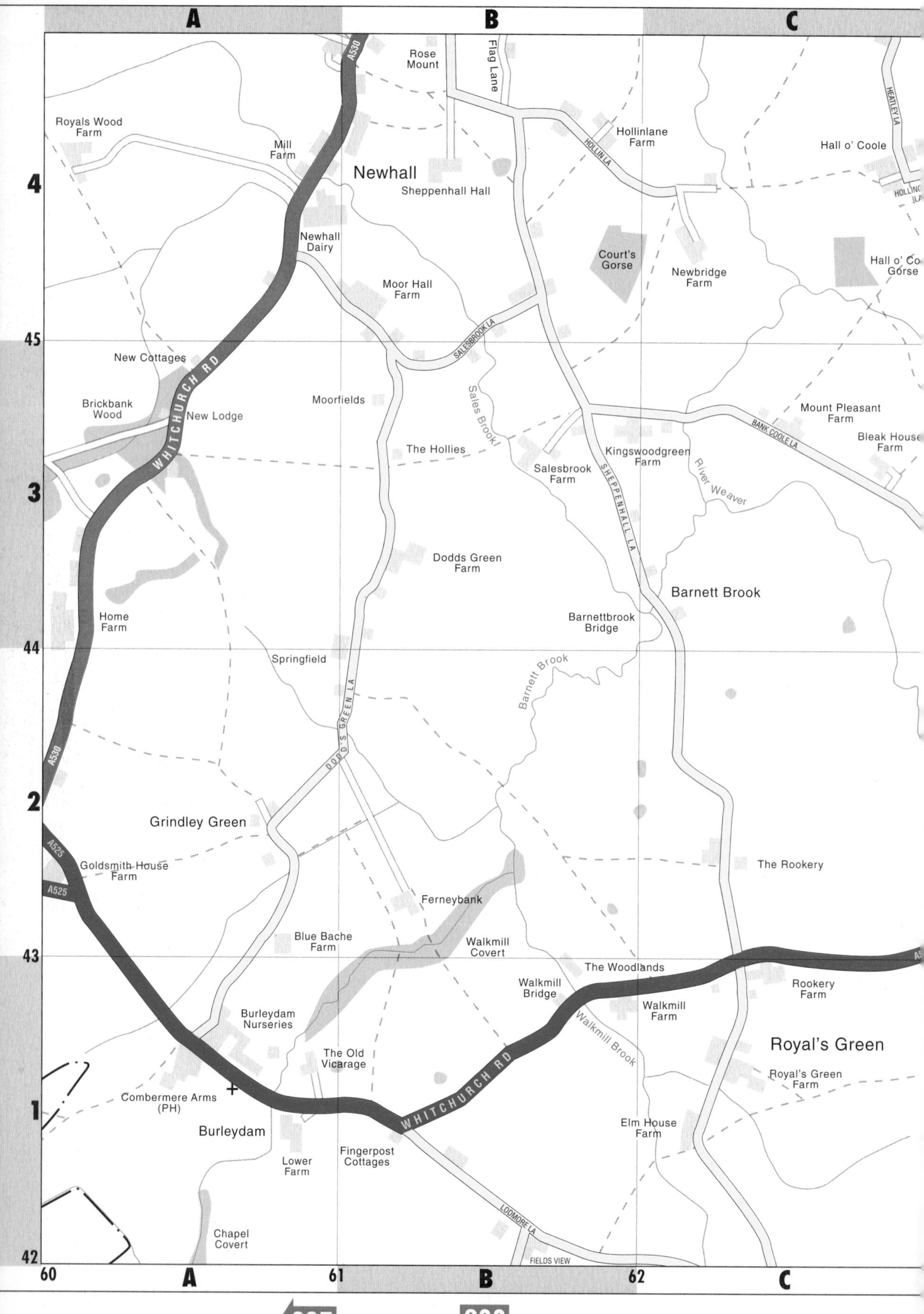
A
B
C
Rose Mount
Flag Lane
Royals Wood Farm
Mill Farm
Newhall
Sheppenhall Hall
Hollinlane Farm
HOLLIN LA
HEATLEY LA
Hall o' Coole
Newhall Dairy
Court's Gorse
Newbridge Farm
Moor Hall Farm
SALESBROOK LA
New Cottages
WHITCHURCH RD
Brickbank Wood
New Lodge
Moorfields
Sales Brook
The Hollies
Salesbrook Farm
Kingswoodgreen Farm
SHEPPENHALL LA
River Weaver
Mount Pleasant Farm
BANK COOLE LA
Bleak House Farm
Dodds Green Farm
Barnett Brook
Barnettbrook Bridge
Home Farm
Springfield
Barnett Brook
DODD'S GREEN LA
A530
Grindley Green
A525
Goldsmith House Farm
The Rookery
Ferneybank
Blue Bache Farm
Walkmill Covert
The Woodlands
Walkmill Bridge
Rookery Farm
Walkmill Farm
Burleydam Nurseries
Walkmill Brook
Royal's Green
The Old Vicarage
Royal's Green Farm
Combermere Arms (PH)
Burleydam
Elm House Farm
Lower Farm
Fingerpost Cottages
LODMORE LA
Chapel Covert
FIELDS VIEW
4
45
3
44
2
43
1
42
60
61
62

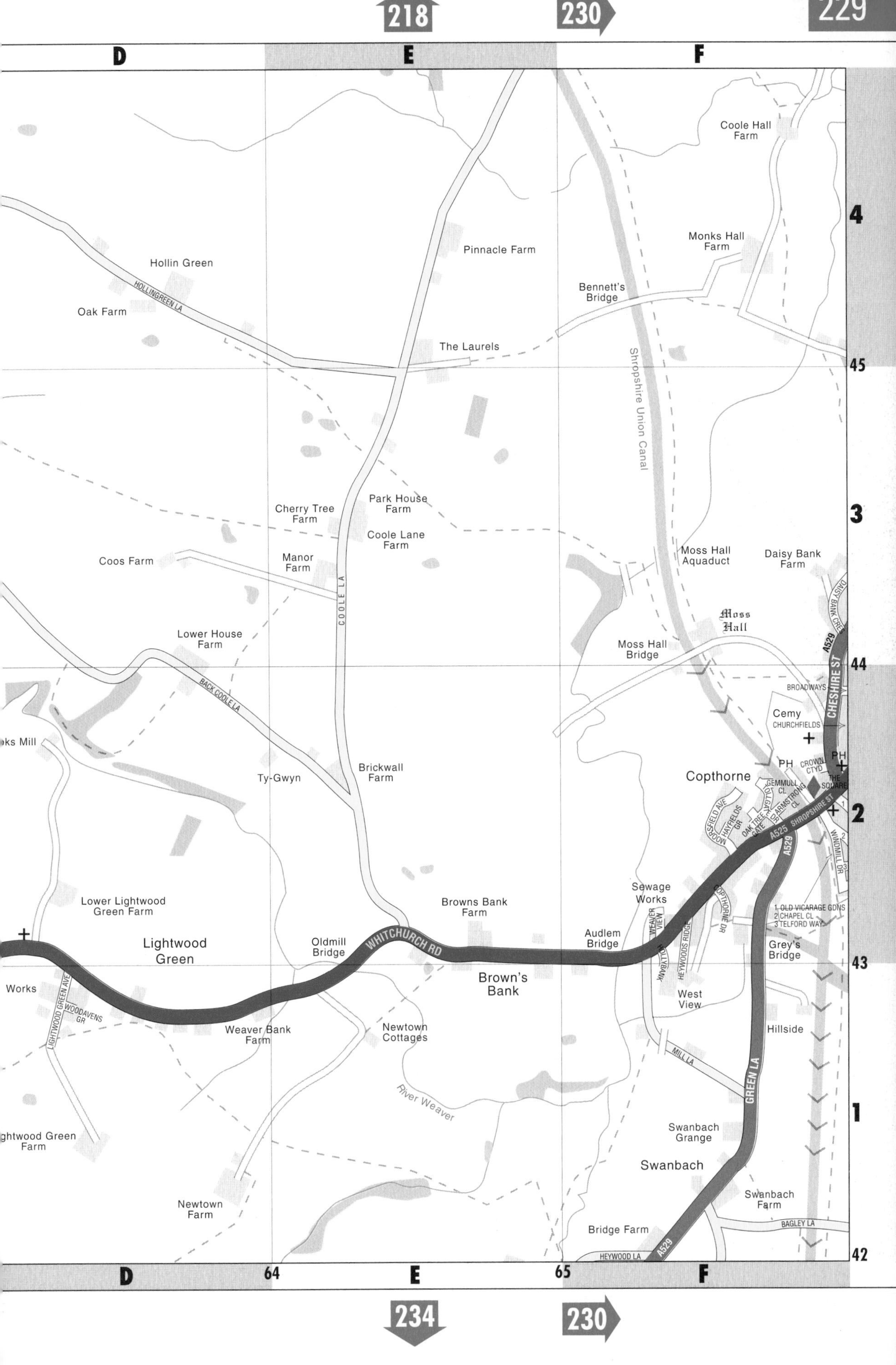
218
230
D
E
F
Coole Hall Farm
Monks Hall Farm
Pinnacle Farm
Hollin Green
HOLLINGREEN LA
Oak Farm
Bennett's Bridge
The Laurels
Shropshire Union Canal
Park House Farm
Cherry Tree Farm
Coole Lane Farm
Coos Farm
Manor Farm
COOLE LA
Moss Hall Aquaduct
Daisy Bank Farm
DAISY BANK CRES
Moss Hall
Lower House Farm
Moss Hall Bridge
A529
CHESHIRE ST
BACK COOLE LA
BROADWAYS
Cemy
CHURCHFIELDS
PH
CROWN CTYD
THE SQUARE
Copthorne
Brickwall Farm
Ty-Gwyn
GEMMULL CL
ARMSTRONG CL
MOORSFIELD AVE
HAYFIELDS GR
OAK TREE GATE
A525
SHROPSHIRE ST
WINDMILL DR
Sewage Works
COPTHORNE DR
1 OLD VICARAGE GDNS
2 CHAPEL CL
3 TELFORD WAY
Lower Lightwood Green Farm
Browns Bank Farm
Lightwood Green
Oldmill Bridge
WHITCHURCH RD
Audlem Bridge
WEAVER VIEW
HOLLYBANK
HEYWOODS RIDGE
Grey's Bridge
Brown's Bank
Works
LIGHTWOOD GREEN AVE
WOODAVENS GR
West View
Weaver Bank Farm
Newtown Cottages
Hillside
MILL LA
River Weaver
GREEN LA
Swanbach Grange
Swanbach
Newtown Farm
Swanbach Farm
BAGLEY LA
Bridge Farm
HEYWOOD LA
64
65
42
43
44
45
1
2
3
4
234
230

229
219

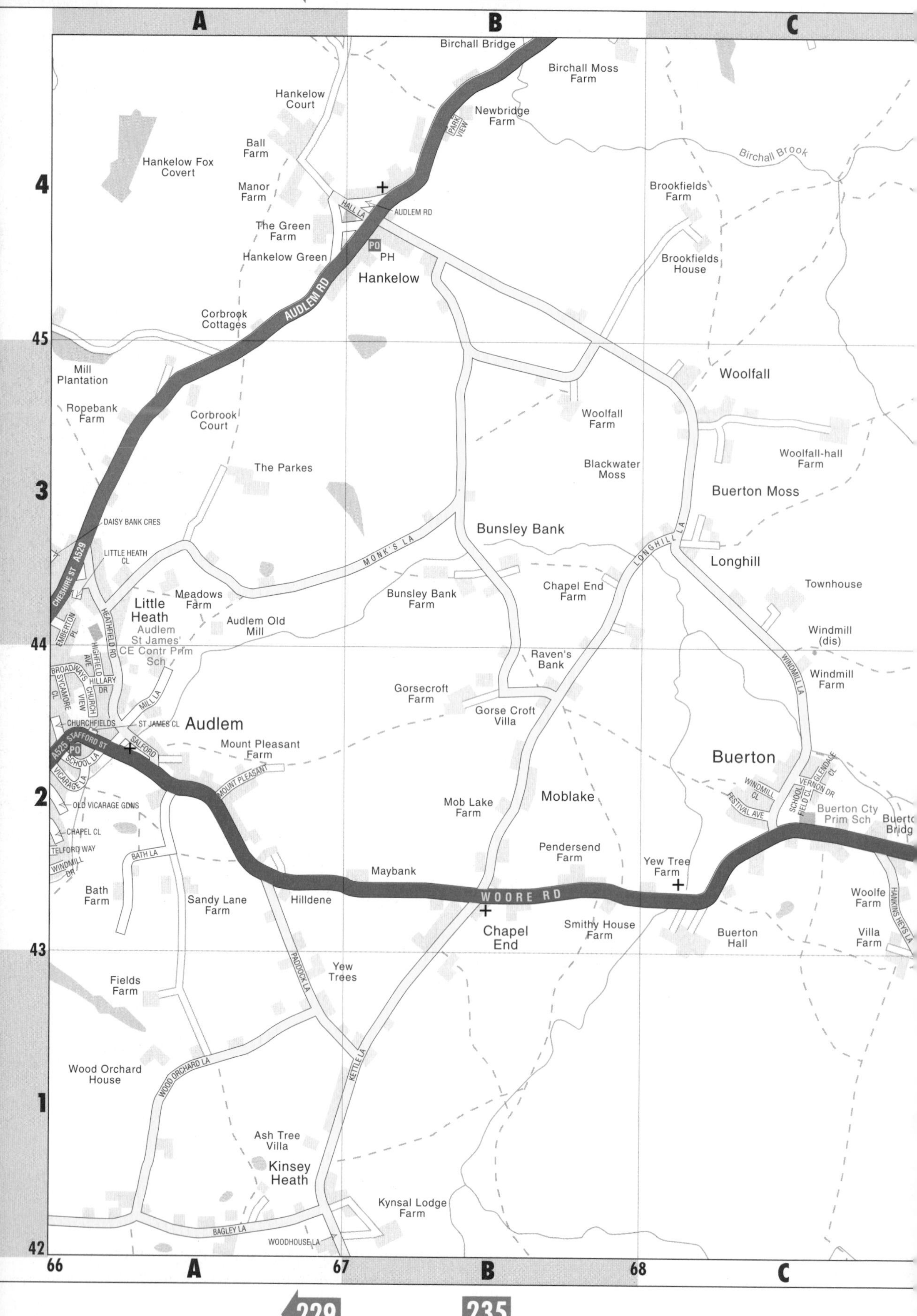
A
B
C
4
45
3
44
2
43
1
42
66
67
68
Birchall Bridge
Birchall Moss Farm
Newbridge Farm
Hankelow Court
Ball Farm
Hankelow Fox Covert
Manor Farm
The Green Farm
Hankelow Green
PH
Hankelow
AUDLEM RD
HALL LA
PARK VIEW
Birchall Brook
Brookfields Farm
Brookfields House
Corbrook Cottages
Mill Plantation
Ropebank Farm
Corbrook Court
Woolfall
Woolfall Farm
Woolfall-hall Farm
Blackwater Moss
The Parkes
Buerton Moss
DAISY BANK CRES
Bunsley Bank
LITTLE HEATH CL
MONK'S LA
LONGHILL LA
Longhill
CHESHIRE ST
A529
Meadows Farm
Bunsley Bank Farm
Chapel End Farm
Townhouse
Little Heath
Audlem Old Mill
Audlem St James' CE Contr Prim Sch
Windmill (dis)
EMBERTON PL
HEATHFIELD RD
Raven's Bank
WINDMILL LA
Windmill Farm
Gorsecroft Farm
BROADWAYS
SYCAMORE CL
HIGHFIELD AVE
HILLARY DR
CHURCH VIEW
MILL LA
Gorse Croft Villa
CHURCHFIELDS
ST JAMES CL
Audlem
Mount Pleasant Farm
A525
STAFFORD ST
SALFORD
Buerton
SCHOOL LA
VICARAGE LA
MOUNT PLEASANT
WINDMILL CL
GLENDALE CL
VERNON DR
Moblake
OLD VICARAGE GDNS
Mob Lake Farm
FESTIVAL AVE
SCHOOL FIELD CL
Buerton Cty Prim Sch
CHAPEL CL
Pendersend Farm
TELFORD WAY
WINDMILL DR
BATH LA
Maybank
Yew Tree Farm
Bath Farm
WOORE RD
Sandy Lane Farm
Hilldene
Chapel End
Smithy House Farm
Woolfe Farm
Buerton Hall
Villa Farm
HANKINS HEYS LA
Yew Trees
Fields Farm
PADDOCK LA
KETTLE LA
Wood Orchard House
WOOD ORCHARD LA
Ash Tree Villa
Kinsey Heath
Kynsal Lodge Farm
BAGLEY LA
WOODHOUSE LA

229
235

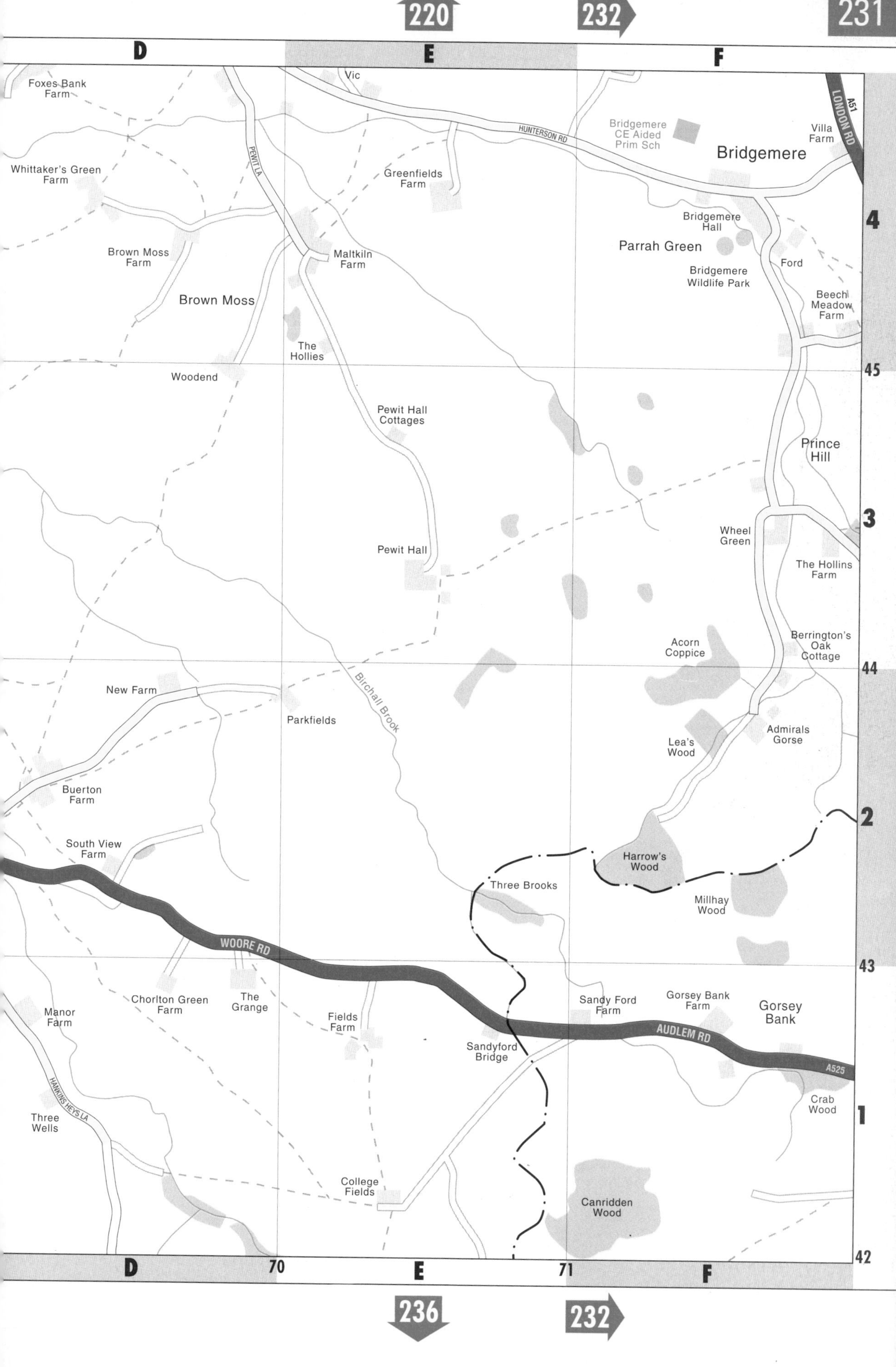

D E F

Foxes Bank Farm

A51 LONDON RD

Vic

HUNTERSON RD

Bridgemere CE Aided Prim Sch

Villa Farm

Bridgemere

Whittaker's Green Farm

Greenfields Farm

Bridgemere Hall

4

Brown Moss Farm

Parrah Green

Bridgemere Wildlife Park

Ford

Maltkiln Farm

PEWIT LA

Beech Meadow Farm

Brown Moss

The Hollies

45

Woodend

Pewit Hall Cottages

Prince Hill

Wheel Green

3

Pewit Hall

The Hollins Farm

Berrington's Oak Cottage

Acorn Coppice

44

New Farm

Birchall Brook

Parkfields

Lea's Wood

Admirals Gorse

Buerton Farm

South View Farm

Harrow's Wood

2

Three Brooks

Millhay Wood

WOORE RD

43

Chorlton Green Farm

The Grange

Fields Farm

Sandy Ford Farm

Gorsey Bank Farm

Gorsey Bank

Manor Farm

AUDLEM RD

A525

Sandyford Bridge

HANKINS HEYS LA

Crab Wood

Three Wells

1

College Fields

Canridden Wood

D E F

70 71

42

231
221

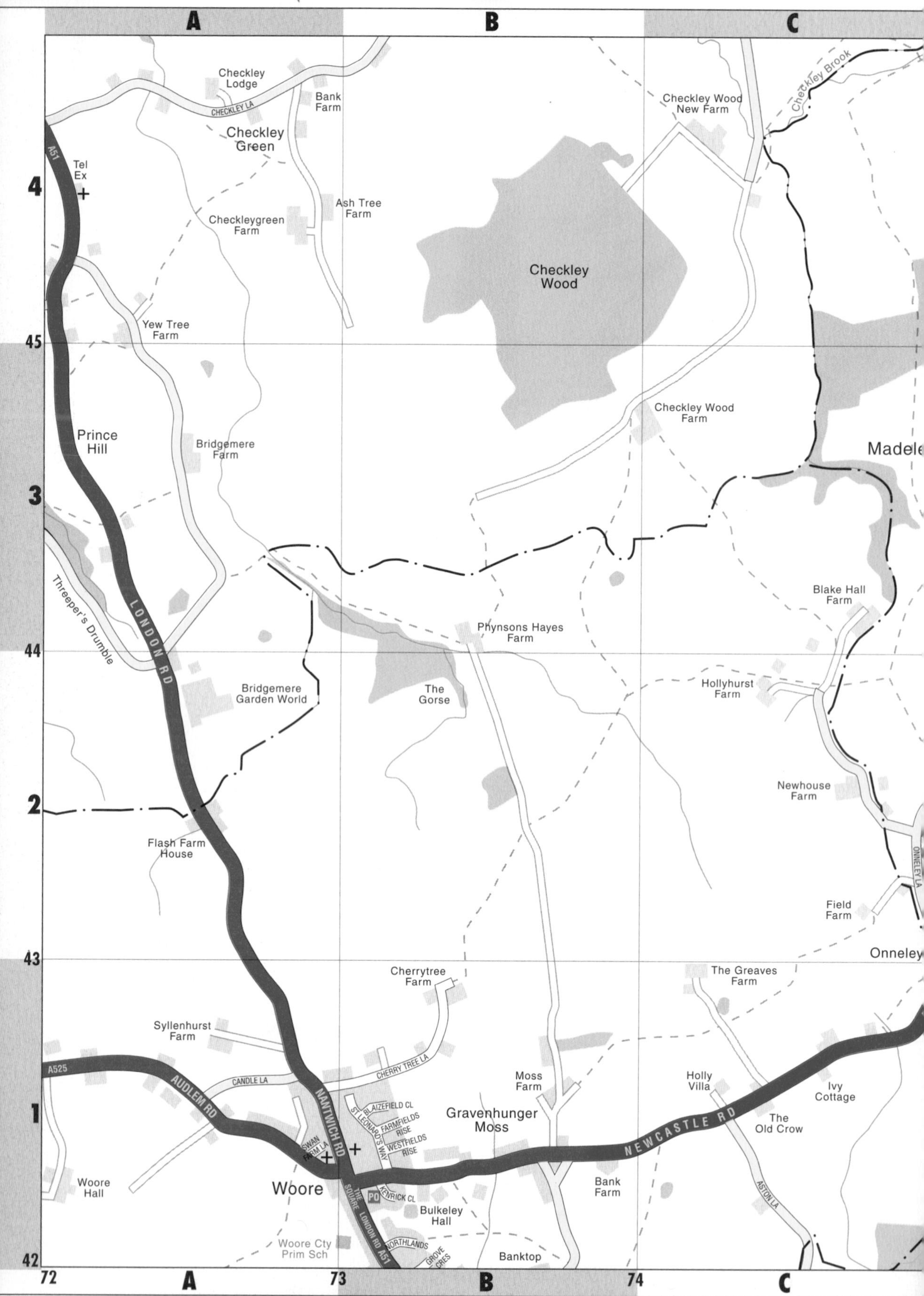
A
B
C
4
3
2
1
45
44
43
42
72
73
74
Checkley Lodge
Bank Farm
CHECKLEY LA
Checkley Green
Checkley Wood New Farm
Checkley Brook
A51
Tel Ex
Ash Tree Farm
Checkleygreen Farm
Checkley Wood
Yew Tree Farm
Prince Hill
Bridgemere Farm
Checkley Wood Farm
Madele
Threeper's Drumble
LONDON RD
Blake Hall Farm
Phynsons Hayes Farm
Bridgemere Garden World
The Gorse
Hollyhurst Farm
Newhouse Farm
Flash Farm House
ONNELEY LA
Field Farm
Onneley
Cherrytree Farm
The Greaves Farm
Syllenhurst Farm
A525
CANDLE LA
CHERRY TREE LA
AUDLEM RD
NANTWICH RD
BLAIZEFIELD CL
FARMFIELDS RISE
ST LEONARD'S WAY
WESTFIELDS RISE
SWAN FARM LA
Moss Farm
Gravenhunger Moss
Holly Villa
Ivy Cottage
The Old Crow
NEWCASTLE RD
Woore Hall
Woore
THE SQUARE
LONDON RD
A51
PO
KENRICK CL
Bulkeley Hall
Bank Farm
ASTON LA
NORTHLANDS
GROVE CRES
Woore Cty Prim Sch
Banktop

231

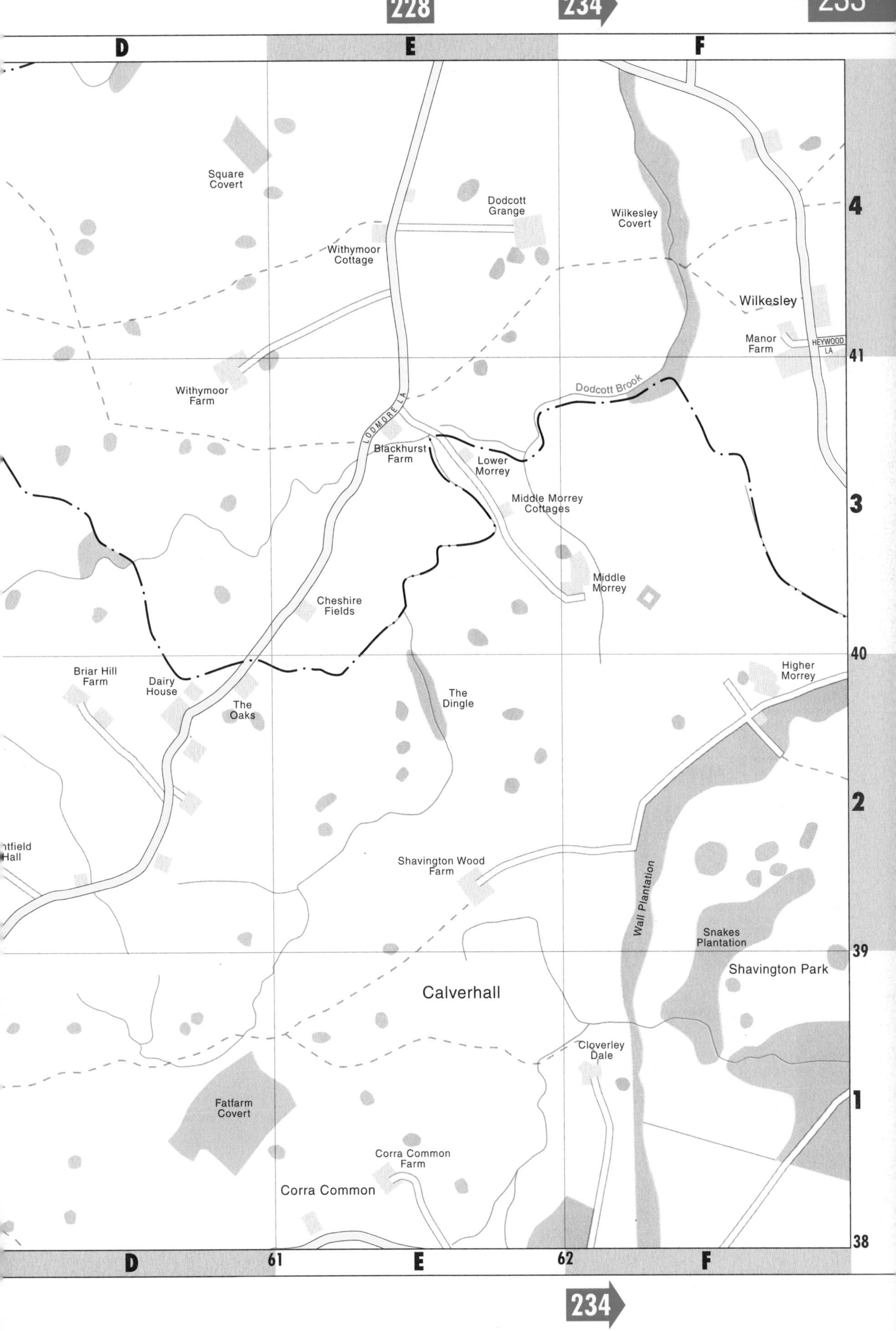

D E F

Square
Covert

Dodcott
Grange

Wilkesley
Covert

4

Withymoor
Cottage

Wilkesley

Manor
Farm

HEYWOOD LA

41

Withymoor
Farm

Dodcott Brook

L'OOMORE LA

Blackhurst
Farm

Lower
Morrey

Middle Morrey
Cottages

3

Cheshire
Fields

Middle
Morrey

40

Briar Hill
Farm

Dairy
House

Higher
Morrey

The Oaks

The
Dingle

...ntfield
Hall

2

Shavington Wood
Farm

Wall Plantation

Snakes
Plantation

39

Shavington Park

Calverhall

Cloverley
Dale

1

Fatfarm
Covert

Corra Common
Farm

Corra Common

38

D E F

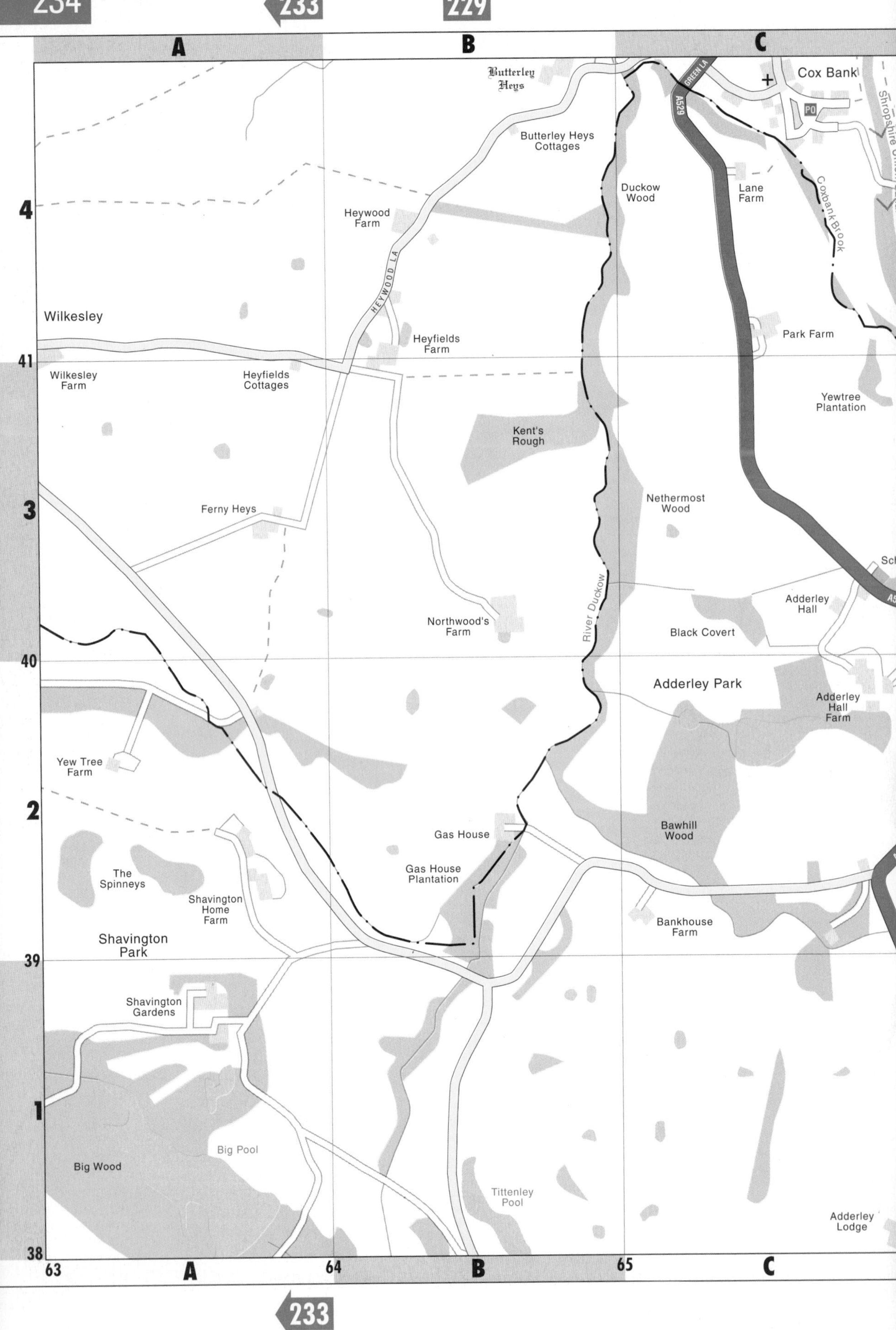

A   B   C

4

Wilkesley

41

3

40

2

1

38

Butterley
Heys

Butterley Heys
Cottages

Duckow
Wood

Lane
Farm

GREEN LA

A529

Cox Bank

PO

Shropshire Union

Coxbank Brook

Park Farm

Heywood
Farm

HEYWOOD LA

Yewtree
Plantation

Heyfields
Farm

Wilkesley
Farm

Heyfields
Cottages

Kent's
Rough

Nethermost
Wood

Sch

A5

Adderley
Hall

Ferny Heys

River Duckow

Black Covert

Adderley Park

Adderley
Hall
Farm

Northwood's
Farm

Yew Tree
Farm

The
Spinneys

Gas House

Bawhill
Wood

Gas House
Plantation

Shavington
Home
Farm

Bankhouse
Farm

Shavington
Park

39

Shavington
Gardens

Big Pool

Big Wood

Tittenley
Pool

Adderley
Lodge

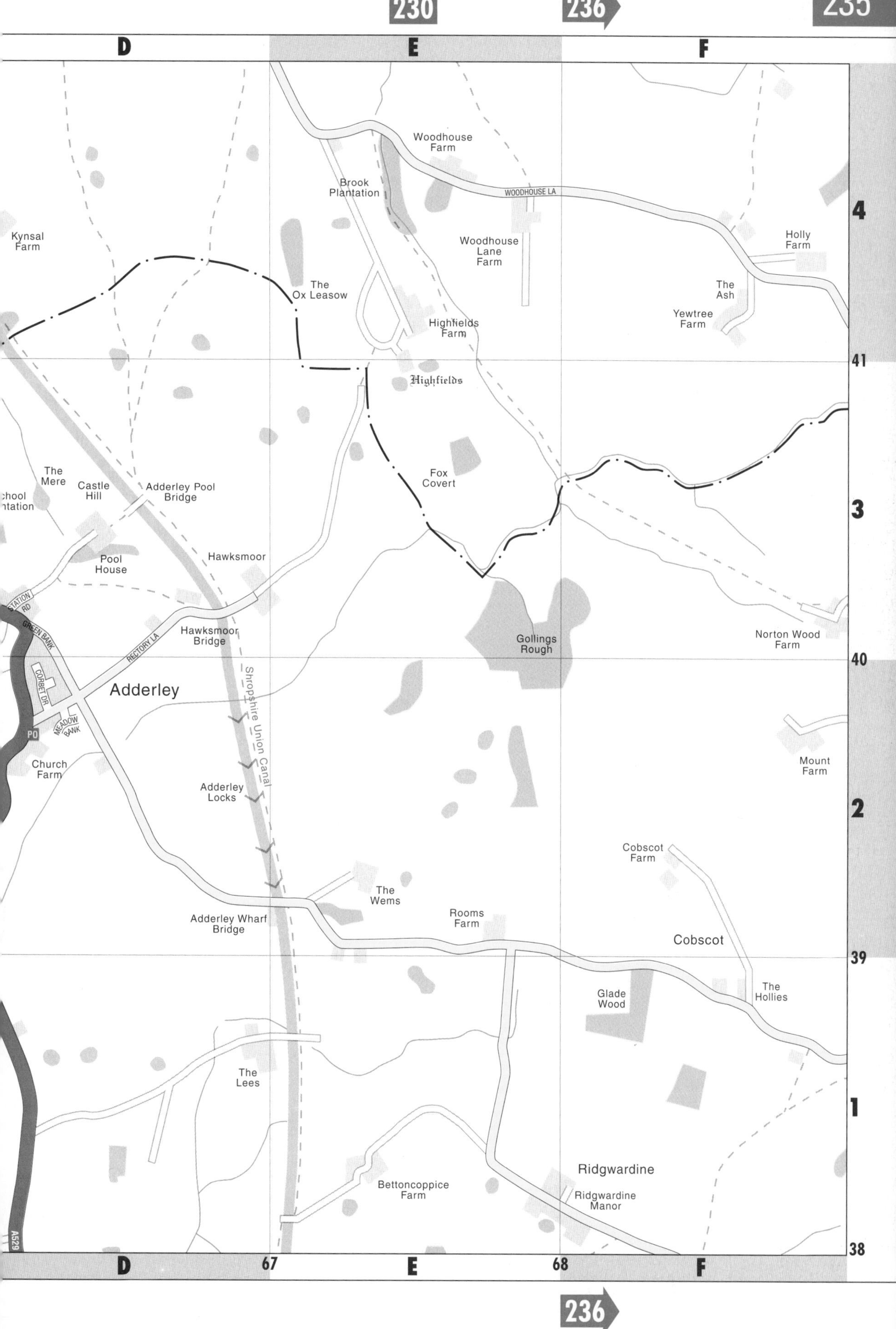

D
E
F

4

Kynsal Farm

Woodhouse Farm

Brook Plantation

WOODHOUSE LA

Woodhouse Lane Farm

Holly Farm

The Ash

Yewtree Farm

The Ox Leasow

Highfields Farm

41

Highfields

The Mere

Castle Hill

School Plantation

Adderley Pool Bridge

Fox Covert

3

Hawksmoor

Pool House

Norton Wood Farm

STATION RD

GREEN BANK

RECTORY LA

Hawksmoor Bridge

Gollings Rough

40

CORBET DR

Adderley

Shropshire Union Canal

MEADOW BANK

PO

Mount Farm

Church Farm

Adderley Locks

2

Cobscot Farm

The Wems

Rooms Farm

Cobscot

Adderley Wharf Bridge

39

Glade Wood

The Hollies

The Lees

1

A529

Bettoncoppice Farm

Ridgwardine

Ridgwardine Manor

38

D
67
E
68
F

A | B | C

4

Long Wood

College Fields

College Fields

College F Cottage

Hankins Heys

Poplars Farm

Square Plantation

HANKIN HEYS LA

41

Mere Cottage

WOODHOUSE LA

Mere Farm

Mere Villa

Bellaport Home Farm

3

New Cottages

Bellaport Old Hall

POPLAR LA

Norton Wood Farm

The Grove

Bellaport Wood

Ladies Wood

40

Wet Butts Plantation

BELLAPORT RD

Greenacre

2

The Croft

Bellaport Lodge

BEARSTONE RD

River Tern

39

Cemy

Brand Hall Farm

CHURCH FIELDS

Napley Farm

BESWICKS LA

ST CHADS WAY

NAPLEY DR

Brook Farm

CHAPEL LA

GRIFFIN CL

PO

CHURCH MEADOW

1

MAIN RD

PH

Napley Lodge

Mucklestone

Norton Hales CE Sch

Norton in Hales

NAPLEY RD

Napley Heath

Brand Hall

FORGE LA

Marlpit Plantation

38

69 | A | 70 | B | 71 | C

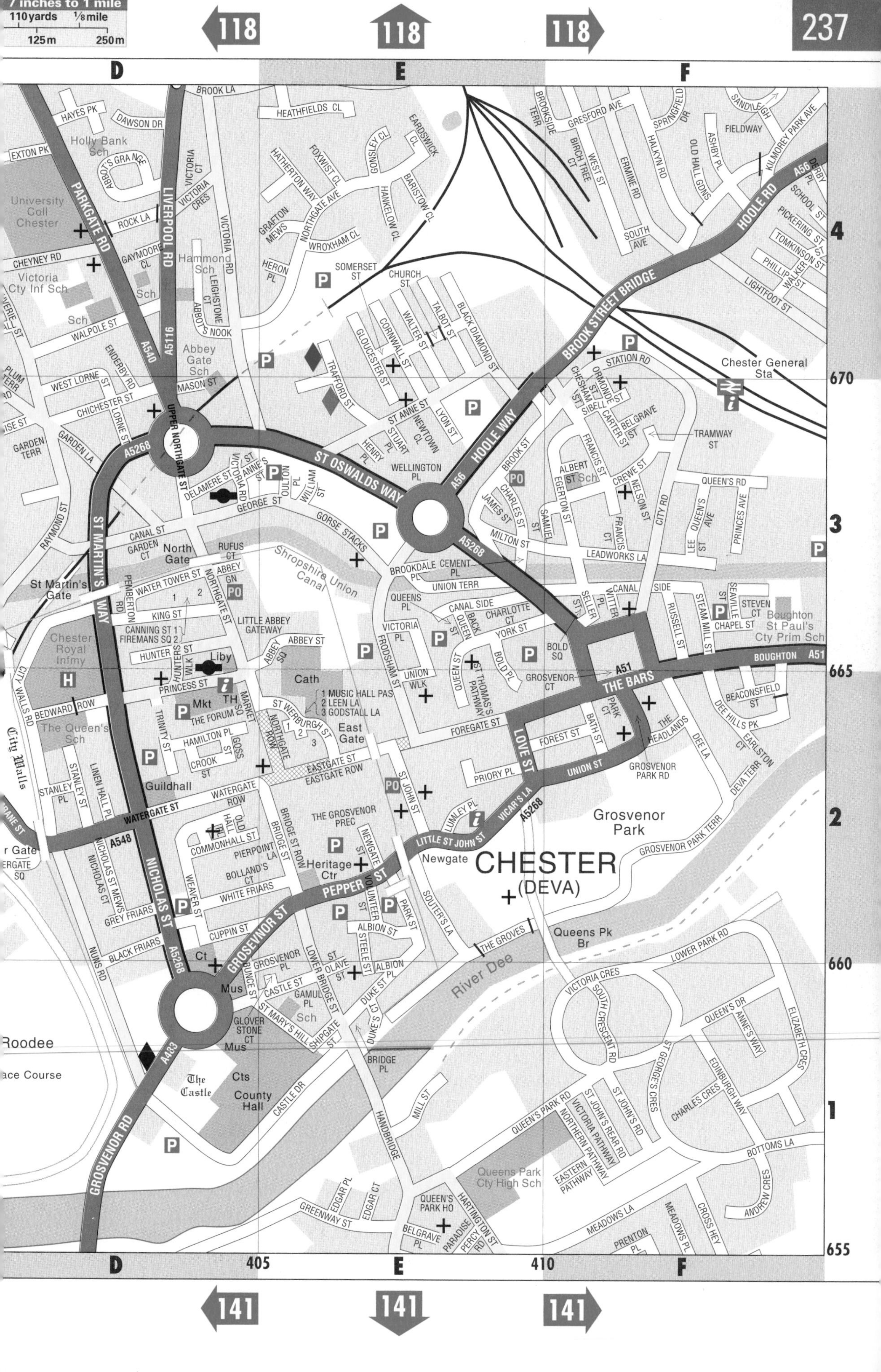

7 inches to 1 mile
110 yards
1/8 mile
125m
250m
118
118
118
D
E
F
BROOK LA
HAYES PK
DAWSON DR
Holly Bank Sch
EXTON PK
ABBOT'S GRANGE
University Coll Chester
PARKGATE RD
LIVERPOOL RD
VICTORIA CT
VICTORIA CRES
VICTORIA RD
ROCK LA
CHEYNEY RD
GAYMOORE CL
Hammond Sch
Victoria Cty Inf Sch
Sch
LEIGHSTONE CT
ABBOT'S NOOK
Sch
WALPOLE ST
ENDERBY RD
A540
A5116
Abbey Gate Sch
WEST LORNE ST
MASON ST
CHICHESTER ST
LORNE ST
GARDEN TERR
GARDEN LA
UPPER NORTHGATE ST
A5268
HEATHFIELDS CL
HATHERTON WAY
FOXWIST CL
GONSLEY CL
EARDSWICK CL
NORTHGATE AVE
HANKELOW CL
BARISTOW CL
GRAFTON MEWS
WROXHAM CL
HERON PL
SOMERSET ST
CHURCH ST
GLOUCESTER ST
CORNWALL ST
WALTER ST
TALBOT ST
BLACK DIAMOND ST
TRAFFORD ST
ST ANNE ST
NEWTOWN CL
LYON ST
STUART PL
HENRY PL
WELLINGTON PL
ST OSWALDS WAY
HOOLE WAY
A56
BROOK STREET BRIDGE
HOOLE RD
BROOKSIDE TERR
GRESFORD AVE
BIRCH TREE CT
WEST ST
ERMINE RD
HALKYN RD
SPRINGFIELD DR
OLD HALL GDNS
ASHBY PL
FIELDWAY
SANDILEIGH
KILMOREY PARK AVE
DERBY PL
SCHOOL ST
PICKERING ST
TOMKINSON ST
PHILLIP ST
WALKER ST
LIGHTFOOT ST
SOUTH AVE
Chester General Sta
STATION RD
CHESHAM ST
ORMONDE ST
SIBELL ST
CARTER ST
BELGRAVE ST
TRAMWAY ST
FRANCIS ST
BROOK ST
ALBERT ST
ST Sch
EGERTON ST
CREWE ST
NELSON ST
QUEEN'S RD
CHARLES ST
JAMES ST
SAMUEL ST
FRANCIS CT
CITY RD
LEE ST
QUEEN'S AVE
PRINCES AVE
MILTON ST
LEADWORKS LA
DELAMERE ST
VICTORIA RD
ANNE'S ST
HOLLY PL
WILLIAM ST
GEORGE ST
GORSE STACKS
RAYMOND ST
CANAL ST
GARDEN CT
North Gate
RUFUS CT
Shropshire Union Canal
BROOKDALE PL
CEMENT PL
UNION TERR
St Martin's Gate
ST MARTIN'S WAY
ABBEY GN
WATER TOWER ST
NORTHGATE ST
PEMBERTON RD
KING ST
CANNING ST
FIREMANS SQ
LITTLE ABBEY GATEWAY
ABBEY ST
ABBEY SQ
QUEENS PL
CANAL SIDE
CHARLOTTE CT
QUEEN ST
BACK QUEEN ST
YORK ST
VICTORIA PL
FRODSHAM ST
BOLD SQ
SELLER ST
WITTER PL
CANAL SIDE
RUSSELL ST
STEAM MILL ST
SEAVILLE ST
STEVEN CT
CHAPEL ST
Boughton St Paul's Cty Prim Sch
BOUGHTON
A51
Chester Royal Infmy
H
HUNTER ST
HUNTERS WLK
Liby
Cath
UNION WLK
QUEEN ST
ST THOMAS'S PATHWAY
BOLD PL
GROSVENOR CT
THE BARS
PARK CT
CITY WALLS RD
PRINCESS ST
TH
Mkt
MARKET SQ
1 MUSIC HALL PAS
2 LEEN LA
3 GODSTALL LA
BEDWARD ROW
TRINITY ST
THE FORUM
ST WERBURGH ST
NORTHGATE ROW
East Gate
FOREGATE ST
LOVE ST
FOREST ST
BATH ST
BEACONSFIELD ST
DEE HILLS PK
THE HEADLANDS
DEE LA
EARLSTON CT
City Walls
The Queen's Sch
HAMILTON PL
GOSS ST
CROOK ST
EASTGATE ST
EASTGATE ROW
PRIORY PL
UNION ST
GROSVENOR PARK RD
DEVA TERR
STANLEY ST
STANLEY PL
LINEN HALL PL
Guildhall
WATERGATE ROW
WATERGATE ST
ST JOHN ST
LUMLEY PL
VICAR'S LA
A5268
Grosvenor Park
THE GROSVENOR PREC
BRIDGE ST ROW
BRIDGE ST
OLD HALL PL
COMMONHALL ST
PIERPOINT LA
BOLLAND'S CT
WATERGATE SQ
A548
NICHOLAS ST MEWS
NICHOLAS CT
NEWGATE ST
LITTLE ST JOHN ST
Newgate
CHESTER (DEVA)
GROSVENOR PARK TERR
Heritage Ctr
WHITE FRIARS
WEAVER ST
PEPPER ST
GREY FRIARS
NICHOLAS ST
VOLUNTEER ST
PARK ST
SOUTER'S LA
CUPPIN ST
GROSVENOR ST
ALBION ST
THE GROVES
Queens Pk Br
BLACK FRIARS
NUNS RD
A5268
Ct
GROSVENOR PL
STEELE ST
OLAVE ST
ALBION PL
LOWER PARK RD
River Dee
Mus
BUNCE ST
CASTLE ST
GAMUL PL
LOWER BRIDGE ST
DUKE ST
VICTORIA CRES
SOUTH CRESCENT RD
QUEEN'S DR
ANNE'S WAY
ELIZABETH CRES
Sch
GLOVER STONE CT
ST MARY'S HILL
SHIPGATE ST
DUKE'S CT
Roodee
Race Course
Mus
A483
The Castle
Cts
County Hall
CASTLE DR
BRIDGE PL
ST GEORGE'S CRES
EDINBURGH WAY
CHARLES CRES
MILL ST
HANDBRIDGE
QUEEN'S PARK RD
ST JOHN'S REAR RD
VICTORIA PATHWAY
NORTHERN PATHWAY
ST JOHN'S RD
EASTERN PATHWAY
BOTTOMS LA
ANDREW CRES
GROSVENOR RD
Queens Park Cty High Sch
EDGAR PL
EDGAR CT
GREENWAY ST
QUEEN'S PARK HO
HARTINGTON ST
PARADISE
PERCY RD
BELGRAVE PL
MEADOWS LA
MEADOWS PL
CROSS HEY
PRENTON PL
1
2
3
4
670
665
660
655
405
410
141
141
141

Altrincham

D5
1 POLICE ST
2 STAMFORD WAY
3 STAMFORD SQ

E6
1 LYNGARTH HOUSE
2 ASTBURY CL
3 THELWALL CL

B5165

Timperley Sta

South Trafford Coll of F Ed

Broadheath Prim Sch

Broadheath

Dairyhouse Farm

Higher House

DUNLIN WLK 1
CHOKEBERRY CL 2

CHOLMONDELEY AVE 1
ATTENBURY S PK EST 2

Cheshire Ring Canal Wlk

Bridgewater Canal

Blue Chip Bsns Ctr

Atlantic Bsns Ctr

Lyon Ind Est

1 MARWOOD CL
2 BURLESCOMBE CL

Century Park Ind Area

Brentwood Sch

PH

Oldfield Brow

Altrincham CE (VA) Prim Sch

Old Market Pl

Altrincham General

Altrincham Sta

Altrincham Golf Course

1 RENSHAW ST
2 AIREDALE CT
3 CLARENDON AVE
4 WOODLANDS LA
5 WOODLANDS CT
6 AMBASSADOR PL
7 OAKFIELD TRAD EST

DUNHAM RD

STOCKPORT RD

WOODLANDS RD

Blessed Thomas Holford RC High Sch

Timperley Brook

The Devisdale

Inglewood Haigh Lawn

Devisdale Grange

Altrincham Gram Sch for Girls

Denzell Gdns

St Anne's

The Downs

HALE RD

Hale Sta

Bowdon

Park Rd

Church Brow

B5160

Rosehill

LANGHAM RD

B5162

Altrincham Prep Sch

SOUTH DOWNS RD

Altrincham Gram Sch for Boys

ASHLEY RD

Liby

B5163

Bow Green Rd

Bollin Prim Sch

Bowdon CE Prim Sch

Bowgreen

1 PRIMROSE COTTS
2 PRIMROSE BANK

C4
1 STAMFORD GRANGE
2 EASINGWOLD

D3
1 ROSTHERNE ST
2 WILLIAM WLK

D4
1 GREENWOOD ST
2 THE CAUSEWAY
3 CROSS ST
4 BREWERY ST
5 GRAFTON MALL
6 LLOYD SQ
7 OSBOURNE PL

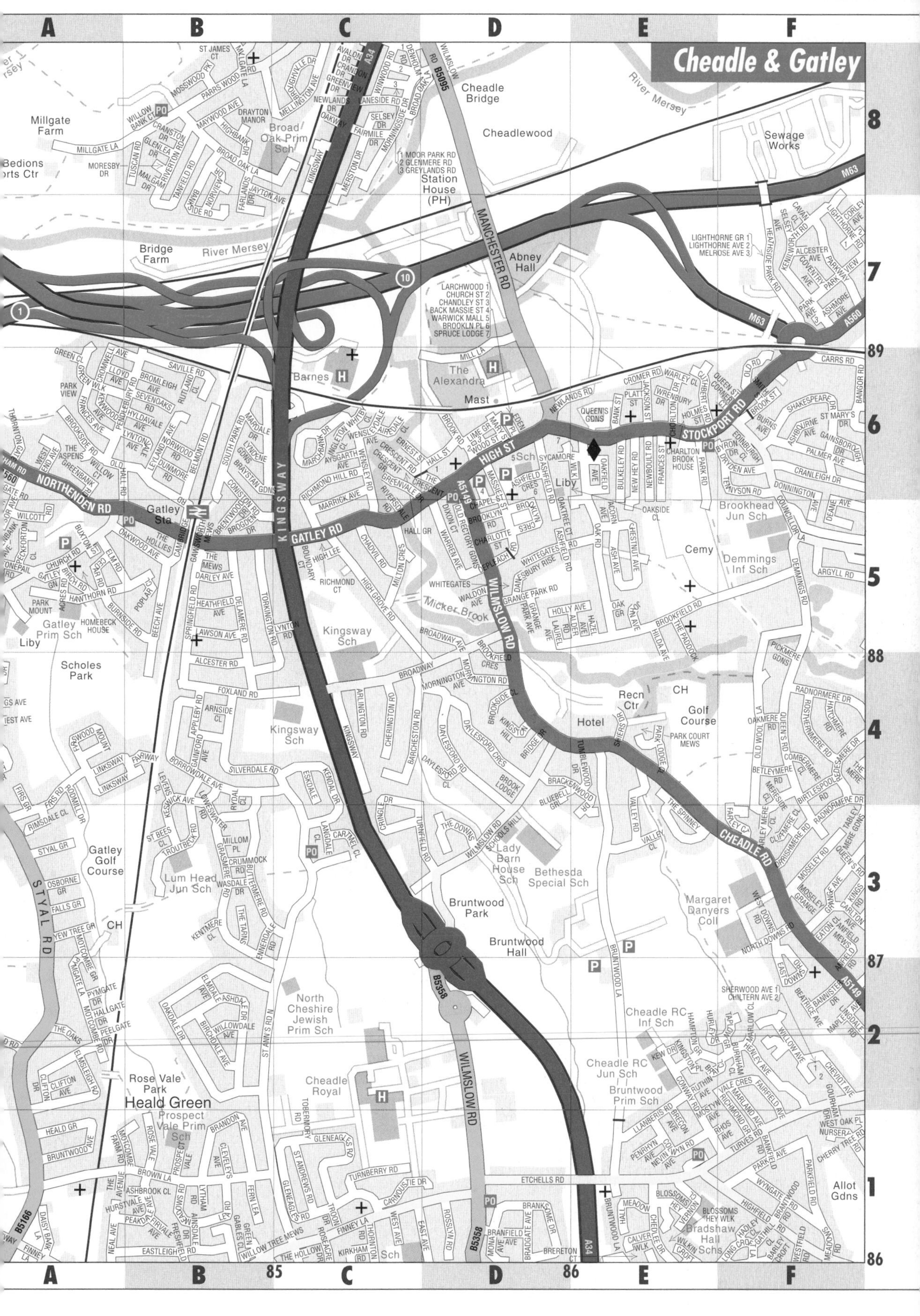
Cheadle & Gatley
Millgate Farm
Cheadle Bridge
Cheadlewood
Sewage Works
Station House (PH)
Bridge Farm
River Mersey
Abney Hall
Broad Oak Prim Sch
Barnes
The Alexandra
Mast
Gatley Sta
Gatley Prim Sch
Scholes Park
Kingsway Sch
Brookhead Jun Sch
Cemy
Demmings Inf Sch
Recn Ctr
Hotel
Golf Course
Gatley Golf Course
Lum Head Jun Sch
Lady Barn House Sch
Bethesda Special Sch
Bruntwood Park
Bruntwood Hall
Margaret Danyers Coll
North Cheshire Jewish Prim Sch
Cheadle Royal
Rose Vale Park
Heald Green
Prospect Vale Prim Sch
Cheadle RC Inf Sch
Cheadle RC Jun Sch
Bruntwood Prim Sch
Bradshaw Hall Schs
Allot Gdns
KINGSWAY
GATLEY RD
HIGH ST
STOCKPORT RD
NORTHENDEN RD
WILMSLOW RD
CHEADLE RD
MANCHESTER RD
STYAL RD
ETCHELLS RD
M63
A34
A560
A5149
B5095
B5358
B5166
A B C D E F
85 86
86 87 88 89

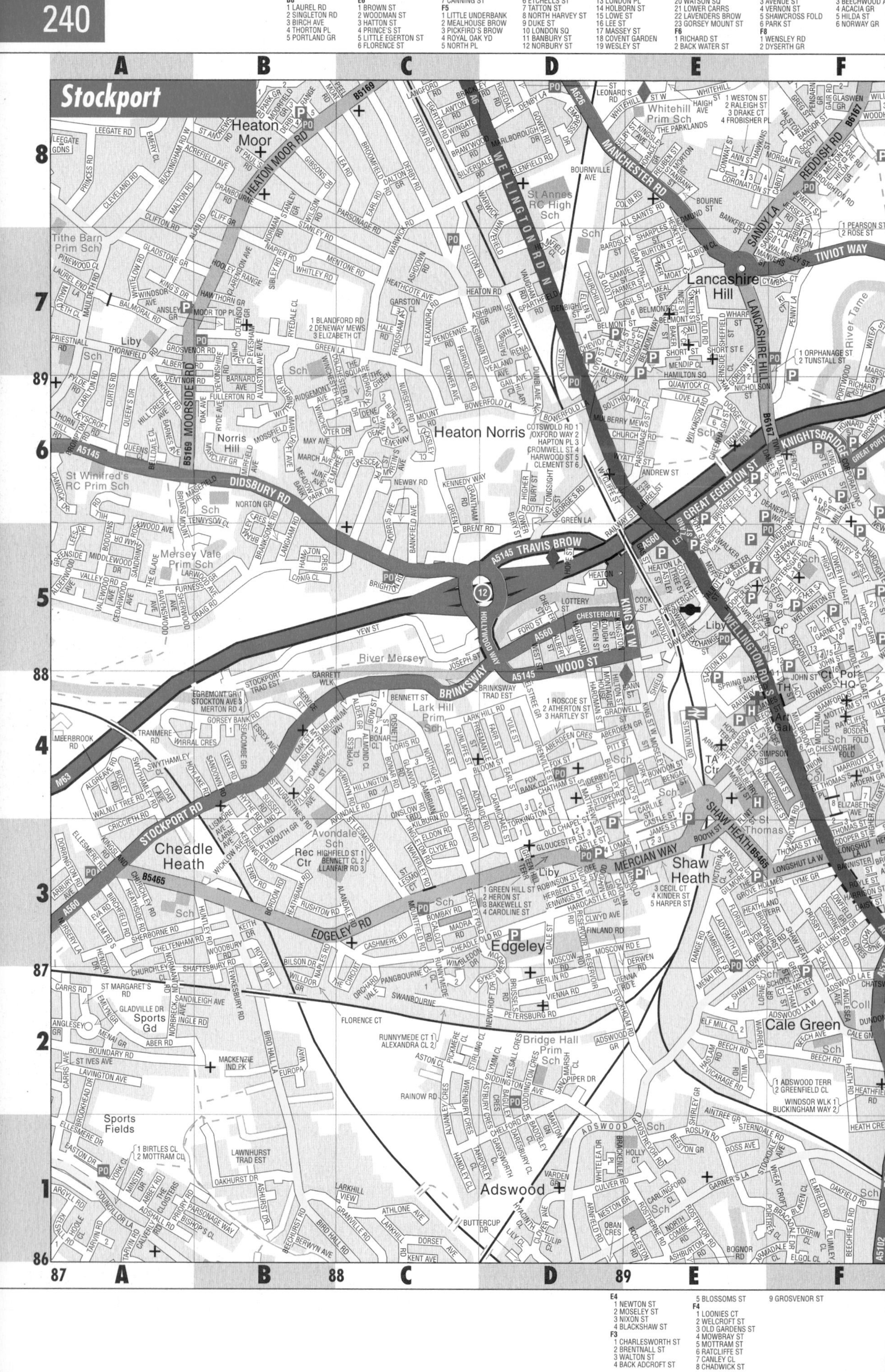
Stockport
B8
1 LAUREL RD
2 SINGLETON RD
3 BIRCH AVE
4 THORTON PL
5 PORTLAND GR
E6
1 BROWN ST
2 WOODMAN ST
3 HATTON ST
4 PRINCE'S ST
5 LITTLE EGERTON ST
6 FLORENCE ST
7 CANNING ST
F5
1 LITTLE UNDERBANK
2 MEALHOUSE BROW
3 PICKFIRD'S BROW
4 ROYAL OAK YD
5 NORTH PL
6 ETCHELLS ST
7 TATTON ST
8 NORTH HARVEY ST
9 DUKE ST
10 LONDON SQ
11 BANBURY ST
12 NORBURY ST
13 LONDON PL
14 HOLBORN ST
15 LOWE ST
16 LEE ST
17 MASSEY ST
18 COVENT GARDEN
19 WESLEY ST
20 WATSON SQ
21 LOWER CARRS
22 LAVENDERS BROW
23 GORSEY MOUNT ST
F6
1 RICHARD ST
2 BACK WATER ST
3 AVENUE ST
4 VERNON ST
5 SHAWCROSS FOLD
6 PARK ST
F8
1 WENSLEY RD
2 DYSERTH GR
3 BEECHWOOD A
4 ACACIA GR
5 HILDA ST
6 NORWAY GR
Heaton Moor
Heaton Norris
Norris Hill
Lancashire Hill
Cheadle Heath
Shaw Heath
Edgeley
Cale Green
Adswood
River Mersey
River Tame
E4
1 NEWTON ST
2 MOSELEY ST
3 NIXON ST
4 BLACKSHAW ST
F3
1 CHARLESWORTH ST
2 BRENTNALL ST
3 WALTON ST
4 BACK ADCROFT ST
5 BLOSSOMS ST
F4
1 LOONIES CT
2 WELCROFT ST
3 OLD GARDENS ST
4 MOWBRAY ST
5 MOTTRAM ST
6 RATCLIFFE ST
7 CANLEY CL
8 CHADWICK ST
9 GROSVENOR ST

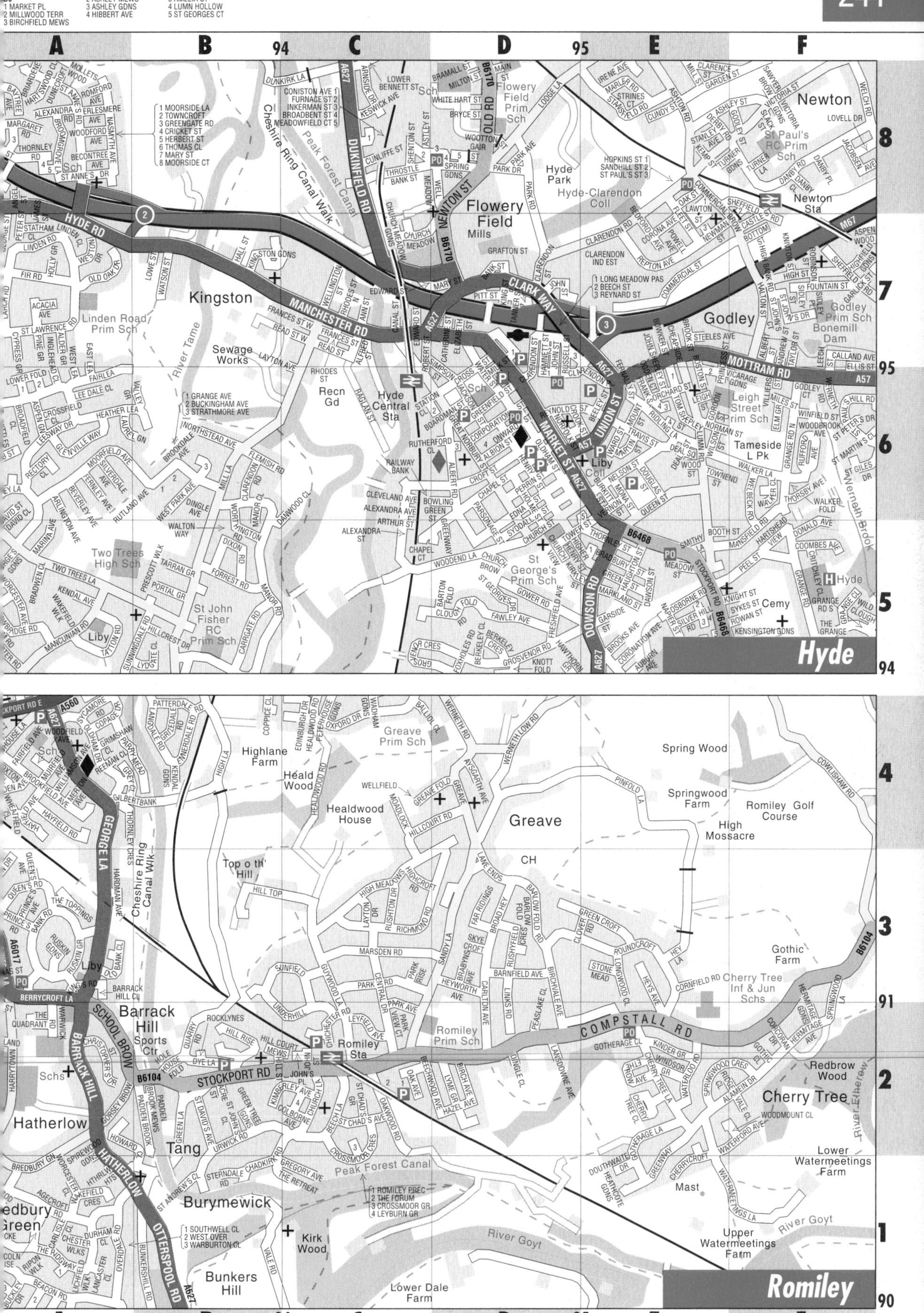

Hyde

Romiley

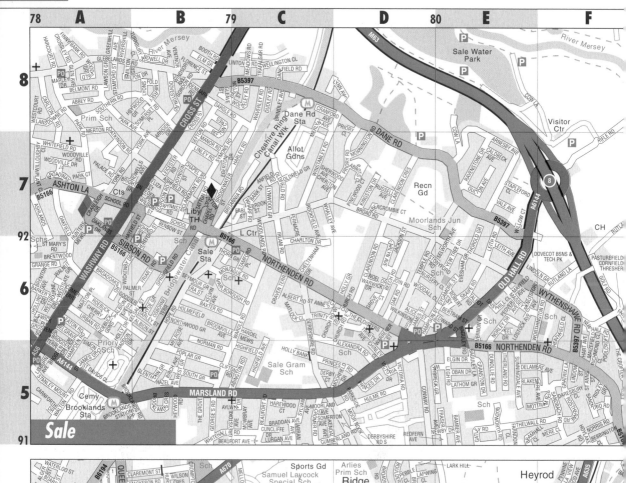

Sale

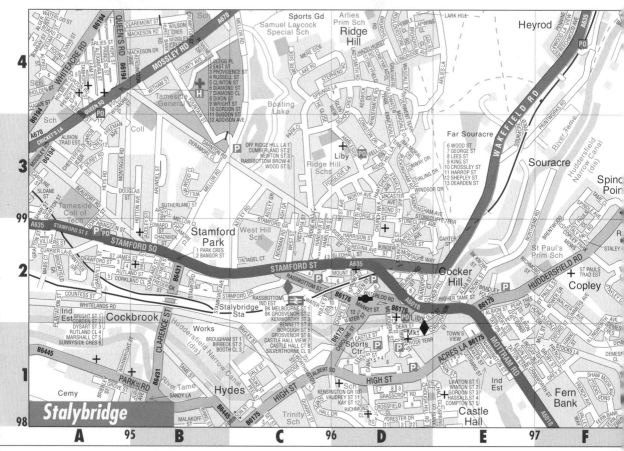

Stalybridge

Street names are listed alphabetically and show the locality, the Postcode District, the page number and a reference to the square in which the name falls on the map page

Grosvenor St **6** Macclesfield SK11 ...... **112** B4

Full street name
This may have been abbreviated on the map

Location Number
If present, this indicates the street's position on a congested area of the map instead of the name

Town, village or locality in which the street falls.

Postcode District for the street name

Page number of the map on which the street name appears

Grid square in which the centre of the street falls

Schools, hospitals, sports centres, railway stations, shopping centres, industrial estates, public amenities and other places of interest are also listed. These are highlighted in magenta

Abbreviations used in the index

App	Approach	Cl	Close	Ent	Enterprise	La	Lane	Rdbt	Roundabout
Arc	Arcade	Comm	Common	Espl	Esplanade	N	North	S	South
Ave	Avenue	Cnr	Corner	Est	Estate	Orch	Orchard	Sq	Square
Bvd	Boulevard	Cotts	Cottages	Gdns	Gardens	Par	Parade	Strs	Stairs
Bldgs	Buildings	Ct	Court	Gn	Green	Pk	Park	Stps	Steps
Bsns Pk	Business Park	Ctyd	Courtyard	Gr	Grove	Pas	Passage	St	Street, Saint
Bsns Ctr	Business Centre	Cres	Crescent	Hts	Heights	Pl	Place	Terr	Terrace
Bglws	Bungalows	Dr	Drive	Ho	House	Prec	Precinct	Trad Est	Trading Estate
Cswy	Causeway	Dro	Drove	Ind Est	Industrial Estate	Prom	Promenade	Wlk	Walk
Ctr	Centre	E	East	Intc	Interchange	Ret Pk	Retail Park	W	West
Cir	Circus	Emb	Embankment	Junc	Junction	Rd	Road	Yd	Yard

Town and village index

ntrim Rd WA2 8 A1
ntrobus St CW12 156 B2
ntrobus St Mark's Sch CW9 53 E2
nvil Cl CH1 94 A1
pple Market St CW9 103 F4
pple Tree Cl L24 21 F1
pple Tree Gr CH1 94 C4
ppleby Cl
Macclesfield SK11 111 F3
Stockport SK3 240 D1
Widnes WA8 22 B4
ppleby Rd Gatley SK8 239 B4
Warrington WA2 8 B2
pplecroft ST5 210 C1
pplecross Cl WA3 10 A3
ppledale Dr CH1 95 D4
pplefield CW8 103 E4
ppleford Cl WA4 26 C4
ppleton Cl CW12 178 C4
ppleton Dr L65 69 F2
ppleton Hall Gdns WA4 26 C3
ppleton Mews WA13 18 B2
ppleton Rd
Altrincham WA15 238 F1
Chester CH2 118 C3
Widnes WA8 13 D1
ppleton St Northwich CW8 78 B1
Widnes WA8 23 D4
ppleton Thorn Cty Prim Sch WA4 27 E2
ppleton Thorn Trad Est WA4 27 E3
ppleton Village WA8 13 D1
ppleton Wlk 15 SK9 34 B1
ppletree Gr WA2 8 C1
ppleyards La CH4 141 F4
pprentice La SK9 33 F2
pril Rise SK10 87 D1
pron Rd M90 33 E3
psley Cl WA14 238 B1
psley Gr WA14 238 B1
psley St SK1 240 F5
ragon Ct WA7 24 B2
ragon Gn CH1 117 F3
ran Cl L24 21 E1
rbour Cl Macclesfield SK10 87 E2
Northwich CW9 104 B4
rbour Cres SK10 87 E2
rbour Mews SK10 87 E2
rbour St ST7 210 B3
rbourhay St SK10 87 F1
rbury Ave SK3 240 A3
rbury La WA2 8 B3
rcade The
Ellesmere Port L65 70 A3
Northwich CW9 103 F4
rcher Ave WA4 16 C1
rcher Cl SK10 87 F4
rchers Way Blacon CH1 118 A2
Ellesmere Port L66 69 F1
rclid Cl 12 SK9 34 C1
rclid Hospl CW11 154 A1
rcon Pl WA14 238 A6
rden WA8 12 A1
rden Cl Cheadle SK8 34 B4
Tarvin CH3 121 E2
Warrington WA3 10 A3
rden Ct CW12 179 D4
rden Dr L64 66 C3
rden St SK22 39 E4
rden Wlk SK1 240 E5
rdenbrook Rise SK10 86 C3
rdern Gr SK1 240 F4
rdern Lea WA6 73 E1
rderne Ave CW2 190 A1
rdleigh Cl CW1 189 F4
rgosy Dr WA15 32 C4
rgyll Ave Bebington L62 43 E2
Chester CH4 141 D4
rgyll Cl SK10 87 D1
rgyll Rd SK8 239 F5
rgyll St OL6 242 B3
rkenshaw Rd WA3 9 D4
rkenstone Cl WA8 12 B1
rkle Ave SK9 34 C2
rklow Dr L24 21 E1
rkwright Cl CW7 149 D4
rkwright Ct WA7 23 F2
rkwright Rd WA7 23 F2
rley Ave WA4 26 B4
rley Cl Alsager ST7 193 E2
Altrincham WA14 238 D8
Chester CH2 118 C3
Macclesfield SK11 112 A4
rley Cty Prim Sch CW9 54 C3
rley Dr WA8 12 A1
rley End WA16 29 E2
rley Hall CW9 54 B3
rley Mere Cl SK8 239 F3
rley Mossend La CW9 54 B1
rley Pl CW2 206 A4
rley Rd Antrobus CW9 54 A4
Appleton CW9 27 E1
Northwich CW9 104 B4
rlies Cl SK15 242 D4
rlies La SK15 242 E4
rlies Prim Sch SK15 242 D4
rlies St OL6 242 A4
rlington Ave M34 241 A6
rlington Cl CW2 206 B4
rlington Cr SK9 59 F3
rlington Dr Goldborne WA3 4 B4
Macclesfield SK11 112 A4
Penketh WA5 14 C2
Poynton SK12 36 B2
rlington Rd SK8 239 C4
rlington Way SK9 59 F3

Armadale Cl SK3 240 F1
Armett St SK11 112 B4
Armitage Rd WA14 238 D3
Armitstead Rd CW11 174 C2
Armour Ave WA2 8 A1
Armoury St SK3 240 E4
Armstrong Cl Audlem CW3 229 F2
Warrington WA3 9 E2
Armthorpe Dr L66 69 E3
Arncliffe Dr WA5 6 C3
Arndale WA7 49 F3
Arnesby Ave M33 242 E7
Arnfield Rd SK3 240 D1
Arnhem Cres WA2 16 B4
Arnhem Way CH3 142 A3
Arnold Pl WA8 22 B4
Arnold St Nantwich CW5 204 C3
Stockport SK3 240 E3
Arnold's Cres CH4 139 D2
Arnside Ave
Congleton CW12 156 A1
Haydock WA11 1 A3
Arnside Cl Gatley SK8 239 B4
High Lane SK6 37 F4
Winsford CW7 126 B1
Arnside Dr SK14 241 C8
Arnside Gr Sale M33 242 B8
Warrington WA4 16 A1
Arpley Rd WA1 16 A2
Arpley St WA1 16 A2
Arradon Ct CH2 118 C3
Arran Ave
Ellesmere Port L65 70 B1
Sale M33 242 C5
Arran Cl
Holmes Chapel CW4 130 B1
Warrington WA2 9 D1
Arran Dr WA6 74 B3
Arrivals Way M90 33 D4
Arron Pl CW2 189 E2
Arrowcroft Rd CH3 119 F3
Arrowsmith Dr ST7 193 D2
Arrowsmith Rd WA11 1 C4
Arthill La WA14 20 A1
Arthog Dr WA15 31 F4
Arthog Rd WA15 31 F4
Arthur Ave L65 70 B3
Arthur St Blacon CH1 118 A1
Crewe CW2 190 B1
Hyde SK14 241 C5
Lostock CW9 80 A1
Runcorn WA7 23 D1
Warrington WA2 16 A3
Artists La SK10 85 E4
Artle Rd CW2 206 B4
Arundel Ave SK7 36 B4
Arundel Cl Knutsford WA16 82 A4
Macclesfield SK10 87 F1
Wistaston CW2 205 F4
Arundel Ct L65 70 C2
Arundel Rd SK8 35 D3
Arundel St OL6 242 B3
Arundell Cl WA5 6 C3
Ascol Dr CW9 80 B2
Ascot Ave WA7 49 D3
Ascot Cl Congleton CW12 156 B2
Macclesfield SK10 87 E2
Warrington, Grappenhall WA4 17 E1
Warrington, Martinscroft WA1 17 F4
Ascot Dr L66 69 F2
Ash Ave Altrincham WA14 238 A5
Cheadle SK8 239 E5
Irlam M44 11 E3
Newton-le-W WA12 2 B1
Ash Cl Ellesmere Port L66 69 F1
Holmes Chapel CW4 130 B2
Malpas SY14 213 E3
Tarporley CW6 146 B1
Ash Gr Altrincham WA15 238 F7
Altrincham, Rosehill WA14 238 C1
Cheadle SK8 34 A4
Chester CH4 141 D3
Congleton CW12 156 A2
Ellesmere Port L66 69 E3
Goldborne WA3 3 D4
Knutsford WA16 57 E1
Macclesfield SK11 112 B2
Middlewich CW10 151 E4
Nantwich CW5 204 C2
Rode Heath ST7 193 F4
Runcorn WA7 49 E4
Stalybridge SK15 242 C3
Warrington WA4 16 B2
Weaverham CW8 102 C4
Widnes WA8 22 B4
Wilmslow SK9 34 B2
Ash Grove Cty Prim Sch SK11 112 B2
Ash Hay La CH2 96 B1
Ash House La CW8 77 E4
Ash La Appleton WA4 26 C4
Widnes L26, WA8 22 A4
Ash Lawn Ct CH2 118 B2
Ash Priors WA8 12 B2
Ash Rd Crewe CW1 190 B3
Cuddington CW8 101 F1
Elton CH2 72 B2
Haydock WA11 1 C4
Hollins Green WA3 11 D1
Lymm WA13 18 B2
Partington M31 11 E2
Penketh WA5 14 C2
Poynton SK12 36 C2
Winwick WA2 8 A3
Ash St Northwich CW9 79 D1
Stockport SK3 240 B4
Ash Terr SK11 112 B2
Ash Way L60 41 D3

Ashbank CW9 104 B4
Ashberry Cl SK9 60 B4
Ashberry Dr WA4 27 D3
Ashbourne Ave
Cheadle SK8 239 F6
Runcorn WA7 49 D3
Ashbourne Cl CH1 94 C4
Ashbourne Dr SK6 37 F3
Ashbourne Mews SK11 111 F4
Ashbourne Rd
Great Sankey WA5 15 D3
Hazel Grove SK7 36 C4
Ashbrook Ave WA7 49 F2
Ashbrook Cl SK8 239 B1
Ashbrook Cres WA2 16 B4
Ashbrook Dr SK10 87 D3
Ashbrook Rd Bollington SK10 87 F4
Nether Alderley SK10 85 F3
Ashburn Gr SK4 240 D7
Ashburn Rd SK4 240 D7
Ashburton Rd SK3 240 E1
Ashbury Cl WA7 24 B1
Ashbury Dr WA11 1 B4
Ashby Dr 15 CW11 174 B3
Ashby Pl CH2 237 F4
Ashcroft SK9 59 F3
Ashcroft Ave CW2 206 A2
Ashcroft Rd WA13 19 D2
Ashdale Cl ST7 193 E3
Ashdale Dr SK8 239 B2
Ashdend Cty Prim Sch SK9 59 F3
Ashdene Rd SK9 59 F3
Ashdown La WA3 10 A3
Ashdown Rd
Manchester SK4 240 C7
Ollerton WA16 82 C3
Ashenhurst Rd ST7 193 F2
Ashenough Rd ST7 210 B3
Ashfield Cl WA13 19 D2
Ashfield Cres Bebington L62 43 E4
Blacon CH1 117 E3
Cheadle SK8 239 D6
Ashfield Dr SK10 87 D1
Ashfield Gr M44 11 F3
Ashfield Rd
Altrincham WA15 238 E3
Bebington L62 43 E4
Cheadle SK8 239 D5
Cheadle SK8 239 D6
Ellesmere Port L65 70 B3
Sale M33 242 B7
Ashfield Rd N L65 70 B3
Ashford Cl SK9 34 B2
Ashford Rd SK9 60 A2
Ashford Way WA8 13 E1
Ashgate La CW9 79 F3
Ashgrove CW7 149 E4
Ashlands Frodsham WA6 74 B4
Sale M33 242 A7
Ashlea Dr CW5 205 F3
Ashleigh Cl CH4 140 C3
Ashley CE Contr Prim Sch WA15 31 F3
Ashley Cl Haslington CW1 191 E3
Warrington WA4 17 E2
Ashley Ct Altrincham WA15 238 E1
Holt LL13 196 B4
Ashley Dr
Cheadle Hulme SK7 35 E3
Hartford CW8 103 D3
Ashley Gdns Clutton CH3 182 B1
High Lane SK6 37 E4
3 Hyde SK14 241 E5
Ashley Grange CW9 103 F2
Ashley Mews 2 SK14 241 E5
Ashley Mill La WA14 31 E4
Ashley Mill Rd N WA14 31 F4
Ashley Rd Altrincham WA15 238 E2
Ashley WA15 31 F4
Mere WA16 56 B4
Rostherne WA14 31 E4
Runcorn WA7 23 E1
Wilmslow SK9 34 A1
Ashley Ret Pk WA8 23 D4
Ashley Sch WA8 12 B1
Ashley St SK14 241 E8
Ashley Sta WA15 31 F3
Ashley Way WA8 23 D4
Ashley Way W WA8 22 C4
Ashleys The SK4 240 B7
Ashmead Cl ST7 193 F2
Ashmead Mews ST7 193 F2
Ashmore Ave SK3 239 F7
Ashmore Cl
Middlewich CW10 151 E3
Warrington WA3 10 A2
Ashmore's La ST7 193 E2
Ashmuir Cl Blacon CH1 117 F2
Crewe CW1 190 A3
Ashness Dr SK7 35 F4
Ashridge St WA7 22 C2
Ashton Ave
Altrincham WA14 238 E6
Macclesfield SK10 86 B1
Ashton Cl Bebington L62 43 F2
Congleton CW12 157 D1
Frodsham WA6 49 E1
Middlewich CW10 151 E3
Runcorn WA7 48 C3
Ashton Dr WA6 49 E1
Ashton Hayes Cty Prim Sch CH3 121 F4
Ashton La Ashton CH3 121 F3
Sale M33 242 A7
Ashton Rd Hyde SK14 241 E8
Manley WA6 99 F2
Newton-le-W WA12 2 B3
Norley WA6 100 A2

Ashton St WA2 16 A3
Ashton's Green Sch WA9 1 A2
Ashton-under-Lyne Sixth Form Coll OL6 242 B3
Ashtree Cl Neston L64 67 D4
Prestbury SK10 87 E4
Ashtree Croft L64 68 A4
Ashtree Dr L64 67 D4
Ashtree Farm Ct L64 68 A4
Ashurst Dr SK3 & SK8 240 B1
Ashville Ct CW2 206 A4
Ashville Ind Est WA7 49 F2
Ashville Rd WA7 49 F2
Ashwood WA14 31 D4
Ashwood Ave Goldborne WA3 3 E4
Warrington WA1 16 C4
Ashwood Cl Barnton CW8 78 A2
Ellesmere Port L66 69 E1
Ashwood Cres CW8 78 A2
Ashwood Ct CH2 119 D2
Ashwood La CH2 96 A3
Ashwood Rd SK12 38 B3
Ashworth Cl WA14 238 B1
Ashworth Pk WA16 81 F4
Askerbank La SK11 159 D1
Askett Cl WA11 1 B4
Askrigg Ave L66 69 D3
Aspen Cl Ellesmere Port L66 69 F1
Heswall L60 41 E4
Kidsgrove ST7 195 F2
Stockport SK4 240 A5
Aspen Gn M34 241 A6
Aspen Gr Saughall CH1 117 D4
Warrington WA1 17 D4
Aspen Way Chester CH2 119 D2
High Lane SK6 38 A4
Aspen Wood SK14 241 F7
Aspens The
Cuddington CW8 101 E3
Gatley SK8 239 A6
Aspinall Cl WA2 9 D2
Aspull Cl WA3 9 E2
Asquith Cl CW1 191 E3
Assheton Wlk L24 21 F1
Astbury CE Aided Prim Sch CW12 178 A4
Astbury Cl
2 Altrincham WA15 238 E6
Goldborne WA3 4 A4
Kidsgrove ST7 195 E2
Astbury Cres SK3 240 D2
Astbury Dr CW8 78 A2
Astbury Lane Ends CW12 178 C4
Astbury St CW12 156 B1
Aster Cres WA7 49 F3
Aster Rd WA11 1 C4
Aster Wlk M31 11 F1
Astle Ct SK11 84 A2
Astley Cl Warrington WA4 16 A2
Widnes WA8 12 B2
Astley Ct M44 11 F4
Astley Gr SK15 242 C3
Astley Rd Irlam M44 11 F4
Stalybridge SK15 242 C2
Astley St Hyde SK14 241 C8
Stockport SK3 & SK4 240 E5
Astmoor Bridge La WA7 23 F1
Astmoor Cty Prim Sch WA7 23 F1
Astmoor East Interchange WA7 24 A2
Astmoor Ind Est WA7 23 F2
Astmoor La WA7 23 F1
Aston Ave CW7 126 A1
Aston Cl SK3 240 C2
Aston Ct WA1 9 E1
Aston Cty Prim Sch WA7 50 B1
Aston Fields Rd WA7 50 C2
Aston Gn WA7 50 C3
Aston La
Aston (nr Runcorn) WA7 50 C1
Runcorn WA7 50 C3
Sutton WA7 50 B1
Woore CW3 232 C1
Aston La N WA7 50 C2
Aston La S WA7 50 C2
Aston Rd ST5 210 B1
Aston Way
Middlewich CW10 128 C1
11 Wilmslow SK9 34 B3
Astule Dr SK11 112 A4
Atcherley Cl CW5 218 C4
Atherton Cty Inf Sch L65 69 F3
Atherton La M44 11 F3
Atherton Rd L65 69 F3
Atherton St SK3 240 D4
Athey St SK11 112 B4
Athlone Ave SK8 240 C1
Athlone Rd WA2 8 A1
Athol Cl L62 43 F3
Athol Dr L62 43 F3
Athol Rd SK7 35 E3
Athol St SK4 240 D7
Atholl Ave CW2 190 B1
Atholl Cl SK10 87 D1
Athy Cl WA12 1 C2
Atkinson Rd M33 242 A7
Atlanta Ave M90 33 D4
Atlantic Bsns Ctr WA14 238 C7
Atlantic St WA14 238 B6
Attenbury's La WA14 238 E8
Attenbury's Pk Est WA14 238 E8
Atterbury Cl WA8 12 B1
Attlee Ave WA3 5 D2
Attwood Cl CW1 191 E2
Attwood St ST7 195 D1
Aubourn Cl WA8 12 B2
Auburn Ave SK14 241 E5
Auckery Ave L66 69 E2

Auckland Rd CH1 117 E2
Audie Murphy Rd WA5 15 D3
Audlem Cl WA7 49 F2
Audlem Dr CW9 104 A3
Audlem Rd Audlem CW3 230 A4
Hatherton CW5 219 E2
Nantwich CW5 204 C2
Woore CW3 232 A1
Audlem St James' CE Contr Prim Sch CW3 230 A3
Audley Cres CH4 141 F3
Audley Rd Alsager ST7 193 F1
Audley ST7 210 A1
Barthomley CW2 208 C3
Kidsgrove ST7 210 A3
Newcastle-u-L ST7 210 A1
Audley St
Ashton-u-L OL6 242 B2
Crewe CW1 190 B3
Audley St W CW1 190 B3
Audre Cl WA5 14 B3
Aughton Way CH4 139 E2
Augusta Dr SK10 87 D2
Austell Rd M22 33 E4
Austen Cl 2 CW11 174 B3
Austin Cl CW7 149 E3
Austin St CW9 79 E1
Austral Ave WA1 17 E4
Australia La WA4 17 E1
Autumn Ave WA16 57 E1
Avalon Dr M20 239 C8
Avebury Cl Goldborne WA3 3 F4
Widnes WA8 13 F2
Avens Rd M31 11 F2
Avenue St 3 SK1 240 F6
Avenue The
Alderley Edge SK9 60 A1
Alsager ST7 193 E2
Altrincham WA15 31 F4
Bebington L62 43 E4
Comberbach CW9 78 B4
Gatley SK8 239 A1
Great Barrow CH3 120 C4
High Legh WA16 29 E3
Kidsgrove ST7 194 C1
Lymm WA13 18 B1
Marston CW9 79 D2
Newton-le-W WA12 2 B2
Sandbach CW11 174 C4
Tarporley CW6 146 B1
Avery Cl WA2 8 C1
Avery Cres WA11 1 B4
Avery Rd WA11 1 B4
Avery Sq WA11 1 B4
Aviemore Dr WA2 9 D2
Avocet Cl Newton-le-W WA12 2 B2
Warrington WA2 8 B2
Avocet Dr Altrincham WA14 238 B8
Winsford CW7 149 E3
Avon WA8 12 A1
Avon Ave WA5 14 C2
Avon Cl Kidsgrove ST7 195 D1
Macclesfield SK10 87 D1
Neston L64 66 C3
Avon Ct ST7 193 E3
Avon Dr Congleton CW12 156 C1
Crewe CW1 191 D3
Avon Rd Altrincham WA15 31 F4
Cheadle SK8 34 B4
Culcheth WA3 5 D1
Avon St SK3 240 E3
Avon Wlk CW7 127 D1
Avondale L65 70 A1
Avondale Ave L62 43 F3
Avondale Dr WA8 12 A1
Avondale Rd Haydock WA11 1 B4
Stockport SK3 240 C4
Avondale Sch SK3 240 B3
Avonlea Cl CH4 140 C3
Avonside Way SK11 112 B3
Avro Way WA15 32 C4
Axminster Wlk SK7 35 F4
Aycliffe Wlk 5 WA8 22 B4
Aylesbury Cl
Ellesmere Port L66 69 E2
Macclesfield SK10 87 E2
Aylesby Cl WA16 57 D1
Aylsham Cl WA8 12 B2
Aylwin Dr M33 242 C5
Ayrshire Way CW12 157 D1
Aysgarth Av CW1 173 D1
Aysgarth Ave Cheadle SK8 239 C6
Romiley SK6 241 D4
Ayshford Cl WA14 238 B6
Azalea Gr WA7 49 F2

Babbage Rd CH5 116 A2
Babbacombe Rd WA5 14 C2
Bache Ave CH2 118 B3
Bache Dr CH2 118 B3
Bache Hall Ct CH2 118 B3
Bache Hall Est CH2 118 B3
Bache Sta CH2 118 B3
Bachefield Ave CH3 142 A3
Bachelor's La CH3 142 A4
Back Adcroft St 4 SK1 240 F3
Back Booth St WA12 2 A2
Back Bridge St WA12 2 A2
Back Brook Pl WA4 16 C2
Back Crosland Terr WA6 73 D1
Back Cross La CW12 179 D4
Back Eastford Rd WA4 16 A1
Back Eddisbury Rd
Macclesfield SK10 113 E4
Rainow SK10 113 E4

eech La Barnton CW8 78 A2
Eaton CW6 147 D3
Macclesfield SK10 87 E1
Norley WA6 75 F1
Romiley SK6 241 C2
Wilmslow SK9 60 A3
eech Lawn WA14 238 C4
eech Rd Alderley Edge SK9 60 A2
Altrincham WA15 238 E3
Common Side CW6 124 B1
Heswall L60 41 E4
High Lane SK6 37 F4
Runcorn WA7 49 E4
Sale M33 242 D6
Stockport SK2 & SK3 240 F2
Sutton WA7 50 A2
Warrington WA4 26 B4
Whaley Bridge SK23 65 F4
eech Rise Crowton CW8 76 A1
Crowton CW8 76 B1
Whaley Bridge SK23 65 E3
eech St Hyde SK14 241 D7
Middlewich CW10 128 B1
eech St W CW1 190 B2
eech Tree Cl CW5 205 E3
eech View Rd WA6 75 E1
eechcroft Ave CW2 206 A4
eechcroft Dr L65 70 A1
eeches The
Altrincham WA14 238 C2
Chester CH2 119 D3
Helsby WA6 73 E2
Nantwich CW5 204 C3
eechfield
Altrincham WA14 238 C3
Moulton CW9 126 C4
eechfield Ave SK9 59 F3
eechfield Cl L60 41 D4
eechfield Dr CW10 128 A1
eechfield Gdns CW8 103 D3
eechfield Rd
Alderley Edge SK9 85 D4
Cheadle Hulme SK8 35 D4
Ellesmere Port L65 70 A3
Stockport SK3 240 F1
Warrington WA4 17 D1
eechfields CW7 150 A4
eechlands Ave CH3 119 D1
eechmill Dr WA3 4 C2
eechmoore WA4 25 D3
eechmuir CH1 117 F2
eechtree Farm Cl WA16 29 E4
eechtree La WA13 29 D4
eechurst Rd SK8 240 B1
eechway Bollington SK10 88 A4
Chester CH2 118 B3
High Lane SK6 37 F4
Wilmslow SK9 60 A3
eechways WA4 26 B3
eechways Dr L64 66 B4
eechwood
Altrincham WA14 238 B1
Knutsford WA16 57 E1
eechwood Ave
Great Sankey WA5 14 C3
Hartford CW8 103 D3
Newton-le-W WA12 2 B2
3 Reddish SK5 240 F8
Romiley SK6 241 D2
Runcorn WA7 49 F3
Stalybridge SK15 242 F4
Warrington WA1 16 C4
eechwood Cty Prim Sch
Crewe CW1 190 B3
Runcorn WA7 49 F3
eechwood Dr Alsager ST7 193 D2
Eaton (nr Congleton) CW12 156 C4
Ellesmere Port L66 69 E1
Higher Wincham CW9 79 F3
Wilmslow SK9 60 C4
eechwood Gr SK8 35 D4
eechwood La
Culcheth WA3 4 B2
Stalybridge SK15 242 F4
eechwood Mews SK10 87 E1
eechwood Rd
Bebington L62 43 E4
Broughton CH4 140 C3
eecroft Cl WA5 7 E1
eeley St SK14 241 E6
eeston Ave WA15 238 F6
eeston Brow SK10 88 A4
eeston Castle CW6 167 F2
eeston Cl Bollington SK10 63 E1
Holmes Chapel CW4 130 A2
Middlewich CW10 151 E3
Warrington WA3 9 E2
eeston Ct WA7 24 B2
eeston Dr Alsager ST7 193 E2
Knutsford WA16 82 A4
Winsford CW7 149 E4
eeston Gn L66 69 F3
eeston Gr SK3 240 E1
eeston Mount SK10 63 E1
eeston Rd Broughton CH4 139 D2
Higher Kinnerton CH4 161 D4
Wilmslow SK9 34 B3
eeston St CW8 103 F4
eeston Terr SK11 111 F3
eeston View CH4 141 F4
eggarman's La WA16 82 A4
eilby Rd WA11 1 C4
elfry Cl SK9 60 B4
elfry Dr SK10 87 E2
elgrave Ave Alsager ST7 193 E3
Broughton CH4 140 C3
Congleton CW12 156 B2
Warrington WA1 16 C4
Belgrave Cl Dodleston CH4 162 A3
Goldborne WN7 4 B4
Widnes WA8 13 F2
Belgrave Cty Inf Sch CH4 141 D3
Belgrave Dr L65 69 F3
Belgrave Pl CH4 237 E1
Belgrave Rd
Altrincham WA14 238 C3
Chester CH3 142 A4
Crewe CW2 190 A1
Irlam M44 11 E3
Macclesfield SK11 112 B2
Northwich CW9 104 A2
Sale M33 242 A6
Belgrave St CH2 237 F3
Belgravia Gdns WA15 31 F4
Bell Ave SK11 112 C2
Bell House Rd WA8 13 E1
Bell La WA4 17 F2
Bell Meadow Ct CW6 146 B1
Bellaport Rd TF9 236 A2
Bellard Dr CH2 119 D2
Belldale Cl SK4 240 A6
Belle Vue Terr CW11 175 D3
Bellemonte Rd WA6 74 B3
Belleville Ave M22 33 F4
Bellhouse La
Higher Walton WA4 25 E4
Warrington WA4 17 E1
Bellingham Dr WA7 49 D4
Bellsfield Cl WA13 18 C1
Bellvue La CH3 119 F2
Belmont Ave
Macclesfield SK10 86 B1
Sandbach CW11 175 D4
Warrington WA4 16 C2
Belmont Cl SK4 240 E7
Belmont Cres WA5 15 D3
Belmont Hall
(Boarding Sch) CW9 53 F1
Belmont Rd
Altrincham WA15 238 E2
Bramhall SK7 35 F3
Gatley SK8 239 B6
Great Budworth CW9 53 F1
Northwich CW9 104 B4
Sale M33 242 A8
Widnes WA8 13 E1
Belmont Sh Ctr SK4 240 E7
Belmont St SK4 240 E7
Belmont Way SK4 240 E7
Belvedere Cl WA6 49 E1
Belvedere Dr CH1 117 F2
Belvedere Rd WA12 2 A3
Belvedere Terr ST7 193 F4
Belvoir Rd Warrington WA4 26 A4
Widnes WA8 13 D1
Bembridge Cl
Great Sankey WA5 14 B4
Widnes WA8 12 C2
Bembridge Ct CW10 151 E4
Bemrose Ave WA14 238 C6
Ben Nevis Dr L66 68 C3
Benbow St M33 242 B7
Benbrook Gr 12 SK9 34 B1
Benbrook Way SK11 111 F1
Bendee Ave L64 67 D4
Bendee Rd L64 67 D4
Bengal St SK3 240 E4
Benja Fold SK7 35 F3
Benjamins Way ST7 209 F1
Bennet Cl L64 68 A4
Bennet Rd CW9 104 B3
Bennett Ave WA1 16 C3
Bennett Cl 4 SK3 240 C4
Bennett St Stalybridge SK15 242 D1
3 Stockport SK3 240 C4
Warrington WA1 16 A3
Bennett's La
Higher Kinnerton CH4 161 D4
Widnes WA8 13 F1
Bennetts La SK11 158 C3
Benson Rd WA3 9 E2
Benson Wlk 6 SK9 34 B1
Bent La Astbury CW12 178 A4
Crowton CW8 101 E4
Culcheth WA3 5 D1
Partington WA13 19 E4
Bentham Ave WA2 8 B2
Bentham Rd WA3 5 D1
Bentinck Rd WA14 238 C4
Bentinck St WA7 22 C2
Bentley Dr CW1 191 D3
Bentley Gr CW7 149 E3
Bentley's Farm La WA4 52 C3
Bentleys The SK5 240 F7
Benton Dr CH2 118 B2
Bentside Rd SK12 38 B3
Benty Heath La
Thornton Hough L64 42 C2
Willaston L64 43 D2
Beresford St WA1 16 C4
Berisford Cl WA15 238 E7
Berkeley Ave ST7 193 E3
Berkeley Cl Goldborne WA3 4 A4
Hyde SK14 241 D5
Berkeley Cres Hyde SK14 241 D5
Wistaston CW2 206 A4
Berkeley Ct WA7 24 B2
Berkeley Rise CW7 149 D4
Berkley Dr CH4 141 E3
Berkshire Cl SK10 86 C1
Berkshire Dr
Congleton CW12 156 B2
Irlam M44 11 E3
Warrington WA1 17 F4
Berlin Rd SK3 240 D2
Bernard Ave WA4 26 B4
Bernisdale Rd WA16 57 F2
Bernsdale Cl CH5 116 A2
Berristal Rd SK10 88 C2
Berry Cl Ellesmere Port L66 69 E2
Wilmslow SK9 60 A3
Berry Dr L66 69 E2
Berry Rd WA8 12 B1
Berrycroft La SK6 241 A3
Berrystead CW8 103 D2
Bertram St
Newton-le-W WA12 2 A2
Sale M33 242 E6
Berwick Ave L62 43 F2
Berwick Cl Macclesfield SK10 86 C1
Warrington WA1 17 F3
Berwick Ct CW4 130 A1
Berwick Gdns L66 69 D3
Berwick Gr L66 69 D3
Berwick Rd L66 69 D3
Berwyn Ave SK8 240 B1
Berwyn Cl L66 69 D3
Berwyn Gr WA9 1 A2
Bessancourt CW4 130 B2
Bessemer Rd M44 11 F3
Beswick St SK11 112 A4
Beswicks La Lindow End SK9 59 E2
Norton in Hales TF9 236 B1
Beswicks Rd CW8 78 C1
Betchton Cres CW11 175 E4
Betchton Rd CW11 175 F1
Betchworth Cres WA7 49 E3
Betchworth Way SK10 87 E2
Bethesda Sage Sch SK8 239 D3
Betjeman Cl WA4 16 C2
Betjeman Way CW1 190 C3
Betley Cl CW9 104 A3
Betley St CW1 190 B2
Betleymere Rd SK8 239 F4
Betsyfield Dr WA3 9 D4
Bettisfield Ave L62 43 E3
Betty's La CW6 168 B1
Bevan Ave ST7 210 C3
Bevan Cl WA5 15 E3
Beverley Ave Appleton WA4 26 B4
Denton M34 241 A6
Beverley Dr L60 41 D3
Beverley Rd WA5 15 E3
Beverley Way
Ellesmere Port L66 69 D4
Macclesfield SK10 87 E2
Bevin Ave WA3 5 D2
Bevyl Rd L64 41 D1
Bewley Ct CH3 142 A4
Bewsey Farm Cl WA5 15 E4
Bewsey Ind Est WA2 16 A4
Bewsey Rd WA5 15 F3
Bewsey St WA2 16 A3
Bexhill Ave
Altrincham WA15 238 F6
Warrington WA2 8 A2
Bexington Dr CW1 190 A4
Bexton Ave CW7 126 A1
Bexton Cty Prim Sch WA16 81 F4
Bexton La WA16 82 A4
Bexton Rd WA16 56 C1
Bibby Ave WA1 16 C3
Bibby St ST7 193 F4
Bickerton Ave WA6 74 B4
Bickerton CE Contr
Prim Sch SY14 200 A4
Bickerton Cl WA3 9 E2
Bickerton Rd WA14 238 B6
Bickerton Way CW9 103 F2
Bickley Cl
Hough Common CW2 206 C1
Runcorn WA7 23 E1
Warrington WA2 8 C2
Bickley Town La SY14 214 C3
Bicknell Cl WA5 15 D4
Bida La CW12 179 D4
Biddulph Common Rd
CW12 179 F4
Biddulph Grange Ctry Pk
ST8 179 F2
Biddulph Grange Hospl
ST8 179 F2
Biddulph Park Rd ST6 179 F3
Biddulph Rd Biddulph ST7 195 F3
Congleton CW12 179 D4
Kidsgrove ST7 195 F3
Biddulph St CW12 179 E4
Biddy's La SK10 88 A1
Bideford Rd WA5 14 C2
Bidston Cl CH2 118 B3
Bidston Dr SK9 34 C1
Bidston Gn L66 69 E2
Bidvale Way CW1 190 B4
Big Field La CW6 146 A4
Biggin Ct WA2 8 C1
Bignall End Rd ST7 210 A2
Billington Ave WA12 2 B3
Billington Cl WA5 14 C4
Billington Rd WA8 12 A2
Bilson Dr SK3 240 B3
Bilton Cl WA8 13 F1
Bilton Way CW1 189 F3
Bings Rd SK23 65 F4
Bingswood Ave SK23 65 F4
Bingswood Ind Est SK23 65 F4
Bingswood Rd SK23 65 F4
Binney Rd CW9 104 A4
Binns St SK15 242 B1
Binyon Way CW1 191 D2
Birch Ave Alsager ST7 193 F1
Crewe CW1 190 C3
Irlam M44 11 E3
Macclesfield SK10 87 D1
3 Manchester SK4 240 B8
Birch Ave continued
Romiley SK6 241 D2
Sale M33 242 B5
Warrington WA2 8 A2
Wilmslow SK9 59 F3
Winsford CW7 127 D1
Birch Brook Rd WA13 19 D3
Birch Cl Crewe CW1 190 C3
Holmes Chapel CW4 130 B2
Birch Cres WA12 1 C2
Birch Ct CW12 155 F2
Birch Fold CW4 107 D1
Birch Gdns CW11 175 E3
Birch Gr Ellesmere Port L66 70 A1
Higher Wincham CW9 79 F3
Knutsford WA16 57 E1
Lostock CW9 105 D4
Warrington, Bruche WA1 16 C4
Warrington, Latchford WA4 16 B2
Birch Heath La CH3 142 C4
Birch Heath Rd CW6 168 B4
Birch House Rd ST5 210 B1
Birch La
Hough Common CW2 206 C1
Winsford CW10 127 F1
Birch Rd Audley ST7 209 F1
Chester CH4 140 C3
Congleton CW12 155 F2
Gatley SK8 239 A5
Haydock WA11 1 C4
Partington M31 11 E2
Poynton SK12 36 C1
Runcorn WA7 49 E4
Widnes WA8 13 D2
Birch Rise CH2 118 B3
Birch Tree Ave SK7 37 D4
Birch Tree Cl WA14 238 C1
Birch Tree Ct CH2 237 F4
Birch Tree La Antrobus WA4 53 D3
Goostrey CW4 107 E1
The Bank ST7 195 D4
Birch Tree Rd WA3 3 F4
Birch Way SK10 86 C3
Birchall Ave WA3 4 C2
Birchall Moss La CW5 219 F1
Birchall St WA3 9 D4
Birchall Wlk CW2 206 B4
Birchdale WA14 238 C2
Birchdale Ave SK8 239 B2
Birchdale Cres WA4 26 B4
Birchdale Rd Appleton WA4 26 B4
Warrington WA1 17 D4
Birchen Rd L26 21 D4
Birchenwood Rd ST7 195 F1
Birches Cl L60 41 D4
Birches Croft Dr SK10 86 C1
Birches La Lach Dennis CW9 105 D4
Lostock CW9 105 D4
Birches The Broughton CH4 139 D2
Crewe CW2 206 B4
Neston L64 41 F1
Birches Way ST7 195 D1
Birchfield Ave
Rode Heath ST7 193 F4
Widnes WA8 13 D1
Birchfield Mews 3 SK14 241 D6
Birchfield Rd Cheadle SK3 240 A3
Great Sankey WA5 15 D3
Lymm WA13 19 D2
Widnes WA8 13 D2
Birchfields WA15 238 F1
Birchgate Cl SK10 86 C1
Birchin Cl CW5 205 D3
Birchin La CW5 205 D3
Birchinall Cl SK11 112 A4
Birchmuir CH1 117 F2
Birchmuir Cl CW1 190 A3
Birchvale Ave SK6 241 D3
Birchway Bollington SK10 88 A4
Cheadle Hulme SK7 35 E4
Heswall L60 41 E3
High Lane SK6 37 F4
Birchways WA4 26 C3
Birchwood Bvd WA3 9 E1
Birchwood CE Aided
Prim Sch WA3 9 F2
Birchwood Cl
Ellesmere Port L66 69 E1
Elton CH2 72 B2
Stockport SK4 240 A5
Birchwood
Comm High Sch WA3 9 E2
Birchwood Dr
Nantwich CW5 204 C3
Peover WA16 106 B4
Wilmslow SK9 60 B4
Birchwood Park Ave WA3 9 E3
Birchwood Sta WA3 9 F1
Bird Hall La SK3 & SK8 240 B2
Bird Hall Rd SK8 240 C1
Bird's La CW6 186 A4
Birds La CH3 166 C1
Birdwell Dr WA5 15 D3
Birkdale Ave L63 43 E3
Birkdale Cl Bramhall SK7 35 F4
Macclesfield SK10 87 E2
Birkdale Ct CW9 104 A4
Birkdale Dr ST7 195 E2
Birkdale Rd Penketh WA5 14 C2
Widnes WA8 13 D3
Birkenhead Rd L64 42 C1
Birkenhead St CW9 104 B4
Birkett Ave L65 70 B1
Birkin Cl WA16 57 E2
Birkinheath La WA14 31 D2
Birley Cl WA15 238 F7
Birley St WA12 2 B2
Birstall Ct WA7 49 E4
Birtles Cl Cheadle SK8 240 A1
Sandbach CW11 175 E4
Birtles La SK10 85 F1
Birtles Rd SK10 86 B1
Birtles Way 6 SK9 34 B3
Birtlespool Rd SK8 239 F4
Birtley Ct WA8 12 A1
Birtwistle Rd CW9 104 B3
Bishop Rd SK10 88 A4
Bishop Reeves Rd WA11 1 C4
Bishop St CH2 118 C2
Bishop's Cl Cheadle SK8 240 A1
Kidsgrove ST7 210 B4
Bishopdale Cl WA5 14 C4
Bishopgates Dr CW9 103 F2
Bishops' (Blue Coat)
CE (Aided) High Sch The
CH3 142 A4
Bishops Cl WA14 238 B1
Bishops Ct Broughton CH4 139 E2
Warrington WA2 7 F2
Bishops Gdns L65 70 A3
Bishops Way WA8 13 E2
Bishops Wood CW5 204 C1
Bishopsfield Ct CH2 118 C2
Bishopton Dr SK11 111 F4
Bispham Rd WA5 15 D2
Bittern Cl Poynton SK12 36 A2
Runcorn WA7 50 B4
Warrington WA2 8 B2
Bittern Gr SK10 87 D1
Bk Adcroft St SK1 240 F3
Bk Grosvenor St SK15 242 D1
Bk Knowl St SK15 242 E2
Bk Melbourne St SK15 242 D1
Black Denton's Pl WA8 13 E1
Black Diamond St CH2 237 E4
Black Firs Cty Prim Sch
CW12 155 F2
Black Firs La CW12 155 F2
Black Friars CH1 237 D2
Black La SK10 87 F1
Black Lion La L66 69 E3
Black Moss Rd WA14 20 C4
Black Park Rd SY13 226 B1
Black Rd SK11 112 C4
Blackacres Cl CW11 174 C3
Blackberry Cl WA14 238 B8
Blackboards La L66 69 D4
Blackbrook Cl WA8 12 B2
Blackbrooke Ave WA2 8 C1
Blackburn Cl WA3 3 F4
Blackburne Ave WA8 22 A3
Blackburne Cl WA2 9 E1
Blackcroft Ave CW8 78 A1
Blackden La Goostrey CW4 108 A2
Siddington SK11 132 C4
Blackden Wlk 9 SK9 34 B1
Blackdown Cl L66 69 D3
Blackeys La L64 66 C4
Blackhill La WA16 81 F4
Blackhurst Brow SK10 61 D1
Blackhurst St WA1 16 A3
Blackledge Cl WA2 9 D2
Blackshaw Cl CW12 157 D1
Blackshaw Dr WA5 7 D1
Blackshaw La SK9 59 F1
Blackshaw St
20 Macclesfield SK11 112 B4
4 Stockport SK3 240 E4
Blackthorn Cl
Broughton CH4 139 D2
Huntington CH3 142 A3
Blackthorn Pl ST5 210 C1
Blackthorn Wlk M31 11 E1
Blackthorne Ave CH1 95 D4
Blackwell Cl CW10 151 E3
Blacon Ave CH1 118 A3
Blacon Cty High Sch CH1 117 E2
Blacon Cty Inf Sch CH1 117 F3
Blacon Hall Cty Jun Sch
CH1 117 F3
Blacon Hall Rd CH1 117 F3
Blacon Point Rd CH1 117 F2
Blagg Ave CW5 204 B2
Blair Cl SK7 36 B4
Blair Dr WA8 12 A2
Blairgowrie Dr SK10 87 D2
Blaizefield Cl CW3 232 B1
Blake Cl Blacon CH1 117 F3
Wistaston CW2 189 F1
Blake La CW8 102 A1
Blake St CW12 156 B2
Blakeacre Rd L26 21 D3
Blakeden La CW7 148 C4
Blakeley Brow L63 43 D3
Blakeley Ct L63 43 D4
Blakeley Dene L63 43 D4
Blakeley Rd L63 43 D3
Blakelow Bank SK11 112 C3
Blakelow Cl CW10 151 D4
Blakelow Cres CW5 205 F2
Blakelow Rd SK11 112 C3
Blakely La WA16 58 C4
Blakemere Ave M33 242 E5
Blakemere Cl SY13 226 A1
Blakemere Ct L65 70 B4
Blakemere La WA6 100 B2
Blakemere Way CW11 174 C4
Blandford Ct SK15 242 D2
Blandford Dr SK11 111 F4
Blandford Rd
Great Sankey WA5 15 D3
Stockport SK4 240 C6
Blandford St SK15 242 D2

Bridge Rd WA1 17 E4
Bridge Row CW12 156 C2
Bridge St Broughton CH4 140 B4
Chester CH1 237 E2
Goldborne WA3 3 D4
Holt LL13 180 C1
Macclesfield SK11 112 B4
Neston L64 66 C4
Newton-le-W WA12 2 A2
Northwich CW9 79 F1
Runcorn WA7 23 D2
Stalybridge SK15 242 C1
Stockport SK1 240 F6
Warrington WA1 16 A3
Whaley Bridge SK23 65 F4
Wybunbury CW5 220 B4
Bridge St Row CH1 237 E2
Bridge Terr CH3 119 D1
Bridge View Cl WA8 23 D2
Bridgedown CW6 146 B1
Bridgefield Ave SK9 34 B1
Bridgefield St SK1 240 E6
Bridgeman Rd CH1 117 F2
Bridgeman St WA5 15 E2
Bridgemere CE Aided Prim Sch CW5 231 F4
Bridgemere Cl CW11 174 C4
Bridgemere Garden World CW5 232 A2
Bridgemere La CW5 219 F1
Bridgemere Way CW9 103 F2
Bridgend CH2 97 D1
Bridgend Cl WA8 12 B2
Bridges Rd L65 70 C3
Bridgeside Dr WA6 73 D2
Bridgestones CW12 156 B1
Bridgewater Ave WA4 16 C2
Bridgewater Cl Cheadle SK8 34 B4
Congleton CW12 157 D1
Bridgewater Cty High Sch (Lower Sch) WA4 26 B3
Bridgewater Cty High Sch Upper Sch & Sixth Form Coll WA4 26 B4
Bridgewater Dr CH3 119 E1
Bridgewater Mews WA4 26 B4
Bridgewater Pl CW7 126 A1
Bridgewater Rd WA14 238 D7
Bridgewater St Lymm WA13 18 C2
Runcorn WA7 23 D1
Sale M33 242 B7
Bridgeway East WA7 24 B1
Bridgeway West WA7 24 B1
Bridgewood Dr L66 69 E1
Bridgfield Cl SK6 37 F4
Bridgnorth Gr ST5 210 C1
Bridle Cl L62 43 F4
Bridle Hey CW5 204 C1
Bridle Pk L62 43 F4
Bridle Rd Bebington L62 43 F3
Crewe CW2 190 A2
Woodford SK7 35 F1
Bridle Way Ellesmere Port L66 69 E2
Woodford SK7 35 F1
Bridlemere Ct WA1 16 C4
Briedden Way L66 69 D3
Brien Ave WA14 238 E7
Brierley Cty Prim Sch CW1 190 B2
Brierley Rd CW12 157 D1
Brierley St Crewe CW1 190 B2
Stalybridge SK16 242 A1
Briers Cl WA2 8 C2
Brieryhurst Rd ST7 195 D2
Briggs Ave CW2 190 B1
Bright St Ashton-u-L OL6 242 A2
Crewe CW1 190 A3
Brighton Cres SK11 113 D2
Brighton Gr [1] Hyde SK14 241 E5
Sale M33 242 B7
Brighton Rd SK4 240 C5
Brighton Road Ind Est SK4 240 C5
Brighton St WA5 15 F3
Brights Ave ST7 195 D1
Brightwell Cl WA5 14 C3
Brimelow Cres WA5 14 C2
Brimstage Cl L60 41 E4
Brimstage Gn L60 41 E4
Brimstage Rd L60 41 E4
Brindley Ave Sale M33 242 C8
Warrington WA4 16 C2
Winsford CW7 126 B1
Brindley Cl ST7 194 C1
Brindley Gr [13] SK9 34 C1
Brindley Hall Rd
Burland CW5 202 C4
Faddiley CW5 186 C1
Brindley La CW11 153 E2
Brindley Pk [4] CW11 174 C2
Brindley Rd WA7 23 F2
Brindley St WA7 22 C2
Brindley Way
Congleton CW12 157 D1
Macclesfield SK11 112 B2
Brindleys Way ST7 209 F1
Brine Leas Cty High Sch CW5 204 C2
Brine Pits La CW5 218 C1
Brine Rd CW5 204 C2
Brinell Dr M44 11 F3
Brinksway SK3 240 C4
Brinksway Trad Est [1] SK3 240 C4
Brinley Cl L62 43 E3
Brinton Cl WA8 22 C4
Brisbane Cl SK7 35 F3
Brisbane Rd CH1 117 E2
Bristol Ave WA7 50 C3
Bristol Cl Blacon CH1 117 F3
Cheadle SK8 34 A4

Bristol Dr L66 69 F1
Bristow Cl WA5 15 D4
Britannia Rd M33 242 C7
Brittania Dr CW9 104 C4
Brittania Gdns WA6 73 D1
Brittania Rd WA6 73 D1
Brixham Ave SK8 34 C4
Brixham Wlk SK7 35 F4
Broad Hey SK6 241 D3
Broad La Altrincham WA15 32 A4
Appleton WA4 27 E4
Burtonwood WA5 1 B1
Heswall L60 40 B4
Holmes Chapel CW4 129 F1
Sproston Green CW4 129 F1
Stapeley CW5 205 D1
Broad Oak Ave
Broughton CH4 139 D2
Haydock WA11 1 A3
Penketh WA5 14 C2
Broad Oak La
Manchester M20 239 B8
Manchester M20 239 C8
Broad Oak Prim Sch M20 239 C8
Broad Rd M33 242 D7
Broad St CW1 190 B3
Broad Street Cty Inf Sch CW1 190 B3
Broad Wlk SK9 59 F4
Broadacre CW9 78 B3
Broadacres CW5 217 F2
Broadbent Ave WA4 16 C2
Broadbent St SK14 241 D8
Broadcar Rd SK11 113 E3
Broadfield Cl M34 241 A6
Broadfields WA7 50 B4
Broadheath Prim Sch WA14 238 C8
Broadheys La WA16 28 B3
Broadhurst Ave
Culcheth WA3 4 C1
Warrington WA5 15 E2
Broadhurst La CW12 156 B2
Broadhurst St SK3 240 F3
Broadlake L64 67 F4
Broadland Gdns L66 69 F1
Broadland Rd L66 69 F1
Broadleigh Way CW2 206 B4
Broadley Ave WA3 3 E4
Broadmead Chester CH3 119 E1
Heswall L60 41 E4
Broadoak Comp Sch M31 11 F1
Broadoak La High Legh WA16 29 E3
Mobberley WA16 57 F3
Broadoaks Rd M33 242 A6
Broadwalk SK10 87 D3
Broadway Altrincham WA15 32 A4
Barnton CW8 78 A2
Cheadle SK8 239 C4
Sale M33 242 A7
Widnes WA8 12 A1
Wilmslow SK9 60 A3
Broadway Ave SK8 239 D5
Broadway E CH2 118 C3
Broadway The CW5 204 C3
Broadway W CH2 118 B3
Broadways CW3 230 A2
Broadwood Cl SK6 37 F4
Broady Ct CW2 190 B1
Brock Gdns L24 21 F1
Brock Rd WA3 9 E2
Brockhurst St CW9 104 A4
Brockhurst Way CW9 104 A3
Brocklehurst Ave SK10 87 F1
Brocklehurst Ct SK10 87 E2
Brocklehurst Dr SK10 87 D4
Brocklehurst Way SK10 87 E2
Brockway E CH3 166 A1
Brockway W CH3 166 A1
Brockwell Cl [2] CW7 149 D4
Brodie Cl CH2 95 E1
Brogden Ave WA3 4 C2
Brogden Dr SK8 239 B5
Brogden Gr M33 242 A5
Brogden Terr M33 242 A5
Broken Banks [21] SK11 112 B4
Broken Cross SK11 111 F4
Broken Cross Cty Prim Sch SK11 111 F4
Brokencross Pl CW9 104 C4
Bromborough Golf Course L63 43 D3
Bromborough Rake Sta L62 43 E4
Bromborough Sta L63 43 E3
Bromborough Village Rd L62 43 F4
Bromleigh Ave SK8 239 B6
Bromley Ave WA3 3 E4
Bromley Cl Crewe CW1 189 F4
Heswall L60 40 C4
Warrington WA2 8 C2
Bromley Dr CW4 130 B1
Bromley Rd
Congleton CW12 156 C2
Macclesfield SK10 111 F4
Brompton Gdns WA5 15 F4
Brompton Rd SK4 240 A6
Brompton Way L66 69 F1
Bronington Ave L62 43 E3
Brook Acre Cty Prim Sch WA2 8 C1
Brook Ave Altrincham WA15 238 E6
Shavington CW2 206 B3
Warrington, Stockton Heath WA4 16 C1
Warrington, Westy WA4 16 C3
Wilmslow SK9 34 B2
Brook Bottom Rd SK22 39 D4

Brook Cl Altrincham WA15 238 E6
Crewe CW1 190 C2
Cronton WA8 12 B3
Brook Ct CW11 175 D3
Brook Dr Cheadle Hulme SK8 35 D4
Great Sankey WA5 15 D3
Kelsall CW6 122 B2
Brook End WA9 1 A1
Brook Farm Sch CW6 168 B4
Brook Furlong WA6 48 C1
Brook Gdns ST6 179 E1
Brook Hey L64 41 D1
Brook House Dr CW2 206 B4
Brook La Altrincham WA15 238 F6
Broughton CH5 139 E4
Burland CW5 203 E4
Chester CH2 118 C2
Knutsford WA16 57 D1
Northwich CW9 104 B4
Warrington WA3 18 A4
Wilmslow SK9 59 F2
Brook Lane Ind Est CW10 151 E4
Brook Lodge SK8 239 D4
Brook Pl WA4 16 C2
Brook Rd Cheadle SK8 239 D6
Ellesmere Port L66 69 E3
Lymm WA13 18 B2
Tarporley CW6 168 B4
Brook Side CW8 102 B4
Brook St Cheadle SK8 239 F6
Chester CH2 237 E3
Congleton CW12 156 C2
Crewe CW2 190 B2
Goldborne WA3 3 D4
Hyde SK14 241 E7
Knutsford WA16 57 D1
Macclesfield SK10 87 E1
Macclesfield SK11 112 B4
Macclesfield SK11 112 C4
Neston L64 66 C4
Northwich CW9 79 D1
Northwich CW9 79 F1
Runcorn WA7 23 D1
Sale M33 242 C7
Widnes WA8 13 D1
Brook Street Bridge CH2 237 F4
Brook Terr CW11 175 D2
Brook Way Great Sankey WA5 15 D3
Nantwich CW5 204 C2
Brook Well L64 66 C3
Brookdale WA8 12 A2
Brookdale Ave Denton M34 241 B6
Knutsford WA16 57 E1
Brookdale Pl CH1 237 E3
Brookdale Way CH3 143 D3
Brooke Ave CH2 118 B4
Brooke Dr SK9 34 B2
Brooke Way [11] SK9 34 B2
Brookes Ave CH4 139 D2
Brookfield CW1 191 E3
Brookfield Ave
Altrincham WA15 238 F8
Poynton SK12 36 B2
Romiley SK6 241 A4
Runcorn WA7 23 F1
Brookfield Cl Lymm WA13 18 B2
Tarporley CW6 168 B4
Brookfield Cres
Cheadle SK8 239 D4
Goostrey CW4 107 F1
Brookfield Dr Alsager ST7 193 E3
Chester CH2 118 C2
Holmes Chapel CW4 130 A2
Brookfield Gr OL6 242 A2
Brookfield La SK11 112 C4
Brookfield Park WA4 17 D1
Brookfield Rd Cheadle SK8 239 E5
Comberbach CW9 78 B4
Culcheth WA3 4 B2
Lymm WA13 18 B2
Brookfield St WA12 2 A2
Brookfields Sch WA8 13 E1
Brookhead Dr SK8 240 A2
Brookhead Jun Sch SK8 239 F5
Brookhouse Cl SK10 86 C1
Brookhouse La
Church Minshull CW10 172 B4
Congleton CW12 157 E1
Duddon CH3 144 B3
Whitley WA4 52 A1
Brookhouse Rd Alsager ST7 193 E2
Sandbach CW11 175 D3
Brookhurst Ave L63 43 E3
Brookhurst Cl L63 43 E3
Brookhurst Prim Sch L62 43 E3
Brookhurst Rd L63 43 E3
Brookkash Rd M22 34 A4
Brookland Ave CW2 205 F4
Brookland Dr CW11 175 F3
Brookland La WA9 1 A1
Brookland St WA1 16 C4
Brooklands Ave SK11 112 A4
Brooklands Cres M33 242 B5
Brooklands Dr
Goostrey CW4 107 F1
Northwich CW9 104 A2
Brooklands Gr CW1 190 A3
Brooklands Mews SK11 112 A4
Brooklands Rd
Congleton CW12 155 F1
Neston L64 41 E1
Sale M33 242 B5
Brooklands Sta M33 242 A5
Brooklands Station App M33 242 A5
Brookledge La SK10 62 C3
Brookln Pl SK8 239 D6
Brooklyn Cres SK8 239 D5

Brooklyn Dr
Ellesmere Port L65 69 F3
Lymm WA13 18 C2
Brooklyn Rd SK8 239 D5
Brooklyn St CW2 190 B1
Brookmere Cl CW11 174 C4
Brooks Ave SK14 241 E5
Brooks Dr WA15 32 B4
Brooks La Bosley SK11 135 F1
Middlewich CW10 128 B1
Brooks St SK1 240 F3
Brookside Ashton CH3 121 F4
Chester CH3 142 A4
Cuddington CW8 101 F2
Kingsley WA6 75 E1
Brookside Ave
Great Sankey WA5 15 D2
Lymm WA13 18 B2
Poynton SK12 36 C2
Sutton Lane Ends SK11 112 C1
Warrington WA4 16 B1
Brookside Cl Cheadle SK8 239 D4
Haydock WA11 1 A4
Brookside Ct SK10 87 D1
Brookside Cty Inf Sch L66 69 E2
Brookside Gn CW2 206 B4
Brookside La SK6 37 F4
Brookside Prim Sch SK6 37 F3
Brookside Rd
Congleton CW12 156 B2
Gatley SK8 239 A6
Brookside Terr CH2 237 F4
Brookside View WA11 1 A4
Brookside Way WA11 1 A4
Brookvale Ave N WA7 50 A3
Brookvale Ave S WA7 50 A3
Brookvale Cl WA5 6 C3
Brookvale Cty Comp Sch WA7 50 B3
Brookvale Cty Inf Sch WA7 50 A3
Brookvale Cty Jun Sch WA7 50 A3
Brookway WA15 238 F7
Brookway La WA9 1 A1
Brookwood Cl WA4 26 A4
Broom Ave WA4 26 C3
Broom Cres CH3 121 D1
Broom Field Cl SK9 60 C4
Broom La WA16 81 F1
Broom Rd Altrincham WA15 238 E3
Partington M31 11 F1
Broom St CW1 190 A3
Broom's La CW6 122 B3
Broome Ct WA7 50 A3
Broomehouse Ave M44 11 F4
Broomfield Cl SK11 84 A2
Broomfield La WA15 238 E3
Broomfield Rd SK4 240 C8
Broomfields Cty Jun Sch WA4 26 C4
Broomfields Rd WA4 26 B4
Broomfields Recn Ctr WA4 26 B4
Broomgrove La M34 241 A8
Broomheath La
Duddon CH3 144 B4
Tarvin CH3 121 E1
Tarvin, Broom Bank CH3 144 B4
Broomhill La
Brown Knowl CH3 199 E4
Great Barrow CH3 120 C4
Broomlands L60 40 C4
Broomsfield La CW8 78 A2
Broomville Ave M33 242 B6
Broseley Ave WA3 4 B2
Broseley La WA3 4 B3
Brotherton Cl L62 43 E4
Brough St W SK11 112 B4
Brougham St SK11 242 C1
Broughton Ave WA3 3 E4
Broughton Cres SY14 211 D1
Broughton Hall Rd CH4 139 E2
Broughton Jun & Inf Sch CH4 139 E2
Broughton La CW2 189 F1
Broughton Mills Rd CH4 139 F3
Broughton Rd Adlington SK10 62 B3
Crewe CW1 190 B4
Reddish SK5 240 F8
Broughville Dr M20 239 C8
Brow Cty Prim Sch The WA7 23 F1
Brow La Antrobus CW9 53 E3
Heswall L60 40 C4
Brow The WA6 75 E1
Browmere Dr WA3 9 D4
Brown Ave
Lawton-gate ST7 194 A3
Nantwich CW5 204 C2
Brown Heath Rd
Christleton CH3 143 D3
Waverton CH3 143 D3
Brown La SK8 239 B1
Brown Lees Cl CW2 190 A1
Brown Lees Rd ST7 195 F2
Brown St Alderley Edge SK9 60 A1
Altrincham WA14 238 D3
Congleton CW12 156 C2
Macclesfield SK11 112 B4
[1] Stockport SK1 240 E6
Widnes WA8 23 E4
Brown's La Chester CH4 141 E4
Wilmslow SK9 60 C4
Brownhill Dr WA1 16 C4
Brownhills Rd CW6 147 E3
Browning Ave WA8 22 C4
Browning Cl Blacon CH1 117 F3
[11] Sandbach CW11 174 B3
Browning Dr L65 69 F2
Browning Gn L65 69 F2

Browning Gr ST7 210 B4
Browning St CW1 190 B2
Browning Way CW7 149 D4
Brownlow Cl SK12 36 C1
Broxton Ave CW10 151 E3
Broxton Cl WA8 12 B2
Broxton Dr CW2 190 A1
Broxton Rd Broxton CH3 182 B1
Clutton CH3 182 B1
Ellesmere Port L66 69 F3
Bruce Ave WA2 8 B1
Bruce Cres L63 43 E3
Bruce Dr L66 69 E2
Bruche Ave WA1 16 C4
Bruche Cty Inf Sch WA1 17 D4
Bruche Cty Jun Sch WA1 17 D4
Bruche Dr WA1 16 C4
Bruche Heath Gdns WA1 17 D4
Bruen The CH3 121 E2
Bruera Rd L65 69 F2
Brunel Rd SK11 112 B2
Brunner Bsns Ctr CW8 78 B1
Brunner Gr CW5 205 D3
Brunner Pl CW7 149 D4
Brunner Rd WA8 23 D4
Brunswick Cres L66 69 F2
Brunswick Hill SK11 112 B4
Brunswick Rd
Altrincham WA14 238 D7
Newton-le-W WA12 1 C2
Brunswick St
[35] Macclesfield SK11 112 B4
St Helens WA9 1 A2
Brunswick Terr SK11 112 B4
Bruntleigh Ave WA4 17 D2
Bruntwood Ave SK8 239 A1
Bruntwood La Cheadle SK8 239 E1
Cheadle SK8 239 E2
Bruntwood Prim Sch SK8 239 E2
Brussels Rd SK3 240 D2
Bryant Ave WA4 16 C3
Bryce St SK14 241 D8
Brymau Four Est CH4 140 B4
Brymau One Est CH4 140 C4
Brymau Three Est CH4 140 B4
Brymau Two Est CH4 140 C4
Brynlow Dr CW10 151 D4
Brynmore Dr SK11 112 C4
Brynn St WA8 23 D4
Brynton Cl SK10 87 E1
Brynton Rd SK10 87 E1
Buchan Cl WA5 15 D4
Buchan Gr CW2 190 A2
Buck La CW2 206 C2
Buckbean Way CW4 107 F1
Buckden Way SK11 112 B4
Buckfast Ave WA11 2 A4
Buckfast Cl
Cheadle Hulme SK8 35 D3
Macclesfield SK10 87 E1
Penketh WA5 14 C2
Poynton SK12 36 B3
Buckfast Ct WA7 24 C2
Buckfast Way CW10 128 A1
Buckingham Ave
Chester CH3 119 D1
Denton M34 241 B6
Widnes WA8 13 D2
Buckingham Cl CW2 205 F4
Buckingham Dr
Davenham CW9 103 F2
Great Sankey WA5 15 E2
Knutsford WA16 57 D1
Winsford CW7 149 E4
Buckingham Rd
Ellesmere Port L65 70 B1
Irlam M44 11 E3
Poynton SK12 36 B2
Stalybridge SK15 242 D3
Wilmslow SK9 59 F3
Buckingham Rd W SK4 240 A8
Buckingham Way SK2 240 F2
Buckland Cl WA8 22 B4
Buckley Ave CW10 128 C4
Buckley Cl CW10 151 D4
Buckley Dr SK6 241 A1
Buckley St
Macclesfield SK11 112 B4
Warrington WA2 16 A3
Bucklow Ave
Mobberley WA16 58 A2
Partington M31 11 F2
Bucklow Gdns WA13 19 D2
Bucklow View WA14 238 A3
Bucklow Wlk [19] SK11 112 C4
Bucklowhill La WA16 30 A2
Buckton St WA1 16 B4
Bude Cl Alsager ST7 193 D2
Bramhall SK7 35 F4
Crewe CW1 190 A4
Bude Rd WA8 12 C1
Budworth Ave
Warrington WA4 16 C2
Widnes WA8 12 B1
Budworth Cl Runcorn WA7 49 E4
Sandbach CW11 174 C4
Budworth Heath La CW9 54 B1
Budworth La
Comberbach CW9 78 C4
Great Budworth CW9 78 C4
Budworth Rd
Bate Heath CW9 54 C1
Ellesmere Port L66 69 F1
Sale M33 242 E5
Tabley WA16 55 E1

Clovelly Ave WA5 14 C4
Clovelly Gr WA7 50 B3
Clover Ave Frodsham WA6 74 B4
Stockport SK3 240 D1
Clover Ct WA7 50 A3
Clover Dr CW7 126 B2
Clover La CH4 140 C3
Clover Pl CH4 140 C3
Clover Rd SK6 241 E3
Cloverdale CW8 103 E4
Cloverdale Rd SK11 112 A3
Cloverfield WA7 50 B4
Cloverfield Gdns L66 69 E4
Cloverfields CW1 191 E2
Clowes Ave ST7 193 F1
Clowes St SK11 112 A4
Clumber Cl SK12 36 C2
Clumber Rd SK12 36 C2
Clutton CE Contr Prim Sch CH3 182 B1
Clwyd Ave SK3 240 D3
Clwyd Cl CH4 139 D3
Clwyd Way L66 69 D3
Clyde Ave ST6 179 F1
Clyde Cres CW7 127 D1
Clyde Gr CW2 190 A2
Clyde Rd SK3 240 C3
Clydesdale L65 70 A2
Clydesdale Ave CW2 190 A2
Clydesdale Rd WA4 26 B4
Coach Rd Bickerton SY14 199 E1
Chowley CH3 183 D2
Edge Green SY14 199 E1
Hampton SY14 199 E1
Little Budworth CW6 147 E4
Coachway SK10 86 C4
Coalbrookdale Rd L64 41 F1
Coalpit Hill ST7 210 B4
Coalpit La Langley SK11 113 E3
Mollington CH1 94 B2
Winsford CW10 127 F1
Coare St SK10 87 E1
Coastguard La L64 41 D1
Cob Hall La WA6 98 B3
Cob Moor Rd
Kidsgrove ST7 195 D2
Lawton-gate ST7 195 D2
Cobal Ct WA6 74 A4
Cobb's La CW5 204 C4
Cobbett's Way SK9 59 F2
Cobblers Cross La CW6 146 C1
Cobblers La LL12 161 D1
Cobbles The Chester CH4 141 E4
Cuddington CW8 101 E2
Lower Peover WA16 81 F1
Cobbs Cty Inf Sch The WA4 26 C4
Cobbs La Appleton WA4 26 C4
Hough Common CW2 206 C1
Cobden St
Ashton-u-L OL6 242 A2
Newton-le-W WA12 2 B2
Warrington WA2 16 A3
Cock Hall La SK11 113 E2
Cock La CW9 78 C4
Cocker Hill SK15 242 E2
Cockhedge Ctr WA1 16 A3
Cockhedge La WA1 16 B3
Cockhedge Way WA1 16 A3
Cockington Cl CW9 104 A2
Cocklade La L24 21 E1
Cockpit La CW8 102 A1
Cocksheadhey Rd SK10 63 E1
Cocksmoss Rd SK11 133 E2
Coe La WA14 30 B4
Coerdon Dr WA4 17 E1
Cogshall La Comberbach CW9 78 A4
Little Leigh CW9 77 F4
Northwich CW9 78 B3
Colborne Ave SK6 241 C2
Colborne St WA12 2 C2
Colchester Pl SK4 240 C7
Colchester Sq CH4 140 C3
Coldmoss Dr CW11 175 E2
Coldstream Cl WA2 8 C2
Cole Ave WA12 2 B2
Colebrook Cl WA3 10 A2
Coleclough Pl WA3 4 C2
Colehill Bank CW12 156 C1
Colehill Pl CH5 91 E1
Colenso Gr SK4 240 B7
Coleridge Cl CH1 118 A3
Coleridge Way CW1 190 C3
Colin Rd SK4 240 E8
Colinwood Ave CH4 139 D2
Collar House Dr SK10 86 C3
College Cl Warrington WA1 16 B3
Wilmslow SK9 59 F4
College Fields CW2 190 A1
College Gn CH4 141 E4
College La CW6 168 C1
College of Law Christleton Hall CH3 142 B4
College Rd ST7 193 D3
College View CH5 91 E1
Colley La
Hassall Green CW11 175 E3
Sandbach CW11 175 E3
Colleys La Nantwich CW2 205 E4
Willaston (nr Nantwich) CW2 205 E4
Collier St WA7 22 C2
Collier's Row WA7 48 C4
Colliers La CW9 54 C1
Colliery Green Cl L64 66 C3
Colliery Green Ct L64 66 C3
Colliery Green Dr L64 66 C3
Collin St WA5 15 F3
Collinbrook Ave CW2 190 A1
Collingham Gn L66 69 D3
Collingham Way CW7 126 B1
Collingtree Ave CW7 127 D2
Collingwood Cl
Macclesfield SK10 87 D1
Poynton SK12 37 D2
Collingwood Rd WA12 2 A2
Collins Green Rd WA5 1 C1
Collins St CW2 190 A2
Collinson Ct WA6 74 A4
Colmere Ct L65 70 B4
Colne Rd WA5 6 C3
Colshaw Cty Prim Sch SK9 34 B1
Colshaw Dr SK9 34 B1
Colshaw La SK11 109 F1
Colshaw Wlk SK9 34 B1
Coltsfoot Dr WA14 238 B8
Columbine Cl
Huntington CH3 142 A3
Widnes WA8 12 A2
Columbine Wlk M31 11 F1
Colveley Way CW7 126 A1
Colville Ct WA2 8 A2
Colville Rd SK11 111 F4
Colwick Ave WA14 238 E6
Colwyn Cl WA5 7 F1
Colwyn Rd Bramhall SK7 35 F4
Cheadle SK8 239 E1
Comber Way WA16 82 A4
Comberbach Cty Prim Sch CW9 78 B4
Combermere Cl SK8 239 F4
Combermere Pl CW1 190 A3
Comboy Dr CW9 104 B3
Combs Cl SK22 39 D4
Comer Terr M33 242 A6
Commercial Ave SK8 34 C3
Commercial Brow SK14 241 E8
Commercial Rd SK10 112 C4
Commercial St SK14 241 E7
Common Farm La SK11 83 F1
Common La Betley CW3 221 F3
Chelford SK11 83 F1
Culcheth WA3 4 C2
Duddon CW6 145 D4
Kelsall CW6 122 B2
Lach Dennis CW9 105 F3
Stretton WA4 52 C4
Tarvin CW6 122 B2
Warrington WA4 16 C1
Waverton CH3 143 D2
Common Rd WA12 1 C2
Common St WA12 1 C2
Common The WA7 49 F4
Commonhall St CH1 237 D2
Commons Mill CW11 175 D4
Commons The CW11 175 D3
Commonside WA6 73 F1
Commonwealth Cl CW7 149 E3
Company's Cl WA7 48 C3
Compass Cl WA7 50 B3
Compstall Rd SK6 241 E2
Compton Cl WA11 1 B4
Compton Pl Chester CH4 141 D3
Ellesmere Port L65 70 A3
Compton St SK15 242 E1
Concord Pl WA2 8 B1
Condliffe Cl CW11 175 E3
Conery Cl WA6 73 E2
Coney Gr WA7 50 A3
Coneymead SK15 242 D4
Congleton Cl SK9 85 D4
Congleton Edge Rd CW12 179 D3
Congleton La
Siddington SK11 109 E3
Withington SK11 109 E3
Congleton Rd
Alderley Edge SK10 85 D3
Astbury CW12 177 F2
Biddulph ST6 179 E1
Biddulph, Mow Cop CW12 178 C1
Broughton CH4 139 E2
Kidsgrove ST7 194 B1
Macclesfield SK11 112 A3
Marton SK11 133 D3
Nether Alderley SK10 85 D3
Sandbach CW11 175 D4
Scholar Green CW12 177 F2
Siddington SK11 110 A3
Smallwood CW11 177 D3
Smallwood, Arclid Green CW11 176 A4
Warren SK11 111 F1
Congleton Rd N
Lawton-gate ST7 194 C3
Scholar Green ST7 194 C3
Congleton Rd S ST7 194 B2
Congleton Sta CW12 157 D1
Congleton War Memorial Hospl CW12 156 C1
Conifer Cl CH1 95 D4
Conifer Gr WA5 14 C4
Conifer Wlk M31 11 E1
Conifers The ST7 193 D2
Coniston Ave
Bebington L63 43 E2
Congleton CW12 155 F1
Dukinfield SK14 241 C8
Penketh WA5 14 B2
Winsford CW7 126 B1
Coniston Cl Hooton L66 44 A1
Nantwich CW5 205 D3
Runcorn WA7 49 E3
Coniston Dr Frodsham WA6 74 B4
Holmes Chapel CW4 130 A2
Stalybridge SK15 242 D3
Wilmslow SK9 34 B2
Coniston Rd Chester CH2 118 C3
Gatley SK8 239 B5
High Lane SK6 37 E4
Neston L64 66 C3
Partington M31 11 F2
Coniston Way SK11 111 F3
Connah's Quay High Sch CH5 91 E1
Connaught Ave WA1 16 C4
Connaught Cl SK9 60 B4
Connaught Dr WA12 2 B1
Conroy Way WA12 7 E4
Consort Pl WA14 238 B3
Constable Dr SK9 60 C4
Constables Cl WA7 24 A1
Constance Rd M31 11 F2
Constance Way WA8 23 D3
Convamore Rd SK7 35 E4
Conway Ave Irlam M44 11 F4
Warrington WA5 7 F1
Winsford CW7 149 E4
Conway Cl Broughton CH4 140 B3
Crewe CW1 190 B4
Great Sankey WA5 14 C3
Knutsford WA16 82 A4
Conway Cres SK10 87 F1
Conway Ct L65 70 B2
Conway Dr Newton-le-W WA12 2 C2
Stalybridge SK15 242 D3
Conway Rd Cheadle SK8 239 E2
Sale M33 242 D5
Conway St SK5 240 E8
Coogee Ave WA5 14 C4
Cook Ave WA11 1 C4
Cook St Ellesmere Port L65 70 B3
Stockport SK3 240 E5
Cooke's La CW9 104 C3
Cooks La SY13 225 E4
Cooksmere La CW11 175 D4
Coole La
French Lane End CW5 218 C2
Newhall CW3 229 E3
Coombe Dr WA7 49 D4
Coombe Park L66 69 E3
Coombes Ave SK14 241 F5
Coope Rd SK10 87 F3
Cooper Ave
Newton-le-W WA12 1 C2
Warrington WA2 8 A1
Cooper La WA11 1 B3
Cooper St Congleton CW12 156 C2
Runcorn WA7 23 D2
Stockport SK1 240 F3
Widnes WA8 13 D1
Cooper's Cft CH3 142 A4
Cooper's La CH5 91 E1
Coopers Opening CW11 175 D4
Cop Meadow SK11 112 C1
Copage Dr SK6 241 A4
Cope Ave CW5 204 B2
Copeland Gr WA7 49 F3
Copeland Rd WA4 16 A1
Copes La CW5 204 B2
Copeswood Cl CH4 139 E2
Copgrove Wlk M22 33 F4
Copley Ave SK15 242 F2
Copley Park Mews SK15 242 F2
Coppenhall Cty High Sch CW1 190 C3
Coppenhall Gr CW2 190 A2
Coppenhall Heyes CW2 190 A2
Coppenhall La CW2 189 E2
Copper Beach Cl CH4 139 E2
Copper St SK11 112 C3
Copper Wood CW8 101 F3
Copperfield Cl WA3 9 E3
Copperfield Rd
Cheadle Hulme SK8 35 D3
Poynton SK12 36 B1
Copperfields Tarporley CW6 146 B1
Wilmslow SK9 60 B4
Copperhill Rd CW12 179 D4
Coppermine La SY14 184 A1
Coppice CW8 101 E3
Coppice Cl Disley SK12 38 A3
Romiley SK6 241 B4
Runcorn WA7 24 A1
Willaston (nr Nantwich) CW5 205 E3
Coppice Dr Disley SK12 38 A3
Middlewich CW10 151 F3
Coppice Gn WA5 7 D1
Coppice Gr WA16 57 D2
Coppice La SK12 38 A3
Coppice Rd
Haslington CW11 192 A4
Kidsgrove ST7 210 B4
Poynton SK12 37 D2
Willaston (nr Nantwich) CW5 205 E3
Coppice Rise SK11 112 B3
Coppice The
Altrincham WA15 32 A4
Nantwich CW5 204 C2
Sandbach CW11 174 C4
Whaley Bridge SK23 65 F3
Coppice Way SK9 34 C2
Coppins Cl Chester CH3 119 D1
Helsby WA6 73 D2
Coppins The Warrington WA2 8 B1
Wilmslow SK9 59 F2
Copse The Altrincham WA15 32 B4
Newton-le-W WA12 2 A2
Runcorn WA7 50 A3
Copthorne Cl CW12 156 C1
Copthorne Dr CW3 229 F2
Corbet Ave WA2 16 A4
Corbet Dr TF9 235 D2
Corbet St WA2 16 A4
Corcoran Dr SK6 241 F2
Cordale Cl WA5 14 C4
Corfe Way CW7 149 E4
Coridor Rd L65 71 D3
Corkland Cl OL6 242 B2
Corkland St OL6 242 B2
Corks La SK12 38 C3
Corley Ave SK3 239 F7
Cormorant Cl CW1 190 C2
Cormorant Dr WA7 22 C1
Cornbrook Rd SK11 112 B2
Corner Croft SK9 60 A2
Corner Ct SK8 239 F6
Cornerhouse La WA8 12 B2
Corners The CW8 102 C4
Cornfield Cl
Ellesmere Port L66 69 F1
Macclesfield SK10 87 E2
Sale M33 242 F5
Cornfield Rd SK6 241 E3
Cornforth Way WA8 12 C2
Cornhill Cl ST5 210 B1
Cornish Cl M22 33 E4
Cornishway M22 33 E4
Cornishway Ind Est M22 33 E4
Cornubia Rd WA8 23 E4
Cornwall Ave WA7 23 D1
Cornwall Cl
Congleton CW12 157 D1
High Lane SK6 37 F4
Macclesfield SK10 86 C1
Runcorn WA7 23 F1
Cornwall Gr CW1 190 A3
Cornwall Rd Cheadle SK8 34 A4
Chester CH2 118 B4
Irlam M44 11 E3
Widnes WA8 13 D2
Cornwall St Chester CH2 237 E4
Warrington WA1 16 C4
Cornwell Cl SK9 60 B4
Corona Ave SK14 241 E7
Coronation Ave
Alsager ST7 193 D2
Glazebury WA3 5 E4
Hyde SK14 241 E5
Warrington WA4 17 E1
Winsford CW7 126 C1
Coronation Bldgs SK10 88 A4
Coronation Cres
Crewe CW1 190 C3
Kidsgrove ST7 194 C1
Sandbach CW11 175 D3
Coronation Dr
Frodsham WA6 49 E1
Haydock WA11 2 A4
Newton-le-W WA12 2 C1
Penketh WA5 14 C2
Widnes WA8 22 A4
Coronation Gr CW8 78 A2
Coronation Rd
Broughton CH4 139 D2
Congleton CW12 156 C2
Ellesmere Port L65 70 B2
Middlewich CW10 151 E3
Runcorn, Higher Runcorn WA7 23 D1
Runcorn, Preston Brook WA7 50 C3
Coronation St Chester CH4 140 C4
Crewe CW1 190 B3
Macclesfield SK11 112 B3
Reddish SK5 240 E8
Coronation Terr CW6 146 B1
Coroner's La WA8 13 D2
Coronet Ave CW9 103 F2
Coronet Way WA8 22 A4
Corporation St Hyde SK14 241 D6
Stalybridge SK15 242 D1
Stockport SK1 240 F6
Correction Brow SK12 37 E3
Corstons La L64 67 D3
Corwen Cl WA5 7 F1
Cossack Ave WA2 8 A1
Cotebrook Dr CH2 118 B4
Cotebrook Rd CW9 104 B4
Cotes Pl CH1 117 F2
Cotesmore Dr L60 41 E4
Cotgreaves Cl CH4 141 D3
Cotswold Ave WA3 3 E3
Cotswold Cl Chester CH2 118 C3
Cuddington CW8 102 A1
Macclesfield SK10 86 C1
Cotswold Gr WA9 1 A2
Cotswold Rd Stockport SK4 240 D7
Warrington WA2 8 A2
Cotswold Way CW7 149 D4
Cottage Cl Bebington L63 43 E3
Neston L64 66 C4
Cottage Dr East L60 40 C3
Cottage Dr West L60 40 C3
Cottage La Heswall L60 40 C3
Macclesfield SK10 112 C4
Cottage Rd CH4 141 D3
Cottage St SK11 112 A4
Cottam Dr WA2 9 D2
Cotterdale Cl WA5 14 C4
Cotterill WA7 49 E4
Cotterill Dr WA1 17 E4
Cotterill St CW2 190 B1
Cottesmore Gdns WA15 32 B4
Cotton La Duddon CW6 145 E4
Runcorn WA7 49 E4
Sandbach CW11 175 D2
Cotton Tree St SK3 & SK4 240 E5
Cottonwood Dr ST7 195 F2
Cottrell Rd WA15 32 B4
Coulton Rd WA8 13 F2
Counce Ave WA12 2 B1
Countess Ave SK8 34 C3
Countess Cl SK11 111 F4
Countess of Chester Hospl CH2 118 A3
Countess Rd SK11 112 A4
Countess St OL6 242 A2
Countess Way CH2 118 B2
Counting House Rd SK12 38 C3
County Ave OL6 242 B4
Courier Row SK10 87 F4
Court La CW8 77 D1
Court The CW12 156 A2
Courtney Gn SK9 34 B1
Courtney Pl WA14 238 A1
Courtney Rd CH4 140 C2
Cousens Way CH1 118 A2
Cove The WA15 238 F3
Covent Garden 18 SK1 240 F5
Coventry Ave Cheadle SK3 239 F7
Ellesmere Port CH1 94 C4
Coverdale Cl WA5 14 B4
Covert Cl CW7 149 D4
Covert Gdns ST7 210 B4
Covert Rise CH3 166 A1
Covington Pl SK9 60 A3
Cow La Ashley WA15 31 F3
Bollington SK10 88 A4
Hargrave CH3 144 A1
Macclesfield SK11 112 B3
Norley WA6 101 D3
Rainow SK10 88 B2
Sale M33 242 E7
Cowanway WA8 12 C3
Cowbrook La SK11 135 D3
Cowdell St WA2 16 A4
Cowfields CW5 204 C3
Cowhey Cl CH4 141 D3
Cowley Way CW1 190 C1
Cowlishaw Rd SK14 & SK6 241 F4
Cowper Cl CW2 206 A4
Cowthorne Dr CH3 143 D2
Coyt Rd SK23 65 F3
Crab La WA2 9 D2
Crabmill Dr CW11 174 C4
Crabmill La Norley WA6 100 C3
Warmingham CW11 173 F4
Crabtree Ave
Altrincham WA15 32 B4
Disley SK12 38 C3
Crabtree Fold WA7 50 B4
Crabtree Gr CW1 190 C3
Crabtree La WA16 29 D3
Crabwall Pl CH1 117 F3
Crackley Bank Prim Sch ST5 210 C1
Cradley WA8 12 B1
Cragside Way SK9 60 B3
Craig Cl Macclesfield SK11 112 A3
Stockport SK4 240 B5
Craig Dr SK23 65 F3
Craig Gdns L66 69 F4
Craig Rd Congleton CW12 156 C2
Macclesfield SK11 112 A3
Stockport SK4 240 B5
Craig Wlk ST7 193 F1
Craigleigh Gr L62 43 F2
Craigside ST6 179 E1
Craithe Rd CH3 119 D1
Crampton Dr WA15 32 B4
Cranage Cl WA7 49 E4
Cranage Hill Hospl CW4 130 A3
Cranage Rd CW2 190 A2
Cranage Way 12 SK9 34 B3
Cranberry Cl WA14 238 B8
Cranberry Cty Inf & Jun Sch ST7 193 D2
Cranberry Dr ST5 210 B1
Cranberry La ST7 193 D2
Cranberry Moss La ST7 193 D2
Cranberry Rd M31 11 F2
Cranborne Rd Crewe CW1 190 B3
Warrington WA4 16 A1
Cranbourne Ct SK4 240 B8
Cranbourne Rd SK4 240 B8
Crandon Dr M20 239 C8
Cranebrook Cl CW1 190 A4
Cranfield Dr ST7 193 D2
Cranford Ave
Knutsford WA16 56 C1
Macclesfield SK11 112 C4
Sale M33 242 C8
Cranford Cl L62 43 F2
Cranford Ct Chester CH4 141 D3
Warrington WA1 17 F4
Cranford Mews ST7 193 D2
Cranford Rd SK9 34 A1
Cranham Ave WA3 3 F4
Cranleigh Cl WA4 26 A4
Cranleigh Cres CH1 118 A2
Cranleigh Dr Cheadle SK8 239 F6
Hazel Grove SK7 37 D4
Sale M33 242 A7
Cranmere Cl CW9 104 A2
Cranshaw La WA8 13 D3
Cranston Dr
Manchester M20 239 B8
Sale M33 242 E5
Cranswick Gn L66 69 E3
Crantock Dr SK8 34 B4
Cranwell Ave WA3 4 C2
Cranworth St SK15 242 E1
Crauford Rd CW12 157 D4
Craven Ave WA3 3 F4
Craven Ct WA2 7 F2
Craven Dr WA14 238 C8

Darwin Gr SK7 35 F3
Darwin Rd CH1 117 E2
Darwin St CW8 103 F4
Darwin Street Cty Prim Sch CW8 103 F4
Daryl Rd L60 41 D4
Daten Ave WA3 9 F3
Dauncey Cl CH2 95 E1
Davehall Ave SK9 60 A4
Daven Cty Prim Sch CW12 156 C1
Daven Rd CW12 156 C1
Davenham Ave WA1 16 C4
Davenham Cres CW2 190 A2
Davenham Ct CW9 104 A2
Davenham Rd
Davenham CW9 104 C2
Lach Dennis CW9 104 C2
8 Wilmslow SK9 34 B2
Davenham Way CW10 151 E3
Davenport Ave Crewe CW2 206 B4
Nantwich CW5 204 C4
Warrington WA1 16 C3
Wilmslow SK9 59 F2
Davenport Cl CW11 175 E4
Davenport La
Altrincham WA14 238 C7
Brereton Green CW11 154 B1
Marton SK11 132 C3
Mobberley WA16 58 B3
Davenport Rd
Altrincham WA14 238 C7
Heswall L60 40 C4
Davenport Row WA7 49 E4
Davenport St
Congleton CW12 156 B1
Crewe CW1 190 B3
Macclesfield SK11 112 C4
Davenport Sta SK3 240 F1
Davey La SK9 60 A1
Daveylands SK9 60 B4
David Cl M34 241 A5
David Lewis Manchester Epileptic Colony The SK9 84 A3
David Rd WA13 18 B2
David St Denton M34 241 A6
Northwich CW8 103 F4
David's Ave WA5 15 D3
Davidson Ave CW12 157 D3
Davies Ave Cheadle SK9 34 A3
Newton-le-W WA12 2 B2
Warrington WA4 16 C2
Davies Cl WA8 23 D2
Davies Way WA13 18 B2
Davis Cl ST7 193 F2
Davy Rd WA7 23 F2
Daw Bank SK3 240 E5
Dawlish Ave SK8 34 C4
Dawlish Cl Bramhall SK7 35 F4
Hollins Green WA3 11 D2
Dawn Cl L64 67 D3
Dawn Gdns L65 70 A2
Dawpool Cl CH2 118 B3
Dawpool Dr L62 43 E4
Dawson Dr CH2 237 D4
Dawson Rd
Altrincham WA14 238 D8
Bollington SK10 88 A4
Cheadle SK8 34 B4
Macclesfield SK11 111 F4
Dawson St SK14 241 E5
Dawstone Rd L60 41 D4
Daylesford Cl SK8 239 D4
Daylesford Cres SK8 239 D4
Daylesford Rd SK8 239 D4
De Lacy Row WA7 24 A1
Deacon Cl Altrincham WA14 238 B1
Croft WA3 9 D4
Deacon Rd WA8 13 D1
Deacon Trad Est WA12 2 A1
Deadman's La CW5 205 D1
Deakin's Rd CW7 127 D2
Deal Sq SK14 241 E6
Deal St SK14 241 E6
Dean Bank CW6 168 B2
Dean Cl Bollington SK10 88 A4
Partington M31 11 F2
Sandbach CW11 174 C4
7 Widnes WA8 23 D4
Wilmslow SK9 34 B1
Dean Cres WA2 8 A1
Dean Ct SK10 88 A4
Dean Dr Altrincham WA14 238 B1
Wilmslow SK9 34 B1
Dean Hollow ST7 209 E1
Dean La SK7 36 C4
Dean Meadow WA12 2 B2
Dean Pk SY14 214 A3
Dean Rd Goldborne WA3 3 D4
Irlam M44 11 F3
Wilmslow SK9 34 C2
Dean Row Cty Jun Sch SK9 34 C1
Dean Row Rd SK9 34 B1
Dean St Middlewich CW10 128 B1
Northwich CW9 104 B4
Stalybridge SK15 242 D1
Widnes WA8 23 D4
Winsford CW7 126 B1
Dean Valley Cty Prim Sch SK10 87 F4
Dean's La ST5 210 B1
Deane Ave SK8 239 F5
Deanery Cl CH2 118 B2
Deanery Way SK1 240 F6
Deans Cl Chester CH2 118 B3
Tarvin CH3 121 D1
Deans La Barthomley CW2 208 B2
Sandbach CW11 174 C3
Warrington WA4 17 F2
Deans Rd L65 70 C2
Deans Way
Higher Kinnerton CH4 161 D4
Tarvin CH3 121 D1
Deansgate L65 70 A3
Deansgate La
WA14 & WA15 238 E7
Deansway WA8 22 B4
Deanwater Cl WA3 9 E2
Deanwater Ct SK8 34 B4
Deanway SK9 34 B1
Dearden St SK15 242 D2
Dearnford Ave L62 43 E3
Dearnford Cl L62 43 E3
Debra Cl L66 69 E2
Debra Rd L66 69 E2
Dee Banks CH4 141 F4
Dee Banks Sch CH3 142 A4
Dee Cl Biddulph ST6 179 F1
Kidsgrove ST7 210 C4
Sandbach CW11 174 C4
Dee Cres CH3 180 C1
Dee Fords Ave CH3 119 D1
Dee Hills Pk CH2 237 F2
Dee La Chester CH2 237 F2
Holt LL13 196 B4
Dee Meadows LL13 196 B4
Dee Park Cl L60 41 D3
Dee Park Rd L60 41 D3
Dee Pk LL13 196 B4
Dee Point Cty Prim Sch CH1 117 E2
Dee Side L60 40 B4
Dee View CH3 180 C1
Dee View Rd
Connah's Quay CH5 91 E1
Heswall L60 40 C4
Dee Way CW7 127 D1
Deepdale WA8 12 B2
Deer Park Ct WA7 49 F3
Deerwood Cl
Ellesmere Port L66 69 E4
Macclesfield SK10 86 C1
Deerwood Cres L66 69 E4
Deeside Ellesmere Port L65 70 A2
Holt LL13 196 C4
Deeside Cl L65 70 A1
Deeside Coll of F Ed (Coleg Glannau Dyfrdwy) CH5 91 E1
Deeside Cres CH1 116 C3
Deeside Ind Est (Parc Ddiwydiannol Glannau Dyfrdwy) CH5 93 D1
Deeside La CH1 116 C2
Deirdre Ave WA8 13 D1
Delafield Cl WA2 8 C2
Delamer Rd WA14 238 C3
Delamere Ave Bebington L62 43 F2
Ellesmere Port L66 69 F3
Goldborne WA3 3 F3
Sale M33 242 E5
Widnes WA8 12 B1
Delamere CE Contr Prim Sch CW6 123 E3
Delamere Cl Bebington L62 43 F2
Sandbach CW11 174 C4
Delamere Ct Alsager ST7 192 C2
Bebington L62 43 F2
Delamere Dr
Ellesmere Port L66 69 F3
Macclesfield SK10 87 F1
Delamere Forest Sch WA6 100 B2
Delamere Gn L66 69 F2
Delamere Park Way E CW8 101 E3
Delamere Park Way W CW8 101 E3
Delamere Rd Ashton CH3 99 D1
Congleton CW12 155 F2
Gatley SK8 239 B5
Nantwich CW5 204 C2
Norley WA6 100 A3
Wilmslow SK9 34 C2
Delamere Rise CW7 126 A1
Delamere St Chester CH1 237 D3
Crewe CW1 190 B2
Warrington WA5 15 F3
Winsford CW7 126 A1
Delamere Sta CW8 100 B1
Delamore's Acre L64 68 A4
Delavor Cl L60 40 C4
Delavor Rd L60 40 C4
Delenty Dr WA3 9 F2
Delery Dr WA1 16 C4
Delford Rd WA16 82 B4
Delfur Rd SK7 35 F4
Delhi Rd M44 11 F4
Dell Cl L63 43 D3
Dell Dr WA2 9 D1
Dell La L60 41 D4
Dell The Cuddington CW8 101 E3
Guilden Sutton CH3 119 F3
Kelsall CW6 122 B2
Delmar Rd WA16 57 E1
Delph La Daresbury WA4 25 D1
Warrington WA2 8 C3
Winwick WA2 7 F3
Winwick WA2 8 C3
Delphfield WA7 50 B4
Delphfields Rd WA4 26 B4
Delphside ST7 209 F1
Delta Ct CH4 140 A3
Delves Ave WA5 15 F4
Delves Cl CW2 206 A2
Delves Wlk CH3 142 A4
Delvine Dr CH2 118 B3
Demage Dr L66 69 E2
Demage La Backford CH1 94 C2
Chester CH2 118 B4
Demage La S CH2 118 B4
Demesne Cl SK15 242 F1
Demesne Cres SK15 242 F1
Demesne Dr SK15 242 F1
Demmings Inf Sch SK8 239 F5
Demmings Rd SK8 239 F5
Den La CW3 221 E2
Denbigh Cl Hazel Grove SK7 36 B4
Helsby WA6 73 D1
Denbigh Cres CW10 151 E4
Denbigh Ct L65 70 B2
Denbigh Dr CW7 149 D4
Denbigh Gdns L65 70 B2
Denbigh St Chester CH1 118 A2
Stockport SK4 240 D7
Denbury Ave WA4 16 C1
Denbury Dr WA14 238 B5
Denby La SK4 240 D8
Dene Ave WA12 1 C2
Dene Ct SK4 240 C6
Dene Dr CW7 149 E4
Denehurst Cl WA5 14 C2
Denehurst Park Way CW8 101 E3
Denesgate CW7 149 E4
Deneside Ave CW1 190 B3
Deneway Cheadle Hulme SK7 35 E4
High Lane SK6 37 F4
Stockport SK4 240 C6
Deneway Cl SK4 240 C6
Deneway Mews SK4 240 C6
Denewood Ct SK9 60 A3
Denford Cl CH4 139 E2
Denford Pl ST7 193 E3
Denhall Cl CH2 118 C3
Denhall La L64 67 D1
Denham Ave WA5 15 D3
Denham Dr SK7 35 E4
Denholm Rd M20 239 C8
Denise Ave WA5 14 C3
Denison Rd SK7 36 C4
Denmark Rd M33 242 B8
Denmark St WA14 238 D4
Dennett Cl WA1 17 F3
Dennis Dr CH4 141 D3
Dennis Rd WA8 23 E4
Dennison Rd SK8 35 D4
Densham Ave WA2 8 A1
Denston Cl CW2 190 A1
Denstone Dr CH4 141 D2
Dentdale Wlk M22 33 E4
Dentith Dr CH1 117 F3
Denton Cl CW7 126 B1
Denton Dr CW9 79 E1
Denton Drive Ind Est CW9 79 E1
Denton St WA8 13 E1
Denver Ave CW2 190 A2
Denzell Gdns WA14 238 A3
Depenbech Cl SY14 213 D2
Depleach Rd SK8 239 D5
Depmore La WA6 75 D1
Deramore Cl OL6 242 B3
Derby Cl Irlam M44 11 E3
Neston L64 66 C2
Newton-le-W WA12 2 A2
Derby Ct M33 242 C5
Derby Dr WA1 16 C4
Derby Pl CH2 118 C2
Derby Range SK4 240 B8
Derby Rd Ashton-u-L OL6 242 A3
Goldborne WA3 3 E4
Hyde SK14 241 E8
Kidsgrove ST7 210 B4
Manchester SK4 240 C8
Warrington WA4 16 B1
Widnes WA8 13 E2
Derby Row WA12 7 E4
Derby St Altrincham WA14 238 E5
Congleton CW12 156 B2
Crewe CW1 190 A3
Newton-le-W WA12 2 A2
Stockport SK3 240 D4
Derbyshire Hill Cty Prim Sch WA9 1 A1
Derbyshire Hill Rd WA9 1 A1
Derbyshire Rd
Partington M31 11 E1
Poynton SK12 37 E3
Sale M33 242 C6
Derbyshire Rd S M33 242 D5
Derek Ave WA2 8 C1
Derrington Ave CW2 190 B2
Derwen Rd SK3 240 E3
Derwen Sch CH4 161 D4
Derwent Ave CW7 127 D1
Derwent Cl Alsager ST7 193 D2
Culcheth WA3 5 D1
Holmes Chapel CW4 130 A2
Macclesfield SK11 112 A3
Partington M31 11 F2
Willaston (nr Nantwich) CW5 205 E3
Derwent Cres ST7 195 E1
Derwent Dr Biddulph ST6 179 F1
Cheadle Hulme SK7 35 E3
Congleton CW12 156 C1
Hooton L66 44 A1
Wilmslow SK9 34 B3
Derwent Rd Chester CH2 118 C3
High Lane SK6 37 F4
Warrington WA4 16 A1
Widnes WA8 12 B1
Derwent Terr SK15 242 D4
Derwent Way L64 66 C4
Desoto Rd WA8 22 C3
Desoto Rd E WA8 22 C3
Desoto Rd W WA8 22 C3
Deva Ave CH4 140 B3
Deva Bsns Pk CH5 116 A4
Deva Cl SK12 36 A2
Deva Ct CH2 118 C1
Deva La CH2 118 B3
Deva Link CH1 118 A2
Deva Rd CW2 189 E2
Deva Stad (Chester City FC) CH1 117 F1
Deva Terr CH2 237 F2
Devisdale Grange WA14 238 B3
Devisdale Rd WA14 238 B4
Devon Cl SK10 86 C1
Devon Gr ST6 179 E1
Devon Pl Congleton CW12 156 C2
Widnes WA8 13 D2
Devon Rd Chester CH2 118 C3
Irlam M44 11 E3
Partington M31 11 F1
Devonshire Dr SK9 60 A1
Devonshire Gdns WA12 2 B1
Devonshire Pl Chester CH4 141 F4
Runcorn WA7 23 D1
Devonshire Rd
Altrincham WA14 238 D6
Broughton CH4 139 E2
Hazel Grove SK7 36 C4
Manchester SK4 240 B7
Warrington WA1 16 C4
Dewar Ct WA7 23 F2
Dewes St CW1 190 A3
Dewhurst Rd WA3 9 E1
Dexter Way CW10 128 B1
Dial La CW12 158 A1
Dial Rd WA15 32 B4
Dial St WA1 16 B3
Diamond Cl OL6 242 A4
Diamond St OL6 242 A4
Dibbins Gn L63 43 D4
Dibbinsdale Rd L63 43 D4
Dickens Cl
Cheadle Hulme SK8 35 D3
6 Sandbach CW11 174 B3
Dickens La SK12 36 C1
Dickenson St WA2 16 B4
Dickinson Cl WA11 1 A3
Dickson Cl WA8 23 D4
Dickson St 2 WA8 23 D4
Dicksons Dr CH2 118 B2
Didsbury Rd SK4 240 B6
Dierden St CW7 127 D1
Dierdens Terr CW10 128 B1
Dig La Acton CW5 203 F2
Frodsham WA6 74 A4
Ravensmoor CW5 203 F2
Shavington CW2 206 A2
Diglake St ST7 209 F2
Diglee Rd SK23 39 E2
Dinas Cl CH1 117 E2
Dingle Ave Denton M34 241 B6
Lindow End SK9 59 E2
Newton-le-W WA12 1 C1
Dingle Bank CH4 141 E4
Dingle Bank Cl WA13 18 C2
Dingle Cl Macclesfield SK10 87 D2
Romiley SK6 241 D2
Dingle Cty Prim Sch The CW1 191 E3
Dingle La Appleton WA4 26 C3
Kelsall CW6 122 C3
Sandbach CW11 175 E3
Winsford CW7 126 B1
Dingle The Barnton CW8 78 A2
Haslington CW1 191 E3
Lymm WA13 18 C2
Dingle Way CW8 101 F3
Dingle Wlk CW7 126 B1
Dinglebrook Gr 2 SK9 34 C1
Dingleway WA4 26 B4
Dinmor Rd M22 33 E4
Dirty La WA14 30 C3
Disley Cty Prim Sch SK12 38 B3
Disley Sta SK12 38 B3
Ditchfield La WA16 29 E2
Ditchfield Pl WA8 22 A4
Ditchfield Rd Penketh WA5 14 C2
Widnes WA8 22 A4
Ditton CE Contr Prim Sch WA8 12 A1
Ditton CE Prim Sch WA8 12 B1
Ditton Rd Widnes WA8 23 D3
Widnes, Ditton Marsh WA8 22 B3
Dixon Ave WA12 2 B3
Dixon Cl WA11 2 A4
Dixon Ct SK8 239 D5
Dixon Dr SK11 84 A2
Dixon Rd Congleton CW12 157 D3
Denton M34 241 B5
Dixon St Ashton-u-L OL6 242 A4
Irlam M44 11 F4
Warrington WA1 16 A3
Dobb Hedge Cl WA15 32 B3
Dobell's Rd CW9 103 F3
Dobers La Frodsham WA6 74 B2
Kingsley WA6 74 B2
Dobson's Sq SY14 213 D2
Dock Rd Northwich CW9 103 F4
Widnes WA8 23 D3
Widnes, Ditton Marsh WA8 22 C3
Dock St Ellesmere Port L65 70 B4
Widnes WA8 23 D3
Dock Yard Rd L65 70 C3
Dodd's Green La SY13 228 A2
Dodd's La Appleton WA4 27 D3
Bradley Green SY14 224 C4
Doddington Cl CW11 175 E4
Doddington Rd CW2 190 A2
Dodds La CW12 178 B3
Doddswood Dr CW12 156 C2
Dodge Hill SK1 & SK4 240 E6
Dodgsley Dr WA6 75 E1
Dodleston CE Contr Prim Sch CH4 162 A4
Dodleston La
Dodleston CH4 162 B2
Pulford CH4 162 B2
Doe's Meadow Rd L63 43 D4
Doeford Cl WA3 4 C3
Dog La Brereton Green CW11 153 F4
Chowley CH3 182 B2
Coddington CH3 182 B2
Nantwich CW5 204 C3
Threapwood SY14 223 E4
Dogmore La CW6 147 E2
Dolly La SK23 39 F2
Dolphin Cres L66 69 F1
Dolphin Ct CH4 141 D4
Dombey Rd SK12 36 B1
Domestic App M90 33 E4
Domville Cl WA13 18 C2
Don Wlk L65 70 A4
Donagh Cl SK10 86 C1
Donald Ave SK14 241 F5
Donkey La SK9 60 A3
Donne Pl CH1 117 F3
Donnington Ave SK8 239 F6
Donnington Way CH4 140 C4
Dooley's Grig SK11 108 C1
Dooley's La SK9 33 E1
Dorac Ave SK8 34 B4
Dorchester Cl SK9 60 B4
Dorchester Pk WA7 24 C2
Dorchester Rd Chester CH4 140 C3
Great Sankey WA5 15 E3
Dorchester Way
Burtonwood WA5 6 C3
Macclesfield SK10 87 E2
Doreen Ave CW12 179 D4
Doreold Dr CW5 204 B3
Dorfold St CW1 190 B2
Dorfold Way CH2 118 A4
Doric Ave WA6 74 B4
Dorin Park Sch CH2 118 B3
Doris Rd SK3 240 C4
Dormer Cl CH3 143 D3
Dorney Cl WA4 26 C3
Dornoch Ct CW4 130 A1
Dorothea St WA2 16 B4
Dorric Way CW1 190 B4
Dorrington Cl WA7 50 B4
Dorrington Rd SK3 240 A3
Dorrit Cl SK12 36 C1
Dorset Ave SK8 240 C1
Dorset Cl CW12 156 C2
Dorset Ct WA7 50 A3
Dorset Dr ST6 179 E1
Dorset Pl Chester CH2 119 D3
Kidsgrove ST7 195 D1
Dorset Rd Altrincham WA14 238 B5
Chester CH2 118 B4
Irlam M44 11 E3
Dorset St OL6 242 A2
Dorset Way WA1 17 D4
Dorset Wlk SK10 86 C1
Douglas Ave WA9 6 A3
Douglas Cl Hartford CW8 103 E3
Widnes WA8 13 F2
Douglas La CW7 171 D3
Douglas Pl CH4 140 C3
Douglas St
Ashton-u-L OL6 242 A3
Hyde SK14 241 E6
Doune Ct L65 70 B2
Dounrey Cl WA2 9 D1
Douthwaite Dr SK6 241 E1
Dove Bank Prim Sch ST7 195 D1
Dove Cl Ellesmere Port L65 70 A4
Helsby WA6 73 E3
Sandbach CW11 175 D4
Warrington WA3 9 F2
Dove Cote Gn WA5 7 D1
Dove Gr ST6 179 E1
Dove Pl CW7 127 D1
Dovecot Bsns & Tech Pk M33 242 F6
Dovecote Cl CW2 206 A4
Dovedale Cl Bebington L62 43 F3
Congleton CW12 157 D2
High Lane SK6 37 F4
Warrington WA2 8 C2
Dovedale Ct WA8 12 A2
Dover Cl WA7 50 C3
Dover Ct L65 70 B1
Dover Dr Ellesmere Port L65 70 B1
Winsford CW7 149 D4
Dover Rd Chester CH4 141 D3
Macclesfield SK10 87 F1
Warrington WA4 17 D2
Dovesmead Rd L60 41 E4
Doveston Rd M33 242 B8
Doward St WA8 13 E1
Downes Cl SK10 87 D1
Downesway SK9 59 F1
Downham Ave WA3 4 C1
Downham Dr L60 41 D4
Downham Pl CH1 117 F2
Downham Rd S L60 41 D4
Downing Cl SK11 112 C2
Downs Dr WA14 238 E8
Downs End WA16 57 E1
Downs Rd WA7 23 D1
Downs The
Altrincham WA14 238 D3
Cheadle SK8 239 D3
Cuddington CW8 101 E3

Downsfield Rd CH4 141 D3
Downside WA8 12 A2
Downswood Ct CH2 118 B2
Downswood Dr CH2 118 B2
Downway La WA9 1 A1
Dowson Rd SK14 241 E5
Dragon Yd WA8 13 D2
Dragon's La CW11 152 A1
Drake Ave M44 11 F3
Drake Cl WA5 7 E1
Drake Ct SK5 240 E8
Drake La Acton CW5 203 F2
Ravensmoor CW5 203 F2
Drake Rd Altrincham WA14 238 B8
Neston L64 41 F1
Drakelow La
Lach Dennis CW10 128 C4
Middlewich CW10 128 C4
Drakes Way SY14 213 D3
Draxford Ct SK9 60 A3
Draycott Dr ST5 210 B1
Drayton Ave SK8 34 A4
Drayton Cl Runcorn WA7 22 C1
Wilmslow SK9 34 B1
Drayton Cres CW1 190 C3
Drayton Manor M20 239 B8
Drenfell Rd ST7 194 C4
Drill Field Rd CW9 103 F4
Drive A CH5 93 D1
Drive B CH5 93 D1
Drive C CH5 93 D1
Drive The Altrincham WA15 32 B4
Holmes Chapel CW4 130 B1
Lymm WA13 19 E1
Drome Rd CH5 93 D1
Drovers Way CW11 175 D3
Drumber La ST7 195 D4
Drumber The CW7 126 B1
Drumble Field SK11 84 A2
Drummond Ave L66 69 E2
Drummond Ct WA8 13 E1
Drummond Way SK10 86 C1
Druridge Dr WA5 14 C2
Drury Cl CW1 190 C3
Drury La Knutsford WA16 57 D1
Warmingham CW1 173 E2
Dryden Ave SK8 239 F6
Dryden Cl CW2 190 A1
Dryden Pl WA2 8 B1
Dryhurst Dr SK12 38 B3
Dryhurst La SK12 38 B3
Dublin Croft L66 69 F1
Duchy Rd CW1 207 D4
Duchy St SK3 240 D3
Duck La CH3 121 F4
Duckworth Gr WA2 9 D1
Duddon Cl Davenham CW9 103 F2
Duddon CW6 145 D3
Duddon Hook La CW6 144 C3
Duddon Rd CW6 145 D3
Duddon St Peter's CE
Contr Prim Sch CW6 145 D3
Dudleston Rd L66 69 D3
Dudley Ave WA7 23 E1
Dudley Cres L62 44 A2
Dudley Rd Ellesmere Port L65 70 A3
Irlam M44 11 E2
Sale M33 242 C8
Dudley St WA2 16 A4
Dudley Wlk SK11 111 F4
Dudlow Green Rd WA4 26 C3
Dufton Wlk M22 33 F4
Duke Ave Cheadle Hulme SK8 34 C3
Glazebury WA3 5 E4
Duke St Alderley Edge SK9 60 A1
Chester CH4 237 E1
Congleton CW12 156 B1
Crewe CW2 190 B2
Macclesfield SK11 112 B4
Newton-le-W WA12 2 A2
Stalybridge SK15 242 C1
9 Stockport SK1 240 F5
Duke's Cres CW11 175 D4
Duke's Ct CH4 237 E1
Dukes Way CW9 103 F2
Dukesway CH2 118 C4
Dukinfield Rd SK14 241 C8
Dulas Ct CH2 118 B4
Dulverton Ave CH3 119 E1
Dumbah La SK10 87 E3
Dumbers SK11 136 A1
Dunbar Cl
Connah's Quay CH5 91 E1
Ellesmere Port L66 69 E3
Holmes Chapel CW4 130 B1
Dunblane Ave SK4 240 D6
Duncan Ave
Newton-le-W WA12 2 B3
Runcorn WA7 23 E1
Duncan St WA2 16 B4
Duncansby Cres WA5 14 C3
Duncansby Dr L63 43 E2
Dundalk La WA8 22 B4
Dundalk Rd WA8 22 C4
Dundee Cl WA2 8 C2
Dundee Ct L65 70 C2
Dundonald Ave WA4 16 B1
Dundonald Rd SK8 35 D4
Dundonald St SK2 240 F2
Dundrennan Cl SK12 36 B3
Dunecroft M34 241 A8
Dunham Cl Bebington L62 43 F2
Sandbach CW11 175 E3
Dunham Cres CW2 206 A4
Dunham Ct WA6 97 F3
Dunham Forest Golf Course
WA14 20 C2
Dunham Lawn WA14 238 B4
Dunham Massey Hall WA14 20 B2
Dunham Pk WA14 20 C2
Dunham Rd
Altrincham WA14 238 B4
Northwich CW9 104 A2
Partington WA13 19 F4
Wilmslow SK9 34 B3
Dunham Rise WA14 238 C4
Dunham Way CH2 118 C3
Dunham-on-Hill Cty Prim
Sch WA6 97 F3
Dunkirk Ave CW7 149 E4
Dunkirk Dr L65 70 A1
Dunkirk La Capenhurst CH1 94 B4
Dukinfield SK14 241 B8
Ellesmere Port L65 70 A1
Dunley Cl WA3 10 A3
Dunlin Ave WA12 2 B2
Dunlin Cl Poynton SK12 36 A2
Runcorn WA7 49 F3
Warrington WA2 8 C2
Dunlin Wlk WA14 238 B8
Dunlop St WA4 16 A2
Dunmore Cl CW10 151 E4
Dunmore Cres L66 69 D3
Dunmore Rd
Ellesmere Port L66 69 D3
Gatley SK8 239 B6
Dunmow Rd WA4 17 E2
Dunn's La CH3 121 F4
Dunnock Cl WA2 8 C2
Dunnock Gr WA3 9 F2
Dunnocksfold Rd ST7 193 D2
Dunnockswood ST7 193 D2
Dunollie Rd M33 242 E5
Dunoon Cl CW4 130 A1
Dunraven Rd L64 67 D4
Dunscar Cl WA3 9 E3
Dunsford WA8 12 B2
Dunsmore Cl WA11 1 B4
Dunstan La L64 67 F2
Dunster Cl CW9 104 A2
Dunster Gr L60 41 D4
Dunster Rd SK10 87 F1
Dunwood Dr ST7 193 E3
Durban Ave CH3 142 B4
Durber Cl ST7 209 E1
Durham Cl
Macclesfield SK10 86 C1
Romiley SK6 241 A1
Warrington WA1 17 F4
Durham Ct L65 70 C2
Durham Dr CW7 149 E3
Durham Gr M44 11 E3
Durham Rd Blacon CH1 117 F3
Widnes WA8 13 D2
Durlston Cl WA8 12 B1
Durrell Way WA3 3 F4
Dutton Cl CW5 204 C2
Dutton Gn L65 70 C2
Dutton La CW8 101 E3
Duxford Ct WA2 8 C1
Dyar Terr CW8 78 B1
Dyberth Rd CH1 117 E2
Dye House La SK22 39 E4
Dye La SK6 241 B2
Dyer St WA3 2 C4
Dyers Cl WA13 19 D2
Dyers La WA13 19 D2
Dykin Cl WA8 13 F2
Dykin Rd WA8 13 F2
Dysart St OL6 242 A2
Dyserth Gr 2 SK5 240 F8
Dystelegh Rd SK12 38 B3

Eadie Gr CW1 190 A4
Eaglaisway SK10 86 C1
Eagland Pl CW12 156 C2
Eagle Brow WA13 18 B2
Eagle La L66 69 E4
Eagles Way WA7 49 F3
Eaglesfield CW8 103 E2
Ealing Rd WA5 15 D3
Eanlewood La WA7 50 B4
Eardley Cres CW12 156 C2
Eardley Pl CW1 190 A3
Eardleyend Rd ST7 209 F4
Eardswick Cl CH2 237 E4
Eardswick La CW1 172 B3
Eardswick Rd CW10 151 E3
Earl Rd Cheadle Hulme SK8 34 C3
Manchester SK4 240 C8
Wilmslow SK8 34 C3
Earl St Sale M33 242 C7
Stockport SK3 240 D4
Warrington WA2 16 A4
Earle Cl WA12 1 C2
Earle Cres L64 41 E1
Earle Dr L64 41 E1
Earle Rd WA8 23 E4
Earle St Crewe CW1 190 B2
Newton-le-W WA12 2 A2
Earle's La CW6 122 B3
Earles La
Higher Wincham CW9 79 F3
Marston CW9 79 F3
Earlestown District CE Jun
& Inf Sch WA12 2 A2
Earlestown Sta WA12 2 A2
Earls Gdns L65 70 A3
Earls Oak CH2 118 B4
Earls Rd CW2 206 A2
Earls Way Davenham CW9 103 F2
Runcorn WA7 49 F3
Earlston Ct CH2 237 F2
Earlsway Chester CH4 141 D4
Macclesfield SK11 111 F4
Earndale WA8 13 D3
Easby Cl Cheadle Hulme SK8 35 D3
Poynton SK12 36 B2
Easenhall Cl WA8 13 E3
Easingwold 2 WA14 238 C4
East Ave Bollington SK10 87 F4
Cheadle SK8 34 B4
Great Sankey WA5 15 D2
Northwich CW9 104 B3
Stalybridge SK15 242 D3
Warrington WA2 16 B4
Warrington, Stockton Heath
WA4 16 B1
Weston CW2 207 E3
East Ct ST7 193 F2
East Dam Wood Rd L24 21 D1
East Downs Rd
Altrincham WA14 238 C2
Cheadle SK8 239 F2
East Dudley St CW7 126 C1
East Gn CH5 116 A3
East La Cuddington CW8 102 A2
Runcorn WA7 49 F4
East Lancashire Rd
Goldborne WA3 3 E3
Haydock WA11 1 B4
East Lea M34 241 A6
East Mains L24 21 D2
East Millwood Rd L24 21 D2
East Park Rd SK11 112 A3
East Rd Halewood L24 21 D3
Middlewich CW10 128 A1
Wythenshawe M90 33 E4
East St Ashton-u-L OL6 242 A4
Widnes WA8 13 E1
East View WA4 17 E1
Eastbury Cl WA8 13 E3
Eastcott Cl CW12 155 F2
Eastdale Pl WA14 238 D7
Eastdale Rd WA1 17 D4
Easter Ct WA5 7 D1
Eastern Pathway CH4 237 F1
Eastern Rd Shavington CW5 205 F3
Willaston (nr Nantwich)
CW5 205 F3
Eastfields Gr CH1 117 D4
Eastford Rd WA4 16 A1
Eastgate Rd CW4 130 B2
Eastgate Row CH1 237 E2
Eastgate St CH1 237 E2
Eastham Ctry Pk L62 44 A4
Eastham Glenburn Cty Inf
Sch L62 43 F3
Eastham Rake Bebington L62 43 F3
Willaston L62 43 F2
Eastham Rake Sta L62 43 E2
Eastham Village Rd L62 44 A2
Eastham Way 9 SK9 34 B3
Eastleigh Rd SK8 239 B1
Easton Dr SK8 240 A1
Eastward Ave SK9 59 F3
Eastway Ellesmere Port L66 69 E4
Widnes WA8 12 B1
Eastwood WA7 24 B1
Eastwood Ave WA12 2 C2
Eastwood Ct CH4 139 D3
Eastwood Rd WA5 6 C4
Eaton Ave CH4 141 E4
Eaton Bank CW12 156 C2
Eaton Bank Ind Est CW12 156 C2
Eaton Cl Broughton CH4 139 E2
Cheadle SK8 239 F3
Poynton SK12 37 D2
Sandbach CW11 175 E4
Eaton Cres CW9 103 F1
Eaton Cty Prim Sch CW6 147 D2
Eaton Dr Alderley Edge SK9 59 F1
Middlewich CW10 151 D4
Eaton Gr CH4 140 C3
Eaton La Davenham CW9 103 F1
Eaton CW6 146 C1
Goostrey CW4 107 E1
Macclesfield SK11 112 B3
Tarporley CW6 168 C4
Eaton Mews CH4 141 E4
Eaton Rd Alsager ST7 193 E2
Altrincham WA14 238 C1
Chester CH4 141 F2
Eccleston CH4 141 F2
Sale M33 242 A6
Tarporley CW6 146 B1
Wettenhall CW7 170 B4
Eaton St Crewe CW2 190 B2
Runcorn WA7 23 D1
Eaton View CW9 126 C4
Eaves Brow Rd WA3 9 D4
Eaves Knoll Rd SK22 39 D4
Ebnal La SY14 213 F2
Eccles Cl SK23 65 E4
Eccles Rd SK23 65 F3
Eccleston Ave Bebington L62 43 E4
Chester CH4 141 E3
Ellesmere Port L66 69 F3
Eccleston CE Aided Prim
Sch CH4 141 F1
Eccleston Cl WA3 9 E3
Eccleston Dr WA7 23 E1
Eccleston Rd CH4 161 D4
Eccleston Way 2 SK9 34 B2
Eccups La SK9 59 E4
Echo Cl CH4 140 C3
Ecton Ave SK10 113 D4
Ecton Cl CW7 127 D2
Edale Cl Altrincham WA14 238 C1
Bebington L62 43 F3
Cheadle SK8 34 B4
Edale Dr CW6 122 B3
Edbury Pl CH4 141 E4
Eddisbury Cl SK11 112 C4
Eddisbury Dr ST5 210 B1
Eddisbury Hill CW8 123 E4
Eddisbury Rd L66 69 F1
Eddisbury Sq WA6 74 A4
Eddisbury Terr SK11 112 C4
Eddisford Dr WA3 4 B2
Edelsten St WA5 15 F3
Edelston Hall La CW5 203 F1
Eden Ave
Fowley Common WA3 5 E2
High Lane SK6 37 F4
Winsford CW7 126 C1
Eden Cl Biddulph ST6 179 F1
Ellesmere Port L66 69 E3
Kidsgrove ST7 195 D1
Wilmslow SK9 59 F3
Eden Dr SK10 87 F1
Eden Pl Cheadle SK8 239 D6
Sale M33 242 B7
Edenbridge Gdns WA4 26 C2
Edendale WA8 12 A1
Edenfield Cl WA16 58 A2
Edenfield Rd WA16 58 A2
Edenhall Cl CW4 130 A2
Edgar Ct CH4 237 E1
Edgar Pl CH4 237 E1
Edgars Dr WA2 9 D1
Edge Gr CH2 118 C1
Edge La SY14 199 E1
Edge View La WA16 59 D1
Edgecroft CH3 166 A1
Edgehill Chase SK9 60 C4
Edgeley Fold SK3 240 C3
Edgeley Park (Stockport
County FC) SK3 240 E3
Edgeley Rd SK3 240 B3
Edgemoor WA14 238 A2
Edgerley La CH3 181 D3
Edgerton Rd WA3 3 F4
Edgeview Rd CW12 179 D4
Edgeway Henbury SK11 111 E4
Wilmslow SK9 60 A3
Edgewell La CW6 147 D2
Edgewood Dr Bebington L62 43 E3
Wistaston CW2 206 A4
Edgworth St WA2 16 A3
Edinburgh Cl SK8 239 F6
Edinburgh Ct L65 70 B2
Edinburgh Dr
Macclesfield SK10 87 D1
Romiley SK6 241 C4
Edinburgh Pl CW12 156 C1
Edinburgh Rd
Congleton CW12 156 C1
Widnes WA8 22 A4
Wistaston CW2 205 F4
Edinburgh Way CH4 237 F1
Edison Rd WA7 23 E2
Edith St WA7 22 C2
Edleston Cty Prim Sch
CW2 190 B2
Edleston Rd CW2 190 B2
Edlestone Gr 9 SK9 34 C1
Edmund Cl SK4 240 E8
Edna St Chester CH2 118 C2
Hyde SK14 241 D6
Edward Gdns WA1 17 F3
Edward Rd WA5 14 B3
Edward St
Ashton-u-L OL6 242 B2
Audley ST7 209 F2
Crewe CW2 190 B1
Ellesmere Port L65 70 B4
Haydock WA11 1 A3
Hyde SK14 241 C7
Macclesfield SK11 112 A4
Northwich CW9 104 B4
Sale M33 242 E6
Stockport SK1 240 F4
Widnes WA8 13 E1
Edwards Ave CW2 206 B3
Edwards Cl CW2 206 B3
Edwards Rd CH4 141 D3
Edwards Way Alsager ST7 193 F2
Widnes WA8 22 B4
Edwin St WA8 13 E1
Egdon Cl WA8 13 F1
Egerton WA16 29 E3
Egerton Ave Hartford CW8 103 D2
Partington WA13 19 E4
Warrington WA1 16 C4
Egerton Ct CW6 122 A3
Egerton Cty Prim Sch
WA16 56 C1
Egerton Dr Chester CH2 118 B3
Sale M33 242 B7
Egerton Moss WA15 31 F3
Egerton Rd Blacon CH1 117 E3
Lymm WA13 18 B1
Wilmslow SK9 34 A1
Egerton Rd S SK4 240 C8
Egerton Sq WA16 57 D1
Egerton St Chester CH2 237 F3
Congleton CW12 156 B1
Ellesmere Port L65 70 B3
Runcorn WA7 23 D2
Warrington, Howley WA1 16 B3
Warrington, Stockton Heath
WA4 16 B1
Egerton Street Sch CH2 237 F3
Egerton Wlk CH4 162 A4
Eggbridge La CH3 143 D3
Egremont Gr 2 SK3 240 B4
Egypt St Warrington WA1 16 A3
Widnes WA8 22 C4
Eisenhower Cl WA5 15 D3
Elaine Cl Ellesmere Port L66 69 E2
Widnes WA8 13 E1
Elaine St WA1 16 B4
Elanor Rd 2 CW11 174 B4
Elcho Rd WA14 238 B3
Elcombe Ave WA3 3 F4
Elder Dr CH4 140 C3
Elderberry Way SK9 60 C4
Elderberry Wlk M31 11 E1
Eldon Rd Macclesfield SK11 111 F4
Stockport SK3 240 C3
Eldon St WA1 16 B3
Eldon Terr L64 66 C4
Eleanor Cl CW1 189 F3
Eleanor St
Ellesmere Port L65 70 B3
Widnes WA8 23 D4
Electra Way CW1 191 D1
Electricity St CW2 190 B2
Elf Mill Cl SK3 240 E2
Elgar Ave L62 43 F3
Elgar Cl L65 69 F2
Elgin Ave
Holmes Chapel CW4 130 A1
Macclesfield SK10 87 D1
Warrington WA4 16 A1
Elgin Cl CH3 119 D2
Elgin Dr M33 242 E5
Elgin St SK15 242 E1
Elgol Cl SK3 240 F1
Eliot Cl CW1 191 D2
Eliza St M33 242 B7
Elizabeth Ave Disley SK12 38 B3
Stockport SK1 240 F4
Elizabeth Cl CW6 122 B3
Elizabeth Cres CH4 237 F1
Elizabeth Ct Kidsgrove ST7 210 B3
Stockport SK4 240 C6
Widnes WA8 23 D4
Elizabeth Dr WA1 17 D4
Elizabeth Rd Haydock WA11 1 C4
Partington M31 11 F2
Elizabeth St
Congleton CW12 156 B1
Crewe CW1 190 A3
Hyde SK14 241 D7
Macclesfield SK11 112 B4
Elizabethan Way CW9 104 C3
Elk View SY14 222 C3
Elkan Cl WA8 13 F1
Elkan Rd WA8 13 F1
Ella Gr WA16 57 D1
Elland Dr L66 69 E3
Ellen Brook Rd M22 33 E4
Ellen St Stockport SK4 240 D7
Warrington WA5 15 F4
Ellerby Cl WA7 50 C4
Ellerton Ave L66 69 E3
Ellerton Cl WA8 12 B2
Ellesmere Ave
Broughton CH4 139 E2
Chester CH2 118 B3
Ellesmere Cl CW11 174 C4
Ellesmere Dr SK8 240 A1
Ellesmere Pl CW1 190 A3
Ellesmere Port Cath
(Aided) High Sch L65 70 A2
Ellesmere Port Hospl L65 70 A1
Ellesmere Port Sta L65 70 B3
Ellesmere Port Stadium
The L65 70 C2
Ellesmere Rd
Altrincham WA14 238 E6
Cheadle SK3 240 A3
Culcheth WA3 4 C2
Northwich CW9 104 A2
Warrington WA4 16 A1
Ellesmere St Runcorn WA7 23 D1
Warrington WA1 16 B3
Ellesworth Cl WA5 15 E4
Elliot St 9 WA8 23 D4
Ellis La WA6 49 E1
Ellis St Crewe CW1 190 A3
Hyde SK14 241 F6
Widnes WA8 22 C4
Ellison St
Warrington, Howley WA1 16 B3
Warrington, Stockton Heath
WA4 16 B1
Elloway Rd L24 21 D2
Ellwood Gn CW2 206 C2
Elm Ave Newton-le-W WA12 2 B1
Widnes WA8 13 D1
Elm Beds Rd SK12 37 E1
Elm Cl Partington M31 11 F1
Poynton SK12 36 C2
Tarporley CW6 146 B1
Wistaston CW2 189 F1
Elm Cres SK9 60 A2
Elm Dr Crewe CW1 190 C3
Holmes Chapel CW4 130 B2
Macclesfield SK10 87 F1
Elm Gn L64 67 F4
Elm Gr Alderley Edge SK9 60 A1
Alsager ST7 193 F2
Broughton CH4 140 C3
Ellesmere Port L66 70 A1
Hyde SK14 241 F6
Sale M33 242 B8
Warrington WA1 16 C4
Wilmslow SK9 34 B2
Winsford CW7 127 D1
Elm Rd Altrincham WA15 238 E3
Congleton CW12 156 A2
Gatley SK8 239 A5
Haydock WA11 1 C4
High Lane SK6 37 F4

m Rd continued
Hollins Green WA3 11 D1
Middlewich CW10 151 E4
Penketh WA5 14 C2
Runcorn WA7 49 E4
Warrington WA2 8 A2
Weaverham CW8 102 B4
Willaston L64 67 F4
m Rd S SK3 240 A3
m Ridge Dr WA15 32 B4
m Rise Frodsham WA6 74 B4
Prestbury SK10 86 C3
m Sq CH4 140 C3
m St Ellesmere Port L65 70 B4
Northwich CW9 79 D1
m Tree Ave Lymm WA13 18 B1
Warrington WA1 16 C4
m Tree Ct CW6 147 D2
m Tree Dr ST7 209 F1
m Tree La CW11 174 B4
m Tree Rd Goldborne WA3 3 F4
Lymm WA13 18 B1
mbridge Prim Sch WA15 32 B4
mdale Ave SK8 239 B2
mfield Cl SK9 60 A1
mfield Rd
Alderley Edge SK9 60 A2
Stockport SK3 240 F1
mir CH1 117 F2
more Cl
Holmes Chapel CW4 130 A2
Runcorn WA7 24 B1
ms The Goldborne WA3 3 F4
Runcorn WA7 22 C1
lmsleigh Rd SK8 239 A2
lmstead Cres CW1 189 F4
lmstead Rd SK11 84 A2
lmsway Altrincham WA15 32 A4
Bollington SK10 88 A4
Cheadle Hulme SK7 35 E4
High Lane SK6 37 F3
lmtree Dr SK4 240 C6
lmwood WA7 24 B1
lmwood Ave Chester CH2 118 C2
Warrington WA1 16 C4
lmwood Cl ST7 194 A2
lmwood Gr CW7 149 F4
lmwood Rd CW8 78 A2
lnor Ave SK23 65 F3
lnor La SK23 65 F2
lsby Rd ST7 193 F1
lston Ave WA12 2 B3
lstree Ave CH3 119 D2
lstree Gr SK3 240 D4
lswick Ave SK7 35 F4
ltham Cl WA8 13 F2
ltham Wlk WA8 13 F2
lton Cl Bebington L62 43 F2
Goldborne WA3 3 F4
Warrington WA3 9 E2
lton Crossings Rd CW11 174 B3
lton Cty Prim Sch CH2 72 A2
lton Dr SK7 36 B4
lton La Elton WA6 72 C2
Haslington CW11 174 B1
lton Lordship La WA6 73 D4
lton Rd CW11 174 B3
lvington Cl WA7 49 F2
lworth Ave WA8 13 D3
lworth CE Contr Prim
Sch CW11 174 C4
lworth Hall Cty Prim Sch
CW11 174 C4
lworth Rd CW11 174 C3
lworth St CW11 175 D4
lworth Way 6 SK9 34 B2
lwyn Dr L26 21 D4
ly Cl CH1 94 C4
ly Ct 6 SK10 112 C4
mbassy Cl CH1 117 E2
mberton Pl CW3 230 A3
mbleton Ct WA7 49 E3
mbridge Cswy SK10, SK17 90 A3
merald Rd M22 33 F4
mery Cl SK4 240 A8
mily St 14 WA8 23 D4
mlyn Gr SK8 240 A2
mmerdale Ave WA2 8 A2
mmett St CW8 78 A2
mpress Dr Crewe CW2 190 A2
Reddish SK4 240 D8
mral Ct SY14 211 D1
mslie Ct L64 66 B4
nderby Rd CH1 237 D3
ndon Av SK10 88 A4
ndsleigh Cl CH2 118 B4
ndsleigh Gdns CH2 118 B4
nfield Cl CW2 206 A2
nfield Park Rd WA2 9 D2
nfield Rd L65 70 A3
ngelsea Brook La CW2 208 A2
nglefield Ave CH4 140 B3
Englefield Cl CW1 190 A4
Englesea Gr CW2 190 A1
nglish Martyrs RC Sch
WA11 1 C4
Ennerdale Chester CH2 118 C3
Macclesfield SK11 111 F3
Ennerdale Ave L62 43 F2
Ennerdale Cl CW7 126 B2
Ennerdale Dr
Congleton CW12 156 A1
Frodsham WA6 74 B4
Ennerdale Rd Crewe CW2 189 E2
Gatley SK8 239 B3
Partington M31 11 F2
Romiley SK6 241 B4
Ennerdale Terr SK15 242 D3
Ennis Cl L24 21 E1
Enticott Rd M44 11 E3
Enville Rd WA14 238 C3
Enville St WA4 16 B2
Epping Dr WA1 17 E4
Epsom Ave SK9 34 C2
Epsom Gdns WA4 26 C4
Epworth Cl WA5 6 C4
Era St M33 242 B6
Eric Ave WA1 16 C4
Eric St WA8 13 E1
Erlesmere Ave M34 241 A8
Ermine Rd CH2 237 F4
Ernest St Cheadle SK8 239 C6
Crewe CW2 190 B1
Errington Ave L65 70 B3
Errwood Cl L24 21 F1
Erskine Rd M31 11 F1
Erwood St WA2 16 A3
Esk Dale Cl CW7 126 B1
Esk Rd CW7 127 D1
Eskdale Ellesmere Port L65 70 A2
Gatley SK8 239 C4
Eskdale Ave
Cheadle Hulme SK7 35 E3
Warrington WA2 8 B2
Eskdale Cl Bebington L62 43 F3
Runcorn WA7 49 E3
Essex Ave SK3 240 B4
Essex Cl CW12 156 C3
Essex Dr Biddulph ST6 179 E1
Kidsgrove ST7 194 C1
Essex Gdns M44 11 E2
Essex Rd CH2 119 D3
Essex Wlk SK10 86 C1
Esther St WA8 13 D1
Esthers La CW8 102 B4
Etchells Prim Sch SK8 239 C1
Etchells Rd SK8 239 D1
Etchells St 6 SK1 240 F5
Ethelda Dr CH2 119 D3
Etherow Ave SK6 241 E2
Etherow Cl CW11 174 C4
Eton Dr L63 41 F3
Eton Rd L65 70 B2
Etterick Pk CH3 119 D1
Ettiley Ave CW11 174 B3
Euclid Ave WA4 17 D1
Europa Bvd WA5 7 E2
Europa Way Cheadle SK3 240 B2
Ellesmere Port L65 70 B3
Eustace St WA2 16 A3
Eva Rd SK3 240 A3
Eva St CW11 174 B4
Evans Cl WA11 1 C4
Evans Pl WA4 16 B2
Evans St Ashton-u-L OL6 242 A4
Crewe CW1 190 B3
Evansleigh Dr CH5 116 A2
Evelyn St WA5 15 E2
Evelyn Street Cty Prim
Sch WA5 15 F2
Everdon Cl CW7 126 C2
Everest Cl L66 69 F2
Everest Rd ST7 195 E2
Everglade Cl SK11 112 A3
Everite Rd WA8 22 A4
Eversley WA8 12 A1
Eversley Cl Appleton WA4 26 C3
Frodsham WA6 74 B3
Eversley Ct CH2 118 B2
Eversley Pk CH2 118 B2
Evesham Ave SK4 240 B7
Evesham Cl
Macclesfield SK10 87 F2
Warrington WA4 26 B4
Evesham Gr M33 242 E6
Ewart St CH4 140 A4
Ewloe Ct L65 70 B1
Ewrin La SK10 89 E3
Excalibur Cty Prim Sch
ST7 193 F1
Excalibur Ind Est ST7 193 F2
Excalibur Way M44 11 F4
Exchange Cl 25 SK11 112 B4
Exchange St
Macclesfield SK11 112 B4
Stockport SK3 240 E5
Exeter Cl SK8 34 C4
Exeter Pl CH1 117 F3
Exeter Rd L65 70 B3
Exeter Wlk SK7 35 F4
Exit Rd W M90 33 D4
Exmouth Cres WA7 50 C3
Exmouth Way WA5 6 C3
Exton Pk CH2 237 D4
Eyam Rd SK7 36 C4
Eyebrook Rd WA14 238 A2
Factory La Disley SK12 38 C4
Widnes WA8 13 D2
Factory Rd CH5 116 A2
Fair Haven's Ct WA8 23 D4
Fair Mead WA16 82 A4
Fair Oak Rd ST5 210 B1
Fair View Cl CW8 77 F2
Fairacre Dr CW10 151 F3
Fairacres Rd SK6 37 F4
Fairbourne Ave
Alderley Edge SK9 60 A2
Wilmslow SK9 59 F2
Fairbourne Cl
Warrington WA5 7 F2
Wilmslow SK9 59 F2
Fairbourne Dr SK9 59 F2
Fairbrook CW2 189 F1
Fairbrother Cres WA2 8 B1
Fairburn Ave CW2 189 F2
Fairburn Cl WA8 13 F2
Fairclough Ave WA1 16 B2
Fairclough Cres WA11 1 A3
Fairclough St
Burtonwood WA5 6 C3
Newton-le-W WA12 2 A2
Fairfax Dr Runcorn WA7 23 E1
Wilmslow SK9 59 F2
Fairfield Ave Cheadle SK8 239 F2
Ellesmere Port L65 70 A1
Romiley SK6 241 A4
Sandbach CW11 175 D3
Fairfield CE Aided Prim
Sch WA1 16 B3
Fairfield Cty High Sch
WA8 13 D2
Fairfield Cty Inf Sch WA8 13 D1
Fairfield Cty Jun Sch WA8 13 D1
Fairfield Gdns WA4 16 C1
Fairfield Rd Broughton CH4 139 D2
Chester CH2 119 D2
Irlam M44 11 E3
Lymm WA13 18 C2
Northwich CW9 104 A2
Warrington WA4 16 C1
Widnes WA8 13 D1
Fairfield St WA1 16 B3
Fairfields ST7 209 F1
Fairford Rd CH4 140 C3
Fairford Way SK9 60 B4
Fairhaven Cl Bramhall SK7 35 F4
Great Sankey WA5 15 D2
Fairhaven Dr L63 43 E3
Fairhaven Rd WA8 13 E1
Fairhills Rd M44 11 F4
Fairholm Rd CW9 127 D4
Fairholme Ave L64 41 E1
Fairholme Cl CH1 94 A1
Fairholme Rd SK4 240 C7
Fairlawn SK4 240 D7
Fairlawn Cl L63 43 D3
Fairlea M34 241 A6
Fairmeadow CH4 162 B1
Fairmile Dr M20 239 C8
Fairoak Ct WA7 50 C2
Fairoak La WA7 50 C2
Fairview LL13 196 C4
Fairview Ave Alsager ST7 193 E2
Weston CW2 207 D3
Fairview Rd
Ellesmere Port L65 70 A1
Macclesfield SK11 112 A3
Fairway Cheadle Hulme SK7 35 E3
Gatley SK8 239 B4
Hawarden CH5 116 A1
Fairway The ST7 193 E2
Fairways Appleton WA4 26 B3
Frodsham WA6 74 B4
Fairways Dr L66 69 E4
Fairy La M33 242 F6
Fairywell Cl SK9 34 B1
Falcon Cl Middlewich CW10 151 E3
New Mills SK22 39 E4
Winsford CW7 149 E3
Falcon Dr CW1 190 A4
Falcon Rd L66 69 F2
Falcondale Rd WA2 8 A3
Falconers Gn WA5 7 D1
Falcons Way WA7 49 F3
Fallibroome Cl SK11 111 F4
Fallibroome High Sch
SK10 86 C1
Fallibroome Rd SK11 111 F4
Fallowfield WA7 23 E1
Fallowfield Cl CW7 125 F1
Fallowfield Ct CW1 190 A3
Fallowfield Gr WA2 9 D1
Falls Gr SK8 239 A3
Falmouth Cl SK10 111 F4
Falmouth Dr WA5 14 C2
Falmouth Pl WA7 50 C3
Falmouth Rd
Congleton CW12 178 C4
Crewe CW1 190 A3
Falstone Cl WA3 10 A3
Falstone Dr WA7 50 C4
Fanner's La WA16 28 B3
Fanny's Croft ST7 193 E1
Fanshawe La SK11 110 C3
Fanshawe Wlk CW2 206 B4
Far Ridings SK6 241 D3
Faraday Rd
Ellesmere Port L65 70 A2
Runcorn WA7 23 E2
Faraday St WA3 9 F2
Farams Rd ST7 193 F4
Farbailey Cl CH4 141 D3
Farfields Cl SK11 111 F1
Faringdon Rd WA2 8 A3
Farlands Dr M20 239 B7
Farley Cl CW10 151 D4
Farley Ct SK8 239 F3
Farm Cl CW8 77 E1
Farm Dr CH5 91 E1
Farm La Appleton WA4 26 C4
Disley SK12 38 A3
Withington SK11 108 C1
Farm Rd Northwich CW9 104 C4
Oakmere CW8 124 A4
Weaverham CW8 77 E1
Farm Way WA12 2 C1
Farmdale Dr CH2 72 A2
Farmer Cl CW2 190 A2
Farmer St SK4 240 E7
Farmer's La WA5 7 D3
Farmers Heath L66 69 E1
Farmfield Dr SK10 87 E2
Farmfields Rise CW3 232 B1
Farmleigh Dr CW1 189 F4
Farmleigh Gdns WA5 15 E3
Farmstead Way L66 69 F1
Farndale Cl CW2 206 A3
Farndon Cl Broughton CH4 139 E2
Cuddington CW8 102 A2
Sale M33 242 E5
Farndon Cty Prim Sch
CH3 180 C1
Farndon Rd L66 69 F3
Farne Cl CH2 95 E4
Farnham Ave SK11 112 A3
Farnham Cl Appleton WA4 26 C4
Cheadle Hulme SK8 35 D4
Farnhill Cl WA7 50 B4
Farnley Cl WA7 24 B1
Farnworth CE Contr Prim
Sch WA8 13 D2
Farnworth Cl WA8 13 D2
Farnworth Rd WA5 14 B2
Farnworth St WA8 13 D2
Farr Hill Dr L60 40 C4
Farr Hill Rd L60 40 C4
Farr St SK3 240 D4
Farrant St WA8 23 D4
Farrell Rd WA4 26 B4
Farrell St WA1 16 B3
Farriers Way CW7 126 A1
Farthing La CW9 79 D4
Farwood Cl SK10 86 C1
Faulkner Dr CW10 151 F3
Faulkner St CH2 118 C2
Faulkner's La
Lindow End WA16 58 C1
Mobberley WA16 58 C1
Faulkners Cl CH4 161 D4
Faulkners La CH3 142 B4
Fawley Ave SK14 241 D5
Fawns Keep SK9 60 B4
Fawns Leap CW8 101 F3
Fearndown Way SK10 87 E2
Fearnhead La WA2 9 D1
Fearnley Way WA12 2 B1
Feather La L60 40 C4
Feilden Ct CH1 94 C1
Felix Rd CW8 103 F4
Fellside Gn SK15 242 D3
Felskirk Rd M22 33 E4
Fence Ave SK10 112 C4
Fence Ave Ind Est SK10 112 C4
Fence La CW12 178 B2
Fenham Dr WA5 14 C2
Fennel St WA1 16 B3
Fenton Cl Congleton CW12 157 D1
Widnes WA8 12 B2
Fenwick La WA7 49 E3
Fenwick Rd L66 69 F1
Ferguson Ave L66 69 F3
Ferguson Dr WA2 8 B1
Ferma La CH3 120 B3
Fern Ave WA12 2 B1
Fern Bank SK15 242 F1
Fern Cl WA3 9 E2
Fern Cres Congleton CW12 157 D2
Stalybridge SK15 242 F1
Fern Ct CW1 190 C2
Fern Lea SK8 239 B1
Fern Lea Dr SK11 112 A4
Fern Rd L65 70 A1
Fern Way CW8 77 E1
Fernacre M33 242 C7
Fernally St SK14 241 E6
Fernbank Cl Crewe CW1 190 C2
Winsford CW7 127 D1
Fernbank Rise SK10 88 A4
Fernbankcl WA3 9 F2
Ferndale Ave CH2 72 A2
Ferndale Cl Bold Heath WA8 13 F4
Sandbach CW11 175 E3
Warrington WA1 17 E4
Weston CW2 207 D3
Ferndale Cres SK11 111 F4
Fernhill Rd CH1 117 F3
Fernhurst WA7 49 E4
Fernilee Cty Inf Sch SK23 65 F2
Fernlea WA15 238 F1
Fernlea Rd Heswall L60 41 D4
Marston CW9 79 D3
Fernleaf Cl ST7 193 F4
Fernleigh CW8 103 E4
Fernley Ave M34 241 A6
Fernwood Gr SK9 60 B4
Ferry Cl CH5 116 A3
Ferry La Sealand CH1 117 E1
Warrington WA4 17 F2
Ferry Rd L62 44 A3
Ferryview Wlk WA7 23 F1
Festival Ave Buerton CW3 230 C2
Warrington WA2 8 B1
Festival Cres WA2 8 B1
Festival Dr SK10 85 F3
Festival Hill CW12 156 C1
Festival Rd L65 69 F3
Festival Way WA7 49 E4
Fiddler's Ferry Rd WA8 13 E1
Fiddlers La CH1 94 B1
Field Ave CW2 189 F1
Field Cl Bollington SK10 87 F4
Cheadle Hulme SK7 35 E2
Northwich CW8 103 E4
Tarvin CH3 121 D1
Field Hey La L64 43 D1
Field La Appleton WA4 26 B3
Tarvin CH3 121 D1
Tattenhall CH3 166 A1
Wistaston CW2 189 F1
Field Side Cl WA16 58 A2
Field St SK6 241 A3
Field View ST6 179 E1
Field View Cl SK11 112 C3
Field Way ST7 193 F2
Field Wlk M31 11 E1
Fieldbank SK11 112 A4
Fieldbank Rd SK11 112 A4
Fieldfare CW7 150 A4
Fieldfare Cl WA3 9 F2
Fieldgate WA8 22 A4
Fieldhead Mews SK9 60 C4
Fieldhead Rd SK9 60 C4
Fieldhouse Row WA7 49 E4
Fielding Ave SK12 36 C1
Fields Cl ST7 193 F2
Fields Cres CW12 156 B1
Fields Dr CW11 175 D3
Fields Rd Alsager ST7 193 F2
Congleton CW12 178 C4
Haslington CW1 191 E2
Fields The CW5 205 E3
Fields View SY13 228 B1
Fields View Cl CW5 220 A4
Fieldsend Dr WN7 4 B4
Fieldside CW6 145 D3
Fieldsway WA7 49 D3
Fieldview Dr WA2 8 B1
Fieldway Chester CH2 118 C2
Ellesmere Port L66 69 D4
Frodsham WA6 74 B4
Saughall CH1 94 A1
Weaverham CW8 77 E1
Widnes WA8 13 E1
Fife Rd WA1 16 C4
Fifth Ave Kidsgrove ST7 194 C1
Runcorn WA7 49 F4
Fiji St WA5 15 F3
Filkin's La CH3 119 D1
Finch La L26 21 D4
Finchdale Gdns WA3 4 A4
Finchett Dr CH1 118 A2
Finchley Rd WA15 238 E3
Findlay Cl WA12 2 A1
Finlan Rd WA8 23 D4
Finland Rd SK3 240 D3
Finlay Ave WA5 14 C2
Finlow Hill La SK10 85 F3
Finney Cl SK9 34 B1
Finney Dr SK9 34 B1
Finney Gr WA11 1 C3
Finney La Cheadle SK8 34 A4
Gatley SK8 239 C1
Wythenshawe SK8 34 A4
Finney's La CW10 128 A1
Finningley Ct WA2 8 C1
Finny Bank Rd M33 242 A8
Finsbury Park WA8 13 E3
Finsbury Wlk CW7 149 D4
Fir Ave Bramhall SK7 35 F4
Halewood L26 21 D4
Fir Cl Halewood L26 21 D4
Poynton SK12 36 C2
Tarporley CW6 146 B1
Fir Ct SK10 86 C1
Fir Gr Macclesfield SK11 112 B3
Warrington WA1 16 C4
Weaverham CW8 102 C4
Fir La CW8 102 A1
Fir Rd Bramhall SK7 35 F4
Denton M34 241 A7
Fir St Irlam M44 11 E3
Stockport SK4 240 E6
Widnes WA8 13 E1
Fir Tree Ave Chester CH4 141 D3
Goldborne WA3 3 F4
Knutsford WA16 82 B4
Fir Tree Cl WA4 26 B1
Fir Tree La Burtonwood WA5 7 D4
Chester CH3 119 F1
Fir Way L60 41 D3
Firbank CH2 72 B2
Firbank Cl WA7 24 B1
Firbeck Cl Broughton CH4 139 D2
Congleton CW12 155 F2
Firbeck Gdns CW2 189 E2
Firdale Rd CW8 103 E4
Firemans Sq CH1 237 D3
Firman Cl WA5 15 D4
Firs Gr SK8 239 A4
Firs La WA4 26 A3
Firs Rd SK8 239 A4
Firs Sch The CH2 118 C3
Firs The WA14 238 B3
First Ave Adlington SK10 36 B1
Crewe CW1 190 C1
Deeside Ind Est CH5 93 D1
Kidsgrove ST7 194 C1
Sandbach CW11 175 D3
First Dig La CW5 219 E4
First Wood St CW5 204 B3
Firswood Mount SK8 239 A4
Firthfields Cl CW9 103 F1
Firths Fields CW9 103 F1
Firtree Ave WA1 17 D4
Firtree Cl CW8 78 A2
Firtree Gr CH1 95 D4
Firvale Ave SK8 239 B1
Firwood Rd ST6 179 F1
Firwood Wlk CW2 190 B1
Fisher Rd CH1 117 F2
Fisher St WA7 23 D2
Fisherfield Dr WA3 10 A3
Fishermans Cl CW11 191 F4
Fishers La CW5 203 E4
Fishpool Rd CW8 123 F2
Fistral Ave SK8 34 B4

Gladstone St continued
Willaston (nr Nantwich) CW5 205 E3
Winsford CW7 149 E4
Gladville Dr SK8 240 A2
Glaisdale Cl CW2 206 A3
Glamis Cl Chester CH3 119 D1
Wistaston CW2 205 F4
Glan Aber Pk CH4 141 D4
Glandon Dr SK7 35 E4
Glanvor Rd SK3 240 C4
Glastonbury Ave
Cheadle Hulme SK7 35 E3
Chester CH2 118 B4
Goldborne WA3 4 B4
Glastonbury Cl WA7 24 C2
Glastonbury Dr
Middlewich CW10 128 A1
Poynton SK12 36 B3
Glaswen Gr SK5 240 F8
Glazebrook La WA3 11 D3
Glazebrook St WA1 16 B3
Glazebrook Sta WA3 11 D3
Glazebury CE (VA) Prim Sch WA3 5 E4
Glaziers La WA3 4 B1
Gleadmere WA8 12 B1
Gleave Av SK10 88 A4
Gleave Rd WA5 6 C3
Gleave St M33 242 B8
Glebe Ave WA4 17 E1
Glebe Cl CW5 220 A4
Glebe Green Dr CW7 149 E3
Glebe La WA8 13 D3
Glebe Meadows CH2 96 C1
Glebe Rd CW8 102 A2
Glebe St ST7 194 B1
Glebe The WA7 23 F1
Glebecroft Av CH2 72 A2
Glebeland WA3 4 C2
Glebelands Rd
Knutsford WA16 57 D1
Sale M33 242 A8
Glebeway Rd L65 70 C3
Gledhall St SK15 242 D2
Glen Aber Dr CH4 140 C4
Glen Ave M33 242 A8
Glen Cl WA3 11 D1
Glen Rd L66 69 E2
Glen The Blacon CH1 117 F3
Runcorn WA7 49 F3
Glenathol Rd L66 69 E2
Glenbourne Pk SK7 35 E3
Glenburn Ave L62 43 F2
Glencoe Cl CW4 130 B1
Glencoe Rd L66 69 E2
Glencourse Rd WA8 13 D3
Glendale Av CH2 72 A2
Glendale Ave CH5 116 A2
Glendale Cl Buerton CW3 230 C2
Wistaston CW2 189 E2
Glendene Ave SK7 35 E3
Glendyke Rd L66 69 E2
Gleneagles Cl Bramhall SK7 36 A4
Chester CH3 119 D2
Wilmslow SK9 60 B4
Gleneagles Dr
Haydock WA11 1 A3
Holmes Chapel CW4 130 A1
Macclesfield SK10 87 E2
Widnes WA8 13 D3
Winsford CW7 126 B1
Gleneagles Rd
Ellesmere Port L66 69 E2
Gatley SK8 239 C1
Glenesk Rd L66 69 E2
Glenfield WA14 238 B4
Glenfield Dr SK12 36 B2
Glenfield Rd SK4 240 D8
Glenholme Rd SK7 35 E4
Glenlea Dr M20 239 B8
Glenmaye Rd L66 69 E2
Glenmere Rd M20 239 C8
Glenn Pl WA8 12 C1
Glenorchy Cl CW4 130 B1
Glenside Cl CH1 117 E3
Glenside Dr SK9 60 B3
Glent View SK15 242 D4
Glenthorn Gr M33 242 B5
Glenton Pk L64 66 C3
Glenville Cl WA7 49 D3
Glenville Way M34 241 A6
Glenwood Cl L66 69 E3
Glenwood Gdns L66 69 E3
Glenwood Rd L66 69 E3
Gleyve WA16 29 E3
Gloucester Ave WA3 3 D4
Gloucester Cl
Ellesmere Port CH1 94 C4
Macclesfield SK10 87 F2
Warrington WA1 17 E4
Gloucester Rd Cheadle SK8 34 B4
Kidsgrove ST7 194 C1
Knutsford WA16 81 F4
Poynton SK12 36 B2
Widnes WA8 13 D2
Gloucester St Chester CH2 237 E4
Stockport SK3 240 D3
Glover Rd WA3 9 E2
Glover St Crewe CW1 190 A3
Newton-le-W WA12 2 B2
Glovers Loom CH3 142 A4
Gloverstone Ct CH4 237 E1
Glyn Ave L62 43 F4
Goathland Way SK11 112 B3
Goddard Rd WA7 23 F2
Goddard St CW1 190 A3
Godfrey St WA2 16 B4
Godley Ct SK14 241 F6
Godley Prim Sch SK14 241 F7
Godley St SK14 241 F8
Godscroft La WA6 73 F3
Godshill Cl WA5 14 B4
Godstall La CH1 237 E2
Godstow WA7 24 C2
Godward Rd SK22 39 D4
Golborne Dale Rd WA3 3 D2
Golborne Rd Goldborne WA3 3 E4
Winwick WA2 8 A4
Golborne St WA1 16 A3
Gold Triangle Complex WA8 22 A3
Goldborne All Saints RC Sch WA3 3 D4
Goldborne Cty Prim Sch WA3 3 D4
Goldborne La WA16 28 C1
Goldcliffe Cl WA5 7 E2
Goldcrest Cl Crewe CW1 189 F4
Runcorn WA7 49 F3
Winsford CW7 149 E3
Golden Sq WA1 16 A3
Goldfinch Cl CW12 156 C1
Goldfinch La WA3 9 F2
Goldford La SY14 199 F3
Goldsmith Dr CW11 174 B3
Golf Rd Altrincham WA15 238 F3
Sale M33 242 F6
Golftyn Dr CH5 91 E1
Golftyn La CH5 91 E1
Gongar La CH3 98 C1
Gonsley Cl CH2 237 E4
Gonville Ave SK11 112 C2
Gooch Dr WA12 2 B1
Goodall St SK11 112 C4
Goodall's Cnr CW2 206 B2
Goodier St M33 242 A6
Goodrington Rd SK9 34 C2
Goodwood Cl Barnton CW8 78 A2
Chester CH1 118 A1
Goodwood Gr L66 69 F2
Goose Gn WA14 238 D4
Goose La WA4 26 A1
Gooseberry La Kelsall CW6 122 C2
Runcorn WA7 24 B1
Goosebrook Cl CW9 78 B4
Goosebrook La WA4, CW9 52 C1
Goosetrey Cl 10 SK9 34 C1
Goostrey Cty Prim Sch CW4 130 C4
Goostrey Cty Prim Sch (The Annexe) CW4 107 F1
Goostrey La Cranage CW4 130 A4
Goostrey CW4 130 A4
Goostrey Sta CW4 131 D4
Gordale Cl CW12 157 D3
Gordon Ave Bebington L62 43 F4
Haydock WA11 1 C4
Warrington WA1 17 D4
Gordon La CH1 95 D3
Gordon Rd M33 242 B8
Gordon St
Ashton-u-L OL6 242 A4
Hyde SK14 241 E6
Stalybridge SK15 242 E1
Stockport SK4 & SK5 240 E7
Gore La SK9 59 E1
Gorse Bank Rd WA15 32 B4
Gorse Cl WA6 101 D3
Gorse Covert Cty Prim Sch WA3 10 A3
Gorse Covert Rd WA3 10 A3
Gorse Hall Cty Prim Sch SK15 242 D1
Gorse Hall Dr SK15 242 C1
Gorse La CW12 178 B3
Gorse Sq M31 11 E2
Gorse Stacks CH1 237 E3
Gorse The WA14 31 D4
Gorse Way CH3 142 A3
Gorsefield CH3 166 A1
Gorsefield Ave L62 43 E3
Gorsefield Cl L62 43 E3
Gorsefield Hey SK9 60 C4
Gorselands SK8 35 D3
Gorsewood Rd WA7 50 B3
Gorsey Bank Cres CW5 220 A4
Gorsey Bank Cty Prim Sch SK9 59 F4
Gorsey Bank Rd SK3 240 B4
Gorsey Brow SK6 241 A2
Gorsey La Altrincham WA14 238 B5
Bold Heath WA9 6 B3
Partington WA13 20 A4
Warrington WA2 16 B4
Widnes WA8 13 F1
Gorsey Mount St 23 SK1 240 F5
Gorsey Rd SK9 59 F4
Gorseywell La WA7 50 C3
Gorsley Cl CW10 151 E3
Gorstage La CW8 102 B4
Gorsthills Cty Prim Sch L66 69 E2
Gorston Wlk M22 33 E4
Gosberryhole La CW12 158 A1
Gosforth Ct WA7 49 F4
Gosforth Pl CH2 118 C2
Gosling Cl WA4 26 A1
Gosling Rd WA3 9 D4
Gosport Dr WA2 8 C1
Goss St CH1 237 D2
Gotherage Cl SK6 241 E2
Gotherage La SK6 241 E2
Gothic Cl SK6 241 F2
Gothurst Ct WA8 22 B4
Gough Ave WA2 8 A1
Gough St SK3 240 D5
Gough's La WA16 82 B4
Goulden St Crewe CW1 190 A3
Warrington WA5 15 F3
Goulders Ct WA7 50 A3
Gourham Dr SK8 239 F2
Gower Rd Hyde SK14 241 D5
Reddish SK4 240 D8
Gowy Cl Alsager ST7 192 C2
Sandbach CW11 174 C4
Wilmslow SK9 34 C1
Gowy Cres CH3 121 D1
Gowy Ct L66 69 F4
Gowy Rd CH2 96 C1
Gowy Wlk CW7 127 D2
Goyt Pl SK23 65 F4
Goyt Rd Disley SK12 38 B3
New Mills SK22 39 E3
Goyt Valley Ind Est SK23 39 E2
Goyt View SK22 39 D3
Goyt's La SK17 90 C1
Grace Ave WA2 16 A4
Grace Cl CW1 191 E2
Gradwell St SK3 240 D4
Grafton Mall 5 WA14 238 D4
Grafton Mews CH2 237 E4
Grafton Rd L65 70 B4
Grafton St Altrincham WA14 238 D4
Ashton-u-L OL6 242 A2
Hyde SK14 241 D7
Newton-le-W WA12 2 A2
Reddish SK4 240 E7
Warrington WA5 15 F3
Graham Ave L66 69 E3
Graham Cl WA8 12 B1
Graham Dr Disley SK12 38 B3
Halewood L26 21 D4
Graham Rd Blacon CH1 117 F2
Widnes WA8 22 B4
Grainger's Rd CW9 103 F3
Grammar School Rd
Lymm WA13 18 C1
Warrington WA4 16 C2
Grampian Way Bebington L62 43 F2
Neston L64 66 C3
Winsford CW7 149 D4
Granby Cl WA7 50 B3
Granby Rd
Cheadle Hulme SK8 35 D4
Warrington WA4 26 A4
Grand Junction Ret Pk CW1 190 B2
Grandford La CW5 217 E1
Grange Ave Barnton CW8 78 A2
Cheadle SK8 & M19 239 F3
Denton M34 241 B6
Warrington WA4 16 C2
Grange Cl Crewe CW1 190 C2
Goldborne WA3 3 E3
Hyde SK14 241 F5
Sandbach CW11 174 C4
Grange Cres L66 44 A1
Grange Ct Altrincham WA14 238 C1
Biddulph ST6 179 E1
Grange Ctr L65 70 A3
Grange Cty Comp Sch The WA7 23 E1
Grange Cty Inf Sch The WA7 23 E1
Grange Cty Jun Sch The WA7 23 E1
Grange Dr Hartford CW8 103 D3
Penketh WA5 15 D2
Thornton Hough L63 42 A4
Widnes WA8 12 B1
Grange Jun Sch The CW8 103 D3
Grange La Edge Green SY14 198 C2
Tilston SY14 198 C2
Weaverham CW8 102 A4
Winsford CW7 126 A2
Grange Lea CW10 128 A1
Grange Park Ave
Cheadle SK8 239 D5
Runcorn WA7 23 E1
Wilmslow SK9 60 A4
Grange Park Rd SK8 239 D5
Grange Rd Altrincham WA14 238 C1
Ashton CH3 99 D1
Barnton CW8 78 A2
Biddulph ST6 179 F2
Chester CH3 119 E1
Chester, Bache CH2 118 B2
Cuddington CW8 101 F1
Ellesmere Port L65 70 B2
Haydock WA11 1 B3
Hyde SK14 241 F5
Macclesfield SK11 112 B3
Northwich, Rudheath CW9 104 B3
Runcorn WA7 23 E1
Sale M33 242 A6
Grange Rd N SK14 241 F6
Grange Rd S SK14 241 F5
Grange Rd W CH3 119 E1
Grange Sch The CW8 103 D3
Grange The Hartford CW8 103 D3
Hyde SK14 241 F5
Grange Valley WA11 1 B3
Grange Valley Prim Sch WA11 1 B3
Grange Way CW11 174 C4
Grangebrook Dr CW7 126 B2
Grangefields ST6 179 F2
Grangeland Dr WA16 83 F2
Grangelands SK10 86 C1
Grangemoor WA7 49 E4
Grangeside CH2 118 B4
Grangeway Runcorn WA7 49 E4
Wilmslow SK9 34 B2
Grangeway Ct WA7 49 E4
Granston Cl WA5 7 F1
Grant Cl WA5 7 E1
Grant Rd WA5 15 D3
Grant St WA12 2 A2
Grantham Ave
Warrington WA1 16 C4
Warrington, Lower Walton WA4 26 A4
Grantham Cl CW9 104 B4
Grantham Rd SK4 240 C6
Granville Dr L66 69 D4
Granville Rd
Cheadle SK3 & SK8 240 C1
Chester CH1 118 A2
Northwich CW9 104 A3
Wilmslow SK9 59 F3
Granville Sq CW7 149 F4
Granville St
Ashton-u-L OL6 242 A2
Runcorn WA7 23 D2
Warrington WA1 16 B3
Winsford CW7 149 F4
Grapes St SK11 112 B4
Grappenhall CE Aided Prim Sch WA4 17 D1
Grappenhall Hall Sch WA4 17 D1
Grappenhall La WA4 27 F3
Grappenhall Rd
Ellesmere Port L65 69 F2
Warrington WA4 16 B1
Grasmere SK11 111 F3
Grasmere Ave
Congleton CW12 155 F1
Crewe CW2 189 F3
Warrington WA2 8 C2
Grasmere Cl
Stalybridge SK15 242 D4
Winsford CW7 126 B1
Grasmere Cres SK7 35 F4
Grasmere Dr
Holmes Chapel CW4 130 A2
Runcorn WA7 49 E3
Grasmere Rd
Alderley Edge SK9 60 A1
Chester CH2 118 C3
Ellesmere Port L65 70 B1
Frodsham WA6 74 B4
Gatley SK8 239 B3
Lymm WA13 18 C2
Neston L64 66 C3
Partington M31 11 F2
Grason Ave SK9 34 B1
Grasscroft Rd SK15 242 D1
Grassfield Way WA16 82 A4
Grassmere Cres SK6 37 F4
Grassmoor Cl L62 43 F4
Grassygreen La ST7 209 F1
Gratrix La M33 242 F5
Gratrix Rd L62 43 E4
Gravel La SK9 59 F3
Graveyard La WA16 58 C3
Gray Ave WA11 1 B3
Gray's Cl ST7 195 D4
Graylag Cl WA7 49 F3
Graysands Rd WA15 238 F3
Greasby Dr L66 69 F2
Great Ashfield WA8 12 B2
Great Budworth CE Contr Prim Sch CW9 79 D4
Great Delph WA11 1 B4
Great Egerton St
SK1 & SK4 240 E6
Great King St SK11 112 B4
Great Norbury St SK14 241 D6
Great Portwood St SK1 240 F6
Great Queen St SK11 112 B4
Great Riding WA7 50 B4
Great Sankey Cty High Sch WA5 14 C4
Great Sankey Cty Prim Sch WA5 15 D3
Great Sankey L Ctr WA5 14 C4
Great Underbank SK1 240 F5
Greatoak Rd ST7 209 F2
Greave SK6 241 D4
Greave Fold SK6 241 D4
Greave Prim Sch SK6 241 D4
Greaves La SY14 222 C4
Greaves Rd SK9 59 F4
Grebe Cl Knutsford WA16 57 D2
Poynton SK12 36 A2
Greeba Ave WA4 16 A2
Greek St Runcorn WA7 22 C2
Stockport SK1 & SK3 240 E4
Green Acre Cl WA16 82 A4
Green Ave Alpraham CW6 169 E2
Barnton CW8 78 A2
Davenham CW9 103 F2
Green Bank Adderley TF9 235 D3
Chester CH4 141 F3
Green Bank Ctr CH4 141 E3
Green Bridge Cl WA7 24 A1
Green Cl SK8 239 A6
Green Coppice WA7 50 B4
Green Courts WA14 238 B3
Green Croft SK6 241 E3
Green Dr Alsager ST7 193 E2
Wilmslow SK9 34 B1
Green Gables Cl SK8 239 B1
Green Hall Mews SK9 60 A3
Green Hill St SK3 240 D3
Green Hill Terr SK3 240 D3
Green Jones Brow WA5 6 C3
Green La Acton CW5 204 A2
Alderley Edge SK9 59 F1
Appleton WA4 27 D3
Audlem CW3 229 F1
Green La continued
Barbridge CW5 187 D4
Bollington SK10 63 D1
Burtonwood WA5 6 C4
Chester CH3, CH4 119 D2
Chester, Lache CH4 140 C2
Chowley CH3 182 C3
Davenham CW9 103 F2
Disley SK12 38 B2
Ellesmere Port L65 70 B2
Ellesmere Port, Sutton Green L66 69 E2
Higher Kinnerton CH4 161 D3
Higher Wincham CW9 79 F2
Horton Green SY14 212 A4
Irlam M44 11 F3
Kelsall CW6 122 B2
Knutsford WA16 56 B2
Lindow End SK9 84 C4
Manchester SK4 240 B7
Peover WA16 83 E1
Picton CH2 96 B2
Plumley WA16 80 C3
Poynton SK12 37 E2
Romiley SK6 241 B2
Sandbach CW11 173 F4
Saughall CH1 117 E4
Shocklach SY14 211 E4
Stockport SK4 240 D6
Stockport, Heaton Norris SK4 240 C6
Warrington WA1 17 D4
Widnes WA8 12 C1
Willaston (nr Nantwich) CW5 205 F3
Wilmslow SK9 60 A4
Winwick WA2 8 A4
Green La Cl WA2 8 A4
Green La E CH5 116 B4
Green La W CH5 93 D2
Green Lane Ind Est SK4 240 D6
Green Lane Sch WA1 17 D4
Green Lawns Dr CH1 94 C4
Green Mdws SK11 111 F3
Green Meadows WA3 3 F3
Green Oaks Path WA8 23 E4
Green Oaks Way WA8 23 E4
Green Pk CW8 102 C4
Green Rd M31 11 F2
Green St Alderley Edge SK9 60 A1
Holt LL13 180 C1
Hyde SK14 241 E5
Knutsford WA16 57 D1
Macclesfield SK11 112 C4
Sandbach CW11 175 D4
Stockport SK3 240 F2
Warrington WA5 15 F3
Green The Cheadle SK8 34 C4
Ellesmere Port L65 70 A1
Hartford CW8 103 D3
Harthill CH3 183 F2
Higher Kinnerton CH4 161 D4
Lawton-gate ST7 194 A2
Middlewich CW10 151 E3
Neston L64 66 B4
Neston L64 66 C3
Stockport SK4 240 C6
Tarvin CH3 121 F1
Thornton Hough L63 42 B2
Wilmslow SK9 34 C2
Green Tree Gdns SK6 241 B2
Green View WA13 19 D3
Green Villa Pk SK9 59 F2
Green Way CH1 94 A1
Green Wlk
Altrincham WA14 238 B3
Cuddington CW8 102 A2
Gatley SK8 239 A6
Partington M31 11 E1
Greenacre Dr L63 43 E4
Greenacre Rd CH4 140 C2
Greenacres Crewe CW1 190 B3
Duddon CW6 145 D3
Frodsham WA6 74 B3
Lymm WA13 19 D2
Sandbach CW11 175 D4
Greenacres Cl WA3 4 A4
Greenacres Rd CW12 155 F1
Greenall Ave WA5 14 B2
Greenall Rd CW9 104 A4
Greenalls Ave WA4 16 B1
Greenbank Ave
Ellesmere Port L66 69 E4
Gatley M22 239 A5
Greenbank Cl CW5 205 E3
Greenbank Dr SK10 88 A4
Greenbank Gdns WA4 16 C1
Greenbank La CW8 103 E3
Greenbank Pk CW11 175 D1
Greenbank Rd
Chester CH2 119 D2
Gatley SK8 239 A6
Warrington WA4 16 C1
Greenbank Residential Sch CW8 103 E3
Greenbank St WA4 16 B1
Greenbank Sta CW8 103 E3
Greenbridge Rd WA7 24 A1
Greencourts Bsns Pk M22 34 A4
Greendale Dr
Middlewich CW10 151 D4
Newcastle-u-L ST5 210 B1
Greendale La SK10 86 A4
Greenfield Ave CH4 161 D4

Greenfield Cl
New Mills SK22 39 D4
Stockport SK3 240 E2
Greenfield Cres CH3 143 D3
Greenfield Gdns CH2 72 A2
Greenfield La
Chester CH2 119 D3
Frodsham WA6 49 D1
Greenfield Prim Sch
SK14 241 D6
Greenfield Rd
Bollington SK10 88 A4
Broughton CH4 139 E2
Congleton CW12 156 A2
Ellesmere Port L66 69 D4
Waverton CH3 143 D3
Greenfield St SK14 241 D6
Greenfield Way CW8 102 A2
Greenfields Chester CH2 95 F1
Winsford CW7 127 D1
Greenfields Ave
Appleton WA4 26 B4
Bebington L62 43 E4
Shavington CW2 206 A2
Greenfields Cl Neston L64 66 C3
Newton-le-W WA12 2 B2
Warrington WA1 17 E4
Greenfields Cres L62 43 E4
Greenfields Croft L64 66 C3
Greenfields Dr L64 66 C3
Greenfields Rd ST7 193 F2
Greengate Rd
Dukinfield M34 241 A8
Lawton-gate ST7 193 F3
Greengates Cres L64 66 C3
Greenhalgh St SK4 240 E6
Greenhill Ave M33 242 A8
Greenhill La WA4 52 A3
Greenhill Wlk SK12 38 B3
Greenhills Cl SK11 112 C4
Greenhouse Farm Rd
WA7 50 A4
Greenhythe Rd SK9 34 B3
Greenland Cl CW6 146 B1
Greenlands CH3 166 A2
Greenlaw Cl CW9 104 A3
Greenlea Cl L65 70 A1
Greenore Dr L24 21 E1
Greensbridge La L26 21 D4
Greenshall La SK12 38 C3
Greenshank Cl WA12 2 B2
Greenside SK4 240 A5
Greenside Ave WA6 74 B4
Greenside Ct CW9 105 E3
Greenside Dr
Altrincham WA14 238 E1
Lostock CW9 105 D4
Greensway CH4 141 D4
Greenvale Dr SK8 239 C6
Greenview Dr M20 239 C8
Greenway Alsager ST7 193 D3
Altrincham WA14 238 A5
Appleton WA4 26 B4
Cheadle Hulme SK7 35 E3
Congleton CW12 156 A2
Crewe CW1 190 B4
Farndon CH3 180 C1
Great Sankey WA5 14 C4
Hyde SK14 241 D5
Romiley SK6 241 E1
Tilston SY14 198 B2
Warrington WA1 16 C4
Wilmslow SK9 60 A3
Greenway Cl Helsby WA6 73 D2
Rode Heath ST7 193 F4
Greenway Dr CW9 104 B4
Greenway Rd
Altrincham WA15 238 F8
Biddulph ST6 179 F1
Cheadle SK9 34 B3
Runcorn WA7 23 D1
Speke L24 21 D2
Widnes WA8 13 D1
Greenway St CH4 237 E1
Greenway Wlk CW9 104 B4
Greenways ST7 209 F1
Greenwell Rd WA11 1 B3
Greenwood Ave
Chester CH4 141 E4
Congleton CW12 156 C2
Greenwood Cl Croft WA3 4 C1
Weaverham CW8 77 E1
Greenwood Cres WA2 8 C1
Greenwood Dr
Newton-le-W WA12 2 B1
Wilmslow SK9 60 B4
Greenwood Rd WA13 18 C1
Greenwood St 1 WA14 238 D4
Greg Ave SK10 87 F4
Greg Mews SK9 34 A1
Gregory Ave SK6 241 C1
Gregory Cl WA5 15 E4
Gregson Rd WA8 13 E1
Grenfell Cl L64 41 E1
Grenfell Pk L64 41 E1
Grenfell St 11 WA8 23 D4
Grenville Cl CW1 191 E3
Grenville Cres L63 43 E4
Grenville Rd L64 41 F1
Grenville St SK3 240 D4
Gresford Ave CH2 237 F4
Gresford Cl WA5 7 F1
Gresham Wlk SK4 240 E7
Gresley Way ST7 209 F1
Gresty Green Rd CW2 206 B4
Gresty La CW2 206 A4
Gresty Rd CW2 190 B1
Gresty Road Football Gd
(Crewe Alexandra FC)
CW2 190 B1
Gresty Terr CW1 190 C2
Greta Ave SK9 34 B3
Greville Dr CW7 127 D1
Grey Cl SK6 241 A4
Grey Friars CH1 237 D2
Grey Rd WA14 238 C5
Grey St Stalybridge SK15 242 F1
Warrington WA1 16 B3
Greyhound Park Rd
CH1 117 F2
Greyhound Pk CH1 118 A1
Greyhound Rd SK10 86 A3
Greylands Rd M20 239 C8
Greymarsh Dr SK12 36 C1
Greymist Ave WA1 17 E4
Greys Ct WA1 9 E1
Greystoke Ave M33 242 B5
Greystoke Dr SK9 60 A1
Greystoke Rd SK10 87 F1
Greystone Heath Sch
WA5 14 C3
Greystone Pk CW1 190 B2
Greystone Rd WA5 14 C2
Greystones L66 69 E2
Greystones Rd CH3 119 E1
Grice St WA4 16 B1
Griffin Cl Blacon CH1 117 F3
Burtonwood WA5 6 C3
New Mills SK22 39 E3
Norton in Hales TF9 236 B1
Griffin Mews WA8 13 D2
Griffiths Dr CW9 104 B3
Griffiths Rd Lostock CW9 79 F1
Northwich CW9 104 C4
Griffiths St WA4 16 C2
Grig Pl ST7 193 E3
Grimsditch La
Daresbury WA4 52 A3
Whitley WA4 52 A3
Grimshaw Ave SK10 88 A4
Grimshaw Cl SK6 241 A4
Grimshaw La SK10 88 A4
Grindley Bank CH2 119 F4
Grindley Gdns L65 70 B1
Grisedale Ave WA2 8 A2
Grisedale Cl WA7 49 F3
Grisedale Rd L62 43 F4
Grisedale Way SK11 112 A3
Grizedale WA8 12 C2
Grizedale Rd SK6 241 B4
Groarke Dr WA5 14 B3
Groby Pl WA14 238 D5
Groby Rd Altrincham WA14 238 C4
Crewe CW1 190 C4
Groby St SK15 242 F1
Grosvenor Ave
Alsager ST7 193 E3
Goldborne WA3 3 E4
Hartford CW8 103 D2
Warrington WA1 16 C4
Grosvenor Cl
Great Sankey WA5 15 E3
Wilmslow SK9 60 A2
Grosvenor Cres SK14 241 C5
Grosvenor Ct Chester CH1 237 F2
Winsford CW7 149 E4
Grosvenor Dr SK12 36 B2
Grosvenor Gdns WA12 2 B1
Grosvenor Nuffield Hospl
CH4 141 E3
Grosvenor Pk Rd CH2 237 F2
Grosvenor Pk Terr CH2 237 F2
Grosvenor Pl CH4 237 E1
Grosvenor Prec The CH1 237 E2
Grosvenor Rd
Altrincham WA14 238 E5
Chester CH4 141 E4
Congleton CW12 156 A2
Haydock WA11 1 A4
Hyde SK14 241 D5
Manchester SK4 240 B7
Tarvin CH3 121 D1
Widnes WA8 13 D2
Grosvenor Sq M33 242 A6
Grosvenor St Chester CH1 237 D2
Crewe CW1 190 A3
6 Macclesfield SK11 112 B4
Runcorn WA7 23 D2
Stalybridge SK15 242 D1
9 Stockport SK1 240 F4
Winsford CW7 149 F4
Grotsworth La SY14 214 C4
Grotto La WA16 108 A4
Grounds St WA2 16 A4
Grove Arc SK9 60 A4
Grove Ave Chester CH3 119 D2
Kidsgrove ST7 194 C1
Lawton-gate ST7 194 A2
Lostock CW9 80 A2
Lymm WA13 18 B2
Wilmslow SK9 60 A4
Grove Cl CW7 149 D4
Grove Cres CW3 232 B1
Grove Ct Alsager ST7 193 F2
Sale M33 242 D6
Grove Gdns CH3 119 F1
Grove La SK8 35 D3
Grove Park Ave ST7 194 A2
Grove Pk WA16 57 D1
Grove Prim Sch The SK8 35 D4
Grove Rd Altrincham WA15 238 E3
Backford CH1 94 C2
Grove Rise WA13 18 C2
Grove St New Mills SK22 39 D4
Runcorn WA7 22 C2
Stalybridge SK16 242 A1
Warrington WA4 16 B2
Wilmslow SK9 60 A4
Grove The
Cheadle Hulme SK8 35 D3
Knutsford WA16 57 E2
Lawton-gate ST7 194 A2
Penketh WA5 14 C2
Sale M33 242 B5
Stockport SK3 240 E3
Grovemount CW9 103 F1
Groves The Chester CH1 237 E2
Ellesmere Port CH1 95 D4
GroveThe SY13 225 F1
Grovewood Mews SK11 112 B3
Grub La CW6 122 B3
Grundy Cl WA8 12 C2
Grundy St WA3 3 D4
Guardian St WA5 15 F3
Guernsey Cl Appleton WA4 26 B4
Congleton CW12 157 D1
Guernsey Dr L65 70 B1
Guernsey Rd WA8 13 F2
Guest St WA8 23 D4
Guests Slack WA6 100 A4
Guilden Gn CH3 119 F2
Guilden Sutton CE Contr
Prim Sch CH2 119 F3
Guilden Sutton La CH2 119 E3
Guildford Ave SK8 35 D3
Guildford Cl WA2 9 D1
Guildford Rd CH4 140 C3
Guillemot Cl CW1 190 C3
Gull Cl SK12 36 A2
Gullane Cl SK10 87 D2
Gullet The CW5 204 C3
Gullivers World Theme Pk
WA5 7 E1
Gulls Way L60 40 C4
Gunco La
Macclesfield SK11 112 C3
Prestbury SK10 87 E4
Gunn Gr L64 66 C4
Gutterscroft CW1 191 E3
Gutticar Rd WA8 12 A1
Guy La Hargrave CH3 143 E3
Waverton CH3 143 E3
Guywood La SK6 241 C3

Hackberry Cl WA14 238 B8
Hacked Way La SK11 113 F3
Haddon Cl
Alderley Edge SK9 59 F1
High Lane SK6 37 F3
Holmes Chapel CW4 130 A2
Macclesfield SK11 112 A3
Wistaston CW2 206 A4
Haddon Dr WA8 12 B2
Haddon Gr
Altrincham WA15 238 F7
Sale M33 242 A6
Haddon La L64 67 E2
Haddon Rd Burton L64 67 E1
Cheadle SK8 34 B4
Hadfield Cl WA8 13 F1
Hadfield St CW9 79 D1
Hadleigh Cl WA5 14 C3
Hadley Ave L62 43 E4
Hadley Cl SK8 239 F1
Hadlow La L64 67 F4
Hadlow Rd L64 67 F3
Hadrian Dr CH1 117 F3
Hadrian Way CW8 102 A1
Hafod Cl Blacon CH1 117 E2
Connah's Quay CH5 91 E1
Hag Bank La SK12 38 B4
Hague Bar Prim Sch SK22 38 C4
Hague Bar Rd SK22 39 D4
Hague Fold SK22 38 C4
Hague St OL6 242 A4
Haig Ave Great Sankey WA5 15 D3
Irlam M44 11 E2
Haig Ct WA16 57 E2
Haig Rd Knutsford WA16 57 E2
Widnes WA8 13 D1
Haigh Lawn WA14 238 B3
Hale Ave SK12 36 B1
Hale Bank Rd WA8 21 F3
Hale CE Contr Sch L24 21 E1
Hale Ct WA14 238 D2
Hale Gate Rd Hale L24 21 F1
Widnes WA8 22 A2
Hale Golf Course WA15 32 A4
Hale Gr WA5 15 D3
Hale Low Rd WA15 238 F3
Hale Prep Sch WA15 238 E3
Hale Rd Altrincham WA15 32 B4
Hale L24 21 D1
Manchester SK4 240 C7
Widnes WA8 22 B4
Hale Road Ind Est WA8 22 B3
Hale St WA2 16 A4
Hale Sta WA14 238 D2
Hale View WA7 48 C4
Hale View Rd WA6 73 E2
Halebank CE Contr Prim
Sch WA8 22 A3
Halewood La Ends L26 21 D4
Haley Rd N WA5 6 C3
Haley Rd S WA5 6 C3
Half St SK11 112 B3
Halfacre La WA4 17 F1
Halghton La SY13 222 A1
Halifax Cl WA2 8 B1
Halkett Cl CH4 140 C3
Halkyn Rd CH2 237 F4
Hall Ave
Altrincham WA15 238 F7
Widnes WA8 12 A1
Hall Cl SK10 87 E2
Hall Dr Alsager ST7 193 E2
Appleton WA4 26 B3
Marston CW9 79 D3
Willaston (nr Nantwich)
CW5 205 E3
Hall Gr Cheadle SK8 239 C6
Macclesfield SK10 87 E2
Hall Hill SK10 87 F4
Hall La Antrobus CW9 53 D1
Appleton WA4 27 D4
Audlem CW3 230 B4
Bold Heath WA9 6 A2
Brown Knowl CH3 199 E4
Cronton WA8 12 B4
Daresbury WA4 25 E1
Haughton Moss CW6 186 B3
Higher Wincham CW9 79 F2
Kelsall CW6 122 B3
Little Leigh CW9 77 F4
Lostock CW9 79 F2
Mobberley WA16 58 B2
Partington M31 11 F2
Pickmere WA16 55 D1
Sandbach CW11 174 A3
Stretton WA4 52 C4
Sutton Lane Ends SK11 112 C2
Utkinton CW6 146 B3
Warmingham CW11 173 F2
Winsford CW7 149 D2
Hall La The CW6 147 E1
Hall Meadow SK8 239 E1
Hall Moss La SK7 35 E2
Hall Nook WA5 14 C2
Hall O'shaw St CW1 190 C2
Hall Rd Altrincham WA14 238 C1
Haydock WA11 1 C4
Warrington WA1 17 E4
Wilmslow SK9 60 A4
Wilmslow, Handforth SK9 34 C2
Hall St Ashton-u-L OL6 242 B2
Audley ST7 209 E1
Cheadle SK8 239 D6
Denton SK14 241 B7
Macclesfield SK11 112 B4
New Mills SK22 39 D4
Warrington WA1 16 B3
Hall Terr WA5 14 C4
Hall Wood Ave WA11 1 C4
Hall Wood Rd SK9 34 C1
Halla Way WA4 16 C2
Hallastone Rd WA6 73 E2
Hallcroft M31 11 F2
Hallcroft Pl WA4 17 D1
Hallefield Cres SK11 112 C4
Hallefield Dr 14 SK11 112 C4
Hallefield Rd 15 SK11 112 C4
Hallfield Dr CH2 72 A2
Hallfield Park L66 69 E2
Hallfields Rd Tarvin CH3 121 E1
Warrington WA2 16 B4
Hallgate Dr SK8 239 A2
Hallgreen La CW12 155 E4
Halliday Cl WA3 9 F2
Halliwell's Brow WA16 29 D2
Hallows Ave WA2 16 B4
Hallows Cl CW6 122 B2
Hallows Dr CW6 122 B2
Hallowsgate Ct CW6 122 B2
Halls Rd Biddulph ST6 179 E1
Mow Cop ST7 195 E4
Hallsgreen La CH2 96 C4
Hallshaw Ave CW1 190 C3
Hallwood Cl WA7 49 D3
Hallwood Dr L66 68 B2
Hallwood Link Rd WA7 49 F3
Hallwood Park Ave WA7 49 F3
Hallwood Park Cty Prim
Sch WA7 49 F3
Halsall Ave WA2 16 B4
Halsall Cl WA7 50 B3
Halston Cl SK5 240 F8
Halstone Ave SK9 59 F2
Halton Brook Ave WA7 23 E1
Halton Coll of F Ed WA8 23 D4
Halton Coll of F Ed
(Annexe) Runcorn WA7 23 F2
Widnes WA8 23 D4
Halton Cres L66 69 F1
Halton Ct WA7 23 E1
Halton Dr CW2 189 E3
Halton General Hospl
WA7 49 F3
Halton Link Rd WA7 49 F4
Halton Lodge Ave WA7 49 E4
Halton Lodge Cty Prim Sch
WA7 49 E4
Halton Rd Chester CH2 118 C3
Ellesmere Port L66 69 F1
Great Sankey WA5 14 B4
Runcorn WA7 23 E1
Halton St Haydock WA11 1 C3
Hyde SK14 241 F7
Halton St Mary's CE Aided
Prim Sch WA7 50 A4
Halton Station Rd WA7 49 F2
Halton View Rd WA8 13 E1
Halton Way L66 69 F1
Hamble Dr WA5 15 D2
Hamble Way SK10 86 C1
Hambledon Cl L66 69 D3
Hambleton Cl WA8 12 B2
Hambleton Rd SK8 34 B4
Hambleton Way CW7 149 D4
Hambletts Hollow WA6 100 C3
Hamilton Ave
Hawarden CH5 116 A2
Irlam M44 11 E2
Hamilton Cl
Haslington CW1 191 E2
Macclesfield SK10 113 D4
Neston L64 41 D1
Hamilton Cres SK4 240 B5
Hamilton Pl CH1 237 D2
Hamilton Rd
Connah's Quay CH5 91 E1
Lymm WA13 18 B2
Hamilton Sq SK4 240 E7
Hamilton St Chester CH2 118 C2
Stalybridge SK15 242 C2
Hammond Sch
Chester CH2 237 D4
Chester, Hoole Bank CH2 119 D4
Hammond St CW2 190 B2
Hamnet Ct WA3 9 F2
Hamnett St SK14 241 D7
Hamon Rd WA15 238 E4
Hampden Rd M33 242 A5
Hampshire Cl CW12 156 B2
Hampshire Rd M31 11 E1
Hampshire Wlk SK10 86 C1
Hampson Ave WA3 4 C2
Hampson Cres SK9 34 B2
Hampson St M33 242 D6
Hampstead Ct 13 CW7 149 D4
Hampton Cl Neston L64 66 C3
Widnes WA8 13 F2
Hampton Cres Neston L64 66 C3
No Man's Heath SY14 214 A2
Hampton Ct WA7 24 B2
Hampton Dr Cronton WA8 12 B3
Great Sankey WA5 15 E2
Hampton Gdns L65 70 A3
Hampton Gr SK8 239 E2
Hampton Rd Chester CH4 140 C3
Irlam M44 11 E2
Hamsterley Cl WA3 10 A3
Hanbury Cl CW2 206 A4
Hancock Rd CW12 156 C2
Hand St SK11 112 A4
Handbridge CH4 237 E1
Handel Mews M33 242 C6
Handford Ave L62 43 F3
Handford Rd CH2 118 C3
Handforth Cl WA4 17 E2
Handforth Hall Cty Prim
Sch SK9 34 B2
Handforth La WA7 49 E3
Handforth Rd Crewe CW2 189 F2
Wilmslow SK9 34 C1
Handforth Sta SK9 34 B2
Handley Cl SK3 240 C1
Handley Hill CW7 149 E4
Handley St WA7 22 C2
Hangman's La CW9 105 E4
Hankelow Cl Chester CH2 237 E4
Middlewich CW10 151 E3
Hankey St WA7 22 C1
Hankins Heys La CW3 231 D1
Hankinson Cl M31 11 F1
Hanley Cl Disley SK12 38 B3
Widnes WA8 12 B1
Hanley Rd WA8 12 B1
Hanns Hall Rd L64 67 E4
Hanover Bsns Pk WA14 238 B7
Hanover Dr CW7 149 E3
Hanover Rd WA14 238 B7
Hanover St
Stalybridge SK15 242 C2
Warrington WA1 16 A2
Hapsford Cl WA3 9 E2
Hapsford La
Dunham-on-t-H WA6 97 F4
Elton CH2 72 B2
Elton, Hapsford WA6 72 C1
Hapton Pl SK4 240 E7
Harbord St WA1 16 B2
Harbour Cl WA7 50 B3
Harbour La SK11 111 E1
Harburn Wlk M22 33 F4
Harcourt Cl WA3 9 F2
Harcourt Rd
Altrincham WA14 238 D6
Sale M33 242 A8
Hardcastle Rd SK3 240 D3
Harden Pk SK9 60 A2
Harding Ave
Tattenhall CH3 166 B1
Warrington WA2 8 C1
Harding Rd Chester CH2 118 A4
Nantwich CW5 204 B2
Hardingswood Rd ST7 194 C1
Hardknott Rd L62 43 F4
Hardman Ave SK6 241 A3
Hardman St SK3 240 D4
Hardwick Cl SK6 37 F3
Hardwick Dr SK11 112 A3
Hardwick Grange WA1 17 F4
Hardwick Rd WA7 23 E2
Hardwicke Rd SK12 36 C2
Hardy Cl Ellesmere Port L66 69 F2
Wistaston CW2 205 F4
Hardy Dr Altrincham WA15 238 F7
Cheadle Hulme SK7 35 E4
Hardy Rd WA13 18 B1
Hardy St Warrington WA2 16 A3
Warrington WA2 16 A4
Hare La CH3 119 F4
Hare's La WA6 73 F4
Harebell Cl CH3 142 A3
Harebell Gr ST7 195 F
Harecastle Ave ST7 194 C
Harefield Dr SK9 60 A

Harefield Rd SK9 34 C2
Harehill Gdn SK10 86 A3
Harewood Ave L66 69 E2
Harewood Cl CW7 126 A1
Harewood Ct M33 242 C5
Harewood Way SK11 112 A3
Harfield Gdns L66 69 E3
Hargrave Ave CW2 189 F2
Hargrave Dr L66 69 F3
Hargrave La L63 42 C3
Hargreaves Ct WA8 13 E1
Hargreaves Rd CW9 104 B4
Harington Cl CH2 95 E1
Harington Rd CH2 118 B4
Harlech Cl WA5 7 F1
Harlech Ct L65 70 B2
Harlech Way L65 70 B2
Harley Rd M33 242 C7
Harlow Cl WA4 17 E2
Harlyn Ave SK7 35 F4
Harlyn Gdns WA5 14 B2
Harn The L66 69 E2
Harold Rd WA11 1 C4
Harper Cl
Ellesmere Port L66 69 E2
Macclesfield SK11 112 B3
Harper Gr CW12 156 C2
Harper St SK3 240 E3
Harpers Rd WA2 9 D1
Harpur Cres ST7 193 D3
Harraps Pl SK11 112 A3
Harrier Cl CW1 189 F4
Harriet St M44 11 F3
Harrington Dr SK11 111 E1
Harrington Rd WA14 238 B5
Harris Cl CW1 173 D1
Harris Rd CW9 80 A1
Harris St WA8 13 E1
Harriseahead La ST7 195 E2
Harrison Dr Allostock CW4 107 D1
Haydock WA11 1 A3
Harrison Gr CH5 116 A2
Harrison Sq WA5 7 F1
Harrison St
Stalybridge SK15 242 D2
Stockport SK1 & SK2 240 F3
Widnes WA8 22 A3
Harrison Way WA12 2 B2
Harrisons Pl CW8 103 F4
Harrogate Cl Bebington L62 43 E2
Warrington WA5 7 D1
Harrogate Rd L62 43 E2
Harrop Rd Altrincham WA15 238 F2
Bollington SK10 88 B4
Runcorn WA7 23 D1
Harrop St SK15 242 D2
Harrow Cl Appleton WA4 26 C3
Crewe CW2 190 A1
Harrow Dr WA7 23 F1
Harrow Gr L62 43 F4
Harrow Rd L65 70 B2
Harrowgate Cl WA5 15 D4
Harrytown SK6 241 A2
Harrytown RC High Sch SK6 241 A2
Hart Ave M33 242 F5
Hart St WA14 238 E5
Hartford Ave SK9 59 F3
Hartford Bsns Ctr CW8 102 C2
Hartford Cl CW11 175 E4
Hartford Cty High Sch CW8 103 E3
Hartford Cty Prim Sch CW8 103 D2
Hartford Dr L65 69 F2
Hartford Manor Cty Prim Sch CW8 103 E3
Hartford Rd CW9 103 F1
Hartford Sta CW8 103 D2
Hartford Way CH1 118 A1
Harthill Cty Prim Sch CH3 183 F2
Harthill La CH3 183 F2
Harthill Rd Blacon CH1 117 F3
Burwardsley CH3 184 A3
Hartington Dr SK7 36 C4
Hartington Rd
Altrincham WA14 238 D8
Bramhall SK7 35 F3
Cheadle SK8 34 B4
High Lane SK6 37 F4
Hartington St CH4 141 F4
Hartland Cl Poynton SK12 36 B3
Widnes WA8 13 D3
Hartley Cl WA13 18 C2
Hartley Gr SK10 87 F4
Hartley Rd WA14 238 C5
Hartley St SK3 240 D4
Hartshead Ave SK15 242 D3
Hartshead View SK14 241 F5
Hartswood Cl
Appleton WA4 26 C2
Dukinfield M34 241 A8
Harty Rd WA11 1 A3
Harvard Cl WA7 24 B1
Harvard Ct WA2 8 A2
Harvest Cl CW9 126 C4
Harvest Rd SK10 87 E2
Harvey Ave Nantwich CW5 205 D3
Newton-le-W WA12 1 C2
Harvey La WA3 3 D4
Harvey Rd CW12 157 D3
Harvey St SK1 240 F5
Harvin Gr M34 241 A6
Harwood Gdns WA4 17 D1
Harwood St SK4 240 E7
Haryngton Ave WA5 15 F4
Haseley Cl SK12 36 C3
Haslam Rd SK3 240 E2
Haslemere Ave WA15 32 B3
Haslemere Dr WA5 14 B2
Haslemere Way CW1 190 B3
Haslin Cres CH3 142 B4
Haslington Cty Prim Sch CW1 191 E2
Hassall Rd Alsager ST7 193 D3
Haslington CW11 192 A4
Hassall Green CW11 192 A4
Sandbach CW11 175 E2
Hassall St SK15 242 E1
Hassall Way 6 SK8 34 C3
Hastings Ave WA2 8 A2
Hasty La Altrincham M90 32 C4
Wythenshawe WA15 32 C4
Hatch Mere WA6 100 B3
Hatchery Cl WA4 27 D2
Hatchings The WA13 18 C1
Hatchmere Cl
Sandbach CW11 174 C4
Warrington WA5 15 F3
Hatchmere Dr CH3 142 A4
Hatchmere Rd SK8 239 F4
Hatfield Ct CW4 130 A2
Hatfield Gdns WA4 26 C2
Hathaway Cl SK8 34 A4
Hathaway Dr SK11 112 B3
Hatherlow SK6 241 A1
Hatherlow Hts SK6 241 A1
Hatherton Cl
Davenham CW9 103 F2
Newcastle-u-L ST5 210 B1
Hatherton Rd CW5 220 A3
Hatherton Way CH2 237 E4
Hatley La WA6 73 F4
Hatter St CW12 156 C2
Hatton Ave L62 43 F2
Hatton La Appleton WA4 26 A1
Hatton WA4 26 A1
Northwich CW8 103 E3
Stretton WA4 26 A1
Hatton Rd CH1 117 F3
Hatton St Macclesfield SK11 112 B4
3 Stockport SK1 240 E6
Haughton Hall Rd M34 241 A7
Haughton St SK14 241 E5
Havana La CW12 157 D3
Havannah Cty Prim Sch CW12 157 D3
Havannah La
Congleton CW12 156 C3
St Helens WA9 1 A2
Havannah St CW12 156 C2
Haven The Altrincham WA15 238 F3
Crewe CW1 190 B4
Havergal St 5 WA7 22 C1
Havisham Cl WA3 9 E3
Hawarden Gdns L65 70 B1
Hawarden Ind Pk CH4 139 D3
Hawarden Rd WA14 238 D6
Haweswater Av CW1 173 D1
Haweswater Ave WA11 1 A3
Haweswater Cl WA7 50 A3
Haweswater Dr CW7 126 B1
Hawick Cl L66 69 D3
Hawk Rd SK22 39 F4
Hawk St CW11 175 D3
Hawke St SK15 242 F1
Hawker Cl CH4 139 E2
Hawkeshead Way CW7 126 B1
Hawkins La SK10 88 B2
Hawkins Rd L64 41 F1
Hawkins St SK5 240 E8
Hawkins View CH3 120 C3
Hawks Ct WA7 49 F3
Hawks Way L60 40 C4
Hawkshaw Cl WA3 9 E2
Hawkshead Rd WA5 6 C3
Hawkstone Gr WA6 73 E2
Hawley Dr WA15 32 A4
Hawley La WA15 32 A4
Hawley's Cl WA5 7 F1
Hawley's La WA2 8 A1
Haworth Ave CW12 157 D3
Haworth Cl SK11 112 A3
Hawthorn Ave
Altrincham WA15 238 F8
Nantwich CW5 204 C3
Newton-le-W WA12 2 B2
Runcorn WA7 23 D1
Widnes WA8 13 D1
Wilmslow SK9 60 A4
Hawthorn Bank SK22 39 D3
Hawthorn Bsns Pk WA2 16 A4
Hawthorn Cl
Altrincham WA15 238 F7
Holmes Chapel CW4 130 B2
Winsford CW7 126 B2
Hawthorn Dr M44 11 E3
Hawthorn Gdns ST7 210 B4
Hawthorn Gr
Cheadle Hulme SK7 35 E3
Crewe CW1 190 B4
Hyde SK14 241 D5
Manchester SK4 240 B7
Warrington WA4 16 B2
Wilmslow SK9 60 A4
Hawthorn La Bebington L62 43 E4
Wilmslow SK9 60 A4
Wistaston CW2 189 F1
Hawthorn Pk SK9 60 A4
Hawthorn Rd
Altrincham WA15 238 E3
Bollington SK10 87 F4
Chester CH4 140 C3
Christleton CH3 142 C4
Ellesmere Port L66 69 E3
Gatley SK8 239 A5
Hawthorn Rd continued
Neston L64 41 E1
Newcastle-u-L ST5 210 C1
Plumley WA16 80 C2
Weaverham CW8 102 B4
Hawthorn Rise SK10 86 C3
Hawthorn St SK9 60 A3
Hawthorn Terr
Manchester SK4 240 B7
Wilmslow SK9 60 A3
Hawthorn View
Deeside Ind Est CH5 116 A4
Wilmslow SK9 60 A4
Hawthorn Villas CW4 130 B2
Hawthorn Way SK10 87 F1
Hawthorn Wlk
Higher Wincham CW9 79 E2
Partington M31 11 E1
Wilmslow SK9 60 A4
Hawthorne Ave Audley ST7 209 F1
Fowley Common WA3 5 E2
Great Sankey WA5 15 D3
Warrington WA1 17 D4
Hawthorne Cl
Congleton CW12 156 A2
Haydock WA11 1 A3
Hawthorne Dr
Sandbach CW11 175 E3
Willaston L64 43 D1
Hawthorne Gr Barnton CW8 77 F2
Poynton SK12 37 E2
Warrington WA4 16 B1
Warrington WA1 16 C4
Winsford CW7 127 D1
Hawthorne Rd WA4 26 B4
Hawthorne St WA2 16 A4
Hawthorns The
Bunbury CW6 185 F4
Ellesmere Port L66 69 F4
Northwich CW8 103 E4
Tarporley CW6 146 B1
Hay Croft SK8 34 C4
Haycastle Cl WA5 7 F1
Haycroft Cl L66 69 E1
Haydock Cl CH1 118 A1
Haydock High Sch WA11 1 B3
Haydock La WA11 1 B4
Haydock Lane Ind Est WA11 1 C4
Haydock Park Golf Course WA12 2 C3
Haydock St
Newton-le-W WA12 2 A2
Warrington WA2 16 A3
Haye's Rd M44 11 F3
Hayes Cres WA6 49 E1
Hayes Dr CW8 78 B2
Hayes Pk CH2 237 D4
Hayfield Ave SK6 241 A4
Hayfield Cl SK10 87 D2
Hayfield Rd New Mills SK22 39 E4
Romiley SK6 241 A4
Warrington WA1 17 E4
Hayfield St M33 242 B7
Hayfields WA16 57 E2
Hayfields Gr CW3 229 F2
Hayhead Cl ST7 195 D1
Hayhurst Ave CW10 151 E4
Hayhurst Cl CW8 103 F4
Hayle Cl SK10 86 B1
Hayling Cl CW1 190 A4
Haymakers Cl CH4 140 C2
Haymakers Way CH1 117 D4
Haymoor Green Rd CW5 205 F2
Hayside Wlk SY14 213 D2
Hayton St WA16 56 C1
Haywood Cres WA7 24 B1
Hazel Ave Cheadle SK8 239 E5
Macclesfield SK11 112 A3
Romiley SK6 241 D2
Runcorn WA7 48 C4
Sale M33 242 B5
Hazel Cl Ellesmere Port L66 69 F1
Kidsgrove ST7 195 D2
Hazel Dr Lymm WA13 18 C1
Poynton SK12 36 C2
Weaverham CW8 102 B4
Winsford CW7 149 E4
Wythenshawe M22 34 A4
Hazel Gr Alsager ST7 194 A2
Crewe CW1 190 B4
Goldborne WA3 3 D4
Warrington WA1 17 D4
Hazel Grove High Sch SK7 36 B4
Hazel Rd Altrincham WA14 238 D6
Chester CH4 140 C3
Hazel St WA1 16 B4
Hazel Wlk M31 11 E1
Hazelbadge Cl SK12 36 B2
Hazelbadge Rd SK12 36 B2
Hazelborough Cl WA3 10 A3
Hazelcroft SK9 85 D4
Hazelehurst Rd WA6 74 B3
Hazelhurst Dr SK10 88 A4
Hazelhurst Rd SK15 242 D4
Hazelmere Cl CW8 103 E3
Hazelshaw La CW11 154 A2
Hazelwood Mews WA4 17 E1
Hazelwood Rd
Altrincham WA15 238 E2
Barnton CW8 78 A2
Wilmslow SK9 60 B4
Hazlemere Ave SK11 112 A3
Headland Cl WA3 3 F3
Headlands The CH2 237 F2
Heald Cl WA14 238 C2
Heald Dr WA14 238 C2
Heald Gr SK8 239 A1
Heald Green Sta M22 34 A4
Heald Rd WA14 238 C2
Heald St WA12 1 C2
Healdwood Rd SK6 241 C4
Healey Cl CW1 190 A4
Hearn's La Burland CW5 202 C3
Faddiley CW5 202 C3
Heary St SK11 112 C3
Heath Ave
Ellesmere Port L65 70 A1
Rode Heath ST7 193 F4
Sandbach CW11 175 F3
Heath Bank CH2 119 E3
Heath Cl Chester CH3 142 A4
Sandbach CW11 175 E3
Tarvin CH3 121 D1
Heath Cres SK2 & SK3 240 F1
Heath Ct L66 69 D3
Heath Cty Comp Sch The WA7 49 D4
Heath Dr Runcorn WA7 49 D4
Tarvin CH3 121 D1
Heath End Rd ST7 193 D3
Heath Gn CW6 146 B2
Heath Gr L66 69 D4
Heath La Allostock WA16 106 C3
Chester CH3 142 A4
Croft WA3 4 A1
Ellesmere Port L66 68 B4
Goldborne WA3 3 E3
Great Barrow CH3 120 C3
Great Budworth CW9 54 A1
High Legh WA16 28 B3
Little Leigh WA4 77 D4
Marbury SY13 226 C3
Peover WA16 106 C3
Stoak CH2 95 F4
Willaston L66 68 B4
Heath Rd
Altrincham, Hale WA14 238 D2
Altrincham, Timperley WA15 238 F8
Bollington SK10 87 F3
Chester CH2 118 B4
Congleton CW12 156 A1
Penketh WA5 14 C3
Runcorn WA7 23 D1
Sandbach CW11 175 E3
Stockport SK2 & SK3 240 F2
Weaverham CW8 77 F1
Widnes WA8 12 C1
Heath Rd S WA7 48 C3
Heath St Crewe CW1 190 B2
Goldborne WA3 3 D4
Warrington WA4 26 B4
Heath Terr CH2 118 B4
Heath Way CW6 168 B4
Heathbank Rd Cheadle SK8 34 C4
Stockport SK3 240 B3
Heathbrook CW9 104 C4
Heathcote Ave SK4 240 C7
Heathcote Cl CH2 118 B2
Heathcote Gdns
Northwich CW9 104 B4
Romiley SK6 241 E1
Heathcote St ST7 195 D1
Heather Ave M44 11 E3
Heather Brae WA12 2 A2
Heather Cl
Ellesmere Port L66 69 F2
Macclesfield SK11 112 B2
Runcorn WA7 49 F2
Warrington WA3 9 E3
Heather Ct CH3 142 A4
Heather Lea M34 241 A6
Heather Rd WA14 238 E1
Heather Wlk M31 11 E1
Heatherfield Ct SK9 60 C4
Heathergate Pl CW2 206 A4
Heathfield SK9 60 A3
Heathfield Ave Crewe CW1 190 B2
Gatley SK8 239 B5
Heathfield Cl
Congleton CW12 155 F2
Nantwich CW5 204 C3
Sale M33 242 F6
Heathfield Cty High Sch CW12 155 F2
Heathfield Dr ST5 210 B1
Heathfield Park WA4 17 D1
Heathfield Pk WA8 12 B2
Heathfield Rd Audlem CW3 230 A3
Ellesmere Port L65 70 A3
Stockport SK2 & SK3 240 F2
Heathfield Sq WA16 56 C1
Heathfields Cl CH2 237 E4
Heathgate Ave L24 21 D1
Heathland Terr SK3 240 E3
Heathlands Rd L66 69 D4
Heathmoor Ave WA3 3 E3
Heaths La CW6 123 E1
Heathside CW5 204 C3
Heathside Park Rd SK3 239 F7
Heathside Rd SK3 240 A3
Heathview CW1 191 E2
Heathview Cl WA8 22 A3
Heathview Rd WA8 22 A3
Heathway L60 41 D4
Heathwood Dr ST7 193 D3
Heathwood Gr WA1 17 D4
Heatley Cl WA13 19 D2
Heatley La CW5 217 F2
Heatley Way SK9 34 B2
Heaton Cl CW10 151 E3
Heaton Ct Manchester SK4 240 B8
Warrington WA3 9 F3
Heaton La SK4 240 E5
Heaton Moor Rd SK4 240 B8
Heaton Rd SK4 240 C7
Heaton Sq CW7 149 E4
Heaward Cl CW2 206 A2
Hebden Ave
Fowley Common WA3 5 D2
Romiley SK6 241 A4
Hebden Green Sch CW7 149 D4
Heber's Cl SY14 213 E3
Hedge Hey WA7 24 A1
Hedge Row SK10 63 E1
Hedgerow Dr CW9 79 E2
Hefferston Rise CW8 102 A4
Heights The WA6 73 E2
Helena Cl WA16 57 E1
Helford St CW12 156 B2
Hellath View CW5 204 C1
Hellyar-Brook Rd ST7 193 D2
Helmsdale Cl CW1 190 A3
Helmsdale La WA5 15 E3
Helmsley Cl WA5 15 F4
Helsby Ave L62 43 F2
Helsby Cty High Sch WA6 73 E3
Helsby Horns Mill Cty Prim Sch WA6 73 D1
Helsby Rd WA6 73 E1
Helsby St WA1 16 B3
Helsby Sta WA6 73 D2
Helsby Way SK9 34 B2
Helston Cl Bramhall SK7 35 F4
Penketh WA5 14 C3
Runcorn WA7 50 A3
Helston Gr SK8 34 B4
Helton Cl CW4 130 A2
Hemlegh Vale WA6 73 D1
Hemming St CW8 78 B1
Hemmingshaw La CW11 176 A4
Hemsworth Ave L66 69 E3
Henbury Cl CW10 151 E4
Henbury High Sch SK10 111 F4
Henbury La SK8 34 C3
Henbury Pl WA7 49 D3
Henbury Rd SK9 34 B2
Henbury Rise SK11 111 E4
Henderson Cl WA5 14 B3
Henderson Rd WA8 22 C4
Henderson St SK11 112 B4
Hendham Dr WA14 238 B5
Hendon Cl CW1 190 C3
Hendon Dr SK3 240 A3
Henley Ave Cheadle SK8 239 F2
Irlam M44 11 F3
Henley Cl Appleton WA4 26 C3
Neston L64 66 C3
Henley Ct WA7 23 E1
Henley Dr Altrincham WA15 238 F7
Winsford CW7 126 C1
Henley Rd Chester CH4 140 C3
Neston L64 66 C3
Henrietta St CW12 156 B2
Henry Pl CH2 237 E3
Henry St Crewe CW1 190 B3
Haslington CW1 191 E2
Hyde SK14 241 D6
Lymm WA13 18 C2
Tarporley CW6 146 B1
Warrington WA1 16 A3
Widnes WA8 13 E1
Henry Wood Ct CH4 140 C3
Henshall Ave WA4 16 C2
Henshall Dr CW11 175 E4
Henshall Hall Dr CW12 157 D1
Henshall La WA14 20 B3
Henshall Rd SK10 87 F4
Henshall St CH2 237 D4
Henshaw La SK11 110 C1
Hepherd St WA5 15 E2
Hepley Rd SK12 37 D2
Herald Pk CW1 190 C2
Heralds Cl WA8 22 A4
Heralds Gn WA5 7 D1
Herbert St Burtonwood WA5 6 C3
Congleton CW12 156 C2
Crewe CW1 191 D3
Dukinfield M34 241 A8
Lostock CW9 80 A1
Stockport SK3 240 D3
Herberts La L60 40 C4
Herdman St CW2 190 B1
Hereford Ave
Ellesmere Port CH1 94 C4
Goldborne WA3 3 D4
Hereford Cl
Macclesfield SK10 86 C1
Warrington WA1 17 E4
Hereford Dr SK9 34 C2
Hereford Pl CH1 118 A3
Hereford St M33 242 B6
Hereford Way CW10 128 B1
Hereward Rd CH3 119 D1
Hermitage Ave SK6 241 F2
Hermitage Ct CH1 117 D4
Hermitage Cty Prim Sch CW4 130 B2
Hermitage Dr CW4 130 B2
Hermitage Gdns SK6 241 F2
Hermitage Green La WA3 3 D1
Hermitage La
Cranage CW4 130 B4
Goostrey CW4 130 B4
Hermitage Rd CH1 117 D4
Hermitage The L60 40 C4
Heron Cl Broughton CH4 139 D2
Farndon CH3 180 C1
Knutsford WA16 57 D2
Winsford CW7 149 E3
Heron Cres CW1 190 C3

Heron Ct Neston L64 66 B4
Northwich CW9 79 E1
Heron Dr SK12 36 A2
Heron Pl CH2 237 E4
Heron St SK3 240 D3
Herons Way WA7 24 C2
Herrick Cl CW2 206 A4
Herries St OL6 242 A4
Hertford Cl
Congleton CW12 156 C2
Warrington WA1 17 F4
Hertford Gr M44 11 E3
Hesketh Cl WA5 14 C2
Hesketh Croft CW1 190 A4
Hesketh Dr CW9 80 A2
Hesketh Meadow La WA3 3 F4
Hesketh Rd L24 21 F1
Hesketh St SK4 240 E7
Hesketh St N WA5 15 E2
Hesnall Cl WA3 5 E4
Hessle Dr L60 40 C4
Heswall Ave WA3 4 C2
Heswall Rd L66 69 E2
Heswall Sta L60 41 E4
Hewitt Dr CW7 150 B4
Hewitt Gr CW9 79 F3
Hewitt St Chester CH2 118 C2
Crewe CW2 190 B1
Northwich CW9 79 E1
Warrington WA4 16 B2
Hewood Cl WA12 7 E4
Hey Lock Cl WA12 7 E4
Hey Shoot La WA3 5 E3
Heybridge La SK10 87 D3
Heyes Ave WA11 1 B3
Heyes Dr WA13 18 B1
Heyes Farm Rd SK11 111 F4
Heyes La Alderley Edge SK9 60 B2
Appleton WA4 26 C4
Heyes Pk CW8 102 C2
Heyes Rd WA8 22 B4
Heyeswood La CW8 103 D2
Heyfield Park Rd L66 69 D4
Heygarth Prim Sch L62 43 F3
Heys Ave Bebington L62 43 E4
Romiley SK6 241 E3
Heys La SK6 241 E3
Heys Prim Sch The OL6 242 A3
Heys Rd OL6 242 A3
Heys The WA7 23 F1
Heysbank Rd SK12 38 B3
Heyscroft Rd SK4 240 A6
Heysham Cl WA7 50 B3
Heysoms Ave CW8 103 E4
Heysoms Cl CW8 103 E4
Heythrop Dr L60 41 E4
Heywood Cl SK9 60 A1
Heywood Gn CW2 206 B4
Heywood Gr M33 242 B8
Heywood La CW3 234 B4
Heywood Rd
Alderley Edge SK9 60 A1
Ellesmere Port L66 69 E3
Sale M33 242 B5
Heywood St CW12 156 B1
Heywoods Ridge CW3 229 F2
Heywoods The CH2 118 B2
Heyworth Ave SK6 241 D3
Hibbert Ave 4 SK14 241 E5
Hibbert St New Mills SK22 39 D3
6 Widnes WA8 23 D4
Hibel Rd SK10 87 E1
Hickhurst La CW6 147 E2
Hickmore Heys CH3 119 F3
Hickory Cl WA1 17 F4
Hickson St CW8 78 A2
Hickton Dr WA14 238 B6
Hidcote Cl CW2 206 A4
Hield Gr CW9 79 E4
Hield La CW9 79 E4
Higginbotham Gn SK11 112 C3
High Bank WA14 238 D5
High Bank Cl M44 11 E3
High Bank Rd SK14 241 F7
High Bank Side SK1 240 F5
High Bent Ave SK8 35 D3
High Cross CH3 182 B1
High Ct SK10 88 A4
High Elm Dr WA15 32 B4
High Elm Rd WA15 32 B4
High Elms SK8 35 D3
High Field WA14 20 A1
High Gates Cl WA5 15 F4
High Grove Rd SK8 239 C5
High Hill Rd SK22 39 E4
High La SK6 241 B4
High Lane Prim Sch SK6 37 F4
High Lea Rd SK22 39 D4
High Lee SK8 239 C5
High Legh Cty Prim Sch WA16 29 E3
High Legh Rd WA13, WA16 29 E4
High Lowe Ave CW12 157 D2
High Meadow SK8 34 C4
High Meadows SK6 241 C3
High St Altrincham WA14 238 D4
Audley ST7 210 A1
Bollington SK10 88 A4
Broughton CH4 140 C4
Cheadle SK8 239 D6
Congleton CW12 156 B1
Crewe CW2 190 B2
Duddon CW6 145 E2
Farndon CH3 180 C1
Frodsham WA6 49 D1
High St continued
Goldborne WA3 3 D4
Great Budworth CW9 79 D4
Hale L24 21 E1
Hyde SK14 241 F7
Kidsgrove, Harriseahead ST7 195 F3
Kidsgrove, Newchapel ST7 195 F1
Kidsgrove, Talke ST7 210 B3
Kidsgrove, The Rookery ST7 195 E2
Macclesfield SK11 112 B3
Malpas SY14 213 D2
Mow Cop ST7 195 E4
Nantwich CW5 204 C3
Neston L64 66 C4
New Mills SK22 39 E4
Newton-le-W WA12 2 B2
Norley WA6 100 C3
Northwich CW8, CW9 103 F4
Runcorn WA7 23 D1
Sandbach CW11 175 D3
Stalybridge, Castle Hall SK15 242 D1
Stalybridge, Hydes SK15 & SK16 242 C1
Stockport SK1 240 F5
Tarporley CW6 146 B1
Tarvin CH3 121 E1
Tattenhall CH3 166 A1
Warrington WA1 16 B3
Weaverham CW8 77 E1
Winsford CW7 126 B1
High View Helsby WA6 73 E2
Mount Pleasant ST7 195 D3
Higham Ave WA5 7 F1
Highbank Cl CW8 78 A2
Highbank Dr M20 239 B8
Highbank Rd
Kingsley WA6 75 E1
Northwich CW8 103 E4
Highcliffe Ave CH1 118 A2
Highcroft Ave CW12 156 C1
Highcroft Rd SK6 241 C3
Higher Ash Rd ST7 210 B4
Higher Ashton WA8 12 C2
Higher Barlow Row SK1 240 F4
Higher Bents La SK6 241 A3
Higher Bury St SK4 240 D6
Higher Carden La SY14 198 B3
Higher Downs
Altrincham WA14 238 C3
Knutsford WA16 57 E1
Higher Fence Rd SK10 87 F1
Higher Ferry CH1 140 A4
Higher Henry St SK14 241 D5
Higher Heyes Dr WA6 75 E1
Higher Hillgate SK1 & SK2 240 F4
Higher La Bollington SK10 88 A3
Dutton WA4 51 E2
Kettleshulme SK23 64 C3
Lymm WA13 19 D1
Higher Rd Halewood L24 21 D3
Widnes WA8 21 E3
Higher Tame St SK15 242 E2
Highfield Elton CH2 72 A2
Prestbury SK10 87 D3
Sale M33 242 C5
Highfield Ave
Appleton WA4 26 B2
Audlem CW3 230 A2
Goldborne WA3 2 C4
Great Sankey WA5 15 D3
Kidsgrove ST7 195 D1
Lostock CW9 80 A2
Highfield Cl L64 66 C4
Highfield Cres
Widnes WA8 13 D1
Wilmslow SK9 34 B1
Highfield Cty Prim Sch CH1 117 F2
Highfield Dr Lymm WA13 18 B1
Macclesfield SK10 87 D1
Nantwich CW5 205 D3
Highfield Est SK9 34 B1
Highfield Gdns SK14 241 F7
Highfield La
Coddington CH3 181 F2
Winwick WA2 8 B4
Highfield Parkway SK7 35 E2
Highfield Pl CW8 103 F4
Highfield Rd Blacon CH1 117 E3
Bollington SK10 88 A4
Cheadle SK8 239 F1
Congleton CW12 156 C1
Ellesmere Port L65 70 B3
Ellesmere Port, Little Sutton L66 69 D3
Lymm WA13 18 B1
Macclesfield SK11 112 B4
Neston L64 66 C4
Northwich CW8 103 E4
Poynton SK12 36 A2
Widnes WA8 13 D1
Highfield Rd N L65 70 B3
Highfield Sch L26 21 D4
Highfield St 2 SK3 240 C4
Highfield Terr SK22 39 E4
Highfields SY13 224 A1
Highfields Cty Prim Sch
Alsager ST7 193 E2
Nantwich CW5 204 C3
Highgate Cl CW1 190 A4
Highgate Rd WA14 238 B4
Highgrove Mews SK9 60 A3
Highland Ave SK6 241 A2
Highland Way WA16 82 A4
Highlands Rd WA7 48 C4
Highlands The CW6 185 F4
Hightown Crewe CW1 190 B2
Middlewich CW10 128 B1
Sandbach CW11 175 D3
Hightree Dr SK11 111 E4
Highwood Rd WA4 26 B4
Higifield Ave M33 242 C5
Hignett Ave WA9 1 A1
Hilary Ave SK8 34 B4
Hilary Cl Chester CH3 119 D1
Great Sankey WA5 14 B3
Stockport SK4 240 D6
Widnes WA8 13 F2
Hilary Rd Bebington L62 43 F3
Wythenshawe M22 33 E4
Hilbre Bank CW6 169 E2
Hilbre Dr L65 70 B1
Hilda Ave SK8 239 E5
Hilda Gr SK5 240 F8
Hilda St 5 SK5 240 F8
Hilden Rd WA2 8 C1
Hill Cl L64 67 D3
Hill Cliffe Rd WA4 26 A4
Hill Court Mews SK6 241 B2
Hill Crest Ave SK4 240 A6
Hill Ct L64 67 D3
Hill Dr SK9 34 C2
Hill Farm Cl WA2 8 C2
Hill Fields Cl CW12 156 B2
Hill La Brown Knowl CH3 199 E4
Burwardsley CW6 184 C3
Peckforton CW6 184 C3
Hill Rd CH4 141 F1
Hill Rd N WA6 73 E2
Hill Rd S WA6 73 E2
Hill Rise
Altrincham WA14 238 A5
Romiley SK6 241 B2
Hill St Altrincham WA14 238 C8
Crewe CW1 190 B2
Macclesfield SK11 112 B3
Romiley SK6 241 B2
Runcorn WA7 23 D1
Sandbach CW11 174 B4
Winsford CW7 126 C1
Hill Terr ST7 209 E1
Hill The
Hassall Green CW11 175 E3
Sandbach CW11 175 E3
Hill Top Altrincham WA15 32 A4
Barnton CW8 78 A1
Romiley SK6 241 B3
Hill Top Ave
Cheadle Hulme SK8 35 D4
Wilmslow SK9 60 A4
Winsford CW7 126 B1
Hill Top La Heswall L60 41 D4
Neston L64 67 D3
Hill Top Rd
Acton Bridge CW8 76 C1
Dutton WA4 51 E1
Warrington WA4 16 C1
Warrington, Woolston WA1 17 E4
Hill Top Rise SK23 65 E4
Hill View Bollington SK10 87 F4
Whaley Bridge SK23 65 E4
Widnes WA8 12 C3
Hill View Ave WA6 73 D1
Hill View Cty Prim Sch WA7 49 F2
Hillary Ave CW12 157 D1
Hillary Dr CW3 230 A2
Hillary Rd ST7 195 D2
Hillberry Cres WA4 16 A2
Hillbre Ave L60 40 C3
Hillbre Way SK9 34 B2
Hillbrook Rd SK7 35 E3
Hillcourt Rd High Lane SK6 37 F4
Romiley SK6 241 C4
Hillcrest CW12 156 B2
Hillcrest Ave CW4 130 A2
Hillcrest Dr Denton M34 241 B5
Ellesmere Port L66 69 D3
Hillcrest Gram Sch SK3 240 F2
Hillcrest Rd
Bollington SK10 87 F4
Ellesmere Port L66 69 D3
Kelsall CW6 122 C3
Warren SK11 112 A2
Hillcroft Rd WA14 238 A5
Hillfield Frodsham WA6 74 A4
Runcorn WA7 50 B4
Hillfield Gdns CW5 204 C2
Hillfield Pl CW5 204 C2
Hillfield Rd L66 69 E4
Hillfield View CW5 204 C2
Hillfields CW12 156 B2
Hillfoot Cres WA4 26 A4
Hillfoot La WA6 74 C2
Hillingden Ave L26 21 D4
Hillington Rd SK3 240 C4
Hillock La WA1 17 E4
Hillsboro Ave WA6 74 B4
Hillsdown Way L66 69 E1
Hillside Lymm WA13 19 F1
Northwich CW8 103 E4
Hillside Ave
Newton-le-W WA12 1 C1
Runcorn WA7 48 C4
Hillside Cl Bramhall SK7 36 A4
Disley SK12 38 B3
Kidsgrove ST7 195 E4
Hillside Ct SK10 88 A1
Hillside Dr Crewe CW1 190 C3
Ellesmere Port L66 69 F4
Macclesfield SK10 88 A1
Hillside Gr WA5 14 C2
Hillside La CW9 126 C4
Hillside Pk WA16 57 E1
Hillside Rd Appleton WA4 26 B2
Blacon CH1 117 F2
Frodsham WA6 74 B4
Heswall L60 41 D4
Kelsall CW6 122 B2
Knutsford WA16 57 D1
Hillside View SK22 39 D4
Hilltop WA7 50 B4
Hilltop Prim Sch ST7 210 B4
Hilltop Rd
Guilden Sutton CH3 119 F3
Lymm WA13 18 B1
Hillview Rise CW8 78 C1
Hilton Ave WA5 15 D3
Hilton Cl Macclesfield SK11 111 F4
Middlewich CW10 151 D4
Hilton Dr M44 11 E3
Hilton Rd New Mills SK6 38 A4
Poynton SK12 37 E3
Hilton St SK3 240 D4
Hinchley Cl CW8 103 D2
Hind Heath La CW11 174 C2
Hind Heath Rd CW11 174 C2
Hinde St CW5 204 B2
Hinderton Dr L60 40 C3
Hinderton La L64 67 D4
Hinderton Rd L64 66 C4
Hinderton Sch L65 69 F2
Hindle Ave WA5 7 F1
Hindley Cres CW8 78 A2
Hindley St SK1 240 F4
Hinton Cres WA4 26 C4
Hinton Rd Crewe CW2 206 B4
Runcorn WA7 23 D1
Hitch Lowes SK11 84 A2
Hitchen's Cl WA7 50 B4
Hitchens La SY14 184 B1
Hob Hey La WA3 4 B2
Hob La Churton CH3 180 C3
Dunham-on-t-H WA6 97 E3
Trafford WA6 97 E3
Hobart Cl SK7 35 F2
Hobart Way CH1 117 E2
Hobb La WA4 25 E3
Hobbs Cl CW1 191 E2
Hobbs Hill La WA16 28 C1
Hobby Ct WA7 49 F3
Hobcroft La WA16 58 A4
Hobson St SK11 112 B3
Hockenhull Ave CH3 121 D1
Hockenhull Cres CH3 121 E1
Hockenhull La CH3 121 D1
Hocker La SK10 85 E2
Hockerley Ave SK23 65 E4
Hockerley Cl SK23 65 E4
Hockerley La SK23 65 E4
Hockley Cl SK12 37 D2
Hockley Rd SK12 37 D2
Hodge La Hartford CW8 103 D3
Weaverham CW8 102 B3
Hodgehill La SK11 132 C3
Hodgkingson Ave WA5 7 F1
Hoghton Rd L24 21 F1
Hogshead La CW8 124 B4
Holbein Cl CH4 141 F3
Holborn St 14 SK1 240 F5
Holbrook Cl WA5 14 C3
Holbury Cl CW1 190 A4
Holcet Dr WA14 238 B5
Holcombe Ave WA3 3 E4
Holcombe Cl WA14 238 B6
Holcombe Dr SK10 87 D2
Holcroft La WA3 5 E1
Holden Pl WA2 16 C4
Holden St OL6 242 A4
Hole House Fold SK6 241 B2
Hole House La CW8 77 F2
Holehouse La
Adlington SK10 62 B1
Langley SK11 113 E2
Scholar Green ST7 194 B4
Holes La WA1 17 D4
Holford Ave Lostock CW9 80 A2
Warrington WA5 15 F4
Holford Cres WA16 57 D1
Holford Way WA12 2 C2
Holgrave Cl WA16 29 E2
Holker Cl SK12 36 C2
Holkham Cl WA8 12 C1
Holland Ave SK15 242 D2
Holland Cl CW11 175 E3
Holland Rd SK7 35 F4
Holland St Crewe CW1 190 A3
18 Macclesfield SK11 112 B4
Hollands La CW6 122 B3
Hollands Pl SK11 112 C4
Hollands Rd CW9 103 F4
Hollies La SK9 60 C4
Hollies Rd L26 21 D4
Hollies The Gatley SK8 239 B5
Manchester SK4 240 B7
Moulton CW9 126 C4
Runcorn WA7 49 E4
Shavington CW2 206 A2
Hollin Green La
Burland CW5 202 C3
Faddiley CW5 202 C3
Hollin La Newhall CW5 228 B4
Styal SK9 33 F3
Sutton Lane Ends SK11 136 B3
Hollin Rd SK10 88 A4
Hollingford Pl WA16 82 A4
Hollingreen La CW5 229 D4
Hollinhey Cty Prim Sch SK11 112 C2
Hollins Cres ST7 194 C1
Hollins Dr WA2 8 A3
Hollins Gr M33 242 A6
Hollins Grange ST7 210 B4
Hollins Hill CW6 146 C4
Hollins La Antrobus CW9 53 F2
Winwick WA2 7 F3
Hollins Rd SK11 112 C3
Hollins Terr SK11 112 C3
Hollins Way WA8 22 A3
Hollinshead Cl ST7 194 C4
Hollinwood Cl ST7 210 C4
Hollinwood Rd Disley SK12 38 B3
Kidsgrove ST7 210 C4
Hollow Dr WA4 16 C1
Hollow La Kingsley WA6 75 D2
Knutsford WA16 57 D1
Hollow Oak La CW8 101 E2
Hollow The Gatley SK8 239 C1
Mount Pleasant ST7 195 D3
Holloway WA7 22 C1
Hollowood Rd SY14 213 D3
Holly Ave Cheadle SK8 239 D5
Newton-le-W WA12 2 B2
Holly Bank M33 242 C5
Holly Bank Rd SK9 34 A1
Holly Bank Sch CH2 237 D4
Holly Bush La WA3 10 B1
Holly Cl Connah's Quay CH5 91 E1
Hale L24 21 E1
Mickle Trafford CH2 119 F4
Holly Ct Helsby WA6 73 E3
Stockport SK3 240 E1
Holly Dr Sale M33 242 A6
Winsford CW7 149 E4
Holly Gr Denton M34 241 A7
Sale M33 242 D6
Tabley WA16 56 A2
Warrington WA1 17 D4
Holly Grange WA14 238 D2
Holly Hedge La WA4 25 E3
Holly La Alsager ST7 193 F2
Kidsgrove ST7 195 F3
Styal SK9 33 F3
Holly Mount CW2 206 C3
Holly Rd Cheadle Hulme SK7 35 F3
Chester CH4 140 C3
Ellesmere Port L65 70 B3
Goldborne WA3 3 E4
Haydock WA11 1 A3
High Lane SK6 37 F4
Lymm WA13 19 D3
Macclesfield SK11 112 A4
Newcastle-u-L ST5 210 C1
Penketh WA5 14 C3
Poynton SK12 36 C2
Weaverham CW8 102 B4
Holly Rd N SK9 60 A3
Holly Rd S SK9 60 A3
Holly Terr Penketh WA5 14 C3
Tilston SY14 198 B2
Holly Tree Dr Biddulph ST6 179 E1
Peover WA16 106 B4
Holly Wlk Northwich CW8 103 E4
Partington M31 11 E1
Hollybank Audlem CW3 229 F2
Moore WA4 25 D3
Hollybank Rd WA7 49 F4
Hollybush Cres CW5 205 E3
Hollyfield Rd L65 70 A3
Hollyfields CW11 191 F4
Hollyheath Cl CW11 175 E3
Hollythorn Ave SK7 35 E4
Hollytree Rd WA16 80 C2
Hollywood WA14 238 D2
Hollywood Way SK3 & SK4 240 D5
Holm Cl CH3 142 C4
Holm Dr CH2 72 B2
Holm Oak Way CH1 94 C4
Holme St Hyde SK14 241 D6
Tarvin CH3 120 C1
Holmefield M33 242 B6
Holmes Chapel Cty Comp Sch CW4 130 A1
Holmes Chapel Cty Prim Sch CW4 130 A2
Holmes Chapel Rd
Allostock WA16 106 A2
Brereton Green CW12 154 B4
Congleton CW12 155 E2
Lach Dennis CW9 105 F2
Middlewich CW10 128 C1
Ollerton WA16 82 B2
Peover WA16 82 B2
Sandbach CW11 153 F1
Sproston Green CW4 129 E1
Withington SK11 109 D4
Holmes Chapel Sta CW4 130 B2
Holmes Ct WA3 9 E2
Holmes St Cheadle SK8 239 E6
Stockport SK2 & SK3 240 E3
Holmesville Ave CW12 156 A2
Holmeswood Cl SK9 60 B4
Holmfield Ave WA7 23 E1
Holmfield Cl SK4 240 D7
Holmfield Dr
Cheadle Hulme SK8 35 D4
Ellesmere Port L66 69 E2
Holmlea Dr CW1 190 C2
Holmlea Way SK10 86 B3
Holmrook WA14 238 B5
Holmsfield Rd WA1 16 B3
Holmshaw La CW1 192 A2
Holmwood WA14 238 A2
Holmwood Dr L65 70 A1
Holt Hey L64 67 D1
Holt La WA7 49 F1
Holt St Altrincham WA14 238 C
Crewe CW1 190 A
Stockport SK1 240 F

Kelsall Ave L62 43 F2
Kelsall Cl Bebington L62 43 F2
Warrington WA3 9 E2
Widnes WA8 12 B1
Kelsall Cres SK3 240 D2
Kelsall Cty Prim Sch CW6 122 B2
Kelsall Rd Ashton CH3 121 F4
Cheadle SK8 240 A1
Tarvin CH3 121 E2
Kelsall St Congleton CW12 156 C2
Sale M33 242 B6
Kelsall Way Audley ST7 209 E1
2 Wilmslow SK9 34 B3
Kelsborrow Way CW6 122 B2
Kelsterton Ct CH5 91 E1
Kelsterton La CH6 91 D1
Kelsterton Rd CH6, CH5 91 D1
Kelvin Ave M33 242 B6
Kelvin Cl WA3 9 E3
Kelvin Gr CH2 118 C2
Kemberton Dr WA8 13 D3
Kemble Cl CW2 206 A4
Kemmel Ave WA4 16 B2
Kemp St SK14 241 E8
Kempsell Way L26 21 D4
Kempton Ave CW1 190 B4
Kempton Cl Chester CH1 118 A1
Newton-le-W WA12 2 B3
Runcorn WA7 49 E3
Kempton Way SK10 87 E2
Kendal Ave Denton M34 241 A5
Sale M33 242 C5
Warrington WA2 8 B1
Kendal Cl Chester CH2 119 D3
Ellesmere Port L66 69 E1
Macclesfield SK11 111 F3
Kendal Ct CW12 156 A1
Kendal Dr
Cheadle Hulme SK7 35 E3
Ellesmere Port L66 69 F1
Gatley SK8 239 C4
Kendal Gdns SK6 241 B4
Kendal Rd
Macclesfield SK11 111 F3
Widnes WA8 12 B1
Kendal Rise WA7 49 E3
Kendrick St WA1 16 A3
Kenilworth Ave
Knutsford WA16 57 E1
Runcorn WA7 49 D4
Wilmslow SK9 34 B2
Kenilworth Cl
Macclesfield SK11 111 F3
Wistaston CW2 206 A4
Kenilworth Ct L65 70 C1
Kenilworth Dr
Hazel Grove SK7 36 B4
Warrington WA1 16 C4
Kenilworth Gdns WA12 2 B1
Kenilworth Gn SK11 111 F3
Kenilworth Rd Cheadle SK3 239 F7
Goldborne WA3 3 F4
Macclesfield SK11 111 F3
Neston L64 66 C3
Kenley Ave WA8 12 B3
Kenmare Bank CW9 104 A3
Kenmore Gr M44 11 E3
Kennard Pl WA14 238 E6
Kennedy Ave SK10 86 C1
Kennedy Cl CH2 119 D3
Kennedy Way SK4 240 C6
Kennel La CW8 102 A1
Kennelwood Rd CW9 78 B4
Kennerley's La SK9 60 A4
Kennet Dr CW12 156 C1
Kennet Rd WA11 1 B3
Kennet Way SK11 111 F4
Kenneth Rd WA8 22 B4
Kenrick Cl CW3 232 B1
Kensington Ave
Ashton-u-L OL6 242 B4
Warrington WA4 17 E1
Kensington Cl CH4 141 D3
Kensington Ct Alsager ST7 192 C2
Wilmslow SK9 60 A3
Winsford CW7 149 E4
Kensington Gdns
Altrincham WA15 238 F1
Hyde SK14 241 F5
Kensington Gn CH4 140 C3
Kensington Gr
Altrincham WA14 238 E8
Stalybridge SK15 242 D1
Kensington Rd Chester CH4 118 A1
Ellesmere Port L65 70 A3
Stockport SK3 240 B3
Kensington St SK14 241 E5
Kensington Way CW9 103 F2
Kent Ave Bollington SK10 87 F3
Cheadle SK8 240 C1
Kent Cl L63 43 D4
Kent Dr CW12 156 B2
Kent Gdn CH2 118 C3
Kent Gr WA7 23 D1
Kent Rd Chester CH2 118 C3
Great Sankey WA5 15 E2
Irlam M44 11 E3
Partington M31 11 F1
Stockport SK3 240 B4
Kent St Warrington WA4 16 B2
Widnes WA8 13 D1
Kent Wlk Macclesfield SK10 86 C1
Newton-le-W WA12 2 B1
Kent's Green La CW11 191 F4
Kent's La CW1 173 E1
Kentmere Ave CW7 126 B1
Kentmere Cl SK8 239 B3
Kenton Rd L26 21 D4
Kentridge Dr L66 69 E2
Kentwell Dr SK10 87 E2
Kenview Cl WA8 22 A2
Kenwick Cl L66 69 E2
Kenwood Ave
Altrincham WA15 238 F2
Cheadle Hulme SK7 35 E3
Gatley SK8 239 A6
Kenworthy St SK15 242 D1
Kenyon Ave WA5 14 C3
Kenyon La WA3 3 F2
Kenyon's La WA11 1 C4
Kenyon's La N WA11 1 C4
Kerfoot Bsns Pk WA2 16 A4
Kerfoot St WA2 16 A4
Keristal Ave CH3 142 A4
Kerridge Cl CW10 151 D4
Kerridge Rd SK10 88 A2
Kerry Cft L66 69 F1
Kershaw Gr SK11 112 A4
Kershaw St WA8 12 B1
Kestrel Ave WA16 57 D2
Kestrel Cl Congleton CW12 156 C1
Middlewich CW10 151 E3
Winsford CW7 149 E3
Kestrel Dr CW1 190 A4
Kestrel La WA3 9 F2
Kestrel Rd Heswall L60 41 E4
Northwich CW8 103 E4
Kestrels Way WA7 49 F3
Keswick Ave Bebington L63 43 E2
Dukinfield SK14 241 C8
Gatley SK8 239 B4
Macclesfield SK11 111 F3
Warrington WA2 8 B1
Keswick Cl Chester CH2 119 D3
Crewe CW2 189 F2
Irlam M44 11 E2
Macclesfield SK11 111 F3
Stalybridge SK15 242 D4
Widnes WA8 12 B1
Winsford CW7 126 B1
Keswick Cres WA2 8 B1
Keswick Ct CW12 156 A1
Keswick Dr
Cheadle Hulme SK7 35 E3
Frodsham WA6 74 B4
Keswick Rd SK6 37 F4
Ketlan Ct CH4 140 C4
Kettell Ave CW1 190 A3
Kettle La CW3 230 B1
Kettleshulme St James Sch SK23 64 C2
Kettleshulme Way SK12 37 D2
Kettleshulme Wlk 7 SK9 34 C1
Kew Dr SK8 239 E2
Keyes Cl WA3 9 F2
Keyes Gdns WA3 9 F2
Keysbrook CH3 166 B1
Keysbrook Ave CH3 166 B1
Kidderton Cl CW5 202 C4
Kidderton La Burland CW5 202 C4
Faddiley CW5 202 C4
Kidsgrove Bank ST7 195 D1
Kidsgrove Sta ST7 194 C1
Kilbuck La WA11 2 A4
Kilburn Ave L62 43 F3
Kilburn Cl SK8 34 A4
Kilburn Rd SK3 240 C3
Kildare Cl L24 21 E1
Kildonnan Rd WA4 17 D1
Kilford Cl WA5 7 F1
Killingworth La WA3 10 A3
Kilmorey Park Rd CH2 118 C2
Kilmorey Pk CH2 118 C2
Kilmorey Pk Ave CH2 237 F4
Kiln Croft La SK9 34 C2
Kiln La CW5 220 A4
Kilncroft WA7 50 A3
Kilsby Dr WA8 13 F1
Kilshaw Rd WA5 6 C3
Kilsyth Cl WA2 8 C2
Kimberley Ave SK6 241 C2
Kimberley Dr WA4 16 B1
Kimberley St Stockport SK3 240 E3
Warrington WA5 15 F3
Kimberley Terr CH2 118 C1
Kinder Dr CW2 189 E2
Kinder Gr SK6 241 E2
Kinder St Stalybridge SK15 242 D2
Stockport SK3 240 E3
Kinder View SK22 39 E4
Kinderton Cl WA16 29 E2
Kinderton St CW10 128 B1
King Arthur's Wlk WA7 24 A1
King Edward Rd 2 SK11 112 B4
King Edward St
Macclesfield SK11 112 B4
Middlewich CW10 128 B1
Warrington WA1 16 C4
King George Ave CW9 104 A4
King George Cres WA1 16 C4
King George Rd WA11 2 A4
King James Ct WA7 49 F3
King Pl CW5 204 C3
King St Audley ST7 209 E1
Chester CH1 237 D3
Congleton CW12 156 C2
Crewe CW1 190 B2
Ellesmere Port L65 70 B3
Hartford CW8 103 D3
Hyde SK14 241 D7
Kidsgrove ST7 195 D1
Kidsgrove, Talke ST7 210 B3
Knutsford WA16 57 D1
King St continued
Lach Dennis CW9 104 C3
Macclesfield SK10 112 C4
Middlewich CW10 128 A3
Newton-le-W WA12 2 A2
Northwich CW9 104 C3
Runcorn WA7 23 D2
Sandbach CW11 174 C4
Stalybridge SK15 242 D2
King St E SK1 240 F6
King Street Trad Est CW10 128 B1
King's Ave WA3 3 F4
King's Cres CW10 128 B1
King's Cres E CH3 119 D1
King's Cres W CH3 119 D1
King's Dr SK4 240 A7
King's La Cranage CW10 106 B1
Lach Dennis CW10 106 B1
Nantwich CW5 204 B3
King's Rd Romiley SK6 241 A3
Wilmslow SK9 59 F4
King's Sch in Macclesfield The SK10 87 E1
King's Sch The
Chester CH4 141 D2
Macclesfield SK10 112 C4
Kingfisher Cl
Congleton CW12 156 C1
Crewe CW1 189 F4
Farndon CH3 180 C1
Nantwich CW5 204 C4
Runcorn WA7 49 F3
Warrington WA3 9 F2
Kingfisher Ct CW9 79 E1
Kingfisher Dr CW7 149 E3
Kingfisher Gr CW9 79 F3
Kingham Cl WA8 13 E1
Kings Acre WA14 238 A1
Kings Ave SK8 239 A4
Kings Cl Chester CH4 140 C3
Wilmslow SK9 60 A3
Kings Ct Nantwich CW5 204 B3
Runcorn WA7 24 B2
Stockport SK5 240 F7
Kings Dr Helsby WA6 73 D2
Wistaston CW2 205 F4
Kings Gate CW8 102 A1
Kings Grove Cty High Sch CW2 190 A2
Kings La CW6 147 E2
Kings Meadow Runcorn WA7 50 B4
Shavington CW2 206 C1
Kings Mews L66 69 E4
Kings Rd Connah's Quay CH5 91 E1
Ellesmere Port L66 69 E4
Goldborne WA3 3 D4
Irlam M44 11 F3
Warrington WA2 9 D1
Kingsbury Cl WA4 26 B2
Kingsdale Rd WA5 14 C4
Kingsfield Ct CH4 141 E2
Kingshead Cl WA7 24 A1
Kingsland Rd SK3 240 A3
Kingsley Ave Bebington L62 43 F2
Reddish SK4 240 E8
Wilmslow SK9 34 B1
Kingsley Cl Hartford CW8 103 E3
Kidsgrove ST7 210 B3
Kingsley Cres WA7 23 D1
Kingsley Dr Appleton WA4 26 B4
Northwich CW9 104 A3
Kingsley Gdns CH3 142 A4
Kingsley Gn WA6 74 C3
Kingsley & Newton Cty Prim Sch WA6 74 C1
Kingsley Rd Chester CH3 142 A4
Congleton CW12 157 D2
Crowton CW8 76 A1
Ellesmere Port L65 70 B3
Frodsham WA6 74 C2
Haslington CW1 191 E2
Kidsgrove ST7 210 B3
Kingsley WA6 74 C2
Runcorn WA7 23 D1
Kingsley St John's CE Aided Prim Sch WA6 75 E1
Kingsley Wlk CW7 126 A1
Kingsmead Chester CH2 118 B4
Davenham CW9 103 F2
Kingsmead Ct WA3 9 D4
Kingston Ave
Great Sankey WA5 14 C3
Macclesfield SK11 112 C4
Kingston Cl WA7 23 F1
Kingston Dr M33 242 D7
Kingston Gdns SK14 241 B7
Kingston Hill SK8 239 D4
Kingston Pl Biddulph ST6 179 F1
Cheadle SK8 239 E2
Kingston Rd SK9 34 B3
Kingston St SK3 240 D5
Kingsway Altrincham WA14 238 D5
Bollington SK10 87 F4
Cheadle M20 & SK8 239 C6
Chester CH2 118 C3
Crewe CW2 190 A1
Frodsham WA6 74 A4
Heswall L60 41 E3
Newton-le-W WA12 2 B1
Northwich CW9 104 A4
Widnes WA8 13 D1
Winsford CW7 126 C1
Kingsway Cty High Sch CH2 118 C3
Kingsway N WA1 16 C3
Kingsway S WA4 16 C2
Kingsway Sch SK8 239 C4
Kingsway W CH2 118 C2
Kingswood Kidsgrove ST7 195 D1
Poynton SK12 36 C2
Kingswood Ave CH1 94 B1
Kingswood Cres CW10 151 F3
Kingswood La CH1 94 B1
Kingswood Rd WA5 7 D1
Kingswood Wlk CW6 122 B3
Kinloch Cl Crewe CW1 190 A3
Halewood L26 21 D4
Kinnerley Rd L65 70 A2
Kinnersley Ave ST7 210 C4
Kinnersley St ST7 195 D1
Kinnerton Cl CH4 140 C3
Kinnerton Hts CH4 161 D4
Kinnerton La CH4 161 D4
Kinnington Way CH1 94 C4
Kinnock Parr WA5 6 C3
Kinross Cl WA2 8 C2
Kinsale Dr WA3 9 E2
Kinsey Rd L65 70 B1
Kinsey St CW12 156 C1
Kinsey's La CH2 71 F3
Kintore Cl L63 43 E2
Kintore Dr WA5 14 B3
Kipling Ave WA2 8 B1
Kipling Cres WA8 22 C4
Kipling Rd CH1 117 F3
Kipling Way CW1 190 C2
Kirby Cl CH2 118 B3
Kircaldy Ave WA5 14 B3
Kirkacre Ave WA12 7 E4
Kirkby Rd WA3 4 C2
Kirkfell Dr SK6 37 F4
Kirkham Ave WA3 3 F3
Kirkham Cl WA5 15 D2
Kirkham Rd Cheadle SK8 34 B4
Widnes WA8 13 E1
Kirkley St SK14 241 E5
Kirkstall Cl SK10 87 D1
Kirkstall Dr SK12 36 B2
Kirkstead Rd SK7 35 E3
Kirkstone Ave WA2 8 B1
Kirkstone Cres WA7 50 A2
Kirkstone Ct CW12 156 A1
Kirkwall Dr WA5 15 D2
Kirkwood Cl CH3 119 D1
Kishfield La SK23 65 D3
Kitchen St CH1 118 A1
Kitchener Ave M44 11 E2
Kite Gr ST7 195 E2
Kitfield Ave CW10 151 E4
Kitt's Moss La SK7 35 E3
Knap The L60 41 D3
Knight Rd WA5 6 C3
Knight St Hyde SK14 241 E5
Macclesfield SK11 112 C4
Knight's Cl SK11 112 C4
Knight's Grange (Sports Complex) CW7 126 B2
Knights La CW6 123 F1
Knights Meadow CW7 126 B2
Knights Way CW2 206 A2
Knightsbridge SK1 240 F6
Knightsbridge Ave
Davenham CW9 103 F2
Warrington WA4 17 E1
Knightwake Rd SK22 39 D4
Knivton St SK14 241 F7
Knole Ave SK12 36 C2
Knoll St SK22 39 D4
Knoll The Altrincham WA14 238 B5
Runcorn WA7 49 F4
Knott Fold SK14 241 D5
Knottingley Dr L66 69 E3
Knotty La CW12 179 F4
Knowe The L64 68 A4
Knowl Hey Rd L26 21 D3
Knowl La CH3 180 C3
Knowl St SK15 242 E2
Knowl The CH3 180 C3
Knowle Cl L66 69 F2
Knowle Gn SK9 34 B2
Knowle Pk SK9 34 B2
Knowles Ind Est SK23 39 E2
Knowles St WA8 13 E1
Knowsley Ave WA3 3 E4
Knowsley La ST7 194 C2
Knowsley Rd Chester CH2 118 C2
Hazel Grove SK7 36 C4
Macclesfield SK11 112 B3
Knutsford Ave M33 242 E6
Knutsford Cty High Sch WA16 56 C1
Knutsford Cty High Sch (Lower Sch) WA16 56 C1
Knutsford Cty High Sch (Upper Sch) WA16 56 C1
Knutsford L Ctr WA16 56 C1
Knutsford Rd Antrobus CW9 53 E2
Appleton WA4 27 F4
Chelford SK11 84 A1
Cranage CW4 130 A3
Great Budworth CW9 54 A1
Holmes Chapel CW4 130 A3
Lawton-gate ST7 193 F3
Lindow End SK9, WA16 59 F2
Mobberley WA16 57 F2
MobberleyKnolls Green WA16 58 C2
Warrington WA4 16 B2
Wilmslow SK9, WA16 59 F2
Knutsford Road Wlk 20 SK11 112 C4
Knutsford Service Area WA16 56 B1
Knutsford Sta WA16 57 D1
Knutsford View WA15 32 B4
Knutsford Way CH1 117 F1
Kohima Cres CH3 142 A3
Kronsbec Ave L66 69 E3
Kynaston Dr CH4 140 A4
Labelia Wlk M31 11 E1
Labernum Farm Cl L64 67 D3
Laburnam Cl
Congleton CW12 156 A2
Kidsgrove ST7 210 C4
Laburnum Ave
Nantwich CW5 204 C3
Warrington WA1 17 E4
Wistaston CW2 189 F1
Laburnum Cres CW8 78 A2
Laburnum Gr
Broughton CH4 140 C3
Crewe CW1 190 B3
Ellesmere Port CH1 95 D4
Runcorn WA7 49 E4
Weaverham CW8 102 B4
Laburnum La
Altrincham WA15 31 F4
Penketh WA5 14 B3
Laburnum Pl ST5 210 B1
Laburnum Rd
Davenham CW9 103 F2
Goldborne WA3 3 F4
Irlam M44 11 E3
Macclesfield SK11 112 C3
Northwich CW9 104 B3
Laburnum Way Holt LL13 180 B1
Stockport SK3 240 B4
Lacey Ave SK9 34 A1
Lacey Ct Widnes WA8 23 D4
Wilmslow SK9 34 A1
Lacey Gn SK9 34 A1
Lacey Gr SK9 34 B1
Lacey Green Cty Prim Sch SK9 34 A1
Lacey St WA8 23 D4
Lache Cty Inf & Jun Sch CH4 141 D3
Lache Hall Cres CH4 140 C2
Lache La Chester CH4 141 D3
Dodleston CH4 140 C2
Lache Park Ave CH4 141 D3
Lacy St SK1 240 F4
Ladies Mile WA16 56 C1
Ladies Wlk L64 66 C4
Lady Barn House Sch SK8 239 D3
Lady Helen Wlk CW5 204 C3
Lady Kelvin Rd WA14 238 C6
Lady La Croft WA3 9 E4
Mobberley WA16 58 B4
Ladybarn Ave WA3 2 C4
Ladybarn Cr SK7 35 F3
Ladybrook Gr 10 SK9 34 B1
Ladybrook Prim Sch SK7 35 F4
Ladycroft Cl WA1 17 F4
Ladyfield St SK9 60 A4
Ladyfield Terr SK9 60 A4
Ladypit Rd SK23 39 F2
Ladypool L24 21 E1
Ladys Cl SK12 36 C2
Ladysmith Rd SK15 242 D4
Ladysmith St SK3 240 E3
Ladythorn Cres SK7 35 F3
Ladythorn Gr SK7 35 F4
Ladythorn Rd SK7 35 F3
Ladywood Rd WA5 7 E1
Lagos Gr CW7 126 C1
Laira St WA2 16 B4
Lake House Cl CW8 77 E1
Lake La WA4 52 C3
Lake Rd SK15 242 C4
Lake View CW12 156 A1
Lakelands Cl SK10 112 C4
Lakeside SK11 158 B4
Lakeside Cl WA8 22 A4
Lakeside Dr Poynton SK12 36 C3
Warrington WA1 16 A2
Lakeside Rd WA13 18 B1
Laleston Cl WA8 22 C4
Lamb La WA14 31 E3
Lamb St ST7 195 D1
Lambert Ct WA8 23 D4
Lambert Way CW8 103 D2
Lambert's La CW12 156 C1
Lamborne Gr CW10 128 B1
Lambourn Ave WA8 12 B3
Lambourn Cl SK12 36 B2
Lambourn Dr CW1 173 D1
Lambourne Cl
Ellesmere Port CH1 94 C4
Wythenshawe M22 33 E4
Lambourne Gr WA9 1 A2
Lambs La WA1 17 D4
Lambsickle Cl WA7 48 C3
Lambsickle La WA7 49 D3
Lampeter Cl WA5 7 F1
Lampits La CH3 120 C
Lamport Cl WA8 13 F
Lanark Wlk SK10 86 C
Lancashire Hill
SK1 & SK4 & SK5 240 E
Lancashire Rd M31 11 F
Lancaster Ave Goldborne WA3 3 E
Runcorn WA7 48 C
Stalybridge SK15 242 D
Widnes L35 12 A
Lancaster Cl Hazel Grove SK7 36 B
Newton-le-W WA12 1 C
Romiley SK6 241 A
Winsford CW7 149 E
Lancaster Ct 9 SK10 112 C
Lancaster Dr CH3 119 D
Lancaster Fields CW1 191 D
Lancaster Gdns L65 70 E

Linkside Ave WA2 ... 8 A3
Linkside Way CH1 ... 94 C4
Linksway Chester CH2 ... 118 B4
Congleton CW12 ... 178 C4
Gatley SK8 ... 239 A4
Linksway Cl CW12 ... 178 C4
Linkway WA7 ... 49 E4
Linley Gr Alsager ST7 ... 193 F2
Stockport SK3 ... 240 D1
Linley La ST7 ... 194 A1
Linley Rd Alsager ST7 ... 193 F1
Cheadle Hulme SK8 ... 35 D4
Kidsgrove ST7 ... 210 B4
Sale M33 ... 242 B7
Linley Trad Est ST7 ... 194 B1
Linnards La
Higher Wincham CW9, WA16 . 80 A3
Plumley CW9, WA16 ... 80 A3
Linnet Cl Newton-le-W WA12 ... 2 B2
Warrington WA2 ... 8 B2
Winsford CW7 ... 150 A4
Linnet Gr Macclesfield SK10 ... 87 D1
Warrington WA3 ... 9 F2
Linnets Way L60 ... 40 C4
Linnett Cl CW1 ... 190 A4
Linton Cl WA16 ... 57 E1
Linton Gdns WA4 ... 26 B2
Linton Rd M33 ... 242 C8
Linwood Ave WA4 ... 26 B4
Linwood Cl WA7 ... 50 B3
Lion St CW12 ... 156 B1
Lisburn Ave M33 ... 242 A5
Liskeard Cl WA7 ... 50 A3
Liskeard Dr SK7 ... 35 F4
Lismore Ave SK3 ... 240 B4
Lismore Wlk M22 ... 33 F4
Lisson Gr WA15 ... 238 E2
Lister Rd WA7 ... 23 E2
Litherland Rd M33 ... 242 E5
Litter La CW7 ... 125 F1
Little Abbey Gateway CH1 237 D3
Little Aston Cl SK10 ... 87 E2
Little Bollington CE Contr Prim Sch WA14 ... 20 A1
Little Budworth Ctry Pk CW6 ... 147 E4
Little Delph WA11 ... 1 B4
Little Egerton St 5 SK1 ... 240 E6
Little Gn L66 ... 69 E2
Little Heath Cl CW3 ... 230 A3
Little Heath La WA14 ... 20 B3
Little Heath Rd
Chester CH3 ... 119 F1
Christleton CH3 ... 142 C4
Little La L64 ... 41 D1
Little Leigh Cty Prim Sch CW8 ... 77 E3
Little Meadow Cl SK10 ... 87 D4
Little Meadow Rd WA14 ... 238 B1
Little Moreton Hall CW12 .. 177 F1
Little Moss Cl ST7 ... 194 C3
Little Moss La ST7 ... 194 C3
Little Roodee CH5 ... 139 D4
Little St Congleton CW12 ... 156 B1
3 Macclesfield SK11 ... 112 B4
Little St John St CH1 ... 237 E2
Little Stanney La CH2 ... 95 F4
Little Sutton CE Contr Prim Sch L66 ... 69 D3
Little Sutton Sta L66 ... 69 E3
Little Underbank 1 SK1 ... 240 F5
Little Wissage L66 ... 69 F1
Littlebourne WA7 ... 50 C4
Littlecote Ave WA4 ... 26 B2
Littledale Rd WA5 ... 14 B4
Littledales La CW8 ... 102 C2
Littlegate WA7 ... 49 F4
Littler Grange Ct CW7 ... 126 A1
Littler Rd WA11 ... 1 A3
Littlestone Cl WA8 ... 13 D2
Littleton Cl Davenham CW9 . 103 F2
Great Sankey WA5 ... 15 E2
Littleton La CH3 ... 119 F1
Littondale Cl CW12 ... 157 D3
Liverpool Pl WA8 ... 12 B1
Liverpool Rd Backford CH1 ... 95 D2
Chester CH2 ... 118 B3
Great Sankey WA5 ... 15 E2
Haydock WA11 ... 1 A4
Irlam M44 ... 11 F3
Kidsgrove ST7 ... 195 D1
Neston L64 ... 41 F1
Newcastle-u-L ST5 ... 210 B1
Warrington WA5 ... 15 E2
Widnes WA8 ... 12 B1
Willaston L64 ... 41 F2
Liverpool Rd E
Kidsgrove ST7 ... 194 C1
Lawton-gate ST7 ... 194 C1
Liverpool Rd W ST7 ... 194 A2
Liverpool Row WA12 ... 7 E4
Liverpool St CW9 ... 104 B4
Livingstone Cl
Great Sankey WA5 ... 15 E4
Macclesfield SK11 ... 111 F4
Livingstone Rd L65 ... 70 B4
Livingstone Way CW10 ... 151 E3
Llanberis Rd SK8 ... 239 E1
Llandaff Cl L66 ... 69 F1
Llandovery Cl CW7 ... 149 D4
Llanfair Rd 7 SK3 ... 240 C4
Lloyd Ave SK8 ... 239 A6
Lloyd Cl CH3 ... 180 C1
Lloyd Cres WA12 ... 1 C2
Lloyd Dr L65 ... 70 B1
Lloyd Gdns WA14 ... 238 D3
Lloyd Pl CH1 ... 117 F2
Lloyd Sq 6 WA14 ... 238 D4
Lloyd St
Altrincham WA14 & WA15 ... 238 D4
Stockport SK4 ... 240 D7
Lloyd's Ct WA14 ... 238 D4
Llyndir La LL12 ... 162 A1
Llys Caer CH4 ... 139 D2
Llys Derwen CH4 ... 161 D4
Loachbrook Ave CW12 ... 156 A1
Lobelia Gr WA7 ... 49 F3
Loch St WA7 ... 23 D2
Lochinvar Ave L66 ... 68 C3
Lochleven Rd CW2 ... 206 A4
Lochmaben Cl CW4 ... 130 A1
Lock La M31 ... 11 F2
Lock Rd Altrincham WA14 ... 238 C6
Bebington L62 ... 44 A4
Warrington WA1 ... 16 C3
Locker Ave WA2 ... 8 A1
Lockerbie Cl WA2 ... 8 C2
Lockett Rd WA8 ... 13 D2
Lockett St WA4 ... 16 C2
Lockgate East WA7 ... 24 B1
Lockgate West WA7 ... 24 A1
Locking Stumps Cty Prim Sch WA3 ... 9 E2
Locking Stumps La WA3 ... 9 D2
Lockitt St CW2 ... 190 B2
Locksley Cl SK4 ... 240 C6
Lockton La WA5 ... 15 F4
Lodge Brow SK10 ... 63 D1
Lodge Cl WA13 ... 19 D2
Lodge Dr Moulton CW9 ... 126 C4
Winsford CW7 ... 127 D1
Lodge Hollow WA6 ... 73 D2
Lodge La Antrobus CW9 ... 54 A3
Cronton WA8 ... 12 A2
Dutton WA4 ... 76 B4
Hartford CW8 ... 103 D2
Hatherton CW5 ... 220 A2
Hyde SK14 ... 241 D8
Lostock CW9 ... 80 A1
Newton-le-W WA11 ... 2 A4
Runcorn WA7 ... 49 F4
Saughall CH1 ... 94 A1
Warrington WA5 ... 15 F4
Lodge Rd Alsager ST7 ... 193 E2
Kidsgrove ST7 ... 210 B3
Knutsford WA16 ... 57 E2
Sandbach CW11 ... 174 C3
Widnes WA8 ... 22 A4
Lodgefields Cty Prim Sch CW2 ... 189 F2
Lodgefields Dr CW2 ... 189 F2
Lodmore La SY13 ... 233 E3
Lofthouse Gate WA8 ... 12 C2
Lomas Sq SK11 ... 112 B3
Lomas St SK3 ... 240 D3
Lomax Rd CW5 ... 205 E3
Lomond Gr L65 ... 69 F2
London Pl 13 SK1 ... 240 F5
London Rd Adlington SK10 ... 62 B3
Alderley Edge SK9 ... 60 A1
Allostock WA16 ... 107 D3
Appleton WA4 ... 26 B3
Blakenhall CW5 ... 220 B2
Brereton Green CW4 ... 130 B1
Bridgemere CW5 ... 232 A3
Davenham CW9 ... 104 A1
Davenham CW9 ... 104 A1
Frodsham WA6 ... 74 A4
Hatherton CW5 ... 220 B2
Holmes Chapel CW4 ... 130 B1
Macclesfield SK11 ... 112 B2
Nantwich CW5 ... 204 C3
Northwich CW9 ... 103 F4
Prestbury SK10 ... 62 A1
Sandbach CW11 ... 174 B4
Stapeley CW5 ... 205 D2
Sutton Lane Ends SK11 ... 112 B2
Warrington WA4 ... 26 B3
Woore CW5 ... 232 A3
London Rd S SK12 ... 36 B2
London Rd Terr SK11 ... 112 B3
London Row WA12 ... 7 E4
London Sq 10 SK1 ... 240 F5
Loney St SK11 ... 112 B4
Long Acre CW8 ... 77 E1
Long Acres Rd L64 ... 41 F1
Long Barn La WA1 ... 17 E4
Long Croft La SK8 ... 34 C4
Long Hill SK23 ... 65 F1
Long La Alpraham CW6 ... 169 F2
Bickerton SY14 ... 199 F2
Bollington SK10 ... 63 D1
Burland CW5 ... 203 D4
Chester CH2 ... 119 D3
Faddiley CW6 ... 186 B2
Hargrave CH3 ... 143 E1
Haughton Moss CW6 ... 186 B2
Huxley CH3 ... 166 B4
Kidsgrove ST7 ... 195 F2
Middlewich CW10 ... 151 E4
Peover WA16 ... 107 E4
Saughall CH1 ... 94 A1
Spurstow CW6 ... 186 B2
Tilston SY14 ... 198 A2
Warrington WA2 ... 8 A1
Waverton CH3 ... 143 E1
Wettenhall CW7 ... 170 B3
Whaley Bridge SK23 ... 65 F2
Long La S CW10 ... 151 E4
Long Lane Cty Prim Sch WA2 ... 8 A1
Long Looms CH3 ... 120 C3
Long Marl Dr SK9 ... 34 C2
Long Meadow L60 ... 40 C3
Long Meadow Pas SK14 ... 241 D7
Long Row ST7 ... 195 D1
Long Shoot Rd SK11 ... 108 C1
Long Spinney WA7 ... 50 B4
Long Valley Rd ST6 ... 179 E1
Long Wlk M31 ... 11 E1
Longacre St SK11 ... 112 B4
Longacres Rd WA15 ... 32 B4
Longbarn Bvd WA2 ... 9 E1
Longbarn Cty Prim Sch WA3 ... 9 D1
Longbenton Way WA7 ... 24 A2
Longburgh Cl CH2 ... 118 C2
Longbutt La WA13 ... 18 C1
Longbutts La SK11 ... 111 F1
Longclough Rd ST5 ... 210 B1
Longcroft Dr WA14 ... 238 B4
Longdale Dr CH1 ... 117 E3
Longden Ct SK7 ... 35 F3
Longden La SK11 ... 113 D3
Longden St SK11 ... 112 C4
Longdin St WA4 ... 16 C2
Longdown Rd CW12 ... 155 F2
Longfield Ave Cheadle SK8 ... 34 B4
Chester CH2 ... 118 B4
Longfield Gdns M44 ... 11 E2
Longford St Crewe CW2 ... 190 B1
Warrington WA2 ... 16 A4
Longhill La CW3 ... 230 C3
Longhorn Cl CW10 ... 128 B1
Longlands Dr SK22 ... 39 D4
Longlands Rd SK22 ... 39 D4
Longley Ave CW6 ... 122 B3
Longlooms Rd L65 ... 70 B1
Longmeade Gdns SK9 ... 60 B3
Longmeadow
Cheadle Hulme SK7 ... 35 E4
Weaverham CW8 ... 102 B4
Longmoss Cl CW10 ... 151 D4
Longmynd Rise CW7 ... 149 D4
Longnor Rd Cheadle SK8 ... 34 B4
Hazel Grove SK7 ... 36 C4
Longridge WA16 ... 57 E2
Longridge Ave SK15 ... 242 D4
Longridge Trad Est WA16 ... 57 E2
Longsdon Cl ST5 ... 210 B1
Longshaw St WA5 ... 7 F1
Longshut La SK1 & SK2 ... 240 F3
Longshut La W SK2 ... 240 F3
Longsides Rd WA15 ... 32 B4
Longsight La SK8 ... 34 C3
Longsight St SK4 ... 240 D6
Longsons The SK5 ... 240 F7
Longston Ave WA3 ... 3 E4
Longstone La CW6 ... 124 C2
Longview Ave ST7 ... 193 F2
Longwood Cl
Middlewich CW10 ... 151 E4
Romiley SK6 ... 241 E3
Longwood Rd Appleton WA4 26 C3
Stretton WA4 ... 26 C3
Lonsdale Cl WA8 ... 22 B4
Looe Cl WA8 ... 12 C1
Looms The L64 ... 41 D1
Loonies Ct 1 SK1 ... 240 F4
Loont The CW7 ... 149 E4
Lord Nelson St WA1 ... 16 B3
Lord St Bollington SK10 ... 88 A4
Chester CH3 ... 118 C1
Crewe CW2 ... 190 B2
Croft WA3 ... 9 D4
Macclesfield SK11 ... 112 B4
Newton-le-W WA12 ... 2 A2
Runcorn WA7 ... 22 C2
Stockport SK1 ... 240 F5
Warrington WA4 ... 16 A2
Lord's St M44 ... 11 E3
Lords La WA3 ... 9 E2
Lords Mill Rd CW2 ... 206 A2
Lordship La WA6 ... 73 D4
Lordshire Pl ST7 ... 195 F1
Loreto Convent Gram Sch WA14 ... 238 C5
Loreto Convent Prep Sch WA14 ... 238 C5
Lorland Rd SK3 ... 240 B3
Lorne Gr SK3 ... 240 E2
Lorne St CH1 ... 237 D3
Lorraine St ST7 ... 195 F1
Lostock Ave Sale M33 ... 242 E6
Warrington WA5 ... 15 F4
Lostock Gralam CE Contr Prim Sch CW9 ... 80 A1
Lostock Gralam Sta CW9 ... 80 A1
Lostock Hall Cty Prim Sch SK12 ... 36 A2
Lostock Hall Rd SK12 ... 36 A2
Lostock Hollow CW9 ... 80 A1
Lostock Rd SK12 ... 36 B1
Lostock Way SK9 ... 34 B2
Lottery St SK3 ... 240 D5
Louise St CH1 ... 237 D3
Loushers La WA4 ... 16 B1
Loushers Lane Day Sch WA4 ... 16 B1
Lovage Cl WA2 ... 9 E1
Lovat Dr WA16 ... 82 A4
Love La Hassall Green CW11 176 B2
Nantwich CW5 ... 204 C3
Stockport SK4 ... 240 E6
Love St CH1 ... 237 E2
Lovel Terr WA8 ... 22 A3
Lovell Dr SK14 ... 241 F8
Lovely La WA5 ... 15 F3
Low Hill WA6 ... 97 E3
Low Leighton Rd SK22 ... 39 E4
Low Meadow SK23 ... 65 E4
Lowcross La SY14 ... 198 B2
Lowe Ave Congleton CW12 .. 156 C1
Warrington WA4 ... 16 C2
Lowe Cres CW9 ... 53 E2
Lowe Dr WA16 ... 57 D1
Lowe St Denton M34 ... 241 B7
Goldborne WA3 ... 3 D4
Macclesfield SK11 ... 112 B4
15 Stockport SK1 ... 240 F5
Lower Ash Rd ST7 ... 194 C1
Lower Bank St 18 SK11 ... 112 C4
Lower Beech Cotts SK10 ... 87 E1
Lower Bennett St SK14 ... 241 C8
Lower Bridge St CH4 ... 237 E1
Lower Brook St CH5 ... 91 E1
Lower Bury St SK4 ... 240 D6
Lower Carrs 21 SK1 ... 240 F5
Lower Church St WA8 ... 23 D3
Lower Cl L26 ... 21 D4
Lower Darwin St CW8 ... 103 F3
Lower Exchange St SK11 ... 112 B4
Lower Field Rd CH4 ... 141 D3
Lower Fold M34 ... 241 A6
Lower Greenshall La SK12 .. 38 C3
Lower Hague SK22 ... 38 C4
Lower Haigh St CW7 ... 149 E4
Lower Hall La CH3 ... 182 B1
Lower Hall Mews CH3 ... 182 B1
Lower Heath CW12 ... 156 C2
Lower Heath Ave CW12 ... 156 C2
Lower High St ST7 ... 195 E4
Lower Hillgate SK1 ... 240 F5
Lower House La WA8 ... 22 C4
Lower La CW6 ... 147 D2
Lower Macclesfield Rd SK23 65 F3
Lower Meadow Rd SK9 ... 34 C2
Lower Mersey St L65 ... 70 B4
Lower Moat Cl SK4 ... 240 E7
Lower Park Cres SK12 ... 36 B3
Lower Park Cty Prim Sch SK12 ... 36 B2
Lower Park Rd Chester CH4 237 F2
Poynton SK12 ... 36 A3
Lower Park St CW12 ... 156 C2
Lower Peover CE Aided Prim Sch WA16 ... 81 F1
Lower Rake La WA6 ... 73 D2
Lower Rd Halewood L26 ... 21 E4
Widnes WA8 ... 21 E3
Lower Robin Hood La WA6 73 D2
Lower Sandy La CH3 ... 199 E4
Lower Wash La WA4 ... 16 C2
Lowerfield Rd SK10 ... 87 F1
Lowerhouse SK10 ... 87 F4
Lowerlea SK12 ... 38 B3
Lowes La SK11 ... 111 F1
Lowes The WA14 ... 238 B1
Loweswater Cl WA2 ... 8 A2
Loweswater Cres WA11 ... 1 A3
Loweswater Rd SK8 ... 239 B3
Lowfield Gdns WA3 ... 5 E4
Lowfield Gr SK2 ... 240 F3
Lowfield Rd SK2 & SK3 ... 240 E3
Lowfields Ave L62 ... 43 F2
Lowfields Cl L62 ... 43 F2
Lowland Way WA16 ... 82 A4
Lowlands Rd 3 WA7 ... 22 C1
Lowry Cl WA5 ... 15 E3
Lowther Ave WA3 ... 4 C2
Lowther St SK10 ... 88 B4
Lowton Gdns WA3 ... 3 D3
Lowton Jun & Inf Sch WA3 .. 4 A4
Lowton Rd WA3 ... 3 E4
Lowton Sch WA3 ... 4 A4
Lowton West Cty Prim Sch WA3 ... 3 E4
Loxdale Dr L65 ... 69 F2
Loxley Cl Great Sankey WA5 .. 15 D4
Macclesfield SK11 ... 112 A4
Loyola Hey L35 ... 12 C4
Lucerne Cl CH3 ... 142 A3
Lucy St SK3 ... 240 E4
Ludford Cl ST5 ... 210 B1
Ludford St CW1 ... 190 B3
Ludlow Ave CW1 ... 190 C2
Ludlow Cl
Macclesfield SK10 ... 87 F1
Winsford CW7 ... 149 D4
Ludlow Cres WA7 ... 49 D4
Ludlow Dr L65 ... 70 C2
Ludlow Rd CH1 ... 118 A3
Ludwell Cl CH4 ... 141 D3
Lugsdale Rd WA8 ... 23 D4
Luke's Ave WA3 ... 3 E4
Lulworth Cl CW7 ... 149 D4
Lum Head Jun Sch SK8 ... 239 B3
Lumb Brook Rd WA4 ... 26 C4
Lumb Cl SK7 ... 35 F3
Lumb La SK7 ... 35 F3
Lumber La WA5 ... 6 C4
Lumley Pl CH1 ... 237 E2
Lumley Rd Chester CH2 ... 118 B2
Macclesfield SK11 ... 111 F4
Lumley Wlk L24 ... 21 F1
Lumn Hollow 4 SK14 ... 241 E6
Lumn Rd SK14 ... 241 E6
Lumpy St CW12 ... 156 B2
Lundy Dr CH2 ... 95 E4
Lune Cl CW12 ... 157 D1
Lune Way WA8 ... 12 B1
Lunehurst WA3 ... 3 F4
Lunt Ave CW2 ... 190 B1
Lunt's Heath Rd WA8 ... 13 D3
Lunts Heath Cty Prim Sch WA8 ... 13 D3
Lupin Dr Haydock WA11 ... 1 C3
Huntington CH3 ... 142 A3
Lupus Way L66 ... 69 F2
Lurgan Ave M33 ... 242 C5
Luscombe Cl L26 ... 21 D4
Lutener St WA14 ... 238 C8
Luther Gr WA9 ... 1 A1
Luton Rd L65 ... 70 A3
Luton St WA8 ... 23 D4
Lutyens Cl SK11 ... 111 F4
Lyceum Cl CW1 ... 190 A4
Lyceum Way CW1 ... 190 A4
Lychgate WA4 ... 25 F4
Lycroft Cl WA7 ... 49 D3
Lydbury Cl WA5 ... 7 E1
Lydden Rd L65 ... 70 A4
Lydgate Cl Denton M34 ... 241 B5
Wistaston CW2 ... 205 F4
Lydiat La SK9 ... 60 A1
Lydiate La Runcorn WA7 ... 48 B4
Willaston L64 ... 42 C1
Lydiate The L60 ... 40 C4
Lydney Ave SK8 ... 34 B4
Lydstep Ct WA5 ... 7 F1
Lydyett La CW8 ... 78 A2
Lymcote Dr CW8 ... 103 D2
Lyme Ave Macclesfield SK11 112 B3
Wilmslow SK9 ... 34 A1
Lyme Comm Inf Sch WA12 ... 1 C2
Lyme Gr Altrincham WA14 ... 238 C4
Lymm WA13 ... 18 B1
Romiley SK6 ... 241 D2
Stockport SK2 & SK3 ... 240 F3
Lyme Green Bsns Pk SK11 112 B2
Lyme Green Settlement SK11 ... 112 B1
Lyme Hall SK12 ... 38 A1
Lyme Park Ctry Pk SK12 ... 38 A1
Lyme Rd Disley SK12 ... 38 A3
Poynton SK12 ... 37 E2
Lyme St Haydock WA11 ... 1 C3
Newton-le-W WA12 ... 1 C2
Lymewood Dr Disley SK12 ... 38 B3
Wilmslow SK9 ... 60 C4
Lymm Cherry Tree Cty Prim Sch WA13 ... 18 B1
Lymm Cl SK3 ... 240 D2
Lymm High (VC) Sch WA13 19 D2
Lymm Rd
Little Bollington WA14 ... 20 A1
Warrington WA4 ... 17 F2
Lymm Statham Cty Prim Sch WA13 ... 18 B2
Lymmhay La WA13 ... 18 C2
Lymmington Ave WA13 ... 18 B2
Lynalls Cl CW12 ... 155 F2
Lynbrook Rd CW1 ... 190 C2
Lyncastle Rd WA4 ... 27 E2
Lyncastle Way WA4 ... 27 E2
Lyncombe Cl SK8 ... 35 D3
Lyndale Ave Bebington L62 ... 43 F2
Warrington WA2 ... 16 B4
Lyndene Gdns SK8 ... 239 B6
Lyndhurst Cl SK9 ... 59 E3
Lyndon Gr WA7 ... 49 D4
Lyngard Cl SK9 ... 34 C1
Lyngarth Ho 1 WA14 ... 238 E6
Lynham Ave WA5 ... 15 D3
Lynn Ave Kidsgrove ST7 ... 210 B4
Sale M33 ... 242 D8
Lynn Cl WA7 ... 49 E4
Lynn Gr SK11 ... 112 B3
Lynndene L66 ... 69 E4
Lynneal Ave L66 ... 69 E1
Lynside Wlk M22 ... 33 F4
Lynthorpe Ave M44 ... 11 E3
Lynton Ave M44 ... 11 F3
Lynton Cl Heswall L60 ... 41 D3
Penketh WA5 ... 14 C2
Lynton Cres WA8 ... 12 C1
Lynton Gr
Altrincham WA15 ... 238 F5
Haslington CW1 ... 191 E3
Lynton La SK9 ... 60 A1
Lynton Park Rd SK8 ... 34 C4
Lynton Pl Alsager ST7 ... 193 E2
Broughton CH4 ... 139 D2
Lynton Rd SK8 ... 239 C5
Lynton Way CW2 ... 206 A4
Lyntonvale Ave SK8 ... 239 B6
Lynwood WA15 ... 32 A4
Lynwood Ave WA3 ... 3 F3
Lynwood Gr M33 ... 242 C7
Lynwood Rd CH1 ... 117 F3
Lyon Ind Est WA14 ... 238 B7
Lyon Rd WA14 ... 238 C7
Lyon St Chester CH2 ... 237 E3
Crewe CW1 ... 190 B2
Macclesfield SK11 ... 112 B4
Warrington WA4 ... 16 C2
Lyon's La WA4 ... 26 C3
Lyons Fold M33 ... 242 B8
Lyons Rd WA5 ... 15 D2
Lyster Cl WA3 ... 9 F2
Lytham Dr SK7 ... 36 A4
Lytham Rd SK8 ... 239 B1
Lytham St SK3 ... 240 F2
Lytherton Ave M44 ... 11 E2
Lythgoes La WA2 ... 16 A3

Mabledon Cl SK8 ... 34 B4
Mablins La CW1 ... 190 A4
Mablins Lane Cty Prim Sch CW1 ... 190 A4
Mabs Ct OL6 ... 242 A2
Macarthur Dr WA5 ... 15 E3
Macclesfield Coll
Macclesfield SK11 ... 112 A3
Macclesfield SK11 ... 112 B4
Macclesfield District General Hospl SK11 ... 112 A4

Macclesfield Rd
Alderley Edge SK9 85 E4
Congleton CW12 156 C3
Eaton CW12 134 A1
Hazel Grove SK7 36 C4
Holmes Chapel CW4 130 C2
Kettleshulme SK23, SK10 64 B2
Nether Alderley SK9 85 E4
Prestbury SK10 86 C2
Rainow SK10 89 D4
Whaley Bridge SK23 65 E3
Wilmslow SK9 60 B3
Macclesfield Sta SK11 112 B4
Macdermott Rd WA8 22 C3
Macdonald Rd M44 11 F4
Mackenzie Ind Pk SK3 & SK8 240 B2
Mackeson Dr OL6 242 B4
Mackeson Rd OL6 242 B4
Macon Ct CW1 190 C2
Macon Ind Pk CW1 190 C2
Macon Way CW1 190 C2
Maddock St ST7 209 E1
Maddocks Hill WA6 100 C3
Madeley Cl Altrincham WA14 31 F4
Broughton CH4 139 E2
Madeley St CW2 190 B1
Madeline McKenna Ct WA8 12 B2
Madras Rd SK3 240 C3
Madron Ave SK10 86 B1
Maelor Cl L63 43 E3
Mag La WA16 28 C3
Magdala Pl CW9 104 B4
Maggoty La SK11 111 E1
Magnolia Cl
Ellesmere Port L66 69 F1
Partington M31 11 F1
Warrington WA1 17 F4
Magnolia Dr WA7 49 F2
Magnolia Rise SK10 86 C3
Magpie Cres ST7 195 D1
Mahood St SK3 240 D3
Maidenhills CW10 128 B1
Maidstone Cl SK10 87 D1
Maidwell Cl CW7 127 D2
Main Cl WA11 1 A3
Main La WA3 3 F2
Main Rd Broughton CH4 139 D2
Goostrey CW4 107 F1
Higher Kinnerton CH4 161 D4
Langley SK11 113 E2
Moulton CW9 126 C4
Norton in Hales TF9 236 B1
Shavington CW2 206 A2
Weston CW2 207 E4
Worleston CW5 188 C3
Wybunbury CW5 220 A4
Main St Frodsham WA6 74 A4
Great Barrow CH3 120 C3
Hyde SK14 241 D8
Runcorn WA7 49 F4
Maintree Cres L24 21 D2
Mainwaring Dr
Broughton CH4 140 B4
Wilmslow SK9 60 B4
Mainwaring Rd WA16 108 A4
Mairesfield Ave WA4 17 D1
Maisterson Ct CW5 204 C3
Maitland Way CH1 117 E2
Maitland Wood Cl CW9 104 B4
Maizefield Cl M33 242 F6
Major Cross St 15 WA8 23 D4
Makepeace Cl CH3 119 E2
Malaga Ave M90 33 D4
Malakoff St SK15 242 B1
Malam Dr CW9 104 B3
Malbank CW5 204 C3
Malbank Rd CW2 189 F2
Malbank Sch CW5 204 B3
Malcolm Ave WA2 8 B1
Malcolm Cres L63 43 E3
Malcolm St WA7 23 D1
Malgam Dr M20 239 B8
Malhamdale Rd CW12 157 D3
Malin Cl L24 21 E1
Maliston Rd WA5 15 D3
Mallaig Cl CW4 130 B1
Mallard Cl Knutsford WA16 57 D1
Runcorn WA7 49 F3
Warrington WA2 8 B2
Mallard Cres SK12 36 A2
Mallard Gn WA14 238 B8
Mallard La WA3 9 F2
Mallard Way CW7 149 E3
Mallory Ct Altrincham WA14 238 C3
Congleton CW12 155 F2
Mallory Rd L65 70 A2
Mallory Wlk CH4 162 A4
Mallow Cl CH3 142 A3
Mallow Wlk M31 11 F1
Mallowdale Cl L62 43 F3
Malmesbury Ave SK8 35 D3
Malmesbury Cl
Middlewich CW10 128 A1
Poynton SK12 36 B2
Malmesbury Pk WA7 24 B1
Malory Cl CW1 190 C3
Malpas Alport Endowed Prim Sch SY14 213 D2
Malpas Bishop Heber Cty High Sch SY14 213 E3
Malpas Cl Northwich CW9 104 B4
Wilmslow SK9 34 C1
Malpas Dr WA5 15 E2
Malpas Rd Ellesmere Port L65 69 F2
Northwich CW9 104 B4
Runcorn WA7 49 E4
Malpas Way WA5 15 E2
Malt Kiln Rd WA16 80 C2
Malt St WA16 57 D1
Malta Rd CH2 95 D1
Maltmans Rd WA13 18 B2
Malton Ave WA3 3 F4
Malton Cl WA8 12 B3
Malton Dr Altrincham WA14 238 A6
Hazel Grove SK7 36 B4
Malton Rd SK4 240 A8
Malvern Ave L65 70 B2
Malvern Cl
Congleton CW12 155 F2
Great Sankey WA5 15 D4
Shavington CW2 206 A2
Stockport SK4 240 D7
Malvern Dr
Altrincham WA14 238 B5
Macclesfield SK10 87 F2
Malvern Rd Blacon CH1 118 A3
Knutsford WA16 81 F4
St Helens WA9 1 A2
Malvern Way CW7 149 D4
Manchester Airport M90 33 D3
Manchester Airport Sta M90 33 D4
Manchester Bridge CW1 190 C2
Manchester Met Univ, Crewe & Alsager Faculty CW1 190 C2
Manchester Met Univ, Crewe & Alsager Faculty, Alsager Campus ST7 193 D3
Manchester New Rd M31 11 F2
Manchester Rd
Altrincham WA14 238 D7
Cheadle M20 & SK8 239 D7
Congleton CW12 156 C3
Denton SK14 241 C7
Hollins Green WA3 11 D1
Knutsford WA16 56 C2
Lostock CW9 79 E1
Macclesfield SK10 87 E2
Northwich CW9 79 E1
Partington M31 11 F2
Reddish SK4 240 E8
Warrington WA3 18 A4
Warrington, Bruche WA1 16 C4
Warrington, Woolston WA1 17 E4
Wilmslow SK9 34 B1
Manchester Row WA12 7 E4
Mancroft Cl WA1 17 F4
Mancunian Rd M34 241 A5
Mandarin Gn WA14 238 B8
Manifold Cl CW11 174 C4
Manifold Dr SK6 37 F3
Manley Cl Antrobus CW9 53 E2
Holmes Chapel CW4 130 A2
Northwich CW9 104 A3
Manley Cty Prim Sch WA6 99 D3
Manley Gdns WA5 15 F3
Manley Gr SK7 35 F3
Manley La
Dunham-on-t-H WA6 97 F3
Manley WA6 98 B2
Manley Rd Alvanley WA6 98 C4
Frodsham WA6 74 A2
Manley WA6 99 D3
Warren SK11 112 A3
Manley View CH2 72 B2
Manna Dr CH2 72 B2
Manners La L60 40 C3
Manning La S CH2 119 D3
Manning St CW2 190 B1
Mannings La CH2 119 D3
Manor Ave Crewe CW2 190 A1
Goldborne WA3 3 E4
Goostrey CW4 107 F1
Marston CW9 79 D3
Newton-le-W WA12 1 C2
Manor Cl Bramhall SK7 35 E4
Broughton CH5 139 E4
Congleton CW12 157 D1
Denton M34 241 B6
Great Barrow CH3 120 C3
Neston L64 66 B4
Warrington WA1 17 E4
Wilmslow SK9 59 F4
Manor Cres Broughton CH4 139 E4
Knutsford WA16 57 D1
Macclesfield SK10 87 E2
Middlewich CW10 151 E4
Manor Ct Crewe CW2 190 A1
Goldborne WA3 3 E4
Manor Dr Barnton CW8 78 A1
Chester CH3 119 E1
Northwich, Rudheath CW9 104 B4
Manor Farm Cl CH2 119 F4
Manor Farm Cres CH1 94 A4
Manor Farm Ct CH5 139 D4
Manor Farm Rd WA7 24 B2
Manor Fell WA7 50 A4
Manor Fields CW10 151 E4
Manor Gdns SK9 60 B4
Manor Gr CW8 103 E3
Manor La Broughton CH5 139 D4
Davenham CW9 104 B1
Ellesmere Port L66 69 E2
Holmes Chapel CW4 130 B2
Middlewich CW10 151 E4
Ollerton WA16 82 C3
Manor Park Ave WA7 24 B2
Manor Park Cty Prim Sch WA16 57 E1
Manor Pk Great Barrow CH3 120 C3
Hawarden CH4 139 D4
Manor Pk N WA16 57 E1
Manor Pk S WA16 57 E1
Manor Pl WA8 12 A1
Manor Rd Altrincham WA15 238 E4
Bebington L62 43 F3
Chester CH4 141 D3
Cuddington CW8 101 F1
Denton M34 241 B5
Frodsham WA6 49 E1
Haydock WA11 1 C4
Lymm WA13 18 C1
Mow Cop ST7 195 E4
Nantwich CW5 204 C3
Runcorn WA7 23 E1
Sale M33 242 B7
Sandbach CW11 175 E3
Sealand CH5 116 A3
Thornton Hough L63 42 A4
Whaley Bridge SK23 65 F3
Widnes WA8 12 A1
Wilmslow SK9 59 F4
Manor Rd N CW5 204 C4
Manor Sq 5 CW7 149 D4
Manor St CW8 103 E3
Manor Way Crewe CW2 190 B1
Sandbach CW11 175 F3
Manora Rd CW9 104 A4
Manorfield Cl CH1 69 D1
Manorial Rd S L64 66 B4
Manse Field Rd WA6 75 D1
Manse Gdns WA12 2 B2
Mansell Cl WA8 13 E3
Mansfield Cl WA3 10 A2
Mansfield Cty Prim Sch L65 69 F2
Mansfield Rd
Ellesmere Port L65 70 A1
Hyde SK14 241 F5
Mansion Ct CW5 204 C3
Mansion Dr WA16 57 D1
Manston Rd WA5 14 C2
Manuel Perez Rd WA5 15 D3
Manvers St SK5 240 E7
Manx St WA4 16 A2
Maori Dr WA6 74 A4
Maple Ave Alsager ST7 193 F1
Cheadle SK8 239 F2
Disley SK12 39 D3
Ellesmere Port L66 69 E3
Goldborne WA3 3 F4
Haydock WA11 1 A4
Kidsgrove ST7 210 B4
Macclesfield SK11 112 B3
Newcastle-u-L ST5 210 C1
Newton-le-W WA12 2 B1
Poynton SK12 36 C2
Runcorn WA7 49 E4
Sutton WA7 50 A2
Widnes WA8 13 D1
Maple Cl
Brereton Green CW11 153 F2
Congleton CW12 155 F2
Holmes Chapel CW4 130 B2
Sandbach CW11 175 E3
Maple Cres WA5 14 C2
Maple Gr Barnton CW8 78 A2
Bebington L62 43 E4
Broughton CH4 140 B3
Chester CH2 119 D2
Crewe CW1 190 C4
Ellesmere Port CH1 95 D4
Northwich, Greenbank CW8 103 E4
Warrington WA4 16 B2
Winsford CW7 127 D1
Maple La CW8 101 F1
Maple Pl ST7 193 F4
Maple Rd Alderley Edge SK9 60 A2
Bramhall SK7 35 F3
Partington M31 11 F2
Warrington WA1 17 F4
Winwick WA2 8 A3
Mapleton Dr WA7 49 F2
Maplewood Gr CH1 117 D4
Maplewood Rd SK9 60 C4
Mapplewell Cres WA5 15 D3
Marble Arch WA16 57 D1
Marbury Ctry Pk CW9 78 C3
Marbury Gdns L65 69 F3
Marbury La CW9 78 C3
Marbury Rd Chester CH3 119 E1
Comberbach CW9 78 B3
Marston CW9 78 B3
Northwich CW9 78 B3
Wilmslow SK9 34 A1
Marbury St WA4 16 B2
March Ave SK4 240 B6
March St CW1 190 C2
Marchbank Dr SK8 239 C6
Marchwiel Rd L65 70 B2
Marcien Way WA8 12 C2
Marcliff Gr Knutsford WA16 57 D1
Stockport SK4 240 B6
Marcross Cl WA5 7 F1
Mardale Ave WA2 8 B2
Mardale Cl Congleton CW12 157 D3
Stalybridge SK15 242 D3
Mardale Cres WA13 18 C2
Mardale Ct CW4 130 A1
Mardale Dr SK8 239 B6
Mardon Cl WA16 57 E2
Marfields Cty Prim Sch CW12 156 B1
Marfords Ave L63 43 E4
Margaret Ave WA1 17 D4
Margaret Ct WA8 23 D4
Margaret Danyers Coll SK8 239 F3
Margaret Rd M34 241 A8
Margaret's La L66 69 D4
Margery Ave ST7 194 C4
Marian Dr CH3 142 A4
Marian Rd WA11 1 C4
Marie Cl CW5 216 C2
Marie Dr WA4 17 E1
Marigold Cl SK11 111 F4
Marina Ave Denton M34 241 A5
Great Sankey WA5 15 E2
Marina Cl SK9 34 B3
Marina Dr Chester CH2 118 C4
Ellesmere Port L65 70 A3
Warrington WA2 8 B1
Marina Gr WA7 23 D1
Marina La WA7 50 C4
Marina Village WA7 50 C4
Marina Wlk L65 70 A3
Marine Ave M31 11 E2
Marine Dr L60 40 B4
Mariner Cl WA7 50 B3
Marion Dr WA7 48 C3
Maritime Cl WA12 2 B3
Mark Ave L66 69 E2
Mark Cl CH2 118 C1
Mark Rake L62 43 E4
Market Cl CW1 190 B3
Market Ct CW6 146 B1
Market Ctr The CW1 190 B2
Market Gate WA1 16 A3
Market Pl Bollington SK10 88 A4
1 Hyde SK14 241 D6
Macclesfield SK11 112 B4
Stockport SK1 240 F6
Winsford CW7 126 C1
Market Sq Chester CH1 237 D2
Congleton CW12 156 C1
Crewe CW1 190 B2
Sandbach CW11 175 D3
Market St
Altrincham WA14 238 D4
Congleton CW12 156 B1
Crewe CW1 190 B2
Crewe CW1 190 B3
Disley SK12 38 B3
Hyde SK14 241 D6
Kidsgrove ST7 195 D1
Nantwich CW5 204 C3
New Mills SK22 39 D4
Newton-le-W WA12 2 A2
Northwich CW9 103 F4
Stalybridge SK15 242 D2
Whaley Bridge SK23 65 F4
Widnes WA8 23 D4
Market Way CW9 103 F4
Markland St SK14 241 E5
Marl Cft CH3 142 A4
Marl Edge SK10 87 D3
Marl Heys CH2 118 C4
Marland Ave SK8 239 F2
Marlborough Ave
Alderley Edge SK9 60 A1
Winsford CW7 126 B2
Marlborough Cl
Knutsford WA16 57 E2
Macclesfield SK10 87 E2
Wistaston CW2 205 F4
Marlborough Cres
Warrington WA4 16 C1
Widnes WA8 13 D3
Marlborough Ct 24 SK11 112 B4
Marlborough Cty Prim Sch The SK10 87 E2
Marlborough Dr
Helsby WA6 73 D1
Macclesfield SK10 87 E2
Reddish SK4 240 D8
Marlborough Rd
Altrincham WA14 238 D2
Ellesmere Port L65 70 B2
Sale M33 242 B6
Marlborough Wlk L65 70 B2
Marlcroft Ave SK4 240 B6
Marler Rd SK14 241 E8
Marley Ave CW1 190 A4
Marley Cl WA15 238 F7
Marley Dr M33 242 A8
Marley Rd SK12 36 C1
Marley Way CH4 140 C4
Marlfield Rd
Altrincham WA15 32 B4
Warrington WA4 17 D1
Marline Ave L63 43 E3
Marling Cl WA6 74 B3
Marling Park WA8 12 A1
Marlow Ave CH2 118 B4
Marlow Cl Cheadle SK8 239 F2
10 Sandbach CW11 174 B3
Warrington WA3 9 E3
Marlow Dr Altrincham WA14 20 C1
Wilmslow SK9 34 B3
Marlowe Cl Blacon CH1 118 A3
Widnes WA8 12 C1
Marlowe Ct SK11 112 B3
Marlowe Dr CW5 204 C2
Marlowe Rd Neston L64 66 C4
Northwich CW9 104 B3
Marlston Ave CH4 141 D3
Marlston Pl WA7 49 D3
Marple Cres CW2 189 F2
Marple Rd CW9 104 B4
Marquis Dr SK8 34 B4
Marrick Ave SK8 239 C5
Marriott Rd CW11 174 C2
Marriott St SK1 240 F4
Marron Ave WA2 8 A1
Marsden Ave WA4 17 D2
Marsden Rd SK6 241 C3
Marsden Terr 16 SK11 112 B4
Marsh Ave ST7 195 F1
Marsh Cl Alsager ST7 193 D2
Stockport SK3 240 D2
Marsh Gr ST6 179 E2
Marsh Green Cl ST6 179 E1
Marsh Green Rd
Biddulph ST6 179 E1
Sandbach CW11 174 C4
Marsh Hall Rd WA8 13 D2
Marsh House La WA2 16 B4
Marsh La Acton CW5 204 A2
Alsager ST7 193 D2
Churton CH3 181 D3
Coddington CH3 181 F2
Crowton CW8 101 D4
Dutton WA4 51 F2
Elton CH2 72 A2
Frodsham WA6 74 A4
Holmes Chapel CW4 130 C1
Mere WA14 30 C2
Nantwich CW5 204 B3
New Mills SK22 39 E3
Penketh WA5 14 B1
Ravensmoor CW5 203 F1
Runcorn WA7 23 F2
Marsh Rd WA4 27 D2
Marsh St Warrington WA1 16 B4
Widnes WA8 23 D3
Marshall Ave WA5 7 F1
Marshall Ct OL6 242 A2
Marshall La CW8 103 E3
Marshall Rd WA1 17 E4
Marshfield Bank CW2 189 E2
Marshfield La ST6 179 E1
Marshfield Rd CW2 189 E2
Marshgate WA8 22 A3
Marshgate Pl WA6 49 E1
Marshlands Rd L64 66 C3
Marsland Rd M33 242 B5
Marsland St SK1 240 F6
Marson St WA2 16 A3
Marston Cl L62 43 F2
Marston La CW9 79 E3
Marten Ave L63 43 E4
Martens Rd M44 11 F3
Marthall La Chelford WA16 83 D4
Ollerton WA16 82 C3
Marthall Way SK8 34 C3
Martham Cl WA4 17 D2
Martin Ave
Newton-le-W WA12 2 B3
Newton-le-W, Newton Common WA12 1 C2
Warrington WA2 8 C1
Martin Cl Chester CH2 118 B4
Culcheth WA3 4 C2
Runcorn WA7 50 A4
Martin Rd Chester CH2 118 B4
Frodsham WA6 74 A4
Martin St SK14 241 E6
Martin's La CH3 143 F2
Martindale Gr WA7 49 E3
Martland Ave WA3 3 E4
Martlet Ave SK12 38 B3
Marton Cl Congleton CW12 156 C3
Hough Common CW2 206 C2
Marton & District CE Aided Prim Sch SK11 133 E3
Marton Gn SK3 240 D1
Marton La Eaton SK11 134 A2
Marton SK11 133 E4
Warren SK11 111 D1
Marton Pl M33 242 A6
Marton Rd CH4 139 E2
Marton Way 4 SK8 34 C3
Marwood Cl WA14 238 B6
Mary Dendy Hospl SK9 83 F4
Mary St Cheadle SK8 239 D6
Crewe CW1 190 C3
Denton M34 241 A8
Hyde SK14 241 D7
Widnes WA8 23 E4
Maryhill Cl ST7 195 D2
Maryhill High & Prim Sch ST7 195 D2
Maryhill Rd WA7 49 D4
Marys Gate CW2 205 F4
Masefield Ave WA8 22 C4
Masefield Dr Blacon CH1 117 F3
Crewe CW1 190 C2
Stockport SK4 240 A6
Maskery Pl CW12 156 B2
Mason Ave Warrington WA1 16 C4
Widnes WA8 13 D2
Mason Cl L66 69 E1
Mason St Chester CH2 237 D3
Runcorn WA7 23 E2
Warrington WA1 16 B3
Masons La SK10 87 F1
Massey Ave Hartford CW8 103 D2
Lymm WA13 18 A1
Warrington WA5 7 F1
Winsford CW7 126 C1
Massey Brook La WA13 18 A1
Massey Rd
Altrincham WA15 238 E4
Sale M33 242 E6
Massey St
Alderley Edge SK9 60 A1
17 Stockport SK1 240 F5
Masseyfield Rd WA7 50 A3
Massie St SK8 239 D6
Mates La SY14 213 D3
Mather Ave Goldborne WA3 3 F3
Runcorn WA7 48 B4
Mather Cl CW10 151 E4

Nelson St continued
Newton-le-W WA12 .... 2 A2
Runcorn WA7 .... 23 D2
Widnes WA7 .... 23 D1
Nemos Cl WA6 .... 73 E1
Neptune Cl WA7 .... 50 B4
Nesfield Cl CW11 .... 191 F4
Nesfield Dr CW11 .... 191 F4
Nessina Gr CW2 .... 205 F4
Neston Cty High Sch L64 .... 41 F1
Neston Cty Prim Sch L64 .... 66 C4
Neston Dr CH2 .... 118 C3
Neston Gn L66 .... 69 E2
Neston Gr SK3 .... 240 D1
Neston Rd Neston L64 .... 67 D2
Thornton Hough L63 .... 41 F3
Willaston L64 .... 67 F4
Neston St Mary's CE Contr Prim Sch L64 .... 41 F1
Neston Sta L64 .... 66 C4
Neston Way 13 SK9 .... 34 B2
Nether Alderley Cty Prim Sch SK10 .... 85 D3
Nether Alderley Old Mill SK10 .... 85 D3
Nether Fold SK10 .... 87 D4
Netherfield WA8 .... 22 B4
Netherfields SK9 .... 85 D4
Netherlea Ct CW4 .... 130 B4
Netherley Rd L35 .... 12 A1
Netherpool Rd L66 .... 69 F4
Netherton Dr WA6 .... 74 A4
Neumann St CW9 .... 104 A4
Neville Ave St Helens WA9 .... 1 A1
Warrington WA2 .... 8 B1
Neville Cres WA5 .... 15 D2
Neville Dr CH3 .... 119 D1
Neville Rd Bebington L62 .... 43 F4
Chester CH3 .... 119 D1
Neville St Crewe CW2 .... 190 B1
Newton-le-W WA12 .... 2 A2
Nevin Ave SK8 .... 239 E1
Nevin Cl SK7 .... 36 A4
Nevin Rd CH1 .... 117 E2
Nevis Dr CW2 .... 189 E2
New Bank Pl WA8 .... 12 A1
New Bank Rd WA8 .... 12 A1
New Barnet WA8 .... 12 C2
New Chester Rd L62 .... 43 F3
New Crane Bank CH1 .... 118 A1
New Crane St CH1 .... 118 A1
New Cut La WA1 .... 17 E4
New Farm Ct CH3 .... 120 C3
New Grosvenor Rd L65 .... 70 A4
New Hall Ave SK8 .... 34 A4
New Hall La Croft WA3 .... 4 C1
Culcheth WA3 .... 5 D1
New Hall Rd M33 .... 242 F6
New Hall St SK10 .... 87 E1
New Hey La L64 .... 68 A3
New Hey Rd SK8 .... 239 E6
New Horwich Rd SK23 .... 65 F4
New Inn La CW11 .... 176 A1
New King St Audley ST7 .... 209 E1
Middlewich CW10 .... 128 B1
New La Appleton WA4 .... 27 D3
Churton CH3 .... 180 C3
Croft WA3 .... 9 D4
Harthill CH3 .... 183 F2
Winsford CW7 .... 149 F2
New Manchester Rd WA1 .... 17 D4
New Manor Rd WA4 .... 51 D3
New Mills Central Sta SK22 .... 39 D4
New Mills Newtown Sta SK22 .... 39 D3
New Mills Sch (Lower Sch) The SK22 .... 39 D4
New Mills Sch The SK22 .... 39 E4
New Moss Rd M44 .... 11 E3
New Pale Rd WA6 .... 99 E3
New Platt La CW4 .... 130 B4
New Rd Anderton CW9 .... 78 B2
Antrobus CW9 .... 27 E1
Astbury CW12 .... 178 A2
Audley ST7 .... 209 F2
Duddon CW6 .... 145 D3
Ellesmere Port L66 .... 69 D4
Lymm WA13 .... 18 C2
Mere WA16 .... 30 C2
News Bank CW12 .... 132 B1
Prestbury SK10 .... 87 D4
Warrington WA4 .... 16 B2
Whaley Bridge SK23 .... 65 F3
Whaley Bridge, Bridgemont SK23 .... 39 F1
Winsford CW7 .... 126 C1
Wrenbury CW5 .... 216 B2
New School La L66 .... 44 A1
New St
Altrincham WA14 .... 238 D4
Congleton CW12 .... 156 C1
Haslington CW1 .... 191 E3
Neston L64 .... 66 C3
New Mills SK22 .... 39 E4
Runcorn WA7 .... 23 D1
Sandbach CW11 .... 174 B4
Widnes WA8 .... 23 D4
Wilmslow SK9 .... 59 F3
New St Cotts CW12 .... 157 D3
New Warrington Rd CW9 .... 79 D1
New Wellington Sch The WA15 .... 238 F6
Newall Cres CW7 .... 127 D1
Newberry Gr SK3 .... 240 D1
Newbold Way CW5 .... 204 C2
Newboult Rd SK8 .... 239 E6
Newbridge Cl
Runcorn WA7 .... 50 B3
Warrington WA5 .... 7 E1
Newbridge Rd L65 .... 70 C2
Newburgh Cl WA7 .... 24 B1
Newbury Ave Crewe CW1 .... 190 B4
7 Winsford CW7 .... 149 D4
Newbury Cl
Cheadle Hulme SK8 .... 35 D3
Widnes WA8 .... 13 D2
Newbury Rd Cheadle SK8 .... 34 B4
Chester CH4 .... 140 C3
Newby Ct CW12 .... 156 A1
Newby Dr
Altrincham WA14 .... 238 D6
Gatley M22 .... 239 A6
Sale M33 .... 242 E5
Newby Rd SK4 .... 240 C6
Newcastle Rd
Astbury CW12 .... 178 A4
Brereton Green CW11 .... 153 F2
Congleton CW12 .... 156 A1
Hassall Green CW11 .... 176 A2
Haymoor Green CW5 .... 205 E2
Hough Common CW2 .... 206 B2
Kidsgrove ST7 .... 210 C4
Shavington CW2 .... 206 B2
Smallwood CW11 .... 176 B3
Woore CW3 .... 232 C1
Newcastle Rd N CW11 .... 153 F3
Newcastle Rd S CW11 .... 153 F3
Newcastle St CW1 .... 190 A3
Newchapel Rd ST7 .... 195 E2
Newchurch Cty Prim Sch WA3 .... 4 C2
Newchurch La WA3 .... 4 C1
Newcombe Ave WA2 .... 16 C4
Newcroft CH1 .... 94 A1
Newcroft Dr SK3 .... 240 D2
Newdigate St Crewe CW1 .... 190 B2
Crewe CW1 .... 190 B3
Newfield Ct WA13 .... 19 D3
Newfield Dr CW1 .... 190 C3
Newfield St CW11 .... 175 D4
Newgate
Macclesfield SK11 .... 112 B4
Wilmslow SK9 .... 59 E4
Newgate St CH1 .... 237 E2
Newhall Ave CW11 .... 175 D3
Newhall Ct CH2 .... 118 C3
Newhall Rd CH2 .... 118 C3
Newham Cl SK11 .... 112 C2
Newhaven Rd WA2 .... 8 A2
Newington Ct WA14 .... 238 B3
Newland Cl WA8 .... 12 B2
Newland Mews WA3 .... 4 C3
Newlands Ave Bramhall SK7 .. 35 F4
Cheadle Hulme SK8 .... 35 D4
Newlands Cl
Cheadle Hulme SK8 .... 35 D4
Frodsham WA6 .... 74 B3
Newlands Dr Goldborne WA3 ... 3 E4
Manchester M20 .... 239 C8
Wilmslow SK9 .... 59 F3
Newlands Rd Cheadle SK8 .. 239 D6
Macclesfield SK10 .... 111 F4
Warrington WA4 .... 16 C1
Newlyn Ave
Congleton CW12 .... 178 C4
Macclesfield SK10 .... 86 B1
Newlyn Cl WA7 .... 50 A3
Newlyn Dr SK6 .... 241 A3
Newlyn Gdns WA5 .... 14 B2
Newman St Hyde SK14 .... 241 E7
Warrington WA4 .... 16 C2
Newman's La CW5 .... 219 E4
Newmoore La WA7 .... 24 C2
Newnham Dr L65 .... 70 B2
Newplatt La
Allostock CW4 .... 107 D1
Cranage CW4 .... 107 D1
Newport Gr ST5 .... 210 C1
Newquay Cl WA7 .... 50 A3
Newquay Ct CW12 .... 178 C4
Newquay Dr Bramhall SK7 .... 35 F4
Macclesfield SK10 .... 111 E4
Newry Ct CH2 .... 118 B2
Newry Pk CH2 .... 118 B2
Newry Pk E CH2 .... 118 B2
Newsham Cl WA8 .... 12 A2
Newsholme Cl WA3 .... 4 C2
Newstead Cl SK12 .... 36 B3
Newstead Terr WA15 .... 238 F7
Newton Bank CW10 .... 128 A1
Newton Bank Sch WA12 .... 2 C2
Newton Comm Hospl WA12 .... 2 A1
Newton Cty Prim Sch CH2 .... 118 C2
Newton Gr WA2 .... 8 C2
Newton Hall Ct CH2 .... 118 C3
Newton Hall Dr CH2 .... 118 C3
Newton Hall La WA16 .... 58 C3
Newton Hall Mews CW10 .... 128 B1
Newton Heath CW10 .... 128 A1
Newton Hollow WA6 .... 74 B1
Newton La Chester CH2 .... 118 C2
Daresbury WA4 .... 51 F4
Newton-le-W WA12 .... 2 C3
Tattenhall CH3 .... 166 B2
Newton Park Dr WA12 .... 2 C2
Newton Park View CH2 .... 118 B2
Newton Pl CW12 .... 156 C1
Newton Rd
Altrincham WA14 .... 238 E7
Ellesmere Port L65 .... 70 B3
Goldborne WA3 .... 3 E3
St Helens WA9 .... 1 A2
Warrington WA2 .... 8 A3
Wilmslow SK9 .... 34 A1
Winwick WA2 .... 8 A3
Newton St Crewe CW1 .... 190 B3
Hyde SK14 .... 241 D8
Macclesfield SK11 .... 112 B4
Stalybridge SK15 .... 242 C2
1 Stockport SK3 .... 240 E4
Newton Sta SK14 .... 241 F8
Newton-le-Willows Cty Prim Sch WA12 .... 2 B2
Newton-le-Willows High Sch WA12 .... 2 B3
Newton-le-Willows Sta WA12 .... 2 C2
Newtons Cres CW11 .... 191 F4
Newtons Gr CW11 .... 191 F4
Newtons La CW11 .... 191 F4
Newtown Kidsgrove ST7 .... 195 F1
Neston L64 .... 66 C4
Newtown Cl CH2 .... 237 E3
Newtown Cty Prim Sch SK22 .... 39 D3
Nicholas Ave CW9 .... 104 B3
Nicholas Ct CH1 .... 237 D2
Nicholas Rd
Weaverham CW8 .... 77 E1
Widnes WA8 .... 22 B4
Nicholas St CH1 .... 237 D2
Nicholas St Mews CH1 .... 237 D2
Nicholls St WA4 .... 17 D1
Nicholson Ave SK10 .... 87 F1
Nicholson Cl SK10 .... 87 F1
Nicholson St
Stockport SK4 & SK5 .... 240 E6
Warrington WA5 .... 15 F3
Nickelby Rd SK12 .... 36 C2
Nickolson Cl CH2 .... 119 F4
Nicol Ave WA1 .... 17 F4
Nidderdale Cl CW12 .... 157 D3
Niddries La CW9 .... 126 C4
Nield Ct CH2 .... 118 B4
Nield's Brow WA14 .... 238 C2
Nigel Gresley Cl CW1 .... 191 D2
Nigel Rd L60 .... 41 E4
Nigel Wlk WA7 .... 24 A1
Nightgale Cl CW1 .... 189 F4
Nightingale Cl
Farndon CH3 .... 180 C1
Middlewich CW10 .... 151 E3
Runcorn WA7 .... 49 F3
Warrington WA3 .... 9 F2
Wilmslow SK9 .... 34 A1
Nightingale Ct CW7 .... 149 E3
Nile St CW2 .... 190 B1
Nitchingham SK9 .... 60 B3
Nixon Dr CW7 .... 126 A1
Nixon Rd CW8 .... 101 F2
Nixon St Crewe CW1 .... 189 F3
Macclesfield SK11 .... 112 A4
3 Stockport SK3 .... 240 E4
No 2 Passage SK3 .... 240 D5
Noahs Ark La WA16 .... 58 C1
Noble Cl WA3 .... 9 F2
Noel Dr M33 .... 242 D6
Nook La Antrobus CW9 .... 53 F3
Goldborne WA3 .... 3 D4
Warrington WA4 .... 17 D2
Warrington, Fearnhead WA2 .... 9 D1
Nook The Broughton CH4 .... 140 C3
Cheadle Hulme SK7 .... 35 E3
Chester CH2 .... 118 C2
Guilden Sutton CH3 .... 119 E2
Noon Ct WA12 .... 2 A1
Nora St WA1 .... 16 B3
Norbreck Ave Cheadle SK8 240 A2
Crewe CW2 .... 190 A1
Norbreck Dr WA5 .... 15 D2
Norbury Ave 4 Hyde SK14 241 D6
Warrington WA2 .... 16 B4
Norbury Cl
Hough Common CW2 .... 206 C2
Knutsford WA16 .... 57 E2
Widnes WA8 .... 13 F1
Norbury Dr Congleton CW12 156 C2
Middlewich CW10 .... 151 D4
Norbury Hollow Rd SK7 .... 37 D4
Norbury St
Macclesfield SK11 .... 112 B4
Northwich CW9 .... 104 A4
12 Stockport SK1 .... 240 F5
Norbury Way 8 SK9 .... 34 B3
Norcott Ave WA4 .... 16 C1
Norcott Dr WA5 .... 6 C3
Norden Cl WA3 .... 9 E3
Norfolk Cl M44 .... 11 E3
Norfolk Dr WA5 .... 14 C3
Norfolk Gr ST6 .... 179 E1
Norfolk Pl WA8 .... 22 B4
Norfolk Rd Chester CH2 .... 118 C2
Congleton CW12 .... 156 C2
Ellesmere Port L65 .... 70 B3
Kidsgrove ST7 .... 194 C1
Norfolk St Hyde SK14 .... 241 D6
Runcorn WA7 .... 23 D2
Norfolk Wlk SK10 .... 86 C1
Norgrove Cl WA7 .... 50 B4
Norland St WA8 .... 13 E1
Norland's La Cronton L35 .... 12 C4
Widnes WA8 .... 12 C4
Norleane Cres WA7 .... 49 D4
Norley Ave Bebington L62 .... 43 F2
Ellesmere Port L65 .... 69 F3
Norley CE Contr Prim Sch WA6 .... 100 C3
Norley Dr Chester CH3 .... 119 E1
Sale M33 .... 242 E6
Norley La Crowton CW8 .... 76 A1
Norley WA6 .... 101 D4
Norley Rd Cuddington CW8 .. 101 F2
Kingsley WA6 .... 75 D1
Kingsley, Commonside WA6 . 100 B4
Norley WA6 .... 100 B4
Norman Ave Haydock WA11 .... 2 A4
Newton-le-W WA12 .... 2 C2
Norman Cl CH1 .... 94 C4
Norman Dr CW7 .... 149 E3
Norman Rd
Altrincham WA14 .... 238 C6
Manchester SK4 .... 240 B7
Runcorn WA7 .... 23 D1
Sale M33 .... 242 B5
Stalybridge SK15 .... 242 C2
Norman St Hyde SK14 .... 241 E6
Warrington WA2 .... 16 A3
Norman Way CH1 .... 117 F3
Norman's La WA4 .... 52 C3
Norman's Pl WA14 .... 238 D4
Normanby Chase WA14 .... 238 B4
Normandy Ave CW7 .... 149 E4
Normandy Rd CH2 .... 95 E1
Normanton Rd SK3 & SK8 .. 240 A2
Norreys Ave WA5 .... 15 F4
Norris Ave SK4 .... 240 C6
Norris Bank Prim Sch SK4 .... 240 B7
Norris Bank Terr SK4 .... 240 C5
Norris Hill Dr SK4 .... 240 C6
Norris Rd Blacon CH1 .... 117 F3
Sale M33 .... 242 F5
Norris St WA2 .... 16 B4
North Ave Stalybridge SK15 242 D3
Warrington WA2 .... 16 A4
North Brook Rd CW6 .... 146 A4
North Cestrian Gram Sch WA14 .... 238 C5
North Cheshire Jewish Prim Sch SK8 .... 239 C2
North Crofts CW5 .... 204 C3
North Downs WA16 .... 57 E1
North Downs Rd SK8 .... 239 F3
North Dr Heswall L60 .... 41 D4
High Legh WA16 .... 29 E2
Northwich CW9 .... 104 C4
North Fields WA16 .... 57 E2
North Florida Rd WA11 .... 1 C4
North Gn CH5 .... 116 A3
North Harvey St 8 SK1 .... 240 F5
North Mead SK10 .... 87 D3
North Parade L64 .... 41 D1
North Park Brook Rd WA5 .... 7 F1
North Pl 5 SK1 .... 240 F5
North Rd Altrincham WA15 .... 32 A4
Ellesmere Port L65 .... 70 A4
Ellesmere Port, Hooton Park L65 .... 44 C1
Halewood L24 .... 21 D3
North St Broughton CH4 .... 140 A4
Chester CH3 .... 119 D1
Congleton CW12 .... 156 B2
Crewe CW1 .... 190 B4
Hawarden CH5 .... 116 A2
Haydock WA11 .... 1 C3
Mount Pleasant ST7 .... 195 D3
North Stafford St CW1 .... 190 B2
North Vale Rd WA15 .... 238 F6
North View Crewe CW1 .... 190 A3
Great Sankey WA5 .... 14 C4
North Way
Holmes Chapel CW4 .... 130 B2
Shavington CW2 .... 206 B3
Northbank Ind Pk M44 .... 11 F3
Northbank Wlk CW2 .... 206 B4
Northbury Rd L66 .... 69 F1
Northcombe Rd SK3 .... 240 E1
Northcote Rd SK7 .... 35 F4
Northdale Rd WA1 .... 17 D4
Northend Rd SK15 .... 242 E2
Northenden Rd
Gatley M22 & SK8 .... 239 A6
Sale M33 .... 242 C6
Sale M33 .... 242 E5
Northern La WA8 .... 12 A2
Northern Pathway CH4 .... 237 F1
Northern Rise L66 .... 69 F2
Northfield Dr Biddulph ST6 . 179 F1
Wilmslow SK9 .... 60 B4
Northfield Pl CW2 .... 206 B3
Northgate CW6 .... 146 A4
Northgate Ave Chester CH2 237 E4
Macclesfield SK10 .... 87 E1
Northgate Rd SK3 .... 240 C4
Northgate Row CH1 .... 237 E2
Northgate St CH1 .... 237 D3
Northlands CW3 .... 232 B1
Northolt Ct WA2 .... 8 C1
Northstead Ave M34 .... 241 B6
Northumberland Rd M31 .... 11 F1
Northward Rd SK9 .... 59 F3
Northway Altrincham WA14 . 238 E6
Chester CH4 .... 141 D4
Lymm WA13 .... 18 B2
Northwich CW8 .... 78 B1
Runcorn WA7 .... 49 F4
Warrington WA2 .... 8 A1
Widnes WA8 .... 12 B1
Northwich Rd
Antrobus CW9, WA4 .... 53 D3
Cranage CW4, WA16 .... 106 C1
Dutton WA4 .... 51 D1
Great Budworth CW9 .... 78 C4
Northwich Rd continued
Knutsford WA16 .... 56 B
Runcorn WA7 .... 50 C
Runcorn, Brookvale WA7 .... 50 B
Stretton WA4 .... 52 C
Tabley WA16 .... 56 B
Weaverham CW8 .... 102 C
Whitley WA4 .... 52 C
Northwich Sta CW9 .... 104 A
Northwood Ave
Middlewich CW10 .... 151 F
Newton-le-W WA12 .... 2 C
Northwood Gr M33 .... 242 B
Northwood La WA16 .... 28 C
Northwood Rd WA7 .... 23 F
Norton Ave Broughton CH4 .. 140 B
Penketh WA5 .... 14 C
Norton Gate WA7 .... 50 B
Norton Gr SK4 .... 240 B
Norton Hales CE Sch TF9 .... 236 B
Norton Hill WA7 .... 24 B
Norton La
Runcorn, Norton WA7 .... 24 B
Runcorn, Town Park WA7 .... 50 A
Norton Priory Cty High Sch WA7 .... 24 A
Norton Rd CH3 .... 119 E
Norton Station Rd WA7 .... 50 B
Norton View WA7 .... 50 A
Norton Village WA7 .... 24 B
Norton Way CW11 .... 174 B
Norton's La
Great Barrow CH3 .... 98 A
Mouldsworth CH3 .... 98 A
Nortons La CW6 .... 122 C
Nortonwood La WA7 .... 24 B
Norview Dr M20 .... 239 B
Norville L66 .... 69 E
Norway Gr 6 SK5 .... 240 F
Norwich Ave WA3 .... 3 E
Norwich Ct 1 SK10 .... 112 C
Norwich Dr CH1 .... 94 C
Norwood Ave
Cheadle Hulme SK7 .... 35 E
Goldborne WA3 .... 3 F
High Lane SK6 .... 37 E
Norwood Dr CH4 .... 141 D
Norwood Rd SK8 .... 239 B
Nottingham Cl WA1 .... 17 F
Nun House Cl CW7 .... 127 D
Nun House Dr CW7 .... 127 D
Nuns Rd CH1 .... 237 D
Nunsmere Cl CW7 .... 127 D
Nursery Ave WA15 .... 31 F
Nursery Cl Kidsgrove ST7 .... 194 B
Sale M33 .... 242 D
Shavington CW2 .... 206 B
Widnes WA8 .... 13 E
Nursery Dr Biddulph ST6 .... 179 E
Poynton SK12 .... 36 B
Nursery La Cheadle SK3 .... 240 A
Congleton CW12 .... 156 C
Nether Alderley SK10 .... 84 B
Siddington SK11 .... 110 A
Wilmslow SK9 .... 59 F
Nursery Rd Barnton CW8 .... 78 A
Haslington CW1 .... 192 C
Scholar Green ST7 .... 194 C
Stockport SK4 .... 240 C
Nursery The CW8 .... 103 E
Nutfield Ave CW1 .... 190 A
Nuthurst Gdns CW5 .... 204 C
Nuttall Ct WA3 .... 9 E
Nuttall St M44 .... 11 F

O'Connell Cl WA11 .... 1 B
O'Leary St WA2 .... 16 B
Oak Ave Alsager ST7 .... 193 F
Disley SK12 .... 39 D
Goldborne WA3 .... 3 D
Haydock WA11 .... 1 C
Irlam M44 .... 11 E
Macclesfield SK11 .... 112 A
Manchester SK4 .... 240 B
Newton-le-W WA12 .... 2 B
Romiley SK6 .... 241 C
Wilmslow SK9 .... 59 F
Winsford CW7 .... 149 E
Oak Bank SK12 .... 39 D
Oak Bank Cl CW5 .... 205 F
Oak Bank Dr SK10 .... 63 D
Oak Bank La CH2 .... 119 E
Oak Cl SK9 .... 59 F
Oak Cotts SK9 .... 33 F
Oak Dr Cheadle Hulme SK7 .... 35 E
Higher Kinnerton CH4 .... 161 D
Middlewich CW10 .... 151 E
Runcorn WA7 .... 49 E
Oak Gr Cheadle SK8 .... 239 E
Ellesmere Port L65 .... 70 A
Nantwich CW5 .... 204 C
Poynton SK12 .... 36 B
Oak House La CW7 .... 149 D
Oak La Bollington SK10 .... 88 A
Cuddington CW8 .... 101 F
Marton SK11 .... 133 E
Wilmslow SK9 .... 59 F
Oak Lea Ave SK9 .... 60 A
Oak Meadow CW8 .... 102 C
Oak Mews SK9 .... 34 B
Oak Rd Altrincham WA15 .... 238 E
Cheadle SK8 .... 239 E
Chelford SK11 .... 84 A
Chester CH4 .... 140 C
Hooton L66 .... 43 F
Lymm WA13 .... 18 B
Mottram St Andrew SK10 .... 86 A

Oak Rd continued
Partington M31 11 E1
Penketh WA5 14 C2
Sale M33 242 D6
Oak St Crewe CW2 190 B2
Croft WA3 9 D4
Ellesmere Port L65 70 B4
Hyde SK14 241 E8
Northwich CW9 79 D1
Rode Heath ST7 193 F4
Sandbach CW11 174 B4
Stockport SK3 240 B4
Oak Tree Cl CW1 190 C3
Oak Tree Dr CW1 190 C3
Oak Tree Gate CW3 229 F2
Oak Tree La CW4, CW10 129 F4
Oak View Knutsford WA16 57 E1
Marton SK11 133 E3
Speke L24 21 D2
Oak Wood Rd WA16 29 F1
Oakdale Ave WA4 16 B1
Oakdale Cl CH4 139 D2
Oakdale Dr SK8 239 B2
Oakdene Ave Cheadle SK8 34 A4
Ellesmere Port L66 69 E3
Warrington WA1 17 E4
Oakdene Cl L62 43 E3
Oakdene Way CW6 168 B4
Oakenclough Cl SK9 34 B1
Oakes Cnr CW5 219 F2
Oakfield M33 242 A7
Oakfield Ave Cheadle SK8 239 E6
Chester CH2 118 B4
Knutsford WA16 57 E2
Wrenbury CW5 216 C2
Oakfield Cl
Alderley Edge SK9 60 A2
Wrenbury CW5 216 C2
Oakfield Ct WA15 238 F6
Oakfield Cty Inf & Jun Sch
WA8 22 A4
Oakfield Dr Chester CH2 118 B4
Widnes WA8 22 A4
Oakfield Rd Alderley Edge SK9 60 A1
Altrincham WA15 238 E4
Bebington L62 43 E4
Blacon CH1 117 E2
Ellesmere Port L66 68 C4
Plumley WA16 80 C2
Poynton SK12 36 C2
Stockport SK3 240 F1
Oakfield Rise CW4 130 A2
Oakfield St WA15 238 E5
Oakfield Trad Est WA15 238 E5
Oakham Rd M34 241 A5
Oakhill Cl SK10 87 D2
Oakhurst Chase SK9 60 A1
Oakhurst Dr
Cheadle SK3 & SK8 240 B1
Wistaston CW2 206 A4
Oakland Ave CW1 191 E2
Oakland St
Warrington WA1 16 C4
Widnes WA8 23 D2
Oaklands CH3 119 F2
Oaklands Ave CH3 166 A1
Oaklands Cl SK9 34 C1
Oaklands Cres CH3 166 A1
Oaklands Cty Inf Sch SK9 34 C1
Oaklands Dr Lymm WA13 18 B1
Sale M33 242 A7
Oaklands Rd Goldborne WA3 3 F4
Ollerton WA16 82 C3
Oaklands Sch CW7 149 D4
Oaklea Ave CH2 118 C2
Oakleigh Knutsford WA16 82 B4
Manchester SK4 240 B7
Oakleigh Ct CW12 155 F2
Oakleigh Rise CW8 78 C1
Oakley Cl CW11 175 D4
Oakley St CW1 190 B3
Oakley Villas SK4 240 B7
Oakmere Cl CW11 174 C4
Oakmere Dr Chester CH3 142 A4
Ellesmere Port L66 69 F1
Penketh WA5 14 C2
Oakmere Rd Cheadle SK8 239 F4
Wilmslow SK9 34 B3
Winsford CW7 125 F1
Oakmere St WA7 23 D1
Oaks Dr The CH2 118 B4
Oaks Pl WA8 23 D4
Oaks The Bebington L62 43 E4
Gatley SK8 239 A2
Oaksdean Ct SK9 34 A1
Oakside Cl SK8 239 E6
Oaksway L60 41 E3
Oaktree Cl Barnton CW8 78 A2
Tarporley CW6 146 B1
Oaktree Ct Cheadle SK8 239 D5
Chester CH2 119 D2
Oakway M20 239 C8
Oakways WA4 26 B3
Oakwood Av SK9 59 F3
Oakwood Ave Gatley SK8 239 B5
Warrington WA1 16 C4
Oakwood Avenue Cty Prim
Schs WA1 16 B4
Oakwood Cl L66 69 E1
Oakwood Cres Crewe CW2 189 F2
Sandbach CW11 175 F3
Oakwood Ct WA14 31 D4
Oakwood Dr SK10 87 E3
Oakwood Gate WA3 9 E2
Oakwood La
Altrincham WA14 238 B1
Barnton CW8 78 A1
Sandbach CW11 174 A4
Oakwood Rd Disley SK12 38 B3
Rode Heath ST7 193 F4
Romiley SK6 241 C2
Oat Market CW5 204 C3
Oathills SY14 213 D3
Oathills Cl CW6 146 B1
Oathills Dr CW6 146 B1
Oatlands SK9 85 D4
Oban Dr Heswall L60 41 D4
Sale M33 242 E5
Oban Gr WA2 9 D2
Ocean St WA14 238 B6
Ocean Street Trad Est
WA14 238 B7
Off Ridge Hill La SK15 242 C2
Offley Ave CW11 175 D4
Offley Cty Inf & Jun Sch
CW11 175 D4
Offley Rd CW11 175 D4
Ogden Ct SK14 241 E6
Ogden Rd SK7 35 E3
Oglet La L24 46 C4
Oil Sites Rd L65 71 E3
Okell St WA7 23 D1
Old Bank Cl SK6 241 A3
Old Bedions Sports Ctr
M20 239 A8
Old Boston WA11 2 A4
Old Boston Trad Est WA11 2 A4
Old Brickworks Ind Est
SK10 63 F2
Old Butt La ST7 194 B1
Old Chapel St SK3 240 D3
Old Cherry La WA13 28 A4
Old Chester Rd
Barbridge CW5 187 E3
Ellesmere Port L66 69 E2
Helsby WA6 73 E2
Higher Walton WA4 25 F4
Old Church Cl L65 70 B4
Old Coach Rd
Broxton SY14 199 D3
Edge Green SY14 199 D3
Kelsall CW6 122 B3
Old Farm Cl L64 68 A4
Old Gardens St [3] SK1 240 F4
Old Gate Cl CW10 151 D4
Old Gorse Cl CW2 189 F2
Old Hall Ave SK23 65 F2
Old Hall Cl WA4 26 A4
Old Hall Cres SK9 34 C2
Old Hall Ct Ashton CH3 121 F4
Malpas SY14 213 D2
Old Hall Cty Prim Sch
WA5 15 E4
Old Hall Dr L65 70 A2
Old Hall Gdns CH2 237 F4
Old Hall La Elton CH2 72 A2
Knutsford WA16 56 A2
Tabley WA16 55 F2
Woodford SK7 61 E4
Old Hall Pk CH3 119 F3
Old Hall Pl CH1 237 D2
Old Hall Rd Gatley SK8 239 A6
Great Sankey WA5 15 E4
Northwich CW9 104 A3
Sale M33 242 E6
Old Hall St SK10 87 E1
Old Hey Wlk WA12 2 B1
Old Higher Rd WA8 21 E3
Old Hutte La L24 21 D3
Old La Acton Bridge CW8 76 C2
Antrobus CW9 53 E2
Davenham CW9 104 B1
Poulton CH4 162 C1
Pulford CH4 162 C1
Old Liverpool Rd WA5 15 F2
Old Man of Mow The
ST7 195 E4
Old Market Pl
Altrincham WA14 238 D5
Knutsford WA16 57 D1
Old Mill Cl L60 41 D4
Old Mill Ct CH2 118 B3
Old Mill La Hazel Grove SK7 37 D4
Macclesfield SK11 112 C3
Whitley WA4 52 C2
Old Mill Rd CW11 175 E3
Old Moss La Leigh WA3 5 F3
Tarvin CH3 144 B4
Old Oak Dr M34 241 A7
Old Orchard Antrobus CW9 53 E2
Wilmslow SK9 60 A4
Old Orchard The CW8 101 F2
Old Park Rd CW1 207 E4
Old Pearl La CH3 119 D1
Old Quay Cl L64 66 B4
Old Quay La L64 66 B4
Old Quay St WA7 23 D2
Old Rd Anderton CW9 78 B2
Audley ST7 209 F2
Cheadle SK8 239 F6
Hyde SK14 241 D8
Stockport SK4 240 E7
Warrington WA4 16 A2
Whaley Bridge SK23 65 F2
Whaley Bridge, Furness Vale
SK23 39 E2
Whaley Bridge, New Horwich
SK23 65 F3
Wilmslow SK9 60 A4
Wilmslow, Handforth SK9 34 B2
Old Rectory Gdns SK8 239 D5
Old School Cl CH3 180 C1
Old School House La
WA2 8 A4
Old Smithy La WA13 18 B1
Old St SK15 242 D2
Old Stack Yd CH3 120 C3
Old Upton La WA8 12 C2
Old Vicarage Gdns CW3 229 F2
Old Vicarage Rd L64 68 A4
Old Wargrave Rd WA12 2 B2
Old Warrington Rd CW9 79 D1
Old Whint Rd WA11 1 A3
Old Woman's La CH3 142 B4
Old Wool La SK8 239 F4
Old Wrexham Rd CH4 141 E4
Oldfield Brow Prim Sch
WA14 238 A5
Oldfield Cres CH4 140 C3
Oldfield Cty Prim Sch
CH3 119 E2
Oldfield Dr
Altrincham WA15 238 F6
Chester CH3 119 E1
Mobberley WA16 58 A2
Oldfield Gr M33 242 C7
Oldfield La WA14 20 C2
Oldfield Mews WA14 238 C5
Oldfield Rd
Altrincham WA14 238 B5
Ellesmere Port L65 70 A3
Lymm WA13 18 B2
Sale M33 242 C7
Sandbach CW11 174 C2
Oldgate WA8 22 B4
Oldhall St SY14 213 D2
Oldham Dr SK6 241 A4
Oldham St Bollington SK10 88 A4
Hyde SK14 241 D6
Warrington WA4 16 B2
Oldham's Rise SK10 87 E2
Oldhams Hill CW8 78 C1
Oldhill Cl ST7 210 C3
Olive Dr L64 66 C4
Olive Gr ST5 210 B1
Olive Rd L64 66 C4
Oliver Cl SK10 87 F4
Oliver La L66 69 E2
Oliver St
Stockport SK1 & SK3 240 F4
Warrington WA2 16 A3
Ollerbarrow Rd WA15 238 E2
Ollersett Ave SK22 39 E4
Ollersett View Hospl SK22 39 E4
Ollershaw La CW9 79 E2
Ollerton Cl WA4 17 D2
Ollerton Inf & Jun Sch
WA16 83 D2
Ollerton Rd [14] SK9 34 B3
Ollier St [19] WA8 23 D4
One Oak La SK9 60 C4
Onneley La CW3 232 C2
Onslow Rd Blacon CH1 117 E2
Stockport SK3 240 C4
Onston La CW8 101 F4
Onward St SK14 241 D6
Openshaw La M44 11 F3
Orange Gr WA2 8 C1
Orange La CW9 79 E1
Orchard Ave
Acton Bridge CW8 76 C2
Lymm WA13 18 C2
Partington M31 11 F2
Whaley Bridge SK23 65 E4
Orchard Brow WA3 11 D1
Orchard Cl Barnton CW8 78 A2
Cheadle Hulme SK7 35 E4
Chester CH2 118 B3
Ellesmere Port L66 69 F1
Frodsham WA6 74 A3
Goostrey CW4 107 F1
Higher Wincham CW9 80 A3
Macclesfield SK11 112 A3
Middlewich CW10 151 E4
Poynton SK12 36 C2
Weaverham CW8 77 E1
Wilmslow SK9 59 F3
Winsford CW7 149 E4
Orchard Cres
Kidsgrove ST7 194 B1
Nantwich CW5 204 C2
Nether Alderley SK10 84 C3
Orchard Croft CH3 119 F3
Orchard Ct Alsager ST7 193 F2
Chester CH3 119 D1
Haslington CW1 191 E2
Orchard Dene CW8 101 E3
Orchard Dr
Little Leigh CW8 77 E3
Neston L64 66 C3
Wilmslow SK9 34 C1
Orchard Gn SK9 60 A1
Orchard Gr CH3 180 C1
Orchard Haven L66 69 F1
Orchard La L66 69 D4
Orchard Park La CH2 72 B2
Orchard Pl WA6 73 E2
Orchard Rd
Altrincham WA15 238 E5
Ellesmere Port L65 70 A1
Lymm WA13 19 D3
Whaley Bridge SK23 65 E4
Orchard Rise CW9 126 C4
Orchard St Chester CH1 237 D3
Crewe CW1 190 B3
Hyde SK14 241 E6
Northwich CW9 104 A4
Stockport SK1 240 F5
Warrington WA1 16 B3
Warrington, Fearnhead WA2 9 D1
Warrington, Hillcliffe WA4 26 B4
Willaston (nr Nantwich)
CW5 205 E3
Orchard Vale SK3 240 C2
Orchard Way
Congleton CW12 156 A2
Kelsall CW6 122 B3
Widnes WA8 12 A2
Orchards The
Broughton CH4 140 B3
Pickmere WA16 79 F3
Shavington CW2 206 B2
Orchid Cl Huntington CH3 142 A3
Irlam M44 11 F4
Orchil Cl L66 69 D3
Ordnance Ave WA3 9 F2
Ordsall Cl CW11 174 C2
Orford Ave Disley SK12 38 B3
Warrington WA2 16 B4
Orford Cl Hale L24 21 E1
High Lane SK6 37 F4
Orford Gn WA2 8 B1
Orford La WA2 16 A4
Orford Rd WA2 16 C4
Orford St WA1 16 A3
Oriel Bank High Sch SK3 240 F1
Orkney Cl Ellesmere Port L65 70 B1
Widnes WA8 13 F2
Orme Cl Macclesfield SK10 87 E2
Prestbury SK10 87 D4
Orme Cres SK10 87 E2
Ormerod Cl Romiley SK6 241 A1
Sandbach CW11 175 E3
Ormesby Gr L63 43 D3
Ormond Cl WA8 12 B1
Ormonde Rd CH2 118 B2
Ormonde St CH2 237 F3
Ormston Ave WA12 2 A3
Orphanage St SK4 & SK5 240 E7
Orrell Cl WA5 15 D3
Orrishmere Rd SK8 239 F3
Orton Cl CW7 127 D2
Ortonbrook Prim Sch M31 11 F1
Orwell Cl SK9 34 B1
Osborne Ave WA2 8 B1
Osborne Gr Gatley SK8 239 A3
Shavington CW2 206 B3
Osborne Rd
Altrincham WA15 238 E5
Goldborne WA3 3 F4
Hyde SK14 241 E5
Stockport SK2 240 F3
Warrington WA4 16 A1
Osborne Terr M33 242 B6
Osbourne Pl [7] WA14 238 D4
Osier Cl CH2 72 B2
Osmere Cl SY13 226 A1
Osprey Ave CW7 149 E3
Osprey Cl
Middlewich CW10 151 E3
Runcorn WA7 49 F3
Warrington WA2 8 C2
Osprey Dr SK9 60 B4
Osprey View ST7 195 E2
Ossett Cl WA7 50 B4
Ossmere Cl CW11 174 C4
Ostler's La WA16 58 C4
Otters Bank CW7 126 A1
Otterspool Rd SK6 241 B1
Oughtrington Cres WA13 19 D2
Oughtrington Cty Prim Sch
WA13 19 D2
Oughtrington La WA13 19 D1
Oughtrington View WA13 19 D2
Oulton Ave Chester CH2 118 B4
Sale M33 242 E7
Oulton Dr CW12 155 F2
Oulton Mill La Eaton CW6 147 D4
Utkinton CW6 147 D4
Oulton Pl CH1 237 E3
Our Lady of Lourdes RC
Prim Sch M31 11 F2
Our Lady of Perpetual
Succour RC Aided Inf Sch
WA8 12 A1
Our Lady of Perpetual
Succour RC Aided Jun Sch
WA8 22 A4
Our Lady's RC Aided Prim
Sch Runcorn WA7 50 A3
Warrington WA4 16 C2
Our Lady's RC Inf & Jun
Sch L65 70 A2
Our Lady's RC Prim Sch
SK3 240 E4
Out La CH3 184 B3
Outwood Dr SK8 34 A4
Outwood La M90 33 D4
Outwood La W M90 33 D4
Outwood Prim Sch SK8 34 B4
Outwood Rd SK8 34 A4
Oval The Cheadle SK8 34 A4
Ellesmere Port L65 70 B2
Ovenhouse La SK10 87 F4
Over Hill Dr CW7 149 E4
Over Rd CW5 172 A4
Overdale La CW8 101 E1
Overdale Rd Disley SK12 38 C3
Romiley SK6 241 A1
Willaston L64 43 D1
Overdene Rd CW7 149 E4
Overfields WA16 57 E2
Overhill Dr SK9 60 C4
Overhill La SK9 60 C4
Overhill Rd SK9 60 B4
Overleigh Ct CH4 141 E4
Overleigh Rd CH4 141 E4
Overleigh St Mary's CE
Contr Prim Sch CH4 141 E4
Overpool Gdns L66 69 F2
Overpool Rd L65 69 F3
Overpool Sta L66 69 F3
Overton Cl
Congleton CW12 156 B2
Middlewich CW10 151 D4
Overton Dr WA6 74 B3
Overton Rd ST6 179 F3
Overton Way [4] SK9 34 B3
Overway CW7 126 C1
Overwood Ave CH1 94 C1
Overwood La Blacon CH1 117 E2
Mollington CH1 94 B1
Ovington Cl WA7 49 F2
Owen Cl CH1 117 F3
Owen St Crewe CW2 190 B1
Stockport SK3 240 D5
Warrington WA2 16 A4
Owley Wood Rd CW8 77 F1
Ox-Hey Cres ST6 179 E1
Ox-Hey Dr ST6 179 E1
Oxborough Cl WA8 12 C2
Oxenham Rd WA2 8 A2
Oxford Cl CH1 94 C4
Oxford Ct [4] SK10 112 C4
Oxford Dr Halewood L26 21 D4
Romiley SK6 241 C4
Thornton Hough L63 41 F3
Oxford Gr M44 11 E3
Oxford Rd Altrincham WA14 238 D3
Chester CH4 140 C3
Macclesfield SK11 112 A4
Runcorn WA7 49 D4
Oxford St Crewe CW1 190 A3
Newton-le-W WA12 2 A2
Stalybridge SK15 242 F1
Oxford St continued
Warrington WA4 16 B2
Widnes WA8 23 D4
Oxford Way SK4 240 D7
Oxhey Fst Sch ST8 179 F1
Oxheys WA7 50 B4
Oxmead Cl WA2 9 D1
Oxmoor Cl WA7 50 A3
Oxney Cl SK11 111 F4
Oxton Cl WA8 12 B2
Oxton Gn L66 69 E2

Pacific Rd WA14 238 A6
Packmoor Prim Sch ST7 195 F1
Packsaddle Pk SK10 86 C3
Padarn Cl CH4 140 B3
Padden Brook SK6 241 B2
Padden Brook Mews SK6 241 B2
Paddington Bank WA1 16 C3
Paddock Brow SK10 87 D3
Paddock Chase SK12 36 C3
Paddock Dr L64 41 E1
Paddock Hill WA16 59 D1
Paddock La Audlem CW3 230 A1
Dunham Town WA13 20 A3
Kettleshulme SK23 64 C2
Partington WA13 19 E4
Whaley Bridge SK23 65 F3
Paddock Rd CH4 141 F1
Paddock Rise WA7 49 F2
Paddock The Cheadle SK8 239 E5
Chester CH4 141 D4
Ellesmere Port L66 69 E2
Elton CH2 72 A2
Hartford CW8 103 E2
Hassall Green CW11 175 F1
Helsby WA6 73 E1
Heswall L60 41 E4
Lymm WA13 19 E2
Tarporley CW6 146 B1
Whaley Bridge SK23 65 F3
Willaston (nr Nantwich)
CW5 205 E2
Wilmslow SK9 34 B2
Paddock Way CH4 161 D4
Paddock Wlk CW8 101 E3
Paddockhill La WA16 59 D2
Paddocks Gn CW12 178 C4
Paddocks The
Nova Scotia CW8 125 D3
Prestbury SK10 87 D3
Padgate Bsns Ctr WA1 17 D4
Padgate Cty High Sch WA2 8 C1
Padgate La WA1 16 C4
Padgate Sta WA1 9 D1
Padgbury Cl CW12 156 A1
Padgbury La CW12 156 A1
Padston Dr ST7 193 D2
Padstow Cl Crewe CW1 190 B4
Macclesfield SK10 111 F4
Penketh WA5 14 C2
Padstow Dr SK7 35 F4
Padstow Sq WA7 50 A3
Padworth Pl CW1 173 D1
Page Gr CW2 206 A2
Page La WA8 13 E1
Paignton Cl WA5 14 C2
Painswick Rd L66 69 F1
Paisley Ave L62 43 F2
Palace Fields Ave WA7 50 A4
Palace Fields Local Ctr
WA7 50 A3
Palace Hey L64 67 D3
Palace Rd M33 242 A7
Palacefields Cty Prim Sch
WA7 50 A3
Palatine Cl CH1 117 E3
Palgrave Cl CH1 118 A3
Palin Dr WA5 14 B4
Pall Mall CW5 204 C3
Pallard Ave WA6 74 B4
Palliser Cl WA3 10 A2

Palm Gr L66 70 A1
Palmer Ave SK8 239 F6
Palmer Cres WA5 15 E4
Palmer Rd CW11 175 E3
Palmer St M33 242 A6
Palmerston Cl CW1 191 E3
Palmerston Rd SK11 112 A4
Palmerston St SK10 88 A4
Palmerston Way ST6 179 E1
Palmerstone Cl CH1 118 A2
Palmyra Sq N WA1 16 A3
Palmyra Sq S WA1 16 A3
Panda Way CW11 175 D3
Pangbourne Cl
Appleton WA4 26 C3
Stockport SK3 240 C2
Panton Pl CH2 118 C2
Panton Rd CH2 118 C2
Parade Rd M90 33 E4
Parade The Blacon CH1 117 F3
Neston L64 41 D1
Paradise CH4 237 E1
Paradise La CW5 171 F4
Paradise Mill (Mus) SK11 112 B4
Paradise St SK11 112 B4
Paragon Cl WA8 13 D3
Parbold Ct WA8 22 B4
Parchments The WA12 2 B2
Parish Cl ST7 193 D2
Park Ave Altrincham WA15 238 F1
Altrincham, Timperley WA14 238 E8
Broughton CH4 140 C3
Cheadle SK8 239 F1
Cheadle SK3 239 F7
Cheadle Hulme SK7 35 E3
Haydock WA11 1 A3
Hyde SK14 241 D8
Kidsgrove ST7 210 C4
Poynton SK12 36 C2
Romiley SK6 241 C2
Sale M33 242 A8
Saughall CH1 94 A1
Tattenhall CH3 166 A1
Warrington WA4 16 B2
Weaverham CW8 77 E1
Whaley Bridge SK23 39 E2
Widnes WA8 13 D1
Wilmslow SK9 60 B4
Winsford CW7 127 D2
Park Ave N WA12 2 B1
Park Ave S WA12 2 B1
Park Bank CW12 156 C1
Park Brook Rd SK11 112 A4
Park Bvd WA1 16 A2
Park Cl Altrincham WA14 238 F8
Stalybridge SK15 242 C3
Tarvin CH3 121 D1
Park Court Mews SK8 239 E4
Park Cres Appleton WA4 26 B3
Ashton-u-L OL6 242 B2
Cuddington CW8 101 F2
Whaley Bridge SK23 39 E2
Wilmslow SK9 34 A1
Park Ct Chester CH2 237 F2
Frodsham WA6 74 A4
Runcorn WA7 49 D4
Sale M33 242 A7
Park Cty Prim Sch The
Runcorn WA7 24 A1
Tattenhall CH3 166 A1
Park Dr Altrincham WA15 238 F1
Chester CH2 119 D2
Ellesmere Port L65 70 A2
Hyde SK14 241 D8
Stockport SK4 240 B6
Wistaston CW2 205 F4
Park Dr S CH2 119 D2
Park Est CW2 206 B3
Park Gn SK11 112 B4
Park Gr SK4 240 B8
Park House Dr
Prestbury SK10 87 D4
Sandbach CW11 175 E4
Park House La SK10 87 D4
Park House Mews CW11 175 E4
Park La Appleton WA4 26 A3
Audley ST7 209 D2
Bate Heath WA16 79 F4
Congleton CW12 156 C1
Frodsham WA6 74 A4
Hargrave CH3 144 C2
Hartford CW8 103 D2
Hatherton CW5 219 F2
Higher Walton WA4 25 F3
Little Bollington WA14 20 A1
Macclesfield SK11 112 B3
Moulton CW9 126 C4
Pickmere WA16 79 F4
Poynton SK12 36 C2
Sandbach CW11 174 C3
Park Lane Sch SK11 112 A3
Park Lodge Cl SK8 239 E4
Park Mount SK8 239 A5
Park Mount Cl SK11 112 A3
Park Mount Dr SK11 112 A3
Park Rd
Altrincham WA15 238 F1
Altrincham, Bowdon WA14 238 A2
Bebington L62 43 F3
Cheadle SK8 239 E6
Congleton CW12 156 C2
Disley SK12 38 A3
Eaton CW12 134 C1
Ellesmere Port L65 70 B2
Goldborne WA3 3 D4
Park Rd continued
Great Sankey WA5 14 B4
Haslington CW1 191 E3
Heswall L60 41 D4
High Lane SK6 37 F3
Hyde SK14 241 D8
Little Budworth CW6 124 C1
Lymm WA13 29 E4
Macclesfield SK11 112 B3
Middlewich CW10 128 B1
Nantwich CW5 204 C2
New Mills SK22 39 E4
Northwich CW8 78 B1
Partington WA13 19 E4
Romiley SK6 241 C3
Runcorn WA7 49 D4
Sale M33 242 A8
Stalybridge SK15 & SK16 242 A1
Tarporley CW6 146 B1
Thornton-le-M CH2 71 F1
Warrington WA2 8 B1
Whaley Bridge SK23 65 E3
Widnes WA8 13 D1
Willaston L64 68 A4
Willaston (nr Nantwich) CW5 205 E3
Wilmslow SK9 59 F4
Park Rd N WA12 2 C2
Park Rd S WA12 2 B1
Park Rd W CH4 141 D4
Park Rise SK6 241 C3
Park Road Cty Prim Sch WA5 14 C3
Park Road Prim Sch
Altrincham WA14 238 E8
Sale M33 242 A8
Park St Bollington SK10 88 A4
Chester CH1 237 E2
Congleton CW12 156 C1
Haydock WA11 1 A3
Macclesfield SK11 112 B4
Neston L64 66 C4
Northwich CW8 103 F4
Stalybridge SK15 242 E1
6 Stockport SK1 240 F6
Park The Christleton CH3 142 C4
Penketh WA5 14 B2
Park Vale Rd SK11 112 B3
Park View Audlem CW3 230 B4
Bebington L62 43 E4
Cheadle SK3 239 F7
Gatley SK8 239 A6
Little Bollington WA14 20 A1
Park View Ct SK6 241 C2
Park View Rd ST7 195 D2
Park W CH1 117 F1
Park Way CH1 94 A1
Park West L60 40 C4
Park Wlk CH2 118 C2
Parkdale Ind Est WA4 16 B2
Parkdale Rd WA1 17 D4
Parker Ave CW8 103 D3
Parker Dr CH3 180 C1
Parker Dr S CH3 180 C1
Parker St Macclesfield SK11 112 C4
Runcorn WA7 23 D2
Warrington WA1 16 A3
Parker's Rd CW1 190 A4
Parker's Row CH3 180 C3
Parkers Ct WA7 49 F3
Parkett Heyes Rd SK11 111 F4
Parkfield L65 70 A1
Parkfield Ave WA4 17 D2
Parkfield Ct WA14 238 C4
Parkfield Dr
Ellesmere Port L65 70 A2
Helsby WA6 73 D2
Nantwich CW5 204 C2
Parkfield Rd
Altrincham WA14 238 C4
Broughton CH4 139 E2
Cheadle SK8 239 F1
Knutsford WA16 82 A4
Northwich CW9 104 B4
Parkfields La WA2 8 C1
Parkgate WA16 57 E2
Parkgate Ave WA16 108 A4
Parkgate Ct CH1 118 A2
Parkgate Cty Prim Sch L64 41 E1
Parkgate La
Knutsford WA16 57 E2
Thornton Hough L63 41 F3
Parkgate Rd Chester CH1 118 A2
Macclesfield SK11 112 B2
Mollington CH1 117 F4
Neston L64 66 B4
Puddington L66 68 B1
Saughall CH1 94 B2
Shotwick CH1 93 F4
Warrington WA4 16 B1
Parkgate Trad Est WA16 57 E2
Parkgate Way Runcorn WA7 50 B4
9 Wilmslow SK9 34 B2
Parkhill Ct WA16 57 D1
Parkhouse Ind Est ST5 210 C1
Parkhouse Rd E ST5 210 C1
Parkhouse Rd W ST5 210 C1
Parkland Cl WA4 27 D2
Parkland Dr CH2 72 A2
Parklands Ellesmere Port L66 69 E3
Kidsgrove ST7 195 D1
Widnes WA8 12 B2
Parklands Cty Prim Sch L66 69 E3
Parklands Dr Elton CH2 72 B2
Heswall L60 41 E3
Parklands Gdns L66 69 E3
Parklands The
Congleton CW12 157 D1
Reddish SK4 240 E8
Parklands View L66 69 E3
Parklands Way SK12 36 C2
Parklea L66 69 E3
Parkroyal Cty Prim Sch SK11 112 B4
Parkside SK6 37 E4
Parkside Cl SK6 37 E4
Parkside Hospl SK10 112 A4
Parkside Rd
Newton-le-W WA3, WA12 3 D1
Sale M33 242 D5
Winwick WA3, WA12 3 D1
Parkstone Dr CW1 190 A4
Parksway WA1 17 E4
Parkview Pk WA13 29 E4
Parkway Cheadle SK3 239 F7
Deeside Ind Est CH5 92 C1
Wilmslow SK9 60 A3
Parkwood Cl Bebington L62 43 F4
Lymm WA13 18 B1
Parliament St CW8 103 F4
Parliament Way CH1 94 C4
Parlington Cl WA8 22 B4
Parnell Sq CW12 157 D1
Parr Flat Comm Jun Sch WA9 1 A2
Parr Gr WA11 1 A3
Parr St Macclesfield SK11 112 B4
Warrington WA1 16 B2
Widnes WA8 13 E1
Parrs Wood Rd M20 239 B8
Parry Dr WA4 17 F2
Parry Mead SK6 241 A4
Parson St CW12 156 B1
Parsonage Ct SK4 240 B8
Parsonage Gn SK9 60 A4
Parsonage Rd
Manchester SK4 240 C8
Widnes WA8 23 D2
Parsonage St Hyde SK14 241 D5
Macclesfield SK11 112 B4
Stockport SK4 240 E6
Parsonage Way
Cheadle SK8 240 B1
Great Sankey WA5 15 D3
Parsons La CH2 118 A4
Partington Prim Sch M31 11 F2
Partridge Cl
Congleton CW12 156 C1
Warrington WA3 9 F2
Winsford CW7 149 E3
Partridge Way CW9 79 F3
Parvey La SK11 112 C1
Pasture Cl Kelsall CW6 122 B2
Macclesfield SK10 87 E2
Pasture Dr WA3 9 D4
Pasture La WA2 9 D1
Pasturefield Cl M33 242 F5
Patch La SK7 35 E3
Patmos La WA16 105 F4
Patrivale Cl WA1 16 C3
Patten La WA1 16 A3
Patterdale Ave WA2 8 B1
Patterdale Rd
Partington M31 11 F2
Romiley SK6 241 B4
Patterson Cl WA3 9 F2
Patterson St WA12 2 A2
Paul Cl WA5 14 B3
Paul St WA2 16 A3
Paulden Rd CW9 80 A1
Pavement La WA16 57 F2
Pavilions The
Davenham CW9 103 F1
Eccleston CH4 141 D2
Paxford Pl SK9 60 A3
Payne Cl WA5 15 E3
Paythorne Cl WA3 4 C2
Peach Field CH3 142 A4
Peach Gr WA11 1 C4
Peach Tree Cl L24 21 F1
Peacock Ave Cheadle SK9 34 A3
Warrington WA1 16 C3
Winsford CW7 149 E3
Peacock Hay Rd ST7 210 C2
Peacock La WA16 29 F3
Peacock Way SK9 34 B3
Peak Rd SK22 39 E4
Peakdale Ave SK8 239 B1
Pear Tree Ave Crewe CW1 190 A4
Runcorn WA7 49 E4
Pear Tree Cl Frodsham WA6 49 E1
Hale L24 21 F1
Winsford CW7 149 E4
Pear Tree Dr
Higher Wincham CW9 80 A3
Stalybridge SK15 242 E2
Pear Tree Farm Cotts CW9 104 C2
Pear Tree La
Acton Bridge CW8 76 C2
Whitchurch SY13 225 E1
Pear Tree Rd ST7 209 F1
Pear Tree Way
Chester CH2 118 C3
Ellesmere Port L66 69 F1
Pearl La CH3 119 D1
Pearl St SK10 87 D4
Pearle St SK10 87 E1
Pearlings The CH3 119 D1
Pearson Ave WA4 16 B1
Pearson St
23 Macclesfield SK11 112 C4
Reddish SK5 240 F7
Peartree Cl CW11 175 F3
Peartree La SY13 222 B1
Peartree Pl WA4 16 B2
Pearwood Cl CW6 146 B1
Peaslake Cl SK6 241 D2
Peasley Cl WA2 9 D1
Pebble Brook Cty Prim Sch CW2 190 B1
Pebble Cl SK15 242 D4
Peck Mill La WA6 98 A4
Peckfield Cl WA7 50 A3
Peckforton Castle CW6 167 F1
Peckforton Cl Gatley M22 239 A5
Sandbach CW11 174 C4
Peckforton Dr
Ellesmere Port L66 69 F2
Runcorn WA7 49 F2
Peckforton Hall La
Peckforton CW6 185 D3
Spurstow CW6 185 D3
Peckforton Rd CW6 168 A1
Peckforton Way
Chester CH2 118 C3
Northwich CW8 103 F4
Peckmill Cl SK9 34 C1
Pedley Hill Adlington SK10 62 C4
Rainow SK10 88 C2
Pedley House La WA16 58 C1
Pedley La Chelford WA16 83 E4
Congleton CW12 157 F2
Pedley St CW2 190 B1
Peebles Cl
Ellesmere Port L66 68 C3
Holmes Chapel CW4 130 A1
Peel Ave WA14 238 D2
Peel Cres CH3 121 F4
Peel Dr Astbury CW12 178 A4
Sale M33 242 E6
Peel Hall La CH3 121 F4
Peel Hollow ST7 209 D1
Peel House La WA8 13 D1
Peel La CW12 178 B4
Peel Rd WA15 238 E3
Peel Sq CW1 190 A3
Peel St Crewe CW1 190 A3
Hyde SK14 241 F5
Macclesfield SK11 112 B3
Newton-le-W WA12 2 A2
Runcorn WA7 22 C1
Stalybridge SK15 242 C1
Stockport SK2 240 F2
Peelgate Dr SK8 239 A2
Peerglow Pk Est WA14 238 E8
Peerswood Ct L64 66 C3
Peewit Cl CW7 149 E3
Peggie's La SK10 62 B1
Pelham Cl CW1 191 E3
Pelham Rd WA4 17 E2
Pelican Cl CW1 191 D3
Pemberton Cl L64 68 A4
Pemberton Rd CH1 237 D3
Pembridge Ct L65 70 C2
Pembridge Gdns L65 70 C2
Pembroke Cl CH4 141 F3
Pembroke Ct WA7 24 B3
Pembroke Dr L65 70 A2
Pembroke Gdns WA4 26 B2
Pembroke Gr M44 11 E3
Pembroke Rd SK11 111 F4
Pembroke Way CW7 149 D4
Pemston Ct L66 69 F4
Penare WA7 50 B3
Penbrook Cl CW2 189 E2
Pendennis Rd SK4 240 C7
Pendine Cl WA5 7 E1
Pendle Cl CW1 191 D3
Pendle Gdns WA3 4 C1
Pendlebury Rd SK8 239 B6
Pendlebury St WA4 17 D2
Penfold Cl CH1 94 A4
Penfold Hey CH2 118 B4
Penfold Way CH4 162 A4
Penfolds WA7 23 E1
Penhale Mews SK7 35 F4
Penistone Dr L66 69 D3
Penkeith's La WA7 23 D2
Penketh Ave WA5 15 F4
Penketh Ct WA7 23 D1
Penketh Cty High Sch WA5 15 D3
Penketh Cty Prim Sch WA5 14 B2
Penketh Rd WA5 15 D2
Penkford La WA5 1 B1
Penkford Sch WA12 1 C2
Penkford St WA12 1 C2
Penkrth South Cty Prim Sch WA5 14 C2
Penlington Ct CW5 204 C3
Penmann Cres L26 21 D4
Penmark Cl WA5 7 E1
Penmon Cl CH1 117 E2
Penn Gdns L65 70 A3
Penn House Cl SK7 35 F4
Penn La WA7 22 C1
Pennant Cl WA3 10 A2
Pennine Ct SK10 87 F1
Pennine Dr
Altrincham WA14 238 B5
Ashton-u-L OL6 242 B4
Pennine Rd WA2 8 C1
Pennine View SK15 242 F4
Pennine Way Biddulph ST6 179 F1
Winsford CW7 149 D4
Pennine Wlk L66 69 D3
Pennington Cl WA6 49 E1
Pennington Flash Ctry Pk WA3 4 A4
Pennington Gn L66 69 E2
Pennington La WA5 1 B1
Penningtons La SK11 111 F3
Penny La Burtonwood WA5 1 B1
Cronton WA8 12 A3
Haydock WA11 2 A4
Rainow SK10 88 B2
Stockport SK5 240 F7
Penny's La
Lach Dennis CW9 105 D3
Northwich CW9 104 C4
Pennyfields Rd ST7 195 E1
Pennymoor Dr WA14 238 B6
Pennypleck La CW9 28 A1
Penrhyn Ave SK8 239 E1
Penrhyn Cres
Hazel Grove SK7 36 B4
Runcorn WA7 49 D4
Penrhyn Rd Northwich CW8 103 F4
Stockport SK3 240 C4
Penrith Ave
Macclesfield SK11 111 F3
Warrington WA2 8 B1
Penrith Cl Frodsham WA6 49 E1
Partington M31 11 F2
Penrose Gdns WA5 14 B2
Penry Ave M44 11 F3
Penryn Cl WA5 14 C2
Pensarn Gdns WA5 7 E1
Pensarn Gr SK5 240 F8
Pensby Ave CH2 118 B3
Pensby Dr L66 69 E2
Pensby Rd L60 40 C4
Penshaw Ct WA7 49 F4
Pentland Ave WA2 8 A2
Pentland Cl Chester CH3 119 D1
Winsford CW7 149 D4
Pentland Pl WA2 8 A2
Pentre Cl CH3 121 F4
Pentre La CH3 121 F4
Penzance Cl SK10 111 F4
Peover Ave M33 242 E6
Peover Hall WA16 107 F4
Peover La Chelford SK11 108 C4
Congleton CW12 157 F3
Peover Rd 3 SK8 34 C3
Peover Superior Endowed Contr Prim Sch WA16 108 A4
Pepper St Appleton WA4 27 D2
Chelford SK11 83 F1
Chester CH1 237 E2
Christleton CH3 142 B4
Hale L24 21 E1
Henbury SK11 111 D4
Lymm WA13 18 C2
Middlewich CW10 128 B1
Mobberley WA16 31 F1
Nantwich CW5 204 C3
Peppers The WA13 18 C2
Percival Cl CH2 118 B4
Percival La Ollerton WA16 83 D2
Runcorn WA7 22 C1
Percival Rd Chester CH2 118 B4
Ellesmere Port L65 70 A3
Percival St WA1 16 B3
Percy James Cl ST7 193 F2
Percy Rd CH4 141 E4
Percy St Northwich CW9 104 A4
Stalybridge SK15 242 E2
Stockport SK1 240 F6
Warrington WA5 15 F3
Peregrine Cl CW7 149 E3
Perimeter Rd CH2 72 B3
Perrey St WA7 23 D1
Perrin Ave WA7 48 C4
Perrin St SK14 241 D6
Perrins Rd WA5 6 C3
Perth Cl Bramhall SK7 35 F3
Holmes Chapel CW4 130 A1
Warrington WA2 8 C2
Peter House Rd SK11 112 C2
Peter Pl CW1 190 A3
Peter Salem Dr WA5 15 D3
Peter St Altrincham WA14 238 D3
Denton M34 241 A7
Goldborne WA3 3 D4
Macclesfield SK11 112 B4
Northwich CW9 79 D1
Peter St W SK11 112 B4
Peterborough Cl SK10 87 D1
Peterhouse Gdns SK6 241 C4
Peters Cl SK10 87 D4
Petersburg Rd SK3 240 D2
Petersfield Gdns WA3 4 C2
Petersgate WA7 50 B4
Petersham Dr WA4 26 C3
Peterstone Cl WA5 7 E1
Petrel Ave SK12 36 A2
Petrel Cl CW7 149 E3
Petunia Cl SK11 112 A3
Petworth Ave WA2 8 A2
Petworth Cl CW2 206 A4
Pevensey Dr WA16 82 A4
Peveril Cl WA4 26 B4
Peveril Dr SK7 36 C4
Peveril Gdns SK12 39 D3
Peveril Mews SK12 39 D3
Peveril Rd WA14 238 C7
Peveril Wlk SK11 111 F4
Pewit La CW5 231 D4
Pewithall Cty Jun Sch WA7 49 D4
Pewterspear La WA4 26 C2
Pexhall Rd CW12 134 B2
Pexhill Ct SK4 240 A6
Pexhill Dr SK10 111 F4
Pexhill Rd Henbury SK11 111 E3
Macclesfield SK11 111 E3
Siddington SK11 110 B2
Warren SK10, SK11 111 E3

ley Bank Mews WA6 74 A1
ley Cl CW11 174 C3
ley Dr WA7 49 D4
leys Way ST7 209 F1
lshaw La CW7 150 A4
lston Ave WA3 4 B2
mington Cl WA3 4 C2
msdale Cl Gatley SK8 239 A3
Wistaston CW2 206 A4
ng Rd CH3 119 E2
ng-o-Bells La SK12 38 B3
ngsfield Rd L24 21 D1
ingstead Cl SK9 34 B1
ingstead Dr SK9 34 B1
ingstone Way SK23 65 E4
ingway Ellesmere Port L66 69 F2
Neston L64 41 F1
Waverton CH3 143 D3
ingway Golf Course WA15 32 B4
ingway Rd Runcorn WA7 23 E1
Wythenshawe M22, M90 33 E4
ingway Rd W M90 33 E4
ingwood Cl WA3 10 A3
ipley Ave SK8 35 D3
ipley Cl SK7 36 C4
ipley St WA5 15 F3
ipon Ave
Ellesmere Port L66 69 E3
Goldborne WA3 3 E4
ipon Cl WA12 2 B3
ipon Dr CW2 206 A4
ipon Row WA7 49 E3
ipon Wlk SK6 241 A1
ise The SK23 65 E3
iseley St SK11 112 B4
iseley's Pas [33] SK11 112 B4
ising Sun Cl SK11 112 A3
ising Sun Rd SK11 112 A2
isley Moss Ctry Pk WA3 10 A2
isley Rd WA3 9 F3
ivacre Brow L66 69 F4
ivacre Rd Bebington L62 44 A2
Ellesmere Port L65 44 B1
ivacre Valley Ctry Pk L66 69 E4
ivacre Valley Cty Prim Sch L66 69 F4
River La Broughton CH4 140 C4
Chester CH4 141 E4
Farndon CH3 180 C1
Partington M31 11 F2
River Rd WA4 16 A2
River St Congleton CW12 156 B2
Macclesfield SK11 112 C3
Wilmslow SK9 60 A4
River View CW7 126 C1
Riverbank Cl
Bollington SK10 87 F4
Heswall L60 40 C3
Nantwich CW5 204 C4
Riverbank Rd L60 40 C3
Riverdane Rd CW12 156 C2
Rivermead Ave WA15 32 B4
Riversdale Frodsham WA6 49 E1
Warrington WA1 17 F4
Riversdale Rd
Cheadle SK8 239 C5
Runcorn WA7 49 F4
Rivershill M33 242 A8
Rivershill Gdns WA15 32 B3
Riverside Nantwich CW5 204 B3
Northwich CW9 104 A3
Riverside Bsns Pk SK9 60 A4
Riverside Cl WA1 16 B2
Riverside Cres CW4 130 B2
Riverside Ct Chester CH4 141 F4
Langley SK11 113 E2
Riverside Dr CW8 103 F3
Riverside Gr CW2 189 E2
Riverside Pk CH5 116 A4
Riverside Ret Pk WA4 16 B2
Riverside Wlk L64 66 B3
Riversmead CH3 142 A3
Riverton Rd M20 239 B8
Riverview Rd L64 66 C3
Rivington Ct WA1 17 F4
Rivington Gr M44 11 E3
Rivington Rd
Altrincham WA15 238 F2
Ellesmere Port L65 70 B3
Runcorn WA7 50 C2
Rixton Ave WA5 15 F4
Roaches The SK11 112 A3
Roachill Cl WA14 238 B5
Road Beta CW10 151 E4
Road Five CW7 127 E1
Road Four CW7 127 D1
Road One CW7 127 D2
Road St CW6 146 A2
Road Three CW7 127 E1
Road Two CW7 127 D1
Roadside Ct WA3 3 E4
Roan Ct SK11 112 C4
Roan House Way SK11 112 C4
Roan Mews SK11 112 C4
Rob Rd WA12 2 C3
Robert Moffat WA16 29 E3
Robert St Hyde SK14 241 C7
Northwich CW8 103 F3
Runcorn WA7 23 E1
Sale M33 242 E6
Warrington WA5 15 F3
Widnes WA8 13 D1
Robert's Terr CH1 118 A1
Roberts Ave WA11 1 A3
Roberts Ct WA7 49 F3
Roberts Dr CW9 104 B3
Roberts Rd CW9 80 A1
Robin Cl Rainow SK10 88 C3
Runcorn WA7 50 B4
Sandbach CW11 175 D4
Robin Cres SK11 112 B1
Robin Hood Ave SK11 112 B3
Robin Hood La WA6 73 D1
Robin La Chelford SK11 84 A2
Sutton Lane Ends SK11 112 B1
Robin's La Bramhall SK7 35 F4
Cheadle Hulme SK7 35 E4
Robins Cft L66 69 F1
Robins Cl SK7 35 F4
Robins La WA3 4 B1
Robins Way SK10 88 A4
Robinsbay Rd M22 33 F4
Robinson St Hyde SK14 241 F7
Stalybridge SK15 242 C1
Stockport SK3 240 D3
Robinsons Croft CH3 142 A4
Robinsway WA14 238 C1
Robson St WA1 16 B3
Roby Gr WA5 15 D3
Roche Gdns SK8 35 D3
Rochester Cl Goldborne WA3 3 D4
Great Sankey WA5 15 E3
Rochester Cres CW1 190 C3
Rochester Dr L65 70 B2
Rochford Ave M22 33 E4
Rock Bank SK23 65 F3
Rock Dr WA6 49 E1
Rock Farm Cl L64 67 D3
Rock Farm Dr L64 67 D3
Rock Farm Gr L64 67 D3
Rock La Burwardsley CW6 184 B3
Chester CH2 237 D4
Widnes WA8 12 C2
Rock Rd CH5 91 F1
Rock St SK22 39 E4
Rock The WA6 73 E1
Rockfield Cl WA8 12 B1
Rockfield Dr WA6 73 E1
Rockford Lodge WA16 57 E1
Rockhouse La ST7 210 B4
Rockingham Cl WA3 10 B3
Rocklands La L63 42 B4
Rocklee Gdns L64 67 D3
Rocklife La CH6 91 D2
Rocklynes SK6 241 B2
Rocksavage Expressway WA7 49 E3
Rockside ST7 195 E3
Rockwood Ave CW2 190 A2
Rocky La Heswall L60 40 C4
Tattenhall CH3 182 C4
Rocky La S L60 41 D4
Roddy La WA6 75 F1
Rode Hall ST7 194 A4
Rode Heath Cty Prim Sch ST7 193 F4
Rode House Cl ST7 193 F4
Rode The ST7 193 E2
Rodeheath Cl SK9 60 B4
Rodepool Cl SK9 34 B1
Rodgers Cl WA6 49 D1
Rodmill Dr SK8 239 A4
Rodney St
Ashton-u-L OL6 242 A4
Macclesfield SK11 112 B4
Warrington WA2 16 A3
Roe Pk CW12 178 C1
Roe St Congleton CW12 156 C1
Macclesfield SK11 112 B4
Roebuck Gdns M33 242 A6
Roebuck La M33 242 A6
Roebuck St CW1 190 B3
Roeburn Way WA5 14 B2
Roedean Wlk CW1 190 B3
Roehampton Dr WA7 49 F4
Roehurst La CW7 126 B1
Roemarsh Ct WA7 49 F3
Roewood La
Macclesfield SK10 88 A1
Macclesfield, Higherfence SK10 113 D4
Roften Ind Est L66 43 E1
Rokeby Ct WA7 24 B3
Rokeden WA12 2 B2
Roland Ave WA7 22 C1
Rolands Wlk WA7 23 F1
Rolleston St WA2 16 A3
Rolls Ave CW1 190 A4
Rolt Cres CW10 151 D4
Roman Cl WA7 23 F1
Roman Ct L64 66 C4
Roman Dr CH1 117 E3
Roman Rd Stockport SK4 240 E6
Warrington WA4 16 B1
Widnes WA8 22 C3
Roman Rise CW8 78 A2
Roman Way CW11 174 C4
Romanes St CW8 103 F4
Romford Ave M34 241 A8
Romiley Prec SK6 241 C2
Romiley Prim Sch SK6 241 C2
Romiley Rd L66 69 F3
Romiley Sta SK6 241 C2
Romney Cl L64 66 C4
Romney Croft L64 66 C4
Romney Way L64 66 C4
Romsey Dr SK7 35 E3
Ronald Dr WA2 9 D1
Ronaldshay WA8 13 F1
Ronaldsway Halewood L26 21 D4
Heswall L60 40 C3
Rood Hill CW12 156 B2
Rood La CW12 156 C2
Rook Rd WA4 16 C2
Rook St CW2 190 B1
Rookery Cl Nantwich CW5 204 C3
Sandbach CW11 174 B3
Rookery Dr Nantwich CW5 204 C2
Tattenhall CH3 166 A1
Rookery Rd Kidsgrove ST7 195 E2
Tilston SY14 198 A2
Rookery Rise CW7 127 D1
Rookery The Broughton CH4 139 D2
Newton-le-W WA12 2 B2
Rookerypool Cl SK9 34 B1
Rookfield Ave M33 242 C7
Rooks Way L60 40 C4
Roome St WA2 16 B4
Rooth St SK4 240 D6
Rope Bank Ave CW2 206 A4
Rope La Shavington CW2 206 A3
Wistaston CW2 206 A3
Rope Wlk CW12 156 B2
Ropewalk The L64 66 B4
Rosam Ct WA7 49 F3
Roscoe Ave
Newton-le-W WA12 2 C2
Warrington WA2 16 B4
Roscoe Cres WA7 48 C4
Roscoe Pk Est WA14 238 E8
Roscoe Rd M44 11 F4
Roscoe St SK3 240 D4
Roscote Cl L60 40 C4
Roscote The L60 40 C4
Rose Ave Haydock WA11 1 C3
Irlam M44 11 F4
Rose Bank WA13 18 C2
Rose Cl WA7 50 B3
Rose Cres WA8 22 C4
Rose Gdns L64 66 C3
Rose Lea Cl WA8 13 D2
Rose St Reddish SK5 240 F7
Widnes WA8 22 C4
Rose Terr Crewe CW1 190 B3
Stalybridge SK15 242 D1
Rose Vale SK8 239 B1
Rose View Ave WA8 13 D1
Rose Wlk M31 11 E1
Roseacre Dr Cheadle SK8 34 B4
Gatley SK8 239 C1
Rosebank Cl CW7 149 F4
Rosebank Rd M44 11 E2
Rosebank Sch CW8 78 A2
Rosebank Wlk CW8 78 A2
Roseberry Way CW1 191 E2
Rosedale Ave Goldborne WA3 3 E4
Warrington WA1 17 E4
Rosedale Rd SK4 240 D8
Rosefield Ave WA13 18 C2
Roseheath Dr L26 21 D3
Rosehill Ave WA9 6 A3
Rosehill Rd CW2 190 A1
Rosemary Ave Runcorn WA7 49 F2
Warrington WA4 16 C1
Rosemary Cl
Broughton CH4 139 E2
Great Sankey WA5 15 E3
Rosemary Dr WA12 2 C2
Rosemary La LL12 161 E1
Rosemary Row CH3 166 A1
Rosemary Wlk M31 11 F1
Rosemere Dr CH1 94 C4
Rosemoor Gdns WA4 26 C3
Rosendale Dr WA3 10 A3
Rosevale Rd ST5 210 C1
Roseville Dr CW12 179 D4
Rosewood Ave
Chester CH2 118 B3
Frodsham WA6 74 B4
Stockport SK4 240 A5
Warrington WA1 16 C4
Rosewood Cl CW1 190 C3
Rosewood Gr CH1 117 D4
Roslyn Rd SK3 240 E1
Ross Ave SK3 240 E1
Ross Cl WA5 15 E4
Ross Dr L66 69 E3
Ross Rd L65 70 A3
Ross St WA8 13 D1
Rossall Cl L24 21 F1
Rossall Dr SK7 35 F3
Rossall Gr L66 69 E3
Rossall Rd Great Sankey WA5 15 D2
Widnes WA8 13 E1
Rossbank Rd L65 70 A4
Rosscliffe Rd L65 70 A3
Rossenclough Rd SK9 34 B1
Rossendale Rd SK8 34 B4
Rossett Ave M22 33 E4
Rossett Cl WA5 7 F1
Rossett Pk CH4 162 B1
Rossett Rd LL13 180 A1
Rossfield Rd L65 70 A3
Rossfield Rd N L65 70 A4
Rosslyn Cl CH5 116 A1
Rosslyn La CW8 102 A2
Rosslyn Rd Chester CH3 119 D2
Gatley SK8 239 D1
Rossmill La WA15 32 A4
Rossmore Bsns Pk L65 70 A4
Rossmore Cty Prim Sch L66 69 E4
Rossmore Gdns L66 69 E3
Rossmore Ind Est L65 70 A3
Rossmore Rd E L65 69 F4
Rossmore Rd W L66 69 E4
Rossmount Rd L65 70 A3
Rosswood Rd L65 70 A3
Rostherne Ave
Ellesmere Port L66 69 F2
Goldborne WA3 3 E4
High Lane SK6 37 F4
Rostherne Cl WA5 15 E2
Rostherne Cres WA8 12 B1
Rostherne Ct WA14 238 D3
Rostherne Rd Sale M33 242 F5
Stockport SK3 240 E1
Wilmslow SK9 59 F3
Rostherne St [1] WA14 238 D3
Rostherne Way CW11 174 C4
Rosthernmere Rd SK8 239 F4
Rostrevor Rd SK3 240 E1
Rothay Dr WA5 14 B2
Rothbury Cl WA7 49 E3
Rother Dr L65 70 A4
Rothesay Cl WA7 23 F1
Rothesay Dr L62 43 F2
Rothesay Rd CH4 141 D4
Rough Bank CW12 179 F4
Rough Heys La SK11 111 D4
Roughlea Ave WA3 4 B2
Roughley Ave WA5 15 E2
Roughlyn Cres CH4 140 C1
Roughwood La CW11 176 A1
Round Gdns SK10 88 A4
Round Hill Meadow CH3 142 A4
Round Meadow SK10 88 C3
Round Thorn WA3 9 D4
Round Way SK22 39 E4
Roundabout The WA8 12 B3
Roundcroft SK6 241 E3
Roundhey SK8 34 B4
Roundway SK7 35 E3
Roundy La SK10 62 C3
Routledge St WA8 13 D1
Rowan Ave WA3 3 F4
Rowan Cl Alsager ST7 193 E2
Great Sankey WA5 14 B4
Middlewich CW10 151 F3
Newton-le-W WA12 2 B1
Runcorn WA7 49 E4
Sandbach CW11 174 C4
Winsford CW7 126 B2
Rowan Dr SK7 35 E4
Rowan Gr CH5 91 E1
Rowan Pk CH3 142 C4
Rowan Pl CH2 119 D2
Rowan Rd CW8 102 B4
Rowan St SK14 241 F5
Rowan Way SK10 87 F1
Rowan Wlk M31 11 E1
Rowans The CH4 139 D2
Rowanside SK10 86 C3
Rowanside Dr SK9 60 C4
Rowcliffe Ave CH4 141 D2
Rowe St WA1 16 A3
Rowland Cl WA2 9 D2
Rowley Bank La WA16 29 D1
Rowley Rd SK7 36 C4
Rowley Way WA16 82 A4
Rowson Dr M44 11 E3
Rowthorn Cl WA8 22 C4
Rowton Brideg Rd CH3 142 C4
Rowton Cl CW9 103 F2
Rowton La CH3 142 C3
Rowton Rd CW2 189 E2
Roxbo Rough Cl WA5 7 D3
Roxburgh Cl SK10 87 D1
Roxburgh Rd L66 68 C3
Roxby Way WA16 82 A4
Roxholme Wlk M22 33 E4
Royal Ave WA8 12 B1
Royal Gdns
Altrincham WA14 20 C1
Northwich CW9 103 F2
Royal George St SK1 & SK3 240 F4
Royal La CW6 147 D2
Royal Meadows SK10 87 D1
Royal Mews CW9 104 B3
Royal Mount CW1 173 D1
Royal Oak Yd [4] SK1 240 F5
Royal Pl WA8 22 A4
Royal Rd SK12 38 B3
Royal Sch for the Deaf The SK8 34 B3
Royce Ave WA15 238 E5
Royce Cl CW1 190 A4
Royden Ave Irlam M44 11 F4
Runcorn WA7 49 D4
Royds Cl CW8 103 D2
Roylands Dr CW10 151 E4
Royle St Congleton CW12 156 B2
Northwich CW9 104 A4
Stockport SK1 240 F3
Winsford CW7 126 C1
Royle's Pl CW8 103 E3
Royleen Dr WA6 74 B3
Royon Dr SK3 240 B3
Royston Ave WA1 17 D4
Royston Cl
Ellesmere Port L65 69 F2
Goldborne WA3 3 F4
Rozel Cres WA5 15 D3
Rudd Ave WA9 1 A1
Rudheath Cl CW2 189 E3
Rudheath Cty High Sch CW9 104 B4
Rudheath Cty Prim Sch CW9 104 B3
Rudheath L Ctr CW9 104 B4
Rudloe Ct WA2 8 C1
Rudstone Cl L66 69 D3
Rudyard Cl SK11 112 A3
Rue De Bohars CW6 168 B4
Rufford Ave SK14 241 F6
Rufford Cl CW2 206 A4
Rufford Ct WA1 17 F4
Rufus Ct CH1 237 D3
Rugby Cl SK10 87 F2
Rugby Dr SK10 87 F2
Rugby House SK10 87 E2
Rugby Rd L65 70 B2
Ruislip Ct WA2 8 C1
Runcorn Docks Rd WA7 22 C1
Runcorn East Sta WA7 50 B4
Runcorn Rd Barnton CW8 78 A1
Little Leigh CW8 77 E3
Moore WA4 25 E3
Runcorn Spur Rd WA7 49 E4
Runcorn Sta WA7 22 C1
Runger La WA15 32 C4
Runnell The L64 41 E2
Runnymede WA1 17 E4
Runnymede Cl SK3 240 C2
Runnymede Ct SK3 240 C2
Runnymede Dr WA11 1 A3
Ruscoe Ave CW11 174 C3
Ruscolm Cl WA5 14 B4
Rushey Cl WA15 32 B4
Rushfield Cres WA7 50 A3
Rushfield Rd
Cheadle Hulme SK8 35 D3
Chester CH4 141 D3
Rushgreen Rd WA13 19 D2
Rushmere La CH3 163 F2
Rushmore Gr WA1 17 D4
Rusholme Cl L26 21 D3
Rushside Rd SK8 35 D3
Rushton Ave WA12 2 A2
Rushton CE Contr Prim Sch SK11 159 D1
Rushton Cl Northwich CW9 104 B4
Widnes WA8 12 C2
Rushton Dr Chester CH2 118 B4
Hough Common CW2 206 C1
Middlewich CW10 151 E4
Romiley SK6 241 C3
Rushton Fold SK10 61 D1
Rushton La Eaton CW6 147 E3
Little Budworth CW6 147 E3
Rushton Rd
Cheadle Hulme SK8 35 D3
Stockport SK3 240 B3
Rushy View WA12 2 A2
Rushyfield Cres SK6 241 D3
Ruskin Ave
Newton-le-W WA12 2 B2
Warrington WA2 8 B1
Ruskin Ct WA16 57 D1
Ruskin Cty High Sch The CW2 190 B1
Ruskin Dr L65 70 B2
Ruskin Gdns SK6 241 A3
Ruskin Gr SK6 241 A3
Ruskin Rd
Congleton CW12 156 B1
Crewe CW2 190 B1
Ruskin Way WA16 57 D2
Russell Ave Alsager ST7 193 E3
High Lane SK6 37 F4
Sale M33 242 D7
Russell Cl CW12 179 D4
Russell Ct WA8 13 D2
Russell Dr CW1 191 E2
Russell Gdns SK4 240 B5
Russell Rd Runcorn WA7 48 C4
Winsford CW7 149 E4
Russell St
Ashton-u-L OL6 242 A4
Chester CH2 237 F3
Hyde SK14 241 D7
Russet Cl CW10 128 A1
Russet Rd CW8 102 B4
Russett Sch The CW8 102 C4
Rutherford Cl SK14 241 D6
Ruthin Ave SK8 239 E2
Ruthin Ct L65 70 B2
Ruthin Wlk WA6 73 D1
Rutland Ave Denton M34 241 B6
Goldborne WA3 3 E4
Halewood L26 21 D4
Warrington WA4 26 A4
Rutland Cl
Ashton-u-L OL6 242 A2
Congleton CW12 156 C2
Gatley SK8 239 B6
[16] Sandbach CW11 174 B3
Rutland Dr
Middlewich CW10 151 E4
Weaverham CW8 77 E1
Rutland La M33 242 F6
Rutland Pl CH2 119 D3
Rutland Rd
Altrincham WA14 238 D6
Hazel Grove SK7 36 C4
Irlam M44 11 E3
Kidsgrove ST7 195 D1
Macclesfield SK11 112 B2
Partington M31 11 F1
Rutland St
Ashton-u-L OL6 242 A2
Runcorn WA7 22 C1
Ryburn Rd SK11 112 A3
Rydal Ave High Lane SK6 37 F4
Warrington WA4 16 A1
Rydal Cl Ellesmere Port L65 70 B1
Gatley SK8 239 B4
Holmes Chapel CW4 130 A1
Neston L64 66 C3
Winsford CW7 126 B2
Rydal Ct CW12 156 A1
Rydal Dr WA15 32 B4
Rydal Gr Chester CH4 141 D3
Helsby WA6 73 D1
Runcorn WA7 49 D4

muel St Chester CH2 237 F3
:rewe CW1 190 A3
Macclesfield SK11 112 B4
Packmoor ST7 195 F1
Stockport SK4 240 D7
Warrington WA5 15 F2
nbec Gdns WA8 12 B3
nd La SK10 84 C3
ndalwood Cl WA2 8 B1
ndbach Cty High Sch CW11 175 D4
ndbach Cty Prim Sch CW11 175 D3
ndbach Golf Course CW11 174 C4
ndbach Rd
Congleton CW12 156 A2
Hassall Green CW11 176 B1
Lawton Heath ST7 193 F3
Rode Heath ST7 193 F4
Sale M33 242 F5
andbach Rd N ST7 193 E2
andbach Rd S ST7 193 E2
andbach Sch - (Ind) (Boys) CW11 175 D3
andbach Service Sta CW11 175 F3
andbach Sta CW11 174 B4
anderling Rd WA12 2 B2
anders Hey Cl WA7 50 A3
anders Sq SK11 112 B3
anderson Cl Crewe CW2 206 B4
Great Sankey WA5 14 B3
andfield Ave CW5 216 C2
andfield Cl WA3 3 F4
andfield Cres WA3 5 E4
andfield Ct Frodsham WA6 74 A4
Wrenbury CW5 216 C2
andfield La
Acton Bridge CW8 76 C1
Hartford CW8 103 E2
andfield Pk L60 40 B4
andfields WA6 74 A4
andford Rd Nantwich CW5 204 C4
Sale M33 242 F5
andgate Rd SK10 87 F1
andham Gr L60 41 E4
andham Rd L24 21 D2
andheys L64 41 E1
andhill St SK14 241 F8
andhole La Chelford WA16 83 E2
Crowton CW8 101 D4
andhurst Ave CW2 190 A1
andhurst Dr SK9 34 B1
andhurst Rd L24 21 D3
andhurst St WA4 16 C2
andicroft Cl WA3 9 E3
andiford Rd CW4 130 B2
andileigh CH2 118 C2
andileigh Ave
Altrincham WA15 238 F3
Cheadle SK8 240 A2
Knutsford WA16 56 C1
andileigh Dr WA15 238 F3
andiway Bebington L63 43 E3
Knutsford WA16 57 D1
andiway Ave WA8 12 A1
andiway Cl CW8 102 A1
andiway Cty Prim Sch CW8 102 A2
andiway Golf Course CW8 102 B1
Sandiway La CW9 53 D1
Sandiway Pk CW8 102 C2
Sandiway Pl WA14 238 D5
Sandiway Rd
Altrincham WA14 238 D6
Crewe CW1 190 A4
Wilmslow SK9 34 B3
Sandle Bridge La WA16 83 F3
Sandle Bridge Rise WA16 83 F3
Sandon Cres L64 66 C3
Sandon Park Gdns CW2 189 E2
Sandon Pl WA8 13 E1
Sandon Rd CH2 118 C2
Sandon St CW1 190 B2
Sandown Cl Culcheth WA3 4 C2
Middlewich CW10 151 E4
Runcorn WA7 49 E3
Wilmslow SK9 60 A4
Sandown Cres CW8 102 A2
Sandown Dr WA15 32 B3
Sandown Pl SK11 111 F4
Sandown Rd Crewe CW1 190 B4
Stockport SK3 240 B4
Sandpiper Cl Crewe CW1 189 F4
Newton-le-W WA12 2 B2
Sandpiper Dr SK3 240 D2
Sandra Dr WA12 2 B2
Sandringham Ave
Chester CH3 119 D1
Helsby WA6 73 D2
Stalybridge SK15 242 D3
Sandringham Cl
Altrincham WA14 20 C1
Davenham CW9 103 F2
Winsford CW7 126 B2
Sandringham Dr
Great Sankey WA5 15 E2
Poynton SK12 36 B2
Stockport SK4 240 A5
Wistaston CW2 205 F4
Sandringham Gdns L65 70 B1
Sandringham Rd WA8 13 D2
Sandrock Rd CH3 142 C4
Sands Rd ST7 195 F3
Sandsdown Cl ST6 179 E1
Sandside Rd ST7 193 D2
Sandstone Wlk L60 41 D4
Sandwell Dr M33 242 B8
Sandwich Dr SK10 87 E2
Sandwood Ave CH4 139 D2
Sandy Brow La WA3 3 F1
Sandy Cl SK10 87 F4
Sandy Gr ST7 193 E2
Sandy La Allostock WA16 106 C3
Astbury CW12 177 F3
Aston CW5 217 E1
Bold Heath WA8 14 A3
Broughton CH4 140 B3
Brown Knowl CH3 199 E4
Bulkeley SY14 184 B1
Chester CH3 119 D1
Congleton CW12 155 E2
Congleton, Astbury Marsh CW12 156 A1
Croft WA3 9 D4
Cronton WA8 12 B3
Goldborne WA3 2 C4
Goldborne, Wash End WA3 4 A4
Goostrey CW4 107 E1
Haslington CW11 192 A4
Hatherton CW5 219 F3
Higher Kinnerton CH4 161 D3
Huntington CH3 142 B2
Lymm WA13 19 D2
Macclesfield SK10 86 B1
Neston L64 67 D3
Nova Scotia CW8 125 E3
Penketh WA5 15 D2
Romiley SK6 241 D3
Runcorn, Preston Brook WA7 50 C3
Runcorn, Weston Point WA7 48 C4
Saighton CH3 142 B2
Sandbach CW11 174 B3
Stalybridge SK15 242 B1
Stockport SK4 & SK5 240 E7
Swettenham CW12 131 F2
Tarvin CH3 121 E2
Threapwood SY14 222 C4
Warrington WA2 8 B1
Warrington, Cobbs WA4 26 B4
Weaverham CW8 77 E1
Widnes WA8 12 B3
Wilmslow SK9 59 F4
Sandy La W WA2 8 A2
Sandy Moor La WA7 24 B2
Sandy Rd ST6 179 E1
Sandyhill Pl CW7 149 E3
Sandyhill Rd CW7 149 E3
Sandylands Cres ST7 193 F3
Sandylands Pk CW2 205 E4
Sankey St Goldborne WA3 3 D4
Newton-le-W WA12 2 A2
Warrington WA1 16 A3
Widnes WA8 23 D3
Sankey Sta WA5 14 C3
Sankey Valley Ind Est WA12 2 A1
Sankey Valley Park WA12 1 B2
Sankey Way
Great Sankey WA5 15 E3
Warrington WA5 15 E3
Sanky La WA4 25 F1
Santon Dr WA3 3 F4
Sapling La CW6 146 C2
Sarra La CH3 184 A3
Sarsfield Ave WA3 3 E4
Saughall Cl CW9 103 F2
Saughall Hey CH1 94 A1
Saughall Rd CH1 117 F3
Saunders St CW1 190 A2
Saundersfoot Cl WA5 7 F1
Saunderton Cl WA11 1 B4
Saville Ave WA5 15 F4
Saville Rd SK8 239 B6
Saville St SK11 112 C3
Savoy Rd CW1 207 D4
Sawley Cl Culcheth WA3 5 D1
Runcorn WA7 50 C4
Sawley Dr SK7 35 E3
Sawpit St WA13 20 A3
Sawyer Brow SK14 241 F8
Sawyer Dr ST6 179 E1
Saxon Crossway CW7 126 A1
Saxon Rd WA7 23 E1
Saxon Terr WA8 13 D1
Saxon Way Blacon CH1 117 F3
Ellesmere Port CH1 94 C4
Sandbach CW11 175 E3
Saxons La Northwich CW8 103 F3
Northwich, Greenbank CW8 103 E4
Sayce St WA8 13 D1
Scafell Ave WA2 8 B2
Scafell Cl Bebington L63 43 E2
High Lane SK6 37 F4
Scaife Rd CW5 204 C3
Scaliot Cl SK22 39 D4
Scar La SY14 198 C1
Sceptre Cl WA12 2 A2
Scholar Green Cty Prim Sch ST7 194 C3
Scholar's Ct L64 66 C4
Scholars' Green La WA13 18 C1
School Ave L64 66 C3
School Bank WA6 101 D3
School Brow Romiley SK6 241 A2
Warrington WA1 16 B3
School Cl Audley ST7 210 A1
Knutsford WA16 56 C1
Marbury SY13 226 C4
Poynton SK12 36 C2
School Cres Crewe CW1 190 C2
Stalybridge SK15 242 D4
School Ct SK3 240 F2
School Field Cl CW3 230 C2
School Gn CH3 182 B1
School Hill L60 40 C4
School La Aldford CH3 163 F1
Antrobus CW9 53 E2
Astbury CW12 178 A4
Audlem CW3 230 A2
Bold Heath WA8 13 F4
Brereton Green CW11 153 F3
Bunbury CW6 168 C1
Burwardsley CH3 184 A3
Cheadle Hulme SK8 35 D4
Cuddington CW8 102 A1
Dunham Town WA14 20 B3
Eaton (nr Congleton) CW12 156 C4
Ellesmere Port L66 69 D4
Elton CH2 72 A2
Frodsham WA6 74 B4
Great Budworth CW9 79 D4
Guilden Sutton CH3 119 F3
Hartford CW8 103 E2
Henbury SK11 111 D3
Hollins Green WA3 11 D1
Irlam M44 11 E3
Lostock CW9 80 A1
Marbury SY13 215 F1
Marton SK11 133 E3
Mickle Trafford CH2 119 F4
Moulton CW9 126 C4
Nantwich CW5 204 C3
Neston L64 66 C3
Neston, Parkgate L64 41 D1
Nether Alderley SK10 86 A3
Norley WA6 100 B3
Ollerton WA16 83 D2
Poynton SK12 36 C2
Runcorn WA7 49 F4
Sandbach, Betchton CW11 175 F3
Sandbach, Ettiley Heath CW11 174 B4
Smallwood CW11 176 C3
Warmingham CW11 173 F4
Warrington WA3 10 B3
Whitley WA4 52 C3
Willaston L64 42 A1
School Mews SK7 35 F4
School Rd Altrincham WA15 238 F3
Ellesmere Port L65 70 A3
Lach Dennis CW9 104 B3
Sale M33 242 A7
Sale M33 242 B7
Warrington WA2 8 B1
Wilmslow SK9 34 B2
Winsford CW7 127 D1
Winsford, Meadowbank CW7 126 C3
School Rd N CW9 104 C3
School Rd S CW9 104 C3
School St Chester CH2 118 C2
Goldborne WA3 3 D4
Haslington CW1 191 E3
Newton-le-W WA12 2 A2
Warrington WA4 16 A2
School Way Northwich CW9 104 A4
Widnes WA8 13 E2
Schools Hill SK8 239 D3
Schooner Cl WA7 50 B3
Scilly Cl L65 70 B1
Scotch Hall La CW9 53 D2
Scotland Rd WA1 16 A3
Scott Ave Crewe CW1 190 C2
Widnes WA8 22 C4
Scott Cl Macclesfield SK10 113 D4
Reddish SK5 240 F8
Rode Heath ST7 193 F4
1 Sandbach CW11 174 B3
Scott Rd SK10 87 D4
Scott St WA2 16 B3
Scott Wlk WA12 2 B1
Scotthorpe Cl SK11 111 F3
Scotton Ave L66 69 D3
Scretton Green Distribution Pk WA4 27 E2
Scroggins La M31 11 F2
Sea Bank CW10 128 B1
Sea La WA7 23 E1
Sea View L64 66 C2
Seabank Rd L60 40 C3
Seabury St WA4 17 D2
Seacombe Dr L66 69 F2
Seacombe Gr SK3 240 B4
Seafield Ave L60 40 C3
Seaford Cl WA7 24 B1
Seaford Pl WA2 8 A2
Seagull Cl CW1 190 C3
Seahill Rd CH1 116 C4
Seal Rd SK7 35 F4
Sealand Cl WA2 8 C1
Sealand Ind Est CH1 117 F1
Sealand Rd Blacon CH1 117 E2
Chester CH1 118 A1
Sealand CH5 116 B3
Sealand Way 1 SK9 34 B2
Seamon's Dr WA14 238 A6
Seamon's Rd WA14 238 A6
Seamons Wlk WA14 238 B5
Seathwaite Cl WA7 49 F3
Seaton Cl CW1 190 A4
Seaton Pk WA7 24 C2
Seaton St CW7 127 E1
Seaview Ave L62 44 A3
Seaville St CH2 237 F3
Secker Ave WA4 16 B1
Secker Cl WA4 16 B1
Second Ave Adlington SK10 36 B1
Crewe CW1 190 C1
Deeside Ind Est CH5 92 C2
Kidsgrove ST7 194 C1
Runcorn WA7 49 F4
Sandbach CW11 175 D3
Second Dig La CW5 219 E4
Second Wood St CW5 204 B3
Sedbergh Gr WA7 49 F3
Sedburgh Cl CW4 130 A2
Seddon Rd WA14 238 D2
Seddon St CW10 128 B1
Sedgefield Cl SK9 34 B1
Sedgefield Rd CH1 118 A1
Sedgewick Cres WA5 6 C3
Sedgmere Ave CW1 190 A4
Sedum Cl CH3 142 A3
Sefton Ave Congleton CW12 157 D1
Widnes WA8 13 D2
Sefton Cres M33 242 B8
Sefton Dr SK9 34 B1
Sefton Rd Chester CH2 119 D2
Sale M33 242 B7
Sefton St WA12 1 C2
Seftons The SK9 34 B1
Selby Cl Poynton SK12 36 B3
Runcorn WA7 24 C2
Selby Gdns SK7 35 E3
Selby Gn L66 69 D3
Selby St Reddish SK4 240 D8
Warrington WA5 15 F3
Selkirk Ave Bebington L62 43 F2
Warrington WA4 17 D2
Selkirk Cl Ellesmere Port L66 68 C3
Macclesfield SK10 86 C1
Selkirk Dr Chester CH4 141 D4
Holmes Chapel CW4 130 A1
Selkirk Rd CH4 141 D4
Seller St CH2 237 F3
Selsdon Ct CH4 141 E4
Selsey Ave SK3 239 F7
Selsey Cl CW1 190 A4
Selsey Dr M20 239 C8
Selworth Ave M33 242 E6
Selworth Cl WA15 238 E6
Selworthy Dr Crewe CW1 190 A4
Warrington WA4 17 E2
Selwyn Cl WA8 13 E2
Selwyn Dr
Cheadle Hulme SK7 35 E4
Sutton Lane Ends SK11 112 C2
Semper Cl CW12 157 D2
Seneschal Ct WA7 49 F3
Senna La Antrobus CW9 53 D1
Comberbach CW9 78 B4
Sennen Cl WA7 50 B3
Sephton Ave WA3 4 C2
Sergeant York Loop WA5 15 D3
Serin Cl WA12 2 B2
Serpentine The CH4 141 D4
Service St SK3 240 B4
Servite Cl L65 69 F3
Set St SK15 242 C1
Sett Cl SK22 39 D4
Seven Sisters La WA16 82 C3
Sevenoaks Cl SK10 87 D1
Sevenoaks Rd SK8 239 B6
Severn Cl Altrincham WA14 238 C6
Biddulph ST6 179 F1
Congleton CW12 156 C1
Macclesfield SK10 86 C1
Warrington WA2 8 C1
Widnes WA8 13 F2
Severn Dr SK7 35 E3
Severn Rd WA3 4 C1
Severn Wlk CW7 127 D1
Severnvale L65 70 A2
Sewell St WA7 23 D1
Sextant Cl WA7 50 B3
Sexton Ave WA9 1 A1
Seymour Chase WA16 82 A4
Seymour Ct WA7 24 B2
Seymour Dr
Ellesmere Port L66 69 F3
Warrington WA1 17 D4
Seymour Gr M33 242 B6
Seymour Rd SK8 35 D4
Shackleton Cl WA5 15 E4
Shadewood Cres WA4 17 D1
Shadewood Rd SK11 112 A3
Shadowmoss Rd M22 33 F4
Shady Brook La CW8 77 E1
Shaftesbury Ave
Chester CH3 119 E1
Penketh WA5 14 C1
Shaftesbury Rd SK3 240 B2
Shaftesbury Way WA5 6 C4
Shaftway Cl WA11 1 C4
Shakerley Ave CW12 156 C2
Shakespeare Cl CW9 104 B4
Shakespeare Dr
Cheadle SK8 239 F6
Crewe CW1 191 D2
Shakespeare Gr WA2 8 B1
Shakespeare Rd
Neston L64 41 F1
Widnes WA8 13 D1
Shalcombe Cl L26 21 D4
Shalford Dr M22 33 E4
Shall Acres L65 69 F3
Shallacres L66 69 F4
Shallcross Ave SK23 65 F2
Shallcross Cres SK23 65 F2
Shallcross Rd SK23 65 F2
Shanklin Cl WA5 14 B3
Shannon Cl Chester CH4 140 C3
Willaston (nr Nantwich) CW5 205 E3
Shargate Cl SK9 34 B1
Sharnbrook Dr CW2 189 E2
Sharon Park Cl WA4 17 E1
Sharp St Warrington WA1 16 B3
Widnes WA8 23 D4
Sharples St SK4 240 E7
Sharpley St SK11 112 B4
Sharston Cres WA16 57 D1
Shavington Ave CH2 118 C2
Shavington Cty High Sch CW2 206 A3
Shavington Cty Prim Sch CW2 206 B2
Shavington Sports Ctr CW2 206 A3
Shavington Way CW9 103 F2
Shaw Dr WA16 57 E2
Shaw Entry WA8 12 A4
Shaw Heath SK2 & SK3 240 E3
Shaw Moor Ave SK15 242 F1
Shaw Rd SK4 240 B8
Shaw Rd S SK3 240 E2
Shaw St Ashton-u-L OL6 242 A3
Culcheth WA3 5 D2
Haydock WA11 1 C3
Macclesfield SK11 112 B4
Runcorn WA7 22 C1
Warrington WA2 16 A3
Shaw's Ave WA2 16 B4
Shaw's Rd WA14 238 D4
Shawcross Fold 5 SK1 240 F6
Shawell Ct WA8 13 F1
Shaws Fold SK9 33 F2
Shaws La
Mottram St Andrew SK10 86 B4
Winsford CW7 126 C2
Winsford CW7 127 D2
Shay La Ashton CH3 122 A4
Hampton SY14 200 A1
Tarvin CH3 121 F2
Shay's La CW6 124 C2
Sheaf Cl CH3 121 E1
Shearbrook La CW4 107 F1
Sheardhall Ave SK12 38 C3
Sheath St CW9 104 A4
Shed La CH3 119 D1
Sheepfield Cl L66 69 E4
Sheerwater Cl WA1 16 C4
Sheffield Cl WA5 15 E3
Sheffield Rd SK14 241 F8
Sheffield Row WA12 7 E4
Sheffield St SK4 240 E7
Sheiling Ct WA14 238 C4
Sheilings The WA3 3 F4
Shelagh Ave WA8 13 D1
Shelbourne Mews SK11 111 F4
Shelburne Dr CW1 191 E3
Sheldon Ave Chester CH3 119 D1
Congleton CW12 157 D1
Sheldon Rd SK7 36 C4
Sheldrake Dr L64 66 C3
Sheldrake Rd WA14 238 B8
Shellbrook Gr 1 SK9 34 B1
Shelley Ave CW9 80 A3
Shelley Cl Crewe CW1 190 C2
Rode Heath ST7 193 F4
Shelley Ct 7 CW11 174 B3
Shelley Dr CW2 189 F1
Shelley Gr WA4 16 C2
Shelley Rd Blacon CH1 117 F3
Widnes WA8 13 D1
Shellow La SK11 134 B3
Shellway Rd L65 71 D2
Shelton Cl WA8 13 F2
Shenton St SK14 241 C8
Shepcroft La WA4 26 B2
Shepherd's Brow WA14 238 A3
Shepherd's La CH2 118 B3
Shepherds Fold Dr CW7 126 B2
Shepherds Row WA7 23 F1
Shepley Cl SK7 36 B4
Shepley St 1 Hyde SK14 241 E6
Stalybridge SK15 242 D2
Sheppard Cl CW1 190 B3
Sheppenhall Gr CW5 217 E1
Sheppenhall La
Newhall CW5 228 B3
Royal's Green CW5 228 B3
Shepperton Cl WA4 26 C3
Shepsides Cl L66 69 E2
Shepton Rd L66 69 F1
Sherborne Cl WA7 24 C2
Sherborne Rd
Cheadle SK3 240 A3
Crewe CW1 190 B3
Sherbourne Ave CH4 141 D3
Sherbourne Cl SK8 35 D3
Sherbourne Rd
Ellesmere Port L65 70 B2
Macclesfield SK11 111 F4
Sherbourne Way WA5 6 C3
Sherbrook Rise SK9 60 B3
Sherbrooke Rd SK12 38 B3
Sheri Dr WA12 2 B1
Sheridan Ave WA3 3 E4
Sheridan Cl CW1 173 D1
Sheringham Cl CH4 140 C3
Sheringham Dr CW1 190 A4
Sheringham Rd WA5 14 C3
Sherlock Ave WA11 1 C4
Sherratt Cl CW12 156 C1
Sherrington's La CH3 199 E4
Sherwin St CW2 190 B1
Sherwood Ave
Cheadle SK8 239 F2
Sale M33 242 D7
Stockport SK4 240 A5
Sherwood Cl WA8 12 B1
Sherwood Cres WA5 6 C3
Sherwood Gr WA6 73 D2
Sherwood Rd SK11 112 B3

Sutton La CW10 ... 151 E4
Sutton Rd Alderley Edge SK9 . 59 F1
Manchester SK4 ... 240 C7
Poynton SK12 ... 37 D1
Sutton St Runcorn WA7 ... 23 D1
Warrington WA1 ... 16 B2
Sutton Way
Ellesmere Port L66 ... 69 F2
1 Wilmslow SK8 ... 34 C3
Sutton Way Cty Jun Sch L66 ... 69 F2
Sutton's La WA8 ... 23 D4
Swaine St SK3 ... 240 E5
Swale Dr WA14 ... 238 C6
Swale Rd L65 ... 70 A4
Swaledale Ave CW12 ... 157 D3
Swaledale Cl Bebington L62 .. 43 F3
Great Sankey WA5 ... 14 B4
Swallow Cl Kidsgrove ST7 ... 195 D1
Macclesfield SK10 ... 113 D4
Warrington WA3 ... 9 F2
Swallow Ct CW7 ... 149 E3
Swallow Dr CW11 ... 175 D4
Swallow St SK1 ... 240 F3
Swallowfield Cl CW2 ... 206 A4
Swallowfield Gdns WA4 ... 26 C3
Swan Ave WA9 ... 1 A1
Swan Bank Congleton CW12 156 B1
Kidsgrove ST7 ... 210 B4
Swan Cl Ellesmere Port L66 ... 69 F2
Kidsgrove ST7 ... 210 B4
Poynton SK12 ... 36 A2
Swan Ct CW8 ... 101 F4
Swan Farm La CW3 ... 232 A1
Swan Gr WA16 ... 106 B4
Swan La Bunbury CW6 ... 185 F4
Cheadle Hulme SK8 ... 35 D4
Swan Rd WA12 ... 1 C2
Swan St Congleton CW12 ... 156 B1
Wilmslow SK9 ... 60 A4
Swanage Cl WA4 ... 16 C1
Swanage Ct CW7 ... 149 E3
Swanbourne Gdns SK3 ... 240 C2
Swanley La CW5 ... 203 E2
Swanlow Ave CW7 ... 149 E3
Swanlow Dr CW7 ... 149 E3
Swanlow La CW7 ... 149 F3
Swanscoe Av SK10 ... 88 A4
Swanscoe Cl CW10 ... 151 D4
Swanscoe La SK10 ... 88 A2
Swanwick Cl CW4 ... 107 E1
Sweet Briar Cres CW2 ... 189 F2
Sweet Brier Cl CW8 ... 78 A2
Sweetenham Cl ST7 ... 193 E2
Sweetfield Gdns L66 ... 69 E4
Sweetfield Rd L66 ... 69 E4
Sweettooth La CW11 ... 175 D4
Swettenham Cl CW11 ... 175 E4
Swettenham Rd
Swettenham CW12 ... 132 A1
Wilmslow SK9 ... 34 B3
Swettenham St SK11 ... 112 C4
Swift Cl Kidsgrove ST7 ... 195 D1
Warrington WA2 ... 8 C2
Wistaston CW2 ... 205 F4
Swinburne Dr CW1 ... 190 C2
Swindale Ave WA2 ... 8 A2
Swinden Cl WA7 ... 24 B1
Swine Market CW5 ... 204 C3
Swineyard La WA16 ... 28 B2
Swinford Ave WA8 ... 13 F1
Swinley Chase SK9 ... 34 C1
Swinleys Hey CH3 ... 142 A4
Swinnerton St CW2 ... 190 B1
Swinton Sq WA16 ... 57 D1
Swireford Rd WA6 ... 73 D1
Swiss Cott SK10 ... 87 D1
Swiss Hill SK9 ... 60 A1
Swithin Rd M22 ... 33 F4
Swynnerton Way WA8 ... 13 D3
Swythamley Cl SK3 ... 240 A4
Swythamley Rd SK3 ... 240 A4
Sycamore Ave Alsager ST7 . 193 F1
Altrincham WA14 ... 238 A5
Congleton CW12 ... 155 F2
Crewe CW1 ... 190 B3
Haydock WA11 ... 1 A3
Newton-le-W WA12 ... 2 B2
Rode Heath ST7 ... 193 F4
Widnes WA8 ... 13 D1
Winsford CW7 ... 149 E4
Sycamore Cl
Ashton-u-L OL6 ... 242 B2
Audlem CW3 ... 230 A2
Biddulph ST6 ... 179 F1
Holmes Chapel CW4 ... 130 B2
Kidsgrove ST7 ... 210 C4
Wilmslow SK9 ... 34 A1
Sycamore Cres
Barnton CW8 ... 78 A2
Hollins Green WA3 ... 11 D1
Macclesfield SK11 ... 112 A4
Sycamore Ct CW5 ... 204 C4
Sycamore Dr Chester CH4 .. 140 C3
Ellesmere Port L66 ... 70 A1
Lymm WA13 ... 18 B2
Middlewich CW10 ... 151 F3
Sutton WA7 ... 50 A2
Sycamore Farm Cl SK10 ... 87 D1
Sycamore Gr
Broughton CH4 ... 139 D2
Sandbach CW11 ... 175 D4
Sycamore La WA5 ... 15 D3
Sycamore Lane Cty Prim Sch WA5 ... 15 D3
Sycamore Rd Partington M31 11 F2
Romiley SK6 ... 241 A4
Runcorn WA7 ... 49 E4
Sycamore Rise SK11 ... 112 A3
Sycamore St Sale M33 ... 242 E6
Stockport SK3 ... 240 B4
Sycamore Wlk SK8 ... 239 D6
Syddal Cr SK7 ... 35 E2
Syddal Gn SK7 ... 35 E3
Syddall Ave SK8 ... 34 B4
Syddall St SK14 ... 241 D6
Sydney Ave M90 ... 33 D4
Sydney Rd Blacon CH1 ... 118 A2
Bramhall SK7 ... 35 F3
Crewe CW1 ... 190 C3
Sydney St Northwich CW8 ... 103 E4
Runcorn WA7 ... 48 B4
Sykes Meadow SK3 ... 240 D2
Sykes St SK14 ... 241 F5
Sylvan Ave Altrincham WA15 238 F8
Sale M33 ... 242 C5
Wilmslow SK9 ... 59 F3
Sylvan Cl CW8 ... 103 E4
Sylvan Gr WA14 ... 238 D5
Symondley Rd SK11 ... 112 C1
Symons Rd M33 ... 242 B7
Synge St WA2 ... 16 B4
Sytch Croft L64 ... 66 C4
Tabley Ave WA8 ... 12 B1
Tabley Cl Knutsford WA16 ... 56 C2
Sandbach CW11 ... 174 C4
Tabley Gr WA16 ... 56 C1
Tabley Hill La
Knutsford WA16 ... 56 A1
Tabley WA16 ... 56 A1
Tabley Ho WA16 ... 81 D4
Tabley Mere Gdns SK8 ... 239 F3
Tabley Rd Crewe CW2 ... 189 F2
Knutsford WA16 ... 56 C2
Wilmslow SK9 ... 34 B3
Tabley St CW9 ... 79 D1
Tabor St SK11 ... 112 C3
Tadgers La WA6 ... 73 E4
Tadman Gr WA14 ... 238 A6
Talbot Ave L64 ... 66 C3
Talbot Cl Neston L64 ... 66 C3
Shavington CW2 ... 206 A2
Warrington WA3 ... 9 F2
Talbot Gdns L64 ... 66 C3
Talbot Rd
Alderley Edge SK9 ... 60 A1
Altrincham WA14 ... 238 B2
Dunham-on-t-H WA6 ... 97 F4
Ellesmere Port L66 ... 69 F2
Sale M33 ... 242 E6
Talbot St Chester CH2 ... 237 E4
Goldborne WA3 ... 3 D4
Stockport SK1 & SK3 ... 240 E5
Talfryn Cl CH5 ... 91 E1
Talisman Cl WA7 ... 50 B4
Talke Rd Alsager ST7 ... 193 F2
Audley ST5 ... 210 C1
Tall Ash Ave CW12 ... 157 D2
Tall Trees Cl CW8 ... 103 E3
Talwrn Green Prim Sch SY14 ... 222 C3
Tamar Cl Congleton CW12 ... 156 C1
Macclesfield SK10 ... 86 C1
Tamar Rd Haydock WA11 ... 1 B3
Kidsgrove ST7 ... 195 D1
Tamar Wlk CW7 ... 127 D1
Tame Cl Biddulph ST6 ... 179 E1
Sandbach CW11 ... 174 C4
Stalybridge SK15 ... 242 F3
Tame St SK15 ... 242 B1
Tame Wlk 13 SK9 ... 34 B1
Tameside Coll of Tech
Ashton-u-L OL6 ... 242 A3
Hyde SK14 ... 241 E6
Tameside General Hospl OL6 ... 242 B4
Tameside L Pk SK14 ... 241 F6
Tamworth Cl SK7 ... 36 B4
Tamworth St WA12 ... 2 A2
Tan House La
Burtonwood WA5 ... 7 D3
Widnes WA8 ... 23 E4
Tanfield Rd M20 ... 239 B8
Tanhouse Ind Est WA8 ... 23 E4
Tankersley Gr WA5 ... 15 D3
Tanner St
Congleton CW12 ... 156 C1
Hyde SK14 ... 241 D7
Tanner's La WA3 ... 3 D4
Tanners La WA2 ... 16 A3
Tannery La Neston L64 ... 66 C4
Penketh WA5 ... 14 B2
Tannery Way WA14 ... 238 E7
Tanyard Dr WA15 ... 32 B4
Tanyard La WA15 ... 32 A3
Tapley Ave SK12 ... 36 C1
Taplow Cl WA4 ... 26 C3
Taplow Gr SK8 ... 239 F2
Target Cl ST7 ... 210 C3
Target Rd L60 ... 40 B4
Tarn Cl CW7 ... 126 B1
Tarn Ct WA1 ... 17 F4
Tarn Mount SK11 ... 112 A3
Tarnbeck WA7 ... 50 B4
Tarns The SK8 ... 239 B3
Tarnway WA3 ... 3 F4
Tarparley Wlk 11 SK9 ... 34 C1
Tarporley CE Contr Prim Sch CW6 ... 146 B1
Tarporley Cl SK3 ... 240 D1
Tarporley Cty High Sch CW6 ... 146 B1
Tarporley Rd
Common Side CW6, CW8 ... 124 B3
Duddon CW6 ... 145 D3
Ellesmere Port L66 ... 69 F2
Little Leigh WA4 ... 52 A1
Stretton WA4 ... 52 B4
Tarvin CH3 ... 121 E1
Utkinton CW6 ... 146 C3
Whitchurch SY13 ... 225 F2
Whitley WA4 ... 52 B2
Tarran Gr M34 ... 241 B5
Tarran Pl WA14 ... 238 E6
Tarrant Ct CH1 ... 94 C1
Tarvin Ave CW2 ... 189 E2
Tarvin Cl Ellesmere Port L65 .. 70 B2
Goldborne WA3 ... 3 F4
Macclesfield SK11 ... 112 C3
Middlewich CW10 ... 151 E3
Runcorn WA7 ... 49 E3
Tarvin Cty Prim Sch CH3 .. 121 D1
Tarvin Rd Alvanley WA6 ... 73 F2
Bebington L62 ... 43 F2
Chester, Boughton CH3 ... 119 D1
Chester, Vicarscross CH3 ... 119 F1
Christleton CH3 ... 120 B2
Frodsham WA6 ... 73 F2
Manley WA6 ... 99 D2
Tarvin CH3 ... 120 C2
Tarvin Sands Industries CH3 ... 121 D2
Tarvin Way SK9 ... 34 B3
Tasman Cl WA5 ... 15 E4
Tate Cl WA8 ... 12 B1
Tate Dr CW1 ... 191 E2
Tattenhall La Beeston CH3 . 167 D1
Beeston CW6 ... 167 F1
Tattenhall CH3 ... 167 D1
Tattenhall Rd CH3 ... 166 B2
Tatton Cl Alsager ST7 ... 193 E2
Chester CH4 ... 140 C3
Davenham CW9 ... 103 F2
Winsford CW7 ... 126 B1
Tatton Ct SK4 ... 240 C8
Tatton Dr CW11 ... 175 E4
Tatton Hall WA16 ... 56 C4
Tatton Lodge WA16 ... 57 D1
Tatton Park WA16 ... 57 D4
Tatton Pl M33 ... 242 B7
Tatton Rd Crewe CW2 ... 189 F1
Denton M34 ... 241 A5
Sale M33 ... 242 B7
Wythenshawe SK8 ... 34 C3
Tatton Rd S SK4 ... 240 C8
Tatton St Knutsford WA16 ... 57 D1
Stalybridge SK15 ... 242 E1
7 Stockport SK1 ... 240 F5
Tatton Stile WA16 ... 58 A2
Tavener Cl L63 ... 43 E3
Tavistock Rd WA5 ... 14 C2
Tavlin Ave WA5 ... 7 F1
Tawney Cl ST7 ... 195 D1
Taxal & Fernilee CE Contr Prim Sch SK23 ... 65 E3
Taxal Lodge Sch SK23 ... 65 E3
Taxal Moor Rd SK23 ... 65 E2
Taxi Rd M90 ... 33 D4
Taxmere Cl CW11 ... 174 C4
Tay Cl ST6 ... 179 F1
Taylor Ind Est WA3 ... 4 C1
Taylor Rd Altrincham WA14 238 A5
Haydock WA11 ... 1 C4
Taylor St Hyde SK14 ... 241 F7
Stalybridge SK15 ... 242 E1
Warrington WA4 ... 16 A1
Widnes WA8 ... 13 E1
Taylor's La WA5 ... 14 A1
Taylors La CW1 ... 192 B1
Taylors Row WA7 ... 23 E1
Teal Ave WA16 ... 57 D1
Teal Cl Altrincham WA14 ... 238 B8
Warrington WA2 ... 8 C2
Warrington, Oakwood WA3 ... 9 F2
Winsford CW7 ... 149 E3
Teals Way L60 ... 40 C4
Tebay Rd L62 ... 43 F4
Tedder Dr M22 ... 33 F4
Tedder Sq WA8 ... 22 B4
Teddington Cl WA4 ... 26 C3
Tees Ct L65 ... 70 A4
Teesdale Cl WA5 ... 14 C4
Teesdale Rd WA11 ... 1 B4
Tefler Ct CW10 ... 151 F3
Tegg's Nose Ctry Pk SK11 . 113 E3
Teggsnose La SK11 ... 113 E3
Tegid Way CH4 ... 140 B3
Tegsnose Mt SK11 ... 113 E2
Telegraph Rd L60 ... 41 D4
Telford Cl Congleton CW12 . 157 D1
Kidsgrove ST7 ... 210 C4
Macclesfield SK10 ... 88 A1
Widnes WA8 ... 12 B2
Telford Gdns 3 CW11 ... 174 C2
Telford Pl CW5 ... 204 B3
Telford Rd L65 ... 70 C2
Telford Way Audlem CW3 ... 229 F2
Chester CH4 ... 140 C3
Middlewich CW10 ... 128 C1
Telford's Quay L65 ... 70 B4
Tempest Rd SK9 ... 60 B1
Temple Moor Inf Sch M33 ... 242 E6
Temple Rd M33 ... 242 D6
Templeton Cl WA14 ... 238 B6
Tenby Cl WA5 ... 7 F1
Tenby Dr WA7 ... 23 E1
Tenby Rd Macclesfield SK11 . 111 F3
Stockport SK3 ... 240 B3
Tennyson Ave CW1 ... 190 C2
Tennyson Cl
Macclesfield SK11 ... 111 F3
Rode Heath ST7 ... 193 F4
Stockport SK4 ... 240 B6
Wistaston CW2 ... 190 A1
Tennyson Dr WA2 ... 8 B1
Tennyson Rd Cheadle SK8 ... 239 F6
Ellesmere Port L65 ... 70 A2
Widnes WA8 ... 13 D1
Tennyson Wlk CH1 ... 118 A3
Tensing Cl WA5 ... 15 D4
Terence Ave WA1 ... 16 C3
Terminal Rd E M90 ... 33 D4
Terminal Rd N M22 ... 33 E4
Terminal Rd S M90 ... 33 D4
Tern Ave ST7 ... 195 E1
Tern Cl Altrincham WA14 ... 238 B8
Widnes WA8 ... 13 D2
Tern Dr SK12 ... 36 A2
Terra Nova Sch CW4 ... 108 B1
Terrace Rd WA8 ... 23 D3
Terrick Rd SY13 ... 226 A1
Tetchill Cl Ellesmere Port L66 69 E1
Runcorn WA7 ... 50 B4
Tetton La CW10 ... 151 F2
Tewkesbury Cl
Cheadle Hulme SK8 ... 35 D3
Chester CH2 ... 118 B4
Ellesmere Port CH1 ... 94 C4
Middlewich CW10 ... 128 A1
Poynton SK12 ... 36 B2
Tewkesbury Dr SK10 ... 87 F2
Tewkesbury Rd
Cheadle SK3 ... 240 B2
Goldborne WA3 ... 3 D4
Thackeray Dr CH3 ... 119 E2
Thames Cl Congleton CW12 156 C1
Warrington WA2 ... 8 B1
Thames Dr ST6 ... 179 E1
Thames Gdns L65 ... 70 A2
Thames Rd WA3 ... 4 C1
Thames Side L65 ... 70 A2
Thamesdale L65 ... 70 A2
Thaxted Wlk M22 ... 33 E4
Theatre Ct CW9 ... 103 F4
Thelwall Cl 3 WA15 ... 238 E6
Thelwall Cty Inf Sch WA4 ... 17 E2
Thelwall Cty Jun Sch WA4 . 17 E2
Thelwall Ind Est WA4 ... 17 E2
Thelwall La WA4 ... 17 D2
Thelwall Massey Hall Sch WA4 ... 17 F1
Thelwall New Rd WA4 ... 17 E2
Thelwall Rd
Ellesmere Port L66 ... 69 F2
Sale M33 ... 242 E5
Theobald Rd WA14 ... 238 D1
Thetford Cl SK10 ... 87 E2
Thetford Rd WA5 ... 14 C3
Thewlis St WA5 ... 15 F3
Third Ave Adlington SK10 ... 36 B1
Crewe CW1 ... 190 C1
Deeside Ind Est CH5 ... 92 C1
Kidsgrove ST7 ... 194 C1
Runcorn WA7 ... 49 F4
Sandbach CW11 ... 175 D3
Thirlmere SK11 ... 111 F3
Thirlmere Ave WA2 ... 8 B2
Thirlmere Cl
Alderley Edge SK9 ... 59 F1
Frodsham WA6 ... 49 E1
Holmes Chapel CW4 ... 130 A2
Thirlmere Ct CW12 ... 156 A1
Thirlmere Dr WA13 ... 18 C2
Thirlmere Rd Chester CH2 . 119 D3
Ellesmere Port L65 ... 70 A1
Neston L64 ... 66 C3
Partington M31 ... 11 F2
Wistaston CW2 ... 190 A1
Thirlmere Way 1 WA8 ... 22 B4
Thirsk Cl WA7 ... 49 E3
Thistle Sq M31 ... 11 F1
Thistle Wlk M31 ... 11 E1
Thistleton Cl SK11 ... 112 B3
Thistlewood Dr SK9 ... 60 B4
Thomas Cl Alsager ST7 ... 193 F2
Blacon CH1 ... 117 F3
Denton M34 ... 241 A8
Ellesmere Port L65 ... 70 A1
Mickle Trafford CH2 ... 119 F4
Thomas Pl CW7 ... 127 D1
Thomas St
Altrincham WA15 ... 238 E4
Biddulph ST6 ... 179 E1
Congleton CW12 ... 156 C2
Crewe CW1 ... 190 B2
Goldborne WA3 ... 3 D4
Kidsgrove ST7 ... 210 B4
Packmoor ST7 ... 195 F1
Romiley SK6 ... 241 A3
Runcorn WA7 ... 23 D2
Stockport SK1 ... 240 F3
18 Widnes WA8 ... 23 D4
Thomas St W SK1 & SK2 ... 240 F3
Thomas Trad Ctr M44 ... 11 F4
Thomas Wedge CE Contr Jun Sch The CH1 ... 94 A1
Thomasons Bridge La WA4 ... 25 F3
Thompson Ave WA3 ... 4 C2
Thompson Cl WA12 ... 2 B1
Thompson St WA3 ... 9 F2
Thomson St SK3 ... 240 E4
Thoresway Rd SK9 ... 59 F3
Thoriby Rd WA3 ... 4 C2
Thorley Gr CW2 ... 190 A1
Thorley La M90 ... 33 D4
Thorley Mews SK7 ... 35 F4
Thorn Cl Penketh WA5 ... 14 C
Runcorn WA7 ... 49 E
Thorn Dr SK8 ... 34 A
Thorn Gr Altrincham WA15 ... 238 E
Cheadle Hulme SK8 ... 35 D
Sale M33 ... 242 B
Thorn La CW8 ... 103 E
Thorn Rd Cheadle Hulme SK7 . 35 F
Runcorn WA7 ... 49 E
Warrington WA1 ... 17 D
Thorn Tree Cl L24 ... 21 F
Thorn Wlk M31 ... 11 E
Thornberry Cl CH1 ... 117 D
Thornbury Ave WA3 ... 3 F
Thornbush Cl WA3 ... 3 F
Thorne Cl SK10 ... 87 D
Thorne Dr L66 ... 69 D
Thorney Dr SK7 ... 35 E
Thorneyholme Dr WA16 ... 57 D
Thornfield Cl WA3 ... 3 E
Thornfield Hey SK9 ... 60 C
Thornfield Rd SK4 ... 240 A
Thornfield Sch SK4 ... 240 A
Thorngrove Dr SK9 ... 60 B
Thorngrove Hill SK9 ... 60 B
Thorngrove Rd SK9 ... 60 B
Thornhills WA8 ... 12 A
Thornleigh Ave L62 ... 43 F
Thornleigh Dr L66 ... 69 F
Thornley Cres SK6 ... 241 A
Thornley Rd Dukinfield M34 241 A
Lymm WA13 ... 18 B
Thornley St SK14 ... 241 E
Thornsgreen Rd M22 ... 33 E
Thornton WA8 ... 22 C
Thornton Ave SK11 ... 112 A
Thornton Bank CW6 ... 169 E
Thornton Common Rd
Bebington L63 ... 43 D
Thornton Hough L63 ... 42 B
Thornton Cres L60 ... 41 D
Thornton Dr Chester CH2 ... 118 B
Wilmslow M22 ... 34 B
Wistaston CW2 ... 206 A
Thornton Gate M22 & SK8 . 239 A
Thornton Green La CH2 ... 96 C
Thornton Hough Cty Prim Sch L63 ... 42 A
Thornton Mews L66 ... 69 D
Thornton Pl 4 SK4 ... 240 B
Thornton Rd Cheadle SK8 ... 34 B
Ellesmere Port L65 ... 70 C
Great Sankey WA5 ... 15 D
Thornton Sq SK11 ... 112 A
Thorntondale Dr WA5 ... 14 C
Thorntree Gn WA4 ... 27 D
Thornway Bollington SK10 ... 88 A
Cheadle Hulme SK7 ... 35 E
High Lane SK6 ... 37 F
Thornwythe Gr L66 ... 69 F2
Thornycroft CW7 ... 126 A1
Thornycroft Cl SK11 ... 111 F1
Thornycroft St 16 SK11 ... 112 C4
Thorold Gr M33 ... 242 E6
Thorp St SK10 ... 112 B4
Thorpe Cl CW1 ... 189 F4
Thorsby Ave SK14 ... 241 F6
Thorsby Rd WA15 ... 238 E5
Thowler La WA14 ... 30 A3
Threaphurst La SK7 ... 37 E4
Three Fields Cl CW12 ... 156 A2
Threeways CW8 ... 101 E2
Thresher Cl M33 ... 242 F5
Throstle Bank St SK14 ... 241 C8
Thurlestone Rd WA14 ... 238 B6
Thurlow WA3 ... 3 F4
Thursfield Ave ST7 ... 195 D2
Thursfield Prim Sch ST7 ... 195 F2
Thurstaston Rd L60 ... 40 C4
Thurston Cl WA5 ... 15 E3
Thurston Gn SK9 ... 60 A1
Thurston Rd CH4 ... 140 C3
Thynne St WA1 ... 16 A2
Tib St SK14 ... 241 A6
Tibb St ST7 ... 209 F1
Tibbs Cross La WA8 ... 13 E4
Tidal La WA1 ... 16 C4
Tideswell Cl SK8 ... 34 B4
Tideswell Rd SK7 ... 36 C4
Tidnock Ave CW12 ... 156 C3
Tiffild Ct CW7 ... 127 D2
Tilbury Pl WA7 ... 50 C3
Tildsley Cres WA7 ... 48 C3
Tile La WA8 ... 12 A3
Tilestone Paddocks CW6 . 168 C3
Tilewright Cl ST7 ... 195 D1
Tillard Ave SK3 ... 240 B4
Tilley St WA1 ... 16 B3
Tilman Cl WA5 ... 15 D4
Tilston Ave WA4 ... 17 D2
Tilston Parochial CE Contr Prim Sch SY14 ... 198 A2
Tilston Rd Edge Green SY14 213 D3
Malpas SY14 ... 213 D3
Tilston Wlk 5 SK9 ... 34 C1
Tilstone Cl
Hough Common CW2 ... 206 C1
Northwich CW9 ... 104 A3
Timber La CW9 ... 103 F4
Timber St SK10 ... 87 F1
Timberfields Rd CH1 ... 117 D4
Timberley Ave WA4 ... 17 D2
Timbersbrook Gr 4 SK9 ... 34 B1
Timberscombe Gdns WA1 .. 17 F3
Timbrell Ave CW1 ... 190 A3
Timmis Cl WA2 ... 9 D2
Timmis Cres WA8 ... 13 D1
Timperley St WA8 ... 23 D4

Victoria Rd
- Altrincham WA15 .... 238 D3
- Broughton CH4 .... 140 B3
- Chester CH1 .... 237 D3
- Chester CH2 .... 237 D4
- Ellesmere Port L65 ...... 70 B3
- Great Sankey WA5 ...... 15 C2
- Macclesfield SK10 ...... 87 D1
- Neston L64 ...... 67 D3
- Newton-le-W WA12 ...... 2 B2
- Northwich CW9 ...... 104 A4
- Penketh WA5 ...... 14 B2
- Runcorn WA7 ...... 23 D1
- Sale M33 ...... 242 D6
- Warrington WA4 ...... 16 C1
- Warrington, Stockton Heath WA4 ...... 16 B1
- Widnes WA8 ...... 23 D3
- Wilmslow SK9 ...... 60 A3

Victoria Road Cty Prim Sch Northwich CW9 ...... 104 A4
- Runcorn WA7 ...... 23 D1

Victoria Sq
- Warrington WA4 ...... 16 B1
- 6 Winsford CW7 ...... 149 D4

Victoria St
- Altrincham WA14 ...... 238 D5
- Crewe CW1 ...... 190 B2
- Hyde SK14 ...... 241 F8
- Knutsford WA16 ...... 56 C1
- New Mills SK22 ...... 39 D3
- Northwich CW9 ...... 79 F1
- Sandbach CW11 ...... 175 D4
- Stalybridge SK15 ...... 242 C2
- Warrington WA1 ...... 16 B3
- Widnes WA8 ...... 23 D4

Victoria Way SK7 ...... 35 E3
Victoria Wlk 2 SK10 ...... 112 C4
Victory Rd M44 ...... 11 E2
Vienna Rd SK3 ...... 240 D2
Vienna Rd E SK3 ...... 240 E2
Viewlands Dr SK9 ...... 34 B1
Villa Rd CH5 ...... 116 A4
Villagate La WA4 ...... 27 E3
Village Cl Lostock CW9 ...... 105 D4
- Runcorn WA7 ...... 50 A4
- Warrington WA4 ...... 17 F2
Village Ct SK9 ...... 34 B1
Village La WA4 ...... 52 B2
Village Rd Christleton CH3 .. 142 C4
- Great Barrow CH3 ...... 120 C3
- Heswall L60 ...... 40 C4
Village The Astbury CW12 .. 178 A4
- Burton L64 ...... 67 E1
- Prestbury SK10 ...... 86 C3
Village Way SK9 ...... 34 B1
Villars St WA1 ...... 16 B3
Villiers Russell Cl CW1 .. 190 B3
Villiers St
- Ashton-u-L OL6 ...... 242 A2
- Hyde SK14 ...... 241 F6
Vincent Cl WA5 ...... 15 E4
Vincent Dr CH4 ...... 141 E3
Vincent St Crewe CW1 ...... 190 C2
- Macclesfield SK11 ...... 112 B4
Vine Bank Rd ST7 ...... 195 D1
Vine Cl SK11 ...... 112 A3
Vine Cres WA5 ...... 14 B4
Vine Rd L66 ...... 69 F1
Vine St Bollington SK10 ...... 88 A4
- Runcorn WA7 ...... 23 D1
- Widnes WA8 ...... 23 D4
Vine Tree Ave Crewe CW2 . 190 A1
- Shavington CW2 ...... 206 A3
Vine Tree Cty Prim Sch CW2 ...... 190 A1
Violet Cl WA3 ...... 9 E3
Violet St Stockport SK2 ...... 240 F2
- Widnes WA8 ...... 23 D4
Virginia Chase SK8 ...... 34 C4
Virginia Dr CH1 ...... 117 E2
Viscount Dr Cheadle SK8 .... 34 B4
- Wythenshawe WA15 ...... 32 C4
Vista Ave WA12 ...... 2 A2
Vista Rd Haydock WA12 ...... 2 A3
- Newton-le-W WA12 ...... 2 A3
- Runcorn WA7 ...... 49 D4
Vista The M44 ...... 11 E2
Vista Way WA12 ...... 2 A2
Volunteer Ave CW5 ...... 204 C3
Volunteer Fields CW5 ...... 204 C3
Volunteer St Chester CH1 ... 237 E2
- Frodsham WA6 ...... 49 E1
Vose Cl WA5 ...... 15 E3
Vulcan Cl Newton-le-W WA12 ... 2 B1
- Warrington WA2 ...... 8 C1
Vyrnwy Rd CH4 ...... 140 B3

Waddington Cl
- Goldborne WA3 ...... 3 F4
- Warrington WA2 ...... 8 C1
Wade Cres CW8 ...... 78 A2
Wade Deacon Cty High Sch WA8 ...... 13 D1
Wade St CW9 ...... 79 D1
Wadebrook Gr 16 SK9 ...... 34 B1
Wades La CW7 ...... 126 B2
Wadeson Way WA3 ...... 9 D4
Wadham Gdns SK6 ...... 241 C4
Wadham St WA5 ...... 238 F1
Wadsworth Cl SK9 ...... 34 C4
Wagg St CW12 ...... 156 B1
Waggs Rd CW12 ...... 156 B1
Wagon La WA11 ...... 1 A3
Waine St CW1 ...... 190 B3

Wainwright Rd WA14 ...... 238 C5
Wainwright St SK16 ...... 242 A1
Waitney Croft SK10 ...... 113 D4
Wakefield Cres SK6 ...... 241 A1
Wakefield Rd
- Ellesmere Port L66 ...... 69 F1
- Stalybridge SK15 ...... 242 E3
Wakefield St WA3 ...... 3 D4
Wakefield Wlk M34 ...... 241 A5
Wakeham Cl SK11 ...... 111 F4
Wakes Meadow CW6 ...... 185 F4
Walden Cl WA4 ...... 17 E2
Walden Dr CH1 ...... 93 E4
Waldon Ave SK8 ...... 239 D5
Waldon Rd SK11 ...... 112 A3
Waldron Gdns CW2 ...... 189 F1
Waldron Rd CW1 ...... 191 E2
Waldron's La CW1 ...... 173 E1
Walfield Ave CW12 ...... 156 B3
Walford Ave CW2 ...... 190 A2
Walgrove Cl CW12 ...... 156 A2
Walker Ave SK15 ...... 242 F2
Walker Cl Haslington CW1 .. 191 E2
- Hyde SK14 ...... 241 F6
Walker Dr CW10 ...... 151 E4
Walker Fold SK14 ...... 241 F6
Walker La Hyde SK14 ...... 241 F6
- Sutton Lane Ends SK11 ...... 112 C1
Walker St Chester CH2 ...... 237 F4
- Crewe CW1 ...... 190 A3
- 7 Macclesfield SK11 ...... 112 B4
- Stockport SK1 ...... 240 E5
- Warrington WA3 ...... 16 A3
Walkers La
- Ellesmere Port L66 ...... 69 E3
- Penketh WA5 ...... 14 C2
- Scholar Green ST7 ...... 177 D1
- Tarporley CW6 ...... 146 B3
Walkersgreen Rd ST5 ...... 210 B1
Wall Fields Rd CW5 ...... 204 C4
Wall Hill Way WA8 ...... 76 C2
Wall La CW5 ...... 204 C3
Wallace Ct CW7 ...... 127 E1
Wallace St Northwich CW8 .. 103 F4
- Widnes WA8 ...... 23 D4
Wallcroft L64 ...... 68 A4
Waller St WA11 ...... 112 C3
Wallerscote Cty Prim Sch CW8 ...... 102 C4
Wallerscote Rd CW8 ...... 102 C4
Walleys La CW5 ...... 203 E4
Wallfields Cl CW5 ...... 204 C4
Wallhill La CW11 ...... 177 E4
Wallingford Rd SK9 ...... 34 B3
Wallis St Crewe CW1 ...... 190 B2
- Warrington WA4 ...... 16 A2
Wallrake L60 ...... 40 C4
Walls Ave CH1 ...... 118 A1
Wallsend Ct WA8 ...... 12 C2
Wallworth's Bank CW12 .. 156 C1
Walmer Pl CW7 ...... 149 E3
Walmoor Pk CH3 ...... 119 D1
Walmsley St
- Newton-le-W WA12 ...... 2 B2
- Reddish SK5 ...... 240 F7
- Widnes WA8 ...... 23 E4
Walnut Ave CW8 ...... 102 B4
Walnut Cl Chester CH2 ...... 118 B4
- Warrington WA1 ...... 17 F4
- Wilmslow SK9 ...... 60 C4
Walnut Croft CW3 ...... 180 C3
Walnut Dr CW7 ...... 127 D1
Walnut Gr
- Ellesmere Port L66 ...... 70 A1
- Sale M33 ...... 242 A6
Walnut La CW8 ...... 103 D3
Walnut Rd M31 ...... 11 E2
Walnut Rise CW12 ...... 156 A1
Walnut Tree La CW11 ...... 153 D2
Walnut Tree Rd SK3 ...... 240 A4
Walpole Cl CW1 ...... 191 E3
Walpole Gr WA7 ...... 8 B1
Walpole Rd WA7 ...... 49 E3
Walpole St CH2 ...... 237 D4
Walsh Cl WA12 ...... 2 B3
Walsingham Dr WA7 ...... 24 B1
Walsingham Rd WA5 ...... 14 C3
Walter St Chester CH2 ...... 237 E4
- Warrington WA1 ...... 16 C4
- Widnes WA8 ...... 13 E1
Walthall St CW2 ...... 190 B1
Waltham Ave WA3 ...... 5 E4
Waltham Ct WA7 ...... 24 C2
Waltham Dr SK8 ...... 35 D3
Waltham Pl CH4 ...... 141 D3
Walton Ave WA5 ...... 14 C3
Walton Gr ST7 ...... 210 B4
Walton Hall WA4 ...... 25 F3
Walton Heath Dr SK10 ...... 87 E2
Walton Heath Rd WA4 ...... 16 A1
Walton Lea Rd
- Higher Walton WA4 ...... 25 F4
- Warrington WA4 ...... 26 A4
Walton New Rd WA4 ...... 26 A4
Walton Pl CH1 ...... 117 F2
Walton Rd
- Altrincham WA14 ...... 238 B5
- Culcheth WA3 ...... 4 C2
- Warrington WA4 ...... 26 B4
Walton St Runcorn WA7 ...... 23 D1
- 3 Stockport SK1 ...... 240 F3
Walton Way Denton M34 ...... 241 B5
- Kidsgrove ST7 ...... 210 B4
Waltons The CW4 ...... 141 F3
Wansfel Pl WA2 ...... 8 A2
War Memorial Hospl CW6 146 B1
Warbreck Gr M33 ...... 242 D5
Warburton Bridge Rd WA3 . 11 D1

Warburton Cl
- Altrincham WA15 ...... 32 B3
- Lymm WA13 ...... 19 D2
- Romiley SK6 ...... 241 A1
Warburton Dr WA15 ...... 32 B3
Warburton La M31, WA13 ...... 11 F1
Warburton Rd 7 SK9 ...... 34 B2
Warburton St WA4 ...... 16 B1
Warburton View WA3 ...... 11 D1
Ward Ave SK10 ...... 88 A4
Ward Cl WA5 ...... 7 D1
Ward La SK12 ...... 38 C2
Ward St SK14 ...... 241 E6
Ward's La CW11 ...... 153 E3
Ward's Terr CH2 ...... 118 C2
Wardle Ave CW5 ...... 187 E4
Wardle Cres SK11 ...... 111 F1
Wardle Mews CW10 ...... 151 E4
Wardle Ind Est CW5 ...... 187 D4
Wardle Rd M33 ...... 242 C6
Wardley Rd WA4 ...... 16 A1
Wardour Cl SK11 ...... 111 F4
Wardour St WA5 ...... 15 F3
Wards La CW12 ...... 179 E4
Wareham Cl WA1 ...... 17 E4
Wareham Dr CW1 ...... 190 A4
Warford Ave SK12 ...... 37 D1
Warford Cres SK9 ...... 84 A4
Warford Hall (Mary Dendy Hospl) SK9 ...... 84 A3
Warford La WA16 ...... 59 D1
Wargrave CE Prim Sch WA12 ...... 2 B1
Wargrave House Sch WA12 ...... 2 B1
Wargrave Mews WA12 ...... 2 B1
Wargrave Rd
- Newton-le-W WA12 ...... 2 B1
- Newton-le-W, Wargrave WA12 2 A2
Warham St CW9 ...... 60 A4
Waring Ave St Helens WA9 .... 1 A1
- Warrington WA4 ...... 16 C3
Warkworth Cl WA8 ...... 12 B2
Warkworth Ct L65 ...... 70 C2
Warley Cl SK8 ...... 239 E6
Warmingham CE Aided Prim Sch CW11 ...... 173 F4
Warmingham La
- Middlewich CW10 ...... 151 E3
- Sandbach CW11 ...... 174 A4
Warmingham Rd
- Crewe CW1 ...... 173 D2
- Sandbach CW1 ...... 173 E2
Warnley Cl WA8 ...... 12 B2
Warren Ave Cheadle SK8 .... 239 D5
- Heswall L60 ...... 40 B4
- Knutsford WA16 ...... 56 C1
- Lostock CW9 ...... 80 A2
Warren Cl Knutsford WA16 ... 56 C1
- Middlewich CW10 ...... 151 D4
- Poynton SK12 ...... 36 A2
Warren Croft WA7 ...... 50 B4
Warren Ct Ellesmere Port L66 69 E2
- Frodsham WA6 ...... 74 B3
Warren Dr Altrincham WA15 .. 32 B4
- Appleton WA4 ...... 26 B4
- Broughton CH4 ...... 139 D2
- Ellesmere Port L66 ...... 69 F4
- Newton-le-W WA12 ...... 2 C2
- Warren SK11 ...... 111 E1
Warren Gr SK11 ...... 111 E1
Warren La Hartford CW8 ...... 103 D2
- Warrington WA1 ...... 17 E4
Warren Lea SK12 ...... 36 C3
Warren Rd Appleton WA4 ...... 26 B4
- Stockport SK3 ...... 240 E2
- Warrington WA2 ...... 8 B1
Warren St SK1 ...... 240 F6
Warren The CW8 ...... 101 E3
Warren Way Tarporley CW6 168 B4
- Wilmslow SK9 ...... 60 C4
Warrener St M33 ...... 242 D6
Warrilow Heath Rd ST5 ...... 210 B1
Warrington Ave
- Crewe CW1 ...... 190 B3
- Ellesmere Port L66 ...... 70 A1
Warrington Bank Quay Sta WA5 ...... 15 F2
Warrington Bsns Pk WA2 .... 8 B1
Warrington Central Sta WA2 ...... 16 A3
Warrington Collegiate Inst Padgate Campus WA2 ...... 9 D2
Warrington District General Hospl WA5 ...... 15 F3
Warrington La WA13 ...... 19 F2
Warrington Rd
- Bold Heath WA8 ...... 13 E4
- Comberbach CW9 ...... 78 B4
- Croft WA3 ...... 9 F4
- Cronton L35 ...... 12 C4
- Cuddington CW8 ...... 102 A3
- Dunham-on-t-H WA6 ...... 97 E3
- Glazebury WA3 ...... 5 E3
- Goldborne WA12 ...... 3 D3
- Hatton WA4 ...... 25 F2
- Little Leigh CW8 ...... 77 D3
- Lymm WA13 ...... 18 A2
- Mere WA16 ...... 56 B4
- Mickle Trafford CH2 ...... 119 F4
- Penketh WA5 ...... 14 C2
- Runcorn, Castlefields WA7 ...... 23 F1
- Runcorn, Manor Park WA7 ...... 24 A2
- Warrington WA3 ...... 9 F4
- Warrington, Locking Stumps WA3 ...... 9 E2
- Widnes WA8 ...... 13 E1
- Widnes, Moss Bank WA8 ...... 23 E4

Warrington Road Cty Prim Sch WA8 ...... 13 E1
Warrington St SK15 ...... 242 E1
Warrington Tech Coll North Campus WA2 ...... 8 A1
Warton Cl Bramhall SK7 ...... 36 A4
- Penketh WA5 ...... 15 D2
Warwick Ave
- Great Sankey WA5 ...... 14 B4
- Newton-le-W WA12 ...... 2 B1
- Warrington WA5 ...... 15 F4
Warwick Cl Kidsgrove ST7 .. 195 D2
- Knutsford WA16 ...... 57 E1
- Macclesfield SK11 ...... 111 F3
- Manchester SK4 ...... 240 D8
- Neston L64 ...... 66 C3
Warwick Ct
- Ellesmere Port L65 ...... 70 C1
- Manchester SK4 ...... 240 C7
Warwick Cty Prim Sch SK11 ...... 111 F3
Warwick Dr
- Altrincham WA15 ...... 238 F1
- Hazel Grove SK7 ...... 36 B4
- Sale M33 ...... 242 D6
Warwick Mall SK8 ...... 239 D6
Warwick Pl CW7 ...... 149 E3
Warwick Rd
- Altrincham WA15 ...... 238 E1
- Blacon CH1 ...... 117 F3
- Irlam M44 ...... 11 E3
- Macclesfield SK11 ...... 111 F3
- Manchester SK4 ...... 240 C7
- Romiley SK6 ...... 241 A2
Warwick Wlk SK11 ...... 111 F3
Wasdale Dr SK8 ...... 239 B3
Wasdale Gr CW1 ...... 173 D1
Wasdale Terr SK15 ...... 242 D4
Wash La Allostock WA16 ...... 106 C2
- Warrington WA4 ...... 16 C2
Washington Cl ST6 ...... 179 E1
Washington Dr WA5 ...... 15 D3
Washway Rd M33 ...... 242 A6
Wasley Cl WA2 ...... 8 C2
Waste La Cuddington CW8 ... 101 F2
- Kelsall CW6 ...... 122 C2
Watch La CW11 ...... 174 A3
Water La WA3 ...... 60 A4
Water Lode CW5 ...... 204 C3
Water Rd SK15 ...... 242 C2
Water St Bollington SK10 ...... 88 A4
- Hyde SK14 ...... 241 D6
- Macclesfield SK11 ...... 112 B4
Water St continued
- Newcastle-u-L ST5 ...... 210 B1
- Newton-le-W WA12 ...... 2 B2
- Northwich CW9 ...... 104 A4
- Runcorn WA7 ...... 23 D2
- Stalybridge SK15 ...... 242 D2
- Stockport SK1 ...... 240 F7
- Widnes WA8 ...... 23 D3
Water Tower (Mus) CH1 .. 118 A1
Water Tower Rd L64 ...... 41 F1
Water Tower St CH1 ...... 237 D3
Waterbank Row CW9 ...... 103 F4
Waterbridge Ct WA4 ...... 26 B4
Waterfoot La SK23 ...... 65 E3
Waterford Ave SK6 ...... 241 F2
Waterford Dr L64 ...... 67 D4
Waterford Pl SK8 ...... 34 A4
Waterford Way WA7 ...... 50 B3
Watergate Row CH1 ...... 237 D2
Watergate Sq CH1 ...... 237 D2
Watergate St CH1 ...... 237 D2
Waterhouse Ave SK10 ...... 87 F4
Waterloo Gr ST7 ...... 195 D1
Waterloo La CW6 ...... 74 C1
Waterloo Rd Bramhall SK7 ... 35 F4
- Chester CH2 ...... 118 B2
- Haslington CW1 ...... 191 E2
- Northwich CW8 ...... 103 F4
- Poynton SK12 ...... 37 D1
- Romiley SK6 ...... 241 E2
- 1 Runcorn WA7 ...... 22 C1
- Runcorn WA7 ...... 22 C2
- Stalybridge SK15 ...... 242 D2
- Stockport SK1 ...... 240 F5
- Widnes WA8 ...... 23 D3
Waterloo St OL6 ...... 242 A4
Waterloo St W SK11 ...... 112 B4
Watermeetings La SK6 ...... 241 F1
Watermill Dr SK11 ...... 112 C4
Waters Edge CW9 ...... 78 B2
Waters Gn SK11 ...... 112 B4
Waters Reach SK12 ...... 36 C3
Waters Reams CH3 ...... 142 A4
Watersedge WA6 ...... 49 E1
Watersfield Cl SK8 ...... 34 C4
Waterside Appleton WA4 ...... 26 B4
- Macclesfield SK11 ...... 112 C4
Waterside Cotts CW5 ...... 216 C3
Waterside Dr WA6 ...... 49 E1
Waterside La WA8 ...... 22 B3
Waterside Mews 5 CW11 174 C2
Waterside Rd Disley SK12 .... 38 C4
- New Mills SK22 ...... 38 C4
Waterside View CW9 ...... 104 C3
Watertower View CH2 ...... 118 C1
Waterway CW3 ...... 143 D3
Waterways WA5 ...... 15 E3
Waterworks La
- Ellesmere Port L66 ...... 68 C4
- Winwick WA2 ...... 8 A4
Watery La Astbury CW12 ... 178 B3
- Winwick WA2 ...... 7 F3

Watkin St Hawarden CH5 116
- Warrington WA2 16
Watking Ave WA12 1
Watkinson Way WA8 13
Watlands Rd ST7 209
Watling Cres CH4 141
Watling Ct CH3 119
Watling Dr CW6 123
Watling St CW9 103
Watson Sq 20 SK1 240
Watson St M34 241
Watson's Cl CH4 139
Watton Cl WA4 17
Wavell Ave WA8 22
Wavells Way CH3 142
Waveney Dr WA14 238
Waverley Ave WA4 26
Waverley Cl SK10 113
Waverley Dr SK8 35
Waverley Rd Sale M33 242
- Stockport SK3 240
Waverley Terr CH2 118
Waverton Cl
- Davenham CW9 103
- Hough Common CW2 206
Waverton Cty Prim Sch CH3 143
Waverton Mill Quays CH3 143
Waverton Rd L66 69
Wavertree Ave
- Scholar Green ST7 194
- Widnes WA8 23
Wavertree Ct L66 69
Wavertree Dr CW10 151
Wavertree Rd CH1 117
Way's Gn CW7 149
Waybutt La Betley CW2 221
- Hough Common CW2 221
Wayfarers Dr WA12 2
Wayford Cl WA6 49
Wayside ST7 193
Wayside Cl WA13 18
Wayside Ct L66 119
Wayside Dr SK12 36
Wayside Rd SK10 112
Waywell Cl WA2 8
Weal Stone La CH2 118
Weald Dr L66 69
Wealstone Ct CH2 118
Wearhead Cl WA3 2
Weaste La WA4 17
Weates Cl WA8 13
Weathercock La CW12 157
Weaver Cl Alsager ST7 193
- Biddulph ST6 179
- Sandbach CW11 174
Weaver Cres WA6 49
Weaver Ct SK11 112
Weaver Cty Prim Sch The CW5 204
Weaver Gr
- Mickle Trafford CH2 119
- St Helens WA9 1
Weaver Grange CW9 126
Weaver La WA6 49
Weaver Park Ind Est WA6 ... 49
Weaver Rd Culcheth WA3 5
- Ellesmere Port L65 70
- Frodsham WA6 49
- Moulton CW9 126
- Nantwich CW5 204
- Northwich CW8 103
- Runcorn WA7 49
Weaver St Chester CH1 237
- Winsford CW7 126
Weaver Vale Cty Prim Sch WA6 49
Weaver View Audlem CW3 .. 229
- Church Minshull CW5 172
- Northwich CW8 103
- Weaverham CW8 77
Weaver Way CW9 78
Weaver's La SK7 35
Weaverhall La CW7 150
Weaverham Cty High Sch CW8 102
Weaverham Forest Cty Prim Sch CW8 77
Weaverham Rd
- Cuddington CW8 102
- Weaverham CW8 102
Weaverham Way 4 SK9 34
Weaverside CW5 204
Weaverside Ave WA7 49
Webb Dr WA5 6
Webb's La CW10 128
Webster Cl CW10 139
Websters La L66 69
Weddell Cl WA5 15
Wedge Ave WA11 1
Wedgwood Ave ST7 210
Wedgwood Dr WA8 13
Wedgwood La ST6 179
Wedgwood Rd ST7 210
Wednesbury Dr WA5 14
Weedon Ave WA12 2
Weighbridge Rd CH5 92
Weir Gr ST7 195
Weir La WA1 17
Weir St Northwich CW9 103
- Warrington WA1 16
Welbeck Cl CW10 128
Welbeck Rd SK14 241
Welch Rd SK14 241
Welcroft St 2 SK1 240
Weldon Rd WA14 238
Welford Ave WA3 3
Welford Cl SK9 60

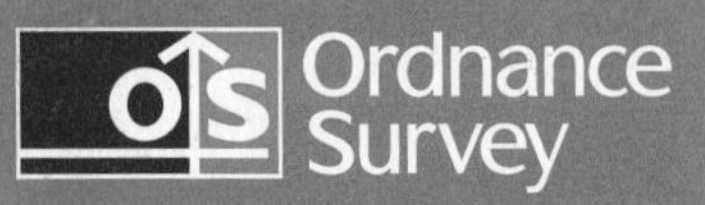

STREET ATLASES ORDER FORM

All Street Atlases contain Ordnance Survey mapping and provide the perfect solution for the driver who needs comprehensive, detailed regional mapping in a choice of compact and easy-to-use formats. They are indispensable and are ideal for use in the car, the home or the office.

The series is available from all good bookshops or by mail order direct from the publisher. Before placing your order, please check by telephone that the complete range of titles are available. Payment can be made in the following ways:

By phone Phone your order through on our special Credit Card Hotline on 01933 443863 (Fax: 01933 443849). Speak to our customer service team during office hours (9am to 5pm) or leave a message on the answering machine, quoting your full credit card number plus expiry date and your full name and address.

By post Simply fill out the order form (you may photocopy it) and send it to: **Philip's Direct, 27 Sanders Road, Wellingborough, Northants** NN8 4NL.

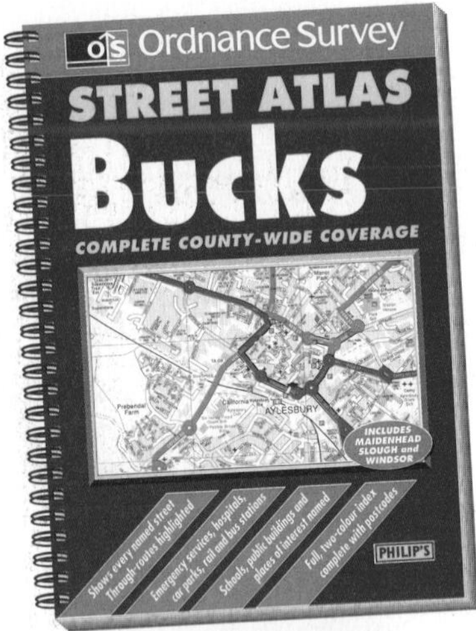

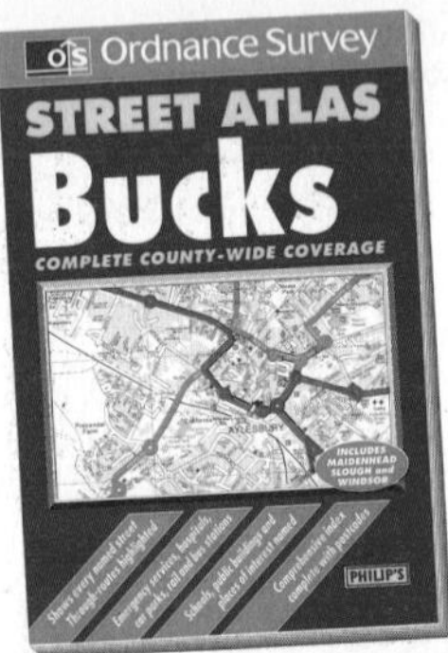

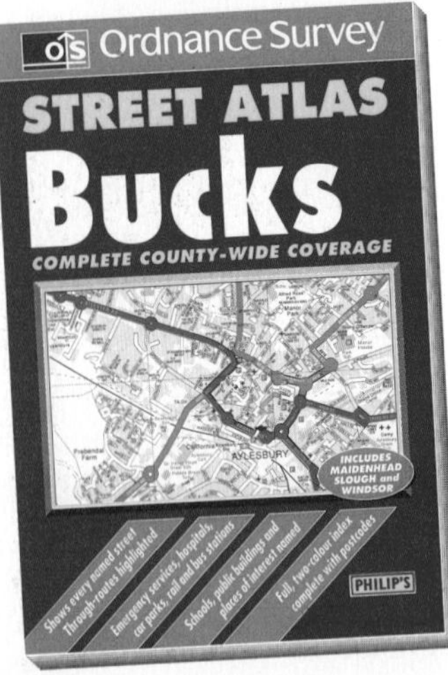

COLOUR EDITIONS

	HARDBACK	SPIRAL	POCKET	£ Total
	Quantity @ £10.99 each	Quantity @ £8.99 each	Quantity @ £4.99 each	£ Total
BERKSHIRE	☐ 0 540 06170 0	☐ 0 540 06172 7	☐ 0 540 06173 5	➤ ☐
MERSEYSIDE	☐ 0 540 06480 7	☐ 0 540 06481 5	☐ 0 540 06482 3	➤ ☐
	Quantity @ £12.99 each	Quantity @ £8.99 each	Quantity @ £4.99 each	£ Total
SURREY	☐ 0 540 06435 1	☐ 0 540 06436 X	☐ 0 540 06438 6	➤ ☐
	Quantity @ £12.99 each	Quantity @ £9.99 each	Quantity @ £4.99 each	£ Total
BUCKINGHAMSHIRE	☐ 0 540 07466 7	☐ 0 540 07467 5	☐ 0 540 07468 3	➤ ☐
DURHAM	☐ 0 540 06365 7	☐ 0 540 06366 5	☐ 0 540 06367 3	➤ ☐
HERTFORDSHIRE	☐ 0 540 06174 3	☐ 0 540 06175 1	☐ 0 540 06176 X	➤ ☐
EAST KENT	☐ 0 540 07483 7	☐ 0 540 07276 1	☐ 0 540 07287 7	➤ ☐
WEST KENT	☐ 0 540 07366 0	☐ 0 540 07367 9	☐ 0 540 07369 5	➤ ☐
EAST SUSSEX	☐ 0 540 07306 7	☐ 0 540 07307 5	☐ 0 540 07312 1	➤ ☐
WEST SUSSEX	☐ 0 540 07319 9	☐ 0 540 07323 7	☐ 0 540 07327 X	➤ ☐
TYNE AND WEAR	☐ 0 540 06370 3	☐ 0 540 06371 1	☐ 0 540 06372 X	➤ ☐
SOUTH YORKSHIRE	☐ 0 540 06330 4	☐ 0 540 06331 2	☐ 0 540 06332 0	➤ ☐
	Quantity @ £12.99 each	Quantity @ £9.99 each	Quantity @ £5.50 each	£ Total
GREATER MANCHESTER	☐ 0 540 06485 8	☐ 0 540 06486 6	☐ 0 540 06487 4	➤ ☐
	Quantity @ £12.99 each	Quantity @ £9.99 each	Quantity @ £5.99 each	£ Total
CHESHIRE	☐ 0 540 07507 8	☐ 0 540 07508 6	☐ 0 540 07509 4	➤ ☐
NORTH HAMPSHIRE	☐ 0 540 07471 3	☐ 0 540 07472 1	☐ 0 540 07473 X	➤ ☐

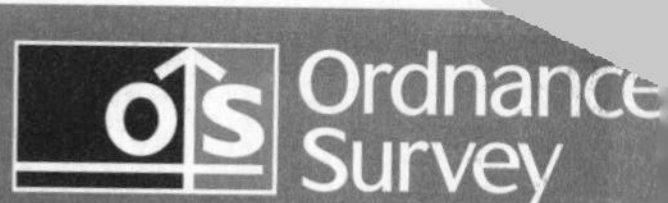

STREET ATLASES ORDER FORM

COLOUR EDITIONS

	HARDBACK Quantity @ £12.99 each	SPIRAL Quantity @ £9.99 each	POCKET Quantity @ £5.99 each	£ Total
SOUTH HAMPSHIRE	☐ 0 540 07476 4	☐ 0 540 07477 2	☐ 0 540 07478 0	➤ ☐
OXFORDSHIRE	☐ 0 540 07512 4	☐ 0 540 07513 2	☐ 0 540 07514 0	➤ ☐
WEST YORKSHIRE	☐ 0 540 06329 0	☐ 0 540 06327 4	☐ 0 540 06328 2	➤ ☐
	Quantity @ £14.99 each	Quantity @ £9.99 each	Quantity @ £5.99 each	£ Total
LANCASHIRE	☐ 0 540 06440 8	☐ 0 540 06441 6	☐ 0 540 06443 2	➤ ☐

BLACK AND WHITE EDITIONS

	HARDBACK Quantity @ £10.99 each	SOFTBACK	POCKET	£ Total
WARWICKSHIRE	☐ 0 540 05642 1	—	—	➤ ☐
	Quantity @ £12.99 each	Quantity @ £9.99 each	Quantity @ £4.99 each	Total
BRISTOL AND AVON	☐ 0 540 06140 9	☐ 0 540 06141 7	☐ 0 540 06142 5	➤ ☐
CARDIFF, SWANSEA & GLAMORGAN	☐ 0 540 06186 7	☐ 0 540 06187 5	☐ 0 540 06207 3	➤ ☐
DERBYSHIRE	—	☐ 0 540 06138 7	☐ 0 540 06139 5	➤ ☐
EDINBURGH & East Central Scotland	☐ 0 540 06180 8	☐ 0 540 06181 6	☐ 0 540 06182 4	➤ ☐
EAST ESSEX	☐ 0 540 05848 3	☐ 0 540 05866 1	☐ 0 540 05850 5	➤ ☐
WEST ESSEX	☐ 0 540 05849 1	☐ 0 540 05867 X	☐ 0 540 05851 3	➤ ☐
NOTTINGHAMSHIRE	—	☐ 0 540 05859 9	☐ 0 540 05860 2	➤ ☐
STAFFORDSHIRE	☐ 0 540 06134 4	☐ 0 540 06135 2	☐ 0 540 06136 0	➤ ☐
	Quantity @ £12.99 each	Quantity @ £9.99 each	Quantity @ £5.99 each	£ Total
GLASGOW & West Central Scotland	☐ 0 540 06183 2	☐ 0 540 06184 0	☐ 0 540 06185 9	➤ ☐

Post to: Philip's Direct,
27 Sanders Road,
Wellingborough, Northants,
NN8 4NL

◆ Free postage and packing

◆ All available titles will normally be dispatched within 5 working days of receipt of order but please allow up to 28 days for delivery

◆ Please tick this box if you do not wish your name to be used by other carefully selected organisations that may wish to send you information about other products and services

Registered Office: 25 Victoria Street, London SW1H 0EX.

Registered in England number: 3396524

I enclose a cheque / postal order, for a **total** of ☐
made payable to *Reed Book Services*, or please debit my
☐ Access ☐ American Express ☐ Visa ☐ Diners

account by ☐

Account no
☐☐☐☐ ☐☐☐☐ ☐☐☐☐ ☐☐☐☐

Expiry date ☐☐ ☐☐

Signature..

Name..

Address..

....

....

....POSTCODE

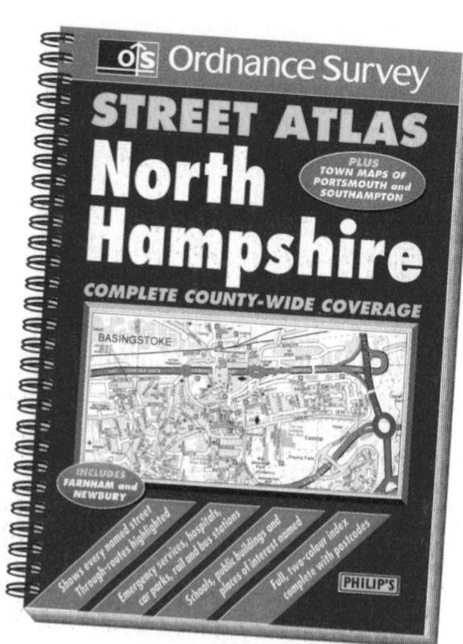

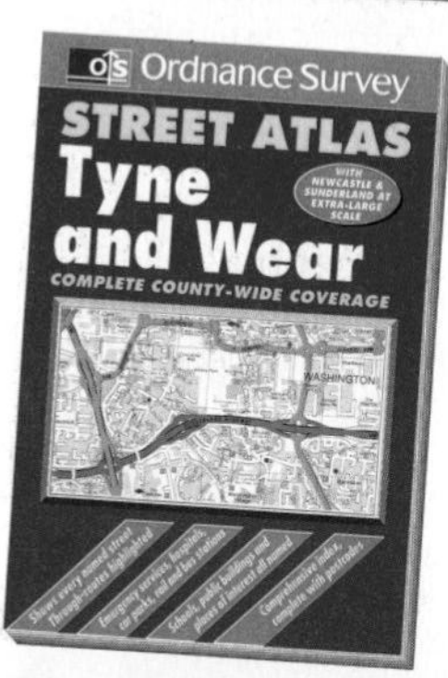

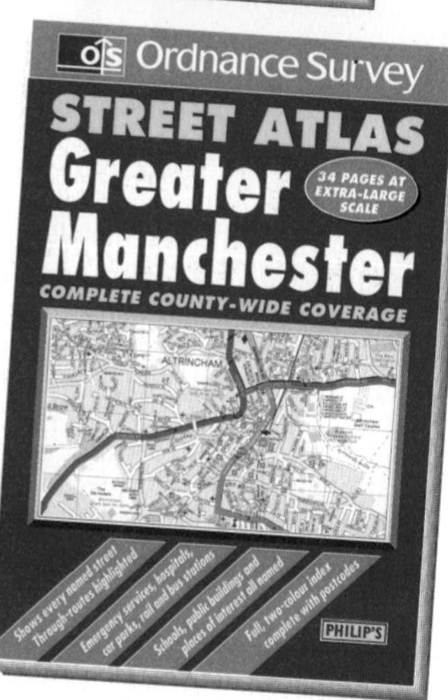